Motivation and Action

Heckhausen and Heckhausen give an extensive and in-depth overview of the diverse lines of research in motivational psychology, in terms of its historical foundations, up-to-date conceptual developments, and empirical research. The major classes of motivated behavior, such as achievement, affiliation, and power, are addressed, and the critical processes involved in motivation and volition are discussed in detail. Different conceptual and empirical lines of research, such as implicit/explicit motivation, intrinsic/extrinsic motivation/volition, causal attribution, childhood and lifespan development, education, personality, and psychopathology, are integrated and analyzed as to the common issues and phenomena they address, thus providing a most useful guideline for understanding debates in current motivational, educational, personality, and social psychology.

Jutta Heckhausen studied psychology at Ruhr University of Bochum in Germany. She wrote her Ph.D. dissertation on mother–infant dyads in joint object-centered action at the University of Strathclyde, Glasgow, in 1985, and her postdoctoral dissertation (Habilitation) on developmental regulation in adulthood at the Free University of Berlin in 1996. She was a postdoctoral Fellow, and then a research scientist, followed by senior scientist and head of the research group Developmental Regulation and Lifespan Development at the Max Planck Institute for Human Development, Berlin. Since 2000, Dr. Heckhausen has been a professor in the Department of Psychology and Social Behavior at the University of California, Irvine. In 1999, Dr. Heckhausen was awarded the Max Planck Research Award for International Cooperation. Her main research interests include motivation and development across the lifespan, goal engagement and disengagement, developmental regulation during major life-course transitions and health problems, and cultural universals and differences in striving for control.

Heinz Heckhausen studied psychology at the University of Münster, Germany, and wrote his doctoral dissertation on task motivation and achievement in 1954, followed by his postdoctoral dissertation (Habilitation) on achievement motivation, hope for success, and fear of failure in 1962. He was a research scientist at the University of Münster until 1962 and then became professor of psychology at Ruhr University, Bochum, where he founded the Department of Psychology. From 1983 until his death in 1988 he was director at the Max Planck Institute for Psychological Research in Munich. Dr. Heckhausen was a Fellow at the Netherlands Institute for Advanced Study in Wassenaar in 1971–1972, and from 1980 to 1982 he was president of the German Psychological Society (DGPs). In 1981, Dr. Heckhausen was awarded an honorary doctorate by the University of Oslo, and in 1988 he received the Order of Merit of the Federal Republic of Germany. Dr. Heckhausen's research interests included achievement motivation, motivation and volition in the course of action, development of motivation, measurement of motives, and causal attribution of action outcomes.

Motivation
and Action

Edited by

Jutta Heckhausen

University of California, Irvine

Heinz Heckhausen

Max Planck Institute for Psychological Research

Munich, Germany, † 1988

CAMBRIDGE
UNIVERSITY PRESS

CAMBRIDGE UNIVERSITY PRESS

Cambridge, New York, Melbourne, Madrid, Cape Town, Singapore, São Paulo, Delhi

Cambridge University Press
32 Avenue of the Americas, New York, NY 10013-2473, USA

www.cambridge.org
Information on this title: www.cambridge.org/9780521852593

First published 2008

Printed in the United States of America

A catalog record for this publication is available from the British Library.

Library of Congress Cataloging in Publication Data

Heckhausen, Jutta, 1957–
[Motivation und Handeln. English]
Motivation and action / Jutta Heckhausen, Heinz Heckhausen.
    p.   cm.
Includes bibliographical references and index.
ISBN 978-0-521-85259-3 (hardback)
1. Motivation (Psychology)   I. Heckhausen, Heinz.   II. Title.
BF503.H413   2008
153.8–dc22   2007024637

ISBN   978-0-521-85259-3 hardback

For Christa Heckhausen

Contents

Preface to the Second English Edition

This is the new edition of *Motivation and Action*. The first English edition, based on the second German edition and published by Springer-Verlag in 1991, was written by Heinz Heckhausen, who died on October 30, 1988. Springer-Verlag and I agreed that a revised edition of this influential textbook on motivational psychology was needed, and Cambridge University Press was ready to publish the international edition of the new book. The edition written by Heinz Heckhausen was already over 15 years old, and it was clear that considerable revisions would be required. Enormous progress has since been made in motivation psychology and its subdomains. There have been major conceptual and empirical innovations, informed and inspired in part by the research perspectives highlighted by Heinz Heckhausen (especially in Chapter 6, "Achievement Motivation," and Chapter 15, "Motivation and Development"), as well as by the study of implicit versus explicit motives, and by the lifespan theory of control. It would be a Herculean task to provide a comprehensive overview of all these developments and to survey the field of motivation psychology in its full range and complexity. No single scientist could now hope to follow in Heinz Heckhausen's footsteps and accomplish this task alone. A collaborative approach was clearly called for, and a look at the ranks of Heinz Heckhausen's students and their students shows that almost every subdomain of motivation psychology is represented by one or several renowned researchers. This new edition of *Motivation and Action* was only possible with the support of these scholars as authors. This book thus represents the intellectual legacy of Heinz Heckhausen in two respects. First, it shows how Heckhausen's approach to motivation psychology has been further developed and refined and that, although much has been retained, there have also been some important changes. Second, the book's chapters have been written by Heinz Heckhausen's intellectual heirs: members of his research groups in Bochum and Munich, their students, and by myself, his daughter.

This new edition pursues the same goals as the earlier edition. It seeks to disentangle convoluted perspectives within the psychology of motivation. It seeks to integrate separate research strands by pointing to common issues and offering a unifying conceptual framework. It seeks to introduce and critically discuss new research findings that have proved particularly fruitful. As in the previous editions, the motivational categories examined are limited to classes of behavior that are characteristic of humans, but not biologically determined needs such as hunger and thirst. The individual chapters build on one another, but each can be read and understood independently.

There are four main parts to the book. The first five chapters provide a broad introduction to the field of motivation psychology, mapping out different perspectives and research traditions. The first chapter gives a brief overview of the main issues addressed and previews the book's contents. The second chapter on the historical development of motivation research remains unchanged from the second edition. Chapters 3 and 4 present two contrasting and one-sided perspectives, focusing exclusively on person factors versus situation factors. In Chapter 5, these perspectives are integrated through the introduction of models that take into account the expectancies and values of different persons in different situations. Chapters 3, 4, and 5 have been thoroughly revised and updated.

The second group of chapters, Chapters 6 to 8 on achievement, affiliation, and power motivation, examine the major themes of human motivation. The chapters on anxiety, altruism, and aggression in the second edition have been dropped to make room for these new chapters and because, from today's perspective, these topics are more relevant to the allied disciplines of social psychology and clinical psychology.

The third group of chapters, Chapters 9 and 10, are completely new and address important foundations of motivated behavior that have more recently become salient topics of motivational research: the distinction between implicit and explicit motives (Chapter 9) and the biological structures and processes involved in motivation (Chapter 10). Thus, the first three groups of chapters provide the conceptual basis for exploring motivated and goal-oriented behavior.

The fourth group of chapters, Chapters 11 to 14, consider the major components of action and its regulation. Chapters 11 to 14 are completely new; Chapter 14 draws on the two attribution chapters in the second edition, but has been entirely rewritten. The topics and research programs covered in Chapters 9 to 14 reflect the recent surge in research activity in international motivation psychology. Issues from current research provide topics of discussion for seminars and promising ideas for researchers and doctoral students are identified.

Finally, Chapter 15 unites the different approaches and strands of research by exploring the relationship of motivation and development from two perspectives: the development of motivation and the motivation of development. This chapter is completely new, though some of it was inspired by parts of the chapter on development in the first edition (the second edition did not include a chapter on the development of motivation).

In terms of authorship, Heinz Heckhausen is cited as coauthor of all chapters that contain parts of his original chapters but have been revised and expanded. This seemed the best way of reflecting Heinz Heckhausen's authorship without suggesting that he authorized the changes and additions himself.

The chapter authors and I have done our best to ensure the reader friendliness that is now expected of academic texts, and textbooks in particular. I think we have succeeded in making the highly complex domain of motivation psychology accessible to students and novices, while ensuring that the text remains informative and stimulating for experts and researchers in the field. These efforts have been facilitated by special formatting elements: boxes, summaries, definitions, and review questions give the reader practical tools for navigating the text.

I am greatly indebted to Susannah Goss, who masterfully translated the German edition into English. Thanks also go to Miriam Geißler at Springer Publishing Company, who edited the German edition and compiled the comprehensive reference list. Finally, I am most thankful to the chapter authors for their readiness to participate in this project and for the outstanding chapters they have produced.

Jutta Heckhausen
Irvine, January 2007

Contributors

Heinz Heckhausen (1926–1988) studied psychology at the University of Münster, Germany. He completed his doctoral dissertation on task motivation and achievement in 1954, and his postdoctoral dissertation on achievement motivation, hope for success, and fear of failure in 1962. He was a research scientist at the University of Münster from 1953 to 1962; professor of psychology at Ruhr University, Bochum, Germany; founder of the Psychological Institute (1964–1982); director of the Max Planck Institute for Psychological Research, Munich, from 1983 to 1988; Fellow at the Netherlands Institute for Advanced Study, Wassenaar, in 1971–1972; president of the German Psychological Society from 1980 to 1982; awarded an honorary doctorate by the University of Oslo, Norway, in 1981; member of the Wissenschaftsrat (German science board; chair 1985–1987); member of the Bavarian Academy of Sciences in 1988; and awarded the Order of Merit of the Federal Republic of Germany in 1988. Dr. Heckhausen's research interests included achievement motivation, motivation and volition in the course of action, development of motivation, measurement of motives, and causal attribution of action outcomes.

Jutta Heckhausen studied psychology at Ruhr University, Bochum, Germany. She wrote her doctoral dissertation on mother–infant dyads in joint object-centered action at the University of Strathclyde, Glasgow, Scotland, in 1985, and her postdoctoral dissertation on developmental regulation in adulthood at the Free University of Berlin in 1996. She was a postdoctoral fellow from 1984 to 1986; research scientist from 1987 to 1996; Fellow at the Center for Advanced Study in the Behavioral Sciences, Stanford, California, in 1995–1996; and senior scientist and head of a research group at the Max Planck Institute for Human Development, Berlin, from 1996 to 2000. She was awarded the Max Planck Research Award for International Cooperation in 1999. Since 2000, she has been a professor at the Department of Psychology and Social Behavior at the University of California, Irvine. Dr. Heckhausen's main research interests are motivation and development across the lifespan, goal engagement and disengagement, developmental regulation during major life course transitions and health problems, and cultural universals and differences in striving for control.

Her web site is located at http://www.seweb.uci.edu/faculty/heckhausen.

Anja Achtziger studied social education with a focus on the education of learning disabled students, at the University of Applied Sciences, Darmstadt, Germany, and psychology with a focus on clinical psychology and social psychology at the Technical University of Darmstadt. She was a research associate in the Decision Research and Social Psychology Center at the Technical University of Darmstadt. She wrote her doctoral dissertation on cognitive aspects of voluntary stereotype control in the Social Psychology and Motivation Center at the University of Konstanz, Germany. Dr. Achtziger's main research interests are psychology of motivation and action, social cognition, decision research, and social cognitive neuroscience, particularly self-regulation.

Jürgen Beckmann was a research scientist in the German Research Foundation's Collaborative Research Center on Decision Research at the University of Mannheim, Germany, from 1980 to 1983. In 1984, he received the Junior Scientist Award of the German Psychology Society. He was a research scientist at the Max Planck Institute for Psychological Research, Munich, from 1984 to 1990 and head of the Intention and Action research group; worked under a stipend at the Max Planck Institute for Psychological Research, Munich, from 1991 to 1996; was visiting scholar at Florida Atlantic University, Boca Raton, in 1993; and was professor of sport psychology at the Institute for Sport Science, University of Potsdam, Germany, from 1997 to 2006. Since 2006, he has been a professor of sport psychology at the Faculty of Sport Science, Technical University of Munich.

Joachim C. Brunstein studied psychology at the University of Giessen, Germany, where he wrote his doctoral dissertation in 1986 and his postdoctoral dissertation in 1993. He was a member of Heinz Heckhausen's research group at the Max Planck Institute for Psychological Research in Munich from 1986 to 1989; lecturer at the Psychological Institute, University of Erlangen-Nuremberg, Germany, from 1990 to 1996; and professor of educational psychology at the University of Potsdam, Germany, in 1998. Since 2004, he has been a professor of educational psychology at the University of Giessen. Dr. Brunstein's research interests include self-regulation of learning, achievement, and development, and his current focuses are self-regulated learning, motivational bases of achievement- and power-related behavior, and the role of life goals for subjective well-being and development in adulthood.

Peter M. Gollwitzer studied psychology at the University of Regensburg and the Ruhr University, Bochum, Germany; received his PhD from the University of Texas at Austin; and wrote his postdoctoral dissertation at the Ludwig Maximilians University of Munich. He was head of the Intention and Action Research Group at the Max Planck Institute for Psychological Research, Munich, from 1989 to 1992. Since 1993, he has been a professor of social psychology and motivation at the University of Konstanz, Germany, and, since 1999, he has taught at both New York University and the University of Konstanz. He is the holder of various research awards (Max Planck Research Award, TRANSCOOP award for transatlantic cooperation in research) and has presented state-of-the-art lectures on goal striving at the conventions of the American Psychological Association, American Psychological Society, International Congress of Psychology, and International Congress of Applied Psychology. Dr. Gollwitzer is a Fellow of the American Psychological Association and Charter Fellow of the American Psychological Society.

Julius Kuhl has been professor of differential psychology and personality research at the University of Osnabrück, Germany, since 1986. He was senior research scientist at the Max Planck Institute for Psychology, Munich, and research scientist at the University of Bochum, Germany. From 1983 to 1984, he was a Fellow at the Center for Advanced Study in the Behavioral Sciences, Stanford, California. Professor Kuhl has overseen the development of innovative instruments and methods to assess and train mental abilities and self-regulatory skills; served as coeditor of the *Enzyklopädie der Psycholoie* (Hogrefe); and, in 2001, published a unifying theory of personality (PSI theory) that integrates theoretical and empirical research from the fields of motivation psychology, cognitive psychology, and neuropsychology. Further information can be accessed at www.diffpsycho.uos.de.

Falko Rheinberg studied psychology at the University of Innsbruck, Austria and the University of Bochum, Germany, from 1967 to 1973. He was a member of Heinz Heckhausen's research group at the University of Bochum from 1973 to 1983, where he wrote his doctoral dissertation on social and individual reference norms in 1977. He then developed and tested methods to enhance motivation in the classroom (in association with Professor Dr. H. Heckhausen and Dr. S. Krug, with funding from the German Research Foundation). This motivation program has been developed continuously and is now also applied to parents (with Dr. S. Fries and Dr. B. Lund). He performed detailed analyses of the structure of learning

motivation, and his findings were presented in a postdoctoral dissertation on purpose and activity in 1983. He was professor of educational psychology and intervention methods at the University of Heidelberg, Germany, from 1983 to 1993; professor of educational psychology (1993–1995); and professor of general psychology since 1995 at the University of Potsdam, Germany.

David Scheffer studied psychology at the University of Osnabrück, Germany, where he first graduated in 1996 and wrote his doctoral dissertation in 2001. He was a research scientist at the University of Osnabrück, taking part in a project testing evolutionary socialization theory funded by the German Research Foundation. Since 1998, he has been an assistant professor at the Helmut Schmidt University of Hamburg, Germany. Dr. Scheffer has conducted numerous research and consultancy projects in the area of employee motivation.

Heinz-Dieter Schmalt studied psychology at the University of Münster, University of Hamburg, and Ruhr University of Bochum, all in Germany. He first graduated in 1969 and wrote his doctoral dissertation in 1974 and his postdoctoral dissertation in 1978 at the Ruhr University of Bochum. Since 1981, he has been professor of general psychology II (motivation, emotion, and learning) at the University of Wuppertal, Germany. His research interests are power motivation, achievement motivation, intrinsic motivation, approach and avoidance, selection and implementation motivation, and measurement of motivation. Dr. Schmalt's book publications include *Motivation* (Kohlhammer, 2000; with Klaus Schneider) and *Achievement Motivation in Perspective* (1985; with Klaus Schneider and Heinz Heckhausen).

Oliver C. Schultheiss received his diploma in 1994 and his doctorate in 1996 from Friedrich-Alexander University in Erlangen, Germany. From 1997 to 1999, he was a postdoctoral student at Harvard University, Boston, Massachusetts, and University of Potsdam, Germany. He was assistant professor (2000–2005) and associate professor (2005–2007) of psychology at the University of Michigan, Ann Arbor, and, since the fall of 2007, he has been a professor at the Friedrich-Alexander University Erlangen, Nürnberg, Germany. His current areas of research include endocrine correlates of implicit motives; effects of implicit motives on brain activation, and cognitive and behavioral responses to perceived facial expressions of emotion; and factors influencing, and outcomes influenced by, the interplay of implicit motives and explicit goals and values.

Kurt Sokolowski studied psychology at Ruhr University, Bochum, Germany, where he received his degree in 1977. He wrote his doctoral dissertation in 1986 and his postdoctoral dissertation in 1992. He was a research scientist at the Institute for Labor Physiology in Dortmund; adjunct professor at the University of Wuppertal, Germany; and visiting professor at the universities in Dortmund, München, Osnabrück, and Wuppertal. Since 2000, he has been a professor of general and differential psychology at the University of Siegen, Germany. Dr. Sokolowski's research interests include psychology of motivation, emotion, and volition and measurement of motivation.

Joachim Stiensmeier-Pelster studied psychology at the University of Bielefeld, Germany, where he received his degree in 1983 and wrote his doctoral dissertation in 1987 and his postdoctoral dissertation in 1992. He was professor of educational psychology at the University of Hildesheim, Germany, in 1996 and has been at the University of Giessen, Germany, since 1999. Dr. Stiensmeier-Pelster's research interests include motivational and emotional determinants of learning behavior and success, particularly the influence of self-concepts of ability and causal attributions. He has also conducted applied research in cooperation with financial services companies on the motivational and emotional determinants of occupational success and the cognitive, emotional, and motivational determinants of accident risk in young drivers.

Michelle M. Wirth received her BA in psychobiology from Swarthmore College, Swarthmore, Pennsylvania, in 1999, and her PhD in psychology from the University of Michigan, Ann Arbor, in 2006. She is currently a postdoctoral Fellow at the University of Wisconsin. Her previous research addressed the neuroendocrine control of hunger and satiety in rats, whereas her more recent research has been focused on issues of emotion and motivation, specifically brain and endocrine involvement in dominance, affiliation, and attachment; the relationship between testosterone and response to signals of social threat (anger faces); progesterone as a putative "tend-and-befriend" (stress-responsive, affiliation-encouraging) hormone; and how the personality trait power motivation affects brain activation and stress hormone responses to social signals (emotional facial expressions) and situations (losing a contest).

1 Motivation and Action: Introduction and Overview

J. Heckhausen and H. Heckhausen

Human life is composed of a continuous flow of activity. Besides the infinite variety of overt actions and expressions that impact the social and physical environment, it also has a more covert side in the mental activities of experiencing, perceiving, thinking, feeling, and imagining. These mental activities are part of the flow, although they cannot be observed directly by others and have no direct impact on the environment. The scope of human activity thus ranges from dreaming (Klinger, 1971) to preplanned, intentional acts. The psychology of motivation is specifically concerned with activities that reflect the pursuit of a particular goal and, in this function, form a meaningful unit of behavior. Motivational research seeks to explain these units of behavior in terms of their **whys** and **hows**.

Questions pertaining to the whys of human activity address its purposes from a variety of perspectives; for example:

- Can different units of behavior be assigned to one and the same class of goals and differentiated from other classes of goals?
- How do these classes of goals evolve in the course of an individual's development, and which individual differences exist in this regard?
- Why is it that specific situational conditions prompt people to choose certain goal-oriented activities over others, and to pursue them with a certain amount of time and energy?

It is only recently that the focus of attention in academic psychology has returned to the hows of human activity; e.g., to how people, having decided on a course of action, actually come to execute (or abandon) it. Questions of this kind have always occupied laypeople – after all, we are all familiar with the difficulties of following through on our intentions in everyday life; for example:

- Why do we find it easy to implement some intentions, but keep losing track of others?
- Why is it that some people find it easier than others to act on their decisions and realize their goals?
- Do people become better at pursuing their adopted goals over the course of life?
- Which situational conditions facilitate or inhibit the resolute pursuit of goals?

1.1 Universal Characteristics of Human Action

Two universal characteristics determine the basic structure and general directionality of motivated human action:

1. the striving for control and
2. the organization of goal engagement and goal disengagement.

These two characteristics of human action are so universal within and indeed far beyond our species that it is hard to imagine human behavior being any different (see the overview in J. Heckhausen, 2000; the first author is solely responsible for the arguments presented in this section). It would seem to be a given that human behavior is geared to effecting change in the environment, and how else might it be directed than either pursuing a goal or withdrawing from a goal? On closer consideration, however, it is clear that these characteristics are in fact an outcome of **behavioral evolution**, and anything but a given. Moreover, the function they fulfill in guiding and organizing the organism's activities is highly adaptive. This is one of the reasons why biopsychological approaches to motivation that predominantly use animal models are so useful for investigating specific functions of the brain to explain motivational phenomena (see Chapter 10).

1

1.1.1 Control Striving

Control striving – i.e., the striving for direct or **primary control** of the physical and social environment – is part of the motivational makeup of our species (White, 1959). In fact, control striving is not unique to humans but is an outcome of behavioral evolution in all mammals, and possibly all species that are mobile and thus in need of general mechanisms of behavioral regulation. Under changing environmental conditions, the organism can thus stay focused on the aimed for outcome as a guideline to modifying its behavior (see the overview in J. Heckhausen, 2000a; Schneider & Dittrich, 1990). Fixed stimulus-response patterns and instinctive behavior are not flexible enough to allow adaptive responses to environmental variation. Open behavioral programs (Mayr, 1974) or behavioral modules (Cosmides & Tooby, 1994; Fodor, 1983; Rozin, 1976), operating in conjunction with domain-general processes of behavioral regulation associated with emotional states and motivational orientations (Hamburg, 1963; Plutchik, 1980; Scherer, 1984), offer a more promising approach. In recent decades there has been a veritable explosion of research on cognitive modules such as risk perception and decision making (e.g., Gigerenzer, Todd, & ABC Research Group, 1999), social exchange (e.g., Cosmides & Tooby, 1992), and foraging (e.g., Krebs, 1980). However, comparative and evolutionary psychology has virtually ignored the motivational and volitional control of behavior. Yet there are both theoretical and empirical reasons for assuming that a set of basic motivational modules regulate control striving and control-related behavior (see also Chapter 15, Section 15.2):

1. In mammals and probably many other species, there seems to be a widespread **preference for behavior-event contingencies** over event-event contingencies: organisms are motivated to engage in behaviors that produce contingent effects (e.g., baby smiles, mother vocalizes).

2. **Exploration** is also a universal motivational system in mammals, and engages the organism with the goal of extending its range of control over the external environment.

3. There is much evidence for an **asymmetric pattern of affective responses to positive and negative events** (Frijda, 1988): organisms soon get used to the positive affect experienced after positive events, whereas the negative emotions elicited by negative events are much longer lasting. This motivates individuals to aspire to new goals rather than resting on their laurels after successes, and prevents them from giving up too soon in the face of setbacks.

The first manifestations of control striving in human ontogenesis can be observed in neonates (Janos & Papoušek, 1977; Papoušek, 1967). Experiences of control are fostered in early parent-child interactions, soon followed by a generalized expectancy of control (Watson, 1966) and – with the development of the self-concept in the second year of life (Geppert & Heckhausen, 1990) – by achievement striving, the

goal of which is to demonstrate personal competence (for details, see Chapter 15).

❶ Human control striving is motivated by both an innate preference for behavior-event contingencies and specifically human anticipatory self-reinforcement, with its attractive and threatening aspects (Chapter 15, Section 15.4)

1.1.2 Goal Engagement and Goal Disengagement

Human action consists of organized behavior and experience. Perceptions, thoughts, emotions, skills, and activities are coordinated to facilitate either the attainment of goals or disengagement from unattainable or futile goals. During periods of **goal engagement**, individuals focus on what is important and ignore irrelevant stimuli. They put key procedures in place, attune their attention and perception to stimuli that trigger or cue behavior, and shield themselves from potential distractions. Expectations of control are optimistic. Research based on the Rubicon model of action phases has provided a wealth of empirical evidence for mental and behavioral resources being orchestrated in this way to facilitate goal pursuit (Chapter 11).

During periods of **goal disengagement**, by contrast, goals are deactivated. This does not imply a gradual decrease in goal engagement; on the contrary, goal disengagement is an active process whereby the processes typical of goal engagement are counteracted (Wrosch, Scheier, Miller, Schulz, & Carver, 2003). It involves degrading the original goal and enhancing the value and attainability of alternative goals, defending self-esteem against experiences of failure and, more generally, seeking to ensure that disengagement from a particular goal does not undermine motivational resources in the long term (J. Heckhausen, 1999).

Goal engagement and goal disengagement can be seen as two motivational modes: **go** and **stop**. In adaptive behavior, at least, the two modes do not overlap, but discretely focus an organism's cognitive, behavioral, and motivational activities on the efficient investment of resources. After all, it is much more efficient to decide on a goal and pursue it resolutely than to dither between options, squandering resources without attaining the aspired goal. Should a goal prove to be unattainable or its costs too high, it makes sense to abandon that goal once and for all, without getting caught up in **postdecisional conflicts** or clinging halfheartedly to old habits, thus wasting mental, behavioral, and temporal resources that could be put to better use in the pursuit of new, attainable goals.

To date, the evolutionary precursors of this form of action regulation remain largely uncharted, but it seems reasonable to assume that animals also redirect their energies into more efficient pursuits wherever appropriate, as can be illustrated by the example of a predator pursuing its prey. Although it begins the chase at top speed, a predator that finds itself

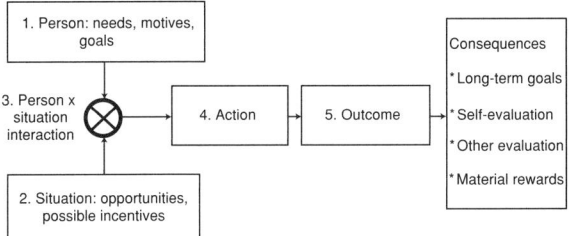

Figure 1.1 The determinants and course of motivated action: General model.

outrun will not slow down gradually, but will stop and turn away from its prey abruptly as soon as it becomes clear that its efforts are futile. In other words, it will save its energy for more worthwhile hunts (see also Chapter 15, Section 15.8.2). Very little previous research on the evolution of behavior (e.g., French, Kamil, & Leger, 2001; Nesse, 2000, 2001) has addressed questions of motivational and volitional psychology. Cross-species studies remain scarce (cf. Bitterman, 1975), although this field of research would doubtless be highly productive, given that the regulation of goal-directed behavior by means of discrete go and stop modes can be assumed to be widespread in the animal kingdom as well (see also the overview in J. Heckhausen, 2000a, and in Chapter 15). In contrast, much progress and innovation has been achieved in research on human motivational and volitional self-regulation in the past 20 years. Chapter 15, Section 1.3 will provide a more in-depth discussion of these issues.

SUMMARY

The two main, universal characteristics of motivated behavior are control striving and the organization of action into phases of goal engagement and goal disengagement.

1.2 Motivation as a Product of Person and Situation

Motivation psychology seeks to explain the direction, persistence, and intensity of goal-directed behavior. The many factors involved can first be classified as pertaining either to the person or to the situation. Throughout this volume, we will draw on the general model of motivation presented in Fig. 1.1 to show how the topics examined are accommodated within a general model, and to illustrate how they relate to one another. The model integrates Heinz Heckhausen's (1977a, b) extended cognitive model of motivation and Rheinberg's representation of the basic model of "classical" motivation psychology (Rheinberg, 1995).

An individual's motivation to aspire to a certain goal is influenced by person factors and by situation factors, including the anticipated outcomes of actions and their consequences. In the following three sections, we will outline these

influences, and show where the relevant chapters of this book fit into the overall model of motivation.

1.2.1 Person Factors: Needs and Implicit and Explicit Motives

Motivational influences that reside within the person (Fig. 1.1, component 1) are crucial to both lay explanations and scientific theories of motivation. In a manner of speaking, they catch the eye at first glance. Three main kinds of person factors can be distinguished:

- universal behavioral tendencies and needs,
- motive dispositions (implicit motives) that distinguish between individuals, and
- the goals (explicit motives) that individuals adopt and pursue.

DEFINITION
By universal behavioral tendencies and needs, we mean basic physical needs and the striving for control that underlies the various motives.

As part of the legacy of early research on motivation and learning, basic needs are covered primarily in the opening chapters of this volume. The focus here is on basic **physiological needs**, such as hunger and thirst, that are shared by all humans (Chapter 3, Section 3.3 and Chapter 5, Sections 5.4.1 to 5.4.3) and that vary according to the situational degree of deprivation (Chapter 4, Section 4.2). The general and universal **striving for control** underlies more specific motivational orientations (Section 1.1.1) and determines motivated action across the entire lifespan (Chapter 15).

Individual **motive dispositions** play a major role in both lay explanations of behavior and the scientific study of motivation (Chapter 3). They seem best able to explain why individual differences in behavior persist across time and situations (see also the excursus on "Kelley's Cube Model of Causal Inferences" on page 5). Nothing would seem more natural than to attribute differences in behavior to individual dispositions: to the person's traits, "factors," habits, motives; in short, to his or her "personality."

The evident heredity of certain characteristics reinforces the tendency to attribute interindividual differences in behavior to underlying dispositions. Beside physical characteristics, these include skills and abilities, behavioral styles, personality, and its development (Plomin, 2004; Plomin, DeFries, Craig, & McGuffin, 2003).

❶ Enduring individual motive dispositions, which have recently been labeled **implicit motives** as distinguished from explicit motives or goals (Chapter 9), are affectively charged preferences for certain kinds of incentives (habitual propensities) that are acquired in early childhood. (McClelland, Koestner, & Weinberger, 1989)

These incentives can be classified according to motivational themes: challenges to personal control in performance situations in the case of the achievement motive (Chapter 6), opportunities for social closeness and social bonding in the case of the affiliation motive (Chapter 7), and opportunities for social control in the case of the power motive (Chapter 8). In this volume, we focus on these "Big Three" motives of achievement, affiliation, and power. It is here that research is most advanced, and where the main concepts of motivation psychology can best be demonstrated.

DEFINITION

In contrast to implicit motives, **explicit motives** reflect the conscious, verbally represented (or representable) self-images, values, and goals that people attribute to themselves. (Chapter 9)

In many cases, implicit and explicit motives do not match: people's conscious impressions of themselves and their motives are not necessarily congruent with their unconscious preferences and habits. In the best case scenario, implicit and explicit motives work together, and the specific goals that people set themselves in given situations (their explicit motives) coincide with their implicit motives. But this is by no means the rule. Implicit and explicit motives are frequently at odds, with detrimental consequences for efficiency, subjective well-being, and even mental health (Chapter 9).

Explicit action goals are the core of action control. They provide directionality of behavior and a criterion for success, and give the individual reason to muster the necessary motivational resources and to shield those resources against distractions. Goals can be more abstract or more concrete in nature, and play a major role in the organization of motivated behavior both in individuals and in groups across many domains of life.

1.2.2 Situation Factors: Intrinsic and Extrinsic Incentives

It soon becomes clear that purely person-centered, dispositional approaches to the explanation of motivated behavior overlook some important aspects. Above all, explanatory models based on enduring personality differences fail to account for the opportunities and constraints of the situation itself. Is the world really divided into thieves and nonthieves, or is it not opportunity that makes a thief?

There are various reasons for focusing on the situation, rather than the person, when seeking to explain behavior:

1. It is only when account is taken of the situation that within-person variations (i.e., intraindividual differences) in behavior can be properly identified.

2. A situation-based approach to behavioral motivation makes it possible to examine common and otherwise unremarkable behaviors that have wide generalizability as caused by a specific situational context.

3. Situations can be controlled and varied systematically in experimental approaches.

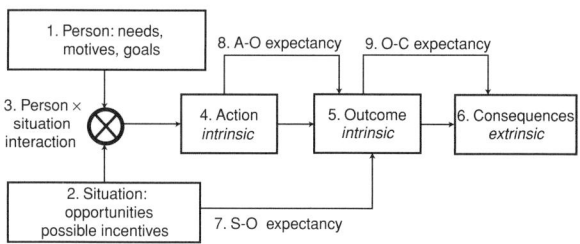

Figure 1.2 Determinants of motivated action: General model with outcome- and consequence-related expectancies.

Early situation-based approaches to the psychology of motivation focused on the organism's need states or drive strengths and on learning experiences; e.g., in experiments with hungry rats that had learned to tolerate an aversive stimulus to obtain food (Chapter 4). As research progressed, attention shifted to the cognitive implications of situational influences; e.g., in Lewin's conflict theory or Festinger's theory of cognitive dissonance. There has recently been a resurgence of interest in nonconscious situational influences; e.g., in how **priming stimuli** activate social stereotypes (Chapter 4).

An approach to situational influences on motivated behavior that is more closely related to Heinz Heckhausen's extended cognitive model of motivation focuses on anticipatory **incentives**.

DEFINITION

Every positive or negative outcome that a situation can promise or signal to an individual is called an "incentive" and has "demand characteristics" for an appropriate action. Incentives may be associated with the action itself, its outcome, or various consequences of an action outcome.

As shown in Fig. 1.2 (see also Fig. 13.1 in Chapter 13), situations can differ in the levels and patterns of **situation-outcome expectancies** (7 in Fig. 1.2), **action-outcome expectancies** (8 in Fig. 1.2), and **outcome-consequence expectancies** (9 in Fig. 1.2). When situation-outcome expectancies are high (i.e., when it is assumed that the situation will automatically lead to the outcome, even without active intervention), there is little incentive to act. But when situation-outcome expectancies are low and action-outcome expectancies are high, the incentive to act is high, particularly if outcome-consequence expectancies are also favorable.

Each component of a course of action has its specific incentives (Chapter 13). Some are **intrinsic**, meaning that they reside in the activity itself (4 in Fig. 1.2) or its outcome (5 in Fig. 1.2). Some are **extrinsic**, meaning that they derive from the consequences of actions and their outcomes – e.g., progress toward long-term goals, self- and other-evaluation, or material rewards (6 in Fig. 1.2). Research interest has long focused on the self-evaluative consequences of action outcomes, particularly in the field of achievement motivation, whereas incentives inherent in the activity itself have

---

EXCURSUS

Kelley's Cube Model of Causal Inferences

The attribution cube model posited by social psychologist Harold Kelley (1967) describes how we as laypeople (and indeed as scientists) determine the extent to which a behavior is attributable to the person or to the environment. Kelley distinguishes three citerion dimensions for the explanation of behavior: consensus, distinctiveness, and consistency (Chapter 14).

1. Consensus: comparison with the behavior of others (individual differences). The less an individual's behavior corresponds with that of most other people in the same situation, the more it seems to be governed by individual factors. If, for example, a crowd of onlookers gathers around an accident victim and only one person kneels down to help, he or she is thought to be very "helpful." Conversely, the more an individual's behavior corresponds with that of most other people in the same situation, the less likely it is to be determined by person factors and the more likely it is to be driven by environmental factors. If, for example, a student regularly attends a compulsory class once a week, and his or her fellow students all do the same, we see no reason to attribute that behavior to a particular personality trait. Rather, it seems to be caused by the situation; specifically, the obligatory nature of the class.

2. Distinctiveness: comparison with behavior in other situations (intraindividual differences across situations). The more consistent a person's behavior is across situations, the more likely it is to be attributed to individual person factors. If, for

example, an employee is not only focused on his work at the office, but continues to talk about it during the company outing and turns every social get-together into a work meeting, he is thought to be highly "achievement motivated." Conversely, the less consistent a person's behavior is across situations, the more that behavior is deemed to be determined by situational factors. If, for example, a student cheats in an exam held in a large auditorium with insufficient invigilation, but not when playing cards with her friends, the assumption might be that she hopes not to be caught cheating in the exam, but considers the risk of being exposed as a cheat by her friends as too high.

3. Consistency: comparison with earlier behavior (stability or intraindividual differences over time). When someone's behavior remains consistent over time, it seems reasonable to attribute that behavior to individual person factors. If, for example, a boy who always did his very best to solve difficult problems at kindergarten is eager to learn to read at school, he is assumed to be highly and consistently "achievement motivated." Conversely, if an individual's behavior fluctuates over time, that behavior can reasonably be attributed to differences in situation factors. If, for example, a girl who always chose particularly difficult tasks at kindergarten and put a great deal of effort in solving them turns out to be bored and distracted at school, it would seem that the tasks set by the teacher are "too easy."

---

tended to be neglected. Recent years have seen a shift in focus, however, with research programs on the experience of flow, willingness to take risks, shared experiences, and achievement-oriented activity incentives providing valuable insights (Chapter 13).

1.2.3 The Interaction of Person and Situation: Subjective Patterns of Incentives

Which is the crucial factor, the person or the situation? Attempts to answer this question are futile, for at least four reasons:

1. It is impossible to isolate the two. We can no more conceive of person factors abstract from a situation than we can of situation factors abstract from a person. In other words, person always assumes "in a situation," and situation always assumes "for a particular person" (Bowers, 1973). In everyday life, individuals are characterized in terms of whether or not their behavioral repertoires are suited to certain situations (Cantor, Mischel, & Schwartz, 1982).

2. Whether situation factors or person factors seem to have the strongest influence on behavior is determined largely by the sampling of variables from each of these domains. Because it is not possible to define comparable units for each domain, it is difficult to determine whether

samples of persons and situations are representative and therefore comparable. If, for example, a sampled group of individuals is very heterogeneous (e.g., in terms of age, mental health, etc.) and the variation in situations is less heterogeneous (e.g., achievement-related demand characteristics only), differences in behavior will quite obviously be more strongly associated with the person factors than with the situation factors. Conversely, if there is more situational variation than variation among persons, situation factors will necessarily dominate (Olweus, 1976).

3. It is not the "situation" in an objective or intersubjective (i.e., consensual) sense that influences behavior, but the individual (subjective, "idiosyncratic") interpretation of it. The situation is always something that is perceived, i.e., the product of an individual's thought, and is thus itself influenced by person factors. The incentives residing in activities, action outcomes, and their consequences are not set in stone; they take shape in the eye of the beholder. What one person sees as an exhilarating motorbike ride, another will see a reckless escapade on a speeding death trap. And what one person scorns as filthy lucre will prompt another to spare no effort at work. In other words, it is not the situation in the "objective" sense of intersubjective consensus among outside observers that prompts action, but the way the situation appears to and exists for the individual.

4. The degree to which behavior is seen to be determined by the person or the situation depends on the observer's perspective. We tend to view our own behavior as influenced primarily by the features of the perceived situation (Jones & Nisbett, 1971), but as observers of the behavior of others, we are more likely to attribute variations to their personal characteristics. The difference can be explained in terms of the salience of figure-ground articulations. When we observe the behavior of others, situational factors constitute the background against which their actions become salient. In self-observation, the reverse is true: situational features are perceived as figures against the background of our own course of action.

Expectancy-value theory permits the systematic integration of person and situation factors in models that yield predictions about behavior (Chapter 5). Although the expectancy of being able to attain a particular goal is largely dependent on situation factors, its value is very much "in the eye of the beholder," and thus conditional on the individual's implicit and explicit motivational state. People are most likely to perform an action when the product of expectancy and value is at its highest. In other words:

❶ The individual aspires to the goal with the highest possible incentive value, taking into account the probability of its attainment. Whether or not a situation acts as an incentive for a specific individual depends on whether or not it corresponds with that person's implicit and explicit motives.

Person and situation interact in these kinds of motivational processes. In addition to the incentive conditions of the situation (e.g., perceived opportunities to attain certain goals), the motives aroused play a decisive role, determining the incentive values of the anticipated outcomes. Depending on the individual motive orientation, situations that appear similar to outside observers may seem radically different to the individual involved. For example, tasks of intermediate difficulty are an irresistible incentive for individuals with a strong achievement motive (high hope for success, low fear of failure), whereas individuals high in fear of failure tend to avoid them (Chapter 6). In other words, whether or not achievement incentives are equivalent in enticing behavior is entirely dependent on the individual's achievement motive. The same holds for other motives (Chapter 7 and Chapter 8).

SUMMARY
A person's motivation to pursue a certain goal is determined by situational stimuli, personal preferences, and the interaction of the two. The resultant motivational tendency is a composite of the various incentives associated with the activity, its outcome, and its internal (self-evaluative) and external consequences, each weighted according to the personal motive profile.

1.3 Motivational and Volitional Action Control

A resultant motivational tendency alone does not compel us to pursue the respective action goal. Before this can happen, the tendency resulting from the situational incentives and their personal evaluation must become an **intention**.

❶ Processes of intention formation determine which of the motivational tendencies that are present at any given time and that swell or subside depending on the specific situation and need state should gain access to action.

Without a superordinate instance to regulate the activation and deactivation of goal intentions, ordered sequences of behavior would be inconceivable. The strongest tendency to emerge at any given moment would be executed directly, causing the ongoing activity to be interrupted. It would be impossible to defer action until a suitable opportunity arises, to pursue a goal doggedly until it has been attained, to break intended actions down into consecutive steps, or indeed to delay gratification of the strongest resultant motivational tendency in favor of a weaker one for which the situation is relatively auspicious. Yet we know from experience that all this is possible, and that individual behavior is not at the mercy of fluctuating motivational processes or constantly changing resultant tendencies.

DEFINITION
Independent regulatory processes determine which motivational tendencies are implemented, at which opportunity, and in what manner. These processes are called "volition."

Motivation psychology, long neglected processes of volition (but see Lewin, Dembo, Festinger, & Sears, 1944), focuses almost exclusively on **motivation**, i.e., the setting or selection of goals. It was left to lay psychologists and the authors of self-help books to consider questions of goal realization or volition. In the early 1980s (Kuhl, 1983), however, the question of how goal implementation is regulated recaptured scientific interest (Halisch & Kuhl, 1986; H. Heckhausen, 1989; Heckhausen, Gollwitzer, & Weinert, 1987; Heckhausen & Kuhl, 1985), paving the way for modern **action-oriented volition research**, which constituted the framework for the development of the **Rubicon Model of action phases** (Chapter 11; H. Heckhausen, 1989), research on the mechanisms underlying **action intentions** (Chapter 11; Gollwitzer, 1999), and a comprehensive **personality psychology model of action regulation and self-regulation** (Chapter 12; Kuhl, 2000a, b).

The action-phase model, also known as the Rubicon model, serves as a useful framework model in research on volition, showing where the various functions of volitional processes come into effect within a sequence of behavior.

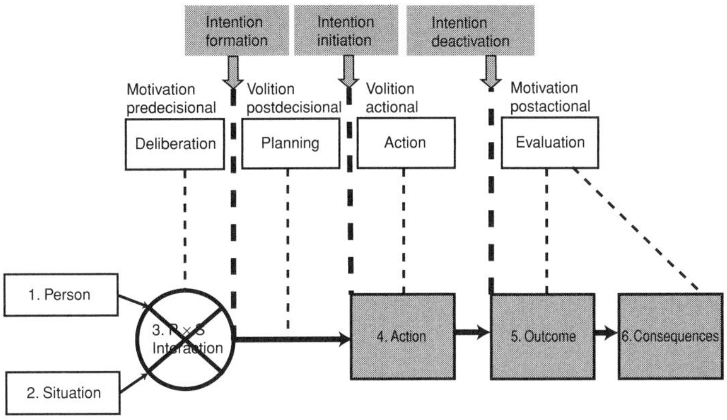

Figure 1.3 Integration of the action-phase model and the general model.

Fig. 1.3 shows the main action phases and their position in our overview model of motivation (see also Chapter 11, Fig. 11.1).

There are two important transitions as the individual moves from motivation to action:

■ The first transition is **intention formation**, which marks the shift from the motivational phase of **deliberation** on motivational tendencies to the volitional phases of **planning** and **action**. It is at this point that the individual determines which motivational tendencies are allowed to pass the threshold, i.e., to acquire the status of an intention that governs behavior as and when appropriate.

■ The second transition is from intention formation to the **initiation of action**, i.e., from the volitional phase of planning to that of acting. It is at this point that the individual determines which existing or newly formed intentions should gain access to action and be put into practice.

■ Once an action has been completed or abandoned, the intention is deactivated. The **deactivation of an intention** marks a third shift: from a volitional to a motivational phase that involves **evaluation** of the action, reflection on its success, and more particularly failure, and **causal attributions** (Chapter 14 "Causal Attribution of Behavior and Achievement").

❶ What is decisive about all of these transitions between different phases of action is that they are ideally discrete shifts rather than gradual changes. Diverse facets of motivational orientation are coordinated and act in concert to facilitate the functioning of each action phase. These motivational facets include conscious and nonconscious processes of attention control and information processing; cognitive processes of interpretation, causal attribution, and prediction; and social cognitive processes of goal and self-evaluation. (Chapter 11 "Motivation and Volition in the Course of Action")

Three major modes of action regulation can be differentiated, each with a specific profile regarding the various facets of action regulation (see following summary box).

Phases of Action Regulation in the Rubicon Model:

1. Goal selection in the predecisional phase before the Rubicon is crossed,

2. goal engagement (go mode) in the postdecisional phase and the action phase once the Rubicon has been crossed, and

3. goal disengagement or intention deactivation (stop mode) in the postactional phase, subsequently leading into a new cycle of action.

The predecisional and postactional phases are regarded as "motivational." Information processing during these phases should be open-minded and impartial, allowing the individual to draw balanced conclusions and make the best possible decisions. During the postdecisional and the actional phases, by contrast, a volitional orientation predominates, and information processing and evaluation are strongly biased in favor of the chosen alternative.

Not everyone is equally skilled at deploying the many facets of volitional regulation of behavior to their best advantage. There are marked **interindividual differences** in the ability (or inability, sometimes pathological) to orchestrate volitional and motivational self-regulation (Chapter 12), and in how these person factors coincide with situational opportunities across the life course (Chapter 15; see also the construct of "motivational competence," Rheinberg, 2002a; and Chapter 13, Section 13.6 and Chapter 15, Section 15.7.4). These individual styles of self-regulation and action control may be the product of early experiences of affective self-regulation. However, much time- and cost-intensive longitudinal studies are needed to identify the early origins of individual styles of self-regulation (Chapter 12, Section 12.6 and Chapter 15, Section 15.7).

SUMMARY

Motivational and volitional regulation of action alternate across an action cycle, thus ensuring a form of information processing that is appropriate to the functioning of each phase of action. Ideally, the transitions between the action phases are discrete and efficient. There are considerable individual differences in the ability to regulate motivation and volition, but research on their developmental origins is scarce.

1.4 Development of Motivation and Motivation of Development: The Dynamic Interaction of Person and Situation Across the Lifespan

The relationship between motivation and development across the lifespan (Chapter 15) can be seen from two perspectives: on the one hand, as the **development of motivation** (Chapter 15, Sections 15.2 to 15.7); on the other hand, as the **motivation of development** (Chapter 15, Section 15.8). In both cases, the regulation of human behavior is largely dependent on the individual capacity for **control** and its stability and change across the life course. The capacity to influence the environment (termed the potential for "primary control" in some conceptual contexts) undergoes radical change as an individual moves through the life course. Following the helplessness and dependence of infancy, the potential for control increases rapidly and universally in childhood and adolescence, plateaus out in adulthood, and declines gradually in old age. The motivational and volitional regulation of behavior must allow for these enormous changes in the potential for control across the lifespan.

The prerequisites for behavior directed at controlling external events are acquired in infancy and early childhood; e.g., generalized control expectancies, orientation toward an intended action goal, planning of steps to achieve that goal, and termination of behavior once it has been attained. The development of achievement-related emotions such as pride and shame imbue control-related behavior with a strong element of self-esteem, and make ambitious undertakings more attractive or (in the case of failure) more threatening. Evaluations of personal achievements and their anticipatory effects on achievement-motivated behavior are further elaborated when children become able to distinguish between task difficulty and their own competence, and indeed between ability, effort, and the combination of the two in predicting and explaining success and failure.

Over the course of this universal developmental process, children see themselves as increasingly competent agents, yet they remain quite dependent on the guidance and support of adult caregivers. Although research in this area is still scarce, there is evidence to indicate that the behavior of these reference persons and their relations to the growing child lay the foundations for interindividual differences in implicit motivational and volitional orientations. Developmental trajectories reach a major crossroads when children start school, where social frames of reference predominate. These may either coincide or conflict with children's implicit motivational orientations, and either promote or inhibit their motivation and development. To date, little is known about

the development of interindividual differences. However, the past two decades of research have shown that the cognitive prerequisites of achievement-motivated self-evaluation are only a small part of the puzzle. Future research must consider the affective dynamics of parent-child dyads and early experiences of control in these contexts.

❗ Investigating the motivation of development broadens our outlook on the development of motivation, opening up a dynamic, interactive perspective on the interaction between motivation and development.

It is only recently that the part individuals play in actively shaping their own development has become a topic of investigation, particularly in lifespan developmental research (Chapter 15, Section 15.8). The same questions might also have emerged from work on the development of motivation itself, which points to increasing levels of independence in the orchestration of action opportunities and developmental contexts. In adolescence and early adulthood, the individual might well have acquired sufficient potential for agency to play a decisive role in the selection of occupational and familial life paths. The question then arises as to what extent individuals remain "true" to these paths, and how much scope they have to shape them along the way. Recent research has shown that developmental goals can organize action cycles into phases of goal engagement and goal disengagement over the course of development, thus regulating the investment and withdrawal of resources. Apart from their long-term nature, these cycles of action have much in common with more short-term actions, and can also be examined within the framework of action-phase models. There is another important aspect, however. Individuals actively influence their environment over the course of development, thus creating their own developmental ecologies and opportunities for future action. Interindividual differences thus lead to increasingly divergent paths, for better or worse. A systems theoretical integration of person and situation across the lifespan can open up an integral perspective on this **dynamic interactionism**. It is not only in the here and now that the **dialectic interaction between person and environment** is operational, but also across the spatial and temporal differences in and effects of lifelong development.

SUMMARY

Research on the development of motivation and research on the motivation of development complement and enrich each other. Many universal developmental achievements in the motivational and volitional regulation of control behavior occur in early childhood and are closely tied to the support and guidance provided by adult caregivers. The active influence that individuals have on their personal development represents a continuation of the striving for control in childhood and adolescence, and gives the dialectic interaction between person and environment across the lifespan a truly dynamic quality.

REVIEW QUESTIONS

1. **What kind of questions does motivation psychology address?**

   Motivation psychology addresses the "whys" and "hows" of activities that reflect the pursuit of a particular goal.

2. **What are the universal characteristics of human behavior and how are they defined?**

   Striving for control: seeking and establishing behavior-event contingencies, or – to use the terminology of control theory – primary control of events in the material and social environment.

   Organizing action into phases of goal engagement and goal disengagement: perceptions, thoughts, emotions, skills, and activities are coordinated to facilitate either the attainment of goals (goal engagement) or disengagement from futile or unattainable goals.

3. **Which factors influence the resultant motivational tendency?**

   The resultant motivational tendency is influenced by personal preferences, situational incentives, and their mutual interaction. It is a composite of the various situational incentives residing in the activity, its outcome, and self- and other-evaluations, each weighted according to the personal motive profile.

4. **What is the difference between motivation and volition?**

   Motivation concerns processes of goal selection and goal setting. Volition concerns regulatory processes that determine which motivational tendencies are implemented, at which opportunity, and in what manner.

5. **How can the development of motivation be defined, in contrast to the motivation of development?**

   The development of motivation involves the development of a universal set of basic motivational modules and of individual differences in motivation. The motivation of development is the active influence that individuals have on their development across their lifespan.

2 Historical Trends in Motivation Research

H. Heckhausen

2.1 Introduction

Attempts to explain human behavior date back to the dawn of time. Questions relating to motives, motivation, and volition, as discussed in Chapter 1, have been addressed from various perspectives under different labels, and have prompted a variety of explanatory models. What is common to all these attempts is that they seek to establish the reasons for actions, their individual differences, and for the activation, control, and persistence of goal-oriented behavior. It would go beyond the scope of this chapter to review the intricate and involved history of this endeavor (see Bolles, 1975, for such a review). What Hermann Ebbinghaus (1850–1909) supposedly said about psychology, namely that it has a long past but a short history, applies equally to the study of motivation.

Once psychology became scientific, i.e., experimental, questions relating to motivation began to emerge in quite different contexts. Labels and definitions differed, reflecting the changing perspectives on the issues. The connotative content of concepts also changed with the biases and assumptions that dominated a particular era, however, increasing or decreasing their popularity. The nomenclature at the beginning of the last century is a case in point. At that time, the battle was between "motives" and "reasons" as directing the choice between alternative courses of behavior or as governing the emergence of a decision to do or not to do something. It was then that volition or "will" took effect to insure that an intention, once formed, would be followed up by the active pursuit of a goal. This applied particularly when resistance was to be overcome, be it in the form of countertendencies within the person or adverse environmental conditions. "Will" was often conceived as the guardian of moral norms and of duty, responsible for prevailing over "baser" tendencies such as "instinct," "drives," and "basic needs."

Just four or five decades later, completely new ideas and concepts had gained currency. Not only had the distinction between the morally good and reasonable on the one hand and the impassioned and impetuous on the other disappeared, but "will" had lost all credibility as a scientific concept. At the same time, "drives" and "needs" had lost their animalistic character and now applied to higher human striving as well.

Moreover, questions of motivation were now being addressed in many other psychological contexts going far beyond the explanation of actions and learning outcomes. "Motivation" was now seen to have explanatory value for apparently automated processes such as perception, imagination, and thought. This brought about the gradual development of the psychology of motivation as an independent field of research with its own concepts, methods, and theories.

At the beginning of the 20th century, motivational questions were still essentially centered on volition (decision making, choice behavior) and the volitional act (intentional behavior). "Motives" were merely seen as justifications for volitional decisions (James, 1890; Ach, 1910; Pfänder, 1911). It was not until 1936, with the publication of P. T. Young's *Motivation and Behavior* that the word "motivation" was first used in a book title. Now it was no longer volition that controlled access to and execution of an action, but needs and tendencies that were assumed to determine behavior in accordance with their strength. Just 20 years later, the numbers of monographs, reviews, and handbooks on questions of motivation had swelled, and continued to do so. With the annual "Nebraska Symposium of Motivation" (first published in 1953) at the forefront, handbooks include Koch (1959–1963) and Thomae (1965), and textbooks providing a more or less comprehensive coverage of the subject were published by Atkinson (1964a), Atkinson and Birch (1978), Bolles (1967, 1975), Cofer and Appley (1964), Madsen (1959, 1974), Heckhausen (1980), Weiner (1972, 1980), McClelland (1985b), and Winter (1996).

At present, the psychology of motivation is still far from being a coherent enterprise in terms of its issues, variables, methods, and theories. This makes it all the more important to trace the historical roots of contemporary research issues from their beginnings, more than a century ago. We start at the beginning of the last century, with a generation of pioneers who initiated many of the approaches that are still being pursued today. On this basis, we track individual strands of research, some with distinct but interconnecting branches, to the present state of the art.

2.2 The Generation of Pioneers

Traditionally, philosophy and theology have viewed humans as organisms endowed with reason and free will. This is what distinguishes us from animals, gives us dignity, and makes us responsible for our actions. This view of humankind leaves barely any scope for questions on the nature of human behavior. Humans are creatures of reason and therefore act rationally, in response to reasonable motives and legitimate values. Because humans are endowed with free will, it would be inappropriate and indeed pointless to explain their behavior in terms of external forces, be these within the environment or within the body. Admittedly, there may be some situations in which rational behavior and free-will decisions are encroached upon by "lower" motives or passions. Over the centuries, and with the development of scientific thought, this general idea of human behavior (of which our coverage here is very simplified) has been repeatedly called into question. Challenges have been raised by those who see human behavior as dependent on physical or physiological features of the organism, as well as by those who posit a hedonistic principle, i.e., behavior is driven by the organism's pursuit of pleasure and avoidance of displeasure. Yet the Cartesian distinction between humans and animals remained: animal behavior does not derive from reason or free will, but is driven by blind natural forces, i.e., instincts.

This dualistic view began to crumble with Darwin's book *The Origin of Species* (1859). According to Darwin (1809–1882), all differences in the physical characteristics and behaviors of organisms can be explained in terms of two principles:

- accidental variation and
- natural selection of the fittest.

Given that both of these principles were causally determined, it seemed reasonable to explain human behavior along deterministic lines as well, i.e., to attribute it purely to natural causes.

Roots in Evolutionary Theory

Aside from this breakthrough, which led to the long held notion of ontological differences between humans and animals being replaced by a deterministic view of human motivation and behavior, the three assumptions outlined below played a major role in the development of research on motivation.

INSTINCTS AND DRIVES. If there is no qualitative ontological difference between species of animals and humans, but rather a gradual progression, then explanations for animal behavior must have certain validity for human behavior as well.

This insight led to a search for the instincts and drives that motivate human behavior. For McDougall, instincts became the major explanatory concept. He published his first list of instincts in 1908, founding the **instinct theory approach** to the study of motivation, which is still reflected in ethology (Lorenz, Tinbergen) and contemporary sociobiology (Dawkins, 1976; Hamilton, 1964; Trivers, 1971). At the same time, Freud was attempting to elucidate apparently irrational phenomena such as the content of dreams (1900/1952) and the behavior of neurotic patients (1915/1952), which he attributed to hidden drives. In so doing, he became the founder of a major branch of the **personality theory** approach to motivation.

To the extent that humankind lost its special status in nature in the wake of evolutionary theory, it also lost its "free will." As a result, the concept of "will" fell out of favor in scientific circles, disappearing completely from the scientific parlance of most psychologists by the 1940s. Some, like Freud and McDougall were quick to accept the deterministic view engendered by Darwinian theory. Others continued to adhere to philosophical traditions and phenomenological approaches, and took another two or three decades to reach this point. This was the case in Germany, where there was a remarkable upswing in the psychology of the will after the turn of the last century.

ADAPTATION TO ENVIRONMENTAL CONDITIONS. Given that an organism's ability to adapt to a changing environment determines its fitness to survive and reproduce on the long term, human intelligence must be seen not as something unique, but as something that has evolved over millennia. Intelligence, i.e., the ability to learn from experience, must have a significant survival function, because it permits rapid adaptation to changed environmental conditions. This would mean that the species of animals still existing today must have rudimentary forms of intelligence.

This view was the basis for the development of comparative psychology in the 1880s, with its endeavors to identify and compare features of species-specific intelligence. Anecdotal observations and speculative comparisons gradually gave way to the systematic and experimental study of learning, pioneered by Thorndike (1874–1949). Thorndike conducted his first animal experiments in the basement of the home of his teacher, William James (Thorndike, 1898, 1911). James (1842–1910) was a remarkable mediator between the old and the new psychology. With his unequaled talent for introspection, he engaged in a phenomenological analysis of volitional acts, examining the role of consciousness. He retained the notion of free will, but held that humans were also endowed with a number of instincts. According to James, consciousness, which is uniquely human, evolved "for the sake of steering a nervous system grown too complex to regulate itself" (James, 1890, Vol. 1, p. 144).

James himself never experimented, but it was he who coined the term "habit," which was to become a central concept of associationist learning theories.

DEFINITION

The term "habit" implies an automated behavioral sequence; James held that these behaviors had, at one time, been under conscious control.

Darwin had already seen instinct as a kind of intelligence-like adaptive mechanism and as a particular case of natural selection. To be able to apply his second principle, accidental variation, to instincts, he considered them to be collections of individual reflex units. Very gradual changes and advances in these collections of reflexes thus became plausible, true to the theory of evolution. This meant that instincts in animal and human behavior no longer had to be seen as global entities. Rather, they could be analyzed in terms of objectifiable stimulus-response associations. The reflex arc subsequently became the basic element of behavior and, around the turn of the last century, the Russian physiologist Pavlov (English translation 1927) laid the foundations for another branch to the experimental study of learning beside Thorndike's. Both continue to influence the study of motivation.

Thorndike and Pavlov were founders of what has been called the **associationist approach** to motivation research. Both dealt with changes in stimulus-response associations. In Thorndike's work, earlier responses are replaced by more successful ones (instrumental or operant conditioning), whereas in Pavlov's approach, the stimuli that originally elicited a response are replaced by formerly neutral ones (classical conditioning).

❶ Thorndike founded the learning branch of the associationist approach to the study of motivation, while Pavlov founded its activation branch.

NATURAL SELECTION AND SURVIVAL OF THE FITTEST. The physical and behavioral characteristics that Darwin hypothesized to represent an advantage for natural selection are not just generalized characteristics specific to the species existing today. Within a species, there must always be individuals that are somewhat better equipped than others for the "fight for survival" under the prevailing environmental conditions.

This conclusion sparked an interest in individual differences and their diagnostic assessment.

Galton (1822–1911), a cousin of Darwin, carried out a number of studies related to heredity and eugenics. Along with the French researcher Binet (1857–1911), who developed the first intelligence test in the early 1900s, Galton founded the psychology of testing, a movement that developed independent of mainstream psychology, particularly in the United States. It was not until the 1930s that the testing movement began to influence the personality theory approach to motivation through the works of Allport (1937), Murray (1938), and Cattell (1950).

SUMMARY

These assumptions, which derived from and/or were supported by the theory of evolution, transformed the old psychology of the human will into a psychology of motivation that accounts for individual differences and that, to a broad degree, also applies to animals. Yet they also led to the psychology of will, which had enjoyed great popularity prior to World War I, being sidelined for some time.

Roots in Psychological Thought

The pioneer generation also advanced a long-established tradition – that of philosophical and psychological speculations about human will. Not only was this tradition relatively immune to Darwinism, it reached its apex at the turn of the last century with the formulation of numerous theories. Along with sensations, ideas, and feelings, there were attempts to establish "volition" as a psychological experiential phenomenon and to determine the effects of "will."

ANALYSIS OF VOLITIONAL PROCESSES IN CONSCIOUSNESS. The volitional act became a central theme for Wilhelm Wundt (1832–1920), the founder of experimental psychology. Wundt (1894) saw the volitional act as the organizing principle behind an individual's experience and actions, as a "psychological causality" to be distinguished from "physical causality," the laws of which were to be investigated by natural scientists.

The analysis of volitional processes through introspection and reaction-time studies led Wundt's contemporaries to espouse differing positions. Significant progress was made by members of the Würzburg school led by Oskar Külpe (1862–1915), a student of Wundt. Their analyses of thought processes failed to identify any conscious underlying processes. This led them to assume that there are unconscious attitudes and tendencies, generated by the task at hand, that control the cognitive processes without awareness, let alone voluntary control. Narziss Ach (1871–1946) interpreted this phenomenon in terms of a psychology of the will and, in 1905, coined the term "determining tendency" ("determinierende Tendenz").

❶ Narziss Ach and the Belgian researcher Albert Michotte (1881–1965), working independently, became the founders of an

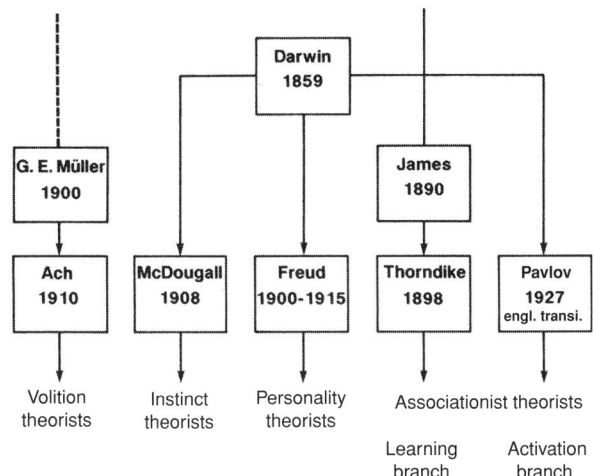

Figure 2.1 Strands contributing to motivation research in the pioneer generation at the turn of the last century. (Based on Madsen, 1974, p. 91.)

experimental psychology of the will. Regrettably, its popularity was short-lived, and it lay dormant for several decades before being revived more recently.

That completes the gallery of those who pioneered the study of motivation at the turn of the last century (for a similar overview, cf. Madsen, 1974). The five members of the pioneer generation are presented in Fig. 2.1:

- Ach, who initiated an experimental approach to the psychology of the will,
- McDougall, who founded the instinct theory approach,
- Freud, who created the conceptual foundation for personality theories,
- and Thorndike and Pavlov, the founders of the learning and the activation branch of the associationist approach.

These five approaches, only four of which have significantly influenced the study of motivation over the past 70 years, present a remarkably one-sided view of the subject. Comparison with the three major areas of motivational research – i.e., "motive," "motivation," and "volition" – shows that only "motivation" is covered in all five approaches. "Motives" are relevant only to the personality theory approach, and the "volition" aspect disappeared with the early demise of the experimental psychology of the will (though, to some extent, it resurfaced and survived elsewhere under different names and in different contexts; e.g., research on decision making). Darwin's theory of evolution cast doubt on the notion of humankind having a special status in nature and heralded a new, deterministic view of human behavior, which could then be studied by scientific methods. This focused attention on characteristics humans share with other species that had previously been overlooked, namely a dependence on the satisfaction of basic needs and the attendant necessity to learn, often under adverse conditions. These characteristics have

since been the subject of much research, as will be shown later. Moreover, motivation research has again begun to consider human capacities for volitional action, i.e., the psychology of the will. It will, however, take some time to make up for past neglect.

In the following, we will trace the individual strands of research and approaches to the study of motivation as they developed over the past century, highlighting the interconnections between them.

2.3 The Psychology of the Will

Since the works of Plato and Aristotle, it has been common practice to assume a triad of psychological functions, distinguishing between thinking, feeling, and willing or, in terms of their respective capacities:

- cognition,
- emotion, and
- motivation.

The functions are sometimes differentiated further – thinking, in particular, has been broken down into sensing, perceiving, and reasoning. Conversely, there have been repeated attempts to subsume willing – although it has always been acknowledged to be an undeniable and unique form of experience – to one of the other two members of the Platonic triad.

There have been few attempts to negate the existence of the will altogether. It was arguably the English empiricist David Hume (1711–1776) who went furthest along this path. Hume strived to avoid using metaphysical or a priori concepts to explain psychological functions, preferring instead to attribute all mental processes to impressions and ideas, and to the associations that link them. The principles of causality and substance seemed to obviate self-awareness and volition as explanatory concepts – these were in fact products of our imagination deriving from experience and association.

Heterogenetic Perspectives

"Heterogenetic" theories of the will were less radical. They did not deny the phenomenal existence of will, but attributed it to manifestations and entities beyond volition itself. Depending on the assumed source of volitional experiences, affective, ideational, sensory, and intellectual theories of the will can be identified. However, those who conceptualized volition as an independent entity, not attributable to other manifestations, were proponents of an "autogenetic" theory of the will.

At the turn of the last century, most psychologists took a heterogenetic position. It is no longer easy to see things from their perspective, but the assumption was that the essential elements of psychological functioning could be studied by means of trained **introspection**. The descriptive identification of what were assumed to be essential classes of experience, capable of being observed introspectively and communicated to others, appeared to be at least as important as the experimental analysis of conditions that permitted inferences to be drawn about underlying but nonobservable processes.

❗ Heterogenetic theories of the will arose from the endeavor to determine the nature of volitional acts by means of introspection alone.

For many, this approach was attractive because it did not require laborious experimentation. Assumptions could be derived from mere armchair speculations. For example, Herrmann Ebbinghaus (1850–1909), the celebrated founder of the experimental psychology of memory, was also a proponent of a heterogenetic affective theory of the will (Ebbinghaus, 1902). Münsterberg (1863–1916) and Wundt's student Külpe (1862–1915) considered sensations to be the basis for volitional experiences. Münsterberg (1888) held that willing consisted of muscular sensations that preceded expected movements. Külpe (1893) conceptualized willing as a "keen organic sensation."

An intellectual theory – today it would be called a cognitive theory – was proposed by Ernst Meumann (1862–1915), another of Wundt's students, who posited that:

> Will is no more than a specific course of intellectual processes, converting our assent to a goal into action. They permit the purely internal psychological experiences to become externalized operators on the environment (Meumann, 1913, p. 347; 1st ed. 1908).

Despite its antiquated terminology, Meumann's approach has much in common with modern notions. It has become increasingly popular to offer cognitive explanations for motivational phenomena and, since the "cognitive revolution" in psychology, efforts have been underway to derive dynamic processes of motivation and volition from the very associative network models that were originally postulated to explain the structure and application of knowledge (Anderson, 1983; Norman, 1980).

Meumann also identified two further points that were rediscovered by and are now emphasized by contemporary motivational psychology:

1. Different temporal aspects of the goal structures of actions: Awareness may focus on the immediate outcome of an action or on its subsequent consequences (the latter were long overlooked as motivational factors, cf. Vroom, 1964; Heckhausen, 1977b).

2. Actors' awareness of being the authors of their actions: The sense of responsibility became a cornerstone of attribution research (Weiner, Heckhausen, Meyer, & Cook, 1972).

To the grand master Wundt, however, volition was not a heterogenetic but an autogenetic phenomenon. For him,

all of the processes involved in what is now known as information processing were driven by volitional acts. This applied to aspects of attention and apperception, in particular, but also to perceptions, thoughts, and memories (Wundt, 1874, 1896; cf. the more recent coverage in T. Mischel, 1970).

SUMMARY

Wundt saw the volitional process as an independent synthesis of antecedent affects that were originally (i.e., in ontogenetic development) dissipated in pantomimic gestures. To this were added combinations of ideas and feelings that he called "motives." He labeled their ideational components "Beweggründe" (underlying reasons) and their affective components "Triebfeder" (driving forces). In other words, Wundt distinguished motivational from volitional processes; he attempted to infer the volitional process from its developmental origins.

Phenomenological Perspectives

While Wundt's volitional theory consists of highly abstract propositions, William James (1890) engaged in a phenomenological analysis of anecdotal material in an attempt to pinpoint the actual volitional act; i.e., the point at which a decision, a "fiat!" or an inner consensus terminates the "deliberative state," and from which point an action is determined by just one of the alternatives available. James was almost surprised to find that it is not always necessary for this point to be reached; sometimes the mental representation of an action is enough to trigger it.

The classic example of getting up on a cold winter's morning illustrates how this **ideomotoric principle** seems to obviate the need for a volitional act.

William James gave an example of the ideomotoric principle from everyday life:

> **EXAMPLE**
>
> If I may generalize from my own experience, we more often than not get up without any struggle or decision at all. We suddenly find that we **have** got up. A fortunate lapse of consciousness occurs; we forget both the warmth and the cold; we fall into some revery concerned with the day's life, in the course of which the idea flashed across us, "Hello! I must lie here no longer" – an idea which at that lucky instant awakens no contradictory or paralyzing suggestions, and consequently produces immediately its appropriate motor effects (James, 1890, pp. 1132-1133).

As convincing as this example of the efficacy of the ideomotoric principle may seem, it does not in fact concern a volitional act, but merely the point in time at which an unquestioned act (getting out of bed on a winter's day) is carried out. Nevertheless, the example points to the existence of something that may govern volitional processes, to a "metavolition"; namely, triggering the execution of an intended action by activating a mental representation. James even presupposes the existence of metamotivations when he postulates that the deliberative motivational process, i.e., the weighing up of two alternative courses of action, is controlled by two opposing tendencies:

1. the "impatience of the deliberative state" and
2. the "dread of the irrevocable."

Beyond this, James identified five types of decisions that mark the point at which the motivational state ends and volition begins. He saw one type associated with the feeling of effort, when all avenues had been explored and considered and the balance was perceived as equal, but a decision had to be made. Because James, unlike his contemporaries in Germany, was not interested in determining the essence of volition, but rather in finding typical situations in which "will" could play a useful explanatory role, he explored all relevant areas of motivational research:

- motivation,
- intention formation, and
- volition.

The study of volitional phenomena evidently remained purely descriptive for such a long time because it was difficult to imagine that manifestations of "higher" mental processes could be studied experimentally, in the same way as perception and memory.

Approaches to an Experimental Psychology of Volition

The late 19th and early 20th century saw three separate approaches to the experimental study of volition. The first two concerned the conceptualization of two different courses of action within a theory of volition. One involved simple reaction-time experiments (L. Lange, 1888; Külpe, 1893), the second addressed processes of association when a specific task was imposed (Müller & Pilzecker, 1900; Ach, 1905, 1910). The third approach involved the experimental induction of a volitional act, with participants having to choose between two possible implementations of an intention (Michotte & Prüm, 1910).

REACTION-TIME EXPERIMENTS. Although not intended to address volition as such, many early endeavors in experimental psychology in the areas of perception, imagination, learning, and thought had a volitional character in terms of the task-centered activities of the respondent. Boring, in his *History of Experimental Psychology* (1929), lists 12 explanatory concepts developed by the psychologists of the era to account for the volitional nature of experimental tasks. These include:

- attention,
- expectation,
- preparation,
- predisposition,
- "Einstellung" (set),
- "Aufgabe" (instruction),

- predetermined, determining tendency (along with G. E. Müller's associative and perseverative tendencies).

In the last three decades of the 19th century, reaction-time experiments were very much in vogue. They were prompted by the discovery of the "personal equation," i.e., individual differences in the timing of stellar transit across the reticle of a telescope. These differences between observers had raised concerns among astronomers, generated much research, and led to the development of new observational methods. It emerged that the original eye-and-ear method (ear to hear the ticking of a clock) involved a "complication," i.e., a mental confounding of the two sensory systems. With this in mind, F. C. Donders (1862), a physiologist from the Netherlands, returned to the study of simple reactions, and complicated these by the successive addition of other mental processes, e.g., by giving two stimuli, each of which required a different response. The lengthened reaction time observed in the two-stimulus condition relative to the single-stimulus condition was attributed to the additional mental process involved – in this case, choice. This "subtractive" procedure led to large-scale studies of "mental chronometry" in Wundt's laboratory. Notably, these procedures have regained currency in contemporary cognitive psychology, where they are used for the analysis of information processing.

In 1888, Ludwig Lange, one of Wundt's students, ran the first experiment in volitional psychology, though without being aware of the fact. His respondents were instructed to attend either to a stimulus or to its motor response. It emerged that reaction times are shorter when attention is focused on the motor response than when it is directed to the stimulus. Wundt speculated that this difference between "muscular" and "sensory" response time arose because in the latter case the stimulus is not just perceived, but also apperceived (interpreted). The temporal difference in favor of the muscular reaction was thought to reflect the duration of the apperception process, namely about 0.1 s. **Mental chronometry** based on Donders' "subtractive procedures" sparked some controversy, however. Külpe (1893) joined in the fray shortly before moving to Würzburg. He aimed to demonstrate that each task imposed results in a corresponding predisposition that determines the focus of the respondent's attention in Lange's experiment, thereby initiating a different process. According to Külpe, the resultant process is an integrated one that is not analyzable in terms of isolated components that can simply be added or subtracted.

❶ Külpe's explanation was thus in line with volitional theory, suggesting that a goal, once accepted by the respondent, governs task-related activities even in those areas that are not, or not directly, under volitional control.

THE WÜRZBURG SCHOOL. A similar conceptualization was apparent in the primary research endeavor of the Würzburg school, namely the introspective analysis of thought

EXCURSUS

Experimental Approaches to Thought Processes

H. J. Watt (1905), a member of the Würzburg school, made a remarkable discovery. His respondents were asked to form associations between nouns (e.g., "bird") and superordinates (e.g., "animal") or subordinates (e.g., "sparrow"). The subsequent introspection was then divided or "fractionated" into four time periods. Oddly enough, it was the third period, the search for the reaction word, that yielded least content, i.e., the least awareness. Watt concluded that the actual intent of an activity remains in awareness only so long as the respondent is taking the experimental instructions on board. After that, the impact of an intention on the cognitive process is unconscious and automatic. In his interpretation of the ideational process in association experiments, Georg Elias Müller (1850–1934) had already postulated a "perseverating tendency" in addition to purely associative tendencies. The adoption of a task results in a corresponding "Einstellung" (set).

Narziss Ach (1905, 1910), who began his research career in 1900 with G. E. Müller in Göttingen and moved to Würzburg in 1904, coined the term "determining tendency," which was also adopted by Watt and other investigators of thought processes, e.g., Otto Selz (1913). It incorporated the concept of "perseverating tendency" introduced by Ach's teacher G. E. Müller. Using reaction-time measures and "systematic experimental introspection" (subtly directed retrospection), Ach (1905) showed that determining tendencies below the level of conscious awareness must be at work in the implementation of an intended goal, and that this holds for both mental and motor tasks.

Ach's (1910) attempt to measure volitional strength also proved to be of great significance. In his ingenious experiment, the associative strength of pairs of syllables, which was varied by manipulating the frequency of presentation, was rivaled by a new instruction for a contrasting task (a different combination of syllables). This meant that a volitional tendency (to carry out the new instruction) competed with an established habit. A triumph of the determining tendency to execute the new task would mean that "associative equivalence" had been reached. In other words, the volitional strength would outweigh the previously established associative strength. The reaction times in this rivalry condition were longer, and there were occasional response errors. In some cases, these errors induced respondents to renew their intention to carry out the task imposed. Ach analyzed this post hoc renewal of the intention and proposed that the "primary volitional act" comprises four elements including a self-reference; e.g., "I really want to do it!"

Selz (1910) was quick to note that Ach had not investigated the original volitional act, but a post hoc renewal of the intention in the face of unsuccessful attempts at its implementation. Nevertheless, the characteristics identified by Ach do seem to provide insight into the components of an intention or determining tendency that direct action. Ach also discovered some volitional metaprocesses (to use modern terminology) using this method of introspection.

---

processes. Here it was not only discovered that much of the thought process is beyond our conscious experience, but also that the process must run an orderly course as the solution to the task set manifests itself directly (see the excursus above).

Narziss Ach was concerned only with volitional processes and paid no heed to motivational issues. There is no doubt that he pioneered the experimental study of volition. Unfortunately, however, this research program withered even within his lifetime. A major contributor to its demise was Kurt Lewin (1890–1947), a young member of the Gestalt school at Berlin, which was founded by Wolfgang Köhler (1887–1967) and Max Wertheimer (1880–1943). In his dissertation, Lewin replicated Ach's attempt at measuring volitional strength, but changed the procedure slightly to show that the mere associative coupling of pairs of syllables as a function of repeated presentation does not give rise to a reproduction tendency unless there is an independent determining tendency to reproduce.

The dispute between Ach and Lewin, which was continued in the works of some of Ach's students, is extremely complex, but soon lost its relevance to research and remains unresolved to this day. A decisive factor in all of this was Lewin's (1926b) influential paper on "Intent, Volition, and Need," in which he expanded productively on several aspects of Ach's volitional act, such as the mental representation of an oppor-

tunity for action and the steps in its implementation,. For Lewin, however, the psychological character of an intention consists of a "quasi need" that derives from "genuine needs." With this, the defined goals of individual intentions became variably objectifiable and generalizable motivational goals (H. Heckhausen, 1987c), and questions of volition became questions of motivation. Of course, these were already dominating the other approaches in motivational research.

That did not keep Lewin and his students from developing a number of experimental paradigms for a psychology of action and emotion. These paradigms were more suited to the study of volitional questions than to motivational issues, and their utility in this respect has by no means been exhausted. They include:

- the retention and resumption of interrupted tasks (Zeigarnik, 1927; Ovsiankina, 1928),
- the discharge value of completing a substitute activity (Lissner, 1933; Mahler, 1933), and
- the forgetting of intentions (Birenbaum, 1930).

THE LEUWEN SCHOOL. This final approach to the experimental investigation of volition was founded by a Belgian, Albert Michotte. In 1905, and again in 1906, Michotte spent a semester with Wundt in Leipzig. In the two years following the 1906 meeting of the German Psychological Society in Würzburg, he spent several months at Külpe's institute, where he was introduced to Ach's work and indeed to the whole of contemporary German thought, which came as a "revelation" to him (Michotte, 1954). In 1908, Michotte and E. Prüm had concluded a lengthy experimental study on volitional choices ("choix volontaire"), the results of which were not published until 1910 because they first had to be translated from German (Prüm's mother tongue) into French. This meant that the Michotte and Prüm monograph appeared – coincidentally and entirely independently – in the same year (1910) as Ach's analysis of the volitional act. In contrast to Ach's post hoc analysis, the Belgian studies succeeded in analyzing the volitional act while it was happening. Admittedly, the actual intention – to follow the experimenter's instructions – had again been formed much earlier. However, there was still a choice to be made between two possible means of implementing each task, as quickly as possible and based on "serious motives."

Once the decision was made, and without waiting for its implementation, there was detailed introspection on the 4–5 seconds in which the choice had been made. The authors found a certain regularity in the sequence of processes:

- a motivation to weigh up the alternatives,
- an inhibition or pause prior to the decision,
- a resolution of the expectancy and muscle tensions once the decision had replaced doubt with certainty and, above all, with a conscious awareness of the action planned.

The authors viewed the latter as the defining characteristic of a volitional act.

Unfortunately, Michotte did not continue his studies on volition (see his overview of 1912); his later research focused on the study of **phenomenal causality**. The tradition of Michotte's and Ach's volitional psychology was continued in England by F. Aveling (1875–1941), who began his research career at Michotte's laboratory. Evidently the only scholar to work in the field of volition outside continental Europe, Aveling (1926) continued the introspective analysis of volitional acts. For him, a crucial feature was in the identification of the self with the motives for the preferred action alternative. For the most part, his work substantiated the findings of Ach and Michotte.

In the USA, volitional issues surfaced only periodically after their phenomenological heyday in the writings of William James. Even then, they emerged in behavioristic contexts in works such as F. W. Irwin's (1971) *Intentional Behavior and Motivation – A Cognitive Theory*. Here, Irwin gives a stringent explanation of how an observer with knowledge about a situation, an act, and its outcome, is able to predict the choice of an act, and hence to infer the intention of the actor. In an essay entitled "From Acts to Dispositions," Jones and Davis (1965) proceeded in an analogous manner, analyzing the mental logic used by an observer of specific acts to infer not intentions, but personality dispositions, i.e., to attribute motives to the actor (Chapter 14).

In Germany, Johannes Lindworsky (1875–1939) collated the findings of volitional research (1923, 3rd ed.). Based on his own observations and on a reanalysis of Ach's findings he, like Selz (1910), doubted that the intensity of a volitional act could enhance the implementation of an intention. Instead, he suggested that what is crucial is keeping the imposed task in mind while it is being executed, and not "squeezing out" a forced intention (Lindworsky, 1923, p. 94).

Three other students of Ach deserve to be mentioned here: Hillgruber, Düker, and Mierke. Hillgruber (1912) discovered what he called the "difficulty principle of motivation," which relates to the implementation of volition during the execution of a task. He found that increasing the difficulty level of a task (in terms of the speed of presentation of syllables to be reversed) increased the number of correct responses. Hillgruber attributed these findings to greater volitional tension. Düker (1931, 1975) reported similar findings, which he held to reflect a "reactive increase in tension."

Locke's more recent goal-seeking theory (1968; Locke & Latham, 1990) also relates to these volitional issues. According to this theory, it is only an apparent paradox that higher goal-setting leads to improved performance. Finally, in 1955, Mierke published a book with the term "will" in the title: *Wille und Leistung* or "Will and Performance."

That was to be the last usage of the term for some time to come. Times have changed once more, however (Chapters 11 and 12), and the terms "will" and "volition" are now acceptable again. Kuhl (1983) found individual differences in the ability to protect an intention that is being implemented against competing intentions or against a subsequent preoccupation with an unsuccessful outcome. He subsumed the processes involved under the term "action control." This signaled a return of the "determining tendency," if not of the volitional act itself, to psychological research. The Würzburg school's work on volition has also made a comeback. It covers aspects such as:

- the "volitional act,"
- the formation of an intention,
- the transition from the motivational to the volitional phase, and
- the initiation of the intended action.

2.4 The Instinct Theory Approach

William James adopted the term instinct as an explanatory concept, but limited it to a particular class of behaviors, which he differentiated from behaviors such as emotion, habit formation, and volitional acts. He defined instinct as

DEFINITION

"the faculty of acting in such a way as to produce certain ends, without foresight of the ends, and without previous education in the performance" (James, 1890, Vol. II. p. 383).

He emphasized the stimulus conditions, which owing to built-in neural structures within the organism, trigger an automated behavioral sequence that is not learned or based on a goal expectation. This compulsive, automatic response to particular situational conditions is vividly described in James's famous description of a broody hen:

> To the broody hen the notion would probably seem monstrous that there should be a creature in the world to whom a nestful of eggs was not the utterly fascinating and precious and never-to-be-too-much-sat-upon object which it is to her (James, 1890, Vol. II, p. 387).

In contrast to James, Wundt's view of instinct remained largely unaffected by Darwin. Wundt (1896) closely linked instinct with drive, and drive with goal-directed behavior. For him, instinctive behaviors derived from previously volitional behaviors that had, at some point, become mechanized.

The Pioneer of Instinct Theory

It was, however, the Anglo-American William McDougall (1871–1938) who pioneered the instinct theory approach within the study of motivation. At the start of his career he was influenced by European psychology, with its introspective analyses of volitional phenomena, as well as by the Darwinian revolution, with its focus on the heredity of behavioral characteristics. His assessment of the relative merits of each approach laid the foundations for Anglo-American motivation research in the 20th century. In his influential work *Introduction to Social Psychology* (1908), which, despite its title, addressed the psychology of motivation, and of which there were more than 30 editions, he argued against the European volitional perspective, and in favor of an approach based on instinct theory. This cleared the path for the study of motivation and blocked off the volitional route. In the introduction to his 1908 book he wrote:

> I will merely sum up on the issue of the work of the nineteenth century as follows: – During the last century most of the workers in the social sciences were in two parties – those on the one hand who with the utilitarians reduced all motives to the search for pleasure and the avoidance of pain, and those on the other hand who, recoiling from the hedonistic doctrine, sought the mainspring of conduct in some vaguely conceived intuitive faculty, instinct, or sense. Before the close of the century the doctrines of both of these parties were generally seen to be fallacious; but no satisfactory substitute for them was generally accepted, and by the majority of psychologists nothing better was offered to fill the gap than a mere word, "the will," or some such phrase as "the tendency of ideas of self realization." On the other hand, Darwin, in the *Descent of Man* (1871) first enunciated the true doctrine of human motives, and showed how we must proceed, relying chiefly upon the comparative and natural history method, if we would arrive at a fuller understanding of them. (McDougall, 1908, p. 14).

McDougall did not completely ignore volition, however. In fact, he devoted an entire chapter to it. He maintained that humans are not mere victims of hedonism, as Darwinian theory dictates, but that they experience conflicts of motives. In his debates with Wundt and James, McDougall rejected the notion of the inhibition of one of two competing motives as the principle underlying volitional decision making. Instead, he proposed that one of the motives is strengthened or reinforced by an impulse deriving from the motive system or the "system of self-regarding sentiment." Applied to the problem of decision making, he defined:

DEFINITION
volition as the supporting or re-enforcing of a desire or connotation by the cooperation of an impulse excited within the system of the self-regarding sentiment (McDougall, 1908, p. 249).

In attributing decision making to a self-regarding motive, McDougall's perspective was consistent with one of the central notions of the volitional psychology of Ach and Michotte, namely the ego- or self-involvement of the process. This was and remained the only point of contact between the two approaches, however. The manifold psychologies of the "self" that have since developed and come to play an important role tend to be seen in terms of motivational and not volitional processes.

McDougall remained fundamentally dissatisfied with the era's introspective studies of consciousness. He wanted to investigate what people actually do, based on sound phylogenetic principles that for him were the instincts, which he defined as follows:

DEFINITION
an inherited or innate psycho-physical disposition which determines its possessor to perceive, and to pay attention to, objects of a certain class, to experience an emotional excitement of a particular quality upon perceiving such an object, and to act in regard to it in a particular manner or, at least, to experience an impulse to such action (McDougall, 1908, p. 25).

To break down this rather complex explanatory construct:
- instincts are innate,
- they have an energizing and piloting function,
- they consist of an ordered sequence of predispositional processes of perceptual processing (cognitive),
- emotional arousal (affective), and
- a readiness to act (conative).

McDougall began by compiling a list of 12 instincts, which he later expanded (see also Chapter 3). He no longer called them "instincts," but "propensities," the defining components of which were less fixed. He thus avoided giving the impression that they are simply highly stereotypical sequences of behavior. What remained was essentially a goal-directed behavioral tendency:

DEFINITION

A propensity is a disposition, a functional unit of the mind's total organization, and it is one which, when it is excited, generates an active tendency, a striving, an impulse or drive towards some goal (McDougall, 1932, p. 118).

THE INSTINCT CONTROVERSY. This work had been preceded by the so-called instinct controversy of the 1920s, one of the few great public controversies in psychology. McDougall's main opponent was J. B. Watson who, as early as 1913, proposed that psychological research should be restricted to phenomena that are objectively observable and can be intersubjectively validated. McDougall's instinct theory had led many psychologists to explain all kinds of behavior in terms of particular instincts. In 1924, Bernard searched the literature for hypothesized "instincts" and found no less than 14,046! It goes without saying that this expansion of the concept turned it into a circuitous construct with very little explanatory value.

McDougall had resisted such expansions – his final list encompassed no more than 18 "propensities" (1932). After a few years, the public lost interest in the instinct controversy, without any clear verdict having been reached (cf. Krantz & Allen, 1967).

SUMMARY

McDougall strongly influenced two other important approaches to the study of motivation:

- First, the strand of research based on personality theories. His lists of instincts or propensities played a key role in endowing personality with motive-like dispositional variables. This was especially apparent in the trait theories of Allport (1937), Philipp Lersch (1938) in Germany, and in H. A. Murray's (1938) formulations, which significantly influenced the development of an approach in motivational research based on personality theory.
- Second, McDougall's work was the direct precursor of a strand of research that focused on the analysis of instinctive behavior and eventually evolved into the study of comparative behavior or ethology.

Forerunners of Ethology

The credit for instigating the study of comparative behavior goes to Konrad Lorenz (1937, 1943), who criticized McDougall's instinct theory for its vague definitions, and instead defined instinctive behavior as limited to a hereditary response sequence, i.e., to the invariant links in a chain of goal-directed behaviors that culminate in a terminal response. This final link, which manifests the actual instinctive behavior, is driven solely by the central nervous system. Triggered by an **innate releaser mechanism**, it is not flexible or modifiable in any way. The antecedent links are still oriented toward the situational context. The earlier they occur in the chain, the more likely they are to be modifiable through

learning. This applies particularly to the preliminary phase of "general activation."

Certain instinctive behaviors (such as the following response in ducklings and goslings) can become imprinted to arbitrary objects if the organism is exposed to these during a short critical period early in its ontogenetic development.

Intensive research efforts were focused on identifying the key stimuli that elicit a certain instinctive behavior in a given species. If these key stimuli are absent over a long period of time, the instinctive behavior may begin without external releasers, in what is known as "idling behavior."

EXAMPLE

The example of a duckling's following response illustrates two aspects of instinctive behavior:

- first, that it is highly stereotyped and not dependent on experience,
- second, that the releaser mechanisms involve internal processes that are subject to critical periods of readiness.

The latter observation led Lorenz (1950) to postulate a kind of "psychohydraulic" model of motivation that resembled Freud's (1895) early conceptualizations. Lorenz assumed that each instinct is powered by an action-specific energy, which is regenerated on an ongoing basis and stored in a reservoir. If the instinctive behavior has not occurred for some time, the reservoir overflows, i.e., the behavior is produced in the absence of the external stimuli (idling behavior).

Nikolaus Tinbergen (like Lorenz, winner of the 1973 Nobel Prize for Medicine), who systematically extended Lorenz's approach, defined instinct in the following terms:

DEFINITION

I will tentatively define an instinct as an hierarchically organized nervous mechanism which is susceptible to certain priming, releasing and directing impulses of internal as well as of external origin, and which responds to these impulses by coordinated movements that contribute to the maintenance of the individual and the species (Tinbergen, 1951, p. 112).

In this definition, a "nervous mechanism" is contrasted with an "impulse" that functions to activate the instinct, i.e., to motivate the behavior.

Although contemporary ethology is beyond the scope of the psychology of motivation, it has again gained increasing attention among motivation researchers, owing to two factors in particular:

1. Its criticism of learning theorists' laboratory experiments, in which animals are placed in artificial environments, rather than in natural ecological ones.

2. Its attempts to apply various ethological findings to human behavior (Eibl-Eibesfeldt, 1973, 1984).

Lorenz's (1966) attempt to apply an instinct-theoretical conceptualization of aggression to humans encountered most criticism from motivation psychologists. Based on his psychohydraulic model of instinct energy, Lorenz postulated that a kind of aggressive energy is constantly being produced within an organism. This energy can build up to dangerous levels unless given occasional opportunities to dissipate in the form of harmless substitute activities.

A more detailed description of instinct theories in ethology can be found in Cofer and Appley (1964), Eibl-Eibesfeldt (1975), Hess (1962), and Hinde (1974). Boyce (1976) presents a critical assessment of Darwin's influence on ethological research under natural conditions and of laboratory research on animals.

Contemporary ethology attempts to explain the relationships between observed situational and behavioral variables by means of neurophysiological constructs or models – in part, with theoretically neutral characteristics in terms of systems theory.

2.5 Personality Theories

This tradition of motivation research addresses the issues solely from the perspective of human psychology. Motivation tends to be seen either as a key domain within which to describe and gain a deeper understanding of personality as such, or as a source for explaining differences between individuals. Yet it can also be seen as a process that can explain actual behavior in terms of individual differences. This is the approach characteristic of motivational psychology as well as cognitive psychology.

The Father of Psychoanalysis

Freud (1856–1939) has already been identified as the pioneer of this approach. He was concerned with explaining apparently unfathomable behaviors by means of clinical observation and procedures designed to elicit and interpret unusual thought processes. Freud was convinced that hidden, unconscious processes guide behavior and influence conscious thought. He considered psychodynamic conflicts to be reflected in unconscious drives, and assumed the fragmentary and indirect manifestation of these drives in behavior and conscious experience to be the key to understanding behavior (see the excursus on p. 21).

Freud applied his analysis of hysteria and other neuroses in many ways, not only to identify the effects of unconscious processes, but also to tap into them directly, to "bring them into consciousness." At first he used hypnosis, later the interpretation of dreams (1900/1952) and free association. Most of all, however, he engaged in ingenious means-end speculations. Like the behavioral psychologists, Freund attempted to identify relationships between antecedent conditions and subsequent manifestations by postulating various hypothetical mediating processes as explanatory concepts (a task that

Freud approached with great flexibility and remarkable openness to continuous self-correction). It was not until 1915 that Freud formulated a comprehensive theory of motivation in his monograph "Instincts and their Vicissitudes," although the roots of this work can be found in "Project for a Scientific Psychology," published in 1895. According to Freud, what the "psychic apparatus" has to contend with are not external, but internal stimuli. Unlike external stimuli, the latter cannot be avoided, because they arise within the organism itself. The organism has manifold needs that result in continuous production and accumulation of drive stimuli, and this accumulated potential has to be discharged on an ongoing basis.

"The nervous system is an apparatus which has the function of getting rid of the stimuli that reach it, or of reducing them to the lowest possible level; or which, if it were feasible, would maintain itself in an altogether unstimulated condition" (Freud, 1915, p. 213).

THE DRIVE REDUCTION MODEL. Freud's theory of motivation represents a drive reduction model. It has much in common with the conceptual model of ethology outlined earlier and, as we will see, forms the basis for the learning branch of the associationist approach to the study of motivation. The drive reduction model incorporates homeostatic and hedonistic ideas. The lower the accumulated drive-stimulus level, the closer the organism comes to equilibrium. Reductions are accompanied by pleasurable sensations, while increases bring about displeasure. Thus, the activity of the psychic apparatus becomes subject to the pleasure-displeasure principle.

Drive, for Freud, is an instance of mind-body dualism, combining the organismic (i.e., energy) with the psychological (i.e., affect) in the form of a mental representation. Furthermore, he differentiates four aspects in every manifestation of a drive:

> If we now apply ourselves to considering mental life from a biological point of view, an "instinct" appears to us as a concept on the frontier between the mental and the somatic, as the psychical representative of the stimuli originating from within the organism and reaching the mind, as a measure of the demand made upon the mind for work in consequence of its connection with the body.
>
> We are now in a position to discuss certain terms which are used in reference to the concept of an instinct – for example, its "pressure," its "aim," its "object" and its "source."
>
> By the "pressure" (Drang) of an instinct we understand its motor factor, the amount of force or the measure of the demand for work which it represents....
>
> The "aim" (Ziel) of an instinct is in every instance satisfaction, which can only be obtained by removing the state of stimulation at the source of the instinct....
>
> The "object" (Objekt) of an instinct is the thing in regard to which or through which the instinct is able to achieve its aim. It is the most variable part of an instinct and is not originally

EXCURSUS

Exploring the Unconscious

Freud was committed to Darwin's biological-empirical determinism, which he saw confirmed by the success of medical science at the time. He rejected the popular notion that mental processes could be investigated by the introspective analysis of mental content. For him, the task was to identify in humans the vital biological drive dynamics that underlie manifest behaviors in all organisms. These he saw as the actual psychological processes operating in a continuous cause-and-effect relationship that, to him, was the unconscious. Examination of the stream of consciousness reveals that unconscious processes are not the exception to the rule, but that the reverse is true. Con-scious mental contents are fragmentary derivatives of the continuous activity of the unconscious. For Freud, all this was the result not of passive reactions to external impressions, but of an active orienting within the organism, its forces and conflicts. If he was influenced by any contemporary school of psychology, it was that of Brentano, whose lectures he had attended in Vienna and who, in contrast to Wundt, saw mental "acts" as characterized by directed intentionality. Incidentally, this was also a position increasingly espoused by the Würzburg school, resulting in controversy between that group and Wundt.

connected to it, but becomes assigned to it only in consequence of being peculiarly fitted to make satisfaction possible . . .

By the "source" (Quelle) of an instinct is meant the somatic process which occurs in an organ or part of the body and whose stimulus is represented in mental life by an instinct (Freud, 1915, pp. 214–215).

Freud viewed mental life as a process of dynamic conflict. In this regard, he was influenced by dualistic principles – an influence that is also reflected in his attempts to solve the problem of classifying motives. He did not attempt to evolve an exhaustive catalog of motives, but kept a decision pending. In 1915, he contrasted ego- or self-preservation drives (e.g., the need for nourishment) with the sexual drives (libido). Later, influenced by World War I, he replaced the former by aggression drives. Nevertheless, his main research interest remained the sexual drives, which he conceptualized in a very broad sense. In his final works he postulated an antagonism between life instincts ("Eros") and death instincts ("Thanatos").

Other major aspects of Freud's drive theory that have influenced more recent work on motivation include the following:

1. Drive impulses become manifest in different ways. If there is high drive intensity without an appropriate object for its satisfaction, the unfulfilled desires continue to take effect by manifesting themselves in consciousness in the form of mental images of earlier drive satisfactions. This notion later had a determining influence on the development of procedures for the assessment of motives (Murray, 1938; McClelland, Atkinson, Clark, & Lowell, 1953). Drive impulses can also be diverted to other objects, they can be sublimated (i.e., directed to nonsexual goals) or suppressed. In the later case, they can influence experience (e.g., in dreams) or behavior (e.g., slips of the tongue or neurotic behavior) in ways that are difficult to decipher.

2. Freud views mental life as a constant conflict between contradictory tendencies within the individual. He proposes a three-level structure of the psyche, in which the pleasure-seeking "id" is subject to the moral control of the "superego," and the reality-oriented "ego" seeks to mediate between the two.

3. The adult personality is an outcome of drives and their vicissitudes in childhood. Interference in drive development, particularly in early childhood, can have very negative effects on an individual's "capacity to work and love." Psychoanalytic therapies make it possible to access the causes of these developmental disturbances and to "rework" them.

4. Drives develop through a number of psychosexual stages, sequentially focused on specific erogenous zones (areas around various body cavities that are sensitive to pleasure) that dominate the pleasure seeking of that stage and provide for its satisfaction. The order is as follows:

- the mouth (oral phase: sucking, swallowing, biting),
- the anus (anal phase: excretion), and
- the genitals (phallic and genital phase: masturbation, homosexual and heterosexual relations).

Drive development can become fixated at any stage. Confronted with traumatic events, it may also revert to an earlier stage (regression).

5. Drive development evolves from a three-person drama involving a married couple and an outsider. The child is cast in the latter role, wanting to become sexually involved with the opposite-sex parent and feeling threatened by the same-sex parent (Oedipus complex). Normally, this conflict is resolved through identification with the parent of the same sex. Thus, even in early childhood there is internalization of moral norms (represented in the parent of the same sex) leading to the formation of conscience (superego) as a controlling authority within the personality structure.

The three last points – the significance of early childhood experiences, the vicissitudes of drive development, and the socializing effects of interactions between family members – continue to influence both theory and research on personality development and the genesis of motives. Since Freud, the descriptive analysis of static components has been supplemented by a dynamic-emotive approach covering processes of development. This approach has affected the study of motivation in many ways. Rapaport (1959, 1960) provides a detailed assessment of its contributions. Toman (1960) expanded the psychoanalytic theory of motivation, focusing on the periodicity and the developmental and biographical aspects of motivational phenomena.

Of course, psychoanalysis was not the only theory of personality at the beginning of the last century. Within "academic psychology," as psychoanalysts called it, there was, for example, Ach's (1910) rather premature identification of personality types, based on the individual differences he observed in his experiments on volition.

Kurt Lewin's Field Theory

A far more productive and influential personality theorist was Kurt Lewin (1890–1947), who focused not on individual differences but on broader psychological principles. Lewin began his critical evaluation of Ach's analysis of volition in his dissertation. In 1926, he replaced Ach's term "determining tendencies" with the term "quasi needs" (see the excursus on page 23) – ostensibly without altering the concept being designated. In retrospect, however, it is clear that the change of terminology was associated with a change in conceptualization. The volitional process, as defined by "determining tendencies," became an issue in motivation. More specifically, the distinction between motivational and volitional concepts disappeared from view once more, and remained obscured until research on volitional issues resurfaced in the 1980s.

Lewin and his students carried out numerous studies on the psychology of action and emotion. Some of his experimental paradigms have become standard procedures for motivational research. This applies particularly to methods of determining and analyzing levels of aspiration (Hoppe, 1930; Jucknat, 1938). Some of the phenomena Lewin investigated by experimental means, such as the substitute value of alternative action for an unfinished task, show an affinity to Freud's theories. Freud's influence on Lewin was probably greater than reflected in the latter's writings, which are critical of Freud's explanations of present behavior in terms of past events in the individual biography. Lewin (1931b) was perhaps the first to propose an interaction between the person and the situation. Nevertheless, his research was focused far more on the effects of situational differences than on individual differences.

Lewin endeavored to conceptualize an existing psychological "total situation" (called the "life space") that incorporated both the person and the subjectively perceived environment in a unified (field theoretical) model. This model represents a momentary interplay of forces, portrayed in terms of a general dynamic. The interplay of forces results in behavior analogous to the sum of the vectors. However, these sophisticated theoretical concepts stood in stark contrast to the lack of techniques available for measuring constructs such as tension, forces, directions, valences,

regions, and distances, or for linking them to observable data.

This is undoubtedly why Lewin's (1936, 1963) field-theory model did not have a great deal of influence on later research. Nevertheless, his thoughtful construction of concepts (e.g., demand character) and functional relationships, his analysis of situational forces (that formed the basis for conflict typologies), and above all his experimental paradigms for inducing motivational phenomena (e.g., level of aspiration) had a significant influence on later motivational research.

Lewin's contribution to research entails a branching of the lines of influence. Lewin indirectly influenced the psychology of learning via Tolman, and the personality psychology approach to motivational research via Allport, as we will see later. He directly influenced the motivation psychology branch within personality theories of motivation through Henry A. Murray in the 1930s, J. W. Atkinson in the 1950s, and V. H. Vroom in the 1960s.

2.5.1 The Motivation Psychology Approach

Instrumentality Theory

Vroom's contribution – although relatively recent – was directly influenced by both Lewin and Tolman. At the beginning of the 1960s, industrial psychology had accumulated a wealth of findings on matters such as job satisfaction and job performance. Vroom (1964) developed what became known as instrumentality theory to shed more light on these findings. It is based on the idea that actions and their outcomes tend to have a series of consequences with differing levels of positive or negative valences for the individual. The individual anticipates these consequences, and this anticipation serves to motivate action. In other words, an action is guided by the instrumentality it has for the occurrence of desirable consequences and the nonoccurrence of undesirable ones.

Significantly, however, this simple idea has had little impact on laboratory research on motivation to date. The actions of participants in laboratory experiments are, after all, of little consequence to them (aside from helping the experimenter or contributing to "science," meeting a course requirement, or making a small amount of money). In real-life settings such as the workplace, much depends on one's actions and their outcomes.

According to instrumentality theory, the individual valences (Lewin's demand characters) of the subjectively perceived consequences of one's actions must first be identified and then multiplied by the action's "instrumentality."

> **DEFINITION**
>
> Instrumentality is the level of expectancy that an action will either produce or preclude certain consequences.

In the latter case, the instrumentality is negative. The sum of the products of valences and instrumentalities for each

The Principles of Lewin's Field Theory

Lewin attempted to explain behavior solely in terms of the (momentarily) existing field of psychological forces. In his "field theory," these psychological forces are cast as vectors (Chapter 5) that emanate from objects and regions of the environment having demand character (valence). These forces affect the individual and determine his or her actions. Lewin attempted to describe the field-theory aspects of his model by means of a topological (later "hodological") analog. Independent of his field theory model of the environment, he had earlier developed a person-oriented model of motivation in terms of an accumulation of single, central, or more peripheral regions (at surface or lower levels). Each region represents a need or quasi need.

Depending on the need condition, each region is a system under more or less tension, striving for release via the executive functions (e.g., motor activities); and using such means as resuming an unfinished task. Dynamic conceptions of this kind are not very far removed from Freud's ideas.

For both Freud and Lewin, the reestablishment of equilibrium is the major principle of motivation.

Lewin explains behavior as a function of the person and his or her (perceived) environment, as reflected in his general equation for behavior: $B = f(P, E)$.

consequence gives the instrumentality-weighted total valence of a possible action outcome, which – provided that the subjective probability of successfully attaining the goal is high enough – will then motivate behavior. Vroom's instrumentality theory is therefore a more precise formulation of the expectancy-value model originally conceptualized by Lewin and Tolman (Lewin, Dembo, Festinger, & Sears, 1944; Tolman, 1932; see also Chapter 5).

Murray's Research Approach

Murray was a key figure in the motivation psychology branch within personality theories of motivation, having been influenced by Darwin, McDougall, and primarily by Freud. In his book *Explorations in Personality* (1938), Murray gave a precise definition of the term "need" that had much in common with psychoanalytic thinking. He distinguished and delineated some 35 different needs (see Chapter 5), determined the situational incentives associated with each ("press"), drew up a detailed taxonomy of behaviors relevant to motivation, compiled questionnaires (or rating scales) to assess individual differences in motives and – together with 27 collaborators – administered these questionnaires, interviews, clinical tests, experimental procedures (level of aspiration), etc., to various samples. In so doing, Murray laid the foundations for a breakthrough by McClelland and Atkinson in the early 1950s that consisted in:

■ the more precise definition of one specific motive, the achievement motive, and

■ the development and validation of a method to assess individual differences on the basis of Murray's Thematic Apperception Test (TAT).

The opportunity to assess individual differences in motives before the event sparked intensive research efforts addressing fundamental issues in motivation research and prompted the development of techniques to measure other motives, such as social affiliation and power (Chapters 7 and 8).

McClelland's Theoretical Assumptions

McClelland was a student of the learning theorist Hull. This academic lineage played a decisive role in the further articulation of what was still a rather global definition of "need" within the personality theory approach to motivation research. Lewin had conceptualized need as a momentary force (or a system under tension within the individual), without paying much attention to its evolution or dispositional character. For Murray needs were more enduring and idiosyncratic entities (analogous to the concept of motive). Although McClelland's theory did not distinguish clearly between motive and motivation – that was accomplished later by Atkinson (1957, 1964a) – it came very close to doing so. McClelland combined elements of associationism with aspects of anticipatory behavior and hedonistic theory. His proximity to Hull is reflected in his 1951 definition:

> A motive becomes a strong affective association, characterized by an anticipatory goal reaction and based on past association of certain cues with pleasure and pain (McClelland, 1951, p. 466).

Two years later (McClelland et al., 1953), he added a fourth component, namely the discrepancy model of adaptation-level theory (Helson, 1948), which he borrowed from the psychology of perception, and which he saw as the psychophysical foundation for the acquisition of all motives in the course of a lifetime. The basic idea is that there are (psychophysically prestabilized, unlearned) adaptation levels for different classes of stimuli or situational conditions, i.e., levels at which the stimuli are perceived as "normal" and neutral. Discrepancies from the adaptation level are experienced as positive, provided that they do not exceed a certain level. Beyond that level, they become increasingly unpleasant. Situational cues and antecedent conditions that are associated with these affective states and affective changes during ontogenetic development become capable of eliciting certain aspects of the original affective situation.

DEFINITION

For McClelland, motivation is the "redintegration" by certain stimulus cues of an experienced change in an affective situation.

This definition is rather complex, as it attempts to explain with a single concept three issues pertaining to motives and motivation:

- the genesis of a motive,
- motive as an acquired individual disposition, and
- the eliciting stimuli as the actual motivation.

McClelland et al. (1953) summarized all this as follows:

> Our definition of a motive is this: A motive is the redintegration by a cue of a change in an affective situation. The word "redintegration" in this definition is meant to imply previous learning. In our system all motives are learned. The basic idea is simply this: Certain stimuli or situations involving discrepancies between expectations (adaptation level) and perception are sources of primary, unlearned affect, either positive or negative in nature. Cues which are paired with these affective states, changes in these affective states, and the conditions producing them become capable of redintegrating a state (A′) derived from the original affective situation (A), but not identical with it (McClelland et al., 1953, p. 28).

With its multipurpose character and fusing of several postulates, this definition was evidently too cumbersome to have a significant influence on the later motivational research spearheaded by McClelland's former collaborator J. W. Atkinson. The discrepancy postulate, in particular, proved unsuccessful, although there were some initial attempts to develop this approach further (cf. Peak, 1955; Heckhausen, 1963a). It is only recently that this postulate has begun to gain increasing significance, particularly in relation to the concept of "self-reinforcement," which is a function of the discrepancy between an action outcome and a performance standard accepted as binding by the individual.

In contrast to Atkinson, McClelland was more interested in individual differences in motives, their genesis, and their consequences than in the motivational phenomena of actual situations. This blending of motivational concepts with personality psychology is reflected in McClelland's well-known analyses of historical change in the motivational climate of nations, and his findings of a pattern of relations between motivational change and economic and political developments (1961, 1971, 1975).

McClelland determined national and historical indices of motivation based on the content analyses of literary documents, analyzed motivational aspects of the entrepreneur personality, and worked on programs for the modification of motives (cf. McClelland, 1965, 1978; McClelland & Winter, 1969).

Atkinson's Approach

Atkinson (1957, 1964a) developed a formal model of motivation – the "risk-taking model" – which, more than any other, stimulated and influenced work on motivation in the 1960s and 1970s (see the excursus on page 25 and Chapters 5 and 8). On the one hand, it elucidated the expectancy component of McClelland's postulates by defining it in terms of the subjective probability of success, i.e., goal attainment (P_s). On the other hand, it related this component to the incentive for success (I_s) by means of multiplication. This product $P_s \times I_s$ builds on an approach previously developed by Lewin's students Sybille Escalona (1940) and Leon Festinger (1942) to explain levels of aspiration, namely the theory of resulting value. It represents a concretization of "expectancy-value theories," which had emerged concurrently but independently as "decision theories," formulated to predict consumer's purchasing decisions in an economic context (von Neumann & Morgenstern, 1944) and bets placed in games of chance in a psychological context (cf. Edwards, 1954).

In decision theory, the product of expectancy and value is the subjectively expected maximum utility of success, which is assumed to govern the decisions of rational individuals. But do all individuals make rational decisions?

Atkinson later turned to the study of changes in and resumption of an action. One of the questions he addressed harkened back to Freud, namely the after-effects of unfulfilled motivations when an action is resumed. Atkinson incorporated these motivational remainders in his risk-taking formula as "inertial tendency" (Atkinson & Cartwright, 1964).

A book coauthored with D. Birch (1970, see also Atkinson & Birch, 1978) reflected a shift in Atkinson's research interest, away from the motivational analysis of individual, "episodic" segments of action to the question of why a particular action tendency ceases to influence behavior, while another commences to do so. His research focus shifted to what might be called the links in the continuous stream of activity. Atkinson's dynamic theory of action is highly abstract; in fact, it postulates so many forces and dependency functions that computer programs are needed to determine the correct predictions for given starting conditions.

Together with J. Raynor – who had previously (1969) expanded the risk-taking model to account for future-oriented actions – Atkinson (1974) attempted to explain the relationships between strength of motive, incentive level of the situation, and (cumulative) short-term and long-term achievement outcomes. This he did on the basis of an explanatory model formulated within the psychology of activation, the Yerkes-Dodson rule.

❶ The Yerkes-Dodson rule states that an intermediate level of activity is most conducive to performance on a task of a given difficulty level.

Heckhausen's Research on Achievement Motivation

In Germany, Heckhausen soon picked up on and expanded the work of McClelland and Atkinson. He developed and validated two independent TAT measures to assess the motive to achieve success and the motive to avoid failure. Together with his colleagues at the University of Bochum, Heckhausen explored various issues relating to the achievement motive:

- development of motives (Heckhausen, 1972, 1982; Trudewind, 1975),
- risk-taking (Schneider, 1973),

EXCURSUS

The Risk-Taking Model

Atkinson (1957) made a considerable step forward by taking account of individual differences in motivation. He added a third, dispositional variable to the product of the probability of success and the incentive for success, namely the motive to achieve success (M_s). This produced the "Atkinson formula" of the risk-taking model (see also Atkinson & Feather, 1966), according to which the current tendency to approach success (T_s) can be predicted if the actor's motive to achieve success, the probability of achieving success under the prevailing conditions, and the incentive value of success are known:

$$[T_s = M_s \times P_s \times I_s]$$

This equation incorporates one of Lewin's ideas, namely, that the demand character (or valence) is a product of motive and goal incentive.

An analogous equation was formulated for the tendency to avoid failure:

Motive to avoid failure $\times$ probability of failure $\times$ incentive of failure. This avoidance tendency is subtracted from the approach tendency to give the resultant tendency to perform.

Owing to its emphasis on individual differences in motives, the risk-taking model stimulated a wealth of research, producing many and diverse findings over a long period of time (see Heckhausen, Schmalt, & Schneider, 1985). This research will be examined in more detail in Chapters 5 and 6.

- occupational choices (Kleinbeck, 1975),
- level of aspiration as a personality parameter (Kuhl, 1978a, b),
- measurement of motives (Schmalt, 1976b),
- regulation of effort (Halisch & Heckhausen, 1977),
- modification of motives (Krug, 1976), and
- applications in educational research (Rheinberg, 1980).

The Bochum group had also shown an early interest in attribution theory within cognitive psychology (see below) – particularly in Weiner's approach (1972) – and its members had contributed to the integration of the two research traditions. Their findings relate to aspects such as the perception of one's own ability as a determinant of the subjective probability of success (Meyer, 1973a, 1976), the motive dependency of causal explanations of success and failure, and the dependency of the affective consequences of an action's outcome and change in expectancy on causal explanations (Meyer, 1973a; Schmalt, 1979). Motive-related biases of causal explanations of success or failure proved to be important determinants of self-evaluation, suggesting that the achievement motive could be conceptualized as a self-reinforcement system (Heckhausen, 1972, 1978).

These multi-faceted approaches led to the construction of more complex models of motivational processes. One such model was designed to predict expended effort on the basis of the perceived relationship between one's own ability and the difficulty of the task (Meyer, 1973a). This approach resembles Ach's (1910) "law of difficulty of motivation." Another such model is the "expanded motivation model" (Heckhausen, 1977a), incorporating elements of attribution theory and, above all, the various consequences arising from the outcome of an action and its incentive values. These effects had been previously neglected in achievement motivation research, but had gained currency in the psychology of work, based on Vroom's (1964) instrumentality theory. Later, Kuhl (1977) showed that different models of motivation can have validity for different groups of individuals; in other words, achievement behavior may be governed more by calculations of required effort for some or by a priori self-evaluations for others.

Kuhl (1982, 1983) was also the first to point out that volitional issues had been neglected for decades. Motivation and volition are now conceptualized as adjacent phases within a course of action (Heckhausen & Gollwitzer, 1987; Heckhausen & Kuhl, 1985). We will come back to this in Chapter 11.

Later chapters will examine the contemporary research generated by the motivation psychology approach. Here, we need only say that Atkinson's work focused research attention on the interaction between person and situation factors. Finally, researchers approaching the subject from this perspective tackled issues relating to motives and motivation systematically, but disregarded volitional issues until the early 1980s.

2.5.2 The Cognitive Psychology Approach

Here, again, we begin with Lewin, whose field-theoretical, topological perspective is clearly apparent in the choice and treatment of the phenomena studied within the cognitive approach. What is more important, however, is the cognitivists' concern with **motive activation**. This concern was alien to both Freud and Lewin, who assumed accumulated drive strengths or existing needs to motivate action. Freud, more than Lewin, would acknowledge that behavior might also consist of cognitions. The cognitive psychology approach reverses the emphasis, postulating that cognitions about an individual's present state can, under certain conditions, activate motivation or influence existing motivations. What motivates us are the imbalances, the contradictions, the incompatibilities of our cognitive representations. Various models have been developed to explain these ideas. They can all be subsumed under the heading **consistency theories** (cf. Zajonc, 1968), and have been characterized as follows:

❶ All have in common the notion that the person tends to behave in ways that minimize the internal inconsistency among his interpersonal relations, among his intrapersonal cognitions, and among his beliefs, feelings and action (McGuire, 1966, p. 1).

This marked the return to motivation research of a notion that had been out of favor since Darwin, namely, that reasoning can instigate motivation. It is also worth noting that cognitivists based their experimental paradigms on approaches from social psychology, as pursued by Lewin in his later years (he died in 1947), and covering:

- interpersonal relationships,
- group dynamics,
- attitude change, and
- person perception.

Consistency Theories

One consistency theory is Fritz Heider's (1946, 1960) theory of cognitive balance.

THEORY OF COGNITIVE BALANCE. According to this theory, the relations between objects or persons can represent balanced or unbalanced cognitive configurations. Heider illustrated his point by reference to triadic personal relationships. If A likes B as well as C, but learns that B does not get on with C, then there is a break in the unity of the triad for A. This motivates A to establish a more balanced relationship within the triad. For example, A might try to find ways to improve the relationship between B and C. This achieved, the configuration of interpersonal relations would attain a "good Gestalt." This postulate, that cognitive processes strive for consistency, balance, and "good Gestalt," is reminiscent of the Gestalt school founded by Wertheimer, Köhler, and Koffka, under whom Heider had studied in the 1920s (as had Lewin earlier).

COGNITIVE DISSONANCE THEORY. This consistency theory was developed by Leon Festinger (1957, 1964), a student of Lewin. It states that cognitive dissonance arises when at least two cognitions that are relevant to self-esteem are mutually incompatible, i.e., contradictory. The individual is motivated to reduce the dissonance by effecting changes in behavior, changes in one of the dissonant cognitions, or by searching for new information or convictions. These postulates about the motivating effects of cognitive dissonance have prompted a wealth of ingenious experiments (Chapter 4).

Most studies pertaining to consistency theory remained rather peripheral to the study of motivation in the stricter sense, primarily because they did not cover enduring motives.

❶ The more general significance of consistency theories is that they drew attention to the role that cognition plays in motivational processes.

ATTRIBUTION THEORY. A further contribution by Heider (1958) not only emphasized the significance of cognition in the psychology of motivation, but also strongly influenced the

mainstream of recent motivational research (Chapter 14). As social psychologists began to study person perception, efforts were made to determine why an observer attributes certain characteristics to the person observed. This prompted several attempts to construct an "attribution theory" (cf. Kelley, 1967; Weiner, 1972). Heider was interested in the genesis of an observer's common-sense explanations for the outcome of another person's behavior. Like Lewin, he distinguished between person forces and environment forces. In contrast to Lewin, however, he analyzed responses to the question of why certain outcomes occur in the context of an observer's experience and behavior. Under which conditions is someone more likely to locate the causes of a behavior or an event within the person or within the situation? Are these causes enduring characteristics (dispositions) of the person, the situation, or the object, or are they temporary states? All observations of behaviors and events seem to involve causal attributions of this kind. Especially if the observed event is, on the face of it, puzzling, there will be a search for causes. Causal attribution is not just a cognitive phenomenon like pure curiosity that has no further implications, however. Its outcomes – e.g., the intentions attributed to an associate – determine any further actions taken.

EXAMPLE

Examples include situations in which actions can lead to success or failure. The major causal factors include the person factors of capability (or knowledge, power, and influence) and the situation factors of difficulty and resistance to the person forces during task performance. The relationship between these two kinds of forces predicts whether a person "can" accomplish the task – this is an enduring causal factor. This "can" must be supplemented by some variable factors if the task is to be accomplished successfully, however, namely intention and effort (exertion, "try"). This simple model of causal factors provides easy explanations for the success or failure of an action. If, for example, somebody did not try hard, but succeeded nonetheless, then his or her ability must be far superior to the difficulty level of the task.

But what does this kind of naive causal attribution, based on perceptions of the behavior of others, have to do with motivation? Quite simply, what holds for the perception of others also holds for the perception of the self. We plan and evaluate our actions according to the causal factors we see as being important – factors like intention, ability, difficulties encountered, amount of effort required, good or bad luck, etc. It makes a big difference whether we attribute a failure to a lack of ability or a lack of effort, for example. In the latter case we are less likely to give up.

B. Weiner (1972, 1974), a student of Atkinson, applied the theory of causal attribution to the study of achievement motivation. This approach triggered a great deal of research activity, which demonstrated that intervening cognitions relating to the causal attribution of success and failure are important mediating processes in the motivational system. At the same time, individual differences associated with differences in motives were revealed. We will examine the motivational research inspired by attribution theory in Chapter 14.

Thus, reason – albeit a "naive" notion of the concept – was again seen as something to be taken into account in psychological interpretations of motivated behavior.

SUMMARY

Various situation factors as well as person factors such as attitudes were at the forefront of attempts to explain motivated behavior from the perspective of cognitive psychology. To date, attitude variables have had little bearing on the study of motivation, partly because their construct character is uncertain with respect to motivation – they are assumed to encompass cognitive, emotional, evaluative, and behavioral components – and partly because there is some doubt about their impact on behavior. Although social psychologists had not intended to engage in studies of motivation along cognitive psychology lines, they made valuable contributions to research on topics such as the following:

- basic issues of motive arousal,
- resumption of motivation,
- motivational conflicts,
- effects of motivation, and above all
- mediating cognitive processes in the self-regulation of behavior.

In recent years, there has been a fruitful exchange about issues of causal attribution between cognitive psychology and motivational psychology (Chapter 14).

In this context, cognitive psychology is not restricted to cognitive science or to methodological approaches based on models of information processing. Nevertheless, these theories and methods are likely to play an important role in future research on volition.

2.5.3 The Personality Psychology Approach

The 1930s saw the emergence of a "personality movement." Its supporters did not consider either psychoanalytic theory or behaviorist learning theories to be capable of providing an adequate interpretation of individual behavior. The movement was spearheaded by the German psychologist William Stern (1871–1938), whose book *General Psychology from a Personality Perspective* was originally published in 1935. Coming from the Wundtian tradition, Stern was not significantly influenced by McDougall. He was a pioneer in differential psychology, using psychometric techniques to examine differences in the capacities and personality characteristics of individuals. What is crucial for this new direction in psychology is that Stern, deviating from Wundt's general psychological approach, was guided increas-

ingly by personalism, the attempt to describe and interpret the individuality of a person in terms of a unitas multiplex.

❗ William Stern's main explanatory mechanisms were traits, which he subdivided into "driving traits" (directional dispositions) and "instrumental traits" (preparedness dispositions), the former having motivational character.

Proponents of Personality Psychology

Stern's most influential student was G. W. Allport (1897–1967). In his book entitled *Personality. A Psychological Interpretation* (1937), Allport extended Stern's basic ideas, adding to them an eclectic variety of contemporary theoretical perspectives.

ALLPORT'S PRINCIPLE OF FUNCTIONAL AUTONOMY. Allport's approach reflects a mixture of German faculty psychology, McDougall's dynamism, and U.S. empiricism. It sees the individual as a unique system that is constantly developing and is oriented toward the future. Accordingly, Allport argued that this system cannot be assessed using "nomothetic" techniques (general abstractions), but requires "idiographic" (concrete, individual) approaches. Allport's definition of a trait is similar to that of Stern:

DEFINITION

A generalized and focalized neuropsychic system (peculiar to the individual), with the capacity to render many stimuli functionally equivalent, and to initiate and guide consistent (equivalent) forms of adaptive and expressive behavior (Allport, 1937, p. 295).

Traits ensure that there is relative equivalence in an individual's behavior across situations. In the 1930s, a lively interactionism debate (cf. Lehmann & Witty, 1934) had been sparked by the findings of Hartshorne and May (1928), which showed that children's honesty/dishonesty behavior differs across situations. Allport's 1937 definition of the trait contained the key to this inconsistency problem, as became amply clear in the more recent interactionism debate. Consistency can only be expected in subjectively equivalent classes of behavior and situations. Thus, an idiographic approach is vital if we are to avoid the "nomothetic fallacy" (Bem & Allen, 1974; see Chapter 3 for a discussion of the consistency paradox).

Allport did not see traits as hypothetical constructs, but as realities within a person that are manifested directly in behavior. Furthermore, Allport, like Stern, distinguished between traits with a more "motivational" character and those with a more "instrumental" character, but without drawing a clear line between them.

Allport's principle of "functional autonomy of motives" became well known. It rejected theories that attribute adult motives to such sources as the vicissitudes of drives in early childhood or to particular classes of instincts or needs, as had been suggested by Freud, McDougall, and Murray. The principle of functional autonomy was designed to account for the uniqueness of individual behavior. Allport writes:

> The dynamic psychology proposed here regards adult motives as infinitely varied and as self-sustaining contemporary systems, growing out of antecedent systems, but functionally independent of them (Allport, 1937, p. 194).

MASLOW'S HIERARCHY OF NEEDS. Allport's approach is the classic among the diverse perspectives on personality research to emerge on the basis of trait theory. This approach was continued in the USA, primarily through humanistic psychology, which was known as the "third force." After World War II, this movement also took European existentialism on board. Its main proponent was Abraham Maslow (1908–1970), along with Carl Rogers, Rollo May, and Charlotte Bühler.

Maslow's book *Motivation and Personality* (1954) was very widely read. It had a far greater influence on attitudes toward applied psychological problems and their solution than it did on empirical research. Maslow postulated a hierarchy of needs, within which lower needs have to be satisfied before higher needs can be addressed. His hierarchical ranking is as follows:

- physiological needs,
- safety needs,
- needs for belongingness,
- esteem needs, and
- needs for self-actualization.

Maslow defined the latter group as "growth needs," in contrast to the "deficiency needs" preceding it (Chapter 3).

CATTELL'S TRAIT THEORY. The final approach to trait theory worth mentioning in this context is based on complex multivariate testing and statistical analyses. Its main proponent was the Anglo-American psychologist R. B. Cattell (1957, 1965, 1974), whose work followed a typically British tradition, unmistakably influenced by Galton's differential psychology and McDougall's dynamic instinct theory. Cattell was taught by Spearman, one of the developers of factor analysis. Using factor analytic methods, Cattell constructed what is probably the most complex model of personality traits in existence, based almost exclusively on correlations between data from questionnaires and tests on a broad variety of areas. Of the factors he extracted, three are considered to have motivational character:

- attitudes,
- sentiments, and
- ergs (drives).

Attitudes consist of dispositions toward particular objects, activities, or situations. They refer to concrete entities; this places them on almost the same level as the data observed. Sentiments comprise groups of attitudes. "Ergs" (from the Greek *ergon*, meaning "work") are viewed as dynamic "source" variables that deliver energy to specific domains of behavior.

DEFINITION
This understanding has much in common with McDougall's original construct of instinct.

Cattell assigned these three factor groups to different levels, distinguishing between surface traits and source traits.

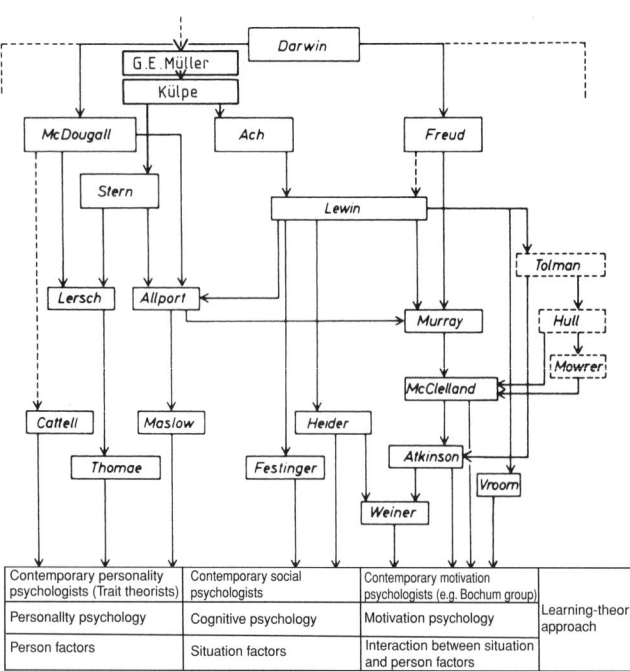

Figure 2.2 Personality theories in the development of motivation research.

He postulated a "dynamic lattice" between individual factors at the different levels, and assumed this lattice to be subject to interindividual variation. For Cattell the factors are not descriptive dimensions that differ according to the method applied, but "the causes" of behavior.

SUMMARY

To conclude, the personality theory approach to the study of motivation is dominated by trait theory and thus addresses just a few fundamental issues in motivation research, primarily:

- the taxonomy of motives,
- motivated goal orientation, and
- the effects of motivations.

This approach presents us with a wealth of dispositional variables, but with few functional variables (e.g., motivation as a process or volition). The orientations and perspectives discussed thus far are outlined in Fig. 2.2.

2.6 Associationist Theories

The associationist approach to the study of motivation can be split into two branches inspired by the work of Thorndike and Pavlov, respectively:

- the learning psychology approach and
- the activation psychology approach.

Both had their origins in Darwinian theory and, more specifically, in a new conception of the old hedonistic principle, modified from the perspective of evolutionary theory.

It was Herbert Spencer (1820–1903) who suggested that those behaviors that facilitate successful interaction with the environment, i.e., that have survival value, must have become associated with pleasurable sensations over the course of evolutionary development. The physiological models of the day held that pleasurable sensations resulted in greater permeability of the nerve tracts, accompanied by an arousal state that allowed better "stamping in" of successful actions, making it easier to reproduce them later. For Spencer, pleasure and displeasure were not goal states to be desired or avoided for their own sake, as had been the postulate of classical hedonism for more than 2,500 years (i.e., since Aristipp). Rather, he viewed them as attendant circumstances that influence the acquisition of new behaviors and increase the probability of previously successful behaviors reoccurring. With these ideas, Spencer anticipated Thorndike's "law of effect," Hull's "drive-reduction theory," and Pavlovian activation theory.

2.6.1 The Learning Psychology Approach

Main Proponents

The experimental psychology of learning had its beginnings in the 1890s. Its founder, Edward Lee Thorndike (1874–1949), was guided by the Darwinian notion that there must be a continuum of intelligence and learning ability in animals and humans. Working with cats, Thorndike sought ways of teaching the animals to solve problems. A cat was deprived of food and placed in a "puzzle box." Food was placed outside the box. The cat, which was restless because it was hungry, would accidentally move certain levers that opened a gate, giving access to the food. As early as the next trial, the animal would show instrumental, goal-directed behavior, i.e., a learning effect.

The analogy to Darwin's notion of evolution is clear. In a given environmental situation, the animal produces a variety of available responses. Under changed environmental conditions, only a few of these responses will lead to success, i.e., have survival value. Responses are selected on the basis of "trial and error," by trying out various possibilities one after the other. To draw an analogy between the available responses and organisms engaged in the "fight for survival," only a few adaptive responses will "survive," while the rest "become extinct." Thorndike (1898) proposed the "law of effect" to explain this pattern:

DEFINITION

Of several responses made to the same situation, those which are accompanied or closely followed by satisfaction to the animal will, other things being equal, be more firmly connected with the situation, so that, when it recurs, they will be more likely to recur; those which are accompanied or closely followed by discomfort to the animal will, other things being equal, have their connections with that situation weakened, so that, when it recurs, they will be less likely to occur. The greater the satisfaction or discomfort, the greater the strengthening or weakening of the bond. (Thorndike, 1898, 1911, p. 2441).

Satisfaction – in this case, of the hunger drive – was seen as creating a new stimulus-response bond for learning, a process that was later called "reinforcement." Thorndike (1898) viewed the observed learning phenomena as analogous to physiological processes, i.e., the bonding of neuronally represented elements of stimulus and response. At first, he was not aware of the motivational factors inherent in the observed behavior. Nevertheless, his learning experiments were also motivation experiments. The animal had to be deprived of food prior to the experiment. How else can they (unlike humans) be motivated to learn? To this extent, experimental learning research with animals, which has now evolved to a major field of research activity, has always incorporated aspects relating to motivation research and produced many very relevant findings. In human research on learning, in contrast, motivational aspects were, at first, largely overlooked.

❶ Stimulus-response bonds (*S–R bonds*) were soon accepted to be the basic units of behavior.

Thorndike did not disregard motivational issues totally. Certain events can only be satisfying if the organism is in a state of "readiness." Thus, food can only lead to a state of satisfaction – and facilitate the formation of new *S–R* bonds – if the organism is hungry. Thorndike (1911) originally referred to this readiness as susceptibility for the formation of a certain stimulus-response element. Later (1913) he introduced the law of "readiness." To avoid any mentalistic connotations, "readiness" was conceptualized as a momentary increase in the conductivity of neurons. Although he was unable to provide a satisfactory solution to the problem of motivation, his influence on the development of learning theories can hardly be overestimated. Learning theories were not only associationist, but also specified what is being associated with what, namely, stimuli with responses. Thorndike labeled the association of a stimulus with a response "habit" (Section 2.2).

> **DEFINITION**
> A "habit" is a pattern of responses that does not involve conscious processes, either because it became automated after having been under conscious control at some earlier point, or because it was acquired without conscious control from the outset.

It was common practice at the time to skirt motivational issues by attributing goal-directed behavior to "instincts." Following the instinct controversy, the term "drive" – first proposed by R. S. Woodworth (1918) – gained currency. Woodworth (1869–1962) also made a fundamental distinction between the "drives" that initiate behaviors and the "mechanisms" that are then activated and that determine the course of the behavior; e.g., stimulus-response bonds. At the same time, he was the first to take the step of inserting a hypothetical construct between S and R, namely, "O" for organism in a particular drive state.

TOLMAN'S INFLUENCE ON THE PSYCHOLOGY OF LEARNING AND MOTIVATION. Edward C. Tolman (1886–1959) was the first to provide a rigorously defined conception of hypothetical constructs, which he called "intervening variables." These must have close conceptual ties to the antecedent manipulations and subsequent observations. To hypothesize a hunger drive of a given strength, for example, the antecedent manipulated period of food deprivation must covary with the subsequently observable behavior of the animal; e.g., general restlessness, running speed, response latency, etc. Tolman (1932) carefully analyzed the criteria of goal-directed behavior.

Tolman was the first to clearly distinguish between motivation and learning. Before that, and indeed thereafter, the two were regularly confounded. For Tolman, learning was essentially the acquisition of knowledge, taking the form of intervening variables such as the cognitive map, means-end readiness, and above all expectancy. For learning to manifest itself in behavior, however, there must be motivation, the efficacy of which is determined by two intervening variables:

- "drive" and
- "demand for the goal object" (analogous to Lewin's demand character; later the term "incentive" was commonly used).

Experiments on "latent learning" provided the crucial demonstration for the need to distinguish between learning and motivation (Chapter 5). Tolman was a "psychological behaviorist," and his notions closely resemble those of Lewin, who later influenced him directly. His is not a purely associationist theory, because he neither postulated fixed stimulus-response bonds on the cognitive side, nor did he invoke drive reduction as the basis for learning on the motivational side. Instead, he drew attention to cognitive intervening variables that direct behavior toward a goal as soon as motivational intervening variables become activated.

❶ Tolman's work forged an important link between the psychology of learning and the psychology of motivation. His influence on the latter was via Atkinson.

HULL'S DRIVE THEORY. Tolman's influence is also apparent in the works of Clark L. Hull (1884–1952), the major theorist of the learning psychology approach. Hull adopted Tolman's theoretical conception of intervening variables (calling them theoretical constructs). Later, the concept of "incentive" also became an important construct in Hull's model. It was used to explain residual behavioral differences in cases of equal drive strength and equal learning outcomes (habit strength). Hull proposed a complex theoretical network consisting of 17 postulates and 133 derived theorems. From the perspective of motivational psychology, he founded drive theory. Essentially, he adopted Thorndike's approach, but elucidated it further and stripped it of mentalistic connotations. "Satisfaction" of a need, which facilitates the formation of *S–R* bonds, became "drive reduction." A distinction was now also made between need and drive.

> **DEFINITION**
> A need is a specific deficiency or disturbance within the organism (e.g., hunger, thirst, or pain) that elicits a nonspecific drive of a certain strength, capable of initiating behavior. For Hull, needs are essentially observable or at least manipulable variables, whereas drives are theoretical (hypothetical) constructs.

Hull's approach is made clear in the following definition – which also reflects a Darwinian perspective:

When a condition arises for which action on the part of the organism is a prerequisite to optimum probability of survival of either the individual or the species, a state of need is said to exist. Since a need, either actual or potential, usually precedes and accompanies the action of an organism, the need is often said to motivate or drive the associated activity. Because of **this** motivational characteristic of needs they are regarded as producing primary animal drives.

It is important to note in this connection that the general concept of drive (D) tends strongly to have the systematic status of an intervening variable or X, never directly observable (Hull, 1943, p. 57). (Author's emphasis.)

In the last revision of his system, Hull (1952) essentially attributed behavior partly to a motivational component and partly to an associative component. The motivational component, which is the product of drive (D) and incentive (K), has a purely energizing function. The associative component determines which of the available S–R bonds ("habits," $_SH_R$) will be implemented in response to the internal and external stimuli of a given situation. The two components are multiplied with each other to determine the behavior tendency, a vectorial concept combining force and direction. This is the **reaction-evocation potential** ($_SE_R$).

$$_SE_R = f(_SH_R \times D \times K)$$

Habit strength ($_SH_R$) is dependent on the number of and delays in preceding reinforcements, i.e., on how often and how quickly a stimulus-response bond has previously been followed by drive reduction.

Kenneth W. Spence (1907–1967) was a student of Hull and later worked with him to advance Hull's theory of motivation and learning in some important respects. Spence was particularly interested in the experimental and conceptual analysis of "incentive" in the light of Tolman's findings. (Incidentally, Hull's use of the symbol "K" for "incentive" in his formula reportedly reflects his appreciation of Kenneth Spence's work.)

Spence (1956, 1960) considered incentives, like habits, to be acquired through learning. His theoretical explanation for the acquisition and manifestation of incentives is associationistic, based on the mechanisms of "fractional anticipatory goal responses" (r_G–s_G) that had been postulated by Hull (1930). The basic idea is that fragments of an earlier goal response (r_G) are elicited by familiar stimuli on the way to reaching (or even perceiving) a goal, and that these are in turn associated with fragments of an earlier goal object (s_G). With this mechanism, Hullian theory can account for Tolman's hypothetical construct "expectancy" and for what cognitive ("mentalistic") theories call anticipation or expectation. This explanation, in terms of associationist theory, endows the fractional anticipatory goal response (r_G–s_G) with motivational characteristics. The response is postulated to produce its own stimulation that – along with the drive stimuli – increases the internal stimulation on the organism. Thus, for Spence, the relationship between drive and incentive is additive, and not multiplicative, as had been suggested by Hull:

$$E = f(D + K) \times H$$

Now there can be an effective response potential (E), i.e., learning, in the presence of incentive stimuli alone, without drive stimuli; in other words, when the organism is not "driven" but "attracted" to a goal. This would be a case of pure incentive motivation.

Spence rejected the learning component of Hull's theory, i.e., habit formation, and the notion that it is drive reduction that enforces the S–R bond. For Spence, drive reduction determines incentive strength (K) that, along with drive (D), governs the intensity with which a learned response is performed. To this extent, drive reduction is a purely motivational issue and cannot explain learning. Spence saw Thorndike's "law of effect" as an indisputable fact ("empirical law of effort"), but not as an explanation for learning. Instead, he reverted to the old associationistic principle of **contiguity**:

DEFINITION
The strength of a habit is solely dependent on the frequency with which a response has been made to a stimulus in temporal or spatial contiguity.

This is also the basic associationistic model for classical conditioning (see Pavlov, page 33), from which the fractional anticipatory goal responses (r_G–s_G) are derived. Spence was the first of the learning psychologists to measure individual differences in motivation and their effects on learning outcomes. This work also inspired researchers taking a motivation psychology approach (e.g., Atkinson and Weiner). The motive examined was "anxiety" (Taylor, 1953), which was assumed to produce a high general drive state or arousal state in the presence of particular tasks. According to "inference theory," this then activates competing responses that interfere with performance, particularly on difficult tasks (Taylor & Spence, 1952).

Applications of the Learning Psychology Approach to Motivation Research
Three of Hull's students and collaborators advanced the learning psychology approach to motivation research by applying it to specific issues:

- Neal E. Miller,
- Judson S. Brown, and
- O. Hobart Mowrer.

Miller and the psychoanalyst Dollard had soon become interested in Freud's psychology of motivation, and applied learning theory to social and psychotherapeutic issues. They developed a "liberalized S–R theory" (Miller & Dollard, 1941; Miller, 1959) and an influential model of conflict behavior (see box on "Classical Learning Experiments" below), which they substantiated by experimental means (1944). Using fear as an example, Miller demonstrated the existence of "acquired drives" (1948, 1951), expanding on Hull's drive theory. He later focused on physiological brain mechanisms, postulating the existence of what he called "go-mechanisms" with an incentive function (1963).

Aside from drives, strong external stimuli can also have a motivating function. In their book *Personality and Psychotherapy* (1950), Dollard and Miller state:

All that needs to be assumed here is (1) that intense enough stimuli serve as drives (but not all drives are strong stimuli), (2) that the reduction in painfully strong stimuli (or of other states of drive) acts as a reinforcement, and (3) that the presence of a drive increases the tendency for a habit to be performed. (Dollard & Miller, 1950, p. 31).

Drive is no longer a uniform, direction-nonspecific, purely energizing factor, as had been suggested by Hull. The drive **cues** associated with it determine which response will be emitted.

> The drive impels a person to respond. Cues determine when he will respond, where he will respond, and which response he will make (p. 32).
>
> To summarize, stimuli may vary quantitatively and qualitatively; any stimulus may be thought of having a certain drive value, depending on its strength, and a certain cue value, depending on its distinctiveness (Dollard & Miller, 1950, p. 34).

Like responses, drives can become associated with previously neutral stimuli.

STUDY

Classical Learning Experiments

In one of their famous experiments (Miller, 1948, 1951) rats were given painful electric shocks through a grid in the floor of a white-walled compartment until they had learned to open the entrance to an adjacent black compartment. After a few trials the animals showed signs of fear as soon as they were placed in the white compartment, even when the grid was not charged. Previously neutral stimuli now aroused fear, a case of classical conditioning. Fear was learned and, at the same time, became a drive state, because the animals now learned new responses to escape to the black compartment even without the presence of electric shocks. These experiments became the prime rationale for the assumption that "higher motives," learned or secondary drives, arise from originally organismic drives, particularly from the fear associated with painful states.

Another classical experiment with rats formed the basis for Miller's (1944) well-known model of conflict resolution. Given the stimulation of a particular drive state, the tendency to approach a positive goal object or to avoid a negative one increases with proximity to the goal. The approach gradient is less steep than the avoidance gradient, however. If the goal region is both positive and negative – e.g., because the hungry animal found food there, but also received a shock – there will be a point, at a particular distance from the goal region, where the approach gradient and the avoidance gradient intersect. This produces conflict. Any further approach results in fear becoming dominant; any further avoidance response results in hunger becoming dominant. The animal shows ambivalent behavior.

This model of conflict has also proved valuable for research on humans; e.g., in the context of psychotherapy. Unlike

Miller, Brown (1961) remained committed to Hullian drive theory. For him, drive was a general, activating, and direction-nonspecific intervening variable. Hence, there is only one drive, and no acquired, secondary drives. There are, however, many sources that contribute to this general and uniform drive; these may be innate and organismic or acquired. There are also secondary motivational systems. All of these are based on the conditioning of certain stimuli with fear states that were originally associated with physical pain. Up to this point, Brown's conceptualization is highly reminiscent of Miller's notion of fear as an acquired drive. Brown goes further, however, postulating that fear can become linked to a whole range of different stimulus constellations, forming unique motivational systems that become energized. Brown's (1953) example of this is the money motive.

EXAMPLE

Brown's money motive example was based on the observation that, when children are injured and suffer pain in the early years of life, their parents display concern and fear. An associative bond is formed between pain and parental concern. If the child now perceives the same concerned expressions when his or her parents talk about money problems (e.g., "We're broke"), the association with pain is reactivated, i.e., fear of pain, anxiety; this results in an association between fear and the word "money." Whenever there is talk of money (e.g., "We've no more money to buy food"), a state of anxiety is induced. This state can be diminished through appropriate instrumental activities (in the same way as the rats in Miller's experiment learned new escape responses to get from the white compartment to the black one even without the presence of shock). A reduction in anxiety can be attained by securing a regular income, for example. This leads to the formation of a "work motive," which, upon closer inspection, serves to reduce the fear of being broke. Although this example seems somewhat contrived, it is consistent with Brown's drive theory.

MOWRER'S THEORY OF AVOIDANCE LEARNING. O. H. Mowrer, the third major learning theorist beside Hull and Spence, also studied the function of fear in motivating avoidance learning. His most significant contribution, in terms of a theory of motivation, was to introduce the emotions of expectancy, hope and fear, as intervening variables mediating between features of the situation and the response. This represents a decisive step within classical S–R theory, leading to a conceptualization of motivation that assigns a central role to such cognitive mediating processes as expectancy. McClelland's theory of motivation (McClelland et al., 1953) clearly shows the influence of Mowrer's position in this respect. In turn, Mowrer was influenced by the work of Young, a representative of the psychology of activation (see later).

Mowrer (1939) began by examining the role of fear or anxiety. He saw the relevance of Freud's (1926) notion that fear is a signal of impending danger, itself an unpleasant state that instigates behavior to avoid the danger. According to Mowrer, fear (or anxiety) is the anticipation of fear. It is a conditioned form of the pain response originally elicited by a strong adverse stimulus. Accordingly, fear has a motivating function, reinforcing all behaviors that serve to reduce it. As Mowrer (1960) himself put it later, this represents a reversal of ideas about "fear learning"; here, learning is reinforced by an expectation of being relieved of fear.

Finally, Mowrer (1960) postulated two basic types of reinforcement mechanisms that underlie all explanations of behavior:

1. Drive induction ("incremental reinforcement"):
Whenever behavior is punished, a conditioned association with the expectancy of fear is produced ("fear learning"),

2. Drive reduction ("decremental reinforcement"):
Whenever behavior is rewarded, a conditioned association with the expectancy of hope is produced ("hope learning").

Correspondingly, there are complementary expectancies of "relief" and "disappointment":

■ Relief occurs when an induced fear state is diminished by the consequences of a response (decremental reinforcement),

■ Disappointment occurs when an induced hope state is diminished by the consequences of a response (incremental reinforcement).

According to Mowrer, these four classes of expectancy emotion (hope and disappointment, fear and relief) and any increases or decreases in their intensity determine, for any given situation, which type of behavior will be chosen and pursued, and thereby learned and reinforced.

Here, Mowrer deviates from the classical *S–R* notion that learning and behavior result from an unmediated association between stimulus and response. Instead, he suggests that expectancy emotions become associated with the stimuli. Stimuli can be either independent of the organism's behavior (and originate externally or internally within the organism), or they can be dependent, i.e., feedback from one's own behavior. Once emotions of expectancy have become associated with such stimuli, they can guide behavior in a flexible and appropriate manner by facilitating responses that increase hope and relief or decrease fear and disappointment.

Mowrer also sees the basic mechanisms of associative learning in classical conditioning. For him, instrumental conditioning – since Thorndike the primary explanatory principle of learning – is a subclass of classical conditioning.

❗ What characterizes explanations of behavior within the learning psychology approach is the focus on situational rather than dispositional, person factors. Behavior is guided by stimuli that can be either external or response-dependent; i.e., internal. Motivational variables such as drive are frequently also conceptualized as "inner" stimuli.

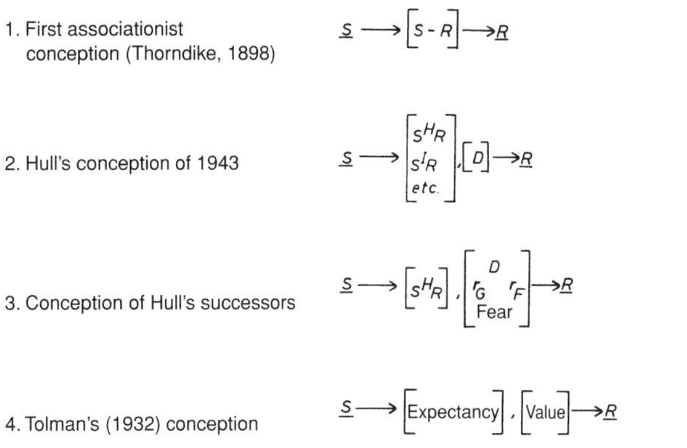

Figure 2.3 Stages in the development of learning theory in terms of the motivational component of behavior. (Based on Bolles, 1974.)

Two types of intervening (construct) variables mediate between a situation ("stimulus") and behavior ("response"):

■ Structural components:
These give behavior direction, goal orientation, and utility. They reflect the effect of learning in terms of Tolman's expectation (what leads to what) or the Hullian concept of habit ($_SH_R$) or conditioned inhibition ($_SI_R$).

■ Motivational components:
These initiate and energize behavior. In Tolman's terms, they are need-dependent demands for the goal object; in Hull's (1943) terms, need-dependent drives (D); in the terms of Hull's successors, other activating mechanisms such as stimulus-evoked fractional goal responses or fear responses (r_G or r_F, respectively).

Fig. 2.3 shows the stages of development of learning theory in simplified form. S and R ("stimulus" and "response") designate the observable situational or behavioral variables. The connecting links shown in square brackets represent the structural and motivational components (in that order). The first stage represents Thorndike's (1898) position at the turn of the last century. It is a purely associationistic and "mechanistic" model with no motivational component. Although Tolman's conceptual model predates that of Hull and his successors, it is in fact a more advanced variant in terms of a theory of motivation, because it contains the foundation for the expectancy-value models that dominate contemporary motivational research.

2.6.2 The Activation Psychology Approach

Main Representatives

Ivan P. Pavlov (1849–1936) was, along with Vladimir Bekhterev (1857–1927), the founder of reflexology, the study of conditioned reflexes. The process by which such reflexes are established was later called **classical conditioning**. It was Ivan Sechenov (1829–1905), the doyen of Russian physiology, who provided the decisive input for Pavlov's work. In 1863 (edited in 1968), Sechenov published his major work

Cerebral Reflexes, which included a discussion of the inhibiting influences of the cortex on the subcortical centers. Working on the "digestive reflex" at the turn of the century, Pavlov demonstrated that unlearned reflex-inducing stimuli (unconditioned, innate stimuli) can be replaced by learned (conditioned) stimuli. This requires the presentation of the stimulus to be conditioned slightly (about half a second) before the unconditioned stimulus. After repeated pairings of the two stimuli, the new conditioned stimulus is sufficient to elicit the response. A typical example of classical conditioning is given below.

EXAMPLE

The classic example is the triggering of the salivary response in dogs, where salivation is measured by means of a fistula implanted in the esophagus. If food (an unconditioned stimulus for salivation) is preceded repeatedly by a formerly neutral stimulus (e.g., a sound, a light signal, or pressure on the skin), then this formerly neutral stimulus will eventually produce salivation without food being presented. Thus, an unconditioned stimulus "reinforces" the association between a formerly neutral stimulus and the response in question.

The concept of reinforcement was first introduced by Pavlov, and alluded to the physiology of the central nervous system in several ways. Reinforcement is the conceptual analog to what Thorndike termed "satisfaction" to explain the law of effect (in **instrumental conditioning**). Pavlov and other Russian physiologists were also able to show that a conditioned stimulus itself has acquired reinforcement characteristics, i.e., can serve to condition a formerly neutral stimulus, producing higher-order conditioning. For Pavlov this was the basis of all higher nervous activity (cf. Angermeier & Peters, 1973).

On the face of it, it would seem unlikely that the study of reflexive behavior of largely immobilized animals in experimental settings would have much to contribute to the study of motivation. Nevertheless, two critical conditions led to Pavlov becoming the founder and instigator of a multifaceted approach to motivation research based on the principle of activation:

■ First, he was a physiologist (he won the Nobel Prize in 1904 for his studies on the physiology of digestion), and attempted to explain the learning phenomena he observed in terms of the underlying neurophysiological mechanisms in the brain.

■ Second, he postulated an interaction between two underlying processes: excitation and inhibition.

For Pavlov, excitation serves to activate behavior; in terms of the traditional idea of motivation, it has an energizing function. Furthermore, **orienting reactions** accompany excitation states and play a part in the genesis of conditioned reflexes. Orienting reactions became the major focus of Russian research on activation.

Pavlov's writings soon became known to US learning psychologists, partly through a lecture that he gave in the US in 1906, and partly through an overview of his work by Yerkes and Morgulis (1909). Pavlov, like the US learning theorists, was opposed to the search for the basic elements of psychological functioning by means of introspection. Instead, he too was interested in finding answers to the question of what leads to what, as reflected by "observables," i.e., changes in external behavior. John B. Watson (1878–1958), who later became the evangelistic spokesman for this antimentalist movement called behaviorism, was strongly influenced by Pavlov's reflexology. Watson's demonstration of experimentally induced avoidance responses in a nine-month-old child by means of classical conditioning became a classic in the field (Watson & Rayner, 1920; for a critical analysis of the impact of the Little Albert study on the psychology textbooks of the next 50 years, see Harris, 1979).

OPERANT CONDITIONING AFTER SKINNER. At first it was difficult to relate conditioned reflexes to Thorndike's "law of effect," the supposed basis of all learning. B. F. Skinner (1935) was the first to propose a fundamental division of all behavior into two categories, response substitution à la Thorndike and stimulus substitution à la Pavlov. Skinner later dubbed the first category "operant behaviors" or "operants" because they act upon the situation, "operate" upon it, and change it. Factors that increase the likelihood of a particular response occurring in the future were labeled "reinforcers." Skinner adopted the term "reinforcement" from Pavlov, finally establishing it in the US psychology of learning. For Skinner, the term reinforcer has no physiological connotations; it simply equates with an increase in the probability that a particular behavior will occur. The process is called **operant conditioning** (analogous to Thorndike's instrumental conditioning). Skinner called the second category of response "respondent behavior" or "respondents" because an available response is simply elicited by a stimulus. The acquisition of new eliciting stimuli is dependent on classical conditioning, as demonstrated by Pavlov.

This was an extremely important distinction for the later development of learning theory; with it Skinner influenced both the Thorndikian and the Pavlovian tradition. However, Skinner (1938, 1953) was more interested in empirical than in theoretical issues. He devoted himself to a detailed empirical analysis of all aspects of operant conditioning and used the knowledge gained to develop a number of applied techniques, including programmed instruction (Skinner, 1968). The influential behavior-therapy movement is also derived directly from his specification of the contingencies of operant conditioning.

It is not easy to categorize Skinner with respect to the evolution of thinking in motivational research; after all, he

Miller's Criticism of Skinner

Miller (1959) pointed out that Skinner's antitheoretical position becomes untenable when behavior is to be explained in terms of any more than two independent and dependent variables. There are, for example, three different manipulations that can serve as independent variables in the manipulation of drinking behavior in rats: hours of deprivation, dry feeding, and injection of a saline solution. Likewise, three different indicators of drinking behavior, the dependent variable, have been used: rate of bar pressing, amount of water consumed, and amount of quinine in the water needed to terminate drinking.

If we were to abandon the hypothetical construct "thirst" as mediating between the three independent variables and the three dependent variables (Fig. 2.4), we would have to postulate nine different if-then relationships. Not only would this be unparsimonious, it would be redundant, because the effect of each of the independent variables can be demonstrated with each of the dependent variables.

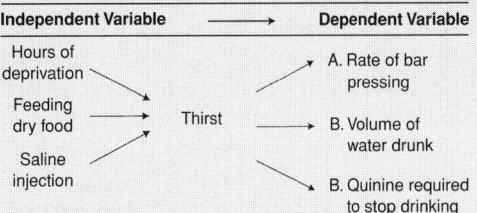

Figure 2.4 Independent and dependent variables related to drinking behavior as an example for the value of taking a hypothetical construct ("thirst") as a mediating (intervening) variable. (Based on Miller, 1959, p. 278.)

rejected all hypothetical constructs and every theoretical construction that goes beyond the formulation of if-then relationships (see the excursus above). He even avoided labels alluding to motivation, such as hunger, referring instead to "deprivation," which was operationally defined in terms of the period of time the animal has been deprived of food, or in terms of the resulting weight loss. Of course, both deprivation and the corresponding "reinforcement" (response consequences that increase the likelihood of the particular response) incorporate motivational aspects identified by learning and motivation theorists as intervening variables, including need, drive or satisfaction, reward or expectation.

Skinner cannot be categorized as belonging to the activation psychology strand of the study of motivation; rather, he forges the link between the research traditions of Thorndike and Pavlov.

The true representatives of the psychology of activation share four major approaches to theory construction:

1. They draw heavily on neurophysiological findings and theories about the functioning of the brain. To this extent, the explanatory constructs hypothesized are not neutral, but have considerable physiological implications. Activating systems in the brain stem are accorded a key role.

2. They make very general statements about the activation and direction of behavior. The emphasis is on finding regular relationships that have general applicability, at the cost of detailed, content-specific determinants of behavior.

3. Affect and emotion are of more relevance than in other theories of motivation.

4. They endeavor to identify the unique structural patterns on the stimulus side that produce generalized, activated behavior and imbue it with an approach or avoidance orientation.

Discoveries and Developments Within the Psychology of Activation

Two discoveries relating to the physiology of the brain proved particularly inspiring for researchers interested in the psychology of activation. One was the discovery of the **ascending reticular activation system** (ARAS).

ARAS AND THE REINFORCEMENT CENTER. Moruzzi and Magoun (1949) found that electrical stimulation of the reticular formation in the brain stem results in a change in the electroencephalogram, in what are known as "activation patterns." The various conditions of activation range from sleep and sleepiness to high levels of excitation. They have been found to be accompanied by changes in performance proficiency on a variety of tasks. This relationship describes an inverted U-function, with intermediate levels of activation being most conducive to performance. Emotions and affects have also been shown to be related to different levels of activation.

Under natural conditions, there are two sources of nonspecific stimulation of the ARAS:

■ the afferent sensory nerves that send collaterals to the reticular formation,

■ as well as efferent cortical impulses arriving at the ARAS. Lindsley (1957) was the major force in calling attention to the significance of these findings on the physiology of the brain for the study of behavior.

The other discovery was the identification of a "reinforcement" or "pleasure center" in the hypothalamus of the rat brain. If this area is stimulated by means of implanted electrodes, rats will learn to produce the responses that preceded this stimulation without previous deprivation or actual drive reduction (Olds & Milner, 1954; Olds, 1955, 1969). The founder of this strand of research was James Olds, a former student of Hebb.

HEBB'S IDEAS OF CELL ASSEMBLIES AND PHASE SEQUENCES. It was the Canadian psychologist Donald O. Hebb who became the most influential mediator between Pavlov's physiological approach and the new psychology of activation. In his book *Organization of Behavior* (1949), he restricted the study of motivation to explanations for the direction and persistence of behavior. From Hebb's perspective, there is no need to explain the energizing of behavior, because the organism is constantly active and metabolizing energy. The only question is why energy is released at particular loci of the organism, and characterized by a particular spatial and temporal pattern of firing. Hebb attributes these effects to "cell assemblies" that are gradually built up through repeated stimulation, forming a closed system that facilitates motor response sequences. A cell assembly is capable of producing other cell assemblies, frequently in concert with other sensory input. This leads to the formation of what Hebb calls "organized phase sequences," for him the physiological equivalent of the cognitive processes that guide behavior.

With a play on words, Hebb later (1953) turned the CNS (central nervous system) into a conceptual nervous system. Drawing on the findings of the ARAS studies, Hebb differentiated between the arousal function and the cue function of all stimulus inputs. Before a sensory input can exercise a cue function (i.e., guide behavior), there must be a certain level of nonspecific activation (Hebb's analog to "drive"), otherwise no integrated phase sequence will occur (e.g., boredom brought on by sensory deprivation is associated with a rapid deterioration in performance on relatively simple tasks).

Conversely, the arousal level can be too high if the information input deviates too sharply from the familiar (or the stimulus is simply too intense), leading to a breakdown in the previously formed phase sequence. This may elicit emotions of displeasure, irritation, and even fear. Minor deviations from previously established phase sequences are pleasurable, however, and motivate the continued pursuit of current behavior. Moreover, they stimulate further formation of phase sequences.

This final postulate corresponds to the processes of **accommodation** that are central to Jean Piaget's (1936) psychology of cognitive development. Here again, we encounter the idea of discrepancy, which – as we saw earlier – plays an affect-producing and therefore motivating role in McClelland's theory of motivation. Small departures from the familiar and the expected have positive emotional valences and motivate approach and persistence; larger discrepancies have negative valences and motivate avoidance, causing a break in the behavioral sequence. In this respect, McClelland's theory (1953) shows the influence of Hebb's conceptualization concerning the effects of discrepant phase sequences.

AROUSAL POTENTIAL AFTER BERLYNE. Daniel E. Berlyne (1924–1976) developed the most extensive theory of motivation based on the principle of arousal. He expanded Hebb's ideas and combined them with the principles underlying the work of Piaget (cognitive accommodation) and Hull (integrative neo-associationism). Based on neurophysiological findings concerning the ARAS and reinforcement centers, Berlyne (1960, 1963b, 1967) investigated the stimulus aspect of activation (arousal), on the one hand, and arousal-dependent motivational effects, on the other. On the stimulus side, it is the nature of the information and the resulting conflict that determine the arousal function. Berlyne used the term "collative variables" to designate these stimulus and conflict characteristics.

DEFINITION

"Collative" means that incoming information is subjected to processes of comparison that can lead to greater or lesser incongruities and conflicts with the familiar and the expected.

Berlyne distinguished four types of collative variables:
- novelty,
- uncertainty,
- complexity, and
- surprise value.

Aside from these collative variables, there are three further types of stimuli that have arousal functions:
- affective stimuli,
- intense external stimuli, and
- internal stimuli arising from need states.

The combination of these stimuli produces what Berlyne called **arousal potential**. In contrast to Hebb, Berlyne was able to present a variety of findings demonstrating the need for a distinction to be made between the arousal potential and the resulting level of activation. The relationship between the two is not linear, but describes a U-function. Both low and high arousal potentials result in high levels of activation, are experienced as unpleasant, and trigger activities serving to reduce the level of activation, i.e., leading to an intermediate level of arousal potential, which is the optimal state.

In Berlyne's (1960) words:

> Our hypotheses imply, therefore, that for an individual organism at a particular time, there will be an optimal influx of arousal potential. Arousal potential that deviates in either an upward or a downward direction from this optimum will be drive inducing or aversive. The organism will thus strive to keep arousal potential near its optimum (Berlyne, 1960, p. 194).

Among the arousal-dependent motivational effects, Berlyne distinguished between exploratory and epistemic behavior (the latter refers to the acquisition of knowledge and insight through cogitation). If the arousal potential is too high, it will motivate focused exploratory behavior, i.e., the closer inspection of the incoming information in order to reduce the arousal potential. If the arousal potential is too low (boredom), it will result in diverse exploration, initiating a search for greater stimulus variety and entertainment, or curiosity.

Young's Attempt to Integrate Psychology and Physiology

Paul Thomas Young founded a unique and independent branch within the motivational psychology of activation. As mentioned earlier, his *Motivation of Behavior* (1936) was the first English-language book to feature the term motivation in its title. Young proposed that physiological and psychological explanations of motivational events represent two different perspectives on the same phenomena. Beginning in the 1940s, Young (1941, 1961) devoted his research activities to food preferences in rats. He showed that even the behavior of satiated animals can be motivated by food, and that the level of motivation depends on the type of food offered. Some substances appear to have intrinsic affective activation value, an incentive (e.g., tastiness) that is independent of the drive strength arising from the organism's need states. Moreover, in postulating "evaluative dispositions" (1959) that are linked to affective activation and therefore capable of reinforcing behavior, Young did not neglect the motivational effects of need states and drive strength.

PSYCHOPHYSIOLOGICAL APPROACHES. Elizabeth Duffy (1932) initiated psychophysiological research in the 1930s, even before the discovery of the ARAS. She was able to correlate indicators of neurovegetative functioning (e.g., muscle tone and galvanic skin responses) with performance measures, and explained the relationships observed by assuming a kind of central activation function (analogous to the present-day concept of arousal), the physiological basis of which she attributed to the autonomic nervous system. Duffy (1934, 1941) also attempted to clarify the concept of emotion in terms of activation phenomena; Young's influence on her work is apparent here. Her book *Activation and Behavior* (1962) reviews the findings of activation research and presents her theoretical models of motivation. She summarizes her main findings on the relationship between activation and performance as follows:

> The degree of activation of the individual appears to affect the speed, intensity, and co-ordination of responses, and thus to affect the quality of performance. In general, the optimal degree of activation appears to be a moderate degree, with the curve expressing the relationship between activation and performance taking the form of an inverted U (Duffy, 1962, p. 194).

A more complete and systematic theory of motivation, covering the findings on activation reported by Duffy and others, was presented by Dalbir Bindra (1959). He began by linking up the conceptualizations of Hebb, Skinner, and Hull. According to Bindra, no distinction can be made between emotional and motivated behavior. Motivated behavior is characterized by its goal directedness:

> Goal direction is thus a multidimensional concept. Appropriateness, persistence and searching . . . can be looked upon as some of the dimensions that are involved in judging behavior as more or less goal-directed (Bindra, 1959, p. 59).

Like Skinner, Bindra attributed goal directedness primarily to reinforcing events. As he saw it, the manifestations of a given motivated behavior result from a variety of interacting factors, including sensory cues, habit strength, arousal level, blood chemistry, and a special "hypothetical mechanism," the "positive reinforcement mechanism" (PRM), which carries out the functions of the reinforcement centers discovered by Olds. In a later version of his theory, Bindra rejected the learning theorists' postulate of associations being formed through reinforcement (1969, 1974). Like Young, he now emphasized the importance of the incentive object, which – along with other stimulus aspects and certain organismic states, the "central motivational states" – induces motivation and initiates and guides behavior.

❶ Along with Bolles (1972), Bindra is the leading proponent of a theory of incentive motivation among the animal learning theorists (Chapter 5). His new conceptualizations of incentive motivation run essentially parallel to the notions developed 40 years earlier by Lewin and Tolman.

SOKOLOV'S ORIENTING REACTIONS. The most prominent representative of the Russian branch of the activation psychology approach to the study of motivation is E. N. Sokolov (1958, English translation, 1963). His work represents an extension to Pavlov's reflexology, incorporating the advances that had been made in neurophysiological measurement techniques and recent findings on brain functioning (e.g., the ARAS). He was primarily interested in the study of orienting and avoidance reactions, identifying their triggering conditions and analyzing their scope and effects. Berlyne incorporated the findings of Sokolov and his colleagues in his theory of motivation, thus establishing their influence on Western activation-oriented research.

DEFINITION

Orienting reactions are complex short-term processes which, in response to a decisive change in the stimulus field, trigger a series of physiological and psychological processes, all of which increase susceptibility to information input and heighten the readiness for action.

They include orienting of the sensory organs to the source of stimulation, exploratory responses, physical and chemical changes in the sense organs that facilitate greater discrimination, increases in the activation of the peripheral (e.g., muscle tone and blood pressure) and central (electroencephalogram) spheres of functioning, etc. After an orienting reaction

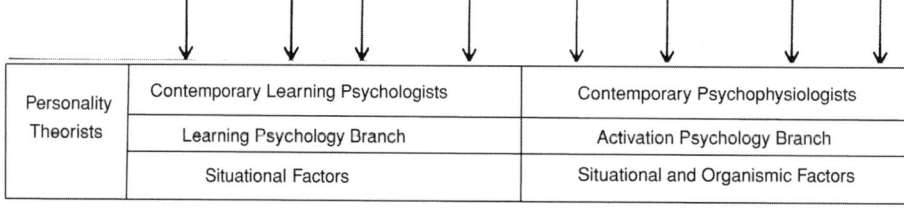

Figure 2.5 Associationist theories in the development of motivation research.

has been triggered repeatedly, it increasingly changes from a generalized to a more specific functional activation. The avoidance reaction encompasses some similar and some distinctly different components. In contrast to the orienting reaction, it decreases susceptibility to information and protects against overstimulation. These detailed analyses of processes lasting only a few seconds are of interest not only to psychophysiologists, they are also relevant to theories of motivation – the processes in question represent prototypes of "advancing" and "retreating" tendencies, which may in turn lead to approach and avoidance behavior.

EYSENCK'S TRAIT THEORY APPROACH. The English psychologist Hans Jürgen Eysenck is known primarily for his trait-oriented research in personality. His use of questionnaire methods and factor analysis was similar to R. B. Cattell's technique. Eysenck's bipolar personality continua of extraversion vs. introversion and neuroticism vs. emotional stability have become standards. According to Eysenck, individual differences along these two mutually independent dimensions are hereditary.

Eysenck (1967) combined this trait-theoretical approach with Pavlov's brain-physiological model of excitation and

inhibition, and particularly with the approaches of Sokolov and Hebb. He was also inspired by the more recent discoveries of activating centers in the brain and the attendant explanatory models of the physiology of activation. He attributed individual differences on the extraversion-introversion dimension to differences in the activation function of the ARAS, postulating higher levels of activation for introverted individuals. Extraverts take longer to develop conditioned reflexes. He characterized the other dimension (neuroticism vs. emotional stability) as an "emotional drive" and attributed it to centers of the limbic system (where Olds had discovered what he called "reinforcement centers"). This led to a unique merger of personality theory and activation-based motivation theory, in support of which Eysenck cited data from numerous tests and experimental studies of the physiology of the brain from both the East and the West.

❶ Many psychophysiologists are now involved in various areas of research on arousal. To the extent that this research is motivation-oriented, it focuses on the influence of situational factors and the effectiveness of organismic factors, particularly specific brain mechanisms.

Fig. 2.5 gives an overview of the two branches of associationist theories within the study of motivation: the learning psychology approach and the activation psychology approach. Both focus on the functional analysis of factors hypothesized to energize and guide observable behavior. Differences in behavior are explained almost exclusively in terms of situational factors, external as well as internal stimuli. Enduring (i.e., dispositional) factors are attributed to biological mechanisms, e.g., organismic homeostatic states that, if disturbed, elicit need states and thus stimulate drives, to mechanisms of the central nervous system such as the ARAS or the reinforcement centers, or to need-independent incentive characteristics of substances such as various types of food. Eysenck was the only proponent of the associationist approach to pay much attention to person factors, i.e., individual differences in motivational dispositions (traits).

There are historical reasons for this. Issues relating to motivation were initially embedded in other theoretical questions and only gradually evolved as questions in their own right. The learning theorists' research was and is primarily focused on learning processes, i.e., on the organism's adaptation to changes in the environment. Arousal-oriented research focuses on the functional analysis of neurological and psychophysiological mechanisms of the responding organism. Both branches made extensive use of animal research. For this reason, and because their actual strength is more easily manipulated, motivation research within the associationist strand is generally restricted to organismic needs or, more accurately, the resulting drives or "primary motives." "Secondary," "higher," or "social" motives that encompass different categories of person-environment interactions were not considered at all, much less as an explanation for individual differences in motivation. Nevertheless, both branches contain some notions that point in that direction:

- fear as a learned, secondary drive (N. E. Miller),
- individual differences in dispositional anxiety (Spence & Taylor),
- exploratory and epistemic behavior (Berlyne),
- personality differences in the perception of the environment and emotional stability (Eysenck).

SUMMARY

The historical overview provided in this chapter was intended to give readers an impression of the variety and scope of the research activities and theoretical models that relate to explanatory concepts like motive (or equivalent concepts) and motivation in one way or another. At the same time, the overview maps out the rather convoluted path that characterizes the study of motivation. The scientific study of motivation is still too young for there to have been a thorough historical analysis of the issues involved.

The subsequent chapters of this book focus more on motivational and cognitive approaches related to the psychology of motivation than on the other strands of motivation research. There are a number of reasons for this:

- These approaches reflect the interplay of influences from the other research traditions, particularly those relating to personality, cognition, and learning.
- They have produced a number of fruitful syntheses of theoretical models and methodological developments.
- They attest to the rapid development of experimental research.
- The study of "higher" human motives not only relates to all the fundamental issues of motivation research, but also demonstrates a variety of approaches to these issues.
- At present, the theory and methods of these approaches are best able to respond to the demand that behavior be regarded as a process of interaction between changing situation factors and dispositional person factors.

Moreover, particular attention will be paid to volitional phenomena, an area of research that is undergoing rapid development. Undoubtedly, the study of volitional processes will play an increasingly significant role in future motivational research.

REVIEW QUESTIONS

1. **Which research traditions can be distinguished in the history of motivation research and who were their founders?**
   - The psychology of the will: founded by Narziss Ach;
   - The instinct theory approach: founded by William McDougall;
   - Personality theories: founded by Sigmund Freud;
   - Associationist theories, the learning psychology approach: founded by Edward Lee Thorndike;
   - Associationist theories, the activation psychology approach: founded by Ivan P. Pavlov.

2. **What are heterogenetic and autogenetic theories of the will?**

   Heterogenetic theories of the will (e.g., Ebbinghaus, Külpe) attribute volitional phenomena to manifestations and entities beyond volition itself (e.g., muscular sensations, intellectual conclusions). These heterogenetic mechanisms were investigated using introspective methods. Autogenetic theories of the will (e.g., Wundt, James), in contrast, conceptualize volition as an independent entity, attributable to volitional processes and not to other manifestations.

3. **What role did Wilhelm Wundt and the members of the Würzburg school consider conscious and/or unconscious processes to play in the development and implementation of volition?**

   Both conscious and unconscious processes are involved in the development and implementation of volition, with unconscious processes playing a particularly important role. For Wundt, all processes of attention, apperception, perception, thought, and memory – i.e., what we now know as information processing – were driven by volitional acts.

4. Who founded experimental psychology, and which were the first experiments conducted?

The founder of experimental psychology was Wilhelm Wundt; his experiments were studies of "mental chronometry." This involved the comparison of reaction times under different experimental conditions. The difference observed ("subtractive procedure") was used as an indicator of the complexity of certain subprocesses of the reaction.

5. What is meant by Narziss Ach's construct of the "determining tendency" and what was the decisive experiment conducted in this respect?

In both mental and motor tasks, determining tendencies below the level of conscious awareness must be at work in order for an intended goal to be implemented. In Ach's decisive experiment to measure volitional strength (determining tendency), respondents had to overcome a strong association (between two syllables) to carry out a new instruction (a different combination of syllables). The more frequent the presentation of the original association, which now had to be overcome in order to execute the new instruction successfully, the stronger the determining tendency was considered to be.

6. What contribution did William McDougall's instinct theory make to the study of motivation?

McDougall saw instincts as inherited psychophysical dispositions that determine people to perceive, and pay attention to, objects of a certain class, and to respond to this experience with a particular quality of emotional excitement and by acting in a particular manner. In the US, this definition paved the way for the selective study of motivational processes (the reasons for action) at the expense of research on volitional processes. McDougall's specification of 18 motivational "propensities" inspired personality psychology (e.g., Allport, Lersch). Finally, McDougall's concepts of instinct and propensities can be seen as direct precursors to the study of comparative behavior or ethology.

7. What was Sigmund Freud's contribution to contemporary motivational psychology?

Freud focused attention on the following aspects, introducing them to the study of psychology: the decisive role of the unconscious; individual drive dynamics as determinants of behavior; drive reduction as the mechanism

underlying motivated behavior. The following assumptions proved particularly influential:
- drive impulses become manifest in different ways;
- the id, the superego, and the ego are involved in permanent conflict;
- the adult personality is an outcome of drives and their vicissitudes in childhood;
- the psychosexual stages of drive development evolve from a three-way drama between mother, father, and child.

8. What influence did Kurt Lewin have on the psychology of motivation?

Lewin's theory did not focus on individual differences, but involved broader psychological principles. His construct of the "quasi need" shifted research interest away from processes of volition (Narziss Ach's "determining tendency"). Lewin explains behavior in terms of the field of psychological forces emanating from the environment and the individual at any point in time: $B = f(P, E)$. Although his model was focused on the environment, Lewin's work influenced the personality theory approach to motivation. His environmental model with its analysis of situational forces (i.e., incentives) informed incentive theories of motivation. Lewin's approach also influenced conflict theory, the theory of level of aspiration, and research on substitute activities. Many of his experimental paradigms are still in use.

9. What are the basic premises of Vroom's instrumentality theory?

Actions and their outcomes have consequences that are associated with positive and negative incentive values. The individual anticipates these action-outcome consequences, and this anticipation serves to motivate action. The valences associated with the positive and negative incentives can vary individually. They are multiplied by the action's instrumentality for attaining the consequences (action-outcome-consequence expectancies). See outcome-consequence expectancies in Chapter 1, Fig. 1.2 to obtain the incentive value.

10. How does McClelland define motivation?

Motivation is the "redintegration" by a stimulus cue of an experienced change in a certain class of affective situation (e.g., achievement situation).

11. How does Atkinson's risk-taking model of achievement motivation represent the interaction between person and situation factors?

$T_s = M_s \times P_s \times I_s$; the motive tendency to approach success is the product of the personal motive to achieve success, the probability of success, and the incentive value of success. This product reflects the interaction between person and situation factors: If any of the factors in the equation is equal to zero, the others will have no effect either. When all factors come together, however, the product, i.e., the motive tendency, increases substantially.

12. **What was the major impact of the cognitive psychology approach (to personality theories of motivation) on the study of motivation? Which research traditions were founded on the basis of this approach?**

The cognitive psychology approach reintroduced the concept of reason to the study of motivation, following a long period during which the field had been dominated by the concepts of drive and instinct. Cognitive processes such as beliefs, perceptions, and expectancies about the courses of action available in a given situation can motivate behavior, as can incentives. The cognitive psychology approach produced consistency theories, which state that motivated behavior is intended to avoid or resolve inconsistencies. These consistency theories include the theories of cognitive balance (Heider) and cognitive dissonance (Festinger). The theory of causal attribution (Heider, Weiner) is also an outcome of the cognitive psychology approach.

13. **What is the basic premise of associationist theories in motivation research?**

The basic idea is that behaviors that facilitate successful interaction with the environment, i.e., that have survival value, became associated with pleasurable feelings over the course of human evolution. Thus, behavior becomes associated with positive affect and thus becomes attractive.

14. **According to Hull, which two components determine behavior? How are these components linked?**

Hull postulates a motivational component ("drive") and an associative ("habit") component. The two components are multiplied to determine a behavior tendency known as the "reaction-evocation potential."

15. **How does B. F. Skinner distinguish between operant responses and respondent behavior?**

In operant responses, behavior is reinforced by being closely followed by a desired stimulus. Behavior causes the outcome and is reinforced by it. In respondent behavior, in contrast, the stimulus eliciting a particular behavior or affect becomes associated with a new stimulus, such that the new stimulus is now also able to trigger the behavior or affect in question.

3 Trait Theories of Motivation

D. Scheffer and H. Heckhausen

3.1 From the Nomothetic to the Idiographic

Motivation emerges from the interaction of situational stimuli and dispositional characteristics. This chapter deals with the latter.

Dispositional factors of motivation are assumed to explain why some people show certain patterns of motivated behavior across situations, whereas others do not. Apart from specific situational stimuli, motivation is thus attributed to stable traits that are rooted in the individual personality, and that distinguish between people across situations and, to a certain extent, over time.

Individual dispositions to show certain patterns of motivation across situations have been given various labels in psychological research, reflecting very different notions of which and how many such dispositions there are, how they develop, and how they influence motivation. Accordingly, theories of motivation differ in terms of the relative importance they attribute to dispositional and environmental influences. Whereas the five-factor model focuses on endogenous dispositions and assumes the environment to play only a minor role, systems theory approaches emphasize the complex interactions between external stimuli and internal dispositions.

In this chapter we start with a simple model and gradually work our way toward a much more complex perspective on the role of dispositional factors in motivation. This does not mean to imply that one model is inherently preferable to another: all scientific theories of motivation aim to explain and predict in the most parsimonious and yet generally valid way possible why different people experience very different levels of tension and energy in similar situations, and why their behavior is directed toward such different goals. The five-factor model pursues these objectives by reference to just five independent dispositions, and meta-analyses have confirmed the validity of this approach. Nevertheless, critics object that this and other models are overly reductionist, and cannot be applied productively to specific situations. They argue that explanations of individual differences should draw on many more variables, and are interested in how the various internal and external factors of motivation are related and interact. Since both approaches unquestionably have their merits, this chapter covers a broad range of perspectives – from the strictly nomothetic to the idiographic.

3.1.1 Key Issues in Trait Theories of Motivation

Person-centered explanations of behavior based on "first-glance" observations provide a natural starting point for the study of motivation. Individual differences in behavior under seemingly equivalent (or unheeded) situational conditions catch the eye immediately. Nothing would seem more reasonable than to attribute these differences to dispositions of varying strengths. That in itself constitutes a trait theory, albeit an incomplete one. When observed behaviors are described in terms of traits, such as "helpfulness" or "pugnacity," they are endowed with motivational characteristics, implying that the individual strives to exhibit that behavior whenever possible.

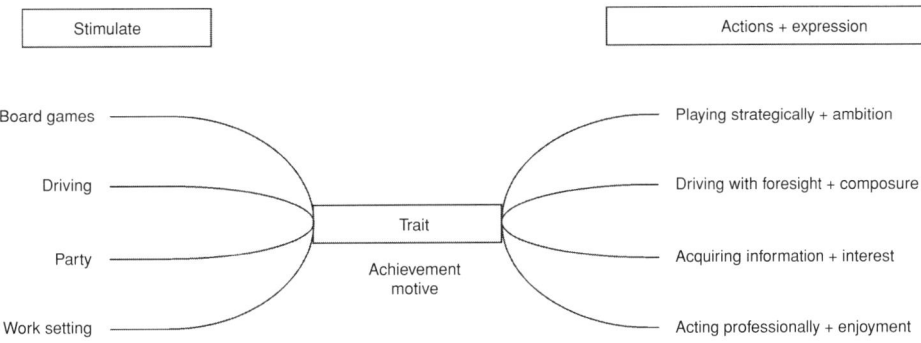

Figure 3.1 The relationship between stimuli (situations), traits, and actions.

Closer examination of the motive-like dispositions that "underlie" certain behaviors inevitably touches on some of the key issues of the motivation concept discussed in Chapter 1. One question to be asked is how individual differences can be objectified. Researchers only began to address this issue, which is essentially one of motive scaling, relatively recently. Their logical first step was to draw up a taxonomy of motives. How can one disposition be distinguished from other potential dispositions, and how many dispositions are there in total? Given that individual differences are not limited to a single behavioral domain such as helpfulness, but are also apparent in many other domains, there must necessarily be numerous dispositions.

These motive dispositions do not all determine processes of motivation at once, however. Instead, one or a few motive dispositions become activated, while the others remain latent. But what are the mechanisms behind this activation process? This question brings us to the key issue of motive arousal: much as it is important to consider person factors in the form of motivational dispositions, it is also vital to be aware of the situational factors that contribute to the arousal of a motive. A taxonomy of motives must therefore take account of the various motives activated across different situations. In other words, how many categories of person-environment relationships can be distinguished on the basis of the motivation processes characteristically activated?

Once these questions have been addressed, a taxonomy of motives can be examined experimentally. The intensity and thematic content of the situational incentives can be varied systematically while observing the extent to which the motivation process remains equivalent, i.e., subject to the same motivational disposition. It is only when the situational incentives of individual motive dispositions have been determined that it is possible to tackle motive scaling by measuring individual differences in behavior, while the intensity and thematic content of situational incentives are held constant.

3.1.2 Definition of a Trait

Allport (1937, p. 295) defined a trait as:

DEFINITION

A generalized and focalized neuropsychic system (peculiar to the individual), with the capacity to render many stimuli functionally equivalent, and to initiate and guide consistent (equivalent) forms of adaptive and expressive behavior.

The "achievement motive" (Chapter 6), e.g., might be defined as an internalized, highly generalized standard of excellence that is applied to stimuli as varied as playing chess, driving a car, chatting at a party, or doing one's job, in such a way that these stimuli are rendered functionally equivalent and lead to corresponding forms of behavior. Consistent (equivalent) forms of adaptive behavior that are congruent with the standard of excellence applied would be a strategic, ambitious approach to the game of chess, foresight and focus when driving, acquisition of useful information at the party, and professionalism at the workplace. Consistent (equivalent) forms of expressive behavior might be dogged determination in the game of chess, calm contemplation when driving, insistent interest at the party, and enjoyment of one's work. This definition of a trait is illustrated in Fig. 3.1.

The more stimuli (or, more generally speaking, situations) a trait can render functionally equivalent, the stronger it is. Extremely strong traits may have detrimental effects. For example, a very strong achievement motive might lead someone to gauge his romantic life with a partner on a standard of excellence and to engage in corresponding forms of adaptive and expressive behavior. It goes without saying that this is unlikely to strengthen the relationship.

Allport's trait definition implies that extremely strong traits lead to uncompromising, inflexible reactions that can only be appropriate or adaptive in the presence of very specific environmental demands. In the course of human evolution many traits have thus come to approximate a normal distribution; in other words, most people have traits of intermediate strength.

Trait theories aim to identify and enumerate the major traits, to determine how they can be measured or inferred, and to establish the forms of adaptive and expressive behavior they can explain and predict. Moreover, they seek to predict how different traits interact with one another and with environmental stimuli.

The first question to be addressed is how many traits there are – or, more specifically, which traits are important enough or seem to be of sufficient practical interest to warrant in-depth investigation. This brings us to the so-called classification problem, with its two potential errors:

1. All too often, people give observed behavior labels such as "helpfulness" or "pugnacity," thus endowing them with the character of a trait, and implying that the individual strives to exhibit that behavior at every opportunity. Although wanting to identify the dispositions underlying behavior seems reasonable, this approach can result in circular reasoning, with every observable behavior being attributed to a corresponding trait. Furthermore, it leads to the "inflation" of traits in behavioral explanations, and thus violates the principle of parsimony.

2. Alternatively, too few traits may be assumed. Although in line with the principle of parsimony, the descriptions and predictions of motivation yielded by this kind of approach are just as invalid as those produced when the first error is committed.

To draw on Albert Einstein, a good trait theory of motivation, like any other theory, must be "as simple as possible, and as complex as necessary."

In this chapter, we will first present theories that aim to explain motivational phenomena on the basis of relatively few variables. The models described will become gradually more complex, encompassing more variables and assuming these to interact with one another. This approach does not mean to imply that any one theory is inherently preferable to another. Simple models are not automatically better than complex ones because they are more parsimonious; complex models are not automatically superior to simple ones because they seem to be more valid and better applicable to specific situations.

3.2 The Lexical Approach or the "Wisdom of Language"

In this section, we present the five-factor model and Cattell's trait theory, both of which focus primarily on the classification problem. The two theories take a similar approach, relying on human intuition in the appraisal of others to generate hypotheses, and using factor analysis to reduce redundancies in empirical data and identify the underlying factors.

Both theories draw heavily on the work of Allport and Odbert (1936), who investigated what is known as the "sedimentation hypothesis," according to which all important interindividual differences that help to predict people's behavior in everyday life have been encoded in language over the course of linguistic evolution. Our ancestors' accumulated knowledge of human personality attributes is thus reflected in a corresponding vocabulary. Allport and Odbert found no less than 17,953(!) English words describing behavioral attributes.

In 1946, Cattell reduced this list to 171 variables, which he classified into bipolar pairs, such as:

- "forward-looking vs. preoccupied with the past," and
- "expressive vs. reserved."

Thus, Cattell did much of the groundwork for the five-factor model. However, because the present chapter proceeds gradually from the nomothetic to the idiographic, we will nevertheless start with the five-factor model. Cattell's theory is broader in scope than the five-factor model, and paved the way for the notion that motivation can be seen as a function of independent, but interrelating endogenous and exogenous systems. Here again, it is important for us to reiterate that our approach should not be interpreted as implying a rank ordering of models: a theory is not automatically any "better" than another, simply because it seeks to consider the complex interplay between environmental and personality factors. Science as an undertaking aims to increase efficiency. As we will see, the five-factor model offers a simple theory that allows individual differences in human motivation to be explained and predicted with great efficiency and methodological stringency.

3.2.1 The Five-Factor Model (The Big Five)

The five-factor model is today seen as the foremost trait theory, especially by practitioners in the field of personnel psychology. It is, in fact, a (relatively simple) model rather than a theory, but psychological research does not always differentiate carefully between the two. Widely used personality tests based on the five-factor model include the **NEO-FFI** (Costa & McCrae, 1985; see also Chapter) and the **Hogan Personality Inventory** (Hogan & Hogan, 1995). The popularity of the five-factor model owes a great deal to its simplicity. It reduces the wealth of personality attributes in human language to just five underlying factors, and thus provides for a clear classification. The statistical procedure of factor analysis is crucial to the model, being used to identify clusters of correlating personality characteristics.

The five-factor model originated from a systematic observation of how people appraise others. The personnel selection psychologists Tupes and Christal, who were responsible for screening applicants for the US Air Force, used the adjective list compiled by Allport and Odbert in their assessment centers. They noticed that five factors always seemed to emerge from factor analyses of appraisal data, even with very different samples of applicants and raters. They concluded that these five factors constitute the underlying structure of the language that observers use to characterize others.

Goldberg (1982) recognized the implications of this work, which was not made available to a general readership until 1992, and disseminated the findings in scientific circles. He developed the general hypothesis that the factors identified by Tupes and Christal reflect the structure of the language that humans use to describe, predict, and control their own and others' behavior in everyday social interactions – processes that social life in groups had rendered indispensable to survival over the course of human evolution (see also Hogan, 1996; Saucier & Goldberg, 1996).

Based on this empirically determined factor structure, Goldberg inferred the existence of certain universal neuropsychological structures or traits, and suggested that humans intuitively screen others (and indeed themselves) for behavioral evidence of these traits. When we meet people for the first time, and know that our interactions with them are likely to be important, we ask ourselves the following questions:

Intuitive Self- and Other-Evaluations on the Basis of the Five-Factor Model

■ Is the other person lively, convincing, optimistic, and sociable (extraverted)?

■ Is the other person friendly, and does he or she adhere to social norms (agreeable)?

■ Is the other person reliable, goal striving, and hardworking (conscientious)?

■ Is the other person well-balanced, robust, and stress-resistant (emotionally stable)?

■ Is the other person flexible, imaginative, and intellectual (open to experience)?

Validity of the Big Five

Goldberg argued that humans are unable to process any more information when appraising others owing to the limited working capacity of the cognitive apparatus. Nevertheless, people seek to gauge the strength of the traits of those around them as accurately as possible. There is one simple reason for this: if we know what makes other people tick, we can predict how they will behave, and this knowledge can help us to succeed in life. We are constantly making predictions about other people's behavior in everyday life: "Will this man be an **emotionally stable** father?"; "Is this **disagreeable** insurance agent trying to take me for a ride?"; "Will this employee be **conscientious** enough to get his/her assignments finished on time?"; and so on. A high score on one of the Big Five factors is not always adaptive, however. For example, some CEOs deliberately promote junior managers who do not seem to be very agreeable, in the belief that they will otherwise not be sufficiently tough in a competitive environment (e.g., in their interactions with subordinates).

❶ The underlying assumption of the five-factor model is that linguistic structures that facilitate valid predictions will be more likely to survive than structures that reliably lead to flawed predictions.

In terms of evolutionary theory, the Big Five can thus be interpreted as a complex form of "memes" – cultural entities that evolve through a process of selection and variation, in the same way as genes.

The behavioral observation methods and questionnaires developed on the basis of the five-factor model have enjoyed widespread application, and meta-analyses have been conducted to examine the validity of the Big Five traits. These meta-analyses unambiguously support the construct and criterion validity of the questionnaires and adjective checklists developed on the basis of the five-factor model (Barrick & Mount, 1991; Meyer et al., 2001). For example, when self-report questionnaires are used to assess the Big Five, extraversion is found to correlate with a good sales record, conscientiousness with positive performance appraisals, agreeableness with a strong customer focus, etc.

Notably, however, the mean, uncorrected correlations of self-reported Big Five with relevant criteria are below $r = .20$. This apparently low validity might be attributable to the limitations of self-evaluation questionnaires. Indeed, assessment center data show that direct other evaluations of behavior exhibit higher mean criterion validity, at $r = .38$ (for a summary, see Meyer et al., 2001).

Yet, even when the uncorrected correlations seem low, relationships between predictors and criteria are often worth taking very seriously. These relationships are often underestimated on account of the low reliability of both the predictor and the criterion (!) variables and their frequently limited variance. The examples from the meta-analysis by Meyer et al. (2001) cited below illustrate this point.

EXAMPLE

Important effects may be concealed behind seemingly low correlations:

Correlation between gender and height	$r = .67$
Correlation between observers' ratings of the attractiveness of cohabiting pairs	$r = .39$
Correlation between the reliability of a test and its construct validity	$r = .33$
Correlation between smoking and the onset of lung cancer within 25 years	$r = .08$
Correlation between chemotherapy and the survival rate in breast cancer patients	$r = .03$

It would hardly be advisable to continue smoking on the basis of the seemingly low correlation between smoking and lung cancer. As this example illustrates, even low validity scores can be of great significance in the real world. Findings showing that significant validities determined for the Big Five can be replicated across numerous different samples testify to the soundness of the approach.

❶ Because the Big Five are empirically independent of one another (i.e., barely intercorrelate), meaningful predictions can be made on the basis of individual trait profiles.

The Big Five and the Structure of Human Temperament

The Big Five traits derived from the five-factor model seem to be relevant to both research and practice for the simple reason that they represent a taxonomy of dimensions of human temperament (Angleitner & Ostendorf, 1994) that evidently also applies to other mammals (McCrae et al., 2000). Extensive international studies suggest that the five factors are basic, biologically rooted, **endogenous** traits, i.e., they are not affected by the environment in any way (McCrae et al., 2000, p. 175). The high heritability of the Big Five, which twin studies generally put at 50% (Loehlin, 1989), is one indication of this endogeneity. However, these estimates include measurement errors caused by the less than perfect reliability of the measures, as well as systematic method factors associated with the use of self-reports. When the method variance is reduced by combining self- and other-evaluations, estimations of heredity are much higher than 50%, at between 66% and 79% (Riemann, Angleitner, & Strelau, 1997).

The remaining 21% to 34% of the variance is explained almost exclusively by influences that siblings do not share, i.e., cannot be traced back to the social background, parenting styles, or similar factors. Harris (1995) argued that, after genetic factors, peers have the most important impact on the development of children's characters. However, it is also possible that the small proportion of variance in the Big Five that cannot be explained by genetic factors is attributable to biological factors; e.g., the prenatal hormonal environment may be influenced by stress during pregnancy (Resnik, Gottesman, & McGue, 1993).

Two further patterns of results support the notion that the Big Five are endogenous personality dimensions:

1. They are remarkably stable. Very accurate predictions of a 70-year-old's personality can be made on the basis of measurements taken 30 years earlier (Costa & McCrae, 1992).

2. There seems to be a universal, cross-cultural process of maturation of the Big Five: extraversion and openness to experience decrease with age, while levels of agreeableness and conscientiousness increase (McCrae et al., 2000). This observation does not contradict the assumption – based on test-retest correlations – that the Big Five are extremely stable. In fact, an individual's rank placement in a sample can remain virtually unchanged over time, with all participants experiencing similar changes in trait strength. The magnitude of this change as a function of chronological age is low, however ($r < .20$, see McCrae et al., 2000). This process of maturation makes perfect sense from the perspective of evolutionary psychology: whereas high levels of extraversion and openness to experience motivate young adults to approach others (an approach that is conducive to the "mating effort"), higher levels of agreeableness and conscientiousness lead to increasing "staidness" with age, thus providing any offspring with the security and routine they need to develop and thrive (an approach that is conducive to the "parenting effort").

The biological rooting of the Big Five brings us back to the sedimentation hypothesis, according to which only genetically anchored traits that remain stable from generation to generation are coded in human language. This process results in a universal grammar for the description of important personality characteristics. Today, this grammar provides a practical **heuristic** that can be used to consolidate observations of oneself and others into valid characterizations of oneself and others. Heuristics are "rules of thumb" that are primarily used when time is short and information is incomplete. Although they have the advantage of being fast and frugal (Fiedler & Bless, 2002), it is important to bear in mind that heuristics like the five-factor model can also lead to errors in the appraisal of others.

Block (1995) identified two potential errors in personality descriptions based on the five-factor model:

1. Neglect of the context: The five-factor model does not define specific situations that activate or deactivate the five "essential" traits. Thus, personality descriptions based on the five-factor model are at risk of being blind to the context, and remain an overly simple form of assessment based on indiscriminate classifications of others.

2. Neglect of less salient, but important characteristics: Based on methodological considerations, Block (1995) argues that factor analysis is not a suitable procedure for examining the decision-making processes underlying personality appraisals. Klein, Cosmides, Tooby, and Chance (2002) have since shown that semantic and episodic memory cooperate in the perception of others, and that the functioning of episodic memory, in particular, does not correspond with the logical structure and sequential approach of factor analysis. Yet episodic memory is thought to be decisive for detailed, finely nuanced personality descriptions. An exclusive focus on factors that explain a large proportion of variance in factor analysis can thus lead to important details being overlooked. And as Block points out, factors that explain a large proportion of variance may have only trivial implications for behavior, if any, whereas residuals with low eigenvalues (i.e., the 6th, 7th, or even 21st factor) may have significant effects.

All things considered, the five-factor model does not seem suited to solve the classification problem. Some personnel psychologists have long maintained that the five factors are much too broad for practical applications and that valid predictions of behavior require considerably larger numbers of better defined traits. Gough (1990) adopted a more differentiated strategy with the **California Personality Inventory**

EXCURSUS

Human Evolution Has Produced a Wealth of Traits: The Swiss Pocket Knife Analogy

Evolutionary psychologists Cosmides (1989) and Cosmides and Tooby (1992) identified a specific psychological mechanism, the function of which is to detect people who are trying to cheat us. This mechanism enables us to solve formal, logical problems that often defeat us in other contexts. Their findings have two implications for the five-factor model:

1. **Psychological mechanisms that develop into differential traits through a process of natural selection seem to be domain specific.** In other words, they only render some potential stimuli functionally equivalent; e.g., all social situations in which cheating may occur. The mechanism is only activated in these situations.

2. **Numerous mechanisms of this kind seem to be needed for survival and reproduction, prompting Cosmides to** compare the human psyche to a Swiss pocket knife. Both have a number of different "tools" that can be applied to certain problems, but that cannot solve others. Although these tools may appear to be similar on the surface, they evolved independently and represent distinct neuropsychological units, each with a specific evolutionary advantage.

Bearing in mind that the number of traits identifiable on the basis of Allport's definition is very high indeed, the five-factor model can nevertheless be put to worthwhile use as a heuristic. Labeling others as "disagreeable" may be interpreted as a product of the mechanism for detecting cheats, for example. After all, we have a vested interest in finding out whether or not the people with whom we interact are likely to abide by social norms.

(CPI). He demonstrated that there are more than a dozen interculturally distinguishable "folk concepts" of traits that are regarded as independent in very different societies, even though their empirical intercorrelations are relatively high. Although dominance and sociability both load on the extraversion factor in the five-factor model, e.g., it is the dissociation of the two that provides the most valuable diagnostic information. The positive correlation between dominance and sociability means that they are relatively few in number, but there are indeed individuals who are both highly assertive and very withdrawn, and who thus seek to avoid public speaking and large crowds. According to Gough (1990), it is precisely this noncorrespondence of correlating traits that is often particularly meaningful for motivation (see also the dissociation-oriented approach presented in Chapter 12, according to which two variables that correlate strongly may be completely independent of each other, meaning that they should be assessed separately).

As the excursus above illustrates, Gough's notion that there is nothing to be gained from reducing a large number of traits to a few underlying factors has received support from researchers with a background in evolutionary psychology. Proponents of the five-factor approach do not claim the Big Five to be the only important human traits, however. They are well aware that there may be other independent personality dimensions, such as the **willingness to take risks** (Andresen, 1995). Indeed, nobody would be genuinely surprised if a Big Six or Big Seven model of endogenous personality dimensions proved to be necessary in the course of time. However, there would have to be very good arguments for the introduction of any new factors to ensure that the principle of parsimony is not violated.

Furthermore, McCrae et al. (2000) distinguish between the biologically anchored dispositions described by the Big Five, and culturally conditioned characteristics, including acquired abilities, habits, values, and motives (McCrae et al., 2000). There can be no doubt that these environmentally determined systems exist, that they influence human motivation, and that they have dynamic characteristics that distinguish them from personality dimensions. Cattell provided factor analytic evidence for the orthogonality of temperament-related and culture-specific traits. He was also the first to point out that dynamic traits should be investigated using methods other than questionnaires (see the distinction between implicit motives, measured by operant tests, and explicit traits, measured by questionnaire methods, in Chapter 9).

3.2.2 R. B. Cattell's Trait Theory

Cattell's theory had a considerable influence on the development of the five-factor model, but is itself much more complex. Cattell first distinguished three types of dispositions as the causes of observable classes of behavior:

- cognitive dispositions (abilities), which are manifest in problem-solving situations of differing complexity,
- temperament dispositions, which are pervasive, i.e., are manifest regardless of the situation, and
- dynamic or motivational dispositions, which increase or diminish in accordance with the incentive strength of the situation.

These three types of dispositions are not distinguished conceptually in the five-factor model, and are thus confounded in the tests based on that model.

The distinction between temperament dispositions ("traits") and dynamic, motivational characteristics is one of Cattell's most significant contributions to research. In a longitudinal study Winter, Stewart, John, Klohnen, and Duncan (1998) showed just how important this distinction is for predicting behavior. Whereas dynamic, motivational characteristics (like the motives covered in Chapters 6–8) describe and predict what a person strives to achieve, temperament dispositions reflect how he or she translates that motive into action.

STUDY

Motives and Traits May Have Interactive Effects on Behavior

In a longitudinal study with two different samples, Winter et al. (1998) showed that implicit motives and traits may have interactive effects on social behavior. Extraverted and introverted individuals (extraversion-introversion was measured using the first vector scale of the CPI by Gough, 1990) only differed on important behavioral criteria if they had scored high on the affiliation and power motives 20 years earlier. For example, women who were high in the affiliation motive 20 years earlier showed high levels of marital instability (more separations and remarriages) if they were later classed as introverted, but not if they were extraverted. This finding makes perfect sense if the trait of extraversion is interpreted as a motive implementation style: given their temperament, introverted individuals find it difficult to open up to others and to experience intimacy. Moreover, they may tend to overreact in marital conflicts. For someone with a high dispositional affiliation motive, responses of this kind must be seen as deficits that can put strain on the relationship (particularly if the partner is also introverted, although this aspect was not tested in the study by Winter and colleagues). For someone without a strong affiliation motive, on the other hand, this temperament-based interpersonal distance need not be seen as a deficit, but can be perceived in positive terms, as a measure of independence. This might explain why introverted women who were low in the affiliation motivation 20 years earlier reported the highest levels of marital stability (although the differences were not significant) in the two samples examined.

Brunstein's distinction between implicit and explicit motives offers an equally plausible explanation for this pattern of results (see Brunstein, Schultheiss, & Grässmann, 1998; Schultheiss & Brunstein, 1999; see also Chapter 9). A questionnaire measure of extraversion can be interpreted as reflecting an explicit affiliation motive. If a person scores low on this measure, but high on a TAT measure of the implicit affiliation motive, the discrepancy is likely to have detrimental effects on well-being.

Asendorpf (2004) has drawn attention to a methodological shortcoming of the Winter et al. study. Whereas implicit motives were measured in young adulthood, the questionnaire measures of extraversion and social behavior were not implemented until 20 years later. Hence, discrepancies between implicit and explicit motives might also derive from experiences that influenced both motive types, but could only logically be picked up by the questionnaires implemented at the second point of measurement. In this case, it would not be a matter of interactions between implicit and explicit motives, but of changes in motive strength in response to social experiences.

This point can be illustrated by reference to two kinds of traits: the temperament disposition of **extraversion**, as contained in the five-factor model, and the motivational disposition of **affiliation**. The goal of the affiliation motive is to experience emotional warmth in social interactions with individuals and groups. It thus describes **what** a person strives to achieve. High extraversion, in contrast, describes the personal behavioral style, or **how** an individual expresses all manner of aspirations (even for power and influence) across very different situations. The following case study illustrates why it makes sense to distinguish between these dispositions, even though they seem so similar on the surface.

EXAMPLE

Ben always sits by himself in the lecture theater. He rarely goes to parties. If his fellow students speak to him, his answers tend to be monosyllabic. His peers conclude that he is introverted and simply not interested in other people, and soon begin to ignore him. They are very much mistaken, however, much to Ben's chagrin. Affiliation is in fact his strongest motive. But because he is so introverted, he does not dare talk to people he does not know very well, and he is at a complete loss for words whenever women speak to him. Consequently, he satisfies his need for social contact on the Internet, where nobody notices how shy and awkward he is. It is only in this context that he can reconcile his need for affiliation with his introverted temperament.

The what and the how of motivation do not correspond in this example. It is very much easier for people who seek to establish a wealth of social contacts to satisfy this need if they are extraverted – particularly in relatively new and unfamiliar situations (Winter et al., 1998). A high achievement motive might be more congruent with Ben's shyness; indeed, satisfying this motive is rather more compatible with an introverted temperament. What we are interested in at the moment, however, is the **independence** of motives and temperament. The contrasting case study that follows provides further illustration of this point.

EXAMPLE

Lisa is always surrounded by a throng of students in the lecture theater. She goes to lots of parties, and is always the center of attention. She loves to engage in lively discussions and has many friends and acquaintances. In time, however, those who get to know her more closely and who observe her carefully realize that she is not really interested in forming meaningful relationships. Other people simply serve her aims of getting ahead and getting her own way. Should they step out of line, she will – in her own charming way – drop them like hot potatoes.

Ben and Lisa are complete opposites in terms of their needs and temperaments. Although Lisa finds it very easy to establish relationships with others, her sociable behavior does not reflect her true motivation. Despite her many contacts with others, she feels no real need for affiliation and social bonding. This makes her very independent and helps her to gain power and influence over others. Ben, on the other hand, is unable to satisfy his most fervent wish of establishing meaningful relationships with others.

Cattell (1957, 1958, 1965) was the first to provide comprehensive empirical evidence for the independence of motivational, cognitive, and temperamental dispositions. In his search for unique, independent dispositions and their mutual boundaries, he did not rely on phenomenological descriptions, the accumulated labels of everyday language, or intuitive insights. Rather, he measured individual differences, often over broad domains of possible classes of reactions, to determine which reactions covary with each other. Unlike the proponents of the five-factor model, he was not content to submit the data obtained from questionnaires measuring motive-related characteristics such as helpfulness or sociability to factor analytic categorization, and to regard the factors extracted as dispositions, with individuals being characterized in terms of their factor scores.

He considered this kind of approach injudicious for two main reasons. First, the factors emerging (the covariation patterns of responses) are largely dependent on the range of variability of responses that can possibly be elicited from the participant by the assessment procedure applied. For example, the factor analyses performed by the proponents of the five-factor model were essentially based on various forms of the almost 200 adjectives that Cattell conceived of as the range of response. It is hardly surprising that factor analyses of a given set of adjectives or behavioral descriptions derived from those adjectives always yield five factors. Measures that encompass representative samples of what occurs outside the test situation (on both the stimulus side and the response side) are needed to overcome the methodological biases inherent in the factors extracted. Second, the questionnaire instruments commonly used to scale the strength of motive dispositions have proved to have limited validity. Responses are based on introspective self-reports that can easily be falsified or influenced by response tendencies, especially since the purposes of the tests are normally quite transparent. Moreover, the extent to which individuals are capable of providing accurate self-reports varies (see Nisbett & Wilson, 1977, and the following excursus). For example, Lisa from the case study above might subjectively interpret her many social activities as indicative of a high affiliation motive, although her behavior is in fact driven by an implicit desire for power and influence. In a self-evaluation, she would not be willing or able to distinguish the what from the how of her motivation.

Cattell (1957) took a two-step approach to sidestep the inherent difficulties of self-report measures:

Step 1. He identified behavioral indices that reflect motive strength in the most direct and "objective" manner, i.e., are not subject to the individual's awareness and do not provide an opportunity for responses to be modified. This involved identifying unitary domains of motive-related interests and attitudes, and constructing objective tests as indices of the corresponding behavior. The motive strength data obtained (for the domains specified a priori) were then subjected to factor analysis and classified according to their "motivational components." These components do **not** represent different motives in themselves, but rather definable manifestations of each motive. The behavioral indices that form the basis of the components can thus be seen as devices by which individual differences in the strength of specific motives might be measured.

Step 2. These scaling devices were employed to determine the covariation patterns of a broad spectrum of different attitudes and interests. For Cattell, the differentiated motivational dispositions that emerged from this process had general psychological validity. Finally, specific criteria were used to categorize these traits in terms of whether they are biological or acquired through sociocultural learning.

To determine the strength of motivational components, Cattell first collated practically all of the behavioral indices that psychologists had ever posited to elicit motive tendencies. At one point, Cattell (1957, pp. 465–471) listed no fewer than 55 such measures of "motive manifestations," originating from areas of psychological research including general knowledge (e.g., information about means-ends relationships), perception, memory, learning, reaction time, fantasy, autonomic responses, prejudice, and resumption of interrupted tasks.

These behavioral indices loaded on six motivational factors that related to motivation in general rather than to a specific motive. Three of these Cattell labeled with the psychoanalytic terms "id," "ego," and "superego." These six factorial components of motive strength were then subjected to second-order factor analysis. From this emerged two second-order factors, an "integrated" and an "unintegrated" motivational component. The integrated component encompasses focused, conscious aspects of a motive disposition ("ego," "superego"). The unintegrated component encompasses "complexes," unconscious predispositions, and physiological reactions. Examples for this are bias and galvanic skin response. In subsequent studies just these two motivational components were employed to measure strength in terms of their combined value, using a set of six principle indices that had proved particularly sensitive.

Cattell had thus created a generally applicable technique for scaling motive strength and could move on to the second

3

EXCURSUS

Telling More Than We Can Know? The Limits of Questionnaire Measures

In 1977, a classic article by Nisbett and Wilson showed that people are often not capable of providing accurate information about the reasons for their behavior. These findings cast doubt on the validity of the questionnaire measures commonly used by psychologists. In the 1980s and 1990s, cognitive psychology thus placed increased emphasis on the experimental investigation of implicit aspects of memory and learning, i.e., aspects that are not accessible to verbal description (Goschke, 1997a; Schacter, 1987). Today, social psychology examines nonconscious attitudes by means of implicit association tests (Bosson, Swann, & Pennebaker, 2000; Greenwald & Banaji, 1995). In particular, the "Implicit Association Test" (IAT), which measures negative attitudes (e.g., toward members of another race) in terms of longer reaction times to specific word cues (e.g., names typical of members of another race, such as Jamel), has stimulated a great deal of theory building and testing in the field (Greenwald et al., 2002). Stable traits can also be investigated by means of implicit measures. Bosson, Swann, and Pennebaker (2000) showed that narcissism is associated with high explicit (conscious) and low implicit self-esteem. In motivation psychology, the distinction between implicit and explicit methods of measurement has a long tradition. For example, it is known that findings from the TAT have much in common with many experimental operationalizations of implicit processes, but do not correlate with questionnaire measures of the same theme. This point is covered in depth in Chapter 9.

step of delineating traits by means of factor analysis. He called this step dynamic calculus: the search for the factors of dynamic structures. Responses to devices covering a wide range of attitudes related to goal-directed behavior were factor analyzed. A number of clear factors emerged and were termed "unitary dynamic source traits." Some of these Cattell labeled "ergs" (from the Greek "ergon," meaning energy or work), which to him represented a sort of biological drive, not unlike McDougall's (1908) original conceptualization of instinct.

Ergic traits can vary in their manifestations depending on situational incentives. Cattell also subjected intraindividual changes in the "level of ergic tension" to factor analysis. He identified two constant components – inherent or constitutional differences and the individual's past history – as well as three variable components: situational incentive, physiological state, and presence or absence of goal satisfaction. He thus demonstrated the dynamic nature of "ergs," which wax and wane according to the incentive strength of the situation at hand. The "ergs" he identified are listed in Table 3.1.

SUMMARY

Cattell used factor analysis to show that the "ergs" he identified are independent of "traits." From today's perspective, however, it is regrettable that he did not continue to investigate "ergs" systematically, and to test their antecedent conditions or consequences in theory-driven experimental analyses. Although the factor analytic approach is a great improvement on a priori definitions, it can only describe mean patterns of relations for the entire population of study participants, and does not allow subgroups to be preselected on the basis of idiographic equivalence classes. This is because of the descriptive rather than explanatory nature of correlational analyses (including factor analysis), which can show which variables are associated and which are not, but are unable to specify causal connections. Few insights into the

key issues of motive arousal and motive development can thus be expected from this approach.

However, Cattell's creative approach to factor analytic trait theory made a substantial contribution to work on the fundamental issue of motive classification by helping to distinguish the motivational dispositions ("ergs") listed in Table 3.1, to which we will return in later sections of this chapter.

3.3 Motives as an Expression of Needs

The three major proponents of need theories are McDougall, Murray, and Maslow. A need can be defined as a discrepancy between an actual state and a desired state (McClelland, Atkinson, Clark, & Lowell, 1953). Actual states are characterized by the presence or absence of certain motive-related incentives, the congruence or fit of which is essential to the trait disposition. For instance, the need for affiliation is activated only when people experience rejection, i.e., when the situation is at variance with the aspired outcome; and it is not deactivated until they have been accepted again. Other positive stimuli do not have the same effect (Shipley & Veroff, 1952).

The various motives activated across different situations must therefore be taken into account in any classification of motives by needs. Need theories investigate how many categories of person-environment relations can be distinguished on the basis of the motivation processes characteristically activated.

3.3.1 Instinct-Based Classification of Motives

To some extent, Cattell's descriptive system of motives was a revival of McDougall's explanatory model of behavior, which dates back to the early 20th century. It was McDougall (1908) who first attempted to attribute all human behavior to motivational dispositions. At that time, these dispositions were

Table 3.1. Action goals, emotions, and example attitude statements for six motive dispositions of the "erg" type (Based on Cattell, 1957, p. 541)		
Action goal	Emotion	Attitude statement
1. Mating	Sex	I want to fall in love with an attractive man/woman.
2. Gregariousness	Loneliness	I want to belong to a social club or team of people with congenial interests.
3. Parenthood	Pity	I want to help the needy, wherever they are.
4. Exploration	Curiosity	I like to read books, newspapers, and magazines.
5. Escape to security	Fear	I want my country to be better protected against terrorism.
6. Self-assertion	Pride	I want to be smartly dressed, with a personal appearance that commands admiration.

commonly labeled "instincts" rather than "motives," which explains why Freud's concept of "Trieb" was rendered as "instinct" (and not "drive") in the original English translation. The 19th century faculty psychologists had already proposed the concept of "instinct" as a counterpart to intelligence. With the increased acceptance of Darwin's theory of evolution, scholars had also begun to draw on instincts to explain human behavior.

James (1892) viewed instinct as the capacity to act intuitively. What for him was just one of several explanatory concepts, McDougall saw as the basic principle for all "dynamic" explanations of behavior. By elevating instincts to such a dominant position, McDougall triggered the great instinct controversy of the 1920s (Chapter 2). The main critics of instinct theory responded with a radical behaviorist position, attributing all behavior to simple reflexes and learning (Watson, 1919). At the same time, Woodworth (1918), who had long envisaged a "motivology," was prompted to reject the term "instinct" once and for all, replacing it by the term "drive." It was Tolman who finally made McDougall's motivational psychology acceptable even to the behaviorists, by rendering it subject to experimental investigation. The concept of instinctive behavior was later investigated and clarified by ethologists such as Lorenz and Tinbergen.

What was McDougall's objective? He was opposed to a psychology limited to the description of mental contents, and to approaches employing "mechanistic" explanations, such as association theory and reflexology. For McDougall, all behavior was "teleological" – directed to the attainment of certain future goal states. He cited seven behavioral characteristics in support of this position:

1. A certain spontaneity of movement.
2. The persistence of activity, independent of the continuance of the impression that triggered it.
3. Directional change of goal-directed activity.
4. Termination of the activity as soon as the desired change in the situation has been brought about.
5. Preparation for the new situation brought about by the present action.
6. Improvement in the behavior's effectiveness when it is repeated under similar circumstances.
7. A reflex action is always a partial reaction, but a purposive action is a total reaction of the organism.

McDougall attributed these characteristics of behavior directed toward specific goal states to instincts. His original definition of instinct was fairly complex, encompassing three consecutive processes:

- a disposition to perceive selectively as a function of specific organic states (e.g., hunger increases sensitivity to edible objects),
- a corresponding emotional impulse (the core of instinct),
- instrumental activities appropriate to attaining the goal (e.g., flight in response to fear).

McDougall's definition of instinct thus integrates very different phenomena. He viewed just one of the three determinants – emotion – as innate and unmodifiable, defining this component to be the core of instinct, but assumed the cognitive and motor components to be subject to change in response to biographical experience, adding to the complexity of the concept.

It was on the basis of this conceptualization that McDougall (1908) drew up a first list of ten instincts, although he was not able to assign clearly defined emotions to the last three (the corresponding emotions are shown in parentheses):

1. flight (fear),
2. repulsion (disgust),
3. curiosity (wonder),
4. pugnacity (anger),
5. self-abasement (subjection),
6. self-assertion (pride),
7. parental instinct (tender emotion),
8. reproduction instinct (-),
9. acquisition instinct (-),
10. construction instinct (-).

Because the term "instinct" came under heavy attack, and occasioned the mistaken idea that behavior is determined largely by innate predispositions, McDougall later adopted the term "propensity." There were no major changes to the concept itself, except for the distinction now made between propensity and tendency, as illustrated by the following quote from McDougall's last book (1932):

A propensity is a disposition, a functional unit of the mind's total organization, and it is one which, when it is excited, generates an active tendency, a striving, and impulse or drive towards some goal; such a tendency working consciously towards a foreseen goal is a desire (McDougall, 1932, p. 118).

Several propensities can combine to form "sentiments." These are cognitive systems that result from learning and experience relating to the evaluation of objects and concepts, as we saw earlier in Cattell's approach. For example, the perception and evaluation of the concept "my country" involves several "propensities." The "self-sentiment" – i.e., the perception of one's self – plays a central, organizational role in these cognitive schemata, which go to shape the "character," i.e., the individual differences existing amid the innate, instinct-like emotional impulses of "propensities."

One question that has remained unanswered is which empirical criteria might be used to infer the number of possible motive dispositions, beyond mere plausibility considerations. This question became perceived as increasingly urgent when – inspired by McDougall's lists of instincts – it became common practice, particularly in neighboring disciplines such as sociology and political science, to attribute all behavioral phenomena to specific instincts. War, for example, was attributed to an aggressive instinct. At the same time, the fact that people fight wars was cited as evidence for the presence of an aggressive instinct. The circularity of this approach (that McDougall himself would never have espoused) was the trigger for the great instinct controversy. The objections could have been countered with clearer criteria for instinctive behavior and systematic studies, but this possibility was overlooked in the heat of the exchange. A second, related reason for the controversy was the suspicion that the instinct concept might be used to revive faculty psychology, and that all that was really being done was to describe and classify behavior. And how might behavior be categorized? As instinct-dependent behavior versus behavior resulting from acquired habits? To this end, it would be necessary to distinguish between interchangeable, instrumental activities and the goal states that are the focal point of behavior.

In the final analysis, opposing metatheoretical positions kept the controversy alive and prevented an objective, empirical resolution of the issues. Its opponents equated the instinct concept with McDougall's assertion that behavior is goal-directed, i.e., structured in terms of a goal. Associationists viewed this approach as unscientific, implying that McDougall had endowed instincts with a kind of mystical force, not unlike the vitalists who preceded him. As far as McDougall was concerned, nothing could have been further from the truth. But these metatheoretical insinuations intensified the controversy and prevented an empirical clarification of the dispute. Because opponents of the instinct concept were unable to offer a better theory, there could be no objective resolution of the issue. The dispute finally petered out as interest in further speculation faded. All of those involved

came to realize that more concrete and detailed experimentation was required, and the early 1930s saw a rapid increase in this kind of research (cf. Krantz & Allen, 1967).

Like Freud, McDougall introduced a thoroughly motivational approach to the explanation of behavior. His questions as to the nature and classification of motives raised central issues, and his descriptive and definitional responses to these issues triggered the controversies that were to determine much of the empirical motivational research of the subsequent decade. Is behavior predominantly the result of previous learning or of innate impulses? Is motivated behavior a function of its energizing or of its direction and selection? And, above all, is behavior to be explained in a mechanistic sense, i.e., in terms of stimulus-response bonds, or in a mentalistic way, in terms of anticipatory cognitions?

It now became taboo to use the term "instinct" to describe a motive disposition. Instead, the terms "drive" and "need" gained currency. The neglected problems of motivational incentives and effects were tackled. Another notable approach to the classification of motives came between McDougall's list of instincts and Cattell's factor-analytically derived catalogs, however, one that was closely linked to attempts at motive scaling.

3.3.2 Person-Environment Relationships

Murray's work *Explorations in Personality* (1938) represents a point of intersection for several important strands of motivational research, particularly those originating from McDougall, Freud, and Lewin. Murray, whose main interest was in clinical and personality psychology, put **needs** at the center of a differentiated conceptual system that was not intended simply to describe behavior or to explain individual differences in responses to standardized situations. Rather, its function was to identify the idiosyncratic aspects of larger (molar) behavioral segments, and to uncover the underlying themes in the cyclical recurrence of idiosyncrasies observed in individuals across situations and time. The individual is seen as an active organism who not only responds to the pressure of situations, but actively seeks out situations and structures them.

Murray attempted to explain the goal-directedness of behavior in terms of a continuous chaining of episodical interactions between individuals and their environments, i.e., a constant interaction of person and situation factors. This explanation went beyond a trait theory of motivation that attributes all behavior unilaterally to dispositional person factors, as the following quotation shows:

> What an organism knows or believes is, in some measure, a product of formerly encountered situations. Thus, much of what is now inside the organism was once outside. For these reasons, the organism and its milieu must be considered together, a single creature-environment interaction being a

convenient short unit for psychology. A long unit – an individual life – can be most clearly formulated as a succession of related short units, or episodes (Murray, 1938, p. 39–40).

Murray thus became the forerunner of the "modern" interactionist position (Bowers, 1973; Magnusson & Endler, 1977):

DEFINITION

The organism (person) and the perceived situation form an interactional unit, mutually influencing each other. The two central and corresponding concepts are "need" on the person side and "press" on the situation side. "Need" and "press" cannot be observed directly, but have to be inferred; they are not descriptive terms, but hypothetical constructs.

But on what basis are they to be inferred? They cannot be read off momentary segments of presently occurring behavior or situations; they have to be inferred indirectly, from their effects. Thus, the motivational concept of "need" (which, incidentally, is not distinguished from "drive") is determined by the goal state to be achieved by means of a person-environment interaction. There is a thematic correspondence between need and press: a press elicits the corresponding need, a need seeks out a corresponding press. The interaction between need and press is called **thema** (hence the "Thematic Apperception Test," see below). It is the "thema" that is the actual unit of analysis in the stream of activity. Each episode in the stream has a thema, a goal-oriented sequence of behavior.

Murray uses the term "need" to refer to both dispositional and functional variables, and classifies needs in terms of a number of attributes. A first distinction is made between primary (viscerogenic) needs (e.g., n(eed)Water, nFood, nSex, nUrination, nColdavoidance) and secondary (psychogenic) needs (Table 3.2). Primary needs arise from organic processes and may be cyclical (like nFood) or regulatory (like nColdavoidance). Further distinctions are made between positive (approach) or negative (avoidance) needs and between manifest and latent needs. Manifest needs are freely expressed in overt behavior ("objectified"); latent needs relate to make-believe or fantasy behavior ("semiobjectified" or "subjectified"). In certain situations, needs can combine to motivate behavior. There can also be conflicts between needs, or one need can become subservient to another.

These conceptual categories are not simply a result of plausibility considerations, speculation, and invention. In fact, the conceptual framework was developed, refined, and tested using data obtained from 50 participants in a variety of research settings at the Harvard Psychological Clinic. The thematic demarcation of the secondary needs is a case in point (Table 3.2). A total of 27 staff, psychologists, and psychiatrists exposed participants to a variety of situations, and observed the recurring manifestations of each participant's more dominant motives. Participants were also confronted with situations in which their less dominant motives were aroused. The research settings included interviews, written biographies,

Table 3.2. Murray's catalog of psychogenic needs (n = need; in alphabetical order)

1.	nAbasement (nAba)
2.	nAchievement (nAch)
3.	nAffiliation (nAff)
4.	nAggression (nAgg)
5.	nAutonomy (nAuto)
6.	nCounteraction (nCnt)
7.	nDefense (nDef)
8.	nDefendance (nDfd)
9.	nDominance (nDom)
10.	nExhibition (nExh)
11.	nHarmavoidance (nHarm)
12.	nInfavoidance (nInf)
13.	nNurturance (nNur)
14.	nOrder (nOrd)
15.	nPlay (nPlay)
16.	nRejection (nRej)
17.	nSentience (nSen)
18.	nSex (nSex)
19.	nSuccorance (nSuc)
20.	nUnderstanding (nUnd)

The following needs were provisionally listed but not investigated systematically:

	nAcquisition (nAcq)
	nBlamavoidance (nBlam)
	nCognizance (nCog)
	nConstruction (nCons)
	nExposition (nExp)
	nRecognition (nRec)
	nRetention (nRet)

childhood memories, various testing procedures, and experiments relating to memory and levels of aspiration.

Murray's (1938) Thematic Apperception Test (TAT), which can be considered one of the most important research instruments in the field of motivational psychology (Chapters 6–9), deserves special mention.

Murray's list of needs leaves much to be desired against the background of the classification problem, however. Does it really make sense to assume the existence of 27 independent needs? Empirical motivation research has offered a more pragmatic solution, providing evidence for the existence of a smaller set of much broader motives, which are presented in detail in Chapters 6–8. Motives can be distinguished from needs in terms of their broader scope. For example, the affiliation motive is not solely directed to satisfying the need for affiliation; seen from the perspective of developmental psychology (Chapter 15), it is clear that the affiliation motive is closely related to the satisfaction of needs for protection, nurturance, and warmth (Ainsworth, 1979; Bowlby, 1982; MacDonald, 1992). Empirical findings show that the affiliation motive is also associated with sexual activity (Scheffer, 2005). However, it is doubtful that the need for sexuality can be subsumed entirely under the affiliation motive, because it is evidently also related to the power motive (McClelland,

1975). Other models even consider sexuality to be an independent motive system in its own right (Bischof, 1985).

SUMMARY

Besides developing the TAT, Murray collated and classified a wealth of ideas from a variety of theoretical approaches, all of which seemed relevant to the explanation of behavior. Drawing on this theoretical background, he developed an inventory of concepts that helped to focus research efforts on the measurement of motives and drew attention to aspects such as the dynamic shift between the interruption and resumption of motivation, the goal-directedness of behavior, and motivational conflict. The TAT provided the basis for later breakthroughs in motive measurement (McClelland et al., 1953) and the dynamic conceptualization of motivation (Atkinson, 1957; Atkinson & Birch, 1970; Kuhl & Blankenship, 1979).

Although the classification problem remains unresolved in many respects, evidence for the existence of some broad-based motives could be provided by developing ways to measure motive differences (e.g., the TAT), validating these findings by reference to individual differences in behavior in seemingly equivalent situations, and demonstrating their universality. In the following, the achievement motive is used to illustrate this approach (McClelland et al., 1953).

The Achievement Motive as a Distinct Motive Class

Allport's definition of traits presented earlier in this chapter raises some important questions, namely which stimuli are rendered "functionally equivalent" and which "forms of adaptive and expressive behavior" are consistent and equivalent. Clearly, determining criteria for these equivalence classes have to be identified. Assuming that such criteria are found, the next step is to determine whether they are universally applicable.

Five determining criteria have been proposed for behavior in achievement-related situations. All five must be present for an action to be experienced or perceived as achievement-oriented by the actor or observer (Heckhausen, 1974a). Specifically, the criteria are as follows:

1. The action must result in a concrete outcome.
2. The outcome must be measurable in terms of standards of quality or quantity.
3. The task must neither be too easy nor be too difficult. In other words, the action must have the potential to result in success or failure and (or at least) require a certain amount of time and effort.
4. The action outcomes must be assessed in terms of a certain standard, which must incorporate a certain binding norm value.
5. The action must have been intended by the actor and the outcome accomplished by him or her.

In short, achievement-motivated behavior is focused on the accomplishment of a task.

If the nature of the task does not reflect an objectifiable outcome, or if its demands are too high or too low, the behavior cannot be characterized as achievement behavior, or only to a limited extent. The same holds if there are no binding standards or norms, if the actor has been forced to do the task, or it has been accomplished without his or her active contribution. Admittedly, an observer does not determine whether all five of these conditions have been met before identifying another person's activities as being achievement-oriented. If one or more of these conditions appear to be present and there is no evidence of the absence of others, then the behavior will be perceived as achievement oriented.

Situations that can elicit such achievement-oriented behavior, i.e., that are congruent with it, have already been alluded to as "tasks." Specifically, they are situations that have the character of a task from the perspective of the actor or an observer. In addition, these situations must offer opportunities for the five criteria of achievement behavior (as defined in the previous section) to be realized.

The third criteria (that the task be neither too easy nor too difficult) plays an important role in individual development. Given that people can perceive only those tasks that appear to be neither impossible nor too easy as achievement-related, the set of achievement-eliciting situations will change over the individual lifespan, especially in childhood and adolescence. Task situations that were once impenetrable but are now within the individual's reach will be included in the set, whereas tasks situations that can now be solved with no effort at all will be excluded.

Some **settings** (in Barker's, 1968, sense) are dominated by situations that require achievement-oriented actions; e.g., school and the world of work in modern industrial societies. There is no question that the societal framework of achievement-arousing situations, their value in relation to other types of settings, and their objective content are, to a large extent, culture and time specific. It is difficult to imagine a culture within human history that did (does) not manifest achievement-orientation. But does this make achievement-oriented behavior universal, i.e., does it manifest itself in all individuals everywhere and at all times?

Authors like Kornadt, Eckensberger, and Emminghaus (1980), and Maehr (1974) have examined the available cross-cultural evidence, and given a tentative positive reply to this question. Considering the abstract and fundamental nature of the five criteria of achievement behavior (and the corresponding achievement-related situations), there can be little doubt as to the universality of achievement-oriented situations and hence the achievement motive.

Kornadt, Eckensberger, and Emminghaus (1980) and Maehr (1974) pointed out that these abstract determining components of achievement-motivated behavior manifest themselves in a tremendous, culture-dependent diversity, becoming concretized only in the context of a "subjective culture" (Triandis, 1972). First, there is the thematic diversity of culture-specific task domains, such as hunting, fishing, commerce, practice of religious rites, artisan and industrial production, buying and selling, scientific research, artistic creation, and much more. Then there are different forms of individual, collective, or cooperative organizations, including the division of labor for the purposes of task accomplishment. Within the thematic sphere of each task, furthermore, there are culture-specific criteria for objectifying achievement-oriented behavior. These include standards of comparison and norm values for assessing achievement, causal explanations of success and failure (e.g., the causal role attributed to higher powers, to fate or "fortuna"), and the consequences of action outcomes, their incentive values, and future orientation.

It would thus appear that – irrespective of the specific historical and cultural framework – the core meanings, i.e., abstractions, of achievement-oriented, person-environment relationships are universal. The historico-cultural context dictates the concrete contents of achievement-related behavior and its potential variation in a specific instance. Having examined the achievement-oriented equivalence class from an external, general perspective, we must now ask whether all individuals in a given cultural epoch perceive this equivalence class in the same manner. This is certainly not the case. Individuals differ in terms of the breadth of situations they perceive to have achievement implications, in the importance they attribute to these situations relative to other types of situations, as well as in other idiosyncrasies.

Returning to Allport's trait definition, we can conclude that the individual's achievement motive depends on the number of "stimuli," i.e., situations, that he or she perceives to be "functionally equivalent" and that thus "initiate and guide consistent and equivalent forms" of achievement-oriented actions.

The question is thus whether there are, or ever were, individuals who, throughout their lifetime, failed to perceive any of the universal situations defined in terms of the previous criteria as eliciting achievement-oriented actions, and who thus omitted to engage in achievement-related behavior. It is hard to imagine this ever being the case. Thus, it would seem that achievement-oriented situations are universal not only among the general population, but also on the individual level. Despite its idiosyncratic variations, and although the concrete situations that elicit achievement-oriented behavior are always specific to the historico-cultural context, it would seem that the achievement motive applies to all individuals.

❗ The logical conclusion to be drawn from this analysis is that the achievement motive is indeed a trait in its own right, and that it encompasses a number of the needs on Murray's list. For example, the need for order can be regarded as a facet of the achievement motive: achievement can often be characterized as a process of creating order from a state of entropy (whether the individual in question is creating an artwork or doing the housework).

Clearly, few motives are as broad and universal as the "Big Three," each of which is covered in a separate chapter of this book (Chapters 6–8). Interestingly, Lawrence and Nohria (2002), who approach the subject from the perspective of economics and business administration, have proposed a classification similar to the one that has emerged from experimental motivational research. They identify four basic motives that cannot be reduced any further:

1. Bonding
2. Defending

    This motive has much in common with the aggression motive, which Kornadt, Eckensberger, and Emminghaus (1980) described as universal, and can also be interpreted as the power motive, which has been thoroughly researched in experimental motivational psychology.

3. Acquiring

    This motive can be likened to the achievement motive defined above.

4. Learning

    Interestingly, this motive is not included in Murray's list. Accordingly, it has not been investigated in experimental motivational research.

Why was learning not identified as a need in its own right by Murray, but included in the economists' much shorter list? In today's political climate, "lifelong learning" is frequently portrayed as a (required) basic motive that provides a particularly powerful index of individual differences.

Upon more careful inspection, however, a subtle difference can be discerned between learning and the other motives. Motivation research sees learning as a general **outcome** of motivation. From this perspective, learning is not a motive in its own right, but a **function** of motives: in the long run, organisms maintain and develop only those adaptive and expressive behaviors that serve to satisfy motives (McClelland, 1985). More generally speaking, certain outcomes of motives may assume the character of general **values** that take on global significance for individuals. Learning can be regarded as such a value – first, because it is an outcome of all motives; second, because it makes the future satisfaction of motives more likely.

3.3.3 Maslow's Hierarchical Model of Motive Classification

Abraham Maslow took an alternative approach in his 1954 book entitled *Motivation and Personality*, classifying motives in terms of needs. Maslow was a founder of "humanistic psychology," a movement that evolved in the USA after World War II, influenced by the existentialist thought of continental Europe. The movement saw itself as a "third force" in psychology, trying to free research from the constraints of either a purely behavioristic or a purely psychoanalytic approach, and to shift the focus of attention in personality theory research to questions relating to the values and purposes of life. In so

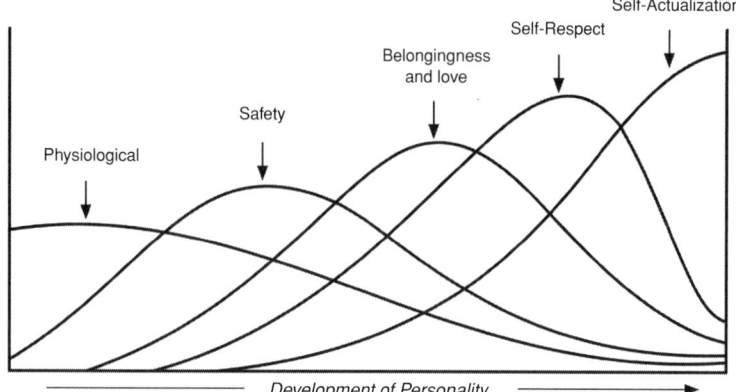

Figure 3.2 Maslow's hierarchical model orders groups of motives according to the relative priority of need satisfaction. (Based on Krech, Crutchfield, & Ballachey, 1962, p. 77.)

doing, the movement picked up on Dilthey's (1894) notions of "analytical psychology," with its partly antiDarwinian stance. True, humans are biologically determined, with innate capacities that unfold during maturation, but we are fundamentally different from infrahuman organisms in our ability, and indeed our need, to achieve self-actualization.

Maslow developed an accessible classification system that differed from earlier taxonomies in two respects. First, it does not identify single needs, but describes whole groups of needs. Second, these groups of needs are arranged in hierarchical order according to their relevance in personality development. This does not imply that the "higher" and "highest" needs are any less "instinctual" or innate than the "lower" needs. A need activates and influences behavior only as long as it remains unsatisfied. In fact, behavior is less "pushed" from within the organism than it is "pulled" by the external consequences of its satisfaction.

❶ Maslow's model is based on the principle of relative priorities in motive activation. It dictates that the lower needs must always be satisfied before higher needs can become aroused and determine behavior.

As illustrated in Fig. 3.2, the hierarchy of needs ranges from existential, physiological needs via security needs, needs for belongingness and love, and esteem needs, to the value of self-actualization.

Self-actualization can become a determinant of behavior only when all other needs have been satisfied. It can thus be seen as an outcome of need satisfaction and, like learning, be defined as a value. Every need is teleologically directed to the attainment of this value, and the satisfaction of every need brings individuals slightly nearer to it. Self-actualization thus "pulls" behavior; the force it develops is qualitatively different from the "pushing" effects of needs.

From the perspective of developmental psychology, the ascending groups of needs portrayed in Fig. 3.2 correspond to the ontological development of the individual (see also Erikson's 1963 research on ego development). The satisfaction of

existential, physiological needs takes priority for infants, and security needs are most urgent for young children, followed by the needs of belongingness and self-esteem. It is not until adolescence that aspects of self-actualization become significant, to be finally realized, if at all, in adulthood.

A hierarchical structure of needs is also congruent with the principles of attachment theory (Ainsworth, 1979; Bowlby, 1982). The need to regulate physiological processes makes young children dependent on the support and protection of familiar others. Over time, this dependency can develop into a deep bond. If physiological needs are not satisfied, however, the development of a trusting relationship between mother and child is jeopardized, underlining the hierarchical relationship between existential needs and security needs. Without feelings of security and trust, it is unlikely that a secure bond will develop. Yet a secure bond is the prerequisite for exploration of the natural environment, which is in turn decisive for the development of self-esteem and autonomy. Children lacking in self-esteem and autonomy cannot really become adults capable of working and engaging in functional relationships; they cannot experience self-actualization. Thus, from the first months of life, human development is determined by sequential developmental tasks that imply a hierarchical **directedness** of needs, as reflected in the concept of "focal times" in developmental psychology (Keller, 1997a, b; see the excursus in the next page).

Empirical support for Maslow's assumption that self-actualization is the highest value was provided by interviews with and biographies of prominent (contemporary and historical) figures, including Lincoln, Beethoven, Einstein, Eleanor Roosevelt, and Aldous Huxley. He saw this sample to be characterized by the following characteristics: superior perception of reality; acceptance of self, of others, and of nature; increased spontaneity; increased problem centering; increased detachment and desire for privacy; increased autonomy and resistance to enculturation; greater freshness of appreciation and richness of emotional reaction; higher frequency of mystic experiences; increased identification with the human species; deeper and more profound

EXCURSUS

Directedness of Development: Contingency, Security, Bonding, and Exploration

Around the second month of life, infants are physiologically able to control their head and body in such a way that they can direct their line of vision. In mastering this physiological need for control, they become able to engage in rudimentary forms of situational control. By about the third month, interactions between babies and their mothers are characterized by a high frequency of eye contact; this age seems to constitute a focal time for this thema, because it soon becomes less important. Researchers interpret the significance of this focal time for development as follows: Because newborn babies have such a short attention span (shorter than 800 ms), they are essentially unable to gauge the effects of their behavior on the environment. When they develop the ability to control their field of vision, parents have the opportunity to mirror their baby's signals – e.g., smiling or the "eyebrow flash" – in face-to-face interactions. If they do so reliably within the baby's short attention span, the baby learns that both his or her own reactions and those of the caregiver are predictable. This experience of contingency gives babies a feeling of security, which helps them to cope with the next developmental thema of establishing a personal bond with primary caregivers, and engaging in exploration beyond their "secure base." Thus, satisfying physiological demands is directly related to satisfying the needs for security, bonding, and exploration in the first year of life (cf. Keller, 1997a, b; Keller et al., 1999).

interpersonal relationships with a few close individuals; more democratic character structure; increased discrimination between means and ends; possessing a sense of humor; creativeness and nonconformity. Maslow further identified a number of major differences between higher and lower needs:

1. The higher need represents a later phyletic or evolutionary development.

2. The higher the need, the less critical it is for sheer survival, the longer its gratification can be postponed, and the easier it is for the need to disappear permanently.

3. Living at a higher need level means greater biological efficiency, longer life, less disease, better sleep, more appetite, etc.

4. Higher needs are experienced as less urgent.

5. Gratification of higher needs produces more desirable and more personal results, i.e., more profound happiness, cheerfulness, and wealth of inner life (1954, pp. 98–99).

Maslow's approach is based on the notion that people are not only driven by needs, but also attracted by their general outcomes. Outcomes with global significance for individuals can be defined as values. The precise definition of a value differs markedly across cultures. A cross-cultural perspective shows that overcoming the egoistic gratification of personal needs is the highest value in many non-western cultures marked by material poverty (Greenfield, Keller, Fuligni, & Maynard, 2002; Keller, 1997c; Markus & Kitayama, 1991). Western industrialized nations, such as the USA, the UK, and Germany are considered individualistic; i.e., people tend to take their personal, individual form of self-actualization very seriously, and to give it priority over group needs. In most Asian, African, and South American cultures, in contrast, the prevailing orientation is more collectivist (more recently labeled "interdependent"). Group needs are given priority over individual needs, and fulfillment of these group needs is seen as true self-actualization (Triandis, 1997).

SUMMARY

Unfortunately, Maslow's definitions of many of his concepts are rather vague, leaving much scope for subjective interpretation, and making it difficult to subject the theory to empirical testing. In fact, no satisfactory empirical tests have been reported to date. Maslow's hierarchical model can be seen to reflect either an individualistic orientation directed at increasing personal need satisfaction, or an interdependent orientation geared toward satisfying the needs of the community. It is quite possible that this "elasticity" of the theory is one of the main reasons for its continued popularity in training programs and seminars.

3.4 Basic Emotions as a Rudimentary Motivation System

Values involve the evaluation of actions, i.e., assessment of the extent to which actions are or are not expedient for motive satisfaction. These evaluations are not solely the product of rational consideration, but are colored by emotions and feelings, the "prerational organs of perception" (Bischof, 1993). Emotions serve as navigational aids to motivation, without which the search for appropriate behavioral options in the vast network of stored, potentially relevant actions would be very protracted, if not hopeless (Damasio, 2000).

Emotions thus play a decisive role in the initiation of goal-directed behaviors designed to have certain effects on the environment and achieve certain outcomes. As psychological organs of perception, they indicate to the organism how close it has come to satisfying a motive and are responsible for the fine tuning of motivational processes. In terms of Murray's theory, emotions can be seen as the point of interface between need and press. As such, they reflect the "thema" that is currently occupying and energizing an individual, and that a practiced observer can "read" fairly accurately from a person's face. Because emotions are involved in the evaluative phase of a motivational sequence (Chapter 11), they are – like values – endowed with the character of global rewards or punishments. The very anticipation of emotions such as joy or love can thus be motivating, even when they are not associated with the motive momentarily aroused.

❶ The emotions can be described as a rudimentary motive system that serves the internal and external communication of motivational sequences.

3.4.1 The Basic Emotions

There are a limited number of basic emotions that can be distinguished on the basis of facial expressions alone. As far back as 1872, Darwin identified the following basic emotions through careful observation of an infant:

1. interest,
2. joy,
3. annoyance/grief,
4. surprise,
5. fear,
6. anger/rage,
7. disgust,
8. shame.

Darwin realized that expressive behavior has a communicative function among social animals, and observed phylogenetic continuity in the facial muscles, from the lower mammals via infrahuman primates to humans.

Aside from this phylogenetic continuity, there is another reason for characterizing basic emotions as innate dispositions, namely, the universality of their evocation (as manifested by facial expressions) and the degree of interobserver agreement in judgments of emotion-specific behavior. The claim that emotional expressions are part of the conventions of a culturally homogeneous population (e.g., Klineberg, 1938) prompted studies of tribes in Borneo and New Guinea who had previously had little contact with other cultures. Members of these tribes were read stories, and then asked to select from several picture cues of the face that most accurately reflected the emotional state of the protagonist (Ekman & Friesen, 1971; Ekman, 1972). In other studies, they were asked to mimic the feelings of the characters in the stories. The facial expressions they produced were videotaped and later evaluated by American students. Interrater agreement was high in all conditions, dispelling any lingering doubts about universality in the production and recognition of emotion-specific facial expressions (only surprise and fear – two emotions frequently expressed in quick succession – were occasionally confused).

To gain a meaningful understanding of emotions, we need to abandon the layperson's view that they are restricted to mere feelings, and stop seeing them as opposites to cognitions in the sense of thoughts, or indeed to cognition in the sense of processing environmental information (Arnold,

1960; Tomkins, 1970, 1981; see also the debate between Zajonc, 1980, and Lazarus, 1984, which in essence seems to have been a battle over semantics).

Functions of Emotions

Some situations are vital to the organism, i.e., to its survival. Typical examples include the threat of a powerful enemy, exposure to an unfamiliar environment, or abandonment at a time when the help or company of others is needed. The perception of such vital situations is triggered partly by innate stimulus cues, which, in humans, are largely overlaid by subsequent experience. Watson (1924) was the first to draw attention to innate triggers, which he assumed to elicit emotions such as fear, rage, or affection in infants. These unconditioned triggers of emotions provide the necessary basis for the emotions to be conditioned to other, previously neutral stimuli (Watson & Rayner, 1920).

For the most part, experiences are overlaid on stimulus cues by means of classical conditioning, i.e., the association of a signal with specific organismic changes that facilitate the initiation of appropriate actions. This bonding process is accompanied by a certain emotional state that may enter into awareness. However, this bond does not constitute a fixed link between stimulus and response, such that a particular stimulus automatically elicits a particular response. Rather, a specific stimulus cue for a particular vital situation elicits changes in the organism's state that prepare it for subsequent expedient action. One component of this change in the organism's state is the experience of an emotion-specific sensation, which in its compressed and holistic form mediates a "feeling" for one's momentary situation. Accordingly, feelings are a kind of in-depth, split-second communiqué about the situation at hand, i.e., the vital situation being encountered. Arnold (1960) proposed a chain of effects comprising three links: perception-appraisal-action.

This chain of effects can be conceptualized as follows: information relating to an emotion-specific vital situation triggers biochemical changes in some areas of the central nervous system (e.g., the limbic system) that, in turn, lead to changes in four different spheres: first, in the peripheral nervous system, including the receptor organs (e.g., increased blood supply or an orienting reflex); second, in experience; third, in expressive movements; and fourth, in action-initiating patterns of behavior. Emotion-specific expressive movements can involve facial expressions, gestures, posture, body orientations, or vocal patterns. As previously mentioned, expressive movements are observable and can provide others with precise information about the actor's momentary emotional state and disposition to act. Admittedly, such expressive movements can be intentionally exaggerated, diminished, controlled, suppressed, or faked in response to "display rules" (Ekman, 1972), i.e., cultural prescriptions for certain social situations. Some expressive movements, especially gestures, may merge with action-initiating behavior patterns.

Table 3.3. Three languages that may be used to describe emotional states		
Subjective Language	**Behavioral Language**	**Functional Language**
Fear, terror	Withdrawing, escaping	Protection
Anger, rage	Attacking, biting	Destruction
Joy, ecstasy	Mating, possessing	Reproduction
Sadness, grief	Crying for help	Reintegration
Acceptance, trust	Pair-bonding, grooming	Incorporation or affiliation
Disgust, loathing	Vomiting, defecating	Rejection
Expectancy, anticipation	Examining, mapping	Exploration
Surprise, astonishment	Stopping, freezing	Orientation

Table 3.3 presents the three different "languages" that can be used to describe the eight basic emotions postulated by Plutchic (1980): "subjective," "behavioral," and "functional."

3.4.2 The Adaptive Value of Emotions

Emotions are adaptive in the phylogenetic sense of having survival value, both in emergencies, where needs must be satisfied urgently, and in situations where they can only be satisfied on the longer term. We need only consider how important it can be to respond both appropriately and quickly in situations that are decisive for an organism's well-being. Although purely reflexive bonds between stimulus and responses would always be quick, they would often be inappropriate, because they would necessarily ignore gradations in meaning and contextual features of the eliciting "stimuli."

If the organism's first reaction is not a motor activity, but an emotion, the stimulus-response bond is "loosened," thus creating the conditions for an appropriate response (Scherer, 1981). At the same time, emotion-specific processing of information can help initiate a prompt response to the situation at hand, or at least induce a state of heightened readiness for action. If people relied solely on the cognitive, argumentative processing of information, involving the analytical elaboration and subsequent integration of incentive and expectancy features, there would be long delays in responding to the situation. Their eventual responses, although fitting, would come too late, and thus be inappropriate to the situational demands.

The phylogenetic development of the basic emotions has facilitated a more flexible response to the demands of a changing and complex environment than could be achieved by simple reflex responses. Furthermore, the communication of emotions via various expressive behaviors can solve problems arising from social interaction within a species; e.g., the bloodless resolution of mating and rank rivalries; cf. Lorenz, 1966.

Scherer (1981) proposed an information-processing model of emotions comprising five consecutive steps (see the following overview) that appear to correspond with phylogenetic and ontogenetic development as well as with the microgenetic sequencing of specific situations.

The Information-Processing Model of Emotions. (Based on Scherer, 1981)

1st step: The incoming information is checked for novelty or entropy (Section 3.5.1 "Zürich Model").

2nd step: Depending on whether the information is found to relate to something pleasant or unpleasant, affects such as pleasure or displeasure, interest or fear/terror are triggered (cf. Schneirla, 1959).

3rd step: The information is screened in terms of its relevance for the goal, i.e., whether it contains cues as to the nature of the situation that might facilitate, interrupt, delay, or hinder the current course of action toward an aspired goal (emotions of joy and fear; in the case of hindrances: frustration, anger, rage).

4th step: Goal-relevant features are analyzed in terms of their requirements and the chances of attaining the goal (emotions: joy, fear, distress, anger).

5th step: Action outcomes are compared with social norms or self-imposed standards (emotions: joy in the sense of pride, shame, guilt, contempt). This last step is probably unique to humans.

A close inspection of these five processing steps reveals that all but the first (checking for novelty) feature aspects of value and expectancy that can be regarded as dispositional, i.e., as traits. Steps 2 and 5 (pleasure/displeasure and comparisons with norms) relate to values; steps 3 and 4 (relevance of situational aspects to goal attainment and available means for attaining the goal) relate to expectancies.

DEFINITION

Emotions are thus prerational forms of values and expectancies that influence the motivational process.

Table 3.4 lists the basic emotions postulated by Darwin, Tomkins, Ekman, Izard, and Plutchic, respectively, arranged in a sequence that approximates Scherer's (1981) processing steps. There is considerable agreement among the diverse theorists who, as the table shows, all postulated between six and nine basic emotions (Ekman, 1972; Izard, 1971; Plutchic, 1980; Tomkins, 1962, 1970) that can be distinguished largely on the basis of facial expressions (cf. Rinn, 1984).

Table 3.4. The basic emotions, in order of the sequential phases of information processing postulated by Scherer (1981)

Darwin	(1877)	Interest	Surprise	Joy	Sadness	Disgust	Fear	Anger	Shame	–
Tomkins	(1981)	Interest	Surprise	Joy	Distress	Disgust	Fear	Anger	Shame	Contempt
Ekman	(1972)	–	Surprise	Joy	Sadness	Disgust	Fear	Anger	–	–
Izard	(1971)	Interest	Surprise	Joy	Distress	Disgust	Fear	Anger	Shame	–
Plutchic	(1980)	–	Surprise	Joy	Sadness	Disgust	Fear	Anger	–	Acceptance

That "interest" is not viewed as a basic emotion by all of the theorists is understandable, given that the corresponding emotional expressions can also be viewed as attention arousal. Some of the authors see shame, and single authors see contempt and acceptance, as products of other basic emotions. All authors assume that the basic emotions can blend together when elicited simultaneously. Tomkins (1981) used the term "affect complexes" to describe potential assemblies of basic emotions with various perceived and conceived causes and consequences.

3.4.3 Personality Traits as "Congealed" Emotions

Having established that all basic emotions are phylogenetically deeply rooted and universal, and that they serve adaptive functions in vital situations in the relationship between the individual (organism) and the environment, we can now consider the implications of these insights for a taxonomy of motive dispositions. The first problem is that emotions tend to be transient **states** that vary across situations. How can these states usefully inform a taxonomy of motive dispositions?

Some research findings indicate that it is worth returning to the five-factor model as previously discussed at this point. In recent years, researchers have increasingly interpreted the Big Five not only as correlating patterns of behavior or as "descriptive labels," but as traits according to Allport's definition. In other words, the Big Five are increasingly seen as mechanisms with the capacity to render many stimuli functionally equivalent and to initiate equivalent forms of adaptive and expressive behavior. From this perspective, extraversion can be seen as a propensity to experience **positive** emotions across situations, and to behave with according optimism, whereas **neuroticism** (the opposite of emotional stability) can be seen as a propensity to experience **negative** emotions across situations, and to behave with according caution (Watson & Clark, 1997; Watson & Tellegen, 1985; Watson et al., 1999). The close connection between emotions and muscular innervation was mentioned in Section 3.4.1. Taking a similarly "proximal" approach, traits can be conceptualized as dispositions based primarily on emotions.

DEFINITION

Traits are the stable, dispositional side of emotions that make certain emotional states more or less probable. Traits can thus be compared to consolidated or "congealed" emotions – previously transient states that have developed into stable and situation-transcending characteristics.

The other traits of the five-factor model can also be interpreted as a dispositionally heightened sensitivity to certain emotions. The **openness to experience** factor is associated with a heightened sensitivity to the emotions of interest and curiosity (McCrae & Costa, 1997). The **agreeableness** factor can be interpreted as a heightened sensitivity to group norms and to the shame that occurs when they are violated (Graziano & Eisenberg, 1997). Likewise the **conscientiousness** factor, the driving force behind integrity and a sense of responsibility, involves a heightened sensitivity to guilt (a strict "superego"); the behavior of conscientious individuals is directed to avoiding feelings of guilt (Hogan & Ones, 1997).

The traits of the five-factor model can thus be interpreted as congealed emotions. This would explain why extraverts are likely to experience joy in a broader range of situations than introverts, and emotionally stable individuals are less likely to experience fear and anxiety than "neurotic" individuals. As such, it makes perfect sense to discuss emotions in a chapter on trait theories. However, it is again important to remember to distinguish between motivational constructs that explain the whats of behavior and those that apply to its hows. Needs and motives (or "ergs") describe the kinds of incentives to which organisms respond; they relate to desired states or behavioral objectives. Traits and the associated emotions serve to direct behavior; they thus describe its hows.

SUMMARY

Emotions play an important role in motivational processes: they indicate to the organism whether progress is smooth or faltering, whether behavior is being supported or stalled, whether unexpected difficulties have arisen or happy coincidences have occurred, whether behavior is being deliberately inhibited, and finally whether or not binding standards can be fulfilled. A taxonomy of motives cannot be established on the basis of emotions, however, because all of the basic emotions listed in Table 3.4 can clearly be combined with any motive. Nevertheless, there do seem to be prototypical combinations of certain motives and emotions. For example, McClelland (1985b) associates the power motive with the emotion of anger, the affiliation motive with the emotion of love, and the achievement motive with the emotion of curiosity/interest.

3.5 Systems Theory Models of Motivation

Systems theory conceptions of motivation had an early heyday in the 1970s (Atkinson & Birch, 1970; Bischof, 1975: Kuhl & Blankenship, 1979), and a parallel strand of research was developed in the context of social-cognitive personality theory (Bandura, 1978; Cervone, 2004; Mischel & Shoda, 1998). Systems theory conceptions are characterized by three main principles:

1. Personality is a complex system involving the interaction of multiple, highly integrated processes.

2. These interacting processes are rooted in basic cognitive and affective systems that initiate and direct behavior.

3. The personality interacts with the environment, and the behavior initiated contributes to shaping the environment (reciprocal interactionism).

The question to be addressed by motivation research is thus how motives and personality traits interact, and by means of which processes (e.g., emotions, self-regulatory styles) they trigger and direct behavior in given situations.

Systems theory approaches to motivation have far-reaching implications; e.g., they call one of the central assumptions of classical test theory into question. Using computer simulations, Atkinson, Bongort, and Price (1977) showed that motive measures can show high construct validity, even when the internal consistency of the TAT scales is very low. In other words, whether a manifest motivation is identified (e.g., in the TAT) is the result of a complex process of interaction between different dispositions (e.g., the affiliation, achievement, and power motives competing to control behavior) and situational stimulus conditions (influenced in part by behavior). For example, a piece of cake may lose its incentive value to someone who has just eaten a large piece. Tuerlinckx, De Boeck, and Lens (2002) have demonstrated that a particular manifest motivation in the TAT is replaced by other forms of motivation in a stochastic "drop-out process." This results in the "behavioral oscillations" described by Atkinson and Birch (1970).

The low consistency with which motives tend to become manifest is nevertheless compatible with Allport's definition of a trait. It is only when a motive is extremely strong that it emerges consistently across different situations; motives of moderate strength do not have such broad impact on the stream of behavior (Scheffer, Kuhl, & Eichstaedt, 2003). This is quite plausible from the perspective of evolutionary and developmental psychology, given that human motivation must be sensitive to the context, and change and develop over the course of ontogenesis. In his model of social motivation, Bischof (1985) shows that this process of change involves an "elemental conflict" between the intimacy (bonding) and autonomy (achievement and power) motives (see section 3.5.1).

3.5.1 The Zürich Model of Social Motivation

Bischof's (1975, 1985) "Zürich model of social motivation" is an ethological systems theory of motivation. Bischof was a student of Konrad Lorenz, and the concept of "imprinting" was central to his work.

❶ Imprinting takes places in sensitive periods during which the organism is especially receptive to environmental information (compare the concept of "focal" times), and has a sustained or even irreversible effect on character.

However, it is not motives that get imprinted, but detectors for certain stimulus characteristics. From the ethological perspective, a distinction can be made between type detectors, which discriminate between conspecifics and other species, and individual detectors, which mark out the boundary of the nuclear family, and thus signal what is perceived as **familiar**. This boundary has a dual function: it suppresses altruistic behavior toward conspecifics beyond it, and it prevents sexual responses to those within it. Both kinds of detectors help to determine the familiarity of an object or situation.

DEFINITION

The familiarity of a stimulus is directly and inversely related to its entropy, that is, its degree of novelty and complexity. Ambivalence, incongruence, and dynamics of a stimulus increase its entropy and decrease its familiarity. Another important input variable in this model is the relevance of an object. Together these input variables influence the felt security and arousal of an organism: a large, strange looking creature making straight for an organism will trigger more arousal and less security than, say, its parents.

Compared to lower animals, like Lorenz's graylag geese, the processes by which type detectors and individual detectors are imprinted on humans are very complex. There is considerable variation across individuals and cultures in what is perceived as familiar or as alien. Phenomena such as customs, dialects, and traditional costumes amplify familiarity and may thus also trigger the individual detectors when we meet people for the first time. In view of these individual differences in the perception and evaluation of what is "familiar" and what is "alien," Bischof's theory – although intended as a general psychological model – is also relevant as a trait theory.

Seen in this way, the first form of learning in ontogenesis is the discrimination between "familiar" and "alien" (Bischof, 1985, 1993). Young children experience familiarity as positive, as a source of security and protection. Unfamiliarity initially implies danger and is experienced as negative. This will change over the course of development when a second guiding principle takes effect: unfamiliarity can then also lead to a positively experienced state of arousal. For both of these guiding principles, the need for security and the need for arousal, individual set points define the ideal degree of unfamiliarity for an organism. There are certain similarities to Murray's list of motives, which are therefore provided here alongside Bischof's concepts:

■ the set point for security ("dependency"), which has conceptual similarities with the affiliation motive, and
■ the set point for arousal ("enterprise"), which comprises facets of the achievement motive.

Four basic motivational tendencies emerge from the interplay of the level of familiarity (as determined by the detectors) and the two set points "dependency" and "enterprise":

■ appetence for, or aversion to, security (bonding vs. surfeit) and
■ appetence for, or aversion to, arousal (exploration vs. fear).

The detectors serve to evaluate the stream of incoming information. If the level of familiarity indicated by the individual detector is below the set point, the organism will experience insecurity, and seek to resolve it. This endeavor is defined in the Zürich model as **attachment motivation**. If, on the other hand, the level of security is above the set point, there is a surfeit response. This motivation, which runs counter to attachment motivation, takes effect most prominently in puberty, when the security parents provide is felt as a

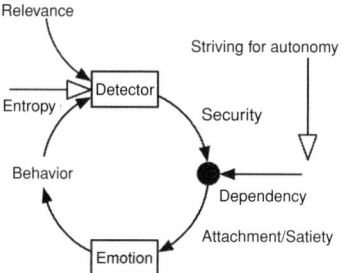

Figure 3.3 The security system of the Zürich Model (cf. Bischof, 1996, p. 501).

surplus to requirements and they become perceived as overly familiar, boring, and overprotective. From the sociobiological perspective, this is an adaptive development that serves to prevent incest. The relations between the variables of the security system are illustrated in Fig. 3.3.

When an object has low entropy, as shown by the unfilled arrow in Fig. 3.3, it triggers security in the organism's detector system (i.e., sensory structures), particularly if a familiar object is also highly relevant. The level of security experienced and desired depends on individual differences that change in the course of development. The older children get, the less security they need, i.e., their dependency decreases. This development seems to be influenced by the quality of early interactions with the primary caregiver (Ainsworth, 1979). The detectors also mature with time; what a small child considers complex and collative, barely triggers any entropy anymore in puberty.

Function of Emotions in the Zürich Model

In addition to detector mechanisms, and needs, the Zürich Model also includes emotions as a decisive factor in motivation. Given a high set point for security, the lower the entropy of a stimulus (i.e., the higher its familiarity), the more positive emotions will be experienced. As the level of entropy increases, negative emotions will begin to set in, leading first to an emotional response and then to avoidance behavior. Emotions make the organism aware of its momentary relationship to the environment. They are, to a considerable extent, muscular innervation, and thus directly related to motor activity.

Given a low individual set point for security, i.e., low dependency, high levels of security are experienced as oppressive and stifling; individuals feel "crushed" by the proximity of familiar others, soon grow tired of them, and seek to escape the situation. Thus, different emotions and behavior can emerge from the interplay of detectors and set points, even when the objective stimuli remain the same. Clearly then, external stimuli cannot be interpreted without reference to an inner set point. Murray had already touched on this idea with his interactionist perspective of the "thema" as a dynamic and developmentally graded interaction of "need" and "press."

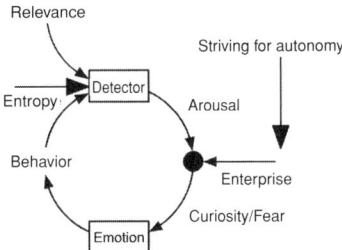

Figure 3.4 The arousal system of the Zürich Model (cf. Bischof, 1996, p. 500).

Fig. 3.4 shows the part of the Zürich Model that explicates the arousal system. It is connected to the autonomy motive, which describes facets of the achievement and power motives. Autonomous behavior is directed at implementing one's goals. It is positively related to the set point "enterprise," because it necessitates direct confrontation with unfamiliar and relevant stimuli, i.e., it involves high entropy. Given a combination of high autonomy and high enterprise, arousal is perceived as pleasant, and prompts diverse exploration and confrontation. The emotion of interest signals that the stimuli acting on the organism have not yet exceeded the set point for enterprise. As soon as this happens, it will be signaled by a feeling of fear, prompting the organism to take steps to remedy the excess of entropy; e.g., by flight, exploration, or aggression.

❶ Thus, emotions, motor activity, and the regulation of social distance differ markedly depending on whether the individual is high or low in the autonomy motive. Even when faced with essentially harmless threats, individuals high in dependency respond with concern, alarm, or even horror. It is only in environments that others find unbearably dull that they feel comfortable. The set points represent the true core of this complex system; they prompt the system to establish a dynamic balance within itself and in relation to the environment.

Here, the Zürich model overlaps with Maslow's hierarchy of needs: high dependency leads to an appetence for security (attachment motivation), i.e., to a focus on the needs shown to the left of Fig. 3.2. This, in turn, is associated with a **preference** for low entropy, which may be reflected in adherence to traditions, community spirit, and a rather predictable way of life. In other words, appetence for security is associated with the values of community and cohesion. In contrast, the more individuals strive for autonomy and seek out opportunities to influence the environment in line with their own goals, the lower their level of dependency, and the sooner they experience uniformity and being part of a collective as repellant. At high levels of enterprise, low security is experienced as freedom, and arousal as challenge. The positive feedback loop assumed in the Zürich model between enterprise and autonomy can also lead to an excessive striving for freedom in

humans: to egotism, isolation, and disproportionate individualism. Conversely, excessively low levels of personal autonomy, and the associated increase in dependency, can lead the individual to "merge" with society. This can have negative repercussions, such as excessive group thought, conformity, and aggression toward members of other groups.

From the perspective of the Zürich model, the type of motivation that serves to promote development and "self-actualization" is the result of a balanced, developmentally graded equilibrium between security and arousal. A certain congruence can be seen here between the Zürich model and Csikszentmihalyi's motivational theory of "flow," which is defined as a state of concentrated absorption in activities (Csikszentmihalyi, 1990; 1997a; see Chapter 13 for details).

The ideal balance between security and arousal can be reinforced by the influence of traits. In his **risk-taking model** of achievement motivation, Atkinson (1957) postulated that only individuals high on the approach component of the achievement motive tend to experience maximally arousing challenges (the demands of which are appropriate to individual ability level, meaning that the probability of success is **moderate**) as attractive and conducive to achievement. Individuals who are afraid of failure tend to choose tasks that are either too easy or too difficult, and experience conditions that elicit arousal (if unsolicited) as less stimulating than alarming.

The achievement motive begins to influence individual choices early in life, thus shaping the social environment and the level of challenge potentially experienced in ways that seem difficult to compensate. Heckhausen and Tomasik (2002) found that males approaching the end of high school in Germany only aspired to a vocational training program that matched their scholastic achievement level if they had a high achievement motive score on the OMT. Given that an early **person-job fit** is vital for the favorable development of job satisfaction and performance (Holland, 1997), a weak achievement motive seems to set young people off on an unfavorable path that is very difficult to change later in life.

THE PRINCIPLE OF FIT. The principle of fit also seems to play a key role in the development of the achievement motive. Heckhausen (1972) saw variables such as sensumotor exploration and "wanting to do it oneself," which can be observed in the striving for control or the pleasure in functioning ("Funktionslust") as early as the second and third years of life, as the precursors of achievement motivation. Heckhausen emphasized the interaction between the parent's expectations of independence and the age appropriateness of these demands ("principle of fit"), assuming that parental encouragement of independent behavior would have positive effects on the achievement motive if it matched the child's level of development, i.e., did not overstretch the child. Drawing on the principle of fit, Cube (2003) attributes many of the problems of modern industrialized societies (drug addiction, listlessness, and apathy) to the tempting, but ultimately destructive approach of providing children with too much security, the outcome of which is often quite the opposite: the ceaseless pursuit of ever stronger "kicks" to compensate for the overriding boredom of school or work. Translated to Kuhl's (2001) concept of "systems configuration," which will be presented in the next section, people are best able to develop their personal resources and to activate **self-development** when the inner set points interact to reach a stable equilibrium, thus putting an early stop to excessive strivings for either security or arousal.

SUMMARY

Basic motivational tendencies reflect the individual approach to entropy or to the complementary dimensions of security and arousal. The regulation of entropy is ultimately determined by a certain system state, a dynamic equilibrium between detectors, set points, emotions, and motor programs, each of which can contribute little to an understanding of the overall state if considered in isolation. A study by Gubler, Paffrath, and Bischof (1994) shows that it is possible to predict human behavior on the basis of these system states, although the difficulties entailed in modeling such complex systems often make it extremely difficult to test them empirically.

3.5.2 Kuhl's Personality Systems Interactions Theory

Personality Systems Interactions (PSI) theory (Kuhl, 2001) is a theory describing motivational systems. It has been developed on the basis of both systematic conceptual inquiry and experimental research (Kuhl & Beckmann, 1985, 1994a), and focuses on two major questions:

■ How does **self facilitation** and growth result from the integration of discrepancies, incongruities, and information that is not understood spontaneously (= entropy)?
■ How is **volitional facilitation** and enactment of intentions realized when obstacles are encountered?

The Self Facilitation System

Two subsystems make up the Self Facilitation System: the low level "object recognition system" (ORS) and the high level "extension memory" (EM). The ORS recognizes objects as single entities, be they external things, internal states, emotions, etc. Because these objects are checked against templates that have been stored in the past, the ORS is oriented toward the past. It further entails a figure-ground sharpening mechanism that makes it inflexible, in the sense that it is ill-equipped to deal with degraded input, unlike intuitive information processing oriented toward the present or the future. EM is an evaluation and decision-making system based on high-level intuition. It has extensive connections to a multitude of subsystems in the brain, drawing on a broad informational base, and including a great number of needs, preferences, values, and other self-aspects.

Comparable to the Zürich Model, PSI theory conceives of self facilitation as a circular system (Fig. 3.5).

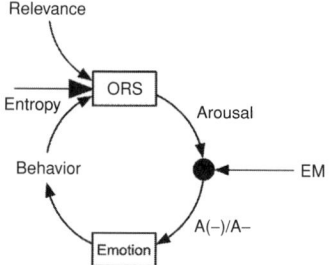

Figure 3.5 The self-development system of PSI theory. *A* –, negative affect; *A*(-), downregulated negative affect; *EM*, extension memory; *ORS*, object recognition system.

A self facilitation cycle is activated when the ORS detects discrepancies or entropy. Highly entropic stimuli are initially associated with negative affect. They are transmitted to extension memory (EM) as "incongruent" or "threatening." Because EM is a parallel memory system that integrates the totality of personal experiences, it is able to integrate information that the ORS cannot handle or interpret by drawing on related experiences. Once the new (discrepant) information has been successfully integrated, negative affect becomes **downregulated** (in the terminology of PSI theory: [A(–)]).

When negative affect (or arousal in the terms of the Zürich model) is not downregulated, however, which may result from individual differences in the activation of this system, negative affect (A–) persists and is translated into consciously accessible negative emotions that in turn trigger avoidance behavior.

Downregulated negative affect elicits a positively experienced emotion such as interest or acceptance, not unlike the concept of negative reinforcement in classical learning theory (Watson & Tellegen, 1985; Watson et al., 1999).

The Volitional Facilitation System

This system comprises two subsystems: the low level "intuitive behavior control" (IBC) system and the high level "intention memory" (IM). IBC has a double function. The first is the intuitive processing of information, involving the integration of contextual information within and across various modalities. The second is to initiate action and spontaneous reaction. Like all intuitive systems, the IBC has a rather rough but, at the same time, robust mode of operation, and overlooks mistakes and incongruence. The **intention memory** is able to form explicit representations of intended actions. Its most important role is to inhibit immediate intuitive reactions in order to facilitate planning and analytical thinking, which would otherwise have to be terminated.

Like Piaget's sensorimotor schemata, intuitive behavior control entails a form of nonconscious perception that does not involve individual objects being extracted from their contexts, but integrates numerous stimuli within parallel networks that simultaneously support intuitive motor programs. The IBC system does not interpret high-entropy

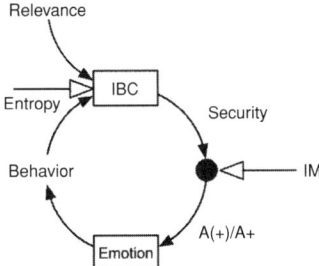

Figure 3.6 The volitional facilitation system of PSI theory. *A+*, positive affect; *A(+)*, inhibited positive affect; *IM*, intention memory; *IBC*, intuitive behavioral control.

stimuli as discrepant and threatening like the ORS would, but finds or constructs some sort of meaning, or familiarity (reflected by the unfilled arrow representing entropy in Fig. 3.6). Familiarity triggers feelings of **security** that can be interpreted as primary positive affect (Bischof, 1993). An adaptive feature of IBC is its speed and "fun" component. As a result of its connectionistic architecture, it is relatively "generous," overlooking mistakes and ignoring dangers. This can be disadvantageous, particularly in the face of potential threats. A further "top-down system," intention memory, is therefore responsible for monitoring and regulating the IBC system.

❶ IM serves to inhibit premature or "irrational" intuitive processing and to delay automatic responding when difficulties arise. This process is called **volitional inhibition**. Intentions that cannot yet be implemented are maintained in IM, to the effect that they can be enacted later.

To facilitate volitional inhibition, primary positive affect (e.g., based on security) is downregulated (in the terminology of PSI theory: A(+)) and transformed into a negative emotion that is not characterized by fear, but by the reduction of positive affect (e.g., frustration or dejection), and that may be expressed as rational, matter-of-fact behavior, listlessness, or even depressive mood. This negative emotion inhibits approach behavior (see Kuhl, 2000, for a more detailed description).

If, on the other hand, IM is unable to inhibit IBC (e.g., because of individual differences in the activation of this system, see Chapter 12), the motivational system remains in the intuitive mode.

SUMMARY

According to PSI theory, motivation can be seen as a function of systems interactions (or configurations). This perspective provides better explanations of complex, recurrent patterns of behavior (e.g., self facilitation, volitional facilitation) than do isolated traits. PSI theory places particular emphasis on the (down-)regulation of affect. Regulation of positive and negative affect can be seen as a volitional act that becomes necessary whenever emotions elicited directly by a situation would not suffice for motivation or would be dysfunctional.

Intuitive behavior control is more appropriate when the information to be processed relates to issues that are very familiar to the individual, however complex they may be; e.g., social interaction. It is also the preferred – and often more efficient – approach when time is short, and in the face of unexpected situations or spontaneous yielding to temptations.

Whenever a critical analysis of objects is required (e.g., because there is a problem to be solved), these intuitive behavioral routines have to be interrupted quickly and the analytical, systematic mode activated. This mode is appropriate when an important decision has to be made, when there is plenty of time, and when it is not yet clear how to proceed.

Scheffer and Kuhl (2006) have described the advantages and disadvantages of each approach for various occupational activities, underlining the practical value that classifications based on systems configurations can have for studies of everyday behavior in occupations and organizations. For some time now, personnel psychologists have emphasized that "compound variables" – e.g., **service orientation** as a combination of the traits of extraversion, agreeableness, and dispositional achievement motivation – have much higher validity than individual traits when it comes to explaining and predicting patterns of behavior that are highly significant at the workplace; e.g., the capacity for teamwork, service orientation, and leadership potential (Schneider, Hough, & Dunnete, 1996).

Finally, it remains to note that systems theory may be criticized to the extent that assuming systems configurations to be the basis for motivation further complicates the classification problem previously discussed. It is then no longer a question of how many universally verifiable traits are involved in human motivation, but of which of these traits universally and verifiably interact with one another to create more complex, higher-order traits of predictive value that direct and guide a broad spectrum of functionally equivalent forms of adaptive and expressive behavior. The functional profiles of the systems and their interactions are nomothetic. Given the multitude of possible combinations, however, the precise "configuration" of a personality system will always be unique. Ultimately, then, investigation of system configurations must take a complementary, idiographic perspective that emphasizes the unique pattern of traits present in each individual and their interactions with environmental variables. This brings us back to an idiographic perspective on individual differences, though on a higher level of systems theory, integrating person and situation across the developmental trajectory of the lifespan.

3.6 Allport's Idiographic Approach

Observers of human behavior intuitively believe that they differ consistently from other people across a broad range of situations. Personality and differential psychologists were, and continue to be, of the same opinion. It thus seemed reasonable to assume that individual differences in behavior in all manner of future situations could be reliably predicted on the basis of individual trait strength. When scholars sought to confirm this assumption in empirical research, however, the consistency of behavior proved to be disappointingly low. Bem and Allen (1974) labeled this phenomenon, which has been the subject of considerable discussion, the "consistency paradox."

Hartshorne and May (1928, 1929) placed children in situations where they had the opportunity to cheat, deceive, or steal. In a test situation, e.g., they could copy from their peers or surreptitiously continue to work after they had been told to stop. The correlation coefficients indicated that the consistency of behavior was rather low (between .20 and .40). Children who cheated in one situation were unlikely to do so in another. Those who cheated in one subject were honest in another. Upon closer consideration, this should not come as a surprise. After all, behavior is determined by the way the individual perceives the situation at hand, and not by the objective perspective of the observing psychologist. Yet it is the latter who assigns the various behaviors to a particular class – defining them, for example, as tempting situations that might induce someone to act dishonestly or deceptively.

To avoid the "nomothetic fallacy" (Bem & Allen, 1974) of this approach, it is first necessary to determine which classes of situations and related behaviors are equivalent from the perspective of each individual. Only then can the consistency of behavior be assessed. In other words, we can only expect consistency in an individual's behavior within subjectively equivalent classes of situations and actions (cf. Bem & Allen, 1974). In the final analysis, equivalence is defined by what the individual perceives as "equifinal," i.e., as producing equivalent outcomes (Brunswik, 1952, 1956). Hence, two or more situations or actions may be seen as equivalent because they promise the same desirable outcomes, or threaten to bring about the same undesirable outcomes. Therefore, a student may decide to cheat in only one of two subjects, because it is here that her grades are in need of improvement. Another student may take the opportunity to carry on working in secret, but decide not to copy from her neighbor, because it would simply be too embarrassing to get caught.

Furthermore, Hartshorne and May found that consistency also depends on the broader context in which opportunities to deceive are embedded. Students who cheat in class will not necessarily do so in competitive sports or at Sunday school. Just these few examples show three things: first, that equivalence classes of situations and actions must be individually determined; second, that they are connected and interrelated; third, that they are shaped and held together by expectations of achieving desirable goals (values) or avoiding undesirable outcomes. Ultimately, then, the outcomes

that people are able to bring about in a given situation determine classes of equivalence and hence consistency. G. W. Allport was already aware of this in 1937, when he defended the trait concept against the situational explanations of Hartshorne and May. He suggested that low consistency correlations proved only that "children are not consistent in the same way, not that they are inconsistent within themselves" (Allport, 1937, p. 250).

The inconsistencies observed are also caused by researchers assuming their respondents consider the same behaviors and situations as they do to be equivalent, and thus pooling them in questionnaire items and manipulated situations. This assumption is highly questionable, however. In his theory of the architecture of personality, Cervone (2004) suggested that both the contents of knowledge (about oneself and others) and the way this knowledge is linked to certain situations vary idiosyncratically; people who describe themselves using the same construct (e.g., "I am extraverted") may relate this construct to very different circumstances. As such, findings of inconsistency do not reflect transsituational inconsistencies in individual behavior as much as a lack of agreement between researchers and study participants on what constitute equivalent situations and equivalent behaviors. Before trait consistency can be studied, respondents would first have to be pretested to determine idiosyncratic equivalence classes of situations and actions, and be divided into groups accordingly. This explains why people do not question the transsituational consistency of traits in everyday life. Unlike empirical psychologists, we do not seem to work on the assumption that there are generally valid (nomothetic) classes of situations and actions. Rather, we proceed idiographically, differentiating and categorizing situations and actions to fit the particularities of each individual case.

McClelland (1985b) illustrated this point with an example that we would like to reproduce here in slightly modified form.

> **EXAMPLE**
>
> What would you think of a dog that barks and bites, howls, scratches, jumps up, rolls on the ground, stretches out its neck, and finally urinates – all within a period of 10 minutes? You might see this behavior as thematically disconnected, inconsistent, or even "disorganized." Looking at the situation from the dog's perspective, however, you would have to revise this interpretation immediately. Only then would you realize that the dog had not been fed for a week, and that the owner was now approaching the kennel with a large piece of meat, but showing no signs of handing it over. Driven by the need for food, the dog applies all of the strategies available in its behavioral repertoire to obtain the food. From the dog's perspective, then, the behavior is entirely consistent.

McClelland (1975) provides an impressive overview of the different strategies that people apply to gain power and status (e.g., accumulating status symbols, ensuring that they are the center of attention, associating with powerful individuals or organizations, helping others without being asked, criticizing others, etc.). In certain situations, people try out all of the strategies available to them in succession. This behavior may seem inconsistent to the outside observer, but is not at all inconsistent from the idiographic perspective – behaviors that seem qualitatively very different are in fact equivalent forms of adaptive and expressive behavior serving to satisfy (in this case) the power motive.

From the perspective of evolutionary psychology, it makes sense to consider motives and behavioral strategies separately. In complex social interactions, a strong autonomy or power motive can rarely be implemented by means of a single behavioral strategy. The more ambiguous situations become and the more often people encounter differently structured situations, the more important it is for them to be able to switch flexibly between different **systems configurations** in order to satisfy their motives. MacDonald (1988) used the term "compartmentalization" to emphasize that people behave very differently in different situations – callously to their rivals and warmly to their friends, for example. High consistency of behavior is not an evolutionary end in itself; like all other behavioral patterns, its adaptive value is tested over the course of natural selection. The fact that flexibility in the application of different behavioral strategies has the appearance of consistency from the subjective perspective is not a contradiction in terms, but accentuates the need for an idiographic approach to complement nomothetic research.

We cannot assume consistency on the motive level, either, because the various motives have to "compete" with one another for access to the stream of behavior, which thus takes a dynamic course that is hard to predict (Atkinson & Birch, 1970; Kuhl & Blankenship, 1979). The resulting "behavioral oscillations" are not necessarily subjectively perceived as inconsistent, however; it can be part of the stable core of a personality to switch from one motive to another in certain situations. Equally, a motive conflict might characterize the consistency of a biography from the idiographic perspective, rendering many different situations equivalent across the life course.

Based on Allport's trait theory presented at the beginning of this chapter, a high consistency of behavior can only be expected when one motive is so strong that it dominates the others. Indeed, in operant tests such as the OMT (Chapter 12), high internal consistencies of thematic responses are found only in groups high or low in one of the three primary motives (Scheffer, Kuhl, & Eichstaedt, 2003). Individuals with average motive strength, in contrast, show inconsistent response behavior across the different picture cues. From the idiographic perspective, these responses are by no means inconsistent, because each individual interprets the ambiguous picture cues on the basis of his or her own prior experience, thus giving them coherent meaning (see Cervone, 2004).

SUMMARY

There are two reasons for complementing the nomothetic perspective by an idiographic approach that emphasizes the unique pattern of traits present within each individual. It is precisely in the "normal" ranges of motive strength that diagnosticians (professionals and laypeople alike) can only usefully describe and characterize individuals by taking an approach that acknowledges the context-dependence and the underdetermined nature of behavioral and biographical trajectories (Baltes & Staudinger, 2000; Sternberg, 2003). In acknowledging the limits of the nomothetic perspective, however, we do not mean to imply that it is entirely without merit, as we aimed to show in this chapter by proceeding gradually from the nomothetic to the idiographic. Both approaches have their advantages and disadvantages, and should therefore be considered complementary. They should ultimately be combined in such a way that the nomothetic approach is able to show how idiographic variety emerges from certain nomothetic regularities.

Longitudinal studies show that highly effective models and theories can be derived from the study of motivation; it is possible to predict behavior in disparate domains over very long time periods (up to 16 years!) on the basis of motives and traits. Domains examined to date include intimate relationships and psychosocial adjustment (McAdams & Vaillant, 1982), number of divorces and jobs (Winter et al., 1998), promotion to top positions in a large company (McClelland & Boyatzis, 1982), and business activities (McClelland, 1965).

Although trait theories only permit the prediction and change of human motivation in a statistical sense, and although predictions are restricted to the probability of a certain behavior occurring later in life, these findings clearly confirm that – to draw on Kurt Lewin – there is nothing more practical than a good theory.

REVIEW QUESTIONS

1. **Define the concept of "trait" and give an example.**

   A trait is a neuropsychic system with the capacity to render many stimuli functionally equivalent, and to initiate and guide equivalent (consistent) forms of adaptive and expressive behavior. Example: the achievement motive (Fig. 3.1).

2. **How can the traits of the five-factor model be interpreted?**

   The Big Five traits can be interpreted as dispositionally heightened sensitivity to certain emotions. The dimensions distinguished are: extraversion, neuroticism, openness to experience, agreeableness, and conscientiousness. These five traits are assumed to be endogenous.

3. **What do the five-factor model and Cattell's trait theory have in common and where do they differ?**

Both theories are based on the "sedimentation hypothesis," the lexical approach, and the method of factor analysis. Cattell's theory is much broader than the five-factor model, however, in that it covers dynamic "ergs" as well as endogenous "traits."

4. **Why did McDougall's instinct-based classification of motives fall into disrepute in scientific circles?**

Attempts to infer instincts that "underlie" behavior can lead to circular reasoning, with every observable behavior being attributed to a corresponding instinct. Inspired by McDougall's list of instincts, it became common practice, particularly in neighboring disciplines such as sociology and political science, to attribute all behavioral phenomena to a specific instinct. For example, war was attributed to an aggressive instinct. At the same time, the fact that people fight wars was cited as evidence for the presence of an aggressive instinct.

5. **What did Murray mean by "thema," and how did he seek to measure individual differences?**

Murray used the term "thema" to describe person-environment relations, which he saw in terms of interactions between need (person) and press (environment). He developed the Thematic Apperception Test to measure individual differences in the relative strength of themas.

6. **Which are the needs identified in Maslow's hierarchical model?**

Maslow's hierarchy ranges from existential, physiological needs via security needs, needs for belongingness and love, and esteem needs, to the value of self-actualization at the very top of the hierarchy.

7. **Discuss the adaptive value of emotions.**

Emotion-specific processing of information can help initiate a prompt response to the situation at hand. If people relied solely on the cognitive, argumentative processing of information, involving the analytical elaboration and subsequent integration of incentive and expectancy features, there would be long delays in responding to the situation.

Their eventual responses, although fitting, would come too late, and thus be inappropriate to the situational demands. The disadvantage of purely emotion-specific information processing is its context-specificity, which may lead to a shortfall in abstract, situation-transcending action strategies.

8. **What are the three basic principles of systems theory models of motivation? What do these principles imply for our understanding of motive dispositions?**

Personality is a complex system involving the interaction of multiple, highly integrated processes. These interacting processes are rooted in basic cognitive and affective systems that initiate and direct behavior. The personality interacts with the environment, and the initiated behavior contributes to shaping the environment. From this perspective, motivational dispositions can be interpreted as systems configurations. In other words, several independent dispositions such as high levels of enterprise, autonomy, and intuitive behavioral control can be interconnected, jointly rendering numerous stimuli functionally equivalent and initiating consistent (equivalent) forms of adaptive and expressive behavior. As the systems configuration takes effect on the environment, the latter can change the system configuration (reciprocal interactionism), such that behavior becomes inconsistent, even though the dispositions involved remained stable.

9. **What is the consistency paradox?**

The inconsistencies frequently observed in behavior are caused by researchers assuming their respondents to consider the same behaviors and situations as they do to be equivalent, and thus pooling them in questionnaire items and manipulated situations. This kind of approach might lead a researcher to assume, for example, that someone who is dominant at work behaves the same way at home. For some respondents, however, assertive behavior in the private sphere will not mean a discernible gain in status. Thus, there is no incentive in this context for their idiographic power motive. From the respondents' own perspective, they are behaving entirely consistently, because dominance in the family circle cannot satisfy their power motive (the reverse case is also conceivable).

4 Situational Determinants of Behavior

J. Beckmann and H. Heckhausen

In Chapter 3, we considered explanations of behavior that draw solely on personality characteristics. Motives are relatively stable personality dispositions. Because the strength of the various motives differs interindividually, they can be invoked to explain differences in behavior. Indeed, motives can be seen as variables underlying predictable differences in individual behavior. In person-centered approaches, motive dispositions are also expected to explain the forces initiating and directing behavior. Seen from this perspective, situational factors serve only to arouse a particular motive. If, for example, someone with a strong achievement motive is invited to play a game of ludo (or Parcheesi), the achievement motive

will take effect immediately, and determine that player's behavior from that moment on. Any differences between the players in this situation would have to be explained by motive-dependent motivational differences. As shown in Chapter 3, however, the explanatory value of models that rely solely on personality variables is limited. An alternative approach is one that focuses on situational variables, on the situational stimuli that trigger and direct behavior. In this chapter, we look at the major theoretical developments that have emerged from situation-centered explanations of behavior.

The early 20th century saw the emergence of a research tradition that took the equally radical approach of focusing on the situation as the sole determinant of behavior. **Behaviorism** turned its back on personality characteristics, and hence on motives, as explanatory variables. Indeed, behaviorists were less interested in individual differences than in the situational specificity of behavior. What initiates a behavioral sequence? What directs it toward a goal? What facilitates its adaptation to situational demands? What brings it to a close? These questions relate to the causes of concrete components of behavior, to functionalist aspects that cannot be attributed to the motive dispositions activated at a particular moment in time. The focus here is on specific processes of motivation.

❶ Behaviorists sought to describe the forces behind the initiation and direction of behavior in more precise terms. One basic assumption was that all instrumental acts are learned. This seemed to make concepts such as instinct and motive redundant. In time, however, the need for an initiating or energizing component was recognized. This energizing component was not specific to certain content domains (equivalent classes of goals), such as achievement, affiliation, or power. Instead, the concept of a general, activating "drive" was introduced (see McDougall, 1932 p. 455).

Behaviorist approaches first shifted the focus of explanatory interest to learning. But how and when is what has been learned implemented in behavior? What is the nature of the link between learning and activation, the relationship between energizing behavior and giving it direction? Complex models were developed to address these questions from the behaviorist perspective. One of these was **Hull's dynamic drive theory,** which, like earlier approaches, attributed **drive** to physiological need states. The later postulates of acquired and derived drives, and of drive as a strong stimulus, prompted attempts to expand the explanatory value of drive theory to include behavior that cannot be attributed directly to physiological need states.

Influenced by psychoanalytic theory, the behaviorists went beyond animal experiments to examine the complexity of human behavioral phenomena. The study of **conflict** phenomena, in particular, led to a fruitful integration of approaches from learning psychology, psychoanalysis, and field theory.

Following an examination of **conflict theory,** we will consider the approaches taken to the situationally motivated determinants of behavior in the psychology of activation and in cognitive psychology. **Activation theories** are, for the most part, physiologically oriented and build on the concepts of drive theory, whereas cognitive theories focus on cognitive interpretations of situations and their effects on behavior, emphasizing the importance of intervening cognitive processes in motivation. Foremost among theoretical approaches incorporating a cognitive interpretation of situational factors is the theory of **cognitive dissonance,** which generated particularly intensive research activity. Originally a theory of motivation based on the assumptions of drive theory, it enjoyed increasing currency as a theory of attitudinal change in social psychology. Eventually, its function was reduced to one of mental hygiene, with processes of dissonance reduction serving solely to produce a conflict-free self. In essence, however, it is a motivational theory that describes processes of self-regulation occurring in response to internal conflicts. Thus, dissonance theory lies at the interface of motivation and volition (Beckmann, 1984).

4.1 The Explanatory Role of the Situation in Motivational Psychology

Information about the current situation is crucial to action control. In the simplest scenario, responses are triggered and controlled by "stimuli" present in the situation. Beside external stimuli, the sources of which are in the environment outside the organism, internal stimuli arise within the organism itself. These internal stimuli may be transient states of the organism such as hunger, or states such as internal conflict.

Early behaviorist approaches did not study the situation within the organism, however, as it was not accessible to direct observation. Scholars were initially concerned only with what could be manipulated on the stimulus side and observed on the response side.

Learned, adaptive behaviors were seen to be based purely on the formation of **associations.** Neither Thorndike nor Pavlov considered it necessary to introduce a motivational concept to explain learned changes in behavior (with the exceptions of the processes of arousal and inhibition).

Nevertheless, both ensured that their animals were hungry before using them in their food-related learning experiments. When Pavlov's dogs were satiated (i.e., not "aroused"), they no longer salivated in response to powdered meat being placed in their mouths; when Thorndike's cats were satiated, they did not engage in food-oriented escape behavior. Both researchers focused on the structural mechanisms of stimulus-response bonds (S-R bonds), and on identifying the temporal relations that would guarantee the best learning outcomes. They were evidently implicitly aware that learning requires a motivational basis, however, and thus manipulated the motivational state of hunger within the organism.

The state within the organism also plays a key role in Thorndike's (1911, 1913) "**Law of Effect,**" according to which it is the achievement of a "satisfying state of affairs" that strengthens the bond between a successful instrumental response and the antecedent stimuli. It was not until 40 years later that underlying motivational states found their rightful recognition as internal situational determinants in the explanation of S-R bonds in Hull's drive reduction theory.

4.2 Need and Drive

Woodworth (1918) disagreed with McDougall's notion of **instincts** being the sole basis for the explanation of behavior. At the same time, he questioned the explanatory value of the simple $S–R$ bonds postulated by the behaviorists. He expanded these simple $S–R$ equations to include the additional determinants of organismic states (O), thus producing $S–O–R$ equations. If the organism is in a need state, a distinction must be made between anticipatory and consummatory responses (terminal actions), as had already been proposed by Sherrington (1906). Whereas anticipatory responses are dominated by external stimuli, consummatory responses reflect the effects of internal stimuli. **Drives,** in particular, propel behavior toward its goal, its satisfaction or satiation. This "dynamic" view of behavior led Woodworth to suggest that the "mechanisms" of behavior (i.e., its structural components) eventually acquire the characteristics of a drive, becoming a motivational force in their own right.

❗ Woodworth (1918) was the first to distinguish between the concepts of "drives" and "mechanisms." In so doing, he differentiated between the dynamic or energetic component and the directive component of motivational phenomena. Tolman (1932) adopted this distinction, introducing it to the psychology of learning. His "intervening variables" were labeled "drive" and "cognition." These theoretical constructs were later used by Hull in his complex drive theory.

Approaches to the Measurement of Internal Stimuli

Whereas behaviorism initially focused exclusively on external effects on the organism, other approaches also considered the internal stimuli that arise from the internal environment of the organism and affect behavior from within. Freud had distinguished between external and internal stimuli as early as 1895, explaining that the latter are those from which the organism cannot escape. On the physiological side, this prompted a search for measurable internal stimuli that provide the incentive for certain behaviors. Cannon and others developed a **localized theory of motivation** for hunger and thirst (Cannon & Washburn, 1912). They measured stomach contractions with the aid of a rubber balloon that was inflated after it had been swallowed. The stomach contractions measured correlated with feelings of hunger. The internal stimuli for feelings of thirst were assumed to arise from a drying of the mucous membrane of the mouth and throat.

Later decades saw intensive research activity in this area (see Bolles, 1967, 1975, for an overview), the findings of which completely undermined the localized theory of motivation. For example, it was shown that dogs engaging in "sham-drinking" (where a fistula is inserted into the esophagus to drain away the water before it reaches the stomach) consumed large amounts of water, even though the oral cavity was kept moist. The regulation of food and liquid intake proved to be extremely complex. Even now, their physiological bases are not entirely understood. Beside peripheral regions of the organism like the gastrointestinal tract, stomach, colon, liver, body cells, arteries, and veins, brain centers have been shown to be involved, exercising a central integrating function (Balagura, 1973; Toates, 1981).

Another line of research, initiated primarily by Curt Richter, focused on the general activity level of experimental animals. Richter's (1927) findings suggest that activity level represents an index of periodic variation in drive that seems to accompany cyclic variation in need as a means of maintaining the organism's metabolic equilibrium (**homeostasis**). Richter used running wheels and stabilimeter cages (see below) to record animals' activity levels automatically over a period of days. Based on the variations in activity observed, he assumed a three-fold causal sequence: (1) need leads to drive [via (2) internal stimulation] and (3) drive leads to linearly increased activity. For a long time, it was thought that physiological indicators of need states were prima facie evidence for the drive in question, which, prior to its satiation, was expressed in increased general activity. At first, it was even thought that homeostatic principles could provide a watertight explanation for all behavior (Raup, 1925). Yet it soon became apparent that basing inferences about the presence of a drive on either antecedent indicators of need or subsequent increases in activity was a risky and overly simplistic strategy.

Here again, matters seem to be far more complicated than first assumed. For example, whether a food-deprived rat displays an above- or below-average level of general activity has far more to do with external stimulus conditions than was originally thought. Various attempts were made to

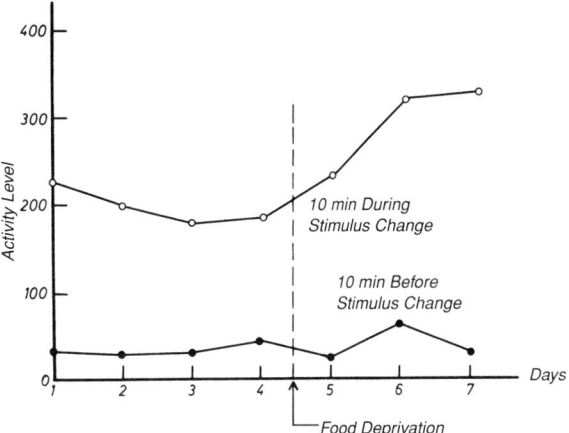

Figure 4.1 Mean activity levels in 10-minute periods prior to and during a stimulus change in satiated (day 1–4) and food-deprived (day 5–7) rats. (Based on Campbell & Sheffield, 1953, p. 321.)

operationalize the internal stimulus, the drive. Campbell and Sheffield (1953) kept rats in stabilimeter cages for seven days. These cages registered the animal's every activity. The laboratory was dark and soundproof; a ventilating fan produced a constant masking noise. Food was provided in the first four days, followed by three days of deprivation. Once a day, the experimenter entered the room for 10 minutes, turning the light on and the fan off. Activity levels were measured in the 10 minutes prior to and during this change in stimulus. Fig. 4.1 shows the mean activity levels in these two 10-minute periods over the seven days of the experiment. The level of activity prior to the stimulus change remains at the same low level, even with increasing hunger in the last three days. During the period of stimulus change, however, the level of activity increases steadily as a function of increasing hunger, supporting Morgan's assumption of an increased general motivational state. These findings, however, challenge Richter's theory that activity increases automatically with an increase in the need state. What increases is evidently the readiness to respond to external stimuli. In another experiment, Sheffield and Campbell (1954) showed that the increase in activity during the deprivation period was particularly pronounced if the change in stimulus was temporally linked to feeding on previous days. It would seem that the animals have learned stimulus cues that precede feeding, suggesting that the periodic variations in drive observed by Richter were the result of food-signaling stimuli that were not controlled in his experiment.

Measurements of general activity are difficult to interpret because there is no way of knowing which specific drives they reflect. Similarly, general activity does not result in drive-specific, goal-directed behavior. Progress was made with the construction of a new experimental apparatus for measuring drive-specific, goal-oriented activity: the **Columbia Obstruction Box**.

4

The Columbia Obstruction Box

Fig. 4.2 shows the layout of the Columbia Obstruction Box. The animal is placed in the entrance compartment (*A*). To reach an incentive object to satisfy a drive, it has to cross an electrically charged grid (*B*) accessed by means of an experimenter-operated door (d_1). Having crossed the grid, the animal reaches the first section of the incentive compartment (*C*). Stepping on the release plate (*E*) opens the door (d_2) to the incentive compartment proper (*D*), which contains a drive-specific incentive object (food, water, or a sex partner).

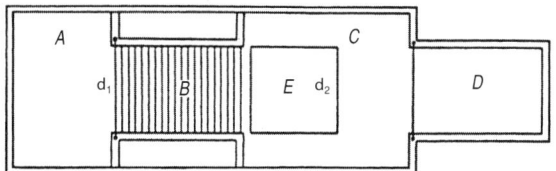

Figure 4.2 The Columbia Obstruction Box designed to measure drive-specific levels of activity. (Based on Jenkins, Warner, & Warden, 1926, p. 366.)

The animals were first given a series of pretrials to acquaint them with the apparatus. The incentive object was present at all times. It was only in the last of the pretrials that the grid was charged. In the main experiment, deprivation of a specific need was varied, and the number of times an animal overcame its aversion to the charged grid to reach the incentive object in each 20-minute observation period was recorded. The aim was to measure the strength or urgency of individual drives, not only as a function of length of deprivation, but also in terms of differences between the various drives.

As shown in Fig. 4.3, thirst seems to have greater drive strength than hunger; and hunger, in turn, seems to have greater drive

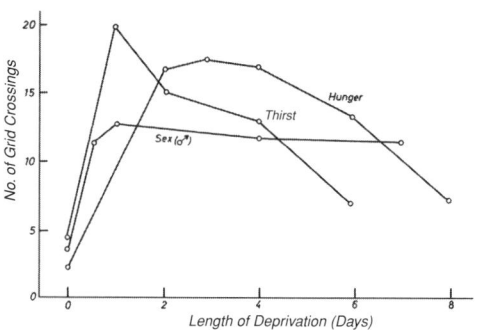

Figure 4.3 Frequency with which rats crossed the electrically charged grid of the Columbia Obstruction Box to make contact with a need-specific incentive object by length of deprivation. (Based on Warden, Jenkins, & Warner, 1936.)

strength than sexuality in males. The number of times the grid was crossed, however, is a questionable measure of drive strength. For one thing, uncontrolled factors in the pretrial phase may have led to different learning outcomes. Likewise, very different results might be obtained if the length of the observational period were changed. It would be difficult to determine which time period would produce the most valid measure of a specific drive strength. Most of all, the attractiveness of the incentive object was not varied systematically. We now know that this can be a motivating factor capable of activating behavior independent of need state. Furthermore, each contact with the incentive object – no matter how fleeting – results in consummatory activities that cannot always be controlled.

4.3 Drive Theory

In the 1920s and 1930s, extensive research relating to the concept of drive produced a broad range of findings and insights. Need states were manipulated; internal and external stimuli, physiological and behavioral indicators of need-dependent **drive strengths,** and instrumental and consummatory reactions were observed, operationalized, measured, and interrelated. This work represented a considerable advance on the speculative concept of **instinct**. However, there was still no clear and cohesive conception of drive beyond the general notion that the motivational state driving behavior increases as a function of need state.

Researchers reconsidered the questions that had already been addressed by instinct theorists. Are there as many drives as there are physiological needs? Or is there just one drive – a generalized incentive function for all behaviors that is not specific to a particular need? Assuming that there are various drives, does a need-specific drive have a selective function (in

terms of stimulus and response) as well as an incentive function; i.e., a directive component as well as an energizing one?

These were the questions addressed by Hull's (1943) **drive theory**. In his complex theory, Hull made a clear distinction between drive and habits. Drive has a purely dynamic function and describes a general state of activation. Habits, in contrast, are learned, associative stimulus-response bonds that give behavior direction.

❶ Hull assumed a single, generalized incentive function, which had no selective function in determining behavior. Thus, the question of motivation was confined to a single drive, or rather to a question of incentive. For Hull, motivation concerned only the energizing of behavior, whereas the selection and goal orientation of behavior were functions of associative learning.

The clear distinction between issues of learning and motivation in the explanation of behavior, however, does not mean that the two components were viewed as mutually exclusive. In fact, one basic tenet of Hull's drive theory is that the motivational component affects the learning component, but that the learning component has no influence on the motivational component. The motivational component, drive (*D*), is – in a manner of speaking – an indigenous source of behavior.

How does drive influence learning? In the late 1930s, Hull began to ask whether stimulus-response contiguity suffices as the sole explanation for learning, i.e., for the formation of new *S–R* bonds. For him, it was not **classical conditioning** that had been invoked to explain Thorndike's trial-and-error learning, that was the primary learning principle, it was **instrumental conditioning**. Stimuli become linked to responses whenever these responses lead to need satisfaction. The subsequent reduction in the existing need or drive serves to reinforce the new *S–R* bond. Thus, *S–R* learning follows the **principle of reinforcement**. This approach to the mechanisms of reinforcement is known as drive-reduction theory (Chapter 2).

According to this approach, the strength of the emerging **stimulus-response bond** ($_sH_R$) is solely dependent on the

STUDY

Experimental Studies on the Drive-Reduction Theory of Reinforcement

In the studies by Williams (1938) and Perin (1942), rats that had been deprived of food for 23 hours learned an instrumental response (lever pressing) that produced food. The frequency of reinforcement of this instrumental response (by provision of the food reward) was varied across four experimental groups during the learning phase. In the subsequent test phase, the animals were again deprived of food (for 22 hours in Williams's study and 3 hours in Perin's study). Lever pressing was no longer reinforced, i.e., the learned response was extinguished. The dependent variable was resistance to extinction, i.e., the number of lever presses prior to a five-minute period of nonresponse. This is a measure of habit strength ($_sH_R$). The results are presented in Fig. 4.4.

The graph shows that the resistance to extinction of the acquired *S–R* bond increases as a function of the number of previous reinforcements. In other words, an animal whose goal responses have more frequently resulted in a reduction of need state in the past will show greater persistence in responding when reinforcement is withheld.

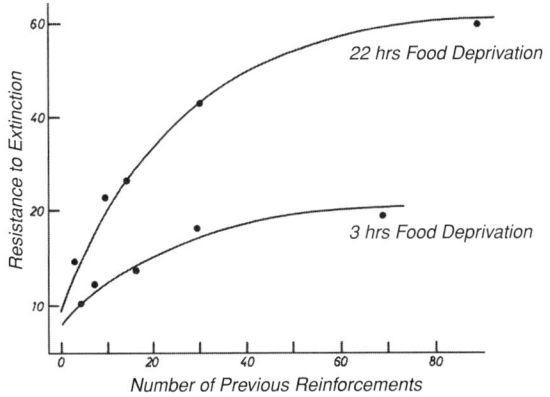

Figure 4.4 Impact of the number of reinforcements and the length of deprivation on resistance to extinction. (Based on Perin, 1942, p. 101.)

frequency of reinforcement. The frequency or strength of learned responses is only dependent on the existing drive strength.

Hull derived his drive-reduction theory of reinforcement (and other concepts of his drive theory) from the two experiments presented in the study box; one by Williams (1938), the other by Perin (1942). The findings of the two studies appear to clearly support the notion of reinforcement being based on **drive reduction**. Furthermore, the two curves in Fig. 4.4 indicate that resistance to extinction increases as a function of hours of deprivation, independent of the number of reinforcements. The higher the frequency of reinforcement, the greater the difference between the two different deprivation conditions, i.e., the two drive strengths, in terms of a resistance to extinction. In other words, where their influence on behavior is concerned, the relationship between frequency of reinforcement and drive strength is multiplicative. Neither habit strength ($_sH_R$), based on the frequency of reinforcement, nor drive strength (*D*), based on hours of deprivation, are the only determinants of behavior (in this case, the extinction of a learned response). Rather, the two must combine to produce the behavior. Thus, behavior is shaped by the product of ($_sH_R$) and (*D*), the so-called reaction potential, $_sE_R$ (Chapter 2, Section 2.6.1).

Performance is not solely a function of learning. A motivational component is also required. Hull makes an explicit distinction between learning and performance to the extent that, once a habit has been formed, performance of a response is determined only by the product of $_sH_R$ and *D*. Although not stated explicitly, however, the same also applies to the preceding acquisition process. For Hull, both learning and performance are behavioral principles. To build up habit strength, the organism has to repeatedly engage in behavior that results directly in the reduction of a specific drive. Regarding the acquisition phase, the distinction between learning components ($_sH_R$) and motivational components (*D*) is problematic. If reinforcement is a necessary prerequisite for learning, then the learning component (habit formation) must necessarily also incorporate a motivational component.

Hull (1943) expanded his drive theory in a number of directions, essentially formulating six postulates. All of these helped to clarify the drive construct. They stimulated research and led to revisions and new conceptualizations. The six postulates relate to:

1. the antecedent conditions of drive,
2. drive stimuli,
3. independence of drive and habit,
4. the energizing effect of drive,
5. the reinforcing effect of drive reduction, and
6. the general nature of drive.

4.3.1 Antecedent Conditions of Drive

Drive strength is a direct function of the organism's existing need state, and is presumably mediated by need-specific receptors within the organism. Empirical studies have focused primarily on the need for food and the resulting drive states. Duration of food deprivation is varied as an antecedent condition of drive, thus serving as operational criterion for drive strength.

The value of deprivation as a criterion for drive strength, however, proved to be limited. In rats, for example, a relationship between length of deprivation and indicators of hunger – e.g., amount of food consumed – was observed only after a period of deprivation exceeding 4 hours (Bolles, 1967, 1975). Because laboratory rats eat about four times during the day and eight times during the night, a given period of deprivation during the night will deprive the animal more than that same period during the day. The four-hour threshold was confirmed by Le Magnen and Tallon (1966) among others, who showed that food intake does not increase as a function of the period of abstinence between two regular feedings, but that it does increase as a function of the time interval following an omitted feeding.

Research (see Bolles, 1967) has shown that reduction in body weight is a better indicator of the strength of a hunger drive than is the period of deprivation. In line with Hull's drive theory, experiments with rats confirmed that the strength of both instrumental and consummatory behavior (in terms of latency, intensity, persistence, and resistance to extinction) increases proportionately to weight loss. It should be pointed out, however, that the quantitative relationship between the induced need states and drive strength (i.e., their behavioral parameters) does not represent an equal-interval scale, but only a rank-order scale. Needs other than food and liquid intake, such as sexuality or exploration, are not "needs" as defined by drive theory, because their deprivation has little effect on behavior. In these cases, the conditions determining behavior are very complex, and the external situation plays a decisive role in providing incentive conditions. For example, certain hormonal states are necessary but not sufficient conditions for copulatory behavior.

4.3.2 Drive Stimuli

Drive states are assumed to be accompanied by specific drive stimuli (S_D). These are attributed to the structural (associative) and not to the motivational components of behavior. Drive stimuli form stimulus-response bonds of their own, and can thus direct behavior. Unlike generalized, unspecific drive strength, however, they cannot motivate behavior of their own accord. Attempts were made to demonstrate the directive functions of drive stimuli in drive-discrimination studies. In one such study, rats learned certain instrumental responses under food-deprived conditions, and others under water-deprived conditions, but otherwise they were subjected to identical external conditions. How easy would it be for them to respond in a manner appropriate to the existent need state? To identify the appropriate response, they needed to "know" whether they were hungry or thirsty. In

other words, specific drive stimuli needed to have formed associations with the instrumental responses.

The data obtained (Bolles, 1967, pp. 254–264) provide little evidence for the significance of drive stimuli. There are other, more convincing explanations for the finding that rats learn the instrumental response appropriate to the momentary need state more quickly – specifically, the incentive mechanism of fractional goal response (r_G), as illustrated by the following two studies. Hull (1933) had rats run through a maze. If they chose one path, they found water in the goal box; if they chose another path, leading to the same goal box, they found food. The animals were alternately food or water deprived when placed in the maze. It was a long time before they were able to discriminate between the two paths, and even then the distinction was weak and not very reliable. Leeper (1935), in contrast, observed rapid discrimination learning when water and food were placed in different goal boxes. If drive stimuli were the crucial factor, this difference in learning outcomes would not have been observed. Something other than drive stimuli evidently controlled the behavior of the rats in Leeper's research design. The consummatory responses of eating and drinking (R_G) are linked to stimuli present in the environment in which they take place. These environmental stimuli become associated with those previously encountered at the crucial fork in the maze. This triggers anticipatory fractional goal responses (r_G) of eating or drinking that steer the animal more strongly in one direction or the other, depending on the momentary need state.

❶ The hypothetical incentive mechanism of **anticipatory fractional goal response** (r_G) is the most serious challenge to drive theory, because it is also better able to explain other aspects of incentive motivation (Chapter 5). It is an especially marked improvement on explanations of behavior based solely on association, which relied heavily on the effectiveness of drive stimuli (e.g., Estes, 1958).

4.3.3 Independence of Drive and Habit

Neither the learning component (habit) nor the motivational component (drive) determine behavior independently; what takes effect is their multiplicative product. Two main approaches have been taken to this issue. The first compares learning curves obtained under different drive conditions but comparable frequencies of reinforcement. Given the multiplicative effect, variations in drive strength should result in the learning curves plateauing out at different levels (cf. the data presented by Williams and Perin in Fig. 4.4); in each case, however, these plateaus should be reached in equal steps. In the second approach, learning takes place under one drive state, and testing under another. The question is then whether behavior is commensurate with the change in the drive conditions or whether transfer effects from the previous drive condition can be observed?

A study by Deese and Carpenter (1951) is an example of the second approach.

> **EXAMPLE**
>
> Deese and Carpenter (1951) ran food-deprived rats under either low or high drive conditions through a runway leading to a goal box that contained food. The authors measured latency of leaving the start box after the gate was opened. Both groups had reached their respective plateaus of response latency after 24 reinforcements. The drive conditions were then reversed, with the group that was previously run under a low drive condition being run under a high one, and vice versa. The findings shown in Fig. 4.5 attest to a peculiarly asymmetrical transfer effect.
>
>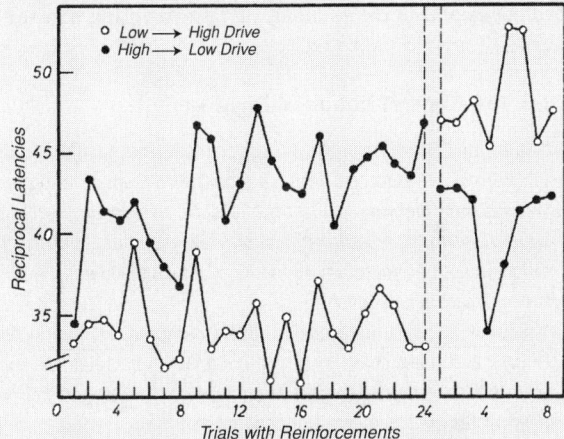
>
> **Figure 4.5** Latencies (reciprocal) of a running response to food under low and high hunger drive conditions and (in the right-hand panel) under reversed drive conditions. (Based on Deese & Carpenter, 1951, p. 237.)

Bolles (1967, pp. 227–242) provides an overview of key findings. In general, it was possible to confirm the independence of habit and drive in the case of food-seeking behavior, as measured in terms of intensity differences. The latter restriction raises the question of whether slow and fast running speed are merely differences in the intensity of one and the same response, or two qualitatively different responses, learned under low or high drive strength.

Furthermore, whether drive and habit are independent of each other is really a question of definition. After all, there are secondary, acquired drives (motives), such as fear, that are activated in the presence of particular stimulus cues. Hull places these in a separate category because, for him, drive (D) encompasses only nonlearned drive states. By contrast, Hull's collaborators and students, such as Spence (1956), Miller (1956), and Brown (1961), categorize everything with motivating characteristics as D, thereby abandoning the postulate of independence of drive and stimulus-response bonds. These extensions of drive theory will be discussed next.

4.3.4 Energizing Effects of Drive

It is a basic hypothetical postulate of drive theory that the motivational component serves exclusively to initiate behavior, but does not give it direction. Here again, however, research findings are inconsistent. The clearest support for the energizing characteristics of drive strength is provided by studies involving learning under drive conditions that are subject to rapid change through instrumental or consummatory responses (Fig. 4.4). On the whole, this applies only to "tissue needs," and not to the "sex drive" (whose drive character was questioned earlier). Parenthetically, if energizing is equated with response frequency, then there are also alternative explanations for these findings; e.g., in terms of purely associative principles or incentive effects. The study by Campbell and Sheffield (1953) presented above is an example of this (Fig. 4.1).

4.3.5 Reinforcement Effects of Drive Reduction

The acquisition of a new stimulus-response bond assumes the existence of a drive state that will be reduced by the response. None of the postulates of drive theory have prompted as much research and testing as this one.

The postulate raises questions about the precise nature of drive reduction. Does it consist in the consummatory activity itself, the effects of the stimulus (e.g., stomach activity after food intake), or the subsequent need reduction within the organism? Is drive reduction not simply a motivational process governing the execution of behavior that has also been acquired in other ways not involving drive reduction? In that case, drive reduction would be a behavioral principle – a matter of motivation – and not a learning principle (see Chapter 5 on latent learning).

To test whether consummatory responses are the critical event facilitating learning, experimenters sought to eliminate parts of the consummatory response sequence. Specifically, they bypassed the oral component by means of a fistula that introduced food directly to the stomach, or the gastric component by means of an esophageal fistula that drained the food before it could enter the stomach (sham feeding). Because limited learning was observed under both conditions, drive reduction must, at least in part, be linked to consummatory activities. Given these findings, the hypothetical drive construct could only be maintained – e.g., by N. E. Miller (1961), who ran numerous experiments with normal and sham feeding – by abandoning Hull's notion that drive reduction is synonymous with a reduction of an organismic need state.

Sheffield went a step further. He showed that neither need reduction nor drive reduction are necessary prerequisites for learning. Sheffield and Roby (1950) demonstrated that thirsty rats will learn an instrumental response in order to obtain a saccharin solution rather than the same amount of water. Because saccharin has no nutritional value, it cannot

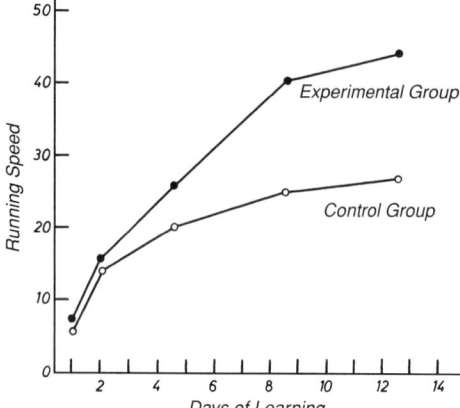

Figure 4.6 Learning gains under the drive condition of copulation without ejaculation in rats. The control group found a male animal in the goal box. (Based on Sheffield, Wulff, & Backer, 1951, p. 5.)

have resulted in higher need satisfaction. Young (1949, 1961) identified numerous taste preferences that prompt learning without providing for the organism's metabolic requirements. Young attributed these findings to differences in the affect-inducing incentive values of the foodstuffs in question.

The findings of a study by Sheffield, Wulff, and Backer (1951) present an even greater challenge to drive-reduction theory. The study involved learning under stimulation of the sex drive. Male rats who had never copulated prior to the experiment learned an instrumental response to gain access to a female in heat, despite the fact that the copulatory process was interrupted prior to ejaculation. It seems reasonable to assume that not only was there no reduction in drive strength in this case, but that – in contrast – drive was increased. There must, then, be certain cases in which learning is the result of drive induction rather than drive reduction. Fig. 4.6 shows the results for the rats in the experimental group in comparison to a control group that found a male animal in the goal box.

❶ Curiosity and exploratory behavior constitute an entire class of learning phenomena that cannot be explained in terms of a reduction in organismic need states.

A final group of studies was based on the remarkable discoveries of Olds and Milner (1954) who electrically stimulated certain lateral regions of the **hypothalamus,** the so-called **pleasure centers**. Rats learned to press a lever or to make another instrumental response when that response was followed by mild stimulation of these brain regions. Olds (1958) observed up to 7,000 responses per hour under this condition, an activity level leading to physical exhaustion. When electrodes were implanted in another region, i.e., one involved in food regulation, the reinforcement effect of electrical stimulation ceased as soon as the animal became satiated. When sexual stimulation was achieved through injection of androgen, the reinforcement effect of stimulating the "hunger region"

was reduced. Evidently, there are interactions between organismic need states and other drives.

Can these findings be reconciled with drive-reduction theory? An inveterate drive theorist might argue that the electrical stimulation of the brain interferes with the complex regulatory mechanism governing need and drive states. Yet it might also be the case that need and drive states are not involved at all, and that the emotional arousal or pleasurable states elicited by a certain behavior in fact reinforce that behavior. Especially the neurotransmitter dopamine seems to play an important role here (see Ikemoto & Panksepp, 1999). In either case, research using brain stimulation raises serious questions about Hull's postulate. In view of these accumulated findings, it would seem advisable – if Hull's theory is not to be abandoned – to divorce drive reduction from antecedent need states and to designate as drives everything that reinforces as a function of its reduction.

4.3.6 The General Nature of Drive

❶ If habit and drive are mutually independent, the habit-activating function of drive must also be independent of different drive sources. Drive is then the summation of all specific drive states, such as hunger and thirst. A response that was learned under hunger conditions must be emitted in an identical stimulus situation, even if the organism is only thirsty.

Some empirical data confirm this assumption; others do not. Hunger and thirst seem to be inappropriate substitutes for each other because the organismic regulatory mechanisms of the two need states are not mutually independent.

The empirical data discussed above indicate that the postulate of a general, nonspecific drive is the exception rather than the rule (cf. Bolles, 1965, p. 265 ff.). Findings from recent neuropsychological research, however, suggest that this old postulate might be worth some reconsideration (cf. Kuhl, 2001, p. 903).

The assumption of a generalized drive also formed the basis for a broad field of research relating to human motivation (Taylor & Spence, 1952). Taylor (1953) developed a questionnaire to measure enduring individual differences in generalized, nonspecific **anxiety** (MAS, "Manifest Anxiety Scale"). Anxiety is viewed not as a function of the situation, but as a motive disposition, an "acquired drive." People with high MAS scores are assumed to have a high generalized drive level, making them more likely to respond.

This has various implications for the acquisition of easy and difficult tasks. The reasoning here is as follows: Tasks are easy if their correct solution involves responses that already possess a measure of habit strength, and if there is little competition with the habit strength of inappropriate responses. Given the multiplicative relationship between $_sH_R$ and D, high-anxiety individuals can be expected to learn easier tasks better and more quickly than low-anxiety individuals, because their higher drive strength raises the dominance of the reaction potential for the correct responses over the incorrect ones even further above the response threshold. The opposite can be expected for difficult tasks. Here, the correct responses have lower habit strength than the incorrect ones. The high-drive strength of high-anxiety individuals serves to exacerbate the unfavorable relationship between competing responses, to the detriment of the correct ones. Moreover, other irrelevant habits are likely to be raised above their response thresholds. Paired-associate tasks were used to test this theory of the interaction between generalized drive strength and task difficulty. Low-difficulty tasks (high associative value between the pairs) were contrasted with high-difficulty tasks (low associative value; other responses are more salient, leading to interference with the prescribed response).

Spence, Farber, and McFann (1956) were able to confirm the hypotheses derived from this model. However, Weiner (1966) and Weiner and Schneider (1971) proposed an alternative explanation based on the frequently reported finding that, in high-anxiety individuals, success leads to improved performance and failure to deterioration, while the reverse holds for low-anxiety individuals. Because easier tasks are more likely to lead to success and difficult ones to failure, Weiner (1966) reasoned that the differential effects found by Spence, Farber, and McFaun (1956) could be attributed to cognitive intervening processes of experiencing success or failure, rather than to response competition (as postulated by drive theory).

To adjudicate between the two explanatory models, Weiner experimentally separated easy tasks from success and difficult tasks from failure. Participants given the task of learning (objectively) easy paired associates were told that their performance was below average, while participants learning difficult syllable pairs were told that their performance was above average. Under these conditions it was indeed possible to show that differential performance was not dependent on the general anxiety level (i.e., "drive strength" as a personality-specific, situation-independent characteristic), but that it was a function of the momentary experience of success or failure. High-anxiety individuals learned a list of difficult trigram pairs (e.g., HOV-MIY) more quickly than low-anxiety subjects when given positive feedback. At the same time, low-anxiety participants learned a list of easy pairs more rapidly than their high-anxiety counterparts when given negative feedback.

A replication study by Weiner and Schneider (1971) produced similar findings for all combinations of participants' anxiety levels, task difficulty, and type of feedback (Fig. 4.7). The interaction between anxiety and feedback of success or failure was more pronounced for difficult tasks than for easy ones (see Chapter 8 on success and failure motives).

SUMMARY

Although empirical findings have undermined hypotheses derived from Hull's drive theory in specific respects, recent

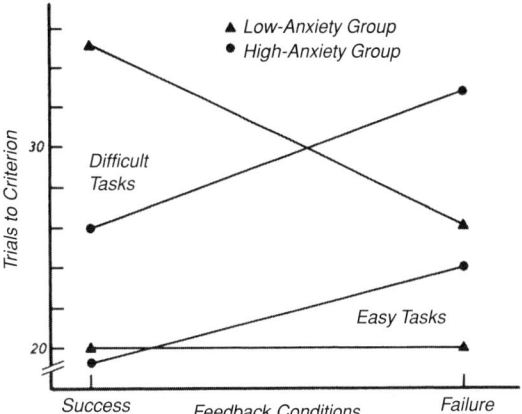

Figure 4.7 Number of trials needed to learn an easy and a difficult list of 13 trigram pairs as a function of success and failure feedback for groups classified as confident of success or anxious about failure. (Based on Weiner & Schneider, 1971, p. 260.)

advances in neuropsychological research have produced findings that partly rehabilitate the generalized model. This applies, for example to the assumption that a generalized drive state serves to energize behavior across situations (Smith, 1971).

Furthermore, Hull's differentiation between energizing (drive) and directive functions (habits) can be tied to specific anatomic structures. For example, LeDoux (1996), has demonstrated that – in the case of fear, in particular – the amygdala, the almond-shaped structure in the center of the brain, causes a generalized activation that first takes effect on brainstem activation systems and subsequently triggers cortical activation. The direction of an activity, in contrast, is mediated by another brain structure, the hippocampus. Models of the situation and of appropriate responses are stored in the hippocampus.

To conclude, this final postulate of drive theory also stimulated research and resulted in insights that advocated the revision, if not the complete abandonment of Hull's drive theory.

4.3.7 Extensions of Drive Theory

When Woodworth (1918) introduced the drive concept and contrasted it with the behavior mechanisms initiated by drive, he pointed out that these mechanisms can themselves acquire an incentive function, meaning that they can become divorced from the energizing function of primary drives. Tolman (1926, 1932) also addressed the question of how secondary drives could evolve and achieve independence from **primary drives**. Allport (1937) introduced the principle of functional autonomy. Although this principle does not deny the historical roots of motives in primary drives, it suggests that they soon become independent of these roots.

Acquired Drives

Co-workers of Hull, particularly Mowrer and N. E. Miller, attempted to expand and develop drive theory to cover more complex motivational phenomena, such as **frustration, conflict**, and nonprimary motivational conditions, particularly in humans. This led them to postulate "acquired drives."

FRUSTRATION. In this context, frustration implies the blocking of responses that lead to drive satisfaction or the blocking of consummatory responses once the goal has been attained. In both cases, animals are observed to respond more vigorously, more frequently, or with greater variation. This frustration effect seems to arise from an increase in the drive whose satisfaction has been thwarted. Dollard et al (1939) assumed that frequent frustration leads to an **acquired drive** that contributes to general drive strength and, in its specific form, becomes tied to aggressive responses. They argued that aggressive behavior is always rooted in frustration, and that every frustration leads to **aggression**. In other words, they saw frustration as a necessary and sufficient condition for aggression. Empirical findings, however, have since refuted these very broad assumptions (cf. Feshbach & Singer, 1971; Bandura, 1971; Zumkley, 1978; Kornadt, 1982b).

The validity of inferring an increase in drive from an increase in frustration is doubtful for several reasons. An animal that does not find the expected food at a goal cannot complete the behavior sequence with consummatory responses. Instead, instrumental goal responses or other behaviors might be intensified; e.g., because past experience has shown that a more vigorous response can lead to success. In other words, an increase in the intensity or variability of behavior might be explained in terms of cognitive factors rather than drive factors. Such an explanation is supported by the results of Holder, Marx, Holder, and Collier (1957), who found that rats can learn to respond more weakly rather than more vigorously following the thwarting of reinforcement.

FEAR AS AN ACQUIRED DRIVE. Although it was not possible to demonstrate acquired drives based on **appetitive needs**, it did seem possible to do so for aversive drives. **Avoidance learning**, where **fear** seems to be the crucial factor, is a case in point.

DEFINITION

Fear can be seen as a conditioned response to pain, and pain as a primary (and aversive) drive state, the reduction of which reinforces instrumental escape and avoidance behavior.

Research has shown that fear and avoidance behavior can also be learned and maintained by means of conditioned fear states, without the pain originally experienced having to be reintroduced. This indicates that fear is an easily acquired drive that soon attains independence and can become attached to a variety of eliciting conditions.

Mowrer (1939) was the first to reason along these lines, referring to the second **psychoanalytic theory of fear** that Freud had formulated in 1926. This theory held that fear, if it is

justifiable fear, represents an effective signal, a warning about real, impending dangers and motivating defense responses. Observations of animals in experimental situations had shown that responses that are learned in order to avoid an electric shock are extremely resistant to extinction. In other words, if an animal is placed in a previously aversive situation, it will continue to display escape behavior, even when the painful stimulus is not present. This would seem to be a typical case of classical conditioning. In actual fact, further reinforcement would have been needed for classical conditioning to occur. Hence, the high resistance to extinction cannot be explained in terms of classical conditioning. Mowrer assumed that fear is elicited by the stimulus cues arising from the originally aversive situation. Although fear was originally a conditioned form of the pain response, it now became an aversive tension state, an independent drive to be reduced by escape behavior.

❗ Thus, the escape response continues to be reinforced by the reduction of fear, even in the absence of pain.

The apparatus that N. E. Miller (1941, 1948) used in his fear experiments was later also adopted in research on the theory of learned helplessness (Seligman & Maier, 1967). Miller's experiment is described in Section 2.6.1 of Chapter 2 in the context of "classical learning experiments."

Based on the results of his experiments, Miller concluded that fear is an (unconditioned) response of the autonomic nervous system to painful stimuli, and that it can therefore be conditioned to other stimuli. Fear is itself also a stimulus, however, because it can form associations with responses. As a stimulus it is also a drive, because every response that removes the organism from the fear-eliciting environment (e.g., flight) results in drive reduction and is thus reinforced.

In contrast to Hull, who hypothesized drives to evolve from primary needs only, Miller and Dollard (1941, p. 66) postulated that any stimulus can become a drive.

Mowrer (1947) introduced limitations to the general validity of the postulate of reinforcement through drive reduction. Initially, he advocated a two-factor theory, which held that all learning is based on either classical or instrumental conditioning. (He abandoned this position in 1960 in favor of an expectancy theory of motivation; see Chapters 2 and 5.) According to Mowrer's two-factor theory, drive reduction is not a general prerequisite for every reinforcing event, but only for instrumentally conditioned responses that are mediated exclusively by the voluntary activity of the skeletal muscles. Classical conditioning (which is restricted to involuntary mechanisms) requires temporal contiguity alone.

❗ Both classical and instrumental conditioning play a role in avoidance learning. First, fear becomes classically conditioned to stimulus cues; then the reduction of fear reinforces the instrumental avoidance response.

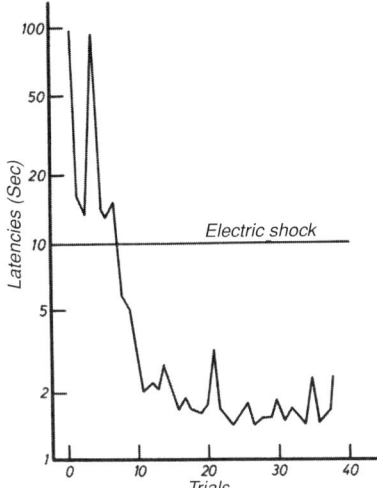

Figure 4.8 An individual acquisition curve (latency time) for an avoidance response to an electric shock delivered after 10 seconds. (Based on Solomon & Wynne, 1953. p. 6.)

Further questions were raised by the experimental findings of Solomon and Wynne (1953), who found that, after several repetitions, an acquired avoidance response was shown more rapidly than a fear response could in fact occur. In their experiment, dogs administered strong electric shocks ten seconds after a conditioned stimulus soon learned the avoidance response of jumping over a hurdle. Fig. 4.8 shows typical response latencies. It took only seven trials for the dog to start jumping the hurdle before the onset of the shock. After three more trials, latencies were reduced to between 1 and 2 seconds, which is too short a time for the occurrence of an intervening fear response. As an autonomic nervous system response, fear generally requires 2–4 seconds to become manifest (cf. Spence & Runquist, 1958). On the occasions that longer latencies were observed, meaning that a fear response may have occurred, the succeeding latencies were often markedly shorter. It would seem that the animal tries to avoid not only pain, but also the fear of pain. Interestingly, under these experimental conditions, resistance to extinction was almost unlimited, with some animals requiring no less than 650 trials for the learned response to be extinguished. These findings seriously challenge the notion that fear reduction results in drive reduction and thus continues to reinforce the acquired avoidance response. The authors explain the high resistance to extinction in terms of a "conservation of fear." Once it abates, response latency increases; fear is then experienced once more and serves to reinforce the avoidance response. Yet even this explanation cannot account for the extreme resistance to extinction.

Schoenfeld (1950) proposed an interpretation of avoidance learning that makes no reference at all to acquired drives. His explanation is simply that there are positive or negative stimuli that have the capacity to reinforce. If these are associated with neutral stimuli, the latter will gradually acquire reinforcing characteristics. Hence, stimuli that were originally neutral acquire negative characteristics, and the organism learns to respond in a manner that will eliminate them.

SUMMARY

Empirical findings have cast doubt on the explanatory value of drive theory, with respect to both its individual postulates and the hypothesis of fear as an acquired drive. Admittedly, drive theory generated a wealth of experimental research findings, but interpretations of these data increasingly drew on factors that related to external, situational determinants rather than to internal, organismic determinants like drive states. In other words, the focus shifted from the internal to the external environment. Stimulus cues, incentive values, and motivating expectations seemed able to provide more plausible theoretical explanations for the activation, direction, and persistence of goal-directed behavior.

Nevertheless, drive theory can be seen as a major step toward the development of the theoretical approaches being used today. For example, social psychologists still draw on the basic assumptions of drive to explain the phenomena of social inhibition and facilitation. Since the 1980s, social psychology has also seen the emergence of neo-associationism, an approach that seeks to overcome the known shortcomings of classical associationism by incorporating cognitive variables.

4.4 Neo-Associationism

Learning theorists increasingly disputed the basic **associationist** approach, and expanded it to include cognitive variables. As shown in studies by Rescorla and co-workers (Rescorla 1968, 1972; Rescorla & Wagner, 1972), even rats are not indiscriminately bound to the law of association; they establish "reasonable" rules. For example, rats do not respond to a contingent sound stimulus if they have already learned that a contingent light stimulus signals the onset of an unconditioned stimulus (e.g., an electric shock). Even if the light stimulus is paired with the sound stimulus in terms of space or time, the sound stimulus will have no effect in its own right – though the principles of associationism would predict otherwise. If light and sound stimuli are presented together from the outset, however, both stimuli will have independent effects (as concomitantly conditioned signals of impending pain, both stimuli are discriminative and thus "salient").

In social psychology, the tradition of the associationist approach is unbroken. Berkowitz (1974) assumed that any stimulus that is repeatedly linked (associated) with certain behaviors becomes capable of eliciting that behavior of its own accord, whether the stimulus is an object or a person. In contrast to the proponents of classical associationism, however, Berkowitz (1974) assumes that these associations are tied to certain mediating conditions, and refers to "mediated associations." Berkowitz's **weapon effect** has become particularly well known. Because weapons are associated with aggression, they become aggressive stimulus cues that can trigger aggression by their very presence. In one experiment (Berkowitz & LePage, 1967), participants were first antagonized by a confederate of the experimenter. They were then given the chance to "get their own back" on the confederate by giving him electric shocks. A gun was visible in the room in one condition, but not in the other. In line with expectations, the participants delivered more shocks to the confederate when they had been antagonized in the presence of a gun than when no gun was present in the room.

Numerous recent experimental studies on nonconscious information processing have shown that different motivations are activated automatically by the perception of certain stimuli (see the following excursus). In these experiments, stimuli such as photographs of people's faces are presented on a computer screen for such a short time (a few milliseconds) that they cannot be consciously perceived or identified. Nevertheless, objective measures of physical responses and behaviors taken in the laboratory have demonstrated that people do in fact process these stimuli (Bargh, Chen, & Burrows, 1996).

Simple, learned stimulus-response bonds cannot provide an adequate explanation for the phenomena described in the excursus. In his cognitive neo-associationist model of impulsive (emotional) aggression, Berkowitz (1990) assumes a developmental mechanism that integrates Leventhal's (1984) theory of emotions and Bower's (1981) **network theory** of memory within an associationist framework. According to this model, frustration and aggressive stimulus cues do not necessarily trigger aggressive behavior. Rather, the intervening conditions determine whether or not aggressive behavior is exhibited. First, there must be a negative evaluation of an event. This negative appraisal triggers a general feeling of displeasure, which in turn activates corresponding thoughts, memories, expressive-motor and physiological responses, and feelings of anger that are linked together associatively in the network of memory. Activation of this network-like system is most likely to spread from an "affect node."

❶ Neo-associationism assumes that – in humans, at least – cognitive and affective processes intervene in the primary association mechanism (Hull's habits) and thus serve to determine the overall response (Berkowitz, 1994). The affective responses elicited within the organism seem to play a key role here.

This aspect has also been considered in research on the activation of stereotypical patterns of behavior, where the role of organismic responses – particularly nonconscious processes of affective evaluation – has been examined. Findings from different paradigms indicate that the affective properties of the stimuli to which individuals are exposed are activated

extremely quickly, without their conscious awareness. This activation of affective connotations can influence their subsequent judgments and behavior (Bargh, 1994, 1997; Fazio et al., 1986; Greenwald & Banaji, 1995; Murphy & Zajonc, 1993).

Affective priming effects are not only apparent in people's evaluations, they have also been observed, e.g., in the pronunciation of target stimuli (Bargh et al., 1996). Consequently, Bargh maintains that there is strong evidence for an unconditional, general process by which all environmental stimuli are evaluated automatically: "It appears that nearly everything is preconsciously classified as good or bad" (Bargh, 1994, p. 19).

❶ Neo-associationism assumes that the association between stimulus and response is mediated by basal organismic processes of evaluation. Thus, affect or emotions are again attributed a key role as intervening variables in the development of motivation and the activation of behavior. The introduction of these organismic processes of evaluation to the equation marked the end of strict associationism (cf. Berkowitz, 1994; Eron, 1994; Bargh & Ferguson, 2000).

4.5 Conflict Theory

Conflict theory represented a significant step along the path to modern conceptualizations of motivation.

4.5.1 Lewin's Conflict Theory

The experimental analysis of conflict behavior was an important facet of drive-related research. Lewin was the first to present fundamental ideas on conflict theory, back in the 1930s.

DEFINITION
According to Lewin, "a conflict is to be characterized psychologically as a situation in which oppositely directed, simultaneously acting forces of approximately equal strength work upon the individual" (1935, p. 122).

Lewin identified three basic categories of conflict situations; Hovland and Sears (1938) later added a fourth. The defining characteristics of the four categories are the situational forces that impinge on the individual, resulting in approach or avoidance behavior as follows:

1. Approach-approach conflict: The individual has to choose between two incompatible situations or goals, both of which have positive valences of approximately equal strength. It is the proverbial case of Buridan's ass starving to death between two stacks of hay.[1]

2. Avoidance-avoidance conflict: Here, the choice is between "evils" of approximately equal strength; e.g., a student has to do his homework or face being set extra work as punishment.

---

[1] In an allegory, Jonathan Buridan is said to have envisioned the impossibility of a logical decision between two solutions of the same value through a donkey starving to death between two stacks of hay.

EXCURSUS

Effect of Stereotypes: The Model of Nonconscious Behavioral Confirmation

Since the 1980s, social psychologists involved in social cognition research have paid particular attention to the more subtle effects of stereotypes (Kunda, 1999). One widespread stereotype in the United States is that African-Americans are especially aggressive. Priming studies have shown that this stereotype can be activated unconsciously, and influence people's judgments of others without their conscious awareness (cf. Devine, 1989).

The model of nonconscious behavioral confirmation proposed by Chen and Bargh (1997) assumes three subprocesses:

1. automatic activation of a stereotype,
2. direct and automatic link between perception and behavior, and
3. automatic behavioral confirmation.

It is assumed that the frequent activation of a stereotype suffices to increase the probability of its unconscious and unintentional activation, i.e., the development of automaticity. The activation of a stereotype (or behavioral schema) is thought to trigger the associated response behavior directly, in the manner of James' (1890) ideomotoric principle. The behavior exhibited is then confirmed by the social responses of those involved in the interaction, whose behavior is consistent with the stereotype. These assumptions were tested in an experiment by Chen and Bargh (1997). Two Caucasian participants worked independently on a computer task. One of them was subliminally (below the threshold of conscious perception) exposed to photos of Caucasian or African American faces. In the second part of the experiment, the two participants interacted (they worked on a verbal task together). Finally, participants were asked to evaluate each other. The authors expected subliminal priming with photos of African American faces to activate a negative stereotype, which was in turn expected to result in more negative evaluations of the experimental partner. Appraisals of the experimental partner were indeed more negative when participants were primed with photographs of African American faces than when Caucasian faces were used. Correlations between .30 and .40 were found, indicating that around 10% of the variance in behavior was explained. These findings confirm the model proposed by Chen and Bargh but, at the same time, show that other variables must be involved in explaining the large residual variance in behavior.

3. Approach-avoidance conflict: One and the same goal is both attractive and repulsive. For example, someone might want to commit to a loved one by marrying them, but at the same time fear the loss of independence that this commitment incurs.

4. Double-approach-avoidance conflict (double-ambivalence conflict): An example would be a choice between two jobs, both of which have positive and negative aspects.

Fig. 4.9 summarizes these four types of conflict situations using the symbols developed by Lewin for his field theory; e.g., the arrows represent directional vectors in the field, originating either from the situation or from within the person. Note that the schema for the avoidance-avoidance conflict is surrounded by a box, representing a psychological forced-choice situation. In other words, the individual considers him- or herself to be inextricably caught between two evils and unable to escape the field of conflict.

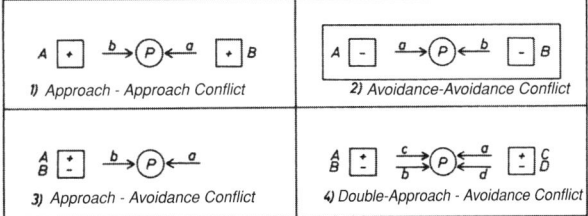

Figure 4.9 The four types of conflict situations [*P*, Person; *A* to *D* positive (+) or negative (−), incentive characteristics of the available objects or goals of behavior; *a* to *d* positive or negative, incentive characteristics of the forces originating from these objects or goals that impinge on the person].

EXAMPLE

Lewin's field-theoretical approach can best be illustrated by the example of a specific conflict situation, such as that represented by the force fields in Fig. 4.10. A three-year-old boy at the beach is trying to retrieve a toy swan that has been swept away by the waves. On the one hand, he is pulled toward his beloved toy. Once he gets too close to the forbidding waves, however, he will be pushed back in the opposite direction. Evidently, there is a subjective barrier running parallel to the shoreline. Once that barrier is crossed, the force pushing the boy away from the waves soon becomes greater than the force pulling him toward the toy swan.

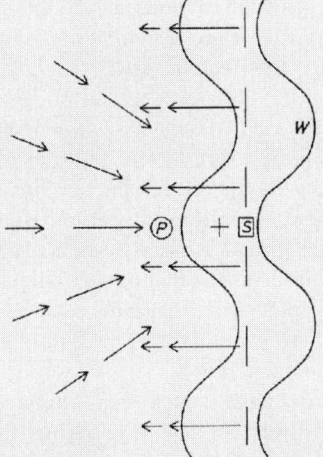

Figure 4.10 The force field occurring in a conflict situation where a goal has both positive and negative valence (*P*, person; *S*, swan; *W*, waves). (Based on Lewin, 1935, p. 92.)

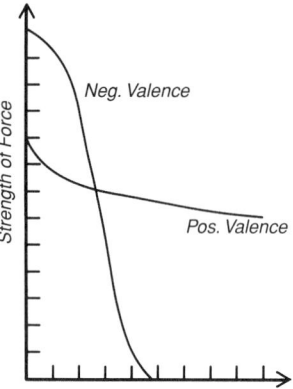

Figure 4.11 Schematic representation of the change in the strength of a force with the distance to a positive and a negative valence. (Based on Lewin, 1946b, p. 812.)

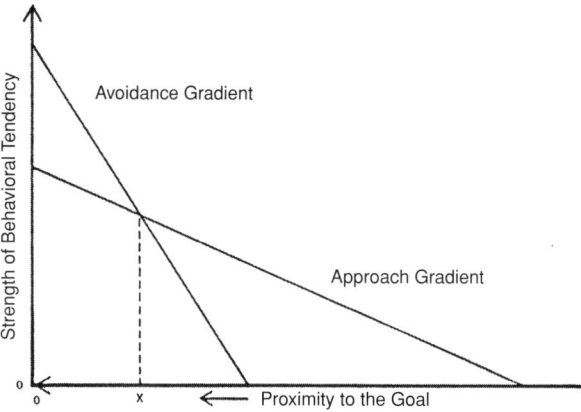

Figure 4.12 Gradients of approach and avoidance when approaching a goal with both a positive and negative valence.

This example led Lewin (1946b) to intuitively postulate that, in an approach-avoidance conflict, the strength of the repelling forces increases more rapidly with increasing proximity to the goal object than does that of the attracting forces. From this it can be deduced that there must be a point some distance from the goal at which equilibrium occurs. This point represents the intercept of the approach and avoidance gradients. Prior to this point, the attracting forces are stronger than the repelling ones, thus pulling the child toward the swan. But once the point of equilibrium is passed, the repelling forces become stronger, pushing the child back again. This results in oscillating behavior. Fig. 4.11 illustrates the fluctuating relationships of the forces in this type of conflict situation as a function of a person's geographical distance to an attractive or feared situation.

According to Lewin, the strength of a behavioral tendency (force) is concomitantly dependent on two quantities: the strength of the **valence** of the goal (object) and the **distance** from the goal. Psychologically speaking, distance can be measured in terms other than geographical units, e.g., in time or in the number of necessary intervening activities, their difficulty, or the amount of effort they require.

4.5.2 Miller's Model of Conflict

Miller (1944) combined Lewin's notion that fluctuations in valence are a function of the distance from the goal with Hull's (1932, 1934) hypothesis of goal gradients. Hull postulated this hypothesis to explain the observations that hungry animals run faster as they approach their goal, and that the correction of errors in maze running begins near the goal and continues in reverse sequence back to the start box.

The goal gradient hypothesis states that stimulus-response bonds are first produced, i.e., habit strength built up, in the immediate proximity of the goal, because it is here that reinforcement is immediate, whereas it is delayed at points further away from the goal. In the acquisition of a new behavior sequence, the development of habit strength thus starts

at the end of the response sequence and rolls slowly back to the beginning of that sequence.

Miller (1951, 1956) formulated six basic assumptions relating to conflict phenomena (see Fig. 4.12):

Basic Assumptions of the Conflict Model (after Miller, 1951, 1956)

1. The tendency to approach a goal becomes stronger, the nearer a person is to it (gradient of approach).
2. The tendency to avoid a feared stimulus becomes stronger, the nearer a person is to it (gradient of avoidance).
3. The gradient of avoidance is steeper than the gradient of approach.
4. When two incompatible responses are in conflict, the stronger one will prevail.
5. The height of the approach and avoidance gradients is dependent on the strength of the underlying drive.
6. The strength of the response tendency being reinforced increases as a function of the number of reinforcements until learning plateaus out at a maximum level. (This assumption was added in 1959.)

Fig. 4.12 illustrates the first four assumptions. As point "x" is crossed on the way to the goal, the avoidance tendency becomes stronger than the approach tendency. At this point, behavior will oscillate between approach and avoidance.

According to the fifth assumption, a change in the relative strengths of the drives underlying the approach and avoidance tendencies can result in a change of the relative strengths of these tendencies, and produce a shift in the point of intersection. For example, increasing the period of food deprivation will increase the pull on an animal to approach a food goal. As a result, the entire approach gradient is raised, placing the intercept of the two gradients closer to the goal.

But what is the reasoning behind the assumption that the avoidance gradient is steeper than the approach gradient? For Miller, the difference lies in the sources of the two tendencies. In the case of hunger, the approach tendency is maintained by a drive stimulus arising from within the organism itself. The

STUDY

Experimental Evidence for Miller's Assumptions

Brown (1948) experimentally confirmed assumptions 1, 2, 3, and 5. Two of his four groups of rats repeatedly found food at the end of a runway; one of these groups had been deprived of food for 48 hours, the other for just one hour. The two remaining groups, which were not deprived of food, received electric shocks at the end of the weak shocks in one group and strong shocks in the other. Following a learning phase, Brown measured the strength with which individual animals pulled toward or away from the goal when placed in the runway. To this end, the animal was placed in a harness permitting the experimenter to stop it at various points on the runway, and to measure the amount of pull exerted. Fig. 4.13 shows the results.

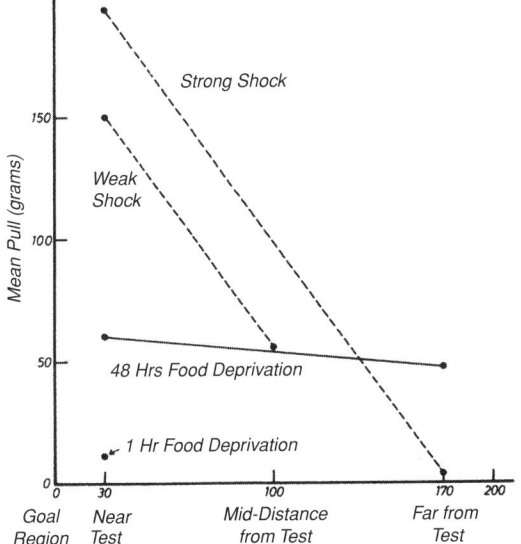

Figure 4.13 Strength of approach and avoidance tendencies at various distances to the goal in four groups of rats: 1 h vs. 48 h food deprivation, strong vs. weak electric shock. (Based on Brown, 1948, pp. 457, 459.)

In a later study, Miller (1959) combined his assumptions 4 (the stronger response prevails) and 5 (the height of the gradient is a function of drive strength) and confirmed them experimentally. The rats were now given both food and electric shocks at the goal, producing a conflict situation. Hours of food deprivation and shock severity were now varied in combination for different groups of rats, thereby producing different levels of drive strengths and permitting the height of the approach and the avoidance gradients to be manipulated independently of each other. The gradients were now expected to intercept at various distances from the goal. Accordingly, the dependent measure was the minimum distance from the goal reached by the animal in the conflict situation. The data confirmed Miller's assumptions. When shock intensity was constant, distance from the goal decreased with hours of food deprivation. Conversely, when hours of food deprivation were kept constant, distance from the goal increased with the intensity of the shock.

drive stimulus remains unchanged, regardless of the organism's distance from the goal where food is available. The avoidance tendency, in contrast, arises from fear, an acquired drive resulting from aversive stimulation (e.g., pain) experienced in the region of the goal. Because fear is not elicited by internal drive stimuli, but by external cues, it becomes closely linked with the original, pain-inducing situation.

This idea also helps to explain the sixth and final assumption. The number of reinforced responses (i.e., habit strength) determines the steepness of the gradient of the respective tendency because habit strength, the associative component of the reaction potential, is dependent on the distance from the goal (at least until learning has reached a plateau on the way to the goal). The avoidance gradient is steeper precisely because, in this case, both components of the reaction potential – drive (i.e., fear) and habit strength – are linked to goal-related stimuli. In the case of the approach tendency, this applies only to the associative component, habit strength. If habit strength were considerably stronger for the approach than for the avoidance tendency, there might be an exceptional case of a steeper approach gradient.

4.5.3 Applications of the Conflict Model

A variety of intriguing applications were derived from Miller's model. The distance from the goal does not necessarily have to be spatial; it may be measured in terms of temporal proximity or similarity to the original goal. A process of decreasing similarity to a conflict-inducing goal often plays a role in the development and treatment of neuroses. For example, an object of aggressive or sexual desire may also elicit fear of negative consequences. In Freud's terms, this can lead to **displacement**. The original object is replaced perceptually by a more or less similar object that elicits less fear or anxiety. Clark (1952) and Clark and Sensibar (1955) were able to experimentally demonstrate this process for sexuality. They induced displacements of imaged projections as a function of sexual motivation.

Displacement corresponds to a generalization of the response to the original object. The more the avoidance tendency outweighs the approach tendency, the less similar the displacement object will be to the original object.

Miller (1948) applied his conflict model to this situation. The gradients of approach and avoidance now signify response strength as a function of degree of similarity to the conflict-inducing stimulus, rather than as a function of spatial or temporal distance. Fig. 4.14 shows the application of this model to the displacement mechanism. It indicates that displacement is most likely to occur at the degree of similarity associated with the highest net strength of the inhibited response. In Fig. 4.14, it would be a degree of similarity falling between C and D.

Murray and Berkun (1955) substantiated these ideas experimentally. After rats had learned to find food at the end

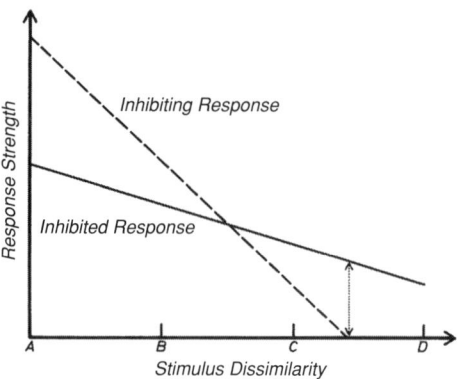

Figure 4.14 Displacement of an inhibited response at the highest net strength of the inhibited response (*dotted arrow*). (Based on Miller, 1944, p. 434.)

of a black runway, they were given electric shocks while eating, resulting in avoidance of the goal box. Two additional runways were then set up parallel to the first. Openings connected the adjacent runways at varying distances from the goal box. The two new runways differed in color from the original one. The one immediately next to the original (black) runway was gray, the other white. This coloring represented a gradient of decreasing similarity from the original, conflict-inducing runway. When an animal was placed in the black runway, it would keep its distance from the goal; this avoidance decreased progressively as the animal escaped first to the gray and then to the white runway. Here, conflict is a function of two mutually exclusive dimensions: spatial distance from the conflict-inducing goal and degree of similarity of the runways.

Both dimensions can be utilized as orthogonal axes in a **three-dimensional model of conflict** in which the gradients no longer represent lines, but planes. Their intercepts become lines of intersection between the two-dimensional axes. In concrete terms, this means that an animal will reduce its distance to the goal if it is willing to accept greater dissimilarity from the original goal (and vice versa). Murray and Berkun were able to demonstrate this empirically. They also found that displacement can have a "therapeutic" effect – the avoidance gradient decreases over time and the animals increasingly approach both the more similar (gray) and the original (black) goal stimulus.

❶ The implication of these findings for psychotherapeutic applications is that the avoidance gradient must be lowered. This can be accomplished by measures altering the degree of similarity to the original cause of conflict. The patient then seems to be able to confront the conflict-inducing situation again. Simply telling a patient to confront the actual source of the conflict at the beginning of a course of therapy would shift the intercept of the two gradients closer to that source, but also raise it, which would increase the level of both conflicting tendencies, resulting in greater internal tension.

CONFLICTING TENDENCIES IN PARACHUTISTS. Threatening but inevitable events that are set to occur at a fixed future date and thus loom ever nearer are prototypical for the conflict model. Examples of such situations are examinations, elective surgery, or childbirth. On the one hand, we dread these situations; on the other hand, we would like to have them over and done with. Fisch (1970) studied conflicting tendencies in the run-up to an exam as a function of temporal proximity and the degree of similarity between the situations portrayed in pictures and the upcoming event.

Epstein (1962) carried out a similar study with people about to do their first parachute jump. Participants were asked to rate their approach tendencies and then their avoidance tendencies at 14 points in the run-up to the jump.

Fig. 4.15 presents the retrospective (mean) self-ratings of 28 novice jumpers at 14 sequential points in time: (1) last week, (2) last night, (3) this morning, (4) upon reaching the airfield, (5) during the training session before the jump, (6) getting strapped into the parachute, (7) boarding the plane, (8) during ascent, (9) at the ready signal, (10) stepping outside (onto the plane's undercarriage), (11) waiting to be tapped, (12) in free fall, (13) after the chute opened, (14) immediately after landing.

Of course, self-reports (especially retrospective ones) are questionable measures of approach and avoidance tendencies. It is quite likely that the parachutists were not able to discriminate between the two tendencies, but in fact experienced mixed feelings of confidence and apprehension. This is also reflected in the fact that the curves represent mirror images of each other. Nevertheless, it is worth noting that the avoidance tendency (apprehension) increases steadily, but then begins to decrease shortly before the critical event of

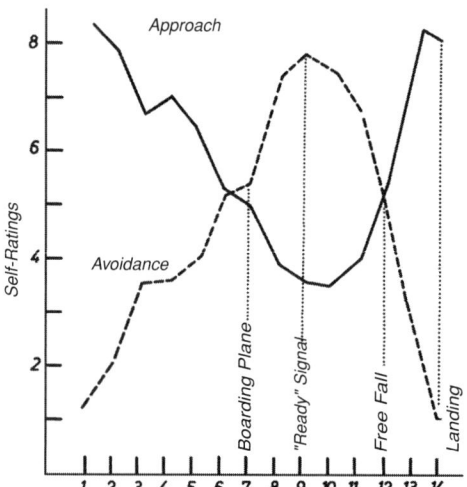

Figure 4.15 Self-ratings of approach and avoidance tendencies as a function of the sequence of events in the run-up to and during the first parachute jump. (Based on Epstein, 1962, p. 179.)

jumping (as if the parachutists gained confidence through the realization that they could no longer turn back).

In subsequent studies, Fenz (1975) measured autonomic indexes of activation during an entire parachute jump. He found that heart rate, respiration, and Galvanic skin response increased steadily until the chute opened. This only applied to beginners, however. Experienced parachutists reached maximum levels at earlier stages in the jump sequence: boarding the plane (heart rate), at the ready signal (respiration), and in free fall (galvanic skin response). In their case, however, the levels of all three indexes remained below the 50% mark of total variation observed among novices. These differences are not solely a function of experience, i.e., the number of previous jumps. Distinguishing between good and bad jumpers reveals that the latter show a sequence of activation similar to beginners, even after many jumps. It would seem that their performance does not equip them to cope as well with the stress of the threatening situation. The relationship between anxiety and performance may (at least in part) be a vicious circle: because they remain anxious, they perform less well, and their poor performance in turn prolongs their anxiety.

4.6 Activation Theories

Early in the 20th century, attention had already been drawn (e.g., Duffy, 1934) to various autonomic activation phenomena and their measurement, particularly in connection with the description and interpretation of emotions. In the 1950s, it was postulated that the hypothetical construct of a general **arousal level**, based on the neurological **ARAS** function (Chapter 2), corresponded to the strength of a generalized drive, and had the potential to replace Hull's D. The main proponents of this position were Malmo (1959) and Hebb (1955), as well as Duffy (1957) and Bindra (1959). Because arousal level can be measured in terms of numerous autonomic indexes, such as galvanic skin response, muscle tone, or electroencephalogram, it was thought to be a more direct indicator of drive strength than those previously used by drive theorists, who relied on deprivation procedures or measures of general activation. Lacey (1969) questioned the validity of general arousal, because the various measures are not highly correlated, and produce profiles that reflect large individual differences (see Walschburger, 1994).

4.6.1 The Construct of Arousal

Yerkes and Dodson (1908) had already found that intermediate levels of arousal (produced by an electric shock) were most conducive to maze learning in animals. The optimal arousal level for easy tasks was higher than that for difficult tasks.

Hebb (1955) interpreted this **inverted U-function** as an interaction between the arousal function and the cue

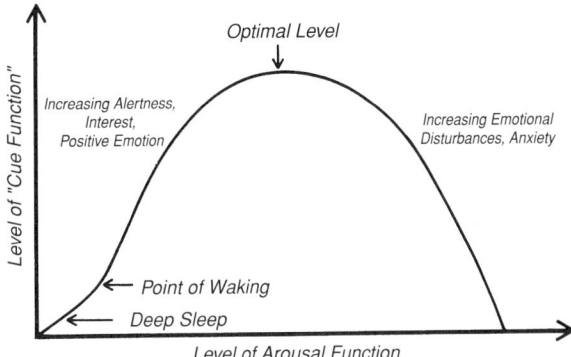

Figure 4.16 Inverted U-function in the relationship between efficacy of behavior (cue function) and level of arousal. (Based on Hebb, 1955, p. 250.)

function. On the one hand, the flow of information picked up by the senses is processed in terms of specific cues; on the other hand, it makes a nonspecific contribution to the generalized arousal level. The cue function requires a certain level of activation of the brain regions involved to reach its optimal level. Fig. 4.16 illustrates Hebb's conceptualization.

A number of questions remain open here. Can arousal level be equated with drive strength? Is there a difference between peripheral and central arousal (in the brain)? Might there even be a differential arousal in the brain? Modern research has provided numerous insights here (e.g., Haider, 1969). As we will see below, both differential arousal and generalized arousal seem to occur. First, however, we address the question of whether arousal can be equated with drive strength.

There are at least two points in which the equation of arousal level with drive strength (D) is difficult, if not impossible, to reconcile with the postulates of classical drive theory:

■ First, the curvilinear relationship between arousal and performance does not tally with the postulate of a monotonic function between drive strength and measures of behavior (with the exception of Hull's exhaustion factor that results from prolonged food deprivation).

Modern research, however, has called this curvilinear relationship between arousal and performance into question (Neiss, 1988; for a summary, see Beckmann & Rolstad, 1997). Dienstbier (1989) advocates a linear function, e.g., whereas Fazey and Hardy (1988) present a complex three-dimensional model in which both a linear and a curvilinear relationship is possible as a function of the three dimensions.

■ The second problem of equating arousal level with drive strength is that arousal level is known to be strongly affected by external stimulation, while the same is not assumed to apply to the classical drive concept (with the exception of aversive drives such as pain).

Investigators have identified relationships with a number of parameters of external stimulation. It is not just stimulus intensity that plays a role, but stimulus variation in time and space. Moreover, not only the physiological or physical aspects of the stimulus are involved but, more importantly, their psychological parameters – e.g., their information content, complexity, and deviation from the expected and familiar.

EFFECTS OF SENSORY DEPRIVATION AND SENSORY FLOODING. At first, research attention focused on dramatic examples of phenomena at the extremes of a hypothesized continuum of stimulation; i.e., sensory deprivation, on the one hand, and situations that induced excitement, alarm, and fear, on the other. Best known among the **sensory deprivation** experiments is that of Bexton, Heron, and Scott (1954).

STUDY

Study on the Effects of Sensory Deprivation

Bexton, Heron, and Scott (1954) hired students at a high rate of pay, and placed them in soundproof rooms. Participants wore translucent goggles eliminating all pattern vision, and gloves and cardboard handcuffs to minimize tactile stimulation. Hallucinations and severe decrements in the participants' intellectual ability were soon observed. After just a few days, the participants terminated the experiment, despite the high pay, because they were no longer able to endure the deprivation condition. When given an opportunity to listen to stock market reports or excerpts from a telephone directory – information in which they would normally not be remotely interested – they now welcomed the prospect, and kept asking for the material to be repeated.

The findings of Bexton, Heron, and Scott (1954) suggest that the organism requires a certain amount of external stimulation to maintain well-being and optimal functioning. As early as 1928, the results of experiments on "psychological satiation" carried out by Lewin's student Anitra Karsten had pointed to similar conclusions. Karsten instructed students to repeat monotonous short tasks for as long as possible; e.g., drawing lines, drawing moon-shaped faces, writing the same sentence over and over. After a while, participants tried to make the tasks more interesting by changing the order of execution. Finally, performance deteriorated into nonsensical subcomponents, accompanied by an increase in errors. Satiation and aversion to the task became increasingly difficult to overcome. When the participants were asked to perform a new task, performance immediately returned to its previous level.

The opposite of sensory deprivation is not **sensory flooding** in the everyday sense of the word, but stimulus input that creates "incongruities," i.e., that can no longer be processed. Such conditions can produce severe emotional reactions, even panic and terror. Hebb (1946, 1949) demonstrated "paroxysms of terror" in chimpanzees who were shown a stuffed head or the lifeless body of an anesthetized fellow chimp, or whose keeper suddenly wore his jacket inside out. Bühler, Hetzer, and Mabel (1928) observed similar severe fright reactions in infants when their mother or another familiar caretaker approached them speaking in a high falsetto voice. It is the sudden change in an otherwise similar and familiar object (Hebb calls it difference in sameness) that elicits severe panic arousal states.

Sensory deprivation and insurmountable incongruities in stimulus input represent the extremes of a broad continuum. Moderate incongruities seem to be experienced as pleasant and entertaining, and to encourage exploratory behavior, curiosity, and manipulatory activities. It is these moderate incongruities within the familiar, the expected, the already mastered, that initiate and control behavior. The endless, apparently purposeless activities of the young child, especially at play, seem to be motivated by external stimulation of this kind (cf. Heckhausen, 1964b; Klinger, 1971; see also Chapter 15). Approaches based on activation theory now have greater currency than those derived from drive theory. Aside from Hebb (1955), the main proponents of the activation theory perspective are Fowler (1971), Walker (1973), and particularly Berlyne (1960, 1963a, b, 1971).

4.6.2 Arousal Potential and Its Effects

Berlyne sought to describe the determinants of arousal level in terms of various properties of the stimulus, particularly its "collative variables." This class of variables includes novelty and change, surprise, complexity, uncertainty, and conflict. The term "collative" refers to the fact that, in order to decide how novel, surprising, etc., a stimulus is, information from two or more sources has to be compared or collated. The collative variables are an important class of antecedent conditions for what Berlyne called **arousal potential**.

DEFINITION

Arousal potential represents a hypothetical totality of all properties of a stimulus pattern. This totality is composed of collative variables, affective stimuli, intense external stimuli, and internal stimuli arising from need states.

Berlyne's concept of arousal potential is covered in more detail in Chapter 2.

It is important to distinguish arousal potential from its effects – the **arousal level,** on the one hand, and positive or negative **hedonic values** resulting in approach or avoidance tendencies, on the other. Berlyne (1971, 1974) used the old Wundt curve – originally introduced by Wundt (1874) to describe the relationship between stimulus intensity and sensations of pleasantness and unpleasantness – to describe the effect of arousal potential. As shown in Fig. 4.17, once an "absolute threshold" has been crossed, positive hedonic value builds to a peak as arousal potential increases. Any subsequent increases in arousal potential lead to a decline in hedonic value and eventually to increasingly negative values.

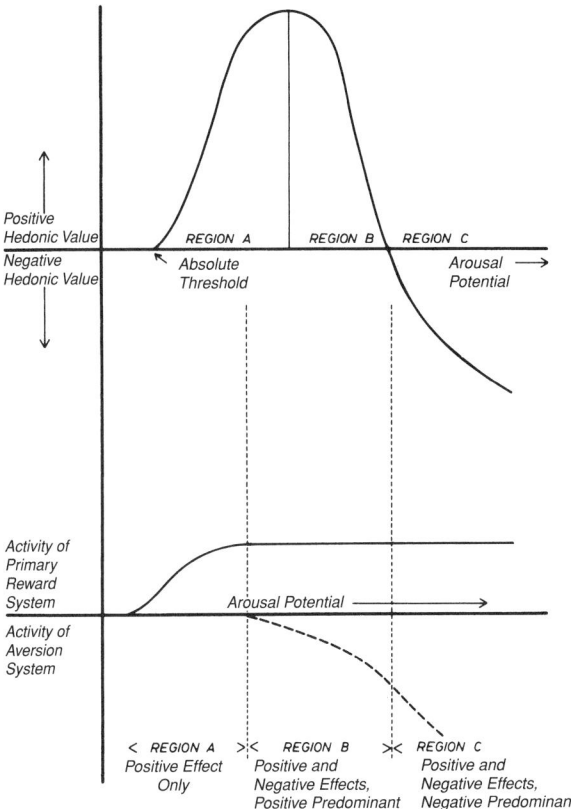

Figure 4.17 The Wundt curve (*above*), broken down into two hypothetical partial curves (*below*) representing the activity of the primary reward system and the aversion system as functions of arousal potential. (Based on Berlyne, 1973, p. 19.)

Berlyne's model was inspired by Olds' neurophysiological findings of positive and negative reinforcement centers in the brain (Olds & Olds, 1965). Berlyne suggested that the Wundt curve reflected the outcome of two opposing systems, a **primary reward system** and an **aversion system**. He interpreted it as a summation curve and split it into two partial curves corresponding to the two hypothesized systems (lower panel of Fig. 4.17). As shown in the figure, three successive regions of the arousal potential can then be identified, each having different effects on behavior. In region A, the arousal potential is low, producing only "positive effects," i.e., pleasant, reinforcing stimulation, eliciting approach behavior. In the middle region (B), there is a mixture of positive and negative effects, the former being dominant. Finally, in the upper region (C), the effects of the arousal potential are predominantly negative.

❶ In contrast to Hebb (1955) or Fiske and Maddi (1961), Berlyne did not see arousal level as a monotonic, linear function of the arousal potential (or stimulus input), but rather as a U-shaped function. This implies that a low arousal potential can serve to increase the activation level, as well as a high one.

Berlyne (1960) further assumed that boredom and stimulus monotony are accompanied by an irritatingly high activation level. That brings us to the postulated reinforcement function of the activation level. Everything that serves to reduce the level of the activation is seen as reinforcing. In this respect, Berlyne's approach is in line with Hull's postulate of reinforcement through drive reduction. At the same time, however, it takes into account the U-shaped relationship between arousal potential and activation, and holds that a low arousal potential will be raised, and a high potential lowered, toward an intermediate level that is experienced as pleasant and positively reinforcing (Berlyne, 1967). Both events result in a reduction in the activation level and, according to Berlyne, both elicit particular types of behavior:

- If the arousal potential is too high, it will prompt "specific exploration" in order to obtain further information from a specific source and thus relieve uncertainty. Berlyne calls this "perceptual curiosity."
- If the arousal potential is too low, it will prompt "diverse exploration" in order to seek out stimulation, regardless of content or source (frequently motivated by boredom).

EXAMPLE

A relevant study was carried out by Berlyne and Crozier (1971). Participants were asked to express their preference for a series of either highly complex or markedly simpler patterns. For one group, presentation of the stimulus patterns was always preceded by a 3.5-second period of near darkness. For the other group, presentation was preceded by exposure to highly complex, i.e., highly stimulating, patterns. Participants in the latter group subsequently preferred patterns containing less information, while their counterparts in the former group, who had previously been exposed to near darkness, preferred the more complex, novel patterns. The stimulation of this group was evidently below the optimal activation level, resulting in a preference for stimulus input that enhanced activation (diverse exploration), while the optimal activation level of the other group had been exceeded, resulting in a preference for patterns that lowered activation (specific exploration).

Berlyne (1971, 1974) compiled these and many other findings to develop a psychology of aesthetics. It states that observers can be pleasantly stimulated by a work of art because it can raise their activation in the direction of an optimal level. A work of art can also be experienced as unattractive, even repellant, however, if the observer finds it too novel or too complex. This negative reaction can be reversed if the observer becomes gradually familiar with the work of art; e.g., by hearing a piece of music again and again. If the work finally becomes so familiar that it no longer has any novelty or surprise value, it will lose its activating function, leaving the observer cold and uninterested.

In contrast to Berlyne, Hebb (1955), as well as Fiske and Maddi (1961), proposed that an intermediate activation level

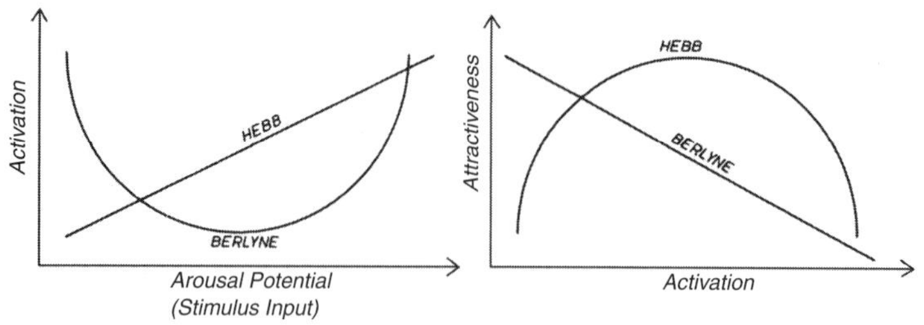

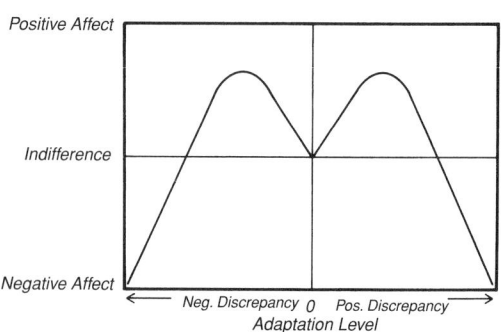

Figure 4.18 Contrasting postulates by Hebb and Berlyne concerning the relationships between arousal potential and activation, and between activation and attractiveness (preferred activation level).

(which for them is the same as an intermediate arousal level) results in an optimum state. All changes in the direction of this intermediate level will be sought out by the organism and will have a positively reinforcing effect. The difference between Hebb's and Berlyne's postulates is elucidated in Fig. 4.18, which shows the relationships that the two authors hypothesized to exist between arousal potential (stimulus input) and activation, on the one hand, and between activation and attractiveness (i.e., preferred activation level), on the other. Their approaches differ primarily with respect to the area of low arousal potential. In general, the empirical data seem to support Berlyne's position. Note that these theoretical notions about activation are closely related to **discrepancy theories of motivation**. McClelland based his theory of motivation on a discrepancy model (McClelland et al., 1953). Discrepancy theories state that relatively small deviations from a norm state are experienced as pleasurable and have motivating characteristics. This applies to deviations in either direction from the norm, or **adaptation level** (Helson, 1964, 1973; see the example below). Adaptation levels represent neutral points in the individual's value system or frame of reference that serve as a basis for all perceptual experiences and judgments. They are constantly shifting in the direction of past experience.

❶ A much cited example for the affective outcomes of deviation from the adaptation level is a study by Haber (1958). Participants first immersed both hands in water at near-body temperature. After they had adapted to this temperature, i.e., come to experience it as neither pleasant nor unpleasant, but neutral, they placed their hands in another bucket containing water that was colder or warmer by varying degrees. Fig. 4.19 shows the results. Small deviations produced a positive affect, whereas larger deviations resulted in an increasingly negative affect, producing what is known as the "butterfly curve."

4.7 Cognitive Appraisal Theories

Situational stimulus events represent pieces of information that must be processed in order to arrive at a cognitive representation of a situation. This endows the situation with meaning, which in turn motivates and influences behavior. Hence, the cognitive interpretation of a situation affects behavior.

The crucial point here is that stimulus events do not determine behavior directly or indiscriminately, but that they are interpreted by the individual, and transformed into a coherent picture of the immediate situation. It would also be wrong to assume that people proceed from a complete representation of the situation, as suggested by Lewin's motivational analysis of conflict situations. There are numerous theoretical models postulating that an appraisal of the situation involves cognitive and motivational processes; the most important of these will be outlined below. First, we will consider emotions, which Schneider and Dittrich (1990) consider to be the organizational core of motivation, both energizing behavior and giving it general direction. Emotions are not simply "internal stimuli." Rather they are the outcome of information processing in which cognitive events play a significant role. Schachter's two-factor theory of emotion and its modifications by Valins, as well as Lazarus' theory of appraisal of threatening situations, are examples of this approach.

4.7.1 Emotion as an Outcome of a Cognitive Appraisal

The psychology of emotion has recently begun to attract a great deal of attention – largely as a result of developments in neuropsychological research (LeDoux, 1996). Subsequent to the cognitive revolution in psychology in the 1960s, research was long dominated by approaches that saw **emotions** primarily in terms of their information content or simply as epiphenomena with no functional significance of their own. The earlier research traditions reported in this chapter, however, had also neglected the subject of emotions. One reason

Figure 4.19 Hypothetical relations between stimulus condition deviating from the adaptation level and hedonic value.

for this neglect was that the theoretical position that emotions might have occupied as an organism-related input of vital importance to behavior was already occupied by the concept of drive.

Emotions can be regarded as the organizational core of motivation or indeed as a rudimentary motivation system (Schneider & Dittrich, 1990) within which different emotions can select, energize, and direct behavior appropriate to the situations in which they arise. The appraisal of a situation, in terms of its potential benefits or threats, is central to Arnold's (1960) **sequential model of emotions**. This model states that it is the "intuitive" appraisal of a situation that elicits emotion and its physiological responses. Appraisal consists of an affective judgment that is experienced as a behavioral approach or avoidance tendency. The concomitant physiological responses determine the emotions expressed. The final step in the sequence is an approach or avoidance response.

From today's perspective, Arnold's positions – and especially her notions about the relationship of emotions to processes within the central nervous system – are rather speculative.

4.7.2 Emotion-Triggering Situations

John Watson (1913), the founder of behaviorism, observed emotional reactions in neonates that were evidently innate rather than learned. These included reactions to strong stimuli, such as sudden noises and loss of physical support, both of which elicited fear. Restrictions of bodily movement elicited anger. Body contact, e.g., stroking of the skin, elicited affection (Watson & Morgan, 1917; Watson, 1924). These unconditioned "stimuli" can be replaced by a variety of previously neutral stimuli by means of classical conditioning (cf. Watson & Rayner, 1920; Harris, 1979), and thus trigger the emotional response formerly evoked by the unconditioned stimuli.

Watson and many others after him, however, were wrong in assuming that any arbitrarily chosen stimulus can be classically conditioned. Research has shown that not every stimulus is equally suitable for eliciting a particular emotion. "Appropriate" stimuli evidently possess a certain unconditioned prepotency that may be conducive – or resistant – to a particular conditioning process (Valentine, 1930).

> **DEFINITION**
> The prepotency of certain stimuli to be paired with particular emotions is called "preparedness" (Seligman, 1971; Schwartz, 1974).

For example, it is easy to condition fear of snakes or spiders (see the following study), despite the fact that there is little opportunity for negative experiences with the two species in many parts of the world. Jones and Jones (1928) observed fear of snakes in four-year-olds who had no cause for such fear, leading them to assume a biogenetic predisposition.

> **STUDY**
> **Preparedness for Conditioning Fear**
> Differences in the unconditioned preparedness of objects for conditioning fear were demonstrated by Öhman et al. (1976). Participants in their study were administered a slight electric shock to the finger tip at the same time as they were shown a picture – either a phobic stimulus (snake or spider) or a neutral stimulus (flower or mushroom). A single presentation of the phobic stimuli proved sufficient to condition the fear response. Although it took longer to condition the fear response with the neutral stimuli, the response was also extinguished much sooner in this condition.

4.7.3 Appraisal of Threatening Situations

Magda Arnold's (1960) sequential model of emotions was the first to assign a central role to the appraisal of a given situation in terms of its potential benefits or threats. This general model of cognitive appraisal of situations was further elaborated and experimentally tested by Lazarus (1968).

Lazarus' Approach to Stress and Coping
According to Lazarus' model, cognitive components relating to situational appraisal and to physiological activation do not simply coexist, they complement each other. Cognitive processes involved in the assessment of a situation can directly influence the physiological activation component, i.e., conditional on the successive intermediate outcomes of such appraisals, there can be a feedback effect on emotions and behavior. Lazarus' experiments focused on **coping** in threatening and **stressful situations**. They were based on a model that assumes two sequential stages of cognitive activity:

1. Primary appraisal of whether and to what extent the situation is threatening.
2. Secondary appraisal of possible means of dealing with the threatening situation.

Essentially, either of two strategies can be applied here: direct action, accompanied by the corresponding emotions, e.g., attack (anger), withdrawal (fear), inactivity (depression); or reappraisal, resulting in a more favorable, less threatening view of the situation, and thus reducing the fear-related emotional arousal level.

Lazarus induced stress in his participants by showing them films with threatening contents: an anthropological film about circumcision rites among Australian aborigines and an accident-prevention film showing close-ups of several accidents in a sawmill (e.g., someone losing his thumb while working with a circular saw). In a study with the latter film, Lazarus et al. (1965) presented participants with two types of cognitive reappraisal before showing them the film. Both reappraisal strategies were designed to make the film less threatening. One involved "denial" (it was only a make-believe film with actors); the other involved

4

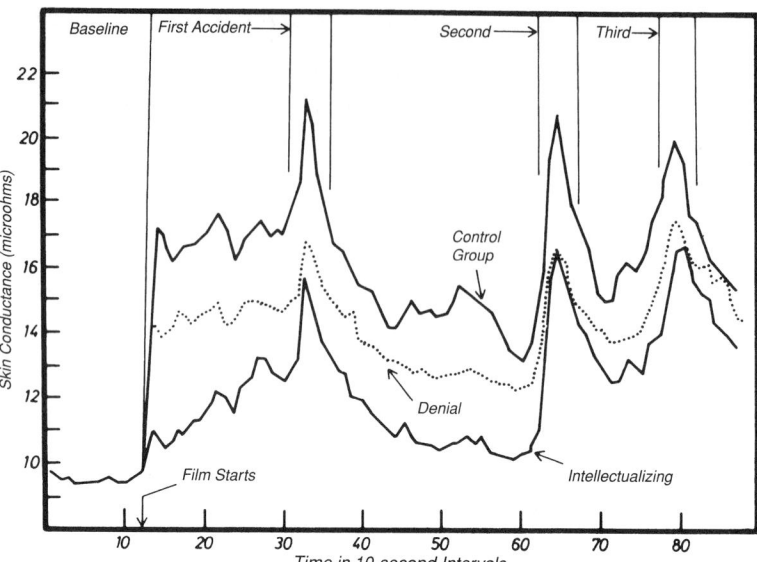

Figure 4.20 Effects of cognitive reappraisal (denial or intellectualizing) on emotional response to an alarming film (measured in terms of galvanic skin response). (Based on Lazarus et al., 1965, p. 628.)

"intellectualizing" (viewing the film in a detached manner). Galvanic skin responses were recorded continuously during the viewing session to serve as a measure of emotional arousal level. Results are shown in Fig. 4.20. Compared with an uninstructed control group, those who were induced to reappraise the situation through denial and especially intellectualization showed a considerable decrease in the autonomic arousal state.

Such results are difficult to interpret within the framework of drive and learning theories. After all, the same fear-arousing stimuli lead to different responses depending on the intervening cognitive appraisals of the situation (for theoretical implications, see Heckhausen, 1973).

Lazarus offered a behavioral explanation assuming a process of interaction between the individual and the situation at hand. In fact, he developed a dynamic **transactional** model assuming a continuous process of reciprocal influences (Lazarus & Launier, 1979).

Lazarus distinguished three different outcomes of stress appraisal:

- harm-loss (i.e., an already experienced impairment),
- threat (i.e., potential and feared loss or injury), and
- challenge (i.e., anticipated opportunities for mastery or gain).

The amount of stress experienced depends on the extent to which an individual feels he or she has been harmed, threatened, or challenged, as well as on the person-environment relations within the particular life sphere. There are two facets to the appraisal of these relations – what is at stake (primary appraisal) and the coping resources and options available (secondary appraisal).

Coping – i.e., dealing with conflicts or coming to terms with difficulties – has two main purposes:

1. Gaining control over or modifying the person-situation variables producing the stress (problem-oriented coping).

2. Gaining control over stress-related emotions (emotion-oriented coping).

STUDY

Study on the Appraisal of Everyday Stressful Events

Folkman and Lazarus (1980) conducted a field study to examine everyday stressful events and the related coping patterns. The authors addressed two main questions. First, do coping responses to everyday stressful events reflect person-specific dispositions, meaning that they remain consistent across events, or are they situation-specific and inconsistent? Second, which of the following five factors influence individual coping responses: type of event (context), persons involved, appraisal of the event, age, and gender?

Over the course of a year, 100 men and women between the ages of 45 and 64 were surveyed on stressful events and how they had attempted to cope with them on repeated occasions. It emerged that stressful events almost always evoked both emotion-focused and problem-focused coping responses. There was a greater tendency toward variability than toward consistency in the coping responses of the individual participants. In fact, it emerged that whether emotion- or problem-focused coping mechanisms were used hinged primarily on the context (family, health, job) and on the appraisal of the event. The work context was conducive to attempts to solve the problem; the health context to emotional control. Contrary to commonly held sex stereotypes, there were no gender differences in the choice of emotion-focused coping mechanisms. However, men did report more problem-focused coping than women in work situations that could not be changed and had to be accepted.

A key finding of this study is that everyday approaches to coping with stress do not reflect person-specific dispositions, but situationally appropriate patterns of behavior.

4.7.4 Cognitive Dissonance

Few approaches within motivation theory generated as much research in the 1960s as did Festinger's (1957, 1964) theory of cognitive dissonance, with more than 1,000 empirical studies being conducted (see Joule & Beauvois, 1998). Recent work has focused primarily on attitudinal change and the establishment of a conflict-free self. Nevertheless, the roots of the theory can be found in the tradition of motivational psychology (Beckmann, 1984).

In formulating his theory of cognitive dissonance, Festinger (1957) was influenced by Lewin's field theory and Heider's cognitive balance theory.

❶ The basic assumption of the theory is that individuals strive for harmony, consistency, and congruence in their cognitive representation of themselves and their environment, insofar as this representation has immediate meaning, i.e., is relevant to the current situation. The theory deals with the relationships between various cognitive elements (knowledge, opinions, values, attitudes) and with the motivational effects mediated by striving for consistency in the face of two conflicting elements.

The first question to be asked is what is meant by "relationships" and "elements." Relationships exist between two elements, i.e., within a pair of elements. The relationship is either irrelevant or relevant – the two elements are either related or they are not. It can be consonant – whereby one element logically follows from the other – or dissonant – whereby the opposite of one element logically follows from the other. The latter state generates a negative affect.

This negative affect, which is triggered solely by the experience of dissonance, and not by factors such as its unpleasant consequences, will motivate the individual to engage in **dissonance reduction** (Harmon-Jones, 2000). Like Lewin's field theory and Heider's cognitive balance theory, Festinger's (1957) conceptualization of the motivational component represents a kind of homeostatic model. Whenever an imbalance is registered, the organism is motivated to restore equilibrium (**homeostasis**). This approach is also consistent with a theory of generalized drive, as proposed by Raup (1925) or Richter (1972). Of course, the criticisms directed at the latter approaches also apply to the present conception of a motivation to reduce dissonance. Beckmann (1984), in contrast, took a functional approach, assuming dissonance reduction to serve the purpose of ensuring that an action is performed effectively and without conflict. Seen from this perspective, processes of dissonance reduction facilitate action control. Harmon-Jones & Harmon-Jones (2002) have recently advocated a similar approach and provided empirical support for their arguments in a series of experiments.

There are three ways to reduce dissonance:

1. by changing one or more elements within dissonant relationships,

2. by adding new elements that are consonant with the existing ones, and

3. by reducing the significance of the dissonant elements.

> **EXAMPLE**
>
> The various possibilities can be illustrated using the example of smokers who find themselves confronted with the information that smoking causes lung cancer. They can achieve reduction of the dissonance by (1) changing an element within the dissonant relationship – by quitting altogether, by reducing the number of cigarettes smoked per day and then seeing themselves as light smokers, to whom the link between smoking and lung cancer does not apply, or by reasoning that the information on lung cancer applies only to cigarettes and not to pipes, which is what they smoke. Alternatively, they can (2) add new elements to reduce the dissonance, by thinking about their many friends who smoke and who are in the best of health, or by reasoning that there are many factors contributing to lung cancer that are beyond individual control. Finally, they can (3) increase the significance of smoking, e.g., by saying that it makes them feel better and increases their performance, or they can reduce the significance of lung cancer, e.g., by saying that it is or soon will be curable, or by doubting the validity of the link between smoking and lung cancer. (Surveys have shown that this skepticism is more widespread among smokers than nonsmokers, and particularly prevalent among heavy smokers.)

The strength of the motivation to reduce dissonance depends on the individual significance of the cognitions standing in dissonant relation to one another and on the number of cognitions involved. People will be more motivated to restore consonance when faced with information that is contrary to their world view than when the cognitions are less relevant to their self-concept.

These postulates have been confirmed for a variety of spheres of action, partly through field studies in real-life settings, but mostly through studies in artificial laboratory situations. Festinger (1957) assumed cognitive dissonance and its reduction to occur in five main spheres, each of which saw intense empirical investigation:

1. postdecision conflicts,

2. forced compliance to do something one would not have undertaken on one's own initiative,

3. selection of information,

4. challenged convictions of social groups, and

5. unexpected outcomes of actions and their consequences.

Postdecision Conflicts

The resolution of a **conflict** by means of a decision can often give rise to cognitive dissonance (Festinger, 1964). Whenever one of two alternatives has been chosen, the positive aspects of the rejected alternative and the negative aspects of the chosen alternative will contribute to the dissonance of the decision. Conversely, the negative aspects of the rejected alternative and the positive aspects of the chosen alternative will increase the consonance of the decision.

The findings reported by Brehm (1956) illustrate this point.

EXAMPLE

Participants in this study were asked to rate household appliances in terms of their attractiveness. In return for their participation, they were allowed to select one of two of these appliances to keep. For one group, the choice was between two products rated to be equally attractive, e.g., a toaster and an electric coffee maker (high dissonance); for another, the choice was between an attractive product and a product rated to be much less attractive (low dissonance). The participants were then asked to rate each product again. In general, these postdecision ratings indicated a marked increase in the attractiveness of the chosen product relative to the rejected product. The net change from the first to the second rating was more pronounced for the high-dissonance group that had to choose between equally attractive alternatives than for the low-dissonance group.

Since Brehm's first study in 1956, there have been numerous empirical confirmations of dissonance reduction in postdecision conflicts. The pattern observed here, in which the balance between the chosen and the rejected alternative is tipped in favor of the former, is known as the **divergence effect**. Generally speaking, the more choices there are, and the less they differ in qualitative terms, the stronger the observed divergence effect will be. Dissonance reduction can also be achieved by retroactive changes in the relative weights of the criteria on which the decision was based. Penner, Fitch, and Weick (1966) asked study participants to rate the importance of eight character traits in a corporate vice president. They were then asked to choose between two candidates on the basis of personality profiles, each of which attributed four of the eight traits to each candidate. After making their choice, participants were again asked to rate the importance of the eight traits. The traits of the chosen candidate were retroactively assigned a higher value.

The opposite of a divergence effect has also been observed: a convergence effect or **effect of regret** in which the chosen alternative is assigned a lower value, and the rejected alternative a higher value (e.g., Walster, 1964). Festinger (1964) sees this self-induced increase in dissonance immediately after a decision as a protective response in people with a low tolerance for dissonance. It represents an attempt to nullify the decision that has just been made.

A dynamic view suggests that the effect of regret may be a short-lived one occurring immediately after a decision has been made, prior to the onset of the divergence effect. Convergence effects seem to be complications that require

individual differences to be taken into consideration; this is highly unusual in dissonance research (see Beckmann & Kuhl, 1984).

Forced Compliance

The sphere of action that has seen the most investigation is that of forced compliance, a particular dissonance-inducing situation in which people are led to do things that do not seem entirely justifiable. Dissonance will occur only from actions entered into voluntarily and to which the individual has made a personal commitment (Brehm & Cohen, 1962).

To reduce the dissonance arising from such situations, the value of the action must be increased retroactively or its negative aspects trivialized. Compliance now appears to have been more reasonable and justifiable.

A number of research techniques have been developed to produce conditions of forced compliance and insufficient justification. In an early study, Festinger and Carlsmith (1959) presented participants with extremely boring tasks. These participants were then asked to tell other potential participants that the experiment was extremely interesting. In return, participants in one group received twenty dollars, while those in another group were given just one dollar. Subsequent ratings showed that participants who received less compensation rated the experiment as more interesting than those who had received high compensation. The greater dissonance of the latter group, which arose from consenting to deceive others for a paltry reward, was reduced in retrospect by falsifying the facts.

It soon emerged, however, that forced compliance does not always lead to dissonance reduction. Brehm and Cohen (1962) postulated two further conditions, in addition to the

---

STUDY

Study on Attitude Change in the Context of Bribery

Frey and Irle (1972) studied the effects of freedom of choice (given vs. not given) and commitment (public vs. anonymous) by means of experimental variation. Participants were paid DM 1 or DM 8 to prepare a discussion paper arguing against lowering the voting age from 21 to 18. For some, the task was obligatory; for others, it was voluntary. Some participants had to present the paper publicly, identifying themselves as the author, others were allowed to present it anonymously. Prior to the experiment, all participants were in favor of lowering the voting age. Findings showed that a reduction in dissonance, i.e., a change of attitude in favor of not lowering the voting age, occurred only in the presence of freedom of choice and public commitment. The absence of both resulted in the "bribery" effect, with attitude change occurring only in the higher-pay condition. In the two other conditions, in which only one facet was present (freedom of choice or public commitment), neither dissonance reduction nor bribery effects were observed.

discrepancy and the importance of relevant cognitions, that are necessary for dissonance reduction:

■ First, the individual must feel that he or she entered into the forced decision voluntarily.

■ Second, a personal commitment to an action alternative is required.

The realization of having made a voluntary commitment to a course of action that is in contradiction with one's own attitudes triggers cognitive dissonance. This dissonance may, in turn, lead to attitudinal change.

The motivational aspects of cognitive dissonance can even modify the effects of organismic needs. Mansson (1969) induced thirst in study participants by giving them crackers topped with a spread that made their mouths feel hot and dry. They were then invited to take part in a 24-hour thirst experiment, and offered either a high or a low reward for their participation. They were given a printed form on which they indicated their consent or refusal to participate in the experiment. Those who did not wish to participate constituted the "refuser" group. There were also two control groups: a high-thirst and a low-thirst control group. Members of these groups were not asked to participate in a thirst experiment. The low-thirst control group was given plain crackers, while the high-thirst control group was given crackers with the thirst-inducing spread. Prior to the expected thirst experiment, which did not in fact take place, data were collected from all groups on a variety of variables relating to the thirst experience. The predictions of dissonance theory were confirmed. Participants who had been prepared to subject themselves to a long period of fluid deprivation without sufficient justification (low reward) behaved as if they were experiencing little thirst, similarly to the low-thirst control group. Relative to the group given a strong justification (high reward) for participating in the experiment, and to the high-thirst control group, these participants rated themselves to be less thirsty. They drank less water, perceived fewer thirst-related words in a recognition task, required more trials to learn thirst-related paired associates, and gave fewer thirst-related responses in the TAT stories they generated. Fig. 4.21 shows the average amount of water consumed by members of the various groups prior to the expected onset of the 24-hour period of deprivation. The amount of water drunk in the high-dissonance group differs significantly from that consumed in all other groups.

Dissonance reduction is thus capable of modifying the effects of organismic drive states, such as thirst and fear, on learning and behavior. These findings emphasize the considerable influence of intervening cognitive processes in otherwise identical conditions.

Selection of Information

Selection of information is a particularly effective way to reduce postdecision dissonance. The individual seeks out and gives preference to information that supports the chosen

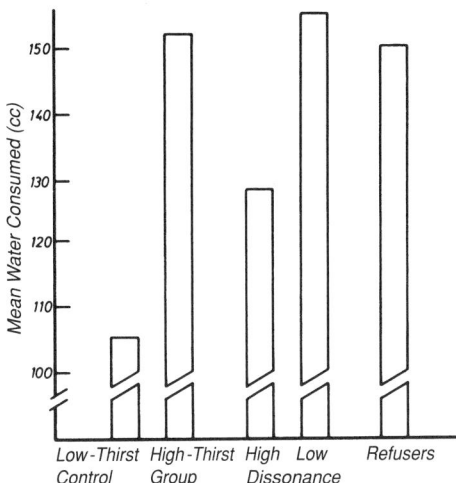

Figure 4.21 Mean amount of water consumed in the low-thirst and high-thirst control groups, the high and low dissonance groups, and the refuser group. (Based on Mansson, 1969, p. 90.)

alternative and devalues the rejected one, while avoiding information that does the reverse. Ehrlich et al. (1957) found that new car owners were more likely to read advertisements for the car they had just bought than for makes they had considered but did not buy.

Subsequent investigations showed that people were more likely to seek support for the chosen alternative than to avoid information casting doubt on their decision (cf. Wicklund & Brehm, 1976). A crucial factor here is the ease with which consonant and dissonant information can be refuted. People tend to prefer consonant information that is hard to refute and dissonant information that is easy to refute – and to avoid easily refutable consonant information and less easily refutable dissonant information. These, in any case, were the findings of a field study conducted by Lowin (1967) during the presidential election of 1964. Supporters of Lyndon Johnson and of Barry Goldwater received promotional materials containing excerpts from the campaign literature of the rival candidates. Some of the arguments were easily refuted, others were hard to refute. The participants were told that they could order additional materials free of charge. It emerged that there were more requests for hard-to-refute than for easy-to-refute consonant messages. The reverse held for dissonant messages.

An interesting case arises when dissonant information may prove beneficial after a decision has been made. If, for example, a student who has already signed up for a course run by a certain professor is given the opportunity to find out more about the examinations set by that professor, he or she will not avoid negative information. In this case, cognitive dissonance is not reduced, but accepted, because the negative information obtained may facilitate the goal of passing the exam (cf. Canon, 1964; Freedman, 1965; Clarke & James, 1967; Frey, 1981).

Challenged Convictions of Social Groups

Festinger, Riecken, and Schachter (1956) introduced this topic with a fascinating field study entitled *When Prophecy Fails* (see the example below).

EXAMPLE

Members of a small sect had gathered in a US town to await a cataclysmic flood that would occur on a certain day in December and would spell the end of the world. The faithful few would be whisked off to another planet in flying saucers. When this failed to occur, the dissonance between their expectations and reality could not be tolerated and had to be reduced. What could have been more logical than to abandon their beliefs about the end of the world and their personal salvation? However, only members of the sect who had been instructed to wait for the inevitable cataclysm on their own elsewhere responded in this way. Those members of the group who experienced the anticlimax together reduced the dissonance in the opposite way. They worked themselves up into a state of even greater fervor and missionary zeal, continuing to inform others that the end of the world was nigh, even though the prophesy had gone unfulfilled. In this case, dissonance reduction was closely linked to social interaction between the members of the group.

Hardyck and Braden (1962) report another field study involving a small religious sect ("True World"), the members of which expected an atom bomb attack on a certain day. They hid in below-ground shelters for 42 days after the assumed catastrophe. When they realized that a bomb had not in fact been dropped, they reduced the dissonance not through increased missionary fervor, but by adding consonant cognitive elements to the dissonant relationship. Specifically, they became convinced that they had passed God's test and prevented the catastrophe from occurring by virtue of their faith.

Unexpected Outcomes of Actions and Their Consequences

There are situational conditions leading to dissonance reduction that were not specified by Festinger (1957) in his original formulation of dissonance theory, but derived from it later. One such category concerns the mismatch between high effort expenditure and disappointing outcomes. Another category concerns the consequences of an action in terms of the self-concept.

MISMATCH BETWEEN EFFORT AND OUTCOME. Having tried hard, but in vain, seems to result in cognitive dissonance. To reduce that dissonance, attempts must be made to justify one's futile efforts retrospectively by increasing the value of the aspired goal (unless the expenditure of effort is trivialized or denied). Most impressive among the studies of this phenomenon are the animal experiments by Lawrence and

Festinger (1962) subtitled *The Psychology of Insufficient Reward*. The authors were able to demonstrate that cognitive dissonance and its reduction is not found only in humans, but can also be observed in infrahuman organisms, suggesting that dissonance theory also applies to nonverbal and noncommunicative behavior.

Hungry rats were trained to run a straight runway to obtain food under conditions that had previously been shown to inhibit learning, and that the animals would avoid if easier or more reliable paths to the goal were made available. Three kinds of difficulty conditions were implemented in the acquisition phase: partial reinforcement, delayed reinforcement, and the requirement of greater effort expenditure (in this case, the rats had to run up an incline of a certain steepness). The dependent measure and indicator of dissonance reduction was resistance to extinction, i.e., the number of nonreinforced trials before the learned behavior was extinguished (in some cases, also its strength).

Lawrence and Festinger designed these experiments to test two implications of dissonance theory:

1. Every dissonance that results from nonreinforcement, delayed reinforcement, or reinforcement only after high effort expenditure will be reduced by attributing "extra attractions" to the goal, deriving from other motives like exploration or sensory stimulation.

2. Because dissonance is cumulative, it must be constantly reduced by a corresponding increase in the strength of these "extra attractions."

Sixteen separate experiments supported both of these hypotheses. In the case of partial reinforcement, the absolute number and relative proportion of nonreinforced trials was varied independently. (Learning theory research generally specified only ratios of nonreinforced to reinforced trials). Fig. 4.22 shows that resistance to extinction after partial reward was not a function of the ratio of reinforced to nonreinforced trials, but increased sharply as a function of the number of nonreinforced trials. This finding supports the postulate that dissonance is cumulative, and has to be constantly reduced by elevating the attractions of the goal. If the dominant drive (hunger) is high in the acquisition phase, however, resistance to extinction increases as a function of the number of nonreinforced trials in the acquisition phase. These results suggest that greater dissonance resulting from the nonoccurrence of the expected reward under conditions of high drive level also leads to increased dissonance reduction in the form of attributing extra attractions to the goal. Findings about the relative expenditure of effort were also in line with these hypotheses. Rats that had to run up an incline of 50° ran faster (Fig. 4.23) during the extinction phase than rats faced with an incline of just 25°. Likewise, resistance to extinction was greater in the former group. These findings on effort proved to be independent of the reinforcement schedule. Varying both the amount of effort required and the number of nonreinforcements independently resulted in a summation

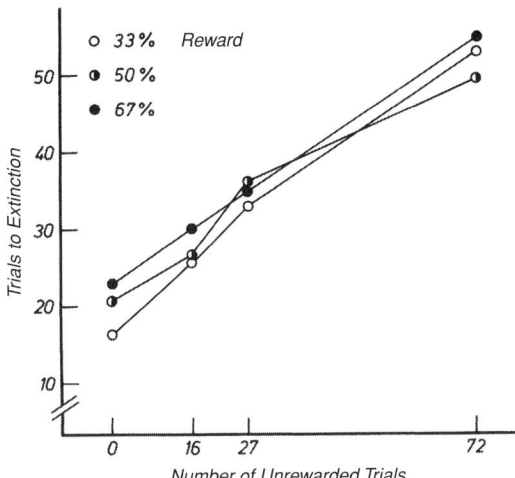

Figure 4.22 Resistance to extinction as a function of the number of unrewarded trials in three conditions with different ratios of reinforced to nonreinforced trials. (Based on Lawrence & Festinger, 1962, p. 91.)

of the effects of the two conditions. These and other findings led Lawrence and Festinger to the following conclusion:

> If an organism continues to engage in an activity while processing information that, considered alone, would lead it to discontinue the activity, it will develop some extra attraction for the activity or its consequences in order to give itself additional justification for continuing to engage in the behavior (Lawrence & Festinger, 1962, p. 156).

DISSONANCE-INDUCING OUTCOMES OF AN ACCOMPLISHED ACTION. Behaving in a way that is inconsistent with one's expectations, i.e., in conflict with the self-concept, is likely to induce dissonance and to result in unambiguous effects of dissonance reduction.

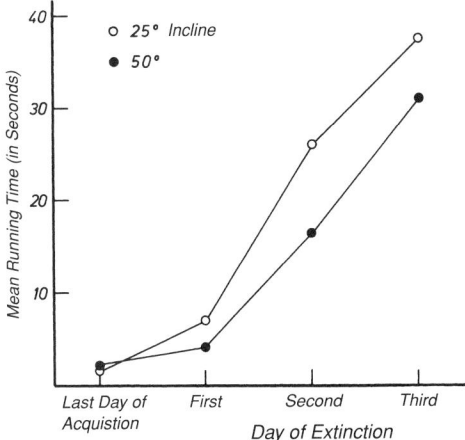

Figure 4.23 Mean running time (in seconds) in the extinction phase by effort condition in the acquisition phase (incline of 25° or 50°). (Based on data from Lawrence & Festinger, 1962, p. 143.)

The experimental paradigm for inducing dissonance with the self-concept was introduced by Aronson and Carlsmith (1962), and is also used in research on achievement motivation and cognitive attribution (Chapters 6 and 14). In this paradigm, participants are set a task that has been designed to result in either success or failure, causing them to adopt either a high or a low self-estimation of their ability on that task. Later they receive feedback on their performance that contradicts their expectations either in a positive or negative direction. According to Aronson, both scenarios will result in cognitive dissonance and initiate attempts to reduce it. Dissonance reduction can be achieved in various ways, the relative effectiveness of which was investigated in a number of subsequent studies.

For example, Irle and Krolage (1973) found that self-esteem increased more in the case of positive discrepancy from the test results than it decreased in the case of negative discrepancy from the results. (These findings are consistent with many others relating to self-serving biases in the attribution of success and failure; cf. Bradley, 1978; Fitch, 1970; Miller, 1976; see also Chapter 14.)

Individuals' ratings of their effort and of the validity of the test were higher in the case of positive discrepancy than they were in that of negative discrepancy. The further the unexpected outcome deviated from the participant's expectations, the less accurately it was remembered. Individuals became convinced that their test score was representative of the mean score expected for the reference group. Interindividual differences in the level of self-esteem also had an effect. This variable interacted with the direction of feedback discrepancy from expectations. The dissonance effects were strongest among participants with high self-esteem and a negative discrepancy from expectations and participants with low self-esteem and a positive discrepancy from expectations.

SUMMARY

Evidently, a remarkable number and variety of phenomena can serve to reduce cognitive dissonance. Most of these relate to changes in attitudes and beliefs when cognitive dissonance arises from postdecision conflicts, forced compliance in actions that one would not otherwise have undertaken, new information about previously chosen alternatives, challenged beliefs, or unexpected outcomes of actions and their consequences. Festinger (1964) postulated that information processing in the run-up to a decision is objective and impartial, but that once a decision has been made, it is biased in favor of that choice. In so doing, he anticipated a volitional specification of dissonance theory and a postulate of the Rubicon model of action phases (Heckhausen, 1987).

The number and theoretical importance of cognitive dissonance studies focused more narrowly on motivational issues, however, has remained limited. Following the resurgence of volitional theory in recent years, dissonance research has again begun to attract increased interest (Beckmann, 1984; Harmon-Jones & Harmon-Jones, 2002).

Indeed, studies such as the animal experiments conducted by Lawrence and Festinger (1962) and Zimbardo's (1969) set of experiments on the cognitive control of drives (cf. Grinker, 1969; Mansson, 1969) have demonstrated the validity of dissonance theory beyond verbal and communicative behavior.

4.8 Cognitive Appraisal Theories and Motivational Psychology

All of the above models concerning the behavioral effects of cognitive appraisals of the situation have contributed to an understanding of motivational issues, even when they neglect individual differences. With respect to their possible role as motives, these theoretical models of cognitive appraisal have remained undeveloped and untested; they are motivational models without motives. This may be the reason why authors such as Festinger and Heider have remained ambivalent and doubtful about the contributions their theories can make to the study of motivation.

According to Festinger (1957):

Cognitive dissonance can be seen as an antecedent condition which leads to activity towards dissonance reduction just as hunger leads to activity oriented towards hunger reduction. It is a very different motivation from what psychologists are used to dealing with, but, as we shall see, nonetheless powerful (Festinger, 1957, p. 3).

From today's perspective, we concur with Festinger to the extent that we see the motivation to reduce dissonance as a motivation that indeed differs from other motivations. Specifically, it is a motivation that serves the realization of actions; a motivation that mobilizes processes to facilitate the implementation of intentions. In other words, it is a volitional process. As mentioned above, the theory of cognitive dissonance can also be seen as a theory of volition. Indeed, Kelly (1962, p. 81) responded to Brehm's approach by pointing out that the aim of dissonance reduction was not to restore balance, but rather "to reconcile force and action."

Beckmann (1984) endorsed this approach. In contrast to Festinger (1964), moreover, he assumed that dissonance reduction – in its function as a volitional process that guarantees the achievement or maintenance of **action control** – may by all means occur before a decision is made if there is no other way of resolving a decisional conflict.

Heckhausen's (1987c) Rubicon model of action phases (Chapter 11) links up with the volitional aspects of the theory of cognitive dissonance. In line with Festinger (1964), Heckhausen assumes that it is, on principle, functional for alternatives to be evaluated objectively and impartially before a decision is made. Once the Rubicon has been crossed,

and a commitment to one alternative made, however, it becomes dysfunctional to dwell on the positive aspects of the alternatives that have been rejected. Such considerations might demoralize the individual and undermine their resolve to pursue the chosen course of action. Consequently, after crossing the Rubicon, people tend to either forget about the alternatives they have rejected, or to play them down. The Rubicon model, however, goes one step further than dissonance theory with respect to the functionality of information processing. The next logical step, once a decision has been made or an intention formed, is to put that intention into practice. Information relating to that action is of the essence here and needs to be taken into account, whether or not it is consonant with the decision that has been made. In fact, in some cases, it may be particularly useful or beneficial to consider information that challenges the choice made. Beckmann and Gollwitzer (1987) tested this assumption in the experiment presented below.

STUDY

Dissonance Reduction or Action Control

In the experiment conducted by Beckmann and Gollwitzer (1987), participants were provided with various pieces of information about two potential partners in a subsequent discussion. Some of the information was positive, some of it was negative. After the information had been presented, a cued-recall memory test was administered. In two conditions, participants were provided with the information before making their decision. In one of these conditions the memory test was administered before the decision was made; in the other, afterward. In the third condition, participants made their decision on the basis of photos of the potential partners, and the additional information was only provided, and its recall tested, after the decision had been made. It was only in this final condition that participants recalled significantly more information about the person they had chosen than about the person they had rejected. In both other conditions, including the typical dissonance condition (information provided before the decision, test administered afterward) participants recalled approximately the same amount of information about both potential partners. Interestingly, participants in the third condition recalled more negative than positive attributes of the partner they had chosen, whereas those in the condition where the test was administered before a decision was made recalled approximately equal numbers of positive and negative attributes. Do these findings disprove the assumptions of cognitive dissonance theory? Viewed from the perspective of volitional theory, the results are by all means in line with expectations. Specifically, participants' ratings of the relevance of the various pieces of information provided showed that information on negative personality attributes was considered much more important than information on positive attributes. When interacting with others, it can be important to know where sensitive points lie, and which topics to avoid to ensure that these do not have a detrimental effect on the conversation.

In other words, the strategy of reinforcing a decision that has already been made by focusing on its positive aspects and overlooking its negative ones can be reversed if negative information is more relevant to the realization of the action than is positive information. In the preactional phase, after a decision has been made, this approach is extremely functional.

SUMMARY

This chapter has dealt with the historical development of a number of quite heterogeneous perspectives on the situational determinants of behavior. The spectrum covers momentary need states and drive strengths, situationally induced conflicts and states of arousal, and emotions and cognitions as outcomes of situational appraisals. The only thing that all these determinants of internal or external situations have in common is that they are intraindividually variable, meaning that they are not linked to interindividual differences in dispositions.

The situational approach is thus just as one-sided as the person-centered approach and does as little justice to the complexity of motivational processes. A whole series of experiments on the theoretical approaches covered in this chapter provide evidence for this point.

Nevertheless, most of the approaches presented in this chapter have undergone further development without any alteration in this basic perspective, i.e., without the inclusion of person variables. This applies particularly to neo-associationism in social psychology.

Overall, however, there has been a discernible convergence on the main problem in motivation, namely how to explain the incentive value of goal states. In the process, it has become increasingly apparent that any clarification of the issue of motivation builds on two basic constructs – expectancy and incentive. We return to this issue in Chapter 5, paying particular attention to the development of Lewin's and Hull's approaches, as well as Tolman's approach, which was, from the outset, concerned with goal-oriented behavior involving the constructs of expectancy and incentive. Approaches from cognitive psychology and their further development have helped to clarify the conditions that determine the levels of anticipatory and incentive variables.

REVIEW QUESTIONS

1. **What is the principle of homeostasis?**

   Organisms endeavor to maintain a state of equilibrium (homeostasis). Whenever an imbalance is registered, the organism is motivated to reestablish the initial state.

2. **How does Hull account for the strength of stimulus-response bonds ($_sH_R$, habits)?**

   According to Hull, the strength of a stimulus-response bond ($_sH_R$) is solely dependent on the frequency of reinforcement. The frequency or strength of learned responses is solely dependent on the existing drive strength.

3. **According to Hull's theory, what energizes behavior and what gives behavior its direction?**

   Hull's theory states that it is generalized drive that energizes behavior, and learned stimulus-response bonds, or habits, that give it direction.

4. **What is affective priming?**

   In affective priming, the affective properties of the stimuli to which individuals are exposed are activated extremely quickly, without their conscious awareness. This activation of affective connotations can influence their subsequent judgments and behavior.

5. **Which are Lewin's three basic categories of conflict situations?**
   1. Approach-approach conflict,
   2. avoidance-avoidance conflict, and
   3. approach-avoidance conflict.

6. **Which six assumptions relating to conflict phenomena were formulated by Miller (1951, 1956)?**
   1. The tendency to approach a goal becomes stronger, the nearer a person is to it (gradient of approach).
   2. The tendency to approach a feared stimulus becomes stronger, the nearer a person is to it (gradient of avoidance).
   3. The gradient of avoidance is steeper than the gradient of approach.
   4. When two incompatible responses are in conflict, the stronger one will prevail.
   5. The height of the approach and avoidance gradients is dependent on the strength of the underlying drive.
   6. The strength of the response tendency being reinforced increases as a function of the number of reinforcements until learning plateaus out at a maximum level.

7. **What happens in cases of displacement?**

   In cases of "displacement," the original object is replaced perceptually by a more or less similar object that elicits less fear or anxiety. Displacement corresponds to a generalization of the response to the original object. The more the avoidance tendency outweighs the approach tendency, the less similar the displacement object will be to the original object.

8. **What are the postulates of Arnold's sequential model of emotions?**

   The appraisal of a situation, in terms of its potential benefits or threats, is central to Arnold's (1960) sequential model of emotions. It is the "intuitive" appraisal of a situation that elicits emotion and its physiological responses. Appraisal consists of an affective judgment that is experienced as a behavioral approach or avoidance tendency.

The concomitant physiological responses determine the emotions expressed. The final step in the sequence is an approach or avoidance response.

9. **According to Berlyne, what are the components constituting the arousal potential of a situation?**

   1. Collative variables (novelty, uncertainty, conflict, complexity, surprise value),
   2. affective stimuli,
   3. intense external stimuli,
   4. internal stimuli arising from need states.

10. **What do dissonance theory and the Rubicon model of action phases have in common; where do they differ?**

    Both dissonance theory and the Rubicon model of action phases work on the assumption that information processing in the run-up to a decision is, on principle, objective and impartial, but that once a decision has been made, it is biased in favor of that choice. However, the Rubicon model further distinguishes between information that is relevant to the decision, and information that is relevant to its realization. Only the processing of the first type of information should be biased after a decision, so as to reinforce and stabilize that decision. Because the latter type of information is relevant to proper execution of the action, the Rubicon model states that it should be processed objectively, even if it contradicts the decision that has been made.

5 Motivation as a Function of Expectancy and Incentive

J. Beckmann and H. Heckhausen

5.1 The Emergence of Incentives as Explanatory Concepts

Like Chapter 4, this chapter deals with the situational determinants of behavior. All of the theories to be discussed assume that the organism is able to anticipate events and that behavior is guided by anticipatory goal states. The underlying assumption is that goal states are involved in the "reinforcement" of behavior. When our actions meet with success, the respective goal states are associated with positive affect. When we fail, or in the case of negative reinforcement, they are associated with negative affect. The anticipation of the affect associated with goal states activates a behavioral tendency to either approach or avoid specific goal states. Situational stimuli that alert the organism to affectively charged goal states are known as **incentives**. Hence, the present chapter deals with **incentive theories** of motivation.

The striving for affectively charged goal states is a core component of motivation. There are evidently two preconditions for this striving. First, it must be possible to anticipate the occurrence of the goal state; there must be an expectation. Second, the goal state must have some subjective significance or value for the organism.

❗ Incentive theories of motivation assume that behavior is goal directed. Its regulation is forward looking, as though the organism were constantly asking itself what leads to what. Behavior is proactive, and is attracted to future goal states by the incentive-like promises and threats of the present situation.

The explanatory models covered in Chapter 4, such as Hull's (1943) reinforcement theory, are rather reactive by comparison. Here, the general energizing of behavior is attributed to a nonspecific drive, and behavior is assumed to be guided by previously established stimulus-response bonds (habits).

Preliminary conceptualizations of incentive theories are found, in one form or another, in the work of the pioneers of motivation research, such as William James, Freud, and McDougall. The first theory of motivation in which the idea of incentives not only plays a central role, but is also developed systematically, is Lewin's field theory. Within his model of the psychological environment, Lewin tried to define the effects of incentives – or, to use his terminology, valences – on behavior.

For Tolman, "expectancy" and "demand for the goal" became the hypothetical constructs of a "psychological behaviorism." These intervening cognitions mediate between the situation and the subsequent behavior. Tolman felt the assumption of rigid, learned stimulus-response bonds ("habits") in Hull's reinforcement theory to be inappropriate for explaining the flexible goal orientation of behavior. Based largely on his experimental findings on latent learning, Tolman was able to draw a distinction between learning and motivation (performance). Reinforcement of behavior has less effect on learning as such than on whether what has been learned is actually put into practice. According to Tolman, reinforcement generates the expectation of an event with incentive character.

The proponents of reinforcement theory, Hull and his students, incorporated Tolman's findings in their work, leading to a gradual transformation of reinforcement theory into an incentive theory of motivation. This applied particularly to Spence (1956) and, even more so, to Mowrer (1960), who used incentives to explain everything that had previously been attributed to drives.

This move toward an incentive-oriented approach further raised the question of whether response reinforcement might not be a superfluous or even inadequate explanation for operant learning. Might it not be better to explain the reinforcer's impact on behavior as a motivational incentive effect rather than as an effect related to the linkage between stimulus and response? This is a position long held by many well-known theorists in learning and motivation; e.g., Walker (1969), Bolles (1972), and Bindra (1974). Theoretical models that expand on Tolman's approaches suggest that it is not stimulus-response bonds that are learned, but **expectations** of contingencies. According to Bolles there are two basic types of expectations:

- situation-consequence contingencies (S–S^*) and
- response-consequence contingencies (R–S^*).

This results in a simple cognitive model of motivation. The probability of a response increases as a function of the strength of S–S^* and of R–S^*, and with the value of S^*. In other words, motivation is a function of expectancy and value.

The 1940s and 1950s saw the development of theoretical models incorporating expectancy and incentive beyond the confines of learning theory. These "**expectancy-value theories**" were invoked to explain decision-making behavior in situations ranging from placing bets in a game of chance to purchasing decisions (von Neumann & Morgenstern, 1944; Edwards, 1954) or setting levels of aspiration for tasks of varying difficulty levels (Escalona, 1940; Festinger, 1942; Atkinson, 1957).

❶ Expectancy-value theory states that, when several action alternatives are available, the one with the highest product of attainable value (incentive) times probability of success (expectancy) will be chosen. In other words, the individual strives for a goal state with the highest possible incentive value, taking into account the probability of its attainment. Expectancy-value theories form an important basis for contemporary motivation research.

Before examining the expectancy-value theories that are paradigmatic of today's motivation research, we will consider the foundations of these theories, starting with the concepts of incentive and expectancy, and then discussing Kurt Lewin's conceptualizations. The latter provided an extremely fertile ground for contemporary theorizing.

5.2 Situational Parameters of Motivation

Behaviorist learning theory assumes the situations in which individuals find themselves to play a crucial role in energizing

and directing behavior. Situational stimuli alert people to goal states that have incentive value for themselves personally. They also provide information permitting individuals to gauge the probability of attaining these goal states. In other words, situations contain stimuli that lead to subjective representations of incentive and expectancy. These subjective representations are not independent of person factors.

5.2.1 The Incentive Concept

DEFINITION
The incentive construct describes situational stimuli that are capable of eliciting a motivational state. Affective responses constituting a fundamental (basal) evaluation are at the core of this construct.

A stimulus can acquire incentive character over the course of an individual's learning history through its association with affect. A ski slope, for example, can trigger positive affective responses, such as pleasure and excitement, in one person, but negative responses, such as fear, in another. These responses depend on the individual's previous experience – in this case, associated with skiing. Learning, however, does not always seem to be a necessary precondition for an object to acquire incentive value. For example, a taste can activate specific receptors for sweet substances, which then trigger specific behaviors without the need for having had any prior experience of the foodstuff in question (Pfaffmann, 1982).

Affect, in its function as a primary evaluative mechanism, is an integral component of the incentive concept. For Schmalt (1996, p. 245), incentives are nothing more than anticipated affect. An object associated with **positive affect** has positive incentive value; an object associated with **negative affect** has negative incentive value. Recent research assumes that positive and negative affect are two mutually independent events (Watson & Tellegen, 1985), meaning that it is possible for strong positive and strong negative affect to occur at the same time.

❶ Crucially, incentives do not describe objective states, but subjective phenomena as perceived and affectively evaluated by the individual.

Particular objects or events that represent or are associated with the goal state, or that threaten to frustrate it, have positive or negative salience. These objects or events (S^*) represent a corresponding positive or negative incentive. They attract or repel the organism. Everything that has "reinforcement qualities," i.e., that can be shown to affect the antecedent behavior, can be attributed incentives. Incentives, like expectancies, are hypothetical constructs, and motivation theorists employ them to differing extents. In particular, their theoretical explanations of the conditions that give rise to incentives differ. The incentive value of objects or events may be seen as learned or innate (independent of experience), and as more or less dependent on momentary need states. Other terms used to designate this value character are **valence** (Lewin) and **demand for the goal** (Tolman).

Perceived or expected objects and events that have incentive character elicit behavior as well as giving it direction. Incentives are assumed to both energize and guide behavior by eliciting and attracting it across space and time.

The association of objects with affects, which endows stimuli with incentive character, occurs at early stages of processing in the **limbic system**. The **amygdala** plays a key role in generating affect, the nucleus accumbens is central in mediating motivational effects including reinforcement, and the prefrontal cortex helps to facilitate action (Wise & Rompré, 1989).

Leaving behind Hull's reinforcement theory, Milner (1970) defined incentives as the mechanisms that trigger behavior in the absence of a biological "drive." More recent research findings indicate that this triggering effect is not independent of the organismic state.

Organismic states influence the effect or salience of incentives. Toates (1986) suggested that organismic states can function as mediators that increase or diminish the salience of incentives, depending on whether excitatory or inhibitory influences predominate. Recent neuropsychological research has confirmed this assumption, showing that the salience of incentives is a function of the motivational state communicated by the central nervous dopamine system (Berridge & Robinson, 1998). It would seem that **dopamine** triggers desires and aspirations that can prompt an active search for cue stimuli. It does not have an impact on affective quality, however, i.e., how much we like something. This explains why we are more likely to notice food when we are hungry, and why – although the range of foods we consider palatable increases as our hunger grows – we would not be any happier to be served a worm for breakfast.

Schneider and Schmalt (1994, p. 16, own translation) see motives and incentives as closely related: "Situational incentives reflect the specific motive goals that people can aspire to or seek to avoid. Motives, in contrast, reflect evaluative dispositions for classes of these goals, the strength of which differs interindividually." In the following, we will show that the first formulations of incentive theories (e.g., Lewin's field theory) were in fact motivation theories without motives, i.e., that they disregarded enduring individual dispositions.

5.2.2 The Expectancy Concept

Another situational determinant of motivation is expectancy, i.e., the perceived probability that a certain goal state will ensue from a situation. This may entail the need for action or occur without the individual's involvement. Like incentive, expectancy is a subjective quality that develops over the course of the individual's learning history (see the overview and Fig. 1.2 in Chapter 1).

Characteristics of the "Expectancy" Variable

1. Expectations of the situation-consequence contingency type ($S–S*$), cf. Bolles, 1972): This type of expectation consists simply in the anticipation of a specific goal state, independent of the organism's own behavior (as in classical conditioning, where a signal precedes the presentation of food).

2. Expectations of the response-consequence contingency type ($R–S*$): This type of expectation entails the need for action on the part of the organism.

3. Expectations can also be differentiated on the basis of the amount of time or the number of behavioral sequences they encompass.

4. Expectations are not directly observable. They must be inferred, and therefore represent hypothetical constructs.

Theories of motivation differ in the extent to which they take the last point in the overview into account, i.e., in how well they are able to interpret the role of expectations as hypothetical constructs that can be used to predict outcomes on the basis of previous learning.

5.3 Linking Incentive and Expectancy

The French philosopher Blaise Pascal (1623–1662) was the first to link the constructs of value (incentive) and expectancy in the attempt to explain behavior. In so doing, he founded a long-standing tradition of expectancy-value theories in behavioral science. These theories form the basis for most contemporary models of motivation (Feather, 1982). The basic idea is that behavior is explained by the linkage between expectancy and value (= individually weighted incentive), which is usually multiplicative in nature. We do not necessarily have to be consciously aware of the two components in order for them to influence our behavior. In fact, they need not even have a conscious representation. It follows that expectancy-value theories can, in principle, also be used to explain animal behavior.

5.4 Lewin's Field Theory

Kurt Lewin's "field theory" was designed to explain behavioral events in comprehensive and concrete terms by tracing them back to the specific conditions of the "field" that existed at the time a behavior occurred.

❶ According to this conception, which is borrowed from physics, a person is located within a force field and subject to its situational forces. These forces emanate from both the "external" situation (the environment) and the "internal" situation (the person). Thus, the field describes all behavior-relevant conditions residing in the existing situation and in the person's internal states, and establishes causal dynamic relationships between them.

Lewin's field theory differs from the explanatory approaches of learning and drive theory, as presented in Chapter 4, in three major respects:

1. It attempts to reconstruct the entire situation as it exists for the individual.

2. The explanatory approach must be psychological.

The internal and external determinants of behavior must be seen from a psychological rather than a quasi-physical perspective. Thus, stimuli – which behaviorists attempt to define in terms of "physical" events – are not among the fundamental units of causal analysis, but rather perceived environmental events that offer the individual a number of behavioral choices. A psychological analysis, however, is not restricted to aspects that are phenomenologically given by internal states or external environmental conditions. It also includes aspects that are not consciously experienced, but that nevertheless influence behavior. These may be affective reactions that are not consciously represented (cf. Kuhl, 2001), for example.

3. Simple connections in the sense of stimulus-response bonds are viewed as insufficient.

All behavior is driven by underlying forces. This dynamic approach to understanding behavior goes beyond the assumption of a general, nonspecific drive. For Lewin (1942), behavior is a function of the field existing at the time the behavior occurs. It is only the present that can determine behavior. Neither past nor future events can be remembered or anticipated in the present, thereby becoming effective determinants of behavior. Past events, such as learning, may have contributed structure to the present field, in terms of the peculiarities of both the person and the environment. But one cannot simply attribute present behavior to earlier events, as is often done in **psychoanalysis**. Lewin was skeptical of dispositional variables such as intelligence or "instinct," because he saw them as inappropriate references to historical abstractions.

❶ Lewin's field theory is distinct from psychoanalysis to the extent that it sees behavior as determined by the present field – by the subjective representations existing at the time it occurs. Childhood experiences can only have an impact on behavior in terms of their present representation.

Furthermore, Lewin (1942) believed that psychological situations should, wherever possible, be presented in terms of mathematical models, "to permit scientific derivations" and "to use a language which is logically strict and at the same time in line with constructive methods" (1942). Mathematical representations do not have to be exclusively quantitative; they can also be qualitative, as is the case in geometry. Lewin's field theory makes extensive use of topology, a form of geometry that refers to adjacent regions, but not to distances and directions. It also involves vectors with three determinants:

■ strength,

■ direction, and

■ point of application.

Lewin (1931a, b, 1935) argued against psychological explanations of behavior in which classifications were based on external appearances, and in favor of analyzing the conditions that gave rise to those appearances, so that explanatory constructs with general validity could be identified. These explanatory constructs emerged to be the basic concepts of general dynamics, as developed in post-Galilean physics; e.g., potential, force, and field (analogous to electromagnetic or gravitational fields).

No less programmatic, but probably more important for the study of motivation, was Lewin's emphasis on an analysis of the total situation, which resulted in the well-known Lewinian equation (1946a).

❶ Behavior (B) is a function of person factors (P) and environmental factors (E): $B = f(P, E)$.

In principle, field theory thus recognizes the interactional relationships between person and situation factors, reflecting their mutual influences. In practice, however, field theory was unable to fulfill this programmatic pretension, because it neglected the dispositional variables among the person factors in favor of the momentarily functional variables. This neglect of individual differences in motivation resulted from the skepticism toward "historical" explanations mentioned above, although field theory is not in principle at odds with this kind of approach. After all, the notion of previously acquired associations does not contradict the rule that behavior must be a function of the present field. They can provide a prestructuring of personal factors against which the present situation is perceived.

Lewin developed two different explanatory models that are, to a certain extent, complementary: the person model and the environment model. The environment model relates to motivational issues; the person model to volitional issues. This despite the fact that Lewin tried to reduce volitional problems to motivational ones.

The two models differ in terms of their dynamic components. The person model involves energies and potentials, i.e., scalar magnitudes. The environment model employs forces and goal-oriented behavior ("locomotion" through behavioral regions), i.e., vectorial magnitudes. In the final analysis, however, both models are based on a homeostatic dynamic system. The states described tend toward the development of a homeostasis of tension or force. It is not the reduction of tension, but its equalization that is the governing principle of the all-encompassing system or field (cf. Lewin, 1926a, pp. 323ff.).

The Person Model

Lewin's theory of motivation was prompted by his dispute with Ach. Lewin (1922) sought to demonstrate that Ach's (1910) "determining tendency" not only explains a particular type of behavior, but that it is the dynamic prerequisite

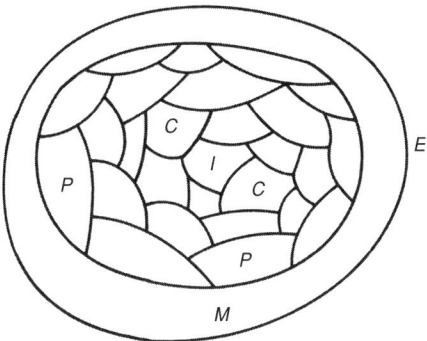

Figure 5.1 Person model. The motor-perceptual region (*M*) mediates between the environment (*E*) and the inner-personal regions (*IP*), which may be either more central (*C*) or peripheral (*P*). (After Lewin, 1936, p. 177.)

for all behavior. Simply establishing a connection between stimulus and response is not sufficient. For learning to manifest itself in behavior, a force should always be present. Most important for Lewin was the question of energizing. This does not mean the use of energy to carry out ongoing cognitive or motor behaviors.

❗ Here, energizing refers to the central question of behavioral determinants. Which of the behavioral tendencies available in a given situation will succeed and ultimately determine behavior?

Lewin attempted to answer this question by postulating changing tension states in various inner-personal regions (cf. 1936). Fig. 5.1 presents the person as a system of separate regions. Each region represents a particular behavioral goal, either an enduring desire that might be labeled a need or a motive, or a momentary intention. The individual regions differ in their proximity to one another, which represents their degree of similarity. It is greatest when two regions share a common boundary.

A further distinction relates to the position of the regions, and whether they are more central or peripheral. Central regions share more boundaries with adjacent regions than do peripheral ones. This indicates "ego-proximity," the personal importance of behavioral goals and activities, as well as their level of influence on other behavioral goals and activities, measured in terms of their number.

Tension Systems in the Person Model
Thus far, the person model represents a purely structural entity with regions, adjacencies, and mediating functions between inside and outside. One more structural characteristic should be mentioned, namely, the nature of the boundaries. These can differ in their "permeability" and can allow "leakage" from one adjacent region to another. This structural characteristic of the boundaries is related to the dynamic component of the person model. It is here that Lewin introduces the concept of tension. Specifically, the tension states of the individual's inner-personal regions can vary. The regions

can be thought of as vessels filled with liquid under varying degrees of pressure. If one region is marked by an increased tension state relative to another, it represents, according to Lewin, a **tension system**. Tension systems strive for the equalization of tension with adjacent regions. This can be accomplished in two ways:

■ The tension system representing an intended action may become discharged if it can access the border region of sensory-motor execution, i.e., if it gains control over behavior and guides it toward the goal.

■ If, however, it does not find such an access, the force will push against the boundary walls of the tension system. How soon there will be an equilibration of tension as a function of its diffusion is now a question of the permeability of the boundaries and the temporal duration.

Both types of tension equalization are quasi-physical conceptualizations rather than genuine explanations. They have heuristic value for analyzing the variables relating to a number of behavioral phenomena addressed by Lewin's students within the "psychology of action and affect." These experiments have become classics in the field. The first type of tension equalization, producing activities that can serve the execution of a purpose, can help clarify the behavior that follows a completed or an interrupted action. Prototypical here is the **Zeigarnik effect**. Lewin's student Bluma Zeigarnik (1927) found that interrupted tasks were more easily remembered than those that had been completed.

The second type of tension equalization, through diffusion to adjacent regions, can serve to explain phenomena such as need satisfaction through goal substitution (Lewin, 1932; Lissner, 1933; Mahler, 1933; Henle, 1944), the role of fatigue, emotionality, anger (Dembo, 1931), and unreality (Brown, 1933) resulting from the discharge of a tension system. Fatigue, emotionality, and unreality are viewed as conditions that change the permeability of the regional barriers, but both types of tension equalization always relate to the implementation of firm intentions.

The structure of the inner-personal sphere is not permanently fixed. It becomes more differentiated as a function of the individual's development and experience. It can be restructured, with each immediate goal forming a region of its own.

❗ As Lewin stated in his fundamental theoretical treatise on *Intent, Volition, and Need* (1926b), action goals represent "quasi-needs," i.e., derived needs. Quasi-needs are transitory in nature. They often arise from the intention to do something that is goal-related; e.g., to mail a letter to a friend. They form a tension system that will disappear only when the goal has been attained.

QUASI-NEEDS. Quasi-needs may also arise without an act of **intention**, e.g., in connection with the intermediate activities leading to a goal associated with "genuine" – i.e., superordinate and enduring – needs. For instance, the instructions given by an experimenter are, as a rule, accepted by a study participant without an actual intentional act. This induces a quasi-need to carry out the imposed task, which is basically the same as a self-initiated intention. In both cases the activity is resumed spontaneously after interruption (cf. Ovsiankina, 1928). According to Lewin, the strength of a quasi-need (or, more specifically, of the corresponding tension system) is not dependent on the presence or intensity of the intention, but on the extent to which the quasi-need is related to or is fueled by real needs (which, for us, represent motives):

> The intention to mail a letter, to visit a friend, even the intention of a subject in an experiment to learn a series of nonsense-syllables, does not represent an isolated entity, even in the case where the action sequence represents a relatively well-defined whole. Instead, it arises from more far-reaching goals, such as the intent to take care of one's business, to make progress in one's studies, or to do a favor for a friend. It is not the strength of an intention, but (apart from other factors) the strength and the vital importance, or more correctly, the degree to which the genuine need – in which the quasi-need is embedded – has become firmly established ("Tiefe der Verankerung"), which determines the effectiveness of an intention (Lewin, 1926b, pp. 369–370).

We will see shortly, when we examine the environment model, that a tension system, whether it represents a need or a quasi-need, is related to specific changes in the perceived environment. Objects that can facilitate a discharge, i.e., serve to satisfy a need, acquire "incentive character," a valence that sets them off from their environment and induces goal-oriented approach behavior. If, for example, you want to mail a letter in an unfamiliar part of town, you are much more likely than usual to notice a mailbox, even if you are not intentionally looking for one. The strength of the valence is dependent on the strength of the tension system. This postulated relationship is the only connection between the two models, which, as we will see later, are totally different.

SUMMARY
Although field theory pays very little attention to individual differences, the person model does incorporate some attempts to describe individual differences in terms of enduring differences in the structural characteristics of the inner-personal space. For one, this applies to different stages of personality development, represented by both the degrees of differentiation (i.e., the number) of inner-personal regions and the permeability of the boundaries of individual regions. For another, Lewin (1935, Chapter VII) used the model to reconstruct and "explain" differences between "normal" and "feeble-minded" individuals, concluding that "feeble-minded" individuals have stronger (less permeable) boundaries between the inner-personal regions and fewer regions than "normal" individuals.

Lewin's concept of tension systems differs from Hull's drive theory in two main respects. First, the tension systems are always goal-specific and do not serve a general incentive function for every conceivable response; second, the tension systems do not simply activate previously established response habits (stimulus-response bonds) that have, in the past, led to the accomplishment of the particular goal. They are focused on achieving goal states by means of flexible actions that are adapted to the situational conditions.

The person model, however, does not specify how this objective is accomplished. In fact, it is not clear how particular tension systems gain access to sensorimotor border regions and how, within these regions, executive processes evolve and are carried out.

The model cannot describe transactions with the environment; they must simply be assumed. The person is totally encapsulated. In other words, the person model does not meet Lewin's requirement of an analysis of the total situation. Neither does it allow for motivating expectancies and incentives (demand characteristics, valences) within the particular person-environment relationship. For this, Lewin developed the environment model.

Despite these limitations, the person model has stimulated a series of important experiments. Because they relate to issues in **volition** rather than motivation, we will examine them below (aftereffects of incomplete tasks).

The Environment Model
From an early stage in his research, Lewin observed the psychological structure of the environment as an action sphere. He found remarkable differences between the psychological and the geographical structure of the environment.

Lewin frequently filmed the behavior of children in free-play situations, typically on a playground, and analyzed their locomotion within the playground's structures as a psychological sphere of action. (One example of this is the conflict-dominated locomotion of the child in Fig. 4.10 in Chapter 4, who wants to retrieve a toy swan from the water but, at the same time, is afraid of the waves.)

To account for such phenomena, the environment model must be able to describe the directions of all possible goal behaviors within a psychological, rather than a geographical space.

The psychological space, the psychological field, consists of a variety of regions. The regions are not literally physical spaces, but psychological potentialities for actions and events. Individual regions represent potentially positive or negative events. They are goal regions with positive valences or repelling regions with negative valences. The remaining regions represent potential instrumental responses, leading toward a goal region or away from a repelling region. In other words, they represent means to an end. One of the regions within the environment model represents the person, usually indicated as a dot or an empty circle. To reach a goal region with a positive valence, the person must traverse,

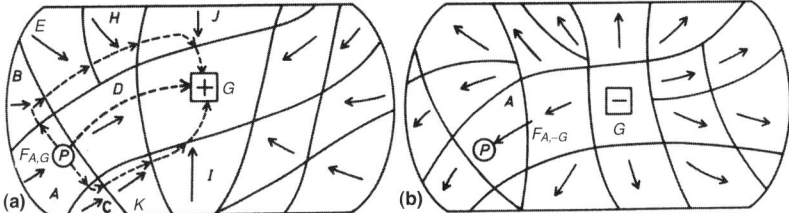

Figure 5.2a,b The environment model illustrated by a positive and a negative force field. All forces within the positive field (**a**) are focused on the goal region *G*. $F_{A,G}$ is the force acting upon the person and corresponds with the positive demand characteristics (valences) of an individual located in region *A* and a goal located in region *G*. There are three possible action paths leading to the goal. They require the individual to pass through different numbers of adjacent regions (actions): *A-D-G*; *A-C-K-I-G*; *A-B-E-H-J-G*. All forces in the negative force field (**b**) gravitate away from region *G*. The force $K_{A,-G}$ represents the negative demand characteristics of *Z*.

i.e., behaviorally attend to, all of the regions between it and the goal region. If, for example, you want to own and drive a car, you must first acquire a driver's license, save money, decide on a make of car, find a dealer, etc.

The environment model represents an attempt to map out the potential actions available in a given life situation that will lead to a desired goal or avert a negative event, rather than an explanation of these actions. It is a cognitive representation of the means-ends relationships that a person perceives with regard to potential behaviors and their outcomes; in other words, the expectations motivating behavior. This is the structural component of the environment model.

The dynamic component is expressed in terms of force fields that have their centers in regions with a positive or negative valence, as shown in Fig. 5.2. Forces with specific intensity act upon the person, and the resultant summation of vectors gives direction and strength to his or her psychological locomotion. Conflict results when opposing forces of approximately equal strength act upon the person. Direction, in this context, means the sequence of individual, purposeful actions. Frequently, different action paths lead to the same goal. In this case, the psychological direction remains unchanged; there is an equifinality of goal-oriented behavior. Thus, the environment model is essentially designed to clarify motivational issues, i.e., the "what" and "how" of approach and avoidance.

Because topological representations consist only of neighboring regions and lack direction, Lewin (1934) sought to expand this approach to a "hodological" conception (from the Greek "hodos" meaning path). Action paths represent connections between the region in which the person is presently located and the goal region. Fig. 5.2a shows three different action paths leading to the same goal. Lewin assumes that there is a "superior" path that is preferred because it traverses the smallest number of regions and is therefore "shortest." Shortness or minimal psychological distance, however, is dependent not only on the number of intermediate regions. It can also be a function of the degree of difficulty, the amount of effort required, and the possible dangers inherent in travers-

ing the various regions, quite independent of their number; e.g., on a battlefield. Topology disregards both directions and distances.

❶ Despite Lewin's efforts (1936, 1938, 1946a), the question of how psychological distance is to be measured and represented remains unanswered to this day. As we will see, however, an answer to this question must be found if we are to determine the strength of forces arising from positive or negative valences and taking effect in various regions of the field.

The Postdictive Environment Model

The environment model cannot explain behavior but can only reconstruct it. It is postdictive not predictive, assuming the conditions that motivate behavior to be given and known. Specifically, these are:

- motivating incentives; i.e., regions of the psychological field that are endowed with valences and
- the cognitive structuring of expectations, i.e., the means-ends relationships of action sequences along the path to the goal.

The latter are depicted as neighboring regions with traversing paths. The heuristic value of this model lies in its analysis of the conditions leading to behavior in a relatively free situation, rather than in an ability to explain it. The model can facilitate the detection and identification of determining factors within the complexity of the psychological total field; e.g., forces, barriers, action paths, and proximity to the goal. Examples of its application are the analysis of reward and punishment (1931a), the typology of conflict (1938; see also Chapter 4), and the simple taxonomy of the direction of behavior presented in Table 5.1. The direction of behavior is determined by whether the valence of the region results in approach or avoidance behavior and whether the person is already in that region or still in another one. The combination of these determinants yields four basic classes of directed behavior, as specified in Table 5.1.

Further variations of the environment model can be found in its application to problems such as:

Table 5.1. Taxonomy of the direction of behavior		
	Direction of behavior	
Position of the person	**Approach**	**Avoidance**
Valence region (A)	(A, A) Consummatory behavior	(A, −A) Escape behavior
Outside the valence region (B) (or C, D, . . .)	(B, A) Instrumental behavior	(B, −A) Avoidance behavior

■ decision-promoting processes of motivation (cf. Cartwright & Festinger, 1943; Lewin, 1943, on food purchases),

■ the social-psychological situation of adolescents (Lewin, 1939),

■ group formation under different leadership styles (Lippitt, 1940),

■ group dynamics (Lewin, 1946b),

■ group decisions (Lewin, 1947), and

■ ecological aspects of large and small school settings and their influence on student activity (Barker & Gump, 1964).

Relative to the person model, however, the environment model generated barely any true experimentation, probably because it assumes relatively free situations rather than the highly controlled ones demanded for experimental design.

Relations Between the Two Models

It is very difficult to reconcile the person model and the environment model, for the simple reason that their dynamic components do not correspond. The person model is based on tension, the environment model on forces. Technically speaking, it is a question of pressure states within vessels as opposed to an all-encompassing force field. This also means that the apparent similarity in the structure of the regions in the two models is only superficial. Furthermore, the adjacency of regions does not have the same meaning in the two models. In the person model it denotes similarity, in the environment model, means-ends relationships (see also Heider, 1960).

There is, however, one major point of correspondence between the two models – the covarying relationship between the need state of the person (tension system) and the valence of an object or action sphere in the environment. In Lewin's words:

> To a certain extent there is an equivalency between the statements "this or that need exists" and "this or that structural region possesses incentive characteristics for these or those actions". After all, a change in the need produces a corresponding change in the incentive characteristics (Lewin, 1951b, p. 353).

This statement raises the question of whether the need of the person and the valence in the environment are, in fact, two perspectives on the same thing. Does it mean that whenever

there is a need, there is also a valence and, conversely, that a corresponding need can be inferred whenever there is a valence? Or would it not be more appropriate to assume a mutual interaction between cause and effect?

The Meaning of Valence

Lewin holds that whenever there is a valence, there must also be a need. What is questionable is whether the reverse is true. A need can emerge in the absence of opportunities within the environment to satisfy it (i.e., in the absence of objects that can take on valence characteristics). In this case, the environment would include wishful thinking at the level of unreality within the life space. One could then say that every need creates a corresponding valence. But Lewin does not accept the reverse, that a valence creates a need. What he does accept is that a portion of the valence is not dependent on the existing need state, but inherent in the valence object itself. For example, we find some types of food more attractive than others, independent of our hunger state. Therefore, valence (Va) has two determinants:

■ it is a function of the need tensions of the person (t) and

■ the perceived "nature" of the goal object (G): $Va(G) = F(t,G)$; (cf. Lewin, 1938, pp. 106–107).

🛈 Lewin's models do not deal with questions of incentive motivation. Rather, his theory of motivation is restricted to the following processes: A tension system (a need or quasi-need) is somehow created within the person. The tension results (under appropriate circumstances) in a corresponding environmental valence. The valence produces a force field in the environment that initiates and gives direction to the organism's behavior. The behavioral sequence is guided by a means-end structuring of the action paths leading to the goal region. Should the goal be attained, the need is satisfied, the tension system dissipates, the valence disappears along with the force field, and the behavior is terminated.

So what, precisely, is valence? According to Lewin, it is the determinant of the psychological force (f, "force") that pushes or pulls the person (P) toward the goal region (G). Lewin further assumes that this psychological force ($f_{P,G}$) is dependent on the relative positions of the person and the goal region, i.e., the psychological distance. For Lewin this dependence is not invariant. In many cases it would appear that the psychological force decreases with increased psychological distance from the goal region (d, distance; $d_{P,G}$). At least that is what

Fajans (1933) observed in infants and toddlers. Lewin's (1938) formulation reads as follows:

$$f_{P,G} = \frac{Va(G)}{d_{P,G}} = \frac{(t, G)}{d_{P,G}}$$

Psychological force according to this definition would today be labeled **motivational strength** or its **resulting motivational tendency**. It is essentially a function of Lewin's hypothetical construction of valence. Lewin went one step further, combining valence multiplicatively with an expectancy construct, labeled potency (P_o).

Potency is a conceptually somewhat ambiguous construct that plays a role in choice situations. It reflects the extent to which a positive or negative outcome of a choice is salient, which in turn is a function of the perceived likelihood of a positive or negative outcome. In this case, the "effective force" is defined as:

$$\text{effective force} = \frac{Va(G) \times Po(G)}{d_{P,G}}$$

This concept, which was developed in the context of setting **levels of aspiration** (Hoppe, 1930), was the direct predecessor of the theories of motivation that remain dominant to this day, namely, expectancy-value theories.

SUMMARY

Lewin's major achievement was a penetrating conceptual analysis, leading to the identification of the constituent elements of a theory of motivation. To this day, the main weakness of field theory is that both the person and the environment model can generate only postdictive "explanations". There is little in the theory that would allow specific, cogent conditions to be identified in advance, and thus permit reliable predictions of behavior. This weakness arises from the field theorists' neglect to tie their theoretical constructs to observable antecedents and outcomes. How can one specify in each individual case the magnitudes of t or G, valence, psychological distance, and force? What determines the means-ends structure of the action path leading to the goal region? Although the relationships among the hypothetical constructs have been carefully defined, their relationships to observable phenomena have been neglected. This deficiency is particularly apparent when this model is contrasted with those of learning and drive theories.

Another deficiency arises from the neglect of individual differences in dispositional variables. This particularly applies to the constructs t and G. The situational factors (G) capable of eliciting specific motives (t) remain largely unspecified, as does the need to at least delineate the essence of individual motives, if not to classify them. All questions relating to motive dispositions are essentially ignored; not only their classification, but also their activation, measurement, and genesis. The main focus is on matters of motivation – goal-orientation, choice, and conflict – as well as on their impact on behavior. Matters of volition, such as the aftereffects of interrupted tasks, in the form of resumption and substitute tasks, are also considered. Self-regulatory processes of intention forming or action control are not postulated, however, probably because the environment model simply assumes the existence of a cognitive representation of a particular situation, without explaining how it arises, e.g., in terms of the adjacent segments of the action path.

Despite its shortcomings, field theory has contributed significantly to the clarification of motivational issues. Unlike laboratory research, which necessarily tends to take a rather one-sided approach, it uncovered a variety of psychological phenomena in human motivation. Furthermore, it generated a series of experimental paradigms that continue to stimulate and enrich motivational research beyond field theory to this day.

Aftereffects of Incomplete Tasks

In the *Psychopathology of Everyday Life* Freud (1901) collected many examples of the aftereffects of unfulfilled desires, i.e., unrealized actions. Even if these are actively suppressed because of their inappropriate or unacceptable nature, they do not just disappear, but become manifest in a variety of covert forms, in free associations, in dreams, or in slips of the tongue, all of which result in an inadvertent interference with an action sequence. These phenomena are commonly known as **Freudian slips**.

Lewin based his model on similar observations, namely the aftereffects of unfinished tasks. His student Bluma Zeigarnik (1927) provided experimental confirmation of his assumptions (see the following excursus). More recent research on **rumination** has returned to this topic area (see Martin & Tesser, 1989).

Aside from these two classical procedures, task retention and resumption, four further behavioral indicators have since been linked to the aftereffects of unfinished tasks:

1. Choice of tasks to be resumed, i.e., the choice between two tasks presented for a second time, one of which was solved at first presentation, while the other was not (Rosenzweig, 1933, 1945; Coopersmith, 1960).

2. Changes in autonomic responses resulting from a casual reference to unfinished materials, while the respondent is working on another task (Fuchs, 1954). It has been observed that task interruption is accompanied by increased muscle tonus (Freeman, 1930; Smith, 1953; Forrest, 1959).

3. Differences in the recognition threshold for words referring to completed or to interrupted tasks (Postman & Solomon, 1949; Caron & Wallach, 1957).

4. Increased attractiveness of a task following its interruption (Cartwright, 1942; Gebhard, 1948).

Lewin said that the idea of investigating unfinished tasks came to him when he realized that he needed to define the concept of tension in the person model in terms of concrete, experimental operations (cf. Heider, 1960, p. 154). There are

The Zeigarnik Effect

Participants were presented with 16 to 20 different tasks, half of which were interrupted before completion by the introduction of the next task. After the experiment, participants were casually asked which tasks they could remember. The aftereffects of the incomplete tasks were manifested as a better retention of these tasks. This finding became known as the "Zeigarnik effect."

A variation of this experiment was carried out by another of Lewin's students, Maria Ovsiankina (1928). Instead of testing task reten-

tion, Ovsiankina observed the spontaneous resumption of interrupted tasks. To this end, participants were left with the task material while the experimenter left the room under a pretext and covertly observed whether or not the participant resumed the tasks. This approach has the advantage of showing more direct effects of unfinished quasi-needs. It avoids the confounding of the demand to recall, which applies equally to finished and unfinished tasks, with the effects arising from unfinished quasi-needs.

a number of hypotheses that can be derived from the person model, each relating to one of the three defining characteristics of that model, namely:

- the tension state of a region (tension system),
- the regional structuring (e.g., central vs. peripheral; degree of differentiation), and
- the nature of the material (i.e., the permeability of the regional boundaries).

An account of the respective hypotheses and results can be found in Heckhausen (1980, p. 189).

Some findings do not relate to the person model, but can be interpreted within the environment model. Instead of positing an inner-personal tension state, this model assumes a psychological force to pull the person in the direction of a particular action. As we have seen, this force depends on the valence of the action goal (G) and the psychological distance (d), while the valence depends on the need strength (t) and on characteristics of the goal (G) that are unrelated to the person:

$$F = \frac{Va(G)}{d_{P,G}} = \frac{t, G}{d_{P,G}}$$

Zeigarnik found that incomplete tasks that have a definite ending are retained better than indefinite serial tasks (like crossing out particular letters in a text) that are highly repetitive. This could be from a factor G, a characteristic of the goal that is independent of the person and that codetermines the strength of the valence. Another finding can only be explained in terms of the other determinant of psychological force, namely psychological distance, $d_{P,G}$.

❗ The closer someone is to their goal when the interruption occurs, the greater the Zeigarnik effect (Ovsiankina, 1928).

It was also shown that it is not the interruption of the action per se that is responsible for the Zeigarnik effect. The determining factor is the psychological situation as it is perceived by the individual; i.e., whether the goal (e.g., solving a task correctly) is perceived as having been accomplished or not. Marrow (1938) demonstrated this effect through a reversal of the experimental design. He informed his participants that he would interrupt them each time they were on the right

path to a solution, but that he would let them continue if they were not. Under these conditions, participants retained the "finished" failed tasks better than the interrupted (successful) ones (cf. also Junker, 1960).

These are the results that support the theory. There are, however, a large number of studies that did replicate Zeigarnik effects where they would have been predicted. These findings did not cast serious doubt on the validity of the postulated aftereffects, however, or lead to the Zeigarnik effect being viewed as a "now you see it, now you don't" phenomenon. Rather, critical analyses of the experimental conditions in question generally raised and/or confirmed suspicions that the necessary psychological conditions had not been established or that the experimental design was flawed (cf. the analyses by Junker, 1960, and Butterfield, 1964). If, for example, the interrupted tasks are much more difficult than the completed ones, participants can easily gain the impression that they are too difficult or even impossible to solve. Because they do not expect to reach the goal, they reject the interrupted tasks and do not develop a quasi-need to solve them.

Most experimental flaws in this context relate to memory factors. Some settings permit over-learning; in others, participants approach the experiment with the intention to learn, as was observed for some of Zeigarnik's participants. Finished tasks frequently provide more opportunity for rehearsal, because the experimenter allows more time for these tasks (in Abel, 1938, it was six times as long as for the interrupted tasks). Alternatively, the order of presentation may facilitate the retention of finished tasks; e.g., if they occur at the beginning or end of a sequence (e.g., in Alper, 1946, or Sanford & Risser, 1948). Finally, the tasks may be overly homogeneous, resulting in the formation of a region that inhibits reproduction.

Complications of the Zeigarnik Effect

Zeigarnik's method entails serious complications for a psychology of memory. Any memory task involves, in three sequential processes:

1. information uptake (learning),
2. storage, and
3. retrieval of stored information (reproduction).

The last two phases of storage and retrieval involve memory. The Zeigarnik effect is assumed to be a phenomenon of memory, rather than of learning. To demonstrate the effect, one would, strictly speaking, first have to show that the finished and unfinished tasks are learned equally well in the acquisition phase, before showing that interruption during the storage process results in differential "fates" for the respective memory traces, which, when recalled, produce the Zeigarnik effect. It is difficult to exclude the possibility that the interrupted tasks are simply learned better in the first place. This would require a test of memory to be implemented before the participant gains the impression of having finished the task (or not). It would, however, be possible to redefine the Zeigarnik effect as a phenomenon of learning, rather than of memory (storage and retrieval). Results indicating that completion of an interrupted task prior to the reproduction phase (retrieval) has no effect on the superior retention of the task but would then represent a serious challenge to the theory of tension systems.

Caron and Wallach (1959) tried to do just that (see the example).

EXAMPLE

Caron and Wallach (1959) informed a group of study participants that they had been misled, and that the unfinished tasks were in fact impossible to solve. According to Lewin's reasoning, these tasks would then be seen as completed, and the experimental group should no longer be able to reproduce them any better than the uninterrupted tasks – in contrast to a control group that was not offered this quasi-therapeutic explanation. However, the data showed that both groups retained approximately the same amount of interrupted material, indicating that there was selective learning during the acquisition phase.

It would appear that the determining factor for the memory trace is not the tension system and its subsequent release, but selective learning during the acquisition phase. But can these results really be said to disprove Lewin's theory of the tension system? Were the interrupted tasks and their associated quasi-needs really as "finished" or discharged as their completed counterparts? Might it not be the case that the explanation given by the experimenter prior to reproduction refreshed the unfinished material, or that the effect of the tension release was offset by an additional learning effect? Because Caron and Wallach found no Zeigarnik effect for the control group, it seems likely that the explanation given to the experimental group provided an additional aid to retention.

Findings that appeared to contradict the hypothesis that the Zeigarnik effect increases in strength as a function of stronger quasi-needs soon began to accumulate as well. A number of studies showed that the more the tasks took on the significance of a test, the more likely the effect was to disap-

pear or become reversed (e.g., Rosenzweig, 1941, 1943; Alper, 1946, 1957; Smock, 1957; Green, 1963). From the perspective of psychoanalytic repression theory, Rosenzweig explained this effect as being a self-defense tendency – despite his observation that increased pressure to perform results in an increased retention of finished tasks, rather than in a decreased retention of unfinished ones (cf. Glixman, 1948; Sears, 1950). All in all, findings are inconsistent and remain confusing. There are also a number of studies showing that test conditions increase the Zeigarnik effect (e.g., Marrow, 1938; Sanford & Risser, 1948; Rösler, 1955; Junker, 1960). Within field theory, it would be quite possible to explain self-defense tendencies as being intervening effects of a central need that cause the Zeigarnik effect to disappear.

STUDY

Zeigarnik Effect or Shielding Self-Esteem?
A Decision Experiment

Participants in studies by Beckmann and colleagues (Beckmann, 1996; Beckmann et al., 2004) were administered an ego-involving intelligence test. For one half of the tasks, they received the feedback "completed successfully" after each task; for the other half, the feedback was "not completed successfully." In one condition, the experimenter induced the motivation for positive self-presentation by explaining that participants were being asked to write down the tasks they had worked on as a basis for the subsequent discussion of their intelligence scores. Participants in the second condition were simply asked to recall the tasks they had worked on. The classic Zeigarnik effect was observed in the latter condition, with participants recalling more unsolved than solved tasks. In the self-presentation condition, the effect was reversed. As a second experiment showed, however, this self-presentation effect only seems to be observed when recall is measured in terms of criteria that can be consciously influenced, such as listing tasks in a test of recall. In other experiments, activation of the tasks was measured in terms of responses that were not subject to conscious control. After completing the test, participants in these experiments were shown tasks they had attempted as well as tasks that had not been administered. They were asked to specify which tasks had been featured in the test, and which had not. The dependent variable was the time taken to make the correct choice. Participants in the non-self-presentation condition recognized unsolved tasks quicker than the tasks they had solved. The unsolved tasks were evidently still more strongly activated than the unsolved tasks. With decision latency as tthe dependent variable, however, the effect was not reversed in the self-presentation condition. Here, too, participants recognized unsolved tasks more quickly than solved tasks. These findings indicate, in fact, that the self-presentation effect is derived from conscious processes of evaluation, and that – independent of this effect – incomplete tasks always remain more strongly activated than completed tasks, as indeed predicted by Lewin's assumption of tension systems.

Greenwald's (1982) work on the Zeigarnik effect is based on the same logic. He assumes, under ego-involving conditions, that a noncompletion of tasks is seen as failure, meaning that the memory of unfinished tasks threatens the maintenance of a positive self-concept. Accordingly, people are more likely to remember completed tasks (successes) than incomplete ones (failures). Beckmann et al. (2004; Beckmann, 1996) tested these assumptions experimentally (see the decision experiment in the study box on previous page).

Individual differences also have a role to play in the Zeigarnik effect. Zeigarnik had already observed stronger effects for "ambitious" than for "nonambitious" participants.

At first, individual differences were used merely as post hoc explanations based on behavioral differences observed during the experiments. Soon, however, researchers began to select groups of participants on the basis of characteristics such as "ego strength" (Alper, 1946, 1957), "need for recognition" (Mittag, 1955), "self-esteem" (Worchel, 1957; Freud; Coopersmith, 1960), and, above all, "achievement motive" (Atkinson, 1953; Moulton, 1958; Heckhausen, 1963b; Weiner, 1965a).

❶ Individuals with a strong, success-oriented achievement motive generally show a stronger Zeigarnik effect than those with a weak, failure-oriented motive.

Substitute Actions

The aftereffects of unfinished tasks also include the possibility of satisfying unsatisfied needs through **substitute actions** that are similar to, or derived from, the unfinished task. Here again, it was Freud who in 1915 first called attention to this form of aftereffect (Freud, 1952). And again it was Lewin (1932) who initiated its experimental analysis. Although inspired by Freud, he was dissatisfied with Freud's speculative inferences based on individual clinical observations.

Lewin analyzed the conditions under which unfinished tasks lose their aftereffects through completion of another task. The intervening activity can be said to have "substitute value" for the original task. Ovsiankina's experimental paradigm of spontaneous **resumption** was ideal for this investigation. The experimenter simply inserts a task that can be completed between the interruption and the resumption of the original task. If the original, interrupted task was resumed, the intervening activity did not have substitute value; if it was not resumed, substitute value can then be inferred.

Again, it was the person model from which the hypotheses were derived, specifically, from its two postulates. First, the relative permeability of the regional boundaries permits an equalization of tension between neighboring regions. Second, the adjacency of regions defines the level of similarity of the respective goals and activities. This would suggest that a release of a tension system is most likely to occur through completion of a similar activity. If region A is a tension system, some of the tension will then flow into neighboring region B. The differential tension is thus equalized.

EXCURSUS

Substitute Actions – Substitute Value of Actions

Lissner interrupted children who were kneading clay figures and asked them to make another figure. The substitute value of the intervening task generally increased as a function of the similarity of the two tasks. One important dimension of similarity proved to be task difficulty level. If the substitute activity was easier than the interrupted task, it had little substitute value, but if it was more difficult, its substitute value was very high, i.e., there was little interest in resuming the original task. Situational factors relating to the individual's action goals also proved to have a strong influence on the substitute value of a task. If, for example, someone wants to construct something for a particular person but, before its completion, is told to construct the same thing for another person, the second task has little substitute value (Adler & Kounin, 1939). The same applies when the experimenter introduces a similar activity, but gives it a completely different label (Lissner, 1933).

Mahler varied substitute activities in terms of their level of reality, i.e., thinking about finishing the task, talking about how to finish it, and actually finishing it. She found that substitute value increased with the degree of reality of the intervening activity or, more specifically, with its level of appropriateness to the interrupted task. (For example, thinking has a higher reality level for problem solving than for motor action.)

Mahler's studies inspired a strand of research focused on the concept of **symbolic self-completion** (Wicklund & Gollwitzer, 1982). Instead of interrupting tasks and leaving them incomplete, the goals, attributes, and competencies inherent in the participant's self-definition were challenged. Individuals who had thus been "made incomplete" now grasped at every opportunity, even if it were only symbolic, to present themselves as "self-completed."

Henle carried out extensive studies attempting to explain substitute value in terms of the environment model rather than the person model, particularly in regards to the relative valences of the interrupted and the substitute activities. In her studies, participants first rated the attractiveness of various activities. Based on these data, Henle generated various combinations of attractive and nonattractive, interrupted and substitute tasks. She found that if the valence of the substitute activity is lower than that of the interrupted activity, the substitute value is low, approaching zero. Conversely, the greater the valence of the intervening activity, the greater its substitute value.

The conditions under which another activity takes on substitute value were investigated primarily by three of Lewin's students (see the excursus below): Lissner (1933), Mahler (1933), and Henle (1944).

5.4.1 Tolman's Analysis of Goal-Directed Behavior

Lewin's explanatory model proceeds from the present conditions in the total situation: the valences within the environment and the structuring of the life space in terms of potential actions leading to the goal. He supposes the prior existence of valences and expectations (response-consequence contingencies), but pays little attention to the questions of how these might be objectified or how they are generated. The restructuring of an individual's life space at any moment in time may have some validity in the case of an empathic relationship between the experimenter and that individual, although even this would not be acceptable to the behaviorists because of its mentalistic nature. When dealing with children or animals, however, the lack of a firm foundation for explanatory concepts, such as valences, incentives, and expectations, is immediately apparent. Doubts may arise about the presence of a particular explanatory factor and its actual effect.

Expectancy and Goal Orientation

Tolman, independent of Lewin, arrived at a rather similar explanatory model in the late 1920s, based on behavior observed in rats. Although Tolman was committed to behaviorism, he believed that nonobservable cognitive processes played an important role in directing an organism's behavior. Instead of simply presupposing such cognitive processes mentalistically, however, he attempted to translate them into observable events, i.e., to expose these internal, nonobservable events by tying them to the antecedent conditions and subsequent outcomes, both of which are observable. Thus, Tolman became the first theorist to define intervening variables in terms of hypothetical constructs, and to recognize the need to anchor them to operations and observations (Chapter 2). Does a rat in a maze know the shortest route to the food box, i.e., have expectations about response-consequence contingencies (R–S^*)? If one follows Tolman in drawing connections between the following observations and operations, the answer is yes:

> Consider a rat, which has completely learned a maze, so that when put in at the entrance, he dashes through like a shot, turning here, there, and yonder, entering no blind alleys and arriving at the food box in only some 4 or 5 seconds from the start. Suppose, now, one of the alleys be considerably shortened between trials. What happens? On the trial after, the animal runs kerplunk into the new end

of the alley. In short, he acts as if the old length of the alley were still going to be present. His behavior postulates, expects, makes a claim for that old length (Tolman, 1926, p. 356).

Tolman pursued a "psychological behaviorism." What distinguished him from other contemporary learning theorists, and brought him closer to Lewin's formulations, were three related approaches to the explanation of behavior (see below).

Tolman's Psychological Behaviorist Perspective on Behavior

1. Molar behavioral units should be observed in preference to molecular ones. It is not single muscle twitches or glandular secretions that signal goal orientation and purpose, but global sequences of behavior.

2. The premature reduction of behavior to physiological and neurological bases contributes little to behavioral explanations if psychological aspects remain unexamined and unspecified.

3. Because behavior is always oriented toward a goal object or goal state, it must be viewed and analyzed in terms of goal orientation.

Tolman insisted that the postulate of goal orientation does not have to remain a mentalistic and highly abstract concept, but that it can be objectified in terms of various aspects of behavior. Indeed, he studied three aspects of goal orientation extensively: **persistence**, **docility**, and **selectivity**. Persistence implies "persistence until," i.e., perseverating until a particular object or state has been reached. Docility means increased learning over time in identical or similar situations. Selectivity implies spontaneous behavior that is not influenced by external pressures; the preference for a particular behavioral option in the face of several choices.

Tolman's approach provided new insights on Thorndike's "law of effect" (Chapter 2), which had, until then, been seen purely as a learning principle.

Because **operant learning** was viewed as dependent on the outcome, the success, the satisfaction of a need, and because the learning process itself was seen as nothing more than an association between stimuli and responses (although this represents a purely hypothetical conceptualization or a quasi-neurological speculation), the motivational conditions of the observed changes in behavior (learning) continued to be ignored. Classical learning experiments were designed to demonstrate the learning process in terms of objectively observable behavior, as measurable performance. There seemed to be no need to distinguish between learning and behavior. Indeed, no clear distinction was made between motivation and learning until Tolman presented the findings of his research.

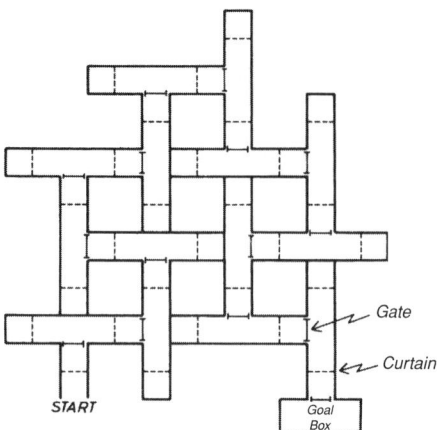

Figure 5.3 Layout of a 14-part T-maze.

Incentive Effects

The narrowly conceived stimulus-response approach was incompatible with Tolman's program of behaviorism, which emphasized the molar and goal-oriented aspects of behavior. Is learning really nothing more than the "stamping in" of static stimulus-response bonds? Could it not also involve the formation of internally represented **cognitive maps** that mediate expectations about what leads to what? Must behavior necessarily be viewed as the final step in a learning program in which the organism is, so to speak, pushed from behind? Could it not be that the organism is more freely pulled toward the goal, guided more flexibly along the way by means-ends expectations, without diversions (i.e., trial and error)?

In the 1920s, some researchers – primarily from Tolman's group – began to vary the incentive characteristics of a goal. These variations resulted in abrupt changes in behavior, totally inconsistent with the notion of a gradual learning process. Behavior and learning now became separate entities, and it was possible to separate the experimental analysis of behavior from learning. In his book *Purposive Behavior in Animals and Men* (1932), Tolman integrated these results into a theory of incentives and expectations. Before considering the individual studies, let us look at the experimental apparatus used in these learning experiments, namely the T-maze. As shown in Fig. 5.3, this maze consists of a number of interconnected T-shaped pathways, one branch leading to a new T-shaped section, the other forming a blind alley.

EXPERIMENTAL EVIDENCE FOR INCENTIVE EFFECTS. An early series of investigations looked at the behavioral effects of different incentive strengths. The first of these investigations dates back to 1924. At that time there was great interest in determining the effect of need strength on activity using the **Columbia Obstruction Box** (Chapter 4, Fig. 4.2). One shortcoming of these studies was that the incentive value of the goal

object was inadequately controlled. Simmons (1924) was the first to focus on incentive factors. She found that the speed of maze learning varies with the incentive value of the food in the goal box. The animals were all equally hungry at the time of the experiment, and did not receive their daily food ration until a few hours after the experiment, when returned to their cages. Before each trial, the rats were permitted a quick nibble on the food in the goal box. They were then placed in the start box. It emerged that the rats' running speed increased and error rate decreased more rapidly in trials with bread soaked in milk than in trials with sunflower seeds. This difference in incentive effect permits two interpretations. Either stronger incentives facilitate more rapid learning; or learning is identical under both incentive conditions, but a lower incentive value of the goal results in a reduced motivation to reach it. The first explanation would be consistent with Hull's (later) reinforcement theory; the second, with Tolman's postulate that – along with the present level of learning – the strength of the demand for the goal object, which derives from incentive strength, directly determines behavior.

The experimental findings of Elliott (1928) provided support for the latter interpretation. Elliot varied the incentive value in learning experiments with rats, and found an increase in the error rate following the switchover to a lesser food incentive. This effect was not attributable to unlearning, but could only be the result of a motivational effect that was unrelated to learning. This implies that learning is not synonymous with behavior and that a distinction must be made between learning and performance. It is clear that the incentive value of the goal object can have an independent effect on behavior.

Latent Learning: The Distinction Between Learning and Motivation

The extreme case of incentive variation is its total absence. In this case, there is no reinforcement and goal-oriented behavior cannot be expected. Can learning still take place under these conditions? Blodgett (1929) was the first to show that it can. In his so-called **latent learning** experiment, three groups of hungry rats were placed in a maze once a day for nine consecutive days. The first group found food in the goal box from the first day on, the second from the third day on, and the third from the seventh day on. As soon as the animal had reached the goal box it was allowed to eat for three minutes (under "food" conditions) or left in the goal box for two minutes before being removed (under "no-food" conditions). Fig. 5.4 shows the rapid decrease in the error rate following the introduction of food in the second and third groups. Both groups immediately reached the performance level obtained by the first group, which had been reinforced from the outset. Tolman and Honzik (1930) later confirmed these findings.

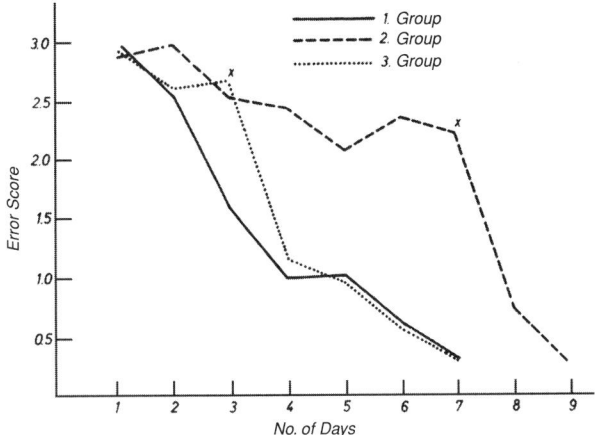

Figure 5.4 The effects of latent learning and of delayed introduction of reinforcement on performance level. Group 1 was given a food reward on every trial. In Group 2, on day 3 (at the points marked *x*); in Group 3, the food reward was not introduced until day 7. (After Blodgett, 1929, p. 120.)

These findings represent a case of learning without reinforcement. Hence, reinforcement cannot be a necessary condition of learning. Learning can remain latent, i.e., not necessarily immediately manifested in behavior. In this particular case, learning must have involved the acquisition of knowledge about the pathways in the maze rather than the establishment of fixed stimulus-response bonds, because the goal-oriented behavior, an efficient approach to the goal, did not occur prior to the introduction of food.

Performance of a learned response becomes observable only if it serves to achieve a goal, i.e., in the presence of motivation. Thus, Thorndike's **law of effect** is not a principle of learning, but of performance. Learning outcomes only manifest themselves in behavior in the presence of motivation and learning, both of which are separate conditional factors.

The goal-oriented motivational state can be enacted only through previously learned responses. That is shown by the difference in the performance of the second and third groups. Seven opportunities to explore the maze led to more efficient goal attainment than three such opportunities.

❶ Thus, behavior is explained by the interaction of two intervening variables, a learning factor and a motivation factor.

The learning factor, according to Tolman, involves knowledge about which path leads to the next maze segment. Under appropriate conditions, this knowledge leads to a goal expectation in the form of response-consequence contingencies. The motivation factor is the demand for the goal, which is dependent on the physiological need state or drive, and on the incentive value of the goal object (i.e., Tolman treated drive and incentive as more or less equal, and did not consider their differential effects or interrelationships). Tolman's two intervening variables, goal expectation and demand for the goal, are not only cognitive in nature, but can also mediate between observable, antecedent conditions and subsequent behavior in a way that permits an explanation of goal-oriented behavior. Fig. 5.5 illustrates the logic of this theoretical formulation.

Belief-Value Matrix

Tolman (1951, 1959) later expanded his theory of motivation to postulate that, apart from need states, there are two intervening cognitive variables that motivate a particular behavior, namely, belief and value. Value equals the incentive of the goal object, the other component of the demand for the goal alongside need (or drive). The two variables, belief and value, are usually not independent, but are linked within a "belief-value matrix" in established systems of beliefs. As a rule, there are a number of possible response-consequence contingencies (*R–S**) leading to the satisfaction of a particular need state, i.e., expectations about choices of action, on the one hand, and accompanying goal states (*S**) of varying value, on the other.

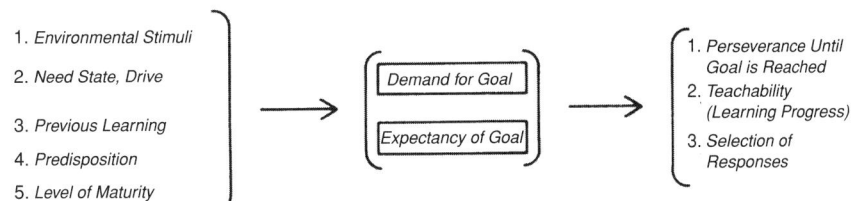

Figure 5.5 Tolman's theoretical construction of two motivational intervening variables: demand for the goal and goal expectation. The variables are conceived to mediate between antecedent, observable conditions and subsequently observable aspects of the goal directedness of molar behavior.

EXAMPLE

This applies particularly in situations involving choices, e.g., a hungry person choosing between two restaurants serving food of differing quality and price on the basis of preferences and pocketbook. The choice between the restaurants and their respective menus involves not only anticipatory choices of action, but also decisions about value. Fig. 5.6 shows the belief-value matrix for a person in such a situation. Tolman's matrix implies an action sequence between the present hunger state (left) and need satisfaction (right). The circuitous lines with arrows indicate the action sequences contemplated; the size of the plus sign denotes the value of each restaurant (means) and the food served there (goal object). All four restaurants offer the most preferred dishes *a* and *b*, but items *c*, *d*, and *e* (although not *f*) would also gratify the person's hunger.

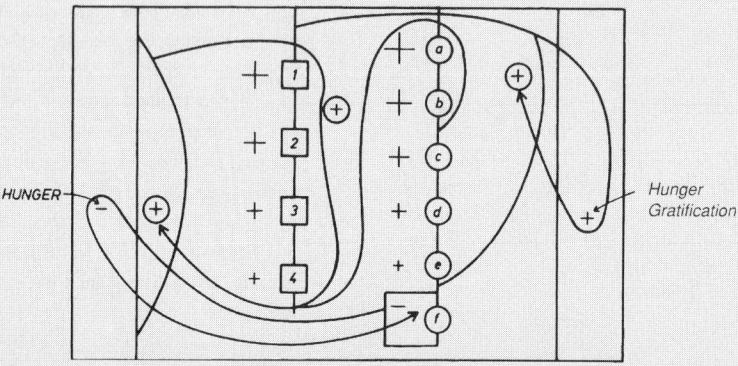

Figure 5.6 Example of a belief-value matrix: cognitive anticipations in the choice between restaurants of different quality (and price) and different dishes in the presence of hunger. (After Tolman, 1952, p. 392.)

5.4.2 Hull's Learning Theory Conception of Motivation

Hull examined whether it was possible to explain motivation in terms of learned stimulus-response bonds, without reference to cognitive variables.

He was particularly interested in whether expectations can be conceptualized within S–R theory. Pavlov's data on classical conditioning, which had been translated into English at the end of the 1920s, offered some clues. Pavlov had shown that previously neutral stimuli could take on a signaling function for impending events. As can be seen in behaviors like salivation, these stimuli seem to create something that is analogous to "knowledge" about the future. There is anticipatory preparation for the actual goal response (eating), although the actual goal object (food) is not yet present. Therefore, there can be no goal response and certainly no goal state (satiation). If one now assumes that the response (R_1) that follows an external stimulus (S_1) brings about a proprioceptive feedback, i.e., results in an internal stimulus (s_1), then this inner stimulus can occur in temporal contiguity with the next external stimulus (S_2), which in turn elicits R_2. Thus, s_1 immediately precedes R_2 and may be associated with it. In the long run, S_1 might suffice to elicit the entire chain of responses, mediated via the internal stimuli produced by these responses. Note that the strengths of the S_n–R_n bonds increase with greater proximity to the goal; the chain is assembled from the end.

Fig. 5.7a–d shows the stages of these associations via internal stimuli.

Thus, a response sequence can literally short-circuit itself via these self-generated, response-dependent, internal stimuli, which can maintain behavior independent of further external stimulation. A conditioned chain of responses of this kind can run its course very quickly, usually faster than the chain of stimuli that represent the changes in the environment in the run-up to the goal. The response sequence is

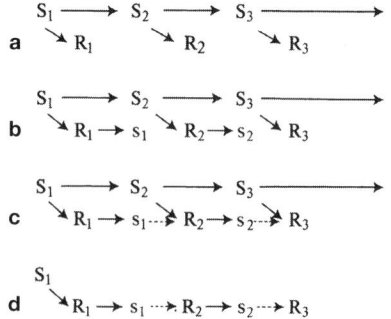

Figure 5.7a–d Basic pattern of how a response sequence (R_1 to R_3) can short-circuit itself via intervening, internal, i.e., response-dependent stimuli (s_1, s_2), thus no longer requiring the external triggering stimulus.

faster than the stimulus sequence; R_3 occurs prior to S_3. In other words:

❶ Events within the organism precede environmental events. This is how the organism can respond to something that has not yet occurred in reality. This is the theoretical basis for **anticipation** (cf. Hoffmann's concept of anticipatory behavioral control: Hoffmann, 1993; Butz & Hoffmann, 2002; Kunde, Koch, & Hoffmann, 2004).

FRACTIONAL ANTICIPATORY GOAL RESPONSES. Along with internal stimuli (as proprioceptive feedback), Hull developed a further concept in his search for an S–R formulation of goal expectations that guide behavior. It was to become even more important to the development of his theory, particularly the part dealing with incentive effects. It concerns a salient group of pure stimulus acts: **fractional anticipatory goal responses**, or r_G–s_G mechanisms. Like Freud before him, Hull assumed that a need state is accompanied by a drive stimulus (S_D) until it becomes satiated. Because the drive stimulus endures, it becomes associated with the whole sequence of responses leading to the goal response. Eventually, the drive stimulus is able to elicit the goal response immediately. It would be premature to trigger the full goal response at this point, however, because it would interfere with the necessary instrumental responses that lead to the goal and provide the basis for a successful goal response. According to the law of effect, such anticipatory goal responses would rapidly be extinguished. What remains is a fragment of the actual goal response, which does not interfere with instrumental responses like biting, chewing, and swallowing (goal response), salivation, licking, and similar components of the eating process.

It is crucial that this fragmentary goal response (r_G) is elicited by the drive stimulus very early on, and that it can, in one leap, bypass the entire chain of responses that has yet to lead to the goal response (R_G). Like all responses, it also results in proprioceptive feedback, S_G, an internal stimulus that Hull calls the goal stimulus. This internal goal stimulus represents the goal event, the satisfaction of the need. Like the drive stimulus, it is present during the entire behavior sequence, accompanying each intervening response. It can therefore serve as the basis for what Tolman called the goal expectation that anticipates behavioral outcomes and guides behavior toward its goal.

It was Crespi (1942, 1944) who provided experimental data showing that Hull's new S–R theoretical formulations could not solve the incentive problem. Rather, he saw incentive as an independent motivational phenomenon. Crespi varied the amount of food given to a hungry rat at the end of a straight runway. Rats provided with more food ran faster in the first 19 trials than those given less food. Fig. 5.8 shows how the plateau of running performance differs in the two incentive conditions. Under both conditions, maximum speed is

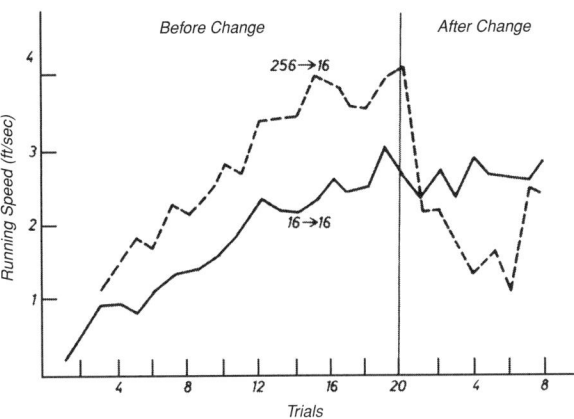

Figure 5.8 Running speed as a function of the amount of food reward. For the first 19 trials, one group of rats was given 16 pellets, the other 256 pellets. From trial 20 on, all were given 16 pellets. (After Crespi, 1942, fig. 2, p. 488, fig. 8, p. 508.)

reached after an equal number of trials, meaning that both groups must have acquired the same habit strength.

Thus far, the findings are congruent with Hull's reinforcement theory. Now, however, Crespi changed the amount of food dispensed to some of the rats. Fig. 5.8 shows the effect of the change from too much to too little food. The high-reward group shows an abrupt decrease in running speed to the level of the low-reward group and even lower. This sudden change in behavior cannot be explained in terms of association theory. Crespi's findings were confirmed by Zeaman (1949), who found that reversing the amount of food reward from .05 to 2.4 grams resulted in a complete reversal of latencies to the level of the high-reward group.

Spence's Extension of Hull's Model

Spence returned to Hull's original concept of the r_G–s_G mechanism. According to Hull's conception, the fractional anticipatory goal response only becomes associated with the drive stimulus (S_D). Spence postulated that it also forms an association with external stimuli (S) and internal, proprioceptive stimuli (s). The anticipatory goal response can now be elicited by the corresponding stimuli and, in turn, serve as a motivator, i.e., increase the strength of the instrumental responses elicited by a particular situation. The anticipatory goal response has thus become an **energizing incentive motivation**.

Spence postulated that anticipatory goal responses could elicit tension states and conflicts that would have a general, nonspecific motivational effect. The true nature of the anticipatory goal response remains clouded to this day. Attempts to observe and record it have been unsuccessful (cf. Bolles, 1967, pp. 352ff.). Because Spence assigned to anticipatory goal responses the status of intervening variables, however, whether or not they are accessible to direct observation is arguably immaterial.

In contrast to Hull, Spence combined the two motivational factors D and K in an additive, not multiplicative manner, resulting in the excitatory potential (E; which is equivalent to Hull's response potential, $_SE_R$; see also Chapter 2):

$$E = (D + K) \times H$$

A number of findings confirm the validity of this modification to the theory (e.g., Reynolds & Anderson, 1961). Another of Spence's modifications to Hull's model, however, was more decisive. Spence (1956) totally abandoned the reinforcement theory of habit formation. For him, the strength of an S–R bond was simply a function of the frequency of association, i.e., contiguity. Reinforcing events – their frequency, strength, nature, and their immediacy or delay – now contribute directly to the level of incentive motivation, K, which is manifested in the fractional anticipatory goal response (r_G–s_G).

This formulation provides a better basis for explaining incentive effects and latent learning than does Hull's earlier revision. The effectiveness of reinforcing events is no longer related to the gradual build up or decrement of habits. After all, it was precisely this sluggishness of the learning process that could not be reconciled with the abruptness of incentive effects. Now the change in incentive value, as manifested by the reinforcing events, is immediately imparted to all responses elicited by the situation via the motivating function of the r_G–s_G mechanism. The r_G–s_G mechanism itself is elicited by the relevant stimuli (external, proprioceptive, and drive stimuli), as in classical conditioning, as a function of their similarity with the actual goal stimulus (S_G). An increase in the temporal or spatial distance from the goal results in a stimulus generalization gradient; i.e., the relevant stimuli lose their similarity to the goal stimulus as distance increases, thereby resulting in a corresponding decrease in the motivational effects of the anticipatory goal responses. Spence's extension of S–R theory into a theory of incentive motivation brings it very close to the conceptualizations of Lewin and Tolman. Viewed in terms of an S–R model, Spence's r_G–s_G mechanism and Tolman's SR–S or R–S^* concepts are closely related.

5.4.3 More Recent Developments

There are many findings and other phenomena that have prompted researchers in motivation to give preference to incentive theories of one kind or another over drive and reinforcement theories (see the following excursus). An examination of the postulates of drive theory presented in Chapter 4 shows that several findings are equally or better explained by incentive theories. The findings of experiments attempting to differentiate among drives, where an animal is given choices corresponding to its relevant drive states, are one example. This choice behavior might be attributable to incentive effects, i.e., anticipatory goal responses, rather than to specific drive stimuli. The revisions of S–R theory by Hull and Spence raise the question of the extent to which energizing effects can be attributed to K.

Various sets of findings reported in Chapter 4 are consistent with Spence's idea that incentive effects result in increased **activation**. There must be a relationship between the strength of the consummatory response (R_G) and the strength of the instrumental response leading to it, because the latter is activated by the r_G, which anticipates the R_G. Sheffield, Roby, and Campbell (1954) confirmed this assumption. Their rats were rewarded with solutions of different sweetness and nutritional value (saccharin or dextrose). The results show an amazingly robust correlation between the amount of liquid consumed and running speed.

Walker's Analysis of the Explanatory Concepts of Learning Theory

Walker (1969) assigned the concepts of learning theory to four categories of hypothetical constructs:

1. Push: including explanatory concepts such as drive, motive, activation, tension, etc.

2. Pull: including valence, incentive, etc.

3. Structure: including cognitive organization, knowledge, habit, strength, etc.

4. Glue: including reinforcement in the sense of a hypothetical process that elicits and reinforces S–R bonds. Where reinforcement implies a goal state representing the satisfaction of a need, it belongs to the "pull" category, along with the concepts of incentive and valence.

Only three of the four categories of concepts are (or can be) manipulated by controlling the antecedent conditions: push through deprivation of need satisfaction, pull through the established incentive value (attractiveness) of a goal object, and structure through previous experience, i.e., the number of learning trials. By contrast, response reinforcement represents a hypothetical process, taking place between two hypothetical constructs. In a manner of speaking, the pull concept exudes a kind of glue within the structure that bonds a response increasingly strongly to a stimulus. Fig. 5.9 illustrates these relationships.

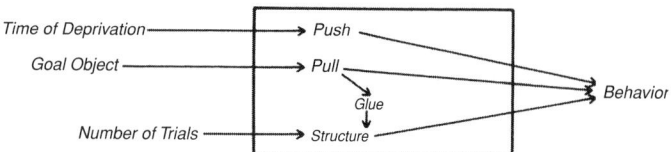

Figure 5.9 Walker's four categories of explanatory concepts of learning theory, one of which ("glue," reinforcement) is superfluous. (After Walker, 1969, p. 51.)

EXCURSUS

Sheffield's Theory of Incentive Motivation

In his theory of incentive motivation, Sheffield goes one step beyond Spence and toward Lewin and Tolman. For him, incentive motivation has a specific, albeit somewhat indirect orienting function. Sheffield assumes that a need state in a situation that is not yet a goal situation can elicit a number of response tendencies. Via proprioceptive stimuli, these arouse fractional goal responses (r_G) of differing strength. The more this occurs in connection with one of the response tendencies, the higher the associated arousal level of that response tendency will become, until it finally brings about a situation in which the goal response (R_G) can occur.

This and similar arguments all lead to the two fundamental questions about the postulates of S–R theory that are raised by every theory of incentive motivation:

1. Is it really necessary to assume two motivational factors, drive and incentive, or can incentive encompass drive?
2. Is the postulate about the habit-forming effects of reinforcement not, in fact, superfluous?

With respect to the first question, drive remains as a variable of need state, but it becomes a determining condition for the strength of the incentive motivation itself.

Seward (1942, 1951) was the first S–R theorist to move in this direction. He spoke of the "externalization of drive" via r_G mechanisms of incentive motivation. Incentive motivation suffices to select and activate appropriate responses, which are elicited by stimuli that have formed an associative bond with the reinforcing goal response.

Two former students of Hull, McClelland, and Mowrer, based their theoretical models on the motivating properties of "excitement," which had previously been emphasized by Sheffield and Young. They endowed it with an emotional component, turning it into an emotion of expectancy. The positions of these authors are outlined in Chapter 2. In an abridged version of McClelland's definition, motivation is defined as an expectation of a previously experienced change in an affectively meaningful situation. This motivating expectancy is elicited by a stimulus cue that partially reactivates the earlier meaningful situation (cf. McClelland et al., 1953).

Mowrer (1960) lists four types of emotions of expectancy (hope, fear, disappointment, and relief) that guide as well as activate behavior. Drive is no longer required, either for the reinforcement of instrumental responses, or for their activation, but it still retains one important function. Its reduction as well as its induction serve to condition the emotions of expectancy. External as well as internal stimulus cues can elicit these emotions. They intensify the sequence of instrumental responses occurring in the run-up to the goal, increasing hope and decreasing fear. Thus, from the inception of a response, there are positive or negative expectancies, mediated by proprioceptive feedback and resulting in reinforcement or inhibition. However, in all this, Mowrer did not answer the question of how an instrumental response is activated before it is intensified or muted by an expectancy.

These and other concepts of incentive and expectancy, as well as their regulatory mechanisms, were incorporated in Heckhausen's (1963a) "systematic theory of motivation." This theory does not use the language of S–R theory; its central concept is the affectively charged "gradient of expectation," which is assumed to motivate approach or avoidance.

The question is now whether reinforcement as a "glue" concept is necessary for explaining changes in behavior. Does a behavior that is followed by reinforcement (in the sense of a need satisfaction) change more than a behavior that is not followed by such reinforcement? If so, can such change not be explained by the constructs of the other three categories of push, pull, and structure? Walker asserts that changes in structure (learning) can always be adequately explained by these three categories, making reinforcement as a glue a superfluous concept. For example, the disappearance of a learned response under conditions of extinction is most parsimoniously explained in terms of the absence of a previous incentive object. There is no longer any pull. Extinction is gradual because the incentive value of situational factors previously associated with the goal object has to be unlearned.

Walker cites a number of findings in support of the assertion that the glue construct is superfluous. Aside from the findings on latent learning and incentive change, he also points to findings showing that habit strength – contrary to the main postulate of reinforcement theory – does not remain at the same level under conditions of continuous reinforcement, but decreases and eventually disappears. The response frequency approaches zero, despite the fact that each occurrence of the particular response has been reinforced.

❶ Walker not only sought to demonstrate that the glue effect of reinforcement remains unvalidated, he also pointed to the need to develop far more complex dependent variables to account for any glue effect between pull and structure.

Bolles' Cognitive Model of Incentive Motivation

Bolles, who was initially (1967) an adherent of the reinforcement view of motivation, later came to prefer a cognitive model based on incentive theory (1972). For him, reinforcement was neither a necessary nor a sufficient condition for instrumental learning. What is learned are not S–R bonds, but two types of expectations:

- The first type of expectation relates to contingencies of external events and their consequences (S–S*; i.e., stimulus-consequence contingencies).

■ The second type relates to contingencies of one's own actions and their consequences ($R–S^*$; i.e., action-consequence contingencies).

The introduction of reinforcement simply provides an opportunity for the learning of both types of expectations. Bolles' model, which was derived from $S–R$ oriented learning research, is more advanced than the other models, and is largely congruent with cognitive approach theories of motivation. It is therefore worth examining this approach to the explanation of behavior, which Bouton and Fanselow (1997) label **functional behaviorism,** in more detail. In examining the reinforcement concept, we must first distinguish (as in Walker's critical analysis) between its two different meanings: reinforcement as an event (manipulated by the experimenter) and reinforcement as a process (habit formation), designated here as the "reinforcement mechanism."

Reinforcing events are often followed by behavior that looks like the kind of learning attributed to the reinforcement mechanism. There are numerous reports of observations, however, where this is not the case. Either there is no learning following reinforcement or, conversely, learning occurs more rapidly or suddenly than can be accounted for by the reinforcement mechanism. Let us look at some of the evidence cited by Bolles. Breland and Breland (1961) reported reinforcement without learning effects in cases of what they called "misbehavior" in animals. Both Brelands were students of Skinner. They sought to apply the principles of operant conditioning to the training of circus animals (see example). These attempts met with remarkable difficulties and failures in various species.

EXAMPLE

For example, a raccoon had learned to take a wooden coin to a piggy bank and deposit it there. This learned behavior broke down completely, however, when it was supposed to be carried out with two coins. Instead, a species-specific food-seeking behavior was initiated. The raccoon rubbed the two coins together, half-inserted them into the piggy bank, and then pulled them out again. This behavior became so dominant that further training had to be abandoned.

One example of learning that occurs too rapidly to be attributed to the reinforcement mechanism is known as "autoshaping." As part of their training, many psychology students used to have to train a pigeon to peck a disc for a food reward. This can usually be accomplished within an hour by rewarding closer and closer approximations to the desired response. But more recent studies show that these students could have saved themselves a lot of effort. All one needs to do is to make the operation of the feeder contingent on the desired pecking response, and to present the pigeon with food every now and then, regardless of what it is doing at that moment (Brown & Jenkins, 1968). Pecking, particularly

pecking an optically distinct object, is a species-specific pattern of behavior and therefore has a high probability of occurrence. An explanation based on reinforcement theory could account for the gradually increasing frequency of the rewarded pecking response. But this explanatory model fails when the reinforcement conditions are reversed, as in the experiments by Williams and Williams (1969). Food rewards were given from time to time on a noncontingent schedule, but never after the desired pecking response. Despite this, the frequency of unrewarded pecking responses increased, and could not (or only to a limited extent) be brought under the control of reinforcement. The experimental animal responds in the same way as any other member of its species when it expects food, emitting need-specific responses that are part of its behavioral repertoire.

Bolles expanded these $S–R$ conceptions into a different type of model, namely, a cognitive one. For him, the answer to the question of what is learned is not the pairing of S and K, but of $S–S^*$ and $R–S^*$ in the form of expectancies. He formulated five corresponding laws of learning (see the following excursus).

All three determinants described in the "law of motivation" are multiplicatively combined in Bolles' model to predict the likelihood of a behavior occurring, or its strength. This conception converges with the expectancy-value theories that emerged from other research orientations (see below). What is new in Bolles' model is that it specifies two determinants of expectation: $S–S^*$ and $R–S^*$. These are distinguished on the basis of whether the goal event, represented by the value (S^*), occurs spontaneously ($S–S^*$) or requires an action ($R–S^*$), and in terms of their respective probabilities. This differentiation also provides the basis for **causal attribution** of action outcomes, which has a determining effect on motivational processes.

Does this imply that $S–R$ bonds play no role at all? Bolles sees these bonds as relevant in two contexts: first, in the innate response patterns of insects in the ethological sense; second, in acquired behavior and skills that have become highly automated.

Bolles' model still needs to be refined in many respects. For example, Dickinson (1997) criticizes the theory's internal consistency. The interrelationship of the theoretical constructs requires further clarification, particularly the conditions under which $S–S^*$ and $R–S^*$ correspond. Moreover, the theoretical constructs have yet to be empirically anchored. Any experimental testing of their predictive value will first require their quantification.

Bindra's Quasi-Physiological Model of Incentive Motivation

Bindra (1969, 1974) proposed a model that is quite similar to Bolles' approach. He also rejected the $S–R$ postulate of response reinforcement, pointing out that learning can occur without opportunities for responding. When animals

EXCURSUS

Laws of Learning in the Form of Expectancies (Based on Bolles, 1972)

■ Primary and secondary laws of learning:

The first two laws deal with learning. They define the two types of expectancies that constitute the essence of learning. The primary law of learning states that learning is a function of the formation of expectancies concerning new contingencies between environmental events. Newly emerging, orderly sequences of events are learned (in other words, stimulus-consequence contingencies). The stimulus signals an event that has significance to the organism, e.g., a potential need satisfaction or a threatening, painful goal object. The notation for this type of expectation is $S–S^*$. Organisms are evidently capable of comprehending not only predictable sequences of environmental events, but also the relationship between their own action and its consequences for the environment. Expectancies belonging to the class of action-consequence contingencies are subsumed under the secondary law of learning and are labeled $R–S^*$ expectancies. They can be observed in the manifold phenomena of instrumental conditioning. $S–S^*$ and $R–S^*$ correspond to Tolman's concept of expectancy ($SR–S$). It is useful to distinguish between the two, however, because it is possible for one type to already be in place in a new learning situation. It could either have been learned previously or have been innately present (see the law of preparatory experience below).

■ Law of execution:

The third law – the law of execution – deals with how these two types of expectation interrelate and determine behavior. Syllogism provides an ideal model here: if $S–S^*$ and $R–S^*$ exist, then S^* can be achieved whenever S is present and R is initiated. A useful experimental investigation would be to determine the extent to which various species (or individuals) are able to carry out such a syllogistic analysis of relationship, in terms of levels of complexity and complication. In any case, as shown by the findings on latent learning, initiation and guidance of behavior hinge on more complex processes than mere $S–R$ pairing. A cognitive theory postulates more exacting processes. Tolman employed the metaphor of a "cognitive map" to "explain" the goal orientation of actions.

■ Law of preparatory experience:

The fourth law – the law of preparatory experience – incorporates innate and acquired expectancies of both types, which an organism may bring to a new situation and which may become dominant. These expectancies explain those situations in which the experimenter's reinforcement procedures do not accomplish anything, as in the case of the raccoon in a study by Breland and Breland (1961), which engaged in unmodifiable, species-specific, food-seeking behaviors. Experience has shown that there are limits to learning that have to be drawn separately for each species. For mammals like rats, the limits soon become apparent when the reinforcing event is delayed: species-specific responses begin to intrude.

■ Law of motivation:

Fifth and finally, Bolles formulated the law of motivation, which states that the likelihood of a response occurring increases with (a) the strength of the $S–S^*$ expectancy, (b) the strength of the $R–S^*$ expectancy, and (c) the value of S^* (Bolles, 1972, p. 405). All three determinants have a motivational component in S^*, a desirable goal (or – if S^* represents a threat – an existing or impending state that is to be changed or avoided). S^*, the value of the goal event, is analogous to Lewin's valence or Tolman's "desire for the goal." It is independent of the need state, which corresponds to Hull's D. $S–S^*$, the expectation that a situation will lead to a goal object or event, is equivalent to Lewin's structure of the life space and to Hull's K. $R–S^*$ gives direction to behavior in the presence of $S–S^*$. This corresponds to Lewin's action path, Tolman's expectations about means-ends relationships, and Hull's purely associative habits.

that have been administered curare, a poison that temporarily paralyzes the effector organs, are presented with an incentive object, they are unable to respond because of their paralysis. Once the paralysis has worn off, however, considerable learning gains become apparent (cf. Taub & Bergman, 1968). Imitation learning or **modeling** (Bandura, 1971) also seriously challenges the postulate of response reinforcement. The mere observation of a model's behavior evidently suffices to alter behavior significantly, without the observers themselves experiencing any form of reinforcement (cf. Bandura, 1971).

The model does not include $R–S^*$ expectancies, because Bindra believes that these can be attributed to $S–S^*$. He argues that $R–S^*$ expectancies are not required because "the specific response form that emerges is a fresh construction created by the momentary motivational state and the spatio-temporal distribution of various distal and contact discriminative-incentive stimuli in the situation" (Bindra, 1974, p. 199).

This conceptualization is reminiscent of Lewin's locomotion within the life space, which is free to follow the given forces and response choices within the field. Bolles (1972, p. 406) doubts the wisdom of excluding $R–S^*$ expectancies, because this would tie the subsequent responses too strongly to the behavioral repertoire of a given motivational state. It would hardly do justice to the flexibility of lower mammalian, not to mention human, behavior. Aside from this point, however, the two authors are in general agreement on the basic issues. Bindra's model is quite specific in many respects and has many physiological corollaries.

According to Bindra, motivation is never solely determined by either an organism's need state or external, incentive stimuli, but by a combination of both. The two aspects generate a "central motive state," as had already been conceptualized by Morgan (1943). From a temporal point of view, primacy is assumed by the incentive objects in the environment.

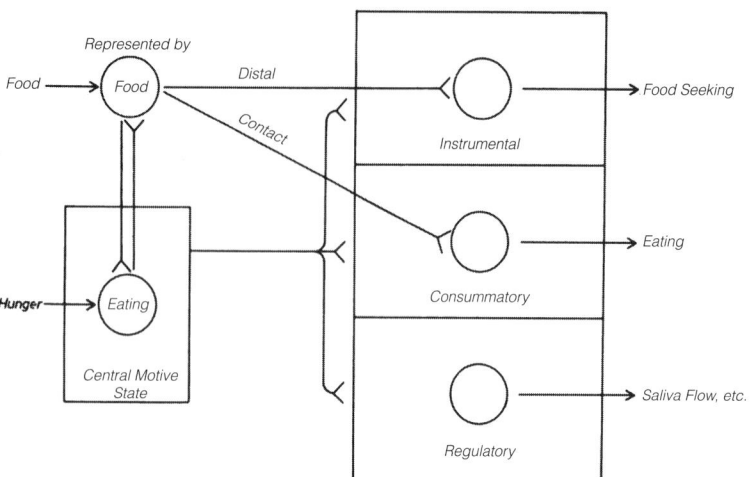

Figure 5.10 Schema of Bindra's model of the motivation process and its influence on three different types of response, as exemplified by unconditioned food-seeking behavior.

They elicit the central motive state, provided there is a state of readiness for it (i.e., the proprioceptive cues are compatible with it, and there is no other competing central motive state). One of the functions of the central motive state is to trigger and intensify sensorimotor functions that expedite approach (or avoidance) behavior. At the same time, it affects autonomic processes (like salivation during food-seeking) and increases the salience of an incentive object's central representation (in the brain). This leads to the mutual enhancement of the central representation of the incentive object and the central motive state.

Changes in behavior (learning) occur with the emergence of central representations of contingencies between situational stimuli and incentive stimuli. Some previously neutral situational stimuli are changed to conditioned incentive-related signals. Fig. 5.10 shows the essence of the model. The arrows indicate the transition from observable events to nonobservable (hypothesized) processes. The forked lines represent the mutual effects of hypothetical variables. Bindra distinguishes between three types of responses:

- instrumental (approach and avoidance),
- consummatory (every response occurring at the point of contact with the goal object), and
- regulatory (internal, organismic responses, such as glandular secretions).

Bindra's model can also explain a number of phenomena and research findings that cannot meaningfully be explained by reinforcement theory.

5.5 Expectancy-Value Theories

There is probably no contemporary theory of motivation that does not incorporate some aspect of what is known as expectancy-value theory. Even theoretical approaches that emerged from completely different backgrounds converge in this respect, as Feather (1959a, b) pointed out

(see the overview in Wahba & House, 1974; and Feather, 1982).

Before we present the most important theoretical models, let us briefly review the convergences that we have observed thus far in this chapter.

As early as Lewin's and Tolman's models, there were references to expectancy and value. Both authors made it quite clear from the outset that value was of pivotal importance to every theory of incentive motivation. For Lewin it was the valence, for Tolman the "demand for the goal." But Tolman was the first to postulate an expectancy variable. He introduced the concept to describe acquired knowledge about means-ends relationships. Later, this evolved into a formalized value-expectancy theory in the form of the belief-value matrix. For Lewin, the expectancy variable remained at first embedded, even hidden, within the regional structure of the environment model, specifically in the perception of the appropriate action path leading to the goal region. Later, with the analysis of goal seeking and levels of aspiration (Lewin et al., 1944), he introduced the independent concept of potency, the perceived probability of reaching the goal. This potency, along with the valence, determines the "effective force" or, in the case of setting levels of aspiration, the "resulting valence," i.e., the choice of task. The theory of resulting valence is one of the expectancy-value theories (see below).

Traditional behaviorism originally had no use for such "mentalistic" constructs as value and expectancy. Nevertheless, their functional equivalents can be detected under the cloak of S–R terminology. The value variable is inherent in the reinforcing experience, in the reduction of drive strength (D), and later in the incentive variable, K. The r_G–s_G mechanism, the fractional anticipatory goal response developed early on by Hull, was invoked to explain how goal objects come to have incentive (K) effects on behavior. The anticipation of the goal object (s_G) incorporates the value variable. At the same time, the r_G–s_G mechanism, through its associative bonding, embodies the expectancy variable, in that the feedback of a particular response (r_G) becomes associated with the representation (s_G) of the future goal event (S_G).

Drawing on Tolman or Lewin, the r_G–s_G mechanism might easily have been conceptualized as a hypothetical construct for the "mentalistic" process of expectancy. Hull, along with Spence and Sheffield, however, omitted to do so. Habit ($_SH_R$) had previously been the only directing structural component. But it no longer sufficed to explain the phenomena of latent learning and incentive change – both easily explained by Tolman's expectancy component. Now, the r_G–s_G mechanism denominating an incentive (K) was added to fill the explanatory gap. What applied to D also applied to K. Its activating effect is nonspecific. According to Spence, it imparts all of its strength to all activated habits. The habit that has been most closely conditioned to the goal response predominates.

Sheffield took this approach one step further in his theory of drive induction. After a few conditioning trials, premature goal responses will be triggered in the run-up to the goal. These result in nonspecific arousal, which in turn increases the response strength of the momentarily dominant habit. If, on the basis of previous learning, the dominant habits are those that lead to the goal, then hesitation and the testing of alternative responses at critical choice points must quickly lead to the identification of the right response, on the basis of increased arousal. As in Spence's model, the activating effect of the fragmentary goal response is nonspecific, an arousing jolt, but it is imparted only to the relevant responses. In this respect, K indirectly attains a behavior-directing function in Sheffield's conceptualization.

Mowrer finally overcame the behaviorists' resistance to the expectancy construct, introducing expectancy emotions that direct behavior. Finally, Bolles made the greatest advance toward a cognitive model by combining two types of expectancy with a goal-related value variable (S^*), namely:

- expectancies about situation-consequence contingencies (S–S^*) and
- expectancies about action-consequence contingencies (R–S^*).

❗ This evolution of the expectancy-value formulation within S-R theory gave it a cognitive character comparable to the cognitive theories of Lewin (1938) and Tolman (1959). In fact, it went beyond them in terms of conceptual precision.

5.6 Decision Theory

This model can be traced back to French philosopher and mathematician Blaise Pascal (1623–1662). When Chevalier de Mérée asked him about the best strategy to adopt in a game of chance, Pascal's advice was to opt for the game that offers the maximum product of potential winnings and probability of winning. In subsequent centuries, the matter of economically expedient decisions acquired great theoretical importance in political economics. Under which conditions it is advisable to buy something; when is it preferable to save one's money (see the review by Edwards, 1954)? This theory assumed the consumer to be an "economic man" who:

- is fully informed,
- can differentiate among an infinite number of alternatives, and
- proceeds rationally.

It gradually became clear, however, that economic decisions are frequently made in conditions of (partial) uncertainty about their consequences. Faced with various combinations of possible gains and their probabilities, people are expected to choose the one that yields the highest product of value and probability of occurrence. This product is termed the **expected value**. In fact, however, decisions related to purchases and games of chance rarely follow this mathematical equation. In place of this expected objective value, David Bernoulli (1738) proposed a subjective one, namely, expected utility.

Bernoulli tried to explain the general reluctance of people to choose a large payoff with a low probability of occurrence over a small payoff with near certainty, even when the expected value is mathematically the same for both – and why this reluctance to take risks lessens with increasing wealth. Bernoulli argued that the subjective value is not a linear, but a concave function of the amount of money, i.e., that the subjective difference between $10 and $20 is greater than that between $110 and $120.

Based on this concept of expected utility, Neumann and Morgenstern (1944) developed a descriptive model of behavior that can be used to determine the utility function for a given individual based on subjective preferences. The individual is asked to choose between alternative combinations of utility and likelihood, and those alternatives that are considered to be equal are identified. If, for example, someone perceives a sure bet of $12 to be equal to a 50% chance of winning $20, then, for him or her, $12 represents half the utility value of $20.

This model of behavior based on decision theory, in which the utility function is determined for each individual, has stimulated a great deal of research (cf. Edwards, 1962). Its application to psychology, i.e., to the prediction of actual behavior, however, has encountered many complications. Just as there are discrepancies between objective and subjective utility, there are also discrepancies between objective and subjective probability. For example, systematic distortions at both ends of the probability scale have been discovered.

❗ High probabilities are likely to be overestimated, while low probabilities are likely to be underestimated (Fig. 5.11). The term "subjectively expected utility" (SEU) is used to reflect subjectively expected probability and utility.

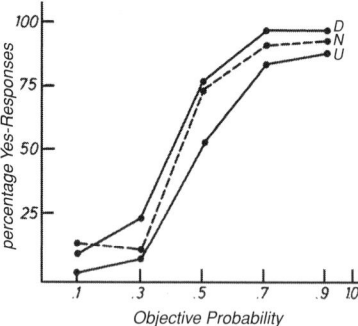

Figure 5.11 Percentage of yes-responses as a function of the objective probability of drawing a marked card under desirable (*D*), undesirable (*U*), and neutral (*N*) conditions. (After Irwin, 1953, p. 331.)

Complexities of Using Decision Theory to Predict Behavior

Even when working on the basis of subjective, rather than objective, probabilities, there are still clearly preferred regions of the probability curve when people are asked to choose between alternatives of equal subjective utility. Where the choice is between alternatives with increasingly higher pay-offs and decreasing probability, combined in such a way that the expected utility of all alternatives is the same, preference will still be given to a 50% probability. The case of negative utility, the chance of losing money, is a different one again. In this case, preference is for the lowest probability coupled with the highest potential loss.

In these cases, we are evidently dealing with psychophysical principles of **risk-taking** primarily investigated by Kahneman and Tversky in a series of experiments (cf. Kahneman & Tversky, 1984). The authors found that it is necessary to distinguish between gains and losses when determining value (in motivational terms, incentive), because the negative value of losing a sum of money is higher than the positive value of winning the same sum. In other words, the value function for losses is steeper than that for winnings. Hence, we can speak of **loss aversion** in cases where an individual is confronted with a loss and gain of the same value, and with equal probabilities.

This irrational bias is consistent with two other inclinations, namely, a tendency toward risk avoidance in the winning sphere, and risk seeking in the losing sphere. Both are predicted by the S-shaped **value function,** which is concave in the winning and convex in the losing sphere. In the first case, this means that if there is a choice to be made between a sure gain and a greater gain with a correspondingly reduced probability (mathematically equal objective value), there will be a reluctance to choose the latter alternative. In the second case, where the choice is between a sure loss and a higher loss with a correspondingly reduced probability (again with equal objective value), preference will be given to the latter. Since the risks of many decision problems can be classified

as either positive or negative, i.e., slotted into a framework of possible gains or possible losses, the preferred alternative can often be determined simply by the way the issue is presented. The inclination to choose the more risky alternative decreases in the first case (gain) and increases in the second (loss).

The positive and negative values attached to an option can also change with differential perceptions of the circumstances, although there is no change in the probabilities associated with the risks. If, for example, the negative consequence of a choice is seen as a necessary cost, the negative value will be lower than if it is seen as a loss. Conversely, positive consequences can decrease in value if other individuals are able to attain even more favorable consequences.

There are many other complications. It is possible that:

■ probability and utility are not simply multiplicatively linked,

■ the probabilities of winning and losing are not complementary, but have to be weighted differentially,

■ the subjective probability of an event can change as a function of temporal delay (Milburn, 1978), and

■ the perceived probability of an event depends on its desirability and, conversely, its desirability depends on its probability.

With respect to the first type of mutual interaction of probability and desirability of an event, Irwin (1953) showed that positive events are perceived as more probable than negative ones. Students were asked to draw a card from a deck containing 10 cards, of which either 1, 3, 5, 7, or 9 were marked. Students were awarded a point for drawing a marked card in the first two trials, and deducted a point for drawing a marked card in the next two trials. For a control group, drawing a marked card had no positive or negative effect. Prior to each draw, participants were told how many of the 10 cards were marked and asked whether they thought it probable that they would draw a marked card. Fig. 5.11 shows the distribution of yes-responses in relation to the objective probability of drawing a marked card for each of the conditions: desirable (point awarded), undesirable (point deducted), and neutral outcomes. Throughout, desirable outcomes were estimated to be most probable, followed by neutral, and finally undesirable outcomes. (Moreover, the graph shows a systematic overestimation of high probabilities and underestimation of low probabilities.)

Conversely, the desirability of an event or object can be influenced by the likelihood of its occurrence. That applies to all "scarce goods," including performance-dependent events. The more unlikely the success, i.e., the more difficult the task, the higher the value assigned to that success. All of these complexities of predicting behavior on the basis of decision theory also present problems for the other expectancy-value theories, which will be examined in the next section.

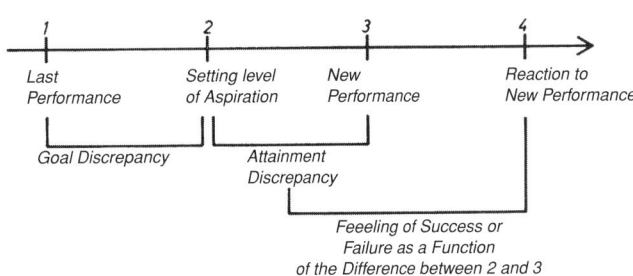

Figure 5.12 Sequence of events in a level of aspiration experiment. (After Lewin et al., 1944, p. 334.)

5.7 Level of Aspiration and the Theory of Resultant Valence

The concept of **level of aspiration** has occupied an important position in the study of motivation since Lewin's student Fritz Hoppe presented his work on success and failure (1930). On the one hand, it implies a specific experimental paradigm; on the other hand, it is a hypothetical construct used in the theory of **achievement motivation** to explain individual differences in performance (Chapter 6).

DEFINITION

As a hypothetical construct, level of aspiration implies the level of performance that will be acceptable to an individual's self-image.

As an experimental paradigm, level of aspiration defines the self-imposed and internalized level of performance communicated by a respondent to the experimenter with respect to a familiar task, which is now to be performed with some degree of mastery (Heckhausen, 1955, p. 119).

The typical procedure presents respondents with a task that can be performed more or less well and more or less quickly, or with several tasks of varying levels of difficulty. After acquiring some insight into their performance level, respondents are asked to set a level of aspiration for each subsequent trial. This results in the sequence of events illustrated in Fig. 5.12.

Hoppe was interested in identifying the factors that determine whether a given level of performance is perceived as a success or a failure. It had been shown that the same performance can be perceived as success by one person and as failure by another. In other words, success and failure are not only dependent on the objectively defined level of difficulty of the task, but also on the previously established level of aspiration. If this level is achieved or exceeded, the individual perceives success. If not, there is a feeling of failure. As shown in Fig. 5.12, the criterion for this self-evaluation is what is known as the attainment discrepancy, i.e., the positive or negative difference between the self-imposed level of aspiration and the actual performance. Feelings of success or failure affect the level of aspiration set for the next performance. Success generally results in an increased level of aspiration, failure in a decreased level, and not the other way round (this is called the "displacement rule"). Displacement of the level of aspiration upward or downward is a function of the intensity of the perceived success or failure, as was shown by Margarete Jucknat's (1938) data presented in Table 5.2.

Feelings of success or failure are concentrated at an intermediate level of subjective difficulty. Success on very easy tasks and failure on very difficult tasks has no effects on self-esteem. However, the more the mastery level exceeds previous performance, the more it will be perceived as a success. Conversely, the more it falls short of previous performance, the more it will be viewed as failure. This **asymmetry of self-esteem** is accompanied by an observable tendency to increase the level of aspiration following improvement in performance. The subjective perception of success does not increase with the level of aspiration, however, but remains more or less the same.

The crucial factor is the **goal discrepancy,** the difference between the last performance and the level of aspiration derived from it (Fig. 5.12). It shows a certain degree of individual constancy over time, and may be positive or negative, i.e., the level of aspiration is always somewhat (or much) higher than the achieved level of performance, or somewhat (or much) lower. One can usually observe a greater readiness

Table 5.2. Percentage of upward and downward displacement of the level of aspiration as a function of the intensity of subjective success or failure (After Jucknat, 1938, p. 99)						
	After success			After failure		
Displacement of the level of aspiration	E!!	E!	E	M	M!	M!!
Upward	96	80	55	22	19	12
Downward	4	20	45	78	81	88
E!! very great success; E! great success; E no significant success; M!! very great failure; M! great failure; M no significant failure.						

to raise the level of aspiration after performance is significantly improved than to lower it after a decrement in performance. There is some – albeit weak – indication of this in Jucknat's data presented in Table 5.2, in the case of very great success and very great failure. As an explanation of this general upward tendency, Hoppe introduced the concept of "ego level," i.e., the tendency to maintain self-confidence at the highest possible level by adopting a high personal standard of performance. Later, this notion became incorporated in the definition of the **achievement motive,** which is defined as the tendency to enhance one's proficiency, or to maintain it at a high level, on all those tasks for which the individual has adopted a standard of excellence, and which can therefore lead to success or failure (Heckhausen, 1965a, p. 604).

Aside from describing and explaining individual differences in the preferred goal discrepancy (which later become an important theme of achievement motivation research, Chapter 6), research on levels of aspiration also examined numerous intraindividual factors that result in pronounced upward or downward shifts in the goal discrepancy (see the example).

EXAMPLE

If, for example, a task is endowed with greater personal importance, there will be a tendency to shift the level of aspiration upward, meaning that positive goal discrepancies become larger, and negative ones smaller (cf. Frank, 1935; Ferguson, 1962). The same holds when goal setting is unrealistic and guided more by wishful thinking than by realistic expectations (Festinger, 1942. The introduction of a performance standard for a socially relevant reference group can bring about a conflict between individual and reference-group norms (between one's own and external performance standards), thereby influencing the setting of levels of aspiration (cf. Heckhausen, 1969, p. 158 ff.). Even the presence, prestige, and behavior of the experimenter or an audience can have an effect, and may result in a splitting of the level of aspiration into one that is publicly stated and one that is privately held.

Overviews of research on the levels of aspiration can be found in Lewin et al. (1944) and Heckhausen (1965a, pp. 647–658).

5.7.1 Success Expectancy and Valence

The **theory of resultant valence** (Lewin et al., 1944), developed in the early 1940s, built on the general findings reported above to explain in more stringent terms why a shift in the level of aspiration occurs in specific cases. Level of aspiration is conceived here as a choice between several alternatives – either between tasks of various difficulty levels (**task choice**) or between different levels of performance on the same task (**goal setting**). In either case, it involves varying difficulty levels. Each level of difficulty has a positive valence in the case

of success and a negative valence in the case of failure. As we saw earlier, the positive valence of success increases as a function of increased difficulty level, up to an upper limit, beyond which success is seen to be totally out of the individual's reach (e.g., an Olympic sprinter wanting to reduce his time of 10 seconds by 2 seconds in the 100-meter dash). Conversely, the negative valence of failure increases with decreasing levels of difficulty. The easier the task, the more embarrassing it is to fail. Again, this holds only up to a point, after which the task is seen as mere "child's play" and failure blamed on the circumstances. By this logic, plotting the difference between the positive and negative valences at each level of difficulty should result in monotonically increasing valences as a function of increasing task difficulty. Likewise, the individual should always choose only the most difficult task that is still humanly possible. This is not the case, however. The choices always fall within a middle range, sometimes above, sometimes below the previous level of performance.

Another factor is clearly in force beside the valence, namely **success expectancy,** the subjective probability of success or failure. Specifically, the valence of success increases as a function of increasing task difficulty and decreasing likelihood of success. This intuitive relationship was empirically confirmed by Feather (1959a, b). He found that the positive valence of success (Va_s) must be weighted by the subjective probability of success (P_s), because success on a difficult task may appear very attractive, but there is also an increased likelihood of failure. This is accounted for by computing the product of valence times probability, $Va_s \times P_s$, the weighted valence of success. The same applies to the negative valence of failure (Va_f) and the subjective probability of failure (P_f) on the same task, which give the weighted valence $Va_f \times P_f$. For any task, the probabilities of success and failure are complementary ($P_s + P_f = 1.00$). If the probability of success is 70%, the probability of failure is 30%. Hence, the formula for the resultant weighted valence (Va_r) is:

$$Va_r = (Va_s \times P_s) + (Va_f \times P_f)$$

There is a resultant weighted valence attached to each alternative task presented. Theoretically, individuals should choose the task with the highest sum of weighted success and failure valences.

If we know the success and failure valences and the probabilities for success and failure for each alternative in a series of tasks of varying difficulties, we can determine where level of aspiration ought to be set on the next trial. It may be set either above or below the previous performance level, depending on changes in the success and failure valences resulting from the subjective probability of success on the tasks in the series. Fig. 5.13 shows a functional relationship, where the maximum resultant valence falls in the region of highest task difficulty, i.e., leads to a positive goal discrepancy in setting the level of aspiration.

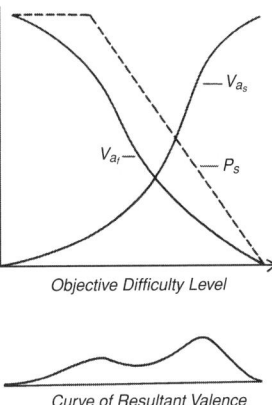

Objective Difficulty Level

Curve of Resultant Valence

Figure 5.13 Derivation of the curve of resultant valence from a set of functions for valence of success (Va_s), valence of failure (Va_f), and subjective probability of success (P_s) as a function of the objective difficulty level of a series of tasks. (After Festinger, 1942 p. 241.)

5.8 Atkinson's Risk-Taking Model

In 1957, Atkinson published an article entitled "Motivational Determinants of Risk-Taking Behavior," which was probably the most cited publication in the field of motivation over the next 15 years. The model, designed to predict individual preferences for task difficulty levels, represents a logical extension to the theory of resultant valence proposed by Lewin et al. (1944). Atkinson added a person component, namely, individual motive strength, to the situational component of value and expectancy (see excursus on the next page).

Aside from assuming an inverse linear relationship between task difficulty and incentive (point 4 of the excursus), Atkinson's crucial modification to the theory of resultant valence was to split Lewin's valence variable, $Va(G) = f(t, G)$ (Lewin, 1938), into a situational component, incentive (I; previously G), a function of task difficulty, and a person component, motive (M; previously t, a motivational variable). He then reconstituted these components to form new valence constructs of his own, success valence (V_s) and failure valence (V_f):

$$V_s = M_s \times I_s; \quad V_f = M_f \times I_f$$

According to this definition of valence, success at a task judged by two individuals to be equally difficult should have a higher valence for a person with a high motive for success (M_e) than for a person with a low motive for success. A similar relationship holds for the failure valence, in the case of individuals with differing levels of the motive to avoid failure. In other words, with increasing task difficulty, the upward slope of the success-incentive gradient should become steeper as the strength of the motive to succeed increases (M_s), and the downward slope should become

steeper as the strength of the motive to avoid failure (M_f) increases.

❶ This motive-weighed valence function of success and failure is the defining element of the risk-taking model. It is in this respect that the model goes beyond the theory of resultant valence and conventional expectancy-value theories.

One might reasonably expect this fundamental component of the theory to have been subjected to extensive empirical tests. Such testing has rarely been undertaken, however (Halisch & Heckhausen, 1988), one reason doubtless being the difficulty of operationalizing and measuring subjective probabilities.

Appending the subjective probability of success (P_s) and probability of failure (P_f) to the success and failure valence of a task – in a sense, a value calculation – gives the approach tendency of success (T_s) and the avoidance tendency of failure (T_f) for that task:

$$T_s = M_s \times I_s \times P_s; \quad T_f = M_f \times I_f \times P_f$$

Success and failure tendency can be summed algebraically to obtain the resulting tendency (T_r) for a given task:

$$T_r = T_s + T_s \text{ or, in more detail}$$
$$T_r = (M_s \times I_s \times P_s) + (M_f \times I_f \times P_f)$$

Because the failure incentive is negative, the failure tendency is also negative (or zero in the extreme case, where $M_f = 0$). Hence, Atkinson viewed the failure motive as an inhibitory force. If the failure motive is stronger than the success motive, the resulting tendencies are negative at all levels of difficulty. Failure-motivated individuals should show a greater tendency to avoid a task as its resultant tendency becomes more negative. If they are set such a task, however they should demonstrate increased effort and persistence (and possibly better performance) – at least, that is what Atkinson (1957) first postulated. Later he rejected this plausible assumption, which corresponds to Hillgruber's (1912) **Difficulty Law of Motivation,** postulating – on theoretical, but not empirical grounds – that a negative resultant valence not only inhibits the choice of a task, but also the effort and persistence applied to it (Atkinson & Feather, 1966).

Predictions of the Risk-Taking Model

Given that the risk-taking model, like any postulate linking value and expectancy, was designed to predict choices or decisions only, it seems unreasonable to assume that the subtractive role of the failure tendency also applies to the parameters of task execution once work on the task has commenced (Heckhausen, 1984b). To date, there is no empirical proof for this. On the contrary, it is quite plausible, as Atkinson (1957) himself originally assumed, that a failure tendency can have a positive effect on task performance, perhaps increasing effort

---

EXCURSUS

Extending the Theory of Resultant Valence in the Risk-Taking Model

Atkinson's risk-taking model extends and revises the theory of resultant valence as outlined below:

1. The two expectancy-weighted values of success and failure are further weighted by person parameters of motive strength. The value of success is weighted by the motive to achieve success (success motive); the value of failure is weighted by the motive to avoid failure (failure motive).

2. In place of Lewin's concept of valence (which was a function of the need tension within a person, "t", and the perceived nature of the goal object, "G"), Atkinson introduced the concept of incentive to reflect the value of success and failure. The incentive of success or failure on a specific task depends only on the perceived difficulty of that task and is not a function of a motive or motivational strength (such as "t"). Of course, as in the theory of the resultant valence, the perceived difficulty of a task is also person dependent, i.e., dependent on the extent to which the person feels capable of carrying out the task (Atkinson, 1964a, p. 254).

3. The subjective probabilities of success and failure are complementary. Probability of success (P_s) and probability of failure (P_f) add up to 1.00:

$$P_s + P_f = 1.00 \text{ (i.e., } P_f = 1 - P_s)$$

4. Value and expectancy do not vary independently of each other. The relationship between subjective probability and incentive is an inverse linear function that reflects everyday experience and empirical data indicating that the feeling of success increases as the perceived probability of success decreases, while the feeling of failure increases as the perceived difficulty of a task decreases (cf. Feather, 1959b; Karabenick, 1972; Schneider, 1973, p. 160). Therefore, the incentives of success (I_s) and of failure (I_f) increase as a function of the decrease in the subjective probability of success (P_s) or failure (P_f), respectively:

$$I_s = 1 - P_s; I_f = 1 - P_f = -P_s \text{ (as } P_f = 1 - P_s)$$

---

to avoid a feared failure or to master the highest possible level of difficulty. (This effect has been confirmed in a number of studies; e.g., Heckhausen, 1963b; Locke, 1968.)

Because success and failure incentives are dependent on the subjective probabilities of success and failure, respectively, and as these two probabilities are complementary, the risk-taking model can make predictions simply on the basis of the two motive parameters and the subjective probabilities. Accordingly, it is possible to express all probabilities and

incentive variables of the resultant tendency (T_r) in terms of P_s:

$$T_r = M_s \times P_s \times (1 - P_s) - M_f \times P_s \times (1 - P_s)$$

or reduced:

$$T_r = (M_s - M_f) \times (P_s - P_s^2)$$

Because of the inverse linear relationship between the success incentive of a task and its probability of success, their

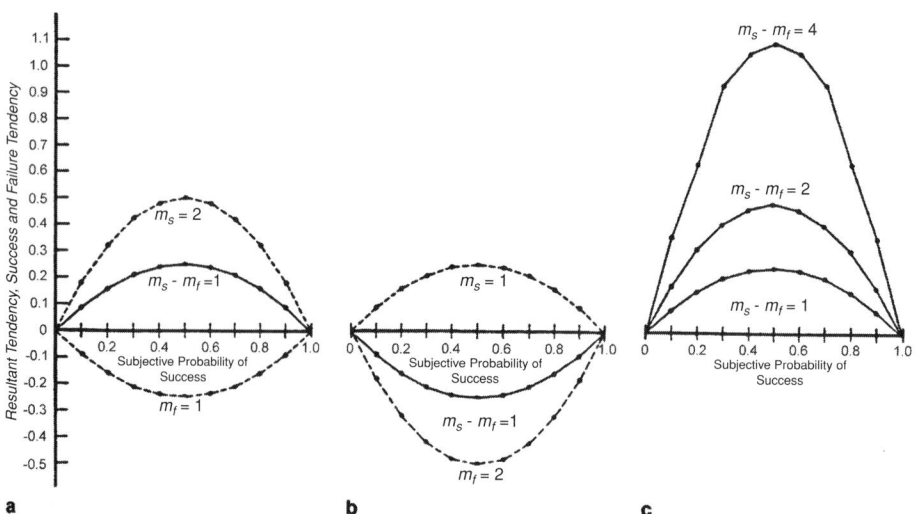

Figure 5.14a–c Strength of the resultant tendency (and the success and failure tendencies – *broken lines*) as a function of subjective probability (**a**) when the success motive is stronger than the failure motive ($M_s - M_f = 1$), (**b**) when the failure motive is stronger than the success motive ($M_s - M_f = -1$), and (**c**) for different individuals where the success motive outweighs the failure motive to varying degrees.

product $-(1 - P_s) \times P_s$ – is a quadratic function whose zero points are at $P_s = 0$ and $P_s = 1$, and whose maximum always lies at the intermediate probability of success ($P_s = .50$). It is a positive (approach) resultant tendency if the **success motive** is stronger than the **failure motive**, and a negative (avoidance) resultant tendency if the failure motive is stronger than the success motive. Fig. 5.14a–c shows the success and failure tendencies as well as the resultant tendencies for a person whose success motive is twice as strong as the failure motive (Fig. 5.14a–ca), and for a person whose failure motive is twice as strong as the success motive (Fig. 5.14a–cb). Fig. 5.14a–c shows that the resultant tendency becomes more pronounced with the dominance of one of the two motives (in this case, the success motive), i.e., that at each sequential step in the probability of success, the difference in the strength of the tendencies increases.

If, for a particular individual, the failure motive is dominant, then the resultant tendency between the success probabilities 0 and 1.00 is always negative. Such a person would theoretically try to get out of doing any task. Because such complete avoidance behavior is barely ever observed, however, Atkinson assumes that other motives, which are not achievement-oriented, may be at work, e.g., affiliation (to please the experimenter). These supplementary motivations persuade the individual to tackle the task despite the resultant avoidance tendency. The efficacy of additional motives is called "extrinsic tendency" (T_{ex}) and is added to the variables constituting the resultant tendencies:

$$T_r = T_s + T_f + T_{ex}$$

SUMMARY

The risk-taking model can be summarized in eight points.

1. It is designed for the "pure case" of a single, purely achievement-related task, i.e., where no other motives are aroused, and the task choice has no further consequences for the actor apart from a direct self-evaluative response to success or failure. The addition of extrinsic tendencies deviates from this pure case in that it specifies a supplemental condition that is not achievement-related. It is only with this addition that failure-motivated individuals can become motivated to approach a task goal.

2. The incentive for achievement behavior – i.e., the motivating agent of a resultant success or failure motivation – consists exclusively in the anticipation of an affective self-evaluation following success or failure (Atkinson speaks of pride or shame, respectively). Aside from these direct consequences, all further achievement-related consequences are ignored, including a superordinate achievement goal for which the present task outcome has something of an instrumentality. Similarly ignored are the incentives of ancillary goals with achievement relevance (except for the occasionally invoked extrinsic tendencies).

3. The incentive values of success and failure on the chosen task – restricted as they are to achievement relevance – depend exclusively on the subjective probability of success on that task. This means that, of the situational variables (expectancy and value), only the subjective probability of success needs to be considered in order to arrive at the weighted incentive (expectancy times value).

4. The risk-taking model applies only to tasks within the same class, i.e., tasks that can be differentiated solely on the basis of their objective probability of success. No prediction can be made for choices between diverse tasks with the same or different subjective probabilities of success. That would require consideration of further incentives related to the types of tasks (e.g., differences in personal importance).

5. Among the family of expectancy-value models, the risk-taking model is the first to contain motive, in the sense of an enduring personality variable. The success motive and failure motive of a person lend weight to the incentive of success and failure in a given situation (or – which amounts to the same thing – to the incentives already incorporated in this probability of success).

6. The failure motive is conceptualized as an inhibiting force, implying that the failure tendency ($T_f = M_f \times I_f \times P_f$) should always lead to an avoidance of task choice (Atkinson & Feather, 1966, p. 19).

7. The model's three variables (motive, incentive, and probability) are mutually related in such a way that intermediate probabilities of success (tasks of intermediate difficulty) produce the strongest motivation to tackle the task, provided that the success motive is stronger than the failure motive. If, on the other hand, the failure motive outweighs the success motive, a task of intermediate difficulty is least likely to motivate, while a very difficult or very easy task should produce relatively high motivation – assuming that the task is not avoided altogether under this condition.

8. Although the risk-taking model was originally applied only to task choice, its application was later expanded to performance variables subsequent to such choices, including effort, persistence, and achievement outcomes. Neither theoretical nor empirical reasons were given for this. It was simply assumed that the maximum net difference between the success and failure tendency determines not only the choice of task difficulty, but also task performance.

The risk-taking model has stimulated decisive research on achievement motivation, particularly research demonstrating that the preferred level of aspiration is motive dependent. Attempts have also been made to use the model to explain parameters of achievement behavior that are unrelated to task choice, e.g., persistence and achievement outcomes. Results were mixed, particularly when parameters of task performance and achievement were predicted. The model has been modified and expanded repeatedly to account for results that are inconsistent with it or to explore new classes of phenomena. Revisions of the model are reviewed elsewhere (Heckhausen, 1980; Heckhausen, Schmalt, & Schneider, 1985). Some major problems (e.g., how to determine the probability of success) and related findings are presented in Chapter on achievement motivation.

5.9 Rotter's Social Learning Theory

Julian Rotter (1954) assumed learned expectations about the relationship between one's actions and their reinforcing consequences to determine behavior, rather than unlearned and stimulus-response bonds resulting in nonspecific arousal. He chose the term **social learning** because "it stresses the fact that the major or basic modes of behavior are learned in social situations and are inextricably fused with needs requiring for their satisfaction the mediation of other persons" (1954, p. 84). According to Rotter (1954, 1955, 1960), a reinforcing event leads to an expectation that a particular behavior or circumstance will, in the future, result in the same reinforcement. Once reinforcement is no longer forthcoming, such acquired expectations about the contingencies of actions and their consequences will be unlearned, i.e., diminished or completely extinguished. Even a small child can increasingly differentiate behaviors in terms of their reinforcing outcomes. The more strongly one has experienced a causal connection between one's actions and a subsequent reinforcement, the greater will be the effect of a nonoccurrence of the expected contingency. Where the expectation is weak, however, nonconfirmation will have comparatively little effect.

This implies that each possible action alternative, in a given situation, has a specific behavior potential (BP). It is a function (1.) of the strength of the expectancy (E) that the particular behavior in that situation (s_1) will lead to the specific reinforcement (R), and (2.) of the reinforcement value (RV) of the reinforcement in that situation. Rotter's (1955) formula states:

$$BP = f(E \ \& \ RV)$$

In a given situation offering a number of action choices, the one with the greatest behavior potential (BP) will prevail. This construct corresponds to the Hullian reaction potential or Lewin's force. Expectancy and reinforcement value clearly correspond to the subjective probability and valence of success or failure, as defined by the theory of resultant valence. The only difference is that Rotter's conception makes fewer assumptions. For example, the relationship between expectancy and reinforcement value is not assumed to be multiplicative, it is left unspecified. Moreover, there are no a priori built-in relationships between the two variables, as is the case for probability of success and valence of success.

Rotter specified the constructs of expectancy and reinforcement values in more detail. The research initiated by his model has focused exclusively on the expectancy variable, however. It is a function of two independent determinants:

- the specific expectancy (E'), on the basis of past experience, that this particular behavior, in this particular situation, will result in a particular reinforcing event; and
- a generalized expectancy (GE) that has become generalized over a broad range of similar situations and behaviors:

$$E = f(E' \ \& \ GE)$$

Rotter's (1954) social learning theory might long have been forgotten had he not added the mediational link of **generalized expectancy** (GE) to facilitate the prediction of expectancy changes. The concept relates to an acting individual's beliefs about the occurrence of the reinforcing consequence being under his or her control. Rotter calls this dimension **internal control** of reinforcement. Generalized expectancies come into play when whole segments of life situations appear to be influenced either by one's own actions (internal control) or by external sources (**external control**). This probably reflects transient cultural beliefs and ideologies about the role of causal agents like fate, luck, or control by powerful others. Rotter assumes that expectancies about one's own control over reinforcement are highly generalized, extending over all life situations, and constituting a personality dimension. He developed an assessment procedure to measure this dimension: the Internal-External (I–E) Scale (Rotter, 1966). The individual's score reflects the generalized expectancy (GE). The scale has continued to play an important role in the research based on Rotter's social learning theory (Rotter, 1966, 1982; Rotter, Chance, & Phares, 1972; Lefcourt, 1976; Phares, 1976).

Empirical Support

Situation-specific expectancies about reinforcing consequences were induced in experiments involving skill-determined vs. chance-determined situations. These studies showed that situations perceived to be chance-determined are less likely to heighten expectancies of further success than are situations perceived to be skill-determined. Likewise, there is less readiness to lower expectancies following failures. In the case of situations perceived to be chance-determined, there is also less readiness to generalize to other, similar situations. Findings related to resistance to extinction are particularly interesting, as they appear to contradict well-established findings from animal experiments, which show that intermittent reinforcement (in approx. 50% of acquisition trials) results in the strongest resistance to extinction. For humans, these results only emerge if the outcome of the task is perceived to be chance-dependent. If it is perceived to be skill-dependent, resistance to extinction after continuous (100%) reinforcement is higher than chance (50%) reinforcement, as shown by the findings of Rotter, Liverant, and Crowne (1961).

Study on Resistance to Extinction as a Function of Specific Expectancies

In the experimental study by Rotter, Liverant, and Crowne (1961), participants were asked to lift a board on which a ball was balanced without dropping the ball. This skill-dependent task was followed by a chance-dependent one involving extra-sensory perception. During the learning phase, the success rate was varied for both groups, to the extent that they received 25, 50, 75, or 100% reinforcement. In the subsequent extinction phase (i.e., constant nonsuccess series), participants were asked to state, prior to each trial, the subjective probability of success. The extinction criterion was reached when the perceived probability was below 10%. Fig. 5.15 shows the number of trials to extinction required for each of the different conditions.

What is the best interpretation of the data plotted in Fig. 5.15? The authors' suggestion that less information is obtained from the reinforcing event in chance-dependent tasks, and that there is consequently less learning than in the skill-dependent tasks, is not very convincing. Looking at the various conditions from the point of view of the study participants, another conclusion appears plausible. Where reinforcement is dependent on skill, the increased success rate leading to a higher expectation of success is accompanied by a growing belief of having the skills necessary for the task at hand. The more firmly this belief becomes established, the more failures must be experienced to challenge and finally abandon it as individuals realize that they have either overestimated their skill level or underestimated the difficulty level of the task. This would explain the monotonic acceleration of the extinction curve as a function of the rate of success.

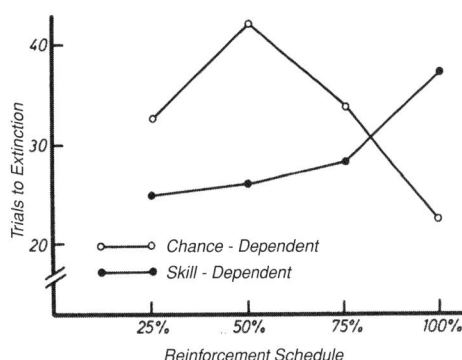

Figure 5.15 Mean number of trials to extinction for a skill-dependent task and a chance-dependent task under four reinforcement schedules. (After Rotter, Liverant, & Crowne, 1961, p. 172.)

But what about the chance-dependent condition? A success rate of 50% will maximize the perception of a chance condition. Participants will never perceive an outcome to be chance-dependent if success is continuous. Instead, they will tend to suspect the experimenter of purposely manipulating the outcomes, and will rapidly abandon all remaining beliefs in chance-dependency during the extinction phase. With a 50% success rate, however, the belief in chance-dependency becomes firmly established, and a greater amount of conflicting experience with 0% success is required before it is abandoned. Success rates of 25 and 75% are intermediate cases falling between the two extremes.

Rotter (1955) also specified the other determinant of the behavior potential, reinforcement value (*RV*), but this specification was not incorporated in the subsequent research generated by his model.

> Reinforcement value *a* in situation 1 is a function of all expectancies that this reinforcement will lead to the subsequent reinforcements *b* to *n* in situation 1, and the values of these subsequent reinforcements *b* to *n* in situation 1. In other words, reinforcements do not occur entirely independently of one another, and the occurrence of one reinforcement may have expected consequences for future reinforcement (Rotter, 1955, pp. 255–256).

Reinforcement value, defined in this manner, can be represented by the following formula:

$$RV_{a,s1} = f[E_{R \to R(b-n)_{s1}} + RV_{(b-n),s1}]$$

The idea that expectancies result from consecutive reinforcements (or valences) is the subject of instrumentality theory.

5.10 Instrumentality Theory

Helen Peak (1955) introduced the concept of instrumentality to the study of motivation to describe the expectation that an action outcome will bring about rewards (reinforcements).

Instrumentality plays a major role in explaining the relationship between attitude and motivation.

❶ The affective component of an attitude about a particular object or situation is a function:

1. of the instrumentality of that object or situation in attaining a desired goal; and
2. the satisfaction to be gained from reaching that goal, which is, after all, dependent on motivation.

In other words, an attitude can determine behavior. On the one hand, it incorporates a subjective probability that the value object can bring about the desired reinforcements (instrumentality); on the other hand, a certain level of satisfaction is expected from these reinforcements.

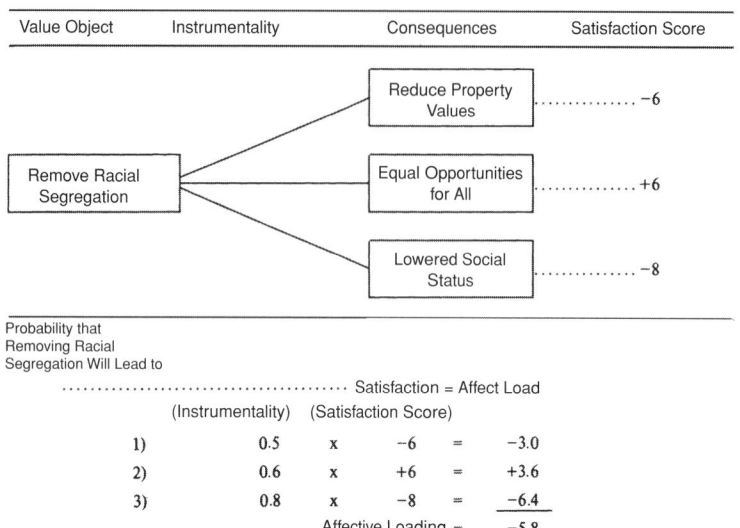

Figure 5.16 Example calculation of the "affective loading" of an attitude object by summing the products of the instrumentalities and reinforcement values of the expected consequence. (After Peak, 1955, p. 155.)

An index of the **affective loading** of a specific value object can be calculated by first multiplying the satisfaction value and instrumentality of each expected consequence of the value object. These products, called "derived affect loads" are then added algebraically to obtain the affective loading of the value object in question. Fig. 5.16 illustrates this procedure for the value object of removing racial segregation.

Numerous studies were conducted in the 1970s to test whether individuals who participate in socio-political activities are more likely to be categorized as "internals" on the *I–E* scale (see Section 5.9). Rotter, Seeman, and Liverant (1962) had made this suggestion on the basis that "externals" are less likely to believe they can change the world. Klandermans (1983), in his literature review, contrasted this efficacy hypothesis with the power-formation hypothesis, which postulates on the contrary that "externals" experience a reduction in their characteristic feelings of powerlessness through socio-political activity. Of the 31 studies reported in the literature, only five confirmed the efficacy hypothesis and only four, the power-formation hypothesis. The criterion behavior of socio-political activists is evidently too complex to be a direct function of either an internal or an external control belief.

Peak's expectancy-value model for determining the affective loadings of an attitude has been confirmed empirically. Rosenberg (1956), for example, was able to predict individual differences in attitudes towards the right of free speech for members of the Communist party, and toward the removal of racial segregation in residential areas, by asking participants to rank a set of value items in terms of their importance as sources of satisfaction and their perceptions of "the extent to which the value tends to be attained or blocked through the instrumental agency of the attitude object" (p. 372). In a related study, Carlson (1956) was able to change an attitude by modifying the level of satisfaction to be derived from the removal of segregation. These approaches to attitude research were continued by Ajzen and Fishbein (1969), who examined behavior in response to actual and anticipated actions of a social partner.

Peak's approaches were first adopted by the industrial psychologists Georgopolous, Mahoney, and Jones (1957) (see study below). Later, Vroom (1964) expanded and formalized them into an **instrumentality theory**. It is not coincidental that industrial psychology, with its applied approach,

STUDY

Applied Research on Instrumentality Theory

Georgopolous, Mahoney, and Jones, (1957) postulated that labor productivity is dependent on the extent to which workers view their productivity as a means (a Lewinian "path goal") of attaining important personal goals. The subjective instrumentality of high or low labor productivity for each of ten personal goals was determined for 621 workers in a factory producing household articles. On the basis of the reported importance of three of these goals – namely, "earning money in the long run," "getting along with coworkers," and "finding a better paying job" – workers were then assigned to one of two groups, one with high and the other with low valence ("need"). Labor productivity was measured in terms of exceeding or falling short of the production quotas set by management and communicated to the workers. The results confirmed the path-goal or instrumentality approach. High productivity was associated with the belief that high productivity is decisive for achieving the three goals. Workers for whom these goals had greater personal importance (i.e., valence) were more likely to perceive such instrumentality.

Hence, labor productivity depends, on the one hand, on its instrumentality value for achieving overall goals and, on the other, on the importance (valence) of these goals for the individual worker.

focused on the instrumentality of action outcomes. The expectancy of the various consequences potentially arising from an action outcome must necessarily play a decisive role in motivating behavior. Only the artificiality of the laboratory experiments that characterized basic research in motivation could have obfuscated the fact that there is an a priori assessment of the instrumentality of future actions and the desirable as well as undesirable consequences of their outcomes.

5.10.1 Vroom's Instrumentality Model

Vroom (1964), in the tradition of expectancy-value theories, combined instrumentality and valence multiplicatively. Valence here means no more than the perceived value of the outcome of an action. The higher the product of valence and instrumentality, the stronger the emerging motivation or action tendency. If there is a choice of alternative actions with equivalent instrumentality, the one with the optimal valence will be chosen. This is accomplished by multiplying the expected valences of the potential outcomes of each action by the expected probability of their occurrence. These products are then summed algebraically, and the action alternative with the greatest sum is chosen.

To clarify Vroom's instrumentality model, it is useful to make some distinctions that remain rather implicit in Vroom's own work. Specifically, a distinction needs to be drawn between action, action outcome, and the ensuing consequences (to be precise, the "consequences of action outcomes"; Vroom labels both "action outcomes").

Whether a chosen action will lead to the desired outcome is more or less probable. In other words, the subjective probability of success can vary between zero and one. (Vroom uses the term "expectancy" (E) rather than subjective probability). Once a particular action outcome has been achieved, it can have more or less appropriate, desirable, or undesirable consequences. On the positive side, it may imply support from co-workers, praise from supervisors, a promotion or pay rise. Vroom does not use the term "probability" to designate the various coefficients between action outcomes and their consequences, as one might have expected. Instead, he uses the term "instrumentality," based on the idea that a given outcome may precede not only the desired consequence, but also its opposite. As such, the respective coefficients can range from −1 to +1, rather than just from zero to one. Vroom defines a positive, a neutral, and a negative instrumentality of an "effective performance" for outcomes with positive and negative valence as follows:

DEFINITION

If effective performance leads to attainment of positively valent outcomes or prevents the attainment of negatively valent outcomes, then it should be positively valent; if it is irrelevant to the attainment of either positively or negatively valent outcomes, it should

have a valence of zero; and if it leads to the attainment of negatively valent outcomes and prevents the attainment of positively valent outcomes, it should be negatively valent (Vroom, 1964, p. 263).

For example, if an action outcome results in a negative consequence, it will have a positive instrumentality for a negative consequence. Because the product of instrumentality and valence is negative, the action will not be initiated. However, if the outcome serves to avoid a negative consequence, both the instrumentality and the consequence will be negative. Their product will thus be positive, resulting in a positive action tendency (see the example).

EXAMPLE

An example here would be a student's fear of failing the year (negative consequence). He is aware that redoubling his efforts in the final weeks of the school year might prevent the feared event from occurring (negative instrumentality of not being promoted to the next grade). Hence, he will put more effort into his school work. In this case, a fear-related arousal leads to an increase in motivation. If instrumentality, like expectancy, varied only between +1 and 0, instead of between +1 and −1, the student's fear of failing the year would result in inactivity, because the product of instrumentality (expectancy) and negative consequences would always be negative.

Generally speaking, the latter approach would imply that fear motivation always leads to a reduction in the action tendency. As we have seen, this is the premise of Atkinson's risk-taking model, in which negative incentives are multiplied by the probability of success (0 to 1). Thus, the fear-related component within the risk-taking model is always negative and always has an inhibitory effect on the resulting action tendency.

Instrumentality, therefore, always concerns the relationship between an action outcome and the ensuing consequences. More generally speaking, it concerns the relationship between the direct outcome of an action and the associated indirect, subsequent effects.

This aspect of action-consequence contingencies has characteristically been overlooked by experimental laboratory research. After all, once the intended action outcome has been achieved, the respondent has completed the imposed task. Activities in the laboratory represent a restricted episode, without further consequences for the manifold life goals of the respondent (save perhaps the desire to make a good impression on the experimenter). It is assumed that there is a valence inherent in the outcome. In Vroom's model, this would mean that a successful outcome always has a full instrumentality of +1, with "rewards" that possesses valence characteristics for the individual respondent (e.g., a feeling of satisfaction with their achievement or other action consequences). The same applies to Atkinson's risk-taking model.

Like other expectancy-value models, its expectancy component does not encompass instrumentalities. It is limited to the likelihood that one's actions will lead to the intended outcome. This is identical to Vroom's expectancy (E). It is the type of expectancy that Bolles called action-outcome contingencies (R–S*), which represent the probability coefficient between one's own efforts and the outcome dependent on those efforts.

5.10.2 The Three-Component Model of Valence, Action, and Performance

Valence Model

As became clear from the discussion above, the valences of potential consequences of actions play a significant role. Collectively they determine – along with their specific instrumentality – the valence of the action outcome.

❶ The valence of the expected action outcome, therefore, is a function of the valences of all further consequences of the action and of the instrumentalities attributed to the action outcome for their occurrence.

The product of valence and instrumentality is computed for each action consequence and these products are then summed algebraically. The action outcome itself has no valence, rather it acquires valence in anticipation of its potential consequences. This relationship can be represented as follows:

$$V_j = f\left[\sum_{k=1}^{n}(V_k \times I_{jk})\right]$$

where V_j = the valence of the action outcome j, V_k = valence of the action consequence k; I_{jk} = the expected instrumentality (-1 to $+1$) of the action outcome j for the occurrence of the action consequence k.

This valence model can serve to explain an individual's assessment of a situation, provided that there has already been action of a specifiable strength in a particular direction, or that action outcomes are already in place. That explains why the model has been used almost exclusively to study **job satisfaction** (Mitchell & Biglan, 1971).

Action Model

The valence model cannot explain which of several action alternatives will be chosen in a particular situation and with what intensity that alternative will be carried out. Like all other expectancy-value theories, such predictions would require consideration of the likelihood that the action will lead to the desired outcome. This is why the instrumentality model of motivation multiplicatively links the expectation that an action will lead to a particular outcome with the valence of that outcome (derived in the manner described above). From this, the resultant action tendency in a choice situation can

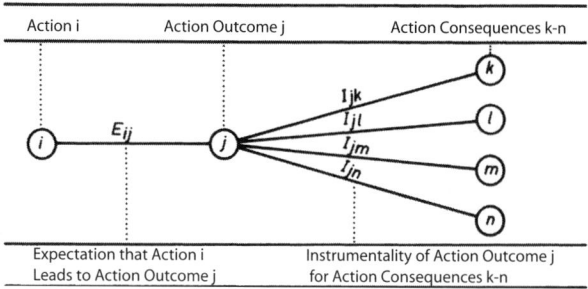

Figure 5.17 Schema of the variables in Vroom's instrumentality model.

be derived. Drawing on Lewin's field theory, Vroom labels it the psychological force (F). Expressed as a formula:

$$F_i = f\left[\sum_{j=1}^{n}(E_{ij} \times V_j)\right]$$

where F_i = the psychological force to perform act i; E_{ij} = the strength of the expectancy (0 to 1) that act i will lead to outcome j; V_j = the valence of outcome j.

In contrast to the valence formula, this formula represents an action model rather than an assessment model for measuring aspects such as job satisfaction. It can explain behavioral differences in performance situations and has been used by industrial psychologists to study productivity or job performance. Vroom (1964) used the model to systematize and analyze a multitude of empirical findings relating to occupational choices, worker turnover, effort, and productivity, thus confirming the explanatory validity of the model. A summary of basic concepts is presented in Fig. 5.17.

Strictly speaking, the action model of psychological force (F) does not predict the action outcome. Vroom himself emphasizes that it predicts the amount of effort invested in the pursuit of a goal. Action outcomes (e.g., job performance) can be interpreted by this action model only insofar as they are dependent on the amount of effort (motivation), but not on other factors, e.g., task-relevant skills. Here, Vroom anticipated an important idea that was later elaborated in causal attribution theory: the motivational process consists, to a large extent, of a **calculation of effort** (Kukla, 1972a; Meyer, 1973a; see also Chapter 14). Different levels of required effort can lead to different levels of action outcomes, and these in turn can lead to consequences with varying valences. According to Vroom, the amount of effort is a function of the algebraic sum of the products of the valences for each level of the action outcome and of the expectancy that each outcome level can be achieved by a particular amount of effort.

Performance Model

To predict the action outcomes actually attained, Vroom (as well as Lawler & Porter, 1967) proposed a third model, the performance model. It states that the attained outcome is a function of a multiplicative relationship between competence and motivation, i.e., psychological force. In other words, action outcome = f(competence × motivation). If we now replace motivation (M) with the action model's formula for psychological force (F), we obtain:

$$\text{Action outcome} = f(\text{competence}) \times \left[\sum_{j=1}^{n} (E_{ij} \times V_j) \right]$$

Individual differences in competence have thus far been largely overlooked (cf. Gavin, 1970). They have not played a significant role in the interpretation of the variance of action outcomes, either by themselves or in conjunction with psychological force (Heneman & Schwab, 1972). This is probably because job performance was assessed by objective psychometric tests rather than self-reports (after all, expectancy, instrumentality, and valence are all subjective in nature).

Action Outcomes and Their Consequences

The fact that Vroom (1964) omitted to distinguish between action outcomes and their consequences led to some confusion between the various levels of outcomes. In fact, these different outcome levels are temporally staggered, and are distinguished by their instrumentality for subsequent "outcomes." Galbraith and Cummings (1967) differentiated between level and level outcomes:

■ Level Outcomes:
According to these authors, a level outcome is one for which an investigator wishes to determine the valence.
■ Level Outcomes:
These include all events that have instrumental meaning for the level outcome and whose valence therefore determines the valence of the level outcome.

Less ambiguous, and arguably psychologically more appropriate, would be our distinction between action outcomes (level outcomes) and action consequences (level outcomes). This distinction raises the question of whether an action outcome receives its valence only through its consequences, or whether it has its own valence. The latter is often referred to as intrinsic valence. In this case, the action outcome is more or less directly tied to significant experiences within the acting individual, without the mediation of any external factors. These experiences are based on self-evaluative processes occurring both during an action and after its outcome. Mitchell and Albright (1972) differentiated five types of intrinsic valences:

Intrinsic and Extrinsic Valences (Based on Mitchell & Albright, 1972)

■ Intrinsic valences:
1. Feelings of self-worth.
2. Opportunity for independent thought and action.
3. Opportunities for self-development.
4. Feelings of self-actualization.
5. Feelings of appropriate accomplishment.
■ Extrinsic valences:
These involve external factors, i.e., action consequences mediated by external forces:
1. 6. Authority.
2. 7. Prestige.
3. 8. Security.
4. 9. Opportunity to make friends.
5. 10. Salary.
6. 11. Promotion.
7. 12. Recognition.

In contrast to the approach taken by Galbraith and Cummings, it might appear reasonable to conceptualize all externally mediated events having extrinsic valences as level outcomes (action consequences), and all events characterized by intrinsic valences as level outcomes (action outcomes). This distinction is also questionable, however, because events with intrinsic valences do not coincide with the accomplishment of a particular action outcome, but are themselves the result of self-assessment processes as a reaction to the desired outcome. Thus, the same action outcomes can have different intrinsic values to the same individual, depending on the extent to which they are attributed to one's own proficiency, to luck, or to the help and support of others.

Furthermore, it is possible that events with external valence (action consequences) serve to initiate self-assessment involving intrinsic valences. A further distinction between level and level outcomes is made by Campbell, Dunnette, Lawler, and Weick (1970) in their **Hybrid Expectancy Model**. They refer to the outcome of an action as the task goal, which has an expectancy I. Attainment of the task goal leads, with an expectancy , to outcomes of the first level with reward characteristics. Their valence is a function of their instrumentality for the satisfaction of needs, and this satisfaction of needs represents level outcomes. This would mean that all action consequences possessing valence would be level outcomes. They can be categorized in terms of the needs assumed to underlie them. What remains is the difficulty of defining level outcomes, i.e., of distinguishing between various needs and measuring their satisfaction.

Empirical Investigations

Vroom's instrumentality theory has proved fruitful for research. It generated a whole series of field studies, most of which confirmed the valence and action models. These models have also been expanded by the addition of variables such as work role, which describes the perceived and assumed demands of the workplace, e.g., expenditure of effort, and which, along with psychological force and competence, is

Vroom's Instrumentality Theory – Three Models in One

Vroom formulated three models: the valence, action, and performance. These three models can be combined to form a process model (Fig. 5.18). This process model contains the individual components determining the valence of the desired action outcome (valence model), the psychological force behind the action (action model), and finally the action outcome achieved (performance model). The process model begins with the interaction between the valence of the action consequences and the instrumentality of the action level for

this valence, which results in the valence of the corresponding action outcome level. This valence interacts with the expectancy that a particular action outcome can be achieved by the action, which results in the psychological force behind the particular action, i.e., the readiness to apply the necessary level of effort. It can also be called the strength of the action tendency or motivation. Finally, the product of psychological force (effort) and level of competence will determine the action outcome achieved.

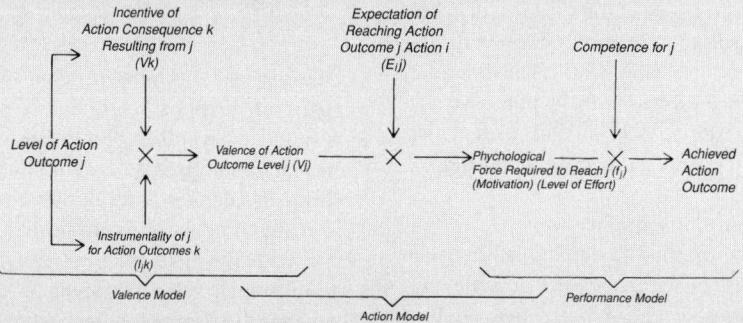

Figure 5.18 Process model of Vroom's instrumentality theory, which links the valence model, the action model, and the performance model.

assumed to determine the action outcome attained (Graen, 1969; Porter & Lawler, 1968). Critical reviews have been published by Mitchell (1974, 1982), Mitchell and Biglan (1971), and Henemann and Schwab (1972). Wahba and House (1974) discussed the theoretical and methodological problems (see also Semmer, 1995).

❶ In general, it has been shown that the multiplicative relationships postulated in Vroom's model are more valid than the additive relationships.

For example, Mitchell and Albright (1972), using the valence model (i.e., the multiplicative combination of valence and instrumentality), were able to account for half of the variance ($r = .72$) in the job satisfaction scores of a sample of navy officers. This general rule does not always apply, however, either to the interaction between the valence of the consequence of an action and the instrumentality of its outcome, or to the interaction between expectancy and the valence of its outcome (cf. Pritchard & Sanders, 1973). In earlier investigations, instrumentality and expectancy were generally not analyzed separately, as required by the model. The two could therefore be confounded, e.g., in studies attempting to determine the degree of relationship between effort and consequences (e.g., Hackman & Porter, 1968), in studies confounding that relationship with the one

between action outcomes and action consequences, i.e., instrumentality (e.g., Gavin, 1970; Lawler & Porter, 1967), or in studies where perceived instrumentality is based on indirect estimates (e.g., Georgopolous, Mahoney, & Jones, 1957; Galbraith & Cummings, 1967; Goodman, Rose, & Furcon, 1970).

All of these studies can be criticized for their operationalizations of the constructs, particularly where instrumentality is concerned. A pertinent example is the study by Pritchard and Sanders (1973), who studied postal workers taking a letter-sorting course that required them to memorize long and complex routes. The valences of 15 different consequences were to be evaluated (e.g., "keeping the job and not getting fired," "getting a raise"; along with more negative valences like "being assigned more work" or "having to work overtime"). The instrumentality scores (I), however, were not operationalized in accordance with the model. They consisted of ratings ranging from +1 to +10 that learning the course material would lead to the 15 consequences. The dependent variables were estimates of the amount of effort invested in the course. (Self-assessment of expended effort appears to be the best measure of the dependent variable, as most of the course program was completed at home.) The best predictions were obtained for the following components of the valence and action models involving multiplicative or additive interrelationships:

$$r = .54\ V \qquad \text{(valence)}$$
$$.52\ V \times E \qquad \text{(valence times expectancy)}$$
$$.50\ V \times 1 \qquad \text{(valence model, multiplicative)}$$
$$.49\ E + (V \times 1) \qquad \text{(action model, additive)}$$
$$.47\ E \times (V \times 1) \qquad \text{(action model, multiplicative)}$$
$$.41\ V + I \qquad \text{(valence model, additive)}$$
$$.36\ E + (V + 1) \qquad \text{(valence and action model, additive)}$$
$$.22\ I \qquad \text{(instrumentality)}$$

The multiplicative valence model seems to be somewhat superior to the additive one (.50 vs. .41), but the same does not hold for the multiplicative and additive action models (.47 vs. .49). The instrumentality measures, whose operationalization is not consistent with the theory, account for little of the variance, but reduce it somewhat when I is added to the other variables. Admittedly, the scale levels of the variables are not suitable for determining whether an additive or multiplicative relationship is more appropriate (Schmidt, 1973).

A further problem consists in the number and types of action consequences to be taken into account by the investigator. Individuals differ in the number and types of action consequences that have relevance for them. Because measures of valence and instrumentality are based on the action consequences chosen by the investigator, there may be an undue restriction of the individual variance in valence and instrumentality, because important consequences are ignored. But if the number and types of consequences are determined for each individual case, then interindividual comparability might be jeopardized by the algebraic summing of all products of valence and instrumentality, as required by the model.

To date, investigations within the framework of instrumentality theory have largely involved field studies in the workplace. Admittedly, this provides them with a high external validity compared with artificial laboratory experiments. There is one disadvantage, however. It is impossible to carry out a causal analysis of simultaneously observed variables without systematic variation of those variables that are presumed to be the determinants. Lawler (1968) thus extended his investigation of 55 industrial managers over a whole year. The valence data consisted of an estimate of the importance of six stated consequences of actions. As mentioned above, his instrumentality data were confounded with expectancy. Participants were asked to estimate the extent to which their own efforts and action outcomes might lead to six action consequences. The actually attained outcomes (dependent variable) were assessed one year later, by means of evaluations by colleagues and superiors and self-evaluation. Multiple correlations between the product of "instrumentality" × valence and the attained action outcome after one year ranged between .45 (colleagues' evaluation), .55 (supervisor's

evaluation), and .65 (self-evaluation). As the correlation of the independent variables and the dependent variables assessed one year later was higher than the correlation between the variables obtained at the beginning of the study, the findings suggest a causal dependence of the performance scores attained, as predicted by Vroom's valence and action models.

The concept of instrumentality introduced an expanded version of the expectancy-value model that has seen widespread use in theoretical and applied research on work motivation (cf. Kleinbeck, 1996; Mitchell, 1982). The expectancy-value theories take a variety of forms in the literature on work motivation (Kanfer, 1990). As Kleinbeck (1996, p. 50, own translation) points out, Vroom's approach, along with Atkinson's risk-taking model, "go a long way to clarifying the emergence of motivation, but always run into problems when it comes to explaining the relationship between motives, motivating potential, and motivation, on the one hand, and performance, on the other." How motivation is translated into action, and maintained effectively until the goal has been achieved, is the subject of volition research.

SUMMARY

Today it is no longer possible to think about research in motivation without taking into account expectancy-value theories (cf. Feather, 1982). If for no other reason, this is because value and expectancy are the two fundamental variables producing motivation tendencies, which in turn provide us with the option to do or not do something. The family of theories has many diverse members, each of which has adjusted itself to a particular problem area. An overview of the whole clan was first provided in a volume by Feather (1982).

Some critical remarks are warranted, however. Heckhausen (1983a) summarized them in five points:

> However fertile motivation models of the family of expectancy and value have been so far, they still exhibit deficiencies in a fivefold respect. The models are (1) too objectivistic in supposing that the actor would use all information on which expectancy and value variables can be based, exhaustively and without errors. Here, cognition-psychological analyses may be helpful. The models are (2) too far generalized supposing a negative correlation between expectancy and value. This appears to be the case only when the value variables belong to the type of scarce goods, which does not hold for large areas of social activities. The models are (3) too rationalistic when they suppose that expectancy and value would always fully be elaborated and integrated. At most, this holds for researchers or consulting groups devoted to a scientific decision analysis; for instance when a site for a nuclear plant has been chosen (cf. Keeney & Raiffa, 1976). Instead of supposing an unproved rationalistic algorithm, one should uncover conditions under which, for instance, only one of the two variables is of influence. An example is task choice in preschool age children where expectancy has a developmental primacy

over incentive (Heckhausen, 1984b). The models are (4) inappropriately formalized when they suppose algebraic relationships at a level at which they cannot be tested, because of the low scale levels of the assessed variables. Instead, algorithms with fewer suppositions are to be employed. Finally, they are (5) too universalistic when they suppose that individual differences within conditions should only be treated as error variance, instead of using them as information as to whether various individuals obey different motivation models and why this may be so (Heckhausen, 1983a, pp. 14–15).

Kuhl and Beckmann (1983) provided experimental evidence for personality differences in the use of expectancy-value algorithms. Studying behavior in a game of chance, they found that action-oriented individuals base their decisions solely on expectancy, and disregard value information, whereas state-oriented individuals make their decisions in accordance with the expectancy-value model. More recently, Stiensmeier-Pelster (1994) has shown that the situational context determines action-oriented individuals' choice of algorithm. When there is a great deal at stake, they too apply the more complex expectancy-value rule.

REVIEW QUESTIONS

1. **What are incentives?**

    Incentives are situational stimuli that alert the organism to affectively charged goal states.

2. **What are the two preconditions for people striving for goal states?**

    It must be possible to anticipate the occurrence of the goal state; i.e., there must be an expectation.

    The goal state must have some subjective meaning; i.e., value.

3. **What are quasi-needs?**

    Quasi-needs are action goals that are derived from "real needs." They form a tension system that disappears only when the goal has been attained.

4. **What is the Zeigarnik effect?**

    The Zeigarnik effect is the finding that incomplete tasks are more easily remembered than completed ones. Lewin's student Bluma Zeigarnik (1927) was the first to demonstrate the effect in an experiment designed to confirm Lewin's theory of tension systems.

5. **How did Kenneth Spence modify Hull's reinforcement theory?**

    Spence extended the theory to cover incentive motivation and, in so doing, totally abandoned the Hullian reinforcement theory of habit formation.

6. **What are emotions of expectancy and what effects do they have?**

    Mowrer (1960) listed four emotions of expectancy: hope, fear, disappointment, and relief. They serve to intensify the sequence of instrumental responses occurring in the run-up to the goal.

7. **What is the major difference between Atkinson's risk-taking model and the theory of resultant valence?**

    In Atkinson's model, the valence function for success and failure is weighted (multiplied) by a person variable, namely, motive.

8. **Why does the risk-taking model predict maximum levels of motivation at intermediate probabilities of success?**

    The values for the incentive of success and the subjective probability of success range from 0 to 1, and there is an inverse linear relationship between the two. Mathematics therefore dictates that, given a probability of success of .5, the incentive of success will be .5. Of all possible combinations of incentive and subjective probability, this one yields the highest product.

9. **How does Vroom's instrumentality theory expand on its predecessors?**

    Vroom's instrumentality theory expands on previous expectancy-value theories of motivation by incorporating the consequences of action outcomes. Motivation is assumed to be influenced by the expectancy of the various consequences potentially arising from an action outcome. Specifically, the probability of the action consequences occurring, the instrumentality, is combined multiplicatively with the perceived value of these consequences.

10. **Which types of intrinsic valence do Mitchell and Albright (1972) distinguish?**

    Mitchell and Albright (1972) distinguish five types of intrinsic valence:

    feelings of self-worth
    opportunity for independent thought and action
    opportunity for self-development
    feelings of self-actualization
    feelings of appropriate accomplishment

6 Achievement Motivation

J. C. Brunstein and H. Heckhausen

Achievement is undoubtedly the most thoroughly studied motive. It was first identified in Henry A. Murray's list of "psychogenic" needs as "n(eed) Achievement," and described in the following terms:

> To accomplish something difficult. To master, manipulate or organize physical objects, human beings, or ideas. To do this as rapidly and as independently as possible. To overcome obstacles and attain a high standard. To excel one's self. To rival and surpass others. To increase self-regard by the successful exercise of talent (Murray, 1938, p. 164).

Murray can also be considered a pioneer of achievement-motivation research in another respect, namely, as the author of the Thematic Apperception Test (TAT). McClelland, Atkinson, Clark, and Lowell (1953) later developed this instrument into one of the best known and most frequently used procedures for measuring people's underlying motives. In their ground-breaking monograph *The Achievement Motive*, McClelland and associates (1953) defined achievement motivation as follows:

DEFINITION

A behavior can be considered achievement motivated when it involves "competition with a standard of excellence."

This definition allows a myriad of activities to be considered achievement motivated, the crucial point being a concern with doing those activities well, better than others, or best of all. The striving for excellence implies quality standards against which performance can be evaluated: people may compare their current performance with their own previous performance ("to excel oneself"), for instance, or with that of others ("to rival or surpass others"), as Murray had already specified (see above). However, an action is only considered to be achievement motivated when the drive to perform emanates from within individuals themselves, i.e., when individuals feel committed to a standard of excellence and pursue achievement goals on their own initiative.

The precise definition of achievement may vary according to the cultural and social context. Fyans et al. (1983) administered a semantic differential instrument to 15–18-year-olds from 30 different language communities to assess their understanding of the achievement concept. Despite the many cultural differences identified, a common semantic core did emerge, reflecting what Max Weber (1904) had termed the "Protestant work ethic." This semantic core covers the life spheres of work, learning, and knowledge. It is associated with an open societal system characterized by personal freedom, and in which individual initiative is considered a precondition for personal success in life. Family values, tradition, and interpersonal relations are all subordinate to this value orientation. The social recognition of an individual hinges primarily on his or her willingness to perform.

Research on achievement motivation has generated an extensive body of findings that can only be outlined in broad brushstrokes in this chapter. More comprehensive and detailed accounts of the development of this research area are available elsewhere (Heckhausen, 1980; Heckhausen, Schmalt, & Schneider, 1985; Weiner, 1985a).

6.1 Evolutionary and Ontogenetic Perspectives

Achievement-oriented behavior is a phylogenetic acquisition unique to humans. It implies commitment to standards of excellence and the evaluation of performance outcomes – two factors necessitating cognitive abilities that only humans possess. This fact does not rule out the possibility of there being evolutionary precursors for human achievement behavior, however.

First, a physiological aspect is worthy of note. For a number of social motives, such as the needs for power and affiliation (Chapters 7 and 8), researchers have been able to identify specific hormones that are released whenever a motive is activated or satisfied, and that are associated with motive-directed behaviors. To date, however, there are no comparable findings for the achievement motive, although there has been no shortage of speculation that this motive, too, has specific neuroendocrine correlates (e.g., arginine vasopressin, a neuropeptide associated with enhanced performance of short-term memory, and involved in the regulation of social behavior; cf. McClelland, 1995; Thompson, et al., 2004). The findings of studies in which the first occurrences of achievement-motivated behavior have been inferred from the emotional expressive reactions of children have shed more light on the subject (Geppert & Heckhausen, 1990; Heckhausen, 1984b, 1987b; Heckhausen & Roelofsen, 1962). This expressive behavior can be analyzed from an ontogenetic, microgenetic, or phylogenetic perspective, as described briefly below (for a more detailed account of motivational development, see Chapter 15).

Self-Evaluative Emotions

Children begin to display self-evaluative reactions to success and failure on activities such as constructing a tower of building blocks between the ages of two and a half and three and a half (for illustrations of pride and shame reactions, see the photographs in Chapter 15, Figs. 15.2 and 15.3). Their first responses are facial expressions: smiling when an activity is successful; turning down the corners of the mouth when it is not. Assuming these two forms of expression to reflect the experience of success and failure, it seems that success is experienced earlier (from the 30th month) than failure (from around the 36th month). This developmental sequence may protect younger children from being discouraged by failure

before they develop the ability needed for success. The emotions of joy vs. sadness signal that the child is concerned with attaining a certain action outcome, and has started to measure his or her actions against a first, simple standard of excellence. However, it is uncertain whether children at this early stage establish a link between the outcomes of their action and their own abilities. There is clear evidence of such a connection being made just a few months later, at the (mental) age of about three to three and a half years, when facial expressions of joy and sadness are supplemented by postural elements that express pride and shame. In pride, the upper torso is stretched and the head thrown back in triumph. Shame reactions are characterized by a lowered head and "crestfallen" torso. These expressions clearly demonstrate that pride and shame are self-evaluative emotions. A causal relationship has been established between the self and the success or failure of one's actions. Children now see themselves as responsible for the outcomes of their actions. Thus, all of the requirements stipulated in the previous definition of achievement-motivated behavior are now met (Heckhausen, 1974a):

DEFINITION

In achievement-motivated behavior, a standard of excellence is applied to evaluate one's actions, and the outcomes of those actions are associated with one's own competence.

In evolutionary terms, joy and sadness are related to expressive behavior observable in primates in the context of affiliation and bonding behavior. Joy and sadness are expressed in response to the acquisition or loss of a desired object, or upon reunification with or separation from a close conspecific (Darwin, 1872; Eibl-Eibesfeldt, 1984; Frijda, 1986; Kaufmann & Rosenblum, 1969; Plutchic, 1980). Pride and shame, on the other hand, are much more closely related to the behavior systems of dominance and submission observable in social primate groups, but also among humans (Eibl-Eibesfeldt, 1984; Lawick-Goodall, 1968; Riskind, 1984, Weisfeld & Beresford, 1982).

In microgenetic terms, it is noteworthy that three- through four-year-old children who win or lose a competitive game first show joy or grief, and that these expressions are then expanded to pride or shame, respectively, as the child establishes eye contact with the (adult) opponent (Geppert & Heckhausen, 1990). Expressions of pride include spellbound fixation on the opponent. Shame prompts an embarrassing smile, as though it were important to appease the superior opponent and to reestablish harmony within the troubled social relationship.

Drawing on these observations on the development of children's expressive behavior, it is possible to speculate on the evolutionary origins of achievement behavior, and to reason that evolution did not need to create a unique affective base for achievement behavior. Instead, two existing pairs of behavioral and expressive systems were combined:

- acquisition vs. loss of a treasured object, linked to emotions of joy vs. grief,
- dominance vs. submission, linked to pride vs. shame and associated gestures of superiority and appeasement.

This combination seems to suffice in providing an independent affective base for achievement behavior. The achievement motive is not biologically anchored, but primarily socioculturally mediated. It can be subjected to various evaluations and take many forms, provided that it is concerned with a binding standard of excellence. Nevertheless, the affective bases for these phenomena are deeply anchored in biological evolution and observable in early phases of ontogenesis.

SUMMARY

In achievement-motivated behavior, people evaluate their actions and competence against a standard of excellence. The first signs of achievement-motivated behavior in human ontogenesis can be observed in the expressive behavior of children (mental age approx. $3\frac{1}{2}$ years) playing competitive games. The expression of self-evaluative emotions such as pride and shame indicates that these children evaluate not only the outcomes of their actions, but also their own competence against a standard of excellence.

6.2 Motive Measurement

One way of finding out more about people's motives is simply to ask. There is no shortage of questionnaire measures that present respondents with statements describing characteristic features of achievement-motivated behavior (e.g., "I often set myself challenging goals" or "I like situations that tell me how good I am at something"). Positive responses are taken to indicate that the respondent has a strong need to achieve. Responses are structured, with participants indicating their agreement or disagreement with each statement on rating scales.

Direct Measurement

McClelland (1980) called the **direct** measurement of motives "respondent," by which he meant that highly standardized stimulus material and structured response formats leave very little scope for participants to provide spontaneous descriptions of their motives. Although this approach has clear advantages, such as its high psychometric quality and ease of analysis, it also has its disadvantages. Responses may be biased by the tendency to present oneself in a socially desirable light. Moreover, statements such as those cited above may assess respondents' evaluations of their own abilities rather than the motives actually driving their actions. Indeed, respondents are not necessarily always in a position to reliably identify the motives governing their behavior. Given his distrust of the validity of self-report measures in general,

McClelland (1980) proposed that "operant" methods be used to measure motives.

Indirect Measurement

Operant methods offer a great deal more scope for differential responses. The test material is much more open and ambiguous than that used in questionnaire measures. Participants do not react to structured statements, but generate their own responses. As a rule, they are not informed that the assessment aims to investigate their motives. The advantages of this kind of **indirect** method of motive assessment are clear: the test situation is more lifelike, specific, and vivid, and offers more opportunity to tap an individual's characteristic ideas and experiences. However, the test situation has to be endowed with stimuli that activate the motive under investigation – only then can this motive be expressed. Furthermore, researchers are faced with the task of filtering out, from the myriad of different responses, those components that provide insights into the nature and strength of the motive aroused. The responses of different individuals can only be compared and contrasted with reference to an objective evaluation system.

❶ The best-known method that has been developed on this basis for the indirect measurement of motives is the TAT.

6.2.1 The Thematic Apperception Test (TAT)

Inspired by the works of Freud (1952) and Murray (1938, 1943; Morgan & Murray, 1935), Morgan and Murray developed the TAT procedure to assess respondents' psychological needs by tapping into the stream of thoughts and fantasies produced in response to picture cues, usually showing one or more people. Respondents are instructed to write a short, spontaneous story about each picture, giving free rein to their imagination. The TAT is one of the family of picture-story tests also known as **projective methods**, in which the respondent describes the actions, thoughts, and feelings of other people – those portrayed in the pictures. The concept of "projection" has a checkered history in psychology (Heckhausen, 1960). Freud used the term to describe a defense mechanism that enables paranoid individuals to attribute the feelings and impulses they cannot accept as their own to other people, thus alleviating the threat posed by these feelings and impulses (e.g., aggressive and sexual needs) by "projecting" them to the outside. Although empirical evidence for such processes has not been found (Murstein & Pryer, 1959), the TAT soon produced very interesting findings with respect to motive measurement. Murray (1933) presented children at a birthday party with pictures of unfamiliar persons both before and after a scary game of murder in the dark. The children were asked to evaluate the maliciousness of the persons portrayed. They judged the strangers to be far more malicious after the scary game than before it. Subsequently, Sanford (1937) found that the frequency of food-related interpretations of TAT pictures increased when respondents were food deprived. These find-ings suggested that the TAT could be used to measure the need states activated at the time of the assessment, such as fear of strangers or need for food.

The next logical step was to use the TAT to measure endur-ing motives. Rather than using self-report measures to tap people's latent psychological needs, these needs were to be inferred from stories generated in response to picture cues. The pictorial material induces a particular motive theme, which then elicits thoughts and fantasies that may differ markedly from person to person. Respondents are instructed to consider a picture cue and to write a story explaining how the situation has arisen, what the people in the pictures are thinking and feeling, and how the story will end. The con-tent of the stories obtained is then evaluated to identify the specific motive activated, e.g., the achievement motive.

Murray's (1943) concept of motive ("need") and his tax-onomy of motives were presented in Chapter 3. Both played a crucial role in the construction of the TAT (see also the excursus below). However, McClelland and colleagues took the decisive step of applying the method to the measurement of motives.

6.2.2 TAT Measurements of the Achievement Motive

In the late 1940s, McClelland and his associates began inves-tigating whether the TAT could be used to measure enduring motives and current need states. They based their work on an experimental paradigm known in the literature as **motive-arousal study**. First, the motive state under investigation is induced through experimental manipulation. For example, the physiologically regulated need of hunger can be activated by temporary food deprivation. Atkinson and McClelland (1948) capitalized on this mechanism in a study with sailors stationed at a submarine base. Depending on their duty schedules, the sailors, who were not informed that they were participating in a psychological experiment, had not eaten for 1, 4, or 16 hours prior to the test. Sailors were shown TAT pic-tures containing food-related cues for 20 seconds and given 4 minutes to write a story about each. As expected, longer deprivation times were associated with an increase in the fre-quency of food-related imagery in the stories. Relative to par-ticipants who had eaten more recently, sailors who had not eaten for 16 hours made more frequent references to themes such as food shortages and efforts to obtain food, and were more likely to have the figures in their stories express hunger.

The questions remained of whether similar findings would be obtained for "higher" motives, such as achievement moti-vation, and whether the TAT could be used to assess enduring personality motives as well as current motive states? McClel-land et al. (1953) addressed precisely the questions in their work on the achievement motive (see also the study presented below). Participants were now shown pictures that suggested achievement-related themes. An example is shown in Fig. 6.1 (other TAT pictures often used to measure motives are repro-duced in Smith, 1992).

Figure 6.1 A picture frequently used to measure the achievement motive: "Two inventors in a workshop." (From McClelland et al., 1953, p. 101.)

STUDY

Arousal of the Achievement Motive (Based on McClelland et al., 1953)

Before participants wrote their stories, achievement-related motiva-tional states of different intensities were induced by administering various tasks under different arousal conditions:

- Relaxed:

The experimenter introduced himself as a graduate student, made an informal impression, and reported that the test items were still in the developmental stage. He explained that the point of the exercise was to test the items, rather than the participants, and said that there was no need for participants to put their names on their forms.

- Neutral:

The experimenter neither played down nor emphasized the test character of the items.

- Achievement-oriented:

The experimenter was introduced as an established researcher administering an important test of intellectual abilities. Partici-pants were urged to do their best.

- Success:

The achievement-oriented instruction was used to introduce the items. Following the test, participants were given the chance to compare their performance with normative scores presented by the experimenter. These norms were fixed at such a level that all participants experienced success.

- Failure:

In this case, the normative scores presented were fixed at such a level that all participants were likely to experience failure.

- Success-Failure:

Success was induced after the first task, and failure at the end of the test battery.

The "relaxed" and "failure" conditions were originally assumed to be the two poles of a motive-arousal continu-um. By analogy with food deprivation and the need for sustenance, Roby and Atkinson (1949) interpreted failure to be

The Route to the TAT: Controversy Between Murray and Allport

As a historical aside, it is interesting to note that the development of the TAT technique sparked a controversy between two Harvard professors: Gordon W. Allport and Henry A. Murray. Whereas Allport (1953) held that non-neurotic individuals experienced no difficulty in reporting their motives; Murray maintained that motives are not readily accessible to introspection and thus cannot be properly measured by self-report methods. He did not attribute this phenomenon so much to repression, as to the very early development of motives in human ontogeny. Whether people are or are not conscious of the motives underlying their actions remains a subject of sometimes lively debate (Wilson, 2002). Indeed, the distinction between "implicit" and "explicit" motives, addressed in more detail in Chapter 9, has recently revived this discussion.

a form of thwarted satisfaction (or deprivation) of the achievement motive. This somewhat questionable analogy ("hunger for achievement") was later abandoned. Instead, McClelland et al. (1953) contrasted the relaxed with the achievement-oriented condition, and sought to find ways of distinguishing between the two, i.e., imagery that occurred more frequently in the achievement-oriented than in the relaxed condition. On this basis, they developed a coding system to measure the strength of achievement-related motivational states in TAT stories.

TAT Coding of Achievement-Related Motive Scores

McClelland and colleagues (1953) based their coding system on the definition of achievement-motivated behavior as involving competition with a standard of excellence. Thus, a story was coded as "achievement-related" (score: +1) only if one of the following criteria was fulfilled:

■ explicit reference to a standard of excellence (e.g., getting a good grade on an exam),
■ reference to a truly exceptional performance outcome (e.g., an invention),
■ reference to long-term achievement goals (e.g., career success).
■ If none of these criteria were satisfied, and any work mentioned was thus of a routine nature, and the story was coded as "achievement-neutral" (score: 0).

If, on the other hand, the story contained only imagery relating to other motives, it was coded as "unrelated" (score: –1).

Stories coded as containing achievement-relevant imagery were then inspected for further content indicative of a strong achievement motive. To this end, McClelland et al. (1953) identified a number of content categories that occurred more frequently in the achievement-oriented than in the relaxed condition. They systematized their search for these categories by applying the schematic representation of an action sequence presented in Fig. 6.2. An action can be said to commence "within" the person with a need (N) to attain a particular goal. This need is accompanied by anticipation of success (Ga+) or failure (Ga–). The instrumental activities undertaken to attain the goal may succeed (I+) or fail (I–). These activities may be facilitated by support from the social environment (nurturant press, Nup), or impeded or thwarted by obstacles or blocks in the world at large (Bw) or within the person him-

or herself (Bp). Positive feelings (G+) are experienced after successes, negative feelings (G–) after failures.

McClelland and colleagues (1953) found that imageries belonging to each of these categories occurred more frequently in the achievement-oriented condition than in the relaxed condition. Finally, each content category was carefully defined and illustrated by examples to ensure that different raters came to the same conclusions. One point was given for every category identified in a story. The total number of points scored across all categories and all stories in a picture series represents a participant's (currently activated) achievement motive. This measure is termed **nAchievement** ("need for achievement") in the literature. Table 6.1 documents the scores that McClelland et al. (1953) measured for nAchievement in each of the arousal conditions described above. As arousal increased, so did the motive scores – a finding that has since been replicated in a number of further studies (Haber & Alpert, 1958; Lowell, 1950; Martire, 1956; Schroth, 1988).

At this stage of its development, the instrument did not, strictly speaking, provide an index for the strength of the **achievement motive**, but reflected the current level of **achievement motivation** induced in the situation at hand. However, it was just one small step to developing a measure of the enduring achievement motive. This decisive step involved standardizing the test situation in the following respects:

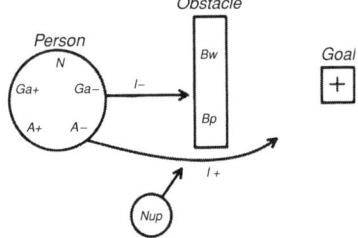

Figure 6.2 Schematic representation of a goal-directed action sequence used to differentiate content categories in TAT stories. *N*, need to attain a goal; *Ga+*, anticipation of success; *Ga–*, anticipation of failure; *G+*, positive affective state; *G–*, negative affective state; *I–*, instrumental activity, unsuccessful; *I+*, instrumental activity, successful; *Nup*, nurturant press; *Bw*, block residing in the situation or the world at large; *Bp*, block residing in the person him- or herself. (Based on McClelland et al., 1953, p. 109.)

Table 6.1. Impact of arousal conditions of various strengths on the frequency of achievement-related imageries in TAT stories (Based on McClelland et al., 1953, p. 184)

Condition	N	Mean	Standard deviation
Relaxed	39	1.95	4.30
Neutral	39	7.33	5.49
Achievement-oriented	39	8.77	5.31
Success	21	7.92	6.76
Failure	39	10.10	6.17
Success-failure	39	10.36	5.67

- the context in which the test was embedded (e.g., the demeanor of the experimenter),
- the instructions given,
- the administration of the test (group vs. one-to-one setting; written vs. oral responses; time limitations),
- the achievement-related content of the pictures,
- the coding system used to analyze the content of the stories.

Three of these components – instructions, administration, and coding – are fixed (for a summary of the respective procedures, see Smith, 1992), leaving the level of arousal induced by the cover story and the achievement-related content of the pictures to be determined.

Extensive studies were conducted to gauge the sensitivity of the nAchievement measure to these two aspects (Haber & Alpert, 1958; Jacobs, 1958; Klinger, 1967). Findings showed that the higher the achievement-related arousal content of the pictures, the higher the nAchievement scores. Nevertheless, pictures low and high in arousal content were found to discriminate almost equally well between respondents high and low in achievement motivation (McClelland et al., 1953, p. 198). Comparable findings were reported for the situational context: the TAT proved to be sensitive to even subtle differences in experimenter behavior (e.g., gestures and facial expressions; cf. Klinger, 1967).

❶ Both arousal factors, pictures and situational context, increase nAchievement scores to approximately the same extent. The question of which combination of the two factors permits the most accurate measurement of individual differences in the strength of the achievement motive was finally resolved in favor of weak situational influences (neutral instructions making no reference to achievement-related issues) and pictures fairly high in arousal content. (Heckhausen, 1964)

6.2.3 Success and Failure Motives

McClelland and Atkinson were aware that their thematic coding system for nAchievement confounded two very different achievement-related tendencies: approaching success and avoiding failure (see the study on the measurement of failure motives described below). In the coding system described

STUDY

A Study on the Zeigarnik Effect

A study conducted by Atkinson (1953) on the Zeigarnik effect (the tendency to remember interrupted actions more easily than actions that have been completed) illustrates early attempts to assess failure motives. Participants were given a test booklet containing 20 tasks to be completed under relaxed, neutral, or achievement-oriented conditions (in the latter condition, they were told that the items tested important abilities). The test booklets were constructed such that only half of the items could be completed in the time available. The participants then wrote TAT stories. At the end of the experiment they were interviewed informally about the tasks, and the number of references to completed vs. incompleted tasks was noted. For the analyses, the sample was split at the median of the nAchievement distribution, and participants assigned to high vs. low achievement motivation groups. No differences were found between the two groups in terms of their ability to recall completed tasks. The groups' patterns of results for incompleted tasks were quite different, however, as shown in Fig. 6.3. Participants high in achievement motivation recalled more incompleted tasks, as predicted

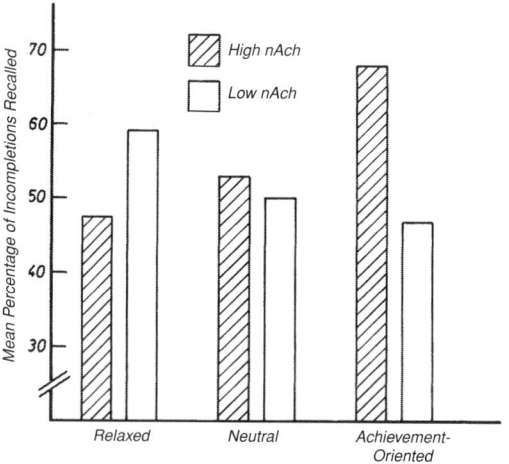

Figure 6.3 Mean percentage recall of incompleted tasks by respondents high and low in achievement motivation (nAchievement) under three arousal conditions. (Based on McClelland et al., 1953, p. 266.)

by Zeigarnik (1927), when they had been exposed to achievement-oriented conditions. Participants with low Achievement scores recalled far fewer incompleted tasks under these conditions. In fact, the percentage of incompleted tasks recalled by participants low in achievement motivation decreased steadily from the relaxed, to the neutral, to the achievement-oriented condition. Atkinson interpreted these findings as indicating that individuals low in nAchievement behaved as might be expected of individuals high in fear of failure, suppressing incompleted tasks from memory, much like an experience of failure. On the same lines, McClelland and Liberman (1949) found that people low in nAchievement take longer to recognize words flashed on a screen when these words are associated with failure. They interpreted this phenomenon as indicative of "perceptual defense" against inimical stimuli.

above, both types of imageries are reflected in a single score. Early attempts to separate success- and failure-related content categories were less than promising (Scott, 1956). Researchers noticed that the behavior of some respondents with moderate to low nAchievement scores was characterized by fear of failure rather than lack of motivation. It was practically impossible to predict how these respondents would behave in performance situations (Sorrentino & Short, 1977).

Assessment of Failure Motives

Moulton (1958) also endeavored to identify the fear of failure as a motive in its own right in TAT stories, but his efforts made little impact on research. Instead, researchers in the US employed anxiety questionnaires such as the "Test Anxiety Questionnaire" (TAQ; Mandler & Sarason, 1952) to assess fear of failure. Atkinson (1964a, 1987; Atkinson & Litwin, 1960) assumed fear of failure to be accessible to introspection, and thus measurable by questionnaire techniques. In the risk-taking model, he defined fear of failure as a motive that undermines and inhibits the success motive. Achievement anxiety questionnaires do not assess motives, however. Instead, they tap behavioral symptoms that may be experienced in overly demanding achievement situations (e.g., a difficult exam). Responses to achievement anxiety questionnaires thus correlate with conceptions of insufficient ability (Nicholls, 1984a, b). Findings soon showed that, apart from feeling more nervous when faced with performance demands, individuals high in achievement anxiety often doubt their abilities to cope with these demands (Liebert & Morris, 1967; Wine, 1971). In the same vein, they rate the subjective difficulty of tasks to be higher than do less anxious individuals (Nicholls, 1984a, b). The TAT measure of the achievement motive does not correlate with self-perceptions of ability in this way. Even individuals who have little confidence in their own abilities may express a strong need for achievement in their imagination (e.g., by having one of the characters in their stories make a pioneering discovery).

❶ In US studies based on the risk-taking model, nAchievement was used as an indicator of the success motive, and TAQ scores as indicators of the failure motive.

In most cases, the two variables have been split at the median, a procedure that is rather questionable from the statistical viewpoint, because it reduces variance and may introduce statistical artifacts. Participants with nAchievement scores above the median and TAQ scores below the median are characterized as being high in "resultant" achievement motive (resultant in the sense that two opposing motives are offset against each other). As mentioned above, the failure motive is conceptualized as an inhibitory force that undermines the success motive (nAchievement) (Atkinson, 1957, 1964a). In

numerical terms, the failure motive is subtracted from the success motive (after both have been standardized within the given sample). The resultant motive is thus calculated by combining a projective measure (nAchievement) with a questionnaire measure (TAQ). It is always difficult to say which of the two variables in difference scores of this kind is responsible for the predicted effects. The hypothesis that the failure motive inhibits achievement in general also remains controversial (Blankenship, 1984; Heckhausen, 1963b, 1968, 1977a, 1984b; Schneider, 1973; Schultheiss & Brunstein, 2005).

6.2.4 TAT Measurements of Hope and Fear

German researchers took a different approach. Heckhausen (1963b; see also Meyer, Heckhausen, & Kemmler, 1965) developed a TAT technique to measure both "hope for success" (HS) and "fear of failure" (FF) using picture stories. The necessary coding system was developed on the basis of TAT stories generated under conditions of neutral instructions (no reference being made to achievement) and picture cues high in arousal content. Three pictures unmistakably depicted hope for success (e.g., a student sitting at a desk and smiling happily), three others fear of failure (e.g., a student being watched by a teacher as he writes something on the board). Behavior in a level of aspiration experiment was used as the criterion for identifying success- or failure-motivated statements, allowing the coding system to be fine-tuned by reference to a validity criterion. Specifically, the TAT stories produced by respondents who set goals that were slightly higher than their previous performance level (indicative of success motivation) were compared with the stories generated by respondents who set excessively high or low goals (both indicative of failure motivation). Content categories that were found to distinguish between these two groups were then used to construct a coding system for HS and FF (Heckhausen, 1963b). The following overview documents the individual content categories (examples are given in parentheses):

Content Categories Used in Heckhausen's TAT Coding System (Based on Heckhausen, 1963b)

- Hope for Success
1. Need for achievement and success (N: "He wants to construct a new piece of machinery").
2. Instrumental activity directed at achieving a goal (I: "The student concentrates on finding a solution to the problem").
3. Anticipation of success (AS: "He is sure his work will be successful").
4. Praise (P: "The foreman praises the workmanship on the component").
5. Positive affect (A+: "He really enjoys doing the homework").

6. Success theme (Th) if the content of the story is predominantly success oriented.

■ Fear of Failure

1. Need to avoid failure (Nf: "He hopes the foreman will not notice his mistake").
2. Instrumental activity directed at avoiding failure (If: "The student hides so the teacher cannot call on him").
3. Anticipation of failure (AF: "He doubts he will be able to manage the task").
4. Rebuke (R: "You'll have to make more of an effort if you want to pass the exam!").
5. Negative affect (A-: "He could kick himself for making the mistake").
6. Failure (F: "The apprentice has ruined the mold").
7. Failure theme (Thf) if content of the story is predominantly failure oriented.

Only one point is allocated per content category per story. Total HS and FF scores are computed by aggregating the points scored across all six stories. The difference between the two scores is termed "net hope" ($NH = HS - FF$); their sum is termed "aggregate motivation" ($AM = HS + FF$). As mentioned above, the coding system was validated using an external criterion, namely, level of aspiration:

- Success-motivated participants (HS) favored goals that slightly exceeded their previous level of performance.
- Failure-motivated participants (FF), in contrast, fell into two subgroups:
    Some opted for excessively low goals, others set themselves unrealistically high targets.

Correlational analyses show that the two motive tendencies, HS and FF, are mutually independent, indicating that there must be people who both strive for success and seek to avoid failure. Neither of the TAT variables correlate significantly with questionnaire measures of achievement motivation (Halisch & Heckhausen, 1988). There is only a slight overlap between FF and TAQ scores, indicating that fear as measured by the TAT is conceptually different from test anxiety (Fisch & Schmalt, 1970). Table 6.2 reports the correlations between nAchievement, as defined by McClelland et al. (1953), and the two variables of Heckhausen's TAT instrument in two samples of college students. Whereas nAchievement shows strong correlations with HS, it does not correlate with FF, confirming that fear of failure is indeed a motive in its own right.

6.2.5 Psychometric Properties of the TAT

Classical test theory (Cronbach, 1990) holds that the quality of a test is a function of the **objectivity** of test administration and coding procedures and the **reliability** of the scores determined. Both objectivity and reliability are considered prerequisites for the **validity** of test scores.

OBJECTIVITY. Because TAT instruments are sensitive to situational influences (cf. Lundy, 1988), the objectivity of test administration is critical. Strict adherence to standardized administration procedures is thus imperative (Smith, 1992).

❗ The objectivity of the TAT coding procedures, measured in terms of the agreement between independent raters, has proved to be satisfactory to high.

Interrater agreement on content categories is at least 85% (only the data of raters who satisfy this criterion are included in empirical analyses); interrater reliability coefficients range between .80 and .95. Coefficients of this magnitude can only be achieved when raters are properly trained; training material and expert ratings are available for this purpose (for nAchievement: Smith & Feld, 1958; for HS and FF: Heckhausen, 1963b). Computer programs have also been developed to analyze the content of TAT stories (for nAchievement: Stone et al., 1966; for HS and FF: Seidenstücker & Seidenstücker, 1974), but despite the parsimony and objectivity of these programs, they have gained little currency in research practice.

RELIABILITY. Reliability is primarily concerned with the stability of test scores over repeated administrations. When compared with questionnaire measures, the test-retest correlations of TAT techniques are relatively modest (Haber & Alpert, 1958; Heckhausen, 1963b; Sader & Specht, 1967), ranging between .40 and .60 at a retest interval of 3–5 weeks. Correlations in the same range are found after a one-year interval (Lundy, 1985). It should be noted, however, that it is impossible to reproduce the original conditions in a TAT retest. Respondents are often able to remember the pictures shown and the stories they told at the first administration, and make a conscious decision to write very different stories at retest. This phenomenon was illustrated for the achievement motive in a study conducted by Winter and Stewart (1977). At retest one week after the first administration of the TAT

Table 6.2. Correlations between nAchievement (McClelland et al., 1953) and the motive variables of Heckhausen's TAT procedure (Based on Heckhausen, 1963b, p. 74)				
	Hope for success	Fear of failure	Net hope	Aggregate motivation
Teacher education students ($N = 71$)	.73**	.15	.32*	.63**
University students ($N = 77$)	.60**	.21	.27*	.62**
*p < .01 **p < .001.				

EXCURSUS

Representativeness of Picture Cues and Participant Samples in Early Studies

The material used by McClelland et al. (1953) and the pictures cues employed in Heckhausen's TAT instrument (1963b) were tailored exclusively to men. Women were not featured at all in the pictures, a shortcoming that would be quite unacceptable from today's perspective. In fact, the results of early studies, particularly in the US, indicated that women's achievement motives were not in line with the traditional feminine role orientations, making behavioral effects difficult to predict. What is particularly embarrassing is that early achievement motivation studies did not even include women participants. Horner (1974a, b) went so far as to postulate "fear of success" as a motive unique to women, suggesting that women associate success in the performance domain with a loss of recognition in the social domain (cf. Stewart & Chester, 1982). This hypothesis proved contentious, and it remains controversial and ultimately unproved to the present day (Hyland, Curtis, & Mason, 1985), whether it is applied to biological or psychological gender (femininity vs. masculinity). It is more likely that women with a traditional role orientation channel their achievement motivation into different domains (e.g., family and child rearing) than career-minded women (career success), as reported by French and Lesser (1964) and Peterson and Stewart (1993). All this implies that gender differences in achievement motivation are located at the behavioral level rather than at the level of the motives driving behavior. Social constraints (blocking the access of certain groups to attractive careers, for example) can impede the expression of the achievement motive in socially recognized productive activities. More recently, researchers have ensured that the picture cues used in TAT studies show as many women as men in achievement situations (Brunstein & Hoyer, 2002; Fodor & Carver, 2000; Thrash & Elliot, 2002). The coding manual and coding system for nAchievement developed by Heckhausen are equally applicable to gender-balanced picture cues.

---

instrument, participants were given one of the following three instructions:

- to think back to the previous week and write stories as similar as possible to their original ones;
- not to worry about whether or not their stories were similar to their original ones;
- to write stories as different as possible from their original ones. The test-retest correlations for each instruction were .61, .58, and .27, respectively.

It seems reasonable to assume that participants in a test measuring imaginative behavior seek to avoid repeating themselves at retest, resulting in the rather low reliability coefficients that are typically reported for the TAT.

HOMOGENEITY. Another way of gauging the reliability of a test is to inspect correlations between scores on the first and second half of the items. This reliability criterion reflects the homogeneity (or internal consistency) of the method.

❶ The homogeneity of the TAT technique has proved to be very low, regardless of whether pictures or content categories form the unit of analysis.

Entwisle (1972) criticized the TAT method on this basis, arguing that it did not produce reliable measurements of the achievement motive, and that it was not suitable for use in research or applied contexts (see also Fineman, 1977). The low internal consistency of TAT techniques is not in fact surprising, however. The authors of the instrument aspired to a certain degree of heterogeneity; the pictures represent different areas of activity, and some of them suggest success, some failure. Atkinson, Bongort, and Price (1977) therefore argued that homogeneity is not a suitable criterion for assessing the construct validity of the TAT (i.e., whether the scores generated are a reliable measure of actual motive levels). Using computer-simulated data, they demonstrated that low internal consistency (measured in terms of the time needed to generate achievement-related imagery per picture) does not mean that TAT results lack construct validity, i.e., that they fail to correspond with theoretically predicted "true" motive scores. Reuman (1982) later confirmed this finding with real-life TAT data. Atkinson (1981) argued that the axioms of classical test theory do not apply to motive measurement because they contradict the basic assumptions of motivation theory; Kuhl (1977) and Schmalt and Sokolowski (2000) came to similar conclusions. In contrast to questionnaires, which prompt respondents to present themselves in a consistent light across a series of usually very similar items, every response to the TAT instrument seems to satisfy the motivational tendency expressed to a certain extent, resulting in marked fluctuation in the achievement-related imagery elicited by a series of picture cues. Atkinson, Bongort, & Price, (1977). were able to show that this fluctuation is by no means random, but exhibits a regularity that can be predicted by "dynamic action theory" (which describes the temporal trajectories of motivational tendencies competing with one another for access to behavior). As compelling as Atkinson's arguments may be, it should be noted that it has not yet been possible to determine, with any degree of accuracy, to what extent TAT picture stories reflect true variance in motive strength and to what extent they are sensitive to random noise in respondents' thoughts and fantasies (Tuerlinckx, De Boeck & Lens, 2002). To date, there have been very few analyses of the TAT with sophisticated test models; one such analysis is presented in the next section. Other aspects that warrant criticism include the lack of published data on the standardization of TAT procedures (cf. Schultheiss & Brunstein,

2001) and the fact that efforts to develop parallel test series have, regrettably, faltered at an early stage (Haber & Alpert, 1958).

6.2.6 The Consistency Problem from the Perspective of Measurement and Construct Validity

Allport (1937) had already reasoned that differences and apparent inconsistencies in a person's behavior do not automatically indicate a lack of consistency in the respective personality trait. A latent personality dimension (e.g., a motive) of a particular strength may be expressed in different ways in different situations (Alker, 1972). Likewise, Mischel and Shoda (1995) argue that personality traits often only become manifest in typical variations of behavior across different situations. A career-oriented person may be competitive in the presence of his colleagues, but obliging and helpful in the presence of his superiors. His different behaviors in the two situations derive from the same motive. Thus, the fact that behavior is specific or adapted to the situation at hand does not yet refute the assumption that it is linked to personality dispositions.

Rasch's (1960) stochastic test model makes it possible to disentangle the strength of manifest reactions (e.g., to the items of an instrument) from the strength of underlying personality traits. This approach links the two theoretical perspectives of measurement and construct validity (see the excursus on the next page). The model tests whether, and to what extent, participants' responses represent a unidimensional continuum of the personality trait under investigation. Responses are unidimensional if they are equivalent across different tasks and situations (e.g., the different TAT pictures) as well as across different groups of respondents (e.g., age and gender groups), i.e., if they yield a comparable index of the personality trait in question in terms of both content and psychometrics.

6.2.7 Other Techniques for Measuring Achievement-Related Motives

Various other techniques have now been developed to measure the achievement motive and its facets. These include adaptations of the TAT method as well as objective tests, most of them questionnaire measures. We do not seek to provide a comprehensive overview of these instruments in the present chapter (cf. Fineman, 1977; Heckhausen, Schmalt, & Schneider, 1985; Rheinberg, 2004a; Stiensmeier-Pelster & Rheinberg, 2003), but outline a selection of the most established.

Adaptations of the TAT

The **French Test of Insight** (FTI) developed by and named for French (1955, 1958a) uses the beginning of stories, rather than pictures, to activate imagery relevant to the motive under investigation ("Don is always trying something new . . ."). The

manual used to categorize the imagery generated is equivalent to the coding system for nAchievement.

❶ The FTI is employed when the investigator deems it appropriate for pictorial cues to be replaced by verbal ones, e.g., when comparing participants from different cultures.

Only recently have systematic attempts been made to develop culture-fair adaptations of the TAT and its picture cues (Hofer & Chasiotis, 2004).

Birney, Burdick, and Teevan (1969) developed another TAT-like technique specifically to assess fear of failure. In contrast to Atkinson, they worked on the assumption that fear of failure is not openly admitted, but becomes manifest indirectly, in perceptions of a hostile and self-threatening environment. The variable assessed by this technique is labeled **hostile press** (HP) and overlaps to some extent with high FF and low nAchievement scores (Birney et al., 1969; Heckhausen, 1968). This projective measure of fear of failure is used as a counterpart to nAchievement, particularly in the US (e.g., Thrash & Elliot, 2002). Schultheiss (2001) has recently translated Heckhausen's (1963b) coding manual into English. Numerous variations on the TAT picture cues and coding system have been proposed. Winter (1991a, b) developed a manual that allows achievement, power, and affiliation motives to be inferred from speeches, school books, and other documents, as well as from TAT stories. It does not permit hope- and fear-related content categories to be assessed separately, however.

THE ACHIEVEMENT MOTIVE GRID. Schmalt (1973, 1976a, b, 1999) took a new approach to measuring the achievement motive. His **Achievement Motive Grid** (AM Grid) is a semiprojective technique that combines the advantages of the TAT method (picture cues) with the merits of questionnaire measures (objective and parsimonious analysis). Respondents are presented with 18 pictures from different areas of activity (sports, school, etc.). The same 18 statements – borrowed from the content categories of Heckhausen's TAT method – are listed below each picture. Respondents are asked to check those statements that, in their opinion, apply to the person shown in the picture (e.g., a student doing his homework: "He feels proud; doesn't think he's capable; is afraid of doing something wrong," etc.). Three different motive tendencies are distinguished:

- HS: The conceptual equivalent of the TAT success motive.
- FF-1: Active failure avoidance; also includes items reflecting a low self-concept of ability.
- FF-2: Fear of failure and its potential social consequences.

The two aspects of fear of failure (active vs. passive avoidance) are thus also clearly apparent in the AM Grid. Schmalt, Sokolowski, and Langens (2000; see also Sokolowski, Schmalt, Langens, & Puca, 2000) have expanded the Grid technique to

Using the Rasch Model to Test the TAT Measures

Kuhl (1977, 1978a) tested whether the TAT measures HS and FF can be scaled according to the Rasch model. He analyzed 6,204 TAT protocols produced by 1,034 respondents of different ages, genders, and educational levels. The consistency of both measures – or, more precisely, their content categories – was tested with respect to the theoretical construct (i.e., the Rasch criterion of "specific objectivity" was applied). The first question to be addressed was whether the frequency of content categories relating to a specific motive (HS or FF) varied proportionally across each pair of picture stimuli. Given this to be true, it should be possible to map all individual content categories to a regression line with a slope of one when two pictures are compared. As Fig. 6.4a shows for FF, the content categories F and R deviate markedly from the regression line. Relative to the other categories, F and R were scored disproportionately more often in stories about picture D than in stories about picture B. Assuming that a motive can be expressed in terms of different content categories depending on the picture, this kind of interaction between the pictures and the response parameters does not necessarily preclude the specific objectivity of a person or an item parameter. For this reason, Kuhl did not view test items as pictures isolated from responses, but conceived of the two as fixed picture-response combinations.

Kuhl subjected the parameters calculated to internal and external model tests. For HS, the parameters of picture-response combinations proved consistent across various subgroups of participants. This finding held whether the groups were divided on the basis of high vs. low HS scores (internal model test) or high vs. low FF scores

(external model test). In other words, the HS content categories yield equivalent and – from the perspective of construct theory – consistent indexes for one and the same personality trait. The same pattern of results did not emerge for FF, however. Rather, the internal model test showed that the FF content categories were not unidimensional. Fig. 6.4b illustrates these findings for picture D in Heckhausen's TAT. Participants low in FF scored disproportionately more often in the categories If, Nf, and Af, whereas participants high in FF scored disproportionately more often in the categories F and R. Thus, the results did not substantiate the assumption that FF is a consistent disposition across situations and reactions. Further analysis revealed that it was not the pictures, but the content categories that caused this inconsistency. Two classes of fear-related imagery were differentiated:

■ a tendency toward expectancy- and action-related failure avoidance (Nf, If, Af) and
■ a tendency to become preoccupied with failure (F) and its affective consequences (R).

Fear of failure (FF), as defined by Heckhausen, thus seems to incorporate active (or "action-oriented") as well as passive (or "state-oriented") approaches to coping with failure (Kuhl, 1983; Schultheiss & Brunstein, 2005). Factor analytic studies yielded very similar results. Whereas HS proved to be unidimensional, two independent factors emerged for FF: the need to avoid failure, on the one hand, and negative affective states occurring in response to failure, on the other (Sader & Keil, 1968).

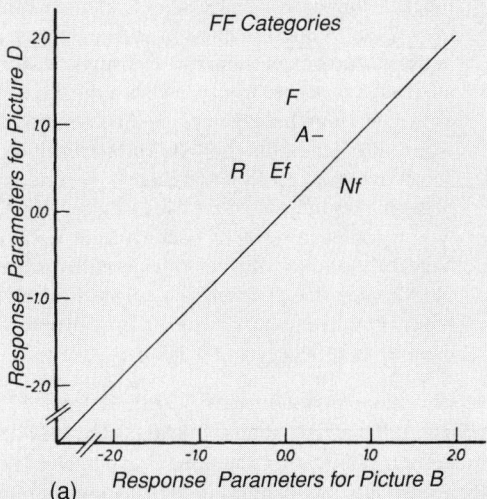

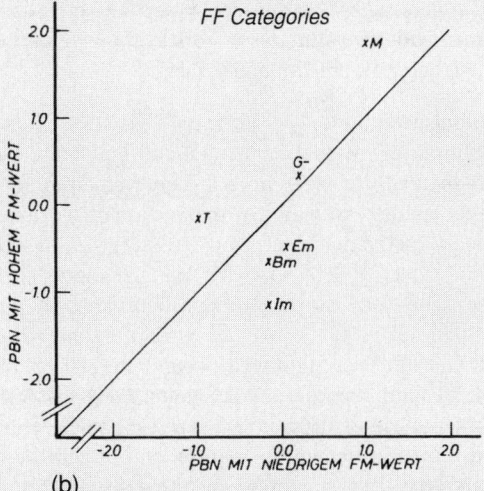

(a)   (b)

Figure 6.4a,b Response parameters for the "fear of failure" (FF) content categories for (**a**) two TAT pictures (pictures B and D from Heckhausen, 1963b) and (**b**) two groups of respondents with high vs. low FF scores. The deviation of the response parameters from the regression line does not challenge the specific objectivity of FF in case **a**, but it does in case **b**. (Based on Kuhl, 1978a, pp. 40, 44.)

cover the power and affiliation motives as well. This Multi-Motive Grid (MMG; Chapter 8) assesses hope and fear components separately for each of the three motives.

❶ The reliability of the AM Grid – unlike that of the TAT – is satisfactory. Besides applications in basic research, it has proved particularly useful in studies on achievement motivation in the school setting (Schmalt, 2003).

Objective Tests

Like projective tests, objective tests do not rely on self-reports as a source of information on motives. Instead, motives are inferred from observable behavioral characteristics. Drawing on Atkinson's risk-taking works (1957, 1964a) and the theory of the dynamics of action (Atkinson & Birch, 1970), Blankenship (1987) has developed a computer-assisted objective method to measure the achievement motive. The following aspects of behavior are tested:

- realistic vs. unrealistic change in levels of aspiration (typical vs. atypical shifts in levels of aspiration in response to success and failure),
- preference for moderately difficult tasks over very easy or very difficult tasks,
- response latencies in choosing between achievement-related activities and neutral activities.

Realistic targets, a preference for moderately difficult tasks, and shorter response latencies in choosing achievement-related activities proved to be intercorrelated behavioral characteristics indicative of a high "resultant" achievement motive. Although its proximity to behavior makes this method seem very convincing, it should be noted that the aspects it is actually supposed to predict (criteria of achievement-motivated behavior) are included in the measurement of the motive itself. In the German-speaking countries, Kubinger and Ebenhöh (1996; see also Kubinger & Litzenberger, 2003) have developed a similar computer-assisted method to assess achievement-oriented attitudes to work in a way that is both proximal to behavior and difficult to fake.

Questionnaire Methods

The multitude of questionnaire methods that have been designed to measure differences in achievement motivation cannot compete with the TAT method's contributions to achievement motivation research (Heckhausen et al., 1985; McClelland, 1980, 1985b; Spangler, 1992). Despite strong correlations between the various questionnaires, they are practically unrelated to the TAT measures of nAchievement or of HS and FF. These findings substantiate McClelland's (1980; McClelland, Koestner & Weinberger, 1989) suspicions that indirect (or operant) and direct (or respondent) procedures for the measurement of motives do not capture the same constructs (see Chapter 9). The three inventories presented below have been chosen to illustrate the many questionnaire measures available because they have been, and remain, closely connected with the development of achievement motivation research.

Questionnaire Methods Tapping Achievement Motivation

■ Mehrabian Achievement Risk Preference Scale (MARPS; Mehrabian, 1969)

  Behaviors characteristic of achievement- or success-motivated individuals:
- realistic targets,
- striving for independence,
- preference for moderately difficult tasks.

■ Achievement Motivation Test (AMT, Hermans, 1970; for a (German) version aimed specifically at children and adolescents, see Undeutsch & Hermans, 1976)

■ Achievement Motives Scale (AMS; Gjesme & Nygard, 1970)

  Two scales tap behavioral characteristics associated with anticipation of success (analogous to HS) vs. failure anxiety (analogous to FF). Items relate to the striving to obtain information about one's competence, and address both cognitive and affective characteristics of achievement-oriented behavior. Sample success item: "I feel pleasure at working on tasks that are somewhat difficult for me." Sample failure item: "I become anxious when I meet a problem I don't understand at once."

It has long been acknowledged that motives measured by questionnaire techniques barely correlate with motives assessed using the TAT method (deCharms, Morrison, Reitman, & McClelland, 1955). This finding has been corroborated by numerous researchers (Halisch, 1986; Halisch & Heckhausen, 1988; Niitamo, 1999; Spangler, 1992; Schultheiss & Brunstein, 2001). Table 6.3 illustrates the typical pattern of results with a dataset that Brunstein and Schmitt (2003) collected from university students enrolled in various majors (psychology students were excluded). The correlations between hope for success as measured by projective (TAT), semiprojective (Grid), and questionnaire (AMS) methods, respectively, all approach zero. There are weak, but significant, correlations between fear of failure as measured by the TAT and by questionnaire measures. Only the correlations between the two questionnaire measures (AMS and MARPS) are really substantial in size. Notably, there is a marked negative correlation between HS and FF in the self-report measure (AMS), but not in the TAT. The correlations reported in Table 6.3 further confirm that there is a considerable overlap between respondents' subjective assessments of their capacities (measured using Meyer's self-concept of ability questionnaire, 1972) and self-attributed achievement orientation. People who describe themselves as success oriented rate their intellectual abilities to be higher than do people who describe themselves as being afraid of failure.

Covington and Omelich (1979), Kukla (1972b), Meyer (1984a, 1987), and Nicholls (1984a) had already drawn attention to this point, and concluded that perceived competence (or ability) is a major component of achievement motivation. However, inspection of the correlations for the TAT measures of HS and FF shows that neither is related to the self-concept of ability, challenging the assumption that achievement-related motives can be equated with self-concepts of ability. These

	1.	2.	3.	4.	5.	6.	7.	8.
Table 6.3. Correlations between different methods of measuring individual differences in achievement motivation (Data from Brunstein & Schmitt, 2003)								
1. HS: TAT	–							
2. FF: TAT	.07	–						
3. HS: MMG	.10	−.03	–					
4. FF: MMG	−.07	.02	−.15*	–				
5. HS: AMS	−.01	−.19**	.04	−.07	–			
6. FF: AMS	−.05	.17**	−.01	.08	−.57**	–		
7. MARPS	−.09	−.19**	.00	−.08	.57**	−.46**	–	
8. Subjective capacity	.05	−.03	.05	−.12	.41**	−.55**	.35**	–

N, 220 students with different majors; *HS*, Hope for Success; *FF*, Fear of Failure; *TAT*, Thematic Apperception Test; *MMG*, Multi-Motive Grid; *AMS*, Achievement Motives Scale; *MARPS*, Mehrabian Achievement Risk Preference Scale; *Subjective capacity*, Self-concept of ability.*p < .05 **p < .01.

findings went unheeded for many years in empirical research. Instead, the same labels (hope for success, fear of failure) were used for measures of achievement motivation that have very little to do with one another on the empirical level. McClelland and his associates (1989; see also Weinberger & McClelland, 1990) finally spelled out the dangers of using the same terms to describe different concepts, and proposed that a clear distinction be drawn between motives measured using indirect (TAT) methods and direct (questionnaire) methods. Their reasoning and findings are presented in Chapter 9.

6.2.8 Anatomy, Mechanisms, and Measurement of the Achievement Motive

According to Atkinson's formula (Chapter 5 and Chapter 2) motivational tendencies result from the interplay of three variables: incentive (I), probability of success (P), and motive (M). For reasons of simplicity, we focus here on the tendency (T) to be successful (s), which Atkinson defines as follows:

$$Ts \times Ms \times Ps \times Is$$

The success motive functions as a weighting factor that is combined multiplicatively with incentive and expectancy. The question arises of which of the two situational factors, incentive or expectancy, is weighted by the success motive (or whether Ms applies to the product of both).

It is impossible to give a formal or mathematical answer to this question on the basis of the formula itself. The fact that Atkinson combined the two situational variables in a subtractive relationship ($Is = 1 - Ps$) complicates the matter further. Approaching the problem on the conceptual level, different achievement motivation researchers have provided very different responses. McClelland, Atkinson, and Heckhausen advocated the view that a strong success motive increases the affective value of success. The product $Ms \times Is$ can thus be interpreted as the **valence** of a success. The amount of pride felt by someone who has mastered a challenging task can be expected to increase as a function of the strength of their success motive (Section 6.4.1). Kukla (1972a, b) and Nicholls (1984a), in contrast, assumed the

achievement motive to have an impact on expectancies. Achievement-motivated individuals are more confident in their abilities, expect to be able to cope with difficult tasks, and are thus more motivated to tackle these kinds of tasks.

Although the issue of affective (or incentive-based) vs. cognitive (or expectancy-based) interpretations of the success motive is at the very core of achievement motivation theory (Section 6.4.2), the debate is still limited to a few insiders. In view of the disparities between motive variables tapped by TAT vs. questionnaire methods, it might be speculated that HS as measured by the TAT has an impact on the incentive of success, whereas HS as measured by questionnaires has an impact on the anticipation of success. This interpretation would converge with the finding that the scores on achievement motive scales are related to the self-concept of ability, whereas TAT scores are not.

Ultimately, however, neither the TAT nor questionnaire methods distinguish carefully between incentive-and expectancy-related information. HS as measured by the TAT – originally defined by Heckhausen (1963b) as "expectancy attitude" – covers both incentives (e.g., positive affect after success) and expectancies (e.g., certainty of success). Much the same can be said for the questionnaires mentioned above. In most cases, the statements to be rated relate to both incentives and expectancies. People who state that they "like working on difficult tasks" indicate not only that they find difficult tasks attractive, but also that they are confident of being able to master them.

A more accurate examination of the mechanisms of achievement motives would require the disentangling of incentive-and expectancy-related components. Global measures of achievement motivation are unsuitable for this purpose. Heckhausen (1977a, b) proposed that the summary concept of "the" achievement motive should be abandoned altogether, and instead split into a number of constituent parts connected with situational variables (incentives, expectancies, instrumentalities, etc.). This approach would certainly help to provide more accurate descriptions of interactions between person and situation characteristics in motivation research. Besides, it seems absurd for a construct as achievement motivation to be reflected by a single summary score on the interindividual level (or by two scores if HS and FF are assessed separately), only to then to be correlated with a broad and diverse range of behavioral criteria.

Multidimensional questionnaire measures of achievement striving have already been successfully developed, as reported by Spence and Helmreich (1978). Schuler and Prochaska (2000) distinguish 17 scales of occupational achievement motivation alone, loading on three factors: ambition, independence, and task-related motivation. Work on projective (or operant) measures is still in its infancy. The **Operant Motive Test** (OMT) developed by Scheffer, Kuhl, and Eichstaedt (2003; see also Scheffer, 2003) on the basis of the TAT procedure is a major step toward this goal. These authors distinguish five facets of the achievement motive: experience of flow, application of standards of excellence, coping with failure, pressure to achieve, and self-criticism. For further details of this technique, see Chapter 12.

Clearly, it is high time to reinvigorate research on the measurement of the achievement motive (or, more specifically, its various components and facets) after a 50-year period of stagnation. Discussion on the measurement of personality traits has recently been revived by the introduction of new chronometric instruments that use a reaction-time paradigm to measure (implicit) attitudes, self-concepts, and motives that people are not able to talk about (because they are not accessible to introspection) or do not want to talk about (because they are socially undesirable; cf. Asendorpf, Banse & Mücke, 2002; Brunstein & Schmitt, 2004; Egloff & Schmukle, 2002; Greenwald et al., 2002; Wilson, Lindsey & Schooler, 2000). This research is still in its early stages, however (cf. Fazio & Olson, 2003).

SUMMARY

The achievement motive can be defined as a recurrent concern to compete with standards of excellence and to exceed previous levels of competence. The TAT procedure was designed to measure this motive, with the achievement-related imagery expressed being interpreted as an indication of motive strength. The method was developed on the basis of empirical criteria: the test's sensitivity to activated motivational states, on the one hand, and strength and change of the level of aspiration, on the other. The TAT method can be used to assess both hope for success and fear of failure. When the criteria of classical test theory are applied, its reliability must be considered low. Rasch model testing showed "hope for success" to be a unidimensional construct, but "fear of failure" to comprise both passive failure avoidance and active coping with failures. Numerous questionnaire measures have been constructed to assess the strength of the achievement motive (or its success- and failure-related subcomponents) directly, by means of self-report. Which of the two methods (TAT or questionnaire) is more suitable for measuring the strength and direction (success vs. failure) of the achievement motive has been the subject of heated discussion. In the final analy-

sis, only the validity of the methods can decide. A procedure that attempts to combine the merits of both methods is the Achievement Motive Grid, which fuses picture-based activation of achievement-related motivational tendencies with a structured response format.

6.3 The Achievement Motive and Behavior

The achievement motive has been related to a range of behavioral characteristics, on the levels of both individual performance and societal productivity indicators. Selected findings are presented in the following two sections.

6.3.1 The Achievement Motive and Individual Performance

The first studies conducted to validate the nAchievement measure investigated the relations between strength of the achievement motive and numerous behavioral criteria, without paying particular attention to situational incentive conditions. Behavior was seen as a direct function of the strength of the motive disposition. Meta-analyses have since shown that such correlations rarely exceed the level of .30 (Collins, Hanges & Locke, 2004; Spangler, 1992). Because these findings have been documented elsewhere (Atkinson, 1964a; Atkinson & Feather, 1966; Heckhausen, Schmalt, & Schneider, 1985), we limit our account to a few examples.

One of the fundamental characteristics attributed to every motive is that it energizes instrumental behavior; a second assumption is that behavior is more easily learned if it serves to satisfy a motive (cf. McClelland, 1980). It thus seemed reasonable to examine the strength of the achievement motive in the context of tasks requiring high levels of effort and concentration, as is generally the case when large numbers of tasks have to be executed as quickly as possible in speeded tests, as Thurstone (1937) was quick to note (see also Thomas, 1983). Other studies tested whether the achievement motive is related to the acquisition of task-specific skills. Lowell (1952) was the first to take this approach. He set participants simple addition problems ("Düker tasks") and scrambled-word tasks (anagrams), and assessed performance at two-minute intervals. Participants high in achievement motivation outperformed those low in achievement motivation throughout on the addition problems (Fig. 6.5a), but only in the middle and last third of the test phase on the anagrams (Fig. 6.5b). In contrast to the (overlearned) addition problems, performance on the anagrams could be improved by practice. Highly motivated participants were evidently better equipped to construct the new learning algorithm necessary than less motivated individuals. Lowell's findings on performance on simple arithmetic problems were replicated in numerous studies (Biernat, 1989; Wendt, 1955), confirming that individuals high in the achievement motive tend to perform better on simple tasks requiring high levels of concentration than do individuals with a relatively weak achievement

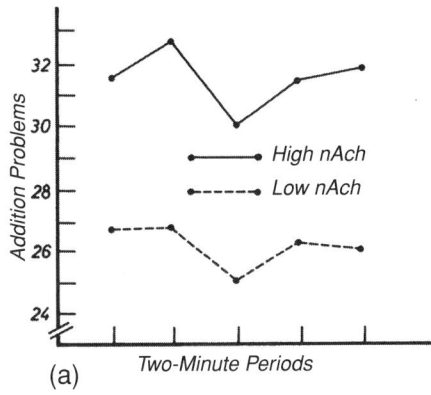 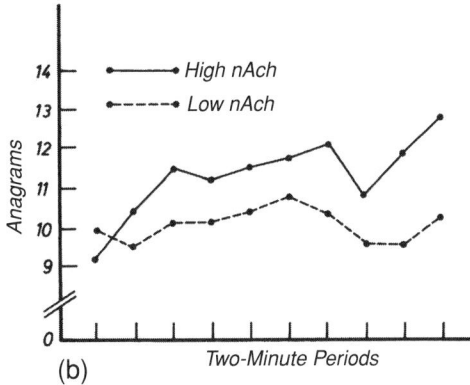

Figure 6.5 Mean performance of individuals high and low in the achievement motive (nAchievement) on (a) simple addition problems and (b) scrambled-word tasks (anagrams) over two-minute periods. (Based on Lowell, 1952, pp. 36, 38.)

motive (Brunstein & Hoyer, 2002). Lowell's findings on the acquisition of problem-solving schemata prompted few follow-up studies, however.

❗ Achievement motivation research has focused on performance (i.e., the application of available competence in a current achievement situation) rather than on the acquisition of competence (i.e., the gradual mastery of skill).

The creativity of research inspired by McClelland's efforts to investigate the effects of the achievement motive on performance outcomes in real-life settings remains unparalleled. Studies carried out in India (Singh, 1979) and Columbia

STUDY

Study on the Achievement Motive and Teamwork

French (1958b) investigated the influence of the achievement and affiliation motives on performance in a teamwork setting. Teams were given the task of constructing a coherent story from a number of phrases. Each of the four members of a team was responsible for putting one set of sentences into logical order. It was only when all four sections of the text were assembled that a coherent text emerged. The team's text coherence score served as the dependent variable (group performance). French varied three factors in the study design:

1. the composition of the groups (either the achievement motive or the affiliation motive was dominant in all members),

2. the task orientation imposed on the groups (in some groups, participants were required to reach consensus on the best solution; in others, they were allowed to insist on their individual solutions), and

3. the type of feedback provided by the experimenter halfway through the experiment (praise for the group's competence or its cooperative spirit).

The study's findings are presented in Table 6.4.

As predicted, groups high in the achievement motive performed better when praised for their competence than for their cooperative spirit. The reverse was true of groups high in the affiliation motive. Task orientation had no effect in groups high in achievement motive, but groups high in the affiliation motive performed somewhat better when the task orientation corresponded with their dominant motive (group orientation). The most favorable constellation was affiliation motivation, group orientation, and feedback focusing on the group's cooperative spirit. In contrast, the combination of individual task orientation and competence feedback had unfavorable effects on performance in affiliation-motivated groups. Likewise, groups high in the achievement motive performed particularly badly when neither the task orientation (group) nor the feedback condition (cooperation) corresponded with their dominant motive. None of the experimental factors alone had a significant main effect on performance, but the interactions between the dominant motive, on the one hand, and task orientation and feedback, on the other, were significant. These findings demonstrate that motives only have a predictable effect on behavior when the situational incentive conditions are taken into account.

Table 6.4. Mean performance of groups of four as a function of dominant motive (achievement vs. affiliation), task orientation (group vs. individual), and type of feedback (competence vs. cooperative spirit) (Based on French, 1958b, p. 404)				
	Achievement motive		Affiliation motive	
	Group task	Individual task	Group task	Individual task
Feedback	orientation	orientation	Orientation	orientation
Competence	40.50	39.38	29.12	25.12
Cooperation	29.25	30.87	38.38	31.50

(Rogers & Svenning, 1969), for example, showed that farmers high in the achievement motive implemented more innovative farming methods, and produced better yields than their less achievement-motivated counterparts. In a longitudinal study, McClelland and Franz (1992) found that the strength of the achievement motive, measured at age 31, predicted income and occupational success at age 41. There is no doubt that findings of this kind are impressive and attest to the criterion validity of the nAchievement measure. However, it remained unclear which mediating processes (more learning, more time devoted to work, higher curiosity levels, higher levels of aspiration, etc.) accounted for the relationships observed.

As mentioned earlier, most early studies seeking to validate nAchievement paid very little attention to situational conditions. There was one notable exception, however, as described in the study box.

Findings similar to those reported by French have been documented by McKeachie (1961), in an analysis of college students' performance, and by Andrews (1967), in an analysis of career advancement in companies. Here again, correspondence between incentives and motives proved to be the decisive factor in educational and occupational success.

6.3.2 The Achievement Motive and Historical and Economic Change

Not only have differences in motive strength been related to individual differences in behavior, differences in the motives of various demographic groups have also been established. This strand of research took the bold, but plausible, approach of using sociological, historical, and economic categories as indicators of achievement-related biases and behaviors. It was initiated by McClelland (1961), based on Max Weber's (1904) hypothesis of an intrinsic relationship between the Protestant work ethic and the spirit of capitalism. According to Weber, the industrial revolution was sparked by the activistic work ethic of postreformation religious movements (e.g., Calvinist teachings of predestination).

The Achievement Motive and Economic Growth

McClelland (1961) reasoned that children brought up in the context of the Protestant ethic are raised to be independent and accountable. This kind of upbringing fosters the development of a high achievement motive, which in turn stimulates entrepreneurial activity, leading to accelerated economic growth, consistent reinvestment of capital gains, and an open-minded approach to technological progress. A comparison of Protestant and Catholic countries around 1950 revealed the former to be wielding greater economic power. McClelland used the per

capita consumption of electricity as an index of economic power, taking into account national differences in natural resources.

How, though, is it possible to test the effects of national differences in collective motives on economic growth? More specifically, how are collective motives measured? McClelland obtained a national motive index by analyzing the content of stories in third grade readers using the nAchievement coding system. He felt that few sources would reflect the national *Zeitgeist* in countries with compulsory schooling as well as these early readers. In a preliminary analysis of a relatively small group of countries, the national nAchievement indexes for the year 1925 were correlated with the per capita consumption of electricity between 1925 and 1950. At .53, the correlation was sensationally high. In a second analysis of a larger group of countries (Table 6.5), McClelland correlated the national nAchievement index with the discrepancy between observed and expected increases in electricity consumption between 1952 and 1958. Differences in the countries' baseline levels of economic growth caused by disparities in the availability of natural resources and the level of industrialization were statistically controlled. The correlation between the motive index for the year 1950 and the increase or decrease in electricity consumption between 1952 and 1958 was .43. Thus, a high national achievement motive indeed seems to be associated with disproportionately high economic growth, while low motive strength predicts below-average growth. Follow-up studies have, on the whole, confirmed this finding. More recently, however, data have shown that the relationship between nAchievement and the level of electricity consumption is no longer as strong as it once was (Beit-Hallahmi, 1980; Frey, 1984; McClelland, 1976, 1984; Orpen, 1983). It seems that the validity of electricity consumption as an indicator of economic development has decreased somewhat.

Content analysis of written documents makes it possible to establish motive indicators for earlier historical periods as well. Samples of datable literary texts were analyzed to examine the currency of achievement-related themes in earlier cultures. These texts included Ancient Greek epigrams, poetry, and funeral orations dating from 900 to 100 BC; Spanish novels, poems, and legends from 1200 to 1730; English dramas, travelogues, and ballads from 1400 to 1830. The respective economic indicators were the extent of Greek olive oil exports, as shown on archeological maps; the tonnage of ships per year departing from Spain for the New World; and annual imports of coal to Greater London. In all cases, periods of economic prosperity were preceded by increases in the nAchievement index, and periods of economic decline by decreases. Fig. 6.6 shows another example of this relationship: deCharms and Moeller (1962) compared the number of patents granted in the USA between 1810 and 1950 with the development of the national motive index (nAchievement as derived from readers). Again, changes in

Table 6.5. National motive index (nAchievement) for the year 1950 and rate of increase in electricity consumption (deviation from the expected growth rate in standard deviations) between 1952 and 1958 (Based on McClelland, 1961, p. 100)					
	National motive index (1950)		Higher consumption than expected	National motive index (1950)		Lower consumption than expected
Countries high in nAchievement	Turkey	3.62	+1.38			
	India	2.71	+1.12			
	Australia	2.39	+0.42			
	Israel	2.33	+1.18			
	Spain	2.33	+0.01			
	Pakistan	2.29	+2.75			
	Greece	2.29	+1.18	Argentina	3.38	-0.56
	Canada	2.29	+0.06	Lebanon	2.71	-0.67
	Bulgaria	2.24	+1.37	France	2.38	-0.24
	USA	2.24	+0.47	South Africa	2.33	-0.06
	West Germany	2.14	+0.53	Ireland	2.29	-0.41
	USSR	2.10	+1.62	Tunisia	2.14	-1.87
	Portugal	2.10	+0.76	Syria	2.10	-0.25
Countries low in nAchievement	Iraq	1.95	+0.29	New Zealand	2.05	-0.29
	Austria	1.86	+0.38	Uruguay	1.86	-0.75
	England	1.67	+0.17	Hungary	1.81	-0.62
	Mexico	1.57	+0.12	Norway	1.71	-0.77
	Poland	0.86	+1.26	Sweden	1.62	-0.64
				Finland	1.52	-0.08
				Netherlands	1.48	-0.15
				Italy	1.33	-0.57
				Japan	1.29	-0.04
				Switzerland	1.20	-1.92
				Chile	1.19	-1.81
				Denmark	1.05	-0.89
				Algeria	0.57	-0.83
				Belgium	0.43	-1.65

nAchievement heralded corresponding changes in the patent index.

Weber's hypothesis suggests that the strength of the achievement motive differs across sociologically defined population groups. Representative findings are available for the US (Reuman, Alwin, & Veroff, 1984; Veroff, Atkinson, Feld, & Gurin, 1960; Veroff, Depner, Kukla, & Douvan, 1980) and Switzerland (Vontobel, 1970). Table 6.6 shows findings reported by Vontobel, who administered Heckhausen's TAT instrument to a sample of German-speaking army recruits in Switzerland. The motive variables were standardized to facilitate comparison ($M = 100$). Findings showed that the success motive diminished with decreasing socioeconomic status, but that the failure motive did not. These differences were particularly pronounced among the urban population. Contrary to what Weber had assumed at the beginning of the 20th century, no differences were found between Protestants and Catholics. Weber had based this assumption on observations made in the US, a country where the Protestant work ethic is still considered to contribute to the higher national economic power relative to most European countries (partic-ularly modern-day Germany, which lacks such a work ethic, as the Oxford economist N. Ferguson maintained on 6 August 2003 in the *New York Times*, substantiating his claim with impressive figures).

SUMMARY

Subsequent to the development of the TAT method of achievement motive measurement, relations between nAchievement scores and a range of behavioral characteristics were investigated. Individuals high in achievement motivation were found to outperform those low in achievement motivation on simple arithmetic problems and learning tasks. High nAchievement scores proved to be associated with innovative and creative outcomes in real-life contexts. Moreover, nAchievement was found to correlate with indicators of economic development and to predict aspects of economic growth and intellectual productivity on the national level. Because situational characteristics (e.g., incentives, instructions, and tasks characteristics) were not taken into consideration in most of these early studies, however, their validity is limited.

Table 6.6. Achievement motivation as measured by Heckhausen's TAT method in a sample of 539 Swiss army recruits, by socioeconomic status and religious denomination. The variables were standardized to have a mean of 100 (Based on Vontobel, 1970, p. 190)

Social background	Hope for success	Fear of failure	Net hope	Aggregate motivation
All regions				
Protestants	100	97	103	98
Catholics	101	107	94	104
Upper class	114	107	108	111
Middle class	108	102	106	105
Lower class	84	108	76	96
Urban regions				
Upper class	132	110	122	121
Middle class	108	98	110	103
Lower class	95	108	87	101

6.4 The Risk-Taking Model as the Dominant Research Paradigm

Atkinson's risk-taking model (1957) has informed achievement-motivation research since the 1960s and dominated it until the late 1970s. Indeed, it is often referred to as the theory of achievement motivation. An introduction to the model can be found in Chapter 5. In this chapter, we examine the empirical data it has generated. The risk-taking model is characterized by the distinction it draws between a directional and an intensity component of motivation. The directional component (dominance of the success or failure motive) determines the preferred level of task difficulty; the intensity component influences the efficiency of task performance.

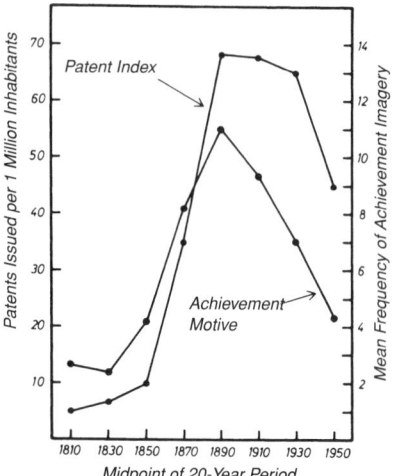

Figure 6.6 National nAchievement index (frequency of achievement-related themes in readers) and number of patents issued per one million inhabitants of the US between 1810 and 1950. (Based on deCharms & Moeller, 1962, p. 139.)

Before we present the empirical findings, let us review the three basic assumptions of the model:

1. The success incentive increases with the subjective difficulty of a task, while the failure incentive decreases.

2. The relationship between incentive and probability of success is multiplicative. It follows from these two assumptions that the resultant motivational tendency (the difference between success and failure tendency) is symmetrical in form as a function of task difficulty:

- Tasks of moderate difficulty maximize the tendency to achieve success or to avoid failure, depending on which of the two motives is dominant.
- For very easy or very difficult tasks, differences in the resultant tendency are relatively small. Thus, the behavior of success-motivated individuals can be expected to differ from that of failure-motivated individuals on tasks of moderate difficulty, but not on extremely easy or difficult tasks.

Atkinson expected this model to apply not only to task choice, but also to persistence and achievement outcomes. He thus explained both decision-making behavior (task choice) and action (task performance) by reference to the same model parameters. The problems involved in equating these two aspects are discussed in more detail in Chapter 5.

3. The valence (V) of a performance outcome is the product of motive strength (M) and incentive (I):

$$V = M \times I$$

This assumption applies to both the valence of success and the valence of failure. The stronger either achievement motive, the stronger its weighting of the respective incentive, producing marked differences in the tendency to approach success or avoid failure. This assumption of the risk-taking model has attracted far less research attention, although it is critical to the logic of the model.

6.4.1 Motive-Dependent Valence Gradients

❶ Another key assumption of the risk-taking model is that valence gradients are motive-dependent.

This assumption can be illustrated for the valence of success. The success incentive increases with the difficulty of a task ($Is = 1 - Ps$). The more difficult a task, the more pride is to be expected upon a successful outcome. According to the logic of the risk-taking model, however, the success motive, which weighs (or multiplies) the incentive associated with success, must also be taken into account in this prediction:

$$Vs = Ms \times Is$$

Thus, success-motivated individuals experience an even higher level of satisfaction upon solving a difficult task than do less success-motivated individuals. It is only in the context of very simple tasks that no differences are to be expected between the two groups, because the incentive here is so low that success is trivial. The same pattern holds for the failure incentive, the only difference being that the failure motive acts as the weighting factor:

$$Vf = Mf \times If$$

In other words, individuals high in failure motivation feel more shame at failing on a simple task ($If = -Ps$) than do less failure-motivated individuals. If the failure incentive is low (i.e., the task is extremely difficult), however, there should be no effect of differences in the strength of the failure motive, as it is no disgrace for anyone to be defeated by a very difficult task. To summarize, as task difficulty increases, the valence of success can be expected to increase more steeply among individuals high in success motivation than among their less success-motivated counterparts. Conversely, as task difficulty decreases, the valence of failure can be expected to increase more steeply among individuals high in failure motivation than among their less failure-motivated counterparts. Taken together, it can be assumed that (distinct) successes are more attractive to success-motivated individuals than to failure-motivated individuals, whereas failure-motivated individuals feel more shame at (distinct) failures than do success-motivated individuals. These effects are not restricted to actual success or failure. Rather, the valences of success and failure take effect in anticipation of these outcomes, even before individuals have begun to tackle the task at hand.

Findings on the Valence of Success and Failure

The assumptions presented above have rarely been tested directly (cf. Halisch & Heckhausen, 1988), however, and no clear picture emerges from the findings of the few available studies. The first study was conducted by Litwin (1966), who measured the valence of hits in a ring toss game in

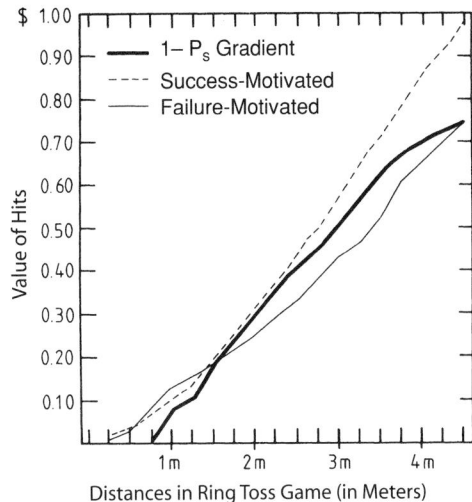

Figure 6.7 Mean monetary value assigned by success- and failure-motivated individuals to hits from various distances in a ringtoss game, as compared with the incentive function calculated on the basis of the estimated probabilities of success alone. (Based on Litwin, 1966, p. 112.)

terms of the prize money participants judged to be appropriate for throws from various distances. After 10 trial throws, participants were asked to specify how much money (from zero to a dollar) should be awarded for hits from each distance. As shown in Fig. 6.7, the valence of success (prize money awarded) increased with the difficulty of the task. Moreover, the slope of the increase was significantly steeper for success-motivated individuals than for failure-motivated individuals (groups were formed by subtracting TAQ from nAchievement scores). The middle (bold) line represents the incentive function ($1 - Ps$), which was plotted on the basis of the probabilities of success estimated by a separate group of participants.

Litwin's (1966) findings seemed to confirm the assumption that valence gradients are motive dependent, although his study only considered the valence of success. However, these findings were only substantiated in one further study, in which Cooper (1983) asked respondents to estimate the valence of easy, moderate, and difficult tasks in terms of the (dis)satisfaction to be expected upon success or failure. However, Cooper's data did not confirm Atkinson's assumptions with respect to the failure valence (i.e., the slope of the valence gradient was not dependent on achievement motivation measures). Neither Feather (1967) nor Karabenick (1972) could confirm success or failure valences to be the product of the interaction ($\times$) of incentive and motive strength. Schneider (1973) did observe such an interaction, but only in one of several experiments.

Despite this disappointing body of findings, it would be premature to abandon the assumption that valences are motive dependent. After all, this assumption only applies to the "pure case," meaning that the variables under investigation must be operationalized with particular care in three respects:

1. the measurement of the two motives (HS and FF),
2. the determination of the subjective probability of success, and
3. the assessment of success and failure incentives.

Shortcomings in all three domains can be identified in the studies cited. With the exception of Schneider's (1973) study, anxiety questionnaires were used to assess the failure motive, thus confounding the tendency to avoid failure with differences in the self-concept of ability. In many studies (including Cooper's), the subjective probabilities of success were gauged by respondents who had no experience of the task. In Feather's study, participants were told that task performance was not dependent on intelligence, which may have reduced the failure incentive.

Halisch and Heckhausen (1988) tried to avoid these methodological pitfalls by taking the following precautions:

1. They used the same instrument (Heckhausen's TAT) to measure the two achievement motives (HS and FF), but also administered questionnaire measures to tap achievement motivation and test anxiety.
2. They used a scaling method that provided a direct and unfalsified measure of the valences of success and failure.
3. They varied task experience systematically to test the dependence of valence estimation on evidence-based expectancy of success.

The participants' task was to track a spot of light moving along a horizontal beam and to push a button activating a video camera at the moment the spot filled a window in the beam. Task difficulty was manipulated by varying the speed of the spot of light.

A psychophysical scaling method was used to measure valence in terms of respondents' anticipated satisfaction or dissatisfaction with their performance. Respondents first identified standards for success and failure by specifying an upper and a lower boundary (or task difficulty level), beyond which they would experience success or failure, respectively. These estimates served as anchors for determining "minimal" success and failure levels (10% of the interval between the upper and lower limits was added to each of these threshold values). Based on these anchor points, participants were asked to specify the difficulty level at which they would experience "twice" as much satisfaction (success) or dissatisfaction (failure). The closer this estimate was to the respective anchor point, the steeper the valence gradient. In this method, slight deviations from the anchor point thus indicate a high level of emotional sensitivity to success or failure (i.e., even small changes in performance are reflected in affective experience). The two achievement motives were assessed with operant TAT (Heckhausen, 1963b) and respondent questionnaire measures (e.g., MARPS, AMS, TAQ; Section 6.2.7). Scores

on the operant and respondent measures were practically unrelated. The questionnaire scores overlapped with scores on Meyer's (1972) questionnaire on the self-concept of ability (Halisch, 1986); the TAT scores did not.

The results revealed a significant relationship between the TAT measures and the slope of the valence gradients for success and failure. The same pattern of results did not emerge for any of the respondent measures. Oddly, it was not the TAT net hope score, but the aggregate motivation score, that interacted with task difficulty. Individuals high in aggregate motivation had a steeper valence gradient for success than for failure; the reverse held for individuals low in aggregate motivation. More detailed analysis of subcomponents of the success motive identified by means of factor analysis showed that the content categories "positive affect," "praise," and "expectancy of success" were associated with steeper valence gradients for success than for failure, in line with the predictions of the risk-taking model (Fig. 6.8a). The findings for the failure motive were not congruent with the risk-taking model, however. Respondents high in the failure motive had steeper valence gradients for success than for failure; the reverse held for those low in failure motivation (Fig. 6.8b). Follow-up analyses showed that these findings were attributable to active failure avoidance (e.g., If). Once more, empirical research had identified a passive, avoidant facet of the failure motive, as well as an active, coping facet associated with higher attraction to success. It may be that success is the clearest indication of having averted failure (cf. Schultheiss & Brunstein, 2005). A coding system separating these two facets of failure is long overdue.

To date, it has been standard practice to use established measurement techniques to examine the motive dependency of failure valence. This approach has not proved very successful. It might instead be worth taking the opposite approach, and using techniques developed to scale failure valence to construct valid measures of failure motives. For example, a measure of passive failure avoidance would have to be capable of identifying people whose failure gradients are steeper than their success gradients. Such research has yet to be carried out. Additionally, new statistical methods of measuring change (e.g., growth curve analysis; cf. Bryk & Raudenbush, 1992) have opened up more effective routes for determining the slope of valence gradients as a function of interindividual differences in motives (Brunstein & Maier, 2005). These developments should prompt new efforts to test the valence assumption of the risk-taking model using more rigorous methods.

Although the valence gradients for the satisfaction/dissatisfaction judgments of success- and failure-motivated individuals identified by means of respondent methods did not differ, valence judgments of another kind were best interpreted in terms of scores on questionnaire methods. This alternative approach involved a reward

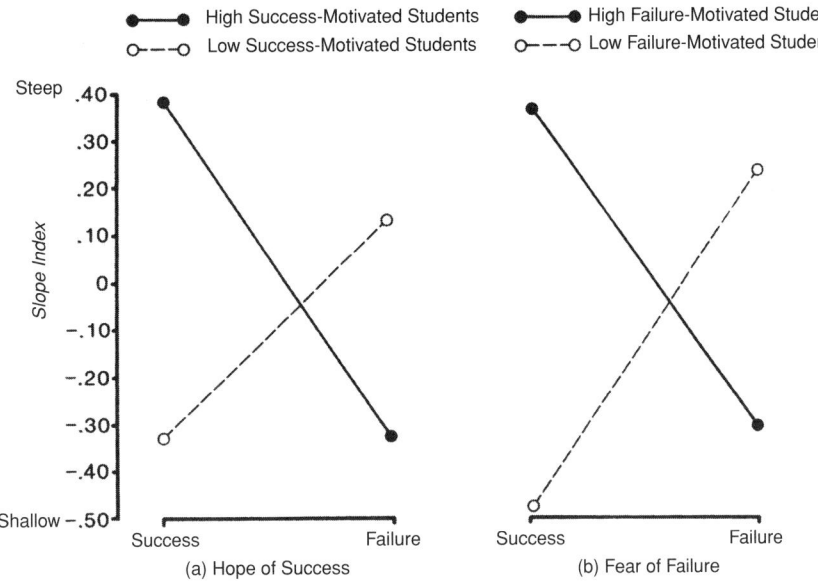

Figure 6.8 Slope indexes of valence gradients for success and failure in (a) individuals high vs. low in success motivation (positive affect, praise, and expectancy of success) and (b) individuals high vs. low in failure motivation (total FF score). (Based on Halisch & Heckhausen, 1988, p. 60.)

schedule based on social comparison norms. Participants were asked to state how many points they would award someone for a success or deduct for a failure. Although there were no differences between success and failure, marked differences emerged in the general intensity with which success was rewarded and failure punished. Findings for a measure of test anxiety (TAQ) are illustrated in Fig. 6.9. Respondents low in test anxiety had steep gradients for both success (awarding points) and failure (deducting points) measured against a social reference norm. Respondents high in test anxiety had shallower gradients; i.e., they did not reward success or punish failure as strongly as their less anxious counterparts. Although this result seems plausible, it contradicts the risk-taking model, which predicts the slopes of the success and failure gradients to differ within the two anxiety groups (steeper success gradients in low anxiety respondents; steeper failure gradients in high anxiety respondents).

SUMMARY

Four overall conclusions can be drawn from the findings of Halisch and Heckhausen (1988):

1. The data go further than previous studies in confirming the assumptions of the risk-taking model. Specifically, the stronger the approach motivation (HS), the stronger the weighting of success and failure with increasing levels of task difficulty. Conversely, the stronger the failure

motive (FF), the stronger the weighting of failure with decreasing task difficulty. The fact that it has proved more difficult to substantiate Atkinson's model for the failure motive than for the success motive appears to be attributable to problems of motive measurement rather than to the assumptions of the model itself. Progress cannot be expected here until a measure capable of isolating the inhibiting component of fear of failure has been developed.

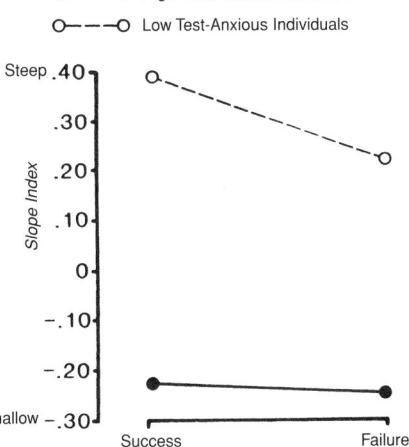

Figure 6.9 Slope indexes of normative valence gradients for high vs. low test-anxious individuals. (Based on Halisch & Heckhausen, 1988, p. 61.)

2. Results differ depending on whether respondents judge their performance against individual or normative standards. Both reference norms have been applied in tests of the motive dependency of valence functions. However, only satisfaction with one's own performance, and not normative judgments on a reward schedule, are consistent with the theoretical principles underlying the risk-taking model.

3. It seems that only TAT variables, and not questionnaire measures, are able to detect motive-dependent differences in the valence of success and failure. Here again, combining a TAT measure of the success motive (nAchievement) with a questionnaire measure of the failure motive (TAQ) seems problematic. Even when using Heckhausen's TAT instrument, active and passive forms of failure motivation can only be disentangled by isolating subcomponents of the FF measure.

4. Parallels can be drawn between valences estimated on the basis of normative assessments of performance and individual differences in ability assessed by questionnaire measures. When normative standards are applied, the valence gradients found for success and failure are not different, as predicted by the risk-taking model, but roughly equally steep. In normative assessments, individuals who consider themselves competent place greater weight on both success and failure than do individuals who consider themselves less competent. Presumably, the latter are less inclined to base their normative judgments on their own experiences.

Overall, findings suggest that operant methods such as the TAT provide more reliable estimates of motives than do questionnaire methods. Questionnaire measures of the achievement motive overlap to a considerable degree with subjective assessments of ability.

6.4.2 Choice: Product of Incentive and Expectancy

We now come to the expectancy aspect of the risk-taking model. Because incentive value hinges on the level of difficulty ($Is = 1 - Ps$; $If = -Ps$) and is in turn multiplied by the probability of success, the function for the resultant motivational tendency peaks at a moderate level of difficulty. This is the point of maximum approach for success-motivated individuals, but the point of maximum avoidance for failure-motivated individuals. The model thus has a symmetrical structure, as described in Chapter 5. The symmetry around the horizontal axis (level of difficulty) is determined by the scores for the two achievement motives. Depending on which of these two motives is dominant, an individual either prefers ($Ms > Mf$) or avoids ($Ms < Mf$) moderately difficult tasks. This symmetry rests on two assumptions:

1. The incentive is a function of the level of task difficulty. This assumption is not only intuitively reasonable, but has also been confirmed in numerous studies (Feather, 1959b, Karabenick, 1972; Schneider, 1973, experiment 2).

2. Approach and avoidance motivation peak at a moderate level of task difficulty ($P = .50$), i.e., the point at which the product of incentive and expectancy is highest.

Studies seeking to confirm this assumption have been dogged by numerous difficulties, as summarized below.

Objective and Subjective Probability of Success

Various methods have been used to measure the probability of success in achievement motivation research. Atkinson (1957) initially worked on the assumption that objective and subjective probabilities of success were congruent. Yet this notion was shattered by his very first study on the subject (Atkinson, 1958a, b). As shown by their performance outcomes, and later substantiated by studies on level of aspiration, highly motivated individuals proved to be most motivated when the objective probability of success was less than 50%. One might therefore speculate that these individuals' judgments of how likely they are to succeed on a task are more optimistic than realistic. Yet it is also possible that, contrary to the predictions of the risk-taking model, achievement-motivated (or, more specifically, success-motivated) individuals prefer tasks of above-average difficulty. Much indicates that task preference indeed deviates from the symmetrical structure assumed in the risk-taking model (Heckhausen, 1963b; Kuhl, 1978b), and that the point of maximum motivation is at $Ps < .50$.

In any test of the risk-taking model, it is vital that the probability of success be assessed accurately by applying one of various standards:

■ absolute standards (e.g., distance from the target in a ring toss game),
■ social comparison standards (how many other people have been able to solve a task), and
■ one's own experience (how well one performed on previous attempts to solve a certain task).

When the same task is presented repeatedly, the subjective probability of success reflects the proportion of successes to failures on previous trials. The performance trend across trials is also taken into account (Jones, Rock, Shaver, Goethals, & Ward, 1968). People who experience success at the beginning of the trials, but failure toward the end, judge their probability of success to be lower than do those whose performance improves over time. Further factors come into play when social comparison standards are applied. In this case, the subjective probability of success is largely dependent on how an individual rates his or her own ability relative to that of others.

Study to Gauge the Objective and Subjective Probability of Success

Schneider (1971, 1973, 1974) investigated the relationship between objective and subjective probabilities of success. Participants were presented with a motor skills task that involved shooting a metal ball through goals of nine different widths. The objective probability of success was calculated on the basis of the relative frequency of successes and failures in previous trials; the subjective probability of being able to score a "goal" at a given difficulty level was obtained from participants. The simplest approach was to ask participants to predict whether or not they would score a goal ("yes"/"no"). Results showed that subjective probabilities of success were considerably higher than objective probabilities of success (Fig. 6.10). Participants' subjective judgments only approached objective task difficulty when tasks were extremely difficult.

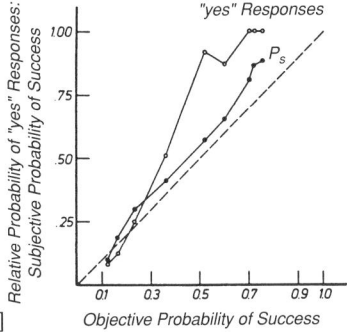

[h]

Figure 6.10 Subjective probability of success (Ps) and relative proportion of predicted goals ("yes" responses) as a function of the objective probability of success on a motor skills task. The *dashed line* shows the results that would be expected if the subjective and objective probabilities of success converged. (Based on Schneider, 1974, p. 162.)

The tendency to overestimate one's performance (see the study above) seems to be characteristic of achievement-related behavior. It is almost as if the desire to improve one's performance outcomes were factored into the expectancy value. At least, this is the pattern observed when a task has already been attempted and performance outcomes are dependent on effort and practice. Expectancies formed without prior exposure to a task may have to be corrected after the first few attempts. The reliability of these expectancies is correspondingly low, and they are not suitable for testing the risk-taking model. Similar problems have emerged for social comparison norms (e.g., "This task was solved by 50% of previous participants"). The divergence of the subjective anticipation of success from the stated norm may be more or less pronounced, depending on how an individual ranks

his or her task-specific ability relative to that of the reference group. Furthermore, research has shown that respondents often have little confidence in probabilities of success or failure reported by an experimenter (Feather, 1963b, 1967). A certain amount of exposure to a task thus seems to be indispensable if reliable data on probabilities of success are to be obtained.

Level of Aspiration: Task Choice and Goal Setting

The risk-taking model was originally developed to explain how levels of aspiration are set. Two experimental paradigms can be used to examine this mechanism:

1. In the task-selection paradigm, participants choose between tasks of the same type representing different levels of difficulty (e.g., throwing from different distances, shooting from the same distance at goals of different widths, or solving increasingly complex labyrinth problems).

2. In the goal-setting paradigm, participants execute repeated trials on a single task. The goal is defined in terms of the time required to execute the task, the number of correct solutions, or the number of mistakes. The goal set by the participant is compared with his or her prior performance to determine goal discrepancy (difference between goal level and previous attainment).

From the outset, a consistent pattern of results emerged. The level of aspiration does not increase steadily with the strength of success-oriented achievement motivation; rather, there is a preference for high, but attainable goals and avoidance of unrealistically high ones. Many of the studies using the task-selection paradigm have involved ring toss games. In a study of kindergarten children, McClelland (1958c) found that success-motivated children preferred "calculated risks," and chose tasks that were neither too easy nor too difficult. Fig. 6.11 shows the distances chosen by success- and failure-motivated students (as measured by nAchievement and TAQ) in a study by Atkinson and Litwin (1960). The preference for intermediate distances was much more pronounced among success-motivated students than among failure-motivated students. Heckhausen (1963b) reported similar findings from an analysis of goal-setting behavior in a labyrinth task. The difficulty of the task was varied by presenting labyrinths of different sizes; the achievement motive was assessed in terms of a TAT measure of net hope (HS–FF). Success-motivated individuals chose goals that were comparable to, or moderately higher than, their previous performance, whereas failure-motivated participants were more likely to set themselves goals that were either extremely difficult or extremely easy relative to their earlier performance (Fig. 6.12).

Most studies designed simply to test whether the most frequently chosen difficulty levels fall into a broadly defined "intermediate" range have produced data substantiating the risk-taking model. Upon closer inspection, however, three

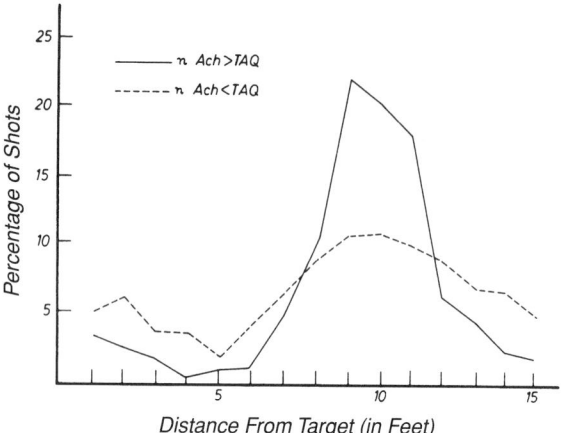

Figure 6.11 Percentage of shots taken from each line by respondents high (nAchievement > TAQ) and low (nAchievement < TAQ) in resultant achievement motive. (Based on Atkinson & Litwin, 1960, p. 55.)

Yet findings similar to those reported above have also been documented for unselected samples of children and school students (McClelland, 1958c).

Besides these two empirical problems, there is a third problem that is inherent in the risk-taking model itself. The model does not predict whether a failure-motivated individual will be more likely to opt for extremely difficult or extremely easy tasks. Heckhausen (1963b) proposed a possible solution to this problem, suggesting that the task choice of failure-motivated individuals depends on the strength of their aggregate motivation ($AM = HS + FF$). If their aggregate motivation is high, so goes Heckhausen's reasoning, they will prefer extremely difficult tasks; if it is low, they will choose very easy tasks. In other words, failure-motivated individuals high in aggregate motivation will tend to expect too much of themselves, and those low in aggregate motivation will not stretch themselves enough. Jopt (1974), Schmalt (1976a), and Schneider (1971) provided empirical evidence for these hypotheses.

It is worth asking whether these discrepancies from the risk-taking model are attributable to shortcomings in the measurements of probability of success or task difficulty. In addition to self-reports, Schneider (1973, 1974; Schneider & Heckhausen, 1981) used an objective index to determine the probability of success, namely, the time it took respondents to decide whether or not they would succeed. Moreover, Schneider asked respondents to state how confident they were in this judgment (confidence rating). Fig. 6.13 shows the three indexes for predictions of hits in a motor skills task (goal-shooting game). The findings for all three indexes were inconsistent with the symmetrical form predicted by the risk-taking model. Decision time peaked well below the objective probability of .50 (when respondents had chalked up as

problems are apparent, two of them empirical, and one theoretical in nature. When the preferred probabilities of success are examined in rather more detail, a marked deviation from the risk-taking model is observed. The maximum preference, whether defined in terms of objective or subjective probability of success, falls below the critical level of $Ps = .50$; as a rule, it is between .30 and .40. In other words, people do not prefer tasks of moderate difficulty, but opt for somewhat more difficult tasks. Moreover, failure-motivated individuals do not choose extremely difficult tasks to anything like the extent predicted by the risk-taking model. Atkinson speculated that too few of his student participants were high in failure motivation (Atkinson & Litwin, 1960; Atkinson & Feather, 1966).

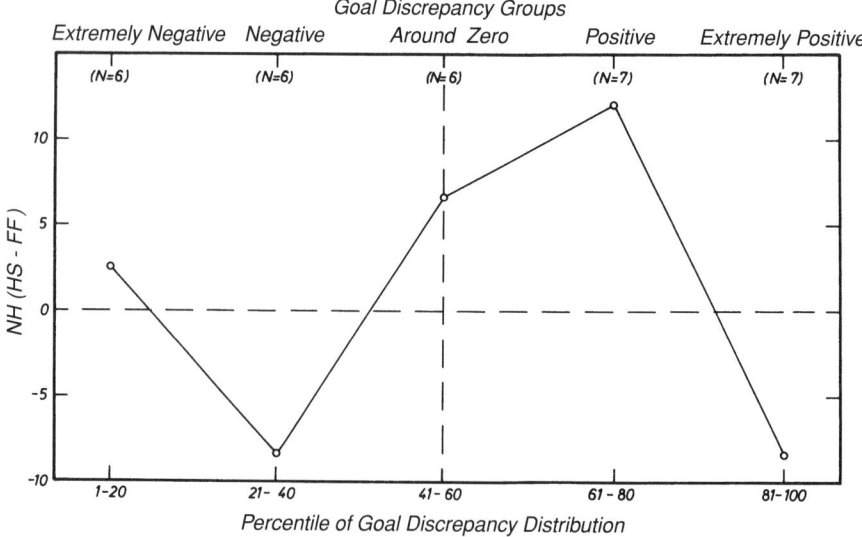

Figure 6.12 Goal discrepancies for labyrinth tasks as a function of net hope (hope for success/fear of failure) in Heckhausen's TAT measure. (Based on Heckhausen, 1963b, p. 95.)

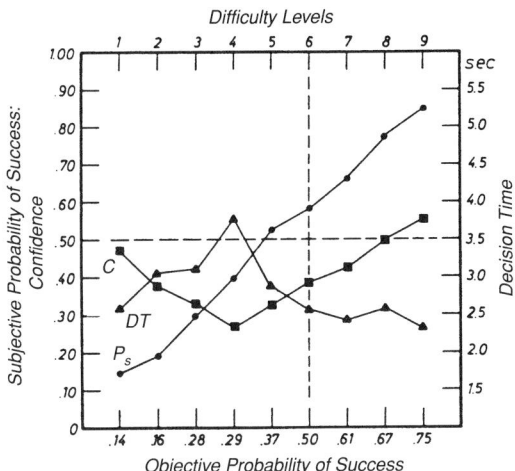

Figure 6.13 Probability of success (Ps), decision time (DT), and confidence (C) in predicting success (hits) in a goal-shooting game as a function of the objective probability of success and absolute difficulty levels. (Based on Schneider, 1974, p. 154.)

many successes as failures on previous trials). Likewise, confidence reached its lowest value well below this point. Subjective assessments of the probability of success were higher than would be expected on the basis of the objective data. Schneider attributes these findings to a "hope bonus" that people add to their performance level when thinking about the future. This "hope bonus" may explain why people tend to tackle tasks that slightly exceed their current level of performance.

There have been many attempts to adapt the risk-taking model to this body of findings (Hamilton, 1974; Heckhausen, 1968; Nygard, 1975; Wendt, 1967). In most cases, additional variables have been specified and incorporated into revisions of the model. Examples of such variables are:

- personal standards defining the difficulty level at which a certain success incentive is reached (Kuhl, 1978b),
- inertial tendencies resulting from previous attempts to complete a task, which afford a kind of additional motivation for future tasks (Atkinson & Cartwright, 1964; Weiner, 1965a, 1970), or
- future-oriented tendencies that take effect when task attainment entails a number of consecutive steps, e.g., in the context of long-term goals (Raynor, 1969, 1974; Raynor & Roeder, 1987).

These attempted revisions are described in detail elsewhere (Heckhausen, 1980; Heckhausen, Schmalt, & Schneider, 1985). None of them proved a resounding success, however.

Typical and Atypical Shifts in the Level of Aspiration

Moulton (1965) took an apparently paradoxical finding from research on the level of aspiration and used it as a test case

for the validity of the risk-taking model. He studied the **atypical shifts** in aspiration levels that are sometimes observed after task accomplishment, namely, increased aspiration levels after failure and decreased aspiration levels after success. The risk-taking model can explain this seemingly rather peculiar behavior in terms of an interaction between the probability of success and the failure motive. Atypical shifts can be expected when failure-motivated individuals experience an unexpected success on a difficult task or a surprising failure on an easy one. In both cases, the probability of success approaches the intermediate range, i.e., precisely the range of difficulty that failure-motivated individuals seek to avoid. As a result, the level of aspiration shows erratic shifts toward the other end of the task difficulty scale. The pattern of results predicted by the risk-taking model is illustrated in Fig. 6.14.

Moulton (1965) tested these inferences by inducing three task difficulty levels (symmetrically distributed probabilities of success of 75%, 50%, and 25%, respectively). Respondents were first instructed to select one of the three tasks, but they were then all administered the moderately difficult task. Moulton induced failure for participants who had chosen the easy task and success for participants who had chosen the difficult task. Participants were then free to choose the next task. As shown in Table 6.7, the results were in line with the assumptions of the risk-taking model. In the free-choice condition, the majority of success-motivated individuals chose moderately difficult tasks, whereas a substantial proportion of the failure-motivated participants opted for easy or difficult tasks. The results also substantiated predictions on change in the level of aspiration. Relatively few participants made atypical choices, and all but one of those who did belonged to the failure-motivated group.

Striving to Maximize Affect or to Obtain Information?

According to the risk-taking model, the preference for moderate levels of difficulty maximizes the anticipated affect, be it pride at success or shame at failure. Success-motivated individuals thus prefer moderately difficult tasks because they promise the highest degree of satisfaction; failure-motivated individuals avoid these tasks because they risk the highest degree of shame. The behavior of the former group is geared at maximizing positive self-evaluative emotions; that of the latter group at reducing negative self-evaluative emotions (Section 6.5). Other authors have pitted the principle of maximizing affect against the principle of obtaining information, based on Festinger's (1954) theory of social comparison processes. According to this second principle, people have a fundamental need to acquire insights into their own attitudes, opinions, and skills, and to evaluate these attitudes, opinions, and skills in social comparison with others. Accordingly, they prefer moderately difficult tasks that split populations into high vs. low ability groups of approximately equal size and thus have the greatest information value with respect

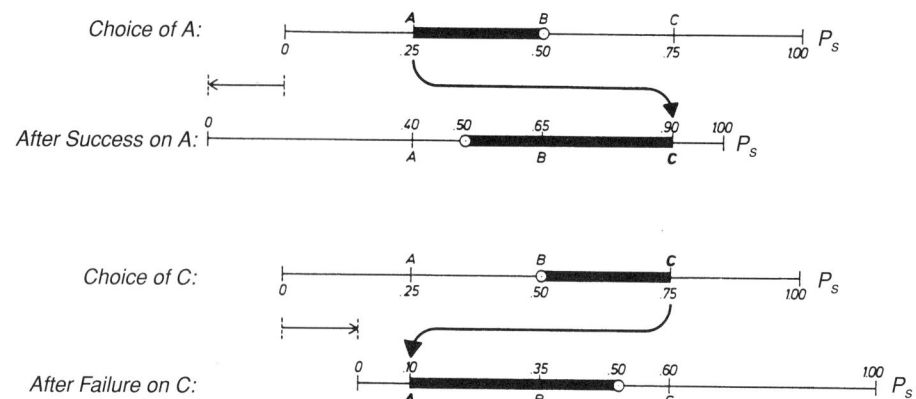

Figure 6.14 Atypical shifts in the aspiration levels of failure-motivated individuals who have succeeded on a difficult task (shift from A to C) or failed on an easy one (shift from C to A), as derived from the risk-taking model.

to one's own ability levels (Meyer, 1973a; Schneider, 1973; Weiner et al., 1971). Both principles (maximizing affect and obtaining information) thus predict a preference for moderately difficult tasks.

Trope (1975, 1980, 1986b; Trope & Brickman, 1975; for overviews, see Trope, 1983, 1986c) compared and contrasted the two principles in an attempt to determine which is decisive for task selection. To this end, he assigned higher diagnosticity for self-evaluation of ability to either easy or difficult tasks. In other words, respondents were told that certain tasks either distinguished very clearly between people high vs. low in ability (high diagnosticity), or barely distinguished between the two groups (low diagnosticity). Trope found that respondents generally preferred high to low diagnosticity tasks. He interpreted these findings as indicating that people strive to reduce uncertainty about their ability levels. Notably, individuals high in achievement motivation are even more likely to choose highly diagnostic tasks than those low in achievement motivation (Trope, 1980).

It follows from Trope's (1986c) interpretation that achievement-motivated individuals seek to obtain realistic and valid information about their abilities as a matter of principle, whether this information proves to be positive (success) or negative (failure; see also Meyer & Starke, 1982). This need for self-assessment – or realistic feedback on one's abilities – can be compared with the need for "self-enhancement," another fundamental motive of self-evaluation (Sedikides & Strube, 1997). Some authors have postulated that achievement-motivated individuals are primarily interested in demonstrating their superior abilities (Kukla, 1972a, b, 1978), implying that they prefer tasks that afford them the opportunity to emphasize positive aspects of the self and thus to enhance their self-esteem.

Consensus has not yet been reached on which of these two needs (self-assessment or self-enhancement) is dom-

inant in determining the tasks selected by achievement-motivated individuals. Sorrentino (Sorrentino & Hewitt, 1984; Sorrentino, Roney, & Hewitt, 1988) reported that both needs influence task choice, but that they are associated with different personality characteristics. The achievement motive (nAchievement) is oriented to maximizing the affective value of a task and predicts how much value individuals attach to obtaining feedback on high abilities (success-motivated individuals) or avoiding feedback on low abilities (failure-motivated individuals). As such, nAchievement can be interpreted as a motive geared to affect maximization. However, Sorrentino identified another motive, labeled **uncertainty orientation** that can also be assessed using the TAT (nUncertainty) (cf. Sorrentino, Hanna, & Roney, 1992).

❶ People high in uncertainty orientation generally strive to obtain information about themselves and their social environment. This cognitive need is expressed in the tendency to choose tasks that promise to provide as much new information as possible, whether it is indicative of high or low ability levels (Sorrentino & Hewitt, 1984). As such, nUncertainty can be interpreted as a motive geared to the self-assessment of abilities.

Attempts have also been made to relate differing needs for self-evaluation to features of the assessment situation (Taylor, Neter, & Wayment, 1995). Brunstein and Maier (2005) found that achievement-motivated individuals act according to the principle of self-enhancement when the ability being tested is socially desirable, and according to the principle of self-assessment in less ego-involving situations. As Sedikides and Strube (1997) have pointed out, the relations between achievement motives – whether assessed by the TAT or by questionnaire measures – and different needs for and standards of self-evaluation warrant careful examination in future research.

6.4.3 Persistence

Persistence is the second major criterion against which the risk-taking model has been tested. Persistence can manifest itself in various forms:

- duration of uninterrupted pursuit of a task,
- resumption of an interrupted or unsuccessful activity, or
- long-term pursuit of a superordinate goal (e.g., career success).

It is no longer taken for granted that the motivation to choose a task can be equated with the motivation that occurs when engaged in a task (cf. Heckhausen & Kuhl, 1985). Where long-term persistence is concerned, Raynor (1969, 1974) was quick to point out that the risk-taking model would have to be extended to yield valid predictions in this domain as well. More specifically, actions would have to be broken down into a series of more or less interconnected subactions, the outcome of each determining whether or not a person is permitted to continue along the path in question (passing academic exams is the prerequisite for entering a graduate career, for example). This model is particularly suited to predicting persistence in long-term, superordinate goals (Raynor & Entin, 1982), and has been discussed in detail elsewhere (Heckhausen, Schmalt, & Schneider, 1985). The notion that ongoing persistence (time spent working on a challenging task) can be equated with the decision to resume work on a previously abandoned task is now also questionable. In the former case, persistence may derive from the incentives residing in the activity without further reflection (e.g., "flow"; Chapter 13); in the latter case, it requires a conscious act of deliberation and decision (e.g., when choosing between various activities). The present section focuses on Feather's persistence studies, which were of particular significance to the risk-taking model.

Feathers Analysis of Persistence Conditions

In the experimental design that Feather (1961, 1962, 1963b) used to analyze motive-dependent differences in persistence (see the studies reported below), participants were first told that the probability of success on a task was either high or low. Failure was then induced on repeated trials of that task. After a certain number of trials, participants were free to decide whether to continue working on the task or switch to another. This procedure allows two factors to be controlled:

- First, the initial probability of success (*Ps*) is steadily reduced by the repeated induction of failure.

  Thus, an initially high probability of success (on a task purported to be easy) will approach $Ps = .50$, and an initially low probability of success (on a task purported to be difficult) will recede from $Ps = .50$. In the former case, approach and avoidance tendencies can be expected to increase (depending on whether the achievement motive is dominated by success or failure tendencies); in the latter case, both tendencies can be expected to decrease,

STUDY

Feather's Studies on Motive-Dependent Differences in Persistence

The student participants in Feather's (1961) first experiment were instructed to retrace a complex figure without lifting their pencils from the paper. What they were not told was that the task was impossible. Participants were presented with four tracing tasks, and told that they could move from the first to the second task at any time. Half of the participants were told that the first task was easy, and half of them that it was difficult. Specifically, they were told that 70% vs. 5% of students had solved the task in a previous trial. In this first experiment, no information was given on the probability of success on the second task. Based on the assumptions of the risk-taking model, Feather predicted that success-motivated individuals would show more persistence on an ostensibly easy task than on an ostensibly difficult task. In the former case, the probability of success approaches $Ps = .50$ after futile attempts to solve it; in the latter case, it recedes from $Ps = .50$. The reverse was expected to hold for failure-motivated individuals, who were expected to show more persistence on an allegedly difficult task than on an allegedly easy task. The avoidance tendencies of failure-motivated individuals were expected to increase as the probability of success on the initially "easy" task approached the critical value of $Ps = .50$. The data presented in Table 6.8 confirm these hypotheses. Two points warrant discussion, however:

- First, Feather found that failure-motivated individuals showed more persistence than their success-motivated counterparts on extremely difficult tasks. This finding is not in line with the risk-taking model, which does not predict the task motivation of failure-motivated individuals to exceed that of success-motivated individuals at any point.
- Second, Feather did not specify the difficulty of the second task. It seems reasonable to speculate that participants expected the second task to be moderately difficult, such that it had an off-putting effect on failure-motivated participants, but was appealing to success-motivated participants. Without knowing the difficulty level of the alternative task, however, this remains uncertain.

In a further experiment, Feather (1963b) specified the probability of success on the second task to be $Ps = .50$. The probability of solving the first task was reported to be 5%. Failure-motivated individuals were expected to be more persistent than their success-motivated counterparts under these conditions. The first task was attractive to them (because it was practically impossible to solve); the second task was threatening, because failure on it would cause great shame. The reverse was expected to hold for success-motivated individuals. In principle, Feather's data confirmed these hypotheses. However, results indicated that the alleged probabilities of success were less influential than the respondents' subjective anticipations of success.

Table 6.7. Initial task preferences and subsequent typical versus atypical shifts in the level of aspiration of success- and failure-motivated individuals (Based on Moulton, 1965, pp. 403–404)

| | Difficulty level of task initially chosen | | | Shift in level of aspiration | |
	Easy	Intermediate	Difficult	Atypical	Typical
	(Ps = .75)	(Ps = .50)	(Ps = .25)		
Success-motivated individuals (N = 31)	1	23	7	1	30
Failure-motivated individuals (N = 31)	9	14	8	11	20

resulting in a reduction of avoidance in failure-motivated individuals, and a reduction of approach in success-motivated individuals.

■ Second, this experimental procedure allows the alternative activity to be varied systematically.

The alternative activity may or may not be a performance-related procedure; the probability of success on this activity can also be varied. In this case, persistence is calculated in terms of the respective probabilities of success.

Overall, Feather's studies succeeded in testing the risk-taking model and, in principle, in confirming its predictions with unprecedented elegance. At the same time, they showed that the possibilities for testing the detailed predictions of the risk-taking model are soon exhausted. The problem remains of how subjective probabilities of success can be reliably induced, controlled, and measured. Nygard (1975, 1977, 1982) took great care in this regard. In one of his studies, participants were presented with very easy or very difficult tasks, and told that they could move on to a moderately difficult task whenever they liked. Relative to failure-motivated participants, success-motivated participants spent longer working on the difficult tasks than on the easy tasks before switching to the moderately difficult task. Considering that both motives were measured with questionnaire measures, meaning that differences in motives reflect differences in self-perceptions of ability, these findings are easy to explain. Individuals who perceive themselves to be more competent (or success-motivated) than others are confident in being able to solve tasks that others find very difficult. If self-concept of ability is not controlled, however, findings such as these are difficult to explain and of little relevance to the validity of the risk-taking model.

Inertial Tendencies of Unfinished Actions

As Feather's analysis showed, persistence on a specific activity is always partly dependent on competing action tendencies. In the same vein, Lewin (1926a, b) had assumed a "system under tension" within the individual, which is not released until a task has been completed. An interrupted action leaves a residual tension that becomes manifest as soon as it is no longer suppressed by another, stronger action tendency.

Atkinson and Cartwright (1964) integrated these ideas into the risk-taking model, adding to the success tendency (Ts) the "inertial tendency" (T_{Gi}) that results from not having completed an earlier achievement-related activity:

$$Ts = Ms \times Ps \times Is + T_{Gi},$$

where T denotes an action tendency, G ("goal") a particular class of action goals (here: achievement), and "i" ("inertial") the fact that the tendency in question derives from an unfinished or failed activity. As soon as the individual embarks on an activity relating to the same theme, this persistent inertial tendency is added to the motivation already activated. In other words, Atkinson and Cartwright (1964) assumed that inertial tendencies can be transferred to the entire spectrum of action tendencies in the same motivational class. Both the classic literature on the substitute value of actions (Henle, 1944; Lissner, 1933; Mahler, 1933) and more recent works on the topic (Wicklund & Gollwitzer; 1982; Brunstein, 1995) suggest that it is unrealistic to assume such a broad level of generalizability. Nevertheless, Atkinson and Cartwright can be commended for expanding the perspective on individual episodes of achievement-related behavior to cover multiple action tendencies. This perspective only came to full fruition in the theory of the dynamics of action, which was developed by Atkinson and Birch (1970; see also Revelle & Michaels, 1976) to explain the interplay of different action tendencies competing for the access to behavior.

Atkinson and Cartwright (1964) only postulated a (positive) inertial tendency for the success tendency. Weiner (1965a, 1970) extended this conceptualization to the tendency to avoid failure. After a failure, the previous success tendency (T_{Gi}) and failure tendency (T_{-Gi}) both continue to exist (the minus sign indicates that the persistent failure tendency has an inhibiting effect on achievement behavior). Building on the original risk-taking model, the following equation can be derived for the resultant motivational tendency (Tr):

$$Tr = (Ms \times Ps \times Is \times T_{Gi} + (Mf \times Pf \times If + T_{-Gi})$$

The resultant inertial tendency increases the motivation of success-oriented individuals to engage in

Table 6.8. Numbers of success- and failure-motivated participants who were high and low in persistence when failure was induced on an allegedly easy vs. difficult task (Based on Feather, 1961, p. 558)

	Difficulty of the first task	Persistence	
		High	Low
Success-motivated participants	Easy	6	2
	Difficult	2	7
Failure-motivated participants	Easy	3	6
	Difficult	6	2

achievement-related activities, and inhibits the motivation of failure-oriented individuals to resume failed activities or related activities. In this point, Weiner's model departs from the Atkinson and Cartwright conception of inertia: after failure, success-motivated individuals are expected to experience a gain in motivation, and failure-motivated individuals to experience a loss. In line with this hypothesis, Weiner (1965b, 1979) found that success-motivated individuals performed better after failure than after success, whereas failure-motivated individuals showed better performance after success than after failure.

6.4.4 Performance Outcomes

It is a daring undertaking to predict not only task choice, but also performance outcomes, on the basis of resultant motivational strength. Motivation is a variable better suited to explaining intraindividual variation in performance than interindividual differences in performance outcomes. These interindividual differences derive primarily from differences in task-related abilities, which often have little to do with motive variables (a highly motivated novice will not be able to match the performance of an expert in a given domain, even if the expert makes no great effort). But even when individual differences in ability are controlled, there is still no coherent theory to explain how achievement motivation influences the individual steps involved in task performance or the associated patterns of information processing.

Krau (1982) noted that the motivation to select a task should not be equated with the motivation that occurs when engaged in a task. Goal setting and goal pursuit are different action phases that are determined by different variables. Specifically, Krau distinguished the following action phases and associated variables:

Action phases	Variables
Goal setting	Estimated task difficulty; strength of the individual achievement motive
Preparation	Planned effort expenditure
Execution	Actual effort expenditure and work-related attitudes

As expected, Krau found that the achievement motive does not have an impact on persistence and performance directly, but that it affects performance outcomes indirectly by increasing the amount of effort that people plan to expend (or are willing to invest). It seems rather rash, in view of these findings, to assume that achievement motivation (or indeed the achievement motive itself) has direct and unmediated effects on task performance. Nevertheless, achievement motivation research has generated various noteworthy models and findings concerning the relationship between motivation and performance. Krau's arguments were later integrated within the **Rubicon model of action phases** (Chapter 11).

School Performance

It would seem logical for researchers to examine the relationship between achievement motivation and school performance. Studies of this type must control for both motivational dispositions (e.g., hope for success and fear of failure) and task difficulty. Researchers can only expect to find substantial relations between motive measures and performance measures when characteristics of the instructional setting and the tasks assigned are taken into account (unless the achievement motivation data also reflect differences in school performance). One way of getting around this problem is to examine ability-based groups. It can be assumed that most students in these classes find the work assigned moderately difficult. O'Connor, Atkinson, and Horner (1966) found that success-motivated students in homogeneous classes showed greater performance gains than their failure-motivated classmates. Weiner (1967) reported comparable data for college students, with success-motivated students benefiting most from ability grouping.

Gjesme (1971) presented similar findings, having taken a somewhat different approach. He assigned students from mixed-ability classes to aptitude groups based on their intelligence scores and found, as expected, that it was only in the moderate-ability group that the success motive was positively, and the failure motive negatively, related to school performance. Assuming that instructional demands fell in the moderate difficulty range for students of moderate intelligence only, these findings are consistent with the risk-taking model.

These data should not be interpreted as supporting ability grouping in schools, however. First, instruction can be individualized to ensure that the tasks assigned are

EXCURSUS

School Performance and the Expectancy-Value Theory of Achievement Motivation

The expectancy-value theory of achievement motivation developed by Eccles and Wigfield (Eccles, Wigfield, & Schiefele, 1998; Wigfield & Eccles, 2000) has inspired a wealth of research on school achievement behavior. Like Atkinson (1957, 1964), Eccles and Wigfield posit that characteristics of achievement-motivated behavior, such as task selection, persistence, and performance, are the product of expectancy variables (e.g., a student's hope for success), on the one hand, and value variables (e.g., the personal incentive of doing well at school), on the other. Their main interest is not in how the dispositional achievement motive is gradually translated into achievement behavior, however. Rather, Eccles and Wigfield assume expectancy and value to have direct and independent effects on achievement motivation. Other characteristics, such as experience, personality, upbringing, and cultural influences are predicted to affect achievement behavior via these two core variables only. Another characteristic feature of the theory is that both the expectancy and value components are assumed to be **task specific**, which accounts for the fact that a student who is highly motivated in mathematics will not necessarily be equally enthusiastic and willing to learn in English.

For Eccles and Wigfield, "value" derives from task incentives that may relate to the aspired outcome and its consequences (e.g., doing well in a mathematics exam and, in consequence, being considered a talented mathematician), or reside in the activity itself (e.g., when a student really enjoys working on tricky mathematics problems). Perceptions of a task's utility (e.g., its relevance to an aspired career) and costs (e.g., having to do mathematics homework instead of meeting up with friends) are also factored into the value attached to it. Eccles and Wigfield assume the expectancy component to be closely related to ability beliefs. Judgments of personal ability in a particular domain

are formed on the basis of previous experience with similar tasks. These judgments in turn have an impact on expectations of success in future tasks in the same domain. Because self-concepts of ability are task- or subject-specific (Marsh, Byrne, & Shavelson, 1988), a student's motivation may vary considerably depending on the task and context (e.g., in mathematics vs. English lessons).

The model's predictions have been confirmed for various aspects of school achievement behavior (cf. Wigfield & Eccles, 2000). Even when controlling for baseline performance, task-specific expectancies and values have been shown to predict learning outcomes (e.g., mathematics grades) as well as students' preferences for certain subjects (e.g., in course selection). One of the best-known – and, in certain respects, most alarming – findings to emerge from this research approach (Eccles, Wigfield, Harold, & Blumenfeld, 1993) is that the mean level of achievement motivation decreases over the elementary school years, and that this negative trend continues across the school career. Eccles and Wigfield reason that the regular and realistic performance feedback provided by teachers, and the inevitable competition with other students, shatters many students' belief in their own capabilities. The value attached to these tasks also decreases, though not as broadly and dramatically.

The Eccles and Wigfield model makes a significant contribution to research by accounting for the task-specificity of expectancy and value variables. Reliable predictions about the achievement behavior of children and adolescents are only possible when task-specific aspects of motivation are taken into account. Moreover, their theory emphasizes the importance of including expectancy- and value-relevant variables other than task difficulty (the classic situation variable in achievement motivation research) in any analysis of achievement motivation.

---

neither too easy nor too difficult ("principle of fit"; Heckhausen, 1969). Second, when cooperative learning methods are applied, heterogeneity of the student body is no impediment to creating realistic, competitive classroom settings that do not over- or understretch students (Slavin, 1995). Moreover, the opportunity to select and work on tasks independently can have positive effects on task motivation, at least when students are predominantly success motivated (and thus choose moderately difficult tasks). McClelland (1980) attributed the low (to nonexistent) correlations found between the achievement motive (nAchievement) and school performance to the fact that the incentives essential for activating the achievement motive (difficulty, novelty, variation, self-determination, informative feedback) are often not present in the classroom, in contrast to occupational settings, where they are either more easily accessible or can be actively sought out. These arguments are all based on the assumption that motives are dispositional variables. However, expectancy-value theories have also been successfully applied to predict school performance, as illustrated in the

excursus on this page based on the research of Eccles and Wigfield.

Motivational Strength and Performance Outcomes: Quantity vs. Quality

The nature of the relationship between motivational strength and performance outcomes has not yet been fully clarified, even when resultant motivational strength, rather than motive strength, is assumed to be the crucial factor. The idea that the intensity of task pursuit (as reflected in speed, i.e., the quantity of tasks completed in a certain time) increases with resultant motivational strength seems unproblematic. What is problematic, however, is the idea that the quality of performance also increases automatically as a function of motivation. Complex tasks cannot be mastered by speed alone; indeed, speed may come at the expense of care and accuracy. The risk-taking model does not distinguish between quantitative and qualitative achievement criteria, and very few studies have tested the model's predictions in the context of complex tasks.

Goal Theory and the Risk-Taking Model

At first glance, the core assumption of Locke's goal theory (1968; Locke & Latham, 1990) – that achievement increases as a function of goal difficulty – seems entirely incompatible with the predictions of the risk-taking model. Yet Locke, Latham, and colleagues have repeatedly found precisely this pattern of results. The relationship between goal level and achievement level has proved to be much stronger for simple than for complex tasks, however (Wood, Mento, & Locke, 1987). Ambitious goals stimulate effort, concentration, and persistence on simple tasks, and thus have direct effects on performance outcomes. In the context of complex tasks (e.g., business strategy games), however, ambitious goals only enhance performance when complemented by a thorough analysis of the problem and strategic planning.

Locke (1975; Locke & Shaw, 1984) pointed out that his findings contradicted the risk-taking model. His data indicated that effort and performance increase with decreasing probability of success (the higher the goal, the more difficult it is), whereas the risk-taking model predicts an inverse U-shaped relationship, with success-motivated individuals making less effort, and thus showing lower performance, as the probability of success recedes from the critical value of $Ps = .50$. In the same vein, Brehm and Wright (see Wright, 1996, for an overview) found that effort expenditure, assessed in terms of physiological measures of cardiovascular response, increases with the difficulty of a task until the point of maximum potential motivation has been reached, at which point it abruptly begins to decrease again.

Bearing in mind that the motivation to select a goal and the motivation to realize that goal are not identical (Chapters 11 and 12), however, it is possible to reconcile these seemingly contradictory findings. The risk-taking model addresses goal setting and task choice, i.e., purely motivational issues. Goal theory, on the other hand, relates to the realization of existing goals, regardless of whether they are self-chosen or imposed by others. It is here that volitional processes come into play. These processes cannot be explained solely by the motivational tendencies that prompted the individual to select the goal in the first place (Heckhausen & Kuhl, 1985). Ach (1910) and Hillgruber (1912) had already drawn attention to this point. In fact, in the "difficulty law of motivation," they postulated that effort expenditure is automatically adjusted to the prevailing difficulty level during task performance, congruent with the findings of Locke, Latham, and colleagues.

Karabenick and Yousseff (1968) used a task that required students to learn a list of paired associates that were objectively equally difficult. They found that success-motivated students (nAchievement > TAQ) performed better on word pairs purported to be moderately difficult. Failure-motivated individuals (nAchievement < TAQ) showed their poorest performance in this condition, and much better performance on paired associates purported to be easy or difficult. These findings are illustrated in Fig. 6.15. The differences in learning outcomes observed were probably the result of differences in effort expenditure, which the risk-taking model predicts to be greatest in the moderate difficulty range. However, it is also conceivable that failure-motivated individuals expended a great deal of effort on the moderately difficult tasks, but made more errors as a result of their fear of failure. More recent research has confirmed that measures of achievement motivation predict performance on paired associates' tasks (Koestner, Weinberger, & McClelland, 1991). The finding that performance is highest on moderately (rather than extremely) difficult tasks remains controversial, however, and was challenged by Locke's goal theory (1968; Locke & Latham, 1990; see the excursus on this page).

Other studies have shown that increased effort expenditure can also have the opposite effect, leading to a decrease in performance. Increasing speed can have detrimental effects on accuracy, a phenomenon known in the literature as the "speed/accuracy trade-off." Schneider and Kreuz (1979) reported one example of this trade-off. Student participants worked on number-symbol tasks once under normal conditions and a second time (one week later) under "record" conditions. The record condition was induced by instructing students to do their very best (based on Mierke, 1955), or by setting high goals (based on Locke, 1968). Two different versions of the number-symbol test were administered, one easy and one difficult. Speed of performance on both easy and difficult tasks increased as a function of the (induced) effort level. The same pattern was not observed for quality of

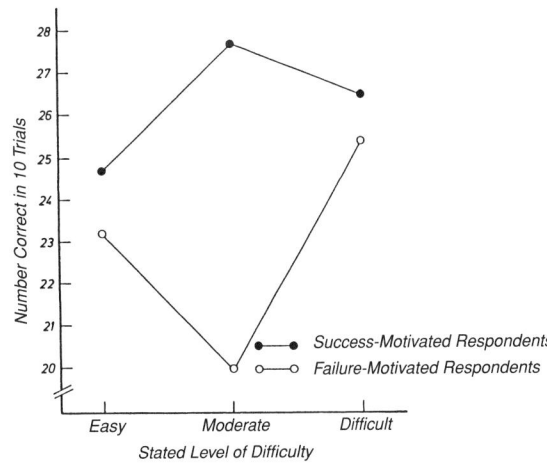

Figure 6.15 Numbers of correct paired associates in 10 trials for word pairs that were purported to be easy, moderately difficult, or difficult, but were in fact equally difficult. Results for success- and failure-motivated respondents. (Based on Karabenick & Yousseff, 1968, p. 416.)

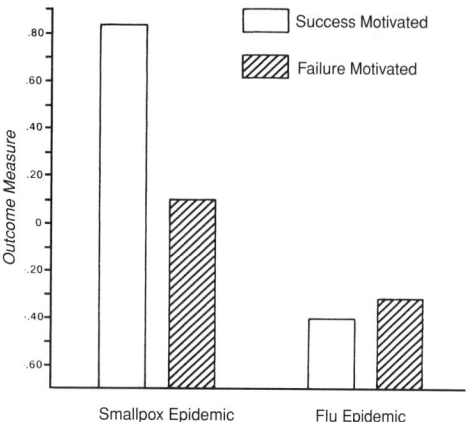

Figure 6.16 Effect of the level of personal involvement on success- and failure-motivated individuals' performance on a complex problem. (Based on Hesse, Spies, & Lüer, 1983, p. 416.)

performance (number of errors). Maximum effort was associated with increased numbers of errors, to a far greater extent on the difficult version of the test than on the easy version. An overly hasty, error-prone approach can thus have counterproductive effects on the quality of performance, particularly on difficult tasks. Accordingly, the quality and quantity of performance may diverge as the strength of motivation increases. Change in motivational strength is only reflected directly in quantity of performance, as Thurstone (1937) had already pointed out. In fact, quality of performance may be impaired by excessively high levels of motivation. It seems that there is an optimal motivational level for any given task, at which performance efficiency is highest (see below).

Nevertheless, a strongly activated achievement motive can also be associated with better performance on complex problems. Fodor and Carver (2000) found that nAchievement (TAT) predicted the creativity and complexity of the suggestions put forward by student participants in a strategy game, the aim of which was to ensure that a pet dog had an adequate supply of water while its owners were away for a few days. However, this effect was only observed when the achievement motive had been activated by feedback on another task. Hesse, Spies, and Lüer (1983) asked their participants to fight a fictional epidemic that had broken out in a small town. They were able to choose between a broad range of measures, some with positive, other with negative consequences. The task was constructed such that the degree of personal involvement was high (serious outbreak of smallpox, high personal responsibility) or low (flu epidemic, low personal responsibility) (Fig. 6.16). When faced with a smallpox epidemic, success-motivated individuals (questionnaire) proved to be much more effective in their approach than failure-motivated individuals. They worked more persistently, asked more questions, and showed a better grasp of the problem.

SUMMARY

Notwithstanding these promising findings, the relationship between motivation and achievement outcomes warrants a theory of its own. This theory should specify the mediating variables – be they motivational, emotional, or cognitive in nature – that intervene between individual, situational, and task-related characteristics, on the one hand, and achievement variables, on the other. To this end, motivational action control during task performance should be examined and carefully modeled in proximal analyses. This approach to the analysis of task performance would require perspectives from differential and general psychology to be combined. It does not suffice to define motivation as an input variable and to measure performance as an output variable, disregarding the intervening motivational influences on information processing. Approaches that satisfy these requirements do exist, but they are few and far between (cf. Boekarts, 2003; Revelle, 1986; Schiefele & Rheinberg, 1997; Schneider, Wegge, & Konradt, 1993; Rheinberg, Vollmeyer, & Burns, 2000), at least in the tradition of achievement motivation theory. Two notable exceptions, both of which draw on the work of Atkinson, are presented in the following sections.

Efficiency of Task Performance

In 1974, Raynor and Atkinson published "Motivation and Achievement," a more detailed analysis of the relationship between motivational strength and quality of performance outcomes that took account of task complexity.

Reminiscent of the Yerkes-Dodson Rule (1908; see also Chapter 2), Atkinson (1974b) did not assume a monotonic relationship between motivational strength and efficiency of task execution. Maximal efficiency derives not from maximal motive strength, but from optimal motive strength, and optimal motive strength decreases as the task and its information processing demands become increasingly complex. People functioning below this optimal level are "undermotivated"; when motivational strength exceeds the optimal level, performance is adversely affected by "overmotivation." These assumptions are illustrated in Fig. 6.17. Performance on a simple task (A in Fig. 6.17) increases continuously as a function of motivational strength; the slope is steep to begin with, and flattens off somewhat later. Performance on a moderately difficult task (B) takes the inverse U-shaped form of the Yerkes-Dodson Rule. When a task is very complex (C), motivational strength reaches its optimal level even sooner. Hence, a given motivational strength can have very different effects on performance outcomes depending on the type of task at hand (in other words, motivation cannot be identified with performance).

The motivational strength to perform a task is determined by three variables:

1. the person's motives,
2. the perceived difficulty of the task (probability of success), and

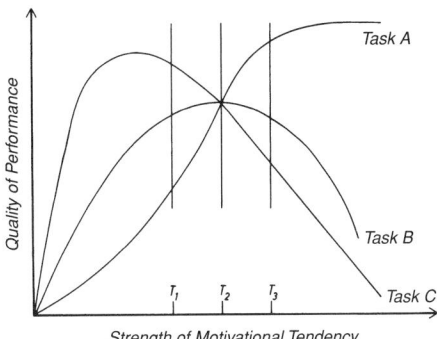

Figure 6.17 Efficiency of task execution (quality of performance) as a function of motivational strength on three tasks (A, B, C) of increasing complexity. Depending on the complexity of the task, the strength of the motivational tendency (T_1, T_2, T_3) may be conducive or inhibitive to quality of performance. (Based on Atkinson, 1974b, p. 200.)

3. the situational incentives (e.g., consequences of self- and other evaluation after success and failure).

These assumptions are largely in line with those of the risk-taking model. Atkinson also continued to assume that the relationship between the tendency to avoid failure and the tendency to approach success is subtractive, leading to the logical, though seemingly paradoxical, hypothesis that high failure motivation can have favorable effects on performance on complex tasks, where (overly) high success motivation would have detrimental effects.

❗ What distinguishes this new approach is the assumption that the effects of motivational strength on performance are moderated by task complexity.

The model was tested with data from empirical studies addressing the effects of multiple motives and incentives on task performance. The idea behind this approach was very simple: the interaction of multiple motives and incentives can soon result in overmotivation and have detrimental effects on performance. Most of these studies are summarized in the volume edited by Atkinson and Raynor (1974) and are based on reanalyses of published data.

Entin (1974) measured the achievement and affiliation motives of student respondents (person characteristics) presented with simple or complex calculations (task characteristics). The situational context was endowed with achievement-related (private feedback) or affiliation-related (public feedback) incentives (situational characteristics). In the private feedback condition, success-motivated students performed better than failure-motivated students, regardless of the complexity of the task. In the public feedback condition, respondents with high scores in both motives (achievement and affiliation) showed marginal performance deficits as a result of overmotivation. Again, no differences were found between simple and complex tasks.

Atkinson's (1974b) reanalysis of studies reported by Atkinson and Reitman (1956) and Reitman (1960) was rather more convincing. Participants were set mathematics tasks in a multi-thematic incentive situation (group competition, encouragement by the experimenter, and the promise of reward). Success-motivated respondents performed less well under these conditions than in a situation with few extrinsic achievement incentives. The reverse held for participants with a low resultant achievement motive, who benefited from the introduction of additional incentives and performed better under these conditions. Findings from further studies confirm that multi-thematic incentives soon lead to performance decrements in success-motivated individuals, whereas less motivated or failure-motivated participants tend to benefit from the provision of additional incentives.

Horner (1974b) asked male students to solve mathematics problems and anagrams, either alone or in competitive situations with a male or a female opponent. Again, the resultant achievement motive and the affiliation motive were assessed. Table 6.9 documents the study's findings for the anagram tasks (the pattern of results for the mathematics task was similar). When working independently, success-motivated students performed much better than failure-motivated students. When competitive incentives were added, a different picture emerged, particularly for respondents competing with a same-sex opponent (i.e., a male). Under these conditions, participants high in both the success and the affiliation motive performed just as poorly as participants low in both of these motives. In the former case, the performance decrement was attributed to the effects of overmotivation; in the latter case, to the effects of undermotivation.

The most convincing evidence to date for overmotivation leading to performance decrements was reported by Short and Sorrentino (1986). Participants worked on a rule-construction task, either alone or in small groups. When the incentive of group work was added, a combination of high success and high affiliation motives predicted a performance decrement, whereas a high failure motive was associated with enhanced performance. This is one of the few studies that has succeeded in demonstrating that the failure motive has a subtractive effect on the achievement tendency and can thus diminish the effects of overmotivation.

Nevertheless, three points of Atkinson's achievement model warrant further consideration:

1. There has been surprisingly little empirical investigation of Atkinson's hypothesis that task complexity moderates the effects of motivational strength on performance. This endeavor would doubtless be facilitated by a taxonomy permitting more precise definitions of task complexity and the associated information processing demands (cf. Wood, 1986). Strictly speaking, the core premise of the achievement model described above remains untested.

2. The performance decrements observed in multi-thematic incentive situations are difficult to interpret.

Table 6.9. Mean number of anagrams solved as a function of the resultant achievement motive (nAchievement – TAQ), affiliation motive (TAT), and three incentive conditions (N = 88 male students; scores were standardized to have a mean of 50 and a standard deviation of 10) (Based on Horner, 1974a, p. 249)

	Condition		
Motive constellation	No competitor (alone)	Female competitor	Male competitor
High affiliation motive			
High success motive	46.5	53.9	48.4
High failure motive	41.8	53.6	56.1
Low affiliation motive			
High success motive	48.4	53.4	53.7
High failure motive	40.8	47.7	46.7

Overmotivation is just one of many possible explanations. In meta-analytic studies, Spangler (1992) found that achievement motive-incongruent incentives, such as material rewards, social recognition, and pressure to perform, reduce efficiency of task performance in individuals high in the achievement motive (nAchievement). Spangler did not interpret this finding as a indicative of overmotivation, however, but as an undermining effect of external rewards. Specifically, he suggested that the intrinsic motivation that achievement-motivated individuals automatically experience in the presence of challenging tasks is undermined by motive-incongruent incentives. It remains unclear which of these two explanations (overmotivation or loss of motivation) is correct.

3. Atkinson's achievement model requires a careful distinction to be drawn between success- and failure-related achievement motives. It is not appropriate to calculate the difference between the two motive scores, because doing so neglects the independence of the two motives. Covington and Roberts (1994) have proposed a more appropriate two-dimensional model of achievement motivation (see the excursus on the following page).

Overmotivation as a Problem of Attention and Effort Control

Beyond the boundaries of achievement motivation research, Baumeister (1984; Baumeister & Showers, 1986) has described and attempted to explain a phenomenon that he terms "choking under pressure." By this he means the decrements in performance sometimes observed at the very moment when peak performance is required (e.g., in an important test). This phenomenon seems to be caused by attention being focused on the action at hand, thus interfering with its automatized and overlearned execution. Self-related cognitions can also interfere with performance, as postulated in the attention thesis of test anxiety (Wine, 1971), in which case attention has to be controlled by volitional means (e.g., by instructing oneself to concentrate on the task).

Typical variables that can easily cause a decline in efficiency are:
■ the presence of critical observers,

■ competition with others,
■ outcome-dependent rewards or sanctions, and
■ ego-relevance of the task.
    Mediating conditions are:
■ high task complexity,
■ expectancies, and
■ individual differences.

Individual differences include the ability to regulate or direct one's effort and attention to be consistent with the demands of a task. Kuhl (1983) described this self-regulatory ability as an essential component of action control, which is vital for ensuring the enactment of intentions, even in difficult or distracting situations with few incentives (Chapter 12). For example, people may visualize incentives that increase their motivation to perform an unpleasant activity; they may reward themselves for completing the activity by doing something more enjoyable afterwards; they may endow the activity itself with playful incentives; they may eliminate environmental distractions that might distract them from the action at hand (for an overview of motivational control strategies, see Wolters, 2003).

Conversely, people faced with very complex and error-prone tasks may have to rein in their motivation in order to avoid rushing into a task with undue haste.

Heckhausen and Strang (1988) investigated the ability of semi-professional basketball players to moderate their effort to an optimal level. In repeated trials, the players were required to perform a difficult dribbling maneuver before shooting a goal under either normal training conditions or "record" conditions. The record condition was induced by instructing players to score a personal best. Two types of measures served as dependent variables: first, physiological indicators of effort (blood lactate levels and pulse rate); second, accuracy of task execution (number of dribbling errors) and completion (number of misses). As expected, a performance decrement (i.e., an increase in the numbers of dribbling errors and misses) was observed in the record condition, although there were marked differences between players. Those (action-oriented) athletes who were able to keep their effort at an optimal level (lactate levels) and who made few errors, even under the stressful record condition, were

EXCURSUS

The Quadripolar Model of Achievement Motivation

Covington and his associates (Covington & Omelich, 1991; Covington & Roberts, 1994) suggested that striving for success and striving to avoid failure should be treated as two independent dimensions of achievement motivation. Unlike Atkinson (1957, 1964a), who reduced these two motives to a single, bipolar dimension (hope for success vs. fear of failure) by computing a difference score, Covington and associates distinguish four types of achievement-motivated individuals (Fig. 6.18):

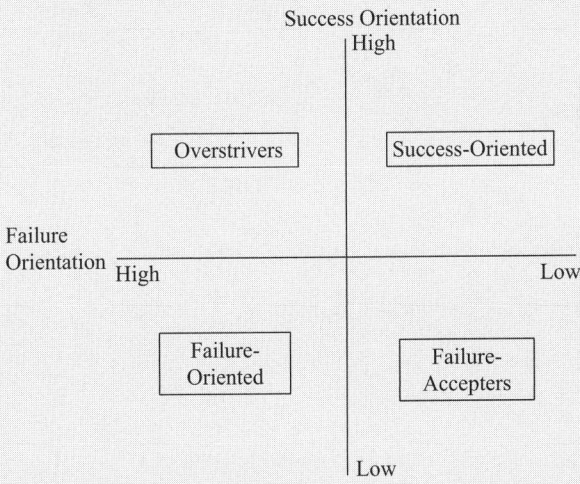

Figure 6.18 Quadripolar model of achievement motivation. (Based on Covington & Roberts, 1994, p. 160.)

Type 1: Success-oriented individuals strive for success without the fear of experiencing failure.

Type 2: Failure-oriented individuals fear failure, but derive little pleasure from success.

Type 3: Overstrivers have high scores on both motives; they strive for success, but also fear failure.

Type 4: Failure accepters do not feel attracted to success, nor are they concerned about possible failure.

This quadripolar (rather than bipolar) model of achievement motivation is based on the finding that correlations between success orientation and failure avoidance are either nonexistent (TAT) or of small to moderate magnitude (self-report). Any imaginable combination of the two motives can be observed within a single individual. The approach traditionally taken in achievement motivation research of subtracting the failure motive from the success motive produces the same neutral score for both overstrivers and failure accepters – both types are characterized by approximately equal (strong vs. weak) levels of the two motives. Yet Covington and Roberts (1994) report that failure accepters differ from overstrivers in numerous respects (see also Martin, Marsh, & Debus, 2001).

Specifically, people who accept failure do not seek to acquire new skills or to improve their performance. Failure accepters actively avoid effort and are rather indifferent to achievement in educational and work settings. In contrast to failure avoiders, their performance does not cause them much anxiety or worry. Covington and Roberts explain these phenomena by reasoning that failure accepters have uncoupled their self-esteem from socially desirable performance outcomes. Overstrivers, on the other hand, work hard to succeed, but their efforts are driven by the fear of failure. They are the students who work incessantly, but whose learning is superficial. In exam situations, they have trouble retrieving the knowledge they spent so much time and energy committing to memory. Their thoughts revolve constantly around achievement-related activities, which they associate with high levels of stress and social pressure. When they do succeed, they experience relief, but rarely real pride and satisfaction. Overstrivers differ from failure avoiders to the extent that their fears have a mobilizing, rather than inhibiting, effect. Because of the value they attach to success, overstrivers see attack as the best means of defense, and try to overcome their fear of failure by stepping up effort expenditure. Unlike success-oriented individuals, whose approach to challenging tasks is inquiring, optimistic, and self-confident, overstrivers often fling themselves into their work without pause for thought. They lack flexibility, sticking instead to established approaches, and tend to get lost in detail. Despite their enormous efforts, they are ineffective and are particularly likely to fail on complex tasks.

Although these findings are more illustrative than explanatory, they demonstrate that a model that conceives of success orientation and fear of failure as two independent characteristics does more justice to the information value of the two achievement motives than an approach based on difference scores (Schultheiss & Brunstein, 2005). A further advantage of the quadripolar model is that individuals whose achievement behavior is characterized by a conflict of motives (overstrivers) can be distinguished from individuals for whom achievement-driven behavior clearly has no incentive at all (failure accepters).

not identified by the level of their achievement motive, but by their scores on a questionnaire devised by Kuhl (1983) to measure action- vs. state-oriented modes of action control.

The study by Heckhausen and Strang (1988) shows that the strength of a motivational tendency alone cannot predict performance. As McClelland (1985a) noted, the risk-taking model has led to rather exaggerated, overly simplistic claims in this respect. What is in fact crucial is whether an individual has the self-regulatory competence to adjust motivational levels to the demands of the task at hand. Schiefele and Urhahne (2000) reported similar findings for academic outcomes: action control (self-regulatory skills) was again found to have a direct effect on examination results, whereas the effects of achievement motivation were indirect (via goal setting).

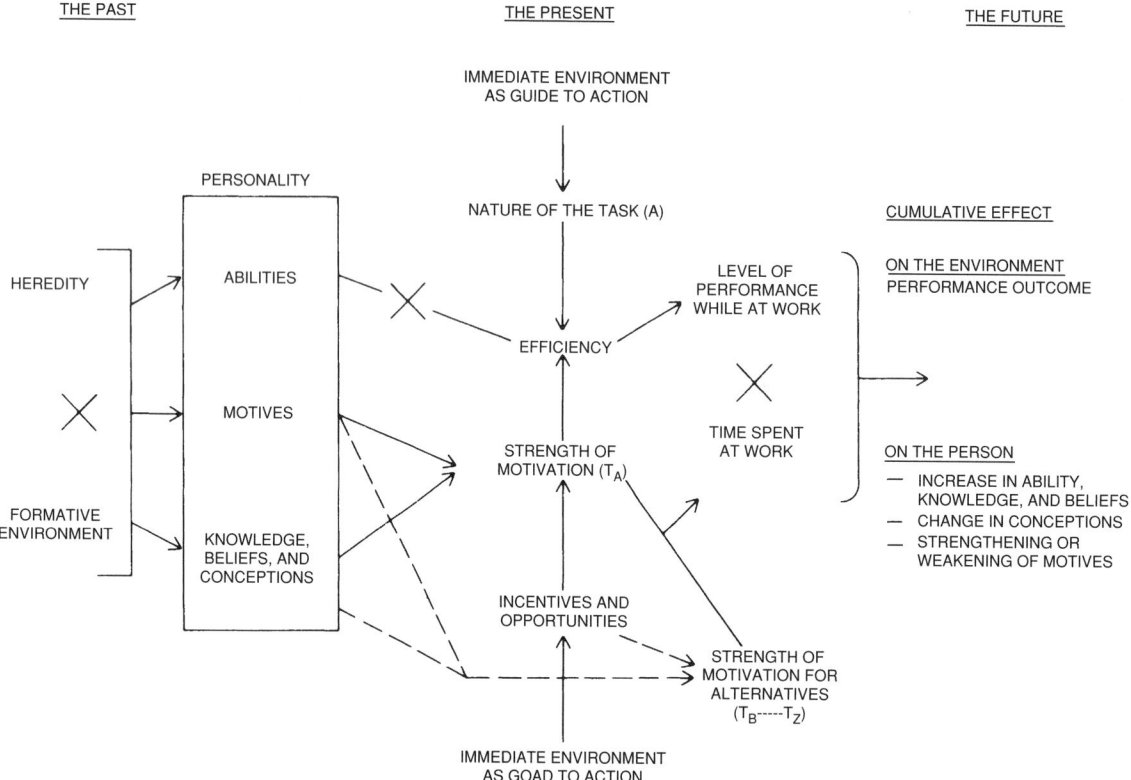

Figure 6.19 The dual role of motivation as a determinant of cumulative achievement. Besides individual ability on a specific task (*A*), strength of motivation (T_A) influences performance gains in two ways. First, together with the specific demands of the task, it determines the efficiency of task performance. Second, strength of motivation has a direct influence on the time devoted to a task, although strength of motivation for alternative activities ($T_B \ldots T_Z$) must also be taken into account here. (Based on Atkinson, Lens, & O'Malley, 1976, p. 51.)

In the final analysis, all of these findings show that achievement motivation is just one of many variables having an impact on quality of performance. It can be the driving force behind efforts to consistently enhance one's performance and achieve ambitious goals, but it cannot compensate for a lack of cognitive or self-regulatory skills. In the following section, we describe a model (Fig. 6.19) developed by Atkinson to account for these phenomena.

Cumulative Achievement

The quality of performance depends not only on the strength of motivation, but also, and indeed primarily, on individual ability. Accordingly, Atkinson (1974a; Atkinson, Lens, & O'Malley, 1976) defined quality of performance as the product (×) of ability and efficiency, where efficiency was the joint function of motivational strength and task demands. Seen from this perspective, an intelligence test (or any other ability test) will only reveal "true" differences in ability if all respondents work on it at the optimal motivational level. Because the multi-thematic incentives involved in test and exam situations both arouse motivation and inhibit performance (e.g., fear), however, this condition is unlikely to be met in real-life situations. Scores on ability tests thus represent a mixture of true ability and motivation-dependent efficiency that is difficult to disentangle. Simply instructing test takers to do their best does not suffice to neutralize these influences, as research showing that scores on concentration tests are influenced by the induction of success- and failure-related motivational states has indeed demonstrated (cf. Brunstein & Gollwitzer, 1996; Brunstein & Hoyer, 2002)

In Atkinson's view, individuals high in motive strength are at particular risk for becoming overmotivated and suffering performance decrements in high arousal situations such as exams. Yet under everyday working conditions, where achievement-relevant incentives are less prevalent, these individuals benefit from high motive strength. In these contexts, their high motivational strength is within the range of optimal efficiency, and fosters the persistent investment of time and effort in successive phases of an activity. Atkinson assumed an almost linear relationship between the strength of the (activated) achievement motive and the time devoted to an activity. In the long run, high efficiency coupled with high time commitment results in a high level of cumulative achievement.

In other words, because quality of performance is dependent on ability and efficiency, it follows that cumulative achievement is the product of performance quality and time invested in a task. The latter is determined by the strength of the success motive, and by the presence of environmental incentives capable of arousing this motive. Of course, incentives and motives relating to alternative activities (e.g., meeting up with friends rather than doing homework) may also take effect. Which activity is performed, and how much time is invested, ultimately depends on the relative strengths of the competing motives. Motivation thus serves a dual function in cumulative achievements. First, it influences the efficiency with which a task is performed. Second, it influences the time invested in that task.

This model has important implications, not only for predicting cumulative achievement, but also for the long-term acquisition of knowledge and skills. Besides having an impact on current performance, the multiplicative interaction between performance quality and time invested affects the individual him- or herself, and facilitates performance gains. As the proverb says, "practice makes perfect." Hence, Atkinson anticipated an idea that was later developed in expertise research (Ericsson, 1996): excellence, in any given area of expertise, is contingent on an extended period of regular study, practice, and application, with a focus on insightful learning ("deliberate practice") rather than routine drills.

Given its complexity, the model has mainly been used as a framework theory for explaining multiply determined performance trajectories (e.g., the development of scholastic outcomes; cf. Helmke & Weinert, 1997). Detailed empirical analyses are scarce, however. Sawusch (1974) tested and confirmed the model's assumptions in a computer simulation. Because these analyses drew on artificial data, their results should be interpreted with caution. Atkinson, Lens, and O'Malley (1976) obtained the resultant achievement motive (nAchievement – TAQ) and intelligence scores of 6th and 9th graders, and compared them with academic performance in grade 12. Overall, differences in intelligence test scores explained more variance in school-leaving grades than did motivational differences. There was also an interaction effect between strength of motivation and intelligence. High motivation predicted better school performance among students in the upper range of the intelligence distribution only. This finding is consistent with Atkinson's concept of cumulative achievement: it is only at high ability levels that motivational strength – mediated by efficiency – can have positive effects on quality of performance. Furthermore, the relationship between motive strength and ability level was more pronounced in grade 9 than in grade 6. This finding might indicate that motive strength – mediated by the time spent on school work – promotes the acquisition of knowledge and skills. Entirely convincing evidence for this hypothesis has yet to be presented, however.

SUMMARY

Most achievement motivation research has drawn on Atkinson's risk-taking model. Although studies of task choice and persistence have produced evidence in support of the model, the insights it provides into achievement levels and learning trajectories are rather limited. Whereas quantity of performance is dependent on strength of motivation, the same only applies to quality of performance under very specific conditions. Atkinson, therefore, developed models to predict the effects of motivational strength and direction on efficiency of task performance at various levels of difficulty. He established that both undermotivation and overmotivation can cause performance decrements. In the case of cumulative achievement, ability levels have to be taken into account as well; it is the interaction between ability and motivation that determines the quality of long-term performance. It has not been possible to confirm the predictions of the risk-taking model for the effects of failure motivation, probably because fear of failure is not purely an avoidance motive.

As yet, there have been relatively few efforts to test the core assumptions of the risk-taking model. Findings on the valence of success and failure and on subjective evaluations of the probability of success indicate either that real-life achievement behavior deviates from the model's assumptions of symmetry (with respondents preferring rather difficult tasks to tasks of moderate difficulty, for example) or that researchers have not yet succeeded in measuring the model's variables (e.g., probability of success) with a sufficient degree of accuracy.

6.5 Achievement Motivation and Self-Evaluation

How can the findings on achievement motivation theory described above best be integrated and interpreted? As impressive and differentiated as these data may be, the question remains of how characteristic patterns of success- and failure-motivated behavior are maintained over time. Heckhausen attempted to answer both of these questions by proposing a self-evaluation model that explains characteristics of success- and failure-motivated behavior in terms of both affective and cognitive aspects of achievement motivation. This model and its applications are discussed in the following sections.

6.5.1 Achievement Motivation as a Self-Reinforcing System

Heckhausen (1972, 1975b, 1977a, b) sees the key to understanding observable differences in the behavior of success- and failure-motivated individuals in the differing directives that govern their behavior, as well as in the contrasting frames of reference (or reference values) that they apply to evaluate the outcomes of their actions. These relationships can best be

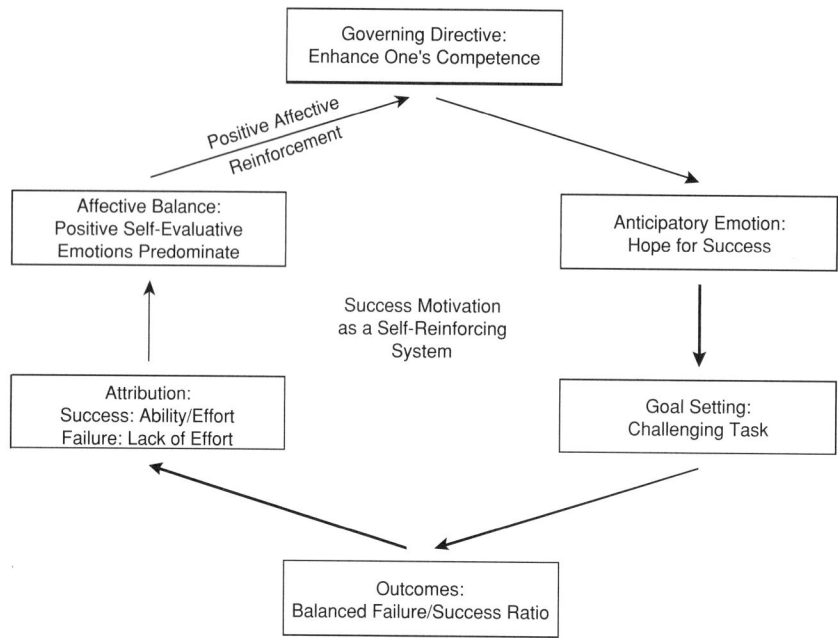

Figure 6.20 Success motivation as a self-reinforcing system.

illustrated by reference to the situation of success-motivated individuals, as illustrated in Fig. 6.20.

The Directive Governing Success-Motivated Individuals

The actions of success-motivated individuals are governed by the directive to enhance their competence, to acquire new skills, and to improve their abilities in specific domains on an ongoing basis. This striving is driven by positive anticipatory emotions (hope for success) that are activated at the beginning of the task situation and that anticipate the affective goal state of pride in one's competence, although not to its full extent. Anticipatory emotions stimulate, but do not satisfy, the need for self-improvement. As a personality trait, hope for success can only be explained against the background of the individual's learning history (e.g., the experience of mastering challenging tasks); for simplicity's sake, this aspect is not considered in detail here (see Chapter 15). At the beginning of an achievement episode, success-motivated individuals act on their hope for success by choosing challenging tasks and setting ambitious goals. They prefer tasks that are slightly more difficult than those they have previously mastered. These kinds of tasks and goals are sensitive to effort investment and afford success-motivated individuals the perfect opportunity to demonstrate their competence. Because the level of aspiration is intermediate or slightly above average difficulty, success-motivated individuals logically experience failure just as often as success; their ratio of failures to successes is more or less balanced. How is it, then, that success-motivated individuals can "afford" to fail just as often as they succeed? According to Atkinson (1957, 1964a), the

pride that success-motivated individuals take in their successes far outweighs the shame they feel at failure. Despite a balanced failure/success ratio, the affective balance of self-evaluation after success or failure – i.e., the ratio of positive to negative self-evaluative emotions – is positive. Although the risk-taking model postulated this phenomenon, no real explanation was given for it. Weiner and colleagues (Weiner et al., 1971; Weiner, 1974) were the first to shed real light on the matter (Chapter 14). Success-motivated individuals tend to attribute success to effort and aptitude, and failure to a lack of effort. Even if they do not succeed, they do not doubt their ability. For them, experiences of failure are associated with the expectation of being able to do better next time. Experiences of success are associated with feelings of joy and pride, and provide confirmation of their ability and effort. Thus, although their failure/success ratio is balanced, the self-evaluations of success-motivated individuals are conducive to achievement-motivated behavior, and evaluations detrimental to self-esteem are rare. This is the critical point in Heckhausen's self-evaluation model: although the directive governing the actions of success-motivated individuals causes them to experience as many failures as successes, their feelings of pride (success) far outweigh their feelings of shame (failure). Heckhausen assumes that affect (here: self-evaluative emotions) serves to **reinforce** achievement-motivated behavior. Rather than each individual element of the model outlined in Fig. 6.20, it is the directive underlying the entire cycle that is reinforced. The behavior of success-motivated individuals is driven by the reference values of improving competence and increasing efficiency of task execution. Because this directive is positively reinforced by achievement-related affect, it can be maintained even in the face of failure.

❶ Like McClelland (1987), Heckhausen thus ascribes to affect a key role in the activation (expectancy emotions) and reward (self-evaluative emotions) of achievement-related behavior. Alongside the governing directive, these emotions play a major role in reinforcing success-oriented behavior.

  Unlike McClelland, however, Heckhausen also specifies the cognitive factors (here, causal attributions of success and failure) that underlie self-evaluations and link them to the corresponding affective reactions.

The Directive Governing Failure-Motivated Individuals

Against the background of this model, the behavior of failure-motivated individuals can be explained from two different perspectives. First, failure-motivated behavior can be conceived of as inhibiting or disrupting the balance of the process depicted in Fig. 6.20. Let us imagine what would happen if failure-motivated individuals also preferred tasks of intermediate difficulty. The ratio of failures to successes would again be balanced. Failure-motivated individuals do not account for success and failure in the same way as their success-motivated counterparts, however. Instead, they attribute failure to a lack of ability, and have no clear preferences for the causal attribution of success (Weiner et al., 1971). And it is precisely because failure-motivated individuals interpret failure as a sign of inadequacy that they experience it as shameful and disheartening. Success cannot compensate for these feelings of failure, because failure-motivated individuals rarely attribute success to ability and effort. Thus, although the failure/success ratio is balanced, the affective balance has an impact from the feelings of threat to the self-esteem. In consequence, if failure-motivated individuals were to prefer tasks of intermediate difficulty, like their success-motivated counterparts, they would be punished by recurrent negative self-evaluative emotions.

Simply describing what failure-motivated individuals do not do cannot provide a satisfactory understanding of failure motivation, however. The adaptive functions of failure-motivated behavior must also be identified. Heckhausen (1975) proposed that the directive governing the behavior of failure-motivated individuals is markedly different from the directive hypothesized for success-motivated individuals. Its ultimate aim is to reduce threats to self-esteem or, if possible, to avoid them altogether. The behavior of failure-motivated individuals is not driven by the goal of self-improvement, but by that of protecting self-esteem. Because these individuals associate achievement-related behavior with negative self-evaluative emotions (fear of failure when embarking on or anticipating an achievement-related activity, and shame when failure occurs), the only possible self-reinforcing fac-

tor is a form of negative reinforcement, namely, reducing experiences that threaten self-esteem. Choosing extremely difficult or extremely easy tasks, low persistence, and abandoning achievement-related activities are just a few of the many measures that can help to diminish or avert threats to self-esteem (see Higgins, Snyder, & Berglas, 1990, for other self-handicapping strategies used to shield self-esteem in achievement situations). All these approaches serve either to minimize the probability of failure (selecting very easy tasks) or to prevent negative self-evaluations after failure (the task was so difficult that failure cannot be attributed to personal inadequacies). Thus, although the behavior of failure-motivated individuals may seem strange and inappropriate from the perspective of the "improve competence levels" directive, it is in fact adaptive and entirely functional from that of the "reduce threats to self-esteem" directive. Nonetheless, the failure-related directive is and remains detrimental to the acquisition of knowledge and skills. It is associated with defensive and sporadic achievement behavior, and is incompatible with the goal of increasing personal competence (see also Covington, 1992, for a clear account of how the conflict between competence striving and threat to self-esteem can have detrimental consequences for student learning).

The self-evaluation model was welcomed as a useful integrative and heuristic framework that unifies and clarifies many of the findings produced in decades of research on achievement motivation. Heckhausen's idea of describing success- and failure-motivated behavior in terms of a self-regulating and self-reinforcing system has since generated much further research, the effects of which are most apparent in applied motivation psychology. One of the model's major implications is that any attempts to transform failure motivation into success motivation (e.g., in training programs) must target three subprocesses at once:

- goal setting,
- causal attributions, and
- achievement-related affect.

A focus on just one of these three subprocesses would risk the intervention's success being compromised by the effects of the neglected elements.

On this basis, Rheinberg and Krug (2005) have developed student training programs that have been shown to bring about a sustained increase in hope for success and a corresponding decline in fear of failure. Furthermore, Fries (2002; Fries, Lund, & Rheinberg, 1999) has reported that a training program targeting all three subprocesses can increase the efficacy of treatments to enhance cognitive skills. Indeed, it is vital that training programs aiming to increase actual performance, as well as motivation, do not overlook the skills necessary for the task at hand. This principle is congruent with Atkinson's model of cumulative achievement outlined above; its effects have already been demonstrated in training programs designed to increase the economic activities of small business entrepreneurs (McClelland & Winter, 1969).

The research presented in the two following sections shows how a change in the reference norm used to evaluate achievement is associated with marked changes in each of the three subprocesses identified above.

6.5.2 The Role of Reference Norms in the Motivation Process

McClelland et al. (1953) and Heckhausen (1963b) defined achievement motivation as the striving to meet standards of excellence. They did not specify which standards are used to evaluate an action outcome, however, because various reference norms may be applied (Heckhausen, 1974a).

Reference Norms (Based on Dickhäuser & Rheinberg, 2003)

1. Individual reference norms:
   Individuals compare their performance outcomes with previous outcomes to determine whether their performance has improved, worsened, or remained unchanged over time. The comparative perspective is temporal change in an individual's development (e.g., learning gains on a new type of task).
2. Social reference norms:
   Individuals compare their performance outcomes with those of others. The comparative perspective is the performance distribution within a social reference group (e.g., a student's position in a class) in temporal cross-section, i.e., the individual's current ranking on a certain task relative to the others in a group.
3. Objective or criterial reference norms:
   Performance outcomes are measured against absolute criteria inherent in the task itself. A solution may be correct or incorrect; an intended outcome may be achieved to a specifiable extent.

Each of these reference norms can also be applied to evaluate the performance of others. This is particularly relevant for occupations involving the routine evaluation of others' performance (e.g., teaching, see below).

The three reference norms are not mutually exclusive, but have been shown to take effect in different phases of skill acquisition (Brackhane, 1976). In Brackhane's study, participants in a dart-throwing task were asked to evaluate their performance. At first, they based their judgments on the characteristics of the task, i.e., on the scores displayed on the rings of the target (criterion norm). As they gained more experience, they developed a personal reference system for assessing change in their performance (individual norm). With increasing practice and experience, the criterion for a good outcome was shifted gradually upward. Finally, some participants inquired about their cohorts' performance (social reference norm), indicating that they were interested in how their performance compared with that of others (social reference norm). The advantages of this sequence of reference norm application are clear (see also Zimmerman & Kitsantas, 1997). At first, attention is focused on the task itself. People then begin to register improvements in their performance, and only start to evaluate that performance in social comparison after gaining enough practice. The reverse sequence of norm application could only lead to frustration and to the swift abandonment of efforts to learn a new skill (unless experts were serving as role models or mentors).

The distinction between different reference norms (or standards of excellence) was long neglected in achievement motivation research, but has attracted increasing attention since the 1980s. It is no coincidence that researchers investigating motivational issues in the context of developmental and educational psychology have played a pioneering role here: Rheinberg (1980; Heckhausen & Rheinberg, 1980) in the German-speaking countries and Nicholls (1984a, b, 1989), Dweck (1986; Dweck & Elliot, 1983), and Ames (1984) in the English-speaking countries, to name just a few.

But how do the different reference norms have an impact on the motivation process?

THE ROLE OF INDIVIDUAL REFERENCE NORMS. Individual reference norms occupy a preeminent position in the psychology of motivation. People assessing their own performance levels on the basis of their previous achievements generally find that effort and persistence, on the one hand, covary with gradual improvements in performance, on the other. Moreover, the performance level attained tends to be in the intermediate range of (subjective) difficulty, which – according to the risk-taking model – is maximally motivating. By contrast, comparison with social reference norms tells an individual only that he or she is better or worse than a certain percentage of others, and does not reflect performance gains (assuming the reference group to be making comparable progress). Individual progress does not imply an improvement in relative ranking, as reflected in the high stability of school grades. Individual reference norms focus attention on improvements in personal performance and the effort made to achieve learning gains. Effort is a factor that is under the voluntary control of the individual, and for which he or she can thus be held responsible. Social reference norms, on the other hand, focus attention on a relative ranking – e.g., relative to the rest of a class – that tends to be relatively stable, and that barely correlates with effort and persistence. Social reference norms thus reflect differences in ability. Especially when assessed in social comparison, ability is generally seen as a determinant of achievement that is very difficult to influence in the short term.

❗ Instructional experiments conducted by Rheinberg and Krug (Rheinberg, 1980; Rheinberg & Krug, 2005) have provided empirical evidence for the assumption that individual reference norms, in terms of both self-evaluations (student ratings) and other-evaluations (teacher ratings), enhance motivation to learn. School classes characterized by individual reference norms show higher levels of hope for success, willingness to exert effort, and student responsibility.

Furthermore, individual reference norms are associated with more realistic levels of aspiration and performance

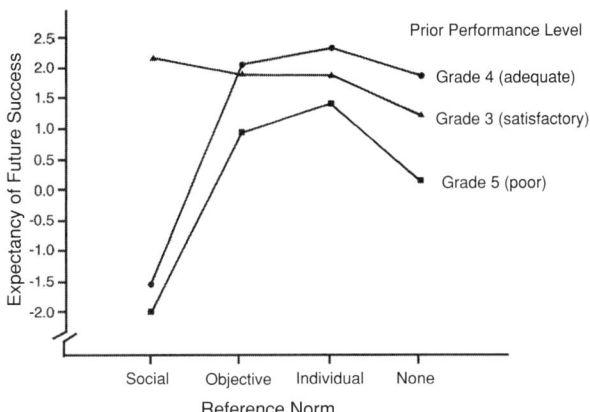

Figure 6.21 Interaction of reference norm and prior achievement on the anticipation of success. (Based on Krampen, 1987, p. 143.)

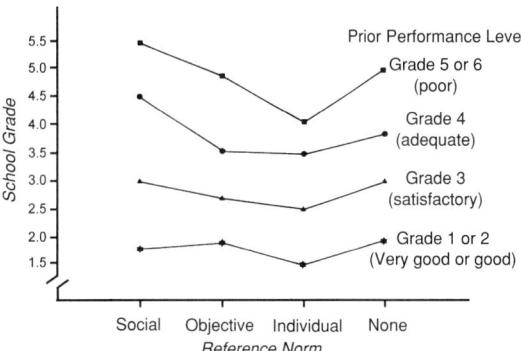

Figure 6.22 Interaction of reference norm and prior achievement on school grades six months later. (Based on Krampen, 1987, p. 144.)

expectations, and with increased effort attributions. Achievement-related affect is dominated by joy and pride rather than by shame and fear of failure. Heckhausen (1975a) even found that people evaluate their own abilities in a more positive light, probably because this appraisal has less to do with social comparison (doing better than others) than with individual learning gains (improving one's own knowledge and skills). Learners who notice the progress they are making see the effects of their efforts at first hand and gain more enjoyment from the learning process (Jagacinski & Nicholls, 1987). This pattern of results has been observed in natural conditions (unaffected by outside influences), as well as in intervention studies in which teachers were trained to apply individual reference norms, and in training studies seeking to modify students' self-evaluations. Transforming a social frame of reference in the classroom to an individual one (or at least enriching it by aspects of intraindividual comparison) creates a motivational climate that has an impact on students' self-evaluations, with favorable effects on precisely those subprocesses (goal setting, causal attribution, and affect) identified above as being relevant to success-motivated achievement behavior (Rheinberg, Vollmeyer, & Burns, 2000).

An impressive study by Krampen (1987) showed that individual reference norms have particularly positive effects on the outcomes of weaker students. Mathematics teachers in 13 ninth and tenth grade classes were trained to provide students with written comments about their work, based on either individual, social, objective (curriculum-based), or no reference norms. The students were assigned at random to one of the four reference-norm conditions. After six months, findings showed significant interactions between the baseline performance level (school grade) and the reference norm on which the teachers' comments were based. As shown in Fig. 6.21, weaker students' expectancies were much higher when feedback was based on individual than on social reference norms (or indeed on objective, curriculum-based feedback, though the effect here was less pronounced). The stu-

dents' performance gains after six months were even more remarkable. Here again, individual reference norms had the most favorable effect; social reference norms had none. The lower the student's baseline performance, the more conducive an individual reference norm was to learning gains (Fig. 6.22).

6.5.3 Reference-Norm Orientation and Achievement Motivation

Both directions of the relationship between reference norms and achievement motivation warrant careful analysis. From one perspective, hope for success can be expected to emerge in conditions characterized by individual reference norms, and fear of failure to develop when social reference norms dominate, particularly when people feel overwhelmed by task demands. From the other perspective, it is worth investigating which reference norms achievement- or success-motivated individuals instinctively use to govern their behavior and evaluate their performance.

Individual Reference Norms as a Developmental Condition for Success Motivation

A wealth of data are available on the first point, particularly from the domain of motivation to learn in schools. Rheinberg (1980) developed a parsimonious test to gauge the relative amount of social comparison information, on the one hand, and information about individual change in achievement, on the other, that teachers take into account when grading their students. Findings consistently show considerable variation in reference-norm orientation across teacher samples, even in equivalent situational contexts. Of course, individual teachers may adapt the reference norm applied to the type and purpose of the evaluation. Teachers with an individual reference-norm orientation have proved to be much more flexible in this respect, however, varying the reference norm applied according to the context of evaluation (e.g., applying objective and social norms when writing report cards, but individual norms in the context of student discussions and everyday feedback). Teachers with a social reference-norm orientation have proved to be less flexible, applying a social frame of reference regardless of the function of the evaluation (report cards, praise for good work, etc.).

The reference norm applied in the classroom also provides a certain amount of insight into teachers' causal attributions of student performance:

■ Teachers with a social reference-norm orientation tend to ascribe success and failure at school to stable, internal factors (e.g., ability), and to form stable expectations of student performance. They only recognize achievements that are above average. They set all students the same tasks, and their praise and criticism is dependent on class-average performance. A "very good" student will be praised even if he could have done better, as long as his performance is above the class average.

■ Teachers with an individual reference-norm orientation attribute students' learning outcomes largely to effort. Their praise and criticism is dependent on learning gains, regardless of students' absolute achievement levels. Progress is consistently rewarded (by praise) and supported by informative feedback. Moreover, these teachers adapt the difficulty level of the tasks set to their students' knowledge levels.

In view of all these correlates, an individual reference-norm orientation in the classroom can be expected to have positive effects on students' learning motivation. Indeed, the empirical data indicate this to be the case. Brauckmann (1976) investigated the relationship between the reference-norm orientation of 16 teachers and the mean success motive of their 492 third-grade pupils, computed separately for each class, and reported a correlation of .54. Rheinberg, Schmalt, and Wasser (1978) found that the failure motive was relatively pronounced in classes whose teachers preferred social reference norms. Interestingly, a longitudinal study by Rheinberg (1980) showed that individualized feedback led to a more pronounced reduction in the initial level of failure motivation in educationally disadvantaged students who could barely compete with their classmates. The sample consisted of fifth graders from the lowest track of the three-tier German secondary system (*Hauptschule*). Students had been allocated to new classes at the beginning of the school year. Half of the classes were assigned a teacher who applied social reference norms; the other half, a teacher who applied individual reference norms. Within each class, students were categorized into three groups based on their scores on an intelligence test. Fig. 6.23 shows change in the failure motive (measured by Schmalt's Achievement Motive Grid, 1976a) over the school year. Students exposed to individual reference norms experienced a reduction in the failure motive, and this effect was most pronounced among students whose intelligence scores were in the lowest tertile.

Corresponding patterns of results were found for test and manifest anxiety. Moreover, students exposed to an individual

reference norm reported an increase in self-perceived ability, regardless of their intelligence. They were also much less likely than students exposed to a social reference norm to attribute failure to a lack of ability. This finding has since been replicated in numerous further studies (Rheinberg & Krug, 2005).

❶ Individual reference norms in the classroom are conducive to the development of students' hope for success, and reduce fear of failure. These effects are not limited to the instructional situation, but extend to the level of personality dispositions as they develop and become increasingly stable.

FAMILY CONTEXT AND ACHIEVEMENT MOTIVATION. Trudewind and Husarek (1979) presented some of the most compelling findings on the relationship between family background and the development of motive dispositions. The authors investigated how mothers' behavior in homework situations was associated with the development of hope for success and fear of failure from first to second grade. Mothers of children who feared failure were found to differ from mothers of children who were confident of success in the following respects:

■ They were more likely to apply social norms than individual and objective norms, and tended to expect too much of their children.

■ They interfered in the homework process and showed little respect for their child's wishes or autonomy.

■ They criticized failure, but responded neutrally to success.

■ They attributed failure to a lack of ability, but success to the ease of the task.

These findings clearly show that fear of failure, as described by Heckhausen (1975b) in his self-evaluation model, is transferred from the (negative) model of the mother to the child. Failure-centered interactions may be internalized in the form of inner dialogs, and thus affect the child's behavior in other situations as well (e.g., at school). As a result, the child experiences fear of failure and helplessness when confronted with scholastic demands, particularly when outcomes are under par. This pattern of results is supported by the findings of Hodoka and Fincham (1995), who studied mother-child interactions in students classified as "helpless" (teacher rating), again in homework situations. Their findings confirm those of Trudewind and Husarek to the letter. A practical conclusion to be drawn from these insights is that interventions designed to combat fear of failure or to boost hope for success must take both the school and family contexts into consideration (for a parent training program of this kind, see Lund, Rheinberg, & Gladasch, 2001).

The Achievement Motive and Preferences for Reference Norms

Extrapolating from these findings, it seems reasonable to assume that people scoring high on success motivation

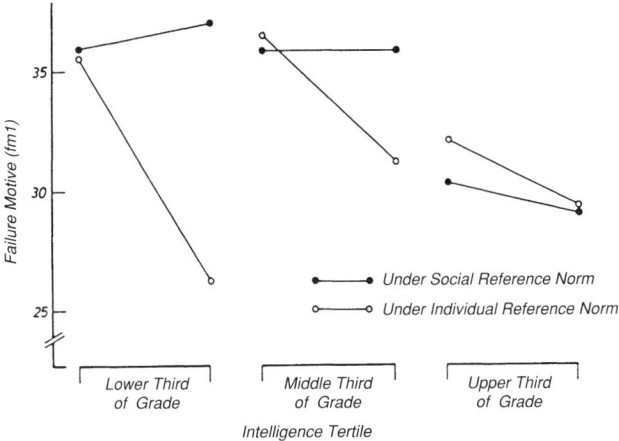

Figure 6.23 Developmental change in the failure motive (FM-1, Grid test) during the fifth grade for classes whose teachers applied individual vs. social reference norms by performance on an intelligence test (in tertiles). (Based on Rheinberg, 1980, p. 148.)

instinctively use individual reference norms to evaluate their performance outcomes. There have been few investigations of this assumption, but at least three studies have provided findings to support it. In a study with 124 students aged between 11 and 13, Rheinberg, Duscha, and Michels (1980) found a significant correlation of $r = .39$ between hope for success (AM Grid; Schmalt, 1976a) and preference for an individual reference norm over a social reference norm in a motor skills game. Brunstein and Hoyer (2002) took a different approach, but their pattern of results was similar. In an experimental study involving a concentration test, student participants were given feedback on both their individual performance gains and their ranking relative to the other participants. The achievement motive was measured by means of the TAT (nAchievement). Change in performance subsequent to the provision of feedback served as the dependent variable. There was no relationship at all between the achievement motive and feedback based on social reference norms. The achievement motive proved highly responsive to feedback on individual change in performance, however. As soon as their performance decreased below the level expected on the basis of their previous performance, participants high in achievement motivation redoubled their efforts, and showed an immediate improvement in performance. Thrash and Elliot (2002) investigated how success and failure motives, assessed by means of projective tests, are related to achievement-related goal orientations, assessed by questionnaire measures. Student participants were asked to state their goals for an upcoming exam:

- outperforming other students (achievement-approach goals),
- avoiding failure (achievement-avoidance goals),
- mastering the tasks as well as possible (mastery goals).

Multiple regression analyses showed that success-motivated students tended to pursue mastery goals, whereas failure-motivated students pursued both achievement-approach goals and achievement-avoidance goals. The latter finding reemphasizes the two sides of the failure-avoidance motive

(active vs. passive coping with failure). Findings were similar, though not identical, when questionnaires were used to assess the two achievement motives. Again, the success motive was associated with mastery goals, and the failure motive with social comparison goals.

Findings on the hierarchical model of motivation (see the excursus) correspond with the ideas of Breckler and Greenwald (1986), who proposed that achievement-motivated individuals, as defined by McClelland et al. (1953), have the capacity to regulate their behavior autonomously. Achievement-motivated individuals strive constantly to improve their knowledge and skills, applying their own standards of excellence, and with no need for social norms and feedback. Against this background, it makes perfect sense that deCharms, Morrison, Reitman, and McClelland (1955) found striving for independence and low conformity to be close correlates of the achievement motive. Failure-motivated individuals, on the other hand, seem to be hounded by concerns about the social evaluation of their achievements and its implications. Failure-motivated individuals are thus dependent on the recognition of others. For them, the striving to achieve is a means to the end of gaining the acceptance and appreciation of the social environment.

To the casual observer, these findings seem to contradict a distinction that Nicholls (1984a, b) made between two forms of achievement motivation. Nicholls proposed the first form of achievement motivation to be activated in situations where the aim is to master a task, make a personal effort, and improve one's performance. In these "task-involving" situations, ability is equated with the capacity to improve one's personal performance. In "ego-involving" situations, in contrast, the main aim is to compare one's ability with that of others and to do as well as possible or, at the very least, to conceal one's weaknesses. There are obvious parallels between Nicholls' distinction between task and ego involvement, on the one hand, and Rheinberg's distinction between individual and social reference norms, on the other. These norms, along with the respective incentives (self-improvement vs.

EXCURSUS

A Hierarchical Model of Motivation

Based on findings such as those presented earlier, Elliot (1997; Elliot & Church, 1997) concluded that approach and avoidance pervade the entire architecture of achievement motivation. In fact, their "hierarchical" model of motivation assumes approach and avoidance goals to be the factors determining performance and affect. The motive dispositions "hope for success" and "fear of failure," by contrast, are regarded as distal factors whose impact on behavior and experience is indirect, via the respective goals formulated.

Avoidance goals are associated with lower levels of efficiency. First, their criteria ("what must not be allowed to happen") are not as clearly defined as those of approach goals ("what is to be achieved"), making the task of planning, executing, and evaluating actions rather more difficult (Schwarz, 1990). Second, people who pursue avoidance goals tend to focus on negative rather than positive events. They are more likely to register their failures than their successes. The opposite holds for people with approach goals. As a result, the former tend to underestimate their successes relative to the latter, even when objective outcomes are comparable (Coats, Janoff-Bulman, & Alpert, 1996). Avoidance goals serve the regulation of negative affect (stress and anxiety), whereas approach goals primarily influence the

intensity of positive affect (energetic arousal and satisfaction) (Carver & Scheier, 1998). As a result, individuals pursuing avoidance goals cannot experience real joy; at most, they feel relief when they succeed in averting or avoiding a threatening state. Their inner participation in achievement-related activities is correspondingly low (Elliot & Harackiewicz, 1996); they are more likely to tackle such tasks under pressure than out of interest.

Although the distinction between approach and avoidance goals is, in many respects, reminiscent of that between success and failure motives, it has provided valuable new insights into how avoidance orientations limit action and emotional experience. Research on family context factors associated with the development of each type of goal orientation is still in its early stages. The results available thus far echo those produced by traditional research on parenting styles (Krohne, 1988): parenting that focuses on rewards and support, and that positively reinforces competence and independence, seems to foster the development of approach goals, whereas parenting that focuses on criticism, discipline, and punishment, and that engenders anxiety and apprehension, tends to promote the development of avoidance goals (see Elliot & McGregor, 2001).

demonstrating one's superior abilities), are indeed key components of both forms of motivational involvement (Butler, 1993). The potential contradiction is that Nicholls assumed classical achievement motivation theory to apply only to ego-involving situations. However, the findings reported above suggest that achievement-motivated individuals – provided that their hope for success outweighs their fear of failure – are in fact attracted to task-related incentives and apply individual, rather than normative standards of excellence. This apparent contradiction is easy to explain, however.

Nicholls' assumptions were based on the awareness that measurements of the resultant achievement motive contain a measure of test anxiety. As described above, test anxiety is associated with low levels of confidence in one's ability. This self-critical outlook has negative implications in social comparison situations, diminishing perceived prospects of success in competition with others. It is only worth people making an effort in ego-involving situations if they have a minimum level of confidence in their abilities (Butler, 1999). Ideally, success materializes without any effort at all, simply as a result of ability. In situations where one's own ability is the only measure of comparison, however, estimations of relative ability are immaterial. Nicholls' argument thus makes perfect sense in the context of the risk-taking model, and in terms of the way the achievement motive was measured (nAchievement – TAQ) and arousal conditions were implemented in the corresponding studies (test items were often purported to be intelligence measures), at least with respect to the anxiety measure. A different picture entirely emerges when the

classical TAT measure of the achievement motive is administered, however, because this measure does not correlate with self-concept of ability (Section 6.2.7).

This discussion again illustrates the point that the theoretical assumptions of achievement-motivation research can only be adequately tested when success- and failure-related motives are properly assessed. Calculating the difference between two (uncorrelated) motives and combining different methods of measurement (TAT and questionnaires) may prove empirically expedient (in the same way as calculating the difference between intelligence and anxiety would probably prove empirically expedient, even though it would mean combining entirely different kinds of constructs). Such an approach can only provide limited insights into the functional mechanisms of achievement-motivated behavior and the underlying motives, however. Nicholls' works have afforded valuable insights into the development of achievement motivation and provided the inspiration for many other models of achievement behavior (Chapter 15).

SUMMARY

Success and failure motivation can be described as two self-reinforcing systems within which behavior is governed by a specific directive, and actions are confirmed or reinforced on an ongoing basis by affective processes (self-evaluative emotions). The directive governing the behavior of success-motivated individuals – to acquire competence and optimize knowledge and skills – is supported by the selection of challenging goals, by attributions conducive to self-esteem, and by positive achievement-related emotions. This kind of directive is most likely to develop when self- and other-evaluations are based on individual reference norms, such that achievement covaries with effort and persistence. Failure motivation, on the other hand, involves negative reinforcement. Specifically, the threat to the self-esteem is reduced by defensive and self-handicapping behaviors (e.g., unrealistic goals and low effort expenditure). The associated directive – to protect self-esteem – is most likely to develop in response to the application of social reference norms and experiences of helplessness. Attempts to transform failure motivation into success motivation must target three aspects: goal setting, causal attributions, and achievement-related affect. In real-life achievement settings, such as the classroom, social comparison norms can be supplemented by individualized feedback.

6.6 The Importance of Achievement-Motivation Research for Motivation and Learning

The theories and data presented in this chapter were inspired by the heroes of achievement motivation research. David McClelland, John Atkinson, and Heinz Heckhausen have shaped our understanding of achievement motivation like few others, and continue to determine our approach to the concept to this day. Because they are discussed in more detail in other parts of this volume, we have touched only briefly on works of Bernhard Weiner and John Nicholls in this chapter. In 1986, Heinz Heckhausen recommended that researchers take time to reflect on this rich legacy before bringing any new ideas into play. Happily, many researchers ignored this advice, which is perhaps precisely the response that Heckhausen had intended to provoke with his remarks. Notable developments in research on goal orientations, self-regulatory processes, and volition can be cited as examples. This chapter does not aim to provide a conclusive overview of research findings on achievement motivation theory; rather, it seeks to identify research questions that address the very core of the human striving for excellence. We conclude this chapter by highlighting three of those questions:

1. Very little is yet known about how achievement motives (or situationally activated states of achievement motivation) influence the acquisition of knowledge and skills. Achievement motivation research has, for decades, focused on performance criteria and neglected to clarify the relationship between motivation and learning. This neglect is surprising, because achievement motivation is often associated or even equated with competence motivation (see Koestner & McClelland, 1990; Schultheiss & Brunstein, 2005). There is much work to be done in this domain, and it is certainly not sufficient – though correct – to note that effort and persistence are important ingredients in the development of excellence. Rather, motivational phenomena must be studied during the learning process itself, and analyzed in the context of the cognitive and emotional processes occurring during task execution.

2. The status of fear of failure in the context of achievement motivation research remains uncertain. The mere attempt to measure "the" failure motive has proven problematic, at least when using the TAT method, which does not distinguish satisfactorily between active and passive forms of coping with failure. Nevertheless, it is fortunate that this important distinction was detected and acknowledged early in achievement motivation research; it helps to prevent unnecessary oversimplification of the "avoidance motivation" concept. Findings on the validity and manifold effects of the failure motive have not yet been integrated within a unifying framework. There is certainly no lack of ideas on how the existing and, in parts, confusing body of findings is to be interpreted. What are now needed are differentiated theories that facilitate accurate predictions about the occurrence and behavioral effects of each form of avoidance. To this end, the focus of research must be shifted to the connections between motivation and strategies for coping with failure.

3. Research questions relating to motive measurement have not yet produced satisfactory responses, but their effects have been stimulating. This is by no means a purely methodological or even technical problem. The habit of interpreting various measures that barely correlate with each other as indicators of hope for success or fear of failure inspires little confidence in outside observers. At the same time, a multifaceted construct such as the achievement motive is too complex to be represented by just one or two numerical values, no matter which instruments are used to determine them. David McClelland and Heinz Heckhausen were also in agreement on this point. Heckhausen suggested splitting the summary motive construct up into expectancy and value components, but this yet to been done – for motive measurement, at least. It may seem comforting to note that the measurement of other latent personality constructs that are not easily accessible poses very similar problems (Bosson, Swann, & Pennebaker, 2000). Researchers would, however, be better advised to act on Heckhausen's suggestion and develop multidimensional tests for the measurement of motive variables.

Review Questions

1. How is the achievement motive defined?

The achievement motive is defined as an enduring striving to compete with standards of excellence and to increase one's competence. Achievement-oriented individuals strive to do well, better than others, or best of all on achievement-related tasks, activities, and skills.

2. **Which empirical criteria were used to develop Thematic Apperception Tests to assess individual differences in achievement motivation?**

The sensitivity of the test to experimentally induced motivational states (McClelland) and strength and change of the level of aspiration (Heckhausen).

3. **What are the advantages and disadvantages of the TAT method of assessing achievement motivation relative to questionnaire methods?**

Advantages: The TAT is immune to response bias tendencies, taps the spontaneous expression of achievement-related motivational tendencies, and does not correlate substantially with self-concepts of ability.

Disadvantages: Despite an objective coding system, the method is sensitive to situational influences (e.g., the behavior of the test administrator), has low internal consistency (reliability), and its implementation and analysis are time- and cost-intensive (parsimony).

4. **Which criteria were used to validate the TAT technique developed to assess the achievement motive?**

Scores on tasks requiring effort and concentration (e.g., adding one-figure numbers); simple learning tasks (e.g., word puzzles); real-life outcomes (e.g., career success, innovation).

5. **How does the risk-taking model define the valence of success and how is it measured?**

The valence of success is defined as the product of the success incentive and the success motive: $Vs = Ms \times Is$. It is measured in terms of satisfaction judgments for achievements at different difficulty levels. The more anticipated satisfaction increases with the difficulty of the task, the higher the valence of success. The gradient of the valence of success (satisfaction across different difficulty levels) is steeper in people high in success motivation than in people low in success motivation. This means that individuals high in success motivation are more sensitive to change in the level of achievement than less success-motivated individuals. Accordingly, their satisfaction is more dependent on the level of achievement attained.

6. **According to the predictions of the risk-taking model, which difficulty levels do success- and failure-motivated individuals prefer when choosing tasks? Outline the actual empirical findings.**

According to the risk-taking model, success-motivated individuals prefer moderately difficult tasks ($Ps = .50$), whereas failure-motivated individuals avoid this range of difficulty, opting instead for extremely difficult or extremely easy tasks. Empirical findings show that success-motivated individuals tend to prefer more difficult tasks falling below the critical level of $Ps = .50$ predicted by the risk-taking model. Failure-motivated individuals are more likely than success-motivated individuals to choose either extremely easy or extremely difficult tasks, but they do not purposely avoid the intermediate range of difficulty.

7. **How does the risk-taking model explain atypical shifts in the level of aspiration in failure-motivated individuals?**

After failure on a simple task or success on a difficult task, the probability of success approaches the critical level of $Ps = .50$, i.e., precisely the range of difficulty that failure-motivated individuals seek to avoid. As a result, there are erratic shifts in the level of aspiration toward the other end of the task difficulty scale (i.e., from very easy to very difficult tasks or vice versa).

8. **Which experimental paradigm did Feather use to predict the level of persistence on the basis of the risk-taking model?**

Two tasks are administered in Feather's experimental paradigm. Participants are told that the first is either difficult or easy, but it is in fact impossible. Over repeated trials, the probability of success thus approaches $Ps = .50$ ("simple" task) or recedes from $Ps = .50$ ("difficult" task). The probability of success on the second task is also stated. Success-motivated individuals are expected to show more persistence when the first task has a moderate probability of success, and the second an extremely high or low probability of success. The reverse is expected to hold for failure-motivated individuals. For them, the more extreme the difficulty level of the second task, and the nearer the probability of success on the first task to $Ps = .50$, the more likely a switch to the second task becomes.

9. **How can the apparent contradiction between the risk-taking model (Atkinson) and goal theory (Locke) in terms of the relationship between task difficulty and performance levels be explained?**

The risk-taking model is primarily concerned with task choice. Tasks of moderate difficulty are generally preferred. Goal theory, in contrast, is concerned with the realization of selected goals. Effort expenditure is automatically adjusted to task difficulty level (difficulty law of motivation) until the point of maximum potential motivation is exceeded.

10. **Name at least two factors that moderate the strength of the relationship between achievement motivation and task performance.**

First, the strength of the relationship depends on the demands of the task. A linear relationship between motivation and performance can only be assumed for very easy, speed-dependent tasks. High levels of motivation on complex, error-prone tasks can lead to decreased performance levels because of the speed/accuracy trade-off.

Second, the individual's cognitive and self-regulatory skills are important. A lack of ability cannot be offset by high motivation. Self-regulatory skills are needed to ensure the optimal level of motivation for the task.

11. How does Covington explain the phenomenon of over-motivation?

By a combination of high-success motivation and high-failure motivation. Covington calls individuals meeting this description "overstrivers." They invest a great deal of time and effort in their work or studies, but because their approach tends to be ill considered and superficial, they remain ineffective.

12. What is the function of motivational strength in Atkinson's model of cumulative achievement?

Motivation fulfills a dual function in this model. Together with ability, it influences the efficiency of task execution. Optimal, rather than maximum, motivation facilitates good performance outcomes.

Motivation also influences the time invested in acquiring skills. From a long-term perspective, high motivation thus also has a positive effect on the acquisition of knowledge and skills.

13. Why might it not be advisable to calculate the "resultant motivation tendency" in terms of the difference between success and failure motivation?

Four arguments can be cited here:

Success and failure motives represent theoretically independent constructs. By calculating difference scores, two dimensions are artificially combined in a single bipolar dimension of achievement motivation.

Difference scores do not reflect which variable (or an interaction of the two) is responsible for the predicted effects.

When difference scores are calculated, individuals high in both motives have the same resultant score as people low in both motives.

Failure motivation does not always undermine the success tendency; it can also facilitate proactive approaches to coping with failure.

14. What is the role of achievement-related affect in Heckhausen's self-evaluation model of achievement motivation?

It reinforces the behavioral directives that govern success- vs. failure-related behavior: to increase competence in the case of success motivation, and to protect self-esteem in the case of failure motivation. Causal attributions provide the link between performance outcomes and the affective reactions of success- vs. failure-motivated individuals. Failure-motivated individuals avoid challenging tasks in order to avoid feelings of failure and attributions that threaten their self-esteem. Success-motivated individuals choose precisely these tasks because their patterns of attribution are conducive to self-esteem and enhanced feelings of competence. For these individuals, even when the ratio of successes to failures is balanced, the affective balance remains positive (with pride outweighing shame).

15. Which reference norms can be used to evaluate a performance outcome?

Individual reference norms: temporal comparison of one's performance with one's own previous performances; social reference norms: comparison of one's performance with the performance of others; objective norms: task-immanent criteria of success, such as solving vs. not solving a task or attaining vs. failing to attain a given learning goal.

16. Individual reference norms are known to be conducive to achievement-motivated behavior. What are the mediating processes involved in this relationship?

Effort attributions of success and failure: individual reference norms emphasize that the level of achievement is contingent on the amount of effort invested.

Realistic goal setting: the goals set are based on individual ability or individual learning trajectories.

A sense of achievement and progress: weaker students, in particular, experience more success when exposed to individual than to social reference norms. The result is increased pride, which in turn reinforces feelings of competence and efficacy.

17. Which characteristics of the mother/child interaction "promote" the development of a strong failure motive in young children?

Trudewind and Husarek (1979) identified the following characteristics in a homework situation:
applying social reference norms;
expecting too much of the child; having unrealistically high goals and expectations;
attributing failure to a lack of ability;
criticizing failure, ignoring success.

18. How do avoidance goals inhibit achievement and enjoyment of learning?

Avoidance goals tend not to have clear criteria; progress on such badly defined goals is inherently difficult to plan and evaluate.

Avoidance goals direct attention to failures; successes are not really registered.

Avoidance goals are associated with negative affect (anxiety, tension), less enjoyment of learning, and less interest in tasks, which are only attempted under pressure (e.g., to avoid experiences of failure, rather than to increase one's competence).

7 Social Bonding: Affiliation Motivation and Intimacy Motivation

K. Sokolowski and H. Heckhausen

7.1 The Development of Social Bonds

People spend much of their lives in the company of others, interacting with their fellow humans. Interpersonal contact can mean mere coexistence at bus stops or in elevators, organized competition in sports contests, or overtly aggressive behavior. Alternatively, it can be helpful, friendly, or purely sociable in nature. In all these situations, **emotions** play an important role in regulating interactions. Generally, emotions serve two communicative functions (Sokolowski, 2002):

- First, expressions of emotion inform members of the same species about the emotional state of the individual (e.g., expressions of anger: "Watch it! Don't come any closer!").
- Second, emotions signal to the individual him- or herself the underlying motivational state (e.g., the feeling of fear when there still is something threatening in the actual situation).

Like other mammals who live in groups, humans are born with the ability to communicate with members of their species. This innate ability is reflected in a baby's contrasting emotional responses to being separated from the mother and to being reunited with her. In adult life, too, most of our emotions are triggered by our dealings with others, and these emotions serve to regulate human interaction in a multitude of respects. Expressions of emotion signal liking/antipathy, dominance/submission, indifference/interest, dependence/autonomy, the need for help, and so on, to those present. However, our subjective emotional experience reflects our overall motivational state with respect to an aspired goal.

Observable behaviors also reflect differences in social relations. The distance between people is reflected in the degree to which they turn toward or away from each other, in the speed of movement, in posture, and in modes of expression (gestures, facial expressions, and intonation). Differences in more subtle forms of nonverbal communication – e.g., duration of eye contact, frequency of head-nodding – can also be discerned, particularly in the initiation of contact and interaction with strangers (Mehrabian, 1972).

Moreover, people differ in their subjective experience of the emotions (e.g., interest and curiosity, affection, disgust, arrogance, insecurity, fear, anger, confidence, etc.) and thoughts that psychological models conceptualize as values and expectancies. People may approach a meeting in a more optimistic or pessimistic frame of mind and feel more or less confident in the meeting itself; they may interpret a lack of response from the other participants as indifference or as diffidence, and their response may be to feel insulted, helpless, or invigorated. The "affiliation motive" construct was introduced to motivational psychology to explain these very different kinds of behavior and experience in similar situations. In essence, the affiliation motive prompts us to make strangers into acquaintances and, eventually, friends and confidants – an endeavor that necessarily involves the risk of rejection. In the 1980s, the "intimacy motive" was identified as a specific facet of this virtually ubiquitous affiliation motive. The goal of the intimacy motive is to experience "a warm, close, and communicative exchange with another person" (McAdams, 1980). This comes closer to what is generally known as "love," a typical dictionary definition of which is: "that disposition or state of feeling with regard to a person which . . . manifests itself in solicitude for the welfare of the object, and usually also in delight in his or her presence and desire for his or her approval; warm affection, attachment" (The Oxford English Dictionary, 2007).

Many goals that can be pursued by forming and maintaining social relationships are not in fact related to the affiliation motive. These include making a favorable impression on others, dominating others, measuring one's own performance against others, seeking or providing assistance, or alleviating fear and insecurity by associating with others. As distinct from these kinds of behaviors, the affiliation motive is defined in the following terms:

DEFINITION

Affiliation (contact, sociability) refers to a class of social interactions that is mundane but fundamental, the goal of which is to seek contact with formerly unknown or little known individuals and to maintain that contact in a manner that both parties experience as satisfying, stimulating, and enriching. The motive is activated whenever we come into contact and interact with unknown or little known individuals.

7.1.1 The Phylogeny of Social Bonding

Over the course of phylogenetic development, various kinds of behavioral systems evolved, each helping the species to adapt to a specific life world, with the ultimate aim of ensuring the reproduction of the species. In essence, these evolved systems gear organisms to certain goals, prompt them to take action, and help them to maintain this behavior – preferably until the goal has been attained. These systems of goal generation and action are among the major evolved psychological mechanisms, and represent an important basis for motivation (Bischof-Köhler, 1985; Buss, 1991; Schneider & Schmalt, 2002). In fact, these evolved goal-generating systems or – in more general terms – **motives** can be considered a defining component of human nature.

There is much to indicate that the motives regulating social life in groups also derive from evolved structures forming the genetic framework upon which later developments were based (Bischof, 1985, 1993; Buss, 1991; McClelland, 1987). These social motives include various forms of social bonding, such as:

- filial love,
- parental love,
- conjugal love,
- friendship, and
- seeking and maintaining positive relationships with unfamiliar others of both sexes and a similar age.

> There is no doubt that these motives form the basis for humans being described as "social beings."

The need for brood care can be regarded as a major breakthrough in the evolution of behavior, having engendered kindness (Eibl-Eibesfeldt, 1984, p. 213). It occurred independently at several stages of evolution, first among insects, then among birds, and finally among mammals. Brood care led to the development of "personal bonding" – the second major evolutionary breakthrough for social relationships – which in turn engendered love (Eibl-Eibesfeldt, 1984, p. 213).

❶ For the anthropologist and evolutionary biologist Lovejoy (1981), the development of the nuclear family, i.e., monogamous pairs engaging in lasting social relationships and providing intensive parental care, was the decisive behavioral and biological step in human evolution.

Family structures of this kind (some with polygamous unions) are still found in aboriginal hunter-gatherer societies, such as the Australian bush people (West & Konner, 1976).

In fact, it is now thought unlikely that hominids and early forms of humans lived in nonfamilial "primal hordes" and engaged in sexual promiscuity. Rather, it would appear that, even during the prehuman transitional period, the enduring bond between a mother and her child – a matrilinear social relationship also found in chimpanzees (van Lawick-Goodall, 1975) – was complemented by a gradual familiarization with the male and a bonding of the child to the father within a matrimony-like union (Konner, 1981). This familial unit of parents and children facilitated the parents' prosocial investment in their own offspring (i.e., kinship selection). For the children, a close and enduring bond with their biological parents provided the requisites for a long childhood, in which they were able to acquire the abilities that distinguish homo sapiens from other species; i.e., abstract representation and thought, temporal representation, and verbal communication.

SUMMARY

Over the course of phylogentic development, the initiation and development of social relationships became increasingly important for survival in animal groups. In mammals, in particular, brood care and personal bonding between mother and child form the basis for other types of social relations.

7.1.2 The Ontogenesis of Social Bonding

Given that close and satisfying social relations have such significance for primates (Harlow, 1958) and for the growing infant (Bowlby, 1969), it can safely be assumed that the affiliation motive has a biological basis (Deci & Ryan, 2000). Indeed, the need for stable and reliable social relationships is so deep-rooted that even the slightest of threats to such relations triggers a whole range of unpleasant emotions (Baumeister & Leary, 1995).

Social bonding in humans presupposes a gradual familiarity with particular individuals, to a much greater extent than in subhuman species. We do not enter into deep bonds with others unquestioningly, in the blind hope that our feelings will be returned. Rather, we first have to get to know and come to trust the other person. Bischof (1985) discerns three types of familiarity, distinguishing different systems that motivate social bonding. He identifies three crucial developmental phases that can be viewed as sensitive stages (see the overview below).

Developmental Stages of Familiarity and Trust (Based on Bischof, 1985)

1. Primary stage:
Children develop trust in the caretakers in their family, particularly the mother.

2. Secondary stage:
Trust is now bestowed on certain individuals outside the family, with friendships, marriage, or marriage-like intimate relationships being established. Secondary trust emerges in adolescence, and presupposes a distancing from the highly familiar, from parents and siblings, in what Bischof (1985) labeled a "surfeit response."

3. Tertiary stage:
This is the relationship that mothers – and, in stable families, fathers – have with their children. For the mother, the act of giving birth seems to be a sensitive situation in its own right.

The same sequence of social bonding and its reference persons (mother, father, peers, partners of the opposite sex) was observed in primates by Harlow and his co-workers, who labeled this relationship "love" (Harlow, 1971).

The social bonding of children to their parents and of parents to their children – Bischof's primary and tertiary stages – seems to create the necessary preconditions for the secondary stage, in which older children establish relationships with people outside the family. From the ontogenetic perspective, Bischof (1975, 1985) observed that older children increasingly develop a "surfeit" response toward the highly familiar members of their family – their parents and siblings – and instead feel more attracted to "outsiders" of their own age. During adolescence, curiosity prevails over the earlier fear and distrust of strangers. Affiliation with strangers is pursued, potentially leading to long-standing friendships.

Bowlby's Attachment Theory Approach
Bowlby's (1958, 1969) biological attachment theory (bonding as a primary drive) is based on the observation that being together with or being reunited with the mother has high incentive value for infants from a very early age. McClelland (1985b) calls innate natural incentives of this kind that originate from the reference person "contact incentives." Bowlby posits that mother and child are phylogenetically predisposed to receive one another's signals, to respond to these signals, and gradually, after the child's first six months of life, to develop a highly individualized mutual attachment. It is not so much the extent of care-taking behaviors on the mother's part that is decisive here, but the provision of love, affection, and security. The child displays a "monotropy," i.e., the desire

to form a personal relationship with a certain individual, usually the mother. As if to complement this attachment to a highly familiar caretaker, a universal fear of strangers begins to emerge around the 8th or 9th month of life ("8-month fear"), and lasts up to two years. Although some developmental psychologists interpret this early fear of strangers as an experience of cognitive dissonance, the assumption of phylogenetic continuity is not easily dismissed (Sroufe, 1977).

Ainsworth elaborated Bowlby's work from the perspective of differential psychology (Ainsworth, Blehar, Waters, & Wall, 1978); Bischof (1975), from that of motivational psychology. According to Ainsworth et al. (1978; see also Sroufe, 1979), the quality of attachment can be observed when young children are separated from and reunited with the mother in different scenarios (in what is known as the "strange situation test"). Based on the behavior observed, two attachment types can be distinguished:

- securely attached infants, and
- insecurely attached infants. Insecurely attached infants either **avoid** the mother or show **ambivalence** toward her when reunited after a period of separation.

Securely attached infants differ from insecurely attached infants in the following respects:

- they are less hesitant in approaching new social situations,
- other children prefer them as playmates,
- they are more likely to propose activities,
- they are less likely to withdraw from social activities and interactions,
- they are more empathic, and
- they are more self-confident.

One reason for these differences is thought to be the mother's sensitivity to her child's nonverbal signals and her ability to respond appropriately (Sroufe, 1979). These differences, which can already be observed in very young children, remain relatively stable over the course of development. Indeed, numerous characteristics distinguishing between adults high and low in affiliation motivation have been identified (see below).

SUMMARY

Three different types of familiarity and bonding can be observed over the course of development. The attachment of young children to their caretakers can assume different forms, known as secure, ambivalent, and avoidant attachment styles. In adolescence, familiarity breeds a surfeit response, which prompts adolescents to seek out and establish contact with strangers.

7.2 Affiliation Motivation

Research on affiliation motivation began with Murray's (1938) attempts to define and measure the concept. His motive classification system, which comprises a total of 44 organismic and acquired needs, includes a "higher" general social need, "positive tropism toward people," of which the need for affiliation, or the affiliation motive, is a subcategory. Murray defined the need for affiliation in the following terms:

DEFINITION

To form friendship and association. To greet, join, and live with others. To cooperate and converse sociably with others. To love. To join groups. (Murray, 1938, p. 83)

As potential goals of the need for affiliation, Murray proposed being in the company of others, cooperating, exchanging views, and being friends with others. Affiliation-related actions include getting to know people, pleasing others, avoiding hurting others, showing goodwill and affection. The emotions associated with the need for affiliation are trust, empathy, love, and liking. Murray used observations of behavior to determine the strength of the need for affiliation, the criteria and categories of which he described in what – from today's perspective – are relatively vague terms of: "friendly feelings, desire to associate, play, and converse, efforts to resolve differences, cooperate and maintain harmony, readiness to trust and confide, and the number, intensity and duration of friendships." (Murray, 1938, p. 175)

The First Phase of Affiliation Motivation Research

The first phase of experimental research on affiliation motivation, in the 1950s, was not based on Murray's approach, but on Hull's drive-reduction model (1943; see Chapter 2). This experimental approach was based on the reasoning that affiliative behavior varies with the need for affiliation, and that the need for affiliation does not exist or evolve in its own right, but is aroused by fear or insecurity (Schachter, 1959). The goal of affiliative behavior was thus thought to be the reduction of fear or insecurity. Festinger's (1954) theory of social comparison provided theoretical backing for this approach; Hardy (1957) introduced the issues of conformity and pursuit of social support in this context.

This approach is reflected in the ways that affiliation motivation was aroused in experiments. Shipley and Veroff (1952) sought to activate the affiliation motive by asking each resident of a student dormitory to stand up in front of the other residents, who then rated him or her on sociometric scales. The TAT was administered immediately after this procedure. Students in the control condition responded to a questionnaire on their food preferences before writing TAT stories. In another experiment, the arousal group consisted of students whose applications to join a fraternity had recently been rejected; the control group of students who had been accepted. Comparing the TAT stories written by the arousal and control groups, Shipley and Veroff (1952) inferred that the need for affiliation was reflected in the frequency of references to separation or impending separation. Participants in the arousal groups scored much higher on these themes

than did their peers in the control groups. Unsurprisingly, the authors concluded that the need for affiliation is primarily determined by the fear of separation or rejection.

In a follow-up study, Atkinson, Heyns, and Veroff (1954) used the same conditions as Shipley and Veroff (1952) to arouse affiliation motivation, with residents of a student dormitory being asked to provide sociometric ratings of each other. The stories produced in response to TAT picture cues were taken as the dependent variable. Atkinson, Heyns, and Veroff (1954) concluded that both their study and the study by Shipley and Veroff measured the same motivational construct. In both studies, participants with high motivation scores were peer-rated to be less popular than were participants with low motivation scores. This finding, which at first glance appears to be paradoxical, begins to make sense when we consider what it is that is actually being measured under these arousal conditions. Byrne (1961a) described it in the following terms:

> The present need for affiliation scoring system identifies those individuals who are made anxious by affiliation threat. (Byrne, 1961a, p. 661).

People with high scores need more reassurance in their relationships and are more likely to bring up the themes of anxiety and social insecurity; they are also more likely to elicit these thoughts and feelings in their relationships and are thus often described as "complicated" or "difficult" (for a summary, see Boyatzis, 1973).

Today, it is assumed that the experiments conducted in this first phase of research on affiliation motivation tended to activate the avoidance component of motivation – "fear of rejection" – rather than the approach component – "hope of affiliation." The latter was the subject of the next phase of research.

Second Phase: Research on Components of the Affiliation Motive

The next phase of research was sparked by the separate measurement of the approach and the avoidance components of affiliation motivation. The approach tendency – the motive component determined by hope rather than fear – was initially measured using French's (1958a) "Test of Insight" (a projective technique similar to the TAT method). Like Murray (see above), French defined the goal of the affiliation motive in positive terms: "affiliation motivation [. . .] is defined as a desire to establish and/or maintain warm and friendly interpersonal relations" (French & Chadwick, 1956, p. 296). Applying this method, French and Chadwick (1956) found that popular individuals scored higher on the approach components of the affiliation motive, and lower on the avoidance components, than did unpopular individuals. French and Chadwick also drew attention to the link between popularity and sensitivity to others. Further evidence for this link was provided by Atkinson and Walker (1956), who found that individuals high in affiliation motivation show higher perceptual sensitivity to faces. Fishman (1966) also found a positive relationship between the strength of the approach component of the affiliation motive and being liked and evaluated as friendly by other members of the group. Furthermore, participants high in the approach component were more likely to engage in positive affiliative behavior within the group. Lansing and Heyns (1959) found that individuals high in affiliation motivation made more private telephone calls, and visited or wrote letters to friends and acquaintances more frequently. In achievement situations, people high in the affiliation motive were shown to differ from those low in the affiliation motive in that they to prefer to work with someone they like, even if that person is not considered to be particularly competent in the task at hand (French, 1956; Walker & Heyns, 1962). Moreover, students high in the affiliation motive were found to be more successful in their studies (measured in terms of the grades attained) when their instructors were warm and likeable (McKeachie, 1961). In competitive situations – e.g., swimming competitions – individuals high in the affiliation motive were observed to perform at their best when swimming for a team (Sorrentino & Sheppard, 1978).

Besides these behavioral variables, perceptual correlates of the approach component of affiliation motivation were also examined. A study by Fishman (1966) showed that **expectancies** have a pronounced moderating effect on affiliative behavior. His findings for residents of a student dormitory show that individuals high in affiliation motivation are friendly toward others when their expectancies relating to the outcomes of this behavior are high. Friendly and obliging behavior could only be adequately explained when both variables – strength of the affiliation motive and strength of related expectancies – were taken into account.

Further important insights into affiliation motivation were gained when Mehrabian (1970) developed two questionnaire measures to assess the approach and avoidance components of the affiliation motive separately. Experiments conducted using these questionnaires showed that expectancies play a key role in the model of affiliation-motivated behavior posited (Mehrabian & Ksionzky, 1974). The approach component ("affiliative tendency") is the manifestation of a generalized expectancy of positive reinforcement in contact with others. The avoidance component ("sensitivity to rejection") can be regarded as a generalized expectancy of negative reinforcement. Individuals high in affiliation motivation are more open, friendly, and confident in their social interactions with strangers, and experience more positive affect than those lower in affiliation motivation. People high in fear of rejection, in contrast, show weak social skills, and feel distressed, anxious, and tense in social situations (Mehrabian & Ksionzky, 1974).

❶ Another important insight of the studies by Mehrabian and Ksionzky (1974) was that the better acquainted the participants were with one another, the weaker the behavioral effects of motive strength proved to be. More specifically, in interactions between close acquaintances or good friends, the direction and strength of the two affiliation motives no longer play a role. Rather, behavior is determined by the "specific reinforcement qualities" or known incentives of the partner.

In interactions with people very close to us, another motive takes effect, namely the intimacy motive (see below). Our dealings with strangers or unfamiliar others are primarily determined by the strength of the two components of the affiliation motive, hope of affiliation and fear of rejection – i.e., generalized expectancies about positive or negative reinforcement.

However, it would be wrong to conclude that individuals high in fear of rejection avoid social contact with people unfamiliar to them. In fact, they have no fewer social contacts than do individuals high in the affiliation motive.

> Contrary to expectations [people with high sensitivity to rejection] were not less affiliative in their behavior and did not report more negative interpersonal attitudes. However, they were found to be less confident, more tense, more anxious, and more distressed in social situations with strangers; and they elicited discomfort and tension from others. They elicited more negative feelings and judged themselves to be less popular and more lonely (Mehrabian & Ksionzky, 1974, p. 143).

The incentive value of being in the company of others is evidently such that it outweighs the fear of rejection. This may be because the affiliation motive is subordinate to the need for "positive tropism toward people" (Murray, 1938; see above), which became prioritized during phylogenetic development. It is on the way to this superordinate goal that different motivational states – driven primarily by hope (goal: to get closer to others) or by fear (goal: not to be rejected) – can be identified. The main differences between the two motivational states reside in people's expectancies of being able to attain the goal of affiliation with others; their concomitant emotions, such as worry, tension, helplessness, or self-assurance; and physiological activation (Sokolowski & Schmalt, 1996).

Higgins (1997) proposed that approach and avoidance motivation be distinguished in terms of their contrasting regulatory focuses, a distinction that can also be profitably applied to the affiliation motive. In approach motivation, the regulatory focus is on attaining a positive state ("promotion focus"); in avoidance motivation, it is on averting a negative state ("prevention focus"). Corresponding differences are observed in the individual's sensitivity to different incentives, in the kinds of action strategies used, and not least in the emotions felt upon reaching the goal: in the former case, joy is experienced; in the latter case, relief (Higgins, 1997). Schüler (2002) incorporated these ideas into her hierarchical model of affiliation motivation, and was thus able to integrate some of the seemingly contradictory findings presented over the history of motivation research. Notably, Schüler (2002) does not presuppose the congruence of motive dispositions and regulatory focus. In other words, she rejects the longstanding assumption that the "hope of affiliation" motive is associated with an approach focus (e.g., to strike up a conversation with somebody) whereas the "fear of rejection" motive triggers an avoidance focus (e.g., to avoid being rejected) that is reflected in individual information processing and behavior. It emerged that, even when pursuing a goal with a "prevention focus" ("You want to avoid being rejected at all costs, and resolve not to make a fool of yourself"), the behavior of individuals high in affiliation motivation is more effective and more appropriate to the situation than is that of individuals high in fear of rejection. Schüler's (2002) findings further indicate that the distinction between individuals high in affiliation motivation and those high in fear of rejection cannot be attributed to a general predisposition to adopt one of the two regulatory focuses. Rather, the groups differ in their capacity to put affiliation-related goals into practice in behavior, as well as in their ability to select and evaluate information relevant to interim goals.

SUMMARY

In the first phase of research into the affiliation motive, it was assumed that insecurity or fear were the main grounds for affiliative behavior. The turning point came with the insight that the motive goal is not, in fact, to alleviate unpleasant states, but to generate pleasant ones. The distinction of two independent motive goals – establishing closer relations with others vs. avoiding rejection – marked the true beginning of research into the affiliation motive and the motivational states that it engenders.

7.3 The Two Sides of the Affiliation Motive – Hope and Fear

Whether in a queue at the supermarket, in a doctor's waiting room, in the carriage of a train, or at a party – all of these situations afford the opportunity to establish contact with unfamiliar others. Yet in each of these situations, marked differences can be observed in the perceptual and behavioral responses of those involved. Some people approach and seek contact with others without a moment's hesitation; others find it difficult to interact with strangers and prefer to take a more passive role. Because differences of this kind are observed repeatedly across a variety of situations, it seems reasonable to assume that they are rooted in dispositional differences. How might differences in the experience and behavior of people in one and the same situation be explained? They may be attributable to differences in the perception and interpretation of the situation or to other

aspects of information processing (retrieval of memories and experiences; expectancies; evaluations; causal attributions). Equally, however, they may be rooted in the arousal of different emotions or the pursuit of different goals.

All of these potential explanations are summarized in the motive construct:

DEFINITION

A motive is an evaluative bias "that gives a stimulus event a meaning – the character of an attraction or a threat – and thus initiates a motivational process that starts with the formulation of goals. [The ensuing] motivation comprises both automatic and conscious processes geared toward effecting a shift from the prevailing emotional state to an anticipated one. Motivation describes the sum total of all internal and external factors that are responsible for generating goals, for energizing behavior, for selective and goal-specific information processing, and for directing experience and behavior" (Schmalt & Sokolowski, 2004).

Motives and motivation thus have great explanatory potential. As mentioned above, the affiliation motive also comprises two contrasting motive components that serve to counter-regulate each other:

- hope of affiliation and
- fear of rejection.

The correlation between the two motive components is weak (Sokolowski, 1992). Fear of rejection urges caution and sensitivity in our dealings with strangers, whereas hope for affiliation prompts us to approach unknown individuals and get to know them better. It is only when one of the two motive components is very dominant that the two antagonistic components' counter-regulatory mechanism of closeness and distance or assurance and apprehension in our interactions with others becomes destabilized. A dominant hope component leads to a rather forward and overly familiar approach to strangers, whereas a dominant fear component in the same situation results in overly cautious and evasive or coolly formal dealings with others.

7.3.1 Hope of Affiliation

Hope, like fear, has a cognitive and an emotional aspect. The emotional aspect can be broken down into subcomponents, such as physiological response patterns or basic behavioral programs (Sokolowski, 2002). From this emotional perspective, hope can be described as a specific affective state relating to the attainment of an anticipated goal state and in a sense provides a guideline for motivated experience and action. From the cognitive perspective, hope can be described as an amalgam of different types of expectancies, as proposed by Heckhausen in the expanded cognitive model (Heckhausen, 1977a; 1977b); see also Chapter 13). According to this model, three types of expectancies can be distinguished in any given situation:

1. Situation-outcome expectancies (How likely is it that the desired outcome will ensue without intervention on my part?),

2. Action-outcome expectancies (How likely is it that my action will lead to the desired outcome?), and

3. Outcome-consequence expectancies (How likely is it that the outcome will have the desired consequences?).

Sokolowski (1992) found that individuals high and low in affiliation motivation show predictable differences in only the first two types of expectancies – i.e., situation-outcome and action-outcome expectancies. Individuals high in hope of affiliation have higher expectancies of a situation being inherently conducive to meeting new people, feel more comfortable in those situations, and endorse these evaluations in a broader range of situations than do individuals low in hope of affiliation. Likewise, where action-outcome expectancies are concerned, individuals high in affiliation motivation are more likely to expect their affiliative actions to succeed in bringing about the desired outcome. These higher expectancies are associated with positive emotions, such as self-assurance, the absence of negative feelings, such as tension (Sokolowski & Schmalt, 1996). Not only do individuals high in the affiliation motive have a more optimistic approach (emotional and cognitive components), their behavior is also more appropriate to affiliative goals than is that of people low in the affiliation motive. Schüler (2002) presented experimental evidence for these behavioral differences in a study of decisions made in an affiliative setting.

The more realistic information processing of individuals high in hope of affiliation in affiliative situations is also reflected in their reactions to social recognition or rejection. In an experimental setting (Sokolowski, 1986), participants high in hope of affiliation showed contrasting responses to acceptance or rejection by a group, feeling very helpless after rejection, but not after acceptance. The lower the participants' hope of affiliation, however, the more "indifferent" their responses to both kinds of feedback. In other words, the emotions of people high in hope of affiliation provide them with "auto-feedback" appropriate to the situation. This emotional auto-feedback can be seen as an effective regulatory mechanism that prompts people to reflect on and optimize their behavior – congruent with Heckhausen's (1975b) conceptualization of motives as a self-reinforcement system.

All of these findings are congruent with the characteristics of individuals high in hope of affiliation ("affiliative tendency") that were identified and summarized by Mehrabian and Ksionzky (1974; see the overview below).

Characteristics of Individuals High in the Affiliation Motive (Based on Mehrabian & Ksionzky, 1974)

- They see others as being more like themselves,
- they see others in a better light,
- they like others more,

- they are more popular with others,
- their friendly manner is infectious and spreads rapidly to others (strangers),
- they are more confident and experience more pleasant affect in their interactions with others,
- the behavioral decisions they make in social contexts are more appropriate to their goals (Schüler, 2002), and
- they have very specific responses to social recognition and rejection (Sokolowski, 1986).

7.3.2 Fear of Rejection

As the natural antagonist of hope of affiliation, fear of rejection urges us to keep a cautious distance to people unfamiliar to us. On the cognitive side, a strong fear of rejection is associated with generalized low action-outcome expectancies, and leads people to doubt the efficacy of their affiliative behavior (Sokolowski, 1992). Moreover, there is an increased tendency to interpret other people's ambiguous or unclear signals as rejection – an observation that prompted Mehrabian to label fear of rejection "sensitivity to rejection" (Mehrabian, 1970). These observations were confirmed in an experiment by Sokolowski and Schmalt (1996) involving an ambiguous social situation. Participants first struck up a pleasant conversation with an unknown individual, who was in fact a confederate of the experimenter. Without warning, the confederate then cut short the conversation and turned to a third person. Despite the ambiguity of the situation, participants high in fear of rejection reacted as if they had been rejected outright. They were plagued by feelings of helplessness, crippling fatigue, and despair. Even a cheerful mood induced earlier in the experiment could not prevent this emotional devastation (Sokolowski & Schmalt, 1996). It is at this point in the social interaction that the vicious circle referred to above takes effect, with the emotional helplessness felt by participants high in fear of rejection impinging on their behavior and nonverbal communication when the confederate turns back to them after the interruption.

Mehrabian and Ksionzky (1974, pp. 142–143) specify further characteristics of people high in fear of rejection ("sensitivity to rejection"; see the overview below):

Characteristics of Individuals High in Fear of Rejection (Based on Mehrabian & Ksionzky, 1974)

- They feel distressed in social situations and elicit similar feelings from others,
- they are less confident, more tense, and more anxious in social situations,
- they judge themselves to be less popular and more lonely (although they do not interact in fact any less with others),
- their social skills are not very well developed and their behavior makes them feel inadequate and incapable of dealing with social situations,

> ■ they have low action-outcome expectancies in their interactions with strangers (Sokolowski, 1992),
> ■ they show strong emotional reactions (helplessness syndrome) to interruptions in social interactions (Sokolowski & Schmalt, 1996), and
> ■ their emotional responses to social recognition or rejection are not very differentiated or specific (Sokolowski, 1986).

In fear of rejection – as in fear of failure (Heckhausen, 1975b) – the effects of a self-reinforcement mechanism that serves to stabilize that fear are clearly apparent. It involves heightened sensitivity to signals of rejection and strong feelings of helplessness in response to infelicitous or ambiguous social interactions. This heightened sensitivity makes it more likely that ambiguous gestures or harmless gaps in the conversation will be (mis)interpreted as rejection, leading to feelings of helplessness that, in turn, render the further course of the interaction more complicated, resulting in a more faltering exchange. Thus, for people high in fear of rejection, their low expectations and heightened caution and insecurity in interactions with strangers are confirmed and reinforced.

Fear of rejection is a motive that overlaps with other social anxieties; i.e., differently motivated states of anxiety that occur in social situations (e.g., shyness) and their associated behaviors. It is important to distinguish **fear of strangers** from **fear of social evaluation**. Fear of social evaluation cannot be traced back to the fear of strangers displayed in the early developmental stage because it presupposes perspective-taking ability (e.g., being able to see ourselves from the point of view of the person we are trying to impress), which has not yet developed when children first begin to show fear of strangers, between the ages of six months and two years.

FEAR OF STRANGERS. This emotion, as expressed in shyness toward strangers, seems to be a genetically predetermined personality variable (Buss & Plomin, 1984). Findings from adoption and twin studies substantiate this view. Correlations have been found between the shyness of adopted two-year-olds and that of their biological mothers, from whom they were separated at birth (Daniels & Plomin, 1985). Moreover, monozygotic twins have been found to display more similar behavior toward strangers (but not toward their mother) than do dizygotic (same-sex) twins (Plomin & Roew, 1979). The genetic substructure of individual differences in fear of strangers points to a phylogenetic legacy. From the perspective of evolutionary biology, it indicates that fear of strangers must have been conducive to survival, at least in early ontogeny.

FEAR OF SOCIAL EVALUATION. Research on fear of social evaluation – i.e., the fear of making an unfavorable impression on others – has taken a number of related approaches. **Fear of self-presentation** (Schlenker & Leary, 1982) involves monitoring the impression that our behavior has on the people we deem to be important. People who experience anxiety in social situations want to avoid making a bad impression on others. At the same time, they are unsure of their ability to present themselves in a favorable light. Hence, fear of self-presentation is closely related to personality traits such as "public self-consciousness" (Buss, 1980) or "anxious self-preoccupation" (Crozier, 1979). This applies not only to the concern that one might not be recognized and appreciated as a social partner by potential affiliates, but more specifically to the fear of failing in the eyes of others – and thus to the extensively researched area of test anxiety (see the overview by Wine, 1982).

Fear of social evaluation may be elicited by either strangers or familiar individuals. However, unfamiliar individuals may trigger fear of strangers without engendering fear of social evaluation at the same time. These two sources of social anxiety must be distinguished because they do not necessarily occur in combination. In a series of experimental social situations, Asendorpf (1984) arranged for his participants to be confronted with strangers and familiar persons. Although levels of social anxiety were very similar in both conditions, strangers elicited fewer cognitions relating to self-presentation, less fear of negative evaluation, and less blushing than did familiar persons. Given that fear of social evaluation does not seem to be strongly activated in interactions with little known individuals or strangers, its influence in the context of affiliation motivation can be assumed to be modest. In fact, it takes effect in the domain of the intimacy motive, to be discussed below, where it has an impact on people's interactions with familiar individuals.

SUMMARY

Individuals high in fear of rejection have generalized low expectancies with regard to the success of their affiliative behavior toward strangers. They are quick to interpret ambiguous behaviors as rejection, and are plagued by feelings of helplessness and resignation. Moreover, their responses to social recognition tend to be rather weak and undifferentiated. Their insecurity is rather infectious, and their manner leads to them often being described as "complicated." Neither fear of social evaluation nor fear of strangers seems to have a great deal in common with fear of rejection.

7.3.3 Conflicts Between Hope and Fear in Affiliative Situations

In his *Letters to Milena*, Franz Kafka wrote of the *longing for people that changes to fear upon its fulfillment* (Kafka, 1986). Kafka was referring to a conflict that reaches its maximum level when the goal is attained, and not before (i.e., during the approach phase). This is the typical course of a conflict between approach and avoidance, as described by Miller (1959), that develops over time as a goal is approached. Because the approach motive is activated before the avoidance motive, this motivation is the first to be implemented (see the following example). Depending on the strength of the avoidance motive, fear will be aroused at some point on the way to the goal. Although the avoidance tendency is activated later, the gradient of avoidance is steeper than the gradient of approach. The maximum **approach-avoidance conflict** occurs at the point where both components are equally strongly aroused.

EXAMPLE

Our interactions with strangers tend to unfold as follows. First, the hope component is activated and, powered by affiliation motivation, contact is initiated. As we get to know the new person, we become closer to them. The closer we become, and the more likeable we find the other person, the more painful it would be if we were rejected. It is now that the fear of rejection is activated, and the effects of this motive on our experience and behavior become increasingly strong. Our sensitivity to relevant signals is heightened – until the point of maximum conflict between approach and avoidance is reached. At the point when fear becomes dominant, we again distance ourselves somewhat from the other person. From this "safe" distance, fear motivation decreases and affiliation motivation becomes dominant once more, and the cycle begins again. These kinds of oscillations in behavior, underpinned by ambivalent emotions, can be observed in interactions between unfamiliar people (e.g., at parties).

Shy people experience similar conflicts in affiliative situations. Not only are they afraid of not appealing to others – or worse still, of being rejected outright – they are, at the same time, driven by the desire to affiliate with others (Cheek & Buss, 1981). Unlike highly introverted people, shy individuals are not loners. When they find themselves in social situations that elicit shyness, they face a typical approach-avoidance conflict. On the one hand, they experience feelings of inferiority in social contexts; on the other hand, they strive for more recognition and closer affiliation with others. These were the results of a large study by Asendorpf (1984), in which students provided self-report data and were then observed in experimentally manipulated social situations. The students also evaluated the extent to which different situations – e.g., a date with a potential partner with whom they were secretly in love, or a job interview – arouse shyness. There were no differences between the evaluations of shy and nonshy individuals – an indication that shy people are not distinguished by the subjective incentives of potential actions in situations involving social evaluation, but by their lack of confidence in being able to cope with the situation. These findings reflect a pattern of behavior in shy individuals that resembles what would be expected for individuals who are high in both hope of affiliation and fear of rejection, and contrasts with the behavior pattern of people with a low-low combination of the two motives.

SUMMARY

Hope of affiliation and fear of rejection regulate the closeness or distance between people. Depending on the relative strength of the two motives, people's interactions with strangers and unfamiliar others are marked by approach-avoidance conflicts at different levels of intensity and at different points in time. Shyness can be seen as a chronic conflict between hope of affiliation and fear of rejection.

7.4 Measuring the Affiliation Motive and Its Behavioral Correlates

---

The first attempts to measure the affiliation motive were in the tradition of the Michigan school of motivation, and based on the work of David McClelland and John Atkinson (Atkinson, 1958a). Motive strength was measured using the projective method of the Thematic Apperception Test (TAT). In the meantime, there have been numerous revisions of the coding system, and the system proposed by Winter (1991a), which is relatively easy to use, is now most frequently implemented in motivation research.

Projective techniques have been the target of harsh criticism, primarily on account of their low levels of reliability and objectivity. As we now know, this criticism is only partially justified (Schmalt & Sokolowski, 2000). Nevertheless, the focus in the 1970s was on the development of questionnaire measures. Mehrabian (1970) proposed two questionnaires to assess the affiliation motive:

- one measuring the hope component ("affiliative tendency") and
- one measuring the fear component ("sensitivity to rejection").

The Grid Technique, which combines characteristics of the TAT method (participants are presented with ambiguous picture cues) with features of questionnaire measures (each picture is accompanied by a set of statements), is a third kind of approach. Because there is great scope for individual conjecture in the interpretation of the pictures, but the statements to be rated are unambiguous, the Grid Technique constitutes a hybrid of the TAT technique and questionnaire measures – it is a semiprojective method (Schmalt & Sokolowski, 2000). A Multi-Motive Grid has now also been developed to measure the achievement, power, and affiliation motives all at once – distinguishing between the fear and hope components in each case (Sokolowski et al., 2000; see also Chapter 8).

7.4.1 The Thematic Apperception Test (TAT)

In the TAT method, participants generate stories in response to ambiguous picture cues. The content of these stories is then screened for imagery relating to the motive under investigation (Chapter 6) – in this case, affiliation. A coding system specifies when affiliation imagery is present, and how this imagery should be scored to provide a measure of motive strength:

> Affiliation Imagery [. . .] is scored when a story contains evidence of concern, in one or more characters, over establishing, maintaining, or restoring a positive affective relationship with another person. (Heyns, Veroff, & Atkinson, 1958, p. 205).

The TAT coding system developed to assess the affiliation motive – which was later documented in detail by Heyns, Veroff, and Atkinson (1958) – has remained essentially unchanged to this day.

Drawing on the "Test of Insight" developed by French (1958a), Boyatzis (1972, 1973) proposed another projective technique to discriminate between fear of rejection and need for affiliation. In contrast to the TAT, Boyatzis' method does not involve ambiguous picture cues (see the example below).

EXAMPLE

Boyatzis' participants were given a story line and asked to continue it; e.g., "John has just started a new job. He and his family have moved to a new neighborhood." Subsequently, participants were informed about a series of possible occurrences in John's life and asked how they thought he would respond to each. For example, John and his wife are invited to dinner by a couple in the neighborhood. Is John pleased about the opportunity to meet his new neighbors (affiliative interest) or does he hope that they will like him (fear of rejection)? It transpired that participants high in affiliative interest had more close friends, whereas participants who feared rejection were only interested in friends whose attitudes corresponded with their own. Moreover, they avoided being alone, indicating that they needed the endorsement of others.

Behavioral Correlates of TAT Measures

Fishman (1966) was the first to observe actual affiliative behavior under realistic conditions, rather than deliberately manipulating arousal states. He used a questionnaire measure to record the mutual popularity and friendliness of female students living in a dormitory. These data were used to derive an index of specific expectancies vis-à-vis each dormitory resident. A TAT was administered immediately before (and not after!) the popularity questionnaire, and the stories produced were analyzed using the coding system by Heyns, Veroff, and Atkinson (1958). The overall affiliation score was then split into "hope for affiliation" (HA) and "fear of rejection" (FR) subscores. Two to four weeks later, a meeting was arranged for groups of four participants living in the same dormitory. The participants were first left to themselves in a comfortably furnished room and then given written instructions to discuss a topical issue. The experimenter was not present in the room, but observed the participants through a one-way mirror, scoring their "positive" and "negative" affiliative

Table 7.1. Correlations of TAT measures of hope of affiliation (HA) and fear of rejection (FR) with the percentage of positive affiliative acts in a group situation by participants' level of affiliation expectancies

	TAT motive measure	
Affiliation expectancy	HA	FR
All	.20	.10
Low (N = 40)	−.19	.24
High (N = 40)	.58**	.16

**p < .01.

behavior. Based on these scores, the percentage of "positive acts" was computed.

The results of Fishman's study, like those of French and Chadwick (1956), confirm the significance of specific expectancies when they are considered in conjunction with TAT scores (Table 7.1). The affiliation motive and hope of affiliation (HA) correlated only weakly with positive affiliative behavior; fear of rejection (FR) did not correlate at all. These weak correlations increased considerably (from $r = .20$ to $.58$ in the case of HA) when computed for only those subgroups with very high specific affiliation expectancies.

STUDY

Study on the Effects of the Affiliation Motive on Operant Behavior

Constantian (1981) gave student respondents electronic pagers and "beeped" them at approximately 2-hour intervals from 9 A.M. until 11 P.M. At each beep, they noted down what they were doing on a checklist. Overall, students high in the affiliation motive (assessed using the TAT coding system by Heyns, Veroff, & Atkinson, 1958) were more likely to be talking or writing to someone when beeped. Besides assessing the affiliation motive as a predictor of operant affiliative behavior, Constantian (1981) collected self-report data on whether participants would prefer to engage in 15 different activities (e.g., working, shopping, going to a museum, eating out, hiking) alone or in company. There was barely any correlation between the strength of the affiliation motive and the number of activities that participants would prefer to do in the company of others. Rather, it transpired that the effects of the affiliation motive and the affiliation-related preferences were complementary. For example, only participants high in the affiliation motive who expressed a preference for company over solitude preferred to hike with others. At the same time, high affiliation participants who expressed a preference for being alone were more likely to engage in that solitary form of affiliative behavior par excellence, namely, writing letters. The beeper method "caught" 60% of participants with high affiliation scores who preferred solitude writing letters, compared with less than 10% of those who preferred company.

In other words, high positive incentive values (high over-all and HA scores on the TAT) combined with high specific expectancies (high mutual popularity), produce the strongest exchange of positive affiliative behavior among individuals who are already acquainted with one another.

In another compelling empirical approach to the effects of the affiliation motive on behavior, Constantian (1981; McClelland, 1985b) assessed spontaneous (operant) behavior in everyday life.

Overall, the behaviors and preferences of individuals high in the affiliation motive reflect efforts to avoid conflicts with others. When participating in group decision making, they are less likely to make proposals that threaten the cohe-sion of the group on the tasks assigned (Exline, 1962). In speeches made by members of the Soviet Politburo, the strength of the affiliation motive was found to correlate sig-nificantly with proposals of détente, at $r = .47$ (Hermann, 1980). Similarly, US presidents such as Eisenhower, Kennedy, Nixon, and Ford, whose inaugural speeches contained dis-tinctly affiliative statements, were intent on effecting recon-ciliation with foreign powers and on obtaining arms limita-tion agreements (Chapter 8). Historians judged these presi-dents to be less effective, however, and their administrations were more frequently involved in scandals (Winter, 1967). In contrast to those low in affiliation motivation, individuals with a medium or high affiliation motive have been shown to make increasingly more suggestions to change the atti-tudes of others as these attitudes differed more from their own (Byrne, 1962). Individuals high in the affiliation motive avoid games of chance such as roulette (McClelland & Watson, 1973), as well as competitive games such as chess (McClel-land, 1975). In games simulating international conflicts, they tend to be more passive and to initiate fewer acts that might spark a conflict. As a result, they also initiate fewer coopera-tive acts, and they use less deceptive propaganda (Terhune, 1968).

Performance situations often also arouse the affiliation motive; e.g., when people cooperate rather than competing, or when a social relationship evolves between the person assigning a task and the person executing it. When affiliation motivation joins forces with achievement motivation in such situations, there may be corresponding changes to the per-formance outcome, without a conflict necessarily occurring between the two motives. French (1958b) found that study participants with a dominant affiliation motive performed best when they work in a group, rather than alone, and when the experimenter praised the group for its cooperative spirit, rather than its proficiency. In another experiment, partici-pants were given the choice of working with a good friend who had previously proved to lack proficiency in the task at hand, or with a less likeable partner, who was known to be proficient. The participants' choices corresponded with their motive profiles: those high in achievement and low in

affiliation motivation prioritized proficiency over friendship, whereas those high in affiliation and low in achievement motivation prioritized friendship over proficiency (French, 1956).

McKeachie (1961) observed similar interactions between the affiliation motive and situational arousal in the academic outcomes of more than 600 students enrolled in 31 intro-ductory psychology, mathematics, and French courses. At the beginning of the semester, the strength of the affilia-tion motive (along with other motives) was determined for all students and their 31 instructors. The extent to which each course provided an affiliation-oriented environment was gauged by the instructor's motive strength and random samples of his or her in-class behavior (e.g., calling students by their names, staying after class to talk to students). As shown in Fig. 7.1, students high in the affiliation motive attained higher grades from high-affiliation instructors than did students low in the affiliation motive. Conversely, students low in the affiliation motive attained higher grades from low-affiliation instructors than did students high in the affiliation motive.

Sorrentino and Sheppard (1978) designed a field exper-iment that was carried out by the swim-team coaches at three Canadian universities. All participants had to swim 200 yards freestyle in both individual and group competi-tion. To ensure that all participants had an equal chance of winning, the coaches determined a handicap for each swim-mer based on their personal best, which was then used to weight the actual time swum. Affiliation-motivated swim-mers were expected to derive additional motivation from the opportunity to help their group to win, and to swim better times in the group than in the individual competition. The opposite was expected to hold for the swimmers who feared rejection – it was hypothesized that they would be demoti-vated by the risk of contributing to their group's defeat and would thus swim better times in the individual than in the group competition. These hypotheses were confirmed fully; in terms of both the opposing shifts in performance between the individual and group competition, and the performance gap between the two motive groups in the group competi-tion. When the swimmers were further categorized in terms of their achievement motive, those who were high in both suc-cess orientation and affiliation motivation showed the largest performance gains from the individual to the group compe-tition.

The motive tendencies for affiliation and achievement were assessed using the coding scheme developed by Heyns, Veroff, and Atkinson (1958); the corresponding negative motive tendencies of fear of rejection and fear of failure were determined using the questionnaires by Mehrabian (1970) and Mandler and Sarason (1952). Notably, the hypotheses were confirmed not only on the basis of the resultant affilia-tion motive score (difference between the HA and FR scores,

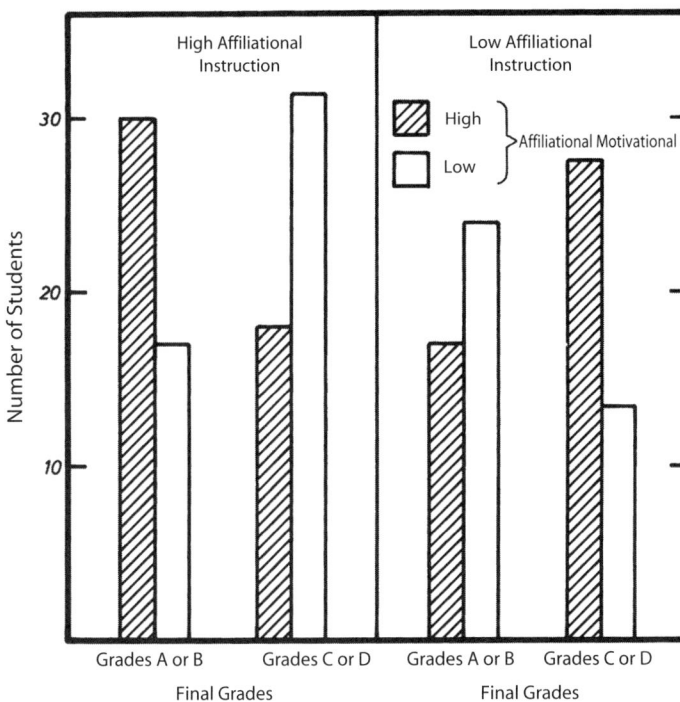

Figure 7.1 Number of students high/low in the affiliation motive obtaining final grades of A/B or C/D in introductory courses with high/low affiliational instruction. (Based on McKeachie, 1961.)

transformed to z-scores), but also for both of the motive tendencies separately.

DEFINITION

These findings provide further support for the notion that the affiliation motive is a dual motive system comprising two independent tendencies: hope of affiliation and fear of rejection.

7.4.2 Questionnaire Measures

Alongside projective methods – now known as implicit measures – the 1970s saw the development of questionnaire measures to assess the affiliation motive by means of self-reports – i.e., by explicit means. In contrast to many other questionnaires, the scales by Mehrabian (1970) were devised within a theoretical context (Mehrabian & Ksionzky, 1974). Mehrabian adopted the postulate of two antagonistic tendencies of the need to affiliate, calling them "affiliative tendency" (R1) and "sensitivity to rejection" (R2). His questionnaires were designed to predict behavior toward unfamiliar others. In situations of this kind, generalized expectancies are more salient than incentive variables, whereas in interactions with familiar others, it is their specific incentive values, rather than generalized expectancies, that are decisive.

The two scores do not correlate with each other and are free of response tendencies indicative of social desirability bias. Upon closer inspection, however, it emerges that neither questionnaire taps generalized expectancies or probabilities so much as the overall potential of affiliation-oriented reinforcers within a given individual's environment ("Having

friends is important to me" for R1 or "I sometimes take criticism too hard" for R2). The abbreviations for the two affiliative tendencies, R1 and R2 (R = reinforcement), are thus well chosen, as the questionnaire measures generalized reinforcement values.

The different combinations of the two measures give four types of affiliation motives:

1st type:	R1 high, R2 low:	One's affiliative needs are fulfilled in most situations.
2nd type:	R1 low, R2 high:	One's affiliative needs remain unfulfilled or are rejected in most situations.
3rd type:	R1 low, R2 low:	Most situations only have a weak positive or negative affiliative reinforcement value.
4th type:	R1 high, R2 high:	One's affiliative needs are either fulfilled or rejected.

These different motive types are seen as developmental outcomes of reinforcements experienced in previous social interactions, particularly in childhood. According to Mehrabian, the fourth type (both R1 and R2 high) provides the motivational foundation for distinctly conformist behavior, and is indicative of a dependency motive. Frequent use of both positive reinforcement and negative sanctions tend to promote dependency in the growing child – and form a corresponding basis for generalized expectancies in adulthood.

Byrne, McDonald, and Mikawa (1963) also proposed four types of affiliation motivation. They cross-classified high and low success and failure expectancies (HA and FR) to produce the following types:

High need to affiliate	HA high	FR low
Fear of rejection	HA low	FR high
Conflict-laden need to affiliate	HA high	FR high (typical of shy individuals)
Low need to affiliate	HA low	FR low

For the most part, Mehrabian and Ksionzky (1974) tested the validity of their questionnaire by observing participants' interactions with unfamiliar others (confederates of the experimenter) in waiting room situations. The variables they examined included the number of utterances per minute, the frequency of head-nodding, the pleasantness of facial expressions, the rate of speech, and the distance from the confederate. One finding of this series of experiments was that information provided about the status of a fictitious unknown other (e.g., social background, economic situation, and academic achievements) had opposite effects on the two motive groups (Mehrabian & Ksionzky, 1974). Participants sensitive to rejection found affiliates whose status was lower than their own to be more attractive than affiliates whose status was superior. The opposite held for participants with high affiliation scores. For them, the attractiveness of the fictitious affiliate increased with his or her social status. In sum, the studies provided numerous indications that affiliation-motivated individuals differ from those who are sensitive to rejection in the hypothesized directions. The findings were not as clear-cut as had been expected, however.

❗ Based the empirical findings, we can conclude that – apart from tapping the two components of the affiliation motive – Mehrabian's two scales assess a personality characteristic that can be labeled "general sociability."

7.4.3 The Grid Technique

Sokolowski (1992) developed a further procedure to measure the affiliation motive. Interactionist models provided the theoretical basis for this semiprojective technique; Schmalt's (1976a) Grid Technique, the methodological basis. Participants are first presented with ambiguous picture cues (Fig. 7.2), analogous to projective methods, but the response format is objective, analogous to questionnaire measures. Specifically, a set of 20 statements relating to the motive under investigation is appended to each picture, and participants are asked to identify those statements that fit each picture best. Motive scores are determined by adding up all of the motive-relevant statements endorsed across the situations illustrated. The pictures show ambiguous affiliation-related scenarios, with age- and gender-specific information being leveled out as far as possible.

Differentiating between action-outcome and situation-outcome expectancies, the 20 statements listed below each picture can be assigned to four stable factors:

■ Hope of affiliation (HA):
   – "optimistic tendency to actively structure situations" (HA 1)
   – "situational optimism" (HA 2)
■ Fear of rejection (FR):
   – "fear of erroneous actions" (FR 1)
   – "resignation/disinterest" (FR 2)

A short form of the affiliation grid has now been devised (Sokolowski, 1992), and the Multi-Motive Grid (Sokolowski et al., 2000) can also be used to measure both components of the motive.

A validation study showed marked differences between the reactions of participants high in hope of affiliation and those high in fear of rejection in a virtual social scenario (presented by means of slides and audio recordings; Sokolowski, 1986). The scenario consisted of three parts:

■ Part 1: Notification that an attractive target person would be at a party in a week's time.
■ Part 2: Final preparations for the party.
■ Part 3: First encounter with the target person at the party.

Participants high in fear of rejection described themselves as being significantly more irritable, nervous, and inhibited than approach-motivated participants after all three parts of the scenario. The heart rate of approach-motivated individuals decreased as the target event drew nearer; that of avoidance-motivated participants increased. This significant interaction effect for changes in heart rate was interpreted as reflecting the approach-avoidance conflict experienced by the affiliation avoiders (Sokolowski & Schmalt, 1996).

In a four-week diary study by Schmalt and Langens (1999), grid scores for the affiliation motive correlated significantly ($r = .35$) with the number of affiliation-related topics produced in free recall in daily diary entries. Abele, Andrä, and Schute (1999) traced the development of 1,216 university students' careers and social lives for one year after graduation. They found that the number of participants living with a long-term partner decreased significantly as a function of the FR grid score. In a laboratory study, Wegge, Quaeck, and Kleinbeck (1996) investigated students' preferences for video games, taking motive measures as predictors. It transpired that participants with high grid scores for the affiliation motive were significantly more likely to prefer an interactive adventure game to a motorbike race game or a combat game. In general, participants with high HA grid scores paid more attention to the color scheme and music of the games, whereas individuals high in the achievement motive preferred games where they could set the difficulty level themselves. In-depth analyses of behavior in an interactive virtual environment have revealed that individuals with high HA grid scores make more effective choices when working toward a

Figure 7.2 Example pictures from Sokolowski's (1992) affiliation grid.

specified goal – regardless of whether that goal has a positive or negative regulatory focus (Schüler, 2002). Indeed, from the moment they register the relevant cues in the virtual environment, affiliation approachers show more effective information processing. Individuals with high FR scores on the affiliation grid, in contrast, are not able to effectively deploy goals as "tools" to direct their behavior – corresponding differences between the two groups can even be discerned on the perceptual level.

Barely any correlations are found between affiliation grid scores and questionnaire scores. In the studies outlined above that also obtained questionnaire data, only the grid scores – and not the questionnaire measures – were significantly related to the criterion variables (see Fig. 7.3).

SUMMARY

Research on the affiliation motive and affiliation motivation began with the development of the first TAT coding system. Because TAT scores do not necessarily correspond with self-attributed motives, the TAT approach to the measurement of motives can be described as "implicit." Despite their various shortcomings, projective or implicit procedures can evidently help to explain spontaneous behavior that is not accessible to conscious awareness.

The next step forward came with the development of questionnaires to assess the approach and avoidance components of the affiliation motive. For the first time, it was possible to pinpoint the typical differences between individuals high in hope of affiliation and those high in fear of rejection. Nevertheless, questionnaire measures can only assess the explicit – i.e., consciously accessible – aspects of motives, meaning that the domains in which these instruments can be applied are rather limited.

The development of the affiliation grid opened up a third way of measuring motives. Inasmuch as this procedure combines characteristics of the TAT method and questionnaire measures, it can be labeled "semiprojective." It has proved particularly useful for explaining and predicting patterns of emotional response and spontaneous preferences in social situations.

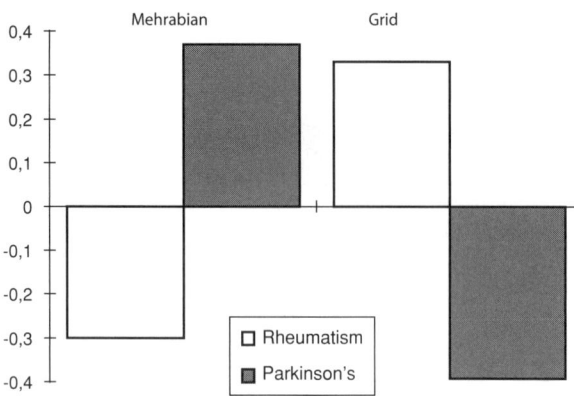

Figure 7.3 Level of the affiliation motive (total motive) as measured by the Mehrabian scales and the affiliation grid (all scores are z-transformed).

7.5 Intimacy Motivation

The affiliation motive is aroused in situations that involve contact with strangers or people we do not know very well, but it plays only a secondary role in our interactions with the people close to us. In fact, motivation research long overlooked our interactions with those near and dear to us, and the joyful state of mutual affection that can be called love, trust, friendship, or intimacy, as a motivating state in its own right. McAdams (1982a) was the first to incorporate these aspects in his research. Based on the observation of marked individual differences in human experience and behavior in interactions with close friends and partners – like those observed in interactions with strangers – McAdams validated a separate TAT coding system for the intimacy motive.

The development of two distinct motive systems governing interactions with others can be traced back to different phylogenetic "roots." The function of the affiliation motive can be seen as facilitating closeness and affiliation to groups, thus providing safety (from predators) and increasing individual chances of survival. The evolutionary roots of the intimacy motive, on the other hand, are to be seen in brood care (see above), which necessitated the development of close social relationships (Eibl-Ebesfeldt, 1997).

In formulating the concept of intimacy motivation, McAdams was inspired by authors writing from the perspectives of theology, philosophy, psychiatry, and psychology, including Martin Buber (1979), David Bakan (1966), Harry Sullivan (1953), and Abraham Maslow (1968).

DEFINITION

McAdams describes intimacy motivation as both the striving and the ability to experience a state described by the following seven facets in close relationships:

- joy and mutual delight (Maslow),
- reciprocal dialogue (Buber, Sullivan),
- openness, contact, union, receptivity (Bakan, Maslow),
- perceived harmony (Buber, Sullivan),
- concern for the well-being of the other (Sullivan),
- renunciation of manipulative control and the desire to dominate the other (Bakan, Buber, Maslow), and
- experience of an encounter with a well-known other as an end in itself (Bakan, Buber, Maslow, Sullivan). (McAdams, 1982a, p. 137 f.).

7.5.1 Measuring the Intimacy Motive

After extensive revisions, McAdams (1980) proposed a coding system for assessing the intimacy motive. It must first be established that at least one of the categories (I) "encounter brought positive affect" or (II) "dialogue" is present in each story generated. Only when this criterion is fulfilled can the remaining subcategories (1–8) be scored (see the overview below).

Content Categories of the Intimacy Motive Scoring Key (Based on McAdams, 1980, p. 423)

I. Encounter brought positive affect
II. Dialogue
  1. Psychological growth and coping
  2. Commitment and concern
  3. Time-space
  4. Union
  5. Harmony
  6. Surrender
  7. Escape to intimacy
  8. Connection with the outside world

Interrater agreement proved to be highly satisfactory, at between 91% and 95% for the two main categories. Test-retest reliability after one year was $r = .48$ among high school students – quite a considerable result for a TAT measure.

McAdams conducted a series of studies to explore the differences between individuals high and low in the intimacy motive. One study involved a psychodrama session, with each participant in turn being asked to direct a minidrama (McAdams & Powers, 1981). TAT stories written before and after the session were analyzed for affiliation and intimacy contents. Of course, only the scores of the stories produced before the drama session were used as measures of individual differences in motives. Analysis of video recordings of the minidramas showed that participants with high intimacy scores sought closer physical proximity to the other participants, needed less introduction time, gave fewer instructions, referred more to "we" than to "I," and laughed more. The latter two behaviors and closer physical proximity were also observed among participants high in the affiliation motive. The topics covered in the psychodrama were also content analyzed and coded in terms of their intimacy content. The correlation with the TAT scores was impressive ($r = .70$). These findings indicate a high level of agreement between fantasy and spontaneous action. Differences were also found in peer ratings on the basis of trait lists: students of both sexes with a high intimacy motive were rated to be more "natural," "warm," "sincere," "appreciative," and "loving," and less "dominant," "outspoken," and "self-centered."

7.5.2 The Intimacy Motive and Memory

Another experiment explored the effects of the intimacy motive on memory. McAdams (1979) projected 30 picture-word combinations onto a screen for a few seconds and then gave participants two minutes to reproduce the words. The picture-word stimuli represented three content categories:

1. personal relationships (e.g., lover, sister, friend),
2. vehicles (e.g., motorbike, submarine), and
3. occupations (e.g., artist, accountant).

As Bonsfield (1953) had already established, reproduction of such material tends to involve its grouping into content categories (a phenomenon known as "clustering"). McAdams' findings indicated that participants with a strong intimacy motive showed a more pronounced tendency for clustering material relating to personal relationships. Autobiographical memory also reflects the effects of dominant motives (McAdams, 1982b). When asked to recall 10 friendship episodes in the past two weeks, participants high in the intimacy motive remembered more dyadic relationships involving mutual openness, listening to the other, and concern for the other's welfare (McAdams, Healy, & Krause, 1984).

Even stronger motivational effects on memory were obtained in studies that required participants to retell a long story that the experimenter had read aloud while projecting a TAT picture (McAdams & McClelland, 1983). In the first study, the experimenter read an intimacy story (a harmonious and friendly 25-year class reunion in the countryside) and a neutral story (a man's long journey from Utah to Mexico, where he finally sets up a restaurant of his own). Both stories were of equal length, and each contained 33 "facts." After distracting the participants with other tasks for an hour, the experimenter showed the two TAT pictures again and, without previous warning, instructed them to write down the respective stories. The stronger the intimacy motive, the more complete was the recall of the intimacy story ($r = .55$), but not of the neutral story ($r = .14$).

SUMMARY

The intimacy motive determines the emotional climate and behavior in close relationships. Unfortunately, this motive is not yet as well researched as the affiliation motive; it is also somewhat more difficult to measure. The intimacy motive is reflected not only in appraisals of close relationships, but also in the ability to trust others and to surrender and relinquish control in relationships, an ability that probably evolves early in ontogenesis.

7.6 Physiological and Neuroimmunological Correlates

Being kicked in the shins hurts – but so does social exclusion. Evidence for the pain of rejection was found in an experiment conducted by Eisenberger, Liebermann, and Williams (2003). Participants were led to believe that they were playing a virtual ball-tossing game with two other players, and could see these "other players" – who did not in fact exist – passing the ball to each another on a computer screen. In the first part of the experiment, they were told that there was a technical hitch, and that they would only be able to watch the other players. After the hitch had been "fixed," they were able to join in the game using a joystick, and the ball was passed to them regularly. In the third part of the experiment, the "other players" stopped passing the ball to the participant, effectively excluding him/her from the game and socially isolating him/her. Throughout the experiment, functional magnetic resonance imaging (fMRI) was used to examine participants' brain activity. It emerged that one area of the brain – the anterior cingulate cortex – was particularly active when social distress was induced. This area is also active during physical pain. An area in the prefrontal cortex showed an opposite pattern of activity: the greater the feeling of social distress, the less active this region was. This finding was attributed to the coping function of the prefrontal cortex, which has been implicated in the regulation of negative affect. Animal experiments confirmed the results found in humans, showing that electrical stimulation of the anterior cingulate cortex and other brain regions belonging to what is known as the "separation distress circuit" can provoke separation cries in mammals (guinea pigs) (Panksepp, 2003).

❶ In short, these midbrain areas seem to be closely associated with social rejection. Social isolation is accompanied by the experience of distress and the secretion of stress hormones (glucocorticoids); these experiences are decreased or inhibited by social reintegration and the release of oxytocin. (Carter, 1998)

IMMUNOGLOBULIN. Back in the late 1970s, McClelland began to study whether the arousal of motives was associated with the secretion of particular hormones, and the consequences that such an association might have for the relevant bodily functions – and ultimately for health (for a summary, see McClelland, 1984a). Jemmott (1982) conducted a one-year longitudinal study of dental students selected on the basis of two motivation profiles – relaxed affiliation (where the motive was translated to behavior) vs. inhibited power (where the motive was not translated to behavior) – that involved measuring immunoglobim levels in their saliva before exams and during vacations. Immunoglobulin A (IgA) is a product of the immune system, and represents the body's first line of defense against viral infections, particularly those of the upper respiratory tract. Affiliation-motivated students had consistently higher immunoglobulin levels than all others, particularly relative to those high in power motivation. Exam stress led to an initial reduction in IgA levels in all students. Overall, the better immune protection of the affiliation-motivated students was associated with fewer respiratory infections.

DOPAMINE. The neurotransmitter dopamine also seems to be associated with the affiliation motive. Dopamine induces dilation of the blood vessels and relaxation of the gastrointestinal system. Along with endorphins, it generates general well-being. Dopamine has been implicated as an important neurotransmitter in the system of positive reinforcement. The relaxing effect of the dopaminergic neuroendocrine system experienced in the context of affiliative behavior can be seen as positive reinforcement of this behavior.

McClelland, Patel, Stier, and Brown (1987) found that arousal of the affiliation motive coincided with the secretion of dopamine (but not of adrenaline, noradrenaline, or cortisone), particularly among individuals high in affiliation motivation who reported their lives to be very stressful. In their experiment, the affiliation motive was aroused by a film – either a romantic love story or the tale of a conflict-ridden marriage – and subsequently assessed using a TAT procedure. Dopamine levels were measured in both saliva and blood serum.

Several independent studies (cf. McClelland, 1985a) have also established that a high affiliation motive is conducive to good health. A longitudinal study of university graduates revealed a negative correlation between the strength of the affiliation motive measured at age 30 and diastolic blood pressure 20 years later (McClelland, 1979). Those who were least susceptible to illness were characterized by relaxed attachments and relationships with others.

Reduced dopamine production resulting in dopamine deficiency is seen as the primary cause of Parkinson's disease. With this in mind, Sokolowski, Schmitt, Jörg, and Ringendahl (1997) tested the hypothesis that the affiliation motive of Parkinson's patients, who suffer chronic dopamine deficiency, is markedly lower than that of a control group with another chronic illness (polyarthritis/rheumatism). The affiliation motive of the two patient groups was assessed by means of implicit (affiliation grid) and explicit (Mehrabian questionnaire) measures. Patients were also questioned about their recent experiences of social interactions. The findings of this study were surprising and apparently contradictory, with the Parkinson's patients scoring much higher on affiliation motive on the Mehrabian scales, and the rheumatism patients scoring much higher on the affiliation grid (Fig. 7.3).

Despite their higher explicit motive scores, indicative of a stronger self-attributed affiliation motive, Parkinson's patients were significantly more likely than rheumatism patients to state that they feel uncertain and insecure in social interactions with others. They find it much more difficult to establish contact with strangers, and are significantly more likely than rheumatism patients to describe these interactions as taxing. The implicit motivational basis for affiliative behavior thus seems to be severely weakened. In Parkinson's patients, behavior in affiliative situations is no longer energized and directed involuntarily by the motives aroused, because the automatic regulation of that behavior is reliant on dopamine, and is thus impaired. The high scores on the Mehrabian scales seem to reflect the patients' aspirations or ideals rather than reality.

OXYTOCIN. Along with the neurotransmitter dopamine, the neuropeptide oxytocin, which is produced in the pituitary gland, plays an important role in social bonding processes. Oxytocin reduces the activity of the sympathetic nervous system (see above), and generally has stress-reducing and calming effects. Oxytocin is also known as the "hormone of motherly love," because it is released in greater quantities during and after childbirth, and is partly responsible for mother-child bonding. Animal experiments have shown that females given oxytocin injections can bond spontaneously with the young of others; conversely, the bonding behavior of a mother animal can be blocked by the administration of oxytocin antagonists. If no young are present, there is an increased readiness to engage in behaviors that establish physical contact – e.g., mutual grooming in primates, which in turn leads to oxytocin secretion in the animal being groomed. Massages have been shown to have comparable effects on humans (Uvnaes-Moberg, 1998). Among mammals living in monogamous relationships, oxytocin is also released during sexual intercourse, thus strengthening the mutual bond.

Dopamine secretion thus seems to be associated with the affiliation motive, whereas oxytocin secretion is more closely related to the intimacy motive. Questionnaire measures are unable to tap relationships between motives and neurotransmitters, however; projective and semiprojective methods (TAT and grid techniques) are required here.

SUMMARY

The precise nature of the relationship between the affiliation and intimacy motives, the evolution of which can probably be traced back to different phylogenetic roots (Eibl-Eibsfeldt, 1997; see above), remains unclear. In many of the studies conducted by McAdams, the differences observed – e.g., in memory – were explained by measures of the intimacy motive, but not by measures of the affiliation motive. The few studies to compute correlations between TAT scores for the two motives report coefficients in the range from .25 to .55. Despite these moderate correlations, the finding that arousal conditions that markedly increased the intimacy-related content of TAT stories had barely any effect on affiliation-related content suggests that intimacy and affiliation are in fact independent motive systems.

A study of behavior in a psychodrama session (McAdams & Powers, 1981) identified much common ground between individuals high in the intimacy motive and those high in the affiliation motive in terms of their physical proximity to other participants, amount of laughter, limited self-references, more balanced dialogue, and positive affect. These behaviors can all be seen as activities seeking to establish and guide social relationships, which are thus relevant to both motives. The intimacy motive involved a further component, however, namely "surrender of control in the process of relating" (McAdams, 1982b, p. 161). Because they have more faith in others, people high in the intimacy motive have the capacity to entrust themselves to the social situation and to relinquish control.

As preliminary experimental research showed, the need to affiliate with others is elicited when fear is aroused (in dangerous situations, exams, evaluations, new and uncertain situations). Beside this reactive tendency to join forces with others as a means of coping with the unpleasant emotions of fear and insecurity, two independent approach motives govern our social interaction with others – the affiliation motive and the intimacy motive. Whereas the former is activated in our dealings with strangers and people we do not know well, the latter takes effect in our interactions with those near and dear to us. The goals of these motives are not to reduce fear, but to achieve positive goal states that are inherent in social intercourse and that are closely associated with production of the neurotransmitters dopamine and oxytocin.

REVIEW QUESTIONS

1. **What is the goal of the affiliation motive?**

   The goal of the affiliation motive is to establish relationships that both parties experience as positive.

2. **In what kind of situations is the affiliation motive activated?**

   The affiliation motive is activated whenever people come into contact and interact with unknown or little known individuals.

3. **What is shyness?**

   Shyness occurs when a high need of affiliation and high fear of rejection are activated at the same time, producing a "stalemate" in the conflict between approach and avoidance.

4. **What are the characteristics of individuals high in the "hope of affiliation" component of the affiliation motive?**

   They see others in a better light, and as being more like themselves;
   They like others more, and are more popular with others;
   Their friendly manner is infectious and spreads rapidly to others (strangers);
   They are more confident and experience more pleasant affect in their interactions with others;
   The behavioral decisions they make in social contexts are more appropriate to their goals;
   They have very specific responses to social recognition and rejection.

5. **What are the characteristics of individuals high in fear of rejection?**

   They feel distressed in social situations and elicit similar feelings from others;
   They are less confident, more tense, and more anxious in social situations;
   They judge themselves to be less popular and more lonely (although they do not in fact interact any less with others);
   Their social skills are not very well developed;
   They have low action-outcome expectancies in their interactions with unfamiliar others;
   They are plagued by feelings of helplessness in ambiguous social situations;
   Their emotional responses to social recognition or rejection are not very differentiated or specific.

6. **Which tests can be used to measure the strength of the affiliation motive?**

   The affiliation motive can be measured using projective methods such as the TAT, questionnaire methods such as the Mehrabian scales, or semiprojective methods such as the Grid Technique.

7. **Which neurotransmitters are particularly relevant to the affiliation motive and to the intimacy motive, respectively?**

   Dopamine is secreted in greater quantities when affiliation-related goals are attained, i.e., when strangers get to know each other better. Oxytocin plays a key role in the establishment and stabilization of close relationships, and is thus closely related to the intimacy motive.

8 Power Motivation

H.-D. Schmalt and H. Heckhausen

8.1 Power: Concepts and Constructs

Before we examine what exactly power motivation might be and how it is commonly conceptualized, we need to have a clear understanding of the phenomena thought to be constitutive of power and the contexts in which they come to bear. Social sciences such as sociology and political science are primarily concerned with the static state of existing power relationships and the role that these relationships play in maintaining and consolidating specific hierarchies. Behavioral sciences such as psychology tend to be more interested in the dynamic process of the exercise of power, its individual determinants and concomitant conditions. Sociobiology focuses on the relationship between power, **status**, and **resources** and the ultimate biological goal of maximizing reproductive fitness, the theory being that organisms with access to power, status, and influence have (or had)

an adaptive advantage over organisms without the benefit of these resources.

Power – and the inequality of its distribution among individuals, social groups, animal societies, and nations – is a multifarious social phenomenon that, like few others, has been the object of explanations, justifications, and objections since time immemorial. In almost all cultures of the world, it is common to describe members of one's group in terms of "dominance"/"submission" and, in so doing, to implicitly acknowledge that group relations are determined by an underlying dimension of power and dominance (Kenrick, Li, & Butner, 2003). It comes as little surprise to learn that dominance has also been observed to be an important "personality variable" in our close relatives, the chimpanzees. King and Figueredo (1997) asked zoo workers to rate 100 chimpanzees on personality dimensions (the "Big Five"). Beside the factors known from human research – neuroticism, extraversion, openness to experience, etc. – dominance proved to play a major role in the chimpanzee personality. Thus, **power** and **dominance** seem to be a major theme in the lives of both human and nonhuman primates. Indeed, no social group would be able to function and survive in the long term without the differential allocation of power. The inequitable distribution of social status and power seems to be one of the universals of human and animal social life (Kenrick, Li, & Butner, 2003). Because power describes relations among groups and nations as well as among individuals, it invites various different levels of analysis and approaches typical of disciplines such as sociobiology, psychology, anthropology, and the social and political sciences.

Motivational Approaches

In this chapter, we analyze power from the perspective of motivational psychology, but drawing on these different levels of analysis and considering both animal and human societies. Nevertheless, the focus of our theoretical analyses is on the individual, with power being conceptualized as a process of exchange between individuals (parties). This focus on the individual entails the investigation of individual motives (Section 8.2); our interest in the process of exchange between two parties draws attention to the behavioral and situational factors that motivate behavior. To use the terminology of motivation theory, we are interested in incentives: Which aspects of behavior, e.g., sources of power (Section 8.1.2), and which contents of communicative exchanges (Sections 8.4.3 and 8.4.4) serve to orchestrate incentives such that one party is able to dominate another? The stated, feigned, or assumed goals of power behavior also serve as important incentives for both parties in power-driven interactions (Section 8.1.3).

DEFINITION

Motives and incentives thus constitute the frame of reference for the present approach. An expectancy variable is added at relevant points (Section 8.1.5) to generate a full expectancy-value model.

Social Approaches

The concept of power often has rather negative connotations, associated as it is with notions of force, oppression, violence, and despotic rule. A position of power is frequently used to justify exploitation and oppression, particularly in the political arena. As noted by the historian Sebastian Haffner (2003; own translation) "power corrupts – often the very path to power, and almost always its absolute possession." Kipnis (1976; Rind & Kipnis, 1999) examined the claim that power corrupts and advocated a conceptualization of power based on these kinds of negative associations. His studies confirmed that the very possession of power causes people to try to influence others more, to value others less, and to form higher opinions of the power person. Moreover, powerful individuals have been shown to have rather stereotypical and simplistic perceptions of others (Keltner & Robinson, 1996, 1997) and to display socially inappropriate behavior in their interactions with them. Yet power is just as often associated with positively connoted phenomena, such as:

- legitimate government,
- authority,
- recognized leadership,
- influence,
- education,
- balancing of interests, and
- group cohesion.

Charismatic leaders who function as role models, pursue a vision that is in the interest of their subordinates, and initiate positive change, growth, and new ideas, represent the positive side of the power spectrum. Through their leader, subordinates are able to experience generalized feelings of strength and efficacy.

Sociobiological Approaches

Besides social scientific approaches, current conceptions of power have been informed by sociobiology, and by findings showing that societies would not be able to function efficiently without asymmetries in the distribution of power, status, and resources. This seems to apply to humans and the nonhuman primates, as well as to many of the higher mammals (White, 1980). It can be assumed that members

of societies based on the equal distribution of power, status, and resources would have become caught up in a permanent state of conflict over the course of evolution, with negative and dysfunctional effects on the chances of survival of the individual, the group, and ultimately the species. Thus, it seems quite reasonable for evolution to have "decided" on a regulatory principle that is conducive to stability in social groups – for certain periods of time, at least. From this perspective, the idea of egalitarian group structures is a social utopia with no basis in primate phylogeny. This assumption has been disputed with reference to primitive societies that appear to be based on principles of equality rather than dominance. One frequently cited example is that of Maori societies, where the possessions of individuals who had accumulated "too much" were free to be plundered by the other members of that society, thus restoring an equal distribution of resources. Upon closer inspection, however, it emerged that this measure actually served to maintain traditional power structures, as tribal chiefs and rulers were exempted from its effects (Eibl-Eibesfeldt, 1988, p. 163).

There is evidently a universal "behavioral glue" that serves to maintain hierarchical group structures: the automatic **complementarity** of dominant and submissive behavior (see the study described below). Dominant or submissive behavior automatically triggers the complementary pattern of behavior in others, and thus serves to stabilize and perpetuate asymmetrical power relations.

STUDY

Studies on the Complementarity Effect

Tiedens and Fragale (2003) conducted two studies in which participants interacted with a confederate whose behavior was either dominant or submissive - as reflected in their posture, for example. In the dominant condition, confederates draped themselves across a chair, one arm over the back of the chair beside them and the right leg crossed over the left such that the chair to the right was "occupied" as well. In the submissive condition, confederates sat with their legs together and hands in their lap. The results show a clear complementarity effect: Participants presented with a dominant confederate tended to display submissive behavior, whereas submissive behavior on the part of the confederate was likely to prompt displays of dominance. Two further observations are worthy of note. First, complementarity of behavior was found to make people feel more comfortable; second, these responses were "automatic" - none of the participants were consciously aware of any effects of the confederate's posture. Given that similar patterns have been observed in nonhuman primates (Wright, 1994), the underlying mechanisms and relationships may have phylogenetic roots.

8.1.1 Power and Power Motivation

Our attempts to define power and power motivation in more precise terms start with a review of how power is conceptualized in various disciplines. The following definitions from the fields of philosophy, sociology, political science, psychology, and biology illustrate the range of perspectives taken.

Definitions of Power

- The sociologist Max Weber: "Power is the probability that one actor within a social relationship will be in a position to carry out his own will despite resistance, regardless of the basis on which this possibility rests" (Weber, 1947, p. 152).
- The sociologist Niclas Luhmann: "Power is the production of effects despite possible resistance; it is, so to speak, causality under unfavorable conditions" (1975, p. 1, own translation).
- The philosopher Bertrand Russel: "Power may be defined as the production of intended effects" (1938, p. 35).
- The political scientist R. A. Dahl: "My intuitive idea of power, then, is something like this: A has power over B to the extent that he can get B to do something that B would not otherwise do" (1957, p. 202).
- The psychologist Kurt Lewin: "We might define power of b over a . . . as the quotient of the maximum force which b can induce on a . . . and the maximum resistance which a can offer" (1951, p. 336).
- The social psychologist Dorwin Cartwright: "The power of O over P, as we conceive it, is concerned with O's ability to perform acts which activate forces in P's life space" (1959, p. 193).
- The organizational psychologist Adam Galinsky: "We define power as the ability to control resources, own and others', without social interference" (Galinsky, Gruenfeld, & Magee, 2003, p. 454).
- The biologists Anderson and Berdahl: "We define power as the ability to provide or withhold valued resources or administer punishments" (2002, p. 1362).

Thus, it would seem that power is at work whenever somebody is in the position to get somebody else to do something that he or she would not otherwise do. Only Russel's definition is more general still. For Russel, power is any attainment of an intended outcome, and does not necessarily involve a social conflict. This conceptualization of power as a general capacity for action (a conglomerate of achievement and power themes) is also prevalent in naive psychology. Any effects that individuals exert on their environment derive from their "power" in the sense of their capacity, ability, and **competence**. As shown by Heider (1958), this approach is in line with a naive action theory that sees every action and the outcome of every action as dependent not only on motivation (the "try" factor), but also on capability (the "can" factor), where the latter reflects the individual's capacity to prevail over environmental forces.

DEFINITION

From the psychological perspective, power can thus be described as a domain-specific dyadic relationship that is characterized by the asymmetric distribution of social competence, access to resources, and/or social status, and that is manifested in unilateral behavioral control.

Power is exercised when behavioral control occurs despite the resistance or inertia of the person it is directed at (B). From the motivational perspective, it would seem important for this set up to have a phenomenological dimension – in other words, for the individual exerting power (A) to have a sense of control.

The sense of control functions as an incentive because it is positively valenced – exerting control results in positive affect (here: a feeling of **self-efficacy**). In other words, the feeling of self-efficacy experienced upon exercising control is, in fact, the motive goal to which we aspire; it is the state that we crave and the absence of which we dread (cf. Schmalt, 1987).

Power motivation can thus be defined in terms of anticipatory emotions and incentive theory, in the tradition of McClelland et al. (1953). McClelland (1975, p. 77) defined the power motive as "the need primarily to feel strong, and secondarily to act powerfully. Influencing others is just one of several ways of satisfying the need to feel strong." In his collection of essays and aphorisms entitled *Human, All Too Human*, Friedrich Nietzsche takes a very similar stance:

> We attack not only to hurt a person, to conquer him, but also, perhaps, simply to become aware of our own strength. (Nietzsche, 1878, p. 249; own translation)

These emotional undercurrents are not assumed to surface in our conscious experience, neither are we assumed to see positive affect as the goal state of our power behavior. In fact, the emotional component of this incentive mechanism, and the regulatory functions it entails, are generally beyond our conscious experience. Explaining power behavior in terms of emotional experience is a purely theoretical approach; indeed if someone asked to explain his or her power behavior replied by citing these emotions, that response would seem rather strange and disconcerting (cf. Fig. 1.2 in Schneider & Schmalt, 2000).

❗ Power relations are motivated by the positive valence of a sense of control. The emotions arising in the context of control can themselves become the object of anticipation, thus constituting an incentive mechanism that serves to motivate power behavior.

A recent study by Anderson and Berdahl (2002) provides empirical support for this conception of power motivation. The authors assessed power as both a personality disposition and a situational variable (i.e., the power a person is assigned to reward or punish others). Both aspects were varied systematically and their relations to a number of cognitive and behavioral outcomes were investigated. Mediation analyses showed that power is linked to positive emotional experience and that participants' sense of power and the related emotions mediated the effects of power on many of its behavioral and cognitive correlates. In other words, the positive emotional experience of power and control plays a major role in mediating the effects of attitudes, opinions, and behaviors pertaining to power (Anderson & Berdahl, 2002, p. 1372).

This approach has its roots in motivational theories that conceptualize the power factor (in the sense of capacity, ability, and competence) either, like White (1959, 1960), as the outcome of a basic effectance motive or, like Alfred Adler (1922), as a motive for power and superiority that develops in response to the underlying shortcomings of the competence factor. For White, competence is the outcome of a basic effectance motive that drives people to keep engaging with their environment as a means of establishing their own efficacy (1960, p. 104). White suggests that at the age of two or three:

> The child has reached a point of understanding where for the first time he can contemplate his place in the family and his relation to other people in general. To some extent he continues to experiment with crude social power, especially with other children whom he may boss, hit, and threaten in various ways (White, 1960, p. 123).

Adler (1922), in contrast, did not see the power motive as directly geared to the goal of exerting power; rather, he proposed a model with more indirect effects, working on the principle of compensation. Essentially, Adler viewed power behavior as the attempt to compensate for one's failings and shortcomings. According to his model, individuals interpret the constitutional lack of power and strength as a lack of competence on their part, and consequently feel inadequate and inferior. They seek to compensate for this perceived **inferiority** (inferiority complex) by striving for perfection, superiority, and social power. These are the two opposing poles between which the approach and avoidance components of the power motive – hope for power and control vs. fear of loss of power and control – take effect.

8.1.2 Sources of Power

To be able to appeal to the motive base of another individual, a power holder must have access to resources that function as reinforcers. The relationship between the holder (A) and the recipient (B) of power must be asymmetrical as regards these resources, which function as "sources of power," providing a basis for power to be exerted in unilateral behavioral control. French and Raven (1959) and Raven (1974) proposed a taxonomy of six **sources of power** (see overview).

Taxonomy of Power (Based on French & Raven, 1959; Raven, 1974)

1. Reward power: The strength of this power source depends on B's estimation of the extent to which A is in a position to satisfy one of B's motives, and the extent to which A makes such satisfaction contingent on B's behavior.

2. Coercive power: The strength of this power source depends on B's estimation of the extent to which A is in a position to punish B for undesirable actions by withdrawing the opportunity to satisfy certain motives, and the extent to which A makes such punishment contingent on B's undesirable behavior. The coercion consists in restricting B's options for action through threat of punishment.

3. Legitimate power: This source of power derives from norms internalized by B, which tell him or her that A is authorized to monitor the adherence to certain behavioral norms and, if necessary, to take actions to ensure such adherence.

4. Referent power: This source of power arises from B's identification with A, i.e., B's desire to be like A.

5. Expert power: The strength of this power source depends on the extent to which B perceives A to have special knowledge, insights, or skills in a particular area.

6. Informational power: This source of power comes into play when A is able to communicate information that prompts B to look at the consequences of his or her behavior in a new light and thus triggers a change in behavior.

Without doubt, the asymmetric distribution of resources originates primarily from the power to reward and the power to punish, both of which are widespread in all primate societies, including humans. In animal societies and in hominid evolution, physical strength and superiority likely gave certain individuals the opportunity to exercise reward and coercive power, and thus to rise in rank and status (Eagly & Wood, 1999). Other sources of power are rooted in a society or culture, and based on mutual agreements and commitments. If, in a group or a party, expertise is not recognized as such, or indeed discredited or disgraced – as can repeatedly be observed in the political arena – that power basis is no longer binding and can be overruled by the reward and coercive power of others – by passing legislation, for example. Once expert opinion has been compromised, potentates can rule "in peace."

Individual differences can also be expected in people's efforts to augment their sources of power. The mere possession of power sources and the sense of power that they convey can be a desirable goal state in its own right; power behavior is not necessarily involved. Indeed, a sense of power and control is often more relevant to personal satisfaction than is actually exerting an influence on others (see above; McClelland, 1975).

Coveted sources of power include, among many others:
- material possessions,
- prestige,
- status,
- leadership,
- control of information, etc.

Winter (1973) found that students holding offices in student government scored higher on power motivation, as did the spokespersons of a local urban renewal program. The same

STUDY

Study on the Ability to Gauge Others' Sources of Power

The ability to gauge other peoples' sources of power quickly and accurately has also been investigated by Schmalt (1987). In this study, pairs of players were led to believe that they were interacting in a kind of prisoner's dilemma game. In actual fact, the responses of the "opponent" were manipulated by the experimenter, such that the opponent made 80% competitive (i.e., confrontational) choices in one condition and 20% competitive choices in the other condition. The basic rules of the prisoner's dilemma game are as follows: Each of the players can choose either cooperation or conflict. Winnings are dependent on the combination of their choices. Players can maximize their winnings by persuading their opponent to cooperate, but then "changing their mind" and choosing conflict, i.e., conning their opponent. Winnings are lowest when both players opt for conflict. If both players decide to cooperate, both receive a moderate sum. Besides measuring the participants' power motive, the intentions of the players were also assessed. Almost all of the participants stated that they intended to cooperate. Expectancy ratings were also obtained as dependent variables over the 30 trials of the game. More specifically, participants were asked how confident they were of being able to put their intentions into practice. The results are shown in Fig. 8.1. Individuals high in power motivation who intended to cooperate and who were paired up with a cooperative opponent, making it relatively easy for them to act on their intentions, became increasingly confident of being able to do so. Those who came up against a competitive opponent became increasingly skeptical about being able to put their intentions into practice – and realistically so. Individuals high in power motivation thus seem to be very sensitive to information relating to their prospects of success, whereas individuals low in power motivation respond to this information slowly, if at all. In other words, individuals low in power motivation do not seem to be very receptive to information that might indicate whether or not their intentions are realistic. It is hardly surprising, then, that individuals low in power motivation make few attempts to influence others, and that their occasional attempts to do so tend to fail.

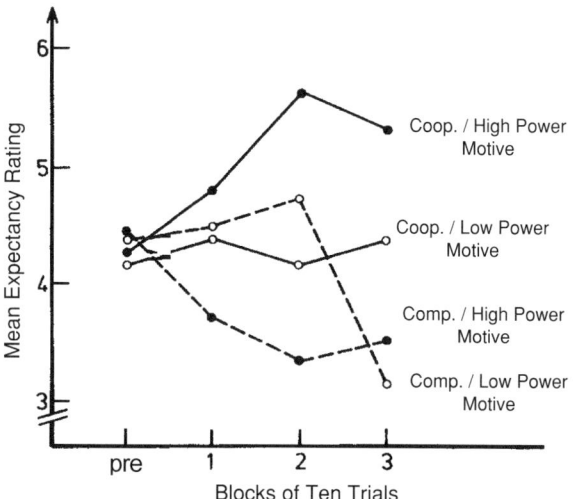

Figure 8.1 Expectancy ratings of individuals high and low in power motivation in the two experimental conditions (*Coop* cooperative; *Comp* competitive). (Based on Schmalt, 1987, p. 111.)

did not hold for party functionaries at various levels of the municipal administration.

There are, however, findings indicating that the mere availability of power sources leads to an increase in power behavior, and to these resources being used to influence others. In a simulation study, Kipnis (1972) invited participants to play the role of managers in an industrial concern. In one condition, they were given a list of sanctions that could be imposed on their workers (power condition); in the other condition, they were simply told to act as managers (nonpower condition). Although the performance of the workers in both conditions was satisfactory, managers in the power condition made more than twice as many attempts to influence their subordinates as managers in the nonpower condition.

The theoretical conceptions of Keltner, Gruenfeld, and Anderson (2003) and Galinsky, Gruenfeld, and Magee (2003) go even further. These authors contend that power, in the sense of the capacity to control resources, suffices to activate approach-related behavior, regardless of the context. At the same time, they assume powerlessness, or the lack of means to control resources, to be associated with behavioral inhibition.

The authors account for this relationship between the power and action by arguing that only those who control resources can afford to turn a blind eye to social norms and conventions. For the powerless, these regulations tend to be all the more binding. Thus, power and the opportunity to exert control can be expected to facilitate more expansive social behavior. In line with this theoretical approach, empirical findings show that powerful individuals whose power motive has been aroused without their knowledge engage in relatively more goal-directed behavior – to their own advantage and to the benefit of others – and that they display more variability in behavior (Galinsky et al., 2003; Guinote, Judd, & Brauer, 2002).

Individual differences can also be expected in efforts to make quick and accurate assessments of other people's motives, goals, and strivings, and to relate these to one's own sources of power, such that the incentives available can be reorchestrated to motivate others in an effective and economic manner. Interestingly, Winter (1973) found teachers, clerics, journalists, and psychologists to be highly power motivated – in contrast to administrators, medical and legal practitioners, for example. Police officers have also been shown to be high in power motivation (Chusmir, 1984). In all five cases, these are decidedly "manipulative" professions aimed at educating, changing, influencing, and even disciplining others. Empirical findings also point to individual differences in the ability to gauge one's own sources of power in a new situation. In a bargaining game ("Con Game"), Schnackers and Kleinbeck (1975) found that players high in power motivation were more aggressive, exerted more influence, were more likely to con other players, and made more winnings from the outset.

8.1.3 Forms and Goals of Power Behavior

We can now give a more accurate description of power behavior from the perspective of power holders:

- On the one hand, power holders have to know which sources of power are available to them – and be determined to deploy them.
- On the other hand, they must be able to assess the motive base of the person to be influenced, and to gauge the effectiveness of their own power sources in the situation at hand.
- Finally, they must select the most effective strategy for deploying their power sources, i.e., the one with the best cost-benefit ratio.

The cost-benefit ratio is important because B may resist A's influence and exert counter-power over A.

For example, the power to reward and the power to punish require A's constant surveillance of B to ensure that A's bases of power are sustainable and stable. This might exhaust A's resources and make B (increasingly) hostile toward A (Anderson & Berdahl, 2002). These costs and risks are not involved in the exercise of referent, expert, or informational power.

Let us assume that A finally succeeds, without using brute force, in exercising power such that B changes his or her behavior in line with A's wishes. This implies that A has managed to reorchestrate the incentive values of the direct and indirect outcomes of the behaviors available to B, such that B becomes motivated to do what A had intended of his or her own accord.

In other words, power and influence imply the reorchestration and manipulation of motives (including the power motive), strivings, and concerns in others. As a rule, this involves the creation of new (positive or negative) incentives. These new incentives do not necessarily address the same motive theme of B's behavior, but represent additional extrinsic, secondary effects of B's actions – in the simplest case, reward or punishment (see above). These forms of power behavior are by no means limited to morally reprehensible acts such as blackmail or corruption. It also covers behaviors such as teaching, the provision of information, and the generation of enthusiasm by a "charismatic" leader. Moreover, a distinction must be drawn between actual and potential

power. It is not always necessary for A to actually demonstrate the sources of power that he or she possesses and intends to bring to bear. Often, B is able to infer this from his or her knowledge of the institutionalized distribution of power and resources.

To integrate and further differentiate what has been said thus far, an extended version of the descriptive model of the individual components of power behavior proposed by Cartwright (1965) and Kipnis (1974) is presented in Fig. 8.2. According to this model, the power motive to influence others must first be aroused within the individual exerting power (point 1 in Fig. 8.2). The reasons for power motivation being aroused may differ greatly, but what is common to them all is the anticipation of positive affect and the final goal of experiencing a sense of strength and **control**. Once power motivation has been aroused, the power holder conveys to the target person the type of behavior expected. This may occur implicitly; e.g., if both parties subscribe to the same social norms and conventions. If the target person complies with these expectations or norms immediately, the power-motivated behavior has already achieved its ends. If, on the other hand, the target person resists (points 2 and 3 in Fig. 8.2), the power holder will review his or her sources of power to determine whether and to what effect each might be deployed in view of the target person's motives and power sources. Depending on the situational context and individual assets, these sources of power can range from physical strength to economic sanctions.

People seeking to deploy power sources such as these may sometimes find that their own inhibitions (point 4 in Fig. 8.2) are not easily overcome, however. These inhibitions include:

- fear of the other person's counter-power,
- insufficient self-confidence, i.e., excessive doubts about one's capacity to influence others,
- competing values,
- long-term costs of exerting power (on the long run, for example, rewards become too expensive and constant surveillance of the target person requires too much effort), and
- institutional or cultural norms that dictate that it would be inappropriate to try to influence certain people in certain ways.

In the animal kingdom, relations between the holder and the recipient of power are regulated by instinctive, fixed "rituals" that regulate the permissible means and sources of power; in humans, cultural conventions and norms often serve the same purpose. It is precisely when these norms are violated that means of exerting power and force often prove particularly contentious – and lend themselves to literary treatment. Prime examples are Goethe's Faust, who made a pact with the devil to seduce poor Gretchen, or Shakespeare's Richard III, who almost wiped out his own family in his quest for power.

In the absence of inhibitions, or if any inhibitions can be overcome, the power holder goes on to utilize various means

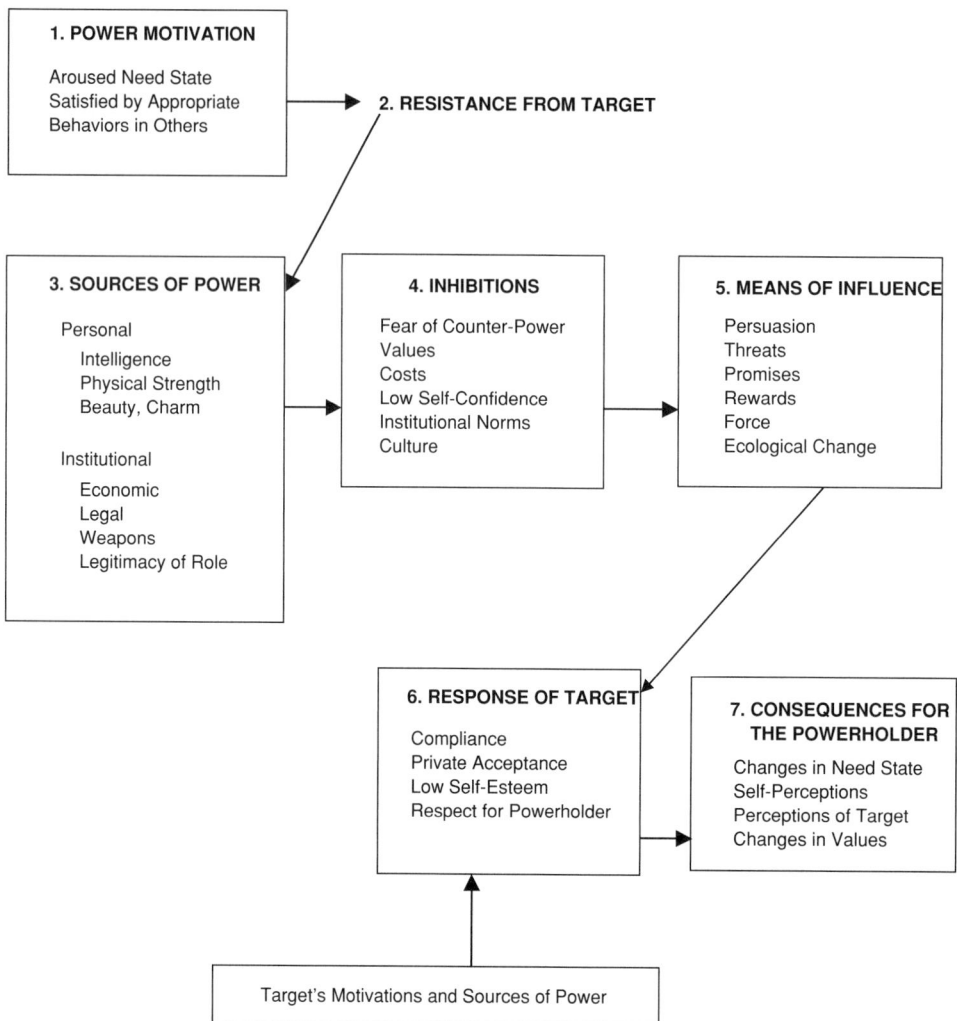

Figure 8.2 A descriptive model of power behavior. (Based on Kipnis, 1974, p. 89, modified and extended.)

of influence (point 5 in Fig. 8.2). Which means of influence are selected depends on various factors: the sources of power available, individual differences among power holders, the power holder's perception of the situation, and the resistance of the target person. As a rule, behavioral routines appropriate to the situation at hand are chosen automatically. It is only in the face of unexpected resistance that a power holder might consciously reflect on his or her means of influence and, if necessary, switch to more severe ones. The larger, more removed, and more anonymous the circle of people to be influenced, the more severe the means of influence applied (cf. Bandura, 1991). Likewise, the less self-confident the power holder is, the stronger the means of influence chosen. When individuals who perceive themselves as weak and externally controlled find themselves in positions of power that afford a wealth of institutional power sources, they are likely to shun personal means of influence, such as persuasion, in favor

of tough institutional measures (Goodstadt & Hjelle, 1973). By the same token, research on nonhuman primates has shown that lower-ranking rhesus monkeys that are thrust into positions of power in their groups by force of circumstance tend to employ malicious and despotic means of influence (Pribram, 1976). They are evidently not accustomed to exerting power in ways appropriate to the individual or the situation at hand.

Let us now turn to the target person, whose response (point 6 in Fig. 8.2) depends on his or her own motives and power sources. There are a number of ways in which a target person can comply with the intentions of the power holder:

■ The target person may give the impression of compliance, but in fact feel resentment.

■ The target person may give the impression of resentful acquiescence, but in fact approve of the power holder's actions.

- The target person's self-esteem may decline.
- The target person may feel more respect for the power holder.

Finally, the act also has implications for the person exercising power. The sense of control, power, and strength is important, as are the feelings of having demonstrated absolute power, made an impression on others, and gained in self-esteem, resources, and status. Similarly, the image of the target person may change – he or she may be considered more dependent and less autonomous, as someone to be kept at more of a distance and accorded less respect (Anderson & Berdahl, 2002). In animal societies, too, a change of rank within a group is a very significant development.

Note that the rationale behind this process of exchange between the power holder and the recipient of power may be simulated and deliberately misinforming. The rules of the power game often imply that the recipient of power is left in the dark, or even deceived, about both the power holder's goals and the power sources available.

In his work *Il Principe* (The Prince), published in 1532, the Florentine statesman and historian Machiavelli wrote that potentates need not be concerned about putting honorable intentions into practice by recognized and accepted means. It is much more important to give the impression of doing so; in other words, to simulate honorable intentions and the availability of appropriate means of influence.

Seen against the background of the complementarity principle of dominant and submissive behavior described above, Machiavelli's strategy makes perfect sense; subjects are likely to accept their leader's claim to dominance, even if it is not really based on honorable intentions and legitimate sources of power.

It should be emphasized that this expanded model of power behavior is descriptive, rather than normative, in nature. It describes the major stages in a cycle of power, without implying that all of them are necessarily involved in each and every power exchange. Conscious deliberation and planning does not necessarily occur at each stage either – appropriate means of influence may be selected and cost-benefit relations assessed automatically, for example. Many components of the process may be interconnected in associative networks and activated instantly upon arousal, thus triggering behavior without the need for conscious processing (Bargh & Chartrand, 1999; Berkowitz, 1990). Incomplete cycles, e.g., which stall because the power holder fails to take into account the target person's counter-power are a case in point.

8.1.4 Approach and Avoidance in Power Motivation

As we have already established, the target person in a power exchange reacts; e.g., he or she may develop resistance or exercise counter-power. Individual differences can thus also be expected in the extent to which power behavior triggers inhibitions and fears, alongside hopes and desires, on the

part of the power holder. Five components of **fear of power** can be distinguished (see overview):

Fear of Power
1. Fear of the augmentation of one's power sources
2. Fear of the loss of one's power sources
3. Fear of exerting power
4. Fear of the counter-power of others
5. Fear of one's power behavior failing

To date, however, neither theoretical nor operational attempts have been made to differentiate these components of fear of power. The components listed represent internal restraints and external obstacles – theoretically described as "inhibition tendencies" – that moderate how the power motive is expressed in behavior. **Inhibition tendencies** moderate the power motive in two ways. On the one hand, a strong power motive coupled with a strong inhibition tendency has detrimental effects on the functioning of the sympathetic nervous system and the immune system, putting people at higher risk for illness (see Section 8.3 for details).

On the other hand, the combination of a strong power motive and strong inhibition tendencies seems to channel the expression of power into socially acceptable behavior, and to the individuals in question enjoying success in the social domain. This can probably be attributed largely to the fact that their power motive is expressed in considerate and socially accepted behavior – e.g., in persuasive communication.

A recent study by Schultheiss and Brunstein (2002) provides compelling evidence for these assumptions. Respondents whose power motives and inhibition tendency had already been assessed were asked to present their point of view on a controversial issue (animal experiments and their ethical justification) to another "participant," who was in fact a confederate of the experimenter. Their presentations were recorded on video and played to external observers, who – without being informed about the study's hypotheses – were asked to rate aspects of the presenter's verbal and nonverbal behavior (e.g., number of arguments presented, frequency of direct address, frequency of eye contact, etc.). Factor analyses of these ratings identified three factors of which "persuasiveness" was the most interesting (Fig. 8.3). The arguments of participants high in both power motivation and inhibition were judged to be far more persuasive than those of participants high in only one of these aspects. Note that this pattern of results emerged only when the power motive was aroused by a goal-imagery exercise. Otherwise, the power motive and inhibition levels had very little effect on persuasiveness ratings.

8.1.5 Connecting Expectancy and Value

Another question with far-reaching theoretical implications is whether and to what extent the expectancy-value model

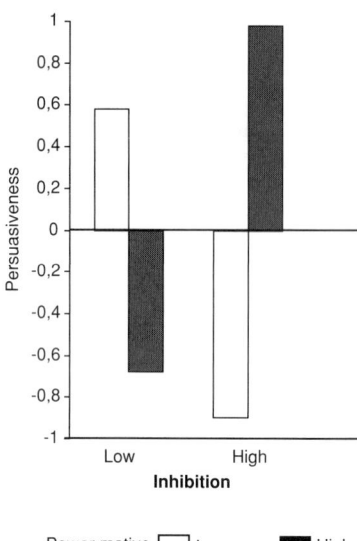

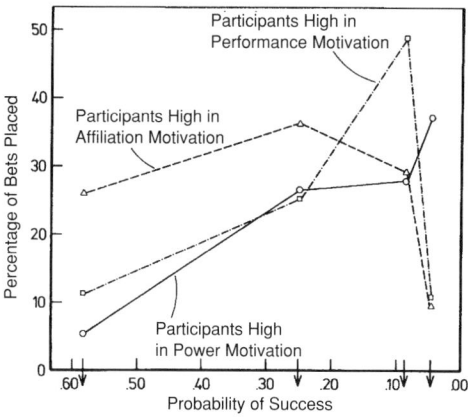

Figure 8.4 Proportion of roulette bets placed at various odds (objective probability of success) by the three motive groups. (Based on McClelland & Watson, 1973, p. 133.)

Figure 8.3 Judged persuasiveness as a function of the power motive and inhibition. (Based on Schultheiss & Brunstein, 2002, p. 569.)

commonly applied in achievement motivation research also holds for power-motivated behavior: How are **incentive values** and **expectancy of success** (or level of task difficulty) related; what is the connection between value (valence) and expectancy? Is the behavioral outcome a product of expectancy and value, as in the **risk-taking model**? Is there an inverse relationship between incentive and expectancy, as in achievement motivation? Assuming that emotions related to the experience of power and control function as incentives, it is quite conceivable that the incentive value of an intended change in B's behavior increases with the amount of resistance that B exerts. On the other hand, the propensity of individuals high in power motivation to engage in virtual and vicarious experiences of control – e.g., under the influence of alcohol – and to experience the associated feelings of strength in this way might indicate that incentive and expectancy are independent.

There are only few empirical findings that cast light on these issues. In one study, McClelland and Watson (1973) had participants play roulette in a casino setting. Participants placed their bets and won or lost chips in front of the whole group – a situation that the authors assumed to entail prestige and power. There were several variants of the game, and the odds of winning ranged between .58 and .04. Participants selected for the experiment were characterized by a dominant power, achievement, or affiliation motive. As illustrated in Fig. 8.4, the power-motivated participants showed a preference for the highest-risk bets, i.e., those with the highest potential winnings but the least likelihood of success. In other words, the size of the incentive had salience for them and they disregarded the low odds of winning. The players high

in affiliation motivation took a very different approach and showed a preference for low-risk bets – almost as if they were actively avoiding public competition. The behavior of participants high in achievement motivation was surprising. In this, a pure game of chance, they showed a preference for high-risk bets (.09). Given the range of odds available, however, these bets might have been interpreted as medium-risk (Fig. 8.4).

In another experiment, McClelland and Teague (1975) confirmed that the expectancy-value model holds in part for power-motivated behavior. Participants in an arm-wrestling competition were given the opportunity to select an equally strong, a stronger, or a weaker opponent, against whom they were then to compete in front of the others. Participants low in power motivation chose only equally strong or weaker opponents, whereas those high in power motivation preferred equally strong or stronger opponents. Thus, individuals high in power motivation chose opponents presenting them with a real challenge, and where the incentive value was high. The anticipated probabilities of success were not dependent on the incentive value of winning. Only in the case of individuals low in power motivation was there an inverse relationship between the probability of success and the strength of the opponent.

In conclusion, there is some evidence to indicate that the strength of satisfaction of the power motive – i.e., the sense of power and strength – depends solely on the level of the incentive value and is unaffected by the probability of success.

8.1.6 Developmental Stages of Power

McClelland returned to the investigation of power-motivated goals and incentives on numerous occasions, placing the issues in a broader cultural and developmental framework (McClelland, 1975). He felt conceptualizations of power-motivated behavior based solely on aspects such as influencing and aggressively imposing one's interests on others to be a rather one-sided notion. Based on extensive analyses in cultural anthropology, he proposed that this one-sided view of power reflects the Western ideal of masculinity, but gives short shrift to other facets of power-oriented behavior, such as those as practiced in Eastern cultures (e.g., India), or those involving more typically feminine forms of exercising power.

As mentioned above, McClelland's definition of power motivation is based on the anticipation of affect, the final motive goal being "to feel strong," and does not, in the first instance, specify how this goal is achieved. Clearly, there are a multitude of power-motivated behaviors that contribute to a feeling of strength that are not rooted in influence, dominance, or control. McClelland based his analyses on a fourfold classification of power behavior, drawing on Erikson's (1963) psychoanalytic theory of ego development. He distinguishes between sources and objects of power pertaining to the self and to others, and thus identifies four consecutive developmental stages of power orientation (Table 8.1):

   I. Intake
  II. Autonomy
 III. Assertion
 IV. Generativity

Although the four stages are conceptualized as a developmental sequence, reaching a higher stage does not mean that the earlier ones are superseded. Rather, they remain available and can be accessed as and when the situation demands. The early mother-child relationship is paradigmatic for Stage I ("It strengthens me"). In later life, it implies maintaining contact with people who provide support and strength, inspiration and enthusiasm. In other words, it means increasing one's own feeling of power by associating with powerful others. Simply belonging to a powerful organization, religious community, or political party engenders a feeling of strength. The paradigm for stage II ("I strengthen myself") is middle childhood, marked as it is by growing independence from the mother and increasing volitional control over one's own behavior. The paradigm for stage III ("I have impact on others") is adolescence, and is characterized by the striving for independence from authorities, by relationships with different romantic partners, and by competing with and prevailing against others. This power orientation, or feeling of strength, derives from asserting oneself in direct confrontation with others (and is typical of competitive sports). Many of the social interactions in which adolescents are involved are of this type. The paradigm for stage IV ("It moves me to do my duty") is the mature adult, who is committed to a permanent relationship and devotes him- or herself to a cause or social group. It describes the power orientation of people who assert their own interests and claims to dominance with reference to the "higher authorities" (God or political leaders) they serve. By virtue of their power, these higher authorities in turn convey a feeling of power and strength to their subordinates (cf. Winter, 1973).

Table 8.1. McClelland's classification of power orientation at four stages of development (1975, p. 36)

	Sources of power	
Objects of power	Others	Self
Self (to feel stronger)	**Stage I: Intake**[a]	**Stage II: Autonomy**
Definition:	"It" (God, my mother, my leader, food) strengthens me	I strengthen, control, direct myself
Action correlates:	Power-oriented reading	Accumulating prestige possessions
Developmental stage:	Oral: being supported	Anal: autonomy, will
Pathology:	Hysteria, drug addiction	Obsessive compulsive neurosis
Occupations:	Client, mystic	Psychologist, collector
Folk tale themes:[b]	Eat, take, leave	I, he, have, go, find
Others (to influence)	**Stage IV: Generativity**	**Stage III: Assertion**
Definition:	"It" (religion, my group) moves me to serve, influence others	I have an impact (influence) on others
Action correlates:	Organizational membership	Competitive sports, arguing
Developmental stage:	Genital: mutuality, principled duty	Phallic: assertive action
Pathology:	Messianism	Criminality
Occupations:	Manager, scientist	Criminal lawyer, politician, journalist, teacher
Folk tale themes:	We, they ascend, fall	Hunt, can

[a] The names of the stages have been added (after McClelland, 1975, p. 36).
[b] Based on word-frequency counts of folk tales (fairy tales, legends, etc.) from 44 cultures on all continents (cf. McClelland et al., 1972).

It is not without reason that politicians – no matter how poorly developed their power motive may in fact be – always claim to be working for the greater good, thus laying claim to the charismatic glow that emanates from selfless commitment to the welfare of others, and intimating that their services are indispensable. Some political leaders really do have this kind of charisma. In his biographies of the Caesars, the Roman historian Suetonius (70–140) reports that Augustus, when sailing around the island of Capri, was cheered by the passengers and crew of another ship "[in] spontaneous homage declaring, as they poured libations, that **to him** they owed life, safe passage on the seas, freedom and fortune" (author's emphasis).

8.1.7 Power and Dominance in Evolution

Once motivational psychology had abandoned the one-sided doctrine of social learning theory that dominated research in the 1960s, more balanced approaches to the biological, i.e., genetically determined origins of motivation became increasingly common (Buss, 2001). Both the individual and the situational conditions under which motives develop and become activated were investigated. Besides motives such as hunger and thirst that regulate an organism's internal environment, research focused on the motives that facilitate people's interactions with the material and social environment and that promote the development and maintenance of social relationships. Indeed, many contemporary theories of motivation consider competence and efficacy motives ("agency, effectance, status, dominance, power, achievement") and motives regulating close social relationships ("affiliation, communion, relatedness, intimacy, sex") to be part of the innate motivational makeup of humans and other, nonhuman primates (Bakan, 1966; Deci & Ryan, 2000; Derryberry & Tucker, 1991; Kenrick et al., 2003; McClelland, Koestner, & Weinberger, 1989; Sheldon, Elliot, Kim, & Kasser, 2001; White, 1959). According to these theories, humans owe their success in the evolutionary development of species to the fact that they were, from the outset, genetically equipped to display certain behaviors in specific situations, and highly unlikely to display other behaviors that – although feasible – fit with the situation.

The idea of motive dispositions being genetically determined seems to have particular currency in the context of power motivation, which takes effect at the interface between personal competence and efficacy, on the one hand, and the establishment and maintenance of social relations, on the other. Observations of nonhuman primates (chimpanzees) in zoos suggest that it is possible to isolate a power motivation factor ("dominance") that is clearly innate (King & Figueredo, 1997; Weiss, King, & Figueredo, 2000). Dominant chimpanzees are more assertive, determined, and resolute in social interactions, more successful at forging alliances with others, better at deceiving others for tactical reasons, and very difficult to intimidate.

An unusual and particularly interesting study by Weiss, King, and Enns (2002) provides additional, more indirect evidence of the role that power and dominance play in the genetic makeup of primates. The authors asked zoo workers to rate 128 chimpanzees in different zoos on measures of dominance and subjective well-being. Because both the genetic relationships among the chimpanzees and the environmental conditions under which they had grown up were known, insights could be gained into the relationship between dominance and **subjective well-being**, as well as into the proportions of variance accounted for by (shared) genetic information. Additive genetic effects accounted for the largest proportion of variance in both variables, and the genetic correlation estimated between the two variables was perfect ($r = 1.00$). The correlation estimated on the basis of the different environmental conditions was meaningless in comparison ($r = .11$).

The main conclusion to be drawn from these findings is that dominance and subjective well-being are controlled by the same genes.

Furthermore, because the ability to experience positive emotions and the ensuing subjective well-being are conceptualized as indicators of fitness, the fact that dominance and well-being are both genetically determined underlines the key role that dominance plays in maximizing fitness.

> **DEFINITION**
> Fitness is the probability of successfully transmitting one's genetic material to the next generation. It is operationally defined in terms of the number of offspring of reproductive age. (Daly & Wilson, 1983; Dawkins, 1976)

Sociobiological research has confirmed that the dominance and rank of male individuals in many species of social-living primates (human and nonhuman) is positively correlated with their reproductive success. High-ranking members of primate societies have greater numbers of offspring than their lower-ranking counterparts (Cowlishaw & Dunbar, 1991; Harcourt, 1987; Kenrick et al., 2003; Kuester & Paul, 1989). The same has been observed for female chimpanzees (Pusey, Williams, & Goodall, 1997). In human societies, high-ranking males evidently have access to more attractive female partners and to larger numbers of females, especially during their fertile period (Pérusse, 1993, 1994). At the same time, women prefer more dominant males for long-term relationships and as fathers for their children. Sadalla, Kenrick, and Vershure (1987) presented fictitious descriptions of potential mates to respondents of the opposite sex, and asked these respondents to rate the target person on sexual attractiveness. The descriptions were varied on the dimensions of dominance (powerful, ascendant), aggression (hostile, violent), and domineering (dictatorial, arrogant). A major finding of this study was that dominance was the only characteristic in men that influenced women's judgments of their sexual attractiveness. Dominance and high status are associated with the possession of material resources. From the biological standpoint, then, it makes sense for women to place dominance and status high on their list of priorities for a mate as a means of promoting their own reproductive success. Likewise, it makes sense for (some) men to flaunt this kind of behavior. A recent follow-up study substantiated these patterns of mate preference in women, and showed that women screening hypothetical long-term mates first aimed to ensure that a potential partner was at least average on social status. Once this was certain, they focused increasingly on the qualities of intelligence and kindness (Li, Bailey, Kenrick, & Linsenmeier, 2002). Viewed from the perspective of motives, one might conclude that women begin their selection of a mate on the basis of power motivation (status). Once the necessary conditions in this domain have been fulfilled, they turn their attention to achievement motivation (intelligence) and affiliation motivation (kindness).

SUMMARY

Power and dominance – and their inequitable distribution among individuals, groups, and states – are among the universals of human social life. The motives behind this behavior seem to have a genetic basis in humans, and very probably in nonhuman primates. Accordingly, the opportunities to exert influence on our fellow humans are many and diverse. They range from the careful consideration of the cost-benefit ratio of an action to the demonstration of power in involuntary gestures and facial expressions. Whatever form power behavior takes, the motive goal to which we aspire consists in its positive affective consequences.

8.2 Measuring the Power Motive

8.2.1 The TAT Method

Having specified some determinants of individual differences in the power motive, we can now examine whether these are congruent with the motive definitions and operationalizations proposed by researchers who have developed instruments to measure the power motive (TAT, Grid Technique).

Murray

First on the list is H. A. Murray, who proposed a definition of the power motive – or, to use his own terminology, "need Dominance" – as early as 1938:

DEFINITION

Desires and Effects: To control one's human environment. To influence or direct the behavior of others by suggestion, seduction, persuasion, or command. To dissuade, restrain, or inhibit. To induce others to act in a way which accords with one's sentiments and needs. To get others to cooperate. Actions: To influence, . . . persuade, . . . organize, . . . govern, . . . supervise, . . . control, . . . dictate terms, . . . make laws, . . . lay down principles of conduct, . . . punish, . . . gain a hearing, . . . be imitated. (Murray, 1938, p. 152)

Murray defines the power motive in terms of a general motivational goal (control) and describes its expression on the behavioral level by listing a number of behaviors that can further that goal – controlling one's social environment.

Veroff

The next definition was proposed by Veroff (1957), who also developed the first TAT measure of the power motive. In the following, Veroff's rather brief definition is fleshed out by some of the content categories from his **TAT coding system**.

DEFINITION

Power motivation will be considered that disposition directing behavior toward satisfactions contingent upon the control of the means of influencing another person(s) (p. 1). Power imagery: . . . affect surrounding the maintenance or attainment of the control of means of influencing a person. . . . Affective concern can also be found in statements of wanting to avoid weakness (Veroff, 1957, p. 3).

Besides the acquisition and maintenance of power sources, Veroff's conception of the power motive covers the fear of losing these resources and the fear of the counter-power of others. The emphasis is split between power behavior, on the one hand, and its affective side-effects and consequences, on the other. The sources of power identified by Veroff are coercive power, legitimate power, informational power, and (arguably) expert power. Overall, Veroff seems to conceptualize power from the perspective of those who fear the loss of their power resources and who are subjected to the power of others, rather than actually exercising power themselves. Accordingly, the goal is not to exercise power and control, but to be free from the control of others (Veroff, 1992, pp. 280–281). Veroff also takes a somewhat different perspective in defining the goal of the power motive not as control over others, but as control of the means of influencing others. This approach might help to explain why even individuals high in power motivation do not seek to dominate others at all times, but simply ensure that the means to do so are in place and can be accessed as and when they are required (Veroff, 1992, p. 278).

The arousal conditions that Veroff (1957) used to validate his TAT coding system were also based on this conception of power. He asked candidates running for offices in student government to write TAT stories during the two hours before the votes were counted and the outcome of the election was announced. It goes without saying that the candidates were in an anxious, tense state – now that the die had been cast, there was nothing they could do but wait for the inevitable. Fear-related contents will certainly have colored their TAT stories. These stories – but not the ones generated by a nonaroused group – were used as the basis for the instrument's coding system, as indicators of a pronounced power motive. This decision biased the direction of subsequent research.

Against this background, it is hardly surprising that a series of investigations using Veroff's instrument have emphasized the individual's powerlessness and fear of the power of others (Veroff & Veroff, 1972). In a nationwide US study carried out in 1957, Veroff, Atkinson, Feld, and Gurin found that respondents with minimal incomes, with little formal education, and from broken homes, as well as Black respondents and widowed respondents aged over 50, showed above-average power motivation. A further indication for fear of powerlessness being at the core of Veroff's conceptualization of the power motive was the finding that high power-motivated fathers whose children are entering adulthood felt particularly uneasy. They seemed to suffer from low self-esteem and reported alcohol problems, yet their ratings of their sex life and social integration were extremely positive (Veroff, Atkinson, Feld, & Gurin, 1960; Veroff & Feld, 1970; Veroff, 1982).

Uleman

The next TAT measure was developed by Uleman (1966) to measure a construct originally termed "need Power" and later (1972) relabeled "need Influence." Uleman's conceptualization of the power motive is not avoidance based; Uleman clearly prefers an offensive conception of power to Veroff's defensive, fear-oriented one, as reflected in the following quotation:

DEFINITION

A party (P1) acts toward a second party (P2) in such a way that it causes P2 to react. . . . The first action must be overt, and intentional or willful (Uleman, 1972, p. 171).

For Uleman, power behavior is an intense, mutually threatening interaction that calls for a courageous approach, rather than a fearful one. He identifies reward power and legitimate power as the major sources of power. In one experiment, Uleman recruited members of a student fraternity to act as experimenters in a study on "the effects of frustration on imagination." The experimenters were first shown how to trick their opponents (e.g., using marked cards) and then instructed to frustrate members of another fraternity by beating them at brainteasers and card games. The "experimenter" and "participant" in each dyad wrote TAT stories before the frustration experiment began. The "experimenters" constituted the arousal group, the "participants" the reference group. Based on the differences in the power imagery generated by the two groups, Uleman devised a coding system that characterizes power behavior in terms of forceful actions that threaten others, and that are unaffected by moral scruples. As yet, there are few validation studies of this measure, though Uleman (1972) reported a positive correlation with self-assessed dominance. In another study, Uleman (1971) asked dyads of participants to discuss a contentious topic with the aim of resolving differences of opinion. He found that, as a rule, the discussant with the higher power motive prevailed.

Winter–McClelland

The final TAT measure was published – after several revisions – by Winter (1973), and incorporated elements of the cod-

ing systems devised by Veroff and Uleman. The correlations between Winter's system and those of Veroff and Uleman range between .39 and .47, indicating that Winter's system covers both the approach and the avoidance components. Winter defines power and power motivation in the following terms:

DEFINITION

Social power is the ability or capacity of O to produce . . . intended effects on the behavior or emotions of another person P (Winter, 1973, p. 5).

On the operational level, a TAT text is scored as containing power imagery when the following criteria are met:

Some person or group of persons . . . is concerned about establishing, maintaining, or restoring his power – that is impact, control, or influence over another person, group of persons, or the world at large . . . 1. Someone shows his power concern through actions which in themselves express his power . . . 2. Someone does something that arouses strong positive or negative emotions in others . . . 3. Someone . . . having a concern for his reputation or position (Winter, 1973, pp. 251–254).

Winter (1988) later incorporated these points in his definition of the power motive:

DEFINITION

The power motive is a concern for having impact on others, arousing strong emotions in others, or maintaining reputation and prestige. (Winter, 1988, p. 510)

Winter (1973) also describes fear of power – the avoidant component of the power motive – on the operational level:

Fear of power . . . (a) The power goal is for the direct or indirect benefit of another (b) The actor has doubt about his ability to influence, control, or impress others (c) The writer of the story suggests that power is deceptive or has a flaw. (Winter, 1973, p. 261, 262)

Winter's coding system covers far more phenomena and components of power motivation than the systems proposed by Veroff or Uleman. Winter also defines the goal of the power motive to be influencing others and exerting control, but he lists a broader spectrum of related behaviors, such as unsolicited assistance. Moreover, Winter is the only one to distinguish a fear component of the power motive, and to go on to differentiate three levels of this component – goals, competency beliefs, and moral considerations.

Winter (1967) developed a procedure for arousing motives without actually intending to measure the power motive. Rather, he was interested in the influence exercised by charismatic leaders, and was likely thinking more in terms of motives such as dependence and submission. His respondents were shown a documentary about John F. Kennedy's 1961 inaugural address. The TAT stories they wrote immediately after the film were compared with the stories produced by members of a control group (who had not seen the Kennedy film) in response to the same picture cues.

Relative to the control group, the TAT responses generated by the aroused group were laden with power imagery. In retrospect, it is hardly surprising that feelings of power and of having an impact on others emerged as the key content criteria for an activated power motive in Winter's measure.

Validation studies have identified a wealth of behavior correlates in a broad range of human activity. In brief, findings paint the following picture:

Behavioral Correlates of High Power Motivation in Students (Based on Winter, 1973)

Students high in power motivation:
- held more offices in student organizations,
- ran for more important committees,
- were more likely to work at university radio stations and in the editorial offices of campus newspapers,
- preferred competitive sports and won more championships,
- were more likely to select "manipulative" professions (e.g., teacher, cleric, psychologist, journalist),
- wrote more letters to the editor,
- were more likely to choose inconspicuous fellow students as friends,
- reported having sexual intercourse relatively early,
- appeared more influential, enterprising, and convincing than others to their fellow members in a discussion group,
- were more likely to be perceived as unhelpful in discussion groups,
- claimed to have higher grades than they actually had,
- were more likely to have prestige possessions and sportier cars,
- drank more beer and hard liquor,
- participated more in competitive sports,
- read more sports and sex magazines (e.g., Playboy).

There are also reports of a predilection for pornographic material (Winter, 1973, p. 139). The fear-oriented component of the power motive, by contrast, had few behavioral correlates. Based on these findings, Winter concluded that individuals high in power motivation have a tendency to draw attention to themselves, to mix with people who are easily influenced, to progressively occupy positions of social influence and formal power, to control channels of information, to acquire and accumulate **prestige possessions** as symbols of power resources, and to indulge in a variety of vicarious activities to satisfy their need for power.

In a reanalysis of existing data, Winter (1988) tested for gender differences in the behavioral and perceptual correlates of the power motive. His results showed that the power motive appears to be expressed in identical behavior in men and women. This applies especially to the formal, institutionalized power acquired through holding office, to power-related careers (teaching, psychology and therapy, journalism, business management, and clergy), and to prestige and visibility management (expressing opinions in public forums, accumulating prestige possessions and resources). Only the cluster of behaviors characteristic of an excessive and **profligate impulsive lifestyle**" (alcohol, drugs, aggression, gambling, and exploitation) was positively related to the power motive in men, but not in women. Responsibility for children – first for younger siblings and later for children of one's own – has proved to be a powerful moderator of the relationship between the power motive and a profligate lifestyle. In fact, the moderating effect of responsibility for children brings men's patterns of power-related behavior and experiences more in line with women's profiles. In women without children, however, the power motive predicts a hedonistic but restless and unhappy lifestyle that has much in common with the profligate behavior of power-motivated men. In other words, whether power motivation is expressed in a "responsible" or a "profligate" lifestyle seems to have more to do with socialization than with biological sex. However, Winter's reanalysis (1988) does not allow any conclusions to be drawn on whether, and to what extent, the agencies of socialization sought out or encountered by males and females are, in themselves, dependent on biological sex, with males and females being exposed to different agencies of socialization.

Several studies have reported differences between individuals high and low in power motivation in terms of the strategies they use to process information and the outcomes of these endeavors. When presented with picture cues depicting power-related situations, participants high in power motivation responded with more pronounced evoked potentials than participants low in power motivation after just 100–150 ms (McClelland, 1984). Highly motivated participants were also better able to recall memorable autobiographical experiences (McAdams, 1982b) and everyday experiences (Woike, 1995) that related to the theme of power. When asked to recall friendship episodes, power-motivated males were more likely to report planned interactions within a large group that were geared toward a specific goal, whereas intimacy-motivated respondents were more inclined to report dyadic relationships involving mutual disclosure, listening to and caring for one's partner (McAdams, Healy, & Krause, 1984). After listening to a story containing 30 power facts and 30 affiliation facts, highly power-motivated individuals were able to retrieve more power facts in an unannounced memory test than were their less motivated counterparts (McClelland, 1984). Woike, Gershkowich, Piorkowski, and Poco (1999; Woike & Poco, 2001) assessed their respondents' agentic and communal motive profiles (combinations of achievement and power motivation and affiliation and intimacy motivation, respectively; cf. Bakan, 1966). They, too, found that participants were better able to process autobiographical memories that were congruent with their dominant motives. It would seem that motives have a decisive effect on how meaningful autobiographical memories are selected, organized, and retrieved. However, it was not possible to confirm the hypothesis that this effect might be mediated by the generation of different kinds of affect – with an agentic motive profile being associated with more negative, aggressive, and tense/angry affect, for example.

An Experimental Game Setting

Winter's TAT technique has been validated in a number of experimental studies, some of which observed the social interactions of power-motivated individuals in power situations and negotiations. In one study (Fig. 8.5; Schnackers & Kleinbeck, 1975), groups of three players, one of whom was high in power motivation, participated in a con game. Players were dealt a number of power cards that could be used to multiply the number shown on the dice they had thrown, thus accelerating their progress toward the goal. Any two players could form a coalition against the third and attempt to finish together. Players then had to decide how to split the winnings. It was possible to disband coalitions and form new ones right up to the last minute.

As expected, players high in power motivation were more likely than those low in power motivation to take the initiative in proposing coalitions. Likewise, they were more likely to be accepted as coalition partners, to enter into and dissolve coalitions, to play off their opponents against each other, and to renege on agreements about the distribution of winnings. Last but not least, they were more likely to win. The correlations between the strength of a player's power motive and his or her winnings increased from .33 in the first to .42 in the second round, and peaked at .45 in the third and final round.

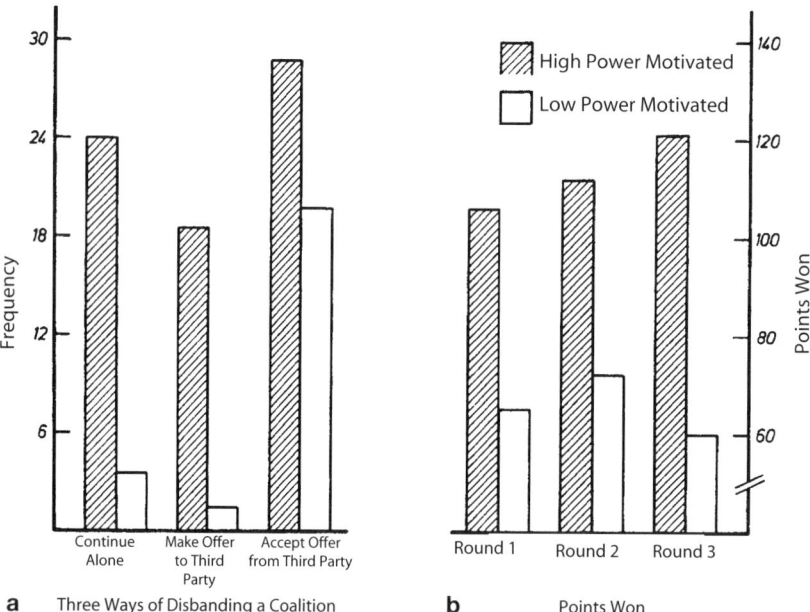

a   Three Ways of Disbanding a Coalition   **b**   Points Won

Figure 8.5 Individuals high and low in power motivation in a bargaining game: (a) Frequency of three ways of disbanding a coalition and (b) points won in three consecutive rounds. (Based on Schnackers & Kleinbeck, 1975, pp. 307, 314.)

In a series of studies, Fodor invited participants high and low in power motivation to participate in group role plays in which disputes were to be resolved, decisions made, or personnel supervised. Electromyogram measures revealed that group leaders high in power motivation showed greater reactivity to a conflict situation that was aroused by asking them to arbitrate a dispute on the production of a new article (Fodor, 1985). In another role-play study, in which participants were required to assume various executive positions within a corporation, executives high in power motivation contributed less factual information to the group discussion than did their colleagues low in power motivation (Fodor & Smith, 1982). In two further studies, participants were asked to act as supervisors for a group of workers who were allegedly working in

an adjoining room. Relative to those low in power motivation, supervisors high in power motivation believed that they had a greater influence on the workers; they also assessed the performance of a worker who had flattered them more favorably (Fodor & Farrow, 1979). When the supervisors were played recordings of comments allegedly made by their workers, supervisors high in power motivation showed higher levels of activation in response to comments that were critical of the work they had assigned (Fodor, 1984).

Individual differences can also be expected in the justifications people give for striving to exert power and influence over others; these justifications may touch on moral values. People may exert power because they enjoy acting in an arbitrary manner, because it renders target persons helpless, or simply for self-aggrandizing purposes. On the other hand, people may exercise power for the sake of a "good cause," to further the aims of a group or an organization, or "in the best interests" of the target person (Table 8.1). With this in mind, McClelland (1970, 1975; McClelland, Davis, Kalin, & Wanner, 1972) distinguished two types of power motives:

- personalized power ("p Power") and
- socialized power ("s Power").

McClelland et al. (1972) found that an indicator of "activity inhibition" (occurrences of the word "not") in TAT stories with otherwise high power-thematic content is characteristic of people in positions of responsibility and associated with reduced alcohol consumption ("s Power"). A lack of activity inhibition coupled with a high power motive ("p Power") was found to be associated with excessive drinking, ostentatious material possessions, need compensation through reading sex and sports magazines, and a propensity to high-risk gambling. In men, the latter motive profile – which McClelland (1975) labeled the "conquistador motive pattern" – has been associated with the tendency to engage in impulsive violent acts.

Mason and Blankenship (1987) investigated the extent to which this motive profile is able to explain the type and frequency of abuse in intimate relationships. They found that men who physically abused their partners were likely to be high in power motivation. Yet women can also be perpetrators. Women who reported high levels of stress in their relationship (e.g., if it was on the verge of breaking down) and scored high on the affiliation motive but low in activity inhibition were more likely to inflict physical and psychological abuse on their partners. These findings correspond with insights gained from evolutionary psychology, which indicate that women respond to their partner's (threatened) withdrawal of resources with extreme **jealousy** (Buss & Schmitt, 1993). Zurbriggen (2000) expanded on research in this area by assuming the existence of both motivational-dynamic and cognitive-associationistic relations between power and sexuality. Her main hypothesis was that the influence of motives on sexual aggression is moderated by the association of power and sexuality in cognitive associationistic networks. In line with the findings of Mason and Blankenship, the power motive proved to be an important predictor of sexual aggression, but only in men. Likewise, Zurbriggen found a link between the affiliation-intimacy motive and aggressive sexual behavior in women. A tentative explanation for this finding is that women interpret sexual refusal on the part of a partner as a threatening act, and that this lowers the threshold for aggressive behavior. Strong power-sex associations on the cognitive level predict more aggressive sexual behavior in intimate relationships, and moderate the motivational effects described. If the cognitive associations between power and sex are weak, the relationships observed between the power motive and sexual aggression fade away.

8.2.2 The Grid Technique

In designing a method to measure the power motive, we drew on the Grid Technique, a tool that had already proved to be a useful and valid measure of the achievement motive (Schmalt, 1973, 1999; see Chapter 7). Respondents are shown a series of picture cues depicting people in situations relating to a specific theme (in this case, power), and a set of statements reflecting various constituent components of the motive construct is listed beneath each picture. Taking a theory-driven approach, we stipulated that both the situational context and personality variables measured should be congruent with our definition of the power motive (Schmalt, 1978, 1986; Schmalt, Sokolowski, & Langens, 2000; Sokolowski, Schmalt, Langens, & Puca, 2000).

The development of our measure assessing the various components of the power motive was thus guided by the following six points:

Regarding the Situation:	1. The situations portrayed must involve an interaction between a central figure and one or more target persons.
	2. These interactions must take place in various social contexts.
	3. The interactions must be varied systematically on the dimensions "control of resources" and "social status."
Regarding the Person:	4. Evaluation of one's own social competence.
	5. Evaluation of the outcome of an action in terms of the exercise of control.
	6. Evaluation of the affective consequences of control.

The grid used to measure the power motive consists of 18 picture cues, most of which depict two interacting figures. Some of these cues were based on pictures used in the TAT method, which covers a relatively broad range of domains of activity. "Control of resources" and "social status" are varied systematically to produce three blocks of six pictures. Each picture portrays a social interaction that is to be evaluated from the perspective of one of the figures involved. This figure, who is identified by an arrow, has high status and resources in one block of situations (situation type A) and low status and resources in another (situation type C). In the third block, it remains ambiguous how social status and resources are distributed among the figures (situation type B).

A sense of control and the affective consequences of this experience have been identified as constitutive elements of the power motive. With this in mind, the statements appended to each picture were devised to reflect positively and negatively valenced concepts of experienced control, based on attribution theory and, more specifically, on a taxonomy of concepts of experienced control (cf. Weiner, 1985a) covering the three dimensions of internality, intentionality, and stability. The statements were further classified according to whether they contain goal anticipations of the type "hope for power" or "fear of power," based on the anticipated positive or negative affective consequences of control.

As mentioned above, the Grid Technique draws strongly on the TAT method. For one thing, many of the ambiguous picture cues that have been chosen to arouse motive dispositions in the various TAT methods were systematized in the grid. For another thing, the contents of the grid statements, which are specific to the motive being measured, cover the evaluation of action outcomes, the affective consequences of control (regarding the aspect of intentionality, in particular) and the perceived social competence – very much in line with Winter's (1973) operational definition of the power motive (Section 8.2.1).

In a first step to validate the method, the statements contained in the grid were subjected to factor analysis for each type of situation separately. It emerged that positively and negatively valenced factors were distinguishable in all types of situations. This indicates that the power motive, as measured with the Grid Technique, can also be described in terms of approach and avoidance tendencies – i.e., "hope of power" and "fear of power."

❗ The Grid Technique permits the psychometrically sound distinction of the hope and fear components of the power motive. Because they are found in all three types of situation, the hope and fear components can be regarded as generalized main dimensions of the power motive.

Moreover, the taxonomy of concepts of experienced control provided valuable insights into the nature of the power motive, particularly in terms of the distinction between internal and external concepts of experienced control. It emerged that a sense of control and the ensuing affective states are contingent upon an action being perceived as intentional and attributable to internal causes. We can thus conclude that power motivation is dependent on a sense of being personally responsible for an action and its consequences.

In one validation study, Schmalt (1986) analyzed this question further by investigating the conditions under which power-motivated individuals judge themselves to be responsible for their actions and, more specifically, to have caused and controlled the direct and indirect outcomes and repercussions of these actions. To this end, short vignettes describing an action and its consequences were prepared, with the amount of information provided on potential causal and influential factors being varied systematically. The vignettes were drawn up on the basis of a model of social responsibility developed by Heider (1958). In this model, which encompasses five consecutive levels of information about an actor's personal responsibility, an event is assumed to have certain desired outcomes. At level I, the actor was essentially just "in the right place at the right time"; by level V he or she took deliberate control of the action and its outcomes. In other words, the increasing levels of information reflect five levels of personal responsibility for an action and its consequences (cf. Fincham & Jaspars, 1979). Individuals high in

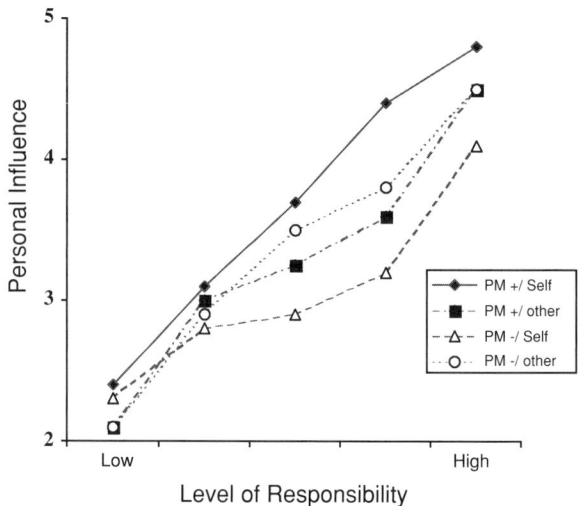

Figure 8.6 Estimated level of personal influence as a function of the power motive (PM+: high; PM–: low) and of the level of responsibility in self-reports and other-reports. (Based on Schmalt, 1986, p. 544.)

power motivation were expected to be more likely to infer personal responsibility for anticipated and desired social events and their outcomes. Fig. 8.6 shows participants' assessments of their personal influence on an outcome as a function of the information available. Individuals high in power motivation tend to believe that they are in control of events and to infer personal responsibility for a desired outcome, even when the information available is patchy. As the level of information provided increases (high level of responsibility), the theme of control becomes particularly salient, and motivational differences become apparent. The fact that these differences are only discernable in self-reports and not in the observations of other-reports suggests that we are dealing with motivational differences in attributional patterns, rather than universal cognitive heuristics (Fig. 8.6).

This finding is particularly interesting because causal knowledge and its functional equivalents in the animal world are among the main prerequisites for successful interaction with complex environments (Dickinson & Shanks, 1995; Kummer, 1995). Moreover, these results replicate one of the key findings from attributional research on achievement motivation, in which the achievement motive was measured using the TAT (Meyer, 1973).

The validity of the Grid Technique has also been confirmed in research employing the Multi-Motive Grid. Wegge, Quaeck, and Kleinbeck (1996) investigated the impact of motives on students' use of video games. With respect to the power motive, they established that fear-motivated individuals tried out and owned most games. Schmalt and Langens (in preparation) found a significant relationship between "fear of power" and the occurrence of power-related themes in daydreams. This suggests that fear of losing control is associated with the tendency to satisfy one's motives vicariously.

This idea was substantiated in a study by Bär (1998), who examined the motive profiles of individuals who consume excessive amounts of pornography. These findings showed that pornophiles are characterized by fear of losing control in combination with high positive affiliation motivation. Research using the TAT had previously shown that individuals high in avoidance power motivation tend to satisfy their power motive by virtual means.

SUMMARY

To date, all methods used to measure motivational differences in the power motive have involved the arousal of that motive by means of picture cues. Research has produced a wealth of insights, ranging from interindividual motivational differences in experimental game settings to differences in the motivational climate of nations.

8.3 The Neurobiology of the Power Motive

More recently, the advent of biological approaches to the psychology of motivation and emotions (Section 8.1.7) has intensified the search for structures and functions of the central nervous system (CNS) that might be at the root of these phenomena. If basal forms of motivation evolved early in human phylogenesis, this development must necessarily be genetically coded and its outcomes evident in the structures and/or functioning of the CNS. This kind of research approach opens up a new level of analysis beside the cognitive and behavioral levels, shifting the focus to neurobiological factors.

8.3.1 Endocrinological Factors

Early on, Steele (1977) was able to show that **adrenaline** and **noradrenaline** are secreted when power motivation is strongly aroused. Steele used inspirational political speeches containing plenty of power imagery (e.g., Churchill's Dunkirk speech, Henry V's speeches from Shakespeare's drama) to activate the power motive. He noted a steep increase in adrenaline and noradrenaline levels, which correlated ($r = .71$) with the strength of the power motive measured immediately after listening to the speech. Control groups who listened to travel descriptions or worked on tasks under ego-involving or relaxed conditions did not show increases in the level of either neurotransmitter; neither was there a correlation between the neurotransmitter levels and the strength of the power motive after arousal.

Two of McClelland's studies indicate that noradrenaline is an action-specific neurotransmitter that favors the processing of power-imagery information. The first of these studies (McClelland, Davidson, Saron, & Floor, 1980) showed that individuals high in power motivation and with high brain noradrenaline turnover were able to learn paired associates involving power imagery comparatively quickly. In another study, participants were read a complicated story containing 30 power facts, 30 affiliation facts, and 18 neutral facts (McClelland, Maddocks, & McAdams, 1985). In free recall, participants high in power motivation again proved better equipped to process information relating to power issues. What is remarkable is the specificity of the interaction between the power motive and the increase in noradrenaline – it was only when both were high that recall of power facts was exceptional.

The male sex hormone **testosterone** is associated with various forms of social behavior in humans and the higher mammals (Christiansen, 1999). Based on their observations of a group of rhesus monkeys, Rose, Holaday, and Bernstein (1971) reported that testosterone levels in males were positively related to dominant and aggressive behaviors and to position in the group hierarchy. Research on humans also indicates that testosterone levels are positively related to dominant behavior, as well as to a propensity to violence and antisocial aggression, and that men with high testosterone levels are more likely to have short-term affairs while involved in long-term relationships (Christiansen, 1999; Mazur & Booth, 1998). These findings are congruent with McClelland's (1987) and Winter's (1973) characterization of an uninhibited power motive as a propensity to engage in antisocial violence and to have sex with multiple partners.

Significant changes in testosterone levels can also be observed in direct dominance-related confrontations – some sports competitions are ritualized forms of such clashes. Testosterone levels tend to increase before a competition, and – in winners – to remain elevated for some time afterward; in losers, testosterone levels tend to fall off again quickly (Bernhardt, Dabbs, Fielden, & Lutter, 1998). This finding is not entirely stable, however. Schultheiss, Campbell, and McClelland (1999) were only able to substantiate it for individuals high in power motivation (personalized power). This pattern of results was replicated and extended by Schultheiss and Rohde (2002), whose findings indicated that increases in testosterone levels were observed among winners high in power motivation, especially those with an uninhibited power motive, and that these increases were associated with the learning of behaviors instrumental to winning the competition. To the extent that they are associated with positive affect, the increased testosterone levels observed in this highly power-oriented subsample might have functioned as rewards; i.e., as motivational (organismic) incentives. Fodor and Carver (2000) showed that positive incentives (rewards) had selective effects on the creativity of participants high in power motivation. It would seem that positive (but not negative) feedback signals to the individual that he or she has succeeded in having an impact on the environment, and that this knowledge serves to activate the power motive.

8.3.2 Psychoimmunological Factors

The next step was to examine the relations between motive strength, inhibition tendencies, immune functions, and susceptibility to certain illnesses. A number of studies have assessed life stress and/or inhibition tendencies alongside the power motive. These external (life stress) and internal (inhibition) factors prevent the unhindered and assertive realization of the need for power and moderate the relationship with various types of illness. The question as to which of the two factors (stress, inhibition) is the most influential has not yet been fully resolved (McClelland, 1989, p. 676).

In one of the first studies on this issue, McClelland and Jemmott (1980) asked respondents to list all the illnesses they had experienced in the previous year. A positive relationship was found between these health records and inhibition of the power motive by internal or external factors – the stronger the inhibition of the power motive and the power stress, as reported in a life-event questionnaire, the more serious the illnesses reported. It seems reasonable to assume that the inhibition of assertive power behavior and exposure to power-related stress leads to chronic arousal of the sympathetic nervous system, with consistently high levels of adrenaline secretion. In time, this can impair the entire immune system. Both component systems of the immune system may be affected:

- First, the specific or cellular defense system, which produces lymphocytes (e.g., killer cells) capable of destroying specific antigens.
- Later, the nonspecific or humoral defense system, which is not cell specific and produces globulins that act as antibodies (IgA, in particular). These are found in body fluids (e.g., saliva) and serve to destroy invading antigens (Jemmott & Locke, 1984).

The studies conducted to date have focused almost exclusively on **immunoglobulin** (IgA) in the humoral defense system, which can be easily measured in saliva samples. A study with male prisoners showed that respondents who reported experiencing the most stress in prison and, at the same time, scored highest on the inhibited power motive had the lowest IgA; they also reported more illnesses than the other prisoners (McClelland, Alexander, & Marks, 1982). McClelland, Davidson, Floor, and Saron (1980) observed an association between adrenaline secretion and immune function. Individuals with inhibited power motivation had higher adrenaline levels and lower levels of immunoglobulin in the saliva. Lower immunoglobulin levels were found to be associated with the number of serious illnesses reported over the previous 6–10 months. Furthermore, opposing shifts in the concentrations of adrenaline and immunoglobulin were observed over the study period – as adrenaline levels increased, immunoglobulin levels decreased. Findings on the concentration of killer cells indicate an analogous pattern in the cellular or specific defense system. People with a pronounced inhibition syndrome (high power, low affiliation motive; high inhibition tendencies) produce fewer killer cells than do people high in affiliation and low in power motivation with lower stress levels. As predicted, the former group report more illnesses and more frequent medical consultations (McClelland, Locke, Jemmot, Kraus, Williams, & Valeri, 1985).

❶ A one-year longitudinal study found examination stress to impair the immune defense system, particularly when several exams are scheduled closely together (Jemmott et al., 1983).

At the beginning of an examination period spanning several months, IgA levels were reduced across the entire group of students. After a short while, however, the IgA levels of a subgroup with inhibited power motivation fell even more steeply and did not return to baseline levels by the end of the exam period. Predictably, there was a dramatic increase in the frequency of illness in this subgroup. It seems that exams imply a high level of power-related stress for individuals with inhibited power motivation, and lead to an impaired immune system.

These findings were confirmed by a further study on acute examination stress (McClelland, Ross, & Patel, 1985) with three points of measurement: immediately after the exam, 1 3/4 hours later, and a few days later, when no more exams were coming up. Students' physiological responses during the exam were appropriate to the situation, i.e., there were short-term increases in IgA and noradrenaline levels. Relative to participants whose affiliation motive was dominant, those with a dominant power motive had lower IgA and higher noradrenaline levels at all three points of measurement, but especially 1 3/4 hours after the exam. The more noradrenaline was secreted during and immediately after the exam, the more pronounced the subsequent drop in IgA. In other words, the stress of the exam stimulated adrenergic activity, which initially led to increased immunoglobulin levels in all individuals. Among students with a dominant power motive, however, IgA subsequently dropped to below baseline level.

McClelland (1989) summarized (Fig. 8.7) the interrelationships that have been tested and confirmed. Empirical findings indicate that stressed power motivation is associated with an increased risk of illness – e.g., respiratory infections – (B in Fig. 8.7). The immediate condition for this susceptibility to illness is a depressed immune function (E), which is directly dependent on the stressed power motive (F), but also mediated by sympathetic activation (A) and noradrenaline/adrenaline secretion (C and D).

SUMMARY

Because the power motive is an "old" motive system in phylogenetic terms, its cognitive and behavioral manifestations are also reflected at the neurobiological level. Uninhibited power motivation tends to be associated with increased biological fitness and well-being, whereas stressed and inhibited power motivation can be detrimental to health.

8.4 An Influential Trio: The Power, Achievement, and Affiliation Motives

When examining the impact of motives in interaction with situational factors, it makes more sense to consider several motives at once than to focus on one at a time – not least because we can consider relative strengths and then

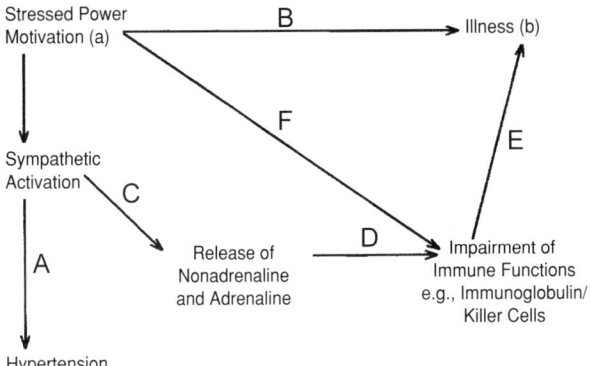

Figure 8.7 Relationships between stressed power motivation, physiological changes, and illness. (Based on McClelland, 1989, p. 676.)

determine which of the motives is dominant. In some experiments, participants are grouped according to a personal profile of two or three motives; in other studies, such motive profiles are ascertained after the experiment. Preexperimental grouping has been employed in mock negotiation and game settings. We will consider these experiments first. Postexperimental determination of motive profiles typically involves criterion groups such as top managers, political leaders, or radicals in student protest movements. This approach has also been taken in studies on historical change in the motivational climate of nations.

8.4.1 Experimental Studies in Game Settings

Terhune conducted studies that involved mock negotiations of varying levels of complexity, with participants being selected according to their motive profiles. In one study (1968a), he used a variation of the prisoner's dilemma game often employed in conflict research (Fig. 8.1). Terhune paired up players such that each player was very high in one of the three motives (achievement, affiliation, or power) and very low in the others. When their chances of winning were balanced, clear differences in cognition and behavior were apparent depending on the participants' dominant motive:

- Players high in the achievement motive were the most cooperative; they also expected their partners to be cooperative.
- Players high in the affiliation motive were the most defensive; they were most afraid of being duped.
- Players high in the power motive were the most profiteering; they tried to dupe their partners but, at the same time, expected them to cooperate.

As the parameters of the game became more threatening, i.e., as both the temptation to dupe one's partner and the fear of being duped increased, the behavior of all participants became more defensive and motivational differences diminished. Very similar findings were reported by Bludau (1976), who paired up participants who were high in achievement, but low in power motivation, with participants exhibiting the opposite profile. Achievement-motivated participants

preferred cooperation and balanced chances of winning. Power-motivated participants tended to be more competitive and preferred more threatening games with a high potential for conflict.

In the rather more complex "international relations" game, several participants with matching motive profiles were grouped together to form a "nation" (Terhune, 1968b). Each of these nations could opt to either increase its defense spending or expand the economy, declare war or sign treaties, spread deceptive propaganda or reveal its true intentions, etc. The results are similar to those of the prisoner's dilemma game. Achievement-motivated participants sought the most cooperation; affiliation-motivated participants, the least – probably because they wanted to keep out of trouble by not getting involved at all (e.g., they sent the fewest messages). Power-motivated participants spent more on defense than the other two groups; achievement-motivated participants had the lowest levels of military expenditure. Power-motivated groups also tried hardest to manipulate others, i.e., to mislead them through overt propaganda and covert messages.

8.4.2 Economic Perspectives

Top managers in business enterprises are an interesting criterion group from the perspective of motivational psychology. Initially, findings accumulated by McClelland (1961) indicated that top management positions tend to be occupied by individuals high in the achievement motive, and that they are generally successful in these posts. This impression later had to be qualified, however. McClelland's findings only seem to apply to the managers of small firms and to lower-level, nontechnical managers (cf. McClelland, 1975; McClelland & Boyatzis, 1982; Stahl, 1983). Managers in large corporations have to delegate tasks, coordinate schedules, and motivate and inspire their staff to work toward the company's global objectives; in short, they must provide leadership. Yet achievement-motivated individuals seem to be lone wolves who seek to do things better than they have been done before, preferably under their own steam. They get sidetracked by details, are unable to delegate, and become caught up in the minutiae of the organization. Individuals taking an achievement-oriented approach are more likely to flourish if managers create organizational climates conducive to their way of thinking and acting, granting them the necessary freedoms within a coherent organizational framework (cf. Litwin & Stringer, 1968).

In a study of two large corporations in Mexico City, both in the same industry, Andrews (1967) demonstrated just how significant the organizational climate is when it comes to eliciting individual motives. Firm A, a branch of a US corporation, was organized according to the principles of achievement. Employees who succeeded in meeting the company's objectives secured rapid promotion, even leapfrogging former superiors who had seniority. Firm B, a Mexican company, was organized along strictly hierarchical lines with an almost patriarchal management structure. Length of service and loyalty to the company were more important criteria for promotion than performance outcomes. A comparison of motive scores obtained from employees at various management levels of the two companies showed clear differences. Higher positions in the organizational hierarchy were correlated with the achievement motive in firm A and with the power motive in firm B.

McClelland (1975) labeled the combination of a high power motive, high activity inhibition, and a low affiliation motive "imperial motive pattern" or the "leadership motive pattern." This motive profile is characterized by the ability to build worker loyalty and commitment to a company's primary objectives. This applies particularly when the power motive has reached the highest developmental stage (IV, generativity) and takes the form of socialized rather than personalized power (see above). McClelland (1975) tested the relationship between managers' motive profiles and their subordinates' ratings of the organizational climate. Relative to the other two motive profiles examined, the **leadership motive pattern** (high power, high achievement, low affiliation) was more strongly associated with a sense of responsibility, organizational clarity, and team spirit, and less closely related to conformity.

❶ An organizational climate that is conducive to economic success can be expected to evolve when a company's top management is characterized by a combination of high power, high achievement, and low affiliation motives.

McClelland and Boyatzis (1982) were able to confirm this assumption at the upper levels of nontechnical management in a large corporation (American Telephone and Telegraph Company). The managers' leadership motive patterns correlated with their promotion records after 8 and 16 years. The achievement motive only correlated with promotion at lower-level positions, where individual performance is more important than leadership qualities.

Wainer and Rubin (1971) found another motive profile to be influential. Fifty-one heads of small, newly established businesses in the technical sector were tested for all three motives. The economic success of the businesses was measured in terms of the growth rate in sales. Analyzing each motive separately, the authors found that a combination of high achievement and low affiliation motive was conducive to economic success, while the power motive appeared to be irrelevant. However, it is important to remember that this study examined only small firms with a simple organizational structure, where strong delegation and leadership skills were not yet required.

STUDY

Predictors of Business Success

Kock (1965, 1974) provided further evidence that a motive profile combining high achievement and power motives with a low affiliation motive is a cornerstone of economic success. He predicted the development of a number of large companies based on previous performance data, and tested the accuracy of those predictions 10 years on. Fifteen comparable firms were selected from a total of 104 Finnish knitwear companies, and various factors of their economic development were tracked over a 10-year period (1952–1961). The achievement, power, and affiliation motives of key managers were then assessed and correlated with the performance data. Table 8.2 shows the correlations between the managers' individual motives (as well as the combination of "achievement plus power minus affiliation,"

Ach + P – Aff) and five criteria of economic success for the period ending 1964. As the table shows, the combination score correlates most strongly with the economic criteria.

In a follow-up study, Kock (1974) predicted the companies' future economic development in the 1962–1971 period based on these motive scores. Most of the seven firms with the lowest motive combination scores Ach + P – Aff ceased to exist during this period. The correlations for the remaining firms essentially confirm the findings of the first study. In contrast to a high power motive or a low affiliation motive, a high achievement motive alone no longer played a decisive role, but the combination of all three motives was again the best predictor of business success.

Table 8.2. Correlations between five criteria of economic development in 15 knitwear companies (1952–1961) and the strength of the management's achievement, power, and affiliation motives, and the combination of achievement plus power minus affiliation motivation (Ach + P – Aff)

	Motive strength			
	Achievement (Ach)	Power (P)	Affiliation (Aff)	Ach + P – Aff
Gross volume of output	.39	.49*	−.61**	.67**
Number of employees	.41	.42	−.62**	.66**
Turnover	.46*	.41	−.53*	.60*
Gross investment	.63*	−.06	.20	.45*
Profit	.27	.01	−.30	.34

*p < .05 **p < .01.
Based on Kock, 1974, p. 215.

Everyday experience suggests that managerial hierarchies based on the power motive tend to perpetuate themselves. This explains why young, aspiring, and career-minded executives strive to move in circles of power and influence. Indeed, successful career guides recommend the following approach: "Move in circles of power and influence – be where the movers and shakers are, not where the work gets done" (Schur & Weick, 1999; Rule 3; own translation).

Sokolowski and Kehr (1999) invited middle managers in a large German car manufacturing company to participate in a training program on "Leadership and Goal Alignment" that offered them the opportunity to enhance their communication skills. Given that the program provided coaching in practical techniques for influencing others, individuals with a strong power motive were expected to show the most positive response to it. The standard three motives were measured using the Grid Technique. As expected, the only significant correlations to emerge were with the power motive:

- Participants high in power motivation reported learning more and rated their intrinsic and extrinsic motivation to be higher.
- Participants high in power motivation also rated their attainment of personal goals in the training program significantly higher, but this relationship was mediated by intrinsic motivation.

Abele, Andrä, and Schute (1999) used the Grid Technique to tap university graduates' aspirations for the future. As expected, and as shown in Winter's (1973) studies using the TAT method, individuals high in power motivation (hope of power) were particularly likely to aspire to high-prestige, high-status jobs.

8.4.3 Political Perspectives

Politicians in governmental office are another salient criterion group of people in positions of power. Donley and Winter (1970) assessed the power motive of the first 12 US presidents in the 20th century, based on content analyses of motive imagery in their inaugural speeches. The strength of the presidents' power motive was then correlated with their political effectiveness (as rated by historians), whether or not war was declared during their administration, and the number of cabinet changes. Although the office of president endows all incumbents with equal and far-reaching powers, it emerged that the presidents low in power motivation (Taft, Harding, Coolidge, Hoover, and Eisenhower) made less use of these powers than did the leaders high in power motivation (F. D. Roosevelt, Truman, Kennedy, and Johnson; see also Winter & Stewart, 1977).

The personality variable of the power motive thus appears to be an influential factor, but what might be the effects of societal conditions and mediating processes? Winter (1987b) analyzed the congruence between **US presidents'** motive profiles and the values of contemporary society. The findings confirmed his main hypothesis: the presidents' motive profiles were largely congruent with the priorities and prejudices of the society of the day in terms of achievement, power, and affiliation. This kind of fit does not guarantee "political greatness," however. The motive profiles of some of those rated by historians as "great presidents" – e.g., Lincoln, Washington, Roosevelt, Truman, and Kennedy – were highly discrepant from that of contemporary American society. One might interpret this finding as indicating that these presidents were capable of inspiring the country to move forward and grasp new opportunities. In a further study by Winter (1987b) and a follow-up study by Spangler and House (1991), the power motive proved to be the most influential single predictor. It correlated significantly with the initiation and ending of wars, as well as with ratings of presidential greatness and effectiveness. In his most recent analysis, Winter (2001) drew up a motive profile for George W. Bush based on his inaugural speech. While Bush's achievement motive was about average, his affiliation and power motives were very strong. Based on his findings, Winter (2001) predicted a very aggressive foreign policy. Given the president's strong affiliation motive, however, Winter also noted that policy would be subject to the approval of the president's friends and advisors. Another striking feature of Bush's speech was the frequent use of negation (the word "not"), particularly when it came to denying aggression or aggressive intentions.

Activists in student protest movements are another interesting criterion group. In the late 1960s, Winter and Wiecking (1971) obtained motive scores from male and female students who, instead of pursuing their studies, worked full time for protest organizations and labeled themselves radicals. At a cursory glance, the results are surprising: the radicals were more achievement motivated and less power motivated than the control group. More specifically, male radicals were higher in achievement motivation and lower in power motivation than the male control group, while female radicals were higher in affiliation and achievement motivation than the female control group.

These results were substantiated by nonreactive data. On 1 May 1969 and 6 May 1969, about 150 students occupied the President's office at Wesleyan University to protest against university policy on military recruitment. At the same time, about 250 students signed a petition repudiating the occupation of the President's office. The authors were able to obtain the names of students in both groups, occupiers and repudiants, from the petitions and "solidarity lists" they had signed. As luck would have it, 55 of the students had participated in an experiment involving TAT assessment of power and achievement motives 3–15 months earlier. A comparison of the two groups showed that the occupiers were significantly lower in power motivation than the repudiators, who were intent on enforcing law and order. The difference in the achievement motive of the two groups was in the expected direction, but was not significant. In the interpretation of their find-

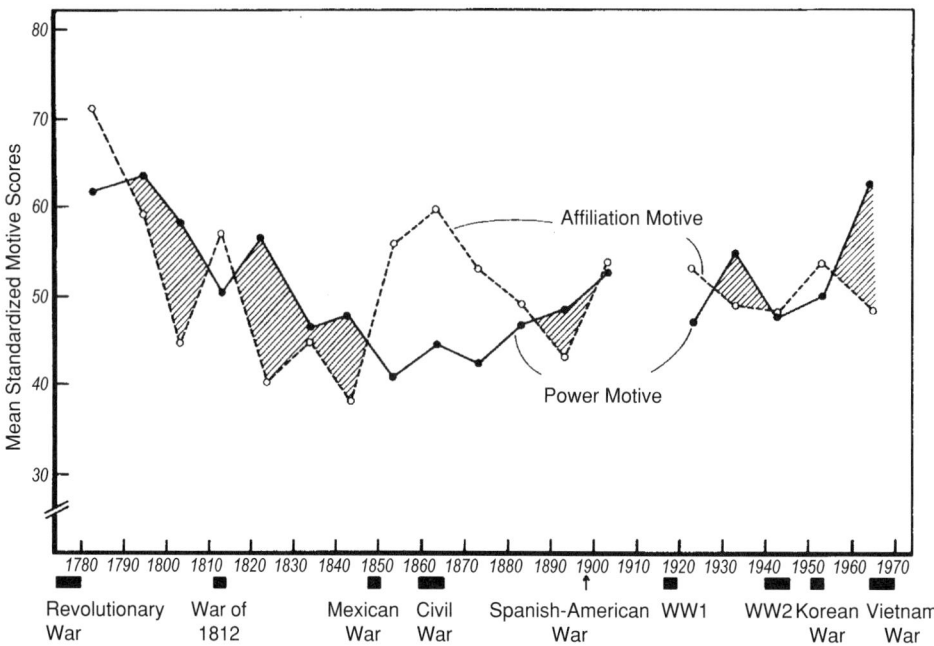

Figure 8.8 Strength of the power and affiliation motive in popular literature in the USA between 1780 and 1970. (Based on McClelland, 1975, p. 336.)

ings, the authors suggested that individuals high in achievement motivation strive for change in established and static institutions, whereas individuals high in power motivation seek to maintain the existing order and to use it to their best advantage.

8.4.4 War and Peace

McClelland (1975) studied historical change in national motive indices and tested the extent to which the relative strength of the power and affiliation imagery prevailing in a country ("imperial motive pattern") is a portent of war and national unrest. His analyses covered United States history from 1780 to 1970 (Fig. 8.8). McClelland examined texts that were popular during the intervals specified in the diagram (children's readers, popular novels and songs, etc.), analyzing their content for achievement, power, and affiliation imagery. He worked on the assumption that these sources would reflect the national *Zeitgeist*, which would in turn warn of imminent periods of armed conflict – or herald phases of peaceful coexistence. The shaded areas in Fig. 8.8 indicate periods of imperial motive patterns, i.e., periods in which the nation's power motive was stronger than its affiliation motive. The strength of the achievement motive was irrelevant here. A certain regularity can be discerned in the sequencing of typical motive patterns and periods of war and peace – phases marked by the imperial motive pattern regularly presage periods of US involvement in armed conflicts. If we accept these correlational relationships to be indicative of causality, and suffi-

ciently stringent to hazard a prediction, we might infer that, in 1970, the psychological stage was set for the USA to enter another conflict. As history showed, these fears soon became reality with the USA's involvement in the first Gulf War only 20 years after the end of the Vietnam War.

As stated above, the power motive of the incumbent president is another factor associated with a country's involvement in armed conflict. This effect is reinforced by media reports. In conflicts between competing politicians, political parties, or social groups, both sides often become involved in a dynamic of escalation, accentuating the power tendency of the opposing side and playing down that of the own side. The affiliative tendencies of the conflict parties is distorted in the opposite direction. These effects have been observed in both the speeches of political opponents and their coverage in the partisan press (Winter, 1987a).

In an ingenious study, Winter (1993) investigated the hypothesis that a societal climate high in power motivation and low in affiliation motivation foreshadows armed conflict between nations. He examined two conflict situations in detail. The first, **World War I,** escalated and ended in catastrophe; the second, the **Cuban Missile Crisis,** deescalated, with a nuclear conflict between the USA and the USSR being averted at the last moment. Winter analyzed exchanges between the respective governments at two points in the crises, scoring them for power and affiliation motive imagery. His results, which are presented in Table 8.3, show a significant increase in power imagery in intergovernmental communications in the run-up to World War I, but a decrease in power

Table 8.3. Motive patterns (standardized power motive imagery minus standardized affiliation motive imagery) in communications between the British and the German governments (*upper panel*) and the US and Soviet governments (*lower panel*) (Based on Winter, 1993, pp. 539–540)

	Early in crisis	Late in crisis	Change
World War I – Power motive minus affiliation motive			
German government	−10.20	5.10	15.30
British government	−6.00	1.13	7.13
Cuba Crisis – Power motive minus affiliation motive			
US government	11.00	−10.67	−21.67
Soviet government	10.33	−10.33	−20.66

imagery coupled with an increase in affiliation imagery in the deescalating Cuban crisis.

These findings confirm the hypothesis that armed conflicts are foreshadowed by a phase of high power and low affiliation motivation. Decreasing national levels of power motivation enhance the prospects of being able to settle a conflict peacefully, and of ongoing conflicts being resolved relatively quickly.

These studies demonstrated that the power motive plays a major role in combination with the affiliation and achievement motives. A motive profile that couples high power with low affiliation motives sets any system to the "expansion" mode. In the economic sphere, a high power motive (plus a high achievement motive) combined with a low affiliation motive paves the way for economic expansion and success. At the national level, a high power motive combined with a low affiliation motive constitutes a highly charged motive profile that heightens the risk of nations entering into armed conflict.

SUMMARY

Because power and the inequality of its distribution is one of the universals of animal and human societies, it can be approached from different levels of analysis – e.g., sociobiology, psychology, sociology, and the political sciences. Analyses approaching the subject from the perspective of motivational psychology logically focus on individual motive patterns and the incentives that trigger power-related behavior, i.e., that prompt the holders of power to exercise that power and/or the recipients of power to comply. A sense of control and its affective consequences has been identified as the main component of the incentive mechanism driving the exercise of power. This emotional component does not surface in our conscious experience, and is thus likely to be a key regulatory principle in both humans and infrahuman species. In humans, those exchanges of power that are not regulated by instantaneous, automatic, and unconscious processes (e.g., glances, facial expressions, gestures) may involve conscious deliberation and planning – a process of weighting up one's own sources of power and resources, the strengths and weaknesses of others, inhibiting and conducive factors and, finally, the outcomes expected – in preparation for the strategic implementation of one's own sources of power.

In almost all examinations of human power motivation, the power motive is first aroused by picture cues, and participants' responses are then analyzed for content reflecting the approach and avoidance tendencies of that motive. These studies have painted a picture of the power-motivated personality as someone who enjoys exerting power and control, is quick to recognize and respond to the intentions of others, but also tends to flaunt his or her resources, and is not averse to an excessive lifestyle (alcohol, sex, gambling). If individuals high in power motivation are prevented from exercising control, whether by internal or external factors, there are often detrimental effects on health, and on the immune system, in particular.

It goes without saying that the power motive plays a major role in the business and political spheres. Individuals high in both power and achievement motivation are especially successful in the business world. It is not surprising that politicians have a very particular relationship to power; indeed, power is often the only thing that politicians are halfway able to deal with. It takes more to make a successful leader, however – **charisma**, or the ability to involve one's supporters and citizens in the feeling of power, efficiency, and control is indispensable. Finally, unless moderated by an affiliation motive, a national climate high in power motivation will put that country at higher risk of involvement in armed conflict.

REVIEW QUESTIONS

1. **What are the defining characteristics of power relations?**

   Power derives from asymmetrical social relationships that are characterized by the inequitable distribution of social competence, access to resources, and/or social status. It is manifested in unilateral behavioral control. (Various definitions of power can be found in Section 8.1.1)

2. **How is power exercised?**

   Power is exercised when a person has access to reinforcers (resources) that can be used to reorchestrate the incentives available, such that others are motivated to comply with the wishes of the power holder. (A list of resources is provided in Section 8.1.2)

3. **What evidence is there to assume that power behavior and dominance behavior are biologically (genetically) determined?**

   The assumption that power behavior and dominance behavior are genetically determined is supported by the following observations:

Lack of cultural specificity.

Comparable behavior in human and nonhuman primates.

Adaptive significance for reproductive success. (See Sections 8.1 and 8.1.7 for details)

4. How is the power motive measured?

First, the power motive is aroused by means of picture cues; respondents then generate stories of their own (TAT) or choose from a set of structured responses (Grid Technique). (See Section 8.2 for details)

5. What are the health risks of an inhibited power motive?

Individuals high in power motivation who are prevented from exercising the power motive by external (e.g., the social situation) or internal (e.g., fears and anxieties) inhibiting factors are susceptible to certain illnesses, owing primarily to a depressed immune function (Section 8.3.2).

6. What are the political dangers of the "power" theme becoming dominant in the thought and cultural expression of a nation?

An imperial motive profile (high–power motive combined with low- affiliation motive) at the national level (as reflected in readers, popular novels and songs, etc.) puts the nation at higher risk of becoming involved in armed conflicts (Section 8.4.4).

9   Implicit and Explicit Motives

J. Brunstein

9.1 Theoretical Concepts and Background

From its beginnings, research into the motives behind people's efforts to be successful (the achievement motive), have an impact on others (the power motive), establish and maintain social contact with others (the affiliation motive), and become involved in affectionate relationships (intimacy motive) has been bound up with the question of which methods are best suited to assessing individual differences in underlying motives (cf. Schmalt & Sokolowski, 2000). As described in Chapter 6 of this volume, McClelland, Atkinson, Clark, and Lowell (1953) developed a version of the Thematic Apperception Test (TAT) to measure the strength of the achievement motive. McClelland and colleagues considered the achievement motive to be an affectively charged need that is activated by challenging tasks and satisfied by the continual improvement of the skills involved and the outcomes achieved. The TAT was devised to allow the achievement motive to be assessed without the influence of:

- response bias tendencies (e.g., social desirability bias),
- cognitive abilities (e.g., the respondent's actual aptitude), or
- situational influences (e.g., external demands).

McClelland (1958b) doubted that methods of **direct** assessment, measures of achievement, or observations of behavior would permit conclusions to be drawn about the strength of the achievement motive. Instead, he worked on the assumption that the achievement motive can only be measured **indirectly**, by tapping into the stream of thoughts and fantasies that people produce in response to motive-arousing picture cues. Soon afterwards, Heckhausen (1963a) presented a comparable, but more differentiated TAT measure of the achievement motive that distinguished between "hope for success" and "fear of failure" (Chapter 6).

DEFINITION
According to McClelland (1980, 1987) a motive that has been activated by environmental stimuli fulfills three functions: it energizes, directs, and selects behavior instrumental for satisfying that motive.

In keeping with this definition, research has shown that the personality variable "need for achievement" as measured by the TAT method predicts criteria of effort expenditure, learning, and attention in achievement situations (Chapter 6). TAT-type procedures were soon developed to assess other motives, such as the needs for power, affiliation, and intimacy, based on the same principles.

Despite the initial success of the TAT approach in explaining both individual (McClelland et al., 1953) and collective achievement behavior (McClelland, 1961), other authors soon began using questionnaires to tap the achievement motive, among others. Questionnaire methods had the advantage of being more parsimonious and reliable than the TAT. However, Atkinson, Bongort, and Price (1977) and Kuhl (1978) were able to show that high reliability as defined by classical test theory is not a necessary condition for the construct validity of TAT-based motive scores (i.e., for high correlations between true and observed motive scores). Moreover, Lundy (1985) reported that the stability of the motive scores generated by the TAT is dependent on the instructions given to respondents. When participants are instructed to write down the first story that comes to mind, regardless of whether they have tackled a similar theme in a previous trial, the reliability of the TAT scores is not high, but by all means respectable, at around $r_{tt} = .50$ at retest after one year. When participants are instructed to think back to their original stories, the coefficients are much higher (Niitamo, 1999, reports coefficients of between .60 and .76 at two-week retest interval).

Many authors seeking to develop questionnaires to measure people's underlying motives have taken Murray's (1938) classification and description of "psychogenic" needs as their starting point. The best-known example of an instrument constructed in this manner is the "Personality Research Form" (PRF) by Jackson (1974). This questionnaire contains scales designed to tap people's strivings for achievement, dominance, and affiliation. However, researchers working on specific scales to capture the achievement motive soon returned to the findings of studies that had used the TAT. Mehrabian (1969) developed a particularly widely-administered questionnaire ("Mehrabian Achievement Risk Taking Scale", MARPS) drawing on Atkinson's risk-taking model (1957). Other authors have based their questionnaires on Festinger's (1954) theory of social comparison processes.

❶ The theory of social comparison processes states that people have a need to assess their abilities by comparing them with the abilities of others.

The "Achievement Motives Scale" (AMS) constructed by Gjesme and Nygard (1970) includes a number of items relating to precisely this need.

From the outset, proponents of the TAT method took a skeptical view of questionnaire methods being used to measure motives. Atkinson (1981), McClelland (1980), and Nicholls (1984), e.g., criticized the fact that the validation of achievement-motive questionnaires was limited to testing the extent to which self-reported achievement behavior (e.g., "I prefer difficult tasks to easy ones") corresponds with the behavior actually displayed in achievement situations (e.g., task choice and goal-setting behavior). Although this approach provides data on the criterion validity of questionnaires, it says little about the construct validity of theories of achievement motivation. These theories are supposed to explain why some people prefer challenging tasks, while others prefer easy ones. Yet the common practice of basing the statements to be rated in questionnaire measures on behavioral characteristics typical of achievement-motivated individuals, and then validating the questionnaires on the basis of the selfsame behavioral characteristics in real-life achieve-

ment situations, provides precious little insight as to how the achievement-motive operates.

Participants in the, at times, lively debate on the reliability and validity of different methods of measuring motives (Entwisle, 1972; McClelland, 1980; Tuerlinckx, De Boeck, & Lens, 2002) have occasionally overlooked the fact that TAT and questionnaire measures of nominally identical motives share virtually no common variance. Since the early 1950s, moreover, evidence has been growing that the motives captured by TAT and questionnaire measures predict different behavioral characteristics, are activated by different situational characteristics, and have had an impact from different factors in development and socialization. McClelland, Koestner, and Weinberger (1989) have integrated these findings in a model that assumes the coexistence of two different types of motives:

- Implicit motives: These are largely inaccessible to introspection, meaning that they can only be measured indirectly (e.g., by interpreting stories produced spontaneously in response to the motive-arousing picture cues of the TAT).
- Explicit (or "self-attributed") motives: These reflect the individual's self-image, as assessed by means of self-report measures.

In the same vein, Stern (1935) had argued that motivation research should distinguish between "phenomotives," which can be deduced from the surface characteristics of observable behavior, and "genomotives," which direct a person's behavior without that person necessarily being consciously aware of them. Whereas phenomotives essentially just describe behavior, genomotives serve to explain what people do.

In the following sections, we will present data providing empirical support for the distinction that McClelland, Koestner, & Weinberger (1989) made between implicit and explicit motives. Furthermore, we will investigate differences in the needs underlying implicit and explicit motives. Even if we assume that the two types of motives are largely independent of each other, this does not rule out the possibility that they have a combined impact on behavior and experience. Accordingly, we will also discuss the interplay between the two motive types – be it in the form of coalitions entered into by implicit and explicit motives or in the form of conflicts arising from contradictory tendencies. Finally, we will give an overview of the theoretical and methodological challenges still facing this field of research.

SUMMARY

The line of thought that prompted David McClelland to distinguish "implicit" from "explicit" motives runs as follows: Implicit motives stem from affectively charged preferences for certain kinds of incentives (e.g., in the case of the achievement-motive, task difficulty) that are learned early in life. Because these preferences develop from early,

Table 9.1. Test correlations between TAT motives and questionnaires tapping motivational self-descriptions (*PRF; N* = 195) and personality traits (*NEO; N* = 111) in two student samples

	TAT		
	Power Motive	**Achievement Motive**	**Affiliation Motive**
PRF: Dominance	.04	−.00	−.02
PRF: Achievement	−.02	.06	.09
PRF: Affiliation	−.06	.15	−.08
NEO: Extraversion	−.01	.00	.01
NEO: Neuroticism	.05	−.11	−.18
NEO: Openness	.04	.00	−.10
NEO: Conscientiousness	−.05	−.00	−.07
NEO: Agreeableness	.06	−.01	−.12

NEO, Five-Factor Inventory, *PRF*, Personality Research Form. Based on Schultheiss & Brunstein, 2001, p. 80.

prelinguistic experiences, they are not represented in the medium of language and cannot be tapped by self-report methods. Neither the activation of an implicit motive nor its translation into instrumental behavior necessitates acts of self-reflection or conscious behavioral control. Explicit motives, in contrast, reflect the self-images, values, and goals that people attribute to themselves and with which they identify. They document people's conscious conceptions of the motives underlying their behavior. Self-attributed motives do not necessarily correspond with the motives that drive people's actions, however. In the following sections, we present data that support these assumptions by demonstrating that the two types of motive have discriminant validity (are empirically independent) and predictive specificity (predict different classes of behavior).

9.2 Evidence for the Independence of Implicit and Explicit Motives

9.2.1 Zero Correlations Between Direct and Indirect Measures of Motives

According to the traditional view on personality assessment, two tests that are supposed to measure the same construct (e.g., a specific motive) must correlate sufficiently with each other, even if their methods differ (Cronbach, 1990). In the TAT method, respondents are presented with ambiguous pictures, and an open-ended response format is used to record their reactions to these pictures (i.e., there are no structured responses; respondents generate stories of their own). In questionnaires, on the other hand, respondents react to structured statements, rating each in terms of how strongly it applies to them. Despite these differences, the scores yielded by the two instruments are expected to correlate substantially if they indeed capture the same characteristic.

❗ This criterion, known as convergent validity, is not met when motives are assessed using TAT and questionnaire measures. Rather, findings indicate that TAT-driven and questionnaire-based measures of motives have discriminant validity, i.e., that they measure different constructs, even when both measurements pertain to the same theme (e.g., achievement, power, or affiliation).

DeCharms, Morrison, Reitman, and McClelland (1955) were among the first authors to report that marked discrepancies often emerge between implicit (TAT) and explicit (questionnaire) motives. They used a TAT measure and self-descriptions (e.g., "I set myself challenging goals") to assess respondents' striving for achievement. None of the self-ratings correlated significantly with the TAT measure of achievement motivation (nAchievement). This was no isolated finding. In a meta-analysis, Spangler (1992) computed a mean correlation of just $r = .088$ for 36 same-sample comparisons of TAT and questionnaire measures of achievement motivation. Thus, someone classified as being high in achievement motivation on the basis of his or her TAT responses might describe him- or herself as being either high or low in achievement motivation on a questionnaire measure.

Similar results have been reported for other motives. Schultheiss and Brunstein (2001) obtained TAT scores for the achievement, power, and affiliation motives from two student samples and correlated these with the students' scores on the nominally similar scales of the "Personality Research Form" (PRF; Table 9.1). The correlations between the TAT and the PRF scores were .06 (achievement), .04 (power), and .13 (affiliation). Schultheiss and Brunstein also administered the German version of the NEO Five-Factor Inventory to one group of participants (Borkenau & Ostendorf, 1993). When motives were measured with the TAT, none of the 15 trait-motive correlations (5 traits × 3 motives) proved to be significant. The correlation between extraversion and the

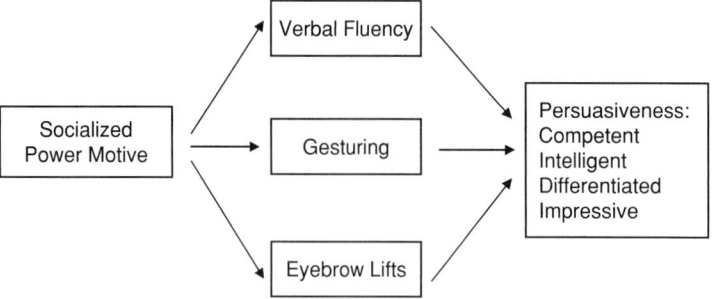

Figure 9.1 Predicting persuasiveness: The effect of (a socially acceptable variant of) the power motive on external ratings of persuasiveness is mediated by paralinguistic and nonverbal behavior. (Diagrammatic representation of the findings of Schultheiss & Brunstein, 2002.)

affiliation motive was. 05; between conscientiousness and the achievement motive, .00; and between agreeableness and the power motive, .06. When motives were measured using questionnaire methods, however, substantial correlations with the scales tapping fundamental personality traits were observed (e.g., power and affiliation correlated with extraversion; cf. Costa & McCrae, 1988).

The methodological variance of the two procedures, i.e., the differences in stimulus material and response formats, might explain why TAT motives share practically no common variance with their nominally similar counterparts in questionnaire measures. However, more recent studies show that the motives measured by TAT procedures are not substantially related to self-reported personal life goals either. Personal goals are assessed using open-ended formats rather than structured questionnaires, with respondents being instructed to describe their most important goals in their own words (Brunstein & Maier, 1996). This material is then coded in terms of dominant themes, similar to TAT picture stories. In four studies, motives (TAT) and goals (free self-reports) relating to the same theme were compared (e.g., the TAT-measured achievement motive was compared with self-reports of achievement goals; the TAT-measured affiliation motive was compared with self-reports of affiliation goals). The relationships discerned between motives and goals in the same domain were moderate (Emmons & McAdams, 1991) to nonexistent (Brunstein et al., 1995; Brunstein, Schultheiss, & Grässmann, 1998; King, 1995). This means that, although some people's explicit goals do correspond with their implicit motives, many others pursue goals that are not congruent with their motives as measured by the TAT.

In the studies reported thus far, all data were derived from a common source, namely, the respondent under investigation. Taking a rather different approach, Schultheiss and Brunstein (2002) explored how well external raters are able to infer an implicit motive, such as the power motive, by observing the behavior of another person. The participants in their experiment were given the task of presenting their

position on animal experiments as persuasively as possible to a person sitting opposite them. According to the ratings of external observers, who were shown video recordings of the participants' arguments, participants high in the power motive (more specifically, a variant of the power motive associated with socially acceptable behavior) performed this task much more convincingly than participants low in the power motive (Fig. 9.1). However, power-motivated participants were not judged to be more dominant, more assertive, or less agreeable than their counterparts. Rather, they were ascribed achievement-relevant attributes such as higher levels of intelligence and competence – characteristics associated with the achievement motive in both self- and other-judgments. The observers formed these impressions primarily on the basis of nonverbal and paralinguistic features of the participants' communicative behavior, i.e., on characteristics that do not tend to be consciously controlled. Participants high in the power motive were characterized by the speed of their speech and by lively gestures and facial expressions. They did not differ from less power-motivated participants in the quality of their arguments, however.

These findings show that the motives driving behavior cannot simply be "read off" overt behavior. This seems to apply to both external observations and self-perception. Depending on the demands of the situation, social norms, and personal abilities and attitudes, one and the same motive may be expressed in quite different behaviors.

For example, Veroff, Depner, Kulka, & Douvan (1980) reported that power-motivated men tend to choose achievement contexts to satisfy their need for social recognition, and interpreted this finding as indicating that other behavioral expressions of the power motive (e.g., social oppression) are increasingly discredited as modern societies embrace the principles of democracy (see also Peterson & Stewart, 1993). The power motive may be expressed in socially competent and responsible behaviors, including achievement-oriented behavior, or in socially unacceptable and self- or other-destructive behaviors (Winter & Barenbaum, 1985; Winter & Stewart, 1978). As Stern (1935) had already pointed out, it is vital to distinguish the purpose of behavior (e.g., striving for personal strength and social recognition) from its expression (e.g., using communicative strategies that give the impression of competence). There is otherwise a danger that the explanations given for the observed behavior are circular. Simply suffixing the attribute "motivated" to the behavior observed may be a common approach in everyday life, but it does not serve the scientific explanation of behavior – the "explanation" is spurious.

Given the weak relationships observed between TAT and questionnaire measures of certain motives, the practice of using the same label (e.g., "the" achievement motive) for both types of measures seems a questionable one. The same terminology is used to describe constructs that should – it seems – be differentiated. As Kagan (1988) and Block (1995) have pointed out, the effects of this linguistic imprecision can contaminate even the level of theorizing. Yet the weak correlations observed between different instruments might equally be due to psychometric shortcomings in one of the two instruments (e.g., the low reliability of the TAT or misleading response tendencies in questionnaire methods).

❶ Correlations between different tests are not a sufficient basis for conclusions to be drawn on the similarities or differences between the constructs they were designed to measure. It is also vital to explore whether the instruments differ in their predictions of relevant behavioral characteristics.

9.2.2 Behavioral Correlates of Implicit and Explicit Motives

McClelland (1980) advanced the hypothesis that implicit and explicit motives influence behavior in different ways. The former are expressed in "operant" behavior, the latter in "respondent" behavior.

DEFINITION

According to McClelland's definition, operant behavior is behavior that a person generates spontaneously, i.e., without premeditation, and that entails recurrent preferences for particular experiences over extended periods of time (e.g., career success). Respondent behavior, on the other hand, is elicited by clearly identifiable environmental stimuli, may be the subject of conscious thought and deliberation, and can be wittingly influenced by a person. This applies, for example, to decisions or appraisals that an individual thinks through carefully or that are imposed from outside.

The following studies illustrate McClelland's argument. Using a time sample method (participants were beeped several times a day via an electronic diary), Constantian (cf. McAdams & Constantian, 1983; McClelland, 1985b) surveyed the affiliative behavior of students in everyday situations, and found that the implicit affiliation motive (TAT) predicted the frequency with which participants were in direct (e.g., engaged in conversation) or indirect (e.g., writing a letter) contact with others when beeped. Questionnaire measures of the same motive did not predict behavior in the same way. Conversely, when asked directly whether they would rather undertake certain activities alone or in company, the students' stated preferences reflected the strength of their explicit, but not of their implicit affiliation motive. In other words, students who described themselves as sociable also reported that they would rather engage in the activities in question with someone else than on their own.

Studies on the achievement motive have produced similar findings. DeCharms et al. (1955) and Biernat (1989) both found that, in contrast to self-reported achievement orientation, the achievement motive as measured by the TAT predicted higher levels of effort expenditure and steeper learning gains when participants were set tasks without being specifically instructed to do well. In both studies, task choice and personal values were predicted by questionnaire measures, but not by the TAT. Individuals who described themselves as achievement oriented were more likely to express views on the quality of paintings that were in line with the opinions of alleged experts. Moreover, they voiced high levels of approval for people who had been successful in their lives, and discredited less successful people. Given the choice of taking on a leadership role in a teamwork setting, they regularly chose to do so. In other words, the behavior of achievement-oriented individuals in situations involving decisions and evaluations was in line with their self-image, and thus also consistent with the expectations made of them.

In an experimental study, Brunstein and Hoyer (2002) contrasted the power of implicit (TAT) and explicit (self-report) achievement motives to predict effort expenditure and task choice as criteria of achievement behavior. They found that the implicit achievement motive predicted effort expenditure (i.e., performance gains on a repetitive task), whereas the explicit achievement motive predicted the choice of an achievement-related task (i.e., the decision to carry on working on that task rather than switching to a neutral activity).

Findings on the Achievement Motive in Academic Settings
Studies conducted in real-life achievement situations have yielded further evidence for the validity of McClelland's (1980) distinction between operant and respondent behavior. One study found that a questionnaire measure of the achievement motive (AMS) predicted whether or not young people considered entering a prestigious competition for young researchers (Dahme et al., 1993). The same questionnaire did not give a

STUDY

Predicting Effort Expenditure and Task Choice by Indirect (TAT) and Direct (Questionnaire) Motive Measures

Brunstein and Hoyer (2002) studied how well implicit (TAT) and explicit (questionnaires) achievement motives predict effort expenditure and task choice as criteria of achievement behavior within a single experimental design. The effort criterion was intended to tap spontaneous achievement behavior, the task choice criterion to tap controlled achievement behavior. Student respondents working on a computerized concentration test were given continuous feedback over a number of trials on change in their achievement relative to their previous performance (individual appraisal) as well as in social comparison (normative appraisal). Feedback was manipulated to signal either an increase or a decrease in achievement. After a scheduled number of tasks, participants were given the choice of continuing with the same kind of task or switching to a neutral activity (judging the aesthetic quality of pictures). The findings are presented in Fig. 9.2.

Task performance (change in working speed on a concentration task relative to a baseline measure without feedback) was predicted by the implicit achievement motive, but not by self-reported achievement motivation. Participants high in the achievement motive (TAT) tended to increase their working speed when informed that their performance fell short of their previous achievement (Fig. 9.2a). Task choice, on the other hand, was predicted by the level of self-attributed achievement motivation. When achievement-oriented participants (questionnaire) were given feedback that was detrimental to their self-image (indicating a drop in performance relative to other participants), they tended to decide to continue working on the task at hand (Fig. 9.2b). Thus, implicit and explicit achievement motives were responsive to different evaluation norms (individualized vs. normative feedback) and predicted different criteria of achievement-oriented behavior (effort expenditure vs. task choice).

These findings are in keeping with the notion that the achievement motive as measured by the TAT energizes behavior aimed at increasing one's competence, whereas the self-reported desire for achievement is influenced by social standards and comparisons and has an impact on people's conscious decisions. What both motives have in common is that they are most responsive to negative achievement trends. When feedback indicated an increase in achievement, neither of the motives significantly predicted either behavioral criteria. Where task choice is concerned, this pattern of results can be explained as follows: People with an achievement-oriented self-image generally have a positive self-concept of their intellectual ability. A decrease in performance relative to others contradicts this self-concept and prompts achievement-motivated individuals to obtain further information about their capacity to perform the task at hand (Trope, 1986c). Positive normative feedback (indicating an improvement in performance relative to others), on the other hand, corresponds with the expectations of achievement-oriented individuals, meaning that there is no further need to sound out their ability on the task. Likewise, people with a high implicit achievement motive (TAT) respond to an alleged decrease in individual performance by mobilizing effort, illustrating that the driving force behind this motive is the need for self-improvement. Effort expenditure is triggered by a status quo considered to be unsatisfactory (decrease in one's performance) and the prospect of being able to turn this situation around by investing more effort (increase in one's performance). When feedback is positive, there is no corresponding reason for the achievement motive (TAT) to trigger an increase in effort.

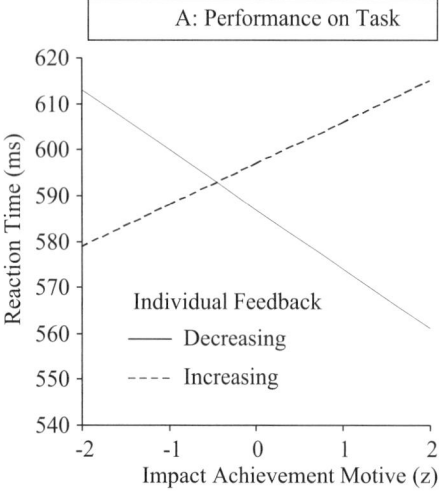
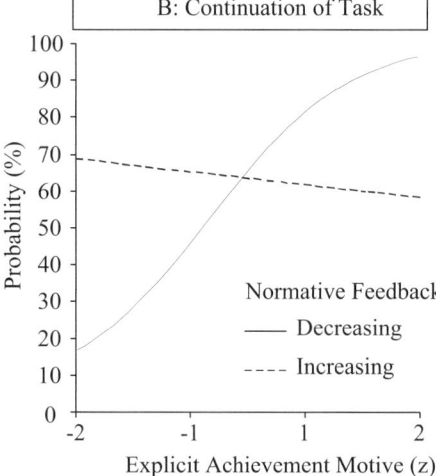

Figure 9.2a,b Effort expenditure and task choice as a function of achievement motivation and feedback. (a) An alleged drop in individual performance (*decreasing* individual feedback) prompts participants high in the implicit achievement motive (TAT) to increase their working speed. (b) An alleged drop in performance relative to the social reference group (*decreasing* normative feedback) increases the likelihood of participants high in the explicit achievement motive (questionnaire) deciding to continue working on the task at hand. (Based on Brunstein & Hoyer, 2002, p. 58.)

reliable prediction of how hard entrants in the competition actually worked on their projects, however. It is in precisely this domain that implicit motives show predictive power:

■ A high achievement motive (TAT) predicts occupational, business, and economic success (Chapter 6) – sometimes independently (McClelland, 1961) and sometimes in combination with a high power motive (McClelland & Boyatzis, 1982). This relationship persists even when controlling for differences in educational level, intelligence, temperament, and socioeconomic status (McClelland & Franz, 1992).

■ Explicit motives do not have comparable validity in predicting aspects of productivity, innovation, and creativity in adulthood.

Educational outcomes, in contrast to occupational outcomes, tend to correlate more strongly with explicit than with implicit achievement motives. McClelland (1980) explained this finding by reasoning that there is little scope for spontaneous and self-determined work and learning to occur in school settings. Rather, tasks are set by teachers and outcomes are evaluated using standardized procedures. McClelland's explanation is something of an overgeneralization in this form, however. It is, in fact, possible to activate the implicit achievement motives of individual students in the classroom setting by tailoring academic demands and achievement feedback to their specific needs (Heckhausen & Rheinberg, 1980; O'Connor, Atkinson & Horner, 1966). For example, achievement-motivated students (particularly those whose confidence of success outweighs the fear of failure) seem to prefer their performance to be measured against individual rather than social reference norms (Rheinberg, Duscha, & Michels, 1980). What is more, gearing task difficulty to individual abilities creates an atmosphere in which all students are able to focus on their own performance (Rheinberg & Krug, 2005).

Although the distinction between operant and respondent behavior provides some insight into the differences between implicit and explicit motives, there is no denying that it is a distinction born of drastic oversimplification, with motives being set in direct relation to behavioral characteristics. In actual fact, the correlations between motive measures and behavioral criteria rarely exceed the level of .30 (Spangler, 1992). Although (simple) correlations of this kind may provide evidence for the specific validity of a given motive measure, it is only possible to establish that substantial relationships exist between motives and behavior by taking the incentives present in the situational context into account as well.

9.2.3 Motive-Arousing Incentives

One of the fundamental principles of motivational psychology is that a motive first has to be activated by a corresponding **incentive** before it can have an impact on behavior. An incentive is defined as a situational characteristic that, based on previous learning experiences, is associated with the possibility of satisfying a motive and, as a result, experiencing positive and rewarding affect (feelings of pride, strength, interpersonal attachment, etc.). The following study by Andrews (1967) on advancement in two types of companies illustrates this principle.

> **EXAMPLE**
>
> One of the companies, known as the Achievement company, offered its employees a broad range of achievement-related incentives, such as autonomy, variety, challenging tasks, and differentiated feedback. The other company, dubbed the Power company, was characterized by a hierarchical management structure. Andrews measured the achievement and power motives of employees in both companies using the TAT method. He then ascertained how often these employees had been promoted in the previous years. A high achievement motive proved to be associated with more rapid advancement in the Achievement company, but not in the Power company. The opposite was true of the power motive, with employees high in the power motive being promoted much more often in the Power company than in the Achievement company. Neither motive was a unique predictor of promotion. Rather, the decisive factor was whether the incentives offered at the workplace coincided with the employees' motives (for similar findings from a more recent study, see Jenkins, 1994). It is only when the environmental incentives – and hence the motivating potential of a situation – correspond with a person's dominant motives that these motives can be expected to have an impact on behavior (Kleinbeck, 1996).

Numerous studies indicate that implicit and self-attributed motives are activated by different classes of incentives. Provided that tasks are tackled in a task-oriented atmosphere, with no pressure beeing exerted by external agents, the implicit acheivement motive triggers high levels of effort and persistence. The incentive resides solely in the difficulty, complexity, or novelty of the task at hand, and the opportunity it affords to do something better, faster, or more effectively. In the presence of external incentives, such as time pressure, assessment, or competition, however, the explanatory power of the achievement motive as measured by the TAT decreases markedly. This has been shown in experimental studies (Entin, 1974; Horner, 1974a; Miller & Worchel, 1956; Wendt, 1955) as well as in real-life achievement settings, as the following example illustrates.

McKeachie (1961) reported that achievement-motivated (TAT) college students do particularly well in seminars if their lecturers refrain from setting goals, voicing demands or expectations, or laying down rules. But precisely these kinds of additional incentives, which are not inherent in the task itself, seem to be needed to activate the explicit achievement motive. People with an achievement-oriented self-image often only really apply themselves when challenged to demonstrate their ability and secure social recognition in competition with others (Patten & White, 1977). These kinds of achievement incentives divert attention from the task at hand and direct it toward the social and personal implications of potential success or failure. For this reason, they are often termed "extrinsic" incentives and contrasted with the "intrinsic" incentives inherent in a task (Chapter 13). In contrast to individuals high in implicit achievement motive, individuals high in self-attributed achievement motivation experience joy, fun, and interest precisely when they are able to measure their abilities in direct competition with others (Tauer & Harackiewicz, 1999).

In the meta-analysis mentioned above, Spangler (1992) undertook a thorough investigation of whether and how different types of incentive predict achievement-motivated behavior. Regarding individual characteristics, Spangler distinguished between indirect (TAT) and direct (questionnaire) measures of the achievement motive; regarding situational characteristics, between activity incentives (challenging tasks) and social incentives (e.g., social recognition as a consequence of success); and regarding behavioral characteristics, between operant criteria (e.g., life-outcome variables) and respondent criteria (e.g., attitudinal measures). Spangler classified studies on achievement motivation along these three dimensions, with the following results:

1. Neither the implicit (TAT) nor the explicit (questionnaire) achievement motive was substantially correlated with criteria of achievement behavior.
2. The implicit achievement motive predicted operant, but not respondent forms of achievement behavior. The validity of questionnaire measures was low, even when the analysis was limited to studies investigating respondent behavior.
3. This rather bleak picture brightened up considerably when the different kinds of incentives that had been used to activate achievement-motivated behavior in the various studies were taken into account. The validity of the TAT achievement motive increased from $r = .22$ to .66 when operant behavior was measured in the presence of activity incentives and without social (or extrinsic) incentives. Likewise, the validity coefficients of the achievement motive questionnaires increased when only studies involving social incentives were considered. The validity coefficients computed for the questionnaires could not compete with those determined for TAT measures of the achievement motive, however.

Based on these findings, Koestner, Weinberger, and McClelland (1991) concluded that only individuals high

in implicit achievement motivation (TAT) are genuinely interested in mastering difficult tasks. For individuals with an achievement-oriented self-image, significant achievements have another function entirely – they serve as a means to the end of gaining the recognition of the social environment.

❶ The main lesson to be learned from Spangler's (1992) findings is that motivation analyses can only produce satisfactory results if different types of incentives are taken into account as well as differences in personality motives when predicting achievement behavior.

9.2.4 Differences in Child-Rearing Practices and Development

Child-Rearing Practices

McClelland et al. (1989) speculated that implicit and explicit motives have different antecedents in child rearing and socialization. McClelland and Pilon (1983; see also McClelland, 1987) reported one of the few studies that has related implicit and explicit motives measured in adulthood to the way that respondents were brought up (for a detailed account of motivational development, see Chapter 15). In a longitudinal study initiated by Sears, Maccoby, and Levin (1957), a total of 379 mothers were interviewed on their child-rearing practices in 1951, when their children were 5 years old. Twenty-six years later, the social motives of the 31-year-old "children" were measured using the TAT and self-descriptions (adjective scales). McClelland and Pilon found that implicit (TAT) and explicit (self-report) motives were associated with different child-rearing practices. Because this only applied to the achievement and power motives, however, the following account is limited to these two motives (Table 9.2).

Adults high in implicit power motive were, according to the mothers' reports, brought up in a permissive atmosphere, characterized by tolerance of both aggressive and sexual behavior on the child's part. Women high in the power motive had even been expressly encouraged by their mothers to fight back in conflict situations. In contrast, adults who described themselves as power oriented had been punished and spanked more often as children, particularly when they showed hostility toward their parents. Adults high in the implicit achievement motive had been toilet trained very early in life, and their mothers had insisted on fixed mealtimes. Self-attributed achievement motives correlated with different parenting practices. Achievement-oriented individuals had been expected to show independence and to succeed on difficult tasks at an early age.

These findings must, of course, be interpreted with caution. Neither do we know what happened in the lives of the "children" between the ages of 5 and 30, nor is it possible to

Table 9.2. Correlations of child-rearing variables (mothers' reports) with implicit (TAT) and explicit motives (self-descriptive adjective checklists) in adulthood ($N = 76–78$)		
Child-rearing practices	Correlations with motive variables	
	Implicit achievement motive (TAT)	Explicit achievement motive (self-report)
Scheduled feeding	.33*	.06
Strict and early toilet training	.41*	−.10
Early and difficult tasks set for child	−.10	.31*
Permissiveness about sex and aggression	.31*	.08
Punishment of aggression toward parents	−.17	.32*
Physical punishment (spanking) by mother	−.07	.39*

*statistically significant.
Based on McClelland & Pilon, 1983, pp. 567, 570; McClelland, Koestner, & Weinberger, 1989, p. 699.

say with any certainty that the child-rearing practices reported by the mothers determined the development of the children's implicit and explicit motives. Despite these limitations, the findings of McClelland and Pilon (1983) are worthy of note in two respects:

1. They lend support to the idea that implicit motives are acquired earlier in life than explicit motives. In the sample examined, toilet training had been completed long before parents began teaching their children to act independently and responsibly. Furthermore, verbal communication is much more relevant to the parenting practices that McClelland and Pilon (1983) found to be associated with the acquisition of explicit motives than to the practices found to correlate with the development of implicit motives. Parental demands, expectations, and even punishments tend to be communicated in words, or at least accompanied by a verbal commentary. Neither the establishment of fixed mealtimes nor permissive child-rearing behavior necessitates a similar degree of verbal communication or language comprehension.

2. The findings presented by McClelland and Pilon (1983) correspond with other observations, as well. It seems that a strong implicit power motive develops only if children are able to enjoy early experiences of efficacy unhindered – though reservations seem warranted where aggressive behavior is concerned. Other studies have shown that a strong power motive can be channeled into prosocial behavior when children are slightly older by teaching them to behave responsibly. The father is an important role model here (Winter & Stewart, 1978). In the study by McClelland and Pilon, a high self-attributed power motive was related to less pleasurable experiences in childhood, at least if the mothers' reports are to be believed. The mothers of dominant adults tended to endorse physical punishment. It is conceivable that self-images characterized by the need for superiority develop as a form of compensation, i.e., in reaction to childhood experiences of inferiority. Without further evidence, however, this interpretation remains pure speculation.

Similar observations can be made for the implicit and explicit achievement motive. The data presented by McClelland and Pilon (1983) indicate that the control of physical needs plays a key role in the development of the implicit achievement motive. This is in line with findings reported by Mischel and Gilligan (1964), who observed that achievement-motivated children are characterized by the ability to resist temptation and delay gratification. Control of physical needs and the capacity to resist competing incentives are important preconditions for people being able to apply themselves to difficult tasks and to work with persistence and concentration.

People faced with stressful situations (e.g., high-stakes exams) sometimes resort to psychotropic drugs to give their performance an artificial boost. Amphetamines, for example, produce a feeling of euphoria as well as acting as appetite suppressants. Bäumler (1975) was able to show that administering Ritalin under experimentally controlled conditions leads to an increase in achievement-related imagery in TAT stories (Bäumler, 1975). Thus, implicit motivational states can be influenced by psychophysical factors that circumvent cognitive processes. High explicit achievement orientation, on the other hand, is socialized in the context of verbally controlled and culturally mediated demands, as shown by the findings of McClelland and Pilon. Besides parenting, experiences in the school setting play a major role here. Students form their assessments of their own ability by engaging in social comparisons with their classmates (Köller, 2000; Marsh, 1989; Stipek, 1996). As early as primary school age, students who describe themselves as achievement oriented rate their mathematical and verbal abilities to be higher than those of their peers (Helmke, 1997).

Development of Achievement Motives

Along the same lines as McClelland (1987), Veroff (1969) suggested that children develop two different kinds of achievement motivation. First, the **autonomous achievement motive** develops at preschool age (or even earlier). At this stage, standards of achievement are personal and the achievement motive is satisfied by gradual gains in mastery. Children with an autonomous achievement motive compete with themselves, aiming to build on their abilities progressively. This description is reminiscent of the concept of the implicit achievement motive introduced later, which is also held to be closely linked to efforts to improve one's self, i.e., one's knowledge and skills (Breckler & Greenwald, 1986; Koestner & McClelland, 1990; Koestner, Weinberger, & McClelland, 1991). At this first stage, then, achievements are evaluated on the basis of (temporal) self-comparisons ("What can I do now that I couldn't do before?" or "What can't I do yet that I'd like to be able to do better?"). Situations characterized by this motive produce a motivational state that Nicholls (1984) termed "task involving": People are completely focused on the challenge posed by the task at hand, and infer their ability from the learning gains they observe as they gradually come to master the task.

It is only later, at primary school age that a **social achievement motive** develops (Veroff, 1969). Standards of achievement are now social; performance is assessed with reference to normative demands and in comparison with one's peers. It is at around the same age that children recognize the concepts of difficulty, effort, and ability as factors having distinct effects on performance (Nicholls, 1978). Only then is it possible for children to draw differentiated conclusions about their own abilities based on their performance (Nicholls, 1984). There are strong parallels between the ensuing efforts to obtain information about one's strengths and weaknesses by systematically comparing one's abilities with those of one's peers and the concept of the explicit achievement motive, as assessed by questionnaire measures or articulated directly (cf. Koestner & McClelland, 1990). Nicholls (1984a) termed this form of achievement motivation "ego involving."

DEFINITION

Ego involvement means that individuals rank their performance relative to the performance of others in order to gauge their relative position on an ability dimension. Ego involvement is intensified when it comes to demonstrating competence in socially desirable activities and gaining social recognition.

The development of a concept of ability based on self-other comparisons prompts a change in the character of achievement-motivated behavior. The focus is no longer on gradually increasing one's personal competence and mastering tasks by means of effort and persistence. Rather, it is now important to seek out information about one's abilities in social comparison and to demonstrate one's command of these abilities in competition with others (Nicholls, 1989). Studies on the development of self-evaluation in children and adolescents (Butler, 1999; Stipek & Gralinski, 1996; Stipek, Recchia & McClintic, 1992) show that the social ranking of abilities becomes the main focus of achievement behavior in

the early and middle school years. The autonomous achievement motive that developed earlier in life becomes less relevant for a while, but it does not disappear altogether. According to Veroff, the two motives can in fact be combined in an integrated system, permitting great flexibility across different situations. Butler (1999) reported that young people with this kind of fully developed self-evaluation system can gauge their abilities either with reference to their own gains in mastery or relative to the abilities of others, as the situation requires. In the following section, we will show that these two forms of self-evaluation reflect the different needs at the root of implicit and explicit motives.

SUMMARY

The motives tapped by picture-story exercises (TAT) and questionnaire measures (self-reports) do not correlate substantially, even when they relate to the same theme. This suggests that the motives captured by the TAT are either not readily accessible to introspection or that they are not easily tapped by self-report measures owing to response bias tendencies (e.g., social desirability bias). Another explanation would be that the TAT does not correlate with other motive measures simply because it is not sufficiently reliable. However, the finding that external observers also ascribe characteristics that do not tend to be associated with a specific motive (as measured by the TAT) to the behavioral expression of that motive (e.g., achievement-related characteristics in the case of the power motive) indicates that this is not the case. Overall, correlational findings suggest that motives assessed by indirect (TAT) and direct (self-report) measures have discriminant validity, meaning that they do not tap the same construct, even though the unfortunate use of identical labels would seem to indicate otherwise.

Three groups of findings provide evidence for the predictive specificity of implicit and explicit motives:

1. The two types of motives are related to different patterns of behavior. Implicit motives predict more spontaneous behavior and behavioral trends over time. Explicit motives, in contrast, have an impact on deliberate choices and conscious responses that can be intentionally attuned to the self-image.

2. Implicit and explicit motives are responsive to different types of incentives – implicit achievement motives are responsive to incentives inherent in an activity or task (difficulty and challenge); explicit achievement motives are responsive to evaluative or social incentives (competition and social recognition).

3. Evidence from developmental psychology suggests that the two types of motives emerge via different socialization experiences. Implicit motives appear to develop via preverbal experiences, whereas explicit motives are acquired somewhat later, as self-concepts become represented in the medium of language. It can be assumed that implicit achievement motives involve internal standards of excellence (competing with oneself), whereas explicit achievement motives involve normative standards of excellence (competing with others). Self-comparisons occur earlier in development than social comparisons, which may explain why the implicit achievement motive is developed earlier than the explicit achievement motive. The question of whether, when, and how the two motives are combined to form an integrated system cannot yet be answered with any certainty. Depending on the demands of the situation, young people can evaluate their abilities on the basis of either self-comparisons (gains in mastery) or social comparisons (relative ability level).

9.3 Cognitive and Affective Needs

The findings reported thus far suggest that the motives captured by the TAT are not rooted in the same needs as the motives tapped by self-report measures. Explicit motives are closely linked to self-concepts. People who describe themselves as achievement-oriented tend to have a positive image of their overall intellectual capacity. In fact, the empirical relationship between questionnaires measuring the achievement motive and self-assessments of intellectual ability is so substantial that many authors consider differences in perceived ability to be the true core of the (explicit) achievement motive (Covington & Omelich, 1979; Kukla, 1972b; Meyer, 1984a; Nicholls, 1984a; Trope, 1986c; Brunstein & Schmitt, 2004). Self-concepts of ability can affect achievement-motivated behavior in a multitude of ways. They are closely related to the anticipated probability of success, which in turn mediates their influence on personal levels of aspiration and hence task choice (Eccles & Wigfield, 2002; Wigfield & Eccles, 2000). The much cited finding that people who are confident of success tend to attribute their performance outcomes to different factors than do people who are afraid of failure also falls into place against this background (Weiner & Kukla, 1970; see also Chapter 14).

In the studies in question, participants were allocated to success- vs. failure-oriented groups based on their scores on the Mehrabian scale (MARPS). Yet responses on this scale also reflect how highly or poorly participants evaluate their abilities (Chapter 6):

- Success-oriented individuals (i.e., people with high scores on the Mehrabian scale) are confident in their capabilities. Thus, it is logical for them to attribute their successes to innate ability, but failures to a lack of effort.

- Failure-oriented individuals (i.e., people with low scores on the Mehrabian scale) are much more skeptical about their abilities relative to those of others. Accordingly, they put their failures down to a lack of ability, but attribute their successes to luck or to the ease of the task.

❶ The same pattern of results does not emerge when the TAT is used to measure the achievement motive. The reason for this is that – as McClelland had intended – the achievement motive tapped by means of the TAT method is not significantly related to the self-concept of ability (Chapter 6).

If interindividual differences in the strength of the achievement motive are reduced to differences in perceived competence or ability, one may well ask whether the concept of motives still has a meaningful part to play. Terms such as "hope for success" and "fear of failure" indicate that what we are dealing with here is not in fact the study of motives, but the analysis of expectancies. Yet the expectancy of being able – or unable – to achieve a goal should not be equated with the motive of aspiring to attain that goal. Trope's (1986c) studies on task choice provided important insights here. His data showed that achievement-motivated individuals are much keener to obtain meaningful information about their abilities than are less achievement-motivated individuals. Like Weiner and Kukla (1970), Trope used the Mehrabian scale to tap differences in the strength of the achievement motive. People scoring high on this scale evidently have a strong need to seek new information about their abilities. Following Sorrentino, Short, and Raynor (1986), these efforts can be interpreted as an expression of a **cognitive need**. In this context, the term "cognitive" means, quite literally that people strive to acquire insights into their abilities, as Festinger (1954) had postulated in his theory of social comparisons. Knowledge of one's own strengths and weaknesses is crucial, e.g., when it comes to choosing tasks or fields of activity (e.g., deciding on a career) where it is of the essence to be competent and successful (Trope, 1986c). The need for self-knowledge may at times be eclipsed by other needs that also relate to self-evaluation of one's abilities (Sedikides & Strube, 1997). For example, some authors argue that achievement-motivated individuals are more interested in demonstrating their abilities than in seeking realistic feedback (Kukla, 1972b; Sorrentino & Hewitt, 1984). The need to obtain accurate information about one's abilities (self-evaluation) does not always prevail over the need to bolster one's self-concept and thus enhance one's self-esteem. This suggests that affective processes associated with the self-esteem that people attribute to themselves are always involved in the evaluation of personal abilities.

In Heckhausen's (1975) self-evaluation model of achievement motivation (Chapter 6), self-evaluative emotions are assumed to play an important role in the self-regulation of achievement-motivated behavior. Individuals who fear failure tend to avoid challenging tasks in order to avoid thoughts and feelings that would be detrimental to their self-esteem and that would ensue from failures being attributed to lack of ability. In general, however, cognitive motivational models tend not to introduce affect until much later phases of operation. For example, in Weiner's (1986) theory of emotion affect first emerges in direct reaction to the evaluation of an outcome; only then is it further elaborated in a multistage process of causal attribution (Chapter 14).

The Function of Affect

McClelland (1987) viewed motives as **affective needs**. In his model, emotions have a dual function (see McClelland et al., 1953; Weinberger & McClelland, 1990; Schultheiss & Brunstein, 2005):

- First, affect serves to satisfy motives and to **reinforce** the behavior executed. Thus, it serves the affective reinforcement of goal-targeted behaviors (e.g., in the form of the pride experienced when a difficult task is mastered).
- Second, affect is the driving force behind motivated behavior.

Cues that previous experience has shown to be associated with the satisfaction of a motive can activate motives in anticipation, i.e., before people begin to act. They trigger affective states that then take on the form of anticipatory emotions (e.g., hope for success or the pride associated with a potential success). Anticipated affect serves to **activate** instrumental behavior. The driving force here is the prospect of effecting a change from a state of low need satisfaction to a state of higher need satisfaction. Differences in the strength of an implicit motive can thus be interpreted as differences in the individual capacity to take pleasure in the incentives present during or after an activity. This links up with Atkinson's (1957) notion that the success motive describes the ability to take pride in success.

❗ For an (implicit) motive to be activated, it is essential that the anticipatory affect be weaker than the affect experienced upon attainment of the desired goal state. There would otherwise be no reason to take action.

Thus, failure leads to the activation, and success to the satisfaction of the (implicit) achievement motive (McClelland et al., 1953; McClelland, 1985b). The tension between an unsatisfactory situation (a difficult task that cannot be solved straight away) and the anticipation of a more satisfactory state of affairs in the future (mastering the difficulty) prompts achievement-motivated individuals to intensify their efforts to achieve that goal state. But it is only when this tension is shored up by positive anticipatory emotions that it has an energizing effect on behavior (see the following example). The incentive to succeed is generated by the experience of failure itself, because individuals know from previous experience that they have the capacity to master even difficult challenges. A success attained only after repeated efforts is worth more to us than one that "comes naturally" (because the task was easy). Thus, the

striving for competence is at the very core of the achievement motive.

> **EXAMPLE**
>
> We are not proud of things that come easy to us, but of things that we work hard to achieve by means of effort, persistence, and resourcefulness. People who do not experience positive anticipatory emotions when faced with difficult tasks are less motivated to invest effort in achieving the desired goal state. For them, achievement is not a way of making the transition from subdued mood to pleasure. This may be the result of people being understretched for lengthy periods of time, or of a lack of encouragement and support being provided for those tackling achievement-related demands (e.g., when children doing their homework are not encouraged to keep trying to solve the problems themselves; Trudewind & Husarek, 1979).

As Kuhl (2001) has argued, these observations imply that achievement-motivated behavior is rooted in the inhibition of positive affect – it is only under this condition that the achievement motive takes effect (Chapter 12). A state of complacency and self-satisfaction is unlikely to activate the achievement motive. However, satisfaction and pride can function as rewards, and – if associated with the experience of attaining success through the exertion of effort – can positively reinforce achievement-motivated behavior. Thus, we come full circle: Based on this experience, positive anticipatory emotions are activated whenever individuals come up against challenges in new situations, or actively seek out such challenges themselves.

Hormonal Correlates of Motives

In his later work, McClelland moved away from the links between implicit motives and the expression of feelings such as pride (achievement), strength (power), and joy (affiliation and intimacy), and instead advocated the hypothesis that each motive is rooted in a specific hormonal process that functions to reward the preceding instrumental behavior. Studies conducted by Schultheiss into the power motive have provided particularly interesting data here (Schultheiss, Campbell, & McClelland, 1999; Schultheiss & Rohde, 2002; for an overview, see Schultheiss, 2007). Schultheiss reported that the gonadal steroid testosterone is directly related to the need for power. He set up a competition in which two respondents sitting opposite each other thought they were performing against each other. In fact, the winner and loser had already been determined by chance. Immediately after the competition, power-motivated (TAT) "winners" showed the highest increase in testosterone, as measured in saliva samples, relative to all other participants. High testosterone scores were also linked to steeper learning gains (the task involved connecting sequences of numbers). Power-motivated "winners" outperformed all other participants on this aspect, as well.

What is more, Schultheiss found that the testosterone levels of power-motivated participants increased even before the competition began. The mere idea of competing with another person and emerging victorious triggered increased testosterone production in power-motivated participants. The increase in testosterone levels observed before the competition began was much smaller than the surge shown by power-motivated participants after "winning" the competition, however. In line with previous testosterone studies (Mazur & Booth, 1998), self-attributed power motives did not predict either testosterone scores or learning gains in the studies by Schultheiss.

Research on autobiographical memories (Conway & Pleydell-Pearce, 2000) shows that implicit motives are closely related to affectively charged experiences. Findings show that when respondents are asked to describe the emotional highlights of their lives, they tend to report events that correspond with their implicit motives. Power-motivated individuals remember experiences of personal strength, whereas intimacy-motivated individuals remember experiences of interpersonal attachment (McAdams, 1982b). Explicit motives are also linked to episodic memories. Unlike implicit motives, however, they are associated with routine experiences. In her extensive studies, Woike (1995, Woike et al., 1999) found that the retrieval of memorable affective experiences was predicted by TAT motives, whereas the retrieval of memorable routine experiences was predicted by self-reported motives. Thus, people's explicit motives are not reflected in their most memorable affective experiences, but in habitual everyday activities, indicating that the motives tapped by self-report measures have much in common with the measurement of traits (Section 9.4).

SUMMARY

The findings summarized in this section suggest that affect is a key factor in the activation and satisfaction of implicit motives. Implicit motives are related to our most memorable affective experiences in life. What is more, they have neuroendocrine correlates that are assumed to reinforce the preceding instrumental behavior (e.g., testosterone in the power motive). Explicit motives, on the other hand, express cognitive needs associated with the formation and maintenance of positive and stable self-concepts, and tend to be expressed in the routines of daily life rather than in particularly memorable experiences. Weinberger and McClelland (1990) speculated that implicit motives are rooted in a system of incentives that developed relatively early in evolution, but was later supplemented and overlaid by a cognitive motivational system. The development of language, and the opportunity it affords to plan and reflect on one's behavior in view of culturally mediated rules, was decisive here. Assuming that two independent motivational systems do coexist side by side, the next question to arise is whether and how these systems coordinate and interact in the regulation of behavior.

9.4 The Interaction of Implicit and Explicit Motives

The findings reported thus far lend support to the notion that implicit and explicit motives constitute two different motivational systems that are activated by different incentives and are expressed in different types of behavior, even within the same content domain (e.g., achievement, power, or affiliation). However, this **duality hypothesis** does not rule out the possibility of the two motive types interacting and having joint effects on human behavior and experience. What evidence is there for such an **interaction hypothesis**? In this section, we first report findings on coalitions observed between implicit and explicit motives, and then move on to the conflicts that may occur between the two systems.

9.4.1 Coalitions

McClelland (1985a) and Biernat (1989) suggested that implicit and explicit motives frequently enter into productive partnerships.

❶ When working in coalition, implicit motives have an energizing function, and explicit motives a directive function in the regulation of behavior.

Implicit motives imply highly generalized preferences for certain forms of incentives that can be present in various domains of life. "Where" (i.e., in which domain) and "how" (i.e., through which behaviors) an implicit motive is expressed hinges largely on a person's conscious goals, values, and attitudes, as well as on the opportunities and constraints of their situation.

First indications that implicit and explicit motives may enter into coalitions were found in a study reported by French and Lesser (1964). The study was designed to investigate the behavioral expression of the achievement motive (as measured by the TAT) in women with a traditional role orientation and in more career-minded women. French and Lesser administered tasks tapping intellectual competence and tasks tapping social competence to both groups of women. Among career-minded women, the strength of the achievement motive predicted achievement on the intelligence tasks. Among women with a traditional role orientation, in contrast, a high achievement motive was associated with higher scores on the social competence tasks. We tend to think of the concept of achievement as being intimately bound up with the demands of academic and working life. Yet the implicit achievement motive is not restricted to school or occupational settings. Rather, it implies increasing efficiency and mastery, regardless of the skills involved. The achievement motive can thus be expressed across a broad variety of

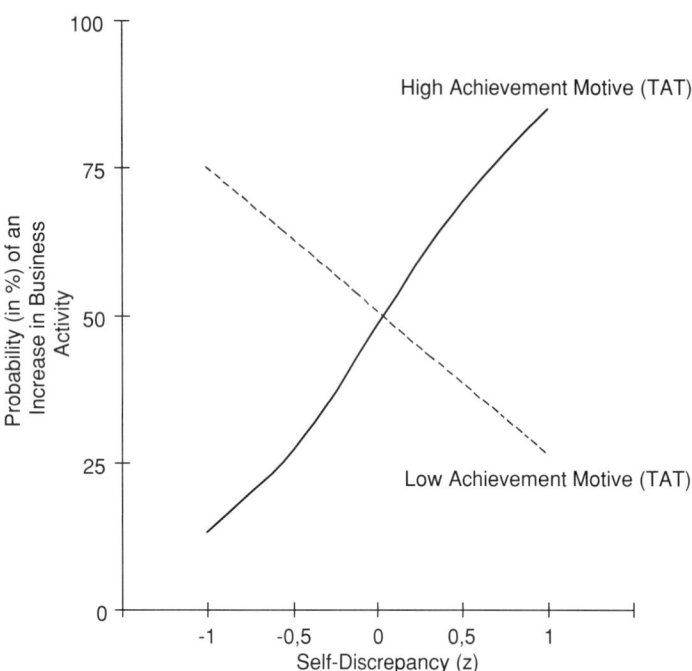

Figure 9.3 Interaction between self-discrepancy and (implicit) achievement motive (TAT) in predicting the business activity of participants in a motivation training program. (Based on Langens, 2001, p. 9.)

behavioral domains, depending on the individual's outlook on life and personal values.

Interaction effects of this kind have not only been observed in laboratory experiments, they also occur in real-life situations (Langens, 2001). In a reanalysis of data collected as part of a motivation training program for Indian businessmen, Langens analyzed how the implicit achievement motive (TAT) interacts with discrepancies between actual and ideal selves (in short: self-discrepancies). The level of business activity after the training program served as the dependent variable. Self-discrepancies (e.g., between actual and desired work-selves) did not prove to have either particularly stimulating or particularly inhibiting effects on business activity. In combination with the achievement motive, however, self-discrepancies predicted marked differences in business activity (Fig. 9.3). Participants who reported a marked discrepancy between their actual and their ideal work-selves, and were high in the achievement motive, turned out to be the most active (further evidence for the "affective shift" hypothesis outlined earlier). In the absence of this motive, a negative correlation was observed between self-discrepancies and business activity. But even a strong achievement motive did not trigger increased business activity among businessmen who were satisfied with themselves. Metaphorically speaking, self-discrepancies act like a lock channeling achievement-motivated behavior. The precondition for this happening – in addition to a high achievement motive – is that the lock gates are open (i.e., that there are

discrepancies between current states and hoped-for future selves).

9.4.2 Conflicts

Implicit and explicit motives do not always interact as harmoniously as in examples reported above. Indeed, the two types of motives can come into conflict with each other, with adverse behavioral and emotional effects. The two examples that follow illustrate this point. Using data from two longitudinal studies, Winter et al. (1998) analyzed how personality traits interact with motives in the personality development of adult women. They focused on the trait of extraversion–introversion and the motives of power and affiliation, both of which were measured by the TAT (remember that power and affiliation constitute facets of extraversion if measured with questionnaires rather than the TAT method). In line with the interaction hypothesis outlined above, Winter and associates assumed that traits determine the ways in which (implicit) motives are expressed in behavior. The criteria they assessed were significant events and outcomes in the domains of personal relationships, careers, and leisure activities. The statistical interactions between extraversion–introversion, on the one hand, and power and affiliation motives, on the other, indeed proved to be significant predictors of the life-outcome variables under investigation. The following example illustrates the research group's findings on the interactions between traits and motives.

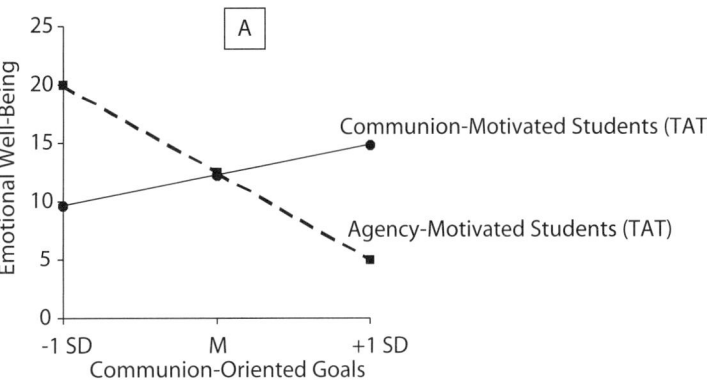

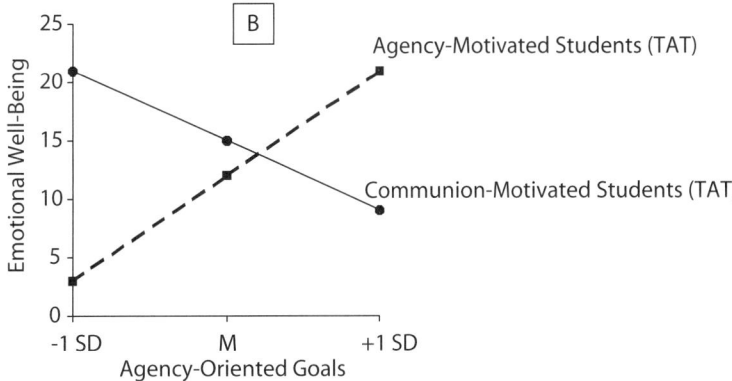

Figure 9.4a,b Emotional well-being as a function of implicit agentic motives (achievement and power) and communal motives (affiliation and intimacy) and self-reported goals in everyday life. (a) Communion-oriented goals (self-report) are associated with high emotional well-being among participants high in implicit communal motive (TAT), but with relatively low emotional well-being among those high in implicit agentic motive. (b) Agency-oriented goals (self-report) are associated with high emotional well-being among participants high in implicit agentic motive (TAT), but with relatively low emotional well-being among those high in implicit communal motive (TAT). (Based on Brunstein et al., 1995, p. 7.)

EXAMPLE

Winter et al. (1998) found that extraverted women high in the power motive had careers associated with high levels of social impact and prestige. They attached great importance to maintaining social relationships at work. Extraverted women high in the affiliation motive, in contrast, were characterized by having achieved satisfying intimate relationships and by involvement in volunteer work. The picture to emerge for introverted women was a different one entirely. For them, the power motive was not linked to having a prestigious career, nor was the affiliation motive associated with the development of satisfying relationships. On the contrary, marital problems and divorces were particularly common among introverted women who were high in the affiliation motive. Relative to extraverted women, it seems to be much more difficult and conflicted for introverted women to express their social needs in interpersonal relationships. Indeed, it is only logical that a person who would rather be alone than with others will find it difficult to fulfill their latent need for close relationships. Yet shy and withdrawn individuals can have a strong need for interpersonal attachment, as illustrated by the findings of Winter and colleagues. The same holds for introverted individuals who crave social recognition. In other words, whether and in what way a motive is expressed in behavior hinges on the personality traits that distinguish a person's actions, thoughts, and feelings.

To summarize, the findings presented by Winter et al. demonstrate that more precise – and arguably more interesting – predictions can be made about social behavior when a combination of different personality characteristics (here: traits and motives) is taken into account than when just only one kind of personality variable is examined.

Incongruence between implicit motives and explicit life goals can trigger emotional problems, as shown by studies conducted into the emotional well-being of students by Brunstein et al. (1995); Brunstein, Schultheiss, & Grässmann, 1998; for an overview, see Brunstein, Schultheiss, & Maier, 1999). In these studies, the participants reported their current agentic (achievement and power) and communal (affiliation and intimacy) goals representing the consciously accessible and personally meaningful objectives, purposes, and projects they were striving for and sought to attain in their present life situation (see also Austin & Vancouver, 1996; Little, 1983; Pervin, 1989). At the same time, the strength of their implicit agentic and communal motives was assessed using the TAT. The participants rated their emotional well-being on scales of positive and negative mood in everyday life, with ratings being taken regularly over a period of several weeks to months. The results can be summarized as follows (Fig. 9.4): The more strongly committed students were to goals that corresponded with their motives (i.e., agency-motivated students to agentic goals and communion-motivated students to communal goals), the higher their emotional well-being. Conversely, participants who were committed to goals that were ill-suited to satisfying their implicit motives or were even in direct opposition to these motives (i.e., communion-motivated students pursuing agentic goals or agency-motivated students pursuing communal goals) reported a marked decrease in positive affect and a corresponding increase in negative affect in everyday life. Even when participants succeeded in realizing goals that did not correspond with their implicit motives, this was not reflected in an increase in emotional well-being. In fact, successes of this kind must be considered Pyrrhic victories: The more intensely participants focused on achieving goals that were incongruent with their needs, the more they neglected other goals that would have been better suited to satisfying their motives (Brunstein, Schultheiss, & Grässmann, 1998).

Winter (1996) distinguishes two kinds of discrepancies that may arise between implicit and explicit motivational tendencies:

- First, a person might set a goal that is not backed up by a corresponding motive (e.g., a career goal despite a weak achievement or power motive).
- Second, achieving a personal goal might come into direct conflict with satisfying a motive in another domain (e.g., forming a harmonious relationship despite a strong need for social impact).

Given discrepancies of this kind, it is all the more important for strategies of self-control to be applied in goal-attainment settings (Kuhl, 2001; Sokolowski, 1993; see also Chapter 12). The first kind of discrepancy may make it necessary to boost the incentive value of a goal that is not very attractive in its own right (e.g., by visualizing the likely positive and negative outcomes of attaining – or failing to attain – that goal). The second kind of discrepancy may make it necessary to control impulses emanating from a latent motive that impede the realization of consciously selected goals, values, and norms (e.g., suppressing one's need for social recognition in order to comply with the value of social equality). However, behavioral regulation of this kind is steered by volitional control rather than emotional preferences, and thus requires effort and mental resources that, to use the analogy introduced by Muraven and Baumeister (2000), resemble a muscle that can become fatigued to the point of exhaustion by constant exertion. Volitional self-control may be indispensable for adaptive behavior, but it can have adverse effects on mental health if accompanied by long-term conflict and stress (Kuhl, 2001). In a study with managers, Kehr (2004a) showed that chronic discrepancies between implicit and explicit motives are associated with the risk of volitional depletion or exhaustion, one effect being reduced well-being.

9.4.3 Harmonization of Implicit and Explicit Motives

The notion that implicit and explicit motives often exist side by side, but that discrepancies between the two types of motives can lead to problems of adaptation raises two further questions:

1. How do people whose implicit and explicit motives are compatible differ from people whose implicit and explicit motives are less well attuned?

2. What can be done to reduce or bridge the gap between implicit and explicit motives?

Both of these questions have been addressed in studies with a primary focus on goal setting in everyday life. To answer the first question, we need to identify personality characteristics that moderate the relationship between implicit motives and explicit goals. The finding that the relationship between implicit motives (TAT) and explicitly stated goals (self-reports) tends not to be significant only really indicates that, although some people commit to need-incongruent goals, there are others whose goals do correspond with their motives. In accordance with their function in statistical analysis, variables that allow these two groups of people to be distinguished are known as **moderators**.

Brunstein (2001) reported that the dispositions of action vs. state orientation (Chapter 12) as described by Kuhl (1983; Kuhl & Beckmann, 1994a) fulfill this kind of moderating function when people formulate goals. They influence the extent to which people commit to motive-congruent goals and reject goals that clash with their inner needs. Specifically, Brunstein's findings were as follows (Fig. 9.5): Action-oriented individuals tended to pursue goals that conformed to their implicit motives. Those of them high in agentic motive were engaged in numerous goals relating to the desire for achievement and power, while those of them high in communal motive tended to select goals involving social contact and interpersonal relations. State-oriented individuals, on the other hand, were more likely to be engaged in goals that deviated from or directly contradicted their implicit motives.

Kuhl (2001, pp. 277ff.) interprets these findings as indicating that action-oriented individuals are able to "tone down" negative emotions, such as those caused by everyday frustrations, relatively quickly. They are, to a certain extent, specialized in transforming states of tension into states of relaxation. According to Kuhl, it is only if people are relaxed when formulating goals that they are able to access memory systems (extension memory) in which their affective preferences are stored in the form of wide-ranging associations (or networks) between actions and emotions. State-oriented individuals are often denied access to precisely these systems. Even the slightest setback seems to provoke long fits of brooding in these individuals, meaning that negative affect persists over extended periods. Because people in a state of ongoing tension are not able to examine their emotional preferences

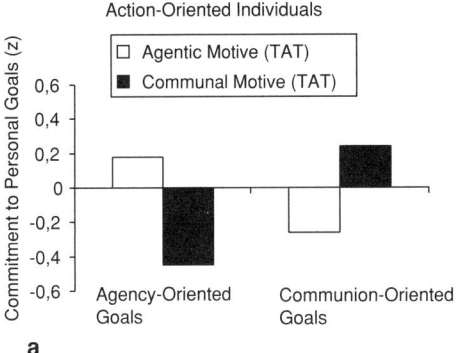

Action-Oriented Individuals

a

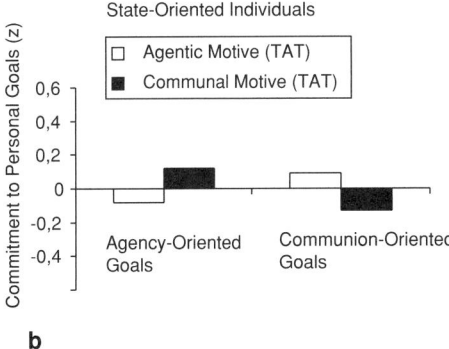

State-Oriented Individuals

b

Figure 9.5 Correspondence between implicit motives (TAT) and the commitment to personal goals (self-report) as a function of action control dispositions. (a) Action-oriented individuals commit more strongly to goals that correspond with their implicit motives. (b) Among state-oriented individuals, there is no systematic relationship between goal commitment and the dominant motive. (Based on Brunstein, 2001, p. 8.)

and select courses of action accordingly, their implicit motives thus have little influence on the goals they select. The upshot of this is that state-oriented individuals tend to adopt goals without sufficient reflection or, paradoxically, to interpret these goals as being self-formulated – without actually having checked that the goals are compatible with their inner needs (Baumann & Kuhl, 2003; Kuhl & Kazén, 1994). Once they have committed themselves, however, state-oriented individuals tend to find it difficult to abandon a goal – even if it contributes little to their quality of life (Maier & Brunstein, 1999).

This interpretation is in line with findings reported by Thrash and Elliot (2002), who found that students high in self-determination showed a high degree of concordance between implicit (TAT) and explicit (self-report) achievement motives. For students who were prone to yield to social pressures, in contrast, they found marked discrepancies between the implicit achievement motive (TAT) and the level of self-attributed achievement orientation (questionnaire).

To answer the second of the questions formulated above, we need to identify processes that act as mediators, increas-

ing the congruence between conscious goals and implicit motives. Schultheiss and Brunstein (1999) reported that **goal imagery** serves this kind of mediating function.

DEFINITION
Goal imagery can be defined as the perception-like mental simulation of the pursuit and attainment of a potential goal.

Goal imagery occurs even before an individual has committed to a particular goal (see the following study). It simulates a course of action, is rich in sensory details and affective experiences, and involves the direct experience of one's (imagined) behavior (e.g., the feelings that occur when engaged in the respective behavior). To use Epstein's (1994) terminology, goal imagery is an experiential form of information processing, to be distinguished from the rational processing of symbolic and linguistic information.

Experiential means that information is processed quickly and intuitively, with people being guided by their previous affective experiences. Rational, on the other hand, means that information is processed analytically, and usually involves conscious deliberation and considered judgments.

STUDY

Study on Goal Imagery
Schultheiss and Brunstein (1999) assumed that the functioning of implicit motives is much better suited to an experiential than to a rational form of information processing (for a detailed account of this model, see Schultheiss, 2001b). Therefore, they hypothesized that implicit motives can only affect the formulation of intentions if a goal is translated from its original format in the medium of language to the experiential format. Goal imagery is ideally suited to this translative function, as Schultheiss and Brunstein (1999) found in two studies. After exploring a specific goal and the actions associated with it in a goal-imagery exercise, participants only felt committed to the goal if it corresponded with their implicit motives (TAT). Without goal imagery, no systematic relationship was observed between participants' implicit motives and their goal commitment. Furthermore, it emerged that participants in the goal-imagery group were more likely to achieve the respective goal than participants who had not engaged in the goal-imagery exercise. Langens (2002) corroborated this finding in a field study that examined the effects of daydreams on the attainment of personal goals. Daydreams led to the "revitalization of goal incentives" in achievement-motivated individuals, with positive effects on the execution of goal-directed behavior.

Goal imagery leads to the activation of implicit motives in the context under consideration. This puts people in a better position to decide whether the goal in question corresponds with their needs – or contradicts them. Moreover, goals can be attained much more effectively if they are backed up by corresponding motives (Kehr, 2004b), on the condition that people are able to visualize clearly and vividly what pursuing and attaining a specific goal will mean to them emotionally.

SUMMARY

Explicit preferences, traits, role images, and values influence the way that motives are expressed in behavior. Certain combinations, such as high extraversion in conjunction with power and affiliation motives, facilitate the satisfaction of implicit motives, whereas other combinations make it harder for implicit motives to be satisfied (e.g., high introversion in conjunction with power and affiliation motives). Discrepancies between implicit and explicit motives in the same behavioral domain can have two kinds of adverse effects:

1. Motivational conflicts can occur, resulting in emotional strain.

2. There is a need for increased self-control (suppression of impulses or intensification of incentives), the effects of which are limited if attempts to harmonize the two types of motives do not succeed. It seems that (action-oriented) individuals with well-honed self-regulatory skills are best equipped in this respect. On the other hand, it is conceivable that the formulation of need-congruent goals is conducive to action-oriented behavioral styles, whereas chronic discrepancies between implicit motives and explicit goals lead to the depletion and eventually exhaustion of volitional resources.

A self-determined approach to goal selection and the ability to visualize the emotional implications of one's future actions are two examples of ways in which explicit goals can be harmonized with implicit motives.

9.5 Theoretical and Practical Implications of the Concept of Dual Motives

---

The data presented in this chapter confirm that there is solid empirical support for McClelland's notion of distinguishing implicit from explicit motives. The two types of motives are associated with specific and distinct behavioral characteristics. They respond to different kinds of incentives and reflect different types of needs. It can also be assumed that the two motive types are influenced by different child-rearing practices, operational in different stages of development. McClelland's **model of dual motives** has already led to more insightful interpretations of empirical findings in the field of motivation psychology. However, it is important not to forget that McClelland's analysis is a post hoc interpretation of studies, few of which were designed to differentiate implicit from explicit motives. In fact, the two motive types have rarely been assessed in the same study, let alone in the same sample.

McClelland's conceptualization has also inspired further research, however. Not only have these studies analyzed the specific effects of the two motive types, they have also explored forms of their interaction. Findings have shown that high levels of coherence between implicit and explicit motives are associated with greater efficiency and adaptiveness, whereas conflicts between implicit and explicit motives have adverse effects on action and are related to lower levels of well-being. What conclusions can be drawn from McClelland's conceptualization for future research in the field of motivational psychology? The following three points are worth considering:

1. First, a new generation of theories might be developed. While it will remain important to analyze the functioning of implicit and explicit motives accurately and thoroughly, new questions will also have to be addressed:

■ How are implicit and explicit motives coordinated in behavioral regulation?

■ How are conflicts between implicit and explicit motives resolved?

■ What kinds of developmental conditions are conducive for the two types of motives being combined in a single harmonious system?

■ Is it possible to differentiate implicit from explicit anxieties and fears in the domain of avoidance motives (e.g., fear of failure)?

Questions such as these can only be answered once multisystemic theories of motivation have been developed, making predictions not only about subsystems, but also about the interplay between them (Brunstein, Maier, & Schultheiss, 1999). Although personality psychology is traditionally tasked with investigating the mental structures driving our actions, including the dynamic and conflicted strivings within these structures (Allport, 1937; Murray, 1938), there is still a dearth of such theories (cf. Buck, 1985; Kehr, 2004b; Kuhl, 2001; Schultheiss, 2001b).

2. In the same vein, it will be important to step up multivariate research approaches in the field of motivational psychology (Brunstein & Maier, 2005; Brunstein, Schultheiss, & Maier, 1999; Cooper, 1983; McClelland, 1985a, b; Winter, 1996). It is only possible to gain insights into dissociations, or indeed potential forms of interaction, between motives if different methods of measuring motives are implemented and different behavioral characteristics are assessed in one and the same study. Motive-activating incentives must also be taken into account in empirical studies (Bornstein, 2002; Rheinberg, 1989; see also Chapter 13). Only when these preconditions are met will it be possible for the particularities of implicit and explicit motives, including the interplay between them, to be systematically investigated and clearly understood, rather than the individual findings of diverse studies being seen very much in isolation.

3. The practical implications of McClelland's conceptualization are clearly apparent. If people have dual motives within a single behavioral domain, it should be possible to

analyze conflicts not only within, but also between motivational systems (e.g., between implicit motives, on the one hand, and explicit goals and motivational self-images, on the other), as well as the resulting problems of adaptation. The ability to attune self-generated goals to both external demands and internal needs is an important precondition for motivational maturity and high levels of adaptability (Brunstein & Maier, 2001; Schultheiss & Brunstein, 2005). As noted by Rheinberg (2002a), this prompts the question of which motivational competences (or meta-motivational skills) serve to foster this ability. Rheinberg's question not only targets basic research, it also entails an important challenge for applied motivational psychology (e.g., in terms of how these competences can be nurtured and taught).

4. Finally, McClelland's conceptualization raises methodological questions. For 50 years now, research into implicit motives has been based primarily on the methods of the TAT and the measures that have been derived from the TAT procedure (Chapter 6). Innovation in empirical research is dependent on progress being made in the way psychological constructs are measured. Which trends can be seen to emerge here? In recent years, objective tests and experimental procedures based on reaction times have become increasingly widespread in research seeking to analyze motivational processes, particularly in studies that have compared the behavioral effects of TAT motives with those of priming methods (Bargh & Barndollar, 1996; Weinberger & Silverman,1987; Zurbriggen, 2000). The parallels observed between the effects of the two methods are further evidence for the view that enduring motives, like motivational states activated for a short time only, can influence behavior without conscious control (Bargh & Gollwitzer, 1994). Priming methods have proved ill-suited to assessing individual differences in motivational preferences, however. For one thing, their effects are too short lived, compared with the long-term effects of motives (Bargh & Barndollar, 1996). For another thing, priming effects are much less reliable than even the TAT (Banse, 2001). A chronometric test that Greenwald, McGhee, and Schwarz (1998) have developed to tap implicit attitudes and self-concepts offers a possible solution to this problem. Their Implicit Association Test (IAT) is both reliable and parsimonious. Like the motives tapped by the TAT, the social attitudes and self-related cognitions (e.g., self-esteem) measured by the IAT show only moderate correlations with self-report measures (Greenwald et al., 2002). Brunstein and Schmitt (2004) have adapted this method to assess automatic associations between achievement-related attributes (e.g., ambitious, competent) and a person's self, and found that the ensuing test scores explained the intensity with which respondents tackled an achievement task. Egloff and Schmukle (2002) have developed a similar method to assess implicit anxiety. The consider-

able efforts currently being undertaken to find ways of measuring attitudes, self-concepts, and motives that are not easily accessible to introspection (Fazio & Olson, 2003; Wilson, Lindsey, & Schooler 2000) can be expected to have inspiring and stimulating effects on future motivational research.

REVIEW QUESTIONS

1. **Which findings lend support to the assumption that implicit and explicit motives are two different constructs?**

McClelland, Koestner, & Weinberger (1989) present four groups of findings:

Measurements of the two types of motives are statistically independent of each other. The correlations between direct (questionnaire) and indirect (TAT) methods of measuring nominally similar motives do not differ significantly from zero.

The two types of motives predict different classes of behavior. Implicit motives predict spontaneous, unprompted behavior and long-term behavioral trends (e.g., investing more effort in difficult tasks; the frequency of engaging in social contact with others in everyday life). Explicit motives predict behavior that is subject to volitional control and that corresponds with the self-concept (e.g., deliberate decisions and considered appraisals).

The two types of motives are activated by different incentives. Implicit motives are activated by incentives inherent in the activity or task itself (e.g., difficulty and novelty in the case of the achievement motive). Explicit motives are activated by social incentives and implications (e.g., the recognition and appreciation of an achievement).

Implicit motives develop via early, affectively charged learning experiences (e.g., increasing mastery of a task; unhindered experience of social efficacy), whereas explicit motives are not developed until later in life, usually hand in hand with the development of self-concepts represented in the medium of language.

2. **Outline an experimental design to test the results of Spangler's meta-analysis. Which factors would have to be varied systematically?**

Three factors would have to be accounted for:

the method used to measure the achievement motive (operant vs. respondent);

the type of behavioral criterion (spontaneous behavior vs. behavior that is under volitional control);

the type of achievement incentive (activity incentives vs. social incentives).

3. **Explain the concept of "affective" needs with reference to the implicit achievement motive.**

The activation of the implicit achievement motive is tied up with anticipatory emotions (hope or fear). These anticipate the self-evaluative emotions (pride or shame) experienced upon reaching the desired goal state (or failing to reach it) and are the driving force behind the behavior instrumental in attaining a goal. The achievement motive specializes in change of affect. It is activated by the prospect of converting an unsatisfactory situation (difficulty mastering a task) into an emotionally more satisfactory one (mastering a difficult task). This is where effort and persistence come in. If the efforts are successful, they are rewarded by satisfaction and pride.

4. **French and Lesser (1964) found that the behavioral expression of the achievement motive is influenced by people's role images. How might the power motive interact with prosocial value orientations?**

Social responsibility might be assessed as a value orientation alongside the power motive (cf. Winter & Barenbaum, 1985). In conjunction with high social responsibility, we can expect the power motive to be associated with prosocial and generative behavior (e.g., involvement in human rights organizations; willingness to assume management duties in groups; support for weaker members of society; choice of a teaching career). In conjunction with low social responsibility, we can expect the power motive to be expressed in egocentric and socially unacceptable behaviors (criminality; physical conflicts; impulsive and inconsiderate behavior toward others; risk-taking behavior in traffic; promiscuity and sexual possessiveness).

5. **Which personality traits have an impact on the extent to which people commit to goals that correspond with their implicit motives?**

High levels of self-determination make it more likely that people will choose goals that are congruent with their needs, and protect them from rashly adopting goals that reflect the interests of others rather than their own needs. The ability to "tone down" negative affect and thus gain access to the affectively charged networks in which one's preferences are stored. This ability is more pronounced in action-oriented than in state-oriented individuals (Chapter 12). Action-oriented individuals are better able to purge their thoughts of the negative consequences of stressful and worrying events.

6. **Schultheiss and Brunstein (1999) reported that goal imagery leads to higher congruence between implicit motives and the goals pursued. What other methods or interventions might help to harmonize implicit and explicit motives? Give examples and explain how they work.**

Possible examples include:

social assertiveness training (to reject goals induced by others);

fantasizing about one's wishes and desires (to explore one's action preferences);

acquiring the necessary skills to self-regulate emotional well-being (and reduce the negative affective states that block access to implicit motives).

10 Biopsychological Aspects of Motivation[1]

O. C. Schultheiss and M. M. Wirth

10.1 A Primer on Biopsychology and Its Methods

DEFINITION

As a discipline, biopsychology aims to explain experience and behavior based on how the brain and the rest of the central nervous system work. Biopsychological approaches to motivation, then, seek to explain motivational phenomena based on an understanding of specific functions of the brain. Most research in this area uses mammalian animal models, such as rats, mice, and sometimes primates, on the assumption that the way motivational processes and functions are carried out by the brain is highly similar across related species, and that findings obtained in other mammals will therefore also hold for humans.

When studying motivational processes, biopsychologists often use lesioning (i.e., selective damaging) techniques to explore the contributions of specific brain areas or endocrine glands to motivational behavior, reasoning that if destroying a specific brain area or gland alters a motivational function, then the lesioned substrate must be involved in that function. Other techniques often utilized in this type of research include direct recordings from neuron assemblies in the behaving animal to determine, for instance, which brain cells fire in response to a reward, and brain dialysis, which allows the researcher to examine how much of a neurotransmitter is released in a behaving animal in response to motivationally relevant stimuli. Finally, biopsychologists frequently use pharmacological techniques; for instance, to increase synaptic activity associated with a specific neurotransmitter by administering a transmitter agonist (which mimics the action of the neurotransmitter) or to decrease synaptic activity by administering a transmitter antagonist (which blocks neurotransmitter activity). This is often done locally in the brain, allowing the researcher to determine the contribution of specific neurotransmitter systems to a function subserved by a circumscribed brain area. These methods are often combined with one another, and they are almost always used in combination with behavioral or learning paradigms designed to reveal the contribution of a brain area, neurotransmitter, or hormone to specific aspects of motivation (e.g., instrumental learning, responding to reward).

One major advantage of the biopsychological approach to motivation is that it can go beyond the circular explanations of motivation that often arise when only behavioral measures are used to infer the causal effects of motivation. For instance, the observation of aggressive behavior (the explanandum) might be explained by the presumed existence of an underlying aggression drive (the explanans), which is in turn inferred from the observation of aggressive behavior. As

[1] Preparation of this chapter was aided by NSF grant BCS 0444301. We wish to thank Jill Becker and Joachim Brunstein for helpful comments and suggestions on a draft of this chapter.

long as there is no independent means of assessing the presumed aggression drive, the explanation for aggressive behavior will remain circular (e.g., "Why is he shouting at Mary?" "Because he has a strong aggressive disposition." "How do you know that?" "Because he's shouting at Mary."). In contrast to purely behavioral accounts of motivation, biopsychologists would argue that activity in certain brain regions or the release of certain transmitters and hormones, in interaction with environmental cues, precedes or causes aggressive behavior, thus separating the explanandum from the explanans. One very successful account of aggressive behavior, Wingfield's challenge hypothesis (Wingfield, Hegner, Dufty, & Ball, 1990), holds that increased levels of testosterone predispose animals to assert their dominance, but only if their dominance is challenged by competitors and in certain situational contexts, such as breeding seasons. Clearly, the explanans here (testosterone) is not only more specific and concrete than a postulated "aggression drive," it is also distinct from the explanandum (aggressive or dominant behavior), and its causal relationship to the explanandum can be studied empirically by, for instance, removing the animal's gonads, administering testosterone, or a combination thereof.

What animal models of motivated behavior can not reveal, however, is the relationship between the brain and the subjective states that accompany and characterize some aspects of motivation. Animal research is therefore increasingly complemented by studies on humans that allow researchers to relate measures of brain activity or physiological changes to both behavior and subjective states. With the advent of sophisticated brain imaging methods, such as functional magnetic resonance imaging (fMRI), that provide relatively high temporal and spatial resolution in assessments of the active human brain, biopsychological research on motivational and emotional processes has both experienced an unprecedented growth spurt and undergone a remarkable transformation, resulting in the new and burgeoning field of affective neuroscience (Panksepp, 1998).

In the present chapter, we will review the current status of biopsychological research, focusing on the key brain systems and processes that have been found to mediate motivational phenomena in studies on animals and humans. Our aim is to provide the reader with an overview of the key substrates of motivation and emotion and to highlight some important recent findings and developments in the field. For more comprehensive and detailed accounts of the biopsychology of motivation, we refer the reader to the excellent books by LeDoux (2002), Panksepp (1998), Rolls (1999), and Toates (1986).

10.2 Hallmarks of Motivation

To make sense of biopsychology's contributions to the understanding of motivation, we feel it is important to first provide an overview of the core phenomena and processes of motivation on which biopsychologists tend to focus. This will equip us with the proper conceptual framework to understand biopsychological contributions to the science of motivation. We will therefore outline what biopsychologists consider to be the hallmarks of motivation in this section, before moving on to describe the key brain structures and processes involved in motivation in Section 10.3.

10.2.1 Motivated Behavior Comes in Two Basic Flavors: Approach and Avoidance Motivation

The first key characteristic of motivated behavior is that it can be aimed either at attaining a pleasurable incentive (reward) or at avoiding an aversive disincentive (punishment). This hallmark of motivation has assumed a central role in the conceptual frameworks proposed by major motivation theorists (e.g., Atkinson, 1957; Carver & Scheier, 1998; Craig, 1918; Gray, 1971; Mowrer, 1960; Schneirla, 1959) and is today an important and active area of research in biopsychology and the affective neurosciences. While an organism in the approach motivation mode works to decrease the distance from a desired goal object (e.g., prey, a food pellet, or a good exam grade) until that object is attained, an organism in the avoidance motivation mode seeks to increase the distance from an aversive goal object or state (e.g., a predator, starvation, or a bad exam grade). Avoidance of a disincentive may take two fundamentally different forms: active avoidance or passive avoidance.

Active avoidance characterizes the behavioral strategy of actively executing behavior that is instrumental in distancing the individual from the disincentive. This behavior can be as simple as fleeing from a dangerous object or as complex as spending a great deal of time studying for a biochemistry exam in order to avoid a bad grade. Some theorists have posited that avoidance motivation is a particularly inefficient form of motivation, because the individual can never be quite sure how far is far enough (Carver & Scheier, 1998). Approach motivation terminates upon contact with the goal object or state, but when does avoidance motivation stop? When a predator is 100 yards away? When it is out of sight? But if the predator is out of sight, how can the organism be sure that it is far enough away? In other words, it could be argued that avoidance motivation is problematic; first, because, it requires the presence of the disincentive as a reference point, enabling the organism to gauge its spatial or psychological distance to the aversive object or state, and, second, because there is no clear-cut criterion of when that distance is far enough for the organism to terminate behavior aimed at avoiding the feared goal object or state.

Based on earlier work by Mowrer (1960), Gray (1971) proposed that one way out of the active avoidance dilemma would be to conceive of objects or places that have been associated with nonpunishment during past learning episodes as safety signals with actual reward value. In other words, instead of running away from a feared object, the individual reframes the situation and, in a sense, switches from avoidance to approach motivation by reorienting his or her behavior with reference to a safe and thus rewarding object or place. This also solves the problem of how far away the individual needs to be from the aversive object in order to feel safe: as soon as the safety object or place is reached, the motivational episode ends.

EXAMPLE

A classic study by Solomon and Wynne (1953) illustrates this switch from avoidance of danger to approach to safety. Solomon and Wynne trained dogs to jump from one compartment of a box to another as soon as a stimulus signaling impending foot shock appeared. Remarkably, most dogs not only learned to avoid the shock by jumping to the safe compartment within very few trials, they were also amazingly resistant to extinction: some continued to jump to the safe compartment upon presentation of the warning signal for more than 600 trials! Equally remarkably, they soon ceased to show any sign of fear once they had learned how to cope with the threat of shock.

The other mode of avoidance motivation is **passive avoidance**. The following are all examples of this behavioral manifestation of motivation: an animal ceasing all foraging behavior and keeping very still when it spots a predator; a rat that learns to stop bar-pressing in the presence of specific discriminatory stimuli, because bar-pressing then reliably produces foot shock; and a student refraining from participating in a class discussion in order not to be ridiculed for saying something stupid. The fundamental difference between passive avoidance, on the one hand, and active avoidance or approach, on the other, is that the former involves the **inhibition** of behavior in order to avoid a certain goal state or object, whereas the latter entails the **execution** of behavior in order to avoid or attain something. Thus, active and passive avoidance represent behaviorally very different solutions for dealing with the same problem, namely, avoiding a punishment.

10.2.2 Motivation Consists of Two Distinct Phases

Biopsychological studies strongly support the view that motivation consists of relatively distinct segments or phases that serve different functions. Most theorists agree that the motivational process features at least two consecutive elements: a **motivation phase** during which the organism works to attain a reward or to avoid a punishment and a **consummation phase** during which the outcome is evaluated – i.e., during which the organism consummates the act and determines the "goodness" of the reward or assesses whether a danger or punishment has been successfully avoided (e.g., Berridge,

1996; Craig, 1918). Thus, an animal may become motivated to eat either because it sees a tasty morsel or because its hunger indicates a state of nutrient depletion (or a combination of the two), and start working toward the goal of obtaining food. The motivation phase can be as simple as taking a few steps toward a food trough and starting to eat or as complex as hunting down an elusive prey in the jungle. Note also that the motivation phase is characterized by observable behaviors (instrumental activity to attain a reward or avoid a punishment) and an affective-motivational state, which in humans can be characterized subjectively by such terms as craving, longing, or being attracted to (or repelled by) the goal object, but in animals can only be inferred from behavior. Berridge (1996) has labeled this phase of the motivational sequence **wanting**, and differentiates it from **liking**, i.e., the evaluation of the hedonic qualities of the reward (or punishment) accompanying the consummation of an incentive.

While most people intuitively assume that you want what you like and vice versa, research indicates that the two phases of motivation are in fact dissociable. For instance, drug addicts feel compelled to take "their" drug, even though there is no longer any pleasure in taking it (wanting without liking; cf. Robinson & Berridge, 2000). Conversely, people subjectively and objectively respond to tasty food with signs of liking, regardless of whether they are hungry or have just eaten a big meal – thus, liking can remain constant despite strong differences in wanting (Epstein, Truesdale, Wojcik, Paluch, & Raynor, 2003). As we will see later, the two phases of motivation are also associated with distinct brain systems.

10.2.3 Many Qualitatively Different Types of Rewards Can Stimulate Motivation

Many different types of rewards (or punishments) can stimulate motivated behavior, and what motivates behavior can vary both across individuals and within an individual across time. Learning psychologists often conceive of rewards as unconditioned stimuli toward which all Pavlovian and instrumental learning is ultimately directed. Types of reward and the associated motivational systems that have enjoyed a long history of research in biopsychology include food in the case of feeding and hunger motivation, water in the case of thirst, orgasm in the case of sexual motivation, social closeness in the case of affiliation motivation, and being on top of the social hierarchy in the case of dominance motivation. Social and personality psychologists, who study humans rather than animals, would add achievement motivation, in which mastery experiences are rewarding; intimacy, in which deepening one's relationship to a specific other is rewarding; and power motivation, in which having an impact on others is experienced as rewarding (similar to, albeit more subtle than, the dominance motivation studied in animals). Another fundamental motivational system, curiosity or exploration, does not seem to be associated with a specific reward, with the possible exception of the discovery of any kind of new and pleasurable unconditioned stimulus. Some of these rewards can be differentiated into several kinds of specific rewards. For instance, research on hunger and feeding reveals that the amounts of protein, fat, or carbohydrates contained in food all represent distinct kinds of rewards to which organisms are differentially sensitive, depending on the kind of nutrient they most urgently need.

While these are all very different kinds of rewards, fulfilling a variety of functions related to the organism's individual and genetic survival, they are also similar in the sense that animals (including humans) want them, feel compelled to attain them repeatedly, and will show invigorated responding in situations in which their behavior could lead to the attainment of a reward. Whether an individual feels more or less wanting for a given reward depends, of course, on his or her need state (e.g., how long has it been since he or she last ate?), as well as on his or her liking of that reward or, in the parlance of human motivational psychology, on whether the individual has a **motive** for attaining a given reward (McClelland, 1987). The more he or she responds with pleasure to obtaining the reward, the stronger the motive to seek it out in the future.

10.2.4 Motivation is Dynamic

Another key feature of motivation emerges from the interplay of wanting and liking, namely, that motivation is a dynamic process. For instance, even the most dedicated glutton will not spend all available time eating, but will switch to the pursuit of a different kind of reward once he or she has eaten to satiety. However, because the glutton enjoys food so much (high liking for the reward), he or she will sooner become motivated to eat again and will thus eat with greater frequency or intensity than a person who takes little pleasure in the reward of tasty food. Moreover, the degree of liking for one and the same reward can change as a function of how much of that reward an individual has already consumed. One piece of chocolate can be quite tasty and rewarding. But even a chocoholic is likely to experience nausea and disgust if forced to eat two pounds of the stuff at once. Cabanac (1971) termed this changing subjective evaluation of the same reward over time **alliesthesia**. This phenomenon is assumed to track the usefulness of a given reward as a function of the changing needs of the organism. Clearly, food is highly useful, and thus very pleasant, for a semistarved individual, but becomes less useful, and thus less pleasant, for someone who has already eaten to satiety.

Thus, motivation for a particular type of reward waxes and wanes, depending on the recency of reward consumption, on the degree to which the reward is experienced as pleasurable, and on other factors, such as the presence or absence of cues in the environment that predict the availability of a particular reward or the strength of competing motivational tendencies. The dynamic nature of motivation, which can even be mathematically modeled (cf. Atkinson & Birch, 1970),

is clear to anyone who studies motivation through observation in humans and other animals, but has frequently been overlooked by personality trait researchers, who emphasize the consistency of behavior over time (for a discussion of this issue, see Atkinson, 1981).

10.2.5 Motivation Can Be Need Driven, Incentive Driven, or Both

Obviously, motivation is often triggered by the physiological needs of the organism. Falling nutrient levels induce hunger; increasing blood saltiness induces thirst. As a consequence, we seek food or drink to quench the need. Somewhat less obviously, however, motivation can also be triggered solely by cues in the environment. These motivation-arousing cues are called **incentives**, and a good illustration of incentive motivation is the salted-peanut phenomenon. Imagine you are sitting in front of the TV after a good, filling dinner. Next to you, there is a bowl of salted peanuts. You are actually full, but why not try one? After you have eaten one and found it quite tasty, your hand goes back to the bowl for more, and half an hour later, you have eaten the entire contents of the bowl, even though you were not at all hungry! In this case, it was something rewarding about the peanuts themselves that made you eat them, rather than an unsatisfied physiological need for nutrients. Thus, how pleasurable a reward is depends not only on our need state, but also on the nature or quality of the reward itself. An enticing reward can sometimes motivate us, even when we are not experiencing any need at all.

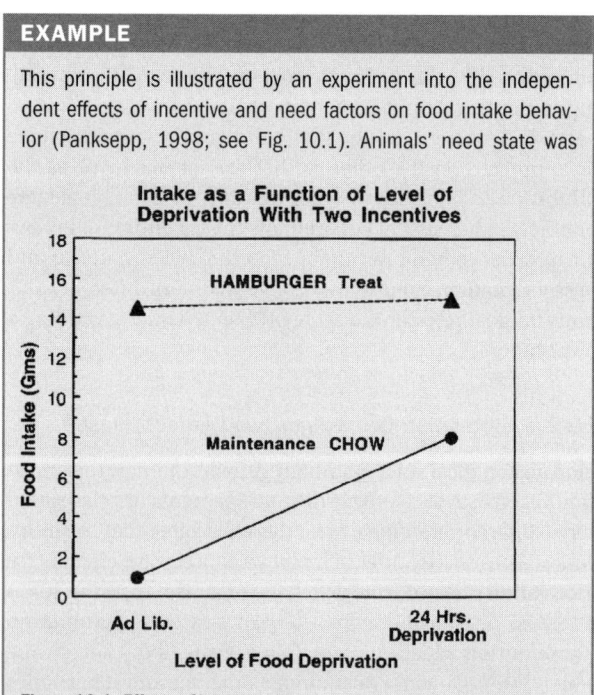

EXAMPLE

This principle is illustrated by an experiment into the independent effects of incentive and need factors on food intake behavior (Panksepp, 1998; see Fig. 10.1). Animals' need state was

Figure 10.1 Effects of incentive (hamburger vs. chow) and need factors (food deprivation vs. ad lib feeding) on food intake. (Adapted with permission from Panksepp, 1998.)

manipulated by allowing them to eat regular lab chow whenever they wanted (ad lib group; low need state) or by starving them for 24 hours (high need state). Half of the animals were then offered regular lab chow (low incentive value), and half were offered a hamburger (high incentive value). Among the animals offered chow, there was a clear effect of need state: hungry, food-deprived rats ate more than did rats that had had constant access to chow. However, the results also document a clear incentive effect on motivation to eat: regardless of need state, all animals gorged themselves on the hamburger treat. These findings illustrate that motivation sometimes reflects differences in need state (in the chow condition) and sometimes reflects differences in the incentive value of a goal object (in the hamburger condition).

Of course, need- and incentive-driven motivation may go hand in hand. Incentives can be more attractive, rewarding, or pleasurable when a person is in a high need state and less so when he or she is in a low need state. For instance, a hungry person may perceive and experience a bland piece of bread as delicious, but consider that same piece of bread to be considerably less attractive when in a state of satiety.

10.2.6 Motivation Is Characterized by Flexibility of Cue-Reward and Means-End Relationships

Motivation drives and, in turn, is influenced by, Pavlovian and instrumental learning processes. Hungry rats are quicker than satiated rats to learn that a certain sound (the conditioned stimulus, or CS) reliably predicts the presentation of a food pellet (the unconditioned stimulus, or US), and anxious people (i.e., individuals who are particularly motivated to avoid punishments) are quicker to learn that a particular face (CS) presented on the computer screen predicts an aversive noise (US) presented on their headphones (Pavlovian conditioning; e.g., Morris, Öhman, & Dolan, 1998). Similarly, hungry rats show better learning of bar-pressing behavior if the bar-pressing produces a food pellet. Anxious people are better at learning to respond to a complex stimulus sequence presented on the computer screen if a speedy response to the stimuli prevents the loss of points or money (instrumental learning; e.g., Corr, Pickering, & Gray, 1997). Finally, power-motivated individuals show enhanced implicit learning of a visuomotor sequence if its execution leads to the presentation of a face with a low-dominance expression, and impaired learning if the sequence is followed by a face with a high-dominance expression (Schultheiss et al., 2005).

Learned cues can, in turn, trigger motivation. This phenomenon is powerfully demonstrated in the case of posttraumatic stress disorder (PTSD; Brewin, Dalgleish, & Joseph, 1996). PTSD is typically acquired during a traumatic episode of life. One key characteristic of the disorder is that any stimulus that happened to be present in the original, PTSD-inducing situation can trigger a stressful reliving of the traumatic event. For instance, a sudden loud noise can elicit a powerful panic response in someone who has been in combat and has learned to associate this noise with the imminent danger of enemy fire, whereas the same noise will only lead to a slight startle response in a person without PTSD. Thus, for the PTSD patient, sudden loud noises are conditioned danger signals that trigger a powerful fear response. On the brighter side, mice and rats that have learned to associate a particular place in their environment with access to a sexual partner will show hormonal changes characteristic of sexual motivation whenever they revisit this place (Graham & Desjardins, 1980). Here, the place is the conditioned cue that elicits the motivational state.

❶ In a sense, Pavlovian and instrumental learning processes make motivation possible in the first place, because they free individuals from fixed, instinctual responses to built-in trigger stimuli, allowing them to become motivationally aroused by wide variety of stimuli that predict the availability of a reward, and to develop an adaptive repertoire of behaviors that are useful for obtaining that reward. Although these learning processes are not entirely unconstrained in many species and domains of behavior (e.g., Seligman, 1970), they nevertheless make goal-directed behavior enormously flexible and adaptive.

10.2.7 Motivation Has Conscious and Nonconscious Aspects

Traditionally, biopsychology has not dealt with the issue of consciousness in the study of motivation, because most research in this field has been carried out in animals that lack the capacity for symbolic language and introspection. Almost by default, then, the majority of biopsychological accounts of motivation assume that consciousness is not a necessary prerequisite for goal-directed, reward-seeking behavior. Researchers working at the intersection of biopsychology, neuropsychology, psychopharmacology, and social psychology have examined the issue more closely, but still come to essentially the same conclusion. For instance, Berridge (1996) reviewed evidence suggesting that, even for as fundamental a motivational system as feeding, humans rarely have accurate insight into what drives their appetites, or what makes them start or stop eating – self-reports of motivation often contradict behavioral data. Similarly, Rolls (1999) has suggested that most of the brain's considerable power for stimulus analysis, cognitive processing, and motor output primarily serves implicit (i.e., nonconscious) motivational processes representing the organism's various needs for physical and genetic survival. Conscious, explicit motivation, by contrast, is the exception to the rule in the brain; it is language dependent and serves primarily to override implicit processes.

Berridge and Robinson (2003) have recently pointed out that implicit/explicit dissociations exist not only in the domain of motivation, but can also be documented for emotion and learning. For instance, learning and memory can be divided into declarative (conscious, explicit) and nondeclarative (nonconscious, implicit) processes, with the former including memory for events and facts and the latter including Pavlovian conditioning and instrumental learning (Squire & Zola, 1996). In this context, it is worth noting that much of the human brain's evolution took place in the absence of symbolic language, that is, without the ability to report on mental states. Accordingly, it is perhaps not surprising that language-based functions are relatively new in an otherwise highly developed and adaptive brain, and that many motivational, emotional, and cognitive functions, which ensured our prelinguistic ancestors' survival, do not depend on or require conscious introspection.

On the other hand, humans are able to formulate goals and to pursue them in their daily lives. If we were governed exclusively by phylogenetically shaped motivational needs, it would be almost inconceivable that any human would ever return to the dentist's after experiencing the pain of a root canal procedure. Of course, conscious regulation of motivational processes is not restricted to overriding raw motivational impulses and needs, but also extends to the formulation of short- and long-term goals and the elaboration of plans to attain them. Traditionally, the brain's contributions to these uniquely human faculties have been studied by neuropsychologists and neurologists, who examined the role of frontal lobe lesions in higher order brain functions in humans. Presently it remains unclear to what extent brain structures subserving conscious self-regulation and goal pursuit are integrated with, dissociated from, or interact with brain structures subserving implicit motivational processes and systems. The elucidation of this issue will be an important task for affective neuroscience in the coming years.

SUMMARY

Biopsychological research focuses on a set of intersecting properties of motivation. Motivation can be directed toward a positive incentive (approach motivation) or away from a negative incentive, through either behavioral approach toward a safe place (active avoidance) or suppression of behavior until the danger is over (passive avoidance). The motivational process consists of two phases, one that involves decreasing (or increasing) the distance from an incentive (wanting) and one that involves evaluating the hedonic qualities of the incentive (liking) once it has been attained. Different types of incentives (e.g., novelty, food, water, sex, affiliation, dominance) can give rise to motivated behavior. Motivated behavior changes its goals dynamically, depending on how recently a given need has been satisfied and what kinds of incentives are available in a given situation. Motivation can reflect the presence of a strong need state (e.g., energy depletion); it can be triggered solely by strong incentives, even in the absence of a profound need (pure incentive motivation); or it can be the product of the confluence of a need state and the presence of

suitable incentives. Motivation is characterized by flexibility of cue-incentive and means-end relationships and drives, and in turn is influenced by Pavlovian and instrumental learning processes. Finally, biopsychological approaches to motivation do not assume that motivation requires conscious awareness, but acknowledge that, in humans, specialized brain systems support the conscious setting and execution of goals.

10.3 Brain Structures Generally Involved in Motivation

While different motivational needs engage different networks of brain areas and transmitter systems, some systems fulfill such general, fundamental motivational functions that they are recruited by almost all motivational needs. This is particularly true of the amygdala, the mesolimbic dopamine (DA) system, and the orbitofrontal cortex (OFC) (cf. Cardinal, Parkinson, Hall, & Everitt, 2002). We will also examine the lateral prefrontal cortex (LPFC), one of several brain structures involved in the regulation of motivational impulses. Figure 10.2 provides an overview of the location of these structures in the human brain.

10.3.1 Amygdala: Recognizing Rewards and Punishments at a Distance

The amygdala is an almond-shaped structure located in the temporal lobes of the brain. Its critical role in motivational processes was first documented by Klüver and Bucy (1937,

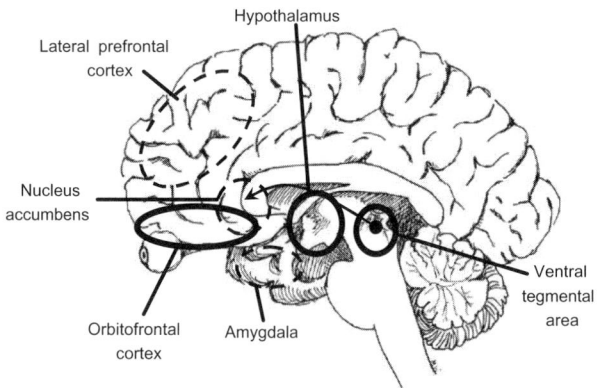

Figure 10.2 Sagittal cut of the brain at the midline, with approximate locations of key structures of the motivational brain. Closed circles represent structures fully or partly visible in a sagittal cut; dashed circles represent structures hidden from view in a sagittal cut. The amygdala is hidden inside the frontal pole of the temporal lobe; the lateral pre-frontal cortex is located on the outer side of the pre-frontal cortex; the nucleus accumbens is a part of the striatum and is situated at the front of the subcortical forebrain. The ventral tegmental area modulates activity in the nucleus accumbens via dopaminergic axons (arrow). Both structures are part of the mesolimbic dopamine system.

1939), who observed a phenomenon that they termed "psychic blindness" in monkeys whose temporal lobes had been lesioned. Klüver and Bucy (1939, p. 984) described what they observed in one monkey as follows: "The [. . .] monkey shows a strong tendency to approach animate and inanimate objects without hesitation. This tendency appears even in the presence of objects which previously called forth avoidance reactions, extreme excitement and other forms of emotional response." Thus, loss of the amygdala leads to an inability to assess the motivational value of an object from afar ("psychic blindness"); the monkey needs to establish direct contact with the object to determine its significance. Also notable is the loss of fear accompanying amygdala lesioning.

Research over the last 60 years has led to a much more nuanced understanding of the "psychic blindness" phenomenon observed by Klüver and Bucy. Specifically, the amygdala been identified as a key brain structure in Pavlovian conditioning. It helps to establish associations between stimuli that do not initially carry any motivational meaning and unconditioned rewards or punishers, provided that the former reliably predict the latter (LeDoux, 1996). Thus, an intact amygdala enables an individual to learn that the sight of a banana (conditioned visual cue) predicts a pleasant taste when the banana is eaten (food reward), whereas the sight of a rubber ball does not predict a rewarding taste if the ball is taken into the mouth. Similarly, the amygdala is necessary for rats or humans to learn that a visual stimulus like a blue light predicts a shock, and thus to express fear upon presentation of the blue light. With an intact amygdala, CS-US associations can be learned within a few trials, and sometimes even on the basis of a single trial; with a lesioned amygdala, humans and animals need hundreds of trials to learn such associations and may even fail to acquire them altogether.

The amygdala consists of several, highly interconnected nuclei (i.e., groups of neuronal cell bodies that serve similar purposes), two of which are particularly important in emotional and motivated responses to CS and US (cf. Fig. 10.3; LeDoux, 1996, 2002). Through its **central nucleus**, the amygdala influences primarily **emotional reactions** mediated by hypothalamic and brainstem structures. For instance, the central nucleus triggers the release of stress hormones (e.g., cortisol) through its effect on the endocrine command centers in the hypothalamus; it increases arousal, vigilance, and

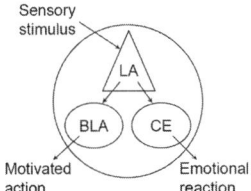

Figure 10.3 A schematic overview of the amygdala and some of its nuclei (LA, lateral nucleus; BLA, basolateral nucleus; CE, central nucleus) and the emotional-motivational functions they mediate. (Based on LeDoux, 2002.)

activation through its projections to major neurotransmitter systems (e.g., dopamine); and it activates various autonomic nervous system responses (e.g., galvanic skin response, pupil dilation, blood pressure). Through the **basolateral nucleus**, the amygdala influences **motivated action** through its projections to the nucleus accumbens, a key structure of the brain's incentive motivation system (see below). If the central nucleus is lesioned, animals are still able to show motivated responses (e.g., bar-pressing for food) in response to a CS, but preparatory emotional responses are impaired (e.g., salivation is lacking). Conversely, if the basolateral amygdala is lesioned, animals will still show an emotional response to a CS, but fail to learn instrumental responses to elicit (or avoid) the presentation of a CS (Killcross, Robbins, & Everitt, 1997).

Another important feature of the amygdala is that it receives input at virtually all stages of sensory processing of a stimulus (LeDoux, 1996). This starts at the earliest stages of stimulus analysis at the level of the thalamus, which can elicit a "knee-jerk" amygdala response to crude stimulus representations (e.g., something that roughly looks like a snake), and extends all the way to highly elaborated multimodal representations from cortical areas that can trigger or further amplify amygdala responses ("It really is a venomous cobra slithering toward me!") or dampen down amygdala responses ("Oh, it was just an old bicycle tire lying on the ground."). The amygdala in turn sends information back to stimulus-processing areas like the visual areas at the occipital lobe, thus influencing stimulus processing and potentially prompting various forms of motivated cognition, such as an enhanced focus on emotionally arousing features of the environment (Vuilleumier, Richardson, Armony, Driver, & Dolan, 2004). The amygdala also influences memory for emotional events (Cahill, 2000).

The involvement of the amygdala in emotion and motivation has frequently been studied using procedures that involve punishments, such as foot shock, because many noxious stimuli are universally aversive, making it relatively easy to elicit fear-related amygdala activation and learning with such procedures (LeDoux, 1996). Despite this research focus on states of fear and other negative emotions, it should not be overlooked that the amygdala also plays a critical role in approach motivation and reward (Baxter & Murray, 2002). For instance, Pavlov's famous dogs would have had a hard time learning to salivate in response to the bell sound (CS) predicting food (US) if their amygdalae had been damaged. Other research shows that an intact amygdala is crucial for second-order reinforcement learning in animals (i.e., learning to bar-press in order to switch on a light that has previously been paired with the presentation of food or a sexual partner; e.g., Everitt, 1990), and that humans depend on the amygdala to generate affective "hunches" that guide their decision making and behavior (Bechara, Damasio, Tranel, & Damasio, 1997).

In summary, the amygdala can be characterized as a motivational "homing-in" device whose activity is influenced by sensory information at all stages of cognitive processing and that allows individuals to adjust their physiological states and overt behavior in response to cues predicting the occurrence of unconditioned rewards and punishers. In the case of rewards, an intact amygdala allows the individual to learn about cues that signal proximity to a desired event or object and to navigate the environment in order to approach the reward, moving from more distal to more proximal reward-predictive cues until the reward itself can be obtained. In the case of punishers, the amygdala enables individuals to respond to punishment-predictive "warning signals," either by freezing, with an increase in vigilant attention or by active avoidance behavior that removes the individual from a potentially harmful situation.

10.3.2 The Mesolimbic Dopamine System: Scaling the "Magnetic" Pull of Incentives

The mesolimbic dopamine (DA) system is a key component in the invigoration of motivated behavior. The system has its roots in DA-producing neuronal cell bodies located in the ventral tegmental area (VTA) of the upper brain stem. The axons of these neurons terminate in the nucleus accumbens, a small cluster of neurons in the ventral striatum, as well as in the prefrontal cortex. The nucleus accumbens receives input from the amygdala and the orbitofrontal cortex (OFC), and has been characterized as a gateway through which sensory information can influence motor response preparation in the basal ganglia (Mogenson, Jones, & Yim, 1980).

Conditioned and unconditioned reward stimuli prompt tegmental DA cells to release bursts of DA in the accumbens and prefrontal cortex, thereby exerting a broad, general influence on synaptic transmission in these structures (Schultz, 1998). Notably, however, it is only at the outset that these DA bursts accompany the actual occurrence of reward. After learning of reward-predictive stimuli has taken place, DA no longer increases in response to the reward itself, but in response to the reward-predictive CS. If that stimulus is itself reliably predicted by another (second-order) predictive CS, the DA burst will ratchet back further and occur in response to the second-order CS, and not in response to the first-order CS or the reward, and so on (cf. Fig. 10.4; Schultz, Dayan, & Montague, 1997).

So what is the function of DA being released into the accumbens? To address this question, researchers have conducted studies in which the mesolimbic DA system was lesioned or DA agonists or antagonists were used to alter the effects of DA release in the accumbens. Results of a typical study of this type are presented in Fig. 10.5 (Ikemoto & Panksepp, 1999). Rats were trained to run down a runway to a goal box filled with a tasty sucrose reward. At each trial, they received either varying amounts of a DA antagonist dissolved

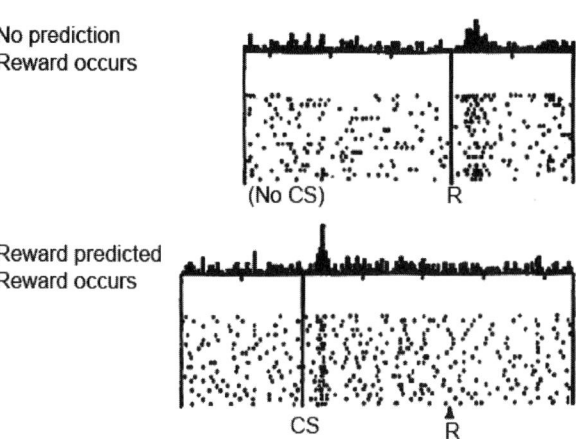

No prediction
Reward occurs

Reward predicted
Reward occurs

Figure 10.4 Recordings from a striatal dopamine (DA) cell of a monkey who received rewarding drops of fruit juice (R) that it learned to associate with a predictive visual or auditory cue (CS). The histogram on top of each panel shows when the cell fired most frequently; single lines of dots below the histogram represent repeated recordings of the time before, during, and after the reward or cue was administered. Each dot indicates when the neuron was firing. (Adapted with permission from Schultz, Dayan, & Montague, 1997.)

in a fluid (vehicle) and injected into the nucleus accumbens or just the vehicle as the control condition. The DA antagonist was intended to block the effects of natural DA release on synaptic transmission in the accumbens; treatment with the vehicle was not expected to interfere with the effects of DA release. After the first trial, rats who had received the highest dose of DA antagonist differed from all other groups in that they traversed the runway to the goal box much more slowly than any other group (left panel of Fig. 10.5). This difference persisted in subsequent trials. Notably, these rats' consumption of the sweet sucrose solution was just as high as all the other rats once they reached the goal box (right panel of Fig. 10.5).

> **EXAMPLE**
>
> A recent study by Pecina, Cagniard, Berridge, Aldridge, and Zhuang (2003) complements these illustrative results. Pecina and colleagues compared hyperdopaminergic rats (i.e., rats that had been genetically engineered to have higher-than-normal DA levels in the brain) with normal rats in terms of their learning of the runway task and their consumption of sucrose solution available in the goal box at the end of the runway. Compared to control rats, hyperdopaminergic rats needed fewer trials to learn that running to the goal box was rewarded with sucrose, showed faster running once they had acquired this knowledge, and were less distractible on their way to the goal box. However, like the DA-impaired rats in the study described above, hyperdopaminergic rats' affective liking responses to sucrose in the goal box did not differ from those of control-group animals.

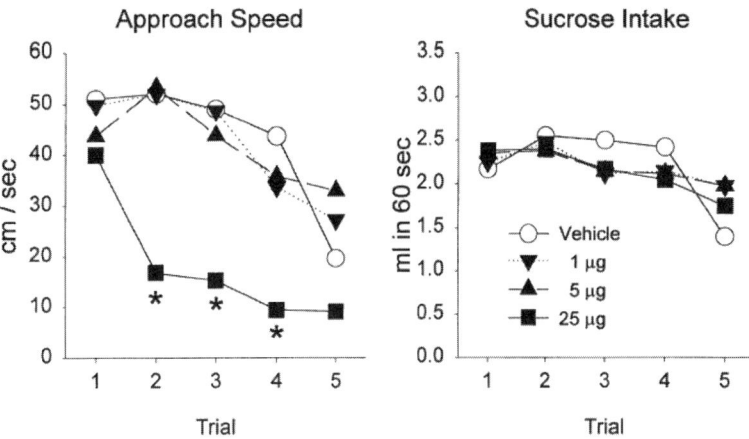

Figure 10.5 An illustration of the dissociation between wanting (running speed to goal box; left panel) and liking (intake of sweet solution; right panel). (Adapted with permission from Ikemoto & Panksepp, 1999.)

❗ These findings illustrate that DA transmission in the accumbens is required for the invigoration of goal-directed behavior (i.e., running toward the goal box), but does not have an impact on the hedonic response to the incentive itself (i.e., consumption of the sucrose solution). In other words, the mesolimbic DA system is highly relevant to **wanting** a reward, but does not mediate its **liking** (Berridge & Robinson, 1998). In a sense, then, the mesolimbic DA system functions like a magnet, pulling the organism closer to a desired goal or object. The findings of Pecina and colleagues suggest that greater availability of DA in the accumbens can be equated with a stronger magnetic pull of incentives.

Brain imaging studies have shown that synaptic activity in the accumbens is also related to incentive seeking in humans. In these studies, accumbens (and sometimes VTA) activation has been observed in response to such varied incentives as beautiful opposite-sex faces, listening to chill-inducing music, or playing computer games (Aharon et al., 2001; Blood & Zatorre, 2001; Koepp et al., 1998). It is notable in this context that the human trait of extraversion seems to be related to the sensitivity of the mesolimbic DA system (see the excursus on the following page).

However, in the same way as the amygdala is often described too narrowly as the substrate of negative emotions; the mesolimbic DA system is often portrayed exclusively as the biological substrate of approach motivation. This view is incorrect. A large body of research shows that the mesolimbic DA system is also involved in active avoidance, that is, in tasks or situations in which the individual has to take action to avoid a punishment (Ikemoto & Panksepp, 1999; Salamone, 1994; but see Ungless, 2004). Animals with a functionally impaired mesolimbic DA system (e.g., through lesions or DA antagonist administration) have more difficulty learning to avoid an aversive stimulus, just as they have difficulty learning how to get to a reward. The mesolimbic DA system is not required for passive avoidance, however, and lesions of this system do not lead to impaired performance on tasks that require the inhibition of ongoing behavior to avoid a punishment. These findings point to a broader conclusion about the function of the mesolimbic dopamine system, namely, that it is involved in the **facilitation** of behavior guided by incentives such as the attainment of reward or relief from punishment (see the excursus on page 257).

10.3.3 The Orbitofrontal Cortex: Evaluating Rewards and Punishments

The OFC is situated directly above the eye orbits, on the ventral (i.e., downward-facing) side of the frontal cortex. It receives highly processed olfactory, visual, auditory, and somatosensory information. It is interconnected with both the amygdala and the mesolimbic DA system, making it one of three major players in the brain's incentive motivation network. The OFC plays a key role in scaling the valence of a broad array of primary and conditioned reinforcers, including perceived facial expressions, various nutritional components of food, monetary gains and losses, and pleasant touch (Rolls, 2000).

Two notable features characterize the OFC. First, different types of reinforcers are represented by anatomically distinct areas of the OFC. Second, each area's activity changes with the motivational value of a given reinforcer. Evidence for the existence of anatomically distinct reward areas comes from studies conducted by Rolls and colleagues (reviewed in Rolls, 2000, 2004). These studies showed that different subregions of the OFC respond to the degree to which a given foodstuff contains glucose, fat, salt, or protein (e.g., de Araujo, Kringelbach, Rolls, & Hobden, 2003). Similarly, brain imaging studies conducted with human subjects show that specific OFC regions are activated in response to monetary gains and losses (O'Doherty, Kringelbach, Rolls, Hornak, & Andrews, 2001). Monetary punishment was associated with activation of the lateral OFC (i.e., toward the side), whereas monetary reward was associated with activation of the medial OFC (i.e., toward the body's midline).

Extraversion: An Incentive-Motivation Trait?

Extraversion is perhaps the most salient personality trait. As early as the AD second century, the Greek physician Galen proposed that individual differences on the continuum from introversion (low extraversion) to high extraversion have a biological basis. The first modern biopsychological account of extraversion was formulated by Hans Eysenck (1967), who mapped individual differences in extraversion onto differences in brainstem arousal systems. Eysenck argued that extraverts suffer from low levels of arousal, and engage in vigorous social and physical activities to achieve a comfortable level of brain arousal at which they can function properly. Introverts, in contrast, have high baseline arousal levels and appear withdrawn because they avoid vigorous activities that would push their arousal level "over the edge" and thus impair their overall functioning.

Although there is evidence supporting the validity of Eysenck's arousal theory of extraversion, it does not seem to tell the whole story. For one thing, as Gray (1981) pointed out, high levels of extraversion resemble a disposition to impulsively seek rewards, whereas high levels of introversion are linked to the avoidance of punishments. Gray's reinterpretation of the extraversion-introversion continuum, which is supported by considerable evidence from animal and human studies, suggests that this trait has less to do with differences in **arousal** than with differences in **motivation** (cf. Matthews & Gilliland, 1999). A second criticism that can be leveled against Eysenck's theory is that the construct of arousal itself is too undifferentiated. Eysenck developed his theory based on pioneering studies conducted in the 1940s on the role of the brainstem in cortical arousal. However, later research indicated that the brain houses several arousal mechanisms that serve a variety of different functions, some supporting sensory processes, others supporting attention and memory, and yet others being involved in motor arousal or activation (e.g., Tucker & Williamson, 1984).

Both criticisms were taken into account in a new theory of the biological basis of extraversion formulated by Depue and Collins (1999). According to these authors, individual differences in extraversion levels are based on variations in the degree to which the mesolimbic dopamine (DA) system, which can be characterized as a motor arousal system, responds to signals of reward with an increase in DA-modulated synaptic transmission. People high in extraversion, like Pecina et al.'s (2003) hyperdopaminergic rats, respond to incentives with greater activation of the mesolimbic DA system, and thus stronger **wanting**, than people low in extraversion. As a consequence, their behavioral surface appears more activated, lively, and invigorated than that of introverts. To test his theory, Depue and colleagues (1994) administered DA agonists or a placebo (i.e., a substance lacking any neurochemically active compounds) to extraverts and introverts and measured hormonal and behavioral indicators of increased DA-dependent synaptic signal transmission, such as the suppression of the lactation hormone prolactin and increased eye blink rate. As expected, after administration of the DA agonist, but not of the

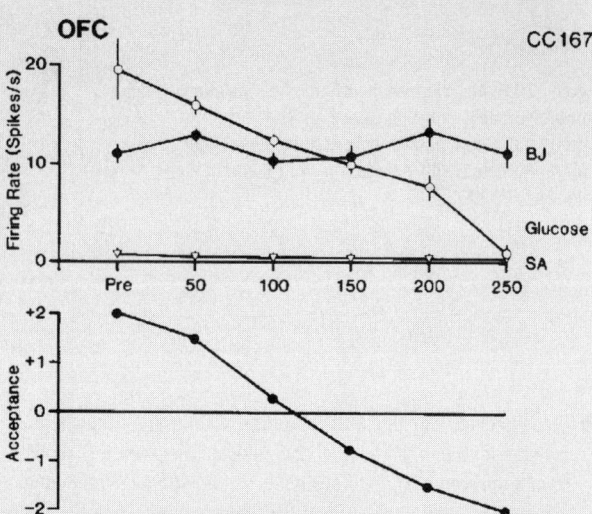

Figure 10.6 Relationship between responses to a DA agonist as assessed by the amount of prolactin suppression relative to placebo (higher levels = greater suppression) and scale scores on Positive Emotionality, a measure of extraversion. Greater DA activation is associated with higher levels of positive emotionality. (Adapted with permission from Depue, Luciana, Arbisi, Collins, & Leon, 1994.)

placebo, extraverts showed more prolactin suppression (Fig. 10.6) and a greater increase in eye blink rate than introverts. These findings suggest that extraverts have a greater capacity for mesolimbic DA system activation, both naturally stimulated by incentive signals and artificially induced by DA agonists, than introverts.

Depue et al.'s (1994) findings also suggest that people do seem to have some insight into the functioning of their motivational brain. Individuals who endorse many extraversion items on personality questionnaires (i.e., extraverts) may have an accurate perception that they are behaviorally engaged by many more things than people who do not endorse such items (i.e., introverts). Yet this does not mean that they can introspectively access the operating characteristics of their mesolimbic DA system; rather, they may perceive in themselves and in their behavior the same things that people who know them well perceive: namely, that they tend to be outgoing, active, and full of energy. However, they seem to be largely unaware of what exactly it is that engages their incentive motivation system in the first place. As Schultheiss and Brunstein (2001; see also Pang & Schultheiss, 2005) have shown, people's implicit motives, which reflect the incentives they **like** and will work for, do not correlate with measures of extraversion. In other words, although people do not have introspective access to what is particularly rewarding for them (determined by their implicit motives), they do seem to have a relatively accurate perception of how strongly they respond to reward-predictive cues when they encounter them (represented by their self-reported extraversion level).

Two Biopsychological Accounts of Approach and Avoidance Motivation

In the introduction to this chapter, we pointed out that the distinction between approach of reward and avoidance of punishment is fundamental in the psychology of motivation. It is perhaps not surprising, then, that a variety of biopsychological accounts for the approach-avoidance distinction have been proposed over the years, not all of which agree on which basic structures and systems in the brain are involved in these motivational states. Two of the most influential models were proposed by the late Jeffrey Gray and by Richard Davidson.

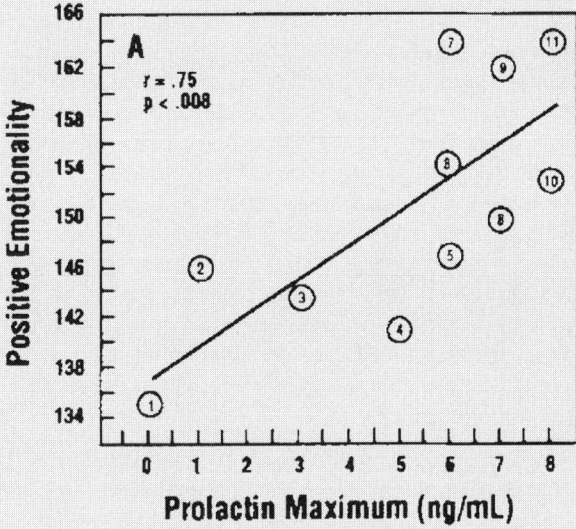

Figure 10.7 Gray's conceptual nervous system model of motivation. Normal arrows represent activating effects, blocked arrows represent inhibiting effects. (Modified with permission from Gray & McNaughton, 2000.)

Gray (1971; Gray & McNaughton, 2000) differentiates between three motivational systems: a behavioral activation system (BAS), a flight-fight-freeze system (FFFS), and a behavioral inhibition system (BIS; cf. Fig. 10.7). The BAS, which Gray associates with the mesolimbic dopamine (DA) system, responds to unconditioned and conditioned reward stimuli, unconditioned and conditioned nonpunishment (safety) stimuli, and novel stimuli that may be rewarding. It is involved in states of approach motivation, but also in active avoidance (e.g., if an individual has to generate certain behaviors in order to reach a safe place in the environment). The FFFS is housed in a system consisting of the periaqueductal gray (a sheath of gray tissue enclosing the channel from the third to the fourth brain ventricle), the medial hypothalamus, and the amygdala. It is activated by unconditioned and conditioned nonreward (frustration) stimuli, unconditioned and conditioned punishment stimuli, and novel stimuli that may be dangerous. The FFFS mediates behaviors that remove the aversive stimulation, such as panicked flight (to escape a predator or harmful situation), freezing (to avoid drawing attention to oneself or to appear dead), or defensive attack (as a last resort, if one has already

been cornered by an enemy or predator). Finally, the BIS is identified with the septohippocampal system consisting of the septum, the hippocampus, and the connections between these structures. It is activated whenever an approach-avoidance conflict occurs and needs to be resolved; i.e., when both the BAS and the FFFS are activated equally strongly by stimuli that predict reward or safety and stimuli that predict punishment or frustration (e.g., if nutritious food is available in an area that is also the prowling ground of predators). In this case, both approach and avoidance responses need to be inhibited for the individual to be able to assess the situation carefully and gain a better understanding of the risks and rewards involved in any further action. At the same time, the individual must be on high alert, and able to respond to changes in the environment within a split second. This is exactly what BIS activation helps achieve: inhibition of prepotent responses from BAS and FFFS and increased arousal, attention, and analysis of the situation. The BIS is also activated by approach-avoidance conflicts of the kind in which a previously rewarded behavior is no longer rewarded or a previously safe behavior is suddenly punished. In both cases, the BIS is a key mediator for decreased frequency of the behavior, enabling the individual to show extinction of behavior in the former case and passive avoidance in the latter. Without an intact septohippocampal system, neither would occur.

Thus, Gray's theory distinguishes not only between approach and avoidance, but also within the latter between active and passive avoidance and escape. Furthermore, it maps these motivational states onto different systems. Approach and active avoidance (as approach to safety) are mediated by BAS activation, escape by FFFS activation, and passive avoidance (and, more generally, approach-avoidance conflict resolution) by BIS activation.

The starting point for Davidson's (2000, 2001) theory is evidence that people who suffer a stroke or lesion in the left frontal cortex are much more likely to subsequently experience severe depression than are individuals who suffer a stroke in the right frontal cortex or other cortex areas. Could the frontal cortices also be involved in affective states and traits in people with an intact, healthy brain? To examine this question, Davidson and colleagues conducted studies on the effects of stimuli (e.g., movies or pictures) that induced strong positive or negative moods on asymmetries in frontal cortex activation, as assessed with electroencephalograms (EEG), positron emission tomography (PET), and other techniques. They found that affectively positive stimuli led to greater left frontal activation than negative stimuli, which elicited stronger activation in the right frontal lobe. These findings were already observable in 10-month-old infants (Fox & Davidson, 1988). Further research indicated that frontal asymmetries could not only be obtained with transiently induced mood states, but also when individual differences in stable traits were measured: individuals who indicated on personality questionnaires that they were prone to approach rewards showed stronger resting left-frontal activation, whereas individuals who characterized themselves as typically moody and prone to motivational withdrawal showed stronger resting right-frontal activation (Sutton & Davidson, 1997; see Fig. 10.8). These findings are not restricted to humans: resting asymmetries in frontal activation also predict hormonal and behavioral indicators of positive and negative affect in monkeys (e.g., Davidson, Kalin, & Shelton, 1993). Davidson (2000) concluded from these findings that, both as a state and as a trait, approach motivation is associated with left-frontal activation and avoidance motivation is associated with right-frontal activation.

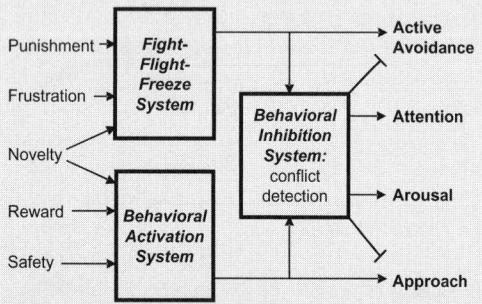

Figure 10.8 Frontal brain asymmetry and approach and avoidance motivation. Higher mid-frontal EEG asymmetry scores represent greater relative left-frontal activation, and higher difference scores on the BIS-BAS scales represent greater relative-approach motivation. (Adapted with permission from Sutton & Davidson, 1997.)

But what exactly is the role of the frontal lobes in approach and avoidance motivation? Do they **generate** these states or reg-

ulate them? Davidson (2000) argues in favor of the latter. Evidence from PET and fMRI studies suggests that increased left-frontal activation leads to decreased activation of the amygdala, a structure that has been implicated in the generation of negative affect. In other words, the left frontal cortex (or specific parts of it) normally keeps the activity of the negative-affect-generating amygdala at bay, and this function can be temporarily weakened by the induction of negative mood states (the amygdala momentarily escapes the control of the left frontal cortex), chronically weakened by a strong avoidance-motivation trait (the left frontal cortex has a generally weak inhibitory effect on the amygdala), and completely abolished in people with a left-frontal stroke or lesion (the amygdala runs unchecked).

Thus, Gray and Davidson present very different accounts of how and where in the brain approach and avoidance motivation become manifest, with Gray's theory being more concerned with the generators of core motivational states and how they contribute to learning and behavior, and Davidson's theory placing more emphasis on the role of the frontal lobes in regulating the experience of positive and negative motivational states. Because both accounts are based on solid and extensive empirical evidence, and because they are not inherently contradictory, it seems possible that the two may eventually become integrated within a more comprehensive theory of how approach and avoidance motivation are generated and regulated in the brain.

The OFC's response to a specific reward is not fixed, but changes dynamically with exposure to or consummation of a given reward and with changes in reward contingencies. Data from responses of single neurons recorded through hair-thin electrodes in primates provide a powerful illustration of the dynamic representation of reward value in the OFC (Rolls, 2000, 2004). If a monkey is given a single drop of glucose syrup (a highly rewarding, energy-rich food substance), glucose-specific cells in the OFC show a strong burst of activity. If the monkey is fed more and more glucose over time, however, the firing rate in these neurons decreases in a fashion that is closely correlated with the monkey's acceptance of further glucose administrations, up to a point at which the OFC neurons stop firing and the animal completely rejects the glucose syrup (cf. Fig. 10.9). If the animal is given sufficient time after it has gorged itself on glucose syrup, however, it will eventually accept more syrup again, and its glucose-specific OFC neurons will resume their vigorous firing in response to the sweet taste. Findings such as these suggest that OFC neurons encode the individual's hedonic response to reinforcers, and that as the individual becomes "satiated" on a given reinforcer, neural responding dies down – a neurobiological manifestation of the alliesthesia effect.

Findings from brain-stimulation reward studies are consistent with this interpretation of OFC functioning (Rolls, 1999). In this type of research, an electrode is implanted in the brain, and the animal can activate the flow of current at the electrode tip by pressing a lever. Depending on where in the brain the electrode is located, the animal is sometimes observed to press the lever frantically, as if that stimulation triggers a pleasurable sensation, and this increase in lever pressing is taken as an indication that a brain reward site has been located. Brain-stimulation reward effects have been documented for many OFC sites, suggesting that pleasurable emotions are indeed experienced when these sites are activated. Notably, for food-related OFC reward sites, it has been observed that lever-pressing varies with the need state of the organism: hungry animals display vigorous lever-pressing at this site, but lever-pressing ceases when they have eaten (Rolls, 1999). This suggests that OFC reward sites are sensitive to the degree of satiation that an organism has reached with regard to a specific reinforcer and must therefore integrate information about the reward's incentive value with the organismic need states.

OFC reward areas can also become activated by conditioned incentives (e.g., sights or sounds that predict food;

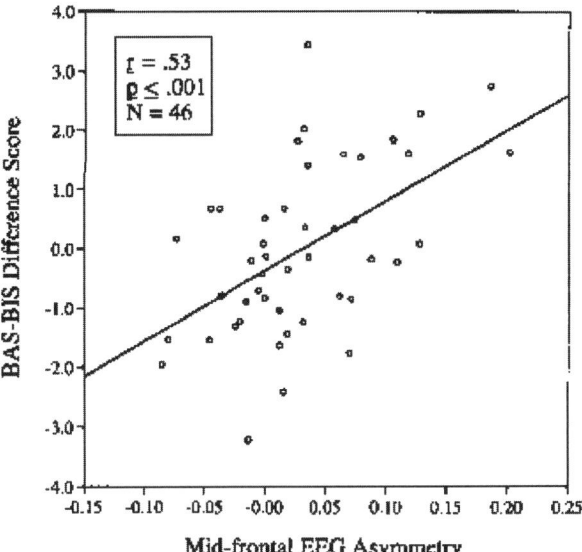

Figure 10.9 An illustration of need-dependent reward evaluation in the OFC. In both panels, the x-axis displays amount of glucose solution fed (in ml). Upper panel: The y-axis displays the firing rate of sweet-responsive neurons in response to glucose, relative to responses to drops of saline (SA) or blackcurrant juice (BJ). Lower panel: Behavioral acceptance of glucose solution. (Adapted with permission from Rolls, 2005.)

Rolls, 2000, 2004). For instance, an area that responds strongly to the taste of food can, through learning, also become activated by the sight of that type of food. Together with the findings on the pleasurable properties of OFC activation, this observation suggests that conditioned incentives can feel just as pleasurable as the "real thing," i.e., the actual reward. This idea is at the core of many modern theories of incentive motivation (e.g., Bindra, 1978). Interestingly, the OFC is also able to break or even reverse learned CS-reward associations very rapidly (Rolls, 2000; 2004). For instance, through learning, OFC neurons will respond to a triangle shape that reliably precedes a food reward, but not to a square shape that is not associated with food. As soon as the relationship is reversed, and the triangle no longer predicts food but the square does, the same OFC neurons will cease responding to the triangle and start responding to the square. Thus, the OFC encodes not only the reinforcement value of rewards, but also of the stimuli associated with them, and it can rapidly change its evaluations as soon as the reward value of a conditioned incentive changes. Not surprisingly, lesions to the OFC abolish the individual's ability to represent changing CS-reward contingencies, and emotional responses may become "unhinged" and persevere for long periods (Damasio, 1994; Rolls, 1999).

The OFC is not the only site of the "incentive motivation network" that codes for the pleasantness of a reward. Some research suggests that portions of the nucleus accumbens and of the ventral pallidum (both parts of the basal ganglia, a subcortical brain structure involved in motor con-

trol and instrumental conditioning) code the pleasantness of food reward (Berridge, 2003). Conversely, the OFC is not only involved in reward evaluation, but also plays a role in response inhibition and the regulation of emotion (Bechara, Damasio, & Damasio, 2000).

10.3.4 The Lateral Prefrontal Cortex: Motivational Regulation and Override

The lateral prefrontal cortex (LPFC) is the portion of the frontal cortex just behind the forehead, extending to the temples. Along with the OFC and the medial PFC, it is one of the last parts of the cortex to appear phylogenetically and is the last to come to maturation, not reaching its full functional capacity until early adulthood (Fuster, 2001). The LPFC supports a host of important mental functions, including speech (Broca's area in left LPFC), working memory, memory encoding and retrieval, and motor control. Most important from a motivational perspective are two specific functions of the LPFC. First, the LPFC is the place in the brain where goals and complex plans to enact them are represented. Second, and related to the first function, the LPFC can regulate the activation of core motivational structures of the brain, such as the amygdala.

Evidence for the key role of the LPFC in goal-directed action comes from neurological case studies (Luria, 1973; Luria & Homskaya, 1964). It is perhaps not surprising that individuals with LPFC lesions that destroy language capability and working memory find it difficult to initiate and execute voluntary behavior, particularly if that behavior is complex. They lack the ability to instruct themselves and to pace themselves verbally through complex action sequences (language center lesion), and may not be able to retain all elements of a complex plan in memory for long enough to execute the plan in its entirety (working memory lesion). More subtle forms of volitional deficits are observed when LPFC lesions do not affect either working memory or speech centers. The Russian neuropsychologist Alexander Luria (1973; Luria & Homskaya, 1964) described people with this type of lesion who were perfectly able to understand and remember a verbal action command, such as "Please take the pencil and put it on the table," and could repeat it to the experimenter, but were unable to use it to guide their behavior. Thus, an intact LPFC is critical for the execution of complex plans that rely on working memory and language for the representation and updating of their elements and to feed these plans to the motor output. Note that the key role of language in the pursuit of complex goals and plans also makes the LPFC a critical point of entry for the social regulation of behavior. Specifically, although people with LPFC lesions may be relatively unimpaired in their ability to respond motivationally to innate or learned nonverbal social cues (e.g., facial expressions, the prosody of spoken language, or gestures), they lose their ability to coordinate flexibly their behavior with that of others through the pursuit of verbally shared goals or to adapt their behavior to the changing demands and expectations of their sociocultural environment.

The LPFC's capacity to represent and enact complex, verbally "programmed" goals implies an ability to regulate and override ongoing motivational needs and impulses, and to resolve conflict between competing behavioral tendencies. Anyone who has ever had to study for an exam on a beautiful sunny day knows that it takes some effort and self-control, often mediated through verbal commands directed at oneself, to focus on one's books rather than jumping up and running outside. The LPFC seems to achieve this feat through its inhibiting effects on activity in structures related to incentive motivation, such as the amygdala. Studies show that nonverbal stimuli with strong incentive properties, such as facial expressions of emotion or pictures with negative affective content (such as depictions of mutilated bodies; Adolphs & Tranel, 2000), cause activation of the amygdala in humans. However, these findings are usually obtained under conditions of passive viewing that do not require LPFC participation in the task. As soon as participants are asked to verbally label the expression of a face or to reappraise a negative scene such that it becomes subjectively less aversive, LPFC becomes activated and amygdala activation decreases (Ochsner, Bunge, Gross, & Gabrieli, 2002). This disrupting effect of LPFC activation on amygdala activity may enable people to refrain from impulsive aversive responses; e.g., to remain seated at their desk to study for an exam instead of giving in to their impulse to engage in motivationally more exciting activities. These findings suggest that engagement of the LPFC's verbal-symbolic functions to deal with an emotionally arousing stimulus dampens down activity in emotion generators such as the amygdala (cf. Lieberman, 2003).

In summary, LPFC supports the planning and implementation of complex behavior through its ability to adopt or formulate explicit (i.e., verbally represented) goals and to keep them activated in working memory, and by controlling activation in the brain's incentive motivation network and thereby inhibiting impulsive responses to motivational cues.

SUMMARY

Many motivational processes make use of what we have termed the brain's incentive motivation network, consisting of the amygdala, the mesolimbic dopamine system, and the orbitofrontal cortex. The amygdala is involved in learning which environmental cues predict the occurrence of a reward or punishment and thereby guiding the organism toward pleasant and away from noxious outcomes. The mesolimbic dopamine system regulates how vigorously the individual engages in reward seeking, but also in active avoidance of punishments, by receiving information about conditioned cues from the amygdala. The orbitofrontal cortex evaluates the "goodness" of primary and secondary rewards, based on the individual's current need state and learning experiences.

Motivational processes rely on these three structures to act in concert, such that cues that predict (amygdala) stimuli that have been experienced as pleasant (orbitofrontal cortex) elicit behavioral invigoration (mesolimbic dopamine system) directed at reward attainment. Behavioral impulses generated by this incentive motivation system are influenced by other functional structures, such as the lateral prefrontal cortex. The lateral prefrontal cortex guides behavior through the formulation of complex, verbally represented goals and plans for their implementation, and can shield explicit goals from the interference of incentive-driven motivational impulses by regulating the output of the brain's incentive motivation network.

We should emphasize at this point that the preceding sections have selectively discussed just some of the most important brain areas involved in motivation and its regulation and omitted other key structures such as the hippocampus (involved in context-dependent modulation of emotional and motivational states) and the medial prefrontal cortex including the anterior cingulate cortex (involved in the regulation of attention, response conflict resolution, and movement initiation). Instead, we will dedicate the remainder of the chapter to the discussion of specific motivational systems that are rooted in hypothalamic structures (cf. Fig. 10.2 for the location of the hypothalamus in the human brain), and that harness the brain's incentive motivation network to guide behavior.

10.4 Specific Motivational Systems

Certain tasks and goals in an organism's life are recurrent. All animals need to find food and eat regularly to get energy; they need to drink so as not to dehydrate; they are driven to find a mate to pass their genes on to their offspring. The attainment of these recurring needs and goals involves challenges such as competing with and dominating other same-sex members of the species. Of course, the tasks and challenges facing currently living beings also occupied their ancestors, reaching back millions of years in evolutionary history. Hence, it is hardly surprising to find that evolution has equipped brains (and bodies) with special systems that ensure that the recurring needs for day-to-day individual survival and the need for genomic generation-to-generation survival are met adaptively and efficiently. Such specialized systems that coordinate and support the attainment of specific classes of incentives have been identified and described in considerable detail for drinking, feeding, affiliation, dominance, and sex. In the following, we take a closer look at how evolution has shaped four of these motivational systems.

10.4.1 Feeding

The primary reason to eat is to provide energy for the body to function. Hunger reflects the need to replenish nutrients. In

Table 10.1. Neuropeptides that affect hunger and feeding			
Neuropeptide	Source	Effect on feeding	Effects on other neuropeptides
Leptin	Fat cells	Decrease	Increases α-MSH; decreases NPY
CCK	Intestine (and brain)	Decrease	Increases α-MSH; decreases NPY
NPY	Brain (hypothalamus)	Increase	
α-MSH	Brain (hypothalamus)	Decrease	
AGRP	Brain (hypothalamus)	Increase	

the modern, developed world, however, where food is over-abundant, there are many other factors that motivate us to eat. These include routine (i.e., "It's noon – it's lunchtime!"), stress, pleasure, and social factors (i.e., when other people are eating). The physiological mechanisms that control the regulation of eating involve interplay between the brain (especially the hypothalamus, a key brain area in the regulation of basic physiological needs) and other organs, such as the liver, stomach, and fat stores. In this section, we will cover some of the neurobiological signals that activate and deactivate the drive to ingest food: the need for energy as well as the desire for the pleasures of taste.

Energy Needs

All organisms need nutrients to provide the energy necessary to sustain the chemical processes of life. Our cells use glucose as their primary energy source. Glucose can be stored as **glycogen** in the liver, and fat is used for the longer-term storage of energy. The body has multiple ways of sensing when more energy might be needed; e.g., when glucose levels drop, fat stores decline, or intestinal motility changes. These conditions trigger activity in brain circuitry that generates a feeling of hunger, or motivation to eat.

Many of the body's systems for sensing energy needs begin in the digestive tract. The stomach contains stretch receptors that send signals of fullness to the brain. The gut also produces many neurohormones that act on the brain to let it know how recently and how much food has been consumed. One such neurohormone is **cholecystokinin** (CCK). The more food enters the gut, the more CCK is released. CCK acts on the vagus nerve, which sends a satiety (i.e., fullness) signal to the brain. Thus, CCK helps to inhibit motivation to eat. High levels of CCK actually induce nausea – a "warning signal" that tells us to stop eating (Greenough, Cole, Lewis; Lockton, & Blundell, 1998).

Another satiety signal comes from fat. Fat cells produce a hormone called **leptin** (see the excursus on the next page), which travels through the blood and acts at the hypothalamus to inhibit food intake. The more fat there is on the body, the more leptin is produced. When leptin levels are low, we feel hungry and eat more; when they are high, we eat less. Leptin thus serves as a signal to the brain, indicating the amount of fat stored in the body, and helps to regulate body weight in the long term. Leptin also acts as a short-term signal: leptin levels in the blood increase at the end of a meal, promot-

ing satiety, and decrease some hours post-meal, promoting hunger (Friedman & Halaas, 1998).

Specialized neurons that monitor levels of glucose in the blood also exist in the brain. These "glucostat" neurons, located in the hypothalamus, react when glucose levels drop, and send a signal to other regions of the hypothalamus to trigger feeding (e.g., Stricker & Verbalis, 2002).

Which are the brain systems to which CCK, leptin, and glucostat neurons communicate? They are numerous, but include neurons in the hypothalamus that produce **neuropeptide Y** (NPY), a potent hunger-inducing molecule. Miniscule amounts of NPY injected into the brains of laboratory animals cause them to eat voraciously. One of the ways that leptin acts is by inhibiting the neurons that produce NPY, and thus staunching hunger. Similarly, CCK overrides NPY production in the hypothalamus (Billington & Levine, 1992; Levine & Billington, 1997).

Neurons producing and responding to a class of neuropeptides called **melanocortins** are also active in the hypothalamus. Peptides that activate melanocortin receptors, such as alpha-melanocyte-stimulating hormone (α-MSH), lead to satiety, whereas peptides that block these receptors, such as Agouti-related protein (AGRP), stimulate hunger (Irani & Haskell-Luevano, 2005; Stutz, Morrison, & Argyropoulos, 2005). In addition to deactivating the hunger signal produced by NPY, leptin and CCK cause α-MSH neurons to increase their firing rate, releasing more α-MSH and thus promoting satiety (see Table 10.1).

Gonadal steroids, whose primary role is to regulate fertility and sexual motivation (see Section 10.4.4), also have an impact on feeding. In female animals, estrogen has a significant restraining effect on food intake. After ovariectomy, which stops the production of estrogen in the ovaries, female rats increase their food intake and gain about 25% of body weight. Progesterone counteracts the effects of estrogen. High levels of progesterone lead to increased food intake and body mass, an effect that is consistent with progesterone's role as a hormone that promotes and safeguards pregnancy, which is characterized by steeply increasing energy needs.

Reward

Need for energy is obviously not the only reason we eat. Eating is pleasurable, and, like other pleasurable activities (sex, addictive drugs, etc.), causes release of dopamine (DA) in the nucleus accumbens, part of the brain's reward learning

Genes and Obesity

Researchers discovered leptin via a mutant mouse strain that overeats and becomes very obese (cf. Fig. 10.10). This strain has a defective gene, which scientists termed the *ob* gene (for obesity). Later, it was

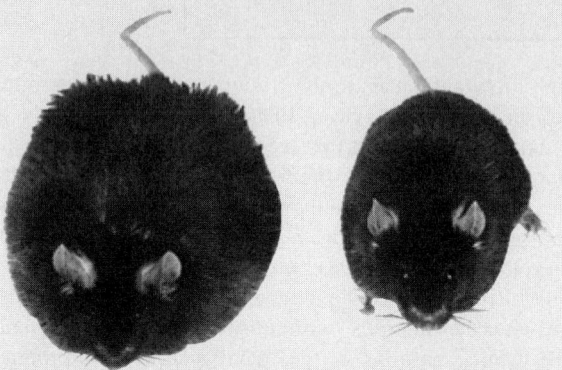

Figure 10.10 The mouse on the left lacks the *ob* gene, which codes for the protein leptin. Without leptin, this mouse overeats and becomes obese. The mouse on the right is genetically "normal." (Photo copyright Amgen Inc., used with permission.)

found that, in normal mice, the *ob* gene codes for the hormone now known as leptin. Without a functioning *ob* gene, the mutant mice cannot produce leptin. Their brains respond as if their bodies contained no fat: the animals act as if they were starving, and eat voraciously. Injections of leptin return the mice's body weight and food intake to normal (Friedman & Halaas, 1998).

Melanocortins were known to affect skin pigmentation in rodents, but their role in food intake was likewise discovered via a mutant mouse strain. This strain also overeats despite extreme obesity, and it has yellow fur – hence its name, the **Agouti mouse** . Researchers found that this mouse strain has a defective gene for a particular melanocortin receptor. The lack of this receptor means that melanocortins like alpha-melanocyte-stimulating hormone (α-MSH) cannot act in the brain or on the skin, resulting in obesity and different pigmentation (Carroll, Voisey, & van Daal, 2004).

Do genetic mutations cause obesity in humans? For most obese people, the answer is no. A melanocortin precursor defect that leads to obesity, a pale complexion, and red hair has been discovered in humans, but this mutation is very rare. Genes may influence the propensity to gain weight, but diet and exercise are the most important factors in human obesity (Martinez, 2000).

---

system (see Section 10.3.2, "The mesolimbic dopamine system"). In particular, sweet and fatty foods are naturally rewarding to humans, rats, and other omnivores. In rats, it has been shown that diets containing extra fat and sugar lead to greater activity in brain structures involved in pleasure and reward (Levine, Kotz, & Gosnell, 2003).

The body's natural opioids contribute to the pleasurable experience of eating. Opioids are released in the brain during intake of sweet and fatty foods, in particular. Injecting laboratory rats with opioids causes them to eat somewhat more regular lab chow, but a great deal more of a palatable sweet or high-fat chow. Unlike NPY, opioids do not seem to be involved in hunger driven by energy needs: injecting NPY to the brain increases animals' intake of bland, yet energy-rich chow, but not of tasty, but energy-dilute sugar-sweetened water. On the other hand, injecting opioids causes a marked increase in sugar-water intake, without having much effect on chow intake (Levine & Billington, 2004).

Sweet and fatty foods are not the only foodstuffs we seek out. A flavor called **umami**, present in meats, sea-foods, and soy, is very rewarding to humans and laboratory animals, possibly because it serves as a good indication that the food is rich in protein (Yamaguchi & Ninomiya, 2000). The food additive monosodium glutamate (MSG) powerfully activates umami taste receptors on the tongue, which is why foods containing MSG taste so good to us.

Finally, we are naturally motivated to seek out a variety of foods. Humans and laboratory animals exposed repeatedly to

a single flavor, even one that is highly rewarding at the start, will rapidly tire of it and consume less of it. However, if they are then exposed to a different flavor, the rewarding nature of the first one will be renewed (Swithers & Martinson, 1998). Because of this phenomenon (alliesthesia), the best way to make a lab rat gain weight is to put it on a "cafeteria diet": a choice of multiple foods (e.g., Gianotti, Roca, & Palou, 1988). That rat will gain considerably more weight than rats offered just one highly tasty food.

Recently, researchers have found that different flavors activate different parts of the orbitofrontal cortex (OFC) in humans. The OFC is a region involved in tracking reward. Thus, different tasty flavors seem to be registered by distinct parts of this brain structure as different kinds of reward. This finding seems to point to the neurobiological basis of the phenomenon that we crave a variety of flavors, rather than just one (Rolls, 2005).

SUMMARY

Hormonal signals from the organs, such as leptin (from fat) and cholecystokinin (from the digestive tract), enter the brain and act on neurons in the hypothalamus to affect hunger and satiety. In the hypothalamus, neuropeptide Y and Agouti-related protein stimulate hunger, whereas alpha-melanocyte-stimulating hormone reduces hunger. Opioids play a role in the pleasurable aspects of eating.

10.4.2 Affiliation and Attachment

While almost all organisms have social interactions with others of the same species, attachments formed between parents and young or between mates are only common in mammals and birds. Parent-offspring attachments, which can be thought of as motivations to be near the parent or the offspring, probably evolved in mammals and birds because these animals require extended parental care, including warmth and nourishment, during immaturity. Mating-pair bonds, which give rise to a long-term motivation to be near the mate, exist in species that cooperate in rearing their offspring. Interestingly, the majority of bird species form mating-pair bonds, but very few mammalian species do – humans being a notable exception.

In this section, we will cover the basic biopsychology of the parent-offspring bond and the mating-pair bond. We will also briefly discuss neurobiological aspects of other kinds of attachments, such as friendships.

Parent-Offspring Attachments

Maternal-offspring attachments have been extensively studied in the rat and the sheep. In these species, there is little or no paternal involvement in brood care – in fact, paternal involvement tends to be restricted to those mammals that form mating-pair bonds.

Rat pups cannot regulate their body temperature in infancy, so the dam (mother) spends much time huddled over them to provide warmth. She also nurses the young and retrieves pups that get separated from the rest of the litter. Male rats and nulliparous females (females that have not borne offspring) do not display these behaviors upon initial contact with pups. In fact, nulliparous females find the odor of rat pups aversive, and avoid them.

How, then, do females develop the motivation to care for their young? Estrogen and progesterone levels are very high during pregnancy, and set the stage for maternal behavior. As the levels of these hormones drop at the end of pregnancy, levels of **prolactin** and **oxytocin** rise – these two hormones released by the pituitary gland are necessary for lactation. The oxytocin surge at the end of pregnancy also induces the uterine contractions of labor. All of these hormones are needed for full expression of maternal behavior (Mann & Bridges, 2001). Nulliparous female rats or castrated male rats treated with progesterone and estrogen followed by prolactin and a jolt of oxytocin – mimicking the hormonal status of the end of pregnancy – engage in maternal behaviors towards pups as frequently as a dam that has just given birth. A major site of action for these hormones is the medial preoptic area (MPOA), a brain region in the hypothalamus that is also important for sexual behavior (Young & Insel, 2002; see section 10.4.4 for more on the MPOA and sexual behavior). The hormones also influence the brain's olfactory system (which handles perception of odor) such that the dams do not mind the odor of pups.

There is evidence that hormones also affect the olfactory system in humans at the end of pregnancy: new mothers rate smells associated with human babies as less unpleasant than do nulliparous women or men (Fleming et al., 1993).

The same hormones are also necessary for maternal behavior in sheep, where oxytocin has an important function in early recognition of young. Sheep live in large herds, and a lactating ewe must allow her own lambs to nurse while keeping other lambs away. Without a sufficient oxytocin surge at the end of pregnancy, however, ewes will reject their own lambs as well. It turns out that oxytocin is needed for the ewe to learn to recognize the smell, sight, and sound of her lambs as distinct from others. Once this learning process is complete, oxytocin is no longer required for offspring recognition (Keverne & Kendrick, 1994; Kendrick, 2004).

In species where fathers help take care of the young, such as Siberian hamsters, tamarin monkeys, and humans, male animals undergo hormonal changes that facilitate paternal behavior toward the end of their mate's pregnancy. Prolactin appears to be important for paternal behavior in many species, including humans, with both mothers' and fathers' prolactin levels increasing at the end of pregnancy. In male wolves, prolactin fluctuates seasonally, increasing in the season in which pups are born. Other hormonal changes also tend to echo those of females in pregnancy. For example, testosterone levels increase in both mothers and fathers in species that need to defend their pups against hostile intruders (Wynne-Edwards, 2001).

Hormones may serve to initiate parental behavior, but the hormones of pregnancy quickly subside, whereas the behavior, once learned, continues. Hormones like oxytocin may cause long-term changes in the nervous system that support attachment to one's young and the motivation to care for them. Rats that have already had litters in the past provide better, faster maternal care than new mothers. In primates, learning may be even more important. Monkeys that have not grown up in a normal social environment show severely deficient maternal behavior in adulthood (Harlow & Harlow, 1966). One famed female chimpanzee raised in captivity had to be trained by humans to provide her infant with proper nursing and care (Matsuzawa, 2003). Clearly, in this species, and most likely in humans, hormones alone do not suffice to produce maternal behavior or a bond to one's offspring.

What about the bond of the infant to its parent(s)? When rat pups are separated from their dams, they show signs of distress, including ultrasonic vocalizations that alert the dam to the fact that the pup has become separated from the litter. Applying warmth to the pups calms them and makes them cease vocalizing. Injections of opioid peptides – brain chemicals involved in pleasure and suppression of pain – achieve the same effect. Similar effects have been seen in young dogs, chickens, and primates: opioid drugs reduce separation distress, even at doses too low to cause sedation or other effects (Nelson & Panksepp, 1998). More evidence for opioid involvement in affiliation and attachment will be addressed in the section on "Other Attachments."

In many of the species studied, opioids and warmth are not the whole story. Rat pups prefer to huddle close to a warm object that smells of their particular dam, indicating that they can recognize their dam by smell (e.g., Sullivan, Wilson, Wong, Correa, & Leon, 1990). In other species, too, the young seem to form a particular attachment to their primary caregiver. For example, young dogs prefer their mother to other dogs, even in adulthood, when they have not had contact to her for two years (Hepper, 1994). In primates, including humans, infants quickly learn to recognize and prefer to be with their primary caregiver(s) (e.g., Porter, 1998). Again, it is thought that hormones like oxytocin may play a role in the formation of these bonds by facilitating long-term changes in the nervous system, which persist (along with the bond) after the hormones have subsided.

Mating-Pair Bonds

The best studied neurobiological animal model of pair bonding is in the prairie vole. When these small rodents mate for the first time, the pair forms an attachment that lasts until one of the animals dies. They live in a nest together, both participate in rearing their young, and they continue to mate with each other and to produce young in subsequent seasons. When separated, the voles exhibit considerable distress, similar to that experienced by infants of many mammalian species during separation from the mother.

Oxytocin and a closely-related hormone, **vasopressin**, are crucial for the formation of this pair bond. Oxytocin and vasopressin levels surge during mating. As in the case of mother sheep learning to recognize their young, these hormones establish an attachment to the mate, which persists – represented in long-term changes in the brain – long after hormone levels have returned to normal. Experimentally blocking oxytocin/vasopressin effects in the brains of voles before their first mating prevents the formation of a pair bond. Conversely, pair bonds can be formed without mating by injecting these hormones into the brains of a pair of animals. Oxytocin seems to be the key hormone in females, and vasopressin in males (Insel 1997; Insel, Winslow, Wang, & Young, 1998), although more recent research implicates oxytocin in pair bonding in both sexes.

While prairie voles form pair bonds, a closely related species, montane voles, do not. Like many other mammals, montane voles mate with multiple partners and only the females care for the young. The difference between these two species lies in the pattern of oxytocin and vasopressin receptors in the brain. Pair-bonding prairie voles have many oxytocin and vasopressin receptors in the nucleus accumbens and ventral pallidum, areas of the brain involved in reward. The oxytocin and vasopressin released when two animals mate for the first time act at these brain sites, permanently changing the dopamine (reward learning) system such that being with the mate becomes rewarding. In a sense, after mating, the brain develops an "addiction" to the mate (Keverne & Curley, 2004).

Does oxytocin underlie pair bonding in other species, such as humans? Although some researchers have speculated this to be the case (e.g., Taylor et al., 2000), conclusive evidence is still lacking. It is clear that humans do not form attachments in the same way as prairie voles: in our species, a single sex act does not lead to a life-long commitment! Nonetheless, oxytocin may play a role in the formation of bonds or attachments in humans. As in other mammals, oxytocin levels rise during sex (in particular, at orgasm) and during massage or other soothing tactile contact (Uvnas-Moberg, 1998). This oxytocin increase may facilitate bonding. Moreover, brain imaging studies have revealed comparatively greater activity in the ventral striatum – a region encompassing reward-related circuitry, such as the nucleus accumbens – when people view photos of their significant other or their own children than when they are shown photos of acquaintances or of other children (Bartels & Zeki, 2000, 2004). Thus, the reward circuitry that is crucial for vole pair bonding also seems to play a role in human attachment.

Other Attachments

Mating bonds and parent-offspring bonds are not the only attachments that animals form. Individuals of many species show signs of stress and pathology if isolated. For example, rodents, canines, and primates tend to live in close-knit groups, and have strong motivations for contact and interaction with others in their group. In primates, in particular, attachments can form between unrelated, non-kin individuals. These are often supported by mutual grooming, which serves to strengthen ties and to soothe distressed apes. Motivation to be groomed seems to involve **beta-endorphin**, a naturally occurring opioid. Levels of this opioid in the nervous system rise during grooming, and individuals seek out grooming when opioid levels are low (Keverne, Martensz, & Tuite, 1989; see also Taira & Rolls, 1996).

Some studies suggest that opioids are involved in human affiliation, as well. After viewing an affiliation-related movie, people high in a "social closeness" trait felt more affiliative and had higher tolerance to heat-induced pain (opioids help to reduce pain). Both of these effects were blocked by naltrexone, an opioid antagonist (Depue & Morrone-Strupinsky, 2005). These findings suggest that the affiliation-related movie caused an increase in opioid release in this group of people.

Oxytocin has social functions beyond parent-infant and pair bonds, including an important role in social memory. When mice lacking the gene for oxytocin encounter a familiar mouse, they behave in the same way as they would with a stranger. When the missing oxytocin is replaced in their brains, they learn who is who in the same way as normal mice (Winslow & Insel, 2002).

EXAMPLE

Recent intriguing studies suggest that oxytocin also plays a role in the trust that humans show toward strangers. Participants in one experiment played an economic game in which Player 1 was given a sum of money, some of which he or she could entrust to Player 2, in whose hands the money would triple. Player 2 then returned an amount of his or her choice (which might be nothing at all) to Player 1. It emerged that Player 2s who received higher sums of money from Player 1s had higher blood levels of oxytocin; likewise, oxytocin levels were related to how much money Player 2s returned to Player 1s (Zak, Kurzban, & Matzner, 2005). In a follow-up study, one group was given a dose of oxytocin intranasally (some small molecules like oxytocin are able to enter parts of the brain, such as the hypothalamus, via the nose) and another group received a placebo. In the oxytocin group, Player 1s entrusted more money to Player 2s (Kosfeld, Heinrichs, Zak, Fischbacher, & Fehr, 2005). In both studies, when people played the game with a computer that allocated money at random, oxytocin had no relationship to money received or given. This suggests that oxytocin actually increases the ability of humans to trust others.

SUMMARY

The hormones estrogen, progesterone, prolactin, and oxytocin are involved in the initiation of maternal behavior. Similar hormones are also involved in paternal behavior. In mothers, oxytocin facilitates early recognition of and bonding with offspring. Oxytocin and vasopressin are also necessary for the formation of pair bonds. Once an attachment has been formed, these hormones are no longer needed to sustain the bond. Opioids are involved in the attachment of an infant to its parent, as well as in affiliation in primates.

10.4.3 Dominance

Most animals not only have to evade predators, find sustenance, and gain access to a mate to survive as individuals and as sets of genes, they also have to compete with members of their own species to secure resources necessary for survival. Behaviors directed at defeating others in resource competitions are called dominance behaviors and they often give rise to relatively stable dominance hierarchies within a group.

Mechanisms and Benefits of Dominance

Dominance issues are most obviously at stake when the males of a species compete with each other for a mate. The competition can be carried out intrasexually, with the aim of defeating other males and keeping them away from females, and/or intersexually, with the aim of attracting the attention of a female by advertising genetic fitness. In Darwin's (1871) own words, this is the difference between "the power to conquer other males in battle" and "the power to charm females." The two often go hand in hand; e.g., when a male's large body size

makes him more likely to win fights with other males, and more attractive to females (Wilson, 1980).

Dominance extends beyond assertiveness and success in the mating game, however, and often involves privileged access to other resources, such as food or protected nest sites. In some species, including many birds, dominance is a relevant attribute only during mating and has to be renegotiated every mating season; in others, particularly animals living in social groups, dominance rank is a more stable individual attribute, determined and changed in occasional violent fights and reinforced frequently by nonviolent signals of dominance (e.g., a warning stare, bared teeth) and submission (e.g., exposure of the throat area in dogs and wolves).

The establishment of stable dominance hierarchies within a social group benefits both the "top dog," the alpha animal at the tip of the hierarchy, and the lower-ranking animals (Wilson, 1980). A stable dominance hierarchy means that all group members can save energy by adhering to a pecking order at the food trough – there is no need to fight over who gets first pick at each feeding occasion. In many species, the dominant animal actively enforces peace among subordinate group members by breaking up fights. Although dominant animals are usually more successful at procreating, subordinate members also get to promote their genes, either by "sneak copulations" or by helping dominant animals with whom they share genetic ties to raise their offspring.

In humans, of course, things are more difficult, because it is much harder to pinpoint one specific dominance hierarchy that is binding for all. A student in a course may be subordinate to the high-expertise professor. Yet that professor may rank rather low among his or her colleagues in the department, whereas the student may be an undefeated ace on the tennis court and excel in the college debating society. Thus, humans' dominance ranks are much more fluid than other animals', reflecting the fact that each of us is a member of many different groups, not just one.

Brain Correlates of Dominance

The biopsychological roots and correlates of dominance have been extensively studied in the rat, biopsychology's favorite animal model (Albert, Jonik, & Walsh, 1992). A male rat tries to establish or maintain dominance by launching an attack that involves pushing an intruder with his hind legs or flank and then chasing him away. He also shows piloerection; i.e., the hair on his body rises to make him look bigger and more intimidating. This pattern of lateral attack and piloerection is also observed in rat mothers trying to protect their pups. A hypothalamic network centered on the anterior nucleus (AN) of the hypothalamus plays a critical role in lateral attack and piloerection and thereby in rats' dominance behavior (Albert, Jonik, & Walsh, 1992; see also Delville, DeVries, & Ferris, 2000). If the AN is lesioned, lateral attack is no longer displayed against intruders; if it is stimulated, lateral attack can be elicited much more quickly and is more intense. This effect is particularly strong in the presence of high levels of testosterone in males or testosterone and estradiol in females. The hypothalamus interacts with other brain areas involved in incentive motivation and reward learning to regulate dominance behavior. For instance, lesions of the nucleus accumbens decrease rats' inclination to attack intruders (Albert, Petrovic, Walsh, & Jonik, 1989). Conversely, elevated levels of gonadal steroids like testosterone and estradiol facilitate motivation to attack intruders in nonlesioned rats by binding to steroid receptors and thereby increasing transmission at dopaminergic synapses in the accumbens (Packard, Cornell, & Alexander, 1997).

Dominance and Aggression

At this point, a word of caution is in order about the relationship between dominance and aggression. First, aggression is just one way of attaining and securing dominance in many species, a fact that may be obscured by a narrow focus on the rat as an animal model of dominance. Aggressive and violent behavior as a means of attaining dominance often backfires in primate groups, and is almost universally outlawed in humans. Work on primates suggests that high levels of the neurotransmitter serotonin, which has a restraining effect on impulsive aggression, promote the attainment of high social rank (Westergaard, Suomi, Higley, & Mehlman, 1999). Thus, considerable social finesse is required to become dominant, and in humans more than most other species nonaggressive means of achieving dominance have become critical for social success.

Second, not all forms of aggression are related to dominance (Panksepp, 1998). Besides the type of offensive aggression associated with dominance in many species, there is also defensive aggression elicited by threat, and predatory attack directed against prey. The latter two are mediated by brain systems other than those we have described for offensive aggression, they serve very different functions, and they are not influenced by hormone levels.

❗ Thus, it would be a mistake to equate dominance with aggression, because many forms of dominant behavior (particularly in higher mammals) are not overtly violent or aggressive and some forms of aggression have nothing to do with dominance.

Hormonal Factors in Dominance Behavior

As indicated by the facilitating effect of gonadal steroids on AN-mediated offensive aggression, hormones play a key role in dominance interactions. In many species, including humans, high levels of testosterone facilitate aggressive and nonaggressive dominance behaviors (Nelson, 2005). For instance, seasonal variations in testosterone levels are strongly associated with seasonal changes in aggression and territorial behavior in many species: when testosterone is high, aggression is high. As testosterone production increases in male mammals and birds around puberty, there is a con-

comitant increase in aggression; castration abolishes both increases. In humans, it has been observed that male and female prisoners high in testosterone are more prone to aggressive behavior and rule infractions (Dabbs, Frady, Carr, & Besch, 1987; Dabbs & Hargrove, 1997). And in most species, those high in testosterone are more likely to engage in battles for dominance.

Success or defeat in dominance contests in turn leads to increased or decreased levels of testosterone. Elevated levels of testosterone have been observed, for instance, in winners of sports competitions, chess matches, and even in simple games of chance, whereas losers' testosterone typically decreases (Mazur & Booth, 1998). These differences in testosterone responses to contest situations even extend to observed dominance. Research has shown that after a soccer match, fans of the winning team have increased testosterone, whereas fans of the losing team have decreased testosterone (Bernhardt, Dabbs, Fielden, & Lutter, 1998). Thus, the relationship between testosterone levels and dominance outcomes is a two-way street, in which testosterone levels influence dominance-seeking behavior and the results affect testosterone levels (Mazur, 1985; Oyegbile & Marler, 2005).

Although basal levels of gonadal steroids like testosterone are usually under hypothalamic control (the hypothalamus regulates release of hormones from the pituitary, which in turn regulates the release of hormones such as testosterone from glands in the body), this mechanism is relatively sluggish and changes can take an hour or more. The testosterone increases and decreases typically observed in winners or losers of dominance contests occur within 10 to 20 minutes, however – much faster than hypothalamic control would permit. So what is it that drives these rapid changes in testosterone levels?

Robert Sapolsky (1987) solved this riddle in a series of elegant field experiments with wild-living baboons in Kenya. He exposed both high-ranking and low-ranking male baboons to stress by darting and immobilizing them (baboons, like many other mammals, experience immobilization as stressful). Sapolsky observed that, within minutes, low-ranking animals showed a drop in testosterone, whereas high-ranking animals' testosterone surged. To find out what explained these differences in testosterone response to a stressor, he next applied a variety of hormone agonists and antagonists and studied their effect on testosterone release. Sapolsky observed a greater increase in the stress hormone cortisol in low-ranking than in high-ranking baboons; moreover, administration of dexamethasone (a cortisol-like substance) suppressed testosterone release in all animals by making the testosterone-producing cells in the testicles less sensitive to signals from the pituitary. In contrast, administration of a substance that inhibited the release of the sympathetic catecholamines epinephrine and norepinephrine (also called adrenaline and noradrenaline) abolished the post-stress testosterone increase in high-ranking baboons, which suggests that these hormones normally have a stimulating effect on testicular testosterone release. Sapolsky concluded from these findings that the balance between cortisol, which is more likely to be released in response to overwhelming stressors, and sympathetic catecholamines, which are released very quickly in response to stressors that are perceived as manageable, has a rapid and direct effect on testosterone. If the cortisol response to a stressor outweighs the catecholamine response, testosterone levels dip quickly – an outcome that is more likely in low-ranking, powerless animals. If the catecholamine response to a stressor outweighs the cortisol response, testosterone increases – a typical outcome for dominant animals that are used to calling the shots.

These findings from a relatively unusual darting-and-immobilization procedure mirror exactly what Sapolsky and others have observed in many mammalian species. Often, dominant and nondominant animals do not differ substantially in their basal testosterone levels (Sapolsky, 1987; Wingfield et al., 1990). When they are challenged, however, dominant animals respond with a rapid increase in testosterone, which increases muscle energy and aggressiveness and thus makes them more likely to win the fight, whereas nondominant animals respond with a testosterone decrease, lowering their pugnacity and thus their likelihood to get hurt in a fight. In humans, high levels of implicit power motivation may be the equivalent to dominant status in animals (Schultheiss, forthcoming). Power-motivated people respond to dominance challenges in which they can keep the upper hand with increased sympathetic catecholamines and decreased cortisol (McClelland, 1982; Wirth, Welsh, & Schultheiss, 2006). The net result is a testosterone increase within 15 minutes of the challenge. In contrast, low-power individuals respond to dominance challenges with increased cortisol levels and low catecholamine levels, suggesting that, even when they are able to keep the upper hand, they feel stressed and uncomfortable with the situation. The result is a drop in testosterone (Schultheiss, et al., 2005).

SUMMARY
Dominance behaviors are aimed at gaining privileged access to resources that ensure the individual's personal and genetic survival. Established dominance hierarchies bestow benefits on dominant and subordinate members of a group by lowering the incidence of energetically costly fights for resources. Dominance is not synonymous with aggression – while offensive, hormone-dependent forms of aggression clearly play a role in the establishment of dominant status, dominance also encompasses nonaggressive behaviors, and predatory and defensive aggression typically are unrelated to dominance. Dominance motivation is supported by the anterior nucleus of the hypothalamus and its interconnections to brain substrates of incentive motivation, and by high levels of gonadal steroids such as testosterone and estradiol, which facilitate signal transmission in brain structures related to dominance

motivation. In many species, high testosterone facilitates dominance and aggression, and the outcomes of dominance encounters cause rapid changes in testosterone, particularly in males, with winners registering an increase and losers a decrease. These testosterone changes are triggered by the effects of stress hormones on the gonads. Elevated cortisol levels inhibit, and elevated sympathetic catecholamine levels stimulate the release of testosterone. In humans, high levels of implicit power motivation predispose individuals to respond to dominance challenges with low cortisol, elevated sympathetic catecholamines, and increased testosterone, whereas low-power individuals respond with increased cortisol, low sympathetic catecholamines, and decreased testosterone.

10.4.4 Sex

The need for sex is at once one of the most potent and most peculiar of all motivational systems. One does not have to be a Freudian to recognize that much of what goes on in the lives of humans and other beings revolves around sexual reproduction. At the same time, not having sex does not threaten our survival as individuals in the same way as not having food, water, or social protection. But given that the transmission of genes to offspring is the ultimate and perhaps most magnificent goal of all sexually reproducing animals, extending an unbroken, billion-year-old chain of life by another generation, it makes sense that evolution ensured that no living being would forget about procreating by making the sexual urge an extremely powerful one. In the following, we review how sexual motivation is shaped by the interaction of biological factors and experience.

Developmental Origins of Sex and Gender
Although for birds and mammals, biological sex initially resides in the genes, the gonads take over fairly early in fetal development. For the rest of our lives, the gonads govern sexual behavior to a large extent, partly through their permanent (organizational) effects on the developing brain, and partly through their temporary (activational) effects on the adult brain (Nelson, 2005). If a gene on the Y chromosome that is present only in males is expressed at conception, testes develop and start producing testosterone and other androgenic hormones, leading to male body morphology (e.g., development of male genitals) and brain organization. If the gene is not activated at conception – as is the case in females, who do not carry the Y chromosome – ovaries develop. Because ovaries release almost no hormones during fetal development, brain and body develop in the female mode. It should be noted that sexual development is not all or none, either male or female. Rather, different parts of the body and of the brain are influenced by the interplay of hormones, hormone-metabolizing enzymes, and the expression of hormone receptors at different times during intra- and extrauterine development, which can lead to variations

in the fit between "brain sex" (sexual identity; sexual preferences) and body sex. Thus, although in many cases male body sex is associated with male sexual identity and a preference for female partners, and female body sex is associated with female sexual identity and a preference for male sexual partners, this is by no means a certain outcome and variations (e.g., transsexuality, homosexuality) do occur (LeVay & Hamer, 1994; Panksepp, 1998).

Hypothalamic Command Centers of Sexual Behavior

The differential "marinating" of the brain in gonadal hormones during fetal development leads to differences in the organization of hypothalamic control of sexual behavior. These differences, and their effect on sexual motivation and behavior, have been most thoroughly studied in rats (Nelson, 2005; Panksepp, 1998). In female rats, the key command center of sexual behavior is the ventromedial nucleus (VMN) of the hypothalamus. If this nucleus is lesioned, female rats will not show any interest in mating with a male, as reflected in the absence of proceptivity (the active solicitation of male sexual interest) and receptivity (the readiness to allow males to mate with them). In rats, receptivity is easily observable as a behavior called lordosis, which consists in the female arching her back and deflecting her tail to allow the male to copulate with her. Electrical stimulation of the VMN, on the other hand, can trigger both proceptivity and receptivity, but only in the presence of the gonadal steroids estrogen and progesterone, which bind to steroid receptors in the VMN and are released during the fertile phase (estrus) of the rat's estrous cycle. Of course, the central coordinating function of the VMN is functionally integrated with the operation of brain structures supporting incentive motivation generally. For instance, female rats in estrus show increased DA release in the nucleus accumbens at the sight of a male rat, and this increased DA release reflects increased motivation to approach the male (Pfaus, Damsma, Wenkstern, & Fibiger, 1995).

The key command center of male sexual behavior is the medial preoptic area (MPOA) of the hypothalamus, which, as a result of organizational effects of gonadal steroids, is larger in males than in females. MPOA lesions in males lead to an inability to copulate, whereas electrical stimulation of the MPOA makes male rats ejaculate earlier than normal. Testosterone treatment in castrated male rats restores normal levels of neuronal firing in the MPOA. As in females, the hypothalamic control of sexual behavior in males is integrated with general-purpose motivational brain systems and hormonal factors. In a series of elegant studies, Everitt (1990) showed that MPOA lesions led to a loss of copulatory ability, while sexual motivation remained intact (e.g., animals continued to bar-press for access to females). Conversely, if the basolateral amygdala was lesioned and the MPOA was spared, animals were no longer motivated to gain access to a female in estrus, but were able to copulate with her once placed on top of her. Likewise, a reduction of DA transmission in the mesolimbic

DA system led to a decrease in sexual motivation, but did not affect copulatory ability. Notably, castration, which leads to an almost complete loss of testosterone, impaired both sexual motivation and copulatory ability.

Hormonal Factors in Sexual Motivation

This last finding suggests that hormones, which bring about differential organization of the hypothalamus in males and females in the first place, later play a key role in sexual motivation. Even with a fully functional brain, sexual behavior in mammals and other species is strongly dependent on sufficient levels of gonadal steroids (i.e., testosterone, estrogen, and progesterone; Nelson, 2005). In females of many species, including our own, initiation of sexual activity coincides with the high-estrogen phase of the reproductive cycle (Wallen, 2001; note, however, that in most other species, females not in estrus show no sexual interest at all). Removal of the ovaries leads to a loss of sexual appetite, which can be restored through the administration of estrogen (Zehr, Maestripieri, & Wallen, 1998). Similarly, male sexual motivation in humans and other species depends on sufficiently high levels of testosterone (Nelson, 2005). Notably, in many parts of the brain, testosterone needs to be converted to estrogen first before it can have an effect on behavior, and studies have shown that male sexual motivation requires the presence of both testosterone and testosterone converted to estrogen in the brain (Baum, 1992).

The release of gonadal steroids does not just fuel sexual motivation, but can itself be the outcome of a motivational process. For instance, research on rats has shown that conditioned sexual cues can trigger the release of testosterone in males (Graham & Desjardins, 1980). By the same token, a study with human subjects revealed that heterosexual men experience a transient testosterone rush when they meet an attractive woman (Roney, Mahler, & Maestripieri, 2003).

Learned Sexuality

Findings about the roles of the hypothalamus and hormone levels in sexual motivation may be taken to suggest that sexual motivation is a purely biological phenomenon that is not influenced by environmental factors.

❶ However, biopsychologists have collected ample evidence that sexual behavior is strongly dependent on social learning processes, to the extent that some researchers even speak of "learned sexuality" (Woodson, 2002).

The conditioned hormone release effect described above is one example of learned sexuality. Moreover, rats reared in social isolation show clear deficits in sexual motivation and copulatory performance later in adulthood, and even animals that were reared socially need to learn, through Pavlovian and instrumental conditioning processes, how to tell male from female, what types of signals are sent by a potentially willing partner, and how to copulate appropriately. Even something as "biological" as male sperm production is amenable to learning: male Japanese quail release more spermatozoa and a greater overall volume of semen during copulation if they have been exposed to a Pavlovian-conditioned sexual cue that stimulated sperm production in the gonads in a preparatory fashion before copulation (Domjan, Blesbois, & Williams, 1998). This dependence of sexual behavior on learning may also explain why, in species whose behavior is particularly open to learning, such as humans, sexual motivation and performance can remain intact even after sudden loss of gonadal function and why the females of our species and some other primates (e.g., the bonobo chimpanzee) show sexual motivation and behavior even during low-estrogen, nonfertile phases of the reproductive cycle.

SUMMARY

Hormonal factors play a critical role in the organization of gendered body morphology and brain structures during development. After maturation, sexual motivation and performance depend on the activational effects of gonadal steroids. The ventromedial nucleus and the medial preoptic area are the hypothalamic control centers for sexual behavior (particularly copulation) in females and males, respectively, and are functionally integrated with the brain's incentive motivation network (i.e., amygdala, mesolimbic dopamine system). Adaptive sexual behavior also depends on learning processes that allow organisms to learn about and discriminate sexual cues and to acquire behaviors that are instrumental for successful mating.

10.5 Conclusion

In this chapter, we have sought to provide an overview of the biopsychology of motivation – an incredibly vast, multifaceted, fascinating, and lively field of study that is often overlooked by social-cognitive motivation psychologists, who tend to rely primarily on self-report and experimental studies with humans. As a consequence, with relatively few exceptions, the biopsychological and social-cognitive approach to the study of motivation have pursued quite separate research agendas for a long time, the former exploring the brain correlates of basal needs such as hunger, sex, or affiliation, and the latter examining people's goals, self-views, attributions, and information-processing biases. However, the fact that we were able to weave numerous studies involving human subjects into this chapter (and we are certain that in just a few years, we will be able to cite many, many more) suggests that the divide between the two fields of motivation research is about to disappear. It is our hope that, as biopsychologists become more interested in the way that fundamental motivational needs play out in the human brain, human motivation researchers will become more interested in how motiva-

tional processes and constructs that are uniquely human are "embrained" and embodied.

REVIEW QUESTIONS

1. **Describe three research strategies that are frequently used in the biopsychology of motivation. What are these strategies almost always combined with?**

   Biopsychological research on motivation often uses: (1) lesioning techniques to study the contributions of specific brain areas to a behavior; (2) recording techniques (e.g., single-cell recording; in-vivo dialysis) to study the behavior of specific neurons; and (3) pharmacological manipulations of synaptic signal transmission to study the role of specific transmitter systems. These strategies are almost always combined with behavioral methods (e.g., Pavlovian or instrumental learning procedures) to illuminate the contributions of specific brain areas or transmitter systems to specific cognitive or behavioral functions.

2. **What are the hallmarks of motivation from the perspective of biopsychology?**

   Motivated behavior can be directed toward the attainment of rewards (approach motivation) or away from punishers (avoidance motivation). Motivation consists of two distinct phases: a motivational phase proper, during which the individual engages in the pursuit of a reward (or avoidance of a punisher) and an evaluation phase, during which the individual consummates the reward and evaluates its "goodness." Although there are many different classes of reward (e.g., food, sex, dominance), they can all engage similar motivational processes (e.g., response invigoration, learning). Motivated behavior changes its goals dynamically, depending on how recently a given need has been satisfied and what kinds of incentives are available in a given situation. Motivation can be induced through a physiological need, the presence of incentive stimuli, or both. Motivation makes use of, and shapes, learning of stimulus-stimulus (Pavlovian conditioning) and means-ends (instrumental conditioning) relationships. Biopsychological approaches to motivation do not assume that motivation requires conscious awareness, but acknowledge that specialized brain systems support the conscious setting and execution of goals in humans.

3. **What is a key function of the amygdala in motivation?**

   The amygdala forges associations between affectively neutral stimuli (CS) and the affectively charged events or stimuli (US) that they reliably predict. In the process, the predictive stimuli take on affective meaning themselves and can induce motivational states. The amygdala thus acts as a motivational "homing-in" device that allows individuals to adjust their physiological states and overt behavior to cues that predict the occurrence of unconditioned rewards and punishers and bring them closer to the former or distance them from the latter.

4. What is the key function of the mesolimbic dopamine system in motivation?

The mesolimbic dopamine system invigorates active behavior directed toward the attainment of reward or safety.

5. What is the key function of the orbitofrontal cortex (OFC) in motivation?

The OFC evaluates the "goodness" of primary and secondary (i.e., learned) rewards based on the individual's current need state, learning experiences, and previous exposure to the reward.

6. What is the key function of the lateral prefrontal cortex (LPFC) in motivation?

The LPFC guides behavior through the formulation of complex, verbally represented goals and plans for their implementation. It also influences behavior by regulating the output of the brain's incentive motivation network and can shield explicit goals from interference by incentive-driven motivational impulses.

7. What is the difference between active and passive avoidance? Which structure of the motivational brain plays a critical role in the former, but not in the latter?

The difference between passive avoidance and active avoidance is that in the former, behavior is inhibited in order to avoid a punisher, whereas in the latter, behavior is executed in order to attain safety. Functions of the mesolimbic dopamine system play a critical role in active, but not passive avoidance.

8. What is alliesthesia? Give an example.

Alliesthesia is the changing subjective evaluation of a reward over repeated exposures or across changing stimulus contexts. For instance, most people experience one piece of chocolate as quite tasty and pleasant, but would respond with nausea and aversion after eating a pound of it.

9. Imagine you have just finished a large meal. Describe the signals sent to your hypothalamus to indicate that you are full, and how neuropeptide systems in the hypothalamus would respond.

Leptin levels increase in the bloodstream; levels of CCK from the gut also rise. CCK sends signals to the vagus nerve. Leptin and CCK (the CCK signal from the vagus nerve) act on the hypothalamus to increase the activity of α-MSH neurons and decrease the activity of NPY neurons.

10. How do opioids and NPY differ in their control of food intake and motivation to eat?

NPY is involved in hunger driven by energy needs. NPY causes animals to prefer the most calorically dense food available, even at the expense of taste. Opioids are involved in motivation to eat for pleasure. Opioids drive animals to choose the tastier option, at the expense of calories (energy).

11. Describe one role of opioids in affiliation or attachment.

Any of the following: a) opioids reduce distress in infant mammals separated from their mothers, implicating opioid systems in infant-to-parent attachment; b) in primates, opioids are involved in motivation to engage in mutual grooming; c) in humans, opioid systems may be involved in feelings of affiliation, as evidenced by higher pain tolerance in people high in a "social closeness" trait after they watched an affiliation-related movie, an effect that was blocked by an opioid antagonist.

12. Describe the role of oxytocin in parent-offspring attachments and pair bonds. Is oxytocin necessary for the initiation of attachment? For the maintenance of the attachment? Is it sufficient?

High oxytocin levels in the bloodstream are necessary for the formation of parent-offspring attachments and pair bonds. However, oxytocin is not sufficient – other hormones and learning factors are also necessary. Oxytocin is not necessary for the maintenance of the attachment once it has been formed.

13. What is the difference between intrasexual and intersexual competition?

Intrasexual competition occurs when members of one gender fight or compete with each other to establish who will be allowed access to members of the other gender, whereas intersexual competition occurs when members of one gender vie, as potential mates, for the attention and acceptance of members of the other gender.

14. What is the relationship between dominance and aggression?

Aggression is one form of dominance behavior. However, not all forms of aggression serve dominance functions (e.g., predatory or defensive aggression are not aimed at dominance), and dominance also encompasses nonaggressive behaviors, which are particularly critical for success in primate species.

15. Which hypothalamic structure plays a critical role in dominance and how can this be demonstrated?

The anterior nucleus (AN) of the hypothalamus plays a critical role in dominance, as assessed by piloerection and lateral attack. If the AN is lesioned, dominance behavior ceases; if the AN is stimulated, dominance behavior is facilitated.

16. **What is the relationship between dominance and gonadal steroid hormones?**

High levels of gonadal steroids (primarily testosterone, but also estradiol) facilitate dominant and aggressive behavior, and success in dominance interactions can in turn increase gonadal steroid levels. Thus, the relationship between dominance and gonadal steroids is reciprocal.

17. **Which mechanism drives the rapid testosterone changes observed in the context of male dominance challenges?**

In males, rapid changes in testosterone release are governed by the stimulatory effects of sympathetic catecholamines (norepinephrine and epinephrine) and the inhibitory effects of cortisol on the testes. In dominant individuals, the effect of sympathetic catecholamines outweighs that of cortisol, producing a net increase in testosterone. In nondominant individuals, the effect of cortisol outweighs that of the sympathetic catecholamines, leading to a net decrease in testosterone.

18. **Which hypothalamic centers regulate male and female sexual behavior, and which specific aspects of sexual behavior are particularly dependent on these centers?**

The ventromedial nucleus (VMN) and the medial preoptic area (MPOA) are the hypothalamic control centers for sexual behavior in females and males, respectively. In females, both proceptivity (active solicitation of male sexual interest) and receptivity (readiness to allow males to mate with them) depend on an intact VMN and sufficiently high levels of estradiol and progesterone. In males, copulatory ability depends on an intact MPOA and sufficiently high levels of testosterone, whereas sexual motivation does not depend on the MPOA.

19. **What evidence is there to suggest that hypothalamic control centers of sexual behavior are functionally integrated with other structures of the brain's incentive motivation network in sexual motivation?**

Female rats in estrous show increased dopamine (DA) release in the nucleus accumbens at the sight of a male rat, and this increased DA release reflects increased motivation to approach the male. In males, a reduction of DA transmission in the mesolimbic DA system leads to a decrease in sexual motivation, but does not affect copulatory ability. Moreover, MPOA lesions lead to a loss of copulatory ability in males, while sexual motivation remains intact. Conversely, if the amygdala is lesioned and the MPOA is spared, then male rats are no longer motivated to gain access to an estrous female but are able to copulate with her once placed on top of her. These findings suggest that sexual motivation depends not just on the hypothalamus for copulatory ability, but also on the amygdala and the mesolimbic DA system for guiding and invigorating an animal's behavior to gain access to a mate.

A. Achtziger and P. M. Gollwitzer

11.1 Characteristics of the Action Perspective

For Kurt Lewin (cf. Lewin, Dembo, Festinger, & Sears, 1944), there was never any doubt that motivational phenomena can only be properly understood and analyzed from an action perspective. Indeed, as he pointed out in support of this claim, processes of goal setting and goal striving are governed by distinct psychological principles. These insights went unheeded for several decades, however, probably for the simple reason that goal setting research based on the expectancy-value paradigm proved so successful (Festinger, 1942; Atkinson, 1957) and captured the full attention of motivation psychologists. It was not until the emergence of the psychology of goals (starting with Klinger's current concerns, 1977, and Wicklund's and Gollwitzer's self-definitional goals, 1982) and the psychology of action control (based on Kuhl's analysis of state vs. action orientation, 1983; see Chapter 12) that the processes and potential strategies of goal striving began to receive the attention that Kurt Lewin had already felt they deserved back in the 1940s (Oettingen & Gollwitzer, 2001). In contrast to the behaviorist approach, an action perspective on human behavior means extending the scope of analysis beyond simple stimulus-response bonds and the execution of learned habits. The concept of **action** is seen in opposition to such learned habits and automatic responses; it is restricted to those human behaviors that have what Max Weber (1921) termed "Sinn" ("meaning" or "sense"). In Weber's conceptualization, "action" is all human behavior that the actor deems to have "meaning." Likewise, external observers apply the criterion of "meaning" to determine whether or not another person's behavior constitutes "action": are there discernible "reasons" for that behavior?

DEFINITION
From this perspective, actions can be defined as all activities directed toward an "intended goal."

The **motivation psychology of action** focuses on questions of **action control**. These issues are important because – as action psychology research has shown repeatedly – a strong motivation to achieve a certain outcome or engage in a certain behavior does not normally suffice for that behavior to be implemented and the goal to be realized (Gollwitzer & Bargh, 1996; Heckhausen, 1989; Kuhl, 1983). In fact, successful goal attainment often requires the skilled deployment of various action control strategies (e.g., formulating "if-then" plans, resuming interrupted actions, stepping up efforts in the face of difficulties; cf. Gollwitzer & Moskowitz, 1996; Sections 11.5–11.7).

11.2 The Rubicon Model of Action Phases

The focus of this section is on the **course of action**, which the **Rubicon model of action phases** understands to be a temporal, horizontal path starting with a person's desires and ending with the evaluation of the action outcomes achieved (Gollwitzer, 1990; Heckhausen, 1987a; 1989; Heckhausen & Gollwitzer, 1987). The Rubicon model seeks to provide answers to the following questions:

- How do people select their goals?
- How do they plan the execution of those goals?
- How do they enact these plans?
- How do they evaluate their efforts to accomplish a specific goal?

❗ The major innovation of the Rubicon model was to define clear boundaries between motivational and volitional action phases. These boundaries mark functional shifts between mindsets conducive to goal deliberation and mindsets conducive to goal achievement. The three most important boundaries are at the transition from the motivational phase before a decision is made to the subsequent volitional phase, at the transition from this planning phase to the initiation of action, and finally at the transition from the action phase back to the motivational (postactional) evaluation phase.

11.2.1 Action Phases

Heckhausen's Rubicon model of action phases was inspired by the necessity to distinguish two major issues in motivation psychology – the **selection** of action goals and the **realization** of those goals (Lewin, 1926b) – and, at the same time, to incorporate both within a single, unifying framework (Heckhausen, 1987a, 1989; Heckhausen & Gollwitzer, 1987). In a manner of speaking, the model examines the transition from wishing to weighing in goal selection and from weighing to willing in actual goal pursuit (Heckhausen, 1987b). Importantly, it highlights the distinctions between goal setting and goal striving, and is careful not to confuse or confound the two. It was precisely that kind of indiscriminate approach that generated confusion in the history of motivation psychology, and resulted in volitional phenomena being neglected for decades (Heckhausen, 1987c, 1989; Kuhl, 1983, Gollwitzer, 1990, 1991). Given that the processes of goal setting and goal striving serve a common function, however, it was important that they should not be seen as isolated, independent phenomena either. The Rubicon model gets around this difficulty by tracking the emergence of a motivational tendency over time – from the awakening of wishes to goal selection and commitment, and finally goal deactivation. It seeks to describe the emergence, maturation, and fading of motivation, dividing a course of action into four natural, consecutive phases separated by clear boundaries or transition points. These four action phases differ in terms of the tasks that have to be addressed before the individual can move on to the next phase. The distinctions the model draws between consecutive action phases are thus both structural and functional in nature.

According to the Rubicon model, a course of action involves a phase of **deliberating** the positive and negative potential consequences of various nonbinding wishes and action alternatives (predecisional phase), a phase of **planning** concrete strategies for achieving the goal selected at the end of the predecisional phase (preactional/postdecisional phase), a phase of **enacting** these strategies (actional phase), and finally a phase of **evaluating** the action outcome (postactional phase; Fig. 11.1; see also Fig. 1.3 in Chapter 1).

❗ The four phases of the Rubicon model differ in terms of the tasks that have to be addressed before the individual can move on to the next phase. Motivational episodes are thus broken down into "natural" and seemingly independent phases. Critically, the Rubicon model seeks to explain both goal setting and goal striving.

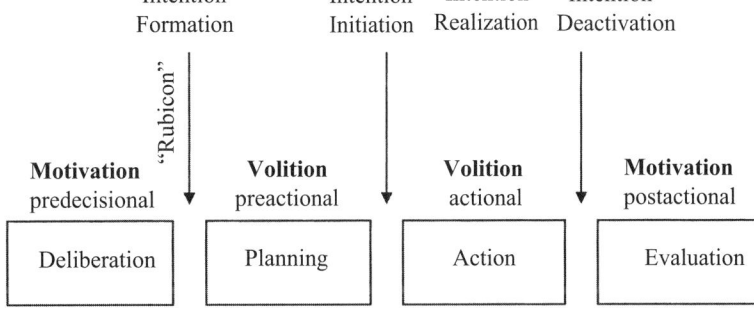

Figure 11.1 The Rubicon model of action phases. (Heckhausen & Gollwitzer, 1987)

The Predecisional Phase

The first phase (predecisional phase) is characterized by deliberation. An individual first has to decide which of his or her many wishes to pursue. A person's motives are assumed to produce certain wishes. For example, a person with a strong achievement motive (Chapter 6) and a weak affiliation motive (Chapter 7) is expected to experience more wishes related to achievement than to affiliation. Yet because people's needs and motives produce more wishes than can possibly be enacted, they are forced to choose among them, committing themselves to certain selected goals. To this end, they weigh the **desirability** and **feasibility** of their many wishes. The objective of the predecisional phase is thus to decide – based on the criteria of feasibility (i.e., the expectancy that the action will succeed) and desirability (i.e., the value of the expected action outcome) – which of their wishes they really want to pursue. Individuals contemplating the feasibility of a potential goal will ask themselves questions such as the following:

- Can I obtain the desired outcomes by my own activity (action-outcome expectancy)?
- Is the situational context facilitating or inhibiting (action-by-situation expectancy)?

The following questions are also crucial:

- Do I have the necessary time and resources to pursue the desired outcome?
- Might favorable opportunities to pursue it arise?

The desirability of a potential goal or desired outcome is determined by reflecting on questions such as the following:

- What are the short- and long-term consequences of pursuing this goal?
- How positive or negative might these consequences be for me?
- How probable is it that these consequences will occur?

In addressing these questions, the individual weighs the expected value of a wish or potential goal; reflects on its positive and negative, short- and long-term consequences; and assesses the probability that achieving the desired outcome or potential goal will bring about these consequences. It is assumed that people do not contemplate their wishes and potential goals in isolation, but see them in relation to other wishes and potential goals. A wish associated with a number of attractive consequences may thus suddenly appear less desirable in the light of a superordinate wish. Conversely, a wish may appear more feasible when contemplated in the context of other wishes than when seen in isolation. The duration of the deliberation process varies from case to case. It is rare for answers to be found to all questions. In fact, many of the questions have no hard and fast answers (e.g., it is difficult to gauge outcome-consequence expectancies when the consequences in question involve external evaluation or progress toward a superordinate goal), and in most cases, there is not even enough time to address all of the questions that might be answered.

The Rubicon model thus postulates the **facit** (i.e., concluding) **tendency** to facilitate predictions of when the motivational task of deliberation will be completed. The more thoroughly an individual has weighed the positive and negative short- and long-term consequences of engaging or not engaging in a particular behavior, the closer he or she comes to the belief of having exhausted all possible routes of action. The chances of gaining new insights into potential consequences decrease, and the facit tendency, i.e., the tendency to decide on a certain wish or potential goal, increases apace. However, a decision is only made when a previously stipulated level of clarification has been attained. This level of clarification is positively correlated with the personal importance of the decision and negatively correlated with the costs incurred in acquiring information on potential consequences and thinking that information through. As shown by Gollwitzer, Heckhausen, and Ratajczak (1990), however, the process of deliberation can be shortened by thinking in depth and detail about how one of the alternatives under consideration might be translated into action. In an experimental design, these authors found that participants who anticipated a decision and planned their subsequent actions were quicker to make a decision.

However, even a wish with a high resultant motivational tendency (i.e., high expected value and hence high desirability) does not necessarily gain access to the executive. Rather, it first has to be transformed into a concrete goal. This transformation is often described as **crossing the Rubicon** in allusion to Julius Caesar's crossing of the stream that once marked the boundary between Italy and Cisalpine Gaul. By leading his army across the Rubicon and marching on Rome, Caesar committed himself irrevocably to civil war. The transformation of a wish into a goal involves a shift from a fluid state of deliberating the value of a potential goal to a firm sense of commitment to its enactment, i.e., to the formation of a "goal intention" (see Section 11.5 for a definition of "goal intention"). Phenomenologically, it results in a feeling of determination and certainty of taking the necessary action (Michotte & Prüm, 1910). The goal specified in the wish thus becomes an end state to which the individual feels committed.

❗ In the predecisional phase, individuals contemplate the feasibility of certain wishes as well as the desirability of potential action outcomes. This process of deliberation culminates in commitment to a specific goal (goal intention) – in crossing the "Rubicon" between wishes and goals. The transformation of a wish into a binding goal or goal intention results in a firm sense of commitment to translate that goal into action.

Preactional Phase

It may not be possible for newly formed goal intentions to be implemented immediately. The individual may first have to complete other activities, or wait for suitable opportunities to arise. Moreover, many goal intentions specify goal states (e.g., spending more time with one's family, graduating from college, etc.) that cannot be achieved instantly. Consequently, people may be forced to wait for favorable opportunities to arise before progressing toward the intended goal state. According to the Rubicon model, individuals in this waiting stage are in the second phase of a course of action – the **volitional** preactional (or postdecisional) phase. The term "volition" indicates that the motivational deliberation of potential action goals has been terminated by crossing the Rubicon, and that the individual is now committed to achieving a specific goal state. The task facing individuals in this postdecisional (but preactional) phase is to determine how best to go about attaining the chosen goal. Thus, it is no longer a question of selecting desirable and feasible goals, but of determining how to facilitate the achievement of the goals chosen; e.g., by means of routine behaviors that are more or less automatic or newly acquired behaviors that require conscious thought. Ideally, people in the preactional phase should also develop plans specifying when, where, and how goal-directed behavior is to be performed (Gollwitzer, 1999). These plans are called **implementation intentions** (Section 11.5). According to the Rubicon model and the theory of intentional action control (Gollwitzer, 1993, 1999), implementation intentions concerning the initiation, execution, and termination of actions help people to overcome the difficulties that can be anticipated as they progress toward their goals. People often find it particularly difficult to get started, instead engaging in extended procrastination and overlooking viable opportunities to initiate goal-facilitating behavior. These are the problems to be overcome in the second phase of action.

How, then, is action initiated when a more or less favorable opportunity arises? The concept of the **fiat tendency** was introduced to answer this question. By crossing the Rubicon, people commit themselves to enacting their chosen goals. The strength of this commitment, which the Rubicon model labels **volitional strength**, is a positive linear function of the strength of the corresponding motivational tendency (i.e., the desirability and feasibility of the intended goal). The strength of a goal intention's fiat tendency is the product of its volitional strength (i.e., the commitment to pursuing the goal state) and of the suitability of the situation for its initiation. The suitability of a situation is not determined in isolation, but relative to other opportunities that might occur in the future (**longitudinal competition**). The fiat tendencies of an individual's other goal intentions also have to be considered. It would be wrong to assume that people always take action to promote a goal with a high fiat tendency. Many situations are conducive to a whole range of intentions, not all of which can be implemented at once (**cross-sectional competition**). In this case, the goal intention with the highest fiat tendency gains access to the executive, and actions seeking to accomplish it are initiated.

❗ In the preactional phase, individuals contemplate how best to pursue the goal to which they committed at the end of the predecisional phase. They choose strategies and formulate plans (e.g., implementation intentions; see also Section 11.5) that seem conducive to attaining the aspired goal state.

Actional Phase

The initiation of action designed to further the plans formulated in the preactional phase signals the transition to the actional phase. In this phase, the individual's efforts are focused on pursuing goal-directed actions and bringing them to a successful conclusion. These efforts are best facilitated by steadfast pursuit of goals, which implies stepping up effort in the face of difficulties, and resuming goal-directed actions after every interruption. Whether or not an action is executed is determined by the volitional strength of the goal intention. The level of volitional strength acts as a kind of threshold value for effort exertion. Although this threshold is primarily determined by the strength of the motivational tendency, it may be spontaneously shifted upward when situational difficulties are encountered. The primary source of increased volition is the extra effort mobilized in response to situational difficulties. In this phase, action implementation is guided by the mental representation of the goal to which the individual has committed, which may well be outside his or her conscious awareness.

❗ In the actional phase, individuals seek to enact the plans made in the preactional phase with the aim of enacting the goal formulated at the end of the predecisional phase. These efforts are best facilitated by steadfast pursuit of the goal and by stepping up the effort exerted in the face of difficulties.

Postactional Phase

The transition to the fourth and final action phase, the postactional phase occurs once the goal-oriented actions have been completed. The task to be addressed at this stage is again a motivational one. Specifically, individuals measure the results of their actions against the goal set at the end of the predecisional phase, asking questions such as the following:

- How well have I succeeded in achieving my goal?
- Did the action result in the positive consequences anticipated?
- Can I now consider my action intention completed?
- If the goal was not attained, do I need to keep working toward it, perhaps by other means?

Individuals in the postactional phase thus look back at the action outcome attained and, at the same time, cast their thoughts forward to future action. If the action outcome corresponds with the aspired goal state, the underlying goal is deactivated. In many cases, shortcomings in the predecisional deliberation of an action's positive and negative, short- and long-term consequences may become apparent at this point. It may, for example, emerge that the desirability of the goal was overrated because certain outcome expectancies were overestimated or overlooked. Of course, not all comparisons between intended and achieved outcomes result in the deactivation of the goal: the action outcome may deviate from the intention in qualitative or quantitative terms. The goal may then be adjusted to the outcome by lowering the level of aspiration. Alternatively, individuals may choose to retain the original goal despite the unsatisfactory outcome, and renew their attempts to achieve it. Deactivation of a goal that has not been achieved seems to be facilitated by the prospect of a new goal taking its place. For example, Beckmann (1994) showed that participants could only detach mentally from a poor score on an intelligence test if they expected a new test to be administered in the next round. Participants who did not have this prospect kept thinking about the poor test result, i.e., engaged in self-evaluative rumination.

❗ In the postactional phase, individuals evaluate the action outcome achieved. If they are satisfied with the outcome, they deactivate the goal set at the end of the predecisional phase. If they are not satisfied with the outcome, they either lower the level of aspiration and deactivate the goal, or retain the original level of aspiration and increase their efforts to achieve the desired goal.

11.2.2 Motivational vs. Volitional Action Phases

Kurt Lewin (1926b) and Narziss Ach (1935) understood **volition** to be the form of motivation involved in goal striving, and goal striving to encompass all processes of motivational regulation that serve the pursuit of existing goals. Thus, volition concerns the translation of existing goals into action and, specifically, the regulation of these processes. **Motivation**, in contrast, concerns the motivational processes involved in goal setting. The focus here is on which goals a person wishes to pursue. People who have to decide between different goals are assumed to weigh the expected value and attainability of the available options very carefully (Gollwitzer, 1990). Classic motivation theories rely on this narrow definition of motivation, assuming the motivation to act to be determined by both the desirability and perceived feasibility of the aspired goal. If someone does not believe him- or herself capable of doing what is needed to attain a goal, or does not consider a goal particularly desirable, he or she will not be motivated to do all she can to pursue it.

In the early 1980s, Kuhl reestablished the distinction between motivation and volition, and drew a clear line between modern volition research and the more philosophical debate on "free will" (Kuhl, 1983; see also Chapter 12). Kuhl was the first modern motivation researcher to draw attention to the contrasting functions and characteristics of "choice motivation" and "control motivation," and strongly advocated that a distinction be made between motivational and volitional issues in research (Kuhl, 1983, 1984, 1987).

SUMMARY

Motivation concerns the processes and phenomena involved in goal setting, i.e., the selection of goals on the basis of their desirability and feasibility. Motivational processes dominate in the predecisional and postactional phases of the Rubicon model. Volitional processes and phenomena, on the other hand, concern the translation of these goals into action. Volitional processes dominate in the preactional and actional phase.

11.3 Action Phases and Mindsets: How Can Psychological Processes Be Incorporated in an Idealized, Structural Model?

The Rubicon model of action phases implies that goal-directed behavior can be broken down into a series of consecutive phases. The premise for this kind of research approach is that the phases identified describe qualitatively different **psychological phenomena** that correspond to the different functions of each action phase. The Rubicon model is thus both structural and functional in nature (Heckhausen, 1987a). The main functions of the four action phases identified are listed in the following overview.

Functions of the Action Phases in the Rubicon Model
1. Predecisional phase: deliberation
2. Postdecisional, preactional phase: preparation and planning
3. Actional phase: action
4. Postactional phase: evaluation

Each of these functions is assumed to be associated with a different mindset; i.e., a form of information processing that is appropriate to the action phase at hand. Based on the terminology of the Würzburg school (Chapter 2), the concept of **mindset** refers to the states of mind that are associated with the assumption and execution of specific tasks (Marbe, 1915; Heckhausen, 1989).

DEFINITION
The term "mindset" describes a certain kind of cognitive orientation that facilitates performance of the task to be addressed in each action phase.

Mindset research is based on the idea that distinct tasks have to be solved in each phase of the Rubicon model (Gollwitzer, 1990).

In their comprehensive research program, Gollwitzer and colleagues (see the overview in Gollwitzer, 1991) have found evidence for qualitative differences between action phases, and they have shown that task-congruent mindsets determine the content and form of information processing in each action phase. Within the research paradigm founded by Gollwitzer, the characteristic task demands of the deliberation, implementation, action, and evaluation phases are first analyzed, allowing hypotheses about phase-specific differences in information processing to then be derived and systematically tested (Gollwitzer, 1990; Gollwitzer & Bayer, 1999). These hypotheses, which are outlined below, concern the cognitive orientations that are functional for addressing phase-specific tasks. It is assumed that each phase is associated with a certain mindset (i.e., with the activation of specific cognitive procedures) that facilitates performance of the task at hand.

Deliberative Mindset

The deliberative mindset is associated with the predecisional phase and thus with the task of **goal setting**. What kind of cognitive orientation characterizes this mindset? How do people in this mindset attend to and process information? Individuals in the predecisional phase are faced with the task of deciding which of their wishes to translate into action; they have to weigh the relative desirability and feasibility of their wishes in order to select comparatively attractive and attainable action goals. Solving this task requires individuals in the deliberative mindset to be primarily concerned with information about the incentives (desirability) of different goals and expectancies (feasibility) of attaining them. The positive and negative incentives and/or potential consequences of specific action outcomes also have to be considered as impartially as possible; it is important that negative consequences should not be overlooked. Likewise, feasibility assessments should be as accurate as possible, i.e., neither overly optimistic nor unnecessarily pessimistic. Only if expectancies and incentives are assessed in an objective and impartial manner can the predecisional task of selecting a comparatively desirable and attainable goal be accomplished successfully.

Implemental Mindset

The implemental mindset is associated with the preactional phase; its task is to prepare for **goal striving**; e.g., by undertaking efforts to initiate appropriate actions. The concrete approach taken depends on the type of goal set. If, upon crossing the Rubicon, the goal was furnished with implementation intentions (Sections 11.5–11.7) specifying when, where, and how actions are to be initiated, all that remains to be done is to wait for an appropriate opportunity to arise (i.e., the "when" and "where" specified in the implementation intention). As soon as a potentially viable opportunity arises, the individual compares it with the opportunity defined as favorable in the implementation intention. If a match is ascertained, goal-directed behavior is initiated immediately. The same holds for goals that do not require implementation intentions because they are habitually initiated in a specific way. Here, too, the individual simply has to wait for a suitable opportunity to arise, and then initiate goal-directed behavior. If neither implementation intentions nor habits that might facilitate goal achievement are in place, corresponding action plans first have to be formulated. Solving these tasks requires individuals to be receptive to and process information that facilitates the initiation of goal-oriented behavior, and that

prevents its postponement. To this end, there is cognitive tuning toward information relevant to where, when, and how to act. At the same time, there should be closed-mindedness in the sense that people should concentrate on information relevant to task performance, and ignore incidental, less relevant information. Thus, attention is focused on a specified opportunity to act, and the individual is shielded from the distractions of competing goals, etc. This shielding function also applies to information about the desirability and feasibility of the goal selected at the end of the predecisional phase, which is irrelevant to the initiation of goal-directed behavior and is, in fact, distracting.

❶ Individuals in the implemental mindset are particularly receptive to information relating to the initiation of goal-directed behavior. At the same time, there is closed-mindedness in the sense that only information that will help to promote the chosen goal is processed.

Actional Mindset

The actional mindset is associated with the actional phase, the task of which can be described as acting toward the goal such that **goal achievement** is promoted. Solving this task requires individuals to avoid disruptions in goal-facilitating behavior, because any halting of the flow of action postpones goal achievement. The actional mindset should therefore evidence characteristics of what Csikszentmihalyi (1975) called "flow experience" and Wicklund (1986) labeled "dynamic orientation." Specifically, individuals in this mindset no longer reflect on the qualities of the goal to be achieved, or on their abilities and skills to achieve that goal. They do not consider alternative strategies, neither do they form implementation intentions or action plans specifying when, where, and how to act. Rather, they are totally absorbed in the actions being executed. Accordingly, they only attend to those aspects of the self and the environment that sustain the course of action, and ignore any potentially disruptive aspects (e.g., self-reflective thoughts, competing goals, or distracting environmental stimuli). The actional mindset is therefore hypothesized to be one of closed-mindedness to any information that might trigger reevaluation of the goal selected at the end of the predecisional phase, reevaluation of the implementation strategy chosen, or any form of self-evaluation (e.g., "Can I be proud of my performance thus far?", "Do I have the necessary skills to achieve the goal?"). Rather, the actional mindset should evidence cognitive tuning toward internal and external cues that guide the course of action toward goal attainment. This information should be as accurate as possible; its evaluation should not be positively biased. The actional mindset should emerge whenever people move effectively toward goal attainment.

Evaluative Mindset

The evaluative mindset is associated with the postactional phase, when the task is to **evaluate** the **action outcome** and its consequences in order to establish whether goal pursuit has led to the intended outcome and desired consequences. Solving this task requires individuals to be primarily concerned with the quality of the action outcome and the actual desirability of its consequences. In other words, individuals in the evaluative action phase compare what has been achieved (outcomes) and obtained (consequences) with what was originally expected or intended. Accurate assessments of the quality of the outcome and objective, impartial views of the desirability of its consequences are thus required. Accordingly, the evaluative mindset should evidence the following characteristics:

- cognitive tuning toward information relevant to assessing the quality of the achieved outcome and the desirability of its consequences,
- accurate and impartial processing of that information, and
- a comparative orientation: the intended outcome and its expected consequences are compared with the actual outcome and its consequences.

SUMMARY

The action phases of the Rubicon model are characterized by four distinct goal-oriented behaviors: deliberating, planning, acting, and evaluating. Because each phase involves a distinct task, each is associated with a mindset conducive to performing that task. The cognitive characteristics of each mindset can be specified by critically analyzing the demands of the tasks addressed in each action phase. For example, the deliberative mindset is characterized by open-mindedness, and by the objective processing of all available information on the potential consequences of an action outcome (desirability) and the viability of the individual's wishes (feasibility). The implemental mindset is characterized by cognitive tuning toward information that facilitates the initiation of goal-oriented behavior, and that prevents its postponement. The actional mindset focuses attention on those aspects of the self and the environment that sustain the course of action; any potentially disruptive aspects (e.g., self-reflective thoughts, competing goals, or distracting environmental stimuli) are ignored. Finally, in the evaluative mindset, there is cognitive tuning toward information that helps to assess the quality of the achieved outcome as objectively and accurately as possible. To this end, the individual compares what has actually been achieved (action outcome) and obtained (consequences of that outcome) with the intended or expected outcomes and consequences.

11.4 Contrasting Effects of the Deliberative and Implemental Mindsets

---

Having discussed the theoretical background to the four mindsets in Section 11.3, we now present empirical findings in

support of the hypotheses formulated about the deliberative and implemental mindsets. We focus on these two mindsets simply because research has yet to examine the actional and evaluative mindsets, or to test the hypotheses derived about information processing and cognitive orientations in these last two phases of the Rubicon model. We begin by describing how the deliberative and implemental mindsets can be induced experimentally.

STUDY

Experimental Design Comparing Deliberative and Implemental Mindsets

- **Induction of the Deliberative Mindset:**

Participants are asked to identify a personal concern (problem) that they are currently deliberating, without yet having decided whether to make a change (i.e., to act) or to let things take their course (i.e., to remain passive). For example, they may be contemplating whether it makes more sense to switch majors or to stick with their current one. Participants are then asked to list the potential short-term and long-term, positive and negative consequences of making or failing to make a change decision, and to estimate the probability of those consequences actually occurring (cf. Gollwitzer & Kinney, 1989, Study 2; Gollwitzer & Bayer, 1999).

- **Induction of the Implemental Mindset:**

Participants are asked to identify a goal (project) that they intend to accomplish within the next three months; e.g., applying for a grant to study abroad. They then list five steps that have to be taken to accomplish that goal, and finally write down concrete plans on when, where, and how to take each step. They thus specify the exact time, place, and manner in which each step toward realizing the goal is to be taken (cf. Gollwitzer & Kinney, 1989, Study 2; Gollwitzer & Bayer, 1999).

- **Alternative Means of Induction:**

Puca (2001) and Puca and Schmalt (2001) induced the deliberative mindset by interrupting the decision-making processes of participants who were poised to make a decision, such that they continued to deliberate on the alternatives available. They induced the implemental mindset by allowing participants to make a decision (between alternatives). Participants were then administered tasks that had nothing to do with the decision task, but served to investigate the effects of the respective mindset on different cognitive processes. Gollwitzer and Kinney (1989, Study 1) had already taken a similar approach, inducing an implemental or a deliberative mindset by presenting participants with a decision task. Specifically, the implemental mindset was induced by asking participants to decide on a certain sequence of trials before the dependent variables were assessed. The deliberative mindset was induced by interrupting participants shortly before they made a final decision on a sequence of trials.

11.4.1 Cognitive Tuning Toward Task-Congruent Information

The implemental mindset is assumed to promote goal attainment by helping people to overcome the classic problems of goal striving; e.g., doubting the attractiveness and hence the desirability of the goal being pursued, the practicability of goal-directed strategies, or the feasibility of the aspired project. Empirical data support these assumptions, showing that the implemental mindset evokes cognitive tuning toward information related to goal attainment. Participants in an implemental mindset report more thoughts relating to the execution of an aspired project (i.e., "implemental" thoughts of the type "I'll start with X and then move on to Y") than participants in a deliberative mindset (who tend to report "deliberative" thoughts of the type "If I do this, it will have positive/negative consequences, if I don't, then X, Y, or Z is likely to happen"; cf. Heckhausen & Gollwitzer, 1987; Taylor & Gollwitzer, 1995, Study 3; Puca & Schmalt, 2001).

In a series of studies, Gollwitzer, Heckhausen, and Steller (1990) induced either an implemental or a deliberative mindset using the procedure described in Section 11.4. Participants were then presented with three fairy tales that were cut short at a certain point in the plot. In what was ostensibly a creativity test, they were asked to continue the story. Participants in the implemental mindset were more likely to have the protagonists of their stories plan how to carry out a chosen goal than were participants in the deliberative mindset. In a second study, participants in an implemental or a deliberative mindset were shown a series of slides, each presenting an image of a person along with sentences reporting that person's thoughts on the pros and cons of a specific course of action and plans to put it into practice. After viewing the slides and working on a short distracter task, participants were administered a cued-recall test of the information presented. Implemental participants were better able to recall information relating to the when, where, and how of goal achievement than information relating to the pros and cons of a change decision. The recall performance of deliberative participants showed the reverse pattern.

SUMMARY

The thoughts of individuals in the deliberative mindset are more attuned to action alternatives than to strategies of goal achievement; likewise, individuals in the deliberative mindset recall information associated with the deliberation of alternatives better than information pertaining to the accomplishment of goal-directed actions. Individuals in the implemental mindset devote more thought to planning goal-directed behavior than to contemplating action alternatives, and find it easier to recall information relating to

the planning of actions than to the contemplation of action alternatives.

11.4.2 Processing of Relevant and Irrelevant Information

Gollwitzer and Bayer (1999) report that the implemental mindset leads to "closed-mindedness," to the extent that individuals in this mindset do not allow themselves to be distracted by irrelevant information, but focus exclusively on information relevant to the accomplishment of their goal. This finding is substantiated by the empirical data of Heckhausen and Gollwitzer (1987, Study 2), who found that implemental participants have shorter noun spans (a good indicator of reduced cognitive processing speed; Dempster, 1985) than do deliberative participants. A set of studies using a modified Müller-Lyer task confirmed that implemental participants' attention is more centrally focused than that of deliberative participants, and that people in a deliberative mindset are more likely to attend to incidental information than people in an implemental mindset (Gollwitzer & Bayer, 1999). In a decision experiment that required respondents to choose between the Rubicon model and Festinger's dissonance theory, Beckmann and Gollwitzer (1987) showed that information relevant to the ongoing action is processed preferentially in the implemental mindset, even when it is not in line with the decisions that have been made.

SUMMARY

Empirical research has shown that people in the deliberative mindset are more likely to be distracted by information that is irrelevant to goal attainment. This finding is in line with the observation that individuals in the deliberative mindset attend to incidental information. The reverse holds for the implemental mindset. Here, processing is attuned to information of direct relevance to goal attainment, and attention is centrally focused.

11.4.3 Biased Processing of Information Relating to Goal Feasibility and Desirability

Mindset research assumes that the implemental mindset fosters a positive evaluation of the chosen goal (i.e., its high desirability) and, at the same time, promotes a highly optimistic assessment of its practicability and attainability. The deliberative mindset, by contrast, is assumed to generate objective assessments of the positive and negative consequences of goal attainment, and a more careful evaluation of the probability of achieving the goal. Various studies (cf. Gollwitzer, 1990) have been conducted to test these hypotheses; one of the classic studies is described on the next page.

STUDY

Classic Study on "Illusionary Optimism" in the Implemental Mindset

In what is known as the "contingency learning task" (Alloy & Abramson, 1979), participants perform a series of trials on a single-stimulus apparatus. Their task is to determine to what degree they can influence the onset of a target light (i.e., the intended outcome) by choosing to press or not press a button. In other words, participants are told that alternative actions (pressing the button/not pressing the button) can lead to the outcome "target light onset." What they do not know is that target light onset is in fact entirely independent of whether or not they press the button; it is determined by a random generator.

The experimenter can vary the apparent degree of control by changing the setting of the random generator, thus manipulating the frequency of target light onset associated with each of the action alternatives (i.e., pressing or not pressing the response button). An extensive body of research using this contingency learning task (cf. Alloy & Abramson, 1988) has shown that nondepressed participants believe themselves to have control over target light onset when this desired outcome occurs frequently (e.g., when the target light comes on in 75% of pressing and 75% of nonpressing responses) as compared to infrequently (e.g., when the target light comes on in 25% of pressing and 25% of nonpressing responses). Given that target light onset is in fact noncontingent to participants' actions, but governed by a random generator, these findings of inaccurate, optimistic judgments of control are remarkable.

Gollwitzer and Kinney (1989) assumed that this unrealistic **illusion of control** over target light onset would be less pronounced in deliberative mindset participants than in the implemental mindset participants. The authors assumed that people in the implemental mindset tend to see themselves and their abilities in a much more positive light than do people in the deliberative mindset (Section 11.4). They therefore modified the contingency learning task by adding a second apparatus and asking participants to work on 5 sets of 20 trials. A single trial consisted of the choice to press or not press the response button followed by task light onset or non-onset. A deliberative mindset was induced by telling participants that their objective in the first part of the experiment was to decide which of the two available apparatuses to work on during the second part of the experiment. Deliberative participants were encouraged to try out both apparatuses before the experiment proper began to ensure an informed decision. The implemental mindset was induced by asking participants to specify which apparatus they would use in each trial *before* starting the first set. After making this decision, they were instructed to try to produce as many light onsets as possible, whether by pressing or not pressing the response button. The participants were thus instructed to "find out" for themselves whether pressing or not pressing the button gave them more "control" over target light onset. Of course, the experimenter knew that target light onset was in fact governed by a random generator, and entirely independent of participants' actions. Besides the two mindsets, a "target light onset" condition was implemented:

- either the "high frequency of target light onset" condition, in which the target light comes on in 75% of pressing and 75% of nonpressing responses
- or the "low frequency of target light onset" condition, in which the target light comes on in 25% of pressing and 25% of nonpressing responses.

Accordingly, both apparatuses presented either noncontingent frequent or noncontingent infrequent onset of the target light. When target light onset was frequent and thus seemed to be "contingent" on participants' actions (pressing/not pressing the response button), implemental mindset participants reported inaccurately high judgments of the degree of control they exerted over target light onset (illusionary optimism), whereas deliberative mindset rated their level of control to be much lower. The deliberative mindset participants evidently recognized that high frequency of an event was not necessarily a valid indicator of their own influence over it. The deliberative mindset thus seems to prevent people from adopting unrealistically optimistic beliefs about how much influence they have over uncontrollable events. When, on the other hand, target light onset was infrequent and thus seemingly noncontingent, both mindset groups showed rather modest control judgments. This finding indicates that people in an implemental mindset can adapt to external constraints if necessary. If environmental feedback tells them otherwise (e.g., a high rate of "non-hits" in the button-press task), they do not cling blindly to a belief of being in control over target outcomes, but abandon this illusion of control.

On the subject of "illusionary optimism" in the implemental mindset, Gagné and Lydon (2001a) report that individuals in an implemental mindset see the future of their current romantic relationship in a more optimistic light than do individuals in a deliberative mindset. Likewise, Puca (2001, Studies 1 and 2) established that the implemental mindset is associated with an optimistic approach to the choice of test materials of varying difficulty (Study 1) and the prediction of future task performance (Study 2). Relative to deliberative participants, implemental participants opted for more difficult tasks and were more optimistic about their chances of success. Finally, Harmon-Jones and Harmon-Jones (2002, Study 2) discerned differences between the deliberative and implemental mindsets in terms of how information on the desirability of chosen and nonchosen alternatives is processed. Dissonance research discovered that, once a choice has been made, the chosen option is seen in a much more positive light than the nonchosen option. Harmon-Jones and Harmon-Jones observed that induction of an implemental mindset increases this effect, whereas induction of a deliberative mindset reduces it.

SUMMARY

Relative to the deliberative mindset, the implemental mindset is associated with increased optimism about the degree of personal control over intended action outcomes and with a preference for difficult tasks. Moreover, the implemental mindset is associated with higher estimations of the probability of success than the deliberative mindset.

11.4.4 Mindsets and Self-Evaluation

Deliberative and implemental mindsets have also been shown to affect the way people see themselves. Experimental findings show that people in a deliberative mindset score much lower on the Rosenberg Self-Esteem Scale (Rosenberg, 1965) than do people in an implemental mindset. Likewise, students judge themselves to be more creative, intelligent, popular, etc., when an implemental mindset is induced than when a deliberative mindset is induced (Taylor & Gollwitzer, 1995). Induction of an implemental mindset evidently boosts people's belief in themselves and their abilities. Where self-ratings of susceptibility to various risks are concerned, moreover, findings show that people in an implemental mindset consider themselves less likely to fall victim to various strokes of fate (e.g., being involved in a plane crash or developing diabetes) than do people in a deliberative mindset. Table 11.1 presents the results of this study.

11.4.5 Moderator Effects in the Deliberative and Implemental Mindsets

Mindset research has now also established that the effects of deliberative and implemental mindsets are moderated by both **individual differences** (see the following overview) and **context variables** (cf. Gollwitzer, 2003).

Individual Differences Found to Moderate the Effects of Deliberative and Implemental Mindsets

1. Level of achievement motivation: only success-motivated individuals show the mindset effects outlined above, failure-oriented individuals do not (Puca & Schmalt, 2001),
2. level of social anxiety: only people low in social anxiety show the mindset effects described, those high in social anxiety do not (Hiemisch, Ehlers, & Westermann, 2002), and
3. positivity of self-concept (Bayer & Gollwitzer, 2005).

Bayer and Gollwitzer (2005) discovered that students with a high self-view of intellectual capability look for both positive and negative information that is highly diagnostic with respect to their achievement potential when in a deliberative mindset, but focus only on positive information, whether its diagnosticity is high or low, when in an implemental mindset. In contrast, individuals with a negative self-view of intellectual capability focus on positive information (irrespective of its diagnosticity) when in a deliberative mindset and look for highly diagnostic information, whether positive or negative, when in an implemental mindset.

Table 11.1. Effects of deliberative and implemental mindsets on different variables (Taylor & Gollwitzer, 1995)

Dependent variables	Mindsets		
	Control	Deliberative	Implemental
Mood	10.05	−2.52	11.30
Risk	6.05	6.00	9.71
Self-esteem	41.77	37.55	41.08
Optimism	30.55	27.36	29.03

Scores measured on the following scales: mood: Multiple Affect Adjective Checklist (MAACL; Zuckerman & Lubin, 1965); risk: Measure of Relative Perceived Risk (Perloff & Fetzer, 1986); self-esteem: Rosenberg Self-Esteem Scale (Rosenberg, 1965); optimism: Life Orientation Test (LOT; Scheier & Carver, 1985).

The situational **context** has also been shown to moderate the effects of deliberative and implemental mindsets. To date, research on this aspect has focused on predictions on the stability of participants' romantic relationships (Gagné & Lydon, 2001a; Gagné, Lydon, & Bartz, 2003). For example, Gagné and Lydon (2001a) found that deliberating on decisions that have already been made can initiate defensive processing of relationship-related information. Participants who were involved in a romantic relationship were asked to consider the positive and negative consequences of a goal decision that was either associated with the relationship or had nothing to do with relationships in general, and the probability that those consequences would occur (see Section 11.4 for details of mindset induction). Gagné and Lydon found that participants gave their partner much higher ratings if the goal decision they had considered was related to the relationship than if it was not. Interestingly, the partner ratings given by participants in a deliberative mindset were more positive than those given by participants in an implemental mindset. Gagné and Lydon (2001a) concluded that deliberation on one's relationship may be perceived as threatening, and that participants evaluated their partner in more positive terms in order to ward off this threat. In a further study, Gagné & Lydon (2001b) assessed the commitment participants felt to their relationship using a questionnaire measure. It emerged that only high-commitment participants boosted their ratings of their partner to defend their relationship against the threat posed by deliberating on a relationship problem; low-commitment participants did not. Thus, commitment to the relationship is another important moderator of the effects of the deliberative and implemental mindset in the context of romantic relationships.

SUMMARY

Self-concept and the context of romantic relationships have been shown to moderate the effects of deliberative and implemental mindsets. Self-concept moderates mindset effects on the processing of high or low diagnostic information about

Table 11.2. Effects of the deliberative and the implemental mindset

	Deliberative mindset	Implemental mindset
Effects on self-concept	Low assessment of self-esteem	High assessment of self-esteem
	Respondents rate themselves somewhat higher on positive characteristics (e.g., intelligence, creativity) than compared to others	Respondents rate themselves much higher on positive characteristics (e.g., intelligence, creativity) than compared to others
	High ratings of own vulnerability to controllable and uncontrollable risks	Low ratings of own vulnerability to controllable and uncontrollable risks
Effects on information processing	Open-mindedness to information of all kinds	Preference for information conducive to the enactment of an intention
	Thoughts tend to focus on "deliberative" behavior	Thoughts tend to focus on "implemental" behavior
	Good recall of others' deliberative behavior	Good recall of others' implemental behavior
	Open-mindedness to incidental information	Attention is centrally focused
Effects on optimism/ pessimism	Low feeling of control over uncontrollable events	Illusionary feeling of control over uncontrollable events
	Realistic view of one's future performance	Optimistic view of one's future performance
	Comparatively negative rating of one's relationship/partner	Comparatively positive rating of one's relationship/partner
Effects on motivation	Lower persistence in putting intentions into practice	Higher persistence in putting intentions into practice

personal strengths or weaknesses. The context and commitment to a relationship moderate mindset effects on people's evaluations of their partners.

11.4.6 Mindsets and Goal Achievement

Studies on the effects of deliberative and implemental mindsets on goal achievement supported the hypothesis that the implemental mindset is more conducive to goal attainment than the deliberative mindset, because both information processing and self-evaluation are focused on the task at hand (Section 11.4).

A good predictor of goal attainment in everyday life is **persistence** of goal-directed behavior, i.e., the tenacity people show in their endeavors to overcome difficulties and master challenges. Accordingly, some authors have investigated the effects of the deliberative and implemental mindsets on persistence of goal striving. Findings presented by Pösl (1994) and Brandstätter and Frank (2002) suggest that people in the implemental mindset show greater persistence when faced with difficult tasks. For example, Brandstätter and Frank (2002, Study 1) found that participants in the implemental mindset persisted longer at a difficult puzzle than did participants in the deliberative mindset.

The findings presented by Pösl (1994) paint a differentiated picture. When both the perceived feasibility of the goal-directed behavior and the perceived desirability of the goal were either high or low, the persistence of goal striving was not influenced by the mindset induced. However, when perceived feasibility and desirability were in opposition (i.e., one was high and the other low), participants in the implemental mindset showed greater persistence in goal-directed behavior than did participants in the deliberative mindset. Importantly, moreover, the persistence of goal-directed behavior

associated with the implemental mindset is not rigid and inflexible. Brandstätter and Frank (2002, Study 2) observed that as soon as a task is perceived to be impossible, or persistence in what was assumed to be goal-directed behavior proves to be aversive, individuals in the implemental mindset are quicker to disengage from goal pursuit than are individuals in deliberative mindset. Thus, the persistence instigated by the implemental mindset seems to be flexible and adaptive.

With respect to the effectiveness of goal striving in the implemental and deliberative mindsets, experimental findings reported by Armor and Taylor (2003) indicate that implemental mindsets are associated with better task performance than deliberative mindsets, and that this effect is mediated by the cognitive orientation of the implemental mindset, e.g., enhanced self-efficacy, optimistic outcome expectations, etc. (Section 11.4.4).

❗ The implemental mindset is more conducive to goal striving than the deliberative mindset.

All effects of deliberative and implemental mindsets identified to date are documented in Table 11.2.

11.4.7 Concluding Discussion: Mindsets and Self-Regulation of Goal Striving

The findings presented above raise questions about the self-regulation of goal striving. Can people intentionally induce a certain mindset in order to increase their prospects of reaching a certain goal, or to facilitate disengagement from a goal, should it prove unrealistic or undesirable? The implemental mindset has proved particularly effective for promoting goal striving (Section 11.4.6). In the study by Armor and Taylor (2003) mentioned above, the optimistic assessments of goal success associated with the implemental mindset led to more effective self-regulation of goal striving and to better outcomes on an achievement-related task than the less optimistic expectations associated with the deliberative mindset. Likewise, Pösl (1994) and Brandstätter and Frank (2002, Studies 1 and 2) showed that induction of an implemental mindset increased the likelihood of goal attainment; this effect seems to be primarily attributable to the greater persistence in goal striving associated with the implemental mindset.

In any discussion of the relationship between the implemental mindset and goal realization, it is important not to forget that the positive effects of this mindset apply primarily to tasks conducted immediately after it has been induced. The more time elapses between the induction of the implemental mindset and task performance, the less pronounced its positive effects on goal attainment, as Gagné and Lydon (2001a) and Puca (2001) have shown.

SUMMARY

Critically, the induction of a mindset does not have a permanent influence on information processing and self-evaluation; the effects of the deliberative and implemental mindsets only apply for a certain time.

11.5 Different Kinds of Intentions: Goal Intentions and Implementation Intentions

Both scientific psychology and naive everyday theories often advocate goal setting as a good strategy for enacting wishes and meeting demands. Yet numerous studies have shown that goal setting alone does not guarantee the accomplishment of those goals – even highly motivated people often find it difficult to translate their goals into action. Sometimes they are simply hesitant to actually take action to achieve their goals, and do not initiate goal-directed behavior for this reason. Sometimes they strive for too many, often competing, goals at the same time, including long-term projects that call for repeated efforts over extended periods. Sometimes the situational conditions are not conducive to goal attainment. For example, someone whose attention is focused on intensive emotional experiences will be distracted and may thus fail to register an opportunity to act on his or her goals.

❶ Contrary to the widespread notion that goal setting is a sufficient condition for the accomplishment of personal goals and projects, an extensive body of research shows that many goals are never actually put into practice.

Drawing on the work of Narziss Ach (1905, 1910, 1935) and Kurt Lewin (1926b), Gollwitzer (1993, 1999) addressed the difficulties of translating goals into action from the perspective

of self-regulation. Gollwitzer concluded that goals can often only be attained when goal pursuit is supported by the self-regulatory strategy of planning. Planning is understood to be the mental anticipation of goal achievement. Against this background, two types of intention are distinguished:
- goal intentions and
- implementation intentions.

The concept of "goal intentions" has much in common with Lewin's (1926b) conceptualization of intentions.

❶ Goal intentions specify desired end states that have not yet been attained. Hence, goal intentions are "goals" in the conventional sense.

Examples of goal intentions are: "I intend to be a good psychologist" or "I intend to be friendly to a certain person."

❶ Implementation intentions are subordinated to goal intentions; they are plans that promote the attainment of goal intentions. In forming implementation intentions, individuals specify the anticipated situations or conditions that will trigger a certain goal-directed response (see the example below). Implementation intentions have the structure "When (if) situation X arises, (then) I will perform response Y," and are often called if-then plans.

EXAMPLE

An implementation intention for someone who would like to improve their diet (in which case the superordinate goal intention might be "I intend to eat healthily") would be: "When my order is taken at a restaurant, I will ask for a salad." Implementation intention research works on the assumption that, once this implementation intention has been formed, the onset of the situation "ordering food" suffices to trigger the behavior "I will ask for a salad."

How, then, do implementation intentions differ from habits? In both cases, behavior associated with a certain situation or stimulus is initiated automatically as soon as that situation or stimulus is encountered.

❶ Implementation intentions differ from habits to the extent that they originate from a single act of will: the conscious pairing of a desired goal-directed behavior with a critical situation or stimulus. By contrast, habits are formed by the repeated and consistent selection of a certain course of action in a specific situation (cf. Fitts & Posner, 1967; Newell & Rosenbloom, 1981).

11.5.1 How Do Implementation Intentions Work?

Numerous studies have investigated the psychological processes underlying the effects of implementation intentions. The focus of research has been on the chronic activation of the situation specified in the implementation intention and on the automatic initiation of the action specified.

The Situation Specified: Chronic Activation

Because forming an implementation intention implies the conscious selection of a critical situation or stimulus as the if-part of the implementation intention, the mental representation of this situation is assumed to be highly activated and thus easily accessible (Gollwitzer, 1999; Gollwitzer, Bayer, & McCulloch, 2003). This heightened cognitive accessibility makes it easier for people to detect and attend to the critical situation in the surrounding environment, even when they are busy with other things. At the same time, it facilitates recall of the critical situation in terms of how, where, and when the goal-directed behavior is to be enacted. Furthermore, speed of perception differs: critical situations are perceived more quickly than situations not specified in implementation intentions. A classic cognitive accessibility study is described below.

STUDY

Classic Study on the Cognitive Accessibility of Situations Specified in Implementation Intentions

Findings from a dichotic listening experiment show that words describing the anticipated critical situation are highly disruptive to focused attention. Mertin (1994) presented participants with words to both ears simultaneously via headphones. Participants were instructed to "shadow" the words presented on one channel, i.e., to repeat these words as soon as they heard them, and to ignore the words presented on the other channel. Attention was thus focused on one channel. It emerged that participants' shadowing performance was much slower when words relating to the critical situation were presented to the nonattended channel than when unrelated words were presented. In other words, critical words attracted attention, even when efforts were made to direct attention to the shadowing task. The same effect was not observed either in a group of participants who had only formulated a goal intention without furnishing it with implementation intentions, or in a group who had not formulated any intentions at all on how to approach the task at hand.

This finding indicates that the critical situations specified in implementation intentions are unlikely to escape people's attention, even when they are busy with other things.

The findings of a study using the Embedded Figures Test (Gottschaldt, 1926) provide further evidence for the enhanced cognitive accessibility of the critical situation. The objective of this test is to detect smaller "*a*-figures" that are concealed within larger "*b*-figures." Participants who had specified the "*a*-figure" in the if-part of an implementation intention were better able to detect these hidden figures than participants who had only formulated a goal intention (Steller, 1992).

In a cued recall experiment, participants had to decide when, where, and how to play certain games by choosing between a number of set options offered by the experimenter. In a surprise memory test administered both immediately and

48 hours later, participants who had specified their choices in an implementation intention recalled these options much more effectively than participants who had formulated goal intentions only (Gollwitzer et al., 2002).

Finally, Aarts, Dijksterhuis, and Midden (1999), using a lexical decision task, provided further support for the assumption that implementation intentions lead to heightened activation of specified situational cues. Participants who had specified critical cues in implementation intentions showed faster lexical decision responses than did participants who had only formed goal intentions.

❶ The chronic activation of the situation specified in the implementation intention is thus reflected in its heightened cognitive accessibility, which in turn facilitates effectively detecting, readily attending to, and successfully remembering critical situational cues.

Implementation Intentions and Action Initiation

As mentioned above, action initiation becomes automatic once an implementation intention has been formulated through a single act of will. In forming implementation intentions, individuals can strategically switch between the conscious and effortful control of goal-directed behaviors and the automatic control of these behaviors in response to selected situational cues. Gollwitzer et al. (2002; e.g., Gollwitzer & Schaal, 1998; Gollwitzer, Fujita, & Oettingen, 2004) call this type of automatic action control **strategic automaticity**. The goal-directed behavior specified in the implementation intention is assumed to be triggered immediately, efficiently, and without conscious intent whenever the critical situation is encountered. Thus, someone who has formed an implementation intention does not have to invest cognitive resources in conscious and effortful control of the goal-directed behaviors specified in an implementation intention; rather, their performance is placed under the direct control of situational cues.

Implementation intentions are thus more effective than goal intentions alone in various respects. For example, it has been shown that participants who have formed implementation intentions respond to the critical situation immediately, even at high levels of distraction. The findings of dual-task experiments attest to the efficiency of automatic action initiation in this context (Brandstätter, Lengfelder, & Gollwitzer, 2001; Achtziger, Michalski, & Gollwitzer, forthcoming). Participants in these experiments have to perform two tasks at the same time. A decrease in performance on one task is interpreted as indicating that the other task taxes cognitive resources. A series of studies using this dual-task paradigm have shown that cognitive resources are not required to initiate the responses induced by implementation intentions. For example, two experiments by Brandstätter et al. (2001, Studies 3 and 4) showed that students working on a task that required them to press the response button as soon as a particular stimuli appeared on the computer screen responded

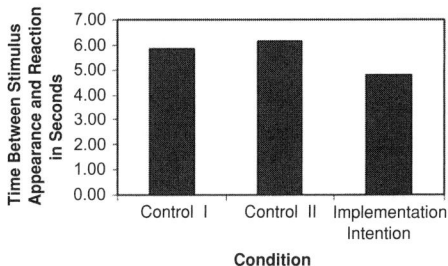

Figure 11.2 Reaction times in a dual-task experiment with and without implementation intentions (Brandstätter, Lengfelder, & Gollwitzer, 2001)

substantially faster if they had formed an implementation intention, even when a dual task had to be performed at the same time. Students who had only formed a goal intention to respond as quickly as possible did not show enhanced reaction times under the dual-task condition. The results of this study are presented in Fig. 11.2.

STUDIES WITH CLINICAL SAMPLES. In further studies, Brandstätter et al. (2001) showed that even patients who have severe problems with action control from chronic cognitive load can benefit from implementation intentions. For example, drug addicts under withdrawal benefited from forming implementation intentions specifying when and where to perform actions that would facilitate their return to "normal" life. Most implementation intention patients succeeded in writing a curriculum vitae to be used in job applications before a set deadline, whereas goal intention participants missed the deadline. In other words, the chronic cognitive load associated with withdrawal did not inhibit goal-directed behavior if an implementation intention had been formed.

Lengfelder and Gollwitzer (2001) tested the hypothesis that implementation intentions automate action initiation in studies with frontal lobe patients. Individuals with frontal lobe injury typically have problems with the conscious control of automated actions or habits. Whenever they see a pair of scissors, for example, they will reach for the scissors and begin cutting, and are not able to consciously and deliberately interrupt that action, no matter how hard they try. In other words, a stimulus associated with the execution of a particular action will involuntarily and inevitably trigger that action in these patients. Against this background, Lengfelder and Gollwitzer (2001) administered a go/no-go task to frontal lobe patients. In this type of task, participants have to respond to selected stimuli (e.g., to press a button when two of five visual patterns appear on a computer screen), but not to others (i.e., selective attention). If implementation intentions are indeed based on automatic processes, as assumed by Lengfelder and Gollwitzer (2001), the patient group should show faster reaction times to the situational cues specified in an implementation intention in the go/no-go task than a control group of healthy individuals. This prediction was con-

firmed, with frontal lobe patients showing significantly faster reaction times than the control group.

ⓘ This finding indicates that the executive functions governed by the frontal lobe are not required in implementation intentions, thus suggesting that implementation intention effects are primarily based on automatic processes.

Further experimental support for this finding has been provided by Achtziger et al. (forthcoming) and Gawrilow and Gollwitzer (2004). Using a procedure that blocks the central executive of working memory (cf. Baddeley, 1996), Achtziger et al. (forthcoming) were able to show that the performance of participants who had formed an implementation intention to support the processing of stereotype-inconsistent information about a target person did not differ depending on whether or not the functions of the central executive had been blocked. However, participants who had not formed an implementation intention proved unable to process stereotype-inconsistent information when the central executive was blocked, and therefore judged the target person in a stereotypical manner. Blocking the central executive puts a heavy load on the frontal lobes (Baddeley, 1996), meaning that automatic processes take precedence. The finding that implementation intentions take effect even when the central executive of working memory is blocked confirms that implementation intention effects do not tax cognitive resources.

Gawrilow and Gollwitzer (2004) demonstrated the effects of implementation intentions in a group of children diagnosed with attention deficit hyperactivity disorder (ADHD). Children with ADHD are known to have important deficits in executive functioning and hence in processes that tax cognitive resources. They consequently find it very difficult to respond quickly and reliably to stop signals. Before being administered a variation of the stop task (cf. Logan, Schachar, & Tannock, 1997), children with ADHD were asked to formulate an implementation intention specifying that they would stop what they were doing as soon as they encountered a certain stimulus. Findings showed that, having formulated this implementation intention, ADHD children managed to inhibit the behavior in question just as well as a control group of healthy children. Thus, the study provided further evidence that implementation intention effects are primarily based on automatic processes, and not on processes that involve central executive functions, and hence tax cognitive resources.

Gollwitzer and Brandstätter (1997, Study 3) demonstrated the immediacy of action initiation as soon as the critical situation is encountered. One group of participants formed implementation intentions that specified viable opportunities for presenting counterarguments to a series of racist remarks made by a confederate of the experimenter; another group formulated goal intentions to the same effect. As expected, the implementation intention participants initiated their counterarguments to the racist comments more quickly than did the goal intention only participants. The study presented below provided empirical evidence that implementation intentions lead to action initiation even in the absence of conscious intent.

STUDY

Study on Action Initiation in the Absence of Conscious Intent

Bayer, Achtziger, Malzacher, Moskowitz, and Gollwitzer (forthcoming) conducted two experiments to test whether implementation intentions lead to action initiation without conscious intent once the critical situation is encountered. In these experiments, the critical situation was presented subliminally (i.e., below the threshold for perception).

In Study 1, Bayer and colleagues investigated whether participants were able to achieve their goal of asserting themselves against a rude experimenter by formulating an implementation intention. Half of the participants were encouraged to set the goal of reprimanding the experimenter by drawing attention to her rude behavior (goal intention condition); the other half were additionally instructed to plan to take this action as soon as they set eyes on her (implementation intention condition). Afterwards, faces of either the experimenter who had showed the rude behavior or a neutral, unknown person were presented subliminally (as primes) to all participants by means of a tachistoscope (presentation times of less than 10 ms). Primes are stimuli that serve to activate associated cognitive contents. These cognitive contents are presented subsequent to the primes and their effects are measured, usually in terms of reaction times. Immediately after each prime, participants were presented with certain words, some of which were associated with rudeness (e.g., offensive, aggressive, arrogant). Participants were asked to repeat all of the words as quickly as possible, and the latencies of their responses were measured by the computer. After the subliminal presentation of the critical primes, participants who had formed an implementation intention to reprimand the experimenter as soon as they set eyes on her showed faster response times to words related to rudeness than did participants who only formed goal intentions.

This finding provides further confirmation that the goal-directed behavior specified in implementation intentions is initiated automatically – i.e., triggered immediately, efficiently, and without conscious intent – as soon as the critical situation is encountered.

THE ROLE OF COMMITMENT IN IMPLEMENTATION INTENTION EFFECTS. Might the effects of implementation intentions be attributable in part or even wholly to an associated increase in goal commitment? If furnishing goals with implementation intentions indeed produces an increase in the level of commitment to superordinate goal intentions, the assumption that implementation intentions automatize the initiation of goal-directed behavior and other cognitive processes would be immaterial. However, this hypothesis has not received any empirical support. For example, Brandstätter et al. (2001, Study 1) found that the positive effect of an imple-

mentation intention to submit a curriculum vitae before a specified deadline was independent of the patients' general commitment to writing a curriculum vitae. Patients in the implementation intention group were no more committed to the goal than were patients in the goal intention group. Analogous results have been reported in numerous studies from domains such as disease prevention (e.g., Orbell, Hodgkins, & Sheeran, 1997), social impression formation (Seifert, 2001, Studies 1 and 2; Achtziger, 2003, Studies 1 and 2), and tennis competitions (Achtziger, Gollwitzer, & Sheeran, in press, Study 2).

All mechanisms known to underlie the effects of implementation intentions are listed in the following overview.

Mechanisms Underlying the Effects of Implementation Intentions

1. Chronic activation of the situation specified in the implementation intention (effectively detecting, readily attending to, and successfully remembering critical situational cues),
2. automaticity of goal-directed behavior (no taxing of cognitive resources),
3. automatic initiation of the action specified in the implementation intention (immediately, efficiently, and in the absence of conscious intent).

11.5.2 Implementation Intentions and the Initiation of Wanted Behavior

Because implementation intentions facilitate attending to, detecting, and remembering situations conducive to goal-directed behavior and, in addition, help to automatize action initiation, people who form implementation intentions can be expected to show higher goal-attainment rates than people who do not furnish their goal intentions with implementation intentions. The results of a host of studies in very different domains provide empirical support for this hypothesis.

Effects of Implementation Intentions on Achievement- and Health-Related Behavior

Research on implementation intentions tends to examine goal intentions that are difficult to attain for reasons already mentioned; e.g., because of external or internal distractions or because the action required is unpleasant or painful. For example, Gollwitzer and Brandstätter (1997) analyzed a goal intention that had to be performed during the Christmas vacation. Students were given the task of writing a report about Christmas Eve no later than 48 hours after the event. As expected, students who had formed a corresponding implementation intention were significantly more likely to write a report within the allotted time than students who had only formed a goal intention.

Orbell, Hodgkins, and Sheeran (1997) found that women who had set themselves the goal of performing regular breast self-examinations greatly benefited from forming implementation intentions. Similar patterns of results have emerged for participation in voluntary cancer screening (Sheeran & Orbell, 2000), resumption of functional activity after hip replacement surgery (Orbell & Sheeran, 2000), and engagement in physical exercise (Milne, Orbell, & Sheeran, 2002). Furthermore, implementation intentions have been found to facilitate the attainment of goal intentions that are otherwise easily forgotten; e.g., regular intake of vitamin tablets (Sheeran & Orbell, 1999) or signing each page of an intelligence test (Chasteen, Park, & Schwarz, 2001).

Significant Moderators of Implementation Intention Effects

The strength of implementation intention effects depends on the presence or absence of various moderators. Some studies (e.g., Gollwitzer & Brandstätter, 1997, Study 1) show that the more difficult it is to initiate a goal-directed behavior, the more pronounced implementation intention effects become. The findings of the study with frontal lobe patients described above (Lengfelder & Gollwitzer, 2001, Study 2; Section. 11.5.1) are relevant here as well. Patients with a frontal lobe injury typically have problems with the conscious control of behavior because their access to executive functions and cognitive resources is limited. Findings show that patients who formed an implementation intention in preparation for a reaction time task outperformed a sample of college students who had formed the same implementation intention. Because the reaction time task can be assumed to be more difficult for the patients than for the healthy students, this finding confirms that forming implementation intentions is particularly beneficial to people faced with difficult tasks.

Commitment to the goal intention also seems to moderate the effects of implementation intentions. Orbell et al. (1997) report that implementation intentions only enhanced compliance in performing breast self-examinations in women who strongly intended to examine their breasts, i.e., who were committed to the superordinate goal intention. Similarly, Gollwitzer et al. (2002, Study 3) found that beneficial effects of implementation intentions on participants' recall of critical situations were only observed when the goal intention had yet to be translated into reality. If it had already been accomplished, no implementation intention effect on memory performance was detected. Furthermore, Sheeran, Webb, and Gollwitzer (2005, Study 1) showed that the beneficial effects of implementation intentions concerning the goal of preparing for an upcoming exam increased as a function of the amount of studying required. In addition to strength of commitment to the goal intention, commitment to the specific implementation intention is required. In the memory study by Gollwitzer et al. (2002), the strength of the commitment to the implementation intention was varied by telling participants (after administering a battery of personality tests) that they were the type of person who would benefit either from strictly adhering to their plans (high commitment condition) or from staying flexible (low commitment condition). Participants in the latter group showed notably weaker implementation intention effects than those in the former group.

Sheeran et al. (2005, Study 2) found that implementation intention effects only occur when the respective superordinate goal intention is activated. The implementation intention to move on to the next item in an intelligence test immediately after finishing the previous one enhanced speed of task processing only when the goal intention of working as quickly as possible was activated. Likewise, in an experiment using the Rogers and Monsell (1995) task-switch paradigm, Bayer, Jaudas, and Gollwitzer (2002) found that implementation intention effects are dependent on the superordinate goal being activated.

Finally, it can be assumed that the strength of the mental link between the if- and then-parts of an implementation intention moderates its effects. For example, if a person invests a lot of time and concentration in encoding an implementation intention in long-term memory and/or mentally rehearsing that intention, stronger mental links should be forged between the two parts, which should in turn produce stronger implementation intention effects. This assumption has not yet been subjected to experimental testing, however.

SUMMARY

The difficulty of initiating goal-directed behavior, the strength of commitment to goal intentions and implementation intentions, and the activation of the goal intention have proved to be significant moderators of implementation intention effects.

11.6 Implementation Intentions and the Control of Unwanted Behavior

To date, research has focused almost exclusively on how implementation intentions can help to translate goals into action by facilitating wanted, goal-directed behavior, and particularly the initiation of goal-directed behavior. Yet merely initiating goal pursuit rarely suffices to achieve a goal. Once initiated, a process of goal striving has to be maintained. People need to shield their goals from distractions or conflicting bad habits. Ways in which implementation intentions can be used to control these "unwanted" effects are outlined below.

Unwanted responses that hamper the successful pursuit of goals can be controlled by different types of implementation intentions. For example, someone who wants to avoid being unfriendly to a friend who is known to make outrageous requests can protect herself from showing the unwanted response by forming the goal intention "I intend to stay friendly" and furnishing it with one of the following three **suppression-oriented implementation intentions**:

- 1st suppression-oriented implementation intention: "And if my friend makes an outrageous request, then I will not respond in an unfriendly manner." The strategy here is to control and suppress unwanted behavior by specifying the critical situation in the if-part of the implementation intention, and ruling out the unwanted response in the then-part. Alternatively, the focus may be on facilitating the initiation of a wanted response:

■ **2nd suppression-oriented implementation intention:** "And if my friend makes an outrageous request, then I will respond in a friendly manner." In this case, the critical situation is again specified in the if-part, and the wanted response that is threatened by disruptive unwanted responses is endorsed in the then-part.

■ **3rd suppression-oriented implementation intention:** "And if my friend makes an outrageous request, then I will ignore it." In this variant, the critical situation is again specified in the if-part of the implementation intention, and the then-part focuses the person away from the critical situation.

Gollwitzer and colleagues have conducted a series of studies using these three types of suppression-oriented implementation intentions. Most of these studies investigated the control of unwanted spontaneous responses to distractions or of automatic activation of stereotypes and prejudice.

11.6.1 Suppression-Oriented Implementation Intentions

When goal pursuit is threatened by distracting stimuli, implementation intentions should be formed to inhibit those distractions, as illustrated by the study described below.

STUDY

Implementation Intentions and Resistance to Distractions

In a computer-based experiment (Gollwitzer & Schaal, 1998) college students performed a series of arithmetic problems while distracting clips of popular commercials were shown at random intervals on a TV screen mounted above the computer monitor. Findings showed that goal intentions ("I will not let myself get distracted") were less effective in protecting participants from the distractions of the commercials than were implementation intentions. Moreover, implementation intentions phrased as distraction-inhibiting ("And if a distraction arises, then I will ignore it") produced better results than those phrased as task-facilitating ("And if a distraction arises, then I will focus my attention on the arithmetic tasks"). Specifically, distraction-inhibiting implementation intentions helped participants to ward off the distractions of the commercials regardless of their motivation to do the tedious arithmetic problems, whereas task-facilitating implementation intentions were effective only when motivation to do the problems was low. When motivation was high, task-facilitating implementation intentions did not shield participants against the distractions of the commercials, and performance on the arithmetic tasks was poor. These findings suggest that task-facilitating implementation intentions may result in overmotivation in distracting conditions and thus undermine performance.

CONTROLLING PREJUDICE. Researchers have also investigated the function of implementation intentions as strategies for controlling unwanted stereotypes in impression formation. In general, models of impression formation (e.g., Brewer, 1988; Devine, 1989) assume that the effects of social stereotypes and prejudices on the way people judge others are governed by processes that require attention, cognitive resources, and conscious effort. Until recently, stereotype research assumed that the application of stereotypes – but not their activation – can be intentionally controlled (cf. Brewer, 1988; Devine, 1989). Stereotype activation was thought to be an unavoidable, automatic process; stereotype use, to be controllable by effortful correctional strategies. Based on the studies of the automaticity of implementation intentions described above, Gollwitzer's research group conducted a series of experiments to test whether implementation intentions can inhibit the automatic **activation** of stereotypes and prejudice, and not just their application. The assumption was that an automatic process such as the activation of a stereotype can be blocked by other automatic processes such as those triggered by implementation intentions. Experiments using different priming paradigms showed that the automatic activation of the stereotype "old person" was inhibited when participants formed an implementation intention ("When I see an old person, then I will tell myself: don't stereotype!"), but was still observed in a group of participants who had formed a goal intention only ("I intend to judge fairly") and in a control group who were simply instructed to form an impression of the people presented (Gollwitzer, Achtziger, & Schaal, forthcoming). Analogous results emerged from a study in which male participants were asked to inhibit the stereotype "women," and studies in which participants of both sexes were asked to inhibit the stereotypes "homeless person" or "soccer fans" (Achtziger & Gollwitzer, 2005).

Other studies investigated the extent to which implementation intentions can prevent the **application** of stereotypes. Seifert (2001, Study 1) tested whether the discrimination of female job seekers applying for jobs in technical domains can be controlled by implementation intentions. Computer science students were presented with a number of applications for the position of computer scientist and a profile of the job's requirements. Half the fictional applicants had a woman's name, the other half a man's name. In a preliminary study, in which all applicants had male names, all applicants were judged to be equally qualified for the job. When male and female names were assigned to the applications at random, however, the computer science students were considerably more likely to hire male candidates, thus discriminating against the female candidates. Only a group of students who had formed the implementation intention "When I evaluate an application, then I will ignore the candidate's gender" managed to overcome this bias. Stereotype research has evidenced that individuals under cognitive load are unable to process stereotype-inconsistent information about unknown others (cf. Macrae, Hewstone, & Griffiths, 1993). Stereotype-inconsistent information is not generally attributed to representatives of certain social categories. For example, "machos" are not usually characterized as "tolerant." Successful processing of stereotype-inconsistent information results in nonstereotypical impressions. In two studies, Achtziger et al. (forthcoming) replicated the finding that stereotype-inconsistent information is poorly processed under cognitive load, and showed that people who formed implementation intentions are able to process stereotype-inconsistent information and hence to evaluate others fairly, even under cognitive load.

SUPPRESSION OF EMOTIONAL RESPONSES. Research has shown that, apart from regulating unwanted behavioral responses (e.g., to distractions) and precluding unfair evaluations of others, implementation intentions can also inhibit unwanted emotional responses. For example, Schweiger Gallo, Achtziger, and Gollwitzer (2003) report a study examining how implementation intentions can be used to inhibit disgust. Female participants were presented with picture cues from the International Affective Picture System (IAPS; CSEA, 1999). Some of these pictures show photographs of injured and mutilated individuals, and activate the emotion "disgust." Participants were able to suppress their disgust by means of an implementation intention, but not by means of a goal intention alone.

SUMMARY

Suppression-oriented implementation intentions have proved effective in inhibiting spontaneous attentional responses, stereotypical and prejudicial responses, and reflexive negative emotional responses.

11.6.2 Blocking Detrimental Self-States by Planning Wanted Behavior

In the research presented in Section 11.6.1, the critical situation specified in the if-part of an implementation intention was linked to a then-part that served to suppress unwanted responses. Implementation intentions may also protect against unwanted responses in another way, however. Instead of focusing on anticipated obstacles and the unwanted responses they trigger, implementation intentions may be designed to stabilize an ongoing goal pursuit. For example, an exchange of opinions can soon develop into an argument if the parties are tired and worn out, even if they did not intend the situation to escalate. However, if the parties planned in advance how to respond constructively to conflicting opinions, the self-states of fatigue and exhaustion should not have a negative impact on the discussion. These assumptions have been tested in a series of studies, one of which is described below.

STUDY

Study on Blocking Negative Self-States

One of the studies on the use of implementation intentions to block negative self-states (Gollwitzer & Bayer, 2000, Study 1) was based on the **theory of symbolic self-completion** (Wicklund & Gollwitzer, 1982) and tested the extent to which the negative effects of self-definitional incompleteness on social sensitivity (cf. Gollwitzer & Wicklund, 1985a) can be attenuated by forming implementation intentions. Participants were law students who were highly committed to becoming successful lawyers. As a cover story, they were told that the study had been designed to analyze how goals affect how people get to know each other. To this end, they would be introduced to another student; their goal was to take that person's perspective during the conversation. Half of the participants were instructed to furnish this goal with the following implementation intention: "And if my partner expresses a preference for a certain topic of conversation, then I will direct the conversation to that topic." They were then administered a questionnaire on how they approached their studies ("no sense of incompleteness" condition) or the same questionnaire with three supplementary questions drawing attention to shortcomings in their current skills and experience (e.g., "Do you have courtroom experience as a judge or district attorney?"). This second questionnaire was designed to create a sense of self-definitional incompleteness.

Finally, all participants were informed that the person they were to meet was called Nadia, and that she had already indicated her preferences for potential topics of conversation. Participants were then handed a sheet of paper listing these preferences. It was quite clear that Nadia did not want to discuss law, but would prefer to talk about her last vacation and popular movies. To assess whether self-definitional concerns would increase the likelihood of participants' choosing law as a preferred topic of conversation despite Nadia's preferences, all participants were asked to note down their own preferred topics for Nadia. In the control condition, a self-completion effect was clearly apparent: participants with an incomplete self-definition were more likely to want to talk about law than participants with a complete self-definition, even though Nadia was clearly not interested in discussing this topic. The same effect was not observed in the group of participants who had formed an implementation intention, however – these participants showed the same low preference for law as a potential conversation topic, whether their self-definitions were complete or incomplete.

These findings show that implementation intentions are able to block the negative effects of the self-state "self-definitional incompleteness" on goal-directed action (specifically, taking someone else's perspective).

Implementation Intentions and Self-Regulatory Performance

According to ego-depletion theory (Baumeister, 2000; Muraven, Tice, & Baumeister, 1998), performing a task that demands a high level of self-regulation will encroach on performance on a second task that also requires self-regulation. Gollwitzer and Bayer (2000, Study 3) were interested in whether this effect could be countered by implementation intentions. In a classic ego-depletion paradigm, participants were first shown a humorous movie and instructed either to express their emotions freely, or to show no emotions at all. They were then presented with a number of difficult anagrams. All participants had formed the goal intention to solve as many anagrams as possible. Half the participants had furnished this goal intention with an implementation intention: "And if I have solved one anagram, then I will move on immediately to the next." Participants who had only formed a goal intention showed the classic ego-depletion effect, with those who had been instructed not to show their emotions during the film performing less well on the anagram task than those who had given free rein to their emotions. This effect was not observed in participants who had furnished the goal intention to perform well with an implementation intention, however.

Webb and Sheeran (2003, Study 2) also demonstrated that implementation intentions can offset ego-depletion effects. First, half the participants were instructed to balance on their "weaker" leg while counting down in sevens from 1,000 (ego-depletion manipulation). Participants in the control condition counted to 1,000 in fives while standing normally on two legs. All participants were then given the goal intention of naming the ink color of words presented in a Stroop test as quickly as possible. Half the participants furnished this goal intention with an implementation intention: "When I see a word, then I will ignore its meaning and name the color in which it is printed." No ego-depletion effect was observed for implementation intention participants; those who had been ego-depleted in the initial task performed as well in the Stroop test as those in the nondepleted control condition. However, participants who had only formed a goal intention showed a marked ego-depletion effect, with those who had been ego-depleted scoring notably lower on the Stroop task than their nondepleted counterparts.

SUMMARY

The negative effects of both self-definitional incompleteness and ego-depletion can be blocked by forming implementation intentions.

11.6.3 Blocking Adverse Contextual Influences by Planning Wanted Behavior

People may see the outcomes of their actions in terms of gains or of losses (Kahneman & Tversky, 1979). Conflict-resolution research suggests that cognitive processes triggered by "loss framing" or "gain framing" have a strong impact on negotiation processes and their outcomes (De Dreu et al., 1994). Loss framing results in comparatively unfair agreements and other negative effects. Trötschel and Gollwitzer (2004) investigated whether these negative loss framing effects can be overcome if prosocial goals, such as finding a fair or integrative solution, are furnished with corresponding implementation intentions. This hypothesis was tested in two experiments, the first of which is described below.

STUDY

Overcoming Loss Framing Effects by Means of Implementation Intentions

Pairs of participants were assigned the roles of heads of state of two rival countries and asked to negotiate the partitioning of a disputed island. The island was made up of 25 regions, each representing one of four terrains: mountains, cornfields, pastures, or forests. Within each pair of negotiators, one participant was subjected to loss framing as follows:

■ **Loss framing condition:** The participant was handed a table listing the four different types of regions, and specifying the loss that would be incurred if each were relinquished to the other participant in terms of a negative score. The other participant in each pair of negotiators was subjected to gain framing.

■ **Gain framing condition:** In this condition, the regions listed in the table were allocated positive scores, indicating the gain that would be incurred if that region were appropriated.

Both participants were told that they had to come to an agreement on the distribution of the 25 regions within 15 minutes. A fairness goal was instilled in some participants by handing them a sheet of paper informing them that fair negotiation outcomes are often very difficult to achieve, and instructing them to set themselves the following goal shortly before entering the negotiations: "I want to find a fair solution." Half the participants with a fairness goal were additionally instructed to furnish this goal intention with an implementation intention: "And if my opponent makes a proposal, then I will make a fair counterproposal." Participants in the control condition were not instructed to specify either a fairness goal or an implementation intention. Outcomes were assessed in terms of individual "profits" within each pair of negotiators. In each of the three conditions, the authors tested whether the difference in profits within each dyad was significantly different from zero.

In both the goal intention condition and the control condition, significant differences in profits were observed as a function of the framing condition. Participants who had been subjected to loss framing made higher profits than those subjected to gain framing. Unfair outcomes of this kind were not observed in the implementation intention condition, where profits were equally distributed between participants.

Intentions and Performance Feedback

Goal attainment can also be negatively affected by unfavorable performance feedback conditions. One example here is the "social loafing" phenomenon often observed at workplaces where employees are given collective, rather than individual performance feedback (cf. Latané, Williams, & Harkins, 1979; Karau & Williams, 1993): people when working in groups where individual performance cannot be monitored have been observed to show lower performance levels. Gollwitzer and Bayer (2000, Study 4) tested whether this phenomenon can be counteracted by means of implementation intentions. Their participants were asked to generate as many uses as possible for a common knife under one of two conditions:

- ■ **"Collective performance feedback" condition:** Participants were told that their responses would be pooled with those of seven other participants, and that the experimenter would not be able to tell how many uses each individual had generated.
- ■ **"Individual performance feedback" condition:** Participants were told that the experimenter would be able to assess each participant's performance separately.

Before beginning the task, all participants formed the goal intention "I intend to name as many uses as possible." Half of the participants furnished this goal intention with the implementation intention: "And when I have noted down a use, then I will immediately go on to the next." The number of uses generated in 12 minutes was taken as the dependent variable. Goal intention participants generated notably fewer uses in the "collective performance feedback" condition than in the "individual performance feedback" condition. This pattern of results, which replicates the classic social loafing effect, was not observed in implementation intention participants, who generated an equal volume of responses, regardless of the feedback condition.

Formation of Implementation Intentions and Competing Goals

Auto-motive theory (Bargh, 1990; Bargh & Gollwitzer, 1994) holds that when goal striving is activated repeatedly and consistently in response to a given situation, this situation will eventually acquire the potential to trigger the critical goal pursuit without conscious intent (Bargh, 1990; Bargh & Gollwitzer, 1994). A goal intention that can be activated in this way is called a "chronic goal." Gollwitzer (1998) conducted two experiments to test whether implementation intentions can shield ongoing goal pursuit against the effects of directly activated chronic goals.

In the first study, participants had to navigate a car along a race track in a simulator. The mean driving speed and number of errors were measured in two baseline circuits. Participants were then given precise instructions on how to drive the next two circuits.

- ■ Participants in the goal intention condition were instructed to set themselves the goal of reaching the finishing post as quickly and with as few errors as possible.
- ■ Participants in the implementation intention condition were additionally instructed to form the following implementation intentions: "And when I enter a curve, then I will reduce my speed. And when I enter a straight section of the track, then I will speed up again."

Before participants were allowed to drive the final two circuits of the track, auto-motive priming was used to activate two goals beyond the participants' conscious awareness. All participants were asked to join the numbered dots presented on different sheets of paper as quickly as possible to produce various shapes (flowers, animals, and other objects). Those in the "move quickly" priming condition were instructed to complete as many figures as possible in five minutes. Those in the "move slowly" priming condition were told to join the dots as carefully and neatly as possible, taking as much time as they needed for each shape. Findings showed that this auto-motive priming had pronounced effects on goal intention participants' driving in the last two circuits: those in the "move quickly" condition drove faster and made more mistakes than those in the "move slowly" condition. No such priming effect was observed for implementation intentions participants, who drove at a moderate speed and made few mistakes in both priming conditions. These findings indicate that goal pursuits furnished with implementation intentions are not affected by competing, nonconscious goals that are activated by situational cues.

Table 11.3 documents all effects of implementation intentions that have been identified to date.

11.7 Potential Costs of Implementation Intentions

As we have shown, implementation intentions facilitate goal pursuit in various ways. It seems reasonable to hypothesize that such an effective means of self-regulation may have certain unforeseen costs. This section examines the three following potential costs of implementation intentions:

1. It is possible that implementation intentions lead to a certain rigidity of behavior that may be detrimental when task performance requires high levels of flexibility.

2. It is possible that implementation intentions cause a high degree of ego-depletion and thus undermine self-regulatory resources.

3. It is possible that thoughts, feelings, and actions may resurface later in a different context (rebound effects), although implementation intentions successfully suppresses unwanted thoughts, feelings, and actions in a given context.

11.7.1 Implementation Intentions and Behavioral Rigidity

Do people who have formed implementation intentions also recognize alternative opportunities to act toward their goal, or do they insist on acting only when the critical situation specified in the implementation intention is encountered? The strategic automaticity created by implementation

Table 11.3. Effects of implementation intentions	
Controlling unwanted behavior	**Promoting wanted behavior**
Suppressing unwanted thoughts, feelings, and actions ("suppression-oriented implementation intentions")	**Fostering the initiation and execution of goal-directed actions**
Inhibiting automatic activation of stereotypes (e.g., age stereotypes, gender stereotypes)	Increasing the latency of counterarguments to racist remarks
Inhibiting prejudice (e.g., discrimination of women in male-dominated professions)	Increasing the probability of participation in cancer screening (e.g., mammography)
Shielding against distraction during complex tasks (e.g., distracting effects of commercials while working on arithmetic problems)	Facilitating the processing of stereotype-inconsistent information despite cognitive load (e.g., on the central executive)
Controlling impulsive behavior in children with ADHD (e.g., enhancing response inhibition in a reaction-time task)	**Fostering persistence of goal-directed actions**
Replacing unwanted behavior by other behavior	Supporting the regular intake of vitamin tablets and essential medication
Inhibiting the automatic activation of prejudice (e.g., toward homeless people)	Helping challenged patient groups to perform difficult everyday actions (e.g., drug addicts under withdrawal to write a CV)
Inhibiting negative emotions (e.g., disgust)	Fostering engagement in physical exercise (e.g., after hip replacement surgery)
Inhibiting behavior that is detrimental to health (e.g., cigarette and alcohol consumption)	
Shielding wanted behavior from unwanted internal and external influences	
Blocking unfavorable contextual influences (e.g., deindividualization, competing goal activations, framing effects)	
Blocking detrimental self-states (e.g., self-definitional incompleteness, mood, ego-depletion)	

intentions – i.e., the delegation of behavioral control to situational cues – can be assumed to free up cognitive resources, thus allowing effective processing of information about alternative opportunities. This assumption has been confirmed in a number of studies showing that individuals who had formed an implementation intention were not blind to changed situational contexts or unexpected opportunities to achieve their goal. Instead of sticking rigidly to their plans, participants responded appropriately to new situations.

For instance, Achtziger (2003, Study 2) showed that participants are able to form implementation intentions that are only applied in certain contexts. A study on prejudice toward soccer fans showed that participants were able to apply the implementation intention "And if I see a soccer fan, then I'll not evaluate him negatively" flexibly, dependent on the context. In this study, the presence of a signal tone indicated that the implementation intention should be applied, whereas the absence of the tone indicated that it should not. In line with the assumption that implementation intentions do not necessarily lead to behavioral rigidity, the inhibition of prejudice toward "soccer fans" was only observed when pictures of soccer fans were accompanied by a signal tone. Likewise, another study (Jaudas & Gollwitzer, 2004) showed that participants who encountered an unexpected opportunity to pursue a goal intention – i.e., an opportunity other than the one specified in the if-part of the implementation intention – were able to recognize and seize this new opportunity. Participants

were shown two symbols (e.g., flower, heart) on a monitor and asked to select the symbol with the highest score. Before the study began, they had been told the score of each symbol, and some participants had formed the implementation intention to select the symbol with the highest score especially quick by pressing the button as soon as it appeared. After a while, a new symbol with an even higher score was presented on the screen. Participants in the implementation intention condition succeeded in selecting this new symbol rather than the one that previously had the highest score.

11.7.2 Implementation Intentions and Ego Depletion

The assumption that implementation intentions automate the control of goal-directed behavior implies efficient and relatively effort-free behavioral control. In other words, the self is not implicated – and should therefore not become depleted – when behavior is controlled by implementation intentions. Empirical support for this assumption has been provided by the studies of Gollwitzer and Bayer (2000) and Webb and Sheeran (2003) reported in Section 11.5.2. Whether the initial self-regulating task was to control one's emotions (Gollwitzer & Bayer, 2000) or to perform well on a challenging task (the Stroop task; Webb & Sheeran, 2003), implementation intentions successfully preserved self-regulatory resources. It would thus seem that self-regulation based on implementation intentions is not costly in terms of self-regulatory resources.

11.7.3 Implementation Intentions and Rebound Effects

Wegner (1994) observed that conscious attempts to control or suppress one's thoughts – e.g., "I will not think about pink elephants!" – lead to rebound effects in the sense that the thoughts controlled become more readily accessible and thus more likely to surface in subsequent thoughts and behavior. Participants in his studies set themselves suppression goals of this kind and were instructed to ring a bell whenever their thoughts turned in the proscribed direction. Participants with the goal of not thinking about pink elephants initially succeeded in suppressing these thoughts. However, findings from a second phase of the experiment, in which participants engaged in free association and wrote down all of their thoughts, showed that participants who had resolved not to think about pink elephants in the first part of the experiment were now considerably more likely to report thoughts relating to pink elephants than participants who had not set a suppression goal. This is effect is termed the **rebound effect**:

❗ The rebound effect involves a marked increase in certain thoughts following the "extinction" of a goal to suppress or inhibit those thoughts.

Against the background of these research findings, it would seem reasonable to hypothesize that suppression-oriented implementation intentions may inhibit unwanted thoughts and feelings to begin with, but that these suppressed thoughts or feelings resurface later, i.e., that rebound effects occur. Gollwitzer et al. (2004) conducted two experiments to test this hypothesis. The participants in these studies were first asked to suppress stereotypical thoughts about a carefully described homeless person in an impression formation task. Rebound was measured either in terms of subsequent expression of stereotypes in a questionnaire tapping participants' evaluation of homeless people in general (Gollwitzer et al., 2004, Study 1) or in a lexical decision task assessing the cognitive accessibility of stereotypical contents regarding homeless people (Gollwitzer et al., 2004, Study 2). It emerged that the participants who had only set themselves the goal of suppressing stereotypical thoughts when forming an impression of the homeless person experienced pronounced rebound effects in both studies, showing more stereotypical judgments of homeless people in general (Study 1) and a higher accessibility of homeless stereotypes (Study 2). Participants who had furnished this goal intention with a corresponding implementation intention did not experience rebound effects.

SUMMARY

Findings on the potential costs of implementation intentions can be summarized as follows:

- implementation intentions do not lead to behavioral rigidity (e.g., in the suppression of prejudice or in performance on choice tasks),
- implementation intentions do not lead to ego-depletion (e.g., performance levels are not reduced when emotions are controlled by means of implementation intentions), and
- implementation intentions do not lead to rebound effects (e.g., when stereotypical thoughts are suppressed).

11.8 Discussion and Future Perspectives

11.8.1 Implementation Intentions: A Foolproof Self-Regulatory Strategy?

Although implementation intentions seem to function effectively without significant costs in terms of behavioral rigidity, ego-depletion, or rebound, they do not always result in the desired outcome. First, the behavior specified in the then-part of an implementation intention may be beyond the person's control. For example, somebody who intends to eat healthily may plan to order vegetarian food, but then find themselves in a restaurant with no vegetarian options. Second, it makes no sense to specify situations that barely, if ever, occur in the if-part of implementation intentions. For example, it would be pointless for someone to plan to eat healthily by ordering vegetarian food the next time they go to a good restaurant if they usually eat in cafeterias or at home. Third, the behaviors specified in the then-part of the implementation intention may not be instrumental to reaching the goal. For example, someone who plans to eat healthily may order a vegetarian meal in a restaurant, not knowing that the dish chosen is full of fatty cheese.

11.8.2 Prospective Memory and Neuronal Substrates

In the past 20 years, implementation intention research has focused on motivational and volitional processes and their effects on impression formation and behavior. In the coming years, the focus should be shifted to **cognitive** and **neuroscientific aspects**. From the cognitive perspective, implementation intention research stands to benefit from prospective memory research (cf. Smith, 2003), which examines the processes by which intentions are stored in and retrieved from long-term memory, as well as from ongoing attempts to examine the different components of working memory (e.g., the central executive, the phonological loop, and the episodic buffer as proposed by Baddeley, 1986; Baddeley, 2000) and their functions in the realization of goal intentions and implementation intentions (Achtziger et al., forthcoming). From the neuroscientific perspective, researchers have already used magnetic encephalography to examine neuronal activity in the deliberative and implemental mindsets, and found that the implemental mindset is associated with higher posterior gamma activity than the deliberative mindset. These findings indicate that more intensive and complex brain activity is involved in planning the implementation of a goal in terms of when, where, and how to perform a specific goal-directed action than in weighing up the positive and negative consequences of a potential course of action and the probability that these consequences will occur. Moreover, the kind of brain activity generated by the implemental mindset seems to be associated with preparation of actions (Achtziger, Rockstroh, Oettingen, & Gollwitzer, 2003). Research has also found the control of negative emotions (e.g., anxiety; Schweiger Gallo, Keil, Mc Culloch, Rockstroh & Gollwitzer, forthcoming) and automatic stereotype activation (Achtziger, Moratti, Jaudas, Rockstroh, & Gollwitzer, forthcoming) by means of implementation intentions vs. goal intentions to involve different electroencephalogram (EEG) responses. Generally speaking, however, there is still much to be learned about the neuronal substrates of action control by means of goal intentions vs. implementation intentions, and indeed about intentional states in general.

SUMMARY

The study of motivation in the course of action has made it possible to distinguish phenomena of goal setting (motivation) from phenomena of goal striving (volition). Whereas research to date has focused on the cognitive orientations associated with the respective action phases (mindset research), the aim of future research will be to identify self-regulatory strategies that facilitate effective accomplishment of the tasks necessary at each phase in the course of action. The theory of intentional action control (Gollwitzer, 1993, 1999) has taken first steps in this direction, showing how implementation intentions can facilitate the performance of tasks that necessitate the initiation of goal-directed behavior, the shielding of that behavior against distractions, the timely termination of goal striving, and measures to ensure that the capacity for action control is not overstretched during goal striving.

Future research should take a two-pronged approach. On the one hand, it should seek to identify further self-regulatory strategies that help to address these kinds of difficulties and thereby help people to attain their goals; on the other hand, the search for effective self-regulatory strategies should be extended to other action phases. The predecisional phase of goal setting has already been examined. Fantasy realization theory (Oettingen, 1996, 2000) distinguishes three different goal setting strategies (mental contrasting of desired future and actual present, indulging in positive fantasies about the future, and dwelling on negative aspects of the present), and has found that only mental contrasting guarantees that the goals people set are in line with their perceived expectations of success. In other words, mental contrasting ensures that people do not pursue goals that are excessively high or low,

but aspire to goals that help them realize their full potential. Future research should examine the postactional phase in which completed goal strivings are evaluated, and seek to identify self-regulatory strategies that are conducive to a person's goal striving in subsequent endeavors. The ultimate goal of this research is to develop intervention programs that will provide individuals with action control strategies that enable them to address the problems that beset goal striving in the different action phases of the Rubicon model more successfully.

REVIEW QUESTIONS

1. **Which four phases are distinguished in the Rubicon model of action phases?**

   The predecisional, preactional, actional, and postactional phase.

2. **At the end of which phase of the Rubicon model does the individual "cross the Rubicon" by committing to a goal intention?**

   At the end of the predecisional phase.

3. **What effects do the deliberative vs. implemental mindsets have on self-evaluation?**

   Studies have shown that an implemental mindset is associated with more positive self-evaluations than a deliberative mindset.

4. **How are the implemental and deliberative mindsets experimentally manipulated?**

   There are two methods of inducing each mindset:
   Implemental mindset: 1. Participants are asked to choose between alternatives, i.e., to make a decision; 2. Participants are asked to plan the steps required to translate a given project into action, specifying when, where, and how to take each step.
   Deliberative mindset: 1. Participants are interrupted during the decision-making process; 2. Participants weigh the positive and negative short- and long-term consequences of making or failing to make a change decision.

5. **What effects do the deliberative vs. implemental mindsets have on information processing?**

   Individuals in the deliberative mindset generally engage in more "deliberative" thoughts, are able to recall deliberative thoughts better than implemental thoughts, and tend to be open-minded (i.e., to process information in an objective and unbiased manner); moreover, their attention is not centrally focused. The opposite effects are observed for individuals in the implemental mindset.

6. **After induction of which mindset are goals more likely to be attained?**

   After induction of the implemental mindset.

7. **What are the effects of a deliberative mindset on people's evaluations of their romantic relationships?**

It depends on the person's commitment to the relationship. If commitment is high, the partner is rated more positively after induction of a deliberative mindset than after induction of an implemental mindset; if commitment is low, the effects are reversed.

8. **What is a "goal intention"?**

Goal intentions specify desired end states that people wish to attain. They have the structure "I intend to reach X."

9. **What is an "implementation intention"?**

Implementation intentions are "if-then" statements that specify the conditions under which goal-directed behavior is to be initiated.

10. **What function do implementation intentions serve?**

Implementation intentions facilitate the enactment of goal intentions that are particularly difficult to attain.

11. **Which factors moderate the effects of implementation intentions?**

The following moderator variables have been identified:

difficulty of the goal intention,

commitment to the goal intention,

commitment to the implementation intention,

degree of activation of the goal intention.

12. **Are cognitive resources required to put implementation intentions into practice?**

Implementation intentions are initiated automatically and thus do not tax cognitive resources.

13. **What positive effects can implementation intentions have on health-related behavior?**

Examples: regular intake of vitamin tablets; participation in cancer screening; regular exercise after hip replacement surgery.

14. **How can implementation intentions inhibit unwanted effects, such as stereotypical views of others?**

Unwanted behavior can be inhibited by forming an implementation intention that inhibits either its activation or its application. The if part of the implementation intention should specify a situation or a stimulus that is likely to trigger activation or application of the stereotype; the then part should specify a goal-directed behavior with the potential to inhibit the stereotype (e.g., by initiating or upholding individualized processes of impression formation).

12 Individual Differences in Self-Regulation[1]

J. Kuhl

Even a casual observer of human behavior can see that there are profound differences in how individuals regulate their actions. Some individuals doggedly pursue a single goal or ideal for many years, making many personal sacrifices and at great personal cost. Others seem to give in to their immediate impulses with barely a thought for the consequences. Some students earn their highest grades under severe stress and in the face of adversity. The same levels of stress and adversity

may lead other students to drop out and abandon their academic goals altogether. Indeed, many students seem to perform best under more relaxed conditions. At the workplace, some employees demonstrate high levels of initiative and set their own agenda, regardless of what others may think. Others prefer to follow the instructions of their superiors, and are eager to learn what is expected of them.

These and other individual differences in self-regulation are the central focus of the present chapter. The following sections offer some preliminary reflections on the neglect of individual differences in psychological research. Next, the chapter considers individual differences in motives and needs, and how global notions of self-regulation and the will can be decomposed into more specific psychological functions and mechanisms. Finally, this chapter shows how this functional analysis of the will can be used to understand a wide array of effects of individual differences in affect regulation (i.e., action vs. state orientation). Throughout the present chapter, the overarching goal is to illuminate the basic psychological functions that may underlie individual differences in self-regulation.

12.1 Reflections on the Neglect of Individual Differences in Psychological Research

There is still no general consensus among experimental psychologists on the significance of individual differences. It therefore seems appropriate to begin this chapter with some reflections on individual differences in self-regulation. Most cognitive psychologists and many social psychologists take no account of individual differences. The reasons for this neglect are not discussed systematically in psychology. In fact, wherever the exclusion of individual differences occurs, it seems to be a tacit a priori assumption rather than an explicitly discussed decision. When asked about their reasons for disregarding individual differences, researchers – particularly those based in the United States – often cite sociopolitical arguments. As they see it, paying attention to dispositional factors risks missing opportunities for social change. This kind of thinking is based on the erroneous assumption that situational influences are always easier to change than

---

[1] Thanks are due to Sander Koole for helpful comments on an earlier version of this chapter.

individual ones. Yet we know from everyday experience that people are often exposed to situational influences that are not easily changed, such as a chronically ill relative, a low income, or a floundering economy.

It is also important to note that personality characteristics are not necessarily fixed and unchangeable. The laws of falling bodies in physics, which take account of individual differences in the mass of falling objects, do not require this variable to remain unchanged across the "lifespan" of an object. The only constraint is that there is no change in the measured mass of an object while each individual measurement is taken and the laws are applied (incidentally, the same applies to situational factors). If the mass of the object changes (e.g., because fragments of the stone under investigation break off), this change is taken into account in the next measurement, before the laws are applied again.

In this respect, neglecting personality characteristics in psychological research is like throwing the baby out with the bath water. Rather than excluding personality dimensions from their work altogether, researchers critical of the static nature of psychological concepts of personality might want to put some thought into the true nature of personality dispositions. Psychology needs a dynamic rather than static conception of personality. One such theory is presented in Section 12.5: The theory of Personality Systems Interactions (PSI) assumes that individual dispositions play a role in the ever-changing exchange of information between psychological systems. Depending on the social context of the interaction, this exchange of information in turn has the potential to influence and change personality functioning.

Besides the sociopolitically motivated reluctance against the study of personality, there is another, even more deeply rooted reason for the widespread neglect of dispositional determinants of behavior. It is based on the misunderstanding that the pursuit of general laws, which is, of course, critical for a young experimental science like psychology, would be impeded if different laws were allowed to apply to different people. If there were idiosyncratic laws for each individual person, so the reasoning, there would be no room for a general psychology. This concern seems to be influenced by the development of experimental psychology in the first decades of the 20th century. Specifically, the beginnings of experimental psychology were characterized by enormous difficulties in abandoning the introspective "observation of the soul" that psychologists associated with "armchair psychology," and that seemed incompatible with the agenda of the newly emerging experimental discipline. The experimental psychologists of the time, who called themselves "behaviorists," only accepted observations that could be made directly and **from an external perspective** as the basis for the development of scientific psychology; they sought to discover **general** psychological laws.

Even today, researchers who take individual differences into consideration are sometimes implicitly suspected of obstructing that agenda, which is of existential importance for scientific psychology. In reality, however, there is no inherent contradiction between personality psychology and a psychological science in search of general law. Again, comparison with laws of nature, such as the laws of falling bodies, helps to illustrate the point. No physicist would ever suggest that averaging the masses of a random sample of objects would produce more general laws of falling bodies. Clearly, the laws of falling bodies are only generally applicable if the individual characteristics (i.e., the mass) of the object in question are included in the equation. The findings on individual differences in self-regulation (e.g., action vs. state orientation) reported in this chapter indicate that – in psychology as in physics – results are only replicable when individual characteristics are taken into account.

❶ Failure to measure unwelcome potential influencing factors – e.g., personality dispositions that are believed to reduce the general applicability of a law – does not constitute scientific rigor; on the contrary, it is a parascientific denial strategy. Scientific "objectivity" requires researchers to consider all potential influencing factors and, if their influence can be established, to incorporate them in psychological "laws." General applicability of a paradigm cannot be achieved simply by ignoring influencing variables. In other words, individual differences whose influence has been established empirically lend general applicability to models that do not a priori include personality parameters (Lewin, 1935).

12.2 Motives as Need-Oriented Self-Regulatory Systems

Motivation psychology is concerned with what motivates people to behave in certain ways. Different approaches offer very different answers to the question of what these motives are. The idea that **cognitive representations** of goals motivate behavior has been popular for some time now (see Brunstein & Maier, 1996; Cantor & Zirkel, 1990; Emmons, 1992; Little, 1989). The advantage of the focus on cognitive motives for behavior is that it coincides with what is currently the most fruitful area of psychological research: In formulating cognitive theories of motivation, researchers are able to capitalize on both the theoretical and the methodological advances of cognitive psychology within the study of human motivation. An exclusive focus on the cognitive determinants of behavior does not paint the whole picture, however. Even if I know which cognitively represented goals an individual is pursuing, I still do not know why this person has set him- or herself those particular goals, and whether a cognitive representation of a goal is a **necessary** condition for motivated behavior, or whether behavior may be motivated by sources other than conscious intentions and other cognitive sources of motivation.

Other sources of motivation we might consider are needs and affects that are not cognitively represented (e.g., if a person starts talking to somebody because of his or her need for closeness, but is unaware of that need and has not consciously set him- or herself the goal of satisfying it). Furthermore, we do not know whether the existence of a goal is a **sufficient** condition for engaging in the corresponding behavior. In fact, as will be discussed in the present chapter, whether or not a cognitively represented goal is translated into action hinges largely on regulatory processes that are described by the terms **self-regulation**, **volition**, or **will**.

12.2.1 Needs: Subaffective Detectors of Discrepancies Between Actual and Desired States

Self-regulatory processes are also investigated in fields of psychology other than motivation psychology; e.g., as "executive processes" in cognitive psychology (Norman & Shallice, 1986), and as central coordinating processes in the frontal lobe in neuropsychology (Damasio, Tranel, & Damasio, 1991; Wheeler, Stuss, & Tulving, 1997). To appreciate the specific perspective that the motivational approach brings to volitional processes, it helps to consider some of the key terms and concepts of motivational theory. To come back to the defining question of motivation psychology introduced above, what are the processes that determine the goals that people set themselves?

> **DEFINITION**
>
> Motivational processes that are not characterized by cognitive representations of a target state can be called **precognitive** or **subcognitive**, because they exist even before cognitive goal representations are generated.

Neurobiology attributes these subcognitive processes to brain structures that, in terms of phylogeny, ontogeny, and indeed brain anatomy, are located "below" the structures mediating cognitive representations. These subcognitive structures may be regarded as detectors of discrepancies between actual and desired states, similar to the detectors in the hypothalamus that are known to monitor blood sugar level, which plays a major role in feelings of hunger and motivating food intake (Leibowitz, Weiss, Walsh, & Viswanath, 1989). These detectors are more comparable with mechanical detectors of discrepancies between actual and desired states (e.g., thermostats) than with cognitive representations (e.g., the thought of a goal or an internal cognitive map).

> **DEFINITION**
>
> Needs may be defined as subcognitive and subaffective detectors of discrepancies between actual and desired states.

Animal experiments show that subcognitive motivational processes can regulate behavior. Specifically, electrical or chemical stimulation of certain nuclei in the hypothalamus has been shown to trigger motivated behavior, such as attacking, suckling, drinking, grooming, etc., independent of the brain structures involved in generating cognitive representations (e.g., when the cortex and hippocampus have been removed; Clemente & Chase, 1973; Himmi, Boyer, & Orsini, 1988; Peck & Blass, 1975).

Freud popularized the assumption that human behavior is motivated by basic (subcognitive) biological needs (drives). Starting from the energetic basis common to all drives (libido), which he associated with the drive to procreate, Freud differentiated needs such as:

- the need to eat (oral),
- the need to exercise control (anal), and
- the need for love (genital).

The psychoanalytic school is known for its propensity to attribute the needs manifested in adulthood to basic drives and the childhood experiences ("vicissitudes") associated with them. Psychoanalysts assumed that individuals whose oral needs are either over- or undersatisfied in childhood will develop a **fixation** not only on needs that are directly linked to the intake of food (drinking, eating), but also on needs associated with the need for food and drink in early infancy; e.g., the needs for skin contact, closeness, and a sense of security (**oral dependency**). The reasoning was that early experiences of feeding are closely linked to the satisfaction of needs for contact and a sense of being cared for.

12.2.2 Affective and Cognitive Systems: Need-Relevant System Configurations

Psychoanalysts were mainly concerned with explaining pathological development, and paid much less attention to **healthy** psychological development. If we were to take a similar approach to inferring the needs that develop from an infant's oral needs in the case of healthy development – i.e., when oral needs are neither over- nor undersatisfied – we might assume these needs to be strongly associated with **independence**, rather than with dependence. In a normally developing child, the need for food can be seen as prototypical of a need that progresses from being satisfied in a dependent manner to being satisfied in an ever more independent manner. The child becomes increasingly independent of the mother – skin contact is no longer necessary during food intake, children learn to feed themselves, and gradually begin to decide what to eat and drink and what to reject. They also find more and more ways to obtain the food they want, even if that food is not actively provided by the mother or is forbidden; i.e., if difficulties (**obstacles**) are to be overcome.

Looking at the **manner** in which a need is satisfied rather than its actual content, we can even discern a gradual progression from the need for food to other needs that likewise imply increasing independence. The prototype here is the **need for achievement**, which centers on the attainment of difficult goals and development of the necessary skills. Early studies on the achievement motive confirmed that independence is indeed a basic prerequisite for the development of the need to achieve. Winterbottom (1953) found that individuals whose mothers emphasized their child's independence from an early stage (e.g., who let them do things without help or interference) tended to produce Thematic Apperception Test (TAT) stories on achievement-related themes. Likewise, Scheffer (2000) found that when adults who associated a large number of achievement-related contents in response to various stimuli (i.e., who had a high **achievement motive**) were administered an indirect test on the structure of the family of origin, they described their mothers as interfering little in their affairs, i.e., as allowing them a great deal of independence.

These mothers do not always show their support for their child, but withhold warmth in certain situations (i.e., they let their child experience the frustration associated with the difficulties encountered). The child then will then seek his or her own solutions to the problem, i.e., engage in **instrumental behavior**.

❶ Instrumental behavior (i.e., behavior that is used as an "instrument" to achieve a certain purpose) is one of the foundations of achievement-related behavior. Accordingly, some researchers have measured the strength of the achievement motive in terms of the frequency of imagined instrumental actions (Atkinson, 1958; Heckhausen, 1963a; McClelland et al., 1953).

Empirical evidence for the assumption that patterns of oral need satisfaction established early in life (e.g., whether or not a child is encouraged from an early age to eat and drink without help) influence the development of the achievement motive is still lacking. However, the fact that animal experiments typically investigate the prototype of achievement-related behavior (i.e., instrumental behavior) in the context of food intake (Carlson, 1994; Skinner, 1953) might point to a link between the two needs.

Needs for Achievement and Power
On the affective level, instrumental behavior is characterized by a typical cycle that begins with the inhibition of positive affect whenever a difficulty or obstacle is encountered. In his influential theory, Gray (1982) describes this frustration effect as an inhibition of the system that facilitates behavior (otherwise known as the reward system). Gray reports numerous experimental findings in support of his theory. If there is no obstacle to be overcome, the system facilitating behavior and the associated positive affect need not be inhibited, and consummatory behavior can be initiated without delay. For example, humans or animals can simply eat the food available without first having to engage in instrumental behavior to obtain it. As soon as instrumental behavior succeeds (e.g., a rat finds food in a maze), the second part of the cycle commences. Inhibition of positive affect can now be released.

The problem with inhibition of positive affect, which this model of achievement motivation sees as the starting point of each instrumental cycle, is that it entails the risk of behavioral inhibition lasting too long. A minimum amount of positive affect seems to be necessary (for many forms of instrumental behavior, at least) to muster the energy needed to facilitate behavior (Gray, 1982). Various models of motivation (see Atkinson, 1964a; Heckhausen, 1989) have proposed a simple solution to the paradox of how an organism can be motivated before the positive affect associated with goal attainment takes effect. The assumption is that moderate levels of positive affect can be generated during the instrumental phase by the **anticipation** of goal states. This effect is described by the concept of **incentive**, according to which the sight or mental image of an aspired object suffices to generate positive affect and to facilitate behavior.

DEFINITION
From a functional perspective, the concept of incentive can be likened to Freud's concept of object cathexis. After repeated positive experiences with an object, the cognitive representation of that object also becomes associated with positive affect (or with negative affect in the case of aversive experiences). What Freud termed object cathexis, Lewin (1935), in his theory of motivation, called "incentive character" or "valence." Today, in the language of learning theory, it is described as the conditioning of an affect onto an object representation (i.e., a stimulus). The term incentive, which is a core concept in motivational theory, denotes the association between a stimulus (or, more specifically, an object representation) and the affective reactions conditioned onto it, which motivate approach or avoidance behavior.

In their **model of affective change** (McClelland et al., 1953), McClelland and associates proposed that the change from inhibited to activated positive affect seen in instrumental behavior corresponds closely with the affective processes characteristic of achievement motivation. Achievement motivation presupposes a minimum degree of difficulty or – as Heinz Heckhausen (1963a) put it – achievement-motivated behavior can only occur "if one can manage a task or fail at it. The shift from inhibited to activated positive affect (i.e., from the perception of difficulty to the anticipation of success) can also apply to power motivation (although not with the frequency typical of achievement motivation): expressing one's feelings and goals in order to influence others (i.e., asserting oneself, showing autonomy, or exercising power) often constitutes a use of instrumental behavior to attain certain goals."

Affiliation Needs
The affective cycle typical of instrumental forms of motivation (i.e., achievement motivation and power motivation) does not apply to all needs. Instrumental behavior is rather untypical when we seek to establish or maintain positive, warm, or even loving relationships with others (i.e., need for affiliation or the

intimacy motive; Chapter 7). Indeed, instrumental behavior may even disrupt the spontaneous exchange of feelings that is characteristic of close interpersonal relationships. Because instrumental behavior is directed toward a specific goal or purpose, it is bound to strike us as manipulative or false – or at the very least as lacking in spontaneity – when exhibited in social interactions.

❗ Positive affect (e.g., agreeableness or warmth) facilitates the establishment of interpersonal relationships; it is also the basis for the expression of negative feelings: Any reduction of positive affect inhibits behavior (including emotional expression). Note that negative affect is not identical to inhibited positive affect, which plays a crucial role in achievement motivation. Inhibition of positive affect is extremely disadvantageous in social interactions, whereas we soon learn that expressing negative feelings prompts others to provide care and to display loving behavior (e.g., when an infant's crying expresses a need that is then satisfied by the mother).

The connection between low positive affect and impaired personal relationships is especially apparent in depression, where the loss of positive affect is extreme. Empirical findings indicate that depression is more closely related to a lack of positive affect (e.g., despondency) than to the presence of negative affect (e.g., agitation or anxiety; Higgins, 1987; Watson & Tellegen, 1985). In fact, depression has much more detrimental effects on social relations than anxiety and other negative feelings (including suicidal feelings; Milana, 1981; Spirito & Hartford, 1990). Satisfying social interactions thrive on the exchange of positive feelings, and the absence of positive emotions can have more harmful effects on relationships than the expression of feelings such as anxiety, discussion of which can in fact strengthen relationships (Gilligan, 1997).

12.2.3 Implicit Motives: Intelligent Needs Serving the Context-Sensitive Regulation of Behavior

To understand how theories of motivation came to incorporate volitional concepts, it is important to appreciate the difference between needs and motives. In the latter half of the 20th century, psychologists addressing the perhaps three most important social needs (i.e., affiliation/intimacy, power/assertiveness, and achievement) essentially studied motives rather than needs, although the lack of distinct measurement methods meant that it was not always possible to differentiate clearly between the two (Atkinson, 1958; H. Heckhausen, 1989; McClelland, 1985b). One major reason for the shift of focus to the motive concept is clear. With the birth of behaviorism in the early 1920s, psychologists adopted a new agenda that emphasized the prediction of **behavior** (as opposed to the traditional experience-based "armchair" psychology), and it was now vital to identify motivational concepts that might further this aim. Simply knowing that a person has a need does not allow conclusions to be drawn on

how he or she will behave. Needs were defined above as subcognitive or precognitive detectors of discrepancies between actual and desired states. In fact, we can go so far as to describe them as sub- and pre-affective. Typically, affect occurs only in **consequence** of a change in either satisfied or unsatisfied needs, i.e., when discrepancies between actual and desired states are reduced or increased (Heckhausen, 1963b):

■ Positive affect can occur when a discrepancy is reduced (e.g., when there is an increase in blood sugar level after a meal).

■ Negative affect can occur when the discrepancy between an actual and a desired state increases.

Needs may trigger behavior without the involvement of higher cognitive structures, as shown by the animal experiments cited above, in which certain nuclei of the hypothalamus were stimulated. The range of behaviors triggered at this subcognitive and subaffective level is rather narrow and inflexible, however (e.g., clinging to anyone available in the case of need for affiliation or sucking movements in the case of hunger). The potential for varied and adaptive behavior in humans is dependent on the involvement of complex cognitive structures, and on the experience of countless previous episodes of need satisfaction. Thousands of experiences of behaviors in different situations are stored in autobiographical memory (Tulving, 1985); these memories include the conditions prevailing at the onset of each episode, the range of behavioral options tested, and the consequences of those behaviors, including the emotions triggered. Comprehensive networks of need-relevant knowledge and behavioral options can be abstracted from these experiences, and may be useful or dangerous, depending on the situation. These networks, commonly known as **motives** (McClelland, 1985b), allow us to predict behavior much more reliably than do the corresponding needs. Given the innumerable experiences an individual gains over the course of a human lifetime, however, these networks are so extensive that most of this knowledge is available only intuitively. Only some aspects of it can be verbally explicated, provided that the individual in question is capable of accurate **self-perception**.

DEFINITION

Motives are extensive, not fully conscious cognitive-emotional networks that have been abstracted from autobiographical experiential knowledge to generate a large number of context-sensitive behavioral options as soon as a need, which constitutes the nucleus of each motive, increases.

This definition of the motive concept is consistent with classical definitions (Atkinson, 1958a; H. Heckhausen, 1989; McClelland et al., 1953). However, these did not always differentiate clearly between motives and needs – partly because methods allowing such a distinction to be made had yet to be developed.

Motives as Implicit Self-Representations

From the definition of motives formulated in the preceding section, it is clear that there is a close connection between motives and self-regulation. Autobiographical experiential knowledge forms the core of self-representations (Wheeler, Stuss, & Tulving, 1997). Indeed, the highest level of representation of an individual's integrated **self** is based on the storing of all experiences that are, directly or indirectly, relevant to that person's current state, needs, and functioning. On the basis of these numerous "self-relevant" experiential episodes, individuals develop a more or less coherent model of themselves that can be updated at any time.

❶ Needs are core components of self-defining states; motives are their cognitive-emotional elaboration. Based on experiential knowledge, motives tell the individual which behavioral options are particularly likely or unlikely to facilitate need satisfaction in specific situations. They can thus be regarded as integral components of the individual's self-system.

The link between a person's self-system and his or her motives has only recently become theoretically explicable. For one thing, the motivation psychology of previous decades focused more on the measurement and validation of motives than on the functional architecture of motivated systems and their mechanisms (Atkinson, 1958a; H. Heckhausen, 1989; McClelland et al., 1953; Winter, 1996). Moreover, the connection between the high-inferential level of the self-system, on the one hand, and motives, on the other, was not evident, because self-representations were studied almost exclusively in terms of **self-concepts**; i.e., consciously held views of one's self. Whether or not researchers are able to capitalize on the great potential of the link between motives and self-regulation will depend on whether these theoretical advances are complemented by advances in the measurement of motives, as discussed in the next section.

Measurement of Motives

From the very beginning of experimental research on motives, these constructs have been assessed by means of **projective** measures (McClelland et al., 1953), and conceived of as largely **unconscious** cognitive-emotional representations. "Cognitive-emotional" means that motives are partly cognitive in nature (e.g., experiential knowledge about behavioral options in various need-relevant situations), but that they also have emotional aspects. Indeed, cognitive representations of need-relevant experiences are practically always associated with emotional experiences, dependent on the degree to which need satisfaction was achieved in the respective situations. From the perspective of learning theory, we could say that emotional responses (e.g., joy about success or sadness about failure) have been conditioned onto cognitive representations of past actions.

Today, neurobiological research sees these emotions, which are integrated in extended cognitive networks, and the bodily perceptions associated with them (somatosensory signals) as **navigational aids** within these cognitive networks (Damasio, Tranel, & Damasio, 1991). Without the guidance of these emotional and somatosensory indicators, the search for appropriate behavioral options within the extensive network of potentially relevant experiences would be a tiresome, if not futile, endeavor (see the example below). The emotional responses encountered while scanning these extended associative networks help the system to focus its attention on promising behavioral options, and to avoid risky ones. It can thus quickly decide which option to pursue.

> **EXAMPLE**
>
> Patients with certain lesions to the brain have been observed to experience great difficulty in making apparently simple decisions (e.g., deciding whether to schedule their next doctor's appointment on a Tuesday or a Wednesday). Research has shown that the connection between areas of the brain important for representing signals from the body (somatosensory, postcentral areas) and areas of the brain important for self-representations (e.g., the right prefrontal cortex) is severed in these patients (Damasio, Tranel, & Damasio, 1991).

Against this background, it seems quite reasonable to interpret motives as components of the self-system that serve to regulate behavior. Whenever a need is aroused, motives generate behavioral options that are embedded in cognitive-emotional representations of appropriate self-relevant experiences. These cognitive-emotional networks, which are postulated to form the functional basis of motives (McClelland, 1985b; Winter, 1996), are so extensive that they cannot possibly be conscious knowledge structures. Indeed, the pioneers of modern motivation psychology realized that it was not possible to measure motives by means of questionnaires, because these methods presuppose conscious knowledge about the subject of inquiry (McClelland et al., 1953). Today, implicit (unconscious) knowledge is measured by implicit memory tests, such as:

- free reproduction ("Just tell me what you can remember of the things you've learned"),
- completing word fragments ("Which word can be formed by filling in the missing letters: COFF _ _?") and similar methods (Goschke, 1997b; Tulving, 1985; Schacter, 1987).

❶ These diverse memory tests have one thing in common – participants do not produce memory contents following a direct cue (or "stimulus," as is the case in recognition tests, cued-recall, or questionnaires), but spontaneously. In other words, the response is self- rather than stimulus-controlled.

The test that was developed to measure motives is based on a principle similar to that of implicit memory tests (see also the excursus on page 304), although it was originally embedded in a different theoretical context entirely. In the Thematic Apperception Test (TAT), participants are asked to write down a "free reproduction" of associations relating to images – in other words, to produce imagined stories based on a series of picture cues.

Today, generating stories is considered to be closely related to functions of the self-system, which is after all based on abstraction from standard features of autobiographical episodes, that is, on "stories" experienced by the individual. The narration of stories thus activates precisely those mental functions that are involved in the representation of one's own "story." There is also empirical evidence to show that narrating one's own experiences in the form of stories ("narrative format") helps people to cope with stress and anxiety (Pennebaker, 1993). Given the close connection between the self-system and the narrative format, the self-system might also be assumed to have stress-reducing functions. Indeed, empirical research shows that individuals with a highly developed, differentiated self-system (i.e., who see themselves as having comparatively many, distinct "self-aspects," both positive and negative) show significantly fewer depressive and physical symptoms under stress (Linville, 1987) and recover more rapidly from negative thoughts than do individuals with a less developed self (Showers & Kling, 1996).

The Operant Motive Test

The Operant Motive Test (OMT) was developed by Kuhl and Scheffer (1999) to preserve TAT features central to motive measurement (production of fantasy stories based on ambiguous picture cues) and to improve on those features with detrimental effects on measurement. Consequently, respondents are not required to write down their invented stories (which takes a long time and, like the relating of dreams, can lead to distortion), meaning that more pictures can be shown (e.g., 15 for the OMT compared with 6 for the TAT). For the purposes of content analysis, it suffices for respondents to note down their spontaneous associations to the following questions, which are also used in the TAT (see overview).

Questions Used for Motive Measurement in the OMT and TAT
- What is important for the person in this situation and what is he or she doing?
- How does the person feel?
- Why does the person feel this way?

The OMT's coding system exploits the theoretical advances that resulted from incorporating self-regulatory processes within motivational theory (H. Heckhausen, 1989; Kuhl, 1981, 1983). Whereas classical motive measurement differentiates between an approach and an avoidance form of each motive only, the OMT distinguishes four different forms of approach motives (in addition to one avoidance component).

When scoring the OMT, the rater first decides whether any of the three basic motives (affiliation, achievement, and power) are present, and whether approach or avoidance motivation is expressed. In the case of approach motivation, the rater then assesses the degree to which either internal, self-regulatory processes (i.e., the "self") or external (situational) stimuli (incentives) are involved. These two "levels" of motive implementation are then evaluated for the presence of positive or negative affect (this affect is not necessarily consciously accessible to the respondent or mentioned explicitly in the associations).

New insights into personality functioning (Kuhl, 2000a, b, 2001) have made it possible to formulate indirect indicators for unconscious affects that influence behavior (Table 12.1). Numerous findings confirm the assumption (2nd modulation assumption of PSI theory, see page 317) that negative affect impairs access to the self and to other forms of high-inferential, intuitive intelligence, and that coping with negative affect facilitates such access (Baumann & Kuhl, 2002, 2003; Kuhl & Kazén, 1994; Rotenberg, 2004). On the basis of these findings, the presence of negative affect can be deduced, even if it is not made explicit in respondents' associations, from a "narrowness" or "rigidity" of motive implementation (e.g., if no creative or socially integrative form of need satisfaction can be identified: rigid implementation of the power motive according to the "all-or-nothing" principle; achievement motivation with a focus on competitiveness or "being better than others"; narrowing of the affiliation motive to a person offering protection rather than an intimate personal exchange). If, on the other hand, negative affect is expressed in the associations and creative solutions are sought, the self-regulated mode of coping with negative affect in implementing the motive in question is scored. In the case of positive affect, a parallel distinction is made between instances in which the self and its volitional mechanisms are involved in need satisfaction and instances in which there is no involvement of the self. Creativity and flexibility of implementation combined with a positive incentive "emanating" from the activity again indicate a variety of motive implementation that involves self-regulatory processes (intimacy for the affiliation motive; flow for the achievement motive; and prosocial, socially integrative influences on others for the power motive).

❶ The intrinsic motivation associated with these motive varieties is attributed to the largely unconscious effects of self-regulatory functions that help to maintain interest in and enjoyment of the activity (self-motivation).

The positive tenor of intrinsic motivation raises an interesting theoretical question: Is intrinsic motivation characterized by an involvement of the self or does it derive solely from the incentives inherent in the activity? Positive affect

Table 12.1. The multilevel model and the motive components of the OMT

Columns define needs ("WHAT")	Affiliation	Achievement	Power
Rows (levels) define mechanisms ("HOW")	Developmental hypothesis:	Developmental hypothesis:	Developmental hypothesis:
	Low family cohesion ("high emotional distance," "low warmth"):	Parental expectations of independence (i.e., exposure to difficulties):	Low paternal influence on the child ("eye level"):
	frustration of the need for closeness	frustration of goal attainment	frustration of the need for structure/hierarchy
Level 1: Self and A+: Self-access and depth	Aff1 Intimacy: Warmth, love, joyful exchange	Ach1 Flow: Being absorbed in a task, learning something	P1 Guidance: Influencing others: explaining, assisting, etc.
Level 2: Incentive objects and A+: Extrinsic (OR)	Aff2 Sociability: Having fun together; entertainment	Ach2 Standards of excellence: Doing something well, positive goals	P2 Recognition: Being the center of attention; status; recognition
Level 3: Self and A(−): Active coping with problems	Aff3 Networking: Identifying and actively overcoming problems within relationships	Ach3 Coping with failure: Identifying errors and problems and actively seeking a solution	P3 Self-assertiveness: Overcoming the resistance of others; making decisions
Level 4: Action and A−: Active avoidance: planning, dogged perseverance (stimulus-free facilitation of IBC)	Aff4 Affiliation: Seeking security; seeking closeness/affiliation	Ach4 Pressure to achieve: Persevering under stress; competing; being better than others	P4 Dominance: Noticing the negative aspects of power; one-sided control
Level 5: Self-inhibition and A−: negative emotions and negative incentives become conscious; paralyzation	Aff5 Dependence: Experiencing loneliness and anxiety; feeling distance; asking for help; "clinging"	Ach5 Self-criticism: Acknowledging one's mistakes; becoming passive after failure; accepting help	P5 Subordination: Experiencing powerlessness; subordinating oneself; yielding to others

A(−), downregulated negative affect; *A+*, positive affect; *A−*, negative affect; *IBC*, intuitive behavior control, *OR*, object recognition system.

alone does not suffice to activate the extended networks of the self-system (see the discussion of the first modulation assumption of PSI theory on page 316). In fact, positive affect facilitates a less extensive activation of the self-system than does **self-confrontational** coping with negative affect. On the other hand, positive affect has a stronger activational effect on low-inferential (automated) intuitive behavioral programs that are much less extensive than the self-system (Kuhl, 2001, p. 183). Indeed, this is how PSI theory explains the corrupting effect of material incentives on intrinsic motivation (Deci & Ryan, 2000; Lepper, Greene, & Nisbett, 1973): Positive affect associated with attractive incentives does not establish deep and lasting connections with the self-system and its self-motivational functions if that affect is short-lived and remains too closely linked to specific objects to reach the extended networks of implicit self-representations (including motives).

Activation of high-inferential intuitive processes (e.g., implicit motives and other implicit self-representations) in the presence of positive affect is more likely to occur if the individual is involved in non-defensive (i.e. self-confrontational) coping with latent negative affect at the same time. In these cases, extended areas of autobiographical experiences and the self-representations inferred from them have to be activated to facilitate coping (e.g., by finding meaning or solutions). Admittedly, this theoretical assumption seems counterintuitive, because "only" positive affect seems to be apparent for the intrinsic variants of motives on the level of observable behavior (Deci & Ryan, 2000; Rheinberg, Iser, & Pfauser, 1997). Importantly, however, Scheffer (2000) found that even the intrinsic forms of phenotypically "purely" positive varieties of the three motives seem to be associated with negative experiences in the satisfaction of the specific needs in childhood. According to Scheffer's findings, certain personality traits determine whether these negative experiences lead to an intrinsic, phenotypically entirely positive form of motivational development. These insights explain why positive affect, which is otherwise short-lived and limited to specific consummatory episodes, "expands" in terms of time and content in the context of intrinsic motivation. Involvement of the self connects positive affect to an extended network of the individual's needs, goals, and values.

SUMMARY

The psychometric properties of the OMT confirm that the new instrument preserves central features of the TAT while making some useful improvements:

■ Although the OMT takes less time to administer and score, and despite theoretical objections to the use of classical reliability measures, interrater agreement after a few days' practice is .85 (using Winter's formula, 1994). In the

12

EXCURSUS

The Measurement of Implicit Self-Representations

On the basis of these theoretical and empirical arguments, the classical TAT would appear to be the ideal instrument for measuring implicit self-representations, and specifically for measuring motives as holistic representations of need-relevant autobiographical experiences. However, the TAT has been criticized for failing to satisfy some of the quality criteria prescribed by classical test theory (Chapter 6). Indeed, the internal consistency and test-retest reliability (i.e., stability) of the TAT's motive scores leave much to be desired, and some studies have found that the instrument's potential to predict school grades is negligible (Entwisle, 1972). According to Winter (1995), however, the instrument's low test-retest reliability can be attributed to the simple fact that participants take the test instructions seriously, and try to produce imaginative and original stories each time the instrument is administered. Hence, the consistency of results obtained from successive tests is low. When respondents are told that they can produce similar stories in the second test, test-retest reliability increases (Winter, 1996).

In psychometric terms, this means that test-retest reliability cannot be considered a fair measure of the TAT's quality. A similar argument applies to the instrument's low internal consistency; e.g., the low correlation of scores from two halves of the test, expressed in terms of Cronbach's α values. The assumptions of classical testing theory (e.g., that errors in the measurement of different items are uncorrelated) simply do not apply to motivational processes, which have a sequential dynamic that violates the principle of independence of subsequent measurements. Because needs become less intense when they have recently been satisfied, someone who has just written a story on the achievement motive is much less likely to produce another story dealing with that motive. The impact of the negative recency effect reported by researchers studying memory and attention may also play a significant role in this context. People telling stories tend to avoid repetitions, and the same holds for other cognitive processes. We try to avoid repeating words in the same sentence, and both human respondents and laboratory animals avoid searching the same area twice when visually exploring a stimulus (Posner & Rothbart, 1992).

In view of the TAT's low reliability (Cronbach's α values approaching zero in many studies), classical test theory would not expect the test to show significant correlations with criteria relating to what it is supposed to measure (because reliability defines the upper limit of validity; Lienert, 1969). After all, why should a test that provides imprecise and unreliable measures have high validity? But if test-retest reliability and Cronbach's α values for internal consistency are indeed inadequate measures of the test's precision because the assumptions of classical test theory simply do not apply in this context, we can expect the validity of the TAT to be much higher than its reliability scores indicate. Research findings confirm the latter assumption: meta-analyses show that the TAT has higher validity than questionnaire measures when it comes to assessing the three basic social motives (achievement, affiliation, and power) in self-initiated behavior, as opposed to behavior initiated by others (Spangler, 1992). When a measurement model that dispenses with some of the unrealistic assumptions of classical testing theory is applied (i.e., Rasch's stochastic model), the homogeneity and unidimensionality of the TAT is superior to that of many questionnaire measures (Kuhl, 1978). Notably, the Operant Motive Test (OMT) has significantly higher internal consistency and test-retest reliability than the TAT (Kuhl & Scheffer, 1999). As explained below, the OMT combines measurement of motives with measurement of components of self-regulation.

upper and lower quartiles of the distribution, Cronbach's α is over .70 (Scheffer, Kuhl, & Eichstaedt, 2003). Lower consistencies are theoretically plausible in the middle range of the distribution because motives (unlike cognitive abilities) compete with each other. Hence, a motive can only be expected to have a consistent influence if its impact is either strong or weak.

■ In terms of its validity, the OMT correlates with implicit measures of early childhood development, as outlined above, and with behavior ratings (Kuhl, 2001, pp. 604ff.; Scheffer, 2003). Moreover, the discrepancy between implicit motives as measured by the OMT and conscious goals predicts the development of psychological symptoms (as discussed later, see Fig. 12.5).

■ Research has confirmed that the OMT is independent of questionnaire measures of motives (Scheffer, 2003).

■ By contrast, the OMT converges with TAT measures, but only when the arousal conditions specific to the motive under investigation are induced (Scheffer, 2000; Scheffer et al., 2003). This finding may indicate that the TAT is more dependent on the induction of arousal conditions than the OMT. Given that the development of the TAT was closely associated with the situational arousal of specific motives, this assumption seems quite plausible.

12.3 Will Without Homunculus: Decomposing Global Concepts of Will

Self-regulatory processes are not only involved in the satisfaction of needs and motives; they also come into play when goals that are not in line with what is currently the dominant motive or strongest need have to be implemented. The following sections are dedicated to the in-depth analysis of processes of self-regulation, independent of the degree to which they serve to satisfy needs or motives in each individual case.

During the era of radical behaviorism, "self-regulation" and other designations for the concept of **will** were banned from experimental psychology as "unscientific," because it was assumed that they could not be measured on the basis of observational data. This same reasoning probably underlies contemporary attempts to deny the will an independent status and to portray volitional phenomena as "perceptual delusions" (Wegner & Wheatley, 1999). Indeed, it is inherently difficult to conceive of "will" as an object of observation for empirical science: precisely those actions that are not caused by external (observable) stimuli, but that originate from within the acting person him- or herself are deemed to be caused by will. Thus, the concept of will seems to describe a form of behavior whose causes cannot be observed. Worse still, "self-caused actions" seem to be a form of behavior that does not obey the rules of cause and effect, and thus eludes experimental analysis.

Today, the **philosophical problems** relating to the concept of will and freedom of will, in particular, can be resolved: Although the internal processes underlying volitional acts are more complex than behavior attributable to simple stimulus-response bonds, this does not necessarily preclude the analysis of their causal conditions. "Freedom" of will does not mean freedom from causal determination, but freedom from a certain form of causal determination; i.e., from determination by factors external to the self (Bieri, 2001; Kuhl, 1996).

Examples of behaviors that are not determined by self-regulated processes include all forms of external control. These include instructions and obligations imposed by external sources (Deci & Ryan, 2000), as well as the compulsive performance of automatized behavioral routines and obsessive fixations on certain stimuli that occur in drug addiction and – in considerably milder form – in "extrinsic" motivation; i.e., when the motivation for performing an action does not reside "within the action" (or a corresponding need of the person performing it), but derives from the desire to attain a certain object.

Habits and incentive-oriented behavior are triggered by external stimuli, whereas acts of will are triggered by high-inferential internal systems, such as the implicit self-system mentioned above, which integrates a huge number of contextually relevant experiences, and the memory for explicit intentions, which might be compared to Freud's ego. Of course, the external and internal causes for a certain behavior may coincide (e.g., when children internalize their parents' expectations). This is not always the case, however.

Even if actions caused by the self or the ego are not seen as free from causal determination, the challenge remains of how to analyze the mechanisms by which these "internal" systems are assumed to trigger behavior. Explanations based on global concepts of will, such as will power, self-regulation, or self-efficacy (Bandura, 1998), are not really explanations at all – they merely attribute behavior to "will," or a similar summary construct which functions as a kind of inner puppet-master, a **homunculus**, the functioning of which remains unexplained.

❗ Global concepts of will are intuitively appealing because they can have enormous predictive power: If we know how people evaluate

their own self-efficacy, we can make fairly accurate predictions about their behavior and performance (Bandura, 1998). However, it is all too easy to forget that high **predictive** power, which radical behaviorism deemed to be so important, does not mean that a variable will have equally high **explanatory** power.

Global concepts of will are no better at explaining volitional phenomena than the high correlation between the inclination of my car's gas pedal and its velocity is able to explain how my car works. Only when the specific processes and functions underlying different volitional acts are identified can we expect to arrive at well-founded explanations of volitional phenomena.

The following section describes a functional design approach to "decomposing" global concepts of will.

12.3.1 Internal Dictatorship vs. Democracy: Self-Control and Self-Regulation

Even the very first step toward decomposing global concepts of will is a difficult one. Everyday experience gives us the sense "that we do things, that we cause our acts, that we are agents" (Wegner & Wheatley, 1999, p. 480) – that our will is a single, undivided entity. How, then, can be it possible for the will to consist of a large number of functional components that we do not even experience consciously? Many empirical findings suggest that the perception of an integrated will that determines our actions in everyday life may be erroneous. For example, research has shown that people sometimes think that they have chosen an activity themselves, when in fact it was imposed by others (Kuhl & Kazén, 1994), and EEG scans of study participants asked to decide for themselves when to make a certain hand movement (Libet, 1985) show that the impulse triggering the movement occurs a few 100 ms before participants actually decide to perform that movement (see Nisbett & Wilson, 1977, for further examples of false self-ascriptions of objectively externally triggered behavior). Against the background of such data, it is all too easy to conclude that there is no such thing as will and that the concept is not worthy of serious investigation (Wegner & Wheatley, 1999), rather than seeing it as one of the true determining sources of behavior or breaking it down into its functional components.

The data on false ascriptions of actions to the will can also be interpreted in a more differentiated way. Even if we were to assume that nonvolitional, i.e., "external," factors caused the behavior observed in the studies cited, it would be premature to generalize these findings, and to assume that volitional processes can never influence behavior. But if we maintain that behavior may be influenced by the will, even if (as the authors assume) nonvolitional causes dominated in the experiments conducted by Wegner and Libet, another interesting possibility opens up: Could it be that volitional processes influence our behavior even if we have no conscious memory of their effects? If there is something to the effect of a higher-order function that coordinates our thinking, feeling, and acting such that it seems consistent, comprehensible, and coordinated to us and to others, then at least some of this coordinating activity must occur without us being consciously aware of it. Language-based consciousness, which is characterized by sequential processing, would be hopelessly overstretched if all factors impinging on complex decisions (which often have to be made within the space of a few seconds) had to be processed, not to mention the associated feelings and needs (one's own and other people's), not all of which can be consciously expressed in language or otherwise. It has thus been proposed that two modes of volition be distinguished:

1. conscious, verbally expressible **self-control**, which operates sequentially and analytically, and

2. self-regulation, which is largely unconscious and not verbally expressible, and which processes and coordinates information from the internal systems (e.g., feelings, beliefs, values, needs) and from the (social) environment largely simultaneously (in parallel) (Kuhl, 1996; Kuhl & Fuhrmann, 1998).

Experiments showing that words relating to a current intention inhibit the processing of words relating to a source of temptation without the respondent's conscious awareness (Fishbach, Friedman, & Kruglanski, 2003) confirm that unconscious processes are involved in shielding intentions against sources of temptation. Many studies show that the **right** ("unconscious") hemisphere is particularly strongly involved whenever self-referential judgments are made (Keenan, Nelson, O'Connor, & Pascual-Leone, 2001), especially when these judgments occur implicitly (Kircher et al., 2002) and when self-relevant feelings are recognized in the faces of others (Pizzagalli, Regard, & Lehmann, 1999) or regulated (Levesque et al., 2003).

❶ There is now little doubt that conscious and unconscious self-representations (e.g., the conscious self or self-concept vs. the unconscious self-image) have different and independent effects on behavior (Greenwald & Banaji, 1995). Accordingly, an unconscious form of will can be assumed to exist alongside conscious will.

Self-Regulation

Self-regulation is a largely unconscious form of volition that involves, and yet goes beyond, the integrative intelligence of motives. Volitional self-regulation draws not only on those networks of experiences that are relevant for one's needs, but on all autobiographical experiences that have contributed to the development of a coherent self-image. Metaphorically speaking, self-regulation is a kind of "internal democracy," within which many, at times contradictory, "voices" are heard (or votes are taken) – one's own feelings, attitudes, and values, and those of others. These internal and external voices "vote" on matters of volition, resulting in a decision that is then implemented by the "government." Implementation may be

facilitated by various measures; e.g., attempts to convince dissenting voices to support the goals adopted. The integration of all relevant experiences permits high levels of flexibility and creativity in behavior. In this respect, the concept of self-regulation is comparable with the concept of **creative will** (Rank, 1945) and with "resilient" forms of ego-control (Block & Block, 1980) that prove extremely adaptable and flexible under pressure.

Self-Control

If the process of integrating "dissenting voices" (corresponding to **self-motivation** at the psychological level) does not work, then it may be time for the second form of volition, namely, self-control, to take over. Persistence in the self-regulatory mode in the face of a task that is necessary, but not at all pleasurable, would mean that we never get the job done, because "internal democracy lends its ear to the voices of protest."

❶ The volitional mode of self-control operates in a very different way from self-regulation. The pursuit of goal attainment no longer involves trying to gather as many positive voices as possible in support of the goal. Instead, all voices that are not directly conducive to goal attainment are "switched to mute mode." At the psychological level, this "internal dictatorship" corresponds to the suppression of the self. The self is no longer the source, author, and agent of behavior, but the object of controlling or even repressive measures preventing any potential distractions from interfering with goal implementation (Kuhl, 1996).

In motivational terms, this mode of volition applies in cases of discrepancy between conscious goals and implicit motives; i.e., when goals that are incongruent with the dominant motive are "introjected." Given the obvious disadvantages of permanently suppressing "self-involvement" in the regulation of behavior, including the risk of psychological disorders (Baumann, Kaschel, & Kuhl, 2005; Kuhl & Kaschel, 2004), it is easy to overlook the advantages of self-control: It is the classic mode of (potentially conscious) volition, and permits many forms of adaptive behavior that are difficult to realize in the more liberal volitional mode of self-regulation. There is empirical evidence for positive effects of self-control on goal attainment – particularly where unpleasant activities are concerned (Gollwitzer & Brandstätter, 1997; Fuhrmann & Kuhl, 1998) – and on readiness to engage in prosocial actions, especially when these require one's own preferences to be set aside (Finkel & Campbell, 2001).

It seems that negative affect is more conducive to self-control than positive affect (Kochanska, Coy, & Murray, 2001; Kuhl & Fuhrmann, 1998). In fact, individuals with a preference for the self-control mode show reduced self-regulatory efficiency (implementation of diet goals) when instructed to motivate themselves through positive affect; e.g., by rewarding themselves mentally for small steps forward rather than punishing themselves for mistakes and weaknesses

(Fuhrmann & Kuhl, 1998). However, the fact that individuals with high (induced or dispositional) self-control achieve higher efficiency by motivating themselves through negative cognitions and emotions (e.g., by imagining the adverse consequences of not implementing an intention) does not mean that they do not experience positive affect once they achieve their goals. In fact, the opposite is true – respondents' satisfaction increases when experimentally induced self-control ("prevention focus") is combined with elements designed to distract attention from the task at hand (Freitas, Liberman, & Higgins, 2002).

Because the conscious form of will (i.e., self-control) is, by definition, more easily accessible to conscious thought, it is hardly surprising that the concept of will has, historically, almost always been reduced to this mode of volition. Today, this traditional conceptualization is reflected in the proposal that conscious action control pertains to self-control only ("imperative will"), whereas unconscious forms of action control are driven by motives (Sokolowski, 1997). If we assume the motive-driven form of action control to have some of the key functional characteristics of self-regulation, however, this approach becomes convergent with the distinction between self-control and self-regulation proposed here.

SUMMARY

Self-regulation is not inherently more satisfying or effective than self-control, or vice versa. What is important is the fit between the dominant mood, the demands of the situation, and the induced or dispositionally preferred mode of self-control or self-regulation.

Self-regulation works better in the context of positive mood and situations emphasizing freedom of choice (Baumann & Kuhl, 2004; Deci & Ryan, 2000), whereas self-control works better in the context of negative mood, controlling instructions (Baumann & Kuhl, 2004; Fuhrmann & Kuhl, 1998), and situations requiring the suppression of distracters or sources of temptation (Freitas, Liberman, & Higgins, 2002).

Self-regulatory functions (e.g., self-determination, attention control to promote goal implementation, and an action-oriented approach to coping with stress) have less impact when individuals experience high levels of social (normative) pressure than when they perceive less normative pressure (Marszal-Wisniewska, 2002; Orbell, 2003).

12.3.2 Progression vs. Regression: Stress-Related Volitional Inhibition and Inhibition of the Self

The differentiation between the integrative and control modes of self-regulation is only part of the story. In everyday life, we often find ourselves in situations where we seem to be less capable of performing and to have less "will power" than usual. This applies particularly to stressful situations in which it is easy to lose track of things. We may lose sight of what we wanted to achieve or have difficulty making decisions, and we may find it impossible to implement our intentions, even

when the opportunity to do so arises (Kuhl & Kaschel, 2004). The latter phenomenon, in which performance of intended behavior is impeded, is termed **volitional inhibition**. The phenomenon of losing track of things in general, and of personal preferences in particular, is called **self-inhibition**, because the information relevant to decision-making can no longer be accessed in the usual way (reduced self-access). These two forms of stress-induced inhibition of the awareness and/or implementation of preferences and intentions correspond to Freud's concept of regression: the rational functioning typical of a healthy adult seems to be suspended by traumatic experiences and acute stressful episodes, such that the system "regresses" to simple ("infantile") processes. Pierre Janet proposed a much more elaborate take on the stress-induced inhibition of self-regulatory functions with his concept of **psychasthenia** ("psychic weakness"), which is currently experiencing a revival (Bühler & Heim, 2002; Hoffmann, 1998).

❶ In practical terms, the fact that volitional inhibition and self-inhibition are induced by stressful situations means that it is not sufficient simply to measure the efficiency of self-regulation and self-control. Rather, the degree to which these functions are available in stressful situations has to be measured separately. In factor-analytic studies, questionnaire scales measuring functional components of self-regulation (e.g., self-motivation, self-relaxation, decision-making competence, etc.) and self-control (e.g., impulse control, planning, etc.) are often orthogonally related to scales measuring self-regulatory competencies under stress (Kuhl & Fuhrmann, 1998).

Neurobiological Findings on Volitional Inhibition

The fact that the stress-induced inhibition of volitional and other high-inferential functions is driven by independent processes has also been demonstrated at the neurobiological level. The sensitivity of the hippocampus to stress seems to be a key factor here (Sapolsky, 1992). At excessive stress levels, the hippocampus is inhibited, leaving its cognitive and emotional functions impaired:

■ The cognitive functions of the hippocampus are implicated whenever numerous pieces of information from different sources have to be linked together (Sutherland & Rudy, 1989); e.g., in spatial orientation (Meaney, Aitken, van Berkel, Bhatnagar, & Sapolsky, 1988), in the memorization and recall of autobiographical episodes (Kirschbaum, Wolf, Wippich, & Hellhammer, 1996; Squire, 1992), and in the perception and recall of stimulus configurations (Metcalfe & Jacobs, 1998).

■ The emotional functions of the hippocampus include its inhibiting influence on cortisol production (Sapolsky, 1992) and its mediation of the inhibiting influences of high-inferential cerebral processes on elemental (subcortical) processes, such as conditioned fear responses (Schmajuk & Buhusi, 1997). Thus, inhibition of the hippocampus might lead to situations in which fear responses cannot be inhibited, even in safe environments (e.g., fear of caged lions at the zoo).

These findings on the neurobiology of the integrative and affect-regulatory functions of the hippocampus (Metcalfe & Jacobs, 1998; Sapolsky, 1992; Schmajuk & Buhusi, 1997) establish a basic framework for psychological theorizing and offer explanations for many regression phenomena. Excessive stress primarily affects the "intelligent" functions and systems. Under stress, we are no longer able to deal with the normal amount of information, meaning that spatial orientation is reduced, that episodes experienced are "forgotten" (although the affects "conditioned" during those episodes are not), and that the broader context (including motives) is neglected. Instead, the focus is on details. For example, we may start to dislike someone for trivial reasons, "forgetting" the good times we have shared with them on account of a single disappointment.

Even the high-inferential experiences that remain accessible cannot influence elementary responses often acquired in early childhood (e.g., knowing that current relationships do not involve the same degree of threat as those experienced in childhood cannot neutralize traumatic early experiences). The discrepancy between motives and behavior, including its unconscious and conscious triggers (e.g., habits, goals, introjects), can thus be seen as a special case of stress-induced regression. When the influence of high-inferential systems is disabled under acute or chronic stress, people simply fail to realize that their conscious goals and behavior are no longer in line with the structures that have evolved from their extensive experience of life (e.g., their motives and self).

The processing of extended experiential networks is evidently very dependent on the parallel mode of processing in the right hemisphere (Beeman et al., 1994; Rotenberg, 1993, 2004). Unlike the "analytic-verbal" left hemisphere, the right hemisphere is very much involved in the perception and regulation of somatosensory and emotional signals from the autonomic nervous system (Dawson & Schell, 1982; Wittling, 1990). We might therefore infer that motive discrepancies deriving from an overemphasis on goals represented analytically and verbally in the left hemisphere, and their isolation from motives and other implicit self-representations in the right hemisphere, might lead to impaired perception of and coping with emotional experiences, with corresponding effects on symptom development. Empirical data have recently confirmed this hypothesis (Baumann, Kaschel, & Kuhl, 2005; Kehr, 2004a).

Findings on the hemispheric lateralization of self-congruent motives and explicit goals (including "introjects") have been applied to striking effect in recent experiments (Baumann, Kuhl, & Kazén, 2004a) demonstrating that other-induced and self-chosen tasks are no longer confounded (self-infiltration) when study participants squeeze a rubber ball with their left hand for three minutes before they classify the tasks, a motor activity assumed to activate the right hemisphere.

12.4 Affect-Regulatory Competencies: Action vs. State Orientation

Investigation of volitional inhibition and its potential neurobiological basis (e.g., stress-induced inhibition of the hippocampus) has shown that whether or not the self-regulatory competencies a person has developed remain available in stressful situations (i.e., under pressure or threat) depends on that person's ability to regulate affect.

❶ Not only do affect-regulation competences provide important protection against unpleasant and disease-inducing affects, they also serve to ensure optimal communication among self-regulatory and cognitive systems.

12.4.1 The Core of the Construct: Self-Regulation of Affect

The construct of **action** vs. **state orientation** was introduced to further the study of individual differences in the regulation of affect (Kuhl, 1981, 1983). In contrast to classical personality dispositions such as extraversion and neuroticism, which focus on differences in sensitivity to positive vs. negative affect, i.e., the ease with which these affects develop (Gray, 1982; Gupta & Nagpal, 1978), state orientation describes the unwanted **persevering** of affect, i.e., the inability to terminate an unwanted affective **state**. It may entail unwanted rumination on an irreversible aversive experience (state orientation after failure: SOF) or a protracted state of indecision, hesitation, or lack of energy, all of which inhibit the implementation of intentions (prospective state orientation: SOP) (Kuhl, 1983).

EXAMPLE

Action and state orientation are measured by items such as the following sample items from the Action Control Scale (ACS-90):

One of the items measuring prospective action orientation, which facilitates decision making and implementation of intentions, reads:

- When I need to solve a difficult problem:
    a. I get started at once.
    b. I think about other things first before starting with the task at hand.

Response a) is scored as action oriented (AOP), response b) as state oriented (SOP).

One of the items measuring the failure-oriented, ruminative form of action orientation reads:

- When I am told that my work is completely unsatisfactory:
    a. I feel paralyzed for quite some time.
    b. I don't get discouraged for long.

Response a) is scored as state oriented (SOF), response b) as action oriented (AOF).

There is much empirical evidence for the reliability and validity of the scales (Diefendorff, Hall, Lord, & Strean, 2000; Kuhl, 1994; Kuhl & Beckmann, 1994a). Although action/state orientation and extraversion/neuroticism share common features, as reflected in the theoretically expected correlations between the constructs, empirical research has also identified a number of differences. In contrast to extraversion and neuroticism, action orientation does not consistently predict mood at the beginning of an experiment; however, it does predict **change in mood** over the course of an experiment (Brunstein, 2001; Kuhl, 1998). These effects and other indicators of the positive influence of action orientation on self-regulation (e.g., compliance with a dietary regimen) persist even when controlling statistically for dispositional sensitivity to affects (e.g., neuroticism; Brunstein, 2001) or current mood (Palfai, 2002).

Counter-Regulation of Negative Affect: Action Orientation after Failure (AOF)

Research on learned helplessness (Hiroto & Seligman, 1975) established that exposing people to unsolvable problems leads them to display performance deficits in a subsequent task. These performance deficits were attributed to reduced expectations of success and to a subsequent decrease in motivation, as assumed in the theory of "learned helplessness" (Abramson, Seligman & Teasdale, 1978). However, the findings of experiments that measured expectations of success did not conform to the predictions of learned helplessness theory: Although respondents faced with loss of control reduced their expectations of success on the unsolvable task, they did not generalize these lowered expectations to other tasks (Kuhl, 1981). In other words, a generalized reduction in control expectations cannot be the cause of the performance deficits observed under failure conditions. How, then, was it possible to explain the finding that state-oriented participants exposed to loss of control (failure) on one task showed performance deficits on new and completely different tasks?

The questionnaire measure for failure-related action orientation, which was designed to measure individual differences in regulation of affect, provided an explanation for these helplessness-related performance deficits. Only state-oriented individuals (SOF), whose questionnaire responses indicated that they had difficulty detaching from unpleasant situations and the thoughts associated with them, showed performance deficits. The helplessness phenomena were not replicated in action-oriented individuals (AOF), who showed no performance deficits after failure (Brunstein & Olbrich, 1985; Kuhl, 1981; Kuhl & Weiß, 1994). There was no question of a generalized decrease in expectations causing the performance deficits observed in state-oriented individuals, because they did not report reduced expectations of success after exposure to failure.

Further studies established that state-oriented rumination was in fact caused by deficits in affect regulation (Kuhl

& Baumann, 2000). Analogous, though much more pronounced, deficits have been documented for state-oriented alcoholics (Stuchlikova & Man, 1999), who have a significantly worse prognosis when it comes to implementing the intention to steer clear of alcohol (Palfai, McNally, & Roy, 2002). Recent findings (Koole, 2004) confirm the hypothesis that uncontrollable rumination in SOF is caused by inhibition of the **implicit self-system**. SOF experience an increase in implicit activation of negative self-related cognitions, as measured by means of a priming method, when confronted with threatening thoughts (imagining a frightening person from their own biography).

❶ Given the many findings showing that the self provides a rather positive "bottom-line" evaluation of one's identity ("self-positivity"; Koole, 2000); the increase in negative evaluations observed in state-oriented individuals supports the hypothesis that self-access becomes inhibited as soon as these individuals are confronted with threatening situations.

Most likely, AOF find it easier than SOF to detach from negative experiences because they check whether new information is potentially threatening and worthy of attention in the **current context** in a "preconscious" phase of information processing. This hypothesis was confirmed by an event-related potentials study in which respondents were presented with a list of words, some of which reminded them of painful life events. The results showed that AOF respondents paid more attention to negative than to neutral words after just 180 ms; SOF respondents did not even differentiate between negative and neutral words at that point (Rosahl, Tennigkeit, Kuhl, & Haschke, 1993). Early "suppression" of information that is of no relevance to the current context or intention seems to be more conducive to efficient coping than later repression of that information. Once the information has reached consciousness, attempts to suppress it take up vital processing capacity and are often unsuccessful: Instructing participants not to think of a white bear for a while can result in an excessive amount of thinking of white bears later on (Wegner, 1994).

Counter-Regulation of the Inhibition of Positive Affect: Prospective Action Orientation (AOP)

In contrast to the studies on learned helplessness, where (lack of) affect-regulatory competence was easily identified as the reason for performance deficits (questionnaire items referred directly to the inability to detach from negative feelings and thoughts), the affect-regulatory core of prospective action vs. state orientation (AOP) was not immediately apparent. Given that positive affect is known to facilitate behavior (Gray, 1982), however, it could be assumed that the hesitation in implementing intentions and the prolonged periods of deliberation reported by prospectively state-oriented individuals were attributable to a lack of behavior-facilitating positive affect.

Although positive affect is not addressed directly in the ACS-90, the experiment by Beckman and Kuhl (1984) described below provided indirect evidence for the assumed affective concomitants of the problems of decision-making and action implementation typically seen in state-oriented individuals.

STUDY

Study on the Regulation of Affect in State- vs. Action-Oriented Individuals

Why is it that negative affect is conscious and directly accessible in questionnaires, whereas behavior-facilitating positive affect (or its inhibition) is not always directly accessible? Theoretical reasons for this difference in the measurement of negative and (inhibited) positive affect have been established, and it is now possible to explain why it makes sense to address negative affect directly in questionnaire measures and to measure positive affect indirectly in terms of its impact. Specifically, positive affect is more closely associated with the intuitive mode of information processing than with conscious, analytical processing (see the first modulation assumption of PSI theory below). It follows that consciously thinking about positive affect may in fact reduce that affect. The opposite is true of negative affect, which is intensified by conscious reflection because, according to the second modulation assumption of PSI theory, negative affect inhibits affect-reducing mechanisms (extension memory, EM). Of course, this does not mean that respondents are unable to report on positive affect at all, but intensive reflection on positive mood may result in its dampening.

In one experiment, Beckmann and Kuhl (1984) asked respondents who were house-hunting to assess the merits of various apartments, and provided them with all the relevant information. Later on, when the respondents were asked to reassess the apartments, state-oriented respondents provided "objective" responses; because they had not been given any additional information, they made few, if any, changes to their previous assessments. Action-oriented participants, on the other hand, assessed the apartments they had favored at first measurement much more positively than the other apartments, even though there had been no change in the information provided. This mental "amplification" of incentives was interpreted as the result of a process of self-motivation, the aims of which were to bring the process of deliberation to a close and to support the implementation of the resulting decision (Beckmann & Kuhl, 1984).

Self-Motivation

PSI theory, as presented in Section 12.5, differentiates self-motivation from other ways of dealing with affect. In contrast to Freud's defense mechanisms and the corresponding coping styles (Folkman & Lazarus, 1988; Janke, Erdmann, & Kallus, 1985; Krohne, 1996), self-motivation (AOP – prospective action orientation) and self-relaxation (AOF – action orientation after failure) are attributed to the affect-regulatory

impact of the implicit self. In other words, positive affect is not based on an impulsive reaction, such as repression of anxiety (e.g., through embellishment), which functions to protect individuals against experiences that would produce anxiety (Byrne, 1961; Krohne, 1996), but is the result of an informed – if largely unconscious – decision, made by a system that takes all self-relevant information on the meaning of various affects into consideration before determining whether an affect is to be admitted or altered in the current context (self-confrontational coping). This form of affect regulation can also be applied to the regulation of negative affect (AOF). In lay terms, it is coping by "looking at the problem instead of looking away." This mode of coping cannot be described in terms of the classical dichotomy of denial ("repression") and sensitization. In fact, it is an **adaptive** form of sensitization that combines tolerance of pain and anxiety (i.e., sensitization) with non-defensive, active coping.

It is difficult to provide empirical evidence for the implicit (unconscious) status of this form of affect regulation. It is even more difficult to demonstrate that the "self" – which PSI theory regards as the source of personal volition – is involved in this form of affect regulation in action-oriented individuals. Nevertheless, a Dutch team has provided empirical evidence for both assumptions with respect to the regulation of positive affect (Koole & Jostmann, 2004).

Koole and Jostmann (2004) were able to show the following:

- Prospectively action-oriented individuals (AOP) do indeed upregulate positive affect, even when that positive affect is measured at the implicit level (e.g., faster reaction times on a task requiring friendly faces to be picked out from a set of faces with negative expressions).
- The differences in reaction time on these tasks are so slight (in the range of milliseconds) that this upregulation cannot have been consciously controlled.
- The upregulation of positive affect is mediated by self-access, measured in terms of the speed with which self-referential questions are answered (e.g., "Does the following word describe you?").

The mediating role of self-access in action-oriented participants (AOP) is shown in Fig. 12.1. The significant association between the experimental induction of "demand or pressure" and the measure for implicit upregulation of positive affect (upper part of Fig. 12.1) decreases significantly when the assumed mediating variable (i.e., self-access) is entered in the regression model (lower part of Fig. 12.1). This pattern of results reveals the mediating status of self-access: When a relationship between two variables (e.g., drinking lots of beer and a hangover on the next morning) disappears after removing a third variable (e.g., drinking alcohol-free beer), this third variable must be the cause of the relationship. If self-motivation is literally generated by the self-system,

Action-Oriented Participants (AOP)

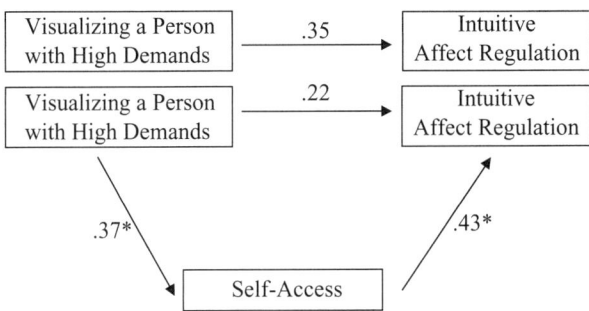

Figure 12.1 In action-oriented individuals (AOP), the effect of visualizing a person with high demands on a measure of unconscious (intuitive) affect regulation is mediated by self-access, measured in terms of reaction times on self-referential judgments; this mediating effect is not observed in state-oriented individuals. (Based on Koole & Jostmann, 2004.)

individuals with highly developed access to the self (high **self-determination**) should be able to motivate themselves better in everyday life and to tackle difficult goals successfully, without having to worry about being permanently discouraged. In fact, there is empirical evidence for the link between self-determination and self-motivation (Kuhl, 2001, p. 613; Lee, Sheldon, & Turban, 2003).

Dibbelt (1997) was able to show that the irresolute behavior of prospectively state-oriented individuals does not derive from a general lack of resolve, but from their failure to muster behavior-facilitating energy from the self-system (see the study below).

12.4.2 Effects of Action and State Orientation

Like many other constructs in personality psychology, the constructs of action vs. state orientation have been validated by way of theoretically predicted and empirically obtained associations with numerous other variables. Research has confirmed that it was the right decision not to combine the two forms of action orientation (i.e., AOP and AOF) in a single scale, even though such an approach might seem quite reasonable given the significant correlations and the higher internal consistency of the combined scale (Kuhl, 1994). Today, the findings on this construct can be seen as an example of the feasibility and utility of a **dissociation-oriented approach** that foregoes the "simplifications" entailed when correlating variables that load on the same factor are aggregated, and instead tests for any differences between the variables in terms of their relations to other variables (an approach that is often only possible within experimental designs).

The classical **aggregation approach**, which is usually based on factor analysis, neglects the dissociation-oriented exploration of relations with other variables whenever there is too strong a focus on the dichotomy between

Study on Self-Motivation in State- and Action-Oriented Individuals

In Dibbelt's (1997) study, participants used the cursor keys to move a cursor from a starting point to a target point on a coordinate grid. As they approached the target point, a new target appeared on the screen. Participants were instructed to switch to the new target if it was closer than the original one, and to keep aiming for the original target if the new one was further away. State-oriented participants did not show a general increase in reaction time when a change in direction was required. However, an increase in their reaction times was observed when the distances between the cursor and the two targets were equal (difference between the target distances is "zero" in Fig. 12.2). In this case, the participants themselves (i.e., their "selves") had to decide which target to aim for; there was no external cue indicating what to do (see Kuhl, 2001, p. 219). However, this increase in reaction time under the "self-determination condition" was observed only when an uncompleted intention was induced prior to the cursor task (e.g. "Could you remind me to save the data at the end of the experiment?"). These findings (Fig. 12.2)

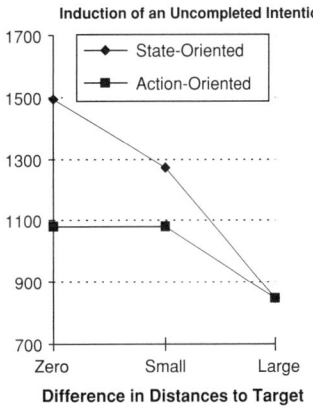

Figure 12.2 Delayed reaction times in implementing a behavioral change in prospectively state-oriented individuals (SOP) after induction of an uncompleted intention. (Based on Dibbelt, 1997.)

are fully congruent with the assumption that positive affect has to be generated before an intention can be implemented. The loading of "working memory" with a behavioral intention leads to inhibition of positive affect that state-oriented individuals are unable to counter-regulate (cf. Koole & Jostmann, 2004). This persevering inhibition has an impact on "self-willed" activities only (i.e., not externally controlled shifts of direction in the cursor task), because activities that need to be regulated by the self also require energy from the self (whose self-motivational ability is impaired in state-oriented individuals). In sum, the mediation analysis by Koole and Jostmann (2004) has shown that action-oriented individuals are able to reestablish positive affect when dealing with difficult "tasks," but that this ability disappears when differences in self-access are statistically removed.

"convergent" and "discriminant" validity (Campbell & Fiske, 1959). This dichotomy makes it easy to overlook cases in which, despite correlating significantly and even strongly, two variables do not measure the same construct, because they have disparate relations with other variables under certain, theoretically predictable, circumstances.

The correlation between prospective and failure-related action orientation is usually significant, and in the range from $r = .30$ to .60 (Kuhl & Beckmann, 1994a), meaning that both variables sometimes load on the same factor (e.g., Kuhl & Goschke, 1994, p. 140). Nevertheless, a number of behavioral correlates are only replicable for AOP. Prospectively state-oriented participants (SOP) are hesitant to switch to subjectively more attractive activities in experimental situations (manifest alienation; Kuhl & Beckmann, 1994b) and seem to maintain uncompleted intentions in memory, even when there is no opportunity to implement them. This increased level of **goal activation** in state-oriented individuals can be inferred from their shorter reaction times on tasks that require words relating to previously formed intentions to be recognized (Goschke & Kuhl, 1993). Paradoxically, frequent thoughts about uncompleted intentions seem to inhibit implementation of those intentions:

- Prospective state orientation (SOP) correlates with delaying uncompleted intentions (procrastination: Beswick & Mann, 1994; Blunt & Pychyl, 1998; Fuhrmann & Kuhl, 1998; Kuhl & Fuhrmann, 1998; Kuhl & Goschke, 1994, p. 141).
- State-oriented individuals (SOP) take longer than action-oriented individuals to make a decision, especially when subjectively unimportant alternatives are available (Stiensmeier-Pelster, 1994; Jungermann, Pfister & May, 1994).
- They are less certain of their decisions (Stiensmeier-Pelster, 1994).
- They generate more complex decision-making contexts (Jungermann et al., 1994).
- Moreover, state-oriented individuals find it more difficult to reduce the number of options in the decision-making process (Niederberger, Engemann, & Radtke, 1987).

Effects of the Prospective Form of Action vs. State Orientation

One explanation for the nonimplementation of intended actions, which seems rather paradoxical given that uncompleted intentions are so strongly activated (Beswick & Mann, 1994; Blunt & Pychyl, 1998; Goschke & Kuhl, 1994), is that the formulation of an intention (and its storage in "intention memory") actually inhibits executive functions in the first instance (see Section 12.5.2 on intuitive behavior control in PSI theory). Normally, this antagonism between inten-

tion formation and behavior control is useful in that it prevents premature implementation of actions. It makes sense for conscious intentions to be formulated whenever it is not yet possible or sensible to put them into practice (e.g., because difficulties have to be overcome or solutions found). When implementation of the intention is imminent (e.g., when the individual sees an opportunity to act), the antagonism between intention memory and behavior control must be overcome by generation of positive affect (Kuhl & Kazén, 1999).

❶ State-oriented individuals (SOP) find it much more difficult than action-oriented individuals to achieve this volitional facilitation (through self-motivation) (Beckmann & Kuhl, 1984; Koole & Jostmann, 2004). This explains the paradox that state-oriented individuals put fewer of their implementations into practice, even though their uncompleted intentions are more strongly activated in intention memory (Goschke & Kuhl, 1993).

In fact, the studies by Dibbelt (1997) outlined above demonstrate that state-oriented individuals only have difficulties implementing their intentions when they are required to load intention memory and the actions have to be initiated by the self, without external triggers. These findings suggest that impaired implementation of one's "own" intentions, i.e., intentions formed by the self-system (volitional inhibition), heightens sensitivity to external influences on one's behavior. Indeed, there are strong connections between the tendency to submit to the expectations of others (tendency to **introjection** and **external control**) and SOP (Kuhl & Fuhrmann, 1998).

According to the theoretical considerations outlined here, these phenomena should be more closely associated with the regulation of positive than of negative affect. Both the aggregation-based factor-analytic approach and the traditional confounding of positive and negative affect as opposite poles of a common bipolar dimension (Russel & Carroll, 1999; Wundt, 1896) would lead us to expect that all of the findings are replicable with variables associated with negative affect (e.g., SOF). In the experiments cited, however, the findings of relationships with variables such as goal activation, procrastination, and overly complex and irresolute decision-making processes were not replicated for the failure-related form of state orientation (SOF).

Effects of the Failure-Related Form of Action vs. State Orientation

The behavioral correlates of the ruminative SOF differ from those identified above. Individuals characterized by SOF tend to engage in uncontrollable rumination that is at odds with their intentions (i.e., irrelevant to the task at hand; Kuhl & Baumann, 2000), to show higher inconsistency when judging their own preferences, and indifferent reaction times when deciding between alternatives of differing attractiveness (latent alienation: Guevara, 1994; Kuhl & Beckmann, 1994b). As shown in Fig. 12.3, state-oriented individuals of the ruminative type often confuse their own wishes with those of others, particularly in the context of negative mood and unpleasant activities (**self-infiltration**: Kuhl & Kazén, 1994; in Fig. 12.3, self-infiltration is reflected in the number of false self-ascriptions of tasks imposed by another person minus the number of self-ascriptions in a baseline condition, i.e., on activities that were neither selected by the participant nor imposed by another person; see also the following study).

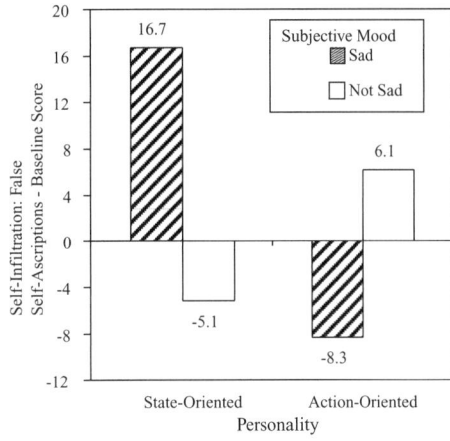

Figure 12.3 Findings on self-infiltration: In the presence of sad mood, individuals characterized by failure-related state orientation (SOF) confuse their own wishes with those of others. (Baumann & Kuhl, 2003)

PSI theory describes such a mechanism (Section 12.5). Essentially, PSI theory holds that the behavior observed in those state-oriented individuals with a propensity to rumination can be explained by inhibited **self-access** in the presence of negative affect. Uncontrollable rumination occurs when self-access is inhibited because, without this access, the system literally does not know what it wants. Without at least an implicitly activated representation of what is wanted (e.g., of activities appropriate to the task at hand or the current self-representation), it is impossible to identify **unwanted** thoughts and feelings, never mind to filter them out and neutralize them. Inhibited self-access also explains why these individuals confuse their own wishes with those of others (self-infiltration), and why they show inconsistencies when asked to state their preferences (alienation): Without self-access one cannot decide whether a wish or a goal has been generated by the self (i.e., is self-determined) nor can one produce consistent judgments of one's own preferences on consecutive occasions.

STUDY

Operationalization of the Self-Infiltration Effect

Self-infiltration is operationalized in terms of false self-ascriptions of other people's instructions or recommendations. In a simulation of a working day in an office, participants are invited to play the role of an office worker, and to select activities they are willing to perform at the end of the experiment. The experimenter, who plays the part of their boss, then assigns a number of activities. Later on, an unexpected memory test is administered, and participants are instructed to classify each activity according to whether it was self-selected or not (i.e., assigned by the experimenter or not chosen at all). Findings show that state-oriented individuals (SOF) often erroneously recall tasks assigned by the experimenter as being self-selected. These individuals are evidently not always consciously aware of this form of internalized external control (misinformed introjection): the conscious self-concept (i.e., the ego) seems to be infiltrated by the wishes and expectations of others. State-oriented self-infiltration is most likely to occur in association with negative affect (Fig. 12.3); e.g., when the activities to be performed are unattractive or when negative mood is induced (Baumann & Kuhl, 2003; Kazén, Baumann, & Kuhl, 2003). These studies have also produced findings indicating that the rumination on unwanted (i.e., task-irrelevant) matters that is characteristic of state orientation is significantly correlated with self-infiltration.

Here again, contrary to what the aggregation approach or a one-dimensional theory of positive and negative emotions would lead us to expect, the findings on the validity correlates of SOF could not be replicated for prospective state orientation in the studies cited. Again, the theoretical challenge was to explain the pattern of results obtained in terms of a simple functional mechanism. Why is it that uncontrollable rumination and self-ascription of others' wishes (self-infiltration) occur in the same people (those characterized by failure-related state orientation) under the same conditions? Is there a common mechanism behind rumination, self-infiltration, and alienation (e.g., inconsistent judgment of one's preferences)?

Neurobiological Foundations of the Relationship Between Self-Perception and Regulation of Affect

The right hemisphere (especially its prefrontal area):

- facilitates self-representations, as measured by self-referential questions ("Does the following word describe you?"; Craik et al., 1999; Keenan et al., 2001; Kircher et al. 2002),

- supports the negative emotional reactions of the "autonomic" nervous system (Davidson, 2000), which are considerably weaker when emotional information is processed in the left hemisphere, (Dawson & Schell, 1982; Wheeler, Stuss, & Tulving, 1997; Wittling, 1990), and

- is directly involved in the downregulation of negative affect (the right hemisphere is activated more strongly

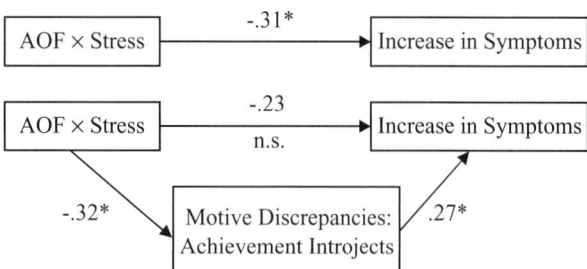

Figure 12.4 Action orientation after failure protects patients with high levels of everyday stress (AOF ×stress) against aggravation of symptoms (increase in symptoms from 1st to 2nd point of measurement). Motive discrepancies mediate the relationship between AOF × stress and aggravation of symptoms. (Based on Baumann, Kaschel, & Kuhl, 2005.)

than the left hemisphere when study participants are asked to downregulate negative affect; Levesque et al., 2003).

❶ Taking all these functions together, we can now explain from a functional design perspective why state orientation (SOF) increases the risk of psychological symptoms (Baumann, Kaschel, & Kuhl, 2005; Hautzinger, 1994; Kuhl, Kazén & Koole, 2007), whereas failure-related action orientation not only protects against stress-induced symptoms, but helps to maintain occupational performance (Kuhl et al., 2007).

Fig. 12.4 reports findings from a mediation analysis carried out in a large sample of patients with various psychological symptoms (e.g., depression, anxiety, eating disorders). The significant **protection** (reflected in a negative regression coefficient) that the interaction between failure-related action orientation and everyday stress (AOF × stress) afforded against aggravation of symptoms (−.31*) decreased significantly (to − .23) when motive discrepancies were included in the regression model. In other words, AOF prevents aggravation of symptoms by suspending the effects of motive discrepancies (for example, the pursuit of introjects, or consciously represented achievement goals that are not supported by a corresponding motive and associated needs). AOP did not have this kind of protective function. It did, however, help to predict overall well-being (in contrast to AOF).

Recent studies show that the stress-resistant self-access of action-oriented individuals can be operationalized by an **objective** index called **autonoetic interference**. In self-infiltration experiments, action-oriented participants show **increased reaction times** when presented with a list of the unattractive activities they chose themselves (e.g., when they were induced to chose among unattractive activities; Kazén, Baumann, & Kuhl, 2003). SOP fail to notice the contradiction between these two incompatible pieces of information from the self-system (i.e., it is an unattractive activity and that they chose it themselves). Because state-oriented individuals are

unable to downregulate negative affect, access to the self is inhibited, which explains why they do not show increased reaction times when recalling facts that should, in fact, give them pause for thought (i.e., the fact of having chosen an unattractive activity) when asked to state which of the activities on a list they chose themselves.

12.5 PSI Theory: Affect-Modulated Interactions of Systems Relevant to Personality

Research findings on stress-induced regression – in terms of inhibition of volition (impaired implementation of intentions) and self-access (e.g., neglect of motives in the formulation of goals) – draw attention to the influence of emotion on the efficiency of high-inferential ("intelligent") psychological systems:

❶ Excessive stress and the associated negative affect inhibit holistic processing, whereas positive affect plays a key role in facilitating behavior.

However, it is difficult to integrate these findings into theories of motivation, which (like personality theories in general) tend not to offer elaborate architectures of psychological functions or processing systems.

Among classic theories of personality, the only exception worth mentioning is Jung's personality theory, which differentiates between two antagonistic modes of processing: analytical thinking and holistic feeling, on the one hand, and intuiting and sensing, on the other. Jung's cognitive typology differs from traditional affective typologies (Hippocrates, Galen), the basic concepts of which continue to play a dominant role in personality psychology, and are now supported by the findings of factor analysis (Eysenck, 1990; McCrae & Costa, 1987). Precisely because he intended to contrast his typology with affective typologies, Jung disregarded the modulatory influence of affect on styles of cognitive processing. Another reason why Jung's four cognitive functions cannot serve as basis for an architecture of the mind in motivation psychology is that – as he noted self-critically in his main typological work (Jung, 1936/1990) – he did not elaborate theoretical concepts of motivation or behavior. The same limitations apply to modern, empirically grounded approaches that aim to revive holistic and analytical forms of information processing in personality psychology (Epstein, Pacini, Denes-Raj, & Heier, 1996).

12.5.1 Psychological Macrosystems

The theory of Personality Systems Interactions (PSI theory) seeks to close the gap in motivation theory in terms of functional design. It is based on the assumption that the functions and systems postulated in the various approaches (e.g.,

Anderson, 1983; Jung, 1936) offered by cognitive or personality psychology (e.g., Jung's main functions of personality; short-term vs. long-term memory; executive functions such as the central, attention-based monitoring system: Norman & Shallice, 1986) do not suffice to answer the questions raised in the preceding paragraphs. Motivation psychology is concerned with the development of need- and behavior-relevant aspects of personal experience, which are expressed in motives and other components of an implicit self-system. It examines the degree to which concrete goals and actions correspond with these motives (self-congruence), and whether or not goals and intentions are implemented in behavior ("volitional facilitation").

❶ According to PSI theory, **volitional facilitation** is dependent on the interaction of an **intuitive behavior control** system (IBC) and a system that is responsible for maintaining difficult intentions (i.e., intentions that cannot or should not be implemented immediately) in memory so that they are not "forgotten" or displaced by competing action tendencies. The main differences between this **intention memory** (IM) and the construct of short-term or working memory in cognitive psychology (Baddeley, 1986) are that the IM stores action-related rather than sensory information, and has an inhibitory component that serves to prevent premature implementation of intended actions (Kuhl & Kazén, 1999).

It is possible to measure the activation of an intended action in IM words relating to uncompleted intentions are recognized faster than neutral words (Goschke & Kuhl, 1993). In recent years, various other methods have been developed to operationalize the persistent activation of intentions (Förster & Liberman, 2002; Koole, Smeets, van Knippenberg, & Dijksterhuis, 1999; Shah, Friedman, & Kruglanski, 2002). Activation of intuitive behavior control can be experimentally induced by asking respondents to imagine where, when, and how they will implement their intentions (Armor & Taylor, 2003; Gollwitzer, 1999; Svenson, Oestergren, Merlo, & Rastam, 2002). Findings show that the implementation of intentions is fostered by the induction of "implementation imagery." IBC dominates social interaction from birth (Meltzoff & Moore, 1994; Papoušek & Papoušek, 1987) into adulthood (Chartrand & Bargh, 1999).

Self-development (including development of motives) and the self-access on which it depends are assumed to be dependent on the interaction of an **object recognition (OR) system** and a high inferential self-system. The self-system is so extensive that it requires a parallel memory system capable of integrating an enormous number of experiences. This **extension memory** (EM) is in turn so extensive that it can only be "felt" implicitly and is not fully accessible to conscious awareness (and might thus be seen as approximating "feeling" in Jung's typology). With its parallel network structure at a high level of integration, extension memory is suitable for representing persons, probably the most complex of the challenges facing the four macrosystems. One of

these persons is the self, which is represented by numerous references to both internal processes (e.g., needs, feelings, values, identity) and other people (Andersen & Chen, 2002).

The OR system supplies the input required for the development of EM and the motives and other self-aspects stored in it. The "objects" in question are not only items that can be perceived visually, but all products of processing that can be extracted from their contexts as single units, and thus recognized and labeled in other contexts. Hence, feelings can be represented as objects, but they must be differentiated from the "emotions" from which they were abstracted.

DEFINITION

Emotions are defined as implicit representations that integrate a large number of both affective and cognitive contents (Ortony, Clore & Collins, 1988), including the relevant contextual information, and that are typically processed at the level of extension memory. An emotion can thus be seen as the experience-centered analogue of a motive, with behavior-relevant representations being more elaborated in the latter.

12.5.2 The First Modulation Assumption: Volitional Facilitation

Affects are subcognitive components of emotions. In neurobiological terms, they are generated on a subcortical level, and may be – but are not necessarily – linked to cognitive elaborations (LeDoux, 1995). In other words, we need to get used to applying terms like "feelings," even when the person concerned is unaware of them: affects are not always consciously accessible. They are generated by changes in the discrepancy between actual and desired states on the level of needs (McClelland et al., 1953), which, as defined at the beginning of the chapter, are subcognitive and subaffective detectors of such discrepancies. To date, however, psychological literature has largely overlooked this important connection between affects and their motivational basis. It implies that each affect is directly or indirectly driven by a "vicissitude"; i.e., a need episode with a positive or a negative outcome. Analogous ideas on the origins of affect have been proposed for attainment of vs. disengagement from personal goals: coming closer to achieve a goal generates positive affect, whereas thwarted attempts to reach a goal generate negative affect (Carver, Lawrence, & Scheier, 1996; Martin & Tesser, 1996). This approach needs to be expanded from a motivational perspective because it does not incorporate subcognitive sources of affects.

The goal- and need-driven basis of affects offers a plausible explanation for the role they are attributed in PSI theory: affects establish that configuration of psychological systems that is most conducive to satisfying a current need or to implementing the respective motive or goal.

Inhibition
(Antagonism)

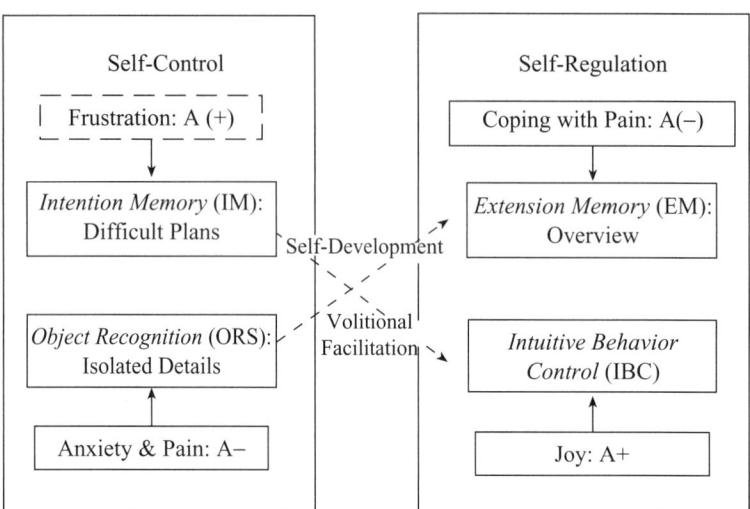

Figure 12.5 Schematic illustration of PSI Theory. (Kuhl, 2001; see text for details.)

Thus, the ability to tolerate phases of inhibited positive affect [A(+)], which necessarily occur in the context of difficult tasks, is postulated to be an integral component of the achievement motive. This "frustration tolerance" can be traced back to the conditions under which the achievement motive develops, as outlined above. In a parenting climate supportive of the child's independence, parents do not always intervene when the child runs into difficulties or experiences frustration [A(+)]. Instead, they allow inhibited positive affect to occur, though not to an excessive degree (Heinz Heckhausen's principle of fit).

❗ The first modulation assumption concerns the functional effects of frustration:

  ▪ The inhibition of positive affect activates intention memory, including its inhibitory component (inhibition of IBC).

  ▪ Release of this inhibition – e.g., when a problem is solved, or when an individual is given encouragement or motivates him- or herself – re-establishes the connection between intention memory (IM) and intuitive behavior control (IBC). Thus, IBC "learns" which behavioral routines are "wanted" at the level of IM (Fig. 12.5).

Positive affect therefore not only has the function of facilitating behavior, it can also **facilitate volition** in the presence of higher-level will. In functional design terms, this occurs when intention memory is loaded with a behavioral intention. The volitional facilitation that occurs in the presence of positive affect permits intuitive behavior control (IBC) to implement conscious intentions more rapidly and accurately, because the release of volitional inhibition reestablishes the connection between IBC and intention memory. The IBC can thus "learn" which of the behavioral routines stored within it correspond with the current intention.

STUDY

Studies on the Volitional Facilitation Effect

Experiments demonstrating that Stroop interference is reduced or completely eliminated when participants are shown positive words such as "success" or "good luck" before presentation of the Stroop stimulus (i.e., color name words printed in nonmatching colors; Kuhl & Kazén, 1999) support the volitional facilitation assumption. According to the first modulation assumption, when intention memory is loaded with the difficult part of the task ("name the color instead of reading the color word"), the positive affect triggered by positive words serves to connect the task with intuitive behavior control, such that the delay in reaction times typically observed for incongruent color words no longer occurs. In the experiment described above, we tried to increase the probability of participants activating the instruction in IM prior to each trial (not necessarily consciously) by having them work on two Stroop tasks per trial, each introduced by a positive, a negative, or a neutral word. We assumed that maintenance of an intention in IM becomes necessary whenever a sequence of more than one action step is to be performed (the next step has to be kept active in memory in order for the sequence to be performed smoothly).

The first modulation assumption provides an explanation for the paradox that performance on the easy task (i.e., naming the color in which a row of Xs is printed) did not improve in trials with a positive prime, but that the difficult task (i.e., naming the incongruent ink color in which a color name word was printed; e.g., responding with "blue" when the word "red" was printed in blue ink) was performed faster when a positive word was presented before the Stroop stimulus. When intention memory is loaded, positive affect does not facilitate simple ("dominant") behavioral routines; rather, it facilitates responses that are difficult, but required and intended.

From a neurobiological perspective (Kuhl, 2001, p. 681ff.), this connection is assumed to be established during affective change from A(+) to A+, when activation of the left hemisphere (IM) caused by A(+) gives way to activation of the right hemisphere (EM) caused by A+. Communication between hemispheres is presumably impaired as long as one of the two affective states dominates. Affective change is of critical importance for the interaction between psychological systems, because it is only during affective change that there is a short "window of opportunity," during which both hemispheres are activated to roughly the same degree and are thus able to exchange the information activated to the best possible effect.

Further studies have confirmed that the effect of volitional facilitation is particularly typical of achievement motivation. A reduction in Stroop interference was found after priming with positive achievement-related words (e.g., "success" or "increase in performance"), but not after priming with words alluding to positive affiliative experiences (e.g., "first love" or "being happy together"; Kazén & Kuhl, 2005). This finding confirms the assumption that affects, together with the currently **dominant need**, establish the configuration of psychological systems that is most conducive to satisfying that need. In the case of achievement behavior, this systems configuration is characterized by a shift from IM to intuitive behavior control. When achievement motivation is aroused, activation of intention memory helps to maintain self-commitment to a difficult task and perseverance until it is completed. Indeed, experimental studies have shown that activation of goal-related information (e.g., by means of experimentally induced priming) can increase perseverance (Shah & Kruglanski, 2003). Volitional facilitation by means of affective change is also crucial, however. In its absence, difficult achievement goals would be maintained for a long time, but concrete efforts to achieve them would be rare ("passive goal fixation").

Beyond the micro-analytical level and the Stroop experiments outlined, experimental evidence for volitional facilitation has also been found on the more everyday macro-analytical level. In numerous experiments, Oettingen and colleagues confirmed that successive contrasting of positive aspects of the desired future (goal attainment) and negative aspects of present reality (difficulties still to be overcome) facilitated implementation of realistic intentions, whereas a focus on just one of these aspects reduced efficiency of implementation (Oettingen, 1997; Oettingen, Pak, & Schnetter, 2001).

Higgins's (1987) findings, according to which inhibited positive affect (e.g., "dejected emotions") is closely associated with a focus on unattained, partly unrealistic ideals – i.e., with discrepancies between the "ideal self" and the "actual self" – can also be explained on the basis of the first modulation assumption. Unrealistic ideals may lead to intention memory being constantly loaded with intentions, without the steps needed to realize those ideals ever being taken. According to the first modulation assumption, fixation on dejected emotions or other forms of the inhibition of positive affect impedes the implementation of the corresponding behavioral intentions (through activation of IBC).

12.5.3 The Second Modulation Assumption: Self-Access and Self-Development

PSI theory also assumes the interaction between the systems relevant to self-development to be modulated by shifts between different affects. As mentioned above, self-development presupposes that new experiences are constantly integrated into the growing network of personal experiences (i.e., into the self-system as part of extension memory). According to the second modulation assumption, this process is made possible by the shift between negative affect (A-), which occurs after painful experiences or experiences that do not fit existing schemata (of EM), and the subsequent downregulation of this negative affect [A(-)] (Fig. 12.5).

❶ The second modulation assumption states that:
  ■ Negative affect activates isolated experiences that are abstracted from their contexts (i.e., "objects" from the OR).
  ■ Negative affect inhibits access to integrated self-representations, motives, and other contents of extension memory.
  ■ Downregulation of negative affect reestablishes access to extension memory.
    During affective change, there is a short "window of opportunity" during which both hemispheres are activated to approximately the same medium degree and are thus able to exchange information to the best possible effect (e.g., to integrate left-hemispheric isolated experiences or "objects" into right-hemispheric extended self-referential networks: self-development).

For self-development to occur, it is thus necessary to overcome the antagonism between the perception of details (i.e., "objects" that are extracted from their contexts) and the extension memory, which unites a huge number of individual perceptions within integrated "experiential landscapes." Fig. 12.5 illustrates the modulating influences of different affects on systems activation, and shows that it is possible to overcome the antagonism between the systems by means of shifts in affect ("emotional dialectic"). For example, rather than a painful experience being suppressed, it is first perceived as an isolated experience ("object"), and later integrated into the self (part of the extension memory), a process that requires tolerance of pain (A−) followed by the ability to cope with that pain [A(−)].

Uncontrollable rumination (Kuhl, 1981; Martin & Tesser, 1989; Nolen-Hoeksema, Parker, & Larsen, 1994) can be attributed to the inhibition of self-access owing to persevering negative affect. Without self-access (e.g., in the presence of excessive negative affect), the system no longer "knows" which cognitions are wanted at a certain time, and which are not. Moreover, it is not possible to apply high-inferential filters that admit only **wanted** thoughts and feelings. A possible neurobiological basis for these relationships was discussed above: the sensitivity of the hippocampus to stress (Section 12.3.2). Animal experiments have shown that inhibition of the hippocampus in the presence of excessive stress inhibits the connectivity between high-inferential processes (e.g., implicit representations in EM, such as "I want to concentrate on the task") and low-inferential processes, such as (inhibition of) distracting thoughts or feelings (Schmajuk & Buhusi, 1997).

The phenomenon of **self-infiltration** can also be attributed to the inhibition of self-access under conditions of persevering negative affect.

DEFINITION
Self-infiltration means confusing one's own wishes and choices with those of others.

Indeed, persevering negative affect leads people to recall tasks that were assigned or recommended by others as being self-selected (Baumann & Kuhl, 2003; Kazén, Baumann, & Kuhl, 2003; Kuhl & Kazén, 1994). What is more, functions of extension memory that do not relate to the implicit self are also adversely affected by negative affect. Performance on coherence tasks ("Do the three words goat, pass, and green have anything in common?") is a good example of this phenomenon – the correct answer (in this example: yes) can only be given intuitively, and not by explicitly seeking a solution (here: mountain) (Baumann & Kuhl, 2002; Bolte, Goschke, & Kuhl, 2003). Intuitive coherence judgments are assumed to be a function of extension memory because they require access to remote semantic networks, such that connections between distantly associated words can be "sensed" implicitly if they cannot be explicated directly. **Summation priming**, which seems to be facilitated more by right- than by left-hemispheric processes (Beeman et al., 1994), represents a similar operationalization of intuitive inferences requiring access to wide semantic networks.

12.6 Development: Determinants of Action and State Orientation

Is it possible to overcome state orientation? In other words, can the stress-induced inhibition of self-perception and the related self-regulatory functions be surmounted? Given the significance of the ability to bring about changes in affective states by means of self-regulation, thus activating the psychological system required at a given point in time, poten-

tial points of intervention for the training or therapy of affect regulation must be of considerable interest. This raises the question as to the conditions under which the ability to self-regulate affect develops. In the context of PSI theory, this developmental process is described by the **systems conditioning model**. Its premise is a simple one. If – in contrast to humanistic approaches to personality psychology (Deci & Ryan, 2000; Rogers, 1961) – the self is no longer regarded as a phenomenological metaphor, but as a real system with a functional profile that is open to investigation, then "self"-regulation of affect means that the self-system has to establish connections with the systems that regulate affects. In neurobiological terms, these might be connections between subcortical affect-generating systems (LeDoux, 1995) and the right pre-frontal cortex, which is activated when participants make self-referential judgments (Craik et al., 1999; Keenan et al., 2001) or try to regulate emotions (Beauregard, Levesque, & Bourgouin, 2001).

How does the brain learn to establish new connections? The best known way is classical conditioning: two stimuli (e.g., the ringing of a bell and the food that triggered salivation in Pavlov's dogs) become linked when they occur sequentially within a certain space of time (contiguity or contingence). Once this connection – for which there is now neurobiological evidence (LeDoux, 1995; Schmajuk & Buhusi, 1997) – has been established, the conditioned stimulus (e.g., the ringing of the bell) triggers a conditioned response (here, the secretion of saliva).

❶ According to the systems conditioning model, the reinforcement of connections between systems is analogous to classical conditioning. For the self-system to be connected to affect-regulating processes, such that the individual is later able to regulate emotions him- or her "self" (i.e., without external help), activation of the self-system must coincide with activation of affect-regulating processes sufficiently frequently in the course of development.

Of course, until affect regulation can be achieved by means of self-regulation, external support is required. For example, a child experiencing negative affect relies on the reassurance or consolation of an attachment figure, and a child experiencing loss of positive affect (e.g., when faced with a difficult task or an experience of loss) needs encouragement. But how can an interaction partner (e.g., father, mother, teacher, partner, therapist) know when a person's self-system is activated, and provide the necessary reassurance or encouragement wwordiithin the appropriate time frame? According to the systems conditioning model, the self is active whenever needs or related feelings are expressed (indeed, one of the primary functions of the self-system is to express feelings and needs). Thus, the attachment figure need only listen out for such references. This attentional focus on personal information is called **responsiveness** or "mind-mindedness" in developmental psychology (Meins, 1999) and "reflection" in the neo-analytical literature (Kohut, 1979). The more differentiated the self becomes throughout its development, the more "exacting" it will be with respect to the feedback expected: At later stages in development the individual needs to feel understood on a personal level for his or her self to remain active. If it does not succeed in communicating self-relevant information – i.e., if the person does not feel "understood" – the self-system becomes inhibited (in accordance with a general principle stating that systems that are not utilized are deactivated or disintegrate). An inhibited self-system cannot be connected to affect-regulating processes, even if the attachment figure succeeds in regulating the feelings of his or her interaction partner.

This might explain why even a very happy childhood by no means guarantees that a child will acquire affect-regulatory autonomy. Children exposed to frequent positive affect (e.g., because their mother is often in a good mood) are more likely to feel happy on a frequent basis (i.e., to find it easier to "enter" positive affective states). According to the systems conditioning model, however, the ability to self-regulate affect will not develop if positive affect is not expressed in response to the child's momentary self-expressions or in an understanding personal context. In adulthood, these individuals may always be reliant on others to provide them with encouragement or reassurance in difficult situations. They tend to have "symbiotic relationships"; i.e., they find it hard to accept that those closest to them have feelings "of their own," and are not always prepared to regulate their feelings (Schülein, 1989).

Empirical Findings on the Systems Conditioning Model

Findings from developmental psychology confirm the assumptions of the systems conditioning model. Even in the first months of a child's life, temporal contiguity of the mother's response to the child's simple self-expressions (e.g., establishing eye contact, smiling, or expressing irritation) is a significant predictor of the child's emotional adaptability later in life. Studies show that children whose mothers do not respond to their child's attempts to establish eye contact within a few hundred ms (i.e., who show low **responsiveness**) during a 30-minute observation period develop significantly more symptoms (bed wetting, physical complaints, aggressiveness, and other adaptive difficulties at preschool age) than children whose mothers respond promptly and appropriately to their child's self-expressions (Keller & Gauda, 1987; Keller, 1997a,b). Like the concept of responsiveness, the concept of **emotional availability** extends beyond the frequency of positive or negative emotional episodes in parent-child interactions. Availability increases the likelihood that parents will respond promptly and appropriately to their child's self-expressions. A recent study showed that the emotional availability of parents (especially the mother) covaries with the child's affect-regulatory competencies at age 12 months (Volling, McElwain, Notaro, & Herrera, 2002). It further provided direct confirmation of the chain of cause and

effect postulated in the systems conditioning model: from parental regulation of affect contingent on the child's self-expressions ("emotional availability") via the development of self-regulatory competencies to the resulting ability to adapt flexibly to changing situations. One feature of self-regulatory competence ("effortful attention") proved to be a mediator for the relationship between the mother's emotional availability and the child's adaptability to new situations four months later.

❶ Emotional availability and responsiveness, operationalized by the construct of "mindfulness," have positive effects on the ability to cope with painful events in adult life as well (Brown & Ryan, 2003). By contrast, repeated confrontation with failure impairs emotional regulation, especially in state-oriented individuals, and can even increase the risk for depressive symptoms (Kuhl & Helle, 1986; Hörhold & Walschburger, 1997).

Studies using imaging techniques show that early mother-child interactions activate the same right-hemispheric system (primarily the right orbito-frontal cortex) that in adulthood provides a (largely unconscious) sense of corporeal and emotional self (Devinsky, 2000) and that is activated when people make self-referential judgments (Keenan et al., 2001). Right-hemispheric activation is observed when infants are shown a woman's face (Tzourio-Mazoyer et al., 2002) or express emotions; e.g., a social smile (Holowka & Petitto, 2002); the mother shows right-hemispheric activation when she hears a crying baby (Lorberbaum et al., 2002. Results of a twin study (Kästele, 1988) suggest that self-regulatory competencies, measured in terms of action vs. state orientation, are significantly more dependent on experience and less genetically determined than are personality dimensions such as extraversion and neuroticism, which pertain more to the primary emotional reaction than to affect-regulatory competencies.

The systems conditioning model explains why the quality of relationships is so important in child-rearing and therapy, even in therapeutic approaches based on learning theory (e.g., behavior therapy), in which relationships play less of a role than in gestalt therapy, for example. Even if we were to limit the theoretical scope to classical conditioning, it is vital to recognize the role of relationships: the conditioning processes necessary for affect regulation will only take effect if sufficiently positive personal relationships are experienced at some phase of development. An inhibited self cannot be connected by means of pedagogical or therapeutic measures, however effective these may be. And it is only when this connection is established that the effects of such measures can, at some point, be initiated independently (i.e., self-regulated).

SUMMARY

This chapter focused on individual differences in basic motivational and self-regulatory competencies. Motives can be defined as capacities to regulate the satisfaction of one's needs by drawing on an increasingly intelligent network of experiences acquired across the lifespan. This extended network organizes all life experiences in terms of their relevance to the satisfaction of needs, but also with reference to other aspects of the **self-system** that are not directly related to need satisfaction (e.g., individual and cultural values, social roles, self-image, and identity). Intelligent need satisfaction adapts to constantly changing contexts and overcomes internal and external conflicts by reconciling seemingly contradictory needs (e.g., achievement at work and affiliation in private relationships) and resolving conflicts with the social environment (e.g., with the needs or cultural expectations of others) in a creative way.

The modulation assumptions of PSI theory and the research they are based upon have shown that affect-regulatory competencies are required for the process of self-development on which motivational intelligence depends. It is only when people have experienced a minimum of closeness and affection in their relationships that they seem able to develop a positive basic mood, which in turn enables them to tolerate, rather than repress, painful experiences. Only those who are able to tolerate negative affect have the capacity to learn from painful experiences. And those who also learn to exit painful experiences in a self-regulated manner (down-regulation of negative affect) are able to activate the extended network of experiences (i.e., extension memory with its self-aspects and motives) into which new experiences must be integrated in order to develop a coherent self. It is this integration of otherwise isolated experiences, and the facility to spontaneously access and process all relevant information in new situations requiring quick decisions rather than prolonged deliberation, that enables people to function as "mature personalities."

REVIEW QUESTIONS

1. **Why does taking individual differences into account make it easier to formulate general laws?**

    The neglect of individual differences can be seen as one of the reasons for the many inconsistent effects found in experimental psychology. If, by way of comparison, scholars had attempted to formulate "general" laws of falling bodies without taking individual differences into account, they would never have arrived at the established laws, the general validity of which resides in the very fact that individual differences in object mass are included in the equation.

2. **What is the difference between needs and motives?**

    Needs are subcognitive and subaffective discrepancies between actual and desired states that can trigger (relatively inflexible) behavior, even if they are not cognitively represented or backed up by affect. Motives are

largely unconscious cognitive representations that have been abstracted from need-relevant autobiographical experiences to generate implicit networks of behavioral options and expected outcomes, and to facilitate context-sensitive, flexible, and creative behavior as a means to satisfy needs.

3. **Which systems configurations (of affects and cognitive functioning) are particularly adaptive for the achievement and affiliation motives?**

    Stable positive affect can be adaptive for the affiliation motive (e.g., because it facilitates the intuitive regulation of behavior on which interpersonal relationships thrive), whereas affective **change** from inhibition to facilitation of positive affect (from "frustration tolerance" to self-motivation) is crucial for the achievement motive. The ability to tolerate a state of reduced positive affect makes it possible to endure difficulties rather than avoiding them (a process that is supported by the retention of difficult goals in intention memory). Once a solution has been found, the acting individual needs to be able to release inhibition of positive affect and to motivate him- or herself to engage in the appropriate behavior.

4. **Why can motives be seen as components of self-regulation?**

    Motives are need-relevant components of the implicit self-system, which involves emotional and somatosensory processes, serves to integrate information, and is characterized by parallel processing – and thus offers a basis for the monitoring and coordination of all cognitive and affective processes that regulate behavior such that it satisfies a wealth of personal needs, goals, values, and other self-defining characteristics.

5. **Why are motives measured by means of "narrative" methods?**

    Motives develop from an extensive web of autobiographical episodes, i.e., from personal "stories." The high level of cognitive integration characteristic of motives is best attained by asking respondents to generate stories of their own. Questionnaire measures assess conscious goals, which may well deviate from implicit needs and motives (e.g., achievement introjects that have not been integrated into the self and can trigger psychosomatic symptoms: Fig. 12.4).

6. **In what respects does the OMT differ from the TAT?**

    In contrast to the Thematic Apperception Test (TAT), the Operant Motive Test (OMT) does not require participants to relate the stories they generate in full. Instead, they are instructed to note down a few key points. Not only does this approach avoid the distortions that may occur when entire stories are written out, it also saves time, meaning that the number of picture cues shown (and hence the reliability of the test) can be increased. Moreover, the OMT coding system distinguishes four different forms of the approach motive in the domains of affiliation, achievement, and power motivation (with the passive-anxious avoidance form as a fifth variant). The four variants of approach motivation result from combining the type of affect that motivated the association reported (i.e., positive vs. negative) with the involvement or noninvolvement of the self (self-regulation vs. incentive-driven motivation; see Table 12.1).

7. What explanation does the functional design approach offer for the observations that intrinsic motivation resides in the activity itself and is reduced by reward or external control?

When behavior is driven primarily by incentives or instructions (i.e., "only" performed because of the reward), the self is less involved in action control. This means that self-regulatory functions such as self-motivation, which help to upregulate enjoyment of an activity, even if it proves difficult or unpleasant, are lacking. Because self-motivation is largely unconscious, the impression is that enjoyment emanates from the activity itself, i.e., that motivation comes "intrinsically" from engaging in the activity ("flow").

8. Which four modes of volition can be differentiated?

The four modes of volition are:

Self-regulation, in which goals that correspond with numerous internal and external needs and values are formulated on the basis of an inner overview (of the self) and positive basic mood; because of their emotional integration with the self, these goals have motivational support.

Self-control, in which the conscious ego focuses on implementing goals despite competing tendencies/alternatives.

Volitional facilitation (vs. inhibition), which provides the energy needed to implement the current action intention, even in the face of difficulties (self-motivation or "prospective action orientation").

Self-facilitation (vs. -inhibition), which maintains access to self-perception, even in painful or frightening situations, by means of nondefensive (i.e., self-confrontative) downregulation of negative affect (self-reassurance or "action orientation after failure").

9. Which findings confirm the hypothesis that prospective action orientation maintains action-facilitating affect under stress and facilitates self- (rather than other-) initiated behavior?

Koole and Jostmann (2004) showed that prospectively action-oriented individuals (AOP) respond more quickly to positive stimuli than state-oriented individuals when exposed to stress, and that this reaction is mediated

by self-access (Fig. 12.1). Dibbelt (1997) showed that prospectively state-oriented individuals only show prolonged reaction times on tasks that require a change in approach after induction of an uncompleted intention (i.e., through loading of "working memory") when that change in approach is "self-willed," and not imposed by an external agent (Fig. 12.2).

10. Why does it not suffice to induce positive control beliefs ("You can do it!") in people who feel helpless or depressed?

Helplessness induced by loss of control on a training task leads to objective performance deficits on different kinds of tasks, even when the subjective loss of control is not generalized to the new task. People evidently display generalized performance deficits after experiencing loss of control because they are unable to cope with the negative affect and the rumination it triggers (Kuhl, 1981). Consequently, there is little point in providing depressive individuals with encouragement ("You can do it!") unless they are also helped to develop the objective abilities needed to regulate affect (see question 15).

11. How is it possible to explain the paradox that ruminating on uncompleted intentions (i.e., activating working memory) actually inhibits their implementation?

Prospectively state-oriented individuals (SOP) are characterized by low levels of action-facilitating affect. This leads to activation of intention memory (Goschke & Kuhl, 1993), which is normally associated with action inhibition (e.g., for the purposes of problem solving) and can be overcome only by means of external encouragement (Kuhl & Kazén, 1999) or self-motivation (AOP) (first modulation assumption of PSI theory).

12. Why is rumination often associated with the confusion of self-selected goals and goals imposed by others?

The negative affect associated with uncontrollable rumination inhibits self-access (second modulation assumption of PSI theory), to the effect that the individuals in question are no longer able to distinguish self-selected from other-imposed goals (Fig. 12.3).

13. How does failure-related state orientation differ from anxiety or neuroticism, and prospective action orientation from extraversion?

Extraversion (E) and anxiety or neuroticism (N) describe the primary emotional reaction (emotional sensitivity), i.e., a person's propensity to experience positive (E) or negative affect (N) in new situations. Action orientation does not describe how people enter negative affect (AOF) or the inhibition of positive (AOP) affect, but how they exit these states.

14. **Why does emotional fixation inhibit goal implementation and self-development?**

Goal implementation requires communication (interaction) between intention memory (IM) and intuitive behavior control (IBC), and thus a shift from the inhibition of positive affect to its release (by means of self-motivation or external encouragement). Self-development requires contact to be established (interaction) between the system responsible for admitting unexpected or painful isolated experiences (object recognition) and the network integrating all personal experiences (i.e., the self as part of EM), which helps people to cope with pain and anxiety (Fig. 12.5). Contact between the left-hemispheric object recognition system (OR) and right-hemispheric self-perception (EM) can only be established by downregulating negative affect (which enables people to deal with difficult experiences), and thus facilitating access to the self-system.

15. **How can emotional fixation be overcome (and affect regulation learned)?**

People learn to regulate their own affects and emotions when the activation of the self coincides sufficiently frequently with the experience of affect being effectively counterregulated by external encouragement or consolation (provided by parents, friends, spouses, teachers, therapists, etc.; "system conditioning"). The self (like the CS in classical conditioning) can only be linked with affect-regulatory processes (the CR), if the individual expresses his or her own feelings and feels understood by the other person (otherwise, the self is "turned off" and cannot be connected, no matter how effective the experiences of encouragement or reassurance may be).

13 Intrinsic Motivation and Flow

F. Rheinberg

13.1 Introduction

DEFINITION
Motivation can be defined as the "activating orientation of current life pursuits toward a positively evaluated goal state". (Rheinberg, 2004a, p. 17)

The purpose of a definition of this kind is to describe the essential qualities of a term as succinctly as possible. Finer points have to be considered separately.

In the present case, at least two points need further elaboration:

1. The "positively evaluated goal state" may be to avoid or prevent undesired events. The qualities of avoidance motivation may differ from those of approach motivation (Chapters 4–9).

2. The second point is rather more complicated, and is the focus of the present chapter. When, as here, the definition of motivation focuses on a goal state, there is a risk of premature conclusions being drawn about where the incentives motivating behavior are located. It is easy to assume that the goal state has incentive value, and that the pursuit of the goal-directed activity is purely instrumental to bringing about that goal state, i.e., that the appeal of an activity resides solely in its intended outcomes. This is the approach taken by scholars such as Heckhausen (1977b) and Vroom (1964).

Unfortunately, this rather rash conclusion sometimes holds and sometimes does not. It is beyond question that people often engage in activities simply because they want to achieve or modify a particular goal state. When winter approaches, for example, a home owner will go down to the basement and light the furnace (= activity) to ensure that the home is comfortably warm (= desired goal state). If the basement is locked and the key is not where it is supposed to be, he or she will invest time and energy in looking for it. It would not occur to anybody to suggest that he or she simply enjoys going down to the basement or looking for mislaid keys. The incentive of the activity resides almost exclusively in the consequences of its intended outcome. The outcome of his or her endeavors is having lit the furnace; the consequence that provides an incentive for his activities is having a nice warm home.

If the incentive of anticipated consequences is high enough, people may even engage in activities that they experience as aversive. A student will finally get around to doing the pile of washing that has been building up all week because he or she wants to cook for friends; a friendly but timid student will muster the courage to complain to his or her noisy neighbor because he or she needs to get a good night's sleep for once.

These last two examples introduce a point that is central to the present chapter: some activities are unpleasant in and of themselves – their incentives are negative. Many people perceive the act of washing up mountains of dirty crockery in a grimy kitchen to be inherently unpleasant, even though the outcome and its foreseeable consequences are attractive. If their volitional competence is low, they will procrastinate until the consequences of their inaction are even more unpleasant than the activity itself. In the second example, the prospect of a power-related confrontation may be so unpleasant and distressing that the timid student puts up with the noise from the next room for months before he or she can finally work him- or herself up to approaching the neighbor about it.

❗ The performance of an activity may possess either positive or negative incentives. When incentives are positive, individuals may engage in an activity purely for the enjoyment of it.

A diary study showed that students who recorded the events of their day in 10-minute intervals spent 46% of their waking time engaged in activities they enjoyed (see Table 10.3 in Rheinberg, 1989). Performing these activities becomes a "goal" in its own right. The word goal is placed in quotes here because it is typically used to describe a desired end state, something that is expected to occur after an action has been completed. Where pleasurable activities are concerned, however, people do not aspire to a specific end state; rather, they want the activity to go on for as long as possible, to occur as often as possible, and to be experienced as intensely as possible. Engaging in the activity is reward in itself.

This incentive structure clearly applies to biologically rewarding activities such as eating or sex, but it can also be demonstrated to apply to countless other activities. People may even enjoy activities known to have very detrimental consequences; this incentive structure is characteristic of behavior patterns such as heavy smoking or overeating.

Of course, the incentives of activities and their results may also share the same valence: an activity that is experienced as positive in its own right may produce desired results.

EXAMPLE

For example, a highly affiliation-motivated student will enjoy striking up a relaxed and friendly conversation during a train journey and feel happy to have made new friends she can soon visit. Likewise, a power-motivated politician will enjoy the experience of making rousing election speeches, and take pleasure in election to an office that secures him lasting influence, respect, and prestige.

Particularly in this kind of single-valence situation, matters are complicated by the fact that people are not always aware of the motives driving their actions. It is easy to forget that a goal-oriented activity is attractive and enjoyable in its own right, particularly when the goal seems very appealing. When this kind of incentive structure applies, people do not tend to celebrate and enjoy the goal state for long after attaining a goal, but soon find themselves on the lookout for a new and worthwhile goal requiring the same form of goal-oriented activity.

A further (unnecessary) complication is caused by a lack of terminological precision. Scientists have long been aware of the issues addressed here. Woodworth (1918) was the first to use the term "intrinsic" to describe incentives residing in the performance of an activity, and to distinguish "intrinsic" from "extrinsic" forms of motivation (Woodworth, 1918, p. 67ff.). As is often the case, however, these early insights went unheeded for some time, and when the terms did re-emerge in later research, it was with different specifications. Motivational psychologists are thus in the unfortunate position of having to work with a pair of terms whose definitions are blurred and inconsistent.

The issues under investigation are complex enough without this added difficulty. The following sections discuss various definitions of "intrinsic motivation" (Section 13.2), explore the qualities and effects of different incentive structures (Sections 13.3 and 13.4), and finally examine a specific component of activity-related motivation, namely, the flow experience, in more detail (Section 13.5).

SUMMARY

Even when activities are clearly goal directed, their incentives may reside in their performance as well as in their aspired outcomes and consequences. The incentives of activities and their results may have the same valence (e.g., when attractive activities produce desired results) or different valences (when aversive activities produce desired results and vice versa). When valences match, the incentives inherent in actually performing the activity are easily overlooked. People can mistakenly believe that their actions are driven by the anticipated consequences alone. Inconsistency in the usage of the key terms "intrinsic" and "extrinsic" presents an additional difficulty.

13.2 Defining "Intrinsic Motivation": In Pursuit of a Phantom

13.2.1 The Problem

Motivational psychologists are not expected to expound on terminological issues, but to cast light on the mechanisms that energize and direct behavior – and rightly so. Their focus should be on content and substance rather than on labels. In the present case, however, any attempt to progress without first examining the various definitions of intrinsic motivation formulated in the literature would necessarily lead to confusion. In fact, rarely in the scientific literature have terms been used as inconsistently and imprecisely as "intrinsic vs. extrinsic."

The problem would be less severe if different labels were used to describe identical contents. Such a difficulty could soon be cleared up by means of conceptual and/or empirical analysis. In the present case, however, the problem is the opposite, with the same labels being used to describe different contents – a surefire way of confusing readers and hampering research progress.

At a perfunctory glance, things seem reasonably clear. "Intrinsic" means "originating or operating from within, belonging naturally, essential or immanent." "Extrinsic" means "originating or operating from without, not belonging, extraneous." Unfortunately, authors differ in what they mean by "within" and "without." Some do not even make this distinction, but characterize intrinsic motivation in terms of underlying needs. In the following, the major definitions of intrinsic are discussed. Further details can be found in H. Heckhausen (1989), Heckhausen and Rheinberg (1980), and Sansone and Harackiewicz (2000). Should readers be left with the impression that the different conceptualizations are "kind of similar," but lack a common core, they will not be mistaken.

13.2.2 Intrinsic in the Sense of "in the Activity"

In view of what was said above about incentives residing in the performance of an activity, it would seem quite reasonable to use the term "intrinsic" in this context – i.e., to describe incentives relating to an activity itself.

❗ According to this definition, incentives that reside in the pursuit of an activity are intrinsic, whereas the incentives of events or changes that occur only once an activity has been successfully completed are extrinsic. This definition of intrinsic vs. extrinsic is based on the structure of an action episode: "intrinsic" pertains to the performance of an activity, "extrinsic" to its intended effects.

A good early example of this kind of structural approach to the incentive concept is found in Bühler (1922). Based on his careful observations in the field of developmental psychology, he distinguished pleasure in functioning and creativity ("Funktionslust" and "Schaffenslust") during an activity from pleasure in satisfaction ("Endlust" or "Befriedigungslust") after an activity. According to the present definition, the former "pleasures" would be intrinsic, and the latter extrinsic in nature. Unfortunately, Bühler did not use these specific terms. Had he done so, much of the later terminological confusion might have been averted.

As is so often the case, however, a true historical account must go back to Aristotle. As Schneider (1996) points out, the **Nicomachean Ethics** distinguish between pleasure that is an essential element of an activity and pleasure originating from outside an activity. Aristotle suggested that the latter may inhibit performance of the activity. Deci (1971) returned to this point a good 2000 years later, and has since investigated it extensively (Deci, Koestner, & Ryan, 1999).

The earliest, and very detailed, analyses of incentives residing in the performance of an activity are found in Groos' (1899) work on the **psychology of play**, which is still worth reading today. Not only does Groos provide an accurate description and classification of these incentives, he uses an evolutionary psychology approach that seems astonishingly modern from today's perspective to derive them (giving an idea of just how severely scientific progress was hampered by the behaviorist-experimental approach that dominated subsequent psychological research; cf. Meyer, Schützwohl, & Reisenzein, 1999). Over 50 years later, Koch (1956) renewed the call for qualitative analyses of the incentives residing in activities. More recently, researchers such as Csikszentmihalyi (1997b) and Rheinberg (1993; Rheinberg & Manig, 2003; Rheinberg & Tramp, 2006) have presented findings from such analyses (see Section 13.4).

Woodworth (1918) was the first to use the terms "**intrinsic/extrinsic**" in his work, albeit rather peripherally. He used the word "intrinsic" to describe "activity running by its own drive" (Woodworth, 1918, p. 70), stipulating that it is only under these conditions that an activity can run "freely and effectively" and result in the absorption on which enduring interest is contingent. When an activity is "driven by some extrinsic motive" (Woodworth, 1918, p. 70), on the other hand, attention is diverted away from the activity, and absorption in it is unlikely.

Woodworth also pointed out that motivation may change over the course of an activity. For example, it is quite possible for someone to take up an activity for extrinsic reasons, but to persist in it for intrinsic reasons. The initial motivation becomes less important as progress is made toward the goal, with the focus shifting to the performance of the activity itself. This process-oriented approach is far in advance of the overly simplistic juxtaposition of extrinsic vs. intrinsic motivation that characterized later research. To be fair, however, we should not forget that Woodworth was free to write about human motivation without having to provide empirical evidence for his conclusions. It is hardly surprising that the theoretical analyses of later authors, who were first obliged to demonstrate their proposed effects experimentally, were at times rather less sophisticated.

Schiefele (1996) made a distinction that has interesting implications for an activity-oriented approach to intrinsic motivation. Because activities generally focus on a certain object, a person's motivation to engage in an activity may be (co)determined not only by the activity itself, but also by that object. For example, a retiree avidly reading an article about J. S. Bach might be interested in the object of "Bach" and/or simply enjoy reading. If the object is the main incentive, this form of intrinsic motivation can be described as **interest**.

DEFINITION

Interest is a form of motivation characterized by a focus on a certain object. ("interest in XY"; cf. Krapp, 2001)

In our example, the retiree would enjoy virtually any activity relating to the object of "J. S. Bach" (listening to Bach's music, singing along with his cantatas, talking about him, visiting the place of his birth, etc.). If, however, the activity of reading is the main incentive, Schiefele (1996) distinguishes another form of intrinsic motivation, driven by **activity-related incentives** (after Rheinberg, 1989, 1993). In this case, the retiree would enjoy reading texts of all kinds. Activity-related incentives are particularly relevant and have been investigated in contexts such as dancing and playing sports and musical instruments (Section 13.4).

SUMMARY

From the very beginnings of theorizing on "intrinsic vs. extrinsic motivation," one conceptualization has focused on the structure of an action episode, with activities whose main incentive resides in the performance of the activity itself, rather than in its expected results, being seen as "intrinsically motivated." Besides pioneers such as Bühler (1922), Groos (1899), and Woodworth (1918), this conceptualization is found in the works of authors such as Harlow (1950), Hunt (1965), Koch (1956), McReynolds (1971), Pekrun (1993), and Schiefele and Köller (2001). Further authors have investigated the same issues, but using terms such as autotelic motivation (e.g., Csikszentmihalyi, 1999; Klinger, 1971) or activity-related (vs. purpose-related) motivation (Rheinberg, 1989, 1993). The intrinsic motivation deriving from an activity may be driven primarily by interest or by activity-specific incentives, depending on whether the object of an activity or its performance provides the main incentive. (Another conceptualization of interest is presented in Section 13.2.4.)

13.2.3 Intrinsic Motivation as the Need for Self-Determination and Competence

In contrast to the conceptualization outlined above, the decisive factor for Deci and Ryan (1980, 1985) was that "intrinsic motivation" derives from the innate psychological needs for competence and self-determination. Because their approach evolved over time, its emphases vary depending on the date of publication.

In an **early phase** of research, they considered intrinsically motivated behavior to be that shown by children in field experiments in the absence of extraneous rewards, and extrinsically motivated behavior to be driven by external rewards (Deci, 1971). In an **intermediate** phase that commanded a great deal of research attention, Deci and Ryan (1980) developed Cognitive Evaluation Theory (CET). This theory distinguishes between intrinsic and extrinsic motivation in terms of whether people perceive their behavior to be self-determined ("I do it because I want to") or as dependent on rewards controlled by others. Thus, the "within/without" distinction does not apply to the activity, but to the self as the perceived locus of causality.

It is only at a casual glance that this **self**-based definition is congruent with the previous **activity**-based one (Section 13.2.2). Granted, we are more likely to engage in activities on our own initiative and without external pressure if they are enjoyable in their own right. Both definitions would classify motivation in cases such as these, where perceived self-determination and enjoyment of an activity coincide, as intrinsic. When actions have important implications, however, we may take a highly self-determined approach to performing aversive activities (e.g., attacking a pile of dishes, Section 13.1) or refraining from attractive ones (e.g., giving up smoking). Such activities might be classified as either extrinsically or intrinsically motivated, depending on the definition applied.

Deci and Ryan (1980) adopted the key concept of **self-determination** (autonomy) from deCharms (1968, 1976). However, deCharms had recognized the risks of definitions and conceptualizations being confounded in the manner outlined above, and warned that it would be overly simplistic to equate "intrinsically motivated" with "self-determined/autonomous" (deCharms, 1979, p. 20). Deci and Ryan (1980) took a different route.

Beside deCharms' need for autonomy, the authors drew on a second motivational concept, namely, **self-efficacy** or the **need for competence**, as described by White (1959). Strictly speaking, this concept had already been introduced by Groos (1899), who described it as "joy in being a cause" (p. 489), "joy in the active production of effects" (p. 489), or a "drive-like need for causation" (p. 488).

Drawing on deCharms' need for autonomy (1968) and White's need for competence (1959), Deci and Ryan (1980) define intrinsic motivation as a form of motivation deriving from the innate needs for competence and self-determination which, when satisfied, typically result in positive feelings of control and perceived causality (Deci & Ryan, 1985, 2000).

In a third phase of theorizing, Deci and Ryan (1985) introduced a third innate psychological need – the need for social relatedness – and formulated Self-Determination Theory (SDT). The need for social relatedness is assumed to motivate people to adopt externally imposed behavioral standards: people adhere to the standards, expectations, and wishes of others in order to belong. After an initial phase of "external regulation," these standards are assumed to be assimilated to the self via a process of integration involving the stages of "introjected regulation," "identification," and finally "integrated regulation," at which point it is barely possible to distinguish what was originally external determination from true self-determination. This form of perceived self-determination is, nevertheless, still defined as extrinsic. Despite the differences in labeling, the assimilation of external behavioral standards to the self is assumed to be facilitated by the same measures that facilitate true intrinsic motivation.

Definitional and conceptual lines are thus likely to become blurred. Moreover, the question arises of why especially the psychological needs for self-determination and competence should make performing an activity so attractive that people keep returning to it, even in the absence of contingent rewards or external pressures. There is no doubt that both these motivational systems are extremely important. Passionate hobby enthusiasts refer to them repeatedly when interviewed about the incentives that induce them to engage in their leisure time activities (Rheinberg, 1993). However, besides these two, several other incentives also play a vital role. These include the excitement of exposure to risk (e.g., extreme sports or illegal graffiti spraying) or unusual physical sensations (e.g., riding a roller coaster or motorcycling), being at one with nature (e.g., hiking or mountaineering), and so on (Rheinberg, 1993, 1996).

SUMMARY

The approach chosen by Deci and Ryan (1980, 1985) is to stipulate two need systems (self-determination and feelings of competence), in terms of which intrinsic motivation is then defined. In the final version of their theory, they propose a developmental continuum of extrinsic motivation which implies that "higher" forms of extrinsic motivation become difficult to distinguish from intrinsic motivation. Both are experienced as self-determined. In spite of these problems, self-determination theory has gained some popularity, particularly among researchers in educational science (Krapp, 1999; for a critical discussion, see Schiefele, 1996). It may be that in the context of education, positively valued goals such as "self-determination," or the assumption of an innate human capacity to assimilate socially mediated norms to the self, render "Self-Determination Theory" particularly attractive.

13.2.4 Intrinsic Motivation as Interest and Involvement

Interest was already mentioned briefly in Section 13.2.2, where it was described as a form of intrinsic motivation deriv-

ing from the performance of an activity in which the object of the activity provides the main incentive (Schiefele, 1996; Schiefele & Köller, 2001).

Individual Interest

The conceptualization of interest as motivation deriving from the performance of an activity does not seem entirely logical from the perspective of an "educational theory of interest," however (Krapp, 1999). After all, one purpose of interest-driven engagement with an object is generally to find out more about that object. But this knowledge gain is a desired **outcome** of the activity. In other words, it ensues from the activity, and would thus be defined as extrinsic in nature. It follows that most interested learning would have to be classified as extrinsically motivated, and intrinsic interested learning would be a rare occurrence in schools and other academic settings (Krapp, 1999, p. 392).

The educational theory of interest proposed by Krapp is not, therefore, based on an activity-related definition of intrinsic motivation, but on the approach taken by Deci and Ryan (1985) described above.

❶ From this perspective, a learning activity is considered to be "intrinsically motivated" if learners identify with the object of study, and hence perceive the learning activity to be self-determined. It is quite possible for the task to be externally imposed, and the learner to be working purposefully toward a specific learning goal. The decisive factor is that learners perceive their actions to be self-determined (self-intentional) and consider the object of study to be worthwhile.

It is beyond doubt that there is more scope for classifying motivation to learn as intrinsic when this definition is applied. But this approach necessarily leads to the inconsistency problems that ensue when intrinsic motivation is defined in the terms of self-determination theory: although the conceptual category is now more applicable to the context of learning and instruction, it subsumes differing phenomena. Readers should therefore be aware that the interest theory literature defines intrinsic motivation in different ways – sometimes in the sense of "in the activity" (Section 13.2.2) and sometimes in the sense of "in the person/the self" after Deci and Ryan (1985) or Krapp (1999).

Current Interest

The importance of disentangling different conceptualizations was further emphasized by the recent emergence of a new approach to the concept of interest in the context of intrinsic motivation: "We consider individuals to be intrinsically motivated when their behavior is motivated by the *actual, anticipated, or sought experience of interest*" (Sansone & Smith, 2000, p. 343).

DEFINITION

Interest is defined as a positively charged cognitive and affective experience that directs attention to and focuses it on the activity or task at hand. People want to engage in the activity here and now ("feel like it") and enjoy doing so.

Sansone and Smith (2000) do not see interest in terms of either an enduring preference for a domain ("individual interest") or underlying needs for self-determination and feelings of competence (Deci & Ryan, 1985; see above), but as a "proximate" positive experience that may be encountered during the activity, but also anticipated and sought.

This understanding of interest and intrinsic motivation is very different from the educational theory of interest outlined above, and has more in common with the activity-related approaches to interest advocated by Schiefele (1996) or Hidi (2000) (Section 13.2.2). In contrast to Schiefele's approach, however, interest is not specified to be object-related, but generalized to *any* form of positively charged engagement motivated by the enjoyment of pursuing an activity. This brings us back to phenomena of activity-related motivation discussed in Sections 13.2.1 and 13.2.2.

Sansone and Smith (2000, p. 344) use the term "interest" to describe this kind of activity-related motivation, and explain their concept of interest in terms of "involvement" and "feeling like it." Of course, it is possible to switch words around in this manner. In the present case, however, it means that the substantive core of the definition of interest, the aspect that distinguishes it from other forms of motivation, is lost – namely, the fact that interest is always focused on a certain object or domain.

SUMMARY

Researchers attempting to define "intrinsic" motivation in terms of interest have taken various approaches. For Sansone and Smith (2000), the concept of interest is synonymous with (positive) activity-related motivation. Schiefele and Köller (2001) limit the scope of this definition to activities whose main incentive is the object of the activity, rather than the activity itself. Finally, Krapp (1999) draws on self-determination theory (Deci & Ryan, 1985). For him, a learning activity is intrinsically motivated if learners experience their interaction with an object of interest to be self-determined – even if that learning activity is purpose-driven, i.e., directed at outcomes and consequences lying beyond the performance of the activity itself.

13.2.5 Intrinsic in the Sense of a Correspondence Between Means and Ends

Another definition of intrinsic motivation focuses on the thematic correspondence of actions and their goals. Kruglanski (1989); Shah and Kruglanski, (2000); and H. Heckhausen (1989) are the main proponents of this kind of approach. It is often possible to work toward a goal in a number of ways. For example, someone wanting to lose weight might decide to eat less, change his eating habits, take up jogging, cycle to

work, start smoking again, take amphetamines, etc. This kind of structure, in which "all roads lead to Rome," is known as the **equifinality** of behavior (e.g., Heider, 1958). Conversely, a single activity may further the pursuit of numerous goals. Someone might study because he seeks to enhance his general knowledge, is interested in a particular topic, aspires to do well in an exam, thinks good exam grades will increase his chances of being offered an interesting job, etc. The term **multifinality** is used to describe structures in which a single activity furthers the attainment of several goals.

Shah and Kruglanski (2000) work on the rather unusual assumption that both equifinality and multifinality diminish intrinsic motivation. In their opinion, intrinsic motivation is characterized by a clear-cut relationship between means and ends, i.e., between an activity and its goal. Goal X can only be attained by performing activity Y, and people performing activity Y aspire to no goal other than X (Shah & Kruglanski, 2000, p. 114). The authors suggest that this kind of one-to-one relationship is vital if intrinsic motivation is to be promoted (p. 123).

Moreover, Shah and Kruglanski (2000) distinguish two kinds of goals:

- First, "specific target goals" that regulate the ongoing activity proximally.
- Second, more general "abstract purpose goals" that provide the reasons for aspiring to the specific target goals in the first place.

❶ Intrinsic motivation is assumed to be facilitated when a specific target goal is clearly assigned to an abstract purpose goal, and both are clearly assigned to a certain activity.

In proposing this threefold correspondence of activity, specific target goal, and abstract purpose, the authors echoed an idea that had already been voiced by H. Heckhausen (1980). Heckhausen assumed intrinsic motivation to ensue when the **action**, the desired **outcome** of the action, and the anticipated **consequences** of that outcome are thematically congruent (Fig. 13.1). A student reads an article carefully (= action) because she wants to understand a certain topic (= outcome). She wants to understand the topic because she hopes it will help her solve a difficult problem (= consequences). According to H. Heckhausen (1980), this is a case of intrinsic achievement motivation because the same motivational theme – concern with a standard of excellence – runs through the entire structure of the action. The activity itself is performed particularly well (= careful reading), the desired outcome is an increase in competence (= gaining a better understanding of a topic), and its consequences are better prospects of mastering a challenge (= solving a difficult problem). If the anticipated consequences had been related to another motivational theme (e.g., altruism: the student wanted to understand the text in order to help a friend prepare for an exam), it would be a case of extrinsic achievement motivation.

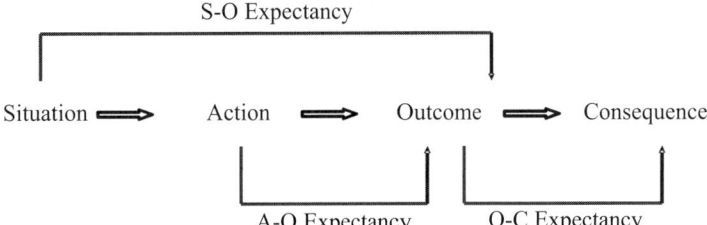

Figure 13.1 Extended cognitive model of motivation. (Based on Heckhausen & Rheinberg, 1980.)

In this conceptualization of intrinsic motivation, the "within/without" distinction reflects whether or not the target goals are located within the same thematic domain as the action itself. In some cases, thematic congruence between an action and its outcome may be a foregone conclusion because the aspired outcome is an inalienable part of the activity. (For example, "restoring something to better condition" is, by definition, an outcome of the activity "repairing.")

The relationship between the outcome of an action and its desired consequences is much more variable. There may be a multitude of reasons for wanting to achieve a particular outcome. "Reasons" are anticipated consequences. For example, a student might make himself a bookshelf in order to have somewhere to put his books and papers and, at the same time, take pride in his do-it-yourself skills. Alternatively, he might make the same bookshelf for somebody else with the aim of earning money, strengthening a relationship, or for any number of other reasons. Because the relationship between the outcome of an action and its intended consequences can be variable and thematically incongruent, it makes perfect sense to specific the motivational structure of an action episode by identifying its aspired consequences and determining the nature of their relationship to the activity. The question remains, however, of whether the use of the term "intrinsic" is actually needed whenever an activity and its intended consequences are thematically congruent.

SUMMARY

Another conception of intrinsic vs. extrinsic motivation found in the literature is based on whether or not an action and its desired consequences are located within the same thematic domain (e.g., gaining competence, helping, exerting power). In the case of thematic congruence, motivation is considered to be intrinsic, in the case of incongruence, it is deemed extrinsic. This conceptualization was advocated by H. Heckhausen (1989) and Kruglanski (1989), in particular.

13.2.6 Goal Orientation and Intrinsic Motivation

Research in the field of learning motivation, in particular, has shown that a desired outcome can be associated with a number of consequences (Heckhausen & Rheinberg, 1980; Rheinberg, 1989). A student may aspire to a good learning outcome for a variety of reasons, as outlined in the description of multifinality earlier (Section 13.2.5).

Especially in the English-speaking countries, two goal orientations have been singled out as particularly relevant:

1. Learning or mastery goal orientation:

Learners with this kind of orientation study because they want to know and understand more about a topic. Their goal is to acquire knowledge and skills.

2. Performance goal orientation (Dweck & Leggett, 1988; Nicholls, 1984a):

Learners with this kind of orientation study in order to demonstrate their competence. Their aim is to show that they are more knowledgeable and skillful than others.

According to Dweck and Leggett (1988), a performance goal orientation is associated with the view that individual ability remains stable across time; whereas a learning goal orientation is characterized by the belief that ability is changeable. Furthermore, a performance goal orientation implies comparison with the achievement of others (**social reference norm**), whereas a learning-goal orientation implies comparison with one's own previous knowledge and skills (**individual reference norm**) or with the demands of the object of study (**objective reference norm**). (The concept of **reference norms** was introduced by Heckhausen, 1974a, and has been examined by Rheinberg, 1980; Chapter 6.)

For students with a learning goal orientation, the learning activity and its aspired outcomes are clearly thematically congruent; these students are concerned with learning and learning gains. According to the arguments presented in Section 13.2.5, this thematic congruence implies "intrinsic motivation to learn." The same does not apply to students with a performance goal orientation. Demonstrating one's superiority over others is not thematically related to the act of learning in any way. The motive of dominating others is associated with other thematic domains of human behavior entirely – most particularly the power motive (Wirth, Welsh, & Schultheiss, 2006). The lack of thematic congruence between the activity and its aspired consequences implies a case of "extrinsic motivation to learn."

This relationship between goal orientation and intrinsic vs. extrinsic motivation to learn has also been established in the literature (e.g., Butler, 2000; Molden & Dweck, 2000). Thus, where motivation to learn is concerned, a further distinction between extrinsic and intrinsic motivation is possible.

SUMMARY

A further distinction can be drawn between intrinsic vs. extrinsic motivation in the context of motivation to learn, with learning goal orientations (serving the acquisition of knowledge and skills) being considered "intrinsic," and performance goal orientations (serving the demonstration of knowledge and skills) being considered "extrinsic." This distinction is a special case of the thematic congruence criterion (Section 13.2.5).

13.2.7 So What Exactly Is Intrinsic Motivation?

The conceptualizations of intrinsic motivation outlined above are by no means exhaustive. A condensed overview of further approaches is provided in H. Heckhausen (1991, p. 403–408). Surprising numbers of authors have felt compelled to formulate their own definitions of intrinsic motivation using their own (or adapted) constructs, perhaps as a consequence of the implicit positive evaluation of "intrinsic" in the sense of natural, immanent, and real. Obviously, it seems tempting for researchers to express this very positive core of motivation in their own terminology, and to go on to identify promising ways of promoting a "true" and "not alienated" form of motivated behavior.

What is unfortunate – for both scientific progress and our understanding of the original literature – is that the products of these attempts to capture intrinsic motivation in words diverge considerably. Furthermore, comparison of the definitions does not disclose a common denominator that could be described as the core of intrinsic motivation (cf. Sansone & Harackiewicz, 2000). The search for "truly intrinsic motivation" thus proves to be the pursuit of a phantom, an undertaking that keeps being revived because people so wants it to succeed.

Consequently, the current debates on whether intrinsic or extrinsic motivation is more conducive to achievement and whether one form of motivation undermines the other will necessarily remain futile (Deci, Koestner, & Ryan, 1999; Eisenberger & Cameron, 1996, 1998; Thierry, 2004). Even the most comprehensive meta-analyses cannot be expected to advance scientific knowledge until theoretical and empirical consensus has been reached on what exactly intrinsic vs. extrinsic motivation is.

The following section describes the ongoing controversy on whether or not extrinsic rewards decrease intrinsic motivation (the undermining effect).

13.2.8 The Undermining Effect of External Rewards: Myth or Reality?

Concerns that the performance and enjoyment of an activity are not always enhanced by the prospect of rewards, but that the opposite is sometimes the case, have a long history. Woodworth (1918), for example, suspected that extraneous rewards would draw attention away from the activity at hand.

A focus on external rewards would necessarily detract from involvement in the activity, with detrimental effects on both achievement and the development of enduring interest in the activity (Woodworth, 1918, p. 69ff.).

The disadvantage of such everyday observations, however, is that it is always possible to find cases in which they apply and cases in which they do not. Deci (1971, 1975) and Lepper, Green, and Nisbett (1973) investigated these effects under experimentally controlled conditions:

- In a first step, the researchers noted what respondents (e.g., preschool children) enjoyed doing of their own accord.
- In a second step, they gave these children rewards for pursuing their favorite activities.
- In a third phase, they stopped giving rewards.

Findings showed that the children now no longer performed the activity as frequently as before the reward phase and that they found it less attractive. The extraneous reward had evidently undermined the value of the activity. This phenomenon was labeled the **undermining effect** or **overjustification effect** (H. Heckhausen & Rheinberg, 1980; Lepper, Green, & Nisbett, 1973; for a summary, see H. Heckhausen, 1989).

Researchers have offered various explanations of this effect, based on their different theoretical approaches. Some maintain that the self-determined motivation experienced at the start of the experiment was weakened by the external rewards, leading to a reduction in "intrinsic motivation" (Deci & Ryan, 1980, 1985). Others attribute the effects observed to processes of self-perception, suggesting that respondents evaluated the motivational basis for their actions and concluded that an activity (now at least partly) contingent on an expected reward could not be all that attractive after all (Lepper et al., 1973).

Experimental evidence showing detrimental effects on motivation of external rewards commanded a great deal of attention – especially in educational practice, but also in developmental psychology – and inspired much research. First, the findings had direct implications for everyday behavior; they imply that rewards and praise should be administered with care. Second, and perhaps more important, they were congruent with the ideas of Rousseau, who believed that, if left to their own devices, humans naturally do what is right. It is only when external desires are imposed on them that they become estranged from their true motivational basis and enter a state of alienation that leaves them open to exploitation and ends in unhappiness. Of course, this beliefs system stood to profit enormously from findings demonstrating the mechanism assumed to underlie these effects under experimental conditions.

Validity of the Undermining Effect

But how "true" is the undermining effect really? It soon became clear that the effect is contingent on certain conditions being in place. For example, it only occurs when people already enjoy pursuing the activity under investigation (Calder & Staw, 1975). In the experiments outlined above, the rewards given were completely unnecessary. How often does this occur in real life? When the activity was not attractive in its own right, rewards often proved to have the opposite – positive – effect (Cameron, Banko, & Pierce, 2001).

This and other findings raised doubts about the validity of the undermining effect. Eisenberg and Cameron (1996) examined the alleged detrimental effects of rewards in a meta-analysis of 61 studies. Their findings indicate that – when the analysis is limited to rewards given under realistic everyday conditions – the undermining effect is more of a myth than reality. They found a (weak) undermining effect only when respondents were given material (not verbal!) rewards simply for tackling a task. Respondents who anticipated these kinds of performance-noncontingent rewards switched to another task sooner after receiving the reward than participants who had not been rewarded.

This publication sparked a scientific controversy, and the body of empirical research covered in subsequent meta-analyses has grown progressively (Deci et al., 1999: 128 studies; Cameron, Banko, & Pierce, 2001: 145 studies). The evidence now suggests that rewards do not have detrimental effects on motivation under ecologically valid, everyday conditions. Particularly when rewards are unexpected or given in the form of verbal reinforcement (praise), and when the tasks to be performed are not attractive in their own right, rewards have been shown to have positive rather than negative effects on motivation. The latest, most extensive meta-analysis by Cameron et al. (2001) indicates that the undermining effect occurs only when:

1. the activity is interesting,
2. the rewards are material (rather than verbal) in nature, and
3. the rewards are expected.

Thus, rewards only seem to have an undermining effect on motivation under very specific conditions that are arguably fairly unlikely to occur in everyday contexts. In all likelihood, it would be difficult to demonstrate the undermining effect reliably in everyday life without making a number of changes to everyday conditions. For instance, researchers seeking to replicate the conditions created in the experiments of Deci (1971) and Lepper et al. (1973) would need to recruit samples of school students and employees engaged in activities that they would enjoy even without any form of reward.

These considerations all seem to be points of detail for Ryan and Deci (2000), however, who see the effects of rewards as a special case of the more general issue of autonomy vs. social control of behavior (Ryan & Deci, 2000, p. 37). They conclude that people who respond to their inner needs and aspire to growth, social relatedness, and community contribution experience greater well-being and better mental health than those who pursue the extrinsic life goals of wealth, fame, and image (p. 48). Given the complexities of research findings about the undermining effect, this conclusion by Ryan and Deci appears perplexing in its simplicity.

FUTURE PROSPECTS. Given the heterogeneity of conceptualizations of "intrinsic," it is hardly surprising that the effect sizes obtained in empirical research tend to be weak, or at best moderate. When respondents are asked to rate the interestingness of a task for which they have been rewarded, for example, there tend to be no effects at all. Rewards are most likely to influence whether, and for how long, participants continue working on a task for which they have been rewarded when given the opportunity to switch to a new task. Until consensus has been reached on the meaning of "intrinsic," scientists cannot expect to find clear patterns of results. A research focus on a clearly defined conceptualization of intrinsic motivation would, on the other hand, permit interesting phenomena to be examined more carefully.

For example, researchers might focus on intrinsic in the sense of "in the activity" (Section 13.2.2), and investigate the probability of undermining effects occurring as a function of the spectrum of activity-related incentives that make an activity attractive (Section 13.4.2). They might, for instance, try to establish why some top-earning football and tennis players give up the game altogether when they retire, whereas some former professional skiers and world cup surfers continue to practice their sports enthusiastically, even without the prospect of material rewards. Insights into the magnitude of such differences between sports, and into the activity-related incentives that make a sport more resistant to the undermining effect, would doubtless further scientific understanding of why people engage in activities of their own accord. A predetermined focus on specific needs (self-determination, feelings of competence, social relatedness) would unnecessarily limit the scope of potential insights.

13.2.9 Terminological Implications

The arguments presented in Section 13.2 raise the question of what, exactly, intrinsic motivation is. This is not the right question to be asking, however. When a term is defined in various ways, and these definitions do not share a common core, the alternatives are either to opt for just one of the definitions, or to abandon the term altogether. The disadvantage of the first alternative is that, no matter how well justified the choice of definition, the term cannot be stripped of its other connotations. The second alternative, which has been recommended elsewhere, is thus preferable: the semantic overload of the term "intrinsic" can be avoided altogether by specifying exactly what is meant in each case (Rheinberg, 1995, 2006). All of the phenomena covered in this section are fascinating and important in their own right. The problem is that, despite their diversity, they have thus far all been given the same label.

The following sections return to the original conceptualization of intrinsic motivation, and examine motivational phenomena residing in the performance of an activity. However, the terms intrinsic (vs. extrinsic) motivation are replaced by activity- (vs. purpose-) related motivation, and individual components of this motivation (e.g., flow) are discussed separately.

13.3 Purpose- and Activity-Related Incentives in the Extended Cognitive Model of Motivation

13.3.1 The Purpose-Oriented Model of Rational Behavior

A more general model suggests itself as a theoretical framework for analyzing the phenomena described and predicting their effects. The extended cognitive model of motivation proposed by Heckhausen (1977a) drawing on Vroom (1964) has previously been applied to the analysis of motivation to learn (Heckhausen & Rheinberg, 1980; Rheinberg, 1989) and seems appropriate for the present purposes.

The model maps out the general structure of goal-directed behavior. A given **situation** presents an individual with various action alternatives, temptations, and potential threats. Any action taken in this situation may bring about a specific **outcome**, which may in turn have certain **consequences** (Fig. 13.1).

The strength of a person's current motivation, i.e., tendency to act, depends on three types of expectancies, as well as on the incentives in place:

1. Situation-outcome expectancies:
These expectancies (S-O expectancies in Fig. 13.1) reflect people's subjective beliefs about how likely it is that a given outcome will ensue without their active involvement. It is highly probable that a red traffic light will change to green (= outcome), whether or not a driver blasts his or her horn (= action). A student who already has a firm grasp of the topics covered in an upcoming exam may feel confident of doing well (= outcome) without the need for further preparation (= action). If a situation is very likely to result in a desired outcome without active involvement on the individual's part, there is no need to take action. High situation-outcome expectancies thus reduce the strength of the tendency to act.

2. Action-outcome expectancies:
The opposite holds for action-outcome expectancies (A-O expectancies). These expectancies reflect people's subjective beliefs about how likely their actions are to bring about or influence a possible outcome. Student A may believe that exams are a matter of pure luck, and that his results will have very little to do with any preparation on his part. If the right questions come up, he will do well; if not, it will just be bad luck. Student B, on the other hand, may

believe that her performance hinges almost entirely on how well she prepares for an exam. Student A has very low action-outcome expectancies; student B has very high action-outcome expectancies.

3. Outcome-consequence expectancies:
These expectancies (O-C expectancies) reflect the certainty of an individual's beliefs that an outcome – assuming that it ensues – will have certain consequences. This link between an aspired outcome and its consequences is also called **instrumentality**. Note that Vroom (1964) had already distinguished these three types of expectancies, but using different terminology. The higher the outcome-consequence expectancy, the more likely the consequences are to influence the tendency to act. All three expectancies are necessary, rather than sufficient, conditions for this influence occurring.

4. Incentives of anticipated consequences:
The incentive value of the anticipated consequences is a further factor in the equation. It is only when the instrumentality and incentive value of the consequences are sufficiently high that these consequences have an impact on the attractiveness of an outcome.

The model has been used to predict phenomena such as whether students who have an important exam coming up in two weeks will do enough preparation.

EXAMPLE

All four of the following conditions must be met if a student is to do sufficient preparation for an exam. The student must be confident that:

1. she will not get the desired grade unless she prepares for the exam,

2. she can influence the grade attained by preparing for the exam,

3. the grade is certain to have consequences, and that

4. these consequences are sufficiently important to her.

The student will not prepare properly for the exam unless all four of these conditions are met. Consequently, four qualitatively different forms of motivational withdrawal can be discerned:

1. it seems unnecessary to study for the exam,

2. it seems pointless to study for the exam,

3. the exam grade is not certain to have consequences, or

4. the possible consequences seem unimportant.

As findings from numerous studies on student preparation for tests and exams have shown, predictions made about whether learners do as much preparation as they consider necessary to achieve a desired outcome are accurate in between 70% and 90% of cases on the basis of this model (Heckhausen & Rheinberg, 1980; Rheinberg, 1989). Of course, whether or not students actually achieve this outcome is another question altogether, and one that is not solely dependent on the amount of motivation and preparation (Engeser, 2004).

13.3.2 The Role of Activity-Related Incentives

On the face of it, the model seems to achieve a high level of accuracy in its predictions. However, it is important to remember that the model predicts a one-off event – preparation for a specific test or exam under given conditions – using episode-specific predictors. Proximal measures such as these are bound to result in more accurate predictions than variables such as general personality traits (e.g., Bowi, 1990). The advantage of the latter approach is that it allows predictions to be made across a variety of situations rather than in a single one.

It thus seems reasonable to ask why the one-off predictions made on the basis of these proximal measures do not apply in more than 70% to 90% of cases. Explorative analyses of motivation to learn have shown that the extended cognitive model of motivation fails to account for an important source of incentives: the incentives involved in the activity itself (Rheinberg, 1989). Activities such as reading, writing, chatting, singing, walking, cycling, and driving may (or may not) have incentives that reside in their outcome-dependent consequences. However, there are also incentives that reside purely in the performance of the activity – no matter what outcome or consequences it may have. Person X prefers walking to sitting – irrespective of where and why he or she is walking. The opposite may hold for person Y.

❶ The incentives that reside in performing an activity are called activity-related incentives. (Rheinberg, 1989)

To return to students' exam preparation, some students experience the act of sitting down at home to work through the material covered in the last few weeks to be highly aversive. Deviations from the model's predictions were largely attributable to this negative activity-related incentive. In some cases, it was so strong that students did very little or no preparation, despite being well aware that this preparation would be highly effective, necessary, and important. The same problem did not arise for students who found exam preparation to be less aversive, or even attractive.

Activity-specific incentives of this kind were not represented in the original extended cognitive model, which assumed the attractiveness of an activity to reside solely in the incentive value of its anticipated consequences. Enjoyment of an activity does not ensue after its completion, however, but during its performance (Section 13.1). In some cases of high positive activity-related incentives, people do not want an activity to end. This presents a theoretical paradox, particularly in the context of achievement motivation (Section 13.4.3). Heckhausen's strictly rationalistic representation of human motivation in the extended cognitive model made it obvious that there must be other sources of incentives inherent in life's activities.

Of course, Heckhausen was perfectly aware of the existence of "purposeless" activities that are pursued for their own

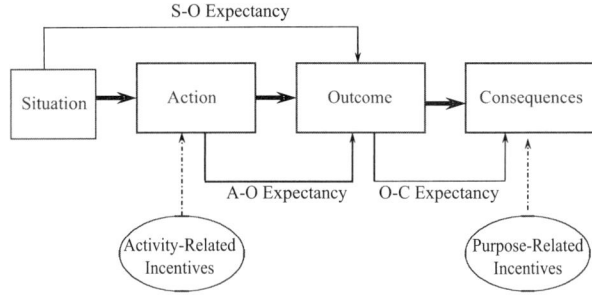

Figure 13.2 Integration of activity- and purpose-related incentives within the extended cognitive model of motivation. (Based on Rheinberg, 1989.)

sake. He had considered motivational structures of this kind in his early work (1964b) on the psychology of play. There was little scope for them within the strictly rationalistic conception of the extended cognitive model, however. Heckhausen and Rheinberg (1980) got around this problem by assuming the three main components of the model – action, outcome, and consequences – to coincide in "purposeless" activities.

This theoretical maneuver made the phenomena of purposeless or activity-related motivation compatible with the extended cognitive model of motivation at a very high level of abstraction. This approach remained too indefinite to be productive, however. The extended model was thus extended further to include activity-related incentives, as independent from purpose-related ones (Rheinberg, 1989). The structure of the resulting model is shown in Fig. 13.2.

Another factor that needed to be included in the equation was a person's propensity to focus on the enjoyment of actually performing an activity or on the value of its potential consequences (activity vs. object-oriented **incentive focus** in the Incentive Focus Scale; Rheinberg, Iser & Pfauser, 1997). When activity-related incentives and this incentive focus factor were taken into consideration, the one-off predictions of the model were almost perfect (Rheinberg, 1989).

❶ The extended cognitive model of motivation permits detailed analyses of motivation in specific situations. A particular strength of the model is that it allows different forms of motivational deficit to be diagnosed. These deficits may be attributable to one or more of the three expectancy types (see the earlier example), or to incentives being insufficient or inappropriate. The latter may apply to purpose-related incentives ("It's not worth it") and/or to activity-related incentives. ("I can't face doing it")

Purpose-related incentives only influence motivation if all three expectancy types are endorsed and the consequences of the action are anticipated to be sufficiently important: The activity is (1) necessary and (2) possible and (3) sufficiently likely to have (4) worthwhile consequences. If any one of these four necessary conditions is not met, purpose-related incentives do not apply. As such, this form of motivation is relatively susceptible to interference and highly sensitive to changes in situational conditions.

The functioning of **activity-related incentives** is comparatively straightforward. A situation must simply offer the prospects of an activity being performed without overly negative consequences. The activity is then very likely to be performed. In this case, then, the motivational basis is relatively robust, which may explain why the concept of intrinsic motivation has proved so attractive in the context of learning and instruction. The purpose- and activity-related conditions of motivation have now been integrated within a unifying framework that can be used to predict motivational outcomes (Rheinberg, 2004a). The following section looks at how activity-related incentives can be assessed and examines the specific features of achievement motivation.

13.4 Qualitative Analyses of Activity-Related Incentives

13.4.1 Standardized Assessment of Quality of Experience

What makes an activity so attractive that an individual will keep returning to it even though it has no tangible benefits, but – quite the opposite – substantial costs in terms of time, money, and effort? This question has been addressed using scales designed to tap affectively charged well-being to measure quality of experience during an activity. Recent studies have focused on the PANAS scales (Watson, Clark, & Tellegen, 1988) and the PANAVA system (Schallberger, 2000).

The PANAVA System
Both the PANAS scales and the PANAVA system are based on the dimensions of **valence** and **activation** that were originally described by Wundt (1896), but using different terminology. In the PANAVA system, Schallberger (2000) rotates these two dimensions or axes of the original system by 45°. The result of this rotation is shown in Fig. 13.3.

The effect of the rotation is to combine the dimensions of valence and activation to produce two dimensions:

- Positive Activation (PA: energetic, wide awake, etc.), and
- Negative Activation (NA: distressed, annoyed, etc.).

The PANAVA system also encompasses the original, i.e., unrotated, Valence dimension (VA). This dimension represents feelings of happiness and satisfaction that seem relevant in their own right and are therefore assessed separately.

The PA dimension is particularly interesting for motivational psychologists. Given our definition of motivation as the "activating orientation of current life pursuits toward a positively evaluated goal state" (Rheinberg, 2006, p. 17), PA is clearly the core component of (approach) motivation. NA has more to do with an avoidance and fear component, although its relationship to motivation is less straightforward.

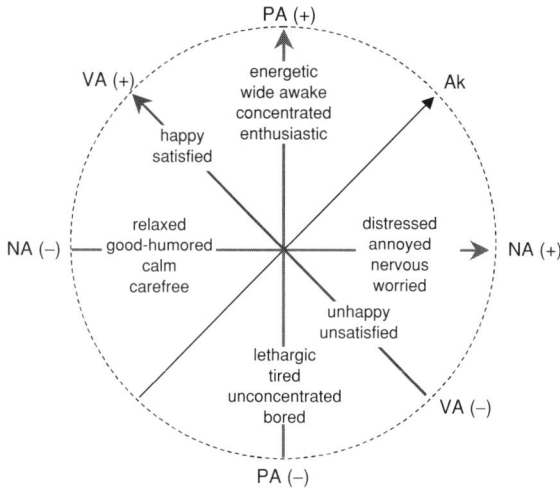

Figure 13.3 The PANAVA system as a circumplex model. (Based on Schallberger, 2000). *Ac*, activation; *PA*, positive activation; *NA*, negative activation; *VA*, positive valence/feelings of happiness; (+), high; (−), low.

In the PANAVA system, quality of experience is rated on just 10 bipolar scales (e.g., "bored 3–2–1–0–1–2–3 enthusiastic") that can be administered while people are actually engaged in an activity. Thus, motivational data can be obtained "online" and compared across different activities, conditions, and points of time. The following study demonstrates the utility of this method.

STUDY

Sampling Experience Data at the Rock Face
When climbers are asked why they spend much of their leisure time scaling rock faces, pushing themselves to the limits in inherently dangerous situations, they often mention "indescribably powerful/enjoyable experiences" or "feelings of exhilaration that are difficult to put into words." Their eyes light up and faces become animated, testifying to the depth and lasting effects of these experiences.

Aellig (2004) equipped rock climbers with a pager and a small block of PANAVA scales, which they wore on a cord around their neck. At each signal of the pager, the climbers got into a relatively stable position and rated their current quality of experience on the PANAVA scales. Although the focus of a climbing trip is on climbing itself, with activities such as leading (the leader is the first in the team to ascend and has furthest to fall) and seconding (the seconder ascends next and is secured from above), it necessarily involves various other activities, such as the journey to the climbing area, the ascent to the rock face, preparing the equipment, abseiling, the descent, the journey home, etc.). Fig. 13.4 illustrates the quality of experience reported by climbers for these different types of activity.

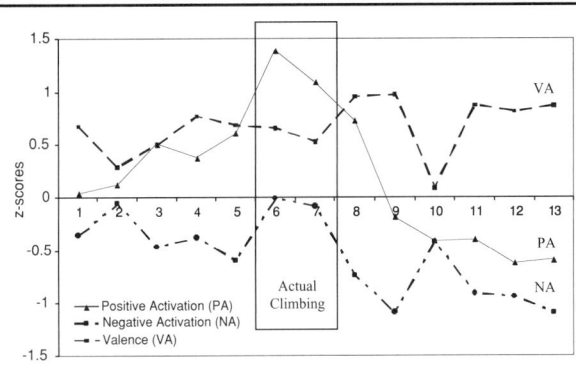

Figure 13.4 Positive (*PA*) and negative (*NA*) activation and feelings of happiness (*VA*) experienced during various activities associated with a climbing trip. (Based on Aellig, 2004, p. 101.)

1   Various activities before departure ($n = 35$ points of time)
2   Journey to the climbing area (by train or car; $n = 26$)
3   Ascent to the rock face, moving to a new crag ($n = 55$)
4   Preparing equipment, packing and unpacking ($n = 37$)
5   Belaying ($n = 87$)
6   Leading ($n = 99$)
7   Seconding ($n = 40$)
8   Abseiling ($n = 47$)
9   During the climb: breaks, eating, drinking, social interaction ($n = 53$)
10 During the climb: waiting, looking for/fetching equipment ($n = 13$)
11 Descent from the rock face, departure ($n = 33$)
12 Journey home ($n = 46$)
13 Various evening activities ($n = 76$)

As the figure shows, PA peaks during the climb itself (leading and seconding). Somewhat surprisingly, however, the same does not hold for feelings of happiness (Valence, VA), which peak subsequent to critical actions (in breaks, when abseiling and making the descent, and at home). The reasons for the decoupling of Positive Activation and feelings of happiness observed in the rock climbers seem to be rooted in the level of Negative Activation (stressed, worried, etc.), which also increases in dangerous situations. PA and NA are thus by no means mutually exclusive in life-threatening situations.

NA may inhibit feelings of happiness during the climb, but precisely this effect is conducive to survival in dangerous situations. During the descent (point 11 in Fig. 13.4), strong feelings of happiness and low NA are reported, even though the risk of serious accidents remains substantial. Having just mastered much more difficult and dangerous situations, the climbers no longer seem sufficiently aware of the dangers facing them. Motivational data assessed directly at the rock face thus provide insights into why even highly professional climbers (e.g., Hermann Buhl, who conquered Nanga Parbat) are prone to accidents when making what would seem to be a straightforward descent – when the worst danger has passed.

Phenomena such as those identified in the study above would be much more difficult to discern by retrospective methods – in retrospect, the whole day would be cast in the positive light of having mastered a difficult challenge (see evening *VA* scores, point 13 in Fig. 13.4). If these findings can be replicated for less dangerous activities, they would considerably further our understanding of what it is that keeps people engaged in activities. The rock climber data suggest that researchers aiming to predict whether or not a respondent will continue to enjoy an ongoing activity should not ask whether the respondent is feeling happy and satisfied, but rather how "enthusiastic," "wide awake," or "energetic" he or she is feeling. Feelings of happiness seem to predominate during breaks or after completion of an activity (Csikszentmihalyi, 1990; Rheinberg & Vollmeyer, 2004), and to correlate more strongly with the absence of Negative Activation than with the presence of Positive Activation (Schallberger, 2000; Schallberger & Pfister, 2001).

13.4.2 Assessing Activity-Specific Incentives

The scales described above have the advantage of being so abstract that they can be applied to any activity, and allow comparisons to be made across activities. When the object of research is to determine what exactly it is that makes pursuing a certain activity so enjoyable, however, this very abstraction becomes a drawback. Researchers seeking to identify the incentives specific to rock climbing – those that distinguish it from, say, driving fast cars or performing on stage – will not learn a great deal by asking respondents about Positive or Negative Activation during the activity. Scores on these scales are likely to be similar or identical for all three activities, even though the quality of the experiences acting as incentives is probably quite different.

With this in mind, Rheinberg (1993, 2004a) developed a special interview technique to elicit verbal descriptions of the experiences that make performing a given activity so attractive. Based on these interview data, standardized incentive catalogues suitable for administration to large samples were compiled for each activity, allowing activity-specific incentive profiles to be drawn up. Table 13.1 gives examples of the incentives verbalized for some of the activities examined.

A broad variety of activities (horse riding, painting, computer hacking, bodybuilding, etc.) have been investigated. Some 30 to 60 categories of incentives that induce enthusiasts to invest time, effort, and money in performing each activity can be identified.

When working with data such as those presented in Table 13.1, it is important to be aware that it is not the experience itself that has been assessed, but a verbal transformation of that experience. Internal affective states, kinetic and other proprioceptive stimulations, changes in perceptions of the outside world occurring during the activity, and the associative enrichments that they trigger tend not to be

Table 13.1. Example verbalizations of activity-specific incentives (Based on Rheinberg, 1989, 1993; Rheinberg & Manig, 2003)	
Experience of power/intensity of feeling (motorcycling)	"You slam your foot down, the bike roars like an animal, and you thunder off at speeds that take your breath away. You can barely hold on. It's pretty wild stuff."
Merging (skiing)	"The experience of beautiful, elegant (esthetic) movements; the merging of the skis with the movements of your body."
Flowing along (music)	"Your fingers run lightly, almost effortlessly, over the instrument. When the melodies soar and flow, time stands still. You forget everything else. I flow along with the music."
Forgetting about everyday problems (graffiti sprayers)	"When you're out spraying, you completely forget all the stress you have at home and at school."
Being alone (surfing in light to moderate winds)	"Not having to talk, being by yourself: silence – just the sound of the board."
Feelings of increasing competence (motorbike)	"The enjoyment of feeling increasingly in control of the bike, of becoming one with it as you ride faster and faster along a stretch of road."

coded verbally. They first have to be translated to a linguistic format, which entails some hermeneutic effort and, accordingly, uncertainty of interpretation (Groeben, Wahl, Schlee, & Scheele, 1988; Rheinberg, 2004a).

The advantage of this method is that it gives people who have never engaged in a certain activity a very good idea of its fascination to others. The value of these insights should not be underestimated. Comparison across activities reveals marked differences in the breadth of the incentive spectrum. For bodybuilding, for example, only a very limited spectrum of activity-related incentives was found. Without the purpose-related incentives of an anticipated change in body shape or fitness, bodybuilders would be unlikely to endure the monotony of their training regimes (Gaugele & Ullmer, 1990). The spectrum of incentives involved in activities such as motorcycling, horse riding, and playing a musical instrument is much broader. Numerous qualitatively different experiences keep these activities attractive and provide a robust, durable motivational basis. Analyses of the incentives involved in socially undesirable leisure pursuits, such as illegal graffiti spraying, have provided insights into why some young people show such commitment and dedication to their unpaid night shifts. These insights may help to channel sprayers' energies elsewhere by focusing attention on the kind of incentives that alternative activities would have to provide.

Going beyond the level of individual experience, factor analysis can be used to identify more general dimensions of incentives residing within each activity (e.g., Rheinberg & Manig, 2003). Classes of incentives that run through very different activities can also be identified by empirical-inductive means (Rheinberg, 1993). This opens up new approaches to the prediction of behavior. If we know what someone enjoys about a certain activity, we can draw on established incentive profiles to predict which other activities are likely to appeal to them, even if they do not yet know that they exist (Rheinberg, 1989).

13.4.3 The Activity-Related Incentive of Achievement Motivation

Many of the activity-related incentives identified in the analyses outlined above reflect motivational concepts that have

already been described in this volume and elsewhere, testifying to ecological validity of those concepts. Beside the power motive (feeling powerful, strong, and dominant when engaged in an activity; Chapter 8), the affiliation motive (experiencing warm and friendly social interaction during an activity; Chapter 7), **sensation seeking** (enjoying exciting, but controlled threats), and so on, many of the activity-related incentives identified are associated with the achievement motive.

DEFINITION

The activity-related incentive of achievement derives from the experience of functioning at the peak of one's abilities when pursuing challenging goals, of complete and unselfconscious immersion in tasks, and of losing all track of time. (Rheinberg, 2002a, 2006)

In other words, feelings of competence during the performance of an activity are combined with complete immersion in that activity (experience of flow, see below). In terms of the examples given in Table 13.1, there is typically a combination of the incentives "feelings of competence," "merging," and "flowing along."

Theoretical models of the activity-related incentive of achievement are as yet lacking. According to McClelland (1999), the incentive of achievement motivation resides in the experience of "doing better for its own sake" McClelland, 1999, p. 228 – a kind of "consumatory experience" that is characteristic of achievement motivation. The quality of this experience is so positive that individuals with the corresponding disposition are repeatedly drawn to cycles of activity offering this kind of "consumatory experience."

However, closer inspection of the relevant phenomena reveals a distinction that, although significant, has attracted little attention to date. Achievement-oriented incentives have thus far been seen as residing in the successful completion of achievement behavior: an action outcome is evaluated against a standard of excellence and thereby classified as a success or a failure. Moderated by causal attributions, successful outcomes have certain consequences – feelings of pride (Atkinson, 1957) or positive self-evaluations (Heckhausen, 1972) – that provide the incentives to act in the first place. Seen from this perspective, the incentive to achieve is clearly purpose-related. A consumatory experience can only occur once a goal has been achieved, i.e., once the goal-oriented activity has been completed. If intrinsic is taken to mean "in the activity," this kind of incentive is clearly extrinsic.

It is also possible to anticipate the consumption of achievement-related incentives. At the level of conscious experience, individuals might, for example, imagine the feeling of having overcome a challenge. Are these anticipated self-evaluative outcomes the source of activity-related incentives to achieve? Probably not.

EXAMPLE

Let us take the example of skiing down a steep slope covered by fresh, untouched snow. As they do so, they enjoy the experience of perfect psychomotor control (combined with the excitement typical of sensation seeking); the positive feeling of functioning at the peak of their abilities, even in the most demanding of conditions. Given the opportunity, the skier would prolong the descent to savor the experience for as long as possible. The pride they feel upon seeing the track they carved out in the untouched snow has a different quality entirely, the major difference being that they do not experience this outcome-dependent affect until the action has been completed. To give an analogous example from the world of work, the feeling of functioning at the peak of one's abilities while making progress on a difficult task is quite different from the feelings experienced once that task has been successfully completed.

The observation that there are two different ways of consuming the experience of "doing better" explains some interesting phenomena. If, for example, someone celebrates a success at length, savoring its outcomes with lasting satisfaction, then these affective consequences clearly have high incentive value for that person. The skier in the example above might relax with friends and a beer on the sun deck, looking up at the mountain every now and then and taking great pleasure in having produced the single track in the snow. If, on the other hand, someone only ever takes pleasure in their successes for a short time before starting to look for new and even more challenging goals, it is clear that the "consumatory experience" they are seeking occurs before the experience of success. In our example, after taking brief pleasure in having mastered the challenge, the skier might head back to the ski lift to look for an even steeper slope. Activity-related incentives are clearly decisive here.

THE PARADOX OF ACHIEVEMENT MOTIVATION. The example above illustrates the paradox of achievement motivation. Achievement-motivated behavior is purpose-related in structure; its purpose is to master a difficult challenge. Once this goal has been achieved, activity-related incentives no longer pertain. In other words, actions resulting in the achievement of an aspired goal undermine their own motivational basis. People are not necessarily aware of this

structure, however, as reflected in phenomena that are, on the face of it, puzzling. Having reflected on the stress of his current lifestyle, for example, an executive may decide to adjust his or her work-life balance. The positive consequences of his or her commitment to the job no longer compensate for the losses incurred to the domains of leisure, family, or health. Nevertheless, he or she may find that he or she keeps getting involved in high-stress projects after all, putting him- or herself in precisely those situations he had resolved to avoid because the rewards were no longer worthwhile.

According to McClelland's (1999) differentiation between nonconscious, **implicit motives** and conscious values or **motivational self-concepts** (Chapter 9), the executive in this example made the decision to slow down at work on the basis of his or her self-attributed motives. But the crucial factor driving his or her actions is in fact the implicit achievement motive. The executive is constantly drawn to situations that give him or her the feeling of functioning at the peak of his or her abilities under challenging conditions. Because implicit motives can take effect without the involvement of higher, conscious processes of evaluation, behaviors of this kind that run counter to conscious decisions are particularly likely to arise when a person's value beliefs and motivational self-concept do not correspond with their implicit motives (see motivational competence, Rheinberg, 2002a, 2006, Section 13.6).

13.5 Flow: Joyful Absorption in an Activity

13.5.1 The Phenomenon

Csikszentmihalyi (1975, 1997b) had already observed the achievement motivation paradox described above in his extensive studies of artists' behavior. He noted that some artists would become entirely caught up in a project, working feverishly to finish it, and no longer seeming interested in anything else. Once the project was finished, however, it seemed to lose all appeal to them. They would put it away in a corner with the products of their previous labors and forget all about it before getting started on a new project.

There is no doubt that, for these artists, the incentive lies in the act of creativity itself. Although most of them had a fairly clear idea of what the end product of their new project would be, their behavior upon goal attainment indicates that they were in fact driven by the pleasure of creative expression; i.e., by activity-related incentives. They did not work to reach a set goal; on the contrary, they set a goal in order to create an opportunity to perform the work they enjoy. Their goal setting served activity-related incentives (Rheinberg, 1989, 2006).

In a large-scale interview study, Csikszentmihalyi (1975, 1997b) attempted to identify what it is that makes performing an activity so attractive that people engage in it repeatedly.

Csikszentmihalyi was not content to document and systematize the incentives associated with certain activities, as has been done in the research on activity-related incentives (Section 13.4.2) outlined above. Realizing that a particular pattern of experience recurred across very diverse activities, he was farsighted enough to focus his work on this state.

❶ The state in question is characterized by unselfconscious and complete immersion in a pursuit that, although requiring high levels of skill and concentration, results in a sense of effortless action and control. Csikszentmihalyi (1975) gave this state the fitting name of "flow."

Flow can be experienced by surgeons performing operations, chess players, musicians, dancers, computer gamers, rock climbers, etc. Although Woodworth (1918) had already described the state of total "absorption" in an activity and noted its importance (Woodworth, 1918, p. 69), he did not go beyond these everyday observations. Csikszentmihalyi recognized just how significant this exceptional state is and examined it closely in an extensive research program.

13.5.2 Qualitative Flow Research

In a first phase of research, Csikszentmihalyi took a qualitative approach, drawing on interview data to specify the conditions and characteristics of flow. Varying numbers of flow components have been identified over the years; the following summary attempts to provide an integrative overview (based on Rheinberg, 2006).

Components of Flow (Based on Csikszentmihalyi, 1975; Rheinberg, 2006)

1. Feeling of optimal challenge; feeling of being in control despite high situational demands (demands and skills are in balance at a high level).
2. The demands of the activity and feedback are perceived as clear and unambiguous; people in flow intuitively know what to do, and how to do it, at any given moment.
3. The pursuit of the action is experienced as smooth. One step flows into the next, as if guided by some inner logic. (This component presumably inspired the term "flow.")
4. There is no need for effortful and volitional concentration; rather, concentration occurs of its own accord, like breathing. Awareness is shielded from all cognitions that do not relate directly to the activity at hand.
5. The sense of time changes. People in flow usually lose all track of time; hours fly by like minutes.
6. People in flow feel a part of what they are doing, and become completely absorbed in it ("merging" of action and awareness); loss of self-reflection and self-consciousness.

The experience of flow is not limited to achievement-related activities. It also occurs in activities without tangible outcomes measurable against a standard of excellence: dancing, horse riding, driving fast cars or motorbikes, singing, juggling, etc. The activity-related incentive to achieve as described above can thus be distinguished as a subform of flow that occurs in achievement-related contexts.

❶ In addition to the general components of flow (see overview), the activity-related incentive to achieve is characterized by the enjoyment of functioning at the peak of one's abilities when pursuing a challenging goal. This component is not necessarily present in the general experience of flow.

Because of the strong preference for objectifiable behavioral data in academic psychology, little attention was initially paid to this phenomenological approach (Csikszentmihalyi & Csikszentmihalyi, 1991, p. 20). It was evidently too far removed from what scientists were prepared to accept as exploitable data sources. Nevertheless, it proved hard to ignore this very telling description of a motivational state that many recognized from their own experience (Weinert, 1991). Since the late 1980s, the flow approach has evoked considerable interest worldwide, far beyond the constraints of academic psychology.

In Germany, opinion pollsters have been collecting annual data on the frequency of flow experiences in representative samples since 1995 (Allensbacher Markt- and Werbeträgeranalyse, 2000). According to these surveys, two thirds of the German population experience flow at least "sometimes." This figure includes approx. 25% who report experiencing flow "often." Only 10% of the population never experience flow.

The strategy of examining the frequency and conditions of flow in terms of its individual components provided first insights into the activities and contexts conducive to the experience of flow. Findings showed flow to be experienced most frequently by people engaged in arts and crafts, intellectual pursuits, or socially interactive (especially sexual) activities (Rheinberg, 1996). These results are in line with findings obtained by other methods (Massimini & Carli, 1991).

Although most flow experiences are reported in the context of hobbies and stimulating leisure pursuits, they also occur in work settings (Csikszentmihalyi & LeFevre, 1989; Pfister, 2002; Schallberger & Pfister, 2001). Activities such as the following have been found to be conducive to flow in office workers:

- working on complicated and unusual tasks,
- working on the computer (e.g., programming), and
- learning new things.

Conditions such as the following have been found to inhibit flow:

- frequent interruptions (e.g., telephone calls),
- having to work superficially owing to time pressures, or
- a negative atmosphere (Triemer, 2001; Triemer & Rau, 2001).

Although certain activities and conditions can thus facilitate or impede the occurrence of flow, there seem to be few activities that rule it out altogether. Even the most mundane activities have been shown to elicit flow occasionally (Csikszentmihalyi, 1975; Rheinberg, 1996). In fact, flow seems to have a lot to do with the individual approach to an activity, and the attention devoted to it. In view of the fact that even concentration camp internees describe flowlike states, Csikszentmihalyi concludes that humans have the inbuilt capacity to turn any situation into one compatible with flow (Csikszentmihalyi, 1975). As mentioned above, however, the success of these endeavors may vary across activities and conditions.

13.5.3 Quantitative Flow Research

The Experience Sampling Method

Measurement of flow is complicated by the fact that people in flow typically have no sense of self. They are so deeply immersed in the activity that there is no room in their awareness for introspection, making it difficult for them to report on the state in retrospect. Methods are thus needed in which data is collected as closely as possible to the execution of the activity. Ideally, flow should be measured directly "online," as the activity is performed.

The development of the experience sampling method (ESM; Csikszentmihalyi, Larson, & Prescott, 1977; Hormuth, 1986) was a major step in this direction. Participants are provided with a "pager" (e.g., a programmable watch or mobile phone) that emits signals at random intervals. At each signal of the pager, they fill out a page in a block of self-report forms, stating what exactly they are doing and describing their quality of experience. As a rule, the assessments run for a week, with participants being paged 5–9 times per day. As in Aellig's study (2004) of rock climbers described above, the ESM collects detailed data that would be practically impossible to obtain by retrospective means (see above) while respondents are actually engaged in an activity. It is admittedly a time- and cost-intensive technique, but has the distinct advantages of high ecological validity and proximity to the action.

The ESM has been used in numerous projects (e.g., Csikszentmihalyi & Csikszentmihalyi, 1991; Csikszentmihalyi & LeFevre, 1989; Delle Fave & Bassi, 2000; Moneta & Csikszentmihalyi, 1996; Rheinberg, Manig, Kliegl, Engeser, & Vollmeyer, 2007; Schallberger & Pfister, 2001). Needless to say, the value of the data produced depends on what exactly respondents are asked, i.e., on the scales administered, and it is here that many ESM-based flow studies have run into problems. The ESM scales were not derived directly from the conceptualization of flow that emerged from the qualitative phase of research (Section 13.5.2). Rather, the ESM became established as a method tapping key for dimensions of optimal experience, and was applied to flow phenomena 10 years later (Csikszentmihalyi, 1991). The scales of established measures tend not to be changed for various reasons and, unfortunately, the ESM scales cover only a selection of the components known to constitute flow.

The flow components most frequently assessed in ESM studies are concentration, the experience of control, and the balance of skills and demands. The rest of the assessment tends to focus on aspects related to "positive experience" that have little to do with the components of flow identified in qualitative research.

Can Flow be Measured in Terms of a Demand/Skill Balance?

Because the ESM scales did not assess all components of flow, researchers had to decide how to measure flow with this restricted pool of variables. Csikszentmihalyi decided to measure flow in terms of just one of its components, namely, the **perceived balance** between demands and skills, on the assumption that people enter flow whenever their skills match the situational demands (e.g., Csikszentmihalyi & LeFevre, 1989).

This approach was parsimonious, but not unproblematic. Indeed, it is always risky to measure a multifaceted concept in terms of just one of its components. Although interview data show that people describing the experience of flow always say that the situational demands were neither too easy nor too difficult, it does not necessarily hold that the reverse is true, and that all those experiencing a balance between their skills and the situational demands enter a state of flow.

Findings presented by Moneta and Csikszentmihalyi (1996) confirm that this reverse conclusion is indeed problematic. The authors found significant interindividual differences in whether or not a demand/skill balance was associated with signs of flow. They did not investigate the reasons for these between-person differences in any depth, however.

❗ There is, however, a theoretical model that predicts marked interindividual differences under precisely these conditions of a balance between demands and skills whenever an activity is geared toward a specific outcome and can thus result in success or failure. Specifically, Atkinson's (1957) risk-taking model of achievement motivation predicts that ability-appropriate demands (that are neither too easy nor too difficult) represent ideal motivational conditions for individuals high in **hope of success**. These individuals are likely to be drawn to activities that match their skills. These same conditions are anything but motivating for individuals high in failure motivation, however, who struggle with a paralyzing **fear of failure**. (Chapter 13)

There is already some empirical evidence for individual differences in the experience of flow. Students were set an intellectually challenging task that was neither too difficult nor too easy for them (an **in-tray exercise** used in personnel recruitment). While working on this task, they were interrupted and asked to complete the **Flow Short Scale** (Rheinberg,

Vollmeyer, & Engeser, 2003), which taps all components of flow as well as current worries (Section 13.5.6). The strength of the achievement motive had already been measured using the Achievement Motives Scale (AMS) by Gjesme and Nygard (1970).

Under these achievement-related and intellectually challenging conditions, the flow scores of students working on the in-tray exercise increased as a function of their hope of success score, as measured by the AMS. At the same time, worry (but not flow) scores increased as a function of fear of failure, as measured by the AMS (Rheinberg, Vollmeyer, & Engeser, 2003). Thus, it would be incorrect to assume that a demand/skill balance is associated with the experience of flow in all individuals and under all conditions.

Can Challenge and Demands be Equated?

When the demands of a task or an activity are compatible with the skills of the person performing it, the situation can be experienced as a **challenge**. If the situational demands are too low for a person's skill, the task becomes a monotonous routine; if they are much too high, a task is unlikely to be attempted in the first place (Heckhausen, 1963a, 1972). Challenge is thus the product of a **skill/demand balance**. Highly skilled persons perceive this challenging balance at objectively high demands, whereas persons with poor skills perceive challenge at objectively low demands. As outlined above, the ESM measures flow in terms of this balance of skills and demands. In other words, flow is conceived to be unlikely whenever an activity is insufficiently challenging. If the concepts of "demands" and "challenges" were confused for any reason, findings might erroneously suggest that it is impossible to experience flow when the demands of a situation are low.

This is precisely what happened with the ESM scales. Csikszentmihalyi's (1975) theoretical model was logically based on demands (e.g., the objective difficulty level of a climbing route). This difficulty level was then set in relation to the respondents' climbing skills. Beginners perceive challenge when tackling low-level climbing routes, experts when tackling high-level routes. In the ESM, however, respondents do not rate the objective demands of an activity, but the result of the skill-demand comparison; i.e., the perceived challenge. It is hardly surprising, then, that flow is barely observed at low challenge scores, even when skill scores are low as well. If the level of challenge is rated to be very low, the individual's skill level in that domain is irrelevant.

A further complication is that respondents seem to have very different ideas of how the demands/challenges of a situation relate to their own skills/ability. For some people, there is a virtually perfect positive relationship between the two ratings (the higher the demands of a situation, the higher my ability). For others, the opposite is the case (the higher the demands of a situation, the lower my ability). The correlations between the two ratings fluctuate between $-.91 < r < .99$, with a standard deviation of SD $= .52$ (Pfister, 2002, p. 123).

❶ Given the marked differences in people's understandings of the concepts to be rated, it seems problematic to measure flow in terms of "challenge" and skills.

13.5.4 A Revision of the Model

These problems with the wording of the ESM scales led to unclear findings and prompted a revision of the flow model. In the original model, demands were plotted on the y-axis and skills on the x-axis of a coordinate system. A diagonal band represented the "channel" in which demands and skills are balanced (**flow channel model**, Fig. 13.5a), and activities can therefore be experienced as challenging.

The revised model (Fig. 13.5b) was the result of demands being equated with challenges (**quadrant model**). To account for findings showing that flow does not in fact occur at low levels of challenge, it was now modeled to occur only when challenges are at an above-average level for the individual and – in accordance with a principle of balance that was no longer entirely clear – skill levels are also above average (Csikszentmihalyi, 1997a). Not surprisingly, this quadrant model also proved unsatisfactory, and further modifications (**octant model**) followed (e.g., Massimini & Carli, 1991).

Research based on the quadrant (or octant) models typically starts by determining which quadrant the respondent is in at each point of measurement (above- vs. below-average skill × challenge; Fig. 13.5b). The quality of experience ratings for each quadrant are then inspected, and mean scores on each scale are reported for each quadrant. For example, Massimi and Carli (1991) found that respondents in the flow segment reported above-average levels of satisfaction, concentration, clarity, creativity, alertness, activity, wanting to perform the activity, and so on.

These findings are clearly indicative of "positive experience," but it is unclear to what extent they reflect the experience of flow. Moreover, the mean profiles are not very clearly defined. It is only in exceptional cases that mean ratings in the flow segment are more than half a standard deviation higher than the mean of all other occasions of measurement (see Massimi & Carli, 1991, p. 297). Given the interindividual differences observed in people's responses to the balance of skills and demands (see above), this pattern of results is hardly surprising.

❶ In conclusion, it seems that the revisions of the flow model are unable to solve the problems inherent in the standard version of the ESM scales, which define flow solely in terms of a demand/skill balance. Nevertheless, one particular effect does, at first glance,

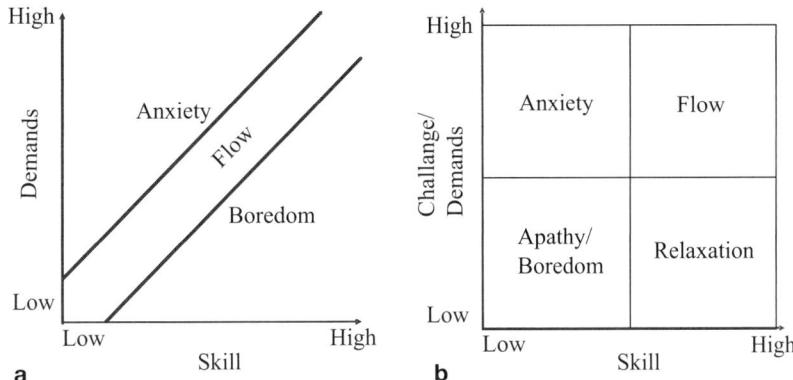

Figure 13.5a,b The original flow channel model (a) by Csikszentmihalyi (1975) and (b) the quadrant model later proposed by Csikszentmihalyi & Csikszentmihalyi (1991) and Csikszentmihalyi (1997a).

seem to provide support for the quadrant model. This effect is considered in the following section.

13.5.5 The Expertise Effect and Resistance to the Undermining of Intrinsic Motivation

The Expertise Effect

When the flow experience is not erroneously equated with a balance between challenge and skill, it is possible to investigate empirically how the balance between demands and skill can influence other aspects of flow. This approach has drawn attention to an interesting phenomenon.

Where certain activities are concerned, it seems reasonable to assume that flow is indeed unlikely to occur when skills and demands are both low. This applies to **complex activities** such as certain sports (e.g., Bieneck, 1991), playing musical instruments (Siebert & Vester, 1990), spraying graffiti (Rheinberg & Manig, 2003), and interacting with a computer (e.g., Schubert, 1986). The apparent effortlessness and smoothness typical of flow is experienced only when the necessary basic operations have become automatic (see component 3 of the overview "Components of Flow" in Section 13.5.2).

Examples would be a novice's faltering attempts to pick out a tune on the piano, or a first-time surfer's vain attempts to stay upright on the board for any length of time. Although low demands undoubtedly coincide with low skills in these cases, the novice's performance is too far removed from smooth, effortless action for flow to occur. Experts are thus more likely than novices to describe experiences of flow in these kinds of complex activities (Bieneck, 1991; Rheinberg & Manig, 2003; Schubert, 1986; Siebert & Vester, 1990).

❗ The expertise effect applies only to complex activities that require several basic skills to become automatic before their performance becomes anything like smooth and effortless. However, in more simply structured activities, such as some computer games, a

state of flow can reliably be induced in absolute beginners when demands and skills are in balance (Rheinberg & Vollmeyer, 2003; Vollmeyer & Rheinberg, 2003). The expertise effect can therefore not be cited as evidence for the universal validity of the quadrant model.

Resistance to the Undermining Effect

Interestingly, the expertise effect also occurs in purpose-related motivational structures. Hentsch (1992) compared "professional artists," who made a living from their art (and art students who aspired to do so), with "hobby artists," who painted in their leisure time for their own enjoyment. The hobby artists are clearly driven by activity-related incentives. For the professional artists, however, the activity and its outcomes have material consequences; they involve purpose-related incentives (external rewards). According to some definitions, this type of motivation would be classified as "extrinsic," and thus incompatible with joyful immersion in the activity (see above; Ryan & Deci, 2000).

However, as experts, professional artists have a much better command of the basic processes required to translate the images in their mind's eye onto canvas. The flow-fostering effect of expertise proved to be stronger than the flow-impeding effect of "extrinsic" motivation just mentioned. Indeed, the professional artists were significantly more likely than the hobby artists to cite aspects of flow as reasons for their creative endeavors. In fact, flow was the strongest incentive category of all for the professional painters (Hentsch, 1992, p. 94). In other words, external rewards do not necessarily prevent people from becoming totally absorbed in an activity. Under certain conditions, people may develop a "resistance" to the undermining effect, becoming absorbed in an activity even when material rewards are expected. A skeptical approach to the overly simplistic contrasts sometimes made in the domain of intrinsic vs. extrinsic motivation (see earlier, Section 13.2.8) is thus warranted.

EXCURSUS

The Flow Short Scale

This method allows the various components of flow to be assessed in 30 to 40 seconds and is thus suitable for completed activities, as well as for ESM-based assessments of ongoing activities. The Flow Short Scale has been translated into several languages. Despite the heterogeneity of the 10 flow items, the consistency of the scale is high (Cronbach's α of around .90 for items 1 to 10). Ratings of items 1 to 10 are aggregated to produce a flow score (F). Ratings of items 11 to 13, which tap worries about the situation, are aggregated to produce a worry score (W; Rheinberg et al., 2003). Both scores are standardized (Rheinberg, 2004a). Each item is rated on a 7-point scale from "disagree" to "agree":

1. I feel just the right amount of challenge. (F)
2. My thoughts/activities run fluidly and smoothly. (F)
3. I don't notice time passing. (F)
4. I have no difficulty concentrating. (F)
5. My mind is completely clear. (F)
6. I am totally absorbed in what I am doing. (F)
7. The right thoughts/movements occur of their own accord. (F)
8. I know what I have to do each step of the way. (F)
9. I feel that I have everything under control. (F)
10. I am completely lost in thought. (F)
11. Something important to me is at stake. (W)
12. I mustn't make any mistakes. (W)
13. I am worried about failure. (W)
    (Items 1–10: flow score; items 11–13: worry score)

13.5.6 Flow and Achievement

A Comprehensive Assessment of Flow

Because the pitfalls of measuring flow in terms of the balance between demands and skills have been recognized, new instruments have been devised to provide comprehensive assessments of the components of flow in different fields of activity. Specifically, instruments have been devised to assess experiences of flow among Internet users (Novak and Hoffman, 1997), computer users (Remy, 2000), and in the context of physical activity (Jackson & Eklund, 2002).

In addition, a 10-item scale has been developed to measure flow in any domain (Flow Short Scale; Rheinberg, Vollmeyer, & Engeser, 2003). A further three items of the scale tap worries that may arise during activity. The method is short enough to be combined with the ESM, meaning that the whole spectrum of flow components plus current worries can be tapped while an activity is ongoing. The method is standardized (Rheinberg, 2004a,) and has been implemented in a broad variety of contexts (Rheinberg, Vollmeyer, & Engeser, 2003). The items of the Flow Short Scale are detailed below.

Flow, Learning, and Achievement

The idea that a state of **absorption** fosters the development of knowledge and skills goes back to Woodworth (1918). In the light of the components of flow listed in the overview in Section **??**, it seems quite reasonable to assume that flow can have positive effects on achievement. Possible exceptions are high-risk activities that are never entirely under the individual's control, and in which total immersion would be too dangerous. A prime example would be motorcycling on the open road, where – relative to the race track – conditions can be unpredictable and beyond the motorcyclist's control. Indeed, a positive correlation has been observed between the intensity of flow experience in these conditions and the frequency of accidents (r = .32; p < .05; Rheinberg, 1991).

With the exception of such dangerous activities, however, flow can be expected to facilitate achievement. Nakamura (1991) found that mathematically gifted but low-achieving students were less likely to experience flow in the classroom than equally gifted, but high-achieving students. Do these findings imply that more frequent flow experiences result in better performance?

The problem with cross-sectional comparisons of this kind is that it is impossible to determine the direction of the causal relationship. In line with the expertise effect of flow discussed above, the results reported by Nakamura (1991) may also be caused by high-achieving students finding it easier to enter flow precisely because they are more proficient. Their lower-achieving peers probably get stuck more often and lack the necessary skills to proceed. In other words, even if flow does foster achievement, the reverse may also hold, with higher levels of competence fostering the experience of flow. In this case, flow would not (only) be the cause, but (also) the consequence of enhanced learning outcomes.

Reciprocal effects of this kind are difficult to disentangle. Empirical evidence indicating that flow fosters academic achievement would help to clarify the situation. Bischoff (2003) investigated university students enrolled in optional language courses. At the beginning of the semester, the students were allocated to different groups depending on their scores on a standardized language test. Over the course of the semester, they were administered the Flow Short Scale a number of times during lessons (Rheinberg et al., 2003). It emerged that achievement at the end of the semester was predicted by the experience of flow during the course (exam grades: r = .38; p < .01; subjective learning gains: r = .44; p < .01). These predictions remained significant when the effects of achievement level on flow were neutralized by using statistical regression techniques to control for test scores at baseline: flow still predicted an additional 10% of variance in achievement at the end of the semester (Engeser et al., 2005).

❗ Thus, research findings indicate that flow can have positive effects on classroom learning gains.

Engeser (2004) reports similar findings for self-directed learning, based on an investigation of psychology students preparing for a statistics exam. Engeser administered the Flow Short Scale (Rheinberg et al., 2003) three weeks before the exam, when the students were working through a set of statistics exercises. Performance-related data were also obtained from the students (prior knowledge of statistics, final school mathematics grade, intelligence data, etc.). Even when statistically controlling for all of the performance-related factors, the flow scores collected while students were working on the exercises predicted an additional 4% of the variance in their exam score. The predictive power of flow experience was approximately equal to that of a test score representing prior knowledge of statistics (Engeser et al., 2005).

Achievement data are now also available from experimentally controlled achievement situations. Rheinberg and Vollmeyer (2003) first showed that it was possible to manipulate the intensity of flow experimentally by varying the difficulty of modified computer games (e.g., Roboguard). The effect sizes observed were large (d > 1). As predicted by the flow channel model (Section 13.5.4, Fig. 13.5a), increasing demands were associated with a linear increase in scores on the Flow Short Scale, up to the point at which the task was perceived to be too difficult, when flow scores began to decrease again.

This finding was replicated with another computer game (Pacman) (Vollmeyer & Rheinberg, 2003) that provided an objective measure of performance (final score). A correlation of r = .63; p < .01 was found between the experience of flow during the game and the score obtained. Although this relationship is substantial, it is important to bear in mind that the influence is bidirectional – flow during the game leads to higher scores and vice versa. Furthermore, worries and fear of failure do not seem to play a discernable role in computer games played on an individual basis. Thus, the motive-dependent differences in response seen in more achievement-related contexts (see the inbox task above; Rheinberg et al., 2003) were irrelevant in these experiments.

13.6 Future Prospects: The Flow Hypothesis of Motivational Competence

DEFINITION

Motivational competence can be defined as a person's ability to reconcile current and future situations with his or her activity prefer-

ences such that he or she can function efficiently, without the need for permanent volitional control. (Rheinberg, 2002a)

There are four components to this definition, the most important being an accurate sense of one's own (implicit) motives (Rheinberg, 2006). Motivational competence implies congruence between a person's implicit motives and his or her motivational self-concept.

This approach essentially specifies and operationalizes Rogers' concept of self-congruence (Rogers, 1961) for the motivational domain, drawing on McClelland's distinction between implicit, nonconscious motives and self-attributed, conscious motives (McClelland, 1999; see also Chapter 9).

It is this theoretical background that distinguishes the concept of motivational competence (based on McClelland, 1999) from the concept of self-concordance proposed by Sheldon and Elliot (1999; based on Deci and Ryan, 1985). Self-concordance concerns the correspondence between the self and a person's **current goals**. Motivational competence might be said to go one level deeper. It concerns the correspondence between an individual's nonconscious motives and the conscious self, and how well that individual's current goals correspond with both.

The pursuit of goals that are not congruent with one's implicit motives does not usually lead to increased emotional well-being. High commitment to motive-incongruent goals may in fact decrease well-being. For people whose goals match their implicit motives, however, well-being increases as progress is made toward the goal (Brunstein, Schultheiss, & Grässmann, 1998). These and similar findings make perfect sense in the light of the assumption that implicit motives do not affect the incentive value of consciously chosen goals as much as the incentive value of engaging in motive-congruent activities (Brunstein, 2003; Spangler, 1992).

For example, research on politicians running in the primaries for the US presidential election has shown that candidates high in power motivation persisted even when it became clear that they had no chance of winning. For them, the run-up to the election with its many speeches and televised debates was a pleasure in itself. Achievement-motivated candidates, on the other hand, stepped down when they no longer had a realistic chance of winning. The incentive structure of the goal-oriented activities did not correspond to their implicit motives (Winter, 1982).

The very low correlations that tend to emerge between implicit motives and the motivational self-concept (Brunstein, 2003; Spangler, 1992) indicate that, for some people, motivational self-concepts correspond with implicit motives, but that, for other people, they do not. For instance, a person who sees him- or herself as persuasive and influential might in fact be achievement rather than power motivated.

EXAMPLE

Individuals whose motivational self-concept and implicit motives do not correspond are especially likely to set motive-incongruent goals when putting a lot of thought into goal selection. When reflecting consciously on a decision, people tend to draw on their motivational self-concept rather than on their implicit motives, and often end up committing themselves to projects that are not in line with their implicit motives. The pursuit of such goals, which are only ostensibly appropriate and "valuable," requires constant monitoring and volitional control, which is of course incompatible with flow (Sokolowski, 1993).

Individuals whose motivational self-concept corresponds with their implicit motives are more likely to select motive-congruent goals. Accordingly, the incentive structure of the situations they encounter when pursuing their goals is much more likely to offer them motivational support. For example, a challenging project will give individuals high in the achievement motive plentiful opportunities to experience the states they find so attractive: joyful absorption in functioning at the peak of their abilities. There is no need for volitional control. Action seems effortless, and flow is very likely (Rheinberg, 2002a, b, 2006, 2004b). Hence, people with high levels of motivational competence can be expected to experience flow more frequently.

Empirical Support for the Flow Hypothesis

The flow hypothesis of motivational competence illustrated in the example above is currently being tested in a large-scale ESM study (Rheinberg, Manig, Kligl, Engeser & Vollmeyer, 2007), but there is already some empirical evidence in its support. Clavadetscher (2003) asked volunteers in a Swiss cultural organization to complete the Flow Short Scale (Rheinberg, Vollmeyer, & Engeser, 2003) for the activities involved in their voluntary work. Additionally, the **Multi-Motive Grid** (MMG; Schmalt, Sokolowski & Langens, 2000) and the **Personality Research Form** (PRF; Stumpf et al., 1985) were used to assess the volunteers' achievement, power, and affiliation motives in terms of motivational self-concepts (PRF) and implicit motives (MMG). The difference between the explicit and implicit measure was computed for each motive; these differences were then aggregated to obtain a rough estimate of motivational competence. In line with the flow hypothesis

of motivational competence, the more the volunteers' motivational self-concepts corresponded with their implicit motives, the more flow they experienced in their chosen projects ($r = .34$; $p < .01$).

The longitudinal study by Engeser (2004) outlined above provides further evidence in support of the flow hypothesis. Engeser assessed the implicit achievement motives (TAT after Winter, 1991a) and motivational self-concepts (PRF; Stumpf et al., 1985) of 266 psychology students enrolled in a statistics seminar. In addition, the scales of the **Volitional Components Inventory** (VCI) by Kuhl and Fuhrmann (1998) were used to assess how the students motivated themselves to achieve their goals.

Motivational competence was examined in terms of the interaction between the implicit achievement motive and motivational self-concept. Students who were high in both the implicit achievement motive and self-attributed achievement motivation were more likely to identify with their work and to become absorbed in the activity ("self-regulation" scale of the VCI). In contrast, students with a high implicit achievement motive but low motivational self-concept reported difficulties in achieving their goals, stating that they often had to force themselves to work ("self-control/volitional inhibition" scale of the VCI). For students with a low implicit achievement motive, the motivational self-concept was of less relevance to the endorsement of the self-regulation scales. This kind of interaction between implicit and explicit motives was also found in sports (Steiner, 2006). In this study, the dependent variable was the Flow Short **Scale** (Rheinberg et al., 2003).

❶ It is particularly important that an individual's implicit motives and motivational self-concept correspond – i.e., that motivational competence is high – when his or her implicit motives are strong.

Although the results of these self-report studies remain to be substantiated for ongoing activities in everyday conditions using ESM, they provide first empirical evidence in support of the flow hypothesis of motivational competence. The hypothesis may provide a relatively parsimonious explanation for the observation that some people are more likely to be found in a state of joyful immersion when engaged in goal-directed activities, whereas for others goal pursuit necessitates permanent volitional control.

STUDY

Flow, Goals, and Happiness: The Paradox of Work

Does flow make people happy? On the one hand, the "positive experience" of flow is directly associated with happiness: "Flow is defined as a psychological state in which the person feels simultaneously cognitively efficient, motivated, and happy" (Moneta & Csikszentmihalyi, 1996, p. 277). On the other hand, empirical studies have estab-

lished a higher frequency of flow when people are at work than at leisure. Yet respondents state that they would rather be doing something else when at work, and report feeling less happy at work than during leisure time. This phenomenon has been termed the "paradox of work" (Csikszentmihalyi & LeFevre, 1989; Schallberger & Pfister, 2001). How might this paradox be explained? Might it be attributable to the way that flow was measured? The studies in question were based on the quadrant model, and assumed flow to occur when both the level of challenge and the level of skill were above average. As discussed above, this definition of flow is very problematic.

Rheinberg et al. (2007) took a different approach to assessing flow in an ESM study of 101 adults. Participants were paged seven times a day for one week. At each signal of the pager, they (a) completed the Flow Short Scale and (b) rated their current happiness/satisfaction (valence). Figure 13.6 plots the mean trajectories of these two scores over the course of the day during the workweek (top panel) and at the weekend (bottom panel).

Although the Flow Short Scale assesses all components of the flow experience, the "paradox of work" was still apparent. On weekdays, flow scores were higher during working hours (09.15–16.15) than during leisure time, whereas happiness and satisfaction were higher in leisure time than in working hours. A different picture entirely emerged at the weekend, when happiness/satisfaction scores were consistently above average and flow scores consistently below average.

How can these findings be explained? Rheinberg et al. (2007) asked respondents to state whether or not their activity was directed toward a specific goal. A goal orientation was expected to foster flow, because goals organize behavior and thus facilitate smoothness of action. Fig. 13.7 shows how goal directedness of behavior was found to affect flow and happiness/satisfaction at work (left panel) and in leisure time (right panel).

As expected, goal-directed activities were associated with higher scores on the Flow Short Scale in work and leisure time. Goal pursuit was associated with lower levels of happiness and satisfaction, however, particularly in leisure time. Why might this be? A goal is a positively evaluated state that has not yet been attained. Accordingly, there is a differential between valence of the present situation and that of the aspired future situation. This differential may activate behavior and facilitate flow, but it is incompatible with current feelings of happiness and satisfaction. Given that respondents were much more likely to pursue goals at work than during leisure time, the finding that goals facilitate flow but reduce happiness/satisfaction resolves the "paradox of work," revealing it to be an effect of greater goal orientation in work-related settings.

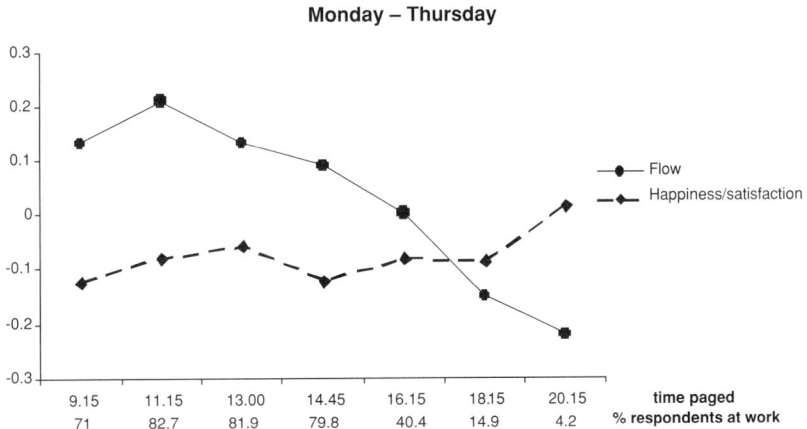

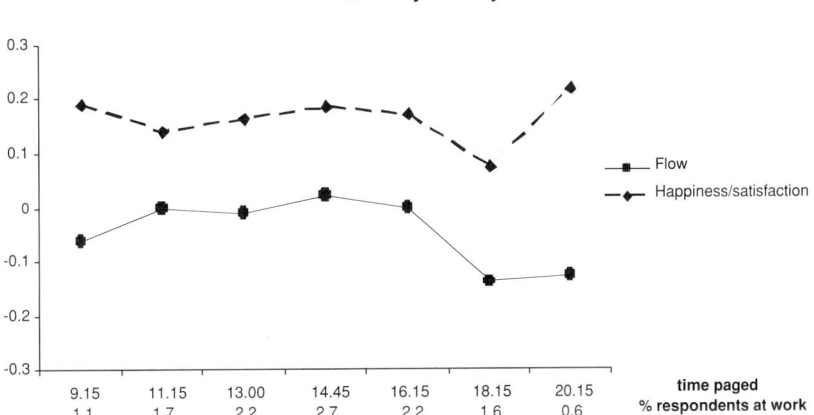

Figure 13.6 Mean trajectories of flow and happiness scores (z-scores) during the working week (upper panel) and at the weekend (lower panel). (Based on Rheinberg et al., 2007.)

Of course, it is quite possible to experience flow without goals, and to be happy at the same time (e.g., when dancing, singing, surfing, taking a long and leisurely motorcycle ride, etc.). In everyday life, goals facilitate flow experience at work. They do not, however, promote happiness and satisfaction. In fact, the opposite tends to be the case.

Interestingly, individuals who had higher flow scores at work scored higher on happiness/satisfaction in the evenings ($r = .57$; $p < .01$). It may be that flow at work contributes to people's subsequent feelings of happiness and satisfaction – even if they did not experience these feelings at work.

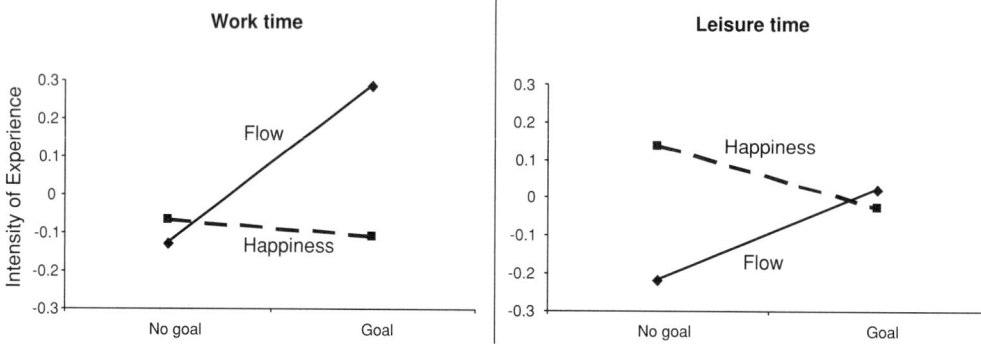

Figure 13.7 The relationship of goal directedness of behavior to flow and happiness at work (left panel) and at leisure (right panel). (Based on Rheinberg et al., 2007.)

SUMMARY

Motivational psychologists are accustomed to thinking of behavior as being energized and directed by the incentives residing in an aspired goal. It is indisputable, however, that incentives also reside in the performance of the activity itself. When incentives are located in the activity itself, rather than in its potential consequences, an activity is often deemed to be intrinsically, as opposed to extrinsically, motivated.

Upon closer inspection, however, different conceptualizations of intrinsic vs. extrinsic can be discerned. Quite apart from the sense of "in the activity," the term "intrinsic" is sometimes applied to motivation deriving from the needs for self-determination and competence, and sometimes equated with interest and involvedness. Another conceptualization focuses on the thematic congruence of means and ends, and is sometimes applied to the distinction between learning goal or mastery orientation vs. performance goal or ego orientation in the context of motivation to learn. Recent meta-analyses indicate that the question of whether intrinsic motivation, whatever its definition, is undermined by extrinsic rewards is not yet entirely settled, but hinges on a number of factors. Current usage of the terms "intrinsic" and "extrinsic" is so inconsistent and imprecise that it would make more sense to give each of the phenomena specified new and more accurate labels.

This type of approach was demonstrated for intrinsic in the sense of "in the activity" with an analysis of activity-related incentives. It was shown that activity-related incentives can be integrated within the extended cognitive model of motivation proposed by Heckhausen (1977a) and its further extension by Rheinberg (1989). The quality of these incentives can be investigated and described at different levels of abstraction. Using proximal measures to assess quality of experience while respondents are engaged in an activity (the experience sampling method, ESM) has proved particularly fruitful.

Two of many activity-related incentives were examined in greater detail, namely, the activity-related incentive to achieve and the experience of flow. Flow research using ESM techniques has the potential to provide substantial insights. However, this approach does have some methodological problems. Specifically, a single component of flow – balance between skills and challenge – is often equated with flow, even though there are both theoretical and empirical reasons for assuming marked individual differences in response to the skill/challenge balance. Enhanced assessment procedures have produced interesting findings on the expertise effect of flow and on the resistance of flow experience to the undermining effects of external rewards. Detailed analyses show that the experience of flow can be conducive to achievement. Of course, this does not rule out the possibility that the reverse also holds (i.e., that a high level of achievement is conducive to flow; see the discussion on the expertise effect above).

Ongoing research on the flow hypothesis of motivational competence was presented according to which individuals whose implicit motives correspond with their motivational self-concepts are more likely to experience flow. Given a free choice of goals, these individuals are more likely to opt for activities with an incentive structure that offers them motivational support. Preliminary findings indicate that it is worth pursuing this hypothesis further.

REVIEW QUESTIONS

1. **What are the different conceptualizations of intrinsic, as opposed to extrinsic, motivation?**

   Intrinsic motivation can be defined in the sense of "inherent in the activity,"
   - as a form of motivation based on self-determination and feelings of competence,
   - as characterized by interest and involvement, or
   - as a form of motivation in which the means and ends of an activity are thematically congruent.

2. **Can you give examples of phenomena that might be classified as either extrinsic or intrinsic, depending on the definition applied?**

   Experiencing great enjoyment and involvement in an activity (e.g., painting, computer programming), even though you know you will be paid for it.

   Taking a self-determined approach to force yourself to do something you know will not be enjoyable.

   Activities that cannot possibly be thematically congruent with an intended outcome – because there is none – can be a source of great enjoyment and performed repeatedly.

3. **Which types of expectancies and incentives are distinguished in Heckhausen's (1977a) extended cognitive model of motivation?**

   Situation-outcome expectancies,
   - action-outcome expectancies,
   - outcome-consequence expectancies, and
   - consequence- (purpose-) related incentives.
   - The model has been further extended to include activity-related incentives.

4. **Apply this model to your current motivation to answer these review questions.**

   Let the situation be that you have read the text up to this point for particular reasons (the consequences of doing so, interest in the topic covered, enjoyment of reading, etc.); let the action be wanting to answer this question now; let the outcome be knowing whether or not you have a sufficient grasp of the material covered; let the direct consequence be a pleasant feeling of being able to turn to other pursuits without jeopardizing further aspired consequences (passing an exam, making a presentation in class, being able to apply the content of the chapter to "real life," etc.). Another expected consequence might be finding out which part(s) of the text you need to think through more carefully.

   Having thus specified the elements of the model, your current motivation to answer these review questions can be determined through the following expectancies and incentives. You do not think that you will be able to gauge how well you have understood the text unless you attempt the questions (low situation-outcome expectancy). However, you do think that answering the questions will help you gauge your understanding of the text (high action-outcome expectancy). Moreover, you believe that this knowledge will allow you to turn to other pursuits with a clear conscience, reduce the general level of uncertainty, or tell you how much and which parts of the text you need to read again (high outcome-consequence expectancy). The incentive value of some or all of these consequences is sufficiently high.

   Alternatively, it may be that you simply enjoy puzzling over questions of this kind or reflecting on the topics covered. In this case, you would be motivated by positive activity-related incentives. Of course, this would not exclude the possibility that the purpose-related incentives outlined above also play a role.

5. **What methods are used to examine the incentives inherent in performing an activity? Give two examples and discuss the advantages and disadvantages of each.**

   Experience sampling methods: Respondents are asked to rate the quality of experience while pursuing the activity. Advantages: Data are obtained "online"; the scales implemented allow comparisons to be made across activities, conditions, and individuals. Disadvantages: Assessments are very abstract, and provide few qualitative insights into the specific incentives of engaging in a particular activity.

   Explorative interviews on the incentives of specific activities. Advantages: Detailed accounts of specific experiences provide insights into what exactly it is that makes performing an activity so attractive. Disadvantages: Data are collected retrospectively and are not easily comparable across activities.

6. **What is meant by the flow experience and what are its characteristic components?**

   Flow is the unselfconscious and complete absorption in a pursuit that, although requiring high levels of skill and concentration, results in a sense of smooth action and effortless control. See the overview in Section 13.5.2 for its components.

7. **What is the difference between qualitative and quantitative flow research?**

In qualitative flow research, retrospective exploratory interviews have been used to identify between 6 and 9 components of flow. In quantitative flow research, the experience sampling method (ESM) is used to assess the occurrence of flow, with respondents rating the quality of their experience on various scales at the signal of a pager or watch. These scales are not congruent with the components of flow identified in qualitative research, however.

8. **How was flow defined in the quantitative phase of research based on the ESM? What problems does this definition entail?**

Flow was defined as occurring when skills and challenges are in balance at a level that exceeds the personal average.

Problems: Flow was defined in terms of just one of its many components.

There are theoretical and empirical reasons for expecting marked individual differences in this very component.

In some cases, demands are confused with challenges; moreover, individual understandings of these concepts vary.

9. **What is the expertise effect of flow and when does it occur?**

In complex activities, the apparent effortless characteristic of flow is experienced only when the necessary basic skills have become sufficiently automatic. The same does not apply to simply structured activities.

10. **Why is the relationship between flow and achievement difficult to interpret?**

The influence is bidirectional. Flow can be conducive to (learning) outcomes, but better (learning) outcomes can also increase the probability of experiencing flow (see the expertise effect in Question 9).

11. **Why can individuals high in "motivational competence" be expected to experience flow more frequently?**

The major component of motivational competence is that a person's implicit motives correspond with his or her motivational self-concept. At a high level of correspondence, people are more likely to set themselves goals that facilitate in motive-congruent activities. When motivational structures are congruent with implicit motives, volitional control becomes less necessary. Action seems effortless, joyful, and flow becomes more likely. To date, however, there are only three pieces of empirical evidence to support these assumptions.

12. **What is the "paradox of work" and how can it be explained?**

Empirical studies have shown that flow is more likely to occur when people are at work than at leisure. Yet people feel happier in leisure time, and are more likely to say they would rather be doing something else when at work. This apparent contradiction is resolved by taking into account that (a) work-related activities are more likely to be goal oriented than leisure activities, and that (b) goals facilitate flow experience, but tend to reduce current happiness/satisfaction. Flow at work is positively related to happiness/satisfaction in subsequent leisure time, however.

14 Causal Attribution of Behavior and Achievement

J. Stiensmeier-Pelster and H. Heckhausen

14.1 Causal Attribution: How Thinking About Causes Influences Behavior

Motivational psychologists are not alone in seeking to understand the reasons for people's behavior and the causes of action outcomes. We all do it; it is an everyday occurrence. We all want to understand what is going on around us. Accordingly, we do not simply observe or note the behavior of others, but seek to understand what motivates them to act the way they do. In other words, we try to identify the reasons for their behavior. Insights into these reasons allow us to predict – and perhaps even influence – how they will behave in the future. We also strive to pinpoint the causes for action outcomes, because only a clear understanding of these causes allows us to reproduce desirable outcomes in the future and to prevent undesirable ones, e.g., by eradicating their causes. The following examples serve to illustrate when and why we analyze the reasons and causes for behavior and action outcomes and how the results of this analysis influence our subsequent behavior.

> **EXAMPLE**
>
> A rather mediocre student unexpectedly gets one of the highest marks in a class test. The teacher might well find herself asking a number of questions: Did the student work particularly hard for the test? Was he lucky? Might he have cheated? Her behavior will differ depending on the cause she infers for the student's surprisingly good test score. She might praise him (if she thinks he has worked particularly hard) or treat him with suspicion (if she thinks he has cheated), etc. Let us assume – to give another example – that someone jostles us as we are getting on a bus. Is she trying to push in to get a good seat or did she trip? Here again, our response will depend on the cause we identify for her behavior. If we decide that the woman wants to push in, we will likely be annoyed and may be tempted to give her a piece of our mind. If, on the other hand, we decide that she stumbled, we will probably keep our thoughts to ourselves.

As these two examples show, **causal attributions** influence our behavior and experience.

Apart from seeking to ascribe causality in an attempt to optimize our own behavior and to predict and potentially influence the behavior of others, we also seek to actively influence the causal attributions of others – because we are well aware that causal attributions do affect behavior. If we bump into someone as we are getting off the bus, for example, we might apologize, because we think an apology will prevent them from thinking we jostled them on purpose, and that this belief will in turn temper their response.

People's explanations for outcomes and events – i.e., the causes they infer and the effects of these causal attributions on their subsequent behavior and experience – soon became the object of theoretical debate and empirical research (see Eimer, 1987, for a summary). There was a huge upsurge in research after Heider (1958), the acknowledged pioneer of the study of attribution processes, published some fundamental ideas on the phenomenon. Kelley and Michela (1980) distinguished two research programs, and hence two groups of theories, within this field of research:

- attribution theories and
- attributional theories (Fig. 14.1).

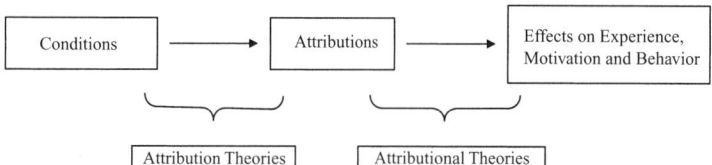

Figure 14.1 Explanatory domain of attribution theories and attributional theories. (Based on Kelley & Michela, 1980.)

Attribution theories are particularly concerned with how causal attributions are reached, and seek answers to the following questions:

- When do attributions occur?
- Do causal attributions necessarily involve the conscious, active analysis of the causal structure of events, or are they based on implicit assumptions about the causes of behavior and action outcomes?
- What kind of information is utilized in causal inferences?
- How is this information sought and how is it processed?
- What are the mechanisms and processes underlying our attributions of actions and outcomes to specific causes?

Attribution theories are discussed in the second part of this chapter, before we turn to attributional theories in the third part. Attributional theories are primarily concerned with the effects of causal attribution on people's subsequent behavior and experience. They play a major role in various subdomains of psychology and are, strictly speaking, what make causal attributions so interesting for the psychology of motivation. The question of how we arrive at causal attributions (attribution theories) is really more a matter for cognitive psychology (although motivational factors of course have some bearing on the attribution process and its outcomes). Nevertheless, because the causes to which outcomes and events are ascribed can have a decisive impact on subsequent motivation, we also cover the more cognitive aspects of causal attribution in this chapter.

One of the most prominent approaches to attribution theory is Weiner's attributional theory of motivation, emotion, and behavior (Weiner, 1986). On the one hand, this theory addresses the processes and mechanisms that are involved in causal search and that terminate in a specific attribution. On the other hand, it provides a comprehensive description of the effects of causal attributions on subsequent behavior and experience. Weiner's ideas form the basis for numerous other attributional theories, such as the attributional theory of depressive disorders (Abramson, Metalsky, & Alloy, 1989; Abramson, Seligman, & Teasdale, 1978; Stiensmeier-Pelster & Schürmann, 1991), the attributional theory of aggressive behavior (Graham, Hudley, & Williams, 1992), and the attributional theory of prosocial behavior (Rudolph, Roesch, Weiner, & Greitemeyer, 2004).

Weiner's ideas have also been incorporated into a number of further theories without the authors always stating this fact explicitly. For example, attributions play a key role in recent theories of learning and achievement (Dweck, 1999; Dweck & Leggett, 1988) and theories of task choice behavior (Dickhäuser & Stiensmeier-Pelster, 2000; Eccles & Wigfield, 1995). The assumptions of Weiner and other authors have also formed the basis for explanations of health-related behavior (Schwarzer, 1994) and sports outcomes (Rethorst, 1994), and for predictions of the sales achieved by financial service providers (Mai, 2004).

14.2 Weiner's Attributional Analysis of Motivation, Emotion, and Behavior

According to Weiner's model, action outcomes are first evaluated in terms of their **valence**, i.e., whether they are positive or negative (Fig. 14.2) (Weiner, 1985b). The result of this evaluation triggers outcome-dependent (and attribution-independent) emotions. A positive evaluation will give rise to general, nonspecific feelings of joy or happiness, whereas a negative evaluation will result in feelings such as sadness or frustration. Under certain conditions, besides evaluating the valence of an outcome, we may undertake **causal search**, i.e., try to identify the causes of an outcome. Weiner posits causal search to occur whenever an outcome:

- occurs unexpectedly,
- is important, or
- is evaluated negatively.

Weiner holds that each of these three conditions is sufficient to initiate causal search. This assumption does not withstand careful theoretical or empirical testing, however, as we will show below. The search for causality culminates in a causal attribution. Which cause is inferred for a particular outcome depends on a number of causal antecedents. As will be discussed in more depth in Section 14.3, specific information about the action outcome in question may be evaluated to arrive at an appropriate causal attribution. Certain causal schemata may also be activated to this end. Hedonic biases, such as the desire to protect one's self-esteem ("I am responsible for successes, but have nothing to do with failures"), may also play a role, as may the perspective taken on the outcome (i.e., whether I was the actor or merely observed someone else's actions). We will consider these causal antecedents and the processes underlying causal attribution in more detail in Section 14.3.

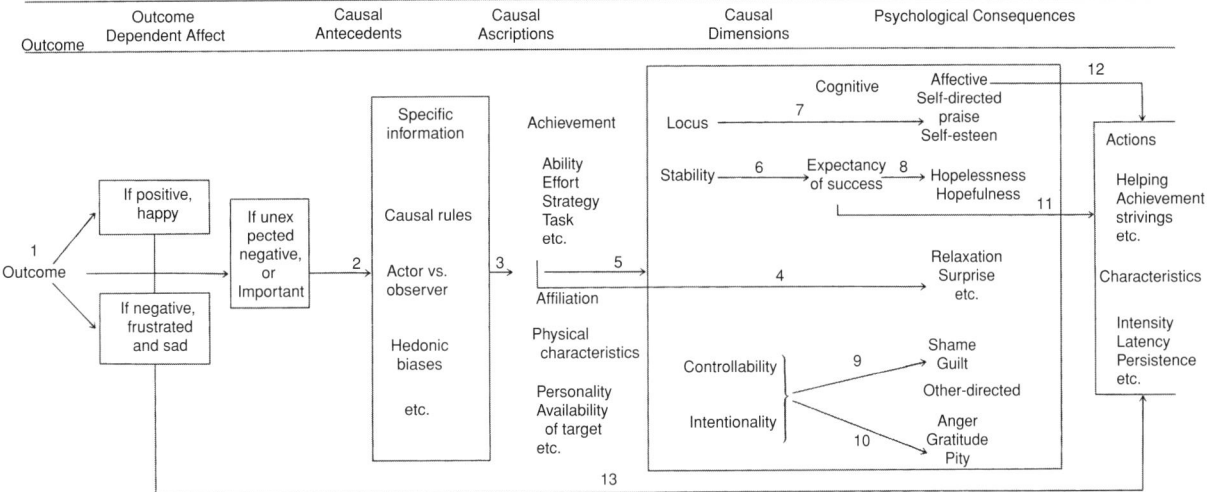

Figure 14.2 Weiner's attributional approach to motivation and emotion. (Based on Weiner, 1985b, p. 565.)

Causal Factors

Attribution theory research has identified a number of **causal factors** (causal attributions) that are regularly cited to explain academic performance, or success and failure in social interactions (i.e., affiliation-related contexts). The causal factors inferred for achievement-related outcomes include high or insufficient ability, high or insufficient effort, task difficulty, and luck. Causal factors that can explain success and failure in affiliation-related contexts include physical characteristics and certain personality features. As shown in the model, these causal factors are then rated along certain dimensions. The most important of these **causal dimensions**, soon identified by Weiner (Weiner et al., 1971), are listed in the following overview.

Causal Dimensions. (Based on Weiner et al., 1971)

1. Locus
   The locus (person-dependence, also termed internality) of a causal factor reflects whether it resides within the actor (internal), or in the environmental conditions or other people (external).
2. Stability
   This dimension reflects stability over time, i.e., whether the causal factor remains stable or changes over time (variable).
3. Steerability
   Rheinberg (1975) proposed this dimension that covers the controllability and intentionality of causal factors:

   - Controllability indicates whether the causal factor was subject to the actor's control (controllable) or beyond it (uncontrollable).
   - Intentionality indicates whether the actor brought about the causal factor deliberately (intentionally) or accidentally. Note that a causal factor or a constellation of causal factors that

was brought about deliberately (intentionality is present) is always controllable, whereas a controllable causal factor was not necessarily brought about deliberately.

The intentionality dimension may in fact be better suited to describe the reason for a certain behavior than it is to characterize the cause attributed to an outcome. Other authors have identified further causal dimensions. For instance, it may, under certain conditions, be important to evaluate causal factors on the globality dimension (e.g., Abramson, Seligman, & Teasdale, 1978): can causal factors be generalized across situational domains (global) or are their effects limited to a particular situation (specific)?

According to the distinction made by Kelley and Michela (1980), Weiner's approach is – up to this point – an attribution theory, concerning solely the process from the perception of an event to the identification of its causes. Weiner, however, goes on to describe the influence of causal attributions on behavior and experience, meaning that his approach is in fact an attributional theory.

Psychological Consequences of Causal Analysis

Causal attributions – and especially their characterization in terms of locus, stability, globality, controllability, and intentionality – have certain cognitive and affective implications (psychological consequences).

❶ The cognitive implications of causal attributions are expectancies of future success (or failure), which in turn elicit feelings of confidence (hope) or hopelessness.

COGNITIVE CONSEQUENCES OF CAUSAL ATTRIBUTIONS. According to Weiner's model, the expectancy of future success or failure largely depends on the attributor's evaluation of the stability and globality dimensions of causality:

■ If a student succeeds (fails) on a task and ascribes this outcome to a cause he perceives to be stable, he will continue to expect to succeed (fail) on that task in the future.

■ Moreover, if he ascribes the outcome to a global cause, he will generalize these expectancies to other tasks as well; the more global the cause is perceived to be, the broader the generalization.

■ If, on the other hand, the student ascribes his success (failure) to a cause he perceives to be unstable (variable), he will anticipate that future outcomes may differ (e.g., failure as opposed to success).

As discussed in greater depth below, however, the relationship between attributions and expectancies of future success is much more complex than assumed by Weiner. As we will show later in this chapter, it is not just a question of the stability and/or globality of the cause to which a success or failure is ascribed, but of its impact on behavior over time. The stability of a cause and its effects on behavior are therefore two distinct phenomena.

Assuming the basic premise of attribution theory – as discussed in Section 14.3 – that the main function of causal attribution is the prediction and control of environmental conditions, then ascriptions to unstable causes must be rather unsatisfactory for the attributor. Unstable causes do not permit reliable predictions of future events or, in consequence, control of the environment. However, this discrepancy is resolved in part by the fact that expectancies of success are also determined by the controllability of their cause. For example, a student who fails because he or she has put little effort into his or her work (unstable, but controllable cause) can still make reliable predictions about future outcomes. Specifically, he or she can expect failure on subsequent tasks if he or she does not put in the necessary effort, and to succeed if he or she commits to working hard. However, the problem remains if an outcome is attributed to an unstable and uncontrollable cause such as luck. Likewise, attributing failure to lack of ability (stable, but uncontrollable cause) is at odds with the assumption that causal ascription serves to predict and to control outcomes. Although this kind of attribution allows us to predict future events (we will expect failure on subsequent tasks), it can scarcely be said to permit their control.

AFFECTIVE CONSEQUENCES OF CAUSAL ATTRIBUTIONS. Causal attributions and the properties ascribed to them not only influence our expectancies, but also our feelings (affect). It is important here to distinguish between self-directed emotions and other-directed emotions, i.e., to specify the object of the affect (Meyer, Schützwohl, & Reisenzein, 1993). For instance, we can be proud of ourselves (the object is our self) or sympathize with others (the object is another person). The causal dimension of locus is associated with the occurrence of self-directed feelings, such as pride or self-respect (or self-esteem). These feelings arise when an outcome is attributed to internal causes, such as ability or effort. For example, we will be especially proud of a good performance if we ascribe it to our superior ability or effort, but are unlikely to feel pride if we attribute our success to luck or the ease of the task. These attributions will not enhance our self-respect, either. By the same token, self-respect is unlikely to decrease if a failure is attributed to bad luck or other external causes. The controllability dimension is associated with both self-directed and other-directed feelings. A failure attributed to causes that are both controllable and internal (e.g., lack of effort) is likely to lead to feelings of guilt, whereas a failure attributed to uncontrollable, internal causes (e.g., lack of ability) will result in feelings of shame.

Other-directed emotions that are determined by the controllability dimension include anger, gratefulness, and sympathy. For example, we may feel anger toward someone whose behavior has harmed us if we consider the causes for the harmful behavior to lie within that person's control.

> ### EXAMPLE
>
> If I lend my car to an acquaintance and he damages it because he was talking on his mobile phone while maneuvering into a parking space (controllable cause), I will doubtlessly be much more annoyed than I would have been had the damage been caused in an accident he could not have averted (uncontrollable cause). We will be particularly angry if somebody causes us harm and if we assume that person to have acted deliberately; i.e., if we consider the reasons for their behavior to be intentional. By the same token, we may feel anger toward people experiencing failure or injury if we consider them to be personally responsible for that outcome (i.e., if we think the cause of their failure or injury was within their control). Teachers whose students perform badly tend to feel anger if they think those students did not work hard enough (controllable cause). If, on the other hand, they consider a student to lack the necessary ability to succeed (an uncontrollable cause for the student), they will more likely show a sympathetic response.

According to Weiner, we are generally more likely to feel sympathy for someone if we see that they are in need of help and, at the same time, assume that they are not responsible for their situation, but that its causes were beyond their control. Likewise, we feel gratitude when we have received help and assume the helper to have acted selflessly (controllable cause for the helper). We are less likely to be grateful if we suspect the helper was simply complying with social norms or was forced to help.

One feeling that is dependent on the causal factor itself, and that is assumed to be independent of that factor's evaluation on the causal dimensions discussed, is surprise. Weiner assumes surprise to occur whenever an outcome is attributed to chance or luck. This assumption does not withstand careful theoretical (see Meyer, 1988, for a summary) and empirical analysis (Stiensmeier-Pelster, Reisenzein, & Martini, 1995), however. Rather than being the affective result of luck attributions, surprise in fact seems to trigger causal search (we will return to this point later).

Weiner postulates the cognitive and affective consequences of causal inferences to determine our subsequent behavior. His model is not limited to a specific context, e.g., achievement behavior, but seeks to explain behavior in all kinds of domains. Weiner himself applied the model to both achievement-related and interpersonal behavior (e.g., assistance or aggression in social interactions). Other authors have used it to explain the emergence of certain types of depressive disorders (e.g., Abramson, Metalsky, & Alloy, 1989), or applied it to health-related behavior (see above). In all cases, the focus has been on three aspects of behavior:

- intensity (e.g., how much effort people make, the lengths to which they go),
- latency (the speed with which action is undertaken), and
- persistence (how long people will keep pursuing a goal, how quickly they give up when difficulties occur).

Looking at Weiner's approach against the background of expectancy-value theories of motivation, it is clear that Weiner's model is no replacement for theories of this kind. In fact, where the proximal determinants of behavior are concerned, Weiner's approach constitutes a typical expectancy-value theory. Specifically, behavior is determined by the expectancy of success (expectancy component), on the one hand, and by affect (incentive component), on the other. In accordance with Atkinson's (1957) risk-taking model, Weiner's approach suggests that people only engage in achievement-related activities if the expectancy of success is sufficient, and if they have previously experienced pride in success, meaning that they can now anticipate renewed feelings of pride. In contrast to the risk-taking model, however, Weiner assumes previously experienced affect to influence behavior more than anticipated affect.

❗ Thus, Weiner's approach explains the conditions for expectancies of success and the experience of pride. Moreover, his model is not limited to achievement behavior, but considers all forms of behavior to be determined by expectancy and value components. For example, the provision of assistance depends on the assumption that our assistance will be effective (expectancy) and a feeling of sympathy (value). Aggression – to give a further example – depends on the experience of anger (value) and the assumption that our aggression will have positive consequences (expectancy).

Following this overview of when and how causal inferences are made, and how they influence our subsequent behavior and experience, the next section addresses the questions of why, when, under what conditions, and how causal attributions are made – in other words, we now turn to attribution theories.

14.3 Attribution Theories

14.3.1 Basic Assumptions

The fundamental idea of attribution theories is that "the man or woman on the street" – i.e., everyone of us – is an intuitive scientist, formulating theories to explain, understand, predict, and influence their own behavior and experience and that of others. Unlike scientific theories, which are generally explicit, these theories tend to be **implicit**. They guide our actions, i.e., we behave in accordance with our theories. Some authors even see the ability to formulate accurate theories about our behavior and experience, and that of our fellow humans, as a type of intelligence. For example, Gardner (1983) postulates the existence of intra-and interpersonal intelligence.

DEFINITION

Intrapersonal intelligence is defined as the ability to faithfully perceive and explain our own behavior and experience, such that we are able to accurately predict and influence it. Interpersonal intelligence, on the other hand, is defined as the ability to perceive, explain, predict, and influence the behavior and experience of others.

Other authors speak of emotional intelligence, with the main characteristics of high emotional intelligence being consistent with those of intra- and interpersonal intelligence (Mayer & Salovey, 1993; Goleman, 1994).

❗ Our motivation to identify the causes for events and to accurately describe these causes derives from our fundamental need for control and predictability. Apart from wanting to know what is going on around us, we seek to influence and control behavior and events (Heider, 1958).

These ideas, originally posited by Heider, were taken up again, and established as the fundamental principle of attribution theory in the 1970s. For example, Kelley (1971, p. 22) pointed out that the causal attribution process is not an end in itself. Rather, we engage in causal attribution with the aim of managing ourselves and our environment more effectively.

To this end, we need to be able to predict events and outcomes. However, we can only make accurate predictions if we understand the causal structure underlying an event. A comprehensive analysis of the situation or event and realistic attributions are two further preconditions. In other words, it is assumed that individuals always strive to behave in a rational manner. The ability to predict events and thus render them controllable also has a value for survival. It enhances the individual's adaption to the environment, thus making it highly functional. "Attributional search as other explanatory behaviors . . . have been accounted for with two different principles: functionalism . . . and mastery. . . . That is, one might explore to promote adaption and survival (functionalism) or to better understand oneself and the environment (mastery)" (Weiner, 1985b, p. 81).

This fundamental postulate has been subject to some criticism. For example, Kuhl (1983) doubts that causal search can be elevated to a general principle of motivation, arguing that people often do not spare a thought for the causes of action outcomes. If they do think about these causes, moreover, this is often an end in itself, which occurs very much as a matter of interest, without the actor drawing any direct consequences for action control. If, for example, someone ruminating on the possible reasons for a failure does so as an end in itself, an attribution of failure to insufficient effort will not necessarily motivate that person to try to solve the problem. Furthermore, Kuhl assumes that causal search can, under certain conditions, be a symptom of a highly dysfunctional state orientation (Chapter 12): "Examples of state-oriented activities may be ... examining the causes for not having reached a goal." (Kuhl, 1981, p. 159).

Kuhl bases this assumption on findings presented by Diener and Dweck (1978), who, in their studies, distinguished helpless from mastery-oriented children. These two groups differed in their level of performance, with helpless children performing at much lower levels than mastery-oriented children. Furthermore, the groups differed in terms of the causes to which success and failure were attributed, and – of particular significance in the present context – in the extent to which they reflected on the causes of their success or failure. The authors interpreted these findings as indicating that helpless children – in contrast to mastery-oriented children – "waste" too much thought on causes, which is why their performance outcomes are poor. The mastery-oriented children, on the other hand, performed well because they were less concerned with the causes of success and failure. Relative to the helpless children, they evidently considered these attributions to be largely irrelevant.

> Attributions may be considered irrelevant to the mastery-oriented child on this task, because the remedy would be the same regardless of the cause of failure (Diener & Dweck, 1978, p. 460).

Kuhl cites the findings of Diener and Dweck in support of his argument that reflecting on the causes of success and failure has negative implications for the effectiveness of behavior, and is therefore dysfunctional. We will come back to the functionality or dysfunctionality of causal search and reflecting on the causes of success and failure in the following section (see the excursus on criticisms of the basic assumptions of attribution theory).

14.3.2 Causal Search: Triggering Conditions, Duration, and Intensity

It is safe to say that we are not engaged in a round-the-clock search for the causes of events or the reasons for behavior. In fact, we make no attempt to establish the origins of most of the things going on around us. This does not imply that we have no idea of their causes, however. Our ideas may be right or wrong, but they guide our behavior, even if we are not always consciously aware of them.

EXAMPLE

If, while waiting at a red traffic light at a busy junction, I notice that the cars approaching from the left and right are stopping, I do not start wondering why this is the case. Rather, based on my previous experience, I implicitly assume – without a second thought – that they are stopping because their lights have just turned red. I further assume that I can safely cross the junction as soon as my lights turn green, because the traffic lights sequence is such that the lights in the other cars' direction remain red for the duration of the green phase in my direction.

As this example illustrates, we have stable beliefs about the reasons why most of the things taking place around us happen. In the words of Kelley and Michela (1980), we have a set of beliefs, schemata, or hypotheses on how certain effects are related to certain causes. On this basis, we formulate (implicit) expectations of how the world works (cf. Meyer, 1988; Stiensmeier-Pelster, Reisenzein, & Martini, 1995). Provided that our experiences correspond with our beliefs, schemata, and expectations, there is no reason to specify the causes of perceived events (in fact, we may not even be consciously aware of events that are congruent with our expectations).

Although attribution theories are based on the fundamental assumption that we seek to identify the causes of events in order to gain a better understanding of the environment and of ourselves, which in turn enables us to exert control over events, there was little research initially into the question of when, how often, and how long we engage in causal attributions. Likewise, there was a dearth of research on the standards of accuracy accepted – i.e., how thoroughly we seek to determine causes – and whether there are individual differences in this respect.

According to Weiner's comprehensive attributional analysis of motivation, emotion, and behavior (see earlier discussion), we seek to establish the causes of any event that is unexpected, negative, or important. Weiner's writings suggest that each of these three conditions is sufficient to initiate causal search. This assumption does not withstand careful scientific analysis, however, as illustrated by the simple example on the next page.

The Stage Model of Attributional Activity

Other questions that remain unanswered by Weiner's attributional analysis of motivation, emotion, and behavior are how long the search for causality lasts and what degree of accuracy is accepted. Drawing on the work of Meyer (1988;

Criticisms of the Basic Assumptions of Attribution Theory: How Functional Is Causal Attribution?

The theoretical reflections above and the empirical findings of Stiensmeier-Pelster et al. (1995) are congruent with the basic assumptions of attribution theory that the search for causality is functional, thus contributing to a better understanding of and adaptation to the environment, and finally to survival. But what about Kuhl's contention (Section 14.1) that causal search is dysfunctional? The results of several studies addressing individual differences in the duration and intensity of attributional activity seem to substantiate Kuhl's criticisms. As mentioned above, Diener and Dweck (1978) conclude that helpless and mastery-oriented children do not differ in the type of attributions they make, but rather in the intensity of their attributional activity. Likewise, Kuhl concludes that action- and state-oriented individuals differ in the extent of their attributional activity rather than in the type of attributions made. Kammer (1983) argues that depressive individuals differ from their nondepressive counterparts in both the quality and the quantity of their attributions, with the former generally thinking about causes of events in more depth and detail. All these findings would seem to indicate that causal attribution is a dysfunctional activity. When the differences found are considered more carefully, however, this apparently plausible assumption collapses.

For all three samples cited above, qualitative differences can be found alongside the quantitative ones. For example, in the study by Diener and Dweck the helpless children also differed from the mastery-oriented children in terms of the kind of attributions they made: mastery-oriented children preferred effort attributions, whereas helpless children tended to ascribe their failures to a lack of ability. Moreover, the quantitative differences observed by Diener and Dweck apply only to lack of ability as the ascribed cause for failure. In other words, there is no general effect in the sense that helpless children think longer and/or more intensively about the causes of any given success or failure than do mastery-oriented children. The only difference is in the frequency of their thinking about lack of effort as the cause for failure. Moreover, we cannot rule out the possibility that the quantitative differences observed do not in fact reflect differences in the extent of causal search. It may be the case that the groups do not differ in the duration and intensity of the causal search, but in the extent to which they ruminate on a cause once they have identified it.

Let us not forget that the helpless and mastery-oriented children in the study by Diener and Dweck also differed in the causes they inferred for their failure. Mastery-oriented children tended to attribute failure to a lack of effort; helpless children were more likely to ascribe it to a lack of ability. It seems reasonable to assume that mastery-oriented children get back to work and redouble their efforts to succeed as soon as they have identified the cause of their failure ("I didn't try hard enough"). It is clear from the attribution what kind of approach is required ("Try harder!"). The helpless children may have completed the causal search just as quickly, but because their causal inference ("I'm no good at this kind of task") does not point to a specific course of action, they might find it harder to return to their work. Indeed, there would be little point in doing so, because someone with no aptitude for the task has few prospects of success anyway. These children thus remain caught up in self-doubts ("I'm no good"), begin to ruminate or to search for meta-attributions ("Why am I no good?"), and try to specify the cause of their failure more closely ("Is it a general lack of ability or do I lack specific skills?"). Thus, whereas the "lack of effort" attribution has direct implications for behavior, behavioral implications can only be derived from the "lack of ability" attribution by specifying its causes more closely. Only then can people decide to address the cause identified in a renewed attempt to achieve their goal, or to abandon the original goal in favor of new ones, because the cause is deemed unchangeable.

A student has received E grades on all previous mathematics tests. Given the stability of his performance over the years, he has come to the firm conclusion that mathematics is simply not his thing. Now his school-leaving exams are coming up. Based on his belief that he is no good at mathematics, he expects to get another E grade. And that is precisely what happens. Will this student try to identify the causes for his poor performance? Most unlikely. The E grade is just what he expected; his causal beliefs are not called into question in any way. According to Weiner's model, however, the student should seek causes for his poor performance, because although the grade was expected, the event was indisputably negative (E grade) and certainly important (school-leaving exam).

Meyer, Niepel, & Schützwohl, 1994), Stiensmeier-Pelster et al. (1995) developed an "expectancy-disconfirmation model" of attributional search, which Stiensmeier-Pelster (2004) recently extended into a stage model of attributional activity (Fig. 14.3). This model seeks to explain when causal search is initiated, how long it lasts, and how intense it is; i.e., its aspired degree of accuracy.

The first question to arise is whether an individual is sufficiently motivated to analyze the causes of an event. Like traditional expectancy-value theories of motivation, the stage model of attributional activity assumes causal search to be motivated by a specific emotion, namely, surprise. As posited by Meyer (1988) and many other authors (e.g., Charlesworth, 1969; Izard, 1977; Ortony, Clore, & Collins, 1988; Scherer, 1984), surprise is assumed to occur when an expected event does not occur, or when the event occurring is unexpected or contrary to expectations (for details, see Stiensmeier-Pelster et al., 1995). It prepares and motivates the individual to engage in epistemic activities (a careful analysis of the situation) as described by Berlyne (1965), of which attributions can be regarded as a specific type (Pyszcynsik & Greenberg, 1987;

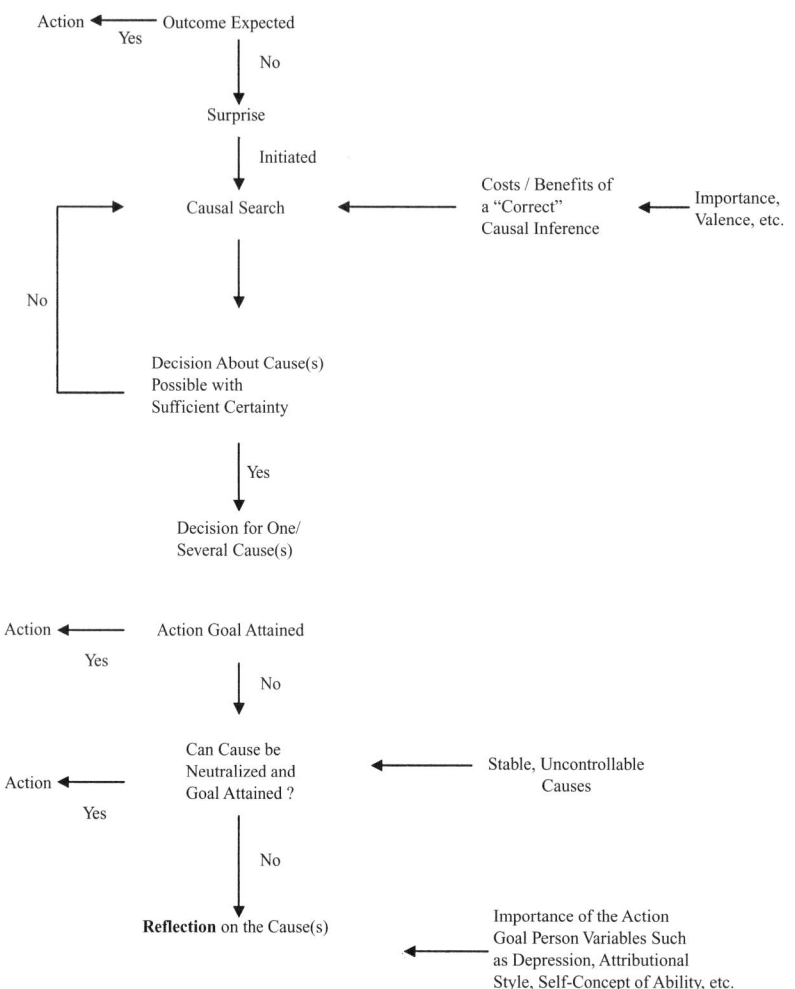

Figure 14.3 Stages of attributional activity and their conditions. (Based on Stiensmeier-Pelster, 2004.)

Weiner, 1985b). Surprise is assumed to prepare the individual to engage in spontaneous epistemic activities (especially causal analysis) by interrupting all ongoing processes (at least briefly) and refocusing the individual's attention on the unexpected event (as demonstrated by Meyer, Niepel, Rudolph, & Schützwohl, 1991), and, at the same time, to motivate the individual to instigate epistemic activities (especially causal analysis). Accordingly, as shown in Fig. 14.3, causal search is only initiated when an event occurs unexpectedly, i.e., when the answer to the question of whether the event was expected is "No." If the answer is "Yes," people continue to pursue their ongoing activities without thinking about their causes.

DURATION OF CAUSAL SEARCH. Surprise is not the only determinant of causal search, although it is sufficient and necessary to initiate the process, and sufficient to generate a corresponding action tendency or desire (epistemic curiosity; see Berlyne, 1960). Other factors also play a role. These factors have less to do with the question of whether causal search is

initiated (as stated above, the decisive point here is whether or not events are expected) than with its duration, intensity, and accuracy. The intensity and duration of causal search, in particular, are assumed to depend on the perceived costs and benefits of the process. According to the stage model of attributional activity, the greater the benefits of a correct causal inference relative to the costs of causal search, the more intense and thorough the search for causes will be (Fig. 14.3). The benefits of a correct causal inference are thought to increase with the importance of the event and the magnitude of its consequences. The valence of the event is also relevant here: the benefits of a correct causal inference can be assumed to be greater after failure than after success. It is only if we are aware of the causes of failure that we can take steps to avoid making the same mistakes again in the future. Thus, the stage model incorporates Weiner's notion that importance and valence are key determinants of causal search.

Table 14.1. Mean duration and intensity ratings of the search for the causes of success and failure by degree of surprise and importance of event

	Surprising/unexpected		Not surprising/expected	
	Unimportant	Important	Unimportant	Important
Success	3.8	3.4	2.5	2.1
Failure	3.3	4.6	1.7	3.2

High scores indicate long and intensive causal search. Scores range from 1 to 5.

The cost of causal search depends on a number of factors, e.g., the effort or exertion it will entail (e.g., to access the necessary information) and the resources the individual can dedicate to it (e.g., time).

Stiensmeier-Pelster et al. (1995, Study 5) examined the influence of the unexpectedness, valence, and importance of an event on causal search. In this study, students were asked to state how long they had needed to determine the causes of a certain event, and how intensive the causal search had been. In all cases, the event in question involved a surprising (unexpected) or unsurprising (expected) success or failure on a test that was either highly important or unimportant to them. Table 14.1 reports the findings of this study. As the data show, the length and intensity of causal search hinges primarily on whether the result was surprising (unexpected) or expected (unsurprising). In the case of failure, moreover, the importance of the test affects the length and intensity of causal search. Failure in important situations stimulates particularly long and intensive searches for causality.

Evidently, the fact of an event being unexpected or contrary to expectations suffices to initiate causal search, and the length and duration of causal search is most pronounced when an unexpected event is negative and important. It is in these cases that the benefits of identifying the causes for failure are greatest.

Accordingly, the stage model of attributional activity proposed by Stiensmeier-Pelster (Fig. 14.3) postulates further stages in the attributional process once the cause of an event or an outcome has been determined. The first question to be addressed is whether the action resulted in the attainment of the aspired goal. If so, the attributional process can be terminated, because the actor is evidently able to pursue his or her actions further. If, however, the goal was not attained, the question arises of whether the cause for that failure can be obviated in the future. If the cause can be neutralized by means of corrective behavior (e.g., increased effort, a new strategy, etc.), the goal-oriented activities can be pursued further, and the attributional process can be terminated. If this is not the case – for instance, whenever a cause is perceived to be stable and uncontrollable – the attributor will continue to reflect on the causes identified. This reflection is further assumed to depend not only on the valence of the

outcome (more pronounced after failure than after success; see above) and the type of cause (more pronounced after stable and uncontrollable outcomes than after variable, controllable ones), but also on the importance of the goal (more pronounced after important events than after unimportant ones).

Causal rumination is also a question of personality, however (Fig. 14.3). Depressive, helpless, and state-oriented individuals and people with low self-concepts of ability seem to put more thought into the reasons for their failures than do nondepressive, mastery- and action-oriented individuals, and people with high self-concepts of ability – presumably because the former tend to ascribe failures to stable and uncontrollable causes, whereas the latter are more likely to infer variable and controllable causes for failure.

Empirical Support for the Stage Model

Aspects of Stiensmeier-Pelster's (2004) model have been tested in several empirical studies. The first aim of these studies was to show the different conditions underlying the processes of causal search, on the one hand, and causal rumination, on the other. Second, the studies sought to demonstrate that the person variables mentioned above (depression, state orientation, etc.) do not influence causal search, but only causal rumination.

INFLUENCE OF UNEXPECTEDNESS, VALENCE, AND IMPORTANCE OF AN ACTION OUTCOME ON CAUSAL SEARCH AND CAUSAL RUMINATION. In one study, students were asked to recall experiences of success or failure and to rate the duration and intensity of causal search, as well as the duration and intensity of rumination on the causes identified. The successes or failures in question were specified to be either important or unimportant; the outcomes, to be either expected or contrary to expectations. Only main effects for three manipulated variables were found (Table 14.2). As Table 14.2 shows, the duration and intensity of causal search hinges solely on the unexpectedness of the outcome. The search for causes is much more thorough after outcomes that are contrary to expectations than after expected outcomes. This finding replicates the results of Stiensmeier-Pelster et al. (1995) presented earlier. The valence and importance of the event had no effect on causal search. By contrast, the duration and intensity of causal rumination proved to be dependent on the valence and the importance of the event, and not on its surprise value. In line with the theoretical assumptions of the stage model outlined above, people are likely to invest more time and effort in reflecting on the causes identified if an outcome or event is negative or particularly important.

INFLUENCE OF UNEXPECTEDNESS AND DEPRESSION ON CAUSAL SEARCH AND RUMINATION ON THE CAUSES OF FAILURE. Stiensmeier-Pelster (2004) conducted two studies to investigate the effects of unexpectedness of failure and respondent depression on causal search and causal rumination. The procedure used in these experiments was that of a typical

Table 14.2. Causal search and causal rumination by degree of surprise, valence, and importance of event

	Degree of surprise Contrary to expectations	Valence			Importance	
		Expected	Success	Failure	Unimportant	Important
Causal search	3.3	2.4	2.7	3.0	2.8	3.0
Causal rumination	3.1	3.3	2.8	3.6	2.8	3.7

High scores indicate long and intensive causal search or causal rumination. Scores range from 1 to 5.

helplessness experiment. In the first phase of the experiment, labeled the "training phase," respondents were administered performance-related tasks, subsequent to which they were given negative feedback. They were then invited to participate in another experiment, the "test phase," which took place in a different university building and was administered by another experimenter. The respondents were again administered performance-related tasks, though of an entirely different kind than those implemented in the first experiment. Immediately after receiving the first set of negative feedback in the training phase, respondents were asked how much thought they had put into the reasons for their failure. These responses served as an indicator for the intensity of causal search. The same question was posed while respondents were working on the new tasks in the second phase of the experiment. Their responses at this point were taken as an indicator for causal rumination. The Beck Depression Inventory (BDI; Beck, 1967) had been administered prior to the experiment to obtain depression scores. The discrepancy between the expectancy of success (expected number of correct answers) and the number of tasks participants were told they had solved correctly served as an indicator for unexpectedness. As shown in Table 14.3, the depression score was significantly correlated with the intensity of causal **rumination** in both parts of the study, but not with the intensity of causal search. Conversely, unexpectedness was significantly correlated with the intensity of causal search in both parts of the study, but not with the intensity of causal rumination.

INFLUENCE OF ATTRIBUTIONS OF SUCCESS AND FAILURE ON CAUSAL SEARCH AND RUMINATION ON THE CAUSES OF SUCCESS AND FAILURE. In an experiment using a procedure similar to that of the study described above, Stiensmeier-Pelster (2004) investigated the intensity of causal search and causal

Table 14.3. Correlations of depression and unexpectedness with causal search and causal rumination

		t1 Causal search	t2 Causal rumination
Depression	Study 1 (N = 35)	.22	.47**
	Study 2 (N = 30)	.30	.55**
Unexpectedness	Study 1 (N = 35)	.29*	.13
	Study 2 (N = 30)	.38*	.09

*p < .05; **p < .01.

rumination as a function of the valence of the event (success vs. failure) and the causes to which success or failure are attributed. In this experiment, the properties of the attribution was assessed after feedback (of either success or failure) using a procedure analogous to the "Attributional Style Questionnaire" (ASQ; Peterson et al., 1982; Poppe, Stiensmeier-Pelster, & Pelster, 2005). Specifically, respondents were first asked to identify the main cause for their performance and then to rate this cause with respect to its locus (internality), stability, and globality. Based on these ratings, the sample was split into two groups: "internal-stable-global attribution" and "external-unstable-specific attribution." Fig. 14.4 presents the findings of this experiment. As the data show, there is little difference in the intensity of causal search, as measured immediately after feedback, as a function of the valence of the outcome (success vs. failure) or the properties of the attribution. In contrast, the intensity of causal rumination, as measured in the test phase, proved to depend on the valence of the outcome and the properties of the attribution. Respondents who were given failure feedback and who attributed this failure to internal-stable-global factors

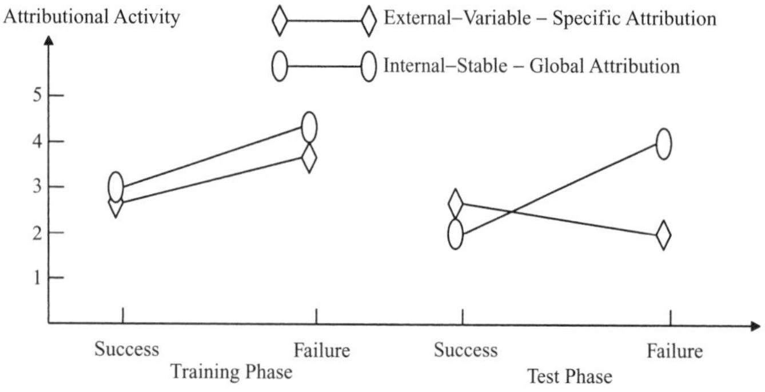

Figure 14.4 Level of attributional activity during the training and test phases as a function of success or failure and attributional style.

put much more thought into the causes of this outcome than did respondents in the other three groups. A comparison of the intensity of attributional activity immediately after feedback and in the second phase of the experiment shows a decrease from the training phase to the test phase for respondents who succeeded on the tasks, as well as for those who failed, and who attributed that failure to external-variable-specific causes. For those who attributed failure to internal-stable-global causes, however, only a very slight decrease in the intensity of attributional activity was identified. These findings are in line with the predictions of the stage model of attributional activity, which states that attributional activity is terminated when a cause is identified, except if failure is attributed to stable and uncontrollable causes, such as lack of ability (an internal-stable cause).

Incidentally, the stage model of attributional activity presented here is congruent with certain assumptions of the **theory of action control** proposed by Kuhl (1983; see also Kuhl & Kazen, 2003). In this model, Kuhl distinguishes two basic modes of action control, which he calls action and state orientation (Chapter 12). Action orientation is present when attention is divided more or less equally between the following four domains:

1. the desired goal state,
2. the current state,
3. the discrepancy between the goal state and the actual state, and
4. potential actions in one's repertoire to overcome this discrepancy.

Causal search is part of the analysis of the current state. It can also help to describe the discrepancy between the current and the goal state, and is certainly important when it comes to exploring potential options for action. Especially if the pursuit of a certain goal has resulted in failure in the past, a thorough analysis of the causes for this failure is vital. Only then will it be possible to identify an appropriate new course of action. If, on the other hand, the cause of the failure has already been established, any further **causal rumination** will no longer be action oriented. Rather, analysis of the actual state will be an end in itself – potential options for action will no longer be subject to feasibility testing, neither will the appropriateness of aspired goal states be evaluated. Attention will be focused entirely on the analysis of the current state; i.e., a failure-centered state orientation will ensue. The following example illustrates this kind of situation. A respondent experiences failure in an experiment, then participates in another experiment that has nothing in common with the first. If, while working on the second experiment, thoughts keep returning to the causes for his or her failure in the first experiment, although there is no way of going back to these tasks, his or her thinking about the causes of failure represents a state orientation. If, on the other hand, the first experiment continued after the failure feedback, and the respondent expected to be administered more of the same kind of

tasks, thinking about the causes of failure (i.e., causal search) would represent an action orientation.

SUMMARY

The conclusions to be drawn from these theoretical reflections and empirical studies on causal search and causal rumination are as follows. If we wish to explain when attributional activity is instigated, its duration and intensity, and the motives underlying it, it makes sense to distinguish between different stages of the attributional process. Moreover, the attributional activity that can be observed at different stages of the process may have different functions. Unquestionably, causal search serves the function of rendering the world we live in controllable and predictable. Thus, like other epistemic activities, it is initiated whenever something happens that is unexpected or contrary to our expectations, whenever our (causal) knowledge fails to provide an accurate prediction of the course of events. It is only once the causes for the unexpected outcome are identified that we are again in a position to make accurate predictions and exercise control. Causal rumination, by contrast, does not serve the primary goal of providing us with a better understanding of the environment. This goal is realized as soon as a causal inference is made. Causal rumination may help us identify new action alternatives or abandon old goals and formulate new ones. We may, however, find it very difficult to accept that we are unable to exert control in certain situations (e.g., after attributions to stable and uncontrollable causes). In these cases, our thoughts may end up "going round in circles," revolving around the causes of certain outcomes. This kind of state is certainly dysfunctional, as it does not lead to a better understanding of the world, or help us to identify productive new courses of action. In other words, it ties up attention that could be put to better use elsewhere for effective action.

14.3.3 Processes of Causal Attribution: Normative Models

Aside from the questions of when and why causal attributions are made, the main concern of attribution theories is to explain precisely how "the man or woman on the street" determines the reasons for an action or the causes of an action outcome. Whereas our focus thus far has been on the extent to which data is collected to arrive at a causal inference, we now turn to questions concerning the type of information gathered, how the information available is weighted, etc. In other words, we now consider the **process of information processing** that underlies causal attribution. Various methods and models have been proposed in this context. Heider (1958) presented some preliminary ideas, which initially failed to attract much research attention. It was not until many years later, in the late 1960s and early 1970s, that there was a veritable surge in the number of publications on matters relating to attribution theory.

Following this incubation period, Heider's (1958) book, *The Psychology of Interpersonal Relations*, stimulated a great deal of research. Attribution theory research was subsequently guided by models of information use and information processing. Aside from Heider's fundamental ideas, these included **correspondent inference theory** (Jones & Davis, 1965), Kelley's (1967) **covariation model** of causal analysis, and his model of **causal schemata** (Kelley, 1972).

These models, which have inspired a wealth of research, specify three facets of the attribution process:

1. the aspects of information utilized,
2. the causal categories available for selection, and
3. the rules for drawing inferences from the information.

The models are highly rationalistic. They are based on straightforward logic and, as research soon showed, are commonsensical (provided that respondents are not too young). Essentially, they are normative theories describing how attributions ought to be made. The models prescribe the approach to be taken by individuals seeking to arrive at "optimal" or "rational" causal inferences, and stipulate how they should decide for or against a cause. In other words, they define standards for causal attribution.

These normative theories can be contrasted with a more descriptive approach to attribution research, which investigates how people actually go about making causal attributions. The latter approach involves describing and explaining the actual process of causal ascription, and deciding whether or not the attributions made are correct. Descriptive attribution theory research has addressed numerous phenomena that explain why, in certain cases, an individual's causal attributions deviate from those made from an outsider's point of view, or those that would have been made had a normative model been applied. These phenomena include differences in the attributions of actors and observers, and apparently self-enhancing attributions. As discussed above, moreover, people do not necessarily look for the most fitting cause, but often – having weighed up the costs and benefits – terminate the attribution process as soon as they have found a causal attribution they personally consider satisfactory.

Heider's "Naive" Analysis of Action

Heider (1958) based his approach on Lewin's general behavioral equation, which states that behavior (*B*) is a function of personal (*P*) and environmental (*E*) forces: $B = f(P, E)$. Heider further subdivided each of these forces – to use his own terminology, the "effective personal force" and the "effective environmental force" – into two components. The effective personal force is composed of "trying" (which might also be called motivation) and "ability" (Heider frequently uses the more generic term "power"). Trying, in turn, is made up of two components, which are related in a multiplicative way: what people want to do (intention) and how intensively they seek to achieve it (exertion).

❗ Hence, trying is the product of intention and exertion; neither is sufficient on its own. Intention requires a minimum of exertion, and exertion requires an intention if any action is to materialize. Trying (intention times exertion) is a variable component of personal force, and ability a fixed component of personal force.

On the environmental side, there is one (fixed) primary dimension: the difficulty to be overcome in order to reach a certain goal. Chance, in the sense of good or bad luck, may have favorable or unfavorable effects from time to time on the efforts to cope with this difficulty. Thus, Heider had already identified the main causal factors cited to explain achievement-related behavior. Later elaborations by Weiner and colleagues (Weiner et al., 1971; Weiner, 1974) did not really add any significant new insights in terms of identifying causal factors relevant to the achievement context. These authors can, however, take the credit for classifying the factors identified by Heider in terms of their locus and stability. Only then was it possible to make accurate predictions of the expectancy and self-directed affect variables, both of which are influential in the context of achievement-related behavior.

❗ An important aspect of Heider's model is that a personal component and an environmental component, namely ability and difficulty, enter into a subtractive relationship, resulting in "can." "Can" is thus a function of ability minus difficulty.

Heider posits that data on all of these variables can be utilized in the analysis of action. Some of these information variables are linked to form superordinate concepts. The product of intention and exertion gives the concept of "trying" (motivation); the difference between ability and difficulty gives the concept of "can." Finally, the unspecified relationship between "trying" and "can" results in the action and its outcome. Heider's model of action analysis is shown diagrammatically in Fig. 14.5. The top row presents information about the components of personal and environmental forces, the middle row the concepts derived from them, and the bottom row the resultant action and its outcome.

THE PURPOSE OF ACTION ANALYSIS. What purpose does the analysis of action serve; which causal criteria are to be distinguished and selected? The question at issue here is whether a behavioral explanation at "first" or "second" glance is appropriate, i.e., whether an action or its outcome is more a result of personal force or environmental force or – to use Heider's distinction – whether there was personal causality (i.e., something was brought about intentionally) or impersonal causality. The answer to this seemingly simple alternative is relevant to any observer interested in rendering future events foreseeable and thus controllable. If the observer concludes that the events observed are because of the personal causality of the actor, i.e., to motives and dispositions (implying the stability of causes), then he or she can predict that the actor will behave in a similar manner in many similar situations in the future. Thus, localizing the cause within the person represents a greater information gain for the observer than

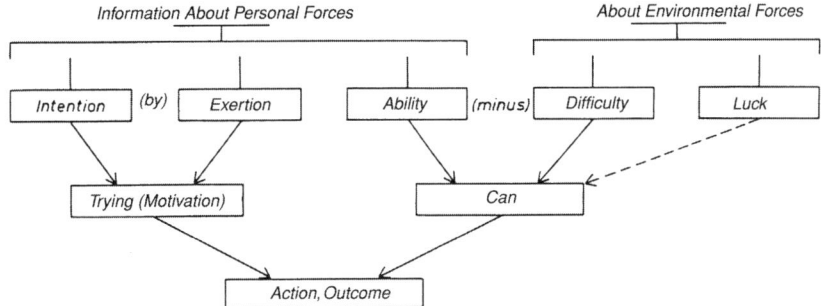

Figure 14.5 Configuration of Heider's action analysis: from information about components of personal and environmental forces (top row) via the concepts derived from them (middle row) to the resulting action and its outcome.

does inferring causality to reside in the particular situation – i.e., impersonal causality. In the first case, the observer can predict future behavior over a whole class of situations; in the second, only in a very specific situation. Therefore, if we have reason to believe that we are justified in attributing (stable) dispositions – especially (stable) motives – to others, then we have made their future behavior more predictable.

Our efforts to render future behavior more predictable might prompt us to favor localizations of causes within personal causality. Instead of the very rational analysis of causes described by Heider, our attributions might then entail a motive-related bias. For example, we may ascribe too much meaning to indications of personal causality and neglect indications of impersonal causality (i.e., that the cause resides in the specific situation). Drawing on the stage model of attributional activity described in Section 14.3.2, it seems plausible to assume that people feel attributions with few benefits (e.g., localizations of causes within specific circumstances) to be unsatisfactory, and therefore continue the causal analysis, whereas they terminate the analysis as soon as indications of personal causality are found (see also Section 14.3.4 on descriptive attribution research).

ATTRIBUTION OF ACTIONS TO PERSONAL CAUSALITY. What are the rules that permit us to infer personal or impersonal causality from the data available about the individual components of Heider's action model? Heider provided only a few vague and general responses to this question – mostly in the form of examples. The models proposed by Jones and Davis (1965) and Kelley (1967) were intended to fill this gap and to present a formalized system of rules.

The first crucial issue in attributing personal causality to an action is whether the actor can be ascribed an intention. Three points are to be considered here:

■ Is the actor merely a marginal entity in a more comprehensive event?
■ Is the action or its outcome merely an unintended side effect or an intermediate phase of a more global intention?
■ Is the intention indeed to be carried out?

It is at this point that information about exertion and ability comes into the picture. An intention can only be inferred via the concept of trying if exertion can be observed. If it is not yet clear what should be done to implement an intention, then it is not regarded as an intention in the sense of a necessary condition for personal causality. Information about the ratio of ability to difficulty is also of major concern, i.e., whether the actor presumes him- or herself to have the necessary ability to accomplish the goal.

Following Brunswik (1952, 1956), Heider emphasized the importance of the observed equifinality of an individual's action for inferring intentions that reflect personal motive dispositions. Such motive-indicative equifinality exists when an individual chooses different action paths in different situational conditions, each leading to the same goal. This approach to inferring intentions and motives was expanded and formalized by Jones and Davis (1965) with their model of correspondent inferences (see the following page).

The inclusion of the environmental factor "difficulty" in the analysis of action presented in Fig. 14.5 risks limiting the analysis to achievement-related behavior. Heider by no means restricted himself to this class of phenomena, however. For example, the attractiveness of a certain object can also represent an environmental force. The extensive quote from Heider's analysis of the "attribution of desire and pleasure" that follows is offered here in support of this point. At the same time, it gives an impression of Heider's way of analyzing phenomena, and explicates another approach – the individual differences approach – that can be used to differentiate between personal and impersonal causality.

To quote from Heider (1958):

We shall start with the data pattern fundamental in the determination of attribution, namely: that the condition will be held responsible for an effect which is present when the effect is present and which is absent when the effect is absent. This principle underlies Mill's methods of experimental enquiry.

Now let us see how this principle operates in the case of the attribution of enjoyment to the object. If I always experience enjoyment when I interact with an object, and something other than enjoyment when the object is removed (longing, annoyance, or a more neutral reaction, for instance), then I will consider the object the cause of the enjoyment. The effect, enjoyment, is seen to vary in a highly coordinated way with the presence and absence of the object.

Now let us see how the principle operates in the attribution of enjoyment to the person. If I sometimes enjoy the object and sometimes do not, then the effect varies, not with the object, but with something within me. I may or may not be able to define that something, but I know that the effect has to do with some fluctuating personal state. It may be my mood, my state of hunger, etc., which, though temporary in character, are often detectable as the conditions highly related to the effect. Notice that in this type of attribution, a temporary state and therefore a more or less nondispositional property of the person is singled out as the source of the pleasure.

When enjoyment is attributed to a dispositional property of the person, additional data pertaining to the reactions of other people are necessary. Concretely, if I observe that not all people enjoy the object, then I may attribute the effect to individual differences. That is to say, the effect, enjoyment in this case, depends upon who the person is. With **o**, enjoyment is present, with **q**, it is absent. We sometimes, then, speak about differences in taste. The important point is that the presence and absence of the enjoyment is not correlated with the presence and absence of the object, but rather with the presence and absence of different people. Therefore, **o** is felt to enjoy **x** and **q** to be dissatisfied with **x** because of the kind of person each is." (Heider, 1958, pp. 152–153)

❶ Interindividual behavioral consistency is thus a crucial key to the localization of cause. Its presence indicates that it is a particular object – an impersonal causality – that has prompted the behavior.

Kelley (1967) picked up on this criterion and formalized it as a critical dimension ("consensus") of his covariation model in which causes are localized on the side of the person or the environment. Kelley's model and the model by Jones and Davis represent a kind of "division of labor" inasmuch as they focus on opposing aspects of causal localization – Jones and Davis on behavioral explanations "at first glance" (the person), and Kelley on behavioral explanations "at second glance" (the situation).

Another difference is also worthy of note. Jones and Davis deal exclusively with attribution of motivation – in other words, not with the causes of action outcomes, but with the reasons for which an action is undertaken. Besides enduring dispositions (which, like motives, represent "personal causes" in the sense of individual differences), these reasons include transitory intentions. Kelley, on the other hand, was less concerned with the actor's reasons (intentions) than with the causal basis for judgment, events, or action outcomes. He was particularly concerned with assigning relative weights to enduring characteristics of the person or the concrete situation (as well as to transitory situational circumstances). But Kelley's model also includes attribution of motivation, namely, in those situations where the "cause" of an action is attributed to an actor's enduring disposition. The two models are presented in more detail below.

Jones' and Davis' Model of Correspondent Inferences

In their paper "From Acts to Dispositions," Jones and Davis (1965) delineated a model articulating how people infer the intentions, motives, and attitudes of others from their actions. Inference of this kind represents the greatest information gain for an observer seeking to predict someone's future activities. Insights into people's intentions are also at the core of explanations and evaluations of past actions, such as those undertaken by parliamentary fact-finding committees or juries in criminal trials. The apportioning of responsibility and punishment hinges on the extent to which the author of the action outcome under investigation can be attributed intent. As a rule, those who judge such actions do not observe them directly, but instead rely on reports about the actions or even just their outcomes.

We thus start from the facts – an action or at least its outcome. Three steps are required to draw retrospective inferences about dispositions; these steps may, but need not, lead to an **attribution of intention**.

FIRST STEP IN THE ATTRIBUTION OF INTENTION. This first step consists in confirming two prerequisites without which the actor cannot have acted with intent. First, he or she must have had prior knowledge about the outcome of the action. Second, he or she must have the ability to bring about the result. If the first condition is not fulfilled, the unforeseen event could not have been intended. If the second condition is not fulfilled, any attribution of this outcome to the actor is doubtful. Looking at Fig. 14.6, what is being confirmed are the two arrows leading from "trying" and from "can" to "action, outcome."

SECOND STEP IN THE ATTRIBUTION OF INTENTION. Once we are certain or can assume that these two prerequisites are met, the second step is to determine which consequences – or effects – of the action outcome might have motivated the actor to bring about this particular outcome. To avoid total reliance on speculation, it may be useful to bear in mind that every action initially involved a choice among various alternatives, at the very least the choice of action or not acting. The assumed effects of such alternatives can then be listed. Those effects that are common to all action alternatives cannot have influenced the actor's choice. Only the "noncommon effects" of the chosen action alternatives can have played

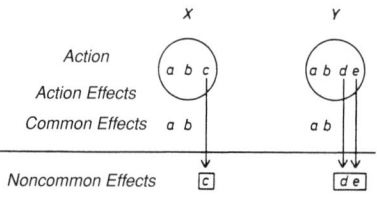

Figure 14.6 Common and noncommon effects of two action alternatives, X and Y.

an influential role. The smaller the number of noncommon effects of the chosen action alternative – in the best case, there will just be one – the less equivocal the inference about the relevant intention will be. Fig. 14.6 illustrates this step for two actions – X and Y – with three and four effects, respectively, where two are common effects. If X is chosen, there is only one noncommon effect, c. It must have been this effect that prompted the choice of X over Y. If, on the other hand, Y is chosen, there are two noncommon effects, d and e, and it remains unclear which of the two was decisive. (This procedure is similar to Irwin's, 1971, analysis of intentional behavior).

Even if we identify a single noncommon effect for the chosen action, however, we cannot presume with certainty that the intention is the manifestation of a personal disposition. It could be an effect favored by all or most individuals in a particular reference group. In this case, the action is motivated by the generally desirable incentive value of its goal object. The action arises more from the peculiarity of the goal object and less from the person's disposition.

For example, we might meet two individuals at an exhibition of modern art: one an art historian, the other a task inspector. Without hesitation, we would attribute the art historian's presence to a typical, "category-based" interest in art, or to the exhibit's unique appeal. Our deductions in the case of the task inspector would be less trivial. Because an interest in art is not typical of this profession, this individual must be personally disposed to appreciate modern art.

❶ In general, actions corresponding to the presumed role repertoire of the actor's group provide no useful information for inferences about dispositions. We do not know whether, along with the role requirement, there was also a relevant individual disposition that precipitated the action. Conversely, knowing that somebody acted contrarily to the situationally appropriate role of his or her social group is very informative for drawing inferences about a disposition.

An example would be two politicians at an election meeting, one who advocates a position favored by those present, the other advocating an unpopular position. Because politicians need voter approval if they are to be elected, we can be more confident that the second politician seriously intends what he says.

THIRD STEP IN THE ATTRIBUTION OF INTENTION. The third and final step involves appraisal of the action outcome's general desirability for the group to which the actor belongs. Of course, such "category-based" inferences from typical members of a reference group to the individuality of the actor are fraught with uncertainty. Jones and McGillis (1976) attempted to specify the third step by splitting desirability into two determinants:

1. what is generally considered desirable by a particular culture, and

2. what is known about what the actor in question considers desirable.

Table 14.4. Correspondence of the inference from an action to the underlying intention (and personality disposition) by the number of noncommon effects of the chosen action alternative and the assumed desirability (or expected valence) of these effects

		Desirability of the noncommon effects (or expected valence)	
		High	Low
Number of noncommon effects	High	Trivial ambiguity	Interesting ambiguity
	Low	Trivial clarity	High correspondence

Based on Jones & Davis, 1965, p. 229.

Furthermore, both types of desirability are weighted in terms of their chances of implementation. Thus, in the sense of expectancy-value theories, desirability is conceptualized as "expected valence."

With these three steps, it is possible to determine the inferred correspondence between the action observed and the underlying intention as an expression of a personal disposition.

❶ The smaller the number of noncommon effects of the chosen action alternative, and the lower the presumed desirability (or expected valence) of the noncommon action effects, the closer the correspondence will be.

The cross-classification in Table 14.4 shows the four possible combinations of high and low levels of the two determinants of inferences. Only one combination results in high correspondence, providing some assurance that inferences made about the actor's intentions and relevant personal dispositions are valid. This is the only case in which the theory of correspondent inferences leads to a clear information gain.

To date, there have been rather few empirical tests of the model. See study on the following page for an illustrative example.

Kelley's Covariation Model

This model takes its name from the notion that an effect covaries with its cause. The effect is present when the cause is present, and absent when the cause is absent.

In his influential 1967 paper, Kelley outlined the differences between his model and that proposed by Jones and Davis. Whereas Jones and Davis wish to determine what inferences can be drawn on the person side, specifically about personal dispositions, Kelley examines the available information to see whether the causes of an action or its outcome can be localized in the environment, or whether it is necessary to see the person as the source of causation – perhaps even the exclusive source. In contrast to Jones and Davis, the information assessed in Kelley's model does not relate to a single person's single action, but to several actions carried out by

STUDY

Study on the Attribution of Attitudes

Jones, Worchel, Goethals, and Grumet (1971) presented their respondents with an essay arguing for or against the use of marijuana. They were asked to assess how deep-seated the author's attitudes were. Two further pieces of information were given, relating to the two determinants of the model:

- The number of uncommon effects was varied by telling participants that the writer had produced the essay voluntarily or under pressure (in the latter case, there were a number of reasons for writing the essay, some related to the issue itself and some that induced the individual to succumb to the pressure).

- The degree of desirability was manipulated by providing additional information about the author's attitudes toward leading his or her own life, being the master of his or her own fate, etc.

If the author strongly subscribes to these kinds of attitudes, he is also likely to be in favor of the free use of marijuana. The results were in line with the correspondence model. If the author had freely chosen to write the essay and had taken a position that deviated from the expected desirability – in other words, if the number of uncommon effects and their desirability was rather low – he was seen as having a more pronounced attitude.

the same person and other persons over time, as well as to actions geared at different goal objects under a variety of circumstances. Because the information material is extended over four dimensions (persons, points in time, goal objects, and circumstances), Kelley can make extensive use of what he calls the "covariation principle," i.e., John Stewart Mill's "method of difference," which holds "that the condition will be responsible for an effect which is present when the effect is present and which is absent when the effect is absent" (Heider, 1958, p. 152).

Hamilton (1980) called attention to another difference between the two models. He sees Kelley's model – which varies persons, entities, and points in time systematically – as a typical scientific analysis, and the model by Jones and Davis – which focuses on just one person and asks whether that person might have acted differently – as a decidedly juridical approach. In other words, we might see Kelley's "intuitive scientist" as a counterpart to Jones' and Davis' "intuitive attorney."

In Kelley's covariation analysis, the cause of a given action (dependent variable) is deduced from the covariation pattern of four criterion dimensions (independent variables; see the following overview).

Criterion Dimensions of Kelley's Covariation Analysis

1. Distinctiveness of entities

    Is the action also triggered by other entities? By entities, Kelley means goal objects or other persons toward whom the action is directed.

2. Consensus between different persons

    Do other persons act in the same manner?

3. Consistency across time

    Does the person always act in this manner?

4. Consistency across modalities

    Does the same action occur when the entity is embedded in other circumstances?

In all cases of high distinctiveness, an individual will respond to the entity in a highly specific manner. If there is a high level of consensus, the individual's reaction to an entity will be similar to that of most other people. If consistency across time is high, the person will react in the same manner whenever that entity is encountered. If there is consistency across modalities, they will act in that manner under varied circumstances.

EXAMPLE

If someone who particularly enjoyed a certain movie recommends that I go and see it, I must decide whether this recommendation is based on the entity (quality of the movie) or attributable to the person (as one who is easily pleased). If I know that this individual reacts very specifically to different movies (distinctiveness), that he has gone to see the movie several times (consistency across time), that he has seen an adaptation for television by the same director (consistency across modalities), and that his judgment is consistent with that of others who have seen the movie (consensus), then I am willing to attribute his recommendation to the entity (i.e., the movie must be worth seeing). If, on the other hand, someone indiscriminately recommends all movies, some of which I like and some of which I do not, and if other people have a different opinion, then I will attribute the recommendations to the peculiarities of the person (e.g., their personal taste).

Kelley likened the procedure resulting in such inferences to a simple and incomplete analysis of the variance of data that can evidently be carried out by anyone. He portrays the potential pattern of covariations (Kelley, 1967) using a variance-analytical cube with three major criterion dimensions: entities, time, and persons (Fig. 14.7). The shaded areas of the left-hand cube (Fig. 14.7a) represent the case in which I attribute the first person's movie recommendation (in the example above) to the entity (E_1) and not to the person (P_1); the shaded areas of the right-hand cube (Fig. 14.7b) represent the case in which I attribute the second person's (P_2) recommendation to that person rather than the entity. (Here, there is inconsistent behavior at one point in time, T_2.)

Kelley continues this analogy to the analysis of variance up to the F-ratio. The distinctiveness variable is the ratio's numerator, representing the between-conditions factor (entities). The denominator – an expression of "error variance" within conditions (entities) – comprises consistency and consensus as indicators of individual stability and interindividual

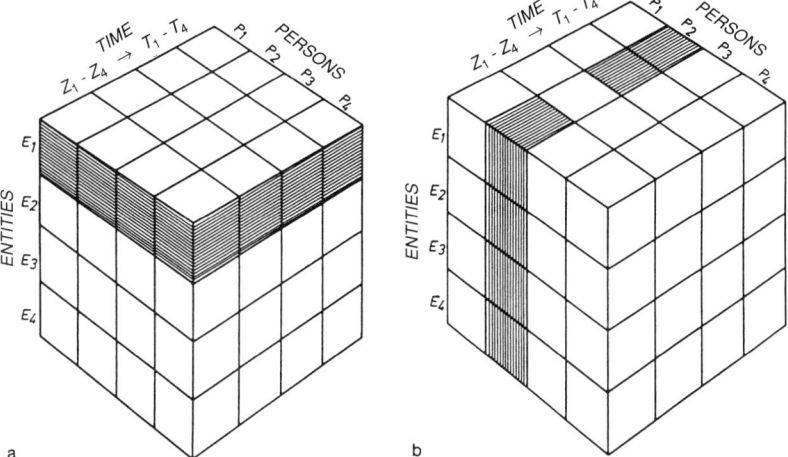

Figure 14.7 Variance-analytical cubes representing information about the covariation of actions across the three dimensions of "entities," "time," and "persons." (a) shows a data pattern indicating attribution of a person's (e.g., P_1) action to the entity E_1; (b) shows a data pattern indicating attribution of the action to the person P_2. (Based on Kelley, 1973, pp. 110, 111.)

replicability of actions. The lower the consistency and consensus (i.e., the higher their variability), the greater will be the denominator, the "error term," and the greater must be the distinctiveness value in the numerator to still localize the cause of the relevant effect within environmental events.

Kelley's conceptual framework is thus focused on possible explanations of behavior "at second glance." If an individual's behavior shows high distinctiveness across entities, and at the same time demonstrates high consensus with other individuals and high consistency over time, we can say that this person has a high "state of information regarding the world" (1967, p. 198). Of course, this would also mean that we could hardly ascribe individual dispositions and motives to that person. Table 14.5 shows the various patterns of information about actions, which, according to Kelley, lead to causes being localized in the entity, the circumstances, or the person.

It is worth noting that Kelley does not just split the causal weight between person and environment. On the side of Heider's environmental force, he distinguishes between the entity itself and the circumstances surrounding it. Whereas an entity is a constant environmental factor, circumstances can vary. For example, if someone who likes a few special movies (high distinctiveness) that others tend to dislike (low consensus), but occasionally cannot stand one of these otherwise favored movies (low consistency), we would tend to suspect that this reaction, which deviates from that person's typical behavior, was brought on by the circumstances.

EMPIRICAL SUPPORT FOR THE COVARIATION MODEL. Kelley's covariation principles assume information processing to be purely logical and statistical. There is no need for psychological contemplation; a simple computer program would suffice. One might well question whether attributors really proceed in such a logical and statistical manner in their localization of causes when presented with an action episode along with covariation information about its consensus, distinctiveness, and consistency. McArthur (1972, 1976) investigated this question empirically. In the first of her studies, McArthur (1972) presented her respondents with an episodic statement such as the following: "George translated the sentence incorrectly." In addition, supplementary information was provided on each of the three criterion dimensions (high or low levels of each were induced, giving a total of eight different combinations or patterns of information).

- Consensus: "Almost everyone (hardly anyone) translates the sentence incorrectly."
- Distinctiveness: "George translates hardly any other (almost every) sentence incorrectly."
- Consistency: "In the past George has almost always (almost never) translated the sentence incorrectly."

Based on this information, respondents had to decide whether it was something about the person, the entity, or the specific circumstance – or a combination of these – that had caused the action outcome (or instigated the reaction in the case of actions, feelings, and opinions).

Table 14.5. Information about actions that, according to Kelley's covariation model, lead to the action's cause being localized in the entity, the circumstances, or the person

Localization of the cause in	Information about distinctiveness (across entities)	Consensus (across persons)	Consistency (across time)
Entity	High	High	High
Circumstance	High	Low	Low
Person	Low	Low	High

Table 14.6. Percentage (rounded) of the total variance in casual attributions to persons, entities, and circumstances accounted for by the three criterion dimensions of distinctiveness, consensus, and consistency

Criterion dimension	Causal attribution				
	Entity	Circumstance	Person	Person and entity	Overall
Distinctiveness	12	8	22	0	10
Consensus	5	0	6	1	3
Consistency	6	41	16	16	20

Based on McArthur, 1972, p. 182.

Interestingly, the results show that the cause was most frequently attributed to the person. The same held for a control group given the statements without the supplementary information. As will be discussed in more depth below, this preference for an explanation "at first glance" typically applies to observations made from the perspective of the observer, as described by Jones and Nisbett (1971). Not infrequently, participants invoked a combination of causes, almost always "person and entity," i.e., an explanation of behavior "at third glance." Because the experiment was limited to attributions of others' behavior, the findings cannot be generalized to self-observations.

A glance at the findings presented in Table 14.6 shows that causal attribution is far more influenced by consistency information (20% of the explained variance) than it is by distinctiveness (10%) or consensus information (3%). The weak influence of consensus information has been confirmed in other studies on the attribution of others' behavior (McArthur, 1976; Nisbett & Borgida, 1975; Orvis, Cunningham, & Kelley, 1975). In a series of studies on self-attribution, moreover, Nisbett, Borgida, Crandall, and Reed (1976), found consensus information to have no effect (see also Feldman, Higgins, Karlovac, & Ruble, 1976). Consequently, Ruble and Feldman (1976) demonstrated that the effects of consensus information are subject to a position effect. When consensus information was provided at the end of the experimental procedure rather than at the beginning (as was the case in the other studies mentioned) it was almost as effective as consistency and distinctiveness information (recency effect). Its salience can also be enhanced by mentioning the representativeness of the reference group in question (Wells & Harvey, 1977).

Thus, previous studies (e.g., Hansen & Stonner, 1978) show that, as predicted by the covariation model, consensus information may be used to attribute the behavior of others if it is salient and seems representative. Consensus information is remarkably neglected in self-attributions, however. This finding touches again on the discrepancy in observational perspectives discussed by Jones and Nisbett (1971).

❗ What is more important in the present context is the impact of the total pattern of information on causal attribution from the observational perspective. Empirical evidence confirms the covariation model, i.e., the relationships portrayed in Table 14.5. Person attribution occurs most frequently in the case of low distinctiveness, low consensus, and high consistency. Distinctiveness information is most decisive here (22% of the total variance, see Table 14.6), followed by consistency information (16%). Entity attribution is most frequent in conjunction with high distinctiveness, high consensus, and high consistency. Attribution to circumstances is most frequent if distinctiveness is high and consistency low; consensus plays no role here.

FÖRSTERLING'S ELABORATION OF THE MODEL. Since it was first proposed several decades ago, Kelley's covariation model (Kelley, 1967, 1973) has been the subject of much theoretical analysis and empirical testing, leading to numerous elaborations and specifications of the model (e.g., Pruitt & Insko, 1980; Cheng & Novick, 1990a, b; Försterling, 1989; for a summary, see Försterling, 2001). The major point of all these elaborations is that Kelley's model – if it is to be regarded as a "naive analysis of variance" – does not include all of the information necessary for an analysis of variance to be performed. Essentially, it permits only an analysis of the main effects:

- Are, for example, stable-person dispositions responsible or not?
- Are stable characteristics of the entity responsible or not?
- Are the specific circumstances prevailing at the time of the event responsible or not?

The analysis of interactions is not possible, however. For example, it would not be possible to determine whether an effect was caused by a combination of certain person factors, on the one hand, and specific properties of the entity, on the other.

Försterling (1989) therefore expanded on Kelley's original idea of regarding the attribution process as a "naive analysis of variance" to propose a full-blown ANOVA model (from Analysis of Variance in statistics; see the study on the next page). This model views the possible causes (person, entity, and circumstance) as independent variables, and the observable effects as dependent variables. In its simplest form, this gives a 2 (persons) × 2 (entities) × 2 (circumstances) experimental design, i.e., two people act with respect to two entities at two points in time. An example would be two students sitting for an exam in two different subjects at two points in time. The dependent variable (the observable effects) would be the students' performance on the two exams at both points in time.

STUDY

Experimental Testing of the ANOVA Model

Försterling (1989) tested his ANOVA model in a study in which students were instructed to imagine they were on a strange planet and did not know how things were causally related. They were asked to imagine they were, for the first time, observing two people playing two different video games on two different days. The students were then informed about both players' performance (success or failure) on both games on both days. To this end, all of the information specified in the ANOVA model was provided in table form. The respondents were instructed to analyze the data carefully and then to gauge the importance of certain causes named by the experimenter (the main effects: person, entity, time; the two-way interactions of person and entity, person and time, and entity and time; and the three-way interaction of person, entity, and time) in explaining the pattern of results presented. The findings of this study were entirely consistent with the predictions of the ANOVA model. If the data were indicative of a main effect, this effect was, for the most part, correctly identified as being particularly important. Likewise, when the data pointed to an interaction effect, this effect was identified correctly. Thus, the attributions made by individuals provided with a full set of covariation information are remarkably consistent with the ANOVA model.

We would not be far off the mark in spontaneously comparing the task administered to Försterling's participants to a brain-teaser. Whether his experiment has ecological validity is an entirely different question. Is it really conceivable that the much cited "man or woman on the street" takes such a logical and statistical approach to establishing the reasons for his or her behavior or that of others, or to determining the causes for the events observed or experienced in everyday life? This would seem unlikely for various reasons:

- the available information is, as a rule, incomplete, and
- we do not tend to observe different people doing different things at different points in time.

Although it may theoretically be possible to procure the necessary information, we are unlikely – unless our interest is professional – to do so, because it would incur a great deal of time and effort. Moreover, if we did go to the trouble of making the necessary inquiries, we would likely be considered highly inquisitive, which is not a socially desirable characteristic.

Unless the anticipated costs of obtaining the necessary information are in reasonable proportion to the expected benefits of making an accurate causal inference, we will be content to make attributions – that may then be less accurate – without access to the full set of covariation information (see Section

14.3.2 on the stage model of attributional activity). This is probably the more functional choice, however. What would be the point of a meticulous causal analysis that takes so long that, by the time it has been completed, the window of opportunity for appropriate action has closed?

SUMMARY

Kelley's covariation model and its various elaborations are normative models describing how people are expected to go about causal search, and the attributions they are expected to make, when certain consensus, distinctiveness, and consistency information is available and the aim is to draw a logical, stringent conclusion. However, it tells us nothing about how the search for causality actually proceeds, or about the attributions actually made, in everyday life. The findings of McArthur and Försterling provide no new insights here. They merely confirm that people are able to make causal attributions that correspond with Kelley's model, i.e., that they are intellectually capable of evaluating the available covariation information and of using it to determine the causes of outcomes and events.

In everyday situations, however, we cannot consult a table (cf. Försterling, 1989) that contains all the necessary covariation information and thus permits unambiguous attributions. Neither do we find ourselves on a strange planet, knowing nothing about the living conditions there; rather, we perceive any available covariation information against the background of years of experience. As a rule, we first have to procure this information, and to invest a certain amount of time and effort in doing so. Moreover, because attributions in everyday life tend to have personal implications (at least for the way we act), the attribution process may be influenced by certain motivational biases. As mentioned above, people may be less interested in a rational explanation of causes than in one that is satisfying to them personally.

Despite these criticisms, Kelley's covariation model has the indisputable advantage of describing a method that can be adopted when we wish to make rational and accurate causal inferences. It has important implications for therapeutic applications, pointing to strategies that might be fruitfully applied in cognitive behavioral therapy with depressive patients or helpless students, for example (Section 14.4.2).

Configuration Concepts: Kelley's Causal Schemata

The covariation analysis of causes for action discussed above presupposes various data inputs. In many everyday situations, these data are not available, or we do not have the time to gather and analyze them (see above). If the information available is incomplete, the attributor can apply specific configuration concepts concerning the coaction of various causes, the "causal schemata" proposed by Kelley (1971, 1972, 1973). For example, if someone has solved a problem that we know was very difficult, we assume their success was from high ability. In other words, the successful action outcome

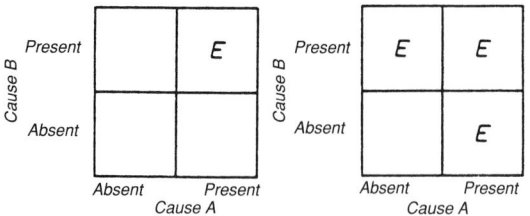

Figure 14.8a,b Causal schemata for (a) "multiple necessary causes" and (b) "multiple sufficient causes" of an effect (E) where two causes (A, B) play a role. (Based on Kelley, 1972, pp. 2, 6.)

has an inhibitory cause, high-task difficulty, and a facilitative cause, high ability. Facilitative and inhibitory causes need not be split among the person and the environment, as in this example; they may both be localized within the person or within the environment.

Aside from distinguishing between facilitative vs. inhibitory and internal vs. external causes, Kelley (1972) introduced two configuration concepts reflecting possible links between causes that can serve to bring about an effect:

- Causal schema of "multiple necessary causes"

   All facilitative causes must be present at the same time if the effect is to occur. Fig. 14.8a,b illustrates this causal schema for two causes, A and B. Effect (E) occurs only in the presence of both A and B (Fig. 14.8a). If this causal schema is salient, we can immediately infer the presence of A and B once the effect has occurred, without having to identify the two causes separately.

- Causal schema of "multiple sufficient causes"

   In this case, only one facilitative cause is required to bring about the effect (Fig. 14.8b), but here, there is no basis for inferring which of the possible facilitative causes is present.

Which causal schema should be invoked when? Attributors evidently develop certain experienced-based rules here. Rare and unusual events (or particularly significant ones; Cunningham & Kelley, 1975) are likely to be attributed to multiple necessary causes. Several causes must coincide and be multiplicatively intertwined for events of this kind to occur. An example would be success on a very difficult task or failure on a very easy one. Two facilitative internal causes, high ability and high effort, must have been simultaneously present in the first, but not in the second case. More common effects, such as success on an easy task or failure on a difficult one, suggest a causal schema of multiple sufficient causes. To succeed on a simple task, just one of the two facilitative causes, either ability or effort, will suffice; to fail on a difficult task, the absence of just one of the two facilitative causes is sufficient to prevent us from overcoming the inhibitory cause (high-task difficulty).

DISCOUNTING PRINCIPLE. How, though, do we determine which of two facilitative causes was present in the case of multiple sufficient causes? Further information about the occurrence of the effect in question does not help us to answer this

question, because one or the other facilitative cause may have been present at every recurrence of the effect (e.g., success on an easy task). According to Kelley (1972, 1973), whenever unidirectional causes are indivisible, the attributor will invoke a **discounting principle**, whereby "the role of a given cause in producing a given effect is discounted if other plausible causes are also present" (1972, p. 113). (This principle is also consistent with the logic of the variance-analytical model.) We are dealing here with the same phenomenon that Jones and Davis (1965), in their model of correspondent inferences, identified as a determinant for attributing an action to an underlying disposition: the number of uncommon effects. The presence of more than one uncommon effect for a chosen action alternative also confronts the attributor with the indivisibility of multiple sufficient causes. It remains uncertain which of the dispositions associated with the various uncommon effects actually instigated the action. A direct correspondence between action and disposition cannot be established.

The greater the number of sufficient causes (or effects), the stronger the discounting of individual causes among several plausible ones (or of an individual uncommon effect among several plausible ones) will be. The only thing that might clarify the situation is a differentiation of the causal schema for the effect in question by multiple observations of covariations among entities, circumstances, times, and persons, i.e., the ongoing formation and testing of psychological hypotheses. Furthermore, it would be interesting to find out which of two possible facilitative causes is more strongly discounted by the attributor, if one of them pertains to the person and the other to the environment. This would show whether attributors tend to use explanations "at first or second glance." Discounting the environmental cause would indicate a preference for explanations "at first glance," the approach typically taken by external observers, as described by Jones and Nisbett (1971; cf. also Jones, 1976). Ross (1977) calls this bias the **fundamental attribution error**. Heider (1958, p. 54) had already called attention to it in stating that "behavior engulfs the field."

AUGMENTATION PRINCIPLE. Causal inferences may also involve the complement of the discounting principle, namely, the **augmentation principle** (Kelley, 1971).

❗ The augmentation principle holds that a facilitative cause gains salience whenever it is confronted by an inhibitory cause; e.g., difficulties, risks, and the need to make sacrifices in the run up to the action goal.

There is an exact analogy to the Jones and Davis model of correspondent inferences here as well, namely, the determinant of desirability. The less socially desirable a pursued goal appears to be (e.g., because it contravenes prescribed roles), the more the relevant internal causes will be augmented and the behavior ascribed to a personal

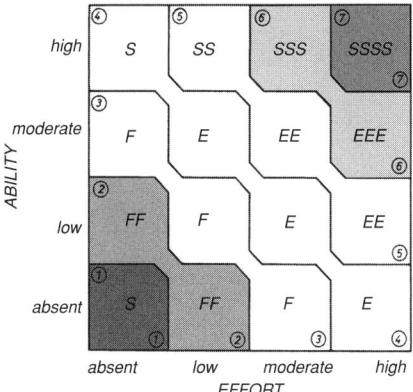

Figure 14.9 Causal schema for graded effects of achievement behavior and compensatory causes, i.e., for success at increasing levels of difficulty (*S*, *SS*, etc.) and for failure at decreasing levels of difficulty (*F*, *FF*, etc.), with four distinct levels of two additive, mutually compensating, causal factors: ability and effort.

disposition rather than to the demand characteristics of the situation.

Experimental demonstrations of causal schemata are usually hypothetical in nature; i.e., they are based on prepared statements from which participants have to select a single cause. Experimental procedures of this kind have justifiably been criticized for their unrealistic presentation of pre-arranged information and their semantic triviality (Fiedler, 1982; and a critique by Shaklee, 1983). Major (1980) gave respondents access to an array of information material before asking them to make an attribution decision for a behavioral event described. Her respondents made only limited use of this information. They much preferred consistency information over distinctiveness and consensus information. Attributions were only moderately consistent with Kelley's covariation model.

CAUSAL SCHEMA FOR GRADUATED EFFECTS. Kelley (1973) went on to analyze further causal schemata. The schemata for necessary and sufficient causes are merely two special cases of a more global schema that is not based solely on the presence or absence of a cause. This schema for graduated (additive or multiplicative) effects has more in common with everyday thinking, because it takes differences in the strength of individual causes into account. Causal schemata of graduated effects are often decisive in achievement behavior, where the effects are success and failure. The graduation of these effects depends on the level of task difficulty. The success effect grows with increasing difficulty level (Fig. 14.9: *S*, *SS*, *SSS*), the failure effect diminishes with decreasing difficulty level (*F*, *FF*, *FFF*). Facilitative causes for success effects are ability and effort, which can be mutually compensating. This also means that both causes are necessary for most effect levels, i.e., neither can be totally absent. Task difficulty, in contrast, is an inhibiting factor for success effects. To this extent, the graded

effects of success and failure correspond to the risk-taking model, i.e., the proportionate relationship between difficulty and success incentive and the inversely proportionate relationship between difficulty and failure incentive.

The matrix in Fig. 14.9 represents a compensatory causal scheme for seven graded effects (*FFF*; *FF*; *F*; *S*; *SS*; *SSS*; *SSSS*) corresponding to seven levels of difficulty, where – at most difficulty levels – neither of the two facilitative causes (ability and effort) is sufficient, but both are required to bring about success (the exception being difficulty level 4). The intensity of each cause has four levels and is additively (not multiplicatively) linked to that of the other cause. At the level of intermediate difficulty, level 4, there are two combinations where the two causes are linked by a scheme of multiple sufficient causes (the cells in the top left and bottom right corners in Fig. 14.9). Here, one cause is absent, while the other is maximally evident. By contrast, success at very high levels of difficulty (levels 6 and 7) and failure at very low levels of difficulty (levels 1 and 2) constitute unusual effects (shaded fields). In both cases, the scheme of necessary causes is particularly pronounced.

Ambiguity arises when the strength of neither causal factor is known. This invites attribution biases (thereby constituting individual differences in motivation, as we will see later). This ambiguity applies to success at various levels of difficulty (levels 4 to 6). For example, individuals can attribute their success at difficulty level 6 (*SSS*) either to high ability and moderate effort or to moderate ability and high effort. The analog holds for failure at various levels of difficulty (levels 2 and 3). A failure at difficulty level 2 (*FF*) can either be ascribed to low ability and lack of effort, or to lack of ability and low effort.

The matrix in Fig. 14.9 can explicate three different schemata of the superordinate causal scheme of graduated effects:

1. Comparison of results at various levels of difficulty (rows or columns) reveals covariation between the intensity of one cause and the strength of the effect, while the other cause remains constant. This can be described as simple covariation (between a single cause and its effect) and holds when a cause (such as ability) remains constant and an improved outcome can only be achieved through increased effort.

2. If clearly unequal effects are compared – i.e., those at least two difficulty levels apart – then both causes can covary with increasing intensity of effect (along the diagonals from lower left to upper right), with both causes contributing proportionately to the increased effect. This can be described as a scheme of combined covariation (with the effect). This combined covariation, like its simple counterpart, serves as a basis for predicting effects when the strength of both causes is known.

3. If, on the other hand, a given effect is to be explained (the diagonals from the top left to the bottom right in Fig. 14.9), then the strength of the two causes is inversely proportionate. This represents a compensatory causal scheme (between two facilitative causes). In the case of effort compensation, given differences in ability are offset by a corresponding increase in the effort to attain a particular effect. In the case of ability compensation, given differences in effort are offset by corresponding differences in ability.

14.3.4 Processes of Causal Attribution: Descriptive Perspectives

Motivational Bias

The findings presented thus far give the impression that causal attribution is a logical and rational affair. The fictitious scenarios commonly presented to participants in experimental settings doubtlessly contribute to this impression. When it comes to establishing the reasons for our own behavior, however, the causes determined affect us personally. If something touches on our self-esteem, self-serving interests may distort the logical and rational use of information.

❶ Motivational biases in attribution have frequently been investigated and ascertained. Such biases are particularly noticeable after success and failure. They are also apparent in the perspective discrepancy between self-assessment and assessment by others, as well as in the use of consensus information. They are reflected in enduring work habits and in "learned helplessness." They influence feelings of responsibility and culpability.

The first finding often cited in support of the argument that attributions of one's own behavior or self-generated outcomes are subject to a self-serving bias is that people tend to take credit for their successes, but to attribute failures to external causes (e.g., Luginbuhl, Crowe, & Kahan, 1975; Stiensmeier-Pelster, Kammer, & Adolphs, 1988; Poppe, Stiensmeier-Pelster, and Pelster, 2005).

In a study by Poppe and colleagues (2005), respondents of different ages and occupational backgrounds were asked how they would attribute success and failure in various real-life situations. The respondents then rated these causes in terms of their locus, stability, and globality. The results are presented in Table 14.7. A tendency toward self-serving attributions emerged for all three attribution dimensions. Specifically, successes are more likely than failures to be attributed to internal, stable, and global causes.

Miller and Ross (1975) cast doubt on the interpretation that this asymmetry in attributions after success and failure derives from self-enhancing or self-protecting tendencies, and proposed three reasons for a rational, nonmotivational bias in information processing:

1. People intend and expect their endeavors to produce success and not failure; accordingly, they are more likely to take responsibility for expected than for unexpected outcomes.

Table 14.7. Means and standard deviations (in brackets) of locus, stability, and globality ratings by positive and negative situations

Attribution dimension	Positive situations	Negative situations
Internality	76.1 (11.0)	65.7 (11.0)
Stability	75.1 (10.7)	61.6 (12.5)
Globality	80.6 (13.5)	59.6 (15.3)

High scores indicate strong endorsement of attribution to internal, stable, or global causes. Scores range from 16 to 112. (Based on Poppe, Stiensmeier-Pelster, & Pelster, 2005.)

2. People perceive stronger covariation between their efforts and increasing successes than under conditions of repeated failure.

3. People have an erroneous conception that there is a tighter contingency between their effort and success than between their effort and failure.

Experimental testing has focused on the validity of the first two explanations (differences in expectations or in invested effort). Results show that these explanations are unable to invalidate a motivational basis for the asymmetry of self-serving attributions (cf. overview by Bradley, 1978). The first of these studies was reported by Miller (1976) himself. His respondents were asked to complete what was purported to be a test of social competence. Before scoring the test and informing participants of their success or failure, Miller told one half of the sample either that it was an extremely valid test, which tapped various desirable traits, or that it was a new test that had not yet been validated. This post hoc induction of a difference in the self-relevance of success and failure excluded the possibility of systematic differences between the experimental groups in terms of both expectations and effort (and thus their covariation with the later results). Miller found that success was attributed more to internal factors and failure more to external ones. This asymmetry was more pronounced when the test results had high self-relevance than when they had low self-relevance.

The analysis by Stevens and Jones (1976) was even more stringent. Working on the basis of Kelley's (1967) purely rational covariation model, they provided respondents with covariation information on all three dimensions. In contrast to McArthur's (1972) study, participants were not asked to interpret the behavior of others based on scenarios presented in a questionnaire, but they themselves – successfully or unsuccessfully – carried out tasks containing distinctiveness, consistency, and consensus information (each at two levels, high vs. low). Findings showed consistent deviation from a purely rational interpretation of the information as posited in Kelley's covariation model. Successful participants were more likely than unsuccessful participants to attribute their outcomes to internal sources (ability and effort) and less likely to attribute them to external sources (luck). The more often participants experienced failure when most others were successful, the more pronounced their self-serving attribution biases were. The results for a data pattern indicative of high consistency, low distinctiveness, and low consensus deviated most blatantly from the assumptions of Kelley's model. This pattern ought to be the most compelling case for a person attribution (Table 14.5). In fact, it was here that ability attribution reached its lowest point and luck attribution its highest.

> ❗ Rational information processing, as posited in Kelley's covariation model, takes place only when causes are attributed to others' behavior. In the case of self-attribution, processing seems to be biased by self-serving tendencies – especially in the case of experiences that threaten to impair self-esteem.

Self-Esteem and Attribution

Self-esteem is often assumed to have strong motivational effects on self-attribution. It therefore seems worth examining the extent to which individual differences in self-esteem or self-concept of ability contribute to the asymmetrical pattern of attribution observed after success and failure. This question has been the subject of several studies.

Taken together, the findings of these investigations show that the self-concept of ability has a marked impact on the attribution of success and failure.

STUDY

Study on Attributional Differences as a Function of the Self-Concept of Ability

In a study by Stiensmeier-Pelster (described in Chapter 6 of Stiensmeier-Pelster, 1988), fifth through seventh graders were asked to state how strongly they would attribute personal successes ("You did very well on a test") and failures ("You got a bad grade on a test") at school to their own (high or low) ability, their own (high or low) effort, task ease or difficulty, or chance (good or bad luck). Findings showed that the lower their self-concept of ability, the less students attributed success to their own (high) ability, and the more they ascribed it to task ease or good luck (Table 14.8).

Table 14.8. Correlations between level of self-concept of ability and attribution of success/failure to ability, effort, task difficulty, and luck

Attribution dimension	Self-concept of ability	
	Success	Failure
Ability	.72**	−.64**
Effort	−.19	−.04
Task difficulty	−.40**	.08
Luck	−.34*	.25*

*p < .05; **p < .001.

The reverse held after failure: the lower the students' self-concept of ability, the more likely they were to attribute failure to their (lack of) ability, and the less likely they were to ascribe it to bad luck.

Findings comparable to those of Stiensmeier-Pelster (1988) have been reported by Schwarzer and Jerusalem (1982), Stroebe, Eagly, and Stroebe (1977), Marsh, Cairns, Relich, Barnes, and Debus (1984), and Stiensmeier-Pelster, Schürmann, Eckert, and Pelster (1994). Thus, empirical research indicates that individuals with a low self-concept of ability tend to attribute failure to a personal lack of ability. By contrast, individuals with a high self-concept of ability tend to ascribe failure to external factors, such as bad luck.

These findings are very difficult to reconcile with the notion of a self-serving bias in information processing that serves to protect self-esteem. If this kind of bias were in operation, individuals with a low self-concept of ability would also tend to attribute success to high ability and failure to bad luck. This is demonstrably not the case, however.

CONSISTENCY THEORY APPROACHES. One approach that seems compatible with the hypothesis of a motivational bias in information processing can, however, is derived from consistency theory (Festinger, 1957; Heider, 1958). The "self-consistency approach" (Jones, 1973) works on the assumption that people endeavor to develop and maintain a consistent image of themselves. Accordingly, they do not necessarily strive to obtain the most complete, accurate, and realistic information about the potential causes for their successes and failures. In fact, they tend to prefer information that leads to attributions consistent with their own self-concept of ability, and to ignore information that would suggest attributions inconsistent with that self-concept.

If someone considers him- or herself very able, it will be consistent with their self-concept of ability to attribute success to high ability, and failure to external causes such as task difficulty or bad luck. If, on the other hand, someone considers him- or herself less able, it will be consistent with their low self-concept of ability to attribute success to external causes, such as luck or the ease of the task, and failure to a lack of ability.

The attributional differences observed between people with high vs. low self-concepts of ability are not necessarily the result of such efforts to achieve consistency, however. These findings can also be explained in purely rational terms, by reference to the covariation model (Kelley, 1967, 1973) described in detail above. Kelley's model predicts that outcomes will be attributed to person factors such as lack of ability when success or failure varies across persons (you succeed/fail where others do not), but remains constant across entities (you succeed/fail on other tasks as well) and time and/or circumstances (you have succeeded/failed in the past as well). Conversely, the model predicts attributions to situational factors (e.g., luck or situational circumstances) when success or failure is constant across persons (everyone else succeeds/fails as well) and entities (you succeed/fail on other tasks as well), but varies across time (in the past or in other circumstances, your outcome would have been different). The attributional differences observed as a function of the self-concept of ability can thus be explained in the following terms:

Table 14.9. Consensus, distinctiveness, and consistency information inferred by individuals with high vs. low self-concepts of ability on the basis of previous experience in the case of failure

	Self-concept of ability	
	High	Low
Consensus	High[a]	Low
Distinctiveness	High	Low
Consistency	Low	High
Cause identified	Circumstances/entity	Lack of ability

[a]For example, a person with a high self-concept of ability will perceive the level of consensus to be high (see text).

❶ In most of the studies described above, respondents were expected to explain action outcomes on the basis of very vague or nonexistent consensus, distinctiveness, and consistency information. When covariation information is lacking, people are assumed to fall back on their own experience, and to infer the missing information by comparing the action outcome in question with earlier outcomes. Because individuals with high and low self-concepts of ability are likely to have different bodies of experience, the covariation information they infer will differ, thus explaining the attributional differences observed.

Table 14.9 presents the covariation information that might be inferred in the case of failure by individuals with high vs. low self-concepts of ability. Considering what goes to make a high or low self-concept of ability, the pattern of information presented seems entirely plausible. People with low self-concepts of ability typically believe that they are not much good at many things, and therefore consider themselves less able than many other people. If they are not provided with any (objective) external covariation information (e.g., by others) in the case of failure, but have to derive it all from their own experience, they are likely to assume that many other people succeeded, and that they were among the few who failed (low consensus). Furthermore, they will see the failure as one in a long line of supposed or real (prior) failures on other tasks (low distinctiveness) as well as on similar tasks (high consistency). Based on this pattern of information, which has been inferred from prior experience, the failure is attributed to a "lack of ability."

Individuals with a high self-concept of ability, by contrast, believe that they are good at many different task domains, in fact often better than many other people. In case of failure, it will therefore be plausible for them to assume that most others failed as well (especially as others seem less able); in other words, they will perceive a high level of consensus. Furthermore, they will see the failure in contrast to earlier experiences with similar or different tasks, which will invoke a perception of high distinctiveness and low consistency. For people with a high self-concept of ability, the pattern of covariation information inferred on the basis on prior

experience makes an attribution of failure to a lack of ability unlikely. It is much more plausible that the outcome will be attributed to the circumstances or the entity (i.e., the type of task).

❶ From this perspective, attributional differences between people with high versus low self-concepts of ability are to be expected only when the covariation information inherent in the situation or provided by another instance is very vague or nonexistent, meaning that attributors have to rely on their prior experience. The more (objective and credible) covariation information people are given, the fewer attributional differences should be observed as a function of self-concept of ability. In the best case scenario, when the attributor has access to a full set of consensus, distinctiveness, and consistency information, such differences should no longer be apparent.

Perspective Discrepancy Between Actor and Observer
Causal attributions have been shown to differ depending on whether they are made from the perspective of the actor or that of the observer. Whereas actors tend to attribute their behavior and its outcomes to situation factors, i.e., to external-variable causes, observers are more likely to attribute (others') behavior to characteristics of the actor, i.e., to internal-stable causes (Jones & Nisbett, 1971). If the actor's preference for situational factors were seen as self-serving, the discrepancy between the actor and observer perspectives (Jones & Nisbett, 1971; Watson, 1982) could be explained in terms of a motivational bias in information processing. However, this explanation is not compatible with the fact that the actor generally has more information to explain his or her behavior and its outcomes than an observer. In this case, the perspective discrepancy is evidently not the result of motivationally determined attribution biases, but of attributional differences deriving from different informational input.

There seem to be two main reasons why behavior is more likely to be attributed to situation factors by the actors themselves and to person factors by observers:
- differences in the focus of attention, and
- differences in the amount of context information.

The actor's attention is focused on aspects of the situation; that of the observer, on the actor. Furthermore, the actor has far more information than the observer about the current situation (distinctiveness); its precedents and background (consistency).

The effects of this perspective discrepancy on attribution can be neatly illustrated by the example of attributional differences in the classroom on the following page.

It is worth noting that teachers who apply **individual frames of reference** (Chapter 6) are much more likely to infer variable causes for student performance than those who apply **social frames of reference**. Teachers who use an individual frame of reference evaluate student performance in terms of whether it represents an improvement or a deterioration

EXAMPLE

Teachers tend to ascribe student learning outcomes to stable student characteristics, such as high vs. low student ability. Students, on the other hand, tend to attribute their performance to internal-variable causes (lack of effort, lack of interest) or external-variable causes (luck). Bearing in mind that the teacher has comprehensive access to consensus information (he knows how all students performed) but has only a limited amount of consistency and distinctiveness information (as a rule, his knowledge of their previous outcomes and their outcomes in other subjects is insufficient), it seems quite plausible for him to attribute learning outcomes to student characteristics. This attribution is also rational within the framework of the covariation principle (the teacher attributes the effect to the cause that is present when the effect is present, and absent when the effect is absent). The student, by contrast, has superior access to distinctiveness information (the grades she obtained in other subjects) and consistency information (her previous grades). She does not, however, have immediate access to consensus information, but would first have to ask the other students how well they did. Given that her performance may differ over time, it seems quite plausible for her to attribute her outcomes to variable causes.

relative to previous outcomes. A social frame of reference, by contrast, implies a focus on how well students perform relative to their classmates. Teachers who apply individual frames of reference take a keen interest in individual students' development; they are highly sensitive to information signaling that a student's performance has improved or declined. Because this kind of approach focuses these teachers' attention on consistency information, they are more likely to attribute learning outcomes to variable factors (for a summary, see Rheinberg, 1980, 2001).

A RECONCEPTUALIZATION OF THE CONDITIONS FOR PERSPECTIVE DISCREPANCY. Monson and Snyder (1977) critically examined the findings on perspective discrepancy and established that all experimental situations in which evidence for perspective discrepancy had been found had in fact fostered its induction. The actors had not themselves brought the situations about, neither did they have the power to shape them; hence, they logically felt subjected to situational influences. Under conditions such as these, it makes perfect sense to give greater weight to situational than to person factors. Because actors are aware of the situational, experiential, and historical context of their current situation, they should be able to make more appropriate attributions than external observers, whether to situational or to person factors. Monson and Snyder postulate as follows:

> Actors should make more situational attributions than should observers about behavioral acts that are under situational control; by contrast, actors' perceptions of behavior that are under dispositional control ought to be more dispositional

than the perceptions of observers (Monson & Snyder, 1977, p. 96).

Actors will likely be more prone than observers to attribute to situational factors if the actor's behavior is:

> (a) elicited by an experimental manipulation; (b) performed in a situational context not chosen or controllable by the actor; (c) performed in the presence of facilitative situational cues provided by those aspects of the experimental manipulation designed to elicit the behavior; (d) dissimilar to previously manifested behaviors because the actor has no prior exposure to the experimental situation; (e) inconsistent with previous self-attributions because the actor has had no prior experience with the particular experimental situation; and (f) not part of an extended causal chain (Monson & Snyder, 1977, p. 101).

However, the actor's self-attributions will be more strongly person centered than those of an external observer when experimentally induced or naturally occurring situations permit the following behavior:

> (a) dispositional; (b) performed in situations chosen and/or controllable by the actor; (c) performed in the presence of neutral or inhibitory situational factors; (d) similar to previously manifested behaviors; (e) consistent with prior attributions, and (f) part of a causal chain with prior dispositional causes (Monson & Snyder, 1977, pp. 101–102).

❶ Monson's and Snyder's reconceptualization of the conditions for perspective discrepancy does not contradict the explanations of Jones and Nisbett (1971), but rather specifies when person factors come to dominate over situational factors in self-attribution. Because of the greater amount of information available to them, actors are generally better able to make appropriate attributions. Observers are always prone to the fundamental attribution error (Ross, 1977) and tend to overestimate person factors.

All conditions of perspective discrepancy analyzed thus far are rooted in information processing and not in motivational circumstances. Therefore, it is only an apparent contradiction that the actor makes fewer attribution errors than the observer in terms of the perspective discrepancy, but displays more bias than the observer in attributing self-relevant actions and their outcomes.

When the two phenomena are considered together, Monson's and Snyder's reconceptualization of perspective discrepancy shows self-serving attribution asymmetry in a new light. The latter phenomenon generally arises in highly controlled experimental situations that expose the actor to a preponderance of situational factors. Thus, the informational input itself favors attribution of unsuccessful outcomes and actions that threaten to impair self-esteem to external causes. Thus, it seems quite reasonable that the self-serving bias of attribution asymmetry should be more pronounced for failure than for success, as reported by Stevens and Jones (1976).

SUMMARY

As a rule, the causal attributions made in everyday life do not comply with the normative models presented in Section 14.3.3. There can be many reasons for this: incomplete information, the desire to protect one's self-esteem, the desire to experience oneself as consistent and the environment as stable, etc. Other possibilities are that there is no time for a careful analysis of the causes of an event, or that there are no clear benefits of an exhaustive causal analysis. Overall, people seem to be less interested in strictly realistic causal attributions than they are in attributions that facilitate their future actions or promote their well-being.

14.4 Attributional Theories

Attributional theories are concerned with the effects that causal attributions have on people's subsequent behavior and experience (Section 14.2). In fact, these are the questions that make the psychology of causal attribution so interesting for motivational psychologists. Moreover, attributional approaches allow more accurate predictions to be made of two key variables in the psychology of motivation: **expectancy** and **value**. In this context, it is less the causal factor itself that guides behavior than the properties (attribution dimensions) ascribed to it – its locus, stability, globality, and controllability or intentionality. The first two of these dimensions were identified by Heider (1958) who, apart from distinguishing internal personal forces from external environmental forces, emphasized the dimension of stability vs. variability. On the person side, ability is stable and motivation (effort) is variable. On the environment side, task difficulty is stable and luck is variable. Weiner combined the dimensions of locus and stability in a four-field schema of causation (Table 14.10). Other authors have since proposed further attribution dimensions. Rosenbaum (1972) utilized the first of Heider's two motivational components, intention and exertion, arguing that causes can also be distinguished in terms of their intentionality. Ability is not intentional, but effort is. Likewise, work habits (stable diligence or stable laziness) are intentional, but the psychophysical state (mood, illness, fatigue) is not (Table 14.11).

"Intentionality" is perhaps not a very fitting label for this distinction, however (quite apart from the fact that

Table 14.11. Classification of internal causes by the dimensions of stability and controllability

Stability	Controllability	
	Controllable	Not controllable
Stable	Work habits (diligence, laziness)	Ability
Variable	Effort (momentary)	Psychophysical state (mood, fatigue)

Weiner, 1979; "steerability," Rheinberg, 1975; "intentionality," Rosenbaum, 1972.

"intentionality" describes the reasons for behavior rather than the causes of an event). Attributing failure to a lack of effort does not mean that the failure was intentional in the sense of purposeful or desired. An intention determines what, if anything, is to be done. It is a precondition for, but not a direct cause of, an action outcome. It therefore makes more sense to label this dimension "controllability" (Rheinberg, 1975; Weiner, 1979).

We feel responsible for causes we have the power to control. Therefore, empirical studies often operationalize controllability in terms of responsibility (for a summary, see Weiner, 1992, 1994). Although a clear theoretical distinction can be drawn between controllability and intentionality, there seem to be strong intercorrelations between the two attribution dimensions (Anderson, 1983).

Abramson, Seligman, and Teasdale (1978) proposed that a further (fourth) dimension – global vs. specific – be considered to account for the generalization of expectancies to other task and/or activity domains that is observed after repeated experiences of failure (see below).

When considering the effects of attributions on behavior in terms of their dimensional ratings, i.e., the properties they are ascribed, the objective properties of the cause – or the properties it is ascribed from an external perspective – are irrelevant. All that matters are the properties ascribed by the attributor him- or herself. The objective causes and the causes ascribed from the external perspective may deviate considerably from the subjective causes. For example, attributional research considers ability to be an internal, stable, and uncontrollable factor (Weiner, 1985a, 1986). Yet Dweck (1986, 1999) showed that people differ in the extent to which they see intelligence and ability as stable and uncontrollable or as changeable (i.e., unstable and controllable), and that this judgment influences their motivation and learning behavior. Likewise, aggression research has shown that aggressive children differ from their less aggressive peers in the extent to which they evaluate the harmful behavior of others as having been caused intentionally (Dodge & Colie, 1987; Dodge, 1993). Aggressive children exhibit a "hostile bias," i.e., they tend to assume that others have hostile intentions and to see harmful behavior as intentional. Finally, research has shown

Table 14.10. Classification scheme for the perceived causes of success and failure

Stability	Locus	
	Internal	External
Stable	Ability	Task difficulty
Variable	Effort	Luck

Based on Weiner et al., 1971, p. 2.

that, as children grow older, parents become more likely to attribute any deviant behavior to causes that are subject to the children's own control (Dix, Ruble, & Zambarano, 1989; for a summary, see Stiensmeier-Pelster, 1995).

❗ Like causal attribution, which often is a subjective rather than a rational process, the evaluation of causal properties tends to be subjective rather than objective.

In the following, we discuss how attributions influence subsequent behavior and experience. Rather than seeking to provide an exhaustive overview, we focus on three major fields of application that remain the subject of intensive conceptual theorizing and empirical testing:

1. the influence of attributions on expectancy,
2. the influence of attributions on the emergence of hopelessness and depression, and
3. the influence of attributions on the emergence of anger and aggression.

Based on the examples of these three fields of application, we will discuss the major theoretical contributions of research into how causal attributions affect behavior and experience. Attributional research has revealed a wealth of further details and stimulated studies in many fields of psychological application (see above). Readers interested in the details of these investigations are referred to the volume by Försterling (2001) and the respective chapters of Weiner's textbook (1992).

14.4.1 Attribution and Changes in Expectancy

Weiner (1985a) formulated an "expectancy principle" to describe the relationship between attribution and expectancies of success. The principle holds that changes in expectancy are influenced by the perceived stability of causes of previously achieved outcomes.

> Changes in expectancy of success following an outcome are influenced by the perceived stability of the cause of the event (Weiner, 1985a, p. 559).

Numerous studies have provided experimental evidence for the assumption that stability attributions influence changes in expectancy of success. Meyer (1973b) was the first to study this relationship empirically (see study).

The relationship between attribution and changes in expectancy is more complex than either Meyer (1973b) or Weiner (1985a) assumed, however. Two strands of argument seem particularly significant here. First, not only can **outcome attributions** determine expectancies of future success but **expectancies of success** can also influence the attribution of future outcomes. The more an outcome deviates from the original expectation, the less likely it is to be attributed to stable factors. This assumption is derived solely from the basic premise of attribution theories, which holds that people

---

STUDY

Relationship Between Expectancy of Success and Attribution

In several trials, Meyer (1973b) induced either consecutive successes or consecutive failures. After every progress report, he asked participants to rate the extent to which the outcome had been caused by ability and task difficulty (Weiner's stable causal factors). Meyer then assigned the participants to two groups based on these attributions: one group of participants who tended not to attribute failures to ability and task difficulty, and one group who were much more likely to do so. As shown in Fig. 14.10, the findings are fully congruent with Weiner's expectancy principle. The participants who tended to attribute failure to the stable factors of task difficulty and ability reduced their expectancies of success with every failure, whereas the other participants barely modified their expectancies of success at all.

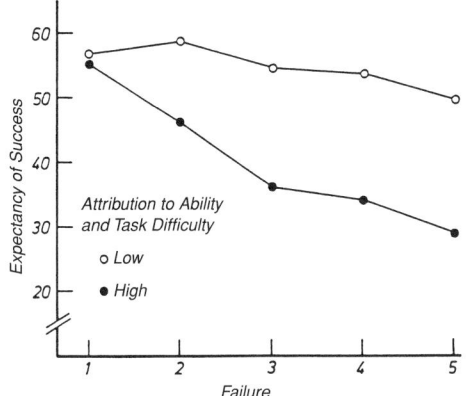

Figure 14.10 Change in the mean expectancy of success within a succession of failures in groups with low vs. high attribution of failure to ability and task difficulty. (Based on Meyer, 1973b, p. 105.)

---

strive to predict and influence the things happening around them, an endeavor that can only succeed if they can assume the world around them to show a certain degree of stability. Thus, it is imperative that we do not revise our view of things every time something happens that is contrary to our expectations. If I consider myself to be good at a certain kind of task, then I will tend to approach it with high expectancies of success. Failure on my first attempt at that task is hardly likely to prompt me to revise my self-concept of ability (and to attribute my failure to lack of ability). As discussed in depth in Section 14.3.4, I am much more likely to attribute my failure to bad luck, a lack of effort, or another variable factor. As mentioned above, an attribution of this kind would also be in line with Kelley's covariation principle. My positive concept of my ability is based on the notion that I succeed more often than others (low consensus) and at many different times (high consistency). If I now experience failure, neither consensus nor consistency takes on an entirely new aspect. Rather, failure is, at first, simply an exception to the rule. In terms of Kelley's model, there is low consistency, suggesting that the outcome might best be attributed to an unstable factor. It is only if failures begin to occur more regularly that there is a change in the covariation information and, along with it, the attribution.

Data in support of these ideas were recently presented by Dickhäuser and Galfe (2004). The authors instructed students to imagine that their score on a test had been as expected, unexpectedly good, or unexpectedly bad. The students were then asked to state whether they would tend to compare this result with worse, equally good/poor, or better results that they had achieved in the past or in other subjects. It emerged that students were more likely to compare unexpectedly poor results with better results achieved in the past or in other subjects and unexpectedly good results with worse results achieved in the past or in other subjects than they were when their results were as expected.

❶ Thus, to draw on Kelley's covariation model, results that are contrary to our expectations are associated with the perception of high distinctiveness and low consistency, suggesting that the outcome can best be attributed to situational factors (variable causes). By contrast, results that are in line with our expectations are associated with the perception of low distinctiveness and high consistency, indicating that they are attributable to stable causes.

The second assumption worth querying is whether it is really the stability of a cause that determines changes in expectancies, as Weiner and colleagues posited, or perhaps its implications for behavior. A distinction must be drawn between the stability of a cause and the stability of its behavioral implications. Imagine the following situation that was used in an empirical study (see details below), for example. You are trying in vain to open a file that has been saved on a floppy disk. Let us assume that you attribute this failure to the disk being faulty. Is this a stable cause? Undoubtedly. Will it have long-term implications for your behavior? Certainly not – you will not bother trying to save a file on that same disk in the future. Causes only have behavioral implications from the actor's perspective when they involve stable properties of the actor him- or herself or stable properties of the entity and it is not possible to change the entity (in this case, the floppy disk).

EMPIRICAL FINDINGS ON THE STABILITY OF CAUSAL FACTORS AND THEIR BEHAVIORAL IMPLICATIONS. The ideas outlined above have been empirically tested by Dickhäuser and Stiensmeier-Pelster (2002, Study 2). Students were asked to imagine both of the following situations: "Imagine you are having difficulty opening a file you have saved on a floppy disk. You know the reason for this a fault with the disk (situation 1) or a lack of knowledge on your part" (situation 2). The students were then asked to rate the stability and controllability of the cause and to state their expectancies of future suc-

Table 14.12. Perceived stability and controllability of the causal factors "faulty floppy disk" and "lack of knowledge" and resulting expectancies of success

	Faulty floppy disk	Lack of knowledge	p
Stable	3.11	1.77	<.001
Controllable	2.71	4.23	<.001
Expectancy of success	3.61	2.69	<.001

High scores indicate strong endorsement of stability or controllability and high expectancy of success. Scores range from 1 to 5. (From Dickhäuser & Stiensmeier-Pelster, 2002.)

cess on opening files from floppy disks. Table 14.12 presents the findings of this study. As the data show, the "faulty floppy disk" causal factor is rated as much more stable and less controllable than the "lack of knowledge" causal factor. Yet, at the same time, the expectancy of future success on opening files from floppy disks is much higher for the "faulty floppy disk" causal factor than for the "lack of knowledge" causal factor. Perceived stability (and perceived controllability) evidently does not determine the expectancy of success in this particular case, because the "faulty floppy disk" causal factor has no long-term implications for behavior.

Another interesting finding to emerge from Stiensmeier-Pelster and colleagues' studies on the stability of causal factors and their implications for behavior was that men were more likely than women to attribute failure on computer-related activities to stable and uncontrollable causes – but, at the same time, they reported higher expectancies of success. When the causes identified were evaluated in terms of their long-term implications for behavior, it emerged that the causes nominated by men had less impact on behavior than those nominated by women, which goes to explain the men's higher expectancies of success (cf. Dickhäuser & Stiensmeier-Pelster, 2002, Studies 1 and 2).

14.4.2 Attributional Analysis of Hopelessness and Depression

In his original formulation of the **theory of learned helplessness**, Seligman (1975) posited that people who are consistently confronted with the experience of failure will develop an expectancy of not being able to achieve success in the future either (generalization of expectancies over time), and that this expectancy will also spread to tasks that have little to do with those that originally resulted in failure (generalization over entities/tasks). Although this hypothesis was confirmed in isolated studies (e.g., Hiroto & Seligman, 1975), doubt was soon cast on the assumption of such extensive generalization (cf. Kuhl, 1981). Instead, researchers working with the theory of learned helplessness drew on Weiner's approach to explain the conditions under which expectancies are or are not generalized. In his studies, Weiner had soon shown that expectancies only generalize over time when an outcome is attributed to a stable causal factor. Drawing on Weiner's theoretical considerations and empirical findings, Abramson, Seligman, and Teasdale (1978) reformulated the theory of learned helplessness from the perspective of attribution theory (see also Abramson et al., 1989; Meyer, 2000; Stiensmeier-Pelster, 1988; Poppe et al., 2005), taking both globality and stability of causal factors into account. They posited that the more stable the cause(s) of failure are judged to be, the more likely it is that the expectancies (of uncontrollability) generated by consistent failure will be generalized over time. Likewise, the more global the cause(s) are judged to be, the more likely it is that the expectancies will be generalized to different tasks.

According to Abramson, Seligman, and Teasdale (1978) and Abramson, Metalsky, and Alloy (1989), however, causal attributions are not classified solely in terms of their stability and globality, but also in terms of their locus or internality. An internal attribution of repeated failures would imply that the attributor is the only person incapable of controlling the outcome, and this would lead to personal helplessness. Attributions of successive failures to an external cause, on the other hand, reflect a belief that few others would be able to control the outcome either, resulting in universal helplessness. Personal helplessness, but not universal helplessness, is assumed to be associated with impairment of self-esteem. This assumption corresponds to Weiner's suggestion that the locus ascribed to a cause governs self-directed affect, including self-esteem. However, empirical findings do not substantiate Weiner's theory-based assumption that locus determines feelings of self-esteem.

❶ Based on their empirical findings, Abramson, Metalsky, and Alloy (1989) later concluded that successive failures or other negative life events lead to impairment of self-esteem only when the cause is judged to be internal, stable, and global (e.g., lack of general ability).

Attribution Dimensions Relevant to the Concept of Learned Helplessness

Abramson, Seligman, and Teasdale (1978) assume orthogonality of the attribution dimensions (properties) of locus (internality), stability, and globality. However, many studies have only been able to substantiate this assumption for the relationship of locus to stability and globality, respectively, but not for that of stability to globality. Rather, almost all investigators who have asked respondents to identify the causes for fictitious or real experiences and then to rate these causes with respect to their locus, stability, and globality, have found that stability ratings correlated closely with globality ratings (for a summary, see Stiensmeier-Pelster et al., 1994; Poppe, Stiensmeier-Pelster, & Pelster, 2005).

Table 14.13. Mean correlations among locus, stability, and globality ratings

	Locus	Stability	Globality
Locus		.12	.15
Stability	.25		.68
Globality	.28	.66	

Correlations for positive situations are presented above the diagonal; correlations for negative situations, below the diagonal. ($N = 854$ students in grades 4–8). (Based on Stiensmeier-Pelster et al., 1994.)

Table 14.13 presents a prototypical pattern of findings. The data stem from a study by Stiensmeier-Pelster et al. (1994), in which children and adolescents were asked to identify the main cause for the outcomes of various positive and negative situations. Using 7-point scales, they then rated this cause in terms of its locus, stability, and globality. As Table 14.13 shows, correlations between locus ratings, on the one hand, and stability and globality ratings, on the other, were weak for both positive and negative outcomes. The relations between stability and globality ratings, by contrast, were very close for both positive and negative situations.

Because stability and globality ratings have repeatedly emerged to be so closely related, the two dimensions are no longer considered separately in research on the power of the attribution theory model of learned helplessness to explain hopelessness depression. Instead, a **generality dimension** has been postulated to comprise the two aspects of stability and globality. The perceived generality – it is now assumed – determines the extent to which expectancies are generalized across time as well as across task domains or situations. Impaired self-esteem is assumed to result from failures or from negative events whose causes are judged to be both internal and general.

Looking at the attribution dimensions relevant to the theory of learned helplessness against the background of Weiner's approach, the controllability dimension is conspicuous by its absence. This may be because the theory originally addressed only the consequences of uncontrollable events, making it pointless to contemplate the controllability of an action outcome or its causes. Had attribution issues not been neglected in the early stages of helplessness research, however, it would have been clear that an attribution process culminating in the action outcome being attributed to an uncontrollable cause is the prerequisite for the perception of uncontrollability.

A look at the empirical research on learned helplessness shows that respondents are generally confronted with uncontrollable **negative** events, and that the uncontrollability of these events is merely assumed by the experimenter. Whether or not the respondents actually perceive these events as uncontrollable is rarely tested. Given the established finding that most respondents (provided they are not suffering

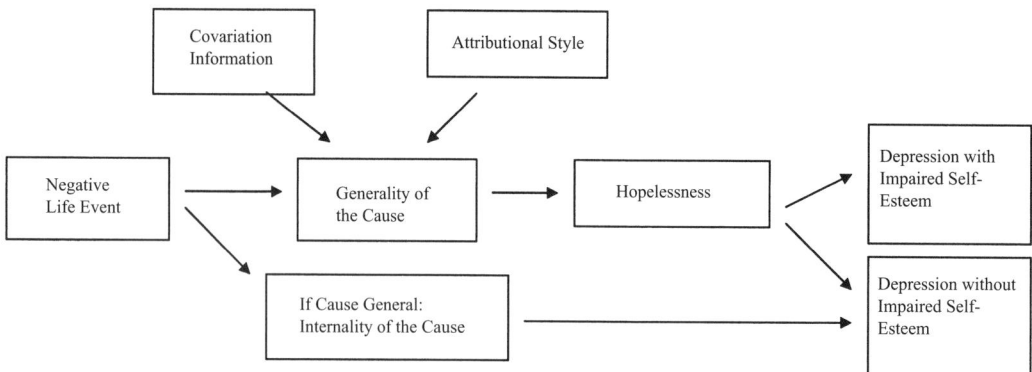

Figure 14.11 Basic principles of the theory of hopelessness. (Based on Abramson, Metalsky, & Alloy, 1989.)

from depression) perceive objectively uncontrollable events as controllable under certain conditions (Alloy & Abramson, 1979; see also Gollwitzer, 1991), this oversight is all the more surprising.

The empirical neglect of the controllability of causes is regrettable in another respect as well. More recent models developed to explain helplessness depression in the tradition of helplessness research no longer see depression as being triggered by uncontrollable events on the situation side; it suffices for a negative event (that may be personally relevant) to occur. Whether the cause of this negative event is perceived to be controllable or uncontrollable is immaterial. At the same time, guilt feelings are an important symptom of depressive disorders.

❶ From the perspective of attribution theory, guilt feelings arise when negative events are attributed to causes that are within the attributor's control. For example, people sometimes experience deep feelings of guilt when a relative dies after a long illness, and they feel that they failed to provide the necessary support because they had other priorities.

The Attribution Theory Model of Depression

Fig. 14.11 summarizes the attribution theory model of depression, which was developed in the tradition of the theory of learned helplessness. First, the model distinguishes between depression with and without impaired self-esteem. Depression without impaired self-esteem is determined by hopelessness. Unlike Weiner, who conceives of hopelessness as affect, this model sees hopelessness as an expectancy. Strictly speaking, the expectancy of hopelessness comprises two expectancies:

1. the expectancy that more negative than positive events will occur; i.e., that aversive events are very probable and desired events rather improbable;

2. the expectancy that no response in one's repertoire will change the likelihood of these outcomes.

In fact, it is a question of a prototypical expectancy of uncontrollability. An expectancy of hopelessness emerges when a (personally significant) negative life event occurs and is

attributed – in the spirit of Weiner – to a stable and global (here: general) cause. Depression associated with impaired self-esteem occurs when the cause of a negative event is additionally located within the attributor's own person (i.e., an internal attribution).

The model also specifies the antecedent conditions of such attributions. On the one hand, they require what is known as a depressive attributional style. People are assumed to have enduring preferences with regard to the causes they infer for positive and negative events. Depressive individuals are assumed to attribute negative events primarily to internal-stable-global causes, and positive events primarily to external-unstable-specific causes, though only the former preference is significant in the present context. Nondepressive individuals are assumed to favor the opposite pattern of attribution (i.e., external-unstable-specific attributions for negative events and internal-stable-global attributions for positive events). Beyond attributional style, the covariation information specified by Kelley (consensus, distinctiveness,

> **EXAMPLE**
>
> ■ Low consensus (e.g., "everyone but me succeeds on a certain task") is assumed to prompt internal attributions (e.g., lack of ability); high consensus (e.g., "it's not just me who fails on the task, everyone else does as well") to prompt external attributions (e.g., task difficulty).
>
> ■ High consistency (e.g., "I'm not just failing on this task at the moment, I have often failed on it in the past as well") is assumed to lead to stable attributions (e.g., lack of ability); low consistency (e.g., "I'm failing at the moment, but in the past I have often succeeded on this task") to variable attributions (e.g., lack of effort).
>
> ■ Low distinctiveness (e.g., "it is not just this task that I fail on, but most other tasks as well") is assumed to generate global attributions (e.g., lack of general ability); high distinctiveness (e.g., "I fail only on this specific task") to generate specific attributions (e.g., lack of mathematical ability).

and consistency) is also assumed to influence concrete attributions of negative events. In line with the theoretical considerations of various authors (e.g., Jackson & Larrance, 1979; Van Overwalle & Heylighen, 1995), it is assumed that the three attribution dimensions of locus (internality), stability, and globality can be derived directly from the covariation information on consensus, consistency, and distinctiveness of a cause (Kelley, 1967, 1973).

It would be interesting to know how the effect of covariation information relates to attributional style, or how these two determinants might interact. For example, does the attributional style only take effect when the covariation information for a given situation is ambiguous, or does it also prevail when the covariation information is unequivocal?

Unfortunately, there have been very few empirical investigations of these questions to date (for a summary, see Poppe, 2002). It would also be interesting to examine whether a depressive attributional style might affect the perception of covariation information. According to the stage model of attributional activity (Section 14.3.2), one of the factors determining the intensity of causal search is the degree of accuracy accepted when identifying a cause. Do I identify the cause (e.g., I lack ability) as soon as I have gathered a few vague clues as to its nature or do I seek to "get to the bottom of things" and decide on a cause only when I have collected a number of valid indications?

Working on the assumption (by all means a plausible one) that our attributional style reflects the concept we have of our abilities, would it not be plausible to accept a causal attribution on the basis of just a few tenuous clues if that attribution is in agreement with our self-concept? In this case, causal search will always be terminated as soon as we come across clues pointing to a cause that is congruent with our self-concept. Let us assume that covariation information is not as coherent in real life as it is in the respective experiments, but that it may be contradictory. If, for example, a student fails a test along with three other students, and only one student passes, it would be plausible to attribute the first student's outcome to an external factor (e.g., task difficulty). To do so, however, the student would require full access to the relevant consensus information. Let us assume that this information is not readily available, but first has to be obtained by the student. He or she asks a classmate, who happens to be the only one who passed the test, how he or she did. If our student tends to attribute failure to internal causes, because he or she considers him- or herself less able, this information matches his or her attributional style and, given that it confirms the image he or she has of him- or herself, he or she will probably not bother asking the others how they did, but assume that his or her failure can be attributed to a lack of ability.

As this thought experiment shows, we are unlikely to fully analyze the myriad of covariation information available in everyday life, but tend to terminate the analysis as soon as we have come up with a subjectively plausible attribution – in all probability, one that conforms with our own attributional style rather than one that contradicts it (in which case, we would probably continue the analysis).

EMPIRICAL FINDINGS ON ATTRIBUTIONAL STYLE AND DEPRESSION. The attribution theory model of depression outlined above has been the subject of numerous empirical studies, most of which have focused on the impact of attributional style on depression. Attributional style is generally assessed by means of questionnaire measures. The "Attributional Style Questionnaire" (ASQ; Peterson et al., 1982; Stiensmeier et al., 1985; Poppe, Stiensmeier-Pelster, & Pelster, 2005) is frequently used in studies with adults. Respondents are presented with equal numbers of successful (positive) and nonsuccessful (negative) situations from performance-related and interpersonal domains. They are then asked to identify the main cause for each event and to rate this cause along the dimensions of locus (internality), stability, and globality.

Numerous cross-sectional studies have established that clinically depressed adults are more likely than nondepressed adults to attribute failure to internal, stable, and global causes (e.g., Raps et al, 1982; Eaves & Rush, 1984; Stiensmeier-Pelster, Kammer, & Adolphs, 1988). Moreover, the failure attribution style typical of depressed adults has also been observed in samples of subclinically depressed adults (e.g., Seligman et al, 1979; Försterling, Bühner, & Gall, 1998).

Apart from these cross-sectional studies, a limited number of longitudinal studies have investigated the relationship between the failure attribution style typical of depressed adults and the onset of symptoms of depression, and sought evidence of causality (for a summary, see Barnett & Gotlib, 1988; Coyne & Gotlib, 1983 for a particularly critical approach; Kammer & Stiensmeier-Pelster, 1987; Peterson & Seligman, 1984; Housten, 1995; Metalsky, Halberstadt, & Abramson, 1987; Metalsky, Joiner, Hardin, & Abramson, 1993; Stiensmeier-Pelster, 1989). For example, Metalsky et al. (1987) found that the students in their study who tended to attribute failure to general (i.e., stable-global) causes reported depressive mood directly after receiving a poor grade (stress), and again two days later. Those who tended to attribute failure to variable-specific causes also reported depressive mood directly after receiving a bad grade, but had recovered completely within two days.

❗ Thus, a tendency to attribute failure to general causes does not determine the onset of depressive mood, but its chronicity. This is precisely what would be expected on the basis of Weiner's attributional analysis – the properties of stability and globality do not determine whether failure triggers negative expectancies (and the associated acute depressive mood), but the extent to which these expectancies remain valid over time or are generalized to other tasks (and thus trigger chronic depressive mood). Strictly speaking, this study shows that a depressive attributional style is not a factor that affects the genesis of depression, but one that determines its chronicity and that may impede recovery.

Empirical research has shown that attributions influence the onset of depressive mood in interpersonal as well as performance-related situations. Stiensmeier-Pelster (1989, Study 1) found that the more students who experienced a negative Christmas vacation tended to attribute failures to general causes, the more pronounced the increase in their level of depressive mood.

THERAPEUTIC APPLICATIONS. Methods of therapy have also been developed on the basis of the attributional analysis of depressive disorders presented by Abramson and colleagues. All of these efforts were based on the notion that depressive individuals distort reality in a typical manner. Specifically, it was assumed that their causal attributions are not in line with Kelley's covariation model, but that they favor internal, stable, and global causes for failure, irrespective of the situational conditions. Accordingly, teaching depressive individuals to make attributions that conform to the covariation model would seem to be a promising therapeutic intervention. In this framework, patients are first asked to describe in detail a specific experience of failure, and then to look for covariation information that contradicts their attributional style; e.g., to make themselves aware of who else failed on the task, of how often they had succeeded on the same task in the past, and of the similar tasks they had already mastered successfully. Such perceptions of high consensus, high distinctiveness, and low consistency in turn point to an external, specific, and variable attribution (for a summary, see Stiensmeier-Pelster & Grüner, 2005).

In general, the success of these training programs was modest. However, when this purely cognitive procedure was combined with operant methods – i.e., when new skills were taught and acquired (see the example) – there were marked improvements in the programs' outcomes.

> **EXAMPLE**
>
> A student who does badly in mathematics attributes his failure to internal, stable, and global causes. In consequence, he will expect to keep getting bad grades, see no reason to make an effort, and may even develop other depressive symptoms (e.g., impaired self-esteem). If it is possible to change that student's failure attributions for the better by means of attribution training, such that he now attributes failure to external, variable, and specific causes, he will respond to the next bad grade by remaining confident of future success and being prepared to keep on trying. If, however, we have not backed up the attribution training program by improving his mathematics skills (e.g., by providing coaching), he will continue to get bad grades, and it will only be a matter of time until he reverts to his old attributional style. We can only genuinely help the student by enhancing his ability as well as modifying his attributional style.

14.4.3 Attributional Analysis of Aggressive Behavior

Aggressive behavior may be either instrumental and proactive (aggression serving the pursuit of goals; e.g., one student hits another to exert power) or reactive and emotional (aggression in response to negative emotional arousal, especially anger or rage, cf. Berkowitz, 1993) in nature. Attributional considerations are relevant in the context of reactive, emotional aggression. One approach that has proved very successful in explaining the emergence of this form of aggression over the past 15 years holds that aggression results from deficits in social information processing (for a summary, see Dodge, 1993). Specifically, reactive-aggressive children and adolescents are assumed to differ from their nonaggressive peers in the way they interpret conflict situations.

❶ Aggressive children are thought to exhibit what is known as a "hostile bias" (see above), i.e., to assume people who cause them harm to have done so on purpose or to see the harmful behavior of others as controllable.

Based on the theoretical ideas and empirical findings of Dodge's research team, and drawing on Weiner's attributional analysis of motivation, emotion, and behavior, Graham, Hudley, and Williams (1992; Graham & Hudley, 1994; Hudley & Graham, 1993; Graham, Weiner, & Benesh-Weiner, 1995) presented an attributional theory of reactive-aggressive behavior, which has generated much research and drawn attention to possible points of intervention (for a summary, see Rudolph et al., 2004).

In principle, like Weiner's model, the theory assumes that a person's behavior and experience in social interactions is conditional on the causes to which the situation's emergence is ascribed, that this causal attribution elicits a certain emotion, and that this emotion in turn motivates a certain behavior. Where reactive-aggressive behavior is concerned, the cause inferred for behavior is less relevant than its perceived controllability and intentionality. What really matters is whether the causes of the damage are perceived as being subject to the actor's control (controllability) and whether the harmful behavior or its consequences were intended by the actor (intentionality).

In fact, in the case of reactive-aggressive behavior, it is assumed that the more strongly people who have been harmed believe that the harmful behavior was subject to the actor's control or even intentional, the more anger they will feel toward the actor. The more anger they feel, the more likely they will be to respond with (reactive-)aggressive behavior (for a summary, see Weiner, 1995).

These hypotheses have been confirmed in several empirical studies (Graham et al., 1992; Stiensmeier-Pelster & Gerlach, 1997; Stiensmeier-Pelster & Assimi, 2002; for a summary, see Rudolph et al., 2004). For example, Stiensmeier-Pelster and Gerlach showed that the anger felt by both aggressive and nonaggressive adolescents toward a peer who had caused them harm, as well as their desire for retribution (i.e., their tendency to engage in reactive-aggressive behavior) increased as a function of their belief that the peer was responsible for the (harmful) behavior. Whether or not the adolescent who inflicted the harm was considered aggressive was immaterial. Congruent with the attributional theory of aggressive behavior (Graham, Hudley, & Williams, 1992), the authors were also able to show that attribution determines anger, and that anger in turn determines the tendency to show an aggressive response. Betancourt and Blair (1992) reported comparable findings from a study with college students. Furthermore, these authors were able to show that anger alone, i.e., anger without the antecedent attribution, does not explain differences in the level of aggression.

The study by Stiensmeier-Pelster and Gerlach (1997) yielded two further important findings:

1. In line with the assumptions of Dodge and Colie (1987), aggressive adolescents were shown to demonstrate a "hostile bias," ascribing far more responsibility than their nonaggressive peers to the person who caused the damage.

2. The person who caused the damage was ascribed less responsibility if he or she produced an excuse for the harm caused than if he or she kept quiet.

The excuse consisted in the actor (a) describing the sequence of events and citing an uncontrollable cause for the damage, and (b) stating that he or she was sorry for the harm caused. When actors provided an excuse for their behavior, not only were they ascribed less responsibility, but the attributors also felt less anger and were less likely to respond with reactive-aggressive behavior.

The following study by Graham, Weiner, and Benesh-Weiner (1995) also examined the role of excuse giving.

STUDY

Relationships Between Attribution, Emotion, and Behavior

Graham, Weiner, and Benesh-Weiner (1995) investigated the extent to which children and adolescents have grasped the relationship between attribution (of controllability and responsibility), emotion (anger), and behavior (reactive aggression), and their appreciation of the effects of excuse giving (citing an uncontrollable cause) on this attribution-emotion-behavior sequence. Awareness of these relationships is an indicator for social competence or, to use Gardner's terminology, interindividual intelligence. Results show that primary school children are largely unaware of these relationships, and that awareness increases with age in nonaggressive children, but not in aggressive children. Hence, aggressive adolescents are less aware of these relationships than are nonaggressive adolescents. Given their insufficient knowledge of the relationship between attribution, emotion, and behavior, and the impact of excuse giving on the attribution-emotion-behavior sequence, aggressive children are less likely than nonagressive children to give excuses for any harm they cause. Consequently, it is often assumed (precisely because they do not give excuses) that these children could have controlled the cause of their harmful behavior. As a result, people show more anger toward them, and they are more likely to become victims of reactive aggression (cf. Graham et al., 1995).

APPROACHES TO PREVENT AGGRESSIVE BEHAVIOR. Graham and colleagues did not stop at investigating the determinants of reactive-aggressive behavior; they went on to derive strategies of conflict prevention from their findings. The core idea of the intervention is to make children and adolescents more aware of how attributions influence emotion and behavior, and to enable them to influence the attributions of others by making effective excuses and apologies, thereby reducing the occurrence of anger and, consequently, aggressive behavior (Hudley & Graham, 1993). These interventions do not necessarily have to be directed solely at those who inflict harm on others, but can also apply to those at the receiving end. It may be possible to overcome the well documented "hostile bias" in aggressive children and adolescents by making them aware of the implications of this attribution tendency and encouraging them to apply a kind of "stop mechanism" ("Stop! Think carefully before you assign hostile intent to others") whenever they notice that they are making a hostile attribution.

Stiensmeier-Pelster and Assimi (2002) used the attributional analysis of aggressive behavior to explain gender differences in levels of aggressive behavior. In their study, students were first asked to describe a situation they had recently experienced in which somebody had caused them harm. They were then asked about certain attributions they had made in that situation (controllability/intentionality), the emotions they had experienced (anger, annoyance), and the behavior they had displayed (direct physical aggression, direct verbal aggression, indirect aggression). In line with the literature (Björkqvist & Niemalä, 1992), it emerged that girls generally responded less aggressively than boys (congruent with the findings of previous studies by Björkqvist, Lagerspetz, & Kaukiainen, 1992, the gender difference in direct aggression was particularly apparent). Furthermore, findings showed that both boys' and girls' aggression levels were explained by the attribution-emotion-behavior sequence postulated in the attributional theory of aggressive behavior.

❶ Hence, the mechanisms that produce reactive-aggressive behavior are the same in both boys and girls.

These results also correspond with the findings of Graham et al. (1992) and Stiensmeier-Pelster and Gerlach (1997). Both research groups found that the mechanisms leading to reactive aggression in habitually aggressive and in nonaggressive children and adolescents do not differ. Thus, there is reason to believe that the gender differences observed in aggression levels can be traced back to attributional or emotional differences.

SUMMARY

Attributions influence behavior and experience in a multitude of ways. For example, the expectancy of success is dependent not only on whether one's previous efforts resulted in success or failure, but primarily on the causes to which that success or failure was attributed. Self-directed emotions are also dependent on attributions. We are not proud when we succeed, for example, but when we succeed and the causes for that success reside within ourselves. Likewise, interpersonal feelings are dependent on attributions. If somebody causes me harm, I am most likely to feel anger or rage if I assume he or she to have acted with intent or believe that he or she could have controlled the cause of his or her behavior. Finally, depressive responses to negative life events are particularly likely if those events are attributed to internal, stable, and global causes.

REVIEW QUESTIONS

1. **What is the difference between attribution theories and attributional theories?**

   Attribution theories are concerned with how causal attributions are reached, whereas attributional theories deal with the effects of these attributions on people's subsequent behavior and experience.

2. **According to Weiner's attributional theory, when is a search for the causes of an action outcome initiated? Has there been any criticism of this assumption?**

   Weiner's model assumes that we seek to establish the causes of any event that is unexpected, negative, or important. Weiner's writings suggest that each of these three conditions is sufficient to initiate causal search. This assumption does not withstand careful analysis, however, as shown by the example of a student who always gets an E grade in mathematics tests. If this student obtains another E grade in his or her school-leaving mathematics exam, the outcome is indisputably important and negative, but it is expected and, as such, highly unlikely to elicit causal search.

3. **Which antecedent conditions can influence causal attributions?**

   Causal attributions can be influenced by antecedent conditions such as:
   - specific information about the action outcome,
   - causal schemata,
   - hedonic bias, and
   - the perspective taken on the outcome (actor vs. observer perspective).

4. **Which causal factors are usually cited to explain academic performance?**

   The causal factors inferred for achievement-related outcomes include:
   - high or insufficient ability,
   - high or insufficient effort,
   - task difficulty, and
   - luck.

5. **Which questions cannot be answered by Weiner's attributional analysis of motivation, emotion, and behavior?**

   Weiner's attributional analysis is unable to answer the questions of how long and intensive the search for causality will be, and of the degree of accuracy accepted in the causal analysis.

6. **Which general equation did Heider use as the basis for his "naive" analysis of action, and how did he elaborate on this equation in the analysis?**

   Heider based his approach on Lewin's general behavioral equation, which states that behavior is a function of personal and environmental forces. He subdivides the personal force into "trying" (variable) and "ability" (fixed), where trying is the product of intention and exertion. On the environmental side, Heider posits one fixed primary dimension – difficulty – which, from time to time, may be influenced by chance (good or bad luck; variable). The difference between ability and difficulty gives the concept of "can."

7. **According to Jones and Davis, which steps may lead to an attribution of intention?**

   Jones' and Davis' model of correspondent inferences identifies three steps that may lead to an attribution of intention:
   - Confirming two prerequisites: the actor must have had prior knowledge about the outcome of the action, and the actor must have the ability to bring about the result.
   - Determining which consequences – or effects – of the action outcome might have motivated the actor to bring about this particular outcome.
   - Estimating the action outcome's general desirability for the group to which the actor belongs.

8. **According to Kelley's covariation model, which are the four criterion or information dimensions used to infer the cause of a given action?**

   Kelley's four criterion dimensions are:
   - distinctiveness of entities,
   - consensus (agreement between different people),
   - consistency of behavior across time, and
   - consistency across different modalities.

9. **What is the precondition for motivational bias in attribution, and when is it particularly apparent?**

   Motivational bias can occur when an attribution touches on self-esteem in which case self-serving interests may distort the logical and rational use of information. It is particularly apparent after success and failure, with success being ascribed to person factors, and failure to external causes.

14

10. **What reasons do Miller and Ross (1975) propose for a rational, nonmotivational bias in information processing in self-attributions? Have their assumptions been confirmed in empirical studies?**

Miller and Ross gave three reasons for rational information processing in self-attributions:

■ People expect their endeavors to produce success rather than failure; accordingly, they are more likely to take responsibility for expected than for unexpected outcomes.

■ People perceive stronger covariation between their efforts and increasing successes than under conditions of repeated failure.

■ People have an erroneous conception that there is a tighter contingency between their effort and success than between their effort and failure. However, studies have shown that these reasons cannot fully invalidate a motivational basis for the asymmetry of self-serving attributions.

11. **How do differences in the self-concept of ability influence the attribution of failure? Are these findings compatible with the hypothesis of a motivational bias in information processing in the attributional process?**

The findings of attribution research indicate that individuals with a low self-concept of ability tend to attribute failure to a personal lack of ability. By contrast, individuals with a high self-concept of ability tend to ascribe failure to external factors, such as bad luck. These findings are difficult to reconcile with the notion of a self-serving bias in information processing that serves to protect self-esteem. If this kind of bias were in operation, individuals with a low self-concept of ability would also tend to attribute success to high ability and failure to bad luck. This is demonstrably not the case, however.

12. **What is the perspective discrepancy and what are the reasons for it?**

The perspective discrepancy describes the observation that actors tend to attribute their actions to situation factors, whereas observers attribute those same actions to person factors. There seem to be two main reasons for this phenomenon:

■ Differences in the focus of attention and differences in the amount of context information. The actor's attention is focused on aspects of the situation; the observer's attention, on the actor.

■ Furthermore, the actor has far more information than the observer about the current situation: its precedents and background.

13. **Which motivational variable is influenced by the attribution dimension of generality? Which dimensions were collapsed to form the generality dimension in research on the explanatory power of the attribution theory model of learned helplessness?**

The perceived generality of a causal factor determines the extent to which expectancies are generalized across time as well as across task domains or situations. Because stability and globality ratings have repeatedly been found to be very closely related, these two dimensions were collapsed to form the generality dimension.

14. **What can be said about the attributional behavior of depressive individuals?**

Depressive individuals seem to distort reality in a typical manner. Their causal attributions do not seem to be in line with Kelley's covariation model; rather they seem to favor internal, stable, and global causes for failure, regardless of the situational conditions.

15. **What mistake do reactive-aggressive people seem to make on a regular basis?**

Reactive-aggressive people often exhibit a "hostile bias," meaning that they tend to assume the people who cause them harm to have done so with intent, and are more likely to assume that the harmful behavior was controllable.

16. **What role do excuses play in reactive-aggressive behavior?**

People who give excuses for any harm they cause are ascribed less responsibility for the outcome, and are thus less likely to be exposed to aggressive behavior. Aggressive children seem to be less likely to give excuses for any harm they cause. Consequently, people often assume that they could have controlled the cause of their harmful behavior. As a result, people show more anger toward them, and they are more likely to become victims of reactive aggression. Excuses and apologies thus serve to stop a conflict from escalating.

15 Motivation and Development

J. Heckhausen and H. Heckhausen

15.1 Development of Control Striving Across the Lifespan: A Fundamental Phenomenon of Motivational Development

This chapter explores the relationship between motivation and development from two perspectives: the development of motivation, on the one hand, and motivational influences on development, on the other. Whether it is a question of the development of motivation or the motivation of development, the regulation of human behavior shifts in accordance with lifespan developmental change in the individual's potential to control the environment. The **lifespan theory of control** (J. Heckhausen, 1999; J. Heckhausen & Schulz, 1995; Schulz & J. Heckhausen, 1996) identifies constructs and articulates hypotheses specifying how individuals respond to the waxing and waning of their potential for effective control at different stages of life and in different areas of functioning, and thus provides a useful conceptual framework for the investigation of development and motivation.

The starting point and conceptual core of the lifespan theory of control is the **functional primacy of primary control** (J. Heckhausen, 1999; J. Heckhausen & Schulz, 1999a). The striving to exert control on the environment (primary control striving) is hypothesized to be a universal and fundamental characteristic of human motivation that evolved over a long phylogeny of behavioral regulation. A preference for self-produced effects on the environment over effects produced by others has been found in various mammals (see overview in J. Heckhausen, 2000a; White, 1959), and may even determine the behavior of all those nonmammalian species with a locomotor system that enables them to influence their environment.

As illustrated in Fig. 15.1, **primary control striving** is expected to remain high and stable throughout the lifespan, despite substantial changes in the potential for effective action. It is **primary control capacity** that undergoes radical change. From a state of almost complete helplessness and dependence on others in infancy, primary control capacity surges in childhood and adolescence, levels out at some point in young or middle adulthood depending on the biographical

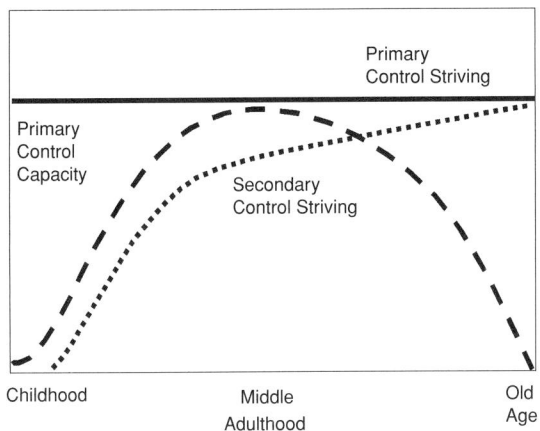

Figure 15.1 Hypothetical lifespan trajectories of the capacity for primary control, primary control striving, and secondary control striving. (Based on J. Heckhausen, 1999.)

path taken, and declines again in old age. This decline is reflected in multiple functional impairments toward the end of life and, finally, death.

The motivational and volitional regulation of behavior must respond to these radical shifts in primary control capacity across the lifespan. To take the example of learning how to walk; it is a major accomplishment for one-year-olds, but soon becomes taken for granted as a basic functional competence – usually until old age, when it once again becomes a challenge, and a competence to be protected against age-related decline. How do humans adapt the goals and challenges they set for themselves to such radical changes in primary control capacity? How do they maintain a functional level of stability in the emotional and motivational prerequisites for effective action? These are the research questions addressed within the framework of the lifespan theory of control.

The rapid growth in control capacity in early life and its decline toward the end of life present young and old with very different challenges and risks, requiring the investment of quite different resources. Although humans seem to start their lives with a built-in readiness for control striving, neonates are so helpless that almost all experiences of control consist in influencing the behavior of their parents (especially the mother). Apart from compensating for children's lack of manual and intellectual proficiency, adult caregivers provide an external scaffold for the motivational (goal-setting) and volitional (persistence and shielding against distraction) regulation of behavior. Early parent-child interactions thus represent the cradle of primary control striving and of action itself (Section 15.5). Given the rapid development of primary control potential from birth to midchildhood, children frequently find themselves able to master difficulties that seemed insurmountable only a short while ago (Parsons & Ruble, 1977). As a result, they are likely to overestimate their capabilities and

may be at risk of setting overly demanding goals. Socialization agents (i.e., parents and teachers) seek to address this risk by setting tasks appropriate to a child's level of cognitive development and by encouraging children to abandon overly ambitious goals that are doomed to failure.

Age-related decline leads to a complementary pattern of effects in old age. The aging individual has to come to terms with an increasing restriction of social roles (e.g., children moving out, retirement, widowhood) as well as biologically determined functional decline (e.g., in cardiovascular health, physical strength, sensory functioning, and memory). These experiences of permanent loss of control can lead to frustration, experiences of helplessness, the risk of depression and despair, and the danger of older people relinquishing the potential for control prematurely and becoming dependent on others too soon. In contrast to young children, who lack experience in emotional and motivational self-regulation, however, older adults can apply **secondary control strategies** (Fig. 15.1), which serve to protect self-esteem and confidence of future success against the negative effects of loss of control, and can help to focus the remaining control capacity on more promising goals instead.

The greater part of this chapter (Sections 15.2 to 15.7) is devoted to the development of control striving and its motivational and volitional regulation. Section 15.8 takes the complementary perspective, examining the motivation of development. Two different approaches to the development of motivation can be distinguished. Researchers can either track the emergence of motivation over child development, or – as was done by Heinz Heckhausen in the original chapter on motivational development and motive change in the first edition of this book (Heckhausen, 1980) – start from the perspective of adult achievement motivation and work back, identifying the necessary components of this highly complex system of behavioral regulation and determining how and when they develop in childhood. Both of these perspectives are considered in Sections 15.2 to 15.7 on the development of motivation. First, we follow the genesis of control behavior through infancy and early childhood, seeking explanations for the development and differentiation of motivated behavior, with a particular focus on achievement- and power-motivated behavior. The key role of parent-child interactions in the development of these behaviors is discussed in detail. Second, we examine the cognitive prerequisites for the development of achievement motivation as conceptualized in the risk-taking model, and map out the developmental milestones in this process. This section is based on a chapter in Heinz Heckhausen's first (German) edition of *Motivation and Action* (Heckhausen, 1980; see Heckhausen, 1982, for an English account) and other works published in the 1980s (Geppert & Heckhausen, 1990; Heckhausen, 1982, 1983b, 1984a, b), and integrates more recent findings published in the last 15 years. The chapter begins by examining newborn babies' striving for control (Section 15.2) and charting the first milestones in the development of intended action and early self-evaluation, as reflected in the emotions of pride and shame (Sections 15.3 to 15.5). Particular attention is paid to the early mother (father)-child dyad, which plays a crucial role in channeling and supporting early action regulation (Section 15.5). Universal patterns in the development of motivated behavior are then investigated in depth, drawing on the example of achievement motivation (Section 15.6).

In the final part of the chapter (Section 15.8), we discuss theoretical conceptions and empirical findings on how individuals seek to influence their development across the life course by means of motivated behavior. Taking a theoretical perspective that integrates lifespan developmental psychology, the psychology of motivation, and action theory, we examine how individuals actively influence their own development and biographies. Finally, we discuss the individual's influence on the social and developmental ecology, and the effects of that ecology on individual development, thus closing the dialectic circle of mutual individual and environmental influence (Section 15.8.4). Although the analysis of these dynamic interactions is still in its infancy, a great deal of progress has been made since Heinz Heckhausen first called for an "explanation of behavior at fourth glance" in 1980.

15.2 Early Control Striving

Humans, and at least some animals, seem to be born with a built-in readiness for **control striving** and for exerting direct or **primary control** on the physical and social environment (White, 1959). Studies on operant learning have shown that many mammals prefer **behavior-event contingencies** to event-event contingencies, even in the absence of consummatory behavior (for an overview, see White, 1959). Chimpanzees favor objects that can be moved, changed, or made to emit sounds and light (Welker, 1956); rhesus monkeys spend hours solving mechanical puzzles (e.g., bolting mechanisms; Harlow, 1953); and both children and rats prefer response-elicited rewards to receiving the same rewards regardless of their behavior (Singh, 1970).

❶ These findings indicate that behavior-event contingency striving is a basic nonconsummatory need in mammals. From the very beginning of life, humans and other mammals are evidently equipped with information-processing strategies and behavioral orientations that help them to detect, strive for, and produce behavior-event contingencies, thus increasing their control of the environment (i.e., primary control). Humans have a natural propensity to focus on self-produced action outcomes. This propensity forms the basis for further developments in the experience of control, such as the ability to compare the effects of an action with an intention or a standard of excellence, or to draw inferences about one's competence on the basis of an action outcome and its evaluation. These two developmental milestones are reached in the first three years of life.

The preadapted, innate behavioral orientations that facilitate individual primary control and that – to draw on Fodor (1983) – can be termed **motivational behavioral modules** (J. Heckhausen, 1999, 2000a, b) also include **exploration striving**, which some authors conceptualize as a "curiosity motive." It may be misleading to classify exploration and curiosity, or indeed anxiety, as motives (Trudewind, 2000), because these behavioral tendencies do not in fact relate to specific content categories. Rather, they are general approach or avoidance orientations that regulate behavior in diverse situations and across the major categories of motivated behavior (achievement, power, affiliation) (Trudewind, 2000; Trudewind & Schneider, 1994). Curiosity and exploration increase individuals' opportunities to test and develop their control of the environment. The striving for new and discrepant experiences ensures that control striving is not limited to constant repetition of what has already been achieved.

> **EXAMPLE**
>
> The psychopathological phenomena of echopraxia (i.e., the pathological repetition by imitation of somebody else's movements) sometimes observed in cases of autism, mental disability, and extreme social deprivation is a negative example for the adaptivity of curiosity. In these cases, contingency striving seems to be running on the spot, and ironically inhibits the development of primary control potential.

Another fundamental regulatory mechanism that promotes primary control striving is the **asymmetry of affective responses** to positive and negative events. As pointed out by Nico Frijda (1988), the fact that individuals soon get used to the positive affect experienced after a change for the better, but experience stronger, longer-lasting negative emotions after a change for the worse, promotes continuous control behavior that does not "rest on its laurels," but strives to overcome setbacks and constraints to control and to change the environment for the better.

Development of Control Striving

The first manifestations of control striving in human ontogeny can be observed in newborn babies (Janos & Papoušek, 1977; Papoušek, 1967). In fact, the ability to engage in operant behavior may develop in the womb. Papoušek found that babies just a few days old learned head movements contingent on acoustic signals and milk reinforcement. Even when they were no longer hungry and the milk had lost its reinforcing potential, the babies continued to respond to the acoustic signal with a turn of the head, and showed positive affect when the milk bottle was presented as expected.

Taking a behaviorist perspective, Watson examined how operant learning can be fostered by providing opportunities for experiences of behavior-event contingency in the first months of life (Watson, 1966, 1972). Watson trained his three-month-old son to fix his gaze on Watson's closed fist, at which point Watson opened his hand. After just a few days of training, the three-month-old showed anticipatory arousal, followed by intense pleasure when the expected effect occurred. Further studies showed that change in the contingencies between behavior and effect (e.g., changing from the right to the left fist; visual fixation on the left fist, opening the right hand) did not lead to extinction of the learned response, but were mastered increasingly quickly. Moreover, success was associated with increased positive affect. Watson hypothesized that infants can already develop **generalized contingency awareness** if exposed to appropriate operant experiences. This assumption was confirmed in a series of studies showing transfer from one contingency experience to another, interference of noncontingent experiences (Finkelstein & Ramey, 1977; Ramey & Finkelstein, 1978; Rovee & Fagan, 1976; Watson & Ramey, 1972), positive affect in response to behavior-contingent outcomes (Barrett, Morgan, & Maslin-Cole, 1993), and negative affect to noncontingent stimulation that had previously been contingent (DeCasper & Carstens, 1981).

DEFINITION

Piaget (1952) labeled this kind of control striving "secondary circular reactions": infants repeat activities that have previously produced certain effects time and again, and respond to the effects with positive affect.

More recently, this kind of **early control striving** has been labeled **mastery motivation** and investigated by two major research groups: the students and associates of Leon Yarrow and of Susan Harter. Harter (1974, 1978) and colleagues have focused on mastery motivation in the early school years, whereas Yarrow and colleagues (e.g., Yarrow et al., 1983) have examined striving for control and mastery in the first three years of life. Their definition of mastery motivation is largely congruent with that of achievement motivation:

> Mastery motivation is viewed as a multifaceted, intrinsic, psychological force that stimulates an individual to attempt to master a skill or task that is at least somewhat challenging for him or her (Barrett & Morgan, 1995, p. 58).

These authors have developed a detailed methodology for the measurement of instrumental (i.e., persistence and curiosity) and expressive (i.e., outcome-related affect) **mastery behavior** and, in a host of studies, have predicted later achievement striving and even cognitive performance itself on the basis of interindividual differences in early mastery behavior (see the overview in MacTurk & Morgan, 1995).

Barrett and Morgan (1995) identify three phases in the development of the multifaceted phenomenon of mastery motivation during infancy and toddlerhood (see following the overview).

Developmental Phases of Mastery Motivation During Infancy and Toddlerhood (Based on Barrett & Morgan, 1995)

Phase 1: This phase corresponds to the early striving for behavior-event contingencies described by Watson. A preference for novelty plays a particularly important role at this age, motivating exploration and curiosity. Curiosity leads infants to challenge themselves, and ensures that control striving is not limited to repetition of known behavior and effects.

Phase 2: At this stage, children vary activities systematically to test whether they produce the intended effect (beginning of Section 15.3).

Phase 3: The intended outcome of an action goal now becomes the yardstick against which the success of an activity is measured (end of Section 15.3).

15.3 Focusing on the Intended Outcome of an Action

Between 9 and 12 months, infants gradually begin to determine which means accomplish particular ends, and enter a new developmental phase of mastery motivation that lasts until the second half of the second year (Barrett & Morgan, 1995; Yarrow et al., 1983). Children of this age experiment with different activities or with modifications of actions that have previously produced certain effects. Indeed, children approaching the end of their first year often get completely carried away by an activity, losing sight of their original goal. For example, Jennings (1991) reports that children of this age enjoy collecting objects in a container. When they have collected all of the available objects, they simply empty the container and start all over again. It is not the outcome of the action – having collected all of the objects – that is the focus of their attention, but the activity of collecting. Children in this phase of development display an impressive level of persistence in their control striving. This stage of development coincides with what Trevarthen (1980; Trevarthen & Hubley, 1978) labeled the "praxic mode" at age 6 to 12 months, when children begin turning away from an overwhelming preference for social interaction to increasing interest in manipulating objects (Section 15.5).

During the second year, the focus of children's attention gradually shifts to the outcomes of their actions, although they do not yet begin to draw inferences about their competence (Section 15.2). The regulatory demands of focusing on an intended action outcome differ depending on the goal in question:

- **Sudden, discrete effects:**
Effects such as banging a drum or dropping an object command attention virtually automatically, making them attractive action goals that give children's activities

directionality early in the second year (Spangler, Bräutigam, & Stadler, 1984; see also Yarrow et al., 1983, on "effect production").

■ **Continuous, action-accompanying effects:**
Regulation of a volitional focus on effects such as the nodding of a pull-along duck is significantly more demanding.

■ **State-related goals in multistep activities:**
Focusing on these goals is particularly demanding. They occur on completion of an action and are only identifiable by the fact that they correspond to the original action intention, e.g., a finished tower of bricks or a tin containing all the available marbles.

■ **"Respecting one's work":**
Hildegard Hetzer (1931) labeled this last type of action goal and the related affect "respecting one's work" (see also Bühler, 1922, on pleasure in satisfaction ["Endlust," "Befriedigungslust"] as opposed to pleasure in functioning and creativity ["Funktionslust," "Schaffenslust"]). From the age of about 18 months, children learn to keep sight of the ultimate goal in a multistep activity (e.g., collecting marbles in a jar) and to terminate the activity no sooner and no later than they have attained that goal. Such state-related action outcomes persist even after an action is completed, and may prompt children who have developed a self-concept to evaluate the effectiveness of their actions and even their competence (Section 15.4).

❗ State-related goals in multistep activities make higher demands of **volitional action control**, which serves to ensure that attention and behavior remain focused on the chosen action goal, even if its outcome can only be attained after the successful completion of a number of subtasks.

Merry Bullock and Paul Lütkenhaus conducted a series of studies to investigate the development of volitional behavior in toddlers (Bullock & Lütkenhaus, 1988; Lütkenhaus & Bullock, 1991). In one study, 14- to 31-month-olds were shown a sequence of actions that involved a doll being fed after various preparations had been made. The children were then asked to copy the sequence of actions, but were not given the doll until 25 seconds later. The children thus had to delay either the entire action sequence or just the final step of actually feeding the doll. None of the children younger than two years were able to delay the entire action sequence, but a good 50% of them succeeded in delaying the last step of feeding.

In another study, Bullock and Lütkenhaus (1988) investigated the development of the focus on self-produced outcomes in tasks that were inherently attractive (building towers, sorting building blocks in a box, cleaning a blackboard). They found that children younger than two years were absorbed in the activity itself, whereas those older than two years were intent on attaining a specific goal (i.e., building a tower by stacking one building block on top of another). But even these children who focused on producing outcomes were not immune to getting carried away and continuing to engage in the activity even after the goal had been attained (e.g., emptying building blocks out of the box in order to start sorting them again). It was only at the age of two and a half years that most children reliably stopped engaging in the activity on reaching their goal. Barrett et al. (1993) report corresponding findings from an observational study of children ages 15 to 30 months. Children older than two years showed greater persistence in the goal-directed, multistep activity of completing a jigsaw puzzle.

Between 18 and 24 months, the development of control (or mastery) motivation thus enters a new phase (see also Barrett & Morgan, 1995). The intended outcome of an action now becomes the yardstick against which its success is measured. It is thus at this point that standards of excellence set by the child or by others take effect as criteria of successful or unsuccessful action. From the age of around 17 to 18 months, children show increasing interest in attaining specific standards when manipulating objects, especially in situations where they feel observed (Kagan, 1982). For example, they can be quite determined to repeat a sequence of actions accurately, to construct a tower with all the available blocks, or to complete a jigsaw puzzle. These standards are often introduced by parents or older children (Section 15.5), but are later adopted by the toddlers themselves.

15.4 Establishment of Personal Competence as an Action Incentive

Anticipatory self-reinforcement is an important motivational resource for achievement-motivated behavior in adults (H. Heckhausen, 1989). An action goal is not attractive because of the intrinsic value of mastering a standard of excellence alone, but also because attaining an action goal allows positive inferences to be drawn about one's competence. It is disputable that these inferences are intrinsic achievement-motivated incentives in the strict sense, because self-evaluation is not activity- or outcome-immanent (Chapter 13). Within the framework of Heinz Heckhausen's (1989) **extended model of motivation**, self-evaluation can be seen as one of many potential **consequences** of an action outcome. Which of these consequences are most important to a given person and in a given situation does not depend on the centrality of the self-concept of ability in a given cultural and social context (see, e.g., Heine et al., 1999). In addition to the incentives of the action outcome (reaching a personal standard of excellence) and its internal (self-reinforcement) and external (recognition of others, educational and career advantages) consequences, incentives residing within the activity itself ("activity-related incentives"; Rheinberg, 1989; see also Chapter 13) may also play a major role in achievement-motivated behavior.

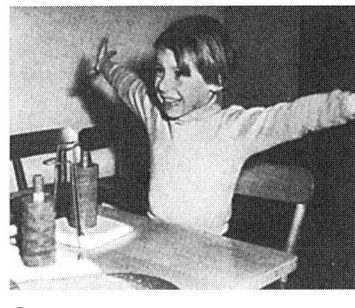  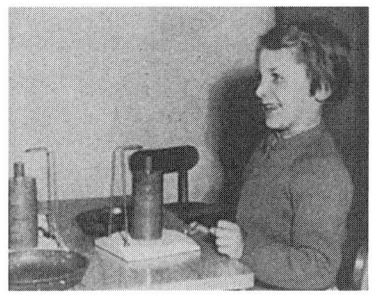

a   b   c

Figure 15.2 Responses to success. (a) Annegret (6;3) spontaneously exclaims, "I [won]!". Triumphant, proud "enlargement of the ego" relative to the experimenter (13th trial). (b) Maria (4;3) spontaneously: "I [won]!". Sits up straight and "enlarges the self" (4th trial). (c) Ursula (5;2) spontaneously: "I finished first again!" Expression of pride: beams at the opponent, upright upper body (2nd trial). (From Heckhausen, 1974, p. 157, Fig. 27, p. 155, Fig. 23, p. 163, Fig. 36.)

15.4.1 Pride and Shame – Emotions Between Achievement and Power

Of the many and diverse incentives for achievement-motivated behavior, three that play a prominent and ubiquitous role in the western industrialized nations, at least, are the exploration of personal competence, the emotional and social-cognitive reinforcement of positive conceptions of personal competence, and the demonstration of personal competence to others.

❗ The predominant conceptual model of achievement-oriented behavior – the risk-taking model and its extensions (Atkinson, 1957; H. Heckhausen, 1989) – specifies self-reinforcement to be the decisive motivational force, and the emotions of pride and shame to be the major positive and negative incentives for achievement-oriented behavior. Accordingly, research on the development of motivation has paid a great deal of attention to the development of emotional responses to success and failure in early life (J. Heckhausen, 1988).

Heckhausen and Roelofsen (1962) examined how two- to five-year-olds responded to success and failure in a tower-building competition. It was clear from the reactions of the younger children (two- to three-and-a-half-year-olds) that their experience was focused on the effects of their action; as a rule, however, they did not yet show the typical **expressions of success and failure** associated with self-evaluation. A few children began to show these responses at 27 months, but most did not do so until 42 months. When these older children won, they raised their eyes from their work, smiled, and gazed triumphantly at the loser (Fig. 15.2). They straightened the upper body, and some of them even threw their arms in the air as if to enlarge their ego. When they lost, they slouched down in their chair, lowered the head, and avoided eye contact with the winner. Instead, their hands and eyes remain "glued" to their work (Fig. 15.3). These postural expressions of pride and shame reflect a close relationship to dominant and submissive behavior (Geppert & Heckhausen, 1990), which seems to have been elicited by the demands of the competitive

  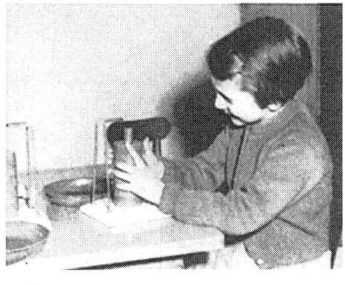

a   b   c

Figure 15.3 Responses to failure. (a) Claudia (4;6), posture expresses deep shame about failure: tries to disappear from view (sixth trial). (b) Franz-Josef (6;0) says, "You [won]", takes hold of his cap, and turns his head away in shame (fifth trial). (c) Ursula (5;2) spontaneously: "Hmm, you finished first." Embarrassed smile of failure, bent posture, fails to disengage from her work (ninth trial). (From Heckhausen, 1974, p. 157, Fig. 28; p. 164, Fig. 40; p. 163, Fig. 37.)

situation. Taking a pluralist view on the activity-related and outcome-specific incentives that may motivate achievement-related behavior, these postural responses of pride and shame seem to express emotions between achievement and power, rather than prototypical achievement-related emotions. The achievement vs. power components may be elicited to differing degrees in different situations, producing hybrid forms dominated by either power or achievement. A systematic investigation of conditions triggering different degrees of achievement- and power-related emotions would be a productive field for future research.

Later studies that did not require some of the cognitive abilities that had been presupposed in the competition study (e.g., the ability to make comparative time judgments; Halisch & Halisch, 1980; Lütkenhaus, 1984) found first pride responses at 30 months and first shame responses somewhat later, at 36 months (Geppert & Gartmann, 1983). Stipek, Recchia, and McClintic (1992) reported similar findings from their competition study: children younger than 33 months smiled and showed pleasure at having completed a tower, regardless of whether they finished first or last, showing that they were simply pleased at having achieved their objective of finishing the tower. Schneider and Unzner (1992) found that children's emotional responses to self-produced effect (without competition) and to success in a competitive situation did not differ until age four. In another study, Stipek, Recchia, and McClintic (1992) observed that even the youngest children in their sample (12 or 13 months) showed positive affect in response to their own successes, but not to the successes of the experimenter. It was not until the age of 22 to 39 months, however, that winning children sought eye contact with the experimenter, meaning that the self-evaluative emotion of pride could not be inferred before the age of around two years. Lütkenhaus (1984) had 36-month-olds do a shape-sorting task with their mothers and noted both positive ("I can do that") and negative ("I can't do that yet") verbal self-evaluative responses at this age.

J. Heckhausen observed even earlier pride responses in a study with mother-child dyads (J. Heckhausen, 1988). By the age of 20 months, almost half of the children responded to success in building a tower or fitting shapes into the appropriate slots by simultaneously making eye contact with the adult and smiling, and in some cases even presenting the product of their work. These responses were associated with intensive and frequent maternal praise at previous points of measurement. The children who showed pride responses at age 20 months had been praised about once every two minutes at age 16 and 18 months. Interestingly, the frequency of praise decreased as the children began to show spontaneous self-reinforcing responses to success (Section 15.5).

The development of the capacity to engage in self-evaluative reflection on the outcomes of one's actions goes hand in hand with an important progression in the child's **self-concept** from the "self as a subject" to the "self as an object" (Geppert & Küster, 1983, see also the study reported below on "wanting to do it oneself"; J. Heckhausen, 1988). At about 18 months of age, children begin to explore the self and to evaluate themselves on descriptive dimensions or in terms of categories. Lewis and Brooks-Gunn (1979) term this the "categorical self." The capacity for self-reflection leads to first experiences of pride in successful action outcomes. The child is now able to interpret information about an action outcome as information about the self – "I'm clever because I can build a tower."

The study by Geppert and Küster (1983) reported in the box below provides insights into the developmental prerequisites for both focusing on a self-produced action outcome

STUDY

Study on "Wanting to Do It Oneself"

Geppert and Küster (1983) observed children ages 9 to 78 months performing various tasks (e.g., playing with Matruschka dolls, completing picture puzzles, throwing balls at cans). The experimenters made offers of help ("Shall I help you?", "I'll help you!") and announcements of intervention ("Please may I do it?", "I'll do it now"), the directness of which was varied systematically. The objective was to examine the relationship between the development of the self-concept and the first occurrence of "wanting to do it oneself" (i.e., rejecting an adult's help and interference). Behavioral tests were administered to assess the development of the self-concept. For example, children were asked to pick up the blanket they were sitting on and give it to the experimenter. Children who have not yet developed a basic self-concept are not able to see themselves in elementary, physical terms, and do not understand that they must step off the blanket in order to pick it up. These children accepted help without protest, evidently because they were indifferent to who actually executed the action. It was only at the age of about one and a half years that children who had developed a concept of self began to protest against any kind of intervention. They did not want their goal-directed activity to be interrupted. If the experimenter intervened immediately before the final step in the task (placing the last building block on the tower), their protest took the form of fits of rage, demonstrating just how outcome oriented children are at this developmental stage.

The older children (age two and a half years and older), who were able to recognize themselves in a mirror, showed another characteristic pattern of behavior. They were more likely to accept interventions and interruptions, but vehemently refused offers of help. Their protests often involved verbal articulations of the wish to do it themselves, with utterances of "me!" or their first name. These children with categorical self-concepts obviously had little difficulty in maintaining a continuous stream of activity despite being interrupted by the experimenter. However, offers of help threatened the attribution of success to their own competence, and thus weakened the major incentive for engaging in achievement-motivated behavior.

and relating that action outcome to one's own competence. The authors investigated the developmental prerequisites for **wanting to do it oneself** – an interesting phenomenon in the development of achievement motivation and a defining characteristic of what laypeople call the "terrible twos" (see Kemmler, 1957, and Goodenough, 1931, on anger in young children).

Because of the prevailing focus on self-evaluative action-outcome consequences, achievement motivation research has largely lost sight of one key issue that warrants mention here. Every achievement-related action is characterized by a multitude of incentives residing in the activity itself, the action outcome (reaching an intended goal) and the internal (self-evaluation) and external (other-evaluation and social or material consequences) action-outcome consequences (Chapter 13). Analogous to the development of cognition (e.g., Siegler, 2002), the development of motivation may be characterized by intraindividual variability in behavior and experience across the developmental trajectory. The sequence of development of motivational and volitional regulatory capacities is relatively fixed, but early forms of control striving – e.g., the "flow" experience of becoming completely absorbed in an activity (Chapter 13; Csikzentmihalyi, 1975) or the focus on a sudden, discrete action effect (Spangler, Bräutigam, & Stadler, 1984) – remain available, and can be used by older children and even adults in concert with more complex patterns of motivation and volition (Jennings, 1991). The system of **mastery motivation** can thus be seen as a hierarchical structure (Harter, 1978) comprising various subcomponents (enjoyment of the activity, joy on achieving a goal, pride in the competence demonstrated by a performance outcome), which allow affective, cognitive, and social aspects to be combined in new and more complex regulatory systems. Individuals can thus respond flexibly to a multitude of situations and differing incentive patterns (e.g., high activity incentive/low self-evaluation incentive, or vice versa). In fact, the regulatory capacity to achieve congruence between one's motivational orientations and motive state across the various situations in which one wishes to exert control (see the concept of motivational competence, Rheinberg, 2006) may itself be an important developmental attribute that is first adopted from adult socialization agents, but increasingly mastered by the child himself or herself.

SUMMARY

The nature of action-related emotions changes and develops in early childhood, with the focus shifting from behavior-event contingencies in early infancy, to achieving a specific outcome (standard of excellence) from about one and a half years of age, and finally to self-evaluation against a certain standard of excellence from the age of about two (playing with the mother) to three (competition) years. Self-related emotions of pride first occur at about the same age, as children acquire the ability to conceive of the self as an object

(Bullock & Lütkenhaus, 1991; Geppert & Küster, 1983; see also "categorical self concept" in Lewis & Brooks-Gunn, 1979). Children who have acquired a self-concept begin to reject adults' offers of help, possibly to ensure that success can be attributed solely to their own competence, Geppert & Küster 1983).

15.4.2 Risks of Self-Evaluative Responses

A **positive evaluation of one's competence** is also considered to be an important motivational resource in theoretical contexts other than achievement motivation – in the present case, for primary control striving. The lifespan theory of control (J. Heckhausen, 1999; J. Heckhausen & Schulz, 1995) highlights the effects of general control, that is, the individual's primary control of the environment, on self-esteem. Although a focus on self-evaluation can have a wealth of positive consequences, it also makes individuals (and their perceptions of their own competence) vulnerable to the negative effects of failure. To the extent that goal-directed actions serve as tests of personal competence, the individual is exposed to the **risk of negative self-attributions** (e.g., low competence, low self-esteem), particularly in social comparison situations with high levels of ego-involvement (Brunstein & Hoyer, 2002; see also Chapter 9). These negative self-attributions can undermine the motivational resources needed for continued control striving, and must be counteracted and compensated by strategies of self-serving interpretation and reevaluation, conceptualized within the theoretical framework of the lifespan theory of control as compensatory secondary control strategies (J. Heckhausen, 1999; J. Heckhausen & Schulz, 1995).

❗ Self-esteem may be protected by compensatory strategies of secondary control such as the following:

  - attributing failure to external factors, thus negating personal responsibility for failure,
  - engaging in "downward" social comparisons with people who are even less successful, and
  - engaging in intraindividual comparisons with domains in which they are personally more competent.

This, and they discuss the development of negative self-evaluations and early forms of compensatory secondary control. Research in this area is still in its early stages, particularly where coping with failure is concerned.

Interestingly, expressions of the self-evaluative emotions of **pride** and **shame** parallel power-related gestures of **dominance** and **submission**, at least in western industrialized societies. Along with the upside of pride-based empowerment, self-evaluation thus involves the downside of shame-based humiliation and **helplessness**, which Dweck (2002) has found to characterize children with a strong orientation to performance goals. Stiensmeyer-Pelster and colleagues have examined processes of increasing helplessness in children exposed to repeated failures in the school setting (see the overview in Stiensmeyer-Pelster, Chapter 14). Their findings indicate that repeated everyday experiences of failure can be a major risk factor in the development of maladaptive long-term motivational and evaluative tendencies (Section 15.7) in the approach vs. avoidance components of achievement motivation, mastery vs. performance goal orientation (Dweck, 2002; Dweck & Leggett, 1988), and state vs. action orientation (Kuhl, 2000b, Scheffer, 2000; see also Chapters 3 and 12).

Negative self-related emotions such as shame and embarrassment are not observed until rather later than pride, however, primarily because children younger than two and a half years respond to failure by changing the task parameters, turning their back on the task, or expressing anger and then abandoning the task (Stipek et al., 1992). In a study of mother-child interactions in task situations, about 30% of children showed anger responses after failure on noncompetitive tasks from the age of 20 months (J. Heckhausen, 1988). The first signs of children beginning to attribute failure to a lack of personal competence at the age of about two years are indirect and implicit in help-seeking behavior after failure, which was observed in some 25% of 22-month-olds (J. Heckhausen, 1988). Geppert and Gartmann (1983) had children ages 18 to 42 months build a tower in four different conditions: success without competition, success with competition (finishing first), failure without competition (tower collapses), and failure with competition (not finishing first). Pride responses to success were observable from the age of 30 months, but shame responses to failure were not seen until 36 months, regardless of whether or not a competitive element was involved. Real shame at failure is evidently not experienced until much later than pride, from three years of age. This developmental sequence shields children against the potentially harmful effects of negative self-evaluation in early childhood.

Moreover, preschool children's conceptions of their own competence do not yet distinguish between the causal concepts of effort and ability. As a result, children of this age tend not to doubt their ability, even in the face of repeated failures (Rholes et al., 1980). Interestingly, they base their judgments more on socioemotional criteria (Is another child nasty or nice?) than on performance criteria (Section 15.6.2). By the age of school entry, children have developed a self-concept of ability that is differentiated from effort, and tend to experience performance decrements after failure (Miller, 1985).

15.4.3 Strategies to Counteract or Avoid Negative Self-Evaluation

As soon as children become aware, at the age of about three and a half years, that action outcomes reflect on their own competence, they begin to shield their self-esteem against the adverse consequences of negative self-evaluations by engaging in behaviors such as the following:

- denying the failure,
- reducing the level of aspiration,
- making self-serving attributions, and
- reinterpreting the action goal (standard of excellence).

In an early study on task choice in preschool and school-age children, Heckhausen and Roelofsen (1962) found that even three and a half-year-olds lowered their aspiration level after experiencing failure, switching to much easier tasks instead. In the competition study mentioned above, in which children between 2 years 3 months and 6 years 10 months of age competed with an experimenter to build a tower by stacking wooden rings on a metal peg as quickly as possible, a variety of failure-related expressions and behaviors were observed when the experimenter won and the children experienced failure. From the perspective of control theory, three major control strategies can be identified from the list of responses provided in Table 15.1. (see the overview in Heckhausen & Roelofsen, 1962, pp. 126, 127):

1. Two components of compensatory secondary control:
   - goal disengagement (categories C.1 and C.2 and D.2.b) and
   - self-protection (categories A.5 and A.9).
2. Primary control striving to overcome obstacles (categories B.1 and B.2 and D.1 and D.2). The strategy of simply denying failure (category A "refusal to accept": all subcategories except 5 and 9) was observed in 8 of the 10 children in the youngest age group (as old as three and a half years), but became increasingly infrequent with age, only being used by 5 of the 13 children older than 5 years.

The cognitively demanding self-protective strategies of excusing failure (example: "My arm's tired now") and recalling earlier successes (example: "But I finished first before") were only used by children older than four and a half years.

Empirical Findings on the Development of Self-Regulatory Strategies

More recent research on the development of compensatory secondary control has focused less on experiences of failure, and more on coping with negative and stressful events (e.g., getting a shot at the doctor's, arguing with a best friend). Findings indicate that numerous **secondary control strategies** become available in childhood and early adolescence (see overview in J. Heckhausen & Schulz, 1995). The account that follows is limited to studies on current and short-term stressors. Studies on coping with death, illness, and other traumatic events are not considered here for space reasons (see, e.g., Compas, 1987; Compas, Worsham, Ey, & Howell, 1996).

Evidence from several studies shows that children of early school age prefer primary control strategies and report very few intrapsychic (secondary) control strategies, even when exposed to uncontrollable stress. One of the most popular

Table 15.1. Overview of children's attempts to cope with failures and conflict situations (Based on Heckhausen, 1974)

A. **Refusing to accept the failure experienced: "refusal to accept"**
   1. Remaining silent in response to the experimenter's question "Who won?"
   2. Denying the failure in response to the experimenter's question
   3. Covering up the failure
   4. Undoing the failure
   5. Excusing the failure ("rationalization")
   6. Restructuring the competitive situation
   7. Verbally distracting the experimenter
   8. Playing down the failure with humor
   9. Recalling earlier successes

B. **Renewing or increasing effort after failure: "compensation"**
   1. Competing in the deconstruction of the tower as a substitute activity
   2. Renewing or increasing effort in the next competition

C. **Avoiding competition after failure: "avoidance"**
   1. Abandoning the competitive activity
      a. Leaving the room
      b. Switching to other activities
   2. Striving to escape the competitive situation
      a. Showing reduced or fluctuating effort
      b. Announcing the abandonment of the game
      c. Introducing other activities

D. **Taking preventative measures to avoid failure: "preventative measures"**
   1. Ensuring success
      a. Not deconstructing the tower fully
      b. Starting to rebuild the tower while deconstructing it
      c. Physically hampering the experimenter
      d. Imposing additional rules on the experimenter
      e. Making the experimenter wait
   2. Avoiding failure
      a. Protesting when the experimenter succeeds
      b. Postponing the next trial or cutting short the ongoing trial
      c. Renouncing potential success

control strategies at this age is to escape the unpleasant situation altogether (Altshuler & Ruble, 1989; Band & Weisz, 1988). As children age, they increasingly use self-distraction techniques (e.g., "I think about something fun"; Wertlieb, Weigel, & Feldstein, 1987) to cope with unpleasant situations (e.g., going to the doctor's). Altshuler and Ruble (1989) confronted 5- to 12-year-olds with hypothetical scenarios of uncontrollable stress that required high levels of self-regulation. The respondents were asked to imagine that a child has to wait patiently for either a positive event (a large piece of a candy after half an hour's wait; a birthday party later in the day) or a negative event (going to the dentist; getting a shot). They were then asked to suggest what the child in the story might do. The 5- to 6-year-olds were far more likely than the 7- to 11-year-olds to recommend escape or avoidance behavior. Nevertheless, children as young as 5 years of age generated behavioral distraction techniques (e.g., do something

else, watch TV), thus demonstrating an elementary understanding of self-regulatory strategies. With increasing age, the children became more likely to propose cognitive distraction (e.g., thinking of something else or fantasizing).

A study on the predictors of childhood depression (Nolen-Hoeksema, Girgus, & Seligman, 1992) provides indirect evidence for the use of even more demanding secondary control strategies to deal with stressful events in childhood. Negative events by themselves predicted depression only in early childhood. In later childhood, causal attribution style (internal, global, stable vs. external, specific, variable) emerged as a major moderating factor. In these more cognitively developed children, stress impact was thus determined by how negative events were explained, and whether these explanations did more to shield the self-image (external, specific, variable) or to damage it (internal, global, stable). However, as shown by Band and Weisz (1988) in a study with young diabetics, secondary control strategies may also be dysfunctional in stressful situations if they mean that opportunities to exert direct influence on events are not taken. Use of secondary control strategies (e.g., "telling myself I can still live a full life") as compared with primary control strategies (e.g., "taking insulin to control my sugar") proved to be more common among children at a formal operational level of cognitive development than among the younger children. However, use of secondary control strategies in the older children was negatively related to compliance with doctor's orders and medical management of diabetes. It may be that secondary control strategies of playing down the condition serve as an excuse for not engaging in vital and effective primary control strategies.

Secondary control strategies seem to proliferate between childhood and adolescence (Compas & Worsham, 1991). Flammer, Züblin, and Grob (1988) found the secondary control strategy of switching to another goal to be the strategy second most frequently endorsed by the 14- to 16-year-olds in their sample (after primary control striving). Under normal circumstances (i.e., unless exposed to exceptional stress), there does not seem to be any further increase in the use of secondary control strategies in young adulthood (Compas & Worsham, 1991).

SUMMARY

Much research is still needed on how strategies for coping with failure and other negative events develop, and particularly on the roots of interindividual and intercultural differences. For example, whether someone prefers the self-serving effect of downward social comparison or tends to attribute unpleasant events to external causes, may hinge largely on the cultural context and on the model provided by the parents. These preferences can have far-reaching implications for behavior and, in turn, for the long-term behavioral consequences of failure. For example, external causal attributions may protect self-esteem, but eventually lead to helplessness; downward social comparisons may allow people to stay active, but fail to provide inspiring role models for control striving.

15.5 Parent-Child Interaction: The Cradle of Action

The first experiences of control do not occur, as Watson had suspected, in experimental manipulations of behavior-event contingencies or in the infant's manipulation of objects, but in natural **interactions** between the infant and the adult caregiver. Long before infants are able to produce direct effects on their environment, they influence their parents' behavior in everyday interactions (see the example below). Papoušek and Papoušek (1987) demonstrated that mothers responses to certain behaviors of their infants show high reliability and low latency, and occur without conscious control.

> **EXAMPLE**
>
> The mother's greeting response to eye contact with her child is a case in point: the mother's mouth is opened, the eyes opened wide, and the eyebrows raised whenever the infant gazes at her face. This reaction is automatized and cannot be suppressed. It provides the infant with repeated, reliable contingency experiences that make minimal demands of the infants' competence to initiate action.

Maternal contingency behavior (also known as responsive behavior) seems to be conducive to the formation of generalized contingency expectations as well as to habituation to redundant stimuli (e.g., Lewis & Goldberg, 1969; Papoušek & Papoušek, 1975, 1987). Furthermore, maternal stimulation and its contingency to the child's behavior seems to be positively related to the development of intelligence (Clarke-Stewart, 1973; Clarke-Stewart, Vanderstoep, & Killian, 1979). Riksen-Walraven (1978) provided compelling evidence for these relationships in a longitudinal study with an experimentally varied intervention design. Mothers were trained either to provide more stimulation for their child, or to be more responsive (i.e., contingent on the child's behavior), or to provide both enhanced stimulation and responsiveness, and to maintain this behavior over a three-month period. Findings showed that enhanced stimulation levels had favorable effects on habituation rate (shorter habituation times) only, and did not have an impact on exploratory behavior or contingency learning. When mothers showed heightened responsiveness in their interactions with their children, thus creating a contingent environment, however, there were very favorable effects on both exploratory behavior and the rate of contingency learning.

Investigation of **exploratory behavior**, another important component of control striving in early social relationships, necessarily raises the issue of mother-child attachment and the metaphor of the mother as a **secure base** (Ainsworth &

Bell, 1970; Ainsworth, Bell, & Stayton, 1974; Sroufe & Waters, 1977). In Harlow's early work (Harlow & Harlow, 1966; Harlow & Zimmermann, 1959) on bonding behavior in rhesus monkeys, the natural mother was replaced by a "surrogate mother" made of either wire mesh or terrycloth, with milk being provided by baby bottles mounted within the models. It emerged that surrogate (terrycloth) mothers provided emotional support, stimulating young rhesus monkeys to engage in more extensive exploratory behavior and even confrontation with unknown objects. Drawing on these and similar findings, leading researchers in the field concluded that infant-mother attachment is based not only on a need for closeness, but on a balanced system of curiosity and caution that permits exploration, but evades dangers (Ainsworth, 1972; Sroufe, 1977). This dyadic behavioral system facilitates the gradual extension of mobility and autonomy throughout the infant's motor and communicative development. By the end of the first year, children are able to withdraw from situations independently and to visually (Carr, Dabbs, & Carr, 1975; Passman & Erck, 1978) and auditorily (Adams & Passman, 1979; Ainsworth & Bell, 1970; Rheingold & Eckerman, 1969) seek reassurance from the caregivers' presence.

❶ A relatively low tendency for maternal interference in the child's exploratory activities (i.e., provision of "floor freedom") has favorable effects on the mother-child bond and was found to be the second strongest predictor of children's intelligence (Ainsworth & Bell, 1970; Stayton, Hogan, & Ainsworth, 1971) after responsiveness (i.e., contingent responses to the child's behavior).

Development of Agency

Infants' early experiences of control are thus bound up with their primary social bonds to caregivers, with their striving for autonomy within these relationships, and the restrictions placed on them. At this early age, experiences of control in the domains of achievement, power, and affiliation are not yet separable. Differentiations in control experiences, control striving, and control behavior soon begin to emerge, however, particularly as infants begin to manipulate objects, and as social (affiliation and power/autonomy) and nonsocial motivations (achievement) become distinguishable and, in some cases, collide. Colwyn Trevarthen's observations on the development of **intersubjectivity** are particularly relevant in this context (Trevarthen, 1980; Trevarthen & Aitken, 2001; Trevarthen & Hubley, 1978). According to Trevarthen children's behavior is driven from birth by two complementary, but sometimes conflicting, motives:

■ the motive to have an active influence on objects and
■ the motive to interact with other humans.

Over the first two years of life, these two motives for object-related control and social relationships alternate and come into mutual conflict. In their first three to four months, infants are focused on other humans, particularly the primary caregiver. Behavioral regulation of aspects such as visual attention and excitability is much smoother and less abrupt in interactions with the mother than in interactions with objects. Furthermore, there is some evidence of mechanisms that foreshadow gestures and language (pregesturing and prespeech; Trevarthen, 1977), indicating that human infants are preadapted to interact with other humans (see also Meltzoff & Moore, 1977).

At about six months of age, in what Trevarthen labels the "praxic mode," children begin to play with objects on their own, and to pay the primary caregiver less attention than before (Trevarthen, 1980; Trevarthen & Hubley, 1978). If the mother is involved in the child's manipulation of objects at all, she tends not to specify the goal of the activity, but rather to be guided by the child's interest in certain objects (see, e.g., Collis & Schaffer, 1975). Conflict often ensues if a caregiver does try to determine the action goal – not because the child rejects the adult per se or prefers the object per se, as Trevarthen suggested, but because the two behavioral intentions are in competition. The child seeks to defend his or her intention against the caregiver's interference and attempts to dominate. In this way, the infant's achievement- and power-related strivings become merged.

In the second year, parent-child interactions with objects become more cooperative at a new level of intersubjectivity, which Trevarthen calls "secondary intersubjectivity" (Trevarthen & Hubley, 1978). The child adopts challenging action goals proposed by the mother, and both work together to achieve them. Cooperation and persistence in pursuing the shared action goal initially relies on the mother keeping the infant's attention focused on the task at hand, thus providing an external scaffold for volitional action control (see the following study and J. Heckhausen, 1987a, b; Kaye, 1977b; Rogoff & Wertsch, 1984; Wood, Bruner & Ross, 1976). As the child becomes increasingly competent, however, the action goal becomes the focus of the joint interaction. Initially, neither party is concerned about who contributes most to

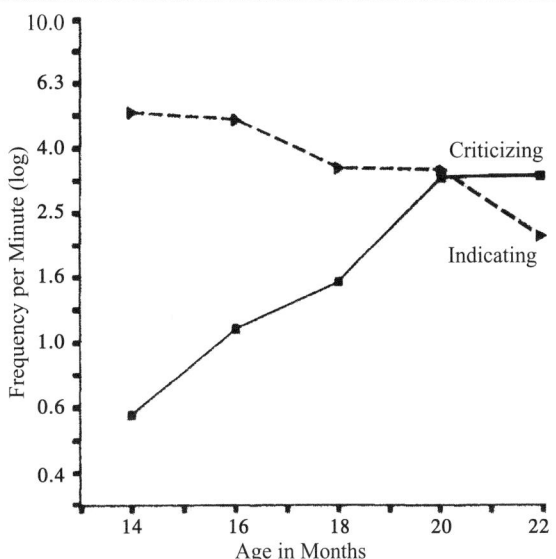

Figure 15.4 Mothers' instruction on the shape-sorting task: indicating the correct solution vs. criticizing the child's slot choice. (Based on J. Heckhausen, 1987a.)

over time from age 14 to 22 months. Early in the study, when the children were just 14 to 16 months and still found the task very difficult, mothers indicated the correct slot at a high frequency per minute. Provision of this kind of direct, nonverbal help decreased as the children grew older. Instead, the mothers increasingly began saying "No, not that one" or otherwise criticizing the child's incorrect choice of slot by verbal means, without showing them the right solution.

At the same time, the mothers fostered the development of positive self-evaluation at age 12 to 18 months by praising the children's successes effusively. As the children's ability to regulate their behavior increased – as reflected in repeated attempts to solve a task (persistence) – the frequency of maternal task-centered motivating attempts decreased; by the end of the second year mothers barely voiced any praise, and frequently refused requests for help. Concurrently, the children became increasingly likely to register their own successes, and to show joy (gazing and smiling at their "work") or even pride (smiling and making eye contact with their mother) at successful outcomes. This higher frequency of pride responses was associated with increased requests for help after experiences of failure from the 18th to 20th month, indicating the children's growing awareness of their own shortcomings, and recognition of the adults' superiority. By the age of 22 months, help-related communication was observed in most mother-child dyads, whether the child asked for help and the mother refused, or the mother offered help and the child rejected it. The shared goal had evidently shifted from a joint focus on completing a task and producing an outcome (e.g., building a tower of blocks) to promoting and demonstrating the child's competence: "I did it myself."

STUDY

Behavioral Regulation in the Mother-Child Dyad: From Apprentice to Master

In a longitudinal study (J. Heckhausen, 1987a, b, 1988) with children ages 14 to 22 months and their mothers, J. Heckhausen investigated change in the joint regulation of behavior in mother-infant dyads. Early in the child's second year, maternal instruction was explicit, specific (e.g., which shape fits which hole), and involved a highly redundant combination of verbal and nonverbal communication. As the children internalized the task intention (e.g., to build a tower, to put all the shapes in the correct holes), the mothers stopped giving explicit instructions, and their guidance became increasingly implicit. In one task, children had to fit geometric wooden shapes into the corresponding slots in a wooden board. Fig. 15.4 shows the change in maternal instruction observed goal attainment. During the second year, the mother increasingly emphasizes the child's competence and expects the child to work toward the goal independently. Once children have acquired a categorical self-concept, they internalize these expectations. From the age of about two years, the shared goal of a task that is challenging but not overly difficult is no longer the action outcome itself (e.g., building a tower), but the development and demonstration of the child's competence (J. Heckhausen, 1988). The shift from a focus on producing outcomes to demonstrating the child's competence is triggered by the mother's refusal to provide help, but later vehemently defended by the child, independent of direct maternal influences (see also the study on "wanting to do it oneself" on page 390; Geppert & Küster, 1983).

SUMMARY

Early parent-child interaction is the cradle of action. It is here that the major, universal foundations for individual action regulation are laid: experience of control; goal setting and persistence; autonomy and resistance to the imposition of external goals; mastery of difficulties; enjoyment of intended action outcomes; ability attributions of successful action outcomes; and finally, defense of ability attributions against the "threat" of outside help. At the same time, the significance of early parent-child interactions necessarily exposes children to certain risks. If parental influences are not appropriate to a child's level of development or are otherwise unfavorable, the development of motivation and behavioral regulation may be misdirected, resulting over time in maladaptive motivational patterns.

15.6 Developmental Preconditions of Achievement-Motivated Behavior

Before favorable and less favorable developmental conditions for motivation and action control are discussed in Section 15.7, this section provides an overview of research on the major milestones in the development of achievement-motivated behavior and, in particular, the cognitive prerequisites for the risk-taking model. The research agenda and review of available findings on the risk-taking model presented in the first version of this chapter (see Chapter 13 of Heckhausen, 1980) remains unsurpassed in its differentiated approach, conclusiveness, and theoretical integration. In the last 20 years, research on the developmental prerequisites of achievement-motivated behavior has been rather heterogeneous – there has been a great deal of interest in some aspects (e.g., the conception of ability, reference norms), but others have been neglected altogether. There has been a strong focus on individual differences in achievement goal orientation (see Dweck, 2003; Elliot, 1999; Nicholls & Miller, 1983; for an overview, see Elliot, 2005), and considerably less interest in the universals of motive development.

15.6.1 Distinguishing Between Degrees of Task Difficulty and Personal Competence

The perception of differences in task difficulty is a prerequisite for the formation of standards of excellence. Task difficulty and competence define each other: the more difficult the task executed, the higher the competence demonstrated. Given that task difficulty cannot be determined independent of the individual's competence,[1] success can just as well be attributed to ease of the task as to high competence, and failure can just as well be attributed to high task difficulty as to low competence. The question to be asked, therefore, is what children do first: Do they first explain success and failure in terms of task difficulty or in terms of competence?

❶ It is not until children are able to process and integrate information relating to individual reference norms (How well did I do on other versions of the task at previous attempts?), on the one hand, and social reference norms (How well do other children do on the task?), on the other, that empirical studies indicate a clear preference for difficulty attributions (in intraindividual comparison) or competence attributions (in interindividual comparison).

Research has shown that three- to five-year-olds are not yet able to alternate flexibly between individual and social **reference norms** (Heckhausen & Wagner, 1965), and that six-year-olds can only do so to a certain extent (DiVitto & McArthur, 1978).

Findings from numerous studies point to a developmental primacy of difficulty attributions – and thus individual reference norms – at preschool age (Falbo, 1975; Heckhausen & Wagner, 1965; Ruble, Parsons, & Ross, 1976). Barrett, Morgan, and Maslin-Cole (1993) observed that even very young children take task difficulty into account, with 15-month-olds already showing more persistence on moderately difficult tasks than on tasks that were too easy or too difficult for them. Preschoolers do not yet draw on social comparison information to assess their personal competence. Ruble and Feldman (1976, Study 1) told the children participating in their study that "almost all" or "very few" children of the same age were able to solve the tasks assigned. The emotional reactions that the eight- and ten-year-olds showed in response to their performance outcomes differed significantly as a function of this information; those of the six-year-olds did not.

School entry affords children increased opportunities to compare their task-specific performance with that of their peers, with the result that social norms become increasingly dominant (Ruhland & Feld, 1977). In the first two years of elementary schooling, children realize that they would have to be particularly clever to solve tasks that few other children are able to answer. This insight is associated with a decreasing self-concept of reading ability (Miller, 1987), but it is not until the age of nine or ten years that children are able to rank

---

[1] The term "competence" is used as a summary construct comprising both ability and effort.

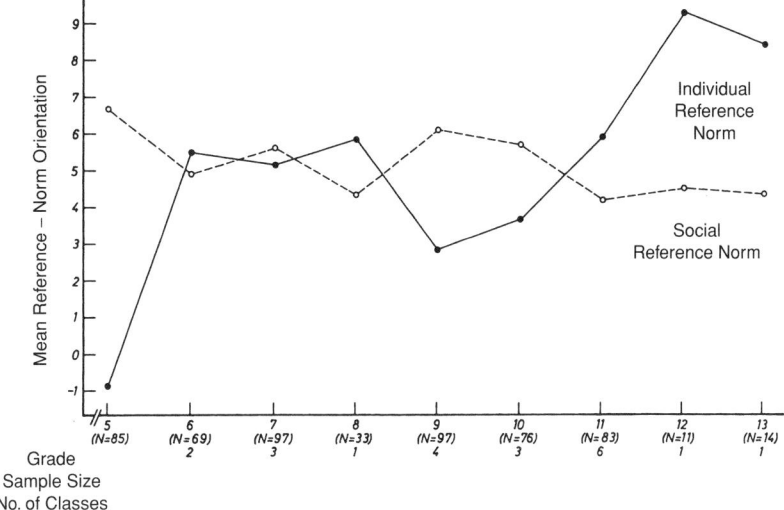

Figure 15.5 Mean preferences for individual and social reference norms in the self-evaluations of secondary students in grades 5 to 13. (After Rheinberg, Lührmann, & Wagner, 1977, p. 91.)

themselves realistically relative to their classmates (Nicholls, 1978). Rheinberg, Lührmann, and Wagner (1977) examined the reference-norm orientations of secondary students in grades 5 to 13. As shown in Fig. 15.5, the importance of individual reference norms soars at the lower end of this age range. They are as important as social reference norms by grade 6, and become increasingly dominant from grade 11 (i.e., about age 17) onward. Aspects of the social ecology of the school and society as a whole were found to have specific effects within this standard developmental trajectory. For example, students in comprehensive schools, where the range of student ability is broader than in tracked schools, were found to prefer social reference norms for longer. Students approaching graduation began to pay more attention to social reference norms, which were likely to be of greater relevance to future employees.

SUMMARY

Children first learn to distinguish different degrees of task difficulty at preschool age, and do not start applying social reference norms to evaluate their competence until starting school. At the transition to secondary level schooling, individual reference norms gain in importance, first drawing level with social reference norms, and becoming very dominant in the last two years of schooling. With the transition to the adult world, social comparison again takes precedence.

15.6.2 Distinguishing Causal Conceptions of Ability and Effort

It is only gradually that differentiated conceptions of ability and effort emerge from a global conception of competence. The conception of effort as a variable causal factor that is

under volitional control seems to develop relatively early. It takes longer for children to recognize ability as an individually constant, but interindividually variable construct. This understanding is complicated by the children's rapid developmental progression, which means that they frequently find themselves able to perform tasks that were impossible only recently.

The assessment of preschoolers' conceptions of effort and ability poses serious methodological challenges, however, because young respondents are not yet able to rate causal factors on a scale. The findings of studies presupposing this ability (e.g., questionnaire studies on control beliefs in the school context) suggest that children do not begin to distinguish between internal and external causal factors until the age of nine years, and between effort and ability conceptions of personal control until the age of ten years (Skinner, 1990; Skinner, Chapman, & Baltes, 1988).

Empirical Assessment of Effort and Ability Attributions

Several ingenious assessment methods have been developed to examine young children's conceptions of effort and ability. Gurack (1978) explored the development of ability attributions by asking children to relate visible indicators of ability (physique, strength, height, age) to different action outcomes. She found a developmental sequence of three increasingly complex "conclusions about ability":

1. Direct conclusions drawn from a visibly relevant physical characteristic (e.g., skinniness – ability to crawl through a small hole in a wall) from the age of three and a half years.

2. Indirect conclusions drawn from a visible physical characteristic about an invisible quality (e.g., height as an index of age – height of a tower constructed) from the age of four years, universally present at five years.

3. Conclusions drawn from an unknown person's previous action outcomes (consistency of competence) about his or her future performance from the age of six years.

The six-year-olds based their assessments of ability primarily on consistency information (across attempts at a task), rather than on the visible physical characteristics of height or age. They did not seem to conceive of ability as a constant personal trait, however; at least, they could not articulate such a concept verbally.

Krüger (1978) examined effort attribution by having children blow cotton balls through miniature houses, a task that required careful dosage of effort. Although this procedure focused the children's experience on effort as the causal factor in success and failure, almost all of the children (three- to six-year-olds) referred only to differences in the degree of difficulty when asked about perceived effort. The developmental primacy of difficulty attribution over competence or even effort attribution thus seems to have a phenomenological basis as well as a psychological one. Even Krüger's three-year-old participants were able to expend effort flexibly, in accordance with task difficulty. From five years of age, intended effort corresponded with actual effort, and most children referred to effort when asked to explain the result attained in freely generated causal attributions.

Nicholls (1978) showed children between 5 and 13 years of age a film of two children sitting next to each other working on mathematics problems. One of the children worked consistently and diligently; the other fooled around, evidently not trying very hard. The participants were told that both children in the film got the same score. They were then asked which of the two children was smarter, why both children had got the same score even though one had tried harder than the other, and whether both children would get the same score if they both tried hard. Findings indicated that five- to six-year-olds do not differentiate between outcome, effort, and ability (naive covariance; see also Heyman, Gee, & Giles, 2003). Children from seven to nine years of age distinguish between effort and outcome, but are unable to say why different effort levels may result in the same outcomes; in other words, they have not yet acquired an independent conception of ability. Between the ages of 9 and 12, children begin to differentiate between effort and ability, but do not really understand the compensatory relationship between the two. It is not until the age of 12 that most children come to understand that high ability can compensate for low effort, and demonstrate an awareness that effort and ability can function as compensatory causal factors (see also Section 15.6.4).

❗ Findings from several early studies using visually represented attributes of competence show that children as young as five to six years old can draw on competence (i.e., not differentiated into effort and ability) factors to explain differences in action outcomes. Effort attributions seem to develop earlier and more quickly than ability attributions.

However, studies that did not provide such clear visual representations of competence have found that preschool children still have very diffuse conceptions of ability (see the overview in Dweck, 2002). When asked how they know whether another child is smart, for example, preschool children often refer to the child's friendliness and good behavior (Stipek & Daniels, 1990; Stipek & Tannatt, 1984). It seems more important for children of this age to determine whether their peers are friendly and well-behaved than whether they are competent and smart in their everyday social comparisons (Frey & Ruble, 1985). Preschool children also tend to confuse behavioral dimensions such as intelligence, good conduct, friendliness, and kindness (Heyman, Dweck, & Cain, 1992; Heyman et al., 2003; Stipek & Daniels, 1990; Stipek & Tannatt, 1984; Yussen & Kane, 1985). Stipek and Daniels (1990) found that many of the preschoolers they surveyed thought that children who are good at reading also share fairly and are able to jump higher hurdles. Moreover, preschool children's estimations of their own competence are typically also very optimistic; most children of this age believe that they are the best in their class (Beneson & Dweck, 1986).

From the age of about seven to eight intellectual and especially scholastic competence and achievement become the focus of attention and of social comparisons (Frey & Ruble, 1985). Children of this age develop domain-specific conceptions of ability, distinguishing between their competence in mathematics, reading, and sports, for example (Wigfield et al., 1997). They see ability as an internal quality (not just mastery of specific tasks) that is normatively defined by comparison with others. For example, Ruble et al. (1980) report that second graders, but not first graders, describe their level of intelligence in social comparison. Significantly, it is at the age of seven to eight years that children first come to see ability and personality traits as enduring person characteristics that permit long-term predictions to be made about performance and behavior (Droege & Stipek, 1993; Rholes & Ruble, 1984; Stipek & Daniels, 1990).

Findings reported by Nicholls and Miller (1983; see the overview in the next section) provide evidence for three stages in the development of conceptions of difficulty and ability.

Development of the Conceptions of Ability and Difficulty (Based on Nicholls & Miller, 1983)

■ Up to about six years of age: Egocentric conception of difficulty; task difficulty is assessed solely in terms of the subjective experience of its demands.

■ From about six to seven years of age: Objective conception of difficulty (or of ability, if the task is mastered); task difficulty is assessed in terms of the objectifiable complexity of its demands (e.g., number of pieces in a jigsaw puzzle).

■ From about seven years of age: Normative conception of difficulty/ability; task difficulty is assessed in terms of the relative number of other people who succeed/fail on it.

STUDIES ON CONCEPTIONS OF ABILITY. Pomerantz and Ruble (1997) investigated several major dimensions of seven- to ten-year-olds' conceptions of ability, namely, perceived uncontrollability, stability, and capacity (i.e., ability makes it possible to succeed without effort, effort exertion leads to especially good outcomes). Whereas perceived uncontrollability remained constant across age groups, conceptions of ability as a stable causal factor increased between seven and nine years of age. The conception of ability as a capacity that can be moderated by effort became established between eight and ten years of age. Children whose conceptions of ability comprised both stability and capacity dimensions evaluated their school learning outcomes in more realistic terms (i.e., congruent with the teacher's evaluation) than did children who had mastered only one or neither of the concepts. Other studies have shown that children from the age of about seven to eight years take success and failure feedback into account when assessing their ability in both individual and social comparison, and use this feedback information to predict their future performance (Entwistle & Hayduk, 1978; Frey & Ruble, 1985; Parsons & Ruble, 1977; Stipek & Hoffman, 1980).

In a fascinating study, Butler (1999) first determined whether fourth to eighth graders have differentiated conceptions of ability and effort, and then compared their information seeking, performance, and interest in a specific task under task- and ego-involving conditions. Students who had already acquired a differentiated conception of ability showed strivings to learn and information seeking under task-involving conditions, and strivings to outperform others and increased interest in social comparison information under ego-involving conditions. They responded to failure with inhibited efforts to learn, restricted information seeking, and subdued interest in the task. In contrast, students who had not yet acquired a differentiated conception of ability were very interested in social comparison information, regardless of whether they succeeded or failed on the task set. The task-involving condition was not conducive to their learning efforts, and the ego-involving condition had no inhibitive effects.

SUMMARY

Between preschool age and second or third grade, independent conceptions of effort and ability slowly emerge from a general, optimistic, and failure-resistant conception of competence. The conception of effort seems to be more closely related to children's experience and thus easier to grasp than the conception of ability. With the transition to school, the conception of effort is consolidated and exposed to the pressures of success and failure in both individual and social comparison. For the first time, ability and effort are set in relation to conceptions of capacity and its limits. These developments lay the foundations for the development of more complex causal schemata for the explanation of success and failure, and for realistic and independent assessments of personal capabilities. At the same time, they make children vulnerable to experiences of loss of control and frustration about the limits of their capabilities (see Section 15.7 on the development of individual differences).

15.6.3 Cognitive Preconditions for Setting Levels of Aspiration

Before moving on to the development of individual differences in achievement motivation, we first have to consider the development of two cognitively demanding aspects of achievement-related information processing:

- the level of aspiration, with its expectancy and incentive components, and
- causal schemata for ability and effort.

Both aspects of achievement-motivated behavior are strongly influenced by individual differences, but they also have some universal cognitive developmental prerequisites, which are discussed in this and the next section. There are two cognitive prerequisites for setting realistic levels of aspiration in the achievement domain: a conception of probability of success, and a connection between expectancy (confidence of success) and the incentive of a given challenge.

We start by discussing research on subjective assessments of the probability of success on a given task, including work on subjective beliefs about control and behavior-event contingencies.

Estimating the Subjective Probability of Success

A fully developed conception of the probability of success presupposes a connection being drawn between two constants: personal ability (corrected for the effects of effort) and objective task difficulty (independent of personal ability and effort). Children acquire the highly complex information integration skills necessary over a long process of development. Before their conceptions of success probability are fully developed, children probably use simplified conceptions that require less complex, shorter-term, and more transparent operations. These less demanding, but functional operations are based on the **principle of covariation** of invested competence (i.e., an undifferentiated combination of effort and ability) and the success or failure experienced on repeated attempts at a task. Such a conclusion was already suggested by the findings of the competition study by Heckhausen and Roelofsen (1962), which found most children younger than four and a half years to be entirely confident of winning, despite an objective probability of 50%, and older children to show signs of conflict when asked to predict the next result. In this study, competence evaluations may have been colored – and enhanced – by the children's hopes and aspirations. Yet, it may not be entirely unrealistic for young children to take an optimistic view of their capacities. Because their competence increases on a daily basis, achievement goals that were out of the question only recently may suddenly prove attainable. Besides, children's optimism about their performance reserves is by no means immune to failure experiences. In a replication of the competition study with three rates of failure (25%, 50%, and 75%), Eckhardt (1968) found that three and a half-year-olds were as uncertain in their predictions of success at a failure rate of 75% as were the older children at a failure rate of 50%. Thus, the three and a half-year-olds were also able to integrate experiences of failure over several trials and, at a failure rate of 75%, were less likely to be unshakably confident in their capabilities and (developmental) reserves.

Such expectations of success are still not very realistic, however, and they remain overly optimistic for the first decade of life. Parsons and Ruble (1977) exposed children up to 11 years of age to a series of successes or failures, and examined their subsequent expectations of success. They found that children three and a half to five years of age remained confident of success, regardless of the type and the number of successes or failures reported. Older children's interpretations of success and failure feedback became increasingly realistic. The girls were some two years ahead of the boys in this respect, probably because boys lag behind girls in general cognitive development. Schuster, Ruble, and Weinert (1998) reported parallel findings from a study with five-, eight-, and nine-year-olds and college students. The authors systematically varied the information that respondents were provided on the consistency over time of a target child's performance in hypothetical failure scenarios (as an indicator of that child's ability; "When Anne played with this game in the past she did not get it right"), as well as on the performance of other children (as an indicator of task difficulty; "The other children did not get it right either").

❗ Significant differences in expectations of success were only observed between the nine-year-olds and the college students, indicating that it is not until adolescence that children learn to predict performance outcomes accurately on the basis of consistency and social comparison information.

Research designs in which the outcome of an action is independent of personal competence and effort make much higher demands of children's conceptions of their prospects of success. Weisz et al. (1982) report a study in which preschool children, fourth graders, eighth graders, and college students were asked to predict the success of two players, one who tried very hard and one who made very little effort, in two versions of a card game. In one version, the players chose cards completely at random; in the other ability-dependent version, they had to remember cards. It emerged that even the preschool children distinguished between different levels of effort in the ability-dependent version; like the older respondents, they predicted that the player who tried harder would be more successful than the player who made little effort. There were marked age differences in predictions concerning the chance-dependent version of the game, however.

Children of preschool age and even fourth graders (although to a lesser extent) believed that players who tried very hard would be more successful than those who did not, even when the outcome was entirely a matter of chance. It was not until eighth grade (i.e., about 14 years of age) that the children seemed to understand that success on chance-dependent tasks is unrelated to effort.

Self-Efficacy and Control Beliefs

Two important research traditions investigating people's expectancies about the success of their actions are Bandura's **self-efficacy** approach (for an overview, see Bandura, 1977, 1986) and the study of control beliefs (for an overview, see T. Little, 1998; Skinner, 1996; Weisz, 1983).

❗ According to Bandura's self-efficacy model, positive beliefs about the efficacy of one's actions in a task situation reinforce effort and persistence, thus increasing the probability of success. The more specific self-efficacy beliefs are to the task at hand, the more accurate the predictions generated by the model.

Seen from the perspective of modern motivation psychology, task-related self-efficacy beliefs – unlike the expectancies of success examined in the risk-taking model – are less a source of information on which challenges to address than motivational resources that make individuals more or less confident of success and thus provide them with more or less energy to implement their intentions (i.e., volition) in an ongoing task situation.

Conceptual models of **control beliefs**, which tend to apply to broader classes of action (e.g., scholastic performance in general), are more general than the construct of self-efficacy beliefs and, at the same time, more differentiated. What control beliefs and self-efficacy beliefs have in common is that they provide volitional resources for action implementation, rather than guiding task selection or goal setting. Modern approaches to control beliefs distinguish between beliefs about the contingency between causal factors and outcomes (e.g., the impact of teacher behavior on grades) and beliefs about individual access to causal factors (e.g., ability) (see Weisz, 1983; Skinner et al., 1988). An individual will consider him- or herself likely to succeed in an activity only if the following two conditions are met:

1. Success must be dependent on conditions or behaviors that people like me can control. Naive theories or beliefs of this kind are termed contingency beliefs (Weisz, 1983), means-ends beliefs (Skinner et al., 1988), or causality beliefs (T. Little, 1998).

2. I personally must be in the position to control these behaviors (e.g., trying hard) or be in the presence of the conditions for success (e.g., being the teacher's pet). Conceptions of this kind are terms competence beliefs (Weisz, 1983), capacity beliefs (Skinner, 1996), or agency beliefs.

Causality beliefs (means-ends beliefs) are beliefs about the controllability of certain events (e.g., getting good grades) and the means by which they can be attained (e.g., effort, ability, being on good terms with the teacher). **Agency beliefs** are individuals' beliefs about whether they personally have access to these means (e.g., access to personal ability or the support of the teacher).

Interestingly, research has consistently shown that overly optimistic expectations of one's general control (combination of causality and capacity) and agency have positive effects on mood, persistence (see, e.g., Weisz, 1983; for adults, see Taylor & Brown, 1988, 1994), and even school learning gains (see also the following excursus). In a two-year longitudinal study with 8- to 11-year-olds in Germany, Lopez et al. (1998) found that children who overestimated their ability and effort (relative to two measures of academic performance) performed better over time. Contrary to expectations, no relationship was found between the magnitude of this action-control bias and school performance. However, the action-control bias was not independent of performance feedback in the form of test results – the longitudinal effects of test results on students' agency beliefs were of the same magnitude as the effects of their agency beliefs on test results. Analogous results were found in a longitudinal study with Russian 2nd to 11th graders. Not only did these students' beliefs about their scholastic ability (i.e., "agency for ability") affect their learning outcomes, their learning outcomes had an impact on their agency beliefs at a subsequent assessment (T. Little, Stetsenko, & Maier, 1999).

Strictly realistic assessments of personal prospects of success clearly do not enhance performance. Findings from self-efficacy research indicate that slight overestimation of self-efficacy has positive effects on the level of aspiration, effort expended, persistence, and resilience to experiences of failure (Bandura, 1977, 1986). Students of different ability levels benefit from high self-efficacy beliefs (see the overview in Pajares, 1996). They complete more tasks, show more persistence on tasks they initially found difficult, and use more effective self-regulation strategies. Pintrich and colleagues (Linnenbrink & Pintrich, 2003; Pintrich & De Groot, 1990; Pintrich & Garcia, 1991) have reported parallel results for college students: undergraduates with higher self-efficacy beliefs use more metacognitive learning strategies, apply these strategies more frequently, and persevere for longer after experiences of failure than do students with lower self-efficacy beliefs. Schunk (1982) manipulated children's self-efficacy beliefs on division tasks by giving them feedback that enhanced self-esteem; this intervention led to improvements in the children's performance on these tasks.

Expectations of success and conceptions about one's competence inform both task deliberation (task choice, level of aspiration) and task implementation (work on tasks). A deliberative, realistic approach is required for the selection of manageable tasks. Overly optimistic expectations of success

or self-efficacy beliefs would be detrimental in this context because they expose students to the risk of failure and frustration. As a matter of fact, however, there is no call for deliberative processes of task choice in school settings. Students are rarely given the opportunity to choose homework assignments or test questions. Rather, they have no choice but to work on tasks set by their teacher, and can thus benefit from high confidence of success. A deliberative, realistic approach is of little help in this context. Because students are obliged to tackle the tasks set by their teacher, they are – to all intents and purposes – permanently in the volitional phase. It is hardly surprising that difficulties arise in the long term. The onset of adolescence, and the concurrent normative transition from elementary to junior high school, marks a pronounced decrease in both the confidence of academic success and the self-concept of ability. Moreover, it can be assumed that students transferring to a school type that gives them more freedom to choose between subjects see the personal significance of the various subjects in more differentiated terms, and thus develop more differentiated concepts of ability in each subject. Students may exit the volitional phase for the subjects they give up, leading to a further decrease in their personal capacity beliefs. In contrast, volitional self-commitment can be expected to be maintained and perhaps even increased in the subjects in which they specialize (Köller, Trautwein, Lüdtke, & Baumert, 2006).

Connection Between Expectancy and Incentive

It is only when children have grasped the multiplicative relationship between the expectancy of success and the success incentive that they are able to set a level of aspiration as formulated in the risk-taking model. The available data confirm that children who understand the covariation between task difficulty and competence (i.e., from the age of about four years to five years at the latest) show more pronounced responses to success (as indicators of incentive) at higher levels of difficulty (as indicators of expectation).

❶ The age at which these phenomena are observed depends on the complexity of the covariation information: visible representations of difficulty (e.g., a much bigger weight to lift, a jigsaw puzzle with many more pieces) are easier to grasp than inferences of difficulty drawn from comparing one's performance with that of other children.

Ruble, Parsons, and Ross (1976) found that social comparison information did not influence the self-evaluations (children could change the expression of a cardboard face accordingly) of six-year-olds, but had a marked impact on those of eight-year-olds. Children's growing ability to process social comparison information is also reflected in task choice, as Veroff (1969) found with a large sample of children of different ages. When presented with three different versions of a task, the majority of four- to seven-year-olds opted for the easy task that "most children your age can do." It was not until the age

School-Related Control Beliefs in International Comparison

Interestingly, international and cross-cultural studies on school-related control beliefs have revealed uniformity in students' means-ends beliefs about academic success but discrepancies in their agency beliefs. In a series of studies, Little and colleagues (Karasawa, Little, Miyashita, & Azuma, 1997; T. Little & Lopez, 1997; T. Little et al., 1995; T. Little, Stetsenko, & Maier, 1999) showed that children in countries as different as East and West Germany, the USA, Japan, the Czech Republic, and Russia acquire very similar conceptions about the major factors influencing academic achievement in the first six years of schooling. As shown in Fig. 15.6, the youngest children's (second graders') importance ratings of all causal factors

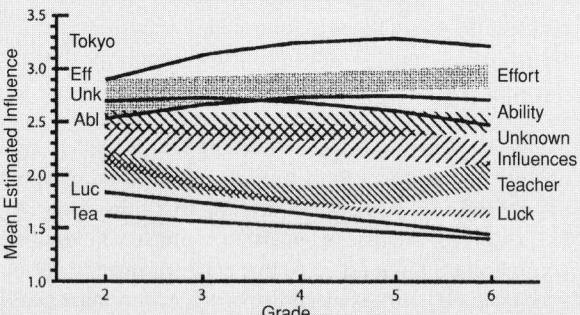

Figure 15.6 Perceived causes of school achievement from second to sixth grade. Causes: **Eff**, effort; **Unk**, unknowns; **Abl**, ability; **Luc**, luck; **Tea**, teacher. The shaded areas represent the variation measured across cultural contexts (East and West Germany, USA, and Russia); the relatively unique trajectories for the sample in Tokyo, Japan, are superimposed on these ranges. (From Little in J. Heckhausen & Dweck, 1998, p. 297, Part B.)

are similar. As the children progress through school, their ratings of the importance of effort increase steadily, peaking in sixth grade. Importance ratings for ability remain stable, coming second in the older children's ranking after effort. Effort and ability are thus increasingly differentiated as causal factors, from almost perfect correlations in secnd grade to correlations of about .50 in sixth grade. Importance ratings for unknown causes and luck decrease steadily, with sixth graders judging luck to be comparatively unimportant for success at school. The perceived importance of teachers declines between second and fourth grade but increases again after fourth grade. Correlations between these causality-related means-ends beliefs and actual school achievement are low.

In terms of beliefs on personal agency (i.e., individual access to important causal factors), however, marked differences emerged across cultures: students in the United States had higher agency estimations for effort and luck than their peers in other nations. At the same time, their personal agency beliefs showed the low-

est correspondence with their actual learning outcomes (correlations between .16 and .32). Before reunification, East German children had the lowest agency beliefs, and the correspondence with their actual performance outcomes was high (correlations over .60, except for teacher influence at .36). Fig. 15.7 illustrates the different patterns of relationship between students' control beliefs and actual school

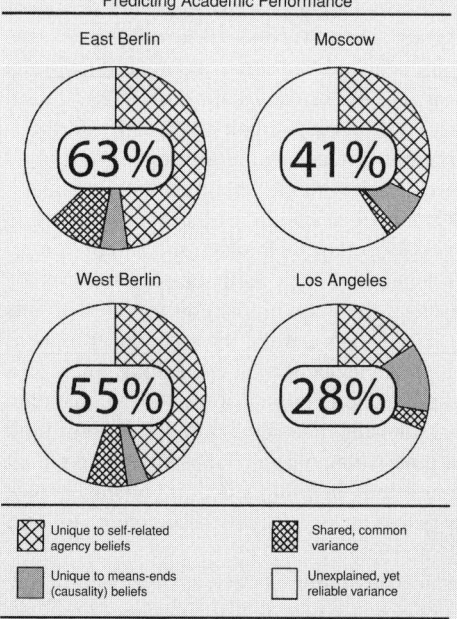

Figure 15.7 Relationship between control beliefs and school performance in East and West Berlin, Moscow, and Los Angeles. (From T. D. Little et al., 1995, p. 695, Fig. 5.)

grades in East Berlin (in the summer of 1990; i.e., shortly before political reunification), West Berlin, Los Angeles, and Moscow. Control beliefs only predict a total of 28% of the Los Angeles students' actual school performance, compared with 63% for the East Berlin students; the figures for West Berlin and Moscow fall in between. Longitudinal follow-ups in East and West Berlin in 1991, 1992, and 1993 showed that the relationship between agency beliefs and school grades in the East Berlin students gradually decreased to the level of their peers in West Berlin as the school system was aligned to that of West Germany. The authors attributed this development to two changes in classroom practice in East Berlin schools: students were now given private, rather than public feedback on their individual performance, and group work was introduced alongside teacher-directed instruction (T. Little, Lopez, Oettingen, & Baltes, 2001).

of eight years that most children preferred the moderately difficult task "that some children your age can do." The preference for this task type increased with age. Complementary relations between task difficulty and failure affect ("the easier the task, the more unpleasant the experience of failure") were not observed in the age groups investigated (up to mid-childhood).

The multiplicative relationship between the expectancy of success and the success incentive seems to be heavily dependent on the salience of those two components in the situation at hand. The experience of repeated successes or failures on a single task, the difficulty of which is varied – as in the weight-lifting study (Heckhausen & Wagner, 1965) – seems to prompt even three and a half- to four and a half-year-olds to set modest levels of aspiration and to avoid very difficult tasks. In the context of new tasks or competitive situations (e.g., in the study by Heckhausen & Roelofsen, 1962), however, children tend to focus on the success incentive and to choose overly demanding goals. First indications of individual differences in the offensiveness versus defensiveness of task choice are apparent from ages as young as four and a half years or even three and a half years (Heckhausen & Wagner, 1965; Wagner, 1969; Wasna, 1970). Some children focus on the expectancy component, others on the incentive component, and yet others alternate between offensive and defensive choices. It is unclear whether these findings can be interpreted as first indications of individual differences in the weighting of the expectancy and incentive components, or whether they simply reflect developmental shortcomings in the cognitive capacity to integrate the two.

SUMMARY

Over the course of development, children must learn to process feedback on their action outcomes in such a way as to generate broadly realistic, but fundamentally optimistic, expectancies of success. This kind of approach is adaptive because it is not usually possible to gauge the exact probability of success, but – in the school setting, at least – it is safe for children to assume that the tasks set are not entirely beyond their capacities and that it is worth investing effort. Research shows that expectancies of success become increasingly realistic until preadolescence. For random events that are not related to ability, such as the random choice of a playing card, developmental gains are still observable even in early adolescence. Interestingly, there are marked individual and cultural differences in how closely children's expectancies of success are related to their actual learning outcomes at school, the major performance domain in childhood and adolescence. Because the developmental context of the school is determined and controlled by adults for the purposes of cultural instruction, with performance demands being set by adult socialization agents rather than chosen by the students themselves, a strictly realistic approach is not in fact necessary and might even inhibit goal striving.

15.6.4 Causal Schemata for Ability and Effort

We now return to the emergence of the ability conception, and thus to the establishment of personal competence as an action incentive (Section 15.4). As the global competence concept gradually begins to differentiate into a conception of ability as a stable causal factor and a conception of effort as a variable causal factor, ambiguities and uncertainties arise in the causal attribution of the outcomes attained. This is because in most cases information about effort exerted, individual ability, or task difficulty is incomplete, or cannot (yet) be correctly integrated. It is impractical even – and indeed especially – for adults to take all potentially relevant information into account in their everyday decisions and behavior (see the critical discussion of Försterling's hyperrational model in Chapter 14, Section 14.3.3, and modern ideas of fast and frugal heuristics, Gigerenzer, 2000). Instead, adults draw on available hypotheses to infer underlying causes, their relationships, and respective weighting. According to Kelley (1972, 1973), these causal schemata (see also the detailed account in Chapter 14) are used to predict ("combined covariation schemata") or causally attribute ("compensatory causal schemata") action outcomes when information is limited. **Compensatory causal schemata** allow success or failure to be attributed to a causal factor about which no information is available if the other factor is given (Kun & Weiner, 1973). For example, it is reasonable to assume that somebody who passes a difficult exam with flying colors despite making little effort is particularly able. **Combined covariation schemata** allow success or failure to be predicted, given a rough idea of an individual's ability and the effort exerted.

❶ Causal schemata thus permit known outcomes to be attributed to unknown causal factors or, when the main causal factors (primarily ability and effort) are known, predictions to be made about future outcomes. Because they are, in essence, conceptions of the causal significance of effort and ability, both schemata are highly relevant to the development of achievement-motivated behavior.

Effort and ability vary in terms of both their perceived controllability (it is often possible to invest more effort, but it is much more difficult to enhance one's ability) and their affective evaluation (effort is laudable, but it is ability that we take pride in; Nicholls, 1976). Causal schemata can thus cognitively accentuate people's tendencies to be more optimistic or pessimistic in their expectancies of success or to prefer a certain pattern of causal attribution, and, in so doing, can amplify individual differences over the developmental trajectory (see also Chapter 14, Section 14.4.1, on the attributional genesis of hopelessness and depression). The development of causal attribution schemata in childhood and adolescence is thus central to the emergence of individual differences in achievement motivation and in other domains of life and behavior. Moreover, it provides a window of opportunity for interventions, including training programs designed to modify patterns of causal attribution (Ziegler & Heller, 2000; Ziegler & Stöger, 2004).

Three preliminary forms of the two causal schemata – proportionate combined covariation in the prediction of outcomes, and inversely proportionate compensation in the causal attribution of a given outcome – have been identified and are specified in the following overview.

Preliminary Forms of Causal Schemata

1. Simple covariation: The magnitude of the effect is proportionate to one of the two causal factors; the other factor is fixed or appears unnecessary.

2. Centered covariation: Only one of the two causes is considered and is brought into simple covariation with the magnitude of the effect.

3. Coupling: The magnitude of the factor to be inferred is judged to be equivalent to that of the given factor. For example, estimations of ability and effort are firmly coupled.

Centered covariation and coupling can easily lead to false conclusions, because the magnitude of only one of the two causal factors is taken into account in the prediction or causal attribution. This shortcoming is gradually overcome; from the age of about eight years, effort attributions no longer rigidly follow ability attributions, and from the age of about nine years, ability can be inferred from effort information (see the overview in Heckhausen, 1982).

Empirical Findings on the Prediction of Performance Outcomes

Empirical research on the development of causal attribution schemata has investigated both the prediction of outcomes when causal factors are known and the explanation of known outcomes (see the detailed reviews in Heckhausen, 1980, 1982, 1983b). We start by considering some of the major results on outcome prediction. Kun, Parsons, and Ruble (1974) informed 6- to 11-year-olds and adults about the levels of effort and ability required to solve various puzzles (three levels of each), and asked them to make predictions of success. The predictions of the six-year-olds evidenced combined covariation; only 31% of these children still centered on effort. Whereas the combined covariation of the six-year-olds was additive, the eight-year-olds showed signs of multiplicative variation: at higher levels of ability, the same increase in effort was predicted to produce a greater effect. Multiplicative covariation predominated among ten-year-olds and adults. In addition, effort increased in importance relative to ability with increasing age. Surber (1980) used clear visual representations of ability and effort in their study with 6-, 9-, and 11-year-olds, and reported similar findings to Kun et al. (1974). In his weight-lifting prediction task, ability was illustrated by bulging muscles and effort by rectangles of different sizes. Even the six-year-olds combined the causal factors of effort and ability in their predictions, if only additively. The predic-

tions of the nine-year-olds and the adults were indicative of multiplicative combination of effort and ability.

Tweer (1976) asked children between five and ten years of age to predict their performance outcomes on a strength task that involved hitting a platform with a hammer, causing a small wagon to slide up a vertical runway. She presented the children with hypothetical scenarios in which either effort ("The first time you don't try at all; the next time you try harder") or ability ("Your right or your left arm" or "You and your father") was varied. When effort was unequal (simple covariation), 60% of the five- to six-year-olds made the correct prediction, but when ability was unequal (intraindividual ability comparison or own ability compared with father's ability) and effort was equal, only 50% of the ten-year-olds made a correct prediction. The rest of the children continued to use coupling as the basis for their predictions, perhaps because ability seems to be the dominant factor in this kind of strength task.

Empirical Findings on the Development of Causal Explanations for Outcomes

Nicholls' (1975, 1978) studies were outlined in Section 15.6.2. In one of his studies, Nicholls showed children between the ages of 5 and 13 films in which the effort expended did not correspond with the outcome (e.g., a child fools around and makes no effort, but still finishes his mathematics problems quicker than a classmate who had worked diligently). These scenarios can only be explained by ability compensation (i.e., the first child completes the assignment quickly because he is especially clever). Nicholls' findings point to a four-stage developmental sequence, which corresponds to Piaget's sequence of development from preoperational thought to formal operations, and is illustrated in Fig. 15.8:

1. Global conception of competence (around five to six years): an undifferentiated coupling of effort, ability, and outcome.

2. Effort covariation: effort alone causes the outcome (around seven to nine years).

3. Ability begins to be seen as an additional and autonomous cause – sometimes still coupled with effort, sometimes in the form of ability compensation (around ten years).

4. Systematic use of ability compensation: ability can compensate for effort in inversely proportionate explanation (ability compensation) and in proportionate prediction of outcomes (around 12 to 13 years).

Research on the development of compensatory schemata in the explanation of outcomes when one of the two causal factors is known (cf. Karabenick & Heller, 1976; Kun, 1977; Surber, 1980; Tweer, 1976) has revealed that compensatory causal attributions are already used by younger children from the age of six to ten years when the following conditions apply:

1. Compensation is required in terms of effort, not ability (someone who is less good at something has to try harder).

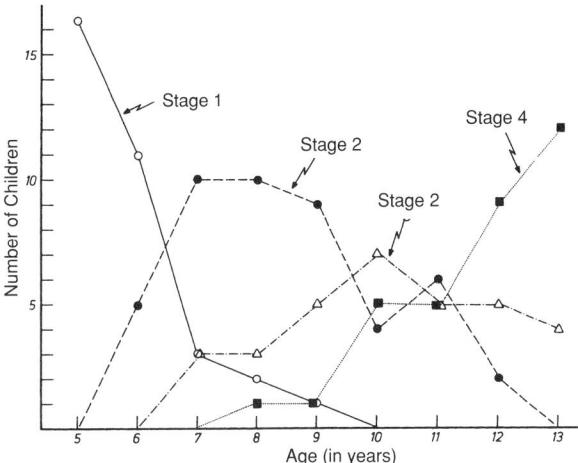

Figure 15.8 Age trends in the development of the ability concept when the performance outcomes of two children were to be explained. The children's work activities were shown on film and contradicted a simple covariation of effort and outcome. Stage 1: global concept of competence; stage 2: effort covariation; stage 3: ability as an independent cause; stage 4: ability compensation. (Based on Nicholls, 1975; from Heckhausen, 1980, Fig. 13.2, p. 661.)

2. The information provided is easy to interpret (e.g., picture cues relieve working memory) and not too complex.
3. Answers are given as paired comparisons (who has to try harder?) rather than on absolute scales (see detailed overview in Heckhausen, 1983b).

SUMMARY

Causal schemata develop in the following sequence:

■ Simple covariation between the effect and one cause from the age of four to five years; effort covariation precedes ability covariation.

■ Combined covariation in the prediction of outcomes at age five to six years when both causal factors are given or two cases of unequal effort are to be compared.

■ Depending on the method and the sample, effort compensation may be observable at five years or not until ten years of age.

■ Ability compensation is obviously more demanding, and is only observed from the age of 6 to 11 years (relatively late when a preconceived ability attribution has to be revised or unequal effort clearly violates covariation with outcomes).

■ Effort and ability compensation schemata develop earlier for experiences of success than for experiences of failure.

Development of Affective Differences Between Effort and Ability Attributions

Affective differences between ability and effort attributions may influence levels of aspiration, the behavioral consequences of failure, and the development of individual differences in motivation and action.

❶ The developmental precondition for affective differences between effort and ability attributions is that affective responses do not simply reflect the action outcome (pride after experiences of success, shame after experiences of failure), but vary depending on the causes ascribed.

This relationship has been investigated in numerous studies asking children between 6 and 13 years of age to state how a target person would feel at succeeding or failing on a task requiring high or low levels of effort and ability (Stipek & DeCotis, 1988; Thompson, 1987; Weiner, Kun, & Benesh-Weiner, 1980). In all cases, findings showed that the focus on the outcome decreased with age, and that the causal factors of effort and ability came to play an increasingly important role in the emotions ascribed. By the age of 13, the respondents referred to pride and shame only when performance outcomes were attributed to ability or effort in the stories (Stipek & DeCotis, 1988). These findings are in line with earlier studies by Weiner and Peter (1973), which showed that the impact of effort attributions on performance evaluations increased with age.

❶ In sum, these findings indicate that instruments assuming a differentiated competence concept (i.e., a clear verbal distinction between the concepts of "effort" and "ability") are not appropriate for children younger than ten years. From the age of about ten, when children have mastered effort and ability compensation as well as simple effort covariation, effort becomes the decisive factor in evaluating the achievements of others. It is at this point that children overcome the coupling schema (effort = ability) and are no longer bound to conclude that success deriving from high ability must be attributable to high effort as well.

Different causes can also have differential effects. For adults, effort is the decisive causal factor in evaluations of others, and ability is the decisive causal factor in self-evaluations. Others are evaluated more highly if they have invested effort, but people tend to see cause for pride in their own achievements if they testify to high ability. In a nutshell, "effort is virtuous, but it's better to have ability" (Nicholls, 1976, p. 306). Ability attributions of failure are problematic because they imply that future attempts have little chance of success either, at least when ability is seen as stable and unchangeable. In contrast, effort attributions of failure spur the individual to try again, investing more energy and care this time to ensure success. We return to the implications that these patterns of causal attribution have for the development and amplification of individual differences in Section 15.7.5 (cf. Dweck, 2002; Heckhausen, 1984a).

FINDINGS ON AFFECTIVE DIFFERENCES IN SELF-EVALUATION. H. Heckhausen (1978) exposed children between 10 and 13 years of age (i.e., the critical age range for the acquisition of effort and ability compensation) to a series of successes or failures. The more these fifth to seventh graders attributed success feedback to their ability, the more satisfaction they reported. Effort attributions had no effect on self-evaluation. Other studies (Nicholls, 1975; Ames, Ames, & Felker, 1977) confirm the importance of ability attributions for self-evaluations from the age of 10 to 11 years upward. First signs of individual motive differences were detected in children's self-evaluations after experiences of failure: negative self-evaluations were found to be associated with effort (in success-motivated individuals; Heckhausen, 1978), with ability (Schmalt, 1978), or with neither of the two (Nicholls, 1975). In a study with children of a similar age, Miller (1985) found that only 11- to 12-year-olds who had already developed a full self-concept of ability (i.e., who were aware that the ability level determines the effects of effort) responded to a series of failures in anagram tasks with performance decrements in a subsequent shape-sorting task.

Developmental Risks of Applying Causal Schemata

What implications do these patterns of causal attribution have for children's interpretations of other people's evaluations of their competence? Overcoming the coupling schema of effort and ability and becoming aware of their compensatory effects can, like other developmental achievements, have detrimental effects. What conclusions are likely to be drawn by a student whose teacher keeps praising him or her for effort or for solving easy tasks? Because the relationship between the two causal factors is compensatory when the outcome is known, inferences can be drawn from the effort factor (which is decisive for other-evaluations) about the ability factor (which is decisive for self-evaluations) as soon as compensation schemata are acquired. The student would then have to conclude that a teacher who praises his or her performance on a simple task enthusiastically considers him or her to have shown (from the teacher's point of view) commendably high effort but (from the student's point of view) shamefully low ability. Conversely, being criticized by a teacher for failure on a difficult task would indicate that the teacher has a high opinion of that student's ability. It is not until the age of 10 to 12 years that children can "decode" these paradoxical messages of praise and criticism because they presuppose that the child's conclusions are based on two premises: that other people praise effort (but not ability) and criticize a lack of effort in their evaluations, and that the relationship between ability and effort is inversely proportionate when the outcome is known (compensation).

This assumes a command of formal operations that can barely be expected of children younger than 10 to 12 years. These empirical findings on the paradoxical effects of praise and criticism are clearly confirmed by the results of Meyer and colleagues, at least when students are shown similar scenarios under experimental conditions and asked to judge who

the teacher thinks is more able – the sanctioned or the non-sanctioned student (Meyer, 1978; Meyer, Mittag, & Engler, 1986).

When the conditions are less specific, however, students tend to interpret teacher sanctions quite differently (e.g., in terms of "niceness/unfairness"; Meyer, Reisenzein, & Dickhäuser, 2004). Furthermore, they make few paradoxical interpretations, especially when their teachers have an individual reference-norm orientation (i.e., precisely those teachers who routinely apply these kinds of sanctions). They are aware that their teachers barely relate school outcomes to the causal factor of ability, and it thus seems pointless for them to draw inferences about the teacher's ability estimations (Rheinberg & Weich, 1988). Findings from real-life classroom settings (Pikowsky, 1988) also show that students rarely or never make paradoxical interpretations under ecologically valid conditions, although they are capable of doing so under experimentally accentuated conditions.

Leon-Villagra, Meyer, and Engler (1990) found that students age 10 to 12 years infer teacher evaluations of student ability from praise and criticism. A study by Miller and Hom (1997) provides even more direct evidence for the developmental prerequisite of a compensatory causal attribution schema for ability and effort: fourth, sixth, and eighth graders were asked to appraise two children who were praised, criticized, or given a material reward for the same test result. Students who understood that greater effort is indicative of lower ability at a given performance outcome stated that the child who was praised and rewarded was less intelligent than the child who was criticized. However, the younger children who did not yet understand the compensatory relationship between ability and effort also seemed to think that children are praised for achievements of which they would not normally be capable.

SUMMARY

From the age of about ten years, ability attributions become decisive for affective self-evaluation. At first, this only applies after experiences of success, and not after experiences of failure. It is at this age, as differentiated conceptions of the two causal factors gradually emerge from a global conception of competence, that children also begin to grasp the compensatory relationship between effort and ability. The more success is attributed to ability and failure to lack of ability, the more satisfied or dissatisfied they are with themselves. Attributions focusing on a lack of personal ability pose first developmental risks. Other people's (e.g., teachers') causal attributions of performance may also involve risks for the development of competence. Excessive praise for mediocre performance can undermine ability attributions; conversely, criticism for failure can be interpreted as indicating that the teacher (mother, friend) had, on the basis of high ability evaluations, expected better outcomes.

15.7 Development of Individual Differences in Motive Strength and Action Regulation Systems

The development of individual differences in motive strength remains a broad and complex field of research, although at a higher level of knowledge than before. It is almost as if motivation researchers had struggled up a steep spiral staircase to reach an observation platform offering panoramic views, only to find themselves overwhelmed by all there is to see. In the past two decades, conceptual development in the field of motivation psychology, and indeed psychology in general, has seen a move away from a strictly cognitive focus toward a perspective that also takes affective dynamics into account. Motivation psychologists now know more and are, at the same time, in the midst of an exciting phase of discovery as to the interactions of implicit and explicit motives, the functions of intrinsic and extrinsic incentives, cognitions adapted to different action phases (e.g., self-efficacy or causation), and individuals' active influences on their own development and its conditions. The development of individual differences cannot be explained solely in terms of cognitive factors such as levels of aspiration or causal attribution styles, neither can it be clarified by an exclusive focus on how differences in the incentive value of success and failure emerge over socialization.

McClelland's comparison of self-attributed (explicit) and implicit (not consciously represented) motives can serve as a useful organizing framework for an overview of research on the development of individual differences in achievement motivation (McClelland, Koestner, & Weinberger, 1989; see detailed discussion in Chapter 9). There is much evidence to indicate that implicit motives (measured by projective tests) and explicit motives (measured by self-report questionnaires) are two independent motive systems that govern different types of behavior and that may be activated in concert or in opposition depending on the situation. **Implicit motives** are activated by incentives residing in the activity itself (to improve one's performance, to master a challenge) and thus generate motivation for more spontaneous behavior that is not prestructured by the environment: the activity itself is attractive to people high in the achievement motive, independent of its outcomes. **Explicit motives**, in contrast, are activated by social incentives (social recognition, reward, status) and thus determine prestructured behavior in socially regulated situations, such as the classroom, where the contingencies for social incentives are transparent (e.g., I have to do my homework carefully to please the teacher and get a good grade).

In this section, we begin by outlining four main strands of research on individual differences in children's motivational processes, namely, research approaches focusing on:

- implicit motives,
- more or less explicit incentives and expectancies,

- explicit goal orientations, and
- processes of action regulation.

In a second step, we discuss developmental processes that can influence individual differences in achievement motivation at critical phases and transitions, present the available empirical findings, and outline perspectives for future research.

15.7.1 Implicit Motives

The foundations for the development of implicit motive strength are laid in early childhood, before verbal instructions and self-reflection give motivational processes the deliberative character that distinguishes higher cognition (Heckhausen, 1980, 1982; McClelland, 1987; Veroff, 1969). Although achievement-motivated behavior comprises both affective (implicit) and cognitive (explicit) processes – in modern terminology, "implicit" and "explicit" components of achievement-motivated behavior – the preverbal development of individual differences in the incentive value of success and failure is decisive. It is at this early stage that children develop a heightened, probably lifelong sensitivity to situational conditions affording them the opportunity to develop and optimize their control of the environment (of objects in the case of achievement motive and of other people in the case of the power motive), or that threaten to reduce or restrict that capacity.

Influence of Parenting on the Development of Implicit Motives

Consensus has not yet been reached on the contextual conditions that promote this individual sensitivity and readiness to act. Longitudinal data are scarce, and results have been mixed. The findings of a longitudinal study by McClelland and Pilon (1983) provide some valuable insights, however. The authors followed up on a 1950s study on parenting styles by Sears, Maccoby, and Levin (1957), using TAT and questionnaire measures to assess the affiliation, power, and achievement motives of the "children," who were now in their early 30s.

❶ Parenting behavior was not found to reliably predict the affiliation motive. Parental behavior and influence did, however, predict the development of the power motive and especially the achievement motive.

The children whose mothers had reported that aggressive and/or sexualized behavior on the child's part was tolerated in the home environment developed a strong power motive. If the father was the dominant influence in the child's upbringing, a strong power motive with activity inhibition emerged (also termed "imperial power motive" or "socialized power motive" by McClelland); if the mother was the dominant influence, an uninhibited power motive was observed (termed "conquistador syndrome" or "personalized power motive" by McClelland, and "Don Juan complex" by Winter, 1973). Further, McClelland and Pilon (1983) found that mothers of boys who had high TAT achievement motive scores at age 30 had insisted on fixed mealtimes and been particularly strict about toilet training. These two influences of early parenting behavior cannot be attributed to the effects of parental strictness or punishment in general: neither of these factors was related to the sons' achievement motivation scores at age 30.

It is difficult to interpret these findings without knowing anything about potential mediating processes between childhood and the age of 30. When the mothers were surveyed in the 1950s, it was – in contrast to current practice – generally considered good parenting to get children used to fixed mealtimes and to begin toilet training as soon as possible; indeed, these challenges were seen as **normative developmental tasks** for the first and second year of life. In other words, mothers who were particularly ambitious in this respect believed – and indeed expected – their children to be capable of achieving these developmental milestones well within time. They therefore generated interaction contexts, even in the preverbal period, in which positive and negative affect was expressed in response to success and failure on self-control tasks (e.g., "Don't ask for food before mealtimes"). Interestingly, the mothers' expectations for school achievement and other early achievement-related outcomes did not predict their children's achievement motives in adulthood. The socialization effects identified by McClelland and Pilon operate on the purely implicit motive level (see also the discussion of these findings in Chapter 9, Section 9.2.4).

A number of cross-sectional studies have also investigated how various socialization variables, parenting practices, and aspects of independence training are related to implicit motive strength in later childhood or adulthood (see the overview in Heckhausen, 1980, 1982; for a more recent review, see Eccles et al., 1998, and Trudewind, Unzner, & Schneider, 1997; see also the following excursus). Winterbottom's (1958) early and influential study extended the findings presented by McClelland and Pilon to children of school age. Mothers of eight-year-old boys high in achievement motivation were found to endorse more requirements for independence and competence than mothers of boys low in achievement motivation, particularly for the age range of five to nine years. Interestingly, these relatively early maternal expectations were not limited to the reliable execution of routine tasks (e.g., getting dressed) to relieve the mother, but included child-centered competence requirements that fostered the child's independence in task choice and execution. Like the requirements for early self-regulation of food intake and excretion identified by McClelland and Pilon, these competence requirements in the early school years may be features of the family environment that foster the development of the

achievement motive. In subsequent studies, however, the features identified by Winterbottom failed to predict the achievement motive in adolescence (Feld, 1967) or in different social classes (Rosen, 1959) and religious orientations (Smith, 1969), casting doubt on the validity of her findings. Some studies even found negative relations between very early expectations of independence and the tendency to approach success (Hayashi & Yamauchi, 1964; Bartlett & Smith, 1966; Teevan & McGhee, 1972).

In the 1970s, a number of studies (Reif, 1970; Heckhausen & Meyer, 1972; Schmalt, 1975; Trudewind, 1975) taking a more systematic approach to parents' expectations of competence and independence confirmed Veroff's (1969) hypothesis that it is not the earliness, but the **developmental adequacy** of independence demands that promotes the development of a success-oriented achievement motive. Fig. 15.9 presents findings from studies by Reif (1970), Trudewind (1975), and Schmalt (1975), showing that child-centered independence training is associated with higher success motives and lower failure motives when it occurs neither early nor late in the child's development. Measuring the earliness of maternal expectations in terms of the child's intelligence level, Heckhausen and Meyer (1972) found a direct relationship between excessive maternal expectations and sons' fear of failure. We return to positive and negative effects on the development of motivation in childhood in Section 15.7.5.

15.7.2 Specific Incentives and Expectancies

The risk-taking model (Atkinson, 1964b) assumes anticipated self-evaluation to be the crucial incentive motivating achievement-oriented behavior. As such, the implicit motive components hope for success and fear of failure, and their relations to the other important motives of power and affiliation, are the only individual characteristics capable of having an impact on achievement-oriented behavior in Atkinson's model (McClelland, 1985b). It soon became clear, however, that achievement-motivated behavior cannot comprehensively be explained in terms of an approach vs. avoidance achievement motive and task difficulty. Eccles showed, for instance, that the gender differences frequently observed in individual preferences for certain school subjects cannot be explained by the risk-taking model (Eccles, 1984, 1987; Eccles, Adler, & Meece, 1984; Eccles, Wigfield, & Schiefele, 1998).

❶ Rather, the choice of subjects and tasks is influenced by the confidence a student has in his or her abilities and by the value of a particular course choice. A wealth of incentives, such as congruence with gender-specific behavioral norms and with the self-concept, and the perceived attitudes of socializers and peers, are thus involved in achievement-related choices.

As described elsewhere, numerous incentives residing in the action itself, its outcomes, and the internal and external

Change in Implicit Motives Across the Lifespan

To date, only a few isolated studies and research groups have investigated change in implicit motives across the lifespan. Veroff, Reuman, and Feld (1984) reported two large-scale studies in which TAT scores for the achievement motive, affiliation motive, hope for power, and fear of weakness (fear component of the power motive) were obtained from US men and women of different ages and educational backgrounds in the years 1957 and 1976. The overall picture was one of great stability across age groups, but three clear patterns of change did emerge:

1. Women showed a steady decrease in the affiliation motive across young (21 to 34 years), middle (35 to 54 years), and older (55 years and above) adulthood. This finding applied to housewives and working women, to married and single women, to mothers, and to women without children (Veroff et al., 1984). The authors reasoned that membership of a peer group, and the reassurance it provides, is crucial for women in young adulthood, but becomes less important as they grow older and increasingly confident in their life choices. Nevertheless, the affiliation theme still seems to have a strong influence on the psychological well-being of older women. Halisch and Gep-

pert (2001a) found that the absence of affiliation-related (but not achievement- or power-related) life events is associated with reduced life satisfaction in 65- to 85-year-old women.

2. The achievement motive of older women is weaker than that of younger and middle-aged women (Veroff et al., 1984). However, careful analysis revealed that this decline applied only to TAT stories generated in response to career-related picture cues (e.g., two women in a laboratory). No age differences were found in stories that involved measuring one's competence in a specific task against a standard of excellence. This finding is in line with the hypothesis that extrinsic and competitive forms of achievement motivation gradually cede to intrinsic and task-oriented forms over adulthood (Maehr & Kleiber, 1981).

3. Men in middle adulthood express more hope for power than young or old men (Veroff et al., 1984). In a study with elderly twins, however, Halisch and Geppert (2001b) found that men's power motive continued to increase even in the seventh decade of life, remaining stable in the eight and ninth decade. Accordingly, even in old age, power-related life events remained more relevant to men's life satisfaction than achievement- or affiliation-related life events.

consequences of those outcomes (see the extended cognitive model of motivation in Chapter 13) influence the choice of achievement-related (and other) activities and the investment of resources in selected goals. Eccles' (2005) general expectancy-value model of achievement choices, presented in Fig. 15.10 (see also Eccles & Wigfield, 2002), provides an overview of the many factors and incentives influencing achievement-related choices.

❶ A major difference between the Eccles and Wigfield model and the risk-taking model is that Eccles and colleagues do not assume the "objective" difficulty of a task (in social comparison) to be the decisive motivating factor (according to the risk-taking model, the more difficult a task is, the higher its attraction), but predict group and individual norms to determine the subjective value of an activity (e.g., how desirable it is for a girl to do well in mathematics, sports, essay writing, football, or cheerleading).

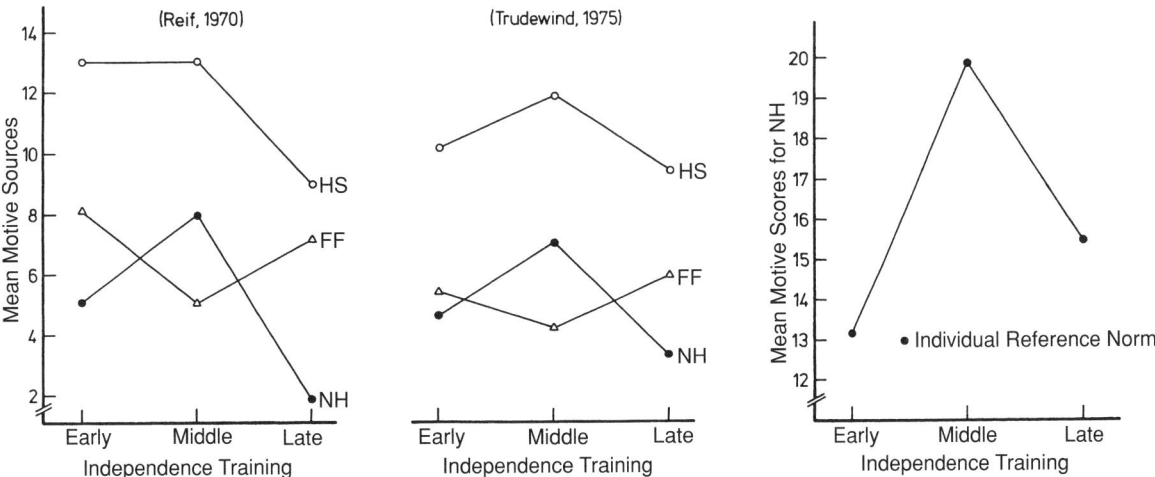

Figure 15.9 (**a**) and (**b**) Mean motive scores (*HS*, hope for success; *FF*, fear of failure; *NH*, net hope: HS–FF) as a function of timing of mothers' child-centered independence training in fourth grade (*left*: Reif, 1970) and fourth and fifth grades (*right*: Trudewind, 1975); (**c**) mean motive scores (NH = HS – FF) in third grade as a function of timing of child-centered independence training in the context of individual reference norms. (Based on Meyer, 1973a, p. 181; Trudewind, 1975, p. 122; Schmalt, 1975, p. 31.)

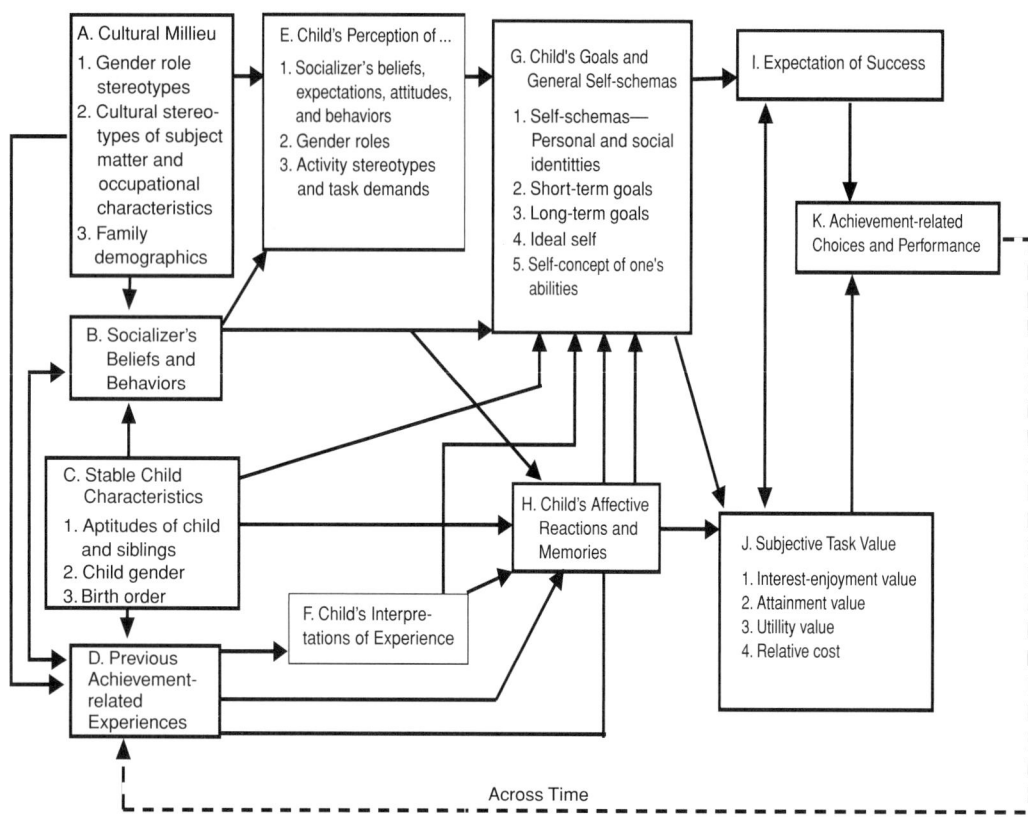

Figure 15.10 Eccles' general expectancy-value model of achievement choices. (From Eccles, 2005.)

Another factor that Eccles (2005) assumes to influence the value of achievement-related choices is their potential **costs**. These include the anticipated threat to self-esteem of failure, the possible negative implications of discrepancies from the self-concept or group norms (e.g., if a girl decides to play football), and the opportunity costs incurred by deciding for one activity and against another. An individual's final choice depends less on the absolute value of an activity than on its relative, subjective value compared with alternatives that must then be abandoned. Empirical findings from a longitudinal study with school leavers show that the values attached to occupational characteristics (e.g., helping others) not only predict plans to enter certain occupations (e.g., nurse, doctor), but also predict not aspiring to others (e.g., natural scientist, business-related profession; Eccles, 2005; Eccles, Barber, & Jozefowicz, 1999).

Furthermore, in the Eccles and Wigfield model, the **expectancy component** (i.e., subjective difficulty) is shaped over time by the individual's experiences and preferences. Students who decide against advanced mathematics and physics courses, for example, in favor of literature and theater studies, will soon feel at home in the world of literature and drama, but have little confidence in their mathematics and physics skills.

❶ The Eccles and Wigfield model emphasizes change in individual preferences and achievement-related cognitions over time, and the impact of that change on long-term competence profiles. The model might thus be described as a dynamic, interactive and inherently developmental psychological approach. The choices an individual makes over time help shape both subjective and objective influences on achievement-motivated preferences, thus leading – "for better or worse" – to canalized development that increasingly accentuates existing differences between individuals or subgroups (e.g., girls vs. boys, different social classes or ethnic groups; J. Heckhausen, 1999; J. Heckhausen & Schulz, 1999b).

Further empirical findings from this research program are discussed in Section 15.8. The construct of **interest** is also worth mentioning in the context of activity-specific incentives, less from the perspective of self-determination (Krapp, 1999; Krapp, Hidi, & Renninger, 1992) than in terms of the differing attraction that particular topics (mathematics, sports, animals) hold for different individuals (see also the discussion in Chapter 13). Some important empirical findings on interest development are also discussed in Section 15.7.5, in the context of canalizing effects in the development of individual differences in motivation.

15.7.3 Generalized Goal Orientations

The Eccles and Wigfield model discussed previously negotiates a middle ground between implicit and explicit motives. On the one hand, the authors (Eccles, 2005; Eccles & Wigfield, 2002) emphasize that there are both conscious and nonconscious components to students' achievement-related value orientations (e.g., culturally mediated value orientations). On the other hand, the research inspired by the model typically uses self-report questionnaires to assess these values, and interprets findings as reflecting on self-concepts (Eccles, Wigfield, & Schiefele, 1998).

The concepts considered in this section are more clearly localized on the side of explicit motives. They relate to the explicit goals pursued in achievement-oriented behavior; the goals that respondents can report on relatively spontaneously (i.e., without first having to construct an answer). In the past 20 years, research on the development of achievement-related motivation has focused almost exclusively on explicit achievement goals (conscious, reportable goals; see the overview in Eccles et al., 1998). Accordingly, attention has been centered on cognitions of personal efficacy and competence and on causal attributions of success and failure. This kind of approach is particularly suitable for the investigation of achievement motivation in school settings – achievement-related behavior in the classroom is highly structured, tends to be evaluated in social comparison, and has far-reaching social consequences (recognition of adults and peers, access to higher education and prized careers). Expectancies relating to these action-event consequences are typically both consciously represented and extrinsically motivated.

Learning/Mastery Goals vs. Performance/Ego Goals

In the late 1970s, a group of researchers including Carol Ames, Carol Dweck, Marty Maehr, and John Nicholls began to exchange ideas on achievement motivation in regular colloquia at the University of Illinois. The new and convergent conceptualizations (see the overview in Elliot, 2005) that they developed became known as the **achievement goal approach**.

❶ Subsequent research on the development of achievement motivation, especially in the field of educational psychology, was strongly influenced by the models of Nicholls and Dweck, in particular. These achievement goal models were originally conceptualized to account for both situation- and person-dependent variation, but the focus has increasingly shifted to individual differences in achievement goal orientations, particularly in recent research developments.

APPROACHES TO ACHIEVEMENT GOAL ORIENTATION. Based on his findings on the emergence of differentiated conceptions of ability and effort from a global concept of competence, and their coordination within causal schemata (see also Sections 15.6.2 and 15.6.4), Nicholls (1985) hypothesized

two contrasting goal orientations: an undifferentiated competence or mastery goal orientation ("task involvement") and a specific performance or ego goal orientation ("ego involvement").

The aim of mastery goals is to improve one's knowledge and skills, master material, and learn new things; the aim of performance goals is to demonstrate one's competence relative to others with as little effort as possible. These two goal orientations lead to contrasting patterns of behavior in achievement situations:

■ Mastery goals are intrinsically motivated; they promote behaviors (e.g., choice of tasks of intermediate difficulty), affect (e.g., joy at success), and cognitions (e.g., learning strategies) conducive to optimizing task mastery.

■ Performance goals are extrinsically motivated; they are geared to maximizing favorable evaluations of the self, and thus elicit less adaptive behaviors (e.g., choice of extremely easy or difficult tasks), affect (e.g., fear of defeat and shame), and cognitions (e.g., causal attributions of failure that threaten self-esteem).

Dweck drew a similar distinction, having approached the issue from another perspective, namely, her work on the helplessness of older school-aged children in achievement situations. In a series of studies, Dweck and colleagues found that, from the age of around 10 to 12 years, children of the same ability level show contrasting responses to failure (Diener & Dweck, 1978; 1980; Dweck, 1975; Dweck & Leggett, 1988; Dweck & Reppucci, 1973). Children who see ability as variable and malleable ("incremental theory of intelligence"; Dweck, 1999), and who thus typically seek to enhance their ability in achievement situations (learning goals), respond to failure by attributing the disappointing outcome to insufficient effort, increasing their effort and persistence, and remaining confident of success. In contrast, children who consider ability to be a stable quantity that is relatively difficult to influence ("entity theory of intelligence"; Dweck 1999), and who thus tend to pursue performance goals, show helpless responses to failure, attributing the outcome to a lack of ability, reducing their effort and persistence, becoming less confident of success, and lowering their level of aspiration.

These contrasting responses to failure are reflected in children's general approaches to achievement situations:

■ Children with a learning goal orientation see achievement situations as opportunities to master challenges and to enhance their knowledge and skills.

■ Children with a performance goal orientation tend to interpret achievement situations as tests of their ability.

Whether this test situation is experienced as threatening or stimulating depends on whether the children consider themselves competent of accomplishing the task (see also the findings of Spinath & Stiensmeyer-Pelster, 2003; Stiensmeyer-Pelster, Balke, & Schlangen, 1996). If their expectations are positive, children high in performance goal orientations aim to demonstrate a high level of ability in order to maximize positive self- and other-evaluations. If not, they try to conceal their lack of ability (e.g., by not trying at all or by choosing less demanding tasks). Ames and Archer (1988) called for research to go beyond goals and concepts of intelligence to see mastery/learning and performance/ego goal orientations as **cognitive-emotional networks** of goals, beliefs, and feelings relating to success, effort, ability, failure, feedback, and evaluation standards (see also Stiensmeyer-Pelster et al., 1996) by integrating their own approach with those of Nicholls and Dweck. Their take on explicit motivational issues thus approaches the levels of complexity and multifunctionality (e.g., for prospective and retrospective, success- and failure-oriented achievement situations) that have been conceptualized for implicit motivational issues (McClelland, 1985).

> ❗ With its focus on optimizing efficiency of task execution, the concept of learning or mastery goals has much in common with intrinsic achievement motivation, and can be seen as an explicit counterpart to the implicit achievement motive. In contrast, the concept of performance goals focuses on extrinsic consequences of actions (i.e., self- and other-evaluation of an individual's competence and characteristics). Individuals tend to be higher in one goal orientation than the other, with the dominant goal orientation determining the choice of goals and other aspects of achievement-oriented behavior, unless overruled by strong situational activation of the nondominant goal orientation (Stipek & Kowalski, 1989).

EMPIRICAL EVIDENCE FOR THE ACHIEVEMENT GOAL APPROACH. Numerous studies on the achievement goal approach have confirmed that a learning goal orientation (i.e., a focus on mastering task demands and improving one's competence) has positive effects on long-term achievement behavior (but not necessarily on actual performance outcomes) under a broad variety of learning and achievement conditions. In contrast, a performance goal orientation has been found to have positive or neutral effects on outcomes when conceptions of personal competence are positive, but negative effects when conceptions of personal competence are negative (see the overview in Harackiewicz & Elliot, 1993; Koestner, Zuckerman, & Koestner, 1987; Miller & Hom, 1990; Sansone, Sachau, & Weir, 1989) and when the individual feels exposed to public evaluation (see, e.g., Witkowski & Stiensmeyer-Pelster, 1998). Findings also indicate that a combination of learning and performance orientations may be particularly motivating (Elliot, 2005) in the workplace (Farr, Hofmann, & Mathieu, 1993), in sports settings (Fox, Goudas, Biddle, Duda, & Armstrong, 1994), and even in educational contexts (Ainley, 1993; Wentzel, 1989).

The motivational value of multiple goal orientations may depend on the individual's ability to activate each at the right moment, thus optimizing the motivational fit with the situational potential for achievement and the potential costs of failure (see also Rheinberg's, 2006, concept of motivational

competence). Butler's (1999) empirical findings show that adolescents are already able to respond to situational conditions by showing incentive-specific strivings, either to master a task or to outperform others. The situation/goal orientation fit hypothesis could prove very productive in future research.

Approach vs. Avoidance Goals

In the early 1990s, Elliot pointed out that research on performance goal orientations had overlooked an important aspect of traditional achievement motivation research, namely, the distinction between approach and avoidance or, to use the terminology of implicit motive research, hope for success vs. fear of failure. The approach-avoidance dimension was expected to be particularly relevant to performance goals, regardless of self-assessed competence:

- At high levels of self-attributed competence, individuals can be expected to choose approach goals, whether mastery oriented (improving one's knowledge and skills) or performance oriented (demonstrating one's competence to others).
- At low levels of self-attributed competence, the focus is likely to be on the risk of failure, and hence on the goal of avoiding public displays of incompetence (Elliot & Church, 1997). Which goal orientation emerges in a given situation evidently depends on individual preferences and vulnerabilities (motive-dependent incentive weighting of success and failure), on the situational opportunities for success and risks of failure, and on the individual's perception of these opportunities and risks, which is – to a certain degree – motive dependent (Elliot, 1997).

THE 2 × 2 ACHIEVEMENT GOAL MODEL. Elliot later extended his trichotomous model of mastery-approach goals, performance-approach goals, and performance-avoidance goals to include mastery-avoidance goals, resulting in a full 2 × 2 achievement goal model (Elliot, 1999; Elliot & McGregor, 2001). When pursuing mastery-avoidance goals, individuals seek to avoid loss or stagnation of competence, forgetting what they have learned, failing to complete a task, or misunderstanding things. Mastery-avoidance goals are probably less common in scholastic contexts and in the first two decades of life than they are in older adulthood, when people struggle with losses in cognitive capacity, particularly in situations with high and multiple demands (J. Heckhausen, 2005).

Numerous empirical studies (see the overviews in Harackiewicz, Barron, & Elliot, 1998; Moller & Elliot, 2006) have tested Elliot's trichotomous model and 2 × 2 achievement goal model in the domains of education, sports, and employment, and substantiated the distinction between approach and avoidance goals for both mastery and performance goals. Performance-avoidance goals (i.e., not revealing oneself to be incompetent) have proved particularly detrimental for achievement outcomes. Furthermore, a host of studies from the United States have found that performance-approach goals (i.e., demonstrating one's competence) are especially conducive to achievement in school and college contexts, whereas mastery-approach goals often seem to have no positive effects on academic achievement (see the overview in Harackiewicz et al., 1998).

SUMMARY

Concepts of generalized goal orientations (i.e., explicit motives) have come to dominate US research on the development of motivation in the past 20 years. Distinctions are made on two dimensions: learning/mastery vs. performance/ego and approach vs. avoidance. The aim of learning or mastery goals is to improve one's competence; the aim or performance or ego goals is to demonstrate one's competence to others and in social comparison. Learning and mastery goals have positive effects on achievement-oriented behavior, but not necessarily on the outcomes attained. Performance and ego goals can induce helplessness in achievement-related contexts at low levels of self-attributed competence. A combination of mastery and performance goals can be particularly motivating under favorable conditions.

Goals can also be distinguished in terms of whether their aim is to approach a desirable action outcome or its consequences or to avoid an undesirable action outcome or its consequences. The approach vs. avoidance orientation determines whether performance/ego goals, in particular, are conducive or detrimental to achievement-related behavior. Goals aiming to minimize displays of incompetence tend to elicit effort avoidance and helplessness responses, especially after failure and when people are exposed to the judgments of others. If the assessment of personal competence is favorable, however, the striving to demonstrate that competence is conducive to effort, and to choosing ambitious, but attainable, levels of aspiration.

15.7.4 Regulation of Motivation and Action

Research at the interface between motivation psychology, personality psychology, and developmental psychology has recently begun to examine interindividual differences in the capacity to regulate motivation and action. Three main strands of research can be distinguished:

- models of self-regulation by means of action control (Brandtstädter, 1998, 2001; Brandtstädter & Rothermund, 2002; Kuhl, 2000b, 2001; see also Chapter 12),
- models of developmental regulation by means of control striving (J. Heckhausen, 1999; J. Heckhausen & Schulz, 1995; Schulz & J. Heckhausen, 1996; Schulz, Wrosch, & J. Heckhausen, 2002; Wrosch, Scheier, Miller, Schulz, & Carver, 2003), and
- models of metamotivational competence (Rheinberg, 2006).

The main approaches to these three strands of research are outlined briefly in the following; the second research strand

is discussed in more detail in Section 15.8, which examines the role of motivation in developmental regulation.

Self-Regulation by Means of Action Control

Models belonging to the first strand of research assume the regulation of the self, its actualization, and its adaptation to available action opportunities to be subject to individual differences in action control. These models include personality systems interactions (PSI) theory by Kuhl and colleagues and the assimilation, accommodation, immunization (AAI) model by Brandtstädter and colleagues.

PSI THEORY. Kuhl's PSI theory (Kuhl, 2000b, 2001; Kuhl & Völker, 1998; see also Chapter 12); establishes connections between different functional levels of implicit and explicit regulation of behavior and the self, which other conceptual models tend to consider in isolation and out of context. PSI theory distinguishes four mental functions:

- intuiting,
- sensing,
- feeling, and
- thinking.

These mental functions are integrated within the framework of two modulation assumptions with differing individual sensitivity to positive or negative affect. Genetically preprogrammed sensumotor schemata (e.g., emotional expression, intuitive parenting programs) associated with certain situational triggers – some evolutionary, some learned over individual ontogenesis – permit **intuitive behavior control**, meaning that behavior can be regulated largely without conscious control. The universal behavioral tools of intuitive behavior control can be applied to different motives as required. The mental function of **intuiting** has more influence on action control and self-experience when positive affect, and thus the reward system, is activated (first modulation assumption). In contrast, the mental function of **sensing** serves to recognize discrepant, isolated experiences, particularly motive-relevant positive or negative incentives (e.g., recognizing situations that involve the chance of success or the threat of failure). Negative affect and activation of the punishment system facilitates the effects of the sensing function (detecting discrepant experiences) on experience (second modulation assumption). The construct of **feeling** represents an individual's access to extensive associative networks of implicit knowledge about action opportunities. In addition to routine situation-action, action-outcome, and action-outcome-consequence expectancies, more unusual approaches, outcomes, and consequences are also stored in parallel networks of the extension memory, and can be implemented in creative behavior, provided that the feeling system is activated. This is, however, typically only the case in the presence of low negative affect and high positive affect, when the reward system is activated (first modulation assumption) and the punishment system is inhibited (second modulation assumption). Kuhl sees the holistic representation of this extensive experiential system as the essence of the self, and the basis of what other theoretical approaches call "intrinsic," self-determined, or autonomous (Deci & Ryan, 1985; Ryan, Kuhl, & Deci, 1997), and what PSI theory terms "**self-regulation**." In contrast, the PSI model conceives of **thinking** as the mental basis for logically and analytically derived, goal-oriented, and volitionally guided activity, which is structured sequentially rather than in parallel. It is less dependent on experiential knowledge and is particularly useful when "**self-control**" is needed to execute goal-directed actions that are at odds with dominant habits or incentives (Kuhl & Völker, 1998).

From the perspective of PSI theory, the emergence of personality styles and disorders can be seen as deriving from individual sensitivities to positive vs. negative affect, which lead to the selective activation and inhibition of the four mental functions (see the two modulation assumptions). The various personality styles and disorders can be distinguished on two dimensions of social interaction: closeness/distance and dominance/subordination.

Whether an individual's behavior tends toward one pole of these dimensions or the other is a consequence of early (preverbal) experiences in the parent-child dyad. Emotional regulation in early parent-child interactions is a major factor here, predestining the child either to strive for independence, recognition, power, and achievement, and hence approaching positive affectivity, or to needs for protection, avoidance of helplessness and failure, and hence avoiding negative affectivity. The early developmental conditions of the action regulation styles conceptualized in PSI theory are discussed as follows.

AAI MODEL. Another action control approach to individual differences in self-regulation is the AAI model of self-regulation proposed by Brandtstädter and colleagues (Brandtstädter, 2001; Brandtstädter & Greve, 1994; Brandtstädter & Rothermund, 2002; Brandtstädter, Wentura, & Rothermund, 1999). According to the AAI model, three processes of goal-related behavior serve to maintain the consistency of the self across the life course:

1. Assimilation, which involves conscious efforts to attain personal goals.

2. Accommodation, by means of which individuals adjust their personal goals to the opportunities available in the given phase of life.

3. Immunization, which involves modification of the criteria for successful attainment of personal goals, thus allowing goal attainment even when opportunities are unfavorable.

The intentional or nonintentional activation of these three processes serves to maintain the integrity of the self, even if it means that goals have to be abandoned or redefined. Individuals differ in the persistence they show in persevering with the goals they have set themselves (assimilation) and in the flexibility they show in adapting their goals to the opportunities available (accommodation). According to Brandtstädter, these two dimensions can vary independently and can be empirically operationalized as independent (near-zero correlations).

❶ Importantly, the personality attribute of high goal flexibility can help to compensate for age-related functional decline. Individuals who are prepared to adapt their goals to the prevailing circumstances are less likely to experience functional impairment as a negative impact to their general well-being and more likely to interpret the experience or threat of functional losses in a more adaptive way.

As yet, there have been no empirical studies of the conditions under which individual differences in the preference for assimilative or accommodative modes of regulation develop in childhood and adolescence.

Lifespan Theory of Control
The lifespan theory of control developed by J. Heckhausen, Schulz, and colleagues (J. Heckhausen, 1999; J. Heckhausen & Schulz, 1995; Schulz & J. Heckhausen, 1996; Schulz, Wrosch, & J. Heckhausen, 2002) addresses similar phenomena as Brandtstädter's AAI model. J. Heckhausen and Schulz do not conceptualize the process of pursuing and adapting long-term developmental goals and life goals as self-regulation, however, but as control striving (see the comparative discussion of the two models in Poulin, Haase, & J. Heckhausen, 2005).

❶ According to the lifespan theory of control, the motivated action of individuals of all ages is determined by primary control striving, that is, the striving to exert control on the environment. The potential for primary control attained across the lifespan (i.e., the potential to control events in the environment) is seen as a criterion of successful lifespan development.

In view of the many and diverse developmental opportunities arising over the course of a human life, **primary control striving** must be focused on certain selected goals. Moreover, because the conditions for goal pursuit and attainment change continuously across the lifespan, goals that are no longer attainable or worth pursuing relative to other goals must be deactivated, freeing the individual to focus on realistic, resource-efficient goals instead. This aspect is discussed in detail in Section 15.8.

Individual differences in various components of the developmental regulation process can influence both objective (e.g., occupational position, marital status) and subjective (e.g., mental health, well-being, emotional balance) developmental outcomes. People differ in the strength of their primary control striving and in their willingness to relinquish unattainable or extremely costly goals or to lower their expectations (see the overview in J. Heckhausen, 1999; see also Brandtstädter's, 2001, findings on tenacious goal pursuit and flexible goal adjustment).

The level of controllability an individual considers necessary for primary control striving to be initiated in the first place is a crucial factor. Accordingly, people also differ in the loss of control they will tolerate in a particular domain (e.g., academic achievement) before distancing themselves from their previous goals in that domain. Moreover, there are probably interindividual differences in the virtuosity with which people apply secondary control strategies of motivational and volitional regulation to goal engagement and disengagement. Studies with adults of different ages (Section 15.8) have found individual differences in the congruence between goals and control striving, on the one hand, and the control potential actually available at a certain age, on the other. When control striving is congruent with the available potential for control, developmental outcomes are much more favorable, particularly with regard to mental health, emotional balance, and well-being (see the overview in J. Heckhausen & Farruggia, 2003; Schulz, Wrosch, & J. Heckhausen, 2002).

Metamotivational Competence

There may also be individual differences in the capacity to regulate motivation, as articulated in Rheinberg's (2006) model of motivational competence.

> **DEFINITION**
>
> This model defines motivational competence as an individual's ability to set goals in such a way that they can be pursued efficiently, without the need for permanent volitional control.

As discussed in Chapter 9, action goals that are accessible to introspection are conceptualized as **explicit motives** or motivational self-concepts (McClelland, 1985). **Implicit motives**, such as the achievement, affiliation, and power motives (Chapters 6, 7, and 8), are typically beyond conscious experience. The correspondence between these two motive systems is low, and it seems reasonable to assume that this low level of correspondence at the group level is a result of many people pursuing explicit goals that are not congruent with their implicit motives, although others – the clear minority – do achieve a high level of correspondence between the two.

❗ The degree of congruence between implicit and explicit motives determines the amount of volitional self-control needed to put goal intentions into practice. At high levels of congruence the metamotivational costs are low, whereas at low levels of correspondence people have to force themselves to translate their intentions into action.

As Brunstein, Schultheiss, and Grässmann (1998) showed, there are also implications for well-being. Goal attainment only enhances emotional well-being when goals and implicit motives are congruent; motive-incongruent goals lead to reduced levels of emotional well-being. Kehr (2004a) showed that chronic discrepancies between implicit and explicit motives are associated with volitional depletion in managers. Moreover, the quality of volitional self-regulation proved to moderate the detrimental effects of discrepancy between implicit and explicit motives. Volitional self-regulatory competence evidently serves a compensatory function when implicit and explicit motives are discrepant or in conflict (Kehr, 2004b).

❗ Rheinberg's model of motivational competence states that individuals can only act joyfully and efficiently without permanent volitional control when their explicit motivational self-concepts are congruent with their implicit motives (Rheinberg, 2006).

Even in the most favorable conditions, however, people sometimes have to do things that are not much fun – things that are incongruent with their implicit motives. In these situations, strategies are needed to bridge the gap between implicit and explicit motives. Individual differences are also apparent in the ability to generate and apply these strategies:

1. People differ in their ability to anticipate the incentive structure of an upcoming situation and to plan in such a way as to avoid motivational gaps (e.g., making a conscious effort to do something they find repellant; see also Sokolowski, 1997).

2. There are individual differences in the capacity to enhance the incentive structure of a situation.

3. People probably differ in their metamotivational knowledge about the thoughts and conceptions that enhance or undermine their motivation to engage in a certain activity.

SUMMARY

Research on individual differences in the competence to regulate one's motivation and action operates at the interface between motivational psychology, personality psychology, and developmental psychology. Three main strands of research can be identified:

1. self-regulation by means of action control, as in Kuhl's PSI model and Brandtstädter's AAI model;

2. developmental regulation by means of control striving for developmental goals, as in the lifespan theory of control by J. Heckhausen and Schulz; and

3. metamotivational competence, as in Rheinberg's research paradigm.

Little is known about the development of individual differences in the regulation of motivation and action, and there is much scope for future research.

15.7.5 Differential Developmental Pathways: Critical Phases, Life-Course Transitions, and Universal Developmental Milestones

In this section, we outline four important factors that **trigger and amplify** the development of interindividual differences in motivation and volition, and show how universal motivational development affords opportunities for individual differentiation and canalization of developmental trajectories, while leaving ample scope for plasticity and intervention. Although a wealth of empirical data have been collected on the development of motivation, many of the conclusions drawn to date must remain speculative, and there is considerable potential for further empirical research. Nevertheless, the data available show that a number of life-course transitions and developmental contexts canalize and accelerate development, intensifying both general and differential motivational development, and thus foster qualitative leaps where general, incremental growth had previously been assumed.

Influence of Parent-Child Interaction on Implicit and Explicit Motive Development

Parental interactional behavior is critical to the development of both implicit motives in early childhood and more explicit components of achievement-motivated behavior, such as self-evaluation and levels of aspiration, in the further developmental trajectory (preschool and school age).

In their comprehensive, cross-cultural psychobiological research program, Keller and colleagues (see the overview in Keller, 2000) identified key dimensions of parental behavior that represent major sources of interindividual variance in early, preverbal, and thus implicit influences. Parents, and especially the primary caregiver (usually the mother), provide infants with their first causal experiences.

❶ Irrespective of the cultural context and parenting style (Keller, Lohaus, Völker, Elben, & Ball, 2003), mothers show contingent responses toward the infant's cues (e.g., the greeting response at eye contact; Papouek, 1967). This behavioral contingency is clearly a defining characteristic of a biologically predetermined, naturally occurring parenting program.

Keller, Lohaus, Völker, Cappenberg, and Chasiotis (1999) found only slight individual differences in the reliability and latency of mothers' responses to their infants' signals, but marked individual differences in the communicative channel used (i.e., visual vs. verbal). These differences in the dominant channel of contingent parental behavior, and differences in the reliability, frequency, and latency of contingent parental behavior that may emerge later (in interactions with postinfancy children, when the influence of evolutionarily determined parenting programs declines) can help explain individual differences in the development of generalized contingency awareness (Watson, 1966).

AFFECTIVE CLIMATE IN THE FAMILY. The affective tone of parent-child interactions is another potentially decisive factor in the development of individual differences in motivation. Various research approaches assume the affective tone (or "warmth"; Keller, 2000; Keller et al., 2003) of the interactional exchange between the primary caregiver and the infant to be an early, preverbal, and nonconscious basis for children's sensitivity to positive and negative affect (Kuhl & Völker, 1998;

see also Chapter 12), and thus for the development of general approach vs. avoidance tendencies (see Section 15.7.3 and Higgins & Silberman, 1998, on the development of promotion and prevention focus). Keller et al. (2003) also found that warmth in maternal interaction behavior is not dependent on maternal attitudes to parenting, but seems to be just as implicit (preconscious) as the regulatory differences that it may foster in infants.

TRANSITION FROM OTHER-REGULATION TO SELF-REGULATION. A crucial point in the development of individual differences in motivation and volition is the gradual transfer of regulatory responsibilities from others (in small children, from the parents, see Vygotsky, 1978) to the self. Such transfers are effected repeatedly across the lifespan. In adaptive mother-child interactions, maternal expectations for child self-regulation and maternal provision of external regulation are closely attuned to the child's current developmental level (J. Heckhausen, 1987a, 1988).

❶ This pattern of behavior in early mother-child interactions corresponds with the findings of studies examining how parenting styles influence the development of the achievement motive. Research has shown that parental autonomy support with respect to task selection, self-regulation (Section 15.7 on the findings of McClelland & Pilon, 1983), and goal-directed behavior fosters the development of an approach-oriented performance motive, as does the provision of opportunities for achievement-related behavior (see Trudewind, 1982a).

Parents have also been found to expect and support growing self-regulation of children's self-reinforcing responses to success. Lütkenhaus (1984) observed that three-year-olds whose mothers displayed positive affect in response to their successes showed more frequent self-evaluations in a second phase of mother-child play. In a longitudinal study of one-year-olds, J. Heckhausen found that children whose mothers had praised the correctness of task action at an early stage of development showed object- or even self-related success responses to successful outcomes (e.g., building a tower) at follow-up 2 months later (J. Heckhausen, 1988). A similar form of maternal support for the development of motivational self-regulation was observed for "wanting to do it oneself," which closely follows mothers' first refusals to provide help in longitudinal development (J. Heckhausen, 1988). Unlike contingent parental responses toward infant signals, these and similar aspects of parental behavior are consciously accessible, and can thus be assumed to more responsive to interventions.

❶ In these transitions from other-regulation to self-regulation at different stages of development, it is crucial that the adult assesses the child's developmental status accurately, rather than on the basis of the child's chronological or apparent age (J. Heckhausen, 1987b). There may be considerable discrepancies between implicit and explicit levels of aspiration when children are consistently over- or underchallenged because of their height. If early developmental conditions are favorable (contingency and warmth of parental behavior), these children may show an approach orientation when acting on their own initiative (when the implicit motive is aroused), but a strong avoidance orientation in response to external performance demands (when the explicit motive is aroused). Empirical studies have yet to investigate these relationships.

In their extension of **PSI theory**, Kuhl and Völker (1998) proposed an integrative perspective on the aspects of parental behavior, experiences of control, affective climate, and transition from other- to self-regulation discussed previously. The authors suggested that the association of early expressions of self-efficacy with the affective warmth experienced in parent-child interactions leads to the development of distinct personality styles and disorders. When parental behavior is characterized by positive affect, but low contingency toward the infant's cues, for example, self-expressions cannot be associated with the reward system. The long-term effects of this dissociation, according to Kuhl and Völker, are a decreased capacity for autonomous self-regulation and inhibited access to the self-constituting extension memory, resulting in a fixation on external rewards, such as social recognition or material values, at the cost of intrinsic motives. Kuhl and Völker assume an early dissociation of negative affect and self-regulation to have corresponding effects. Specifically, an early interaction climate characterized by negative affect (e.g., irritability of the mother, frequent separation) that affords the infant little or no opportunity to terminate negative experiences by means of its own behavior (e.g., expressing negative affect such as fear, thus eliciting a reassuring response from the mother), weakens the connection between the system regulating negative affect and the self-system. According to Kuhl and Völker, the infant then becomes helpless and dependent on outside help to downregulate negative affect.

EMPIRICAL EVIDENCE FOR PARENTAL INFLUENCES ON THE DEVELOPMENT OF THE ACHIEVEMENT MOTIVE. As children develop, the implicit potential of the home environment to stimulate achievement-related behavior begins to play a role, as do the explicit expectations that parents make of their children. In detailed interviews with the parents of fourth graders, Trudewind (1975) investigated the home and family factors influencing the development of achievement motivation, and sought to organize these factors within a taxonomy. A broad range of variables were used to assess three major dimensions of the developmental ecology of the family:

- potential for intellectual and achievement-related stimulation (e.g., scope of potential experiences; stimulation afforded by toys, arts and crafts, books, and pets; help with homework assignments; intensity of speech training; variety of social contacts; frequency and quality of parent-child interactions);
- parental achievement pressure (e.g., expectations for scholastic achievement, homework control, sanctions for school grades); and

- the child's cumulative experience of success and failure.

It emerged that the higher the potential for intellectual stimulation in the family environment, and the earlier parents allowed their children freedom to make decisions, the lower the boys' fear of failure. However, a combination of high intellectual and achievement-related stimulation in the home and high parental achievement pressure proved particularly unfavorable for motivational development. Children in this kind of home environment are evidently exposed to all too frequent, negatively sanctioned experiences of failure. In less intellectually stimulating households, high parental expectations were not found to foster fear of failure.

❶ Home environments giving children plenty of opportunity to try out their competence independently seem particularly conducive to the development of a success-oriented achievement motive. Generalized personal standards appropriate to the current developmental status are able to emerge as children interact with the environment without parental achievement pressure. The weight of parental other-evaluations, and the detrimental effects they have when children are over- or underchallenged, are thus moderated at an early stage, as children develop implicit motive systems based on self-regulation and self-evaluation.

In a four-year longitudinal study with the entire cohort of children entering grade 1 in the German city of Bochum, Trudewind and colleagues assessed the characteristics of the home environment specified in their taxonomy at three points of measurement. Findings showed that the general achievement-related stimulation potential of the home environment continued to covary with the development of a success-oriented implicit achievement motive during the elementary school years (Trudewind, 1982a, b, 1987), and that parents' academic expectations, control of schoolwork, and sanctions increasingly influenced the development of failure orientation (Trudewind, Brünger, & Krieger, 1986; Trudewind & Windel, 1991).

Finally, parent-child interaction can be assumed to play a key role in the childhood development of behavioral regulation strategies (J. Heckhausen & Schulz, 1995; Brandtstädter, 2001). Through subtle control of task-related interactions, parents can involve their child in goal-oriented behavior if a task matches the child's developmental level or, if a task is too difficult, either help the child or distract it from the task (J. Heckhausen, 1987a, 1988). The child thus learns to "switch" from goal engagement to goal disengagement, depending on the controllability of goal attainment (e.g., the developmental adequacy of the task), and parental other-regulation gradually cedes to self-regulation. The longitudinal study by Lütkenhaus, Grossmann, and Grossmann (1985) described in the next section provides interesting insights into the effects of infants' predispositions and parental interaction styles in early childhood.

STUDY

Study on the Effects of Infants' Predispositions and Parental Interaction Styles in Early Childhood

Lütkenhaus, Grossmann, and Grossmann (1985) studied the relations between infants' orienting ability, maternal cooperation when playing with the child at age three years, and situational adequacy of the three-year-olds' effort regulation during a tower-building competition. Three-year-olds who had shown greater orienting ability as babies proved better able to downregulate their effort when lagging behind in the tower-building task. Three-year-olds whose mothers were particularly cooperative in play situations proved better able to increase their building speed when they were about to win. These findings suggest that an innate capacity for reorientation (goal disengagement in the case of failure), on the one hand, and maternal action optimization (optimization of success striving), on the other, foster the development of regulatory behavior that corresponds to the demands of the situation (acceleration when success beckons, deceleration when failure looms).

Parental behavior and explicit parental instruction may also influence the secondary control strategies that can help buffer motivational resources against the negative effects of failure. Parents may teach their children – either by model learning or by direct instruction – to bear in mind that other children did not necessarily do very well either (strategic social comparison) or to focus on extenuating circumstances (self-serving causal attributions), thus communicating a preference for particular secondary control strategies (J. Heckhausen, 1993). As yet, however, the conditions under which interindividual differences in control strategies, behavioral regulation strategies, or motivational competence emerge (Rheinberg, 2006) have not been the subject of empirical study.

SUMMARY

The early developmental conditions of implicit and explicit motives are complex, and many pieces of the puzzle are still missing. Three major dimensions of parental behavior, and their fit with the child's developmental status, are particularly influential in early childhood:

- the contingency of parental responses toward the infant's cues,
- the warmth and affective tone of the interactional exchange, and
- the developmental adequacy of (parent-initiated) transitions from other-regulation to self-regulation.

The achievement-related characteristics of the family environment continue to play a decisive role throughout childhood. Developmental ecologies combining high potential for stimulation and experimentation with autonomy support and low parental achievement pressure are particularly favorable to the development of an implicit achievement motive. In this kind of family environment, children are encouraged to set themselves tasks that are within their capabilities, to

master those tasks, and, in so doing, to become confident of succeeding in a wealth of achievement domains. As yet, little is known about how parenting practices promote or inhibit the development of flexible behavioral regulation strategies that facilitate the switch from goal engagement to goal disengagement, or the acquisition of secondary control strategies for dealing with failure.

Transition to Explicit Social Reference Norms at School Entry

In this section, we examine the effects of the school setting on the development of achievement motivation. Unlike the home, the school context is a developmental environment in which other-regulation and other-evaluation are institutionalized as the dominant conditions stimulating achievement-related behavior. Despite attempts to promote individualized and autonomy-supportive instruction, the school context, as an institution of general education, is by definition determined by norm-oriented instruction and performance evaluation.

Children do not typically choose what they are taught at school, which assignments to do for homework, or which skills to master for a class test. It is not up to them to decide between tasks of different difficulty levels. Rather, it is the teacher who sets the level of aspiration by specifying certain achievement goals (which tasks will I try to master?).

Consequently, students' levels of aspiration at school typically relate to their aspired grades, that is, to other people's evaluations of their achievement. These other-evaluations are defined by social rather than individual standards of comparison. Although all children make learning gains over the school year, only those who improve their relative position in the class can actually improve their grades. Even if grades are not given in the first years of schooling, it is impossible for the parties involved – teachers, students, and parents – to ignore the salience of social comparisons in everyday school life. Parents want to know how well their child is doing relative to his or her classmates. Teachers cannot help classifying their students as good, poor, or mediocre. Children soon learn whether they are one of the "good" or the "bad" students in a class, even if this assessment is not made explicit in grades in the first years at school.

🔴 At school entry, social reference norms suddenly become extremely relevant to children's evaluations of their achievement.

The lack of freedom for students to choose their own tasks and set their own levels of aspiration, along with the dominance of social reference norms, make the school an inhospitable developmental ecology for the implicit achievement motive. There are few opportunities for students to select achievement-related activities independently, and intraindividual comparison (e.g., have I improved?) is difficult, if not impossible. Other-evaluation is dominant, and may even cancel out the incentive effects of anticipated self-evaluation and the enjoyment of engaging in an activity, especially when grades have important long-term implications (e.g., for admittance to vocational training or higher education). Apart from influencing the development of explicit performance motives (e.g., aspired grades), these factors can also have adverse effects on the development of the implicit performance motive, leading to the emergence of strong fear of failure or patterns of helplessness (Dweck, 2002) and stress response (Lewis & Ramsay, 2002). The influence of negative preconditions (e.g., slight developmental delays relative to peers) on motivational development may be amplified at school entrance, meaning that the children in question soon lag even further behind their classmates. The longitudinal study by Trudewind and Husarek (1979) described in the next section provides valuable insights into this amplification of negative developmental influences at the critical transition to school.

STUDY

School Entry, Parental Behavior, and Consequences for Children's Hope for Success and Fear of Failure

As part of the Bochum longitudinal study on the development of the achievement motive at elementary school age, Trudewind and Husarek (1979) investigated how parental influences on the development of the motive's approach and avoidance components are amplified at school entry. Their observation study, which was carried out in the first half of the second grade, showed how parent-child interactions at home can be influenced by the transition to school, with favorable or detrimental effects on motive development. Of the 3,465 children participating in the longitudinal study, the authors selected two groups of 20 boys who did not differ with respect to demographic or other ecological characteristics or intellectual development at school entry, or in terms of their school grades in second grade. The boys selected were not strongly motivated by either success or failure when they started school, but their motive strengths differed dramatically by the end of first grade. The boys in one group had developed a strong success motive; those in the other group had acquired a strong fear of failure. The two groups' motives had clearly developed in diametrically opposed directions over the first year of schooling. So, what had happened? What had triggered this divergent motive change in boys whose backgrounds seemed so similar? The authors sought answers to these questions by examining an ecological key situation at the transition to school, namely, mother-child interactions as children worked on their homework. In this context, implicit motive tendencies that have developed at home in infancy and preschool age collide with the explicit performance demands of the school on a daily basis. The mothers' approach to this critical situation during this vulnerable period proved decisive for the boys' motive development. Mothers whose children developed a strong fear of failure during their first year at school differed from mothers whose children became increasingly confident of success in the following respects:

1. They tended to apply social rather than individual or objective reference norms, had higher levels of aspiration for their child, and were less satisfied with the child's homework performance, although the report card grades of the two groups did not differ.
2. They were more likely to structure and control the homework situation, and granted the child little freedom to make his or her own decisions. They gave less encouragement, and their support – although more frequent – took the form of direct intervention rather than indirect pointers that respected the child's independence (see also the findings of Rosen & D'Andrade, 1959).
3. In an interview, they were less likely to attribute their child's homework success to ability and more likely to attribute failure to lack of ability. In the homework situation, they were more likely to criticize their child for lack of ability or effort and to ascribe success to the ease of the tasks.
4. They responded neutrally to success and were less likely to provide praise or encouragement, but were more likely to criticize or scold the child when outcomes were poor.

Through a detailed analysis of an ecological key situation, Trudewind and Husarek (1979) succeeded in identifying socializing influences that can explain the divergent patterns of motive change observed at the transition to school. Because the boys' achievement motives did not differ when they began school, it seems reasonable to assume that school entry is a **critical phase** for motive development. It is possible that the mothers' interactions with their children did not differ markedly before school entry (although no data are available to confirm this). It was only when external levels of aspiration based on social comparison were adopted in the school setting that achievement pressure and negative other-evaluations of failure were introduced to the home environment as well. Some mother-son pairs did not allow these outside influences to affect their hope for success and learning-oriented interactions; in others, the fear of failure became dominant. A strong failure motive is often associated with the development of explicit performance goals that focus on minimizing negative other-evaluations, and that lead to helpless patterns of failure avoidance rather than to efforts to improve competency levels, even more so after failure (see the overview on learning and performance goals in Section 15.7.3; for details, see Dweck, 2002).

OPPORTUNITIES TO INFLUENCE EXPLICIT ACHIEVEMENT GOALS. Teachers are another major factor in the emergence of dominant fear of failure. Rheinberg and colleagues found considerable differences in the **reference-norm orientations** of elementary school teachers, and showed that a preference for individual versus social comparison has significant implications for students' motive orientations and learning motivation (Rheinberg, 1980; Rheinberg, Schmalt, & Wasser, 1978). Children in classes whose teachers tend to apply social reference norms are more afraid of failure, experience higher test anxiety and generalized anxiety, and express higher levels of school aversion. Fortunately, these effects seem to be reversible. A series of intervention and training studies with teachers have shown that students systematically exposed to individual reference norms in the classroom become more confident of success (Rheinberg & Krug, 2005). A training program in which parents were taught to encourage their (third-grade) children to apply individual reference norms, set realistic goals, and make self-serving causal attributions (Lund, Rheinberg, & Gladasch, 2001) had similar effects. The third graders showed an increase in the approach component of the achievement motive and more realistic levels of aspiration on both the short and the long term (six months after the intervention).

Another consequence of the focus on social comparison standards and standardized levels of aspiration in the school context is that children are no longer motivated to develop realistic expectations or to set appropriate task-related goals. Rather, the teacher sets the same tasks for all students. This arrangement fosters unrealistically high expectations that have little to do with task difficulty and that are only loosely related to the children's scholastic achievement. This trend is particularly pronounced in the school-related self-efficacy beliefs of children in the United States (T. Little, 1998; T. Little et al., 1995), most likely promoted by the cultural norm of high positive self-esteem that has gained increasing currency in recent decades (Twenge & Campbell, 2001).

However, the standardized achievement goals of the school developmental context, based as they are on a social comparison and value system, also fulfill important regulatory functions. The school domain is determined by explicit, extrinsic achievement goals, such as earning good grades, pleasing the teacher, and getting good qualifications to improve one's chances finding of an apprenticeship or earning a place on a sought-after undergraduate program at a good university. Performance-approach goals such as these, which focus on other-evaluations, social comparison, self-representation, and grades, are better predictors of learning outcomes (grades) than are mastery-approach goals (e.g., learning to understand the material better), which predict interest in the subject (Harackiewicz, Barron, Tauer, & Elliot, 2002; see also Schöne, Dickhäuser, Spinath, & Stiensmeyer-Pelster, 2004, on the relationship between mastery and performance goals and individual vs. social reference norms).

❗ Explicit achievement goals are needed to regulate the pursuit of worthwhile goals (Barron & Harackiewicz, 2001; Harackiewicz, Barron, & Elliot, 1998) with long-term developmental consequences for socially regulated educational and occupational careers (J. Heckhausen, 1999; J. Heckhausen & Schulz, 1999b). Furthermore, volitional pursuit of explicit achievement goals can compensate, at least in part, for adverse developments in implicit motives (see also Brunstein & Maier, 1996, and Chapter 9). Ensuing experiences of success may, in turn, have favorable effects on the development of implicit motives (e.g., reduced fear of failure). Moreover, explicit achievement goals give the implicit achievement motive a structured field of activity by helping attune the equivalence class of achievement-relevant situations to individual skills and abilities, values, personality characteristics, and interests.

In this context, the research group led by Eccles and Wigfield (Eccles, 2005; Eccles et al., 1998; see also Section 15.7.2 and the excursus on "School Performance and the Expectancy-Value Theory of Achievement Motivation" in Section 6.4.4) has shown that membership of a group (e.g., gender [Eccles, Adler, & Meece, 1984] or youth subgroup) has considerable effects on the achievement-related values, expectations of success, and self-concepts that develop during middle childhood (13 to 14 years, transition from elementary to junior high or middle school) and especially early adolescence (15 to 16 years, transition to high school), thus focusing the achievement-motivated behavior of children, adolescents, and finally adults on certain domains (e.g., languages and arts for girls), often at the cost of others (e.g., mathematics, science, information technology). This individual differentiation in the contexts that elicit students' achievement motive corresponds with institutional opportunities to drop certain subjects and specialize in others in secondary and postsecondary education in the industrialized world. Interindividual differences are further emphasized here, leading to increasingly divergent developmental trajectories of motivational investment.

The subject- or object-related differentiation of achievement-motivated behavior thus involves the development of interests. Object-related interests probably begin to emerge with early preferences for physical objects or the world of people (Roe & Siegelman, 1964), continue with gender role identification (Ruble & Martin, 2002), and go on to determine educational and occupational decisions in adolescence and young adulthood. These decisions are based partly on gender roles (Eccles, 1987; Gottfredson, 1981), but increasingly reflect adolescents' idiosyncratic self-concepts, subgroup affiliations, and personal aspirations for achievement and upward social mobility. In a study with seventh to ninth graders (junior high school), MacIver, Stipek, and Daniels (1991) found that changes in students' conceptions of their ability in different subjects predicted corresponding changes in interest much better than the other way around.

SUMMARY

The transition to school exposes children – and, indirectly, their parents – to an achievement context that is dominated by other-regulation and other-evaluation, social comparisons, and extrinsic incentives. Expectations and evaluations are strongly standardized, leaving little scope for the implicit, self-regulated achievement motive and its focus on intraindividual improvement. At the same time, explicit achievement goals, social comparison and competition with peers, and long-term, extrinsic consequences for educational and occupational careers suddenly become extremely relevant. Children exposed to repeated experiences of failure, parental autonomy suppression, and parental achievement pressure can soon develop chronic fear of failure. However, explicit achievement goals also serve important regulatory functions. For most children, motivation is optimized over the course of development by a combination of implicit and explicit achievement motives. Explicit achievement goals also serve to attune the equivalence class of achievement-relevant situations to individual skills and abilities, values, personality characteristics, and interests.

Consequences of Cognitive Differentiation for Achievement-Related Beliefs

The two examples presented in the following illustrate how cognitive development can amplify or, in some cases, reduce interindividual differences in achievement-motivated behavior.

The first example concerns the differentiation of **conceptions of competence and self-esteem** in different domains of behavior. Determining factors here are, first, the ability to distinguish causal conceptions of ability and effort (Section 15.6.2) and, second, the emergence of domain-specific incentives and expectancies (Section 15.7.2). Significant progress in these respects is seen between preschool age, when dimensions such as intelligence, good conduct, strength, and friendliness are still confounded (see the overview in Dweck, 2002), and the elementary school years. From seven or eight years of age, notions of intellectual and academic competence begin to emerge from a diffuse conception of competence and self-esteem, and are even differentiated according to school subjects (Wigfield, Eccles, Yoon, & Harold, 1997). A stable conception of ability, adjusted for differences in effort, does not begin to develop until the age of nine years at the earliest (Nicholls, 1978). In other words, competence and self-esteem are distinguished, and the conception of intellectual competence is further differentiated, long before children have developed stable concepts of ability. Accordingly, children's early, diffuse ideas of their value or lack thereof (Heyman, Dweck, & Cain, 1992) cannot simply be transferred to their conceptions of intellectual and scholastic competence. The increasing cognitive differentiation of different achievement domains makes children more resilient to generalized conceptions of competence that, if negative, can induce helplessness and resignation (Dweck, 1999). Instead, children exposed to failure in one domain can focus on their successes in other domains, thus protecting their self-esteem (see J. Heckhausen, 1999, on self-protective secondary control strategies).

❗ Despite the availability of these mechanisms for shielding motivational resources, less able children and/or children experiencing developmental delays remain vulnerable to long-term damage to self-esteem once a stable conception of ability has developed. They are at risk of attributing failure to the stable factor of low ability, the potential consequences of which are avoidance of challenges and failure, impaired self-esteem, and resignation.

A second example of a process of cognitive differentiation that has implications for the development and amplification of interindividual differences in achievement-motivated behavior is the acquisition of patterns of **causal attribution**. H. Heckhausen (1984a) proposed a detailed developmental model describing the emergence of preferred causal attributions of success or failure. The model postulates a number of stages in the development of two contrasting patterns of causal attribution: positive attributional style and depressive attributional style.

This approach converges with related research programs (see also Chapter 14, Sections 14.3.4 and 14.4.2) on internal vs. external control (Rotter, 1966), depression (Abramson, Seligman, & Teasdale, 1977), learned helplessness in school students (Dweck & Repucci, 1973), low self-concept (Ames, 1978; Nicholls, 1976), and fear of failure (Heckhausen, 1977a). Individuals with a positive attributional style attribute success to the stable, internal factor of high personal ability, and failure to a lack of effort or task difficulty. Individuals with a depressive attributional style, in contrast, attribute success to external (e.g., the test was easy), variable (e.g., I was lucky), and specific (e.g., the teacher explained this task type particularly well) causes, and failure to a lack of ability.

CONDITIONS ASSOCIATED WITH THE DEVELOPMENT OF FEAR OF FAILURE. The foundations for the development of this pattern of causal attribution are laid in preschool age, when children start to show preferences for patterns of causal attribution that leave high ability attributions intact (e.g., I didn't manage the task because it was too hard even for me) or, in the case of a depressive attributional style, attributions of low ability. Even at this early stage, the former attributional pattern encourages children to continue selecting challenging tasks and making as much effort as possible, whereas the latter prompts them to lower their level of aspiration and reduce effort investment. When children start school, social reference norms become more salient, accelerating the development of a more stable conception of ability and inverse-compensatory patterns of causal inferences about the role of ability and effort in known achievement outcomes (Section 15.6.4). Differences in the fear of failure and in helplessness seem to develop particularly quickly during this transitional period, not least under the influence of parents who have a strong social reference-norm orientation and who see their child's ability in stable and negative terms (Hokoda & Fincham, 1995; Trudewind & Husarek, 1979). After the first few years at school, most 10- to

11-year-olds have developed either a positive or a depressive attributional style, and the corresponding beneficial or detrimental influences on their achievement-motivated behavior are apparent. Thus, normative cognitive development leads to individual differences in causal attribution really taking effect, with consequences for behavior that cause further divergence in the differential developmental trajectories of success- vs. failure-oriented children. Because attributional patterns are consciously accessible, however, they may provide a means of influencing expectancies and behavior in targeted interventions. In other words, they may offer an opportunity to positively influence the implicit motive system by way of the explicit motive system. Weinberger and McClelland (1990) argued that intervention programs could capitalize on the fact that the cognitive system is more explicit and modifiable and has an impact back on the implicit system. Therapeutic interventions may thus be able to increase the congruence between implicit and explicit motive systems.

The amplification of individual differences prompted by the acquisition of compensatory causal schemata has another detrimental consequence for competence and achievement motivation, namely, **effort avoidance**. If effort investment in a given action outcome is indicative of low ability, children and adolescents might decide that it is a better idea to avoid effort – or at least to give others the impression of not having tried (see also Jagacinski & Nicholls, 1990, on the concept of "self-handicapping"). For example, Covington and Omelich (1979) found that undergraduate students report low effort investment after failure, and consider failure after effort investment to be particularly embarrassing and indicative of inability. However, Jagacinski and Nicholls (1987, 1990) concluded that, although retrospective attributions of failure to a lack of effort are widespread, there is no evidence for strategic reductions in effort as a means of protecting self-esteem against these kinds of attributions. Their findings indicate that strategic effort reduction occurs only when social comparison information about other people's performance and effort is salient (Jagacinski & Nicholls, 1987) – as is often the case in the classroom. Students who use effort avoidance as a strategy to buffer self-esteem may become increasingly disengaged in achievement situations and, as a result, increasingly marginalized in terms of motivation and missed learning opportunities.

SUMMARY

Normative developments in cognitive differentiation may accelerate the development of interindividual differences or help reverse them. They thus offer points of intervention for training programs and developmental plasticity. The differentiation of conceptions of ability and effort, as well as the development of domain-specific incentives and expectancies, make children more resilient to overly general self-appraisals of their competence and characteristics. At the same time, these developments allow conceptions of ability as stable and potentially low to emerge in the first place. The normative development of more complex patterns of causal attribution can make ascriptions of failure to low ability seem inevitable, exposing children to the risk of helplessness and to increased fear of failure. Development in the available patterns of causal attribution can thus consolidate and amplify individual differences by means of cognitive canalization, sometimes leading to resignation. Finally, individuals may use effort avoidance to color others' perceptions of their competence, acting as though an outcome has been attained despite low effort investment, and can thus be ascribed to high ability. This kind of strategy can be expected to have negative consequences for both motivation and the acquisition of knowledge and skills.

Increasing Independence in the Orchestration of Action Opportunities and Contexts of Development

The increasing independence that children, adolescents, and adults have to orchestrate their action opportunities, levels of aspiration, and contexts of development across the lifespan can also amplify existing interindividual differences. This section leads directly into a longer section on the motivation of developmental regulation (Section 15.8) and is thus kept brief.

The normative development of control behavior (or primary control striving) progresses from dominant other-regulation in infancy to high levels of self-regulation (see Vygotsky, 1978) in social institutions (school, college, workplace, family, etc.). Parents are the first (co)producers of experiences of self-efficacy (Section 15.5). In granting – and indeed expecting – increasing independence in children's problem-solving behavior and achievement-oriented behavior in general, they have a decisive influence on the development of achievement-motivated behavior and the associated positive and negative emotions (Sections 15.5 and 15.7; see the overview in Trudewind et al., 1997).

With increasing age, partly prompted by their parents, but partly on their own initiative ("wanting to do it oneself"; Geppert & Küster, 1983), children begin to actively strive for independence in their achievement-oriented behavior. In addition, with the gradual expansion of the developmental-ecological life space (Bronfenbrenner & Morris, 1988) from the home to the neighborhood, and later to the school and recreation sites, children are exposed to new and more diverse influences and, at the same time, play an increasingly active role in selecting social contexts and interaction partners. This increasing involvement in the orchestration of opportunities, social relations, and networks – in other words, developmental contexts – is associated with the stabilization and accentuation of conscious and unconscious preferences, values, beliefs, and self-images (Lang & J. Heckhausen, 2006). Young people's life goals and developmental goals become increasingly individualized, leading to divergent developmental trajectories that become increasingly stable, unique, and irreversible as a result of developmental canalization.

This brings us to the transaction between the individual and the developmental ecology, which Heinz Heckhausen sought to address with his call for an "explanation of behavior at fourth glance" (Heckhausen, 1980; see also Chapter 1). From the perspective of action theory and developmental psychology, more can now be said – in specific terms – about this transactional relationship. This is the objective of Section 15.8, which examines the dynamic interaction between biological and societal opportunity structures and individual developmental regulation.

SUMMARY

It is as a function of the progressive shift from other- to self-regulation that interindividual differences really begin to take effect on the developmental trajectory. Beginning in parent-child dyads in early childhood, this development gradually extends to other developmental ecologies as the child gets older and plays an increasingly active role in choosing developmental opportunities and contexts (within the framework of what is biologically and socially possible). This increasing self-regulation leads to progressive divergence in interindividual developmental trajectories, and to differences in motive dispositions, values, and goals becoming increasingly stable and less reversible with age.

15.8 The Motivation of Developmental Regulation

This section complements the research on the development of motivation presented in Sections 15.2 to 15.7 by investigating the motivation of development, and thus opening up a dynamic, interactive perspective on the interaction between motivation and development. It is only recently that the part individuals play in actively regulating their own development across the lifespan has emerged as an important theme on the research agenda, particularly in lifespan developmental psychology (Baltes, Lindenberger, & Staudinger, 1998; Brandtstädter, 1984, 1998, 2001; Brandtstädter & Lerner, 1999; Freund & Baltes, 2000; J. Heckhausen, 1999, 2000b; J. Heckhausen & Farruggia, 2003; J. Heckhausen & Schulz, 1993, 1995; Lang & J. Heckhausen, 2006; Schulz & J. Heckhausen, 1996; Schulz, Wrosch, & J. Heckhausen, 2002). The regulation of development is in fact the core concern of lifespan developmental psychology. Particularly in adolescence and adulthood – when cognitive and socioemotional development has reached a certain level, biological maturation processes become less influential, and occupational and family careers open up a wealth of biographical permutations – the question of how individuals choose and adhere to specific occupational and family career paths becomes especially

compelling. The force of social constraints and sanctions is decreasing progressively in the developed world (J. Heckhausen, 1990; Kohli, 1981), and high levels of social mobility between generations and within the individual lifespan, coupled with diversified lifestyles and biographies, give individuals unparalleled freedom to regulate their own developmental trajectories (Dannefer, 1989; Wrosch & Freund, 2001; Grob, Krings, & Bangerter, 2001; J. Heckhausen, 1990; J. Heckhausen & Schulz, 1999b; Held, 1986). In modern societies characterized by high levels of social mobility and flexible life choices, individuals play a key role as **producers of their own development** (Brandtstädter & Lerner, 1999; Lerner & Busch-Rossnagel, 1981). Nevertheless, account must still be taken of the constraints and age-graded structures of both biological maturation and aging (e.g., the "biological clock" and childbearing) and societal institutions (e.g., the age-graded structure of the education system). This age-sequenced structuring of developmental potential provides a framework for developmental regulation (J. Heckhausen, 1990, 1999). Individuals' movements within this framework, the paths chosen, and the consistency of goal pursuit, depend largely on the direction and effectiveness of individual motivation and its implicit and explicit motive components. In the following, we first present the lifespan as a field of action within which individuals strive to optimize their development. We then discuss developmental goals as organizers of developmental regulation, the congruence between developmental regulation and age-graded opportunities across the lifespan, and the control strategies involved in goal pursuit or abandonment, before examining the role of individual differences. Finally, we discuss the dynamic, interactive nature of motivation and action directed at regulating one's own development, which brings us to the dialectic transaction between the individual and her or his environment.

15.8.1 The Life Course as a Field of Action

Assuming lifelong development to be an active process that individuals influence by means of their actions, the question arises of what opportunities individuals have to act on their own development, and how these opportunities are distributed across the lifespan. To draw on Lewin (1943), the lifespan can be regarded as a field of action. As in Lewin's environmental model, the distance between the individual's current position and desired and undesired states may differ. In the present context, a temporal dimension (age and chronological time) can be added to Lewin's topological one. Developmental milestones such as the transition to higher education acquire incentive character (see the following example) that endows behavior with direction and persistence over time and space (see also the discussion of the concept of incentive in Chapter 5), although this effect becomes weaker with increasing distance from the goal (see the discussion of goal gradients in Chapter 4).

At the beginning of secondary education, for example, students who need good grades to be accepted at college may still be so far from the transition to higher education that the incentive of a college place does not yet motivate them to do their homework carefully. As graduation approaches, however, the attraction of being admitted to college becomes increasingly powerful.

Another interesting feature of Lewin's field theory in the context of **developmental action theories** is the assumed structure of the psychological sphere of action. The individual's current position and the goal region are not necessarily adjacent; rather, the action paths leading to goals may first have to navigate intermediate goals. Lewin (1934) took a "hodological" perspective (from the Greek *hodos*, meaning "path"), assuming that the individual will take the action path providing the shortest connection between the current position and the goal region. Psychological distance depends not only on spatial distance, however; it is also a function of any difficulties and dangers to be overcome (Chapter 5).

❗ This kind of hodological perspective on the effects of aspired goal states in guiding actions is particularly relevant to research on developmental regulation, the goals of which can rarely be accessed directly. People have to ensure that their action paths stay on track over time, despite delays and detours caused by the constraints and complexities of human life. Strivings that span whole phases of life or even an entire life course require huge regulatory efforts, but once an individual has embarked on a particular developmental and life-course trajectory, these efforts are scaffolded to a considerable degree by societal institutions (e.g., channels of admission to educational institutions and careers).

At the simplest level, the lifespan can be seen as a field of action in which control potential first increases rapidly, reaches a temporary plateau in midlife, and declines again with age, especially advanced age. Fig. 15.1 illustrates the inverse U-shaped trajectory described by primary control potential, beginning with almost complete helplessness and dependence on others in infancy; surging in childhood and adolescence; leveling out at some point in adulthood, depending on the biographical path taken; and declining again in old age under the effects of impaired biological functioning and restricted social roles, finally resulting in death.

The level of **primary control striving** is typically maintained throughout these radical age-related changes in primary control potential (J. Heckhausen, 1997). What changes are its objectives, which can be adapted to the waxing and waning of control potential by setting more or less challenging goals or shifting one's focus to another domain of functioning (e.g., focusing on career goals rather than starting a family, or on health rather than career goals). These shifts in the objectives of developmental regulation are determined by individuals themselves or adopted from others against the

background of biological processes of maturation and aging, societal and institutional structures, and social and cultural norms. We return to this point in the section on developmental goals later in this chapter.

Biological Changes Across the Life Course

Patterns of biological change across the life course generally follow the inverse U-shaped trajectory depicted in Fig. 15.1. In the first half of life, processes of maturation and acquisition dominate, gradually extending the individual potential for control of the material and social environment. Even at this relatively early stage, however, a few domains of functioning are subject to age-related decline. Some can easily be compensated by technical aids (e.g., by wearing sunglasses to respond to the decreased ability to constrict the pupils). Others are not so easily offset. Performance in domains that rely heavily on high-level physical functioning begins to decline long before middle adulthood, leaving only a narrow age window for world-class athletic careers, for example (Schulz & Curnow, 1988; Schulz & J. Heckhausen, 1996; see J. Heckhausen, 2005, on the psychological implications of age-related decline in peak performance).

Middle adulthood sees the onset of various sensory and physiological processes of decline that can typically be offset relatively easily by compensatory strategies (e.g., fitness training) or technical aids (e.g., reading glasses). However, first losses of control potential that are difficult or impossible to overcome are also experienced in midlife (e.g., the ticking of the "biological clock" and the deadline it imposes on childbearing). The control strategies used to deal with these regulatory challenges are discussed in detail as follows.

Finally, in old age, processes of physical decline come to dominate. In very old age (beyond 75 years), in particular, it becomes increasingly difficult to offset this decline using aids or special strategies. These functional losses seem to be the costs of evolutionary selection, which sought to maximize functioning during the early, reproductive stages of life, but neglected the postreproductive phase, meaning that late onset malfunctions and disease were not eliminated from the gene pool (Rose, 1991; Williams, 1957; see also the overview in J. Heckhausen & Schulz, 1999b). Toward the end of life, most people struggle with multiple chronic illnesses and the associated functional impairments (Brock, Guralnick, & Brody, 1990; Schneider & Rowe, 1990).

Societal and Institutional Structures

The societal scaffolding of the life course provides an age-graded structure, on the basis of which individuals form **normative expectancies** about life-course events. These may take the form of situation-outcome expectancies (What happens at what age without my active involvement? – e.g., school entry, retirement), action-outcome expectancies (What can I achieve by my active involvement? – e.g., a valued career, a fulfilled family life), or outcome-consequence expectancies (Which options will be opened up/rendered inaccessible if I don't achieve X? – e.g., graduating from school with good grades, forming a stable relationship). Some of these structures are provided by societal institutions (e.g., the education system, promotion guidelines, matrimonial and divorce laws) and the sociostructural differentiation of educational and occupational trajectories (e.g., certain qualifications are required for certain jobs). Others derive from normative conceptions about the life course, important life goals, and their age-dependent deadlines, which are internalized by the individual members of a society. These age-normative conceptions are playing an increasingly important role in scaffolding the life course as societal institutions become less constraining (J. Heckhausen, 1999).

Institutionalized and Structural Constraints

Age-chronological constraints determining the beginning and end of certain phases of the life-course (e.g., school attendance) structure developmental pathways, as do the regulations on educational, occupation, and family-related transitions (e.g., the educational qualifications needed to pursue certain occupational careers) that are institutionalized in state legislation and company guidelines (e.g., Mayer, 1986; Mayer & Carroll, 1987; Mayer & Müller, 1986).

❶ These institutionalized constraints provide **age-graded opportunity structures** for certain life-course events. Optimal conditions are provided for those who are "on time"; those who are "off time" have to contend with numerous difficulties (J. Heckhausen, 1990, 1999).

One example is the provision of university grants, summer jobs, and cheap accommodation for students in their early twenties, but not in middle adulthood. Society makes it far easier for younger adults than for older adults to get a degree.

Once a particular life-course track has been chosen, institutionalized opportunity structures can have a **channeling or canalization effect**. Some educational pathways lead almost automatically to certain occupational careers, for example, and the first major steps in starting a family (e.g., getting married) pave the way for subsequent developments in that domain (e.g., buying a home together, parenthood). Individuals can thus follow age-sequential paths that have been carved out by society (Blossfeld & Mayer, 1988; Hogan, 1981; Marini, 1984; Sørensen, 1986) to reach important life goals (J. Heckhausen, 1990, 1999) without the need for permanent volitional control and decision making. The regulatory effects of these institutionalized paths through the life course can be compared with those of the canalization phenomena known from developmental biology, in which cells specialize according to genetically controlled programs of development that apply to whole complexes of characteristics, meaning that

they are better protected against disorders and malfunctions than if every characteristic had to be developed individually and independently (Alberch, 1980; Gottlieb, 1991; Oster & Alberch, 1982; Waddington, 1957). In Waddington's (1957) terminology, the process of development takes place in an "epigenetic landscape," a system of valleys and ridges that may start close together, but diverge considerably over the course of development. People from similar origins may make different decisions at a critical points of transition (e.g., whether to pursue higher education), thus opening up different developmental pathways and resulting in different developmental outcomes later in life.

Normative Conceptions About the Life Course

Besides institutionalized and structural constraints, normative societal conceptions about the life course are coming to play an increasingly important role in regulating lifespan development (J. Heckhausen, 1990, 1999). The flexibility and "Weltoffenheit" (openness to the world) of human behavior (Gehlen, 1958) has long given sociological anthropologists reason to see the regulatory function of social groups and their norms as anthropological constants of human life (Berger & Luckmann, 1967; Claessens, 1968). Human behavior is not biologically or genetically predetermined, and tends not to be externally enforced by society. Rather, individuals regulate their own behavior on the basis of the social norms and conventions they internalize (Elias, 1969) during socialization, which make this regulation seem natural and inevitable (Berger & Luckmann, 1967; Douglas, 1986). The same reasoning seems to apply to the regulation of life course, and would help explain why normative life-course patterns and the age timing of life transitions remain valid for most members of modern societies (Hogan, 1981; Marini, 1984; Modell, Fürstenberg & Hershberg, 1976; Modell, Fürstenberg, & Strong, 1978; Uhlenberg, 1974), even when societal frameworks are weakened (Dannefer, 1989; Held, 1986; Neugarten, 1979; Rindfuss, Swicegood, & Rosenfeld, 1987). Life-course sociologists have shown that, during crises such as World War II, the Great Depression, and the postwar years in Germany, the age timing of major life transitions (e.g., graduation from school, marriage) remained largely unchanged (Blossfeld, 1987, 1988), as did normative conceptions about the ages at which people should leave school, get married, and reach other major milestones in life (Modell, 1980).

❶ Age-normative conceptions about the life course are resilient and powerful regulators of developmental processes and life-course decisions, even and indeed especially when external societal and institutional scaffolds are weakened.

Findings from studies on normative conceptions about psychological development across the lifespan are presented in the next section (J. Heckhausen, 1990, 1999; J. Heckhausen & Baltes, 1991; J. Heckhausen, Dixon, & Baltes, 1989; J. Heckhausen & Krüger, 1993; Hundertmark & J. Heckhausen, 1994;

Krüger & J. Heckhausen, 1993; Krüger, J. Heckhausen, & Hundertmark, 1995).

STUDY

Study on Normative Developmental Change Across the Life Course

J. Heckhausen and colleagues asked young, middle-aged and old adults to specify the psychological characteristics (e.g., friendly, forgetful, wise, adventurous) that change over adulthood, and to state when this happens and whether it is desirable (J. Heckhausen, 1990; J. Heckhausen et al., 1989) or controllable (J. Heckhausen, 1990; J. Heckhausen & Baltes, 1991). Fig. 15.11 shows the developmental gains (desirable developmental changes) and losses (undesirable developmental changes) identified by the adult respondents throughout adulthood and old age. The diagram clearly shows how the relationship of expected developmental gains to losses shifts over the life course, with gains predominating in early adulthood, but losses gradually increasing in middle and especially old age, and finally coming to dominate in very old age.

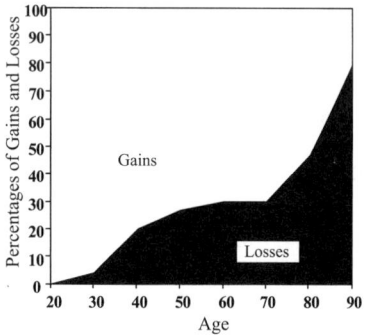

Figure 15.11 Expectations about developmental gains and losses in adulthood. (Based on J. Heckhausen, Dixon, & Baltes, 1989.)

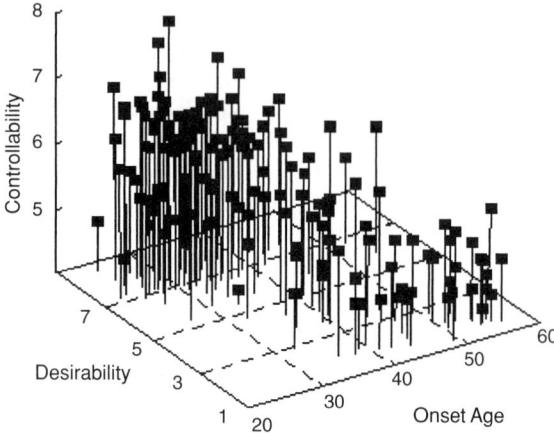

Figure 15.12 Expectations about the desirability, controllability, and age-related timing of developmental changes in adulthood. (Based on J. Heckhausen & Baltes, 1991.)

Interestingly, another study found the perceived controllability and desirability of developmental changes to be closely related (Fig. 15.12), with fewer desirable and fewer controllable psychological changes being expected as people get older (J. Heckhausen & Baltes, 1991). Relative to young adults, moreover, older people are more likely to see undesirable developmental changes as less controllable than desirable ones. More recent findings on the effects of development-related control beliefs on subjective well-being indicate that feelings of personal responsibility for undesirable change or regrettable decisions and life events can diminish older adults' well-being (Lang & J. Heckhausen, 2001; Wrosch & J. Heckhausen, 2002).

AGE DIFFERENCES IN NORMATIVE CONCEPTIONS. Comparison of the age-normative conceptions of psychological development across the lifespan held by adolescents and adults of different ages shows that layperson's conceptions continue to develop from childhood through adolescence and on into old age (J. Heckhausen et. al., 1989; J. Heckhausen & Hosenfeld, 1988; Hosenfeld, 1988). Eleven-year-olds already have relatively detailed conceptions of how people change over adulthood and old age (comprising 40 to 60 psychological attributes). These conceptions become increasingly differentiated in adolescence. Interestingly, contact with older people is just as conducive to the differentiation of the age-normative knowledge system as increasing age. In adulthood and old age, developmental conceptions become increasingly elaborate, multifaceted, and differentiated, with older adults endorsing more attributes as change sensitive than middle-age adults, who in turn endorse more attributes than younger adults (J. Heckhausen et al., 1989).

Age-normative conceptions also serve as a frame of reference for evaluating the life-course position of others. As soon as someone deviates from internalized norms on the family or career status considered appropriate at a certain age, there is internal (and, in the social group, external) pressure for biographical justification. Krüger, Heckhausen, and Hundertmark (1995) found that age-inappropriate family or career status (e.g., not having a steady job by the age of 40) elicited surprise and rather extreme evaluations in their respondents (positive evaluations of advanced development; negative evaluations of delayed development).

❶ Age-normative conceptions provide social frames of reference that individuals use to assess when and to what extent they and others are "on-time" or "off-time" in reaching the major milestones of lifespan development, whether their progress is delayed or accelerated, and whether they need to intervene and make adjustments (see the section on developmental goals later in this chapter) to bring their life back in line with internalized conceptions of a successful life course.

Finally, age-normative conceptions can serve to protect self-esteem by allowing people to see the losses they experience in middle and old age as relatively mild variants of age-related decline (J. Heckhausen & Brim, 1997; J. Heckhausen, 1991; J. Heckhausen & Krüger, 1993). J. Heckhausen and Krüger (1993; J. Heckhausen, 1991) asked young, middle-age, and old adults to rate a large number of psychological attributes with respect to the developmental gains and losses they expected for themselves and for "most other people." As shown in Fig. 15.13, although age-graded developmental expectations for the self and for most other people were generally congruent across the lifespan, there was increasing divergence with advanced age. In fact, people see their own developmental prospects in old age in a much more positive light than they do the prospects of others. This discrepancy, which helps buffer self-esteem, was larger for the middle-aged adults than for the young adults, and most salient for the old participants. Moreover, when asked which age group they identified with most strongly, both old and middle-aged adults believed that they had more in common with younger adults than with people of their own age.

In a large-scale survey study with more than 2,000 participants between 18 and 85 years of age, participants were asked to rate the seriousness of problems in various domains of life (e.g., money, health, loneliness, marriage, stress, work, children) for both themselves and most others of their age (J. Heckhausen & Brim, 1997). All age groups rated most other people's problems to be more serious than their own, with the largest self-other discrepancies being observed for the groups between 34 and 59 years of age. The relationship between participants' ratings of their own problems in a specific domain and the perceived problems of most other people of their age is particularly interesting: the more seriously affected respondents felt by problems in a certain domain, the more serious were the problems they attributed to other people of their age in that domain. In other words, participants downgraded the age-normative reference group to protect their own self-esteem. If the area of functioning in which individuals experience problems is perceived to be a general trouble spot for people of their age, they need not feel as personally responsible for that problem.

SUMMARY

The human life course provides an **age-graded field of action** for individual developmental regulation. Individuals can adapt their goal-related behavior and control striving to the opportunity structures of the life course. In general, the individual potential for control of the environment undergoes radical changes across the lifespan, increasing steeply in childhood, leveling out in middle adulthood, and declining in old age. Biological processes of maturation and aging are one of the main factors determining this inverse U-shaped trajectory. Furthermore, societal opportunities and constraints in the form of institutional and social structures or age-normative conceptions about the life course scaffold important life-course transitions. Sociostructural canaliza-

tion effects narrow down individuals' options along given life-course tracks, but help them stay on track for long-term goals. Normative conceptions about psychological development across the lifespan develop early in life and become increasingly differentiated in adolescence and adulthood. They provide a frame of reference for evaluating one's own development and that of others, and can protect the self-esteem of individuals confronted with developmental losses and other stressors in middle and advanced adulthood.

15.8.2 The Action-Phase Model of Developmental Regulation

The **action-phase model of developmental regulation** has been developed in the context of the lifespan theory of control (Section 15.1) to generate specific predictions about the control strategies used to pursue or deactivate goals at different phases in the lifespan (J. Heckhausen, 1999, 2002a, b; J. Heckhausen & Farruggia, 2003; Schulz, Wrosch, & J. Heckhausen, 2002). The model is based on three major principles, which are presented in this section:

- developmental goals as organizers of developmental regulation;
- the adaptive developmental principle of congruence between developmental goals and developmental opportunities; and
- the sequence of action phases in a cycle of action directed at a developmental goal: goal selection, goal engagement, and goal disengagement.

Developmental Goals as Organizers of Developmental Regulation

Individuals' active attempts to regulate their own development can be conceived of as motivated action. Developmental regulation is directed at goals relating to one's future development and important life-course transitions (Brandtstädter, 2001; see also the following excursus; Brunstein, Schultheiss, & Maier, 1999; J. Heckhausen, 1999). These developmental goals organize action into distinct phases – from the selection of a developmental goal to a phase of active goal pursuit, followed by goal deactivation and finally evaluation of the action outcome – that constitute a development-related cycle of action (see Section 15.8.2 below; J. Heckhausen, 1999; J. Heckhausen & Farruggia, 2003).

The concept of developmental goals has had numerous precursors over the history of research. The goal concepts assumed in these models have been located at different levels of abstraction, differed in their assumed conscious accessibility and universality vs. individuality, and spanned different periods of the life course. One of the first models was proposed by Charlotte Bühler (1933; Bühler & Marschak, 1969), who postulated four basic life tendencies, each comprising a number of specific life goals: need satisfaction (life goals: need satisfaction, love and family, sexuality, self-satisfaction),

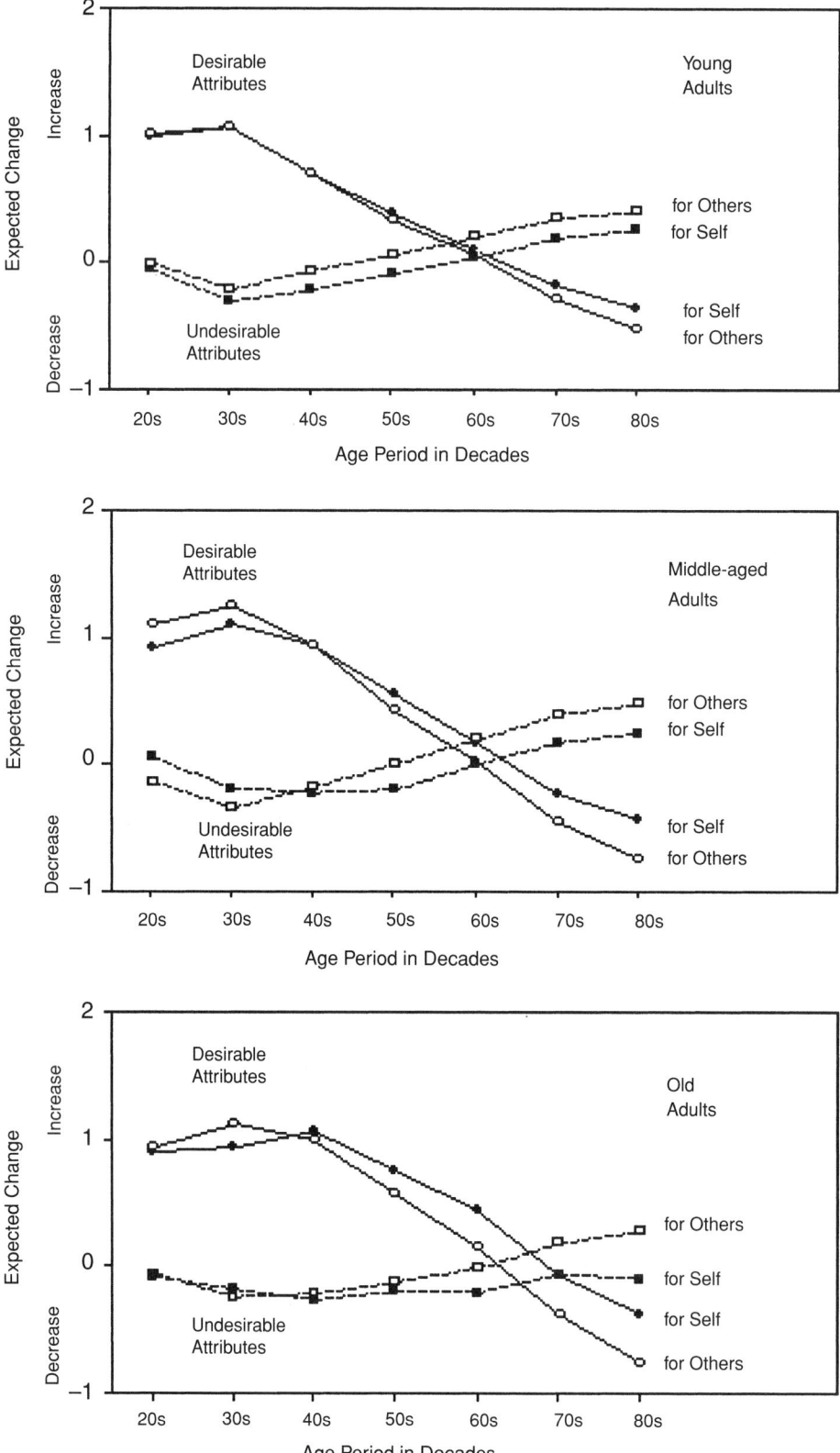

Figure 15.13 Expected developmental change in desired and undesired characteristics for oneself and for "most other people"; respondents in (a) early, (b) middle, and (c) late adulthood. (Based on J. Heckhausen & Krüger, 1993.)

adaptive self-limitation (life goals: self-limitation, caution, adaptability and submission, difficulty avoidance), creative expansion (life goals: self-development, power, fame), and establishment of inner order (life goals: moral values, political and/or religious devotion, success). The basic tendencies and goal categories are universal, but their strengths vary interindividually.

❗ Like implicit motives, Bühler's basic tendencies and life goals are only partly conscious. Unlike implicit motives (McClelland, 1985a), however, Bühler's life goals are age specific to the extent that need satisfaction and adaptive self-limitation predominate in childhood, creative expansion and establishment of inner order become salient in adolescence and adulthood, and old age sees either the continuation of the tendencies dominant in adulthood or a regression to need satisfaction.

Havighurst (1953) drew on normative developmental milestones, rather than individual differences, to formulate his concept of **developmental tasks**. In taking this approach, he sought to reflect the complex interplay between the individual's striving for growth, on the one hand, and the demands, opportunities, and constraints of the social environment, on the other.

DEFINITION

Developmental tasks are age-normative challenges to individual development that derive from processes of biological maturation; cultural traditions; and individual desires, aspirations, and values.

For Havighurst, successful mastery of developmental tasks is conducive to further growth and success in subsequent developmental tasks, whereas failure in a developmental task has negative implications for future development.

Other goal concepts are less specific to development, but related rather to individuals and their motivation; they are on a similar level of abstraction as implicit motives, but are more accessible to conscious introspection. They include "current concerns" (Klinger, 1975, 1977), "life themes" (Csikszentmihalyi & Beattie, 1979), "personal strivings" (Emmons, 1986, 2003), "identity goals" (Gollwitzer, 1987; Gollwitzer & Kirchhof, 1998; Gollwitzer & Wicklund, 1985b), and "terminal values" (Rokeach, 1973). These longer-term goal orientations and personal concerns motivate people to keep generating new and specific objectives that concretize their general goal orientations and set a timeframe for action. Short- or midterm, specific personal goals capable of regulating behavior directly have been investigated in research programs on "personal projects" (B. Little, 1983, 1999), "personal goals" (Brunstein, 1993, 1999; Brunstein, Schultheiss, & Maier, 1999; Wadsworth & Ford, 1983), "life goals" (Nurmi, 1992; Nurmi & Salmela-Aro, 2002; Nurmi, Salmela-Aro, & Koivisto, 2002), and "personal life tasks" (Cantor & Fleeson, 1991; Cantor, Norem, Niedenthal, & Brower, 1987).

Crucially, specific mid-range personal goals endow an individual's everyday behavior with direction, coherence, and

meaning. Their presence alone may enhance psychological well-being (Brunstein et al., 1999). Furthermore, congruence between explicit personal goals and implicit motives (see also Chapter 9) is central to the efficiency of action and to psychological well-being (see the overview in Brunstein et al., 1999).

In a series of studies on the congruence between explicit personal goals and implicit motives in the domains of achievement and power ("agency") versus affiliation and intimacy ("communion"), Brunstein and colleagues found that explicit and implicit motives were not significantly correlated, that the degree of goal attainment on explicit goals influenced emotional well-being only if the goal was congruent with the individual's implicit motives, and that pursuit of motive-incongruent goals had negative implications for attainment of motive-congruent goals and hence for emotional well-being (Brunstein, 1993; Brunstein, Lautenschlager, Nawroth, Pöhlmann, & Schultheiss, 1995; Brunstein, Schultheiss & Grässmann, 1998).

Finally, psychological well-being also depends on whether the goal pursued is perceived to be attainable and controllable (Brunstein, 1993). The pursuit of attainable goals has positive effects on psychological well-being, whereas the pursuit of goals classified as unattainable tends to have adverse effects on subjective well-being and may even be associated with depressive symptoms (Lecci, Karoly, Briggs, & Kuhn, 1994; Röhrle, Hedke, & Leibold, 1994). This pattern of results has been replicated in studies with students (Brunstein, 1993), middle-aged housewives (Brunstein et al., 1991), and older adults (Brunstein et al., 1999).

CONGRUENCE BETWEEN DEVELOPMENTAL GOALS AND NORMATIVE CONCEPTIONS. In a series of studies, our research group has examined whether the developmental goals of adolescents and adults of different ages are congruent with age-normative conceptions about developmental gains and losses (e.g., J. Heckhausen, 1997; J. Heckhausen & Tomasik, 2002; J. Heckhausen, Wrosch, & Fleeson, 2001; Hundertmark, 1990; Hundertmark & J. Heckhausen, 1994; Wrosch & J. Heckhausen, 1999). J. Heckhausen (1997) asked young, middle-age, and old adults to generate developmental goals (e.g., "Please state your five most important personal hopes, plans, and goals for the next 5 to 10 years") and classified these goals into six categories: work, family, health, finances, leisure time, and community (e.g., peace). The age differences found reflect the relevance and controllability of specific goals at different times of life: nominations of goals in the domains of work, family, and finances decreased over adulthood, whereas goals relating to health, leisure, and community became increasingly common. The goals nominated were also coded in terms of whether they were directed at achieving a desirable state (gain-striving goals; e.g., harmonious family life, career success) or avoiding an undesirable one (loss-avoiding goals; e.g., unemployment, health problems). As shown in Fig. 15.14, young adults generated more gain-striving goals than middle-aged adults, who in turn reported more gain-striving goals

The AAI Model of Intentional Self-Development

Developmental goals play a major role in the model of intentional self-development proposed by Brandtstädter (1986, 1998, 2001). For Brandtstädter, the main function of development-related action and thought is to stabilize the individual's construction of self across the lifespan, and to protect it against age-related challenges. This personal continuity depends on the construction and stabilization of self-representations, many facets of which are open to development and thus exposed to dynamic processes of gains and losses across the lifespan. Individuals are motivated to offset any discrepancies arising between self-representations and the associated developmental goals, on the one hand, and the self-states that are actually attained or attainable at a given age, on the other. According to the AAI model, this may be done in three ways:

1. Assimilation: The individual may engage in self-referential activities aiming to bring personal development in line with his or her self and life goals. The discrepancy between actual and desired states is addressed by changing the actual state.

2. Accommodation: The individual may adjust self-referential goals to bring his or her self and life goals in line with the given opportunities and constraints. In this case, the desired state is adjusted.

3. Immunization: The individual may modify self-referential evaluation criteria to stabilize his or her self-representations and protect them against the threat of loss. In other words, the measurement indicators for the desired state are adjusted.

These assimilative, accommodative, and immunizing processes of intentional self-development serve to maintain personal continuity and identity over time. All three processes are activated when developmental losses lead to discrepancies from the self-image (e.g., in an older adult whose self-image includes a good memory for numbers). The three processes are antagonistic, meaning that the activation of one process inhibits that of the other two. For example, a woman who signs up for a memory training course because she is having trouble remembering telephone numbers (assimilation) will not, at the same time, lower her expectations with respect to memory capacity (accommodation) or decide that it is not important to be able to remember telephone numbers after all (immunization).

In their extensive research program, Brandtstädter and colleagues have demonstrated the functioning of these three self-regulatory processes and their adaptive effects on self-esteem and psychological well-being in various contexts (Brandtstädter, 1998, 2001; Brandtstädter & Greve, 1994; Brandtstädter & Rothermund, 2002; Brandtstädter, Wentura, & Rothermund, 1999; Greve & Wentura, 2003; Rothermund & Brandtstädter, 2003a, b).

than older adults. Conversely, the frequency of loss-avoiding goals increased with age.

❗ These age-related trends in gain- and loss-oriented developmental goals reflect normative expectations about the pattern of developmental gains and losses over adulthood (Fig. 15.11). The findings thus confirm that normative conceptions act as guidelines and timetables regulating individual decisions on when to pursue which goals in which domain of life.

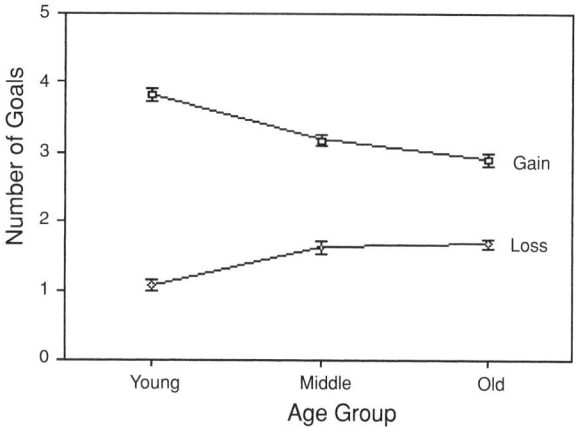

Figure 15.14 Gain- and loss-oriented developmental goals in young, middle, and late adulthood. (Based on J. Heckhausen, 1997.)

This conclusion is further substantiated by a study showing that the developmental goals of adults of different ages correspond with their normative conceptions about psychological development (Hundertmark, 1990; Hundertmark & J. Heckhausen, 1994). Other studies conducted within our research program have addressed specific developmental goals that are subject to age-graded decline in opportunities for goal attainment, and thus expose the individual to the urgency of a developmental deadline (J. Heckhausen & Tomasik, 2002; J. Heckhausen, Wrosch, & Fleeson, 2001; Wrosch & J. Heckhausen, 1999). These studies are discussed later in this chapter.

SUMMARY

Developmental goals organize individual developmental regulation. A number of related approaches have addressed mid- and long-term personal goals and concerns from the perspectives of motivation psychology, personality psychology, and social psychology, and shown that these goals endow an individual's everyday behavior with direction, coherence, and meaning. Personal goals can have positive or negative effects on emotional well-being, depending on whether their attainment can be controlled by the individual, and thus has good prospects of success. Furthermore, pursuit of personal goals that are in conflict with an individual's implicit motives tends to have detrimental effects because it inhibits the attainment of motive-congruent goals. A number of studies have shown that developmental goals reflect age-normative expectations about the relevance, urgency, and controllability of developmental changes. Age-normative conceptions are thus important in the selection of developmental goals. They serve as guidelines and timetables governing individuals' efforts to influence their development favorably.

Congruence Between Developmental Goals and Developmental Opportunities

To ensure successful and efficient investment of personal and social resources, goal striving should be synchronous with the age-graded opportunity structures to attain developmental goals across the life course (J. Heckhausen, 1999; Schulz & J. Heckhausen, 1996; J. Heckhausen & Farruggia, 2003). In other words, developmental goals should be pursued when the biological and societal conditions for their realization are favorable. As discussed in Section 15.8.1, age-normative conceptions about development across the lifespan assume developmental gains to decrease over adulthood and developmental losses to increase (Fig. 15.11). Patterns of gain-striving versus loss-avoiding goals reflect these changes in action opportunities, with more loss-avoiding goals being reported with age, at the cost of gain-striving goals (Fig. 15.14). This general shift to fewer gain-oriented and more loss-oriented goals thus follows the age-graded opportunity structure. But does the same apply to the fit between specific goals and age-differentiated opportunities?

Realization of most developmental goals depends on a number of biological, social, and biographical (in the sense of the canalization effect) conditions being in place. Opportunities to realize important developmental goals, such as starting a family or establishing oneself in a career, are thus not distributed at random across the age axis, but vary systematically with age. These waxing and waning curves of opportunity each have ideal timing periods, when opportunities for goal attainment are at a maximum (J. Heckhausen, 2002a; J. Heckhausen & Farruggia, 2003). Fig. 15.15 shows hypothetical opportunity curves for a selection of major developmental goals (e.g., school graduation, first child) with different gradients of increasing and decreasing opportunities, and phases of maximum opportunity of differing lengths. Some opportunity trajectories are steep and have only a short window of opportunity (e.g., graduation from school, first job); others span much longer periods (e.g., first child).

DEVELOPMENTAL DEADLINES. Research on age-normative conceptions about psychological change (see the overview in J. Heckhausen, 1999, and Section 15.8.1) and findings from life-course sociology (Fallo-Mitchell & Ryff, 1982; Neugarten, Moore & Lowe, 1965; Plath & Ikeda, 1975; Zepelin, Sills & Heath, 1986–87) have shown that most adults have detailed ideas about when in life certain opportunities are favorable and from which point on goal pursuit no longer seems advisable (Settersten & Hagestad, 1996). The age-graded sequencing of phases of maximum opportunity for

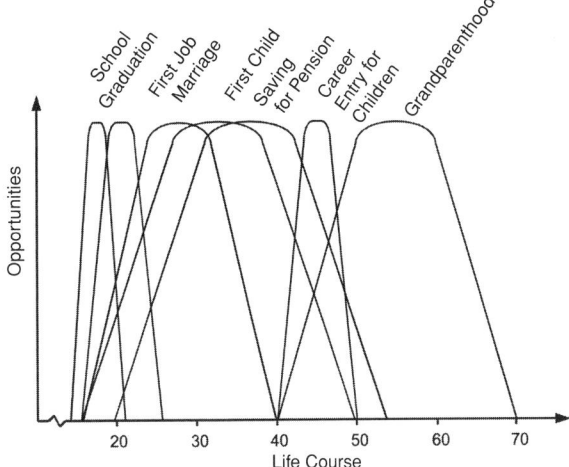

Figure 15.15 Age-graded sequencing of opportunity curves for different developmental goals. (Based on J. Heckhausen, 2002a.)

major life goals can thus provide a timetable organizing developmental regulation. Age-normative conceptions give individuals a good idea of when it is appropriate to contemplate particular developmental goals and to invest substantially in their attainment, and when there is no longer a point in wasting energy on a goal (see the following example). Of course, individuals may decide to deviate from the developmental timetable and pursue goals at unfavorable times (e.g., to study for a degree in middle age). This deviation has its costs, however; goal pursuit under unfavorable biological or social conditions requires far greater investment of energy and resources, which are then no longer available for other goals (J. Heckhausen, 1989). Fig. 15.16 shows the age-graded opportunity structure for a developmental goal, and the investment required as opportunities increase, plateau, and decline.

> **EXAMPLE**
>
> Individuals who have postponed a particular developmental goal, such as childbearing, may miss the ideal "age window" for that goal, but still not want to abandon it. As opportunities for goal attainment decrease, they feel an increasing sense of urgency. They may even be able to foresee a point at which opportunities for goal attainment are so slight that any further goal striving will be in vain. This is the developmental deadline.

Developmental deadlines mark the point at which it no longer makes sense to invest resources in goal pursuit, and when the time has come to disengage from that goal. These timing constraints in goal attainability can be anticipated by the individual and elicit phases of urgent goal striving immediately before the developmental deadline is reached, as illustrated by the steep increase in the goal engagement

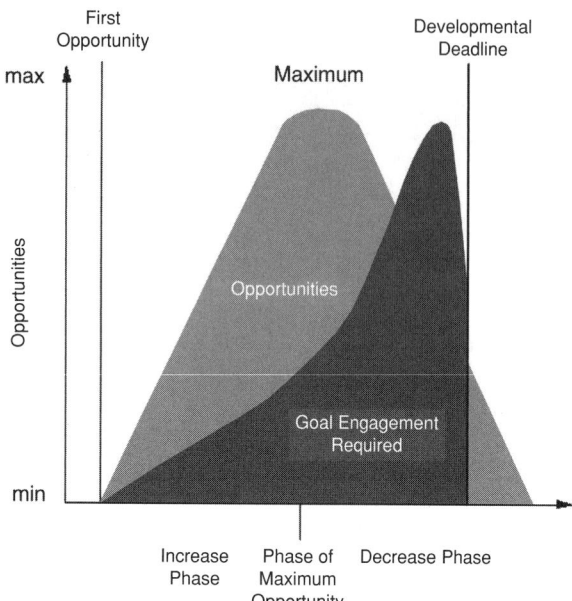

Figure 15.16 Age-graded opportunity structure and goal striving for developmental goals. (Based on J. Heckhausen, 2000b.)

curve in Fig. 15.16. As soon as the developmental deadline has been passed, however, individuals need to disengage from the now futile goal and invest their energy in other, more fruitful projects.

❶ Developmental deadlines make extraordinary demands of an individual's regulatory capacities; they require a switch from urgent, intensive goal engagement in the immediate run-up to the deadline to goal disengagement and protection of self-esteem as soon as the deadline has been passed. Developmental transitions involving developmental deadlines are thus particularly suitable for testing the potentials and limits of individual developmental regulation.

Before presenting empirical findings and the action-phase model itself in the, we discuss the optimization heuristics that help individuals select the right goals at the right time across the life course.

OPTIMIZATION HEURISTICS. As reported previously, the lifespan theory of control assumes the functional primacy of primary control (i.e., the striving to exert control over the environment) over secondary control. It is not always easy to tell which goals are most conducive to long-term **optimization of primary control potential** across the lifespan, however. Because resources are limited, not all goals can be pursued at once, and those that become prohibitively costly or impossible to achieve as opportunities wane should be abandoned. Which goals are selected at any given point depends on the results emerging from the application of the following three **optimization heuristics** (J. Heckhausen, 1999; J. Heckhausen & Schulz, 1993):

1. adaptation to age-graded opportunity structures,
2. consideration of short- and long-term consequences, and
3. maintenance of diversity.

Age-appropriate goal selection capitalizes on phases of maximum opportunity, when goal attainment is highly controllable and requires relatively few personal resources because biological and/or societal conditions are conducive to goal attainment. For example, starting school at the age of 5 or 6 or retiring from working life at the age of 60 to 65 requires little individual regulation. However, individuals who deviate from these age-graded transitions and seek early retirement at the age of 55, for example, may meet with fierce resistance.

A second optimization heuristic implies the **consideration of short- and long-term consequences** of goal selection within and between domains. Investing in one goal can have positive or negative implications for the pursuit of other goals. For example, young men and women who plan to pursue a demanding career need to be aware of the potential consequences of their choice for starting a family and, if they want to have children, find ways to beat the biological clock. Intensive investment in one domain often leads to the neglect of others. However, goal attainment in a given domain (e.g., career success) can have positive long-term implications for other domains (e.g., the financial assets to start a family).

❶ In general, broad and general abilities have more positive consequences in the long term and across domains, whereas too narrow specializations, especially if they occur early in life, often mean that individual potential in other domains is not developed.

The third optimization heuristic involves **maintenance of diversity** across lifespan development. People who specialize early in life risk limiting their developmental potential to a single domain (e.g., sport, music), which puts them in a rather vulnerable position should this domain become unavailable for any reason (e.g., injury). Diversified investment in more than one goal domain can provide the "raw material" for new developmental advancements in the future, in the same way as variability in a population's gene pool provides the raw material on which evolutionary selection can work. Finding the right level of diversity is like walking a tightrope. A very high level of diversity enables individuals to adapt flexibly to new conditions arising over the lifespan, but generally means that they do not develop real expertise in any domain. Ideally, children should be exposed to a variety of domains of functioning early in life, as is indeed the case in the general education systems of industrialized nations. In adulthood, selectivity increases in terms of occupational contexts and the social network.

SUMMARY

To be successful and efficient, goal striving must be synchronous with the age-graded opportunity structures to attain developmental goals across the life course. The rising and falling curves of opportunity for developmental goals such as finding a first job or starting a family have phases of maximum opportunity, during which relevant control striving is most effective. Because these age-graded opportunity curves are represented in age-normative conceptions, they can be anticipated and taken into account in adolescents' and adults' developmental regulation. As adults get older, there is a general shift away from pursuing developmental gains and toward avoiding developmental losses.

Developmental regulation is particularly intensive in the run-up to and immediately after a developmental deadline. As soon as the deadline has been passed, individuals have to switch from a phase of urgent goal engagement to goal disengagement and protection of self-esteem. Three optimization heuristics can be used to regulate the selection of goals for engagement versus disengagement: age-graded goal selection, consideration of short- and long-term consequences, and maintenance of diversity.

Action Phases in the Pursuit of Developmental Goals: Goal Selection, Goal Engagement, and Goal Disengagement

How can the action cycle of goal engagement and goal disengagement be conceptualized against the background of increasing and decreasing opportunities to attain important goals across the life course? A key proposition of the action-phase model of developmental regulation (J. Heckhausen, 1999; J. Heckhausen & Farruggia, 2003) is that the transitions to goal engagement and from goal engagement to goal disengagement are not gradual and progressive, but sudden and discrete, and affect multiple aspects of motivated behavior. The underlying assumption is that the individual can be either in a "go" mode or in a "stop and retreat" mode. The phases of the action cycle and the associated control strategies are presented in Fig. 15.17. The following excursus examines these control strategies in more detail.

THE SEQUENCE OF ACTION PHASES. The action-phase model of developmental regulation (J. Heckhausen, 1999) expands and modifies the Rubicon model of action phases proposed by Heinz Heckhausen (H. Heckhausen, 1991; Heckhausen & Gollwitzer, 1987). Specifically, the Rubicon model has been expanded to include the concept of the developmental deadline, the point at which opportunities to achieve a certain goal decline below a critical level. This developmental deadline is hypothesized to be preceded by an **urgency phase** and followed by a phase of goal disengagement. To track the timeline of the model shown in Fig. 15.17 from left to right, an action cycle starts with the predecisional phase before the Rubicon is crossed (see also Chapter 11, Section 11.2). During this predecisional phase, the individual evaluates developmental alternatives (e.g., different career paths) in terms of their advantages and disadvantages, controllability and feasibility, and costs and utility for other goals (including long-term goals). During this deliberative phase

(Chapter 11), information processing should be open-minded and impartial. As soon as the Rubicon has been crossed and a decision made, however, there is a discrete shift to a mind-set suitable for maximizing primary control striving toward the chosen goal. Strategies of selective primary and selective secondary control are applied to this end. As the individual approaches the developmental deadline for a chosen goal, primary control striving enters an urgency phase, and the application of goal-engagement control strategies is intensified. If internal behavioral resources are insufficient, recourse may be taken to compensatory primary control strategies. As soon as the developmental deadline has been passed, however, goal engagement becomes dysfunctional. The transition from favorable to radically reduced opportunities for goal attainment necessitates a discrete shift from goal engagement to goal disengagement. This change of gear can be illustrated using the analogy of a lion pursuing an antelope. The lion begins the chase at top speed. As soon as it realizes that it is being outrun, however, and that the distance to the antelope is increasing, the lion will stop and turn away abruptly, rather than slowing down gradually.

Active goal disengagement (see also Wrosch, Scheier, Miller, Schulz, & Carver, 2003) facilitates a rapid and radical shift from goal engagement to goal distancing. Strategies of active goal disengagement are thus an important component of compensatory secondary control, preventing behavioral and motivational resources from being invested in vain. Moreover, self-protective secondary control strategies help the individual deflect the long-term negative effects that missing a developmental deadline may have on motivational resources (e.g., self-esteem, hope for success in the future). Individuals who succeed in attaining a goal before the deadline expires can either build on their success in that domain (e.g., work toward their next promotion, have another baby) or apply their control strategies to a domain that may have been neglected while pursuing the more urgent goal. One example is the shift from a focus on career goals to family goals as soon as a major age-dependent move up the career ladder has been made (e.g., tenure in an academic career). Wiese (2000; see also Wiese & Freund, 2000) reported that this kind of "career first, then family" pattern of goal engagement is endorsed by a substantial subgroup of respondents in early adulthood (ca. 25%).

Empirical Studies on Goal Engagement and Disengagement Before and After Developmental Deadlines

Our ongoing research program explores the regulatory strategies that people of different ages and in different sociocultural contexts adopt when confronted with developmental challenges during important life-course transitions. The general research paradigm is to use marked life-course changes in opportunities to attain particular life goals (e.g., having children, climbing the career ladder) as testing grounds for

Control Processes Involved in Goal Engagement and Goal Disengagement

The lifespan theory of control distinguishes two kinds of control striving: primary and secondary control striving. Primary control striving is directed at the external world and serves to produce direct effects of behavior in the environment. Examples include building a Lego house, studying for an exam, applying for a job, or trying to sell someone a house. Secondary control striving, in contrast, is directed at the internal world and serves to influence one's motivational resources, either by increasing volitional commitment to a chosen goal or by shielding self-esteem and other motivational resources against potential threats. Examples of secondary control strategies directed at volition include imagining the benefits of goal attainment, avoiding tempting distractions, or convincing oneself that the prospects of success on an ongoing project are good. Primary and secondary control striving work hand in hand throughout the goal engagement phase to ensure that both behavioral and motivational resources are mobilized.

Goal Engagement Involves Three Kinds of Control Strategies

1. Selective primary control strategies involve the investment of behavioral resources (time, effort, skills) in goal pursuit (example: "I'm going to work hard to succeed in my career.").
2. Selective secondary control strategies use volitional self-regulation to enhance motivational commitment to selected goals (example: "I often imagine how happy I'll be when I've found a good job.").
3. Compensatory primary control strategies include seeking other people's help or advice when one's own primary control resources are insufficient and external assistance is required (example: "If I run into problems with my career plans, I'll ask others for advice.") or taking detours or unusual approaches (example: "I'd accept a less attractive job if it meant I'd get the position I want in the long run.").

Goal Disengagement and Protection of Motivational Resources

If circumstances make goal attainment prohibitively difficult or impossible, goal disengagement is an adaptive response that prevents behavioral and motivational resources that could be more productively applied to other goals from going to waste. Goal disengagement relies on strategies of compensatory secondary control that serve either of two key functions:

1. Goal disengagement: Disengagement from unattainable (or prohibitively difficult) goals allows resources to be invested in other, more feasible goals. Goal disengagement may involve devaluation of the original goal (example: "If I don't succeed in my job, I'll know that it wasn't the right thing for me anyway.").
2. Protection of motivational resources: Strategies serving to protect motivational resources help shield individual self-esteem and action-related optimism against the negative effects of experiences of failure or loss. Self-protective strategies include attribution to external rather than internal factors (example: "If there are problems at school, I tell myself it's not all my fault.") and strategic social comparison (example: "If I don't succeed in my job, I'll tell myself that other people are even worse off.").

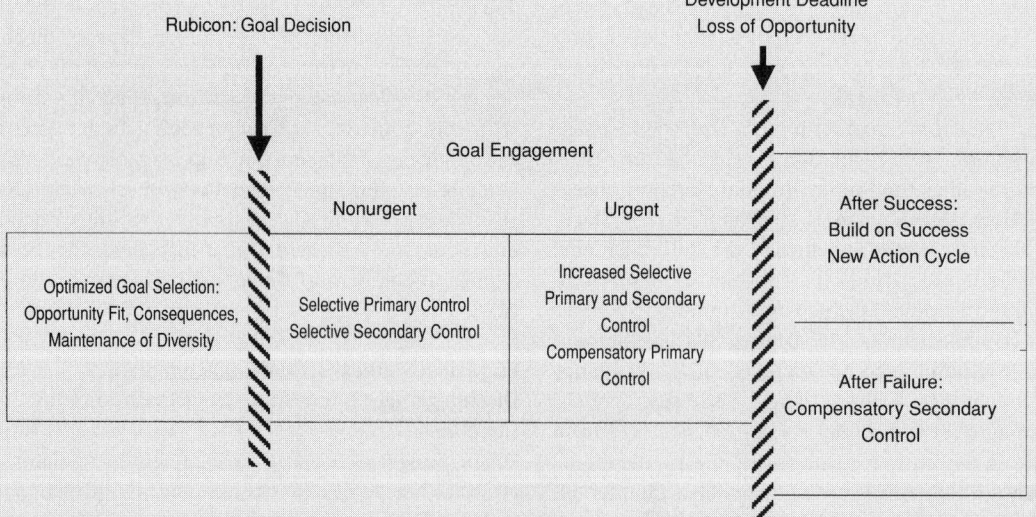

Figure 15.17 Action-phase model of developmental regulation. (Based on J. Heckhausen, 1999.)

Studies on Childbearing as a Developmental Goal

Both studies compared childless women before (age: 30 to 35 years) and after (age: 40 to 45 years and 50 to 55 years) the developmental deadline for childbearing, which most people consider to fall around the age of 40 (J. Heckhausen, Wrosch, & Fleeson, 2001). To this end, the Optimization in Primary and Secondary Control (OPS) scales (J. Heckhausen, Schulz, & Wrosch, 1998) were adapted to the life goal of childbearing.

Sample items from the control strategy questionnaire were as follows:

- selective primary control: "I will do whatever I can to have children of my own";
- selective secondary control: "I will not let anything distract me from my goal of having children ";
- compensatory primary control: "If I have problems conceiving, I will seek assistance (e.g., from a doctor)";
- goal disengagement component of compensatory secondary control: "If I can't have children, I'll have to forget the whole idea";
- self-protective component of compensatory secondary control: "It's not my fault if I don't have children."

Findings show that the childless women in the urgency condition (women in their early 30s) felt strongly committed to the developmental goal of childbearing. They reported using all three control strategies of goal engagement – selective primary control, selective secondary control, and compensatory primary control – more frequently than the older women (see the excursus on "Control Processes Involved in Goal Engagement and Goal Disengagement"). Conversely, the 40- and 50-year-old women reported using compensatory secondary control strategies more frequently than the predeadline women. Thus, both premenopausal women approaching the developmental deadline and women in the age group of rapidly decreasing fertility showed a pattern of goal engagement or disengagement that was congruent with their age-graded opportunities for childbearing.

We then examined how phase congruence (i.e., congruence of goal engagement and opportunities for goal attainment) relates to psychological well-being measured in terms of the absence of depressive symptoms to determine whether congruence is associated with more adaptive developmental outcomes. The findings presented in Fig. 15.18 indicate that strong selective primary control striving in predeadline women was associated with particularly low scores on the depression scale. The reverse holds for postdeadline women (in their 40s and 50s). The more committed these postdeadline women felt to childbearing, the more depressive symptoms they reported. Mental health thus reflects the congruence between control opportunities and control striving; greater congruence is associated with fewer reported depressive symptoms, and low congruence with elevated levels of depressive symptomatology.

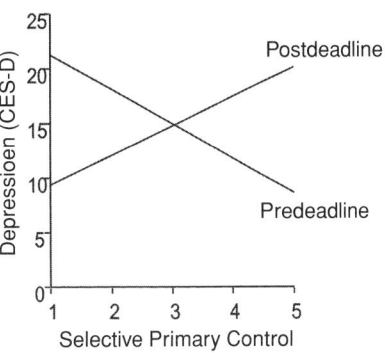

Figure 15.18 Selective primary control as a predictor of depressive symptoms in childless women before and after the developmental deadline. (Based on J. Heckhausen, Wrosch, & Fleeson, 2001.)

In another study on developmental deadlines for childbearing, we investigated whether goal engagement and disengagement lead to change at the information-processing level, and thus have implicit or subintentional effects beyond conscious control strategies. An incidental memory test was used to assess implicit bias in information processing in terms of recall of goal-relevant and goal-irrelevant information. Respondents were again childless women before and after the developmental deadline. They were first asked to name five developmental goals for the next 5 to 10 years (Developmental Goals Questionnaire based on J. Heckhausen, 1997), and then to rate their agreement with sentences about children and babies and sentences about other topics. After the Positive and Negative Affect Scale (PANAS; Watson, Clark, & Tellegen, 1988) had been administered, participants were finally instructed to recall as many as possible of the sentences presented in the rating task. Participants had not been expecting this memory test. The results replicated the findings of the first study on childbearing, to the extent that the developmental goals nominated reflected the age-graded opportunity structures for childbearing. Predeadline women reported more developmental goals relating to children than did postdeadline women. Moreover, for the postdeadline women, negative affect was found to be strongly associated with remembering relatively many sentences relating to the positive aspects of life with children, the personal responsibility for not having children, and the implications of childlessness for other goals (becoming a grandparent) in the incidental memory test.

This study thus provided evidence at both the explicit intentional level (developmental goals nominated) and the implicit subintentional level (selective memory) to confirm that goal engagement and goal disengagement follow age-graded opportunity structures. Moreover, the findings showed that incongruence of implicit goal orientations and opportunities for goal attainment is associated with negative affect.

individuals' regulatory capacity. Specifically, we explore how individuals with different (cultural, sociostructural, individual personality) backgrounds respond to such changes in opportunities with congruent or incongruent goal engagement or goal disengagement.

The two studies described as follows investigated the transition from favorable to fading opportunities for the developmental goal of childbearing. Both of the studies were cross-sectional; changes in the opportunity structure itself (in this case, age-graded female fertility) are too gradual for a longitudinal approach to be feasible.

Another study on developmental regulation before and after a developmental deadline investigated intimate relationship goals (Wrosch & J. Heckhausen, 1999). Partnership formation is, in principle, possible at any time in adulthood, so it might seem surprising that there should be a deadline for this developmental goal. The probability of finding a new partner after a separation is known to decrease rapidly over adulthood, however, from around 80% in early adulthood to 20% in late middle adulthood (Braun & Proebsting, 1986; Teachman & Heckert, 1985). Individuals have to come to terms with this sharp decline in opportunities to find a partner, presumably by distancing themselves from the goal at some point between early and late middle adulthood. In his dissertation study, Carsten Wrosch examined men and women aged 20 to 35 years and 50 to 60 years who had recently separated from a long-term partner or entered a new relationship. It was assumed that the goal of finding a partner would be urgent in early adulthood, especially after a separation, but that adults in their 50s would find it difficult to form a new relationship and that goal disengagement would be the more advisable course of action for this group. In line with the action-phase model, the young respondents reported more goals relating to intimate relationships and more frequent use of the associated goal engagement strategies (selective primary and selective secondary control, compensatory primary control), whereas participants between 50 and 60 years of age nominated relatively few partnership goals and reported more frequent use of compensatory secondary control strategies of goal disengagement and self-protection.

Again, an incidental memory task was used to examine a potential information-processing bias. It emerged that the young adults were better able to recall adjectives describing the positive aspects of intimate relationships (e.g., happy, supportive), whereas the 50- to 60-year-olds remembered adjectives associated with the more negative aspects (e.g., unfaithful, stressful). The respondents in the relationship study were contacted again 18 months after the first wave of data collection and asked to report on their psychological well-being. As shown in Fig. 15.19, strong endorsement of compensatory secondary control strategies (e.g., "I can live a fulfilled life without a partner," "It's not my fault that I don't have a partner") tended to have detrimental effects on the psychological well-being of young, recently separated participants. They

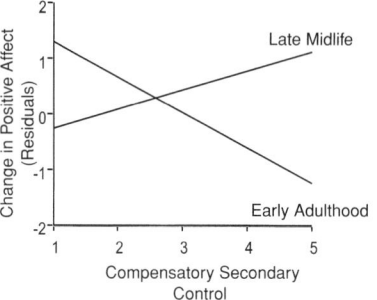

Figure 15.19 Compensatory secondary control as a predictor of change in positive affect over 18 months in recently separated individuals in early adulthood and late midlife. (Based on Wrosch & J. Heckhausen, 1999.)

experienced a decline in positive affect over time. In the older respondents, by contrast, strong endorsement of compensatory secondary control strategies was associated with enhanced positive affect over time. In other words, abandoning the goal of forming a new relationship after separation is problematic in early adulthood, but adaptive in late midlife. Research has not yet examined the nature of the transition from goal commitment to goal disengagement in this particular context. Based on the action-phase model of developmental regulation, we assume that goal engagement does not decrease gradually as the chances of finding a partner fade. Rather, we hypothesize that individuals faced with steadily worsening prospects of finding a mate set themselves a developmental deadline, investing heavily in the goal of finding a partner in the run-up to that deadline, and abandoning it once and for all when the deadline has passed (e.g., devaluing or ignoring the positive aspects of a relationship). It remains for future research to determine whether there really is such a radical shift in priorities at a self-generated developmental deadline.

URGENCY PHASE. Having demonstrated motivational reorientation before and after developmental deadlines in these cross-sectional studies, we now turn to another aspect of the action-phase model of developmental regulation that goes beyond the assumptions of Rubicon model, namely, the **urgency phase** immediately before a developmental deadline is reached. This phase, during which primary control striving is exposed to enormous time pressure, can only be examined in longitudinal studies. Even then, the long time periods involved, as well as the heterogeneity of developmental trajectories and life-course transitions in adulthood, pose considerable challenges for research. We thus chose a transition involving a developmental deadline that is relatively strictly regulated in Germany, namely, the transition from school to vocational training in the dual educational system (on-the-job training combined with general and vocational education at a vocational school). The major challenge of this transition is to find an apprenticeship position, preferably before leaving school. In other countries, such as the United States, the transition from high school to the world of work is far less strictly regulated. Many young people end up "floundering" (Hamilton, 1990) and at risk for downward social mobility (for details on international variation in the school-to-work transition, see J. Heckhausen, 2002b; Heinz, 1999; Paul, 2001). The transition to vocational training is also a challenging and critical step for young people in Germany, however, because the number and quality of apprenticeships (within a single company or at multiple sites; commercial vs. trade apprenticeships) by no means matches the demand. During their final year at school (typically 10th grade), students not wanting to continue their general education have to find an apprenticeship (Heinz, Krüger, Rettke, Wachtveitl, & Witzel, 1985; Heyn, Schnabel, & Röder, 1997) that opens up relatively positive long-term career prospects (J. Heckhausen & Tomasik, 2002; Tomasik, 2003) given their individual capacities. Navigating between the Scylla and Charybdis of over- and under-aspiration under urgency conditions is thus a considerable challenge to developmental regulatory capacities of 16-year-old school leavers.

We investigated students in their final year at four high schools located in lower and lower middle-class residential areas in the eastern and western part of Berlin, Germany. Data on students' goals, control strategies, and vocational aspirations were collected twice in 9th grade and five times at two-month intervals in 10th grade. Findings showed that the adolescents adjusted their vocational aspirations, measured in terms of the social prestige, to their grades (i.e., their educational resources on the labor market). The adolescents even adjusted their ideas of a "dream job" to the apprenticeships they could realistically hope to be offered (J. Heckhausen & Tomasik, 2002), such that the vision of a dream job did not prevent them from investing in the search for an appropriate position. In the United States, under different societal conditions where the transition after high school leaves more options open, the youth aspired to uniformly high educational and vocational goals (J. Heckhausen, Chang, Chen, & Greenberger, 2007). In both societies, high goal engagement was found to be beneficial for subjective well-being, mental health, and sociobehavioral outcomes (Haase, J. Heckhausen, & Köller, 2007; J. Heckhausen et al., 2007).

Empirical Studies on Goal Engagement and Disengagement in the Context of Health Problems

Other studies have investigated goal engagement and disengagement and the associated control processes in the context of health problems in middle adulthood and old age (Wrosch, J. Heckhausen, & Lachman, 2000; Wrosch, Schulz, & J. Heckhausen, 2002).

❶ Health impairments are normative developmental challenges in older age that put the capacity for developmental regulation to the test.

Deteriorating health as a result of chronic illness and progressive sensory (e.g., loss of vision associated with macular degeneration) or motor (e.g., arthritis) impairment leads to a reduction in control potential, and necessitates appropriate control striving strategies. When health problems in old age are reversible and controllable, primary control striving is suitable for overcoming their effects, but abandonment of primary control striving is associated with the development of depressive symptoms, which in turn weaken primary control striving over time (Wrosch, Schulz, & J. Heckhausen, 2002, 2004; Wrosch, J. Heckhausen, & Lachman, 2000). When health outcomes are less controllable, compensatory strategies of secondary control, such as acknowledging the positive side effects of illness, seem to be most conducive to physical and psychological well-being (Affleck, Tennen, Croog, & Levine, 1987; Thompson, 1987). Chipperfield, Perry, and Menec (1999) found that primary control striving (e.g., active persistence, effort) in the "young old" (younger than 80 years) and compensatory secondary control striving (e.g., lowering one's expectations, accepting limitations) in the "old old" (older than 80 years) was associated with higher subjective health ratings. A study on life regrets produced analogous findings. It is more conducive to the psychological well-being of older, but not younger, adults to abandon the goal of making up for past actions, and instead to see those actions as having been beyond their control (Wrosch & J. Heckhausen, 2002).

Several research groups are currently testing the lifespan theory of control and its action-phase model of developmental regulation in longitudinal studies with diverse samples (e.g., patients with macular degeneration, young adults at the transition from one educational institution to another, cancer patients before and after a treatment decision, older adults dealing with interpersonal conflict). These studies are examining patterns of causation between changing opportunities for goal attainment and the control strategies of goal engagement or disengagement applied by the individuals in question, the influence of the social context and personality factors on the fit between opportunities and control behavior, and the objective and subjective developmental consequences of this fit.

SUMMARY

Cross-sectional and longitudinal studies on developmental regulation before and after a developmental deadline have provided evidence in support of two key assumptions of the action-phase model of developmental regulation:

1. a discrete shift from goal engagement to goal disengagement once the developmental deadline has been passed, and

2. a phase of urgent goal engagement in the immediate run-up to the developmental deadline.

Cross-sectional studies on childbearing and intimate relationships have shown that adults surveyed shortly before a developmental deadline are strongly committed to the goal at hand and use corresponding control strategies. Once the developmental deadline has been passed, however, most respondents distance themselves from the goal and use compensatory secondary control strategies to protect the self against the negative consequences of failure experiences. Evidence for congruence between goal engagement/disengagement and opportunities for goal attainment has been found using both explicit measures (goals nominated, control strategies) and implicit indicators of selective information processing. The greater the congruence between goal engagement/disengagement and opportunities for goal attainment, the higher the levels of subjective well-being and mental health recorded (lower levels of depressive symptomatology).

A longitudinal study on the transition from school to vocational training showed that adolescents' capacity for developmental regulation at this precarious transition to adulthood is impressive, with vocational ideals increasingly being adjusted to more realistic aspirations. A combination of selective primary and selective secondary control strategies proved particularly adaptive at this difficult developmental transition. The study also underlined the importance of the urgency phase in the action cycle, and showed that orchestrated application of primary and secondary control strategies is particularly effective at this time.

The action-phase model of developmental control has also been used to investigate the control striving of patients with acute and chronic illnesses. In line with the findings of studies on developmental goals, the investigations conducted to date have observed positive developmental outcomes when health-related goal engagement and disengagement are congruent with the available control potential, and negative implications for well-being when goal striving vs. goal distancing and control potential are incongruent.

15.8.3 Individual Differences in the Capacity for Developmental Regulation

Because research on individual differences in the capacity for developmental regulation is still in its infancy, the main objective of this section is to identify directions for future research. Based on the assumptions of the action-phase model of developmental regulation, individual differences in the following dimensions can be expected to determine the adaptivity of developmental regulation across the lifespan:

1. Knowledge of one's control potential and the opportunities to attain developmental goals within the developmental ecology afforded by the existing biological and societal conditions plays a key role in optimized goal selection, as does the ability to obtain this information.
2. The willingness and ability to adjust processes of developmental regulation to the opportunities and constraints of the developmental ecology determine whether individuals are able to establish congruence between the biological and societal opportunity structures and

their own developmental goals. The construct of motivational competence proposed by Rheinberg (2006; see also Section 15.7.4) is probably decisive in the fine-tuning of environment-action fit. Moreover, the willingness to achieve congruence is probably closely related to the two aspects that follow.

3. Strong primary control striving, characterized by persistence and resilience, is the fundamental motivational resource for developmental regulation. Persistence and resilience may prove excessive, however, if they are not in line with the actual potential for control.

Initial findings on the age-graded adaptivity of primary control striving in the context of childbearing (J. Heckhausen et al., 2001) indicate that individuals who continue to strive for a particular life goal when it is no longer attainable tend to develop depressive symptoms. However, studies on coping with reversible health problems (Wrosch et al., 2000, 2002, 2004) have shown that it is maladaptive to relinquish primary control striving when control potential is still available. Findings presented by Halisch and Geppert (2000) for a sample of 65- to 85-year-olds show that the persistent pursuit of personal goals only has positive effects on life satisfaction if those goals are judged to be attainable. Intensive investment in goals with low feasibility ratings has pronounced negative implications for life satisfaction. Goal striving must therefore be calibrated to the control potential available in a given situation.

4. The willingness and ability to deactivate and disengage from a goal influences both objective and subjective developmental outcomes. Objectively speaking, individuals who cling to unattainable goals are unable to invest the resources tied up in pursuit of those goals in more feasible projects, and thus relinquish control potential. First findings even indicate that deficient disengagement from unattainable goals influences secretion of the stress hormone cortisol over the course of the day and is likely to make these individuals more susceptible to illness (Wrosch, Miller, Scheier, & de Pontet, 2007).

The subjective costs of deficient goal disengagement are also considerable, as shown in a series of studies by Wrosch et al. (2003). The ability to disengage from unattainable goals has been found to have positive effects on subjective well-being (e.g., perceived stress, depressive symptoms) in young and middle adulthood, especially among individuals who have been exposed to high stress (e.g., having one's child undergo treatment for cancer).

5. Because experiences of failure and loss of control are inevitable across the human life course, strategies of compensatory secondary control that serve to protect motivational resources (e.g., self-esteem, avoidance of self-blame, confidence in the success of future endeavors) are indispensable.

Very little is yet known about interindividual differences in people's preferences for and skill in applying these different strategies (e.g., self-serving patterns of attribution and social comparison, devaluation of unattained goals). Research into cross-cultural differences in the acceptance of strategies serving to protect motivational resources is also warranted.

6. Another major dimension of the capacity for developmental regulation that varies interindividually is the willingness and ability to reengage in a new goal when an existing goal seems unattainable.

Wrosch et al. (2003) found that goal reengagement varies interindividually and independently of the willingness to disengage from a goal, and is associated with enhanced psychological well-being (e.g., perceived stress, meaning in life, depressive symptoms). Interindividual differences in the willingness to both disengage from old goals and reengage in new ones show age-differential effects. In young adulthood, those who find it difficult to abandon unattainable goals benefit most from the willingness to pursue new goals. In older adulthood, in contrast, those who are easily able to relinquish unattainable goals have most to gain from high willingness for goal reengagement. The crucial point is evidently that deficient goal disengagement should not stop people from engaging in new and worthwhile goals in early adulthood, when a multitude of opportunities are available to them. In advanced age, in contrast, it is important to be engaged in goal striving at all, even if the goals are unattainable.

7. Finally, the orchestration of primary and secondary control strategies at transitions between action phases – specifically, from goal deliberation to goal engagement (crossing the Rubicon), from goal engagement to the urgency phase before a developmental deadline, and from urgent goal engagement to goal disengagement (crossing the developmental deadline) – is another key determinant of the capacity for developmental regulation.

In this context, the conceptualization of processes of action control and self-regulation proposed by Kuhl in his model of action vs. state orientation and its elaboration in the PSI model (Kuhl, 2000b, 2001; see also Chapter 12 and Section 15.7.4 in this chapter) provides a promising framework that can guide future research.

SUMMARY

The exploration of interindividual differences in the capacity for developmental regulation is still in its infancy and promises to be a fruitful new field of research. Dimensions warranting study include individuals' knowledge about age-graded change in the opportunities for goal attainment over the life course and the corresponding fit between personal goals and the developmental ecology, the strength and resilience of primary control striving, the willingness and ability to disengage from goals for which controllability is low, access to compensatory secondary control strategies serving to protect motivational resources, the willingness and ability to reengage in new and attainable goals when previous goals

become unattainable or prohibitively costly, and finally the orchestration of primary and secondary control strategies at the transition between action phases.

15.8.4 Motivated Development: Dynamic Interaction Between Development and Motivation Across the Lifespan

The dynamic interactions between individuals and their environment have attracted increasing attention in personality psychology and lifespan developmental psychology in recent years (Asendorpf, 2004; Caspi, 1998; Lang & J. Heckhausen, 2006; Lerner, 2002; Roberts & Caspi, 2003; Sameroff, 1983; Scarr & McCartney, 1983). From the perspective of developmental and motivational psychology, it is possible to distinguish three prototypical forms of person/environment transactions that contribute to fit being established over time between the individual and his or her environment: **selective**, **evocative**, and **manipulative transactions** (see also Asendorpf, 2004; Buss, 1987):

- Through their **selection** of environments and situations (e.g., choice of career, choice of partner), individuals can influence the fit of competencies and motivational preferences with the environment, and thus play an active role in testing, developing, and optimizing that fit.

- The **evocation** of environments or situations is usually an unintentional result of individuals with certain personality characteristics (e.g., strong approach or avoidance affiliation motivation) repeatedly eliciting similar outcomes or responses (e.g., friendliness, rejection) in the social environment.

- **Manipulation** occurs when an individual shapes the environment directly and intentionally.

The following example illustrates these dynamic person/environment interactions in the developmental process:

EXAMPLE

Because of his unusual height, a boy keeps being asked whether he plays basketball (evocation). He decides to ask his parents to enroll him in the local basketball league (selection). The more he plays the game, the more he enjoys it. He reads up on the game, watches basketball on TV, and practices shooting baskets at home (selection) in the hope of being selected for a better team next season (manipulation). He eventually plays so well that a professional basketball team offers him a professional contract (manipulation) that he signs (selection). Unfortunately, he has failed to consider the implications of one-sided investment in a career as a basketball player: once he has retired from the game, few career options remain open (unintentional selection) and he feels depressed given the lack of meaningful perspectives and a purpose in life. At the age of 35, he therefore decides to go back to school to earn a biology degree (manipulation). After graduating, he finds a laboratory job in the pharmaceutical industry (selection).

In their longitudinal studies with adolescents and young adults, Eccles and colleagues discovered mutual influences between the individual and the self-selected environment (e.g., in the choice of subjects at school). These authors found that, influenced by the gender role norms prevailing in their peer group, girls may show a dislike for mathematics and physics, and consequently make less effort in these subjects, causing their performance outcomes to fall below those of others over time, which in turn leads to reduced confidence in their ability in these subjects (Eccles, 2005; Eccles et al., 1999). These studies thus show that dynamic interactions between the person and the environment do not always lead to optimized developmental outcomes. When conditions are unfavorable (e.g., adverse gender role norms, educational disadvantaging of the family, developmental delay), the developmental dynamics between person and environment can have either negative or positive implications for development. The decisive point here is whether the influences of biological development and socialization agents in the immediate environment (parents, teachers) suffice to bring development back on track. The further the dysfunctional canalization of the developmental trajectory has progressed, and the weaker the normative regulatory effects of biological and societal structures in the developmental ecology, the more difficult this will be.

Selection and **manipulation** of the environment play a major role in individual developmental regulation, as outlined in Section 15.8. In a field of action mapped out by biological and societal structures, selection is by far the most frequent form of transaction between the individual and the life-course ecology. For example, developmental paths are selected at the transition from school to vocational training (Haase et al., 2007; J. Heckhausen & Tomasik, 2002). Real manipulation of the environment occurs primarily in the context of social relationships with romantic partners, children, parents, friends, colleagues, and neighbors. Not only do individuals decide who to spend more or less time with and who to include in their social networks (Lang, 2001, 2004), but they also play an active role in shaping the quality of their relationships and daily interactions with social partners (Lang & J. Heckhausen, 2006; Lang, Reschke, & Neyer, 2006; Rook, Sorkin, & Zettel, 2004). These social relations come to constitute the everyday social environment, and thus have a ubiquitous influence on the individual's future development through model learning (for better or worse), conformity, contrast, and contradiction. The emergence of subgroups with shared value beliefs and normative ideas about the nature of a successful life course, key aspects of which may differ from the conceptions of society as a whole, is an important aspect in the selection and shaping of social networks. If these subgroups become strong enough, they can create their own social developmental ecologies. The student movement of the late 1960s and early 1970s is one example of this phenomenon. Although these ideological subgroups do not, by

any means, create real countersocieties, they can shape the life courses of their members and the perspectives of society in general to such an extent that they instigate social change, and ultimately lead to long-term transformation of societal institutions (e.g., marriage and divorce legislation). At political and social turning points, the dynamic transactional efforts of individuals, coupled with the leverage of the collective, can develop enormous – although rare – power that changes the societal conditions of lifespan development lastingly and irreversibly, far beyond the individual's immediate social ecology.

SUMMARY

Individuals' motivated influencing of their own development goes far beyond a mere person/situation interaction. Individuals must navigate their way through the opportunity structures dictated by biological and societal influences, and commit to action paths that open up certain opportunities and put others out of reach. In so doing, individuals not only shape their own future, but also have an active influence on the developmental ecology, and thus on their future scope for action. Although the biological (e.g., genetic makeup, biological maturity or age) and societal (e.g., social mobility within a society, individual social background) circumstances determine and limit their developmental potential, individuals not only have the freedom to make the best of the given conditions, but they can also seek to actively shape the conditions of their development by means of selection, evocation, and manipulation. These transactions are not always conscious, or indeed to the advantage of the individual, whose choices (e.g., of a career or a partner) shape the social environment, for better or worse. Nevertheless, individuals can and do become agents in shaping the social ecologies for their own development and thus exert powerful influences on their developmental potential and future life course.

REVIEW QUESTIONS

1. **What is meant by the functional primacy of primary control striving?**

   The striving to exert primary control on the environment is a universal and fundamental characteristic of human motivation. It is a product of behavioral evolution, and has been observed in various mammals and nonmammalian species.

2. **How does the potential for primary control change over the lifespan?**

   The potential for primary control describes an inverse U-shaped trajectory across the lifespan. It begins at a very low level at infancy, increases rapidly in childhood and adolescence, peaks and levels out in early to middle adulthood, and declines in old age, especially advanced old age.

3. **Does control striving develop gradually, or is it already present in neonates?**

Newborn babies already show a clear preference for behavior-event contingencies. They repeat behaviors that regularly lead to certain events (e.g., presentation of a milk bottle), even in the absence of consummatory interest in that event (i.e., when they are satiated), and show positive affect when an expected event occurs as a result of their behavior.

4. **How does the ability to focus on an intended action outcome develop?**

Toward the end of the first year, children gradually begin to distinguish between actions and action goals. During the second year, their attention comes to focus increasingly on the outcomes of their actions. First sudden, discrete effects; then continuous, action-accompanying effects; and finally state-related outcomes in multistep activities become attractive action goals.

5. **What are the main emotional incentives for achievement-oriented behavior, and what is their order of development?**

The main incentives for achievement-oriented behavior are pride and shame: pride is manifested in an upright posture, smiling, and triumphant eye contact with the loser, whereas shame is expressed in slouching, lowering the head, and avoiding eye contact with the winner. Pride develops first, in the second and third year; shame is not observed until the end of the third year or until the fourth year.

6. **What is meant by the phenomenon of "wanting to do it oneself"?**

"Wanting to do it oneself" is observed in the second year, as the self-concept develops. It is at this point that the child begins to reject adults' offers of help or interference in their activities.

7. **What are the benefits and risks of self-evaluative responses?**

The major benefit is anticipated positive self-evaluation, which motivates achievement behavior. The major risk is attribution of failure to a personal lack of ability, which may inhibit future achievement behavior.

8. **How can people avoid negative self-evaluations after experiences of failure?**

Negative self-evaluations can be avoided by applying strategies of compensatory secondary control. Preschoolers are already able to use simple compensatory secondary control strategies (e.g., denying failure, self-distraction). More complex compensatory strategies, such as switching to another goal and self-serving attributions, are not developed until adolescence.

9. **What role do parents play in the early development of action?**

Parents (especially mothers) are the source of the first behavior-event contingency experiences, intentionally or unintentionally providing contingent responses to the infant's behaviors (e.g., eye contact, opening the mouth). The parent-child bond offers a secure base from which to explore the environment. In the second year, actions are initiated and regulated in natural object-related parent-child interactions. It is within this apprenticeship framework that the child gradually acquires the competence to act independently.

10. **Which concepts must children grasp before they can engage in achievement-motivated behavior in the classic sense?**

They must be able to distinguish task difficulty and personal competence as independent factors; to apply individual and social reference norms; to distinguish the ability and effort components of the global conception of competence (and thus generate expectancies of success); to grasp the multiplicative relationship between the expectancy of success and the success incentive (and thus set appropriate levels of aspiration); and to use compensatory causal schemata to infer the causes of success and failure.

11. **Which cross-cultural differences and similarities have been found in children's school-related control beliefs?**

Empirical data show uniformity in causality (means-ends) beliefs in the school context. Students' ratings of the importance of effort increase steadily until sixth grade and are consistently higher than the corresponding ratings for ability. Cross-national differences have been found in students' perceptions of their personal capacities (agency beliefs). Students in the United States have the highest agency beliefs, but the relationship between these beliefs and their actual learning outcomes is the weakest in international comparison.

12. **What are the affective consequences of effort and ability attributions of success and failure in school-age children?**

Ability attributions are associated with positive affect in the case of success and with negative affect in the case of failure; effort attributions have much less of an impact on affect.

13. **Which interactive behaviors, parenting practices, and home environments are conducive to the development of an approach-oriented achievement motive?**

Parental behavior that is contingent with the child's behavior, emotional warmth, developmental adequacy of independence requirements, child-centered independence training, and a stimulating home environment that affords children diverse opportunities to test their competence on their own initiative.

14. How does the general expectancy-value model of achievement choices proposed by Eccles and Wigfield differ from Atkinson's risk-taking model?

Self-evaluation is not the only motivating (value-giving) factor in the Eccles and Wigfield model. Rather, the value component is assumed to be influenced by task-intrinsic and instrumental incentives, as well as by the costs of goal pursuit. Both the value and the expectancy components are assumed to be influenced by the norms and beliefs of social and cultural subgroups, as well as by individual self-concepts.

15. What is the achievement goal approach?

Conceptual models and research programs relating to explicit achievement motives (i.e., achievement goals) have become known as the achievement goal approach. These research programs distinguish achievement goals on one or both of two dimensions: (1) learning or mastery goals vs. performance or ego goals; and (2) approach vs. avoidance goals. Learning/mastery goals and approach goals are preferable to performance/ego goals and avoidance goals in many, but not all achievement conditions. In many real-life achievement contexts, it seems advisable to combine different goal orientations flexibly.

16. How does the transition to school affect the development of achievement-motivated behavior?

The school context emphasizes other-regulation and other-evaluation by the teacher, social comparisons with peers, and extrinsic incentives. This focus is rather unfavorable for the development of implicit achievement-motivated behavior, particularly when children are exposed to frequent experiences of failure and parental achievement pressure. The development of explicit achievement goals is fostered at school, however, and can facilitate the development of a flexible and multifaceted repertoire of achievement-motivated incentives.

17. Which normative developments in the ability to make differentiated causal attributions can aggravate the negative effects of experiences of failure, and thus induce helplessness?

The development of a stable concept of ability that is independent of effort, and compensatory causal attributions of the role of ability and effort in known outcomes.

18. As a function of which development do interindividual differences really begin to take effect on the developmental trajectory, especially in adolescence and adulthood?

The progressive shift from other- to self-regulation, as the individual starts to play an active role in shaping his or her developmental ecology.

19. Which influences determine the opportunities and constraints that the lifespan offers as a field of action for developmental regulation?

Biological processes of maturation and aging (inverse U-shaped trajectory);
the age-graded societal scaffolding of the life course by means of institutions and prescribed age transitions (school entry, retirement);
the canalization of occupational and family careers;
socially learned, normative conceptions about age-appropriate behavior and changes in (occupational, family) status.

20. What role do developmental goals play in individual developmental regulation?

Developmental goals organize developmental regulation, endowing behavior with direction, coherence, and meaning on the medium and long term. Incongruence between implicit motives and developmental goals is maladaptive.

21. Are individuals completely free in the choice of the developmental goals they pursue?

No. If the developmental goals selected are not in line with the opportunities to attain them at a given age or in a social group, goal attainment will be impossible or, at the very least, extremely difficult. Adaptive choices are characterized by congruence between developmental goals and the opportunities for their attainment.

22. What are the major conceptual differences between the AAI model proposed by Brandtstädter and colleagues and the lifespan theory of control developed by Heckhausen and Schulz?

The AAI model sees developmental regulation as self-regulation, whereas the lifespan theory of control conceptualizes developmental regulation as optimization of control (primary control) across the lifespan. For Brandtstädter and colleagues, the criterion for successful development is a consistent self; for Heckhausen and Schulz, it is the maximization of control potential across the life course.

23. Which phases are distinguished in the action-phase model of developmental regulation?

Predecisional phase and goal selection using optimization heuristics → the Rubicon of decision → nonurgent goal engagement, changing to urgent goal engagement as a developmental deadline approaches, with strategies of selective primary and secondary control as well as compensatory primary control → goal disengagement and self-protection in cases of failure, with strategies of compensatory secondary control. One of the main assumptions of the action-control model is that, to ensure the efficient use of resources, the transitions from the predecisional to the postdecisional phase of goal engagement, and from the goal-engagement phase to goal disengagement are not gradual or continuous, but discrete, rapid, and comprehensive.

24. What is a developmental deadline?

Developmental deadlines are points or stages in life at which the prospects of achieving an important developmental goal decrease sharply, such that continued goal pursuit is either futile or requires heavy investment of resources that are then no longer available for other important domains of primary control. One example of a developmental deadline is the "biological clock" for childbearing in middle adulthood.

25. What are the effects of incongruence between goal engagement/disengagement and opportunities for goal attainment across the lifespan?

Incongruence of developmental goals and opportunities for their attainment leads to deterioration in psychological well-being and can result in depressive mood and inhibit primary control striving. This pattern of relationships has been found in different domains of life (e.g., family, education) and has also been observed to apply to behavior in the context of health impairments.

26. To what extent can individual developmental regulation be seen as a dynamic interaction between development and motivation?

It is as a result of the individual's active influence on his or her own development through goal pursuit that the opportunities and constraints of the situation really come to bear. Not only are individuals producers of their future, they actively influence their own future developmental ecology by means of selection, evocation, and manipulation, thus setting the stage for their future developmental regulation.

References

Aarts, H., Dijksterhuis, A. P., & Midden, C. (1999). To plan or not to plan? Goal achievement or interrupting the performance of mundane behaviors. *European Journal of Social Psychology, 29*, 971–979.

Abel, T. M. (1938). Neuro-circularity reaction and the recall of unfinished and completed tasks. *Journal of Psychology, 6*, 377–383.

Abele, A. E., Andrä, M. S., & Schute, T. (1999). Wer hat nach dem Hochschulexamen schnell eine Stelle? Erste Ergebnisse der Erlanger Längsschnittstudie (BELA-E) [Who enters a job quickly after graduating? Results of a longitudinal study (BELA-E)]. *Zeitschrift für Arbeits- und Organisationspsychologie, 43*, 95–101.

Abramson, L. Y., Metalsky, G. I., & Alloy, L. B. (1989). Hopelessness depression: A theory-based subtype of depression. *Psychological Review, 96*, 358–372.

Abramson, L. Y., Seligman, M. E. P., & Teasdale, J. D. (1978). Learned helplessness in humans: Critique and reformulation. *Journal of Abnormal Psychology, 87*, 49–79.

Ach, N. (1905). *Über die Willenstätigkeit und das Denken* [On the activity of will and on thinking]. Göttingen, Germany: Vandenhoeck & Ruprecht.

Ach, N. (1910). *Über den Willensakt und das Temperament* [On acts of will and temperament]. Leipzig, Germany: Quelle & Meyer.

Ach, N. (1935). Analyse des Willens [Analysis of the will]. In E. Abderhalden (Ed.), *Handbuch der biologischen Arbeitsmethoden* (Vol. 6, Part E 460). Berlin, Germany: Urban & Schwarzberg.

Achtziger, A. (2003). *Kognitionspsychologische Aspekte der willentlichen Stereotypkontrolle* [Cognitive aspects of voluntary stereotype control]. Unpublished doctoral dissertation, University of Konstanz, Germany.

Achtziger, A., & Gollwitzer, P. M. (2005). *Controling stereotypes and prejudice by implementation intentions*. Paper presented at the Small Group Meeting of the EASP, Jena, Germany.

Achtziger A., Rockstroh, B., Oettingen, G., & Gollwitzer, P. M. (2003, September). *Neurophysiologische Korrelate verschiedener handlungsvorbereitender mentaler Zustände* [Neurophysiological correlates of goal setting strategies]. Paper presented at the 9th meeting of the Fachgruppe Sozialpsychologie, Heidelberg, Germany.

Achtziger, A., Gollwitzer, P. M., & Sheeran, P. (in press). Implementation intentions and shielding goal striving from unwanted thoughts and feelings. *Personality and Social Psychology Bulletin.*

Achtziger, A., Michalski, V., & Gollwitzer, P. M. (forthcoming). Processing stereotype-inconsistent information under cognitive load.

Achtziger, A., Moratti, S., Jaudas, A., Rockstroh, B., & Gollwitzer, P. M. (forthcoming). The control of automatic stereotype activation by means of implementation intentions in the EEG.

Adams, R. E., & Passman, R. H. (1979). Effects of visual and auditory aspects of mothers and stranger on the play and exploration of children. *Developmental Psychology, 15*(3), 269–274.

Adler, A. (1922). *Über den nervösen Charakter* [The neurotic constitution] (3rd ed.). Munich, Germany: Bergmann.

Adler, D. L., & Kounin, J. S. (1939). Some factors operating at the moment of resumption of interrupted tasks. *Journal of Psychology, 7*, 255–267.

Adolphs, R., & Tranel, D. (2000). Emotion recognition and the human amygdala. In J. P. Aggleton (Ed.), *The amygdala: A functional analysis* (pp. 587–630). New York: Oxford University Press.

Aellig, S. (2004). *Über den Sinn des Unsinns. Flow-Erleben und Wohlbefinden als Anreize für autotelische Tätigkeiten* [The sense in not being sensible: Flow experience and well-being as motivation for autotelic activities]. Münster, Germany: Waxmann.

Aharon, I., Etcoff, N., Ariely, D., Chabris, C. F., O'Connor, E., & Breiter, H. C. (2001). Beautiful faces have variable reward value: fMRI and behavioral evidence. *Neuron, 32*(3), 537–551.

Affleck, G., Tennen, H., Croog, S., & Levine, S. (1987). Causal attribution, perceived benefits and morbidity after a heart attack: An 8 year study. *Journal of Consulting and Clinical Psychology, 55*, 29–35.

Ainley, M. D. (1993). Styles of engagement with learning: Multidimensional assessment of their relationship with strategy use and school achievement. *Journal of Educational Psychology, 85*(3), 395–405.

Ainsworth, M. D. (1972). Attachment and dependency: A comparison. In J. Gewirtz (Ed.), *Attachment and dependency* (pp. 251). Washington, DC: Winston.

Ainsworth, M. D. (1979). Infant-mother attachment. *American Psychologist, 34*, 932–937.

Ainsworth, M. D., & Bell, S. M. (1970). Attachment, exploration and separation: Illustrated by the behavior of one-year-olds in a strange situation. *Child Development, 41*(1), 49–67.

Ainsworth, M. D., Bell, S. M., & Stayton, D. J. (1974). Infant mother attachment and social development: Socialisation as a product of reciprocal responsiveness to signals. In R. P. M. Richards (Ed.), *The integration of a child into a social world*. Cambridge, UK: Cambridge University Press.

Ainsworth, M. D., Blehar, M. C., Waters, E., & Wall, S. N. (1978). *Patterns of attachment: A psychological study of the strange situation*. Hillsdale, NJ: Erlbaum.

Ajzen, I., & Fishbein, M. (1969). The prediction of behavioral intentions in a choice situation. *Journal of Experimental Social Psychology, 5*, 400–416.

445

Alberch, P. (1980). Ontogenesis and morphological diversification. *American Zoologist, 20*, 653–667.

Albert, D. J., Jonik, R. H., & Walsh, M. L. (1992). Hormone-dependent aggression in male and female rats: Experiential, hormonal, and neural foundations. *Neuroscience and Biobehavioral Reviews, 16*(2), 177–192.

Albert, D. J., Petrovic, D. M., Walsh, M. L., & Jonik, R. H. (1989). Medial accumbens lesions attenuate testosterone-dependent aggression in male rats. *Physiology & Behavior, 46*, 625–631.

Alker, H. A. (1972). Is personality situationally specific or intrapsychically consistent? *Journal of Personality, 40*, 1–16.

Allensbacher Markt- and Werbeträgeranalyse (AWA). (1995–2000) (2000). *Berichtsband I. Markstrukturen* [Technical reports I. Market structures]. Allensbach, Germany: Institut für Demoskopie.

Alloy, L. B., & Abramson, L. Y. (1979). Judgment of contingency in depressed and nondepressed students: Sadder but wiser? *Journal of Experimental Psychology, 108*, 441–485.

Alloy, L. B., & Abramson, L. Y. (1988). Depressive realism: Four theoretical perspectives. In L. B. Alloy (Ed.), *Cognitive processes in depression* (pp. 223–265). New York: Guilford Press.

Allport, G. W. (1937). *Personality: A psychological interpretation*. New York: Holt.

Allport, G. W. (1953). The trend in motivation theory. *American Journal of Orthopsychiatry, 23*, 107–119.

Allport, G. W., & Odbert, H. S. (1936). Traitnames: A psycholexical study. *Psychological Monographs, 47*(211).

Alper, T. G. (1946). Task-orientation vs. ego-orientation in learning and retention. *American Journal of Psychology, 59*, 236–248.

Alper, T. G. (1957). Predicting the direction of selective recall: Its relation to ego strength and n achievement. *Journal of Abnormal and Social Psychology, 55*, 149–165.

Altshuler, J. A., & Ruble, D. N. (1989). Developmental changes in children's awareness of strategies for coping with uncontrollable stress. *Child Development, 60*, 1337–1349.

Ames, C. (1978). Children's achievement attributions and self reinforcement: Effects of self concept and competitive reward structure. *Journal of Educational Psychology, 70*, 345–355.

Ames, C., & Ames, R. (1984). Systems of student and teacher motivation: Toward a qualitative definition. *Journal of Educational Psychology, 76*, 535–556.

Ames, C., Ames, R., & Felker, D. W. (1977). Effects of competitive reward structure and valence of outcome on children's achievement attributions. *Journal of Educational Psychology, 69*, 1–8.

Ames, C., & Archer, J. (1988). Achievement goals in the classroom: Students' learning strategies and motivational processes. *Journal of Educational Psychology, 80*(3), 260–267.

Anderson, C., & Berdahl, J. L. (2002). Examining the effects of power on approach and inhibition tendencies. *Journal of Personality and Social Psychology, 83*, 1362–1377.

Anderson, C. A. (1983). Imagination and expectation: The effect of imagining behavioral scripts on personal intentions. *Journal of Personality and Social Psychology, 45*, 293–305.

Anderson, J. R. (1983). *The architecture of cognition*. Cambridge, MA: Harvard University Press.

Andersen, S. M., & Chen, S. U. (2002). The relational self: An interpersonal social-cognitive theory. *Psychological Review, 109*, 619–645.

Andresen, B. (1995). Risikobereitschaft (R): Der sechste Basisfaktor der Persönlichkeit: Konvergenz multivariater Studien und Konstruktexplikation ["Risk preference" (R) – The sixth basic factor of personality: Convergence of multivariate studies and construct explication]. *Zeitschrift für Differentielle und Diagnostische Psychologie, 16*, 210–236.

Andrews, J. D. W. (1967). The achievement motive and advancement in two types of organizations. *Journal of Personality and Social Psychology, 6*, 163–168.

Angermeier, W. F., & Peters, M. (1973). *Bedingte Reaktionen* [Conditioned reactions]. Berlin, Germany: Springer.

Angleitner, A., & Ostendorf, F. (1994). Temperament and the Big Five factors of personality. In C. F. Halverson, G. A. Kohnstamm, & R. P. Martin (Eds.), *The developing structure of temperament and personality from infancy to adulthood* (pp. 69–90). Hillsdale, NJ: Erlbaum.

Armor, D. A., & Taylor, S. E. (2003). The effects of mindset on behavior: Self-regulation in deliberative and implemental frames of mind. *Personality and Social Psychology Bulletin, 29*, 86–95.

Arnold, R. M. (1960). *Emotion and personality: Vol. I: Psychological aspects, Vol. II: Neuro-logical and psychological aspects*. New York: Columbia University Press.

Aronson, E., & Carlsmith, J. M. (1962). Performance expectancy as a determinant of actual performance. *Journal of Abnormal and Social Psychology, 65*, 178–183.

Asendorpf, J. B. (1984). Shyness, embarrassment, and self-presentation: A control theory approach. In R. Schwarzer (Ed.), *The self in anxiety, stress, and depression* (pp. 109–114). Amsterdam: North Holland.

Asendorpf, J. B. (2004). *Psychologie der Persönlichkeit* [Psychology of personality]. Berlin, Germany: Springer.

Asendorpf, J. B., Banse, R., & Mücke, D. (2002). Double dissociation between implicit and explicit personality self-concept: The case of shy behavior. *Journal of Personality and Social Psychology, 83*, 380–393.

Asendorpf, J. B., Weber, A., & Burkhardt, K. (1994). Zur Mehrdeutigkeit projektiver Testergebnisse: Motiv-Projektionen oder Thema-Sensitivität? [On the multiple meaning of projective tests: Motive projection or thematic sensitivity?] *Zeitschrift für Differentielle und Diagnostische Psychologie, 15*, 155–165.

Atkinson, J. W. (1953). The achievement motive and recall of interrupted and completed tasks. *Journal of Experimental Psychology, 46*, 381–390.

Atkinson, J. W. (1957). Motivational determinants of risk-taking behavior. *Psychological Review, 64*, 359–372.

Atkinson, J. W. (Ed.). (1958a). *Motives in fantasy, action, and society*. Princeton, NJ: Van Nostrand.

Atkinson, J. W. (1958b). Towards experimental analysis of human motivation in terms of motives, expectancies and incentives. In J. W. Atkinson (Ed.), *Motives in fantasy, action, and society* (pp. 288–305). Princeton, NJ: Van Nostrand.

Atkinson, J. W. (1964a). *An introduction to motivation*. Princeton, NJ: Van Nostrand.

Atkinson, J. W. (1964b). Some neglected variables in contemporary conceptions of decision and performance. *Psychological Reports, 14*, 575–590.

Atkinson, J. W. (1974a). Motivational determinants of intellective performance and cumulative achievement. In J. W. Atkinson & J. O. Raynor (Eds.), *Motivation and achievement* (pp. 389–410). Washington, DC: Winston.

Atkinson, J. W. (1974b). Strength of motivation and efficiency of performance. In J. W. Atkinson & J. O. Raynor (Eds.), *Motivation and achievement* (pp. 193–218). Washington, DC: Winston.

Atkinson, J. W. (1981). Studying personality in the context of an advanced motivational psychology. *American Psychologist, 36,* 171–128.

Atkinson, J. W. (1987). Michigan studies of fear of failure. In F. Halisch & J. Kuhl (Eds.), *Motivation, intention, and volition* (pp. 47–59). Berlin, Germany: Springer.

Atkinson, J. W., & Birch, D. (1970). *The dynamics of action.* New York: Wiley.

Atkinson, J. W., & Birch, D. A. (1978). *Introduction to motivation* (2nd ed.). New York: Van Nostrand.

Atkinson, J. W., Bongort, K., & Price, L. H. (1977). Explorations using computer simulation to comprehend TAT measurement of motivation. *Motivation and Emotion, 1,* 1–17.

Atkinson, J. W., & Cartwright, D. (1964). Some neglected variables in contemporary conceptions of decision and performance. *Psychological Reports, 14,* 575–590.

Atkinson, J. W., & Feather, N. T. (Eds.). (1966). *A theory of achievement motivation.* New York: Wiley.

Atkinson, J. W., Heyns, R. W., & Veroff, J. (1954). The effect of experimental arousal of the affiliation motive on thematic apperception. *Journal of Abnormal and Social Psychology, 49,* 405–410.

Atkinson, J. W., Lens, W., & O'Malley, P. M. (1976). Motivation and ability: Interactive psychological determinants of intellective performance, educational achievement, and each other. In W. H. Sewell, R. M. Hauser, & D. L. Featherman (Eds.), *Schooling and achievement in American society* (pp. 29–60). New York: Academic Press.

Atkinson, J. W., & Litwin, G. H. (1960). Achievement motive and test anxiety conceived as motive to approach success and motive to avoid failure. *Journal of Abnormal and Social Psychology, 60,* 52–63.

Atkinson, J. W., & McClelland, D. C. (1948). The projective expression of needs: II. The effect of different intensities of the hunger drive in thematic apperception. *Journal of Experimental Psychology, 33,* 643–658.

Atkinson, J. W., & Raynor, J. O. (1974). *Motivation and achievement.* Washington, DC: Winston.

Atkinson, J. W., & Reitman, W. R. (1956). Performance as a function of motive strength and expectancy of goal attainment. *Journal of Abnormal and Social Psychology, 53,* 361–366.

Atkinson, J. W., & Walker, E. L. (1956). The affiliation motive and perceptual sensitivity to faces. *Journal of Abnormal and Social Psychology, 53,* 38–41.

Austin, J. T., & Vancouver, J. B. (1996). Goal constructs in psychology: Structure, process, and content. *Psychological Bulletin, 120,* 338–375.

Aveling, F. (1926). The psychology of conation and will. *British Journal of Psychology, 16,* 339–353.

Baddeley, A. (1986). *Working memory.* Oxford, UK: Clarendon Press.

Baddeley, A. (1996). Exploring the central executive. *Quarterly Journal of Experimental Psychology, 49,* 5–28.

Baddeley, A. (2000). The episodic buffer: A new component of working memory? *Trends in Cognitive Sciences, 4,* 417–423.

Bakan, D. (1966). *The duality of human existence.* Boston: Beacon Press.

Balagura, S. (1973). *Hunger: A biopsychological analysis.* New York: Basic Books.

Baltes, P. B., Lindenberger, U., & Staudinger, U. M. (1998). Life-span theory in developmental psychology. In W. Damon & R. Lerner (Eds.), *Handbook of child psychology* (pp. 1029–1143). New York: Wiley.

Baltes, P. B., & Staudinger, U. M. (2000). Wisdom: A metaheuristic (pragmatic) to orchestrate mind and virtue toward excellence. *American Psychologist, 55,* 122–135.

Band, E. B., & Weisz, J. R. (1988). How to feel better when it feels bad: Children's perspectives on coping with everyday stress. *Developmental Psychology, 24,* 246–253.

Bandura, A. (1971). Vicarious and self-reinforcement processes. In R. Glaser (Ed.), *The nature of reinforcement* (pp. 228–278). New York: Academic Press.

Bandura, A. (1977). Self-efficacy: Toward a unifying theory of behavioral change. *Psychological Review, 84,* 191–215.

Bandura, A. (1978). The self system in reciprocal determinism. *American Psychologist, 33,* 344–358.

Bandura, A. (1982). Self-efficacy mechanisms in human agency. *American Psychologist, 37,* 122–147.

Bandura, A. (1986). *Social foundations of thought and action: A social cognitive theory.* Upper Saddle River, NJ: Prentice Hall.

Bandura, A. (1991). Self-regulation of motivation through anticipatory and self-reactive mechanisms. In R. A. Dienstbier (Ed.), *Nebraska Symposium on Motivation: Vol. 38. Perspectives on motivation* (pp. 69–164). Lincoln: University of Nebraska Press.

Bandura, A. (1998). *Self-efficacy: The exercise of control.* New York: Freeman.

Banse, R. (2001). Affective priming with liked and disliked persons: Prime visibility determines congruency and incongruency effects. *Cognition and Emotion, 15,* 501–520.

Bär, R. (1998). *Pornographie: Motive, Meinungen, sexuelle Phantasien und situative Kontexte* [Pornography: Motives, opinions, sexual fantasies, and situational contexts]. Unpublished Diplom thesis, University of Wuppertal, Germany.

Bargh, J. A. (1990). Auto-motives: Preconscious determinants of social interaction. In E. T. Higgins & R. M. Sorrentino (Eds.), *Handbook of motivation and cognition: Foundations of social behavior* (pp. 93–130). New York: Guilford Press.

Bargh, J. A. (1994). The four horsemen of automaticity: Awareness, intention, efficiency, and control in social cognition. In R. S. Wyer & T. Srull (Eds), *Handbook of social cognition: Vol. 1. Basic processes* (2nd ed., pp. 1–41). Hillsdale, NJ: Erlbaum.

Bargh, J. A. (1997). The automaticity of everyday life. In R. S. Wyer (Ed.), *The automaticity of everyday life: Advances in social cognition* (Vol. 10, pp. 1–61). Mahwah, NJ: Erlbaum.

Bargh, J. A., & Barndollar, K. (1996). Automaticity in action: The unconscious as repository of chronic goals and motivation. In P. M. Gollwitzer & J. A. Bargh (Eds.), *The psychology of action: Linking cognition and motivation to behavior* (pp. 457–481). New York: Guilford Press.

Bargh, J. A., Chaiken, S., Raymond, P., & Hymes, C. (1996). The automatic evaluation effect: Unconditional automatic attitude activation with a pronunciation task. *Journal of Experimental Social Psychology, 32,* 104–128.

Bargh, J. A., & Chartrand, T. L. (1999). The unbearable automaticity of being. *American Psychologist, 54,* 462–479.

Bargh, J. A., Chen, M., & Burrows, L. (1996). Automaticity of social behavior: Direct effects of trait construct and stereotype priming on action. *Journal of Personality and Social Psychology, 71,* 230–244.

Bargh, J. A., & Ferguson, M. L. (2000). Beyond behaviorism: On the automaticity of higher mental processes. *Psychological Bulletin, 126,* 925–945.

Bargh, J. A., & Gollwitzer, P. M. (1994). Environmental control of goal-directed action: Automatic and strategic contingencies between situations and behavior. In W. D. Spaulding (Ed.), *Nebraska Symposium* on Motivation: Vol. 41. Integrative views of motivation, cognition, and emotion (pp. 71–124). Lincoln: University of Nebraska Press.

Barker, R. G. (1968). Ecological psychology. Stanford, CA: Stanford University Press.

Barker, R. G., & Gump, P. (Eds.). (1964). Big school, small school: High school size and student behavior. Stanford, CA: Stanford University Press.

Barnett, P. A., & Gotlib, I. C. (1988). Psychological functioning and depression: Distinguishing among antecedents, concomitants, and consequences. Psychological Bulletin, 104, 97–126.

Barrett, K. C., & Morgan, G. A. (1995). Continuities and discontinuities in mastery motivation during infancy and toddlerhood: A conceptualization and review. In R. H. MacTurk & G. A. Morgan (Eds.), Mastery motivation: Origins, conceptualization and applications (pp. 57–93). Westport, CT: Ablex.

Barrett, K. C., Morgan, G. A., & Maslin-Cole, B. (1993). Three studies on the development of mastery motivation in infancy and toddlerhood. In D. Messer (Ed.), Mastery motivation in early childhood: Development, measurement and social processes (pp. 83–108). London: Routledge.

Barrick, M. R., & Mount, M. K. (1991). The Big Five personality dimensions and job performance: A meta-analysis. Personnel Psychology, 44, 1–26.

Barron, K. E., & Harackiewicz, J. M. (2001). Achievement goals and optimal motivation: Testing multiple goal models. Journal of Personality and Social Psychology, 80, 706–722.

Bartels, A., & Zeki, S. (2000). The neural basis of romantic love. NeuroReport, 11(17), 3829–3834.

Bartels, A., & Zeki, S. (2004). The neural correlates of maternal and romantic love. NeuroImage, 21(3), 1155–1166.

Bartlett, E. W., & Smith, C. P. (1966). Childrearing practices, birth order and the development of achievement-related motives. Psychological Reports, 19, 1207–1216.

Baum, M. J. (1992). Neuroendocrinology of sexual behavior in the male. In J. B. Becker, S. M. Breedlove, & D. Crews (Eds.), Behavioral endocrinology (pp. 97–130). Cambridge, MA: MIT Press.

Baumann, N., Kaschel, R., & Kuhl, J. (2005). Affect regulation and motive-incongruent achievement orientation: Antecedents of subjective well-being and symptom formation. Journal of Personality and Social Psychology, 89, 781–799.

Baumann, N., & Kuhl, J. (2002). Intuition, affect and personality: Unconscious coherence judgments and self-regulation of negative affect. Journal of Personality and Social Psychology, 83, 1213–1223.

Baumann, N., & Kuhl, J. (2003). Self-infiltration: Confusing assigned tasks as self-selected in memory. Personality and Social Psychology Bulletin, 29, 487–497.

Baumann, N., & Kuhl, J. (2004). How to resist temptation: The effects of external control versus autonomy support on the dynamics of self-regulation. Journal of Personality, 73, 443–470.

Baumann, N., Kuhl, J., & Kazén (2004). Hemispheric activation and self infiltration: Testing a neuropsychological model of internalization. Motivation and Emotion, 29, 135–163.

Baumeister, R. F. (1984). Choking under pressure: Self-consciousness and paradoxical effects of incentives on skillful performance. Journal of Personality and Social Psychology, 46, 610–620.

Baumeister, R. F. (2000). Ego-depletion and the self's executive function. In A. Tesser & R. B. Felson (Eds.), Psychological perspectives on self and identity (pp. 9–33). Washington, DC: American Psychological Association.

Baumeister, R. F., & Leary, M. R. (1995). The need to belong: Desire for interpersonal attachments as a fundamental human motivation. Psychological Bulletin, 117, 497–529.

Baumeister, R. F., & Showers, C. (1986). A review of paradoxical performance effects: Choking under pressure in sports and mental tests. European Journal of Social Psychology, 16, 361–383.

Bayer, U. C., Achtziger, A., Malzacher, J. T., Moskowitz, G. B., & Gollwitzer, P. M. (under review). Strategic automaticity by implementation intentions: Action initiation without conscious intent.

Baxter, M. G., & Murray, E. A. (2002). The amygdala and reward. Nature Reviews Neuroscience, 3(7), 563–573.

Bayer, U. C., & Gollwitzer, P. M. (2005). Mindset effects on information search in self-evaluation. European Journal of Social Psychology, 35, 313–327.

Bayer, U. C., Jaudas, A., & Gollwitzer, P. M. (2002, July). Do implementation intentions facilitate switching between tasks? Poster presented at the International Symposium on Executive Functions, Konstanz, Germany.

Beauregard, M., Levesque, J., & Bourgouin, P. (2001). Neural correlates of conscious self-regulation of emotion. Journal of Neuroscience, 21, 6993–7000.

Bechara, A., Damasio, H., & Damasio, A. R. (2000). Emotion, decision making and the orbitofrontal cortex. Cerebral Cortex, 10(3), 295–307.

Bechara, A., Damasio, H., Tranel, D., & Damasio, A. R. (1997). Deciding advantageously before knowing the advantageous strategy. Science, 275(5304), 1293–1295.

Beck, A. T. (1967). Depression – Causes and treatment. Philadelphia: University of Pennsylvania Press.

Beckmann, J. (1984). Kognitive Dissonanz: Eine handlungstheoretische Perspektive [Cognitive dissonance: An action theory perspective]. Heidelberg, Germany: Springer-Verlag.

Beckmann, J. (1994). Rumination and deactivation of an intention. Motivation and Emotion, 18, 317–334.

Beckmann, J. (1996). Self-presentation and the Zeigarnik effect. In T. Gjesme & R. Nygard (Ed.), Advances in motivation (pp. 35–45). Oslo, Norway: Scandinavian University Press.

Beckmann, J., Bobka, K., Fehrenbach, H., Hellebrandt, M., & Rost, K. (2007). The perseverance of complete and incomplete intentions in memory: Zeigarnik effect or self serving recall? Manuscript submitted for publication.

Beckmann, J., & Gollwitzer, P. M. (1987). Deliberative versus implemental states of mind: The issue of impartiality in predecisional and postdecisional information processing. Social Cognition, 5, 259–279.

Beckmann, J., & Kuhl, J. (1984). Altering information to gain action control: Functional aspects of human information processing in decision making. Journal of Research in Personality, 18, 224–237.

Beckmann, J., & Rolstad, K. (1997). Aktivierung, Selbstregulation und Leistung: Gibt es so etwas wie Übermotivation? [Activation, self-regulation, and performance: Is there such a thing as overmotivation?] Sportwissenschaft, 27, 23–37.

Beeman, M., Friedman, R. B., Grafman, J., Perez, E., Diamond, S., & Lindsay, M. B. (1994). Summation priming and coarse coding in the right hemisphere. Journal of Cognitive Neuroscience, 6, 26–45.

Beit-Hallahmi, B. (1980). Achievement motivation and economic growth: A replication. *Personality and Social Psychology Bulletin, 6*, 210–215.

Bem, D. J., & Allen, A. (1974). On predicting some of the people some of the time: The search for cross-situational consistencies in behavior. *Psychological Review, 81*, 506–520.

Beneson, J., & Dweck, C. S. (1986). The development of trait explanation and self-evaluations in the academic and social domains. *Child Development, 57*, 1179–1189.

Berger, P., & Luckman, T. (1967). *The social construction of reality.* New York: Doubleday.

Berkowitz, L. (1974). Some determinants of impulsive aggression: Role of mediated associations with reinforcements for aggression. *Psychological Review, 81*, 165–176.

Berkowitz, L. (1990). On the formation and regulation of anger and aggression: A cognitive-neoassociationistic analysis. *American Psychologist, 45*, 494–503.

Berkowitz, L. (1993). *Aggression: Its causes, consequences, and control.* New York: MacGraw-Hill.

Berkowitz, L. (1994). Is something missing? Some observations prompted by the cognitive-neoassociationist view of anger and emotional aggression. In L. R. Huesmann (Ed.), *Aggressive behaviour: Current perspectives* (pp. 35–57). New York: Plenum.

Berkowitz, L., & LePage, A. (1967). Weapons as aggression-eliciting stimuli. *Journal of Personalitiy and Social Psychology, 7*, 202–207.

Berlyne, D. E. (1960). *Conflict, arousal, and curiosity.* New York: McGraw-Hill.

Berlyne, D. E. (1963a). Complexity and incongruity variables as determinants of exploratory choice and evaluative ratings. *Canadian Journal of Psychology, 17*, 274–290.

Berlyne, D. E. (1963b). Motivational problems raised by exploratory and epistemic behavior. In S. Koch (Ed.), *Psychology: A study of a science* (Vol. V, pp. 284–364). New York: McGraw-Hill.

Berlyne, D. E. (1965). *Structure and direction in thinking.* New York: Wiley.

Berlyne, D. E. (1967). Arousal and reinforcement. In D. Levine (Ed.), *Nebraska Symposium on Motivation, 1967* (pp. 1–110). Lincoln: University of Nebraska Press.

Berlyne, D. E. (1971). *Aesthetics and psychobiology.* New York: Appleton-Century-Crofts.

Berlyne, D. E. (1973). The vicissitudes of aplopathematic and thelematoscopic pneumatology (or the hydrography of hedonism). In D. E. Berlyne & K. B. Madsen (Eds.), *Pleasure, reward, preference* (pp. 1–34). New York: Academic Press.

Berlyne, D. E. (Ed.). (1974). *Studies in the new experimental aesthetics.* New York: Wiley.

Berlyne, D. E., & Crozier, J. B. (1971). Effects of complexity and prechoice stimulation on exploratory choice. *Perception and Psychophysics, 10*, 242–246.

Bernhardt, P. C., Dabbs, J. M., Jr., Fielden, J. A., & Lutter, C. D. (1998). Testosterone changes during vicarious experiences of winning and losing among fans at sporting events. *Physiology & Behavior, 65*, 59–62.

Bernoulli, D. (1738). Specimen theoriae novae de mensura sortis. *Commentarii Academiae Scientiarum Imperialis Petropolitanae, 5*, 175–192.

Berridge, K. C. (1996). Food reward: Brain substrates of wanting and liking. *Neuroscience and Biobehavioral Reviews, 20*, 1–25.

Berridge, K. C. (2003). Comparing the emotional brains of humans and other animals. In R. J. Davidson, K. R. Scherer, & H. H. Goldsmith (Eds.), *Handbook of affective sciences* (pp. 25–51). New York: Oxford University Press.

Berridge, K. C., & Robinson, T. E. (1998). What is the role of dopamine in reward: Hedonic impact, reward learning, or incentive salience? *Brain Research Review, 28*, 309–369.

Berridge, K. C., & Robinson, T. E. (2003). Parsing reward. *Trends in Neurosciences, 26*(9), 507–513.

Beswick, G., & Mann, L. (1994). State orientation and procrastination. In J. Kuhl & J. Beckmann (Eds.), *Volition and personality: Action versus state orientation.* Seattle, WA: Hogrefe.

Betancourt, H., & Blair, I. (1992). An attribution-emotion model of violence in conflict situations. *Personality and Social Psychology Bulletin, 18*, 343–350.

Bexton, W. H., Heron, W., & Scott, T. H. (1954). Effects of decreased variation in the sensory environment. *Canadian Journal of Psychology, 8*, 70–76.

Bieneck, A. (1991). *Tätigkeitszentrierte Anreize des Skifahrens für Behinderte und Nichtbehinderte in Abhängigkeit vom Fähigkeitsstand* [Activity-related incentives of skiing for disabled and nondisabled individuals as a function of ability level].

Unpublished Diplom thesis, University of Heidelberg, Germany.

Bieri, P. (2001). *Das Handwerk der Freiheit: Die Entdeckung des eigenen Willens* [The craft of free time: Discovering one's own will]. Munich, Germany: Hanser.

Biernat, M. (1989). Motives and values to achieve: Different constructs with different effects. *Journal of Personality, 57*, 69–95.

Billington, C. J., & Levine, A. S. (1992). Hypothalamic neuropeptide regulation of feeding and energy metabolism. *Current Opinion in Neurobiology, 2*(6), 847–851.

Bindra, D. (1959). *Motivation: A systematic reinterpretation.* New York: Ronald.

Bindra, D. (1969). The interrelated mechanisms of reinforcement and motivation, and the nature of their influence on response. In W. J. Arnold & D. Levine (Eds.), *Nebraska Symposium on Motivation, 1969* (pp. 1–38). Lincoln: University of Nebraska Press.

Bindra, D. (1974). A motivational view of learning, performance, and behavior modification. *Psychological Review, 81*, 199–213.

Bindra, D. (1978). How adaptive behavior is produced: A perceptual-motivational alternative to response-reinforcement. *Behavioral and Brain Sciences, 1*, 41–91.

Birenbaum, G. (1930). Untersuchungen zur Handlungs- und Affektpsychologie. VII. Das Vergessen einer Vornahme [Studies on the psychology of action and emotion. VIII. The forgetting of instructions]. *Psychologische Forschung, 13*, 1930, 218–288.

Birney, R. C., Burdick, H., & Teevan, R. C. (1969). *Fear of failure motivation.* New York: Van Nostrand.

Bischof, N. (1975). A systems approach towards the functional connections of attachment and fear. *Child Development, 46*, 801–817.

Bischof, N. (1985). *Das Rätsel Ödipus: Die biologischen Wurzeln des Urkonfliktes von Intimität und Autonomie* [The enigma of Oedipus: Biological roots of the basic conflict between intimacy and autonomy]. Munich, Germany: Piper.

Bischof, N. (1993). Untersuchungen zur Systemanalyse der sozialen Motivation I: Die Regulation der sozialen Distanz – Von der Feldtheorie zur Systemtheorie [Social distance regulation – From "field" to "system"]. *Zeitschrift für Psychologie, 201*, 5–43.

Bischof, N. (1996). Untersuchungen zur Systemanalyse der sozialen Motivation IV: Die Spielarten des Lächelns und das Problem der motivationalen Sollwertanpassung [The varieties of smiling and the problem of motivational acclimatization]. *Zeitschrift für Psychologie, 204*, 1–40.

Bischoff, J. (2003). *Lernmotivation, Flow-Erleben und Leistung in universitären Fremdsprachkursen* [Motivation to learn, flow experience, and achievement in university second language courses]. Unpublished Diplom thesis, University of Potsdam, Germany.

Bischof-Köhler, D. (1985). Zur Phylogenese menschlicher Motivation [On the phylogeny of human motivation]. In L. H. Eckensberger & E.-D. Lantermann (Eds.), *Emotion und Reflexivität* (pp. 3–47). Munich, Germany: Urban & Schwarzenberg.

Bitterman, M. E. (1975). The comparative analysis of learning. *Science, 188*, 699–709.

Björkqvist, K., Lagerspetz, K. M. J., & Kaukiainen, A. (1992). Do girls manipulate and boys fight? Developmental trends in regard to direct and indirect aggression. *Aggressive Behavior, 18*, 117–127.

Björkqvist, K., & Niemelä, P. (Eds.). (1992). *Of mice and women: Aspects of female aggression.* San Diego, CA: Academic Press.

Blankenship, V. (1984). Computer anxiety and self-concept of ability. In R. Schwarzer (Ed.), *The self in anxiety, stress, and depression* (pp. 151–158). Amsterdam, Netherlands: Elsevier Science.

Blankenship, V. (1987). A computer-based measure of resultant achievement motivation. *Journal of Personality and Social Psychology, 53*, 361–372.

Block, J. (1995). A contrarian view of the five-factor approach to personality description. *Psychological Bulletin, 117*, 187–215.

Block, J. H., & Block, J. (1980). The role of ego-control and ego-resiliency in the organization of behavior. In W. A. Collins (Ed.), *Development of cognition, affect, and social relations: The Minnesota Symposia on Child Psychology* (Vol. 13, pp. 39–101). Hillsdale, NJ: Erlbaum.

Blodgett, H. C. (1929). The effect of the introduction of reward upon the maze performance of rats. *University of California Publications in Psychology, 4*, 113–134.

Blood, A. J., & Zatorre, R. J. (2001). Intensely pleasurable responses to music correlate with activity in brain regions implicated in reward and emotion. *PNAS, 98*(20), 11818–11823.

Blossfeld, H. P. (1987). Labor market entry and the sexual segregation of careers in the Federal Republic of Germany. *American Journal of Sociology, 93*, 89–118.

Blossfeld, H. P. (1988). Sensible Phasen im Bildungsverlauf – Eine Längsschnittanalyse über die Prägung von Bildungskarrieren durch den gesellschaftlichen Wandel [Critical phases in educational careers – A longitudinal study on the influence of societal changes on educational careers]. *Zeitschrift für Pädagogik, 34*, 45–63.

Blossfeld, H. P., & Mayer, K. U. (1988). Labor market segmentation in the Federal Republic of Germany: An empirical study of segmentation theories from a life course perspective. *European Sociological Review, 4*, 123–140.

Bludau, H. F. (1976). *Mobilitätstendenzen im Gefangenen-Dilemma-Spiel* [Mobility tendencies in the prisoner's dilemma game]. Unpublished Diplom thesis, University of Bochum, Germany.

Blunt, A., & Pychyl, T. A. (1998). Volitional action and inaction in the lives of undergraduate students: State orientation, procrastination and proneness to boredom. *Personality and Individual Differences, 24*, 837–846.

Boekaerts, M. (2003). Towards a model that integrates motivation, affect and learning. *British Journal of Educational Psychology, Monograph Series II, Part 2 (Development and Motivation: Joint Perspectives)*, 173–189.

Bolles, R. C. (1965). Readiness to eat: Effects of age, sex and weight loss. *Journal of Comparative Physiological Psychology, 60*, 88–92.

Bolles, R. C. (1967). *Theory of motivation.* New York: Harper & Row.

Bolles, R. C. (1972). Reinforcement, expectancy, and learning. *Psychological Review, 79*, 394–409.

Bolles, R. C. (1974). Cognition and motivation: Some historical trends. In B. Weiner (Ed.), *Cognitive views of human motivation* (pp. 1–20). New York: Academic Press.

Bolles, R. C. (1975). *Theory of motivation* (2nd ed.). New York: Harper & Row.

Bolte, A., Goschke, T., & Kuhl, J. (2003). Emotion and intuition: Effects of positive and negative mood on implicit judgments of semantic coherence. *Psychological Science, 14*, 416–421.

Bonsfield, W. A. (1953). The occurrence of clustering in the recall of randomly arranged associates. *Journal of General Psychology, 49*, 229–240.

Boring, E. G. (1929). *A history of experimental psychology.* New York: Appleton-Century-Crofts.

Borkenau, P., & Ostendorf, F. (1993). *NEO-Fünf-Faktoren-Inventar (NEO-FFI) nach Costa und McCrae: Handanweisung* [The Neo Five-Factor Inventory (NEO-FFI) by Costa and McCrae: Manual]. Göttingen, Germany: Hogrefe.

Bornstein, R. F. (2002). A process dissociation approach to objective-projective test score interrelationships. *Journal of Personality Assessment, 78*, 47–68.

Bosson, J. K., Swann, W. B., & Pennebaker, J. W. (2000). Stalking the perfect measure of implicit self-esteem: The blind men and the elephant revisited? *Journal of Personality and Social Psychology, 79*, 631–643.

Bouton, M. E., & Fanselow, M. S. (1997). *Learning, motivation and cognition.* Washington, DC: American Psychological Association.

Bower, G. H. (1981). Emotional mood and memory. *American Psychologist, 36*, 129–148.

Bowers, K. S. (1973). Situationism in psychology: An analysis and a critique. *Psychological Review, 80*, 307–336.

Bowi, U. (1990). *Der Einfluss von Motiven auf Zielsetzung und Zielrealisation* [The influence of motives on goal setting and goal implementation]. Unpublished doctoral thesis, University of Heidelberg, Germany.

Bowlby, J. (1958). The nature of the child's tie to his mother. *Interactional Journal of Psychoanalysis, 39*, 350–373.

Bowlby, J. (1969). Attachment and loss. In M. M. Khan (Ed.), *Attachment 1.* London: Hogarth.

Bowlby, J. (1982). *Attachment and loss: Vol. 1. Attachment* (2nd rev. ed.). New York: Basic Books.

Boyatzis, R. E. (1972). *A two factor theory of affiliation motivation..* Unpublished doctoral dissertation, Harvard University, Cambridge, MA.

Boyatzis, R. E. (1973). Affiliation motivation. In D. C. McClelland & R. S. Steele (Eds.), *Human motivation: A book of readings* (pp. 253–276). Morristown, NJ: General Learning.

Boyce, R. (1976). In the shadow of Darwin. In R. G. Green & E. C. O'Neil (Eds.), *Perspectives in aggression* (pp. 11–35). New York: Academic Press.

Brackhane, R. (1976). *Bezugssysteme im Leistungsverhalten* [Reference systems in achievement behavior]. Unpublished doctoral dissertation, University of Münster, Germany.

Bradley, G. W. (1978). Self-serving biases in the attribution process: A reexamination of the fact or fiction question. *Journal of Personality and Social Psychology, 36*, 56–71.

Brandtstädter, J. (1984). Personal and social control over development: Some implications of an action perspective in life-span developmental psychology. In P. B. Baltes & O. G. Brim (Eds.), *Life-span development and behavior (Vol. 6)* (pp. 1–32). Orlando, FL: Academic Press.

Brandtstädter, J. (1986). Personale Entwicklungskontrolle und entwicklungsregulatives Handeln: Überlegungen und Befunde zu einem vernachlässigten Forschungsthema [Personal control and regulative action in development: Thoughts and findings on an underrated issue of research]. *Zeitschrift für Entwicklungspsychologie und Pädagogische Psychologie, 18*, 316–334.

Brandtstädter, J. (1998). Action perspectives on human development. *Handbook of Child Psychology, 1*, 807–863.

Brandtstädter, J. (2001). *Entwicklung, Intentionalität, Handeln* [Development, intentionality, action]. Stuttgart, Germany: Kohlhammer.

Brandtstädter, J., & Greve, W. (1994). The aging self: Stabilizing and protective processes. *Developmental Review, 14*, 52–80.

Brandtstädter, J., & Lerner, R. (Eds.). (1999). *Action and self development: Theory and research through the life span.* Thousand Oaks, CA: Sage.

Brandtstädter, J., & Renner, G. (1990). Tenacious goal pursuit and flexible goal adjustment: Explication and age-related analysis of assimilative and accommodative strategies of coping. *Psychology and Aging 5*, 58–67.

Brandtstädter, J., & Rothermund, K. (2002). The life-course dynamics of goal pursuit and goal adjustment: A two process framework. *Developmental Review, 22*, 117–150.

Brandtstädter, J., & Rothermund, K. (2003). Intentionality and time in human development and aging: Compensation and goal adjustment in changing developmental contexts. In U. M. Staudinger & U. Lindenberger (Eds.), *Understanding human development: Dialogues with lifespan psychology* (pp. 105–124). Dordrecht, Netherlands: Kluwer.

Brandtstädter, J., Wentura, D., & Rothermund, K. (1999). Intentional self-development through adulthood and later life: Tenacious pursuit and flexible adjustment of goals. In J. Brandtstädter & R. Lerner (Eds.), *Action and self development: Theory and research through the life span* (pp. 373–400). Thousand Oaks, CA: Sage.

Brandstätter, V., & Frank, E. (2002). Effects of deliberative and implemental mindsets on persistence in goal-directed behavior. *Personality and Social Psychology Bulletin, 28*, 1366–1378.

Brandstätter, V., Lengfelder, A., & Gollwitzer, P. M. (2001). Implementation intentions and efficient action initiation. *Journal of Personality and Social Psychology, 81*, 946–960.

Brauckmann, L. (1976). *Erstellung und Erprobung eines Lehrerverhaltenstrainings zur Veränderung der motivanregenden Bedingungen des Unterrichts*[Development and testing of a teacher training program targeting the motivating conditions of instruction]. Unpublished Diplom thesis, University of Bochum, Germany.

Braun, W., & Proebsting, H. (1986). Heiratstafeln verwitweter Deutscher 1979/82 und geschiedener Deutscher 1980/83 [Marriage tables of widowed, 1979/82, and divorced, 1980/83, Germans]. *Wirtschaft und Statistik*, 107–112.

Breckler, S. J., & Greenwald, A. G. (1986). Motivational facets of the self. In R. M. Sorrentino & E. T. Higgins (Eds.), *Handbook of motivation and cognition* (pp. 145–164). New York: Guilford Press.

Brehm, J. W. (1956). Post decision changes in the desirability of alternatives. *Journal of Abnormal and Social Psychology, 52*, 384–389.

Brehm, J. W., & Cohen, A. R. (1962). *Explorations in cognitive dissonance.* New York: Wiley.

Breland, K., & Breland, M. (1961). The misbehavior of animals. *American Psychologist, 16*, 681–684.

Brewer, M. B. (1988). A dual process model of impression formation. In T. K. Srull & R. S. Wyer, Jr. (Eds.), *A dual process model of impression formation* (pp. 1–36). Hillsdale, NJ: Erlbaum.

Brewin, C. R., Dalgleish, T., & Joseph, S. (1996). A dual representation theory of posttraumatic stress disorder. *Psychological Review, 103*, 670–686.

Brock, D. B., Guralnick, J. M., & Brody, J. A. (1990). *Demography and epidemiology of aging in the United States: Handbook of the biology of aging* (Vol. 3, pp. 3–23). New York: Academic Press.

Bronfenbrenner, U., & Morris, P. A. (1988). The ecology of developmental processes. In W. Damon & M. Lerner (Eds.), *Handbook of child psychology* (Vol. 1, pp. 993–1028). New York: Wiley.

Brown, J. F. (1933). Über die dynamischen Eigenschaften der Realitäts- und Irrealitätsschichten [On the dynamic properties of the levels of reality and unreality]. *Psychologische Forschung, 18*, 1–26.

Brown, J. S. (1948). Gradients of approach and avoidance responses and their relation to model of motivation. *Journal of Comparative and Physiological Psychology, 41*, 450–465.

Brown, J. S. (1953). Problems presented by the concept of acquired drives. In J. S. Brown & A. Jacobs (Eds.), *Current theory and research in motivation: A symposium* (pp. 1–21). Lincoln: University of Nebraska Press.

Brown, J. S. (1961). *The motivation of behavior.* New York: McGraw-Hill.

Brown, K. W., & Ryan, R. M. (2003). The benefits of being present: Mindfulness and its role in psychological well-being. *Journal of Personality and Social Psychology, 84*, 822–848.

Brown, P. L., & Jenkins, H. M. (1968). Autoshaping of the pigeon's key-peck. *Journal of Analysis of Behavior, 11*, 1–8.

Brunstein, J. C. (1993). Personal goals and subjective well-being: A longitudinal study. *Journal of Personality and Social Psychology, 65*, 1061–1070.

Brunstein, J. C. (1995). *Motivation nach Misserfolg: Zur Bedeutung von Commitment und Substitution* [Motivation following failure: The role of commitment and substitution]. Göttingen, Germany: Hogrefe.

Brunstein, J. C. (1999). Persönliche Ziele und subjektives Wohlbefinden bei älteren Menschen [Personal goals and subjective well-being among older adults]. *Zeitschrift für Differentielle und Diagnostische Psychologie, 20*, 58–71.

Brunstein, J. C. (2001). Persönliche Ziele und Handlungs- versus Lageorientierung: Wer bindet sich an realistische und bedürfniskongruente Ziele? [Personal goals and action versus state orientation: Who builds a commitment to realistic and need-congruent goals?]. *Zeitschrift für Differentielle und Diagnostische Psychologie, 22*, 1–12.

Brunstein, J. C. (2003). Implizite Motive und motivationale Selbstbilder: Zwei Prädiktoren mit unterschiedlicher Gültigkeit [Implicit motives and motivational self-concepts: Two predictors with differing validity]. In J. Stiensmeier-Pelster & F. Rheinberg (Eds.), *Diagnostik von Motivation und Selbstkonzept* (Tests and Trends Vol. 2, pp. 59–88). Göttingen, Germany: Hogrefe.

Brunstein, J. C., Ganserer, J., Maier, H. & Heckhausen, H. (1991). Persönliche Anliegen in Alltagssituationen [Personal concerns in everyday situations]. *Memorandum No. 82.*

Brunstein, J. C., & Gollwitzer, P. M. (1996). Effects of failure on subsequent performance: The importance of self-defining goals. *Journal of Personality and Social Psychology, 70*, 395–407.

Brunstein, J. C., & Hoyer, S. (2002). Implizites versus explizites Leistungsstreben: Befunde zur Unabhängigkeit zweier Motivationssysteme [Implicit versus explicit achievement strivings: Empirical evidence of the independence of two motivational systems]. *Zeitschrift für Pädagogische Psychologie, 16*, 51–62.

Brunstein, J. C., Lautenschlager, U., Nawroth, B., Pöhlmann, K., & Schultheiss, O. C. (1995). Persönliche Anliegen, soziale Motive und emotionales Wohlbefinden [Personal goals, social motives, and emotional well-being]. *Zeitschrift für Differentielle und Diagnostische Psychologie, 16*, 1–10.

Brunstein, J. C., & Maier, G. W. (1996). Persönliche Ziele: Ein Überblick zum Stand der Forschung [Personal goals: A state-of-the-art review]. *Psychologische Rundschau, 47*, 146–160.

Brunstein, J. C., & Maier, G. W. (2001). Das Streben nach persönlichen Zielen: Emotionales Wohlbefinden und proaktive Entwicklung über die Lebensspanne [Striving for personal goals: Emotional well-being and proactive development across the lifespan]. In G. Jüttemann & H. Thomae (Eds.), *Persönlichkeit und Entwicklung* (pp. 155–188). Weinheim, Germany: Beltz.

Brunstein, J. C., & Maier, G. W. (2005). Implicit and self-attributed motives to achieve: Two separate but interacting needs. *Journal of Personality and Social Psychology, 89*, 205–222.

Brunstein, J. C., Maier, G. W., & Schultheiss, O. C. (1999). Motivation und Persönlichkeit: Von der Analyse von Teilsystemen zur Analyse ihrer Interaktionen [Motivation and personality: From the analysis of subsystems to the analyses of their interactions]. In M. Jerusalem & R. Pekrun (Eds.), *Emotion, Motivation und Leistung* (pp. 147–167). Göttingen, Germany: Hogrefe.

Brunstein, J. C., & Olbrich, E. (1985). Personal helplessness and action control: An analysis of achievement-related cognitions, self-assessments, and performance. *Journal of Personality and Social Psychology, 48*, 1540–1551.

Brunstein, J. C., & Schmitt, C. H. (2003). *Prüfung der konvergenten, diskriminanten und prädiktiven Validität von Leistungsmotiv-IATs, -TATs und -Fragebögen* [Testing the convergent, discriminant, and predictive validity of the achievement motive IAT, TAT, and questionnaires] (DFG Report). Potsdam, Germany: University of Potsdam.

Brunstein, J. C., & Schmitt, C. H. (2004). Assessing individual differences in achievement motivation with the Implicit Association Test. *Journal of Research in Personality, 38*, 536–555.

Brunstein, J. C., Schultheiss, O. C., & Grässmann, R. (1998). Personal goals and emotional well-being: The moderating role of motive dispositions. *Journal of Personality and Social Psychology, 75*, 494–508.

Brunstein, J. C., Schultheiss, O. C., & Maier, G. W. (1999). The pursuit of personal goals: A motivational approach to well-being and life adjustment. In J. Brandtstädter & R. M. Lerner (Eds.), *Action and self-development: Theory and research through the life span* (pp. 169–196). London: Sage.

Brunswik, E. (1952). *The conceptual frame work of psychology.* Chicago: The University of Chicago Press.

Brunswik, E. (1956). *Perception and representative design of psychological experiments.* Berkeley: University of California Press.

Bryk, A., & Raudenbush, S. W. (1992). *Hierarchical linear models for social and behavioral research: Applications and data analysis methods.* Newbury Park, CA: Sage.

Buber, M. (1979). *I and thou.* New York: Scribner's.

Buck, R. (1985). Prime theory: An integrated view of motivation and emotion. *Psychological Review, 92*, 389–413.

Bühler, C. (1933). *Der menschliche Lebenslauf als psychologisches Problem* [The human life course as a topic of psychology]. Leipzig, Germany: Hirzel.

Bühler, C., Hetzer, H., & Mabel, F. (1928). Die Affektwirksamkeit von Fremdheitseindrücken im ersten Lebensjahr [The emotional effects of unfamiliarity in the first year of life]. *Zeitschrift für Psychologie, 107*, 30–40.

Bühler, C., & Marschak, M. (1969). Grundtendenzen des menschlichen Lebens [Basic tendencies of human life]. In C. Bühler & F. Massarik (Eds.), *Lebenslauf und Lebensziele* (pp. 78–88). Stuttgart, Germany: Fischer.

Bühler, K. (1922). *Die geistige Entwicklung des Kindes* [The mental development of the child] (3rd ed.). Jena, Germany: Fischer.

Bühler, K.-E., & Heim, G. (2002). Psychisches Trauma und fixe Ideen [Psychic trauma and fixed ideas]. *Zeitschrift für Klinische Psychologie, Psychiatrie und Psychotherapie, 50*, 394–408.

Bullock, M., & Lütkenhaus, P. (1988). The development of volitional behavior in the toddler years. *Child Development, 59*, 664–674.

Bullock, M., & Lütkenhaus, P. (1991). Who am I? Self understanding in toddlers. *Merrill-Palmer Quarterly, 36*, 217–238.

Buss, A. H. (1980). *Self-consciousness and social anxiety.* San Francisco: Freeman.

Buss, D. M. (1987). Selection, evocation and manipulation. *Journal of Personality and Social Psychology, 53*, 1214–1221.

Buss, D. M. (1991). Evolutionary personality psychology. *Annual Review of Psychology, 42*, 459–491.

Buss, D. M. (2001). Human nature and culture: An evolutionary psychological perspective. *Journal of Personality, 69*, 955–978.

Buss, D. M., & Schmitt, D. P. (1993). Sexual strategies theory: An evolutionary perspective on human mating. *Psychological Review, 100*, 204–232.

Buss, H. H., & Plomin, R. (1984). *Temperament: Early developing personality traits.* Hillsdale, NJ: Erlbaum.

Butler, R. (1993). Effects of task- and ego-achievement goals on information-seeking during task engagement. *Journal of Personality and Social Psychology, 65*, 18–31.

Butler, R. (1999). Information seeking and achievement motivation in middle childhood and adolescence: The role of conceptions of ability. *Developmental Psychology, 35*, 146–163.

Butler, R. (2000). What learners want to know: The role of achievement goals in shaping information seeking, learning, and interest. In C. Sansone & J. M. Harackiewicz (Eds.), *Intrinsic and extrinsic motivation* (pp. 162–194). San Diego, CA: Academic Press.

Butterfield, E. C. (1964). The interruption of tasks: Methodological, factual and theoretical issues. *Psychological Bulletin, 62*, 309–322.

Butz, M. V., & Hoffmann, J. (2002). Anticipations control behavior: Animal behavior in an anticipatory learning classifier system. *Adaptive Behavior, 10*, 75–96.

Byrne, D. (1961a). Anxiety and the experimental arousal of affiliation need. *Journal of Abnormal and Social Psychology, 63*, 660–662.

Byrne, D. (1961b). The repression-sensitization scale: Rationale, reliability, and validity. *Journal of Personality, 29*, 334–349.

Byrne, D. (1962). Response to attitude similarity-dissimilarity as a function of affiliation need. *Journal of Personality, 30,* 164–177.

Byrne, D., McDonald, R. D., & Mikawa, J. (1963). Approach and avoidance affiliation motives. *Journal of Personality, 31,* 21–37.

Cabanac, M. (1971). Physiological role of pleasure. *Science, 173*(2), 1103–1107.

Cahill, L. (2000). Modulation of long-term memory in humans by emotional arousal: Adrenergic activation and the amygdala. In J. P. Aggleton (Ed.), *The amygdala: A functional analysis* (pp. 425–446). New York: Oxford University Press.

Cahill, L., Prins, B., Weber, M., & McGaugh, J. L. (1994). Beta-adrenergic activation and memory for emotional events. *Nature, 371,* 702–704.

Calder, B., & Staw, B. M. (1975). The interaction of intrinsic and extrinsic motivation: Some methodological notes. *Journal of Personality and Social Psychology, 31,* 76–80.

Cameron, J., Banko, K. M., & Pierce, W. D. (2001). Pervasive negative effects of rewards on intrinsic motivation: The myth continues. *The Behavior Analyst, 24,* 1–44.

Campbell, B. A., & Sheffield, F. D. (1953). Relation of random activity to food deprivation. *Journal of Comparative Physiological Psychology, 46,* 320–322.

Campbell, D. T., & Fiske, D. W. (1959). Convergent and discriminant validation by the multitrait-multimethod matrix. *Psychological Bulletin, 56,* 81–105.

Campbell, J. P., Dunnette, M. D., Lawler, E. E., & Weick, K. E. (1970). *Managerial behavior performance and effectiveness.* New York: McGraw-Hill.

Cannon, W. B., & Washburn, A. L. (1912). An explanation of hunger. *American Journal of Physiology, 29,* 441–454.

Canon, L. K. (1964). Self-confidence and selective exposure to information. In L. Festinger (Ed.), *Conflict, decision, and dissonance* (pp. 83–95). Stanford, CA: Stanford University Press.

Cantor, N., & Fleeson, W. W. (1991). Life tasks and self-regulatory processes. In M. L. Maehr & P. R. Pintrich (Eds.), *Advances in motivation and achievement* (Vol. 7, pp. 327–269). Greenwich, CT: JAI Press.

Cantor, N., Mischel, W., & Schwartz, J. C. (1982). A prototype analysis of psychological situations. *Cognitive Psychology, 14,* 45–77.

Cantor, N., Norem, J. K., Niedenthal, M., & Brower, A. (1987). Life tasks, self-concept ideals, and cognitive strategies in a life transition. *Journal of Personality and Social Psychology, 53,* 1178–1191.

Cantor, N., & Zirkel, S. (1990). Personality, cognition, and purposive behavior. In L. A. Pervin (Ed.), *Handbook of personality research: Theory and research* (pp. 135–164). New York: Guilford Press.

Cardinal, R. N., Parkinson, J. A., Hall, J., & Everitt, B. J. (2002). Emotion and motivation: The role of the amygdala, ventral striatum, and prefrontal cortex. *Neuroscience and Biobehavioral Reviews, 26,* 321–352.

Carlson, E. R. (1956). Attitude change through modification of attitude structure. *Journal of Abnormal and Social Psychology, 52,* 256–261.

Carlson, N. R. (1994). *Physiology of behavior* (5th ed.). Boston: Allyn & Bacon.

Caron, A. J., & Wallach, M. A. (1957). Recall of interrupted tasks under stress: A phenomenon of memory or learning? *Journal of Abnormal and Social Psychology, 55,* 372–381.

Caron, A. J., & Wallach, M. A. (1959). Personality determinants of repressive and obsessive reactions to failure stress. *Journal of Abnormal and Social Psychology, 59,* 236–245.

Carr, S. J., Dabbs, J. M., & Carr, G. (1975). Mother-infant attachment: The importance of the mother's visual field. *Child Development, 46*(2), 331–338.

Carroll, L., Voisey, J., & van Daal, A. (2004). Mouse models of obesity. *Clinics in Dermatology, 22*(4), 345–349.

Carter, C. S. (1998). Neuroendocrine perspectives on social attachment and love. *Psychoneuroendocrinology, 23,* 779–818.

Cartwright, D. (1942). The effect of interruption, completion and failure upon the attractiveness of activity. *Journal of Experimental Psychology, 31,* 1–16.

Cartwright, D. (1959). A field theory conception of power. In D. Cartwright (Ed.), *Studies in social power* (pp. 183–220). Ann Arbor: The University of Michigan.

Cartwright, D. (1965). Influence, leadership, and control. In J. G. March (Ed.), *Handbook of organizations* (pp. 1–47). Chicago: Rand McNally.

Cartwright, D., & Festinger, L. (1943). A quantitative theory of decision. *Psychological Review, 50,* 595–621.

Carver, C. S., Lawrence, J. W., & Scheier, M. E. (1996). A control-process perspective on the origins of affect. In L. L. Martin & A. Tesser (Eds.), *Striving and feeling: Interactions among goals, affect, and self-regulation* (pp. 11–52). Mahwah, NJ: Erlbaum.

Carver, C. S., & Scheier, M. F. (1998). *On the self-regulation of behavior.* New York: Cambridge University Press.

Caspi, A. (1998). Personality development across the life course. *Handbook of Child Psychology, 3*(5), 311–388.

Cattell, R. B. (1950). *Personality: A systematic, theoretical, and factual study.* New York: McGraw-Hill.

Cattell, R. B. (1957). *Personality and motivation: Structure and measurement.* Yonkers, NY: World Book.

Cattell, R. B. (1958). Extracting the correct number of factors in factor analysis. *Educational Psychological Measurement, 18,* 791–838.

Cattell, R. B. (1965). *The scientific analysis of personality.* Baltimore: Penguin Books.

Cattell, R. B. (1974). *Handbook of modern personality theory.* Englewood Cliffs, NJ: Prentice Hall.

Cervone, D. (2004). The architecture of personality. *Psychological Review, 111,* 183–204.

Charlesworth, W. R. (1969). The role of surprise in cognitive development. In D. Elkind & J. H. Flavell (Eds.), *Studies in cognitive development* (pp. 257–314). Oxford, UK: Oxford University Press.

Chartrand, T. L., & Bargh, J. A. (1999). The chameleon effect: The perception-behavior link and social interaction. *Journal of Personality and Social Psychology, 76,* 893–910.

Chasteen, A. L., Park, D., & Schwarz, N. (2001). Implementation intentions and facilitation of prospective memory. *Psychological Science, 12,* 457–461.

Cheek, J. M., & Buss, A. H. (1981). Shyness and sociability. *Journal of Personality and Social Psychology, 41,* 330–339.

Chen, M., & Bargh, J. A. (1997). Nonconscious behavioral confirmation processes: The self-fulfilling consequences of automatic stereotype activation. *Journal of Experimental Social Psychology, 33,* 541–560.

Cheng, P. W., & Novick, L. R. (1990a). Where is the bias in causal attribution? In K. J. Gilholey, M. T. K. Kayne, R. H. Logie, & G. Erdos (Eds.), *Lines of thinking* (pp. 181–197). New York: Wiley.

Cheng, P. W., & Novick, L. R. (1990b). A probabilistic contrast model of causal induction. *Journal of Personality and Social Psychology, 58,* 545–567.

Chipperfield, J. G., Pery, R. P., & Menec, A. (1999). Primary and secondary control-enhancing strategies: Implications for health in later life. *Journal of Aging and Health, 11*, 517–539.

Christiansen, K. (1999). Hypophysen-Gonaden-Achse (Mann) [Hypophyse-gonad axis (male)]. In C. Kirschbaum & D. Hellhammer (Eds.), *Enzyklopädie der Psychologie, Biologische Psychologie, Band 3: Psychoendokrinologie und Psychoimmunologie* (pp. 141–222). Göttingen, Germany: Hogrefe.

Chusmir, L. H. (1984). Motivational need pattern for police officers. *Journal of Police Science & Administration, 12*, 141–145.

Claessens, D. (1968). *Instinkt, Psyche, Geltung: Bestimmungsfaktoren menschlichen Verhaltens. Eine soziologische Anthropologie* [Instinct, psyche, status: Determining factors in human behavior. A sociological anthropology]. Köln (Cologne), Germany: Westdeutscher Verlag.

Clarke, P., & James, J. (1967). The effects of situation, attitude intensity and personality on information-seeking. *Sociometry, 30*, 235–245.

Clark, R. A. (1952). The projective measurement of experimental induced levels of sexual motivation. *Journal of Experimental Psychology, 44*, 391–399.

Clark, R. A., & Sensibar, M. R. (1955). The relationship between symbolic and manifest projections of sexuality with some incidental correlates. *Journal of Abnormal and Social Psychology, 50*, 327–334.

Clarke-Stewart, K. A. (1973). Interactions between mothers and their young children: Characteristics and consequences. *Monographs of the Society for Research in Child Development, 38*(153), 6–7.

Clarke-Stewart, K. A., VanderStoep, L. P., & Killian, P. (1979). Analysis and replication of mother-child relations at two years of age. *Child Development, 50*(3), 777–793.

Clavadetscher, C. (2003). *Motivation ehrenamtlicher Arbeit im Verein Mahogany Hall, Bern* [Motivation for voluntary work in the Mahogany Hall Society, Berne, Switzerland]. Unpublished final thesis, Berne University of Applied Sciences, Switzerland.

Clemente, C. D., & Chase, M. H. (1973). Neurological substrates of aggressive behavior. *Annual Review of Physiology, 35*, 329–356.

Coats, E. J., Janoff-Bulman, R., & Alpert, N. (1996). Approach versus avoidance goals: Differences in self-evaluation and well-being. *Personality and Social Psychology Bulletin, 22*, 1057–1067.

Cofer, C. N., & Appley, M. H. (1964). *Motivation: Theory and research.* New York: Wiley.

Collins, C. J., Hanges, P. J., & Locke, E. A. (2004). The relation of achievement motivation to entrepreneurial behavior: A meta-analysis. *Human Performance, 17*, 95–117.

Collis, G. M., & Schaffer, H. R. (1975). Synchronization of visual attention in mother-infant pairs. *Journal of Child Psychology and Psychiatry, 16*, 315–320.

Compas, B. E. (1987). Coping with stress during childhood and adolescence. *Psychological Bulletin, 101*, 393–403.

Compas, B. E., & Worsham, N. L. (1991, April). *When mom or dad has cancer: Developmental differences in children's coping with family stress.* Paper presented at the Society for Research in Child Development meeting, Seattle, WA.

Compas, B. E., Worsham, N. L., Ey, L., & Howell, B. (1996). When mom or dad has cancer II: Coping, cognitive appraisals, and psychological distress in children of cancer patients. *Health Psychology, 15*, 167–175.

Constantian, C. A. (1981). *Attitudes, beliefs, and behavior in regard to spending time alone.* Unpublished doctoral thesis, Harvard University, Cambridge, MA.

Conway, M. A., & Pleydell-Parker, C. W. (2000). The construction of autobiographical memories in the self-memory system. *Psychological Review, 107*, 261–288.

Cooper, W. H. (1983). An achievement motivation nomological network. *Journal of Personality and Social Psychology, 44*, 841–861.

Coopersmith, S. (1960). Self-esteem and need achievement as determinants of selective recall and repetition. *Journal of Abnormal and Social Psychology, 60*, 310–317.

Corr, P. J., Pickering, A. D., & Gray, J. A. (1997). Personality, punishment, and procedural learning: A test of J. A. Gray's anxiety theory. *Journal of Personality and Social Psychology, 73*(2), 337–344.

Cosmides, L. (1989). The logic of social exchange: Has natural selection shaped how humans reason? Studies with the Wason selection task. *Cognition, 31*, 187–276.

Cosmides, L., & Tooby, J. (1992). Cognitive adaptations for social exchange. In J. H. Barkow, L. Cosmides, & J. Tooby (Eds.), *The adapted mind: Evolutionary psychology and the generation of culture* (pp. 163–228). New York: Oxford University Press.

Cosmides, L., & Tooby, J. (1994). Origins of domain-specificity: The evolution of functional organization. In L. A. Hirschfeld & S. A. Gelman (Eds.), *Mapping the mind: Domain specificity in cognition and culture* (pp. 85–116). Cambridge, UK: Cambridge University Press.

Costa, P. T., & McCrae, R. R. (1985). *The NEO Personality Inventory manual.* Odessa, FL: Psychological Assessment Resources.

Costa, P. T., & McCrae, R. R. (1988). From catalogue to classification: Murray's needs and the five-factor model. *Journal of Personality and Social Psychology, 55*, 258–265.

Costa, P. T., & McCrae, R. R. (1992). *Revised NEO Personality Inventory (NEO-PI-R) and NEO Five-Factor Inventory (NEO-FFI) professional manual.* Odessa, FL: Psychological Assessment Resources.

Covington, M. V. (1992). *Making the grade: A self-worth perspective on motivation and school reform.* New York: Cambridge University Press.

Covington, M. V., & Omelich, C. L. (1979). Are arousal attributions causal? A path analysis of the cognitive model of achievement motivation. *Journal of Personality and Social Psychology, 37*, 1487–1504.

Covington, M. V., & Omelich, C. L. (1991). Need achievement revisited: Verification of Atkinson's original 2×2 model. In C. D. Spielberger, I. G. Sarason, Z. Kulcsár, & G. L. van Heck (Eds.), *Stress and emotion: Anxiety, anger, and curiosity* (Vol. 14, pp. 85–105). Washington, DC: Hemisphere.

Covington, M. V., & Roberts, B. W. (1994). Self-worth and college achievement: Motivational and personality correlates. In P. R. Pintrich, D. R. Brown, & C. E. Weinstein (Eds.), *Student motivation, cognition, and learning* (pp. 157–188). Hillsdale, NJ: Erlbaum.

Cowlishaw, G., & Dunbar, R. I. M. (1991). Dominance, rank, and mating success in male primates. *Animal Behavior, 41*, 1045–1056.

Coyne, J. C., & Gotlib, I. C. H. (1983). The role of cognitions in depression: A critical appraisal. *Psychological Bulletin, 94*, 472–505.

Craig, W. (1918). Appetites and aversions as constituents of instincts. *Biological Bulletin of Woods Hole, 34*, 91–107.

Craik, F. I. M., Moroz, T. M., Moscovitch, M., Stuss, D. T., Winocur, G., Tulving, E., & Kapur, S. (1999). In search of the self: A positron emission tomography study. *Psychological Science, 10*, 26–34.

Crespi, L. P. (1942). Quantitative variation of incentive and performance in the white rat. *American Journal of Psychology, 55,* 467–517.

Crespi, L. P. (1944). Amount of reinforcement and level of performance. *Psychological Review, 51,* 341–357.

Cronbach, L. J. (1990). *Essentials of psychological testing* (5th ed.). New York: Harper-Collins.

Crozier, W. R. (1979). Shyness as anxious self-preoccupation. *Psychological Reports, 44,* 959–962.

Center for the Study of Emotion and Attention. (1999). *International Affective Picture System (IAPS): Technical manual and affective ratings.* Gainesville: NIMH Center for the Study of Emotion and Attention, University of Florida.

Csikszentmihalyi, M. (1975). *Beyond boredom and anxiety.* San Francisco: Jossey-Bass.

Csikszentmihalyi, M. (1990). *Flow.* New York: Harper & Row.

Csikszentmihalyi, M. (1991). Das Flow-Erlebnis und seine Bedeutung für die Psychologie des Menschen [The flow experience and its significance for human psychology]. In M. Csikszentmihalyi & I. S. Csikszentmihalyi (Eds.), *Die außergewöhnliche Erfahrung im Alltag. Die Psychologie des Flow-Erlebens* (pp. 28–49). Stuttgart, Germany: Klett-Cotta.

Csikszentmihalyi, M. (1997a). *Dem Sinn des Lebens eine Zukunft geben* [The evolving self: A psychology for the third millennium]. Stuttgart, Germany: Klett-Cotta.

Csikszentmihalyi, M. (1997b). *Finding flow.* New York: Basic Books.

Cskiszentmihalyi, M., & Beattie, O. (1979). Life themes: A theoretical and empirical exploration of their origins and effects. *Journal of Humanistic Psychology, 19,* 45–63.

Csikszentmihalyi, M., Larson, R., & Prescott, S. (1977). The ecology of adolescence acivity and experience. *Journal of Youth and Adolescence, 6,* 281–294.

Csikszentmihalyi, M., & LeFevre, J. (1989). Optimal experience in work and leisure. *Journal of Personality and Social Psychology, 56,* 815–822.

Cube v., F. (2003). *Lust auf Leistung* [Appetite for achievement]. Munich, Germany: Piper.

Cunningham, J. D., & Kelley, H. H. (1975). Causal attributions for personal events of varying magnitudes. *Journal of Personality, 43,* 74–93.

Dabbs, J. M., Frady, R. L., Carr, T. S., & Besch, N. F. (1987). Saliva testosterone and criminal violence in young adult prison inmates. *Psychosomatic Medicine, 49,* 174–182.

Dabbs, J. M., & Hargrove, M. F. (1997). Age, testosterone, and behavior among female prison inmates. *Psychosomatic Medicine, 59,* 477–480.

Dahl, R. A. (1957). The concept of power. *Behavioral Sciences, 2,* 201–215.

Daly, M., & Wilson, M. (1983). *Sex, evolution, and behavior* (2nd ed.). Belmont, CA: Wadsworth.

Damasio, A. R. (1994). *Descartes' error: Emotion, reason, and the human brain.* London: Papermac.

Damasio, A. R. (2000). *Ich fühle also bin ich: Die Entschlüsselung des Bewusstseins* [I feel, therefore I am: Decoding consciousness]. Munich, Germany: List.

Damasio, A. R., Tranel, D., & Damasio, H. C. (1991). Somatic markers and the guidance of behavior: Theory and preliminary testing (pp. 217–229). In H. S. Levin, H. M. Eisenberg, & A. L. Benton (Eds.), *Frontal lobe function and dysfunction* (pp. 230–255). Oxford, UK: Oxford University Press.

Daniels, D., & Plomin, R. (1985). Origins of individual differences in infant shyness. *Developmental Psychology, 21,* 118–121.

Dannefer, D. (1989). Human action and its place in theories of aging. *Journal of Aging and Health, 3,* 1–20.

Darwin, C. (1859). *Origin of species by means of natural selection.* London: John Murray.

Darwin, C. (1871). *The descent of man, and selection in relation to sex.* New York: Appleton.

Darwin, C. (1872). *The expression of the emotions in man and animals.* London: John Murray.

Davidson, R. J. (2000). Affective style, psychopathology, and resilience: Brain mechanisms and plasticity. *American Psychologist, 55*(11), 1196–1214.

Davidson, R. J. (2001). Toward a biology of personality and emotion. *Annals of the New York Academy of Sciences, 935,* 191–207.

Davidson, R. J., Kalin, N. H., & Shelton, S. E. (1993). Lateralized response to diazepam predicts temperamental style in rhesus monkeys. *Behavioral Neuroscience, 107,* 1106–1110.

Dawkins, R. (1976). *The selfish gene.* New York: Oxford University Press.

Dawson, M. E., & Schell, A. M. (1982). Electrodermal responses to attended and nonattended significant stimuli during dichotic listening. *Journal of Experimental Psychology: Human Perception and Performance, 8,* 315–324.

de Araujo, I. E., Kringelbach, M. L., Rolls, E. T., & Hobden, P. (2003). Representation of umami taste in the human brain. *Journal of Neurophysiology, 90*(1), 313–319.

DeCasper, A. J., & Carstens, A. A. (1981). Contingencies of stimulation: Effects of learning and emotion in neonates [Special issue: Variability in infancy]. *Infant Behavior and Development, 4*(1), 19–35.

deCharms, R. (1968). *Personal causation.* New York: Academic Press.

deCharms, R. (1976). *Enhancing motivation: Change in the classroom.* New York: Irvington.

deCharms, R. (1979). *Motivation in der Klasse* [Motivation in the classroom]. Munich, Germany: MVG.

deCharms, R., & Moeller, G. H. (1962). Values expressed in American children's readers: 1800–1950. *Journal of Abnormal and Social Psychology, 64,* 136–142.

deCharms, R., Morrison, H. W., Reitman, W., & McClelland, D. C. (1955). Behavioral correlates of directly and indirectly measured achievement motivation. In D. C. McClelland (Ed.), *Studies in motivation* (pp. 414–423). New York: Appleton-Century-Crofts.

Deci, E. L. (1971). Effects of externally mediated rewards on intrinsic motivation. *Journal of Personality and Social Psychology, 18,* 105–115.

Deci, E. L. (1975). *Intrinsic motivation.* New York: Plenum.

Deci, E. L., Koestner, R., & Ryan, R. M. (1999). A meta-analytic review of experiments examining the effects of extrinsic rewards on intrinsic motivation. *Psychological Bulletin, 125,* 627–668.

Deci, E. L., & Ryan, R. M. (1980). The empirical exploration of intrinsic motivational processes. In L. Berkowitz (Ed.), *Advances in experimental social psychology* (pp. 39–80). New York: Academic Press.

Deci, E. L., & Ryan, R. M. (1985). *Intrinsic motivation and self-determination in human behavior.* New York: Plenum.

Deci, E. L., & Ryan, R. M. (2000). The "what" and "why" of goal pursuits: Human needs and the self-determination of behavior. *Psychological Inquiry, 11,* 227–268.

De Dreu, C. K. W., Carnevale, P. J. D., Emans, B. J. M., & van de Vliert, E. (1994). Effects of gain-loss frames in negotiation: Loss aversion, mismatching, and frame adoption. *Organizational Behavior and Human Decision Processes, 60,* 90–107.

Deese, J., & Carpenter, J. A. (1951). Drive level and reinforcement. *Journal of Experimental Psychology, 42*, 236–238.

Delle Fave, A., & Bassi, M. (2000). The quality of experience in adolescents' daily lives: Developmental perspectives. *Genetic, Social, and General Psychology Monographs, 126*, 347–367.

Delville, Y., DeVries, G. J., & Ferris, C. F. (2000). Neural connections of the anterior hypothalamus and agonistic behavior in golden hamsters. *Brain, Behavior and Evolution, 55*, 53–76.

Dembo, T. (1931). Der Ärger als dynamisches Problem [Anger as a dynamic problem]. *Psychologische Forschung, 15*, 1–44.

Dempster, F. N. (1985). Proactive interference in sentence recall: Topic-similarity effects and individual differences. *Memory and Cognition, 13*, 81–89.

Depue, R. A., & Collins, P. F. (1999). Neurobiology of the structure of personality: Dopamine, facilitation of incentive motivation, and extraversion. *Behavioral and Brain Sciences, 22*, 491–569.

Depue, R. A., Luciana, M., Arbisi, P., Collins, P., & Leon, A. (1994). Dopamine and the structure of personality: Relation of agonist-induced dopamine activity to positive emotionality. *Journal of Personality and Social Psychology, 67*(3), 485–498.

Depue, R. A., & Morrone-Strupinsky, J. V. (2005). A neurobehavioral model of affiliative bonding: Implications for conceptualizing a human trait of affiliation. *Behavioral and Brain Sciences, 28*(3), 313–350; discussion 350–395.

Derryberry, D., & Tucker, D. M. (1991). The adaptive base of the neural hierarchy: Elementary motivational controls on network function. In R. A. Dienstbier (Ed.), *Nebraska Symposium on Motivation* (pp. 289–342). Lincoln: University of Nebraska Press.

Devine, P. (1989). Stereotypes and prejudice: Their automatic and controlled components. *Journal of Personality and Social Psychology, 56*, 5–18.

Devinsky, O. (2000). Right cerebral hemisphere dominance for a sense of corporeal and emotional self. *Epilepsy & Behavior, 1*, 60–73.

Dibbelt, S. (1997). *Wechseln und Beibehalten von Zielen als Subfunktionen der Handlungskontrolle* [Changing and keeping goals as subfunctions of action control]. Unpublished doctoral dissertation, University of Osnabrück, Germany.

Dickhäuser, O., & Galfe, E. (2004). Besser als . . ., schlechter als . . . – Leistungsbezogene Vergleichsprozesse in der Grundschule [Better . . ., worse . . . – Achievement-related comparison processes in elementary school]. *Zeitschrift für Entwicklungspsychologie und Pädagogische Psychologie, 36*, 1–9.

Dickhäuser, O., & Rheinberg, F. (2003). Bezugsnormorientierung: Erfassung, Probleme, Perspektiven [Reference norm orientations: Measurement, problems, perspectives]. In J. Stiensmeier-Pelster & F. Rheinberg (Eds.), *Diagnostik von Motivation und Selbstkonzept* (pp. 41–55). Göttingen, Germany: Hogrefe.

Dickhäuser, O., & Stiensmeier-Pelster, J. (2000). Geschlechtsunterschiede im Lern- und Leistungsverhalten am Computer: Ein theoretischer Rahmen [Gender differences in learning and achievement behavior on the computer: A theoretical framework]. In F. Försterling, J. Stiensmeier-Pelster, & L. Silny (Eds.), *Kognitive und emotionale Aspekte der Motivation* (pp. 53–76). Göttingen, Germany: Hogrefe.

Dickhäuser, O., & Stiensmeier-Pelster, J. (2002). Erlernte Hilflosigkeit am Computer? Geschlechtsunterschiede in computerspezifischen Attributionen [Learned helplessness at the computer? Gender differences in computer-specific attributions]. *Psychologie in Erziehung und Unterricht, 49*, 44–55.

Dickinson, A. (1997). Bolles's psychological syllogism. In M. E. Bouton & M. S. Fanselow (Eds.), *Learning, motivation and cognition* (pp. 345–367). Washington, DC: American Psychological Association.

Dickinson, A., & Shanks, D. (1995). Instrumental action and causal representation. In D. Sperber, D. Premack, & A. James Premack (Eds.), *A causal cognition* (pp. 3–25). Oxford, UK: Clarendon Press.

Diefendorff, J. M., Hall, R. J., Lord, R. G., & Strean, M. L. (2000). Action-state orientation: Construct validity of a revised measure and its relationship to work-related variables. *Journal of Personality and Social Psychology, 85*, 250–263.

Diener, C. I., & Dweck, C. S. (1978). An analysis of learned helplessness: Continuous changes in performance, strategy, and achievement cognitions following failure. *Journal of Personality and Social Psychology, 36*, 451–462.

Dienstbier, R. A. (1989). Arousal and physiological toughness: Implications for mental and physical health. *Psychological Review, 96*, 84–100.

Dilthey, W. (1894). Ideen über eine beschreibende und zergliedernde Psychologie [Ideas on a descriptive and analytical psychology]. In *Sitzungsberichte der Königlichen Preußischen Akademie der Wissenschaften zu Berlin (Phil. hist. Classe)* (pp. 1309–1407). Berlin, Germany: LIII.

DiVitto, B., & McArthur, L. Z. (1978). Developmental differences in the use of distinctiveness, consensus, and consistency information for making causal attributions. *Developmental Psychology, 14*, 474–482.

Dix, T., Ruble, D. N., & Zambarano, R, (1989). Mothers' implicit theories of discipline: Child effects, parent effects, and the attribution process. *Child Development, 60*, 1373–1391.

Dodge, K. A. (1993). Social-cognitive mechanism in the development of conduct disorder and depression. *Annual Review of Psychology, 44*, 559–584.

Dodge, K. A., & Colie, J. D. (1987). Social information processing factors in reactive and proactive aggression in children's peer groups. *Journal of Personality and Social Psychology, 53*, 1146–1158.

Dollard, J., Doob, L., Miller, N. E., Mowrer, H. O., & Sears, R. R. (1939). *Frustration and aggression.* New Haven, CT: Yale University Press.

Dollard, J., & Miller, N. E. (1950). *Personality and psychotherapy: An analysis in terms of learning, thinking, and culture.* New York: McGraw-Hill.

Domjan, M., Blesbois, E., & Williams, J. (1998). The adaptive significance of sexual conditioning: Pavlovian control of sperm release. *Psychological Science, 9*, 411–415.

Donders, F. C. (1862). Die Schnelligkeit psychischer Prozesse [The speed of mental processes]. *Archiv für Anatomie und Physiologie*, 657–681.

Donley, R. E., & Winter, D. G. (1970). Measuring the motives of public officials at a distance: An exploratory study of American presidents. *Behavioral Sciences, 15*, 227–236.

Douglas, M. (1986). *How institutions think.* Syracuse, NY: Syracuse University Press.

Droege, K. L., & Stipek, D. J. (1993). Children's use of dispositions to predict classmates' behavior. *Developmental Psychology, 29*, 646–654.

Duffy, E. (1932). The relationship between muscular tension and quality of performance. *American Journal of Psychology, 44*, 535–546.

Duffy, E. (1934). Emotion: An example of the need for reorientation in psychology. *Psychological Review, 41*, 184–198.

Duffy, E. (1941). An explanation of "emotional" phenomena without the use of the concept "emotion." *Journal of General Psychology, 25*, 283–293.

Duffy, E. (1957). The psychological significance of the concept of "arousal" or "activation." *Psychological Review, 64*, 265–275.

Duffy, E. (1962). *Activation and behavior.* New York: Wiley.

Düker, H. (1931). *Psychologische Untersuchungen über freie und zwangsläufige Arbeitsweise: Experimentelle Beiträge zur Willens- und Arbeitspsychologie* [Psychological studies of free and inevitable work: Experimental contributions on the psychology of volition and work]. Leipzig, Germany: Barth.

Düker, H. (1975). *Untersuchungen über die Ausbildung des Wollens* [Studies on the development of volition]. Berne, Switzerland: Huber.

Dweck, C. S. (1975). The role of expectations and attributions in the alleviation of learned helplessness. *Journal of Personality and Social Psychology, 31*, 674–685.

Dweck, C. S. (1986). Motivational processes affecting learning. *American Psychologist, 41*, 1040–1048.

Dweck, C. S. (1999). *Self-theories: Their role in motivation, personality, and development.* Philadelphia: Psychology Press.

Dweck, C. S. (2002). The development of ability conceptions. In A. Wigfield & J. S. Eccles (Eds.), *Development of achievement motivation* (pp. 57–88). San Diego, CA: Academic Press.

Dweck, C. S. (2003). Clarifying achievement goals and their impact. *Journal of Personality and Social Psychology, 85*(3), 541–553.

Dweck, C. S., & Elliott, E. S. (1983). Achievement motivation. In E. M. Hetherington (Ed.), *Socialization, personality, and social development* (pp. 643–691). New York: Wiley.

Dweck, C. S., & Leggett, E. I. (1973). Learned helplessness and reinforcement responsibility in children. *Journal of Personality and Social Psychology, 25*, 109–116.

Dweck, C. S., & Leggett, F. L. (1988). A social-cognitive approach to motivation and personality. *Psychological Review, 95*, 256–273.

Dweck, C. S., & Repucci, N. D. (1973). Learned helplessness and reinforcement responsibility in children. *Journal of Personality and Social Psychology, 25*, 109–116.

Eagly, A. H., & Wood, W. (1999). The origins of sex differences in human behavior. *American Psychologist, 54*, 408–423.

Eaves, G., & Rush, A. J. (1984). Cognitive patterns in symptomatic and remitted unipolar major depression. *Journal of Abnormal Psychology, 93*, 31–40.

Ebbinghaus, H. (1902). *Abriß der Psychologie* [Summary of psychology]. Leipzig, Germany: Veit.

Eccles, J. S. (1984). Sex differences in achievement patterns. In T. Sonderegger (Ed.), *Nebraska Symposium of Motivation: Vol. 32* (pp. 97–132). Lincoln: University of Nebraska Press.

Eccles, J. S. (1987). Gender roles and women's achievement-related decisions. *Psychology of Women Quarterly, 11*, 135–172.

Eccles, J. S. (2005). Subjective task value and the Eccles et al. model of achievement related choices. In A. J. Elliot & C. S. Dweck (Eds.), *Handbook of competence and motivation* (pp. 105–121). New York: Guilford Press.

Eccles, J. S., Adler, T. F., & Meece, J. L. (1984). Sex differences in achievement: A test of alternate theories. *Journal of Personality and Social Psychology, 46*(1), 26–43.

Eccles, J. S., Barber, B., & Jozefowicz, D. (1999). Linking gender to educational, occupational and recreational choices: Applying the Eccles model of achievement related choices. In W. B. Swann & J. H. Langlois (Eds.), *Sexism and stereotypes in modern society* (pp. 153–192). Washington, DC: American Psychological Association.

Eccles, J. S., & Wigfield, A. (1995). In the mind of the actor: The structure of adolescents' achievement task values and expectancy-related beliefs. *Personality and Social Psychology Bulletin, 21*(3), 215–225.

Eccles, J. S., & Wigfield, A. (2002). Motivational beliefs, values, and goals. *Annual Review of Psychology, 53*(1), 109–132.

Eccles, J. S., Wigfield, A., Harold, R., & Blumenfeld, P. B. (1993). Age and gender differences in children's self- and task perceptions during elementary school. *Child Development, 64*, 830–847.

Eccles, J. S., Wigfield, A., & Schiefele, U. (1998). Motivation to succeed. In W. Damon (Series Ed.) & N. Eisenberg (Volume Ed.), *Handbook of child psychology* (Vol. 3, 5th ed., pp. 1017–1095). New York: Wiley.

Eckhardt, G. (1968). Die entwicklungspsychologische Abhängigkeit der Konfliktreaktion vom Grad der Misserfolgswahrscheinlichkeit [A developmental perspective the dependence of conflict responses on the

likelihood of failure]. Unpublished pre-Diplom thesis, University of Münster, Germany.

Edwards, W. (1954). The theory of decision-making. *Psychological Bulletin, 51*, 380–417.

Edwards, W. (1962). Utility, subjective probability, their interaction, and variance preferences. *Journal of Conflict Resolution, 6*, 42–51.

Egloff, B., & Schmukle, S. C. (2002). Predictive validity of an Implicit Association Test for assessing anxiety. *Journal of Personality and Social Psychology, 83*, 1441–1455.

Ehrlich, D., Guttmann, I., Schönbach, P., & Mills, J. (1957). Postdecision exposure to relevant information. *Journal of Abnormal and Social Psychology, 54*, 98–102.

Eibl-Eibesfeldt, I. (1973). *Der vorprogrammierte Mensch* [The preprogrammed human]. Vienna, Austria: Molden.

Eibl-Eibesfeldt, I. (1975). *Krieg und Frieden aus der Sicht der Verhaltensforschung* [The biology of peace and war: Men, animals, and aggression]. Munich, Germany: Piper.

Eibl-Eibesfeldt, I. (1984). *Die Biologie des menschlichen Verhaltens: Grundriß der Humanethologie* [The biology of human behavior: Outline of human ethology]. Munich, Germany: Piper.

Eibl-Eibesfeldt, I. (1988). *Der Mensch – das riskierte Wesen: Zur Naturgeschichte menschlicher Unvernunft* [On the natural history of human folly]. Munich, Germany: Piper.

Eibl-Eibesfeldt, I. (1997). *Die Biologie menschlichen Verhaltens – Grundriss der Humanethologie* [Human ethology – Foundations of human behavior]. Munich, Germany: Piper.

Eimer, M. (1987). *Konzepte von Kausalität* [Concepts of causality]. Berne, Switzerland: Huber.

Eisenberger, N. I., Liebermann, M. D., & Williams, K. D. (2003). Does rejection hurt? An fMRI study of social exclusion. *Science, 302*, 290–292.

Eisenberger, R., & Cameron, J. (1996). Detrimental effects of reward: Reality or myth? *American Psychologist, 51*, 1153–1166.

Eisenberger, R., & Cameron, J. (1998). Reward, intrinsic interest, and creativity: New findings. *American Psychologist, 53*, 676–679.

Ekman, P. (1972). Universals and cultural differences in the facial expressions of emotion. In J. R. Cole (Ed.), *Nebraska Symposium on Motivation, 1971* (pp. 207–283). Lincoln: University of Nebraska Press.

Ekman, P., & Friesen, W. V. (1971). Constants across cultures in the face and emotion. *Journal of Personality and Social Psychology, 17*, 124–129.

Elias, N. (1969). *Über den Prozess der Zivilisation: Soziogenetische und psychogenetische Untersuchungen* [On the process of civilization: Sociogenetic and psychogenetic investigations]. Berne, Switzerland: Francke.

Elliot, A. J. (1997). Integrating the "classic" and "contemporary" approaches to achievement motivation: A hierarchical model of achievement motivation. In M. Maehr & P. Pintrich (Eds.), *Advances in motivation and achievement* (Vol. 10, pp. 243–279). Greenwich, CT: JAI Press.

Elliot, A. J. (1999). Approach and avoidance motivation and achievement goals. *Educational Psychologist, 34*, 169–189.

Elliot, A. (2005). A conceptual history of the achievement goal construct. In A. J. Elliot & C. S. Dweck (Eds.), *Handbook of competence and motivation* (pp. 52–72). New York: Guilford Press.

Elliot, A. J., & Church, M. (1997). A hierarchical model of approach and avoidance achievement motivation. *Journal of Personality and Social Psychology, 72*, 218–232.

Elliot, A. J., & Harackiewicz, J. (1996). Approach and avoidance achievement goals and intrinsic motivation: A mediational analysis. *Journal of Personality and Social Psychology, 70*, 461–475.

Elliot, A. J., & McGregor, H. A. (2001). A 2×2 achievement goal framework. *Journal of Personality and Social Psychology, 80*, 501–519.

Elliot, E. S., & Dweck, C. (1988). Goals: An approach to motivation and achievement. *Journal of Personality and Social Psychology, 54*, 5–12.

Elliott, M. H. (1928). The effect of change of reward on the maze performance of rats. *University of California Publications in Psychology, 4*, 19–30.

Emmons, R. A. (1986). Personal strivings: An approach to personality and subjective well-being. *Journal of Personality and Social Psychology, 51*, 1058–1068.

Emmons, R. A. (1992). Abstract versus concrete goals: Personal striving level, physical illness and psychological well-being. *Journal of Personality and Social Psychology, 62*, 292–300.

Emmons, R. A. (2003). Personal goals, life meaning and virtue: Wellsprings of a positive life. In C. L. Keyes & J. Haidt (Eds.), *Flourishing: Positive psychology and the life*

well-lived (pp. 105–128). Washington, DC: American Psychological Associaton.

Emmons, R. A., & McAdams, D. (1991). Personal strivings and motive dispositions: Exploring the links. *Personality and Social Psychology Bulletin, 17*, 648–654.

Engeser, S. (2004). *Lernmotivation und volitionale Handlungssteuerung: Eine Längsschnittstudie beim Statistik Lernen im Psychologiestudium* [Learning motivation and volitional action regulation: A longitudinal study on learning elementary statistics]. Unpublished doctoral dissertation, University of Potsdam, Germany.

Engeser, S., Rheinberg, F., Vollmeyer, R., & Bischoff, J. (2005). Motivation, Flow-Erleben und Lernleistung in universitären Lernsettings [Motivation, flow-experience, and performance in learning settings at universities]. *Zeitschrift für Pädagogische Psychologie, 19*, 159–172.

Entin, E. E. (1974). Effects of achievement-oriented and affiliative motives on private and public performance. In J. W. Atkinson & J. O. Raynor (Eds.), *Motivation and achievement* (pp. 219–236). Washington, DC: Winston.

Entwisle, D. R. (1972). To dispel fantasies about fantasy-based measures of achievement motivation. *Psychological Bulletin, 77*, 377–391.

Entwistle, D., & Hayduk, L. (1978). *Too great expectations: Young children's academic outlook.* Baltimore: The John Hopkins University Press.

Epstein, L. H., Truesdale, R., Wojcik, A., Paluch, R. A., & Raynor, H. A. (2003). Effects of deprivation on hedonics and reinforcing value of food. *Physiology & Behavior, 78*, 221–227.

Epstein, S. (1962). The measurement of drive and conflict in humans: Theory and experiment. In M. R. Jones (Ed.), *Nebraska Symposium on Motivation, 1962* (pp. 127–206). Lincoln: University of Nebraska Press.

Epstein, S. (1994). Integration of the cognitive and psychodynamic unconscious. *American Psychologist, 49*, 709–724.

Epstein, S., Pacini, R., Denes-Raj, V., & Heier, H. (1996). Individual differences in intuitive-experiential and analytical-rational thinking styles. *Journal of Personality and Social Psychology, 71*, 390–405.

Ericsson, K. A. (Ed.). (1996). *The road to excellence.* Mahwah, NJ: Erlbaum.

Erikson, E. H. (1963). *Childhood and society* (Rev. ed.). New York: Norton.

Eron, L. D. (1994). Theories of aggression. From drives to cognitions. In L. R. Hues-

mann (Ed.), *Aggressive behaviour: Current perspectives* (pp. 3–11). New York: Plenum.

Escalona, S. K. (1940). The effect of success and failure upon the level of aspiration and behavior in manic-depressive psychoses. *University of Iowa Studies: Child Welfare, 16*, 199–302.

Estes, W. K. (1958). Stimulus-response theory of drive. In M. R. Jones (Ed.), *Nebraska Symposium on Motivation, 1958* (pp. 35–69). Lincoln: University of Nebraska Press.

Everitt, B. J. (1990). Sexual motivation: A neural and behavioural analysis of the mechanisms underlying appetitive and copulatory responses of male rats. *Neuroscience and Biobehavioral Reviews, 14*(2), 217–232.

Exline, R. V. (1962). Need affiliation and initial communication behavior in problem solving groups characterized by low interpersonal visibility. *Psychological Reports, 10*, 79–89.

Eysenck, H. J. (1967). *The biological basis of personality.* Springfield, IL: Charles C Thomas.

Eysenck, H. J. (1990). Biological dimensions of personality. In L. Pervin (Ed.), *Handbook of personality theory and research* (pp. 244–276). New York: Guilford Press.

Falbo, T. (1975). Achievement attributions of kindergarteners. *Developmental Psychology, 11*, 529–530.

Fallo-Mitchell, L., & Ryff, C. D. (1982). Preferred timing of female life events. *Research on Aging, 4*, 249–267.

Fajans, S. (1933). Die Bedeutung der Entfernung für die Stärke eines Aufforderungscharakters beim Säugling und Kleinkind [The meaning of distance for the degree of variance as experienced by the infant]. *Psychologische Forschung, 17*, 215–267.

Farr, J. L., Hofmann, D. A., & Mathieu, J. E. (1993). Job perception, job satisfaction relations: An empirical comparison of three competing theories. *Organizational Behavior and Human Decision, 56*(3), 370–387.

Fazey, J. A., & Hardy, L. (1988). The inverted-U hypothesis: A catastrophe for sport psychology. In *British Association for Sports Sciences Monograph no. 1.* Leeds, England.

Fazio, R. H., & Olson, M. A. (2003). Implicit measures in social cognition research: Their meaning and use. *Annual Review of Psychology, 54*, 297–327.

Fazio, R. H., Sanbonmatsu, D. M., Powell, M. C., & Kardes, F. R. (1986). On the automatic activation of attitudes. *Journal of Personality and Social Psychology, 50*, 229–238.

Feather, N. T. (1959a). Subjective probability and decision under uncertainty. *Psychological Review, 66*, 150–164.

Feather, N. T. (1959b). Success probability and choice behavior. *Journal of Experimental Psychology, 58*, 257–266.

Feather, N. T. (1961). The relationship of persistence at a task to expectation of success and achievement related motives. *Journal of Abnormal and Social Psychology, 63*, 552–561.

Feather, N. T. (1962). The study of persistence. *Psychological Bulletin, 59*, 94–115.

Feather, N. T. (1963b). The relationship of expectation of success to reporter probability, task structure and achievement-related motivation. *Journal of Abnormal and Social Psychology, 66*, 231–238.

Feather, N. T. (1967). Valence of outcome and expectation of success in relation to task difficulty and perceived locus of control. *Journal of Personality and Social Psychology, 7*, 372–386.

Feather, N. T. (Ed.). (1982). *Expectations and actions: Expectancy-value models in psychology.* Hillsdale, NJ: Erlbaum.

Feld, S. C. (1967). Longitudinal study of the origins of achievement strivings. *Journal of Personality and Social Psychology, 7*, 408–414.

Feldman, N. S., Higgins, E. T., Karlovac, M., & Ruble, D. N. (1976). Use of consensus information in causal attribution as a function of temporal presentation and availability of direct information. *Journal of Personality and Social Psychology, 34*, 694–698.

Fenz, W. D. (1975). Strategies for coping with stress. In I. G. Sarason & C. D. Spielberger (Eds.), *Stress and anxiety* (Vol. 2, pp. 305–336). Washington, DC: Hemisphere.

Ferguson, E. D. (1962). Ego involvement: A critical examination of some methodological issues. *Journal of Abnormal and Social Psychology, 64*, 407–417.

Feshbach, S., & Singer, R. D. (1971). *Television and aggression: An experimental field study.* San Francisco: Jossey-Bass.

Festinger, L. (1942). A theoretical interpretation of shifts in level of aspiration. *Psychological Review, 49*, 235–250.

Festinger, L. (1954). A theory of social comparison processes. *Human Relations, 7*, 117–140.

Festinger, L. (1957). *A theory of cognitive dissonance.* Evanston, IL: Row Peterson.

Festinger, L. (1964). *Conflict, decision, and dissonance.* Stanford, CA: Stanford University Press.

Festinger, L., & Carlsmith, J. M. (1959). Cognitive consequences of forced compliance. *Journal of Abnormal and Social Psychology, 58*, 203–210.

Festinger, L., Riecken, H. W., & Schachter, S. (1956). *When prophecy fails.* Minneapolis: University of Minnesota Press.

Fiedler, K. (1982). Causal schemata: Review and criticism of research on a popular construct. *Journal of Personality and Social Psychology, 42*, 1001–1013.

Fiedler, K., & Bless, H. (2002). Soziale Kognition [Social cognition]. In W. Stroebe, K. Jonas, & M. Hewstone (Eds.), *Sozialpsychologie* (4th ed., pp. 125–164). Berlin, Germany: Springer.

Fincham, F., & Jaspars, J. (1979). Attribution of responsibility to the self and other in children and adults. *Journal of Personality and Social Psychology, 37*, 1589–1602.

Fineman, S. (1977). The achievement motive construct and its measurement: Where are we now? *British Journal of Psychology, 68*, 1–2.

Finkel, E. J., & Campbell, W. K. (2001). Self-control and accommodation in close relationships: An interdependence analysis. *Journal of Personality and Social Psychology, 81*, 265–277.

Finkelstein, N. W., & Ramey, C. T. (1977). Learning to control the environment in infancy. *Child Development, 48*, 806–819.

Fisch, R. (1970). *Konfliktmotivation und Examen* [Conflict motivation and examinations]. Meisenheim, Germany: Hain.

Fishbach, A. U., Friedman, R. S., & Kruglanski, A. W. (2003). Leading us not into temptations: Momentary allurements elicit overriding goal activation. *Journal of Personality and Social Psychology, 84*, 296–309.

Fishman, D. B. (1966). Need and expectancy as determinants of affiliative behavior in small groups. *Journal of Personality and Social Psychology, 4*, 155–164.

Fiske, D. W., & Maddi, S. R. (1961). A conceptual framework. In D. W. Fiske & S. R. Maddi (Eds.), *Functions of varied experience* (pp. 11–56). Homewood, IL: Dorsey.

Fitch, G. (1970). Effects of self-esteem, perceived performance, and choice on causal attributions. *Journal of Personality and Social Psychology, 16*, 311–315.

Fitts, P. M., & Posner, M. I. (1967). *Human performance.* Oxford, UK: Brooks(Cole.

Flammer, A., Züblin, C., & Grob, A. (1988). Sekundäre Kontrolle bei Jugendlichen [Secondary control in adolescents].

Zeitschrift für Entwicklungspsychologie und Pädagogische Psychologie, 20, 239–262.

Fleming, A. S., Corter, C., Franks, P., Surbey, M., Schneider, B., & Steiner, M. (1993). Postpartum factors related to mother's attraction to newborn infant odors. *Developmental Psychobiology, 26*(2), 115–132.

Fodor, E. M. (1984). The power motive and reactivity to power stresses. *Journal of Personality and Social Psychology, 47*, 853–859.

Fodor, E. M. (1985). The power motive. *Journal of Personality and Social Psychology, 49*, 1408–1416.

Fodor, E. M., & Carver, R. A. (2000). Achievement and power motives, performance feedback, and creativity. *Journal of Research in Personality, 34*, 380–396.

Fodor, E. M., & Farrow, D. L. (1979). The power motive as an influence on use of power. *Journal of Personality and Social Psychology, 37*, 2091–2097.

Fodor, E. M., & Smith, T. (1982). The power motive as an influence on group decision making. *Journal of Personality and Social Psychology, 42*, 178–185.

Fodor, J. (1983). *The modularity of mind.* Cambridge, MA: MIT Press.

Folkman, S., & Lazarus, R. A. (1980). An analysis of coping in a middle-age community sample. *Journal of Health and Social Behavior, 21*, 219–239.

Folkman, S., & Lazarus, R. S. (1988). *Ways of coping questionnaire: Manual.* Palo Alto, CA: Consulting Psychologists Press.

Forrest, D. W. (1959). The role of muscular tension in the recall of interrupted tasks. *Journal of Experimental Psychology, 58*, 181–184.

Förster, J., & Liberman, N. (2002, June). *Introducing a motivational priming model.* Paper presented at the 13th general meeting of the European Association of Experimental Social Psychology, San Sebastian, Spain.

Försterling, F. (1989). Models of covariation and attribution: How do they relate to the analogy of analysis of variance? *Journal of Personality and Social Psychology, 57*(4), 615–625.

Försterling, F. (2001). *Attribution: An introduction to theories, research and applications.* Hove, England: Psychology Press.

Försterling, F., Bühner, F., & Gall, S. (1998). Attributions of depressed persons: How consistant are they with the covariation principle? *Journal of Personality and Social Psychology, 75*(4), 1047–1061.

Ford, M. E., & Nicholls, C. W. (1987). A taxonomy of human goals and some possible applications. In M. E. Ford & D. H. Ford (Eds.), *Humans as self-constructing systems: Putting the framework to work* (pp. 289–311). Hillsdale, NJ: Erlbaum.

Forrest, D. W. (1959). The role of muscular tension in the recall of interrupted tasks. *Journal of Experimental Psychology, 58*, 181–184.

Fowler, H. (1971). Implications of sensory reinforcement. In R. Glaser (Ed.), *The nature of reinforcement* (pp. 151–195). New York: Academic Press.

Fox, N. A., & Davidson, R. J. (1988). Patterns of brain electrical activity during facial signs of emotion in 10-month-old infants. *Developmental Psychology, 24*, 230–236.

Fox, K., Goudas, M, Biddle S., Duda, J. L., & Armstrong, N. (1994). Children's task and ego goal profiles in sport. *British Journal of Educational Psychology, 64*, 253–261.

Frank, J. D. (1935). Individual differences in certain aspects of the level of aspiration. *American Journal of Psychology, 47*, 119–128.

Freedman, J. L. (1965) Preference for dissonant information. *Journal of Personality and Social Psychology, 2*, 287–289.

Freeman, G. L. (1930). Changes in tonus during completed and interrupted mental work. *Journal of Genetic Psychology, 4*, 309–334.

Freitas, A. L., Liberman, N., & Higgins, E. T. (2002). Regulatory fit and temptation during goal pursuit. *Journal of Experimental Social Psychology, 38*, 291–298.

French, E. G. (1955). Some characteristics of achievement motivation. *Journal of Experimental Psychology, 50*, 232–236.

French, E. G. (1956). Motivation as a variable in workpartner selection. *Journal of Abnormal and Social Psychology, 53*, 96–99.

French, E. G. (1958a). Development of a measure of complex motivation. In J. W. Atkinson (Ed.), *Motives in fantasy, action, and society* (pp. 242–248). Princeton, NJ: Van Nostrand.

French, E. G. (1958b). Effects of the interaction of motivation and feedback on task performance. In J. W. Atkinson (Ed.), *Motives in fantasy, action, and society* (pp. 400–408). Princeton, NJ: Van Nostrand.

French, E. G., & Chadwick, I. (1956). Some characteristics of affiliation motivation. *Journal of Abnormal and Social Psychology, 52*, 296–300.

French, E. G., & Lesser, G. S. (1964). Some characteristics of the achievement motive in women. *Journal of Abnormal and Social Psychology, 68*, 119–128.

French, J. A., Kamil, A. C., & Leger, D. (Eds.). (2001). Evolutionary psychology and motivation. In *Nebraska Symposium on Motivation: Vol. 47* (p. 221). Lincoln: University of Nebraska Press.

French, J. R. P., & Raven B. H. (1959). The basis of social power. In D. Cartwright (Ed.), *Studies in social power* (pp. 150–167). Ann Arbor: University of Michigan.

Freud, S. (1895). Entwurf einer Psychologie [Outline of a psychological science]. In: S. Freud (Ed.), *From the beginnings of psychology* (pp. 370–466). London: Imago Publishing.

Freud, S. (1901). Zur Psychopathologie des Alltagslebens [The psychopathology of everyday life]. In *Gesammelte Werke, Vol. IV (1952)*. Frankfurt, Germany: Fischer.

Freud, S. (1915). *Triebe und Triebschicksale* [Drives and their fate]. Gesammelte Werke, Bd. X. Frankfurt: Fischer, 1952.

Freud, S. (1926). *Hemmung, Symptom, Angst* [Inhibition, symptom, anxiety]. Gesammelte Werke, Bd. XIV. Frankfurt: Fischer, 1952.

Freud, S. (1952). Die Abwehrneuropsychosen [The neuropsychoses of defense]. In *Gesammelte Werke, Vol. I (1894)*. Frankfurt, Germany: Fischer.

Freud, S. (1952). Die Traumdeutung [The interpretation of dreams]. In *Gesammelte Werke, Vol. II–III (1900)*. Frankfurt, Germany: Fischer.

Freud, S. (1952). Hemmung, Symptom, Angst [Inhibition, symptoms and anxiety]. In *Gesammelte Werke, Vol. XIV (1926)*. Frankfurt, Germany: Fischer.

Freud, S. (1952). Triebe und Triebschicksale [Instincts and their vicissitudes]. In *Gesammelte Werke, Vol. X (1915)*. Frankfurt, Germany: Fischer.

Freud, S. (1961). Drei Abhandlungen zur Sexualtheorie [Three essays on the theory of sexuality]. In *Gesammelte Werke, Vol. V (3rd ed.) (1905)*. Frankfurt, Germany: Fischer.

Freud, S. (1963). Das Unbehagen in der Kultur [Civilization and its discontents]. In *Gesammelte Werke, Vol. XIV (3rd ed.) (1930)*. Frankfurt, Germany: Fischer.

Freund, A. M., & Baltes, P. B. (2000). The orchestration of selection, optimization and compensation: An action-theoretical conceptualization of a theory of developmental regulation. In W. J. Perrig & A. Grob (Eds.), *Control of human behavior, mental processes, and consciousness: Essays in honor of the 60th birthday of August Flammer* (pp. 35–58). Mahwah, NJ: Erlbaum.

Frey, D. (1981). *Informationssuche und Informationsbewertung bei Entscheidungen* [The search for and evaluation of information in decision making]. Stuttgart, Germany: Huber.

Frey, D., & Irle, M. (1972). Some conditions to produce a dissonance and an incentive effect in a "forced-compliance" situation. *European Journal of Social Psychology, 2*, 45–54.

Frey, K. S., & Ruble, D. N. (1985). What children say when the teacher is not around: Conflicting goals in social comparison and performance assessment in the classroom. *Journal of Personality and Social Psychology, 48*, 550–562.

Frey, R. S. (1984). Does n-achievement cause economic development? A cross-lagged panel analysis of the McClelland thesis. *Journal of Social Psychology, 122*, 67–70.

Friedman, J. M., & Halaas, J. L. (1998). Leptin and the regulation of body weight in mammals. *Nature, 395*(6704), 763–770.

Fries, S. (2002). *Wollen und Können* [Volition and ability]. Münster, Germany: Waxmann.

Fries, S., Lund, B., & Rheinberg, F. (1999). Lässt sich das Training induktiven Denkens durch gleichzeitige Motivförderung optimieren? [Does simultaneous motive modification optimise the teaching of inductive reasoning?]. *Zeitschrift für Pädagogische Psychologie, 13*, 37–49.

Frijda, N. H. (1986). *The emotions*. Cambridge, UK: Cambridge University Press.

Frijda, N. H. (1988). The laws of emotion. *American Psychologist, 43*, 249–358.

Fuchs, R. (1954). *Gewißheit, Motivation und bedingter Reflex* [Certainty, motivation, and conditioned reflex]. Meisenheim, Germany: Hain.

Fuhrmann, A., & Kuhl, J. (1998). Maintaining a healthy diet: Effects of personality and self-reward versus self-punishment on commitment to and enactment of self-chosen and assigned goals. *Psychology and Health, 13*, 651–686.

Fuster, J. M. (2001). The prefrontal cortex – an update: Time is of the essence. *Neuron, 30*(2), 319–333.

Fyans, L. J., Salili, M., Maehr, M. L., & Desai, K. A. (1983). A cross-cultural exploration into the meaning of achievement. *Journal of Personality and Social Psychology, 44*, 1000–1013.

Gagné, F. M., & Lydon, J. E. (2001a). Mind-set and close relationships: When bias leads to (in)accurate predictions. *Journal of Personality and Social Psychology, 81*, 85–96.

Gagné, F. M., & Lydon, J. E. (2001b). Mindset and relationship illusions: The moderating effects of domain specificity and relationship commitment. *Personality and Social Psychology Bulletin, 27*, 1144–1155.

Gagné, F. M., Lydon, J. E., & Bartz, J. A. (2003). Effects of mindset on the predictive validity of relationship constructs. *Canadian Journal of Behavioral Science, 35*, 292–304.

Galbraith, J., & Cummings, L. (1967). An empiric investigation of the motivational determinants of past performance: Interactive effects between instrumentality-valence, motivation, and ability. *Organizational Behavior and Human Performance, 2*, 237–257.

Galinsky, A. D., Gruenfeld, D. H., & Magee, J. C. (2003). From power to action. *Journal of Personality and Social Psychology, 85*, 453–466.

Gardner, H. (1983). *Frames of mind.* New York: Basic Books.

Garland, H. (1984). Relation of effort-performance expectancy to performance in goal-setting experiments. *Journal of Applied Psychology, 69*, 79–84.

Gaugele, H., & Ullmer, C. (1990). *Zur Anreizstruktur des Bodybuildings* [The incentive structure of body building]. Unpublished manuscript, University of Heidelberg, Germany.

Gavin, J. F. (1970). Ability, effort, and role perception as antecedents of job performance. *Experimental Publication System (Manuscript no. 190A), 5.*

Gawrilow, C., & Gollwitzer, P. M. (2004, April). *Inhibition fortlaufender Reaktionen durch Vorsätze bei ADHS Kindern* [Inhibition of continuous reactions in ADHD children]. Paper presented at the symposium "Recent developments in research on implementation intentions" at the 46th meeting of the Tagung experimentell arbeitender Psychologen (TeaP), Giessen, Germany.

Gebhard, M. (1948). Effects of success and failure upon the attractiveness of activities as a function of experience, expectation, and need. *Journal of Experimental Psychology, 38*, 371–388.

Gehlen, A. (1958). *Der Mensch: Seine Natur und seine Stellung in der Welt* [The human being: His nature and status in the world]. Bonn, Germany: Athenäum.

Georgopolous, B. S., Mahony, G. M., & Jones, N. W. (1957). A path-goal approach to productivity. *Journal of Applied Psychology, 41*, 345–353.

Geppert, U., & Gartmann, D. (1983, July). *The emergence of self evaluative emotions as consequences of achievement actions.* Paper presented at the meeting of the International Society for the Study of Behavioral Development, Munich, Germany.

Geppert, U., & Heckhausen, H. (1990). Ontogenese der Emotion [Ontogenesis of emotion]. In K. R. Scherer (Ed.), *Enzyklopädie der Psychologie: Psychologie der Emotion* (Vol. IV, No. 3, pp. 115–213). Göttingen, Germany: Hogrefe.

Geppert, U., & Küster, U. (1983). The emergence of "wanting to do it oneself": A precursor of achievement motivation. *International Journal of Behavioral Development, 6*, 355–370.

Gianotti, M., Roca, P., & Palou, A. (1988). Body weight and tissue composition in rats made obese by a cafeteria diet: Effect of 24 hours starvation. *Hormone and Metabolic Research, 20*(4), 208–212.

Gigerenzer, G. (2000). *Adaptive thinking: Rationality in the real world.* London: Oxford University Press.

Gigerenzer, G., Todd, P. M., & the ABC Research Group. (1999). *Simple heuristics that make us smart.* New York: Oxford University Press.

Gilligan, S. G. (1997). *The courage to love: Principles and practices of self-relations psychotherapy.* New York: Norton.

Gjesme, T. (1971). Motive to achieve success and motive to avoid failure in relation to school performance for pupils of different ability levels. *Scandinavian Journal of Educational Research, 15*, 81–99.

Gjesme, T., & Nygard, R. (1970). *Achievement-related motives: Theoretical considerations and construction of a measuring instrument.* Unpublished manuscript, University of Oslo, Norway.

Glixman, A. F. (1948). An analysis of the use of the interruption-technique in experimental studies of "repression." *Psychological Bulletin, 45*, 491–506.

Goldberg, L. R. (1982). From ace to zombie: Some explorations in the language of personality. In C. D. Spielberger & J. N. Butcher (Eds.), *Advances in personality assessment* (Vol. 1, pp. 203–234). Hillsdale, NJ: Erlbaum.

Goleman, D. (1994). *Emotional intelligence.* London: Bloomsbury.

Gollwitzer, P. M. (1987). Suchen, Finden und Festigen der eigenen Identität: Unstillbare Zielintentionen [Searching, finding, and consolidating of one's own identity:

Unsaturatable goal intentions]. In H. Heckhausen, P. M. Gollwitzer, & F. E. Weinert (Eds.), *Jenseits des Rubikon: Der Wille in den Humanwissenschaften* (pp. 176–189). Berlin, Germany: Springer.

Gollwitzer, P. M. (1990). Action phases and mind-sets. In E. T. Higgins & R. M. Sorrentino (Eds.), *Handbook of motivation and cognition: Foundations of social behavior* (Vol. 2, pp. 53–92). New York: Guilford Press.

Gollwitzer, P. M. (1991). *Abwägen und Planen* [Consideration and planning]. Göttingen, Germany: Hogrefe.

Gollwitzer, P. M. (1993). Goal achievement: the role of intentions. *European Review of Social Psychology, 4*, 141–185.

Gollwitzer, P. M. (1998). *Implicit and explicit processes in goal pursuit.* Paper presented at the annual meeting of the Society of Experimental Social Psychology, Lexington, KY.

Gollwitzer, P. M. (1999). Implementation intentions: Strong effects of simple plans. *Journal of Personality and Social Psychology, 73*, 186–197.

Gollwitzer, P. M. (2003). Why we thought that action mind-sets affect illusions of control. *Psychological Inquiry, 14*, 261–269.

Gollwitzer, P. M., & Bargh, J. A. (Eds.). (1996). *The psychology of action: Linking cognition and motivation to behavior.* New York: Guilford Press.

Gollwitzer, P. M., & Bayer, U. (1999). Deliberative versus implemental mindsets in the control of action. In S. Chaiken & Y. Trope (Eds.), *Dual-process theories in social psychology* (pp. 403–422). New York: Guilford Press.

Gollwitzer, P. M., & Bayer, U. (2000). *Becoming a better person without changing yourself.* Paper presented at the Self and Identity Pre-conference of the annual meeting of the Society of Experimental Social Psychology, Atlanta, GA.

Gollwitzer, P. M., Bayer, U., & McCulloch, C. (2003). The control of the unwanted. In R. Hassin, J. Uleman, & J. A. Bargh (Eds.), *The new unconscious* (pp. 485–515). Oxford, UK: Oxford University Press.

Gollwitzer, P. M., Bayer, U., Steller, B., & Bargh, J. A. (2002). *Delegating control to the environment: Perception, attention and memory for preselected behavioral cues.* Unpublished manuscript, University of Konstanz, Germany.

Gollwitzer, P. M., & Brandstätter, V. (1997). Implementation intentions and effective goal pursuit. *Journal of Personality and Social Psychology, 73*, 186–199.

Gollwitzer, P. M., Fujita, K., & Oettingen, G. (2004). Planning and the implementation of goals. In R. Baumeister & K. Vohs (Eds.), *Handbook of self-regulation* (pp. 211–228). New York: Guilford Press.

Gollwitzer, P. M., Heckhausen, H., & Ratajczak, H. (1990). From weighing to willing: Approaching a change decision through pre- or postdecisional mentation. *Organizational Behavior and Human Decision Processes, 45*, 41–65.

Gollwitzer, P. M., Heckhausen, H., & Steller, B. (1990). Deliberative and implemental mind-sets: Cognitive tuning toward congruous thoughts and information. *Journal of Personality and Social Psychology, 59*, 1119–1127.

Gollwitzer, P. M., & Kirchhof, O. (1998). The willful pursuit of identity. In J. Heckhausen & C. S. Dweck (Eds.), *Motivation and self-regulation across the life span* (pp. 389–423). New York: Cambridge University Press.

Gollwitzer, P. M., & Kinney, R. F. (1989). Effects of deliberative and implemental mind-sets on illusion of control. *Journal of Personality and Social Psychology, 56*, 531–542.

Gollwitzer, P. M., & Moskowitz, G. B. (1996). Goal effects on action and cognition. In E. T. Higgins & A. W. Kruglanski (Eds.), *Social psychology: Handbook of basic principles* (pp. 361–399). New York: Guilford Press.

Gollwitzer, P. M., & Schaal, B. (1998). Metacognition in action: The importance of implementation intentions. *Personality and Social Psychology Review, 2*, 124–136.

Gollwitzer, P. M., Trötschel, R., Bayer, U., & Sumner, M. (2004). *Potential costs of self-regulation by implementation intentions: Rebound and ego-depletion effects?* Unpublished manuscript, University of Konstanz, Germany.

Gollwitzer, P. M., & Wicklund, R. A. (1985a). Self-symbolizing and the neglect of others' perspectives. *Journal of Personality and Social Psychology, 48*, 702–715.

Gollwitzer, P. M., & Wicklund, A. (1985b). *The pursuit of self-defining goals. Action control: from cognition to behavior* (pp. 61–85). Berlin, Germany: Springer.

Goodenough, F. L. (1931). *Anger in young children.* Minneapolis: University of Minnesota Press.

Goodman, P. S., Rose, J. H., & Furcon, J. E. (1970). Comparison of motivational antecedents of the work performance of scientists and engineers. *Journal of Applied Psychology, 54*, 491–495.

Goodstadt, B. E., & Hjelle, L. A. (1973). Power to the powerless: Locus of control and the use of power. *Journal of Personality and Social Psychology, 27*, 190–196.

Goschke, T. (1997a). Zur Funktionsanalyse des Willens: Integration kognitions-, motivations- und neuropsychologischer Perspektiven [On the functional architecture of volitional action: Integration of cognitive, motivational, and neuropsychological perspectives]. *Psychologische Beiträge, 39*, 375–412.

Goschke, T. (1997b). Implicit learning of perceptual and motor sequences: Evidence for independent learning systems. In M. Stadler & P. French (Eds.), *Handbook of implicit learning* (pp. 401–444). Thousand Oaks, CA: Sage.

Goschke, T., & Kuhl, J. (1993). The representation of intentions: Persisting activation in memory. *Journal of Experimental Psychology: Learning, Memory, and Cognition, 19*, 1211–1226.

Gottfredson, L. S. (1981). Circumscription and compromise: A developmental theory of occupational aspirations. *Journal of Counseling Psychology, 28*(6), 545–579.

Gottlieb, G. (1991). Experiential canalization of behavioral development theory. *Developmental Psychology, 27*, 4–13.

Gottschaldt, K. (1926). Über den Einfluss der Erfahrung auf die Wahrnehmung von Figuren [On the influence of past experience on perception]. *Psychologische Forschung, 8*, 261–317.

Gough, H. G. (1990). The California Psychological Inventory. In C. E. Watkins & V. L. Campbell (Eds.), *Testing in counselling practice* (pp. 37–62). Hillsdale, NJ: Erlbaum.

Graen, G. (1969). Instrumentality theory of work motivation: Some experimental results and suggested modifications. *Journal of Applied Psychology Monographs, 53*, 1–25.

Graham, J. M., & Desjardins, C. (1980). Classical conditioning: Induction of luteinizing hormone and testosterone secretion in anticipation of sexual activity. *Science, 210*, 1039–1041.

Graham, S., & Hudley, C. (1994). Attributions of aggressive and nonaggressive African-American male early adolescents: A study of construct accessibility. *Developmental Psychology, 30*, 365–373.

Graham, S., Hudley, C., & Williams, E. (1992). Attributional and emotional determinants of aggression among African-American and Latino young adolescents. *Developmental Psychology, 28*, 731–740.

Graham, S., Weiner, B., & Benesh-Weiner, M. (1995). An attributional analysis of the development of excuse giving in aggressive and nonaggressive African American boys. *Developmental Psychology, 31*(2), 274–284.

Gray, J. A. (1971). *The psychology of fear and stress.* New York: McGraw-Hill.

Gray, J. A. (1981). A critique of Eysenck's theory of personality. In H. J. Eysenck (Ed.), *A model for personality* (pp. 246–276). Berlin, Germany: Springer.

Gray, J. A. (1982). *The psychology of fear and stress.* Cambridge, UK: Cambridge University Press.

Gray, J. A., & McNaughton, N. (2000). *The neuropsychology of anxiety* (2nd ed.). Oxford, UK: Oxford University Press.

Graziano, W. G., & Eisenberg, N. H. (1997). Agreeableness: A dimension of personality. In R. Hogan, J. Johnson, & S. Briggs (Eds.), *Handbook of personality psychology* (pp. 793–825). San Diego, CA: Academic Press.

Green, D. (1963). Volunteering and the recall of interrupted tasks. *Journal of Abnormal and Social Psychology, 66*, 397–401.

Greenfield, P. M., Keller, H., Fuligni, A., & Maynard, A. (2002). Cultural pathways through universal development. *Annual Review of Psychology, 54*, 461–490.

Greenough, A., Cole, G., Lewis, J., Lockton, A., & Blundell, J. (1998). Untangling the effects of hunger, anxiety, and nausea on energy intake during intravenous cholecystokinin octapeptide (cck-8) infusion. *Physiology & Behavior, 65*(2), 303–310.

Greenwald, A. G. (1982). Ego task analysis: An integration of research on ego-involvement and self-awareness. In A. Hastorf & A. Isen (Eds.), *Cognitive social psychology* (pp. 109–147). New York: Elsevier.

Greenwald, A. G., & Banaji, M. R. (1995). Implicit social cognition: Attitudes, self-esteem, and stereotypes. *Psychological Review, 102*, 4–27.

Greenwald, A. G., Banaji, M. R., Rudman, L. A., Farnham, S. D., Nosek, B. A., & Mellott, D. S. (2002). A unified theory of implicit attitudes, stereotypes, self-esteem, and self-concept. *Psychological Review, 109*, 3–25.

Greenwald, A. G., McGhee, D. E., & Schwartz, J. L. K. (1998). Measuring individual differences in implicit cognition: The Implicit Association Test. *Journal of Personality and Social Psychology, 74*, 1464–1480.

Greve, W., & Wentura, D. (2003). Immunizing the self: Self-concept stabilization through reality-adaptive self-definitions. *Personality and Social Psychology Bulletin, 29*, 39–50.

Grinker, J. (1969). Cognitive control of classical eyelid conditioning. In P. G. Zimbardo (Ed.), *The cognitive control of motivation* (pp. 126–135). Glenview, IL: Scott, Foresman.

Grob, A., Krings, F., & Bangerter, A. (2001). Life markers in biographical narratives of people from three cohorts: A life span perspective in its historical context. *Human Development, 44*(4), 171–190.

Groeben, N., Wahl, D., Schlee, J., & Scheele, B. (1988). *Das Forschungsprogramm Subjektive Theorien. Eine Einführung in die Psychologie des reflexiven Subjekts* [Research on subjective theories. An introduction to the psychology of the reflexive subject]. Tübingen, Germany: Francke.

Groos, K. (1899). *Die Spiele des Menschen* [The play of man]. Jena, Germany: Fischer.

Gubler, H., Paffrath, M., & Bischof, N. (1994). Untersuchungen zur Systemanalyse der sozialen Motivation III: Eine Aestimationsstudie zur Sicherheits- und Erregungsregulation während der Adoleszenz [An estimation study of security and arousal regulation during adolescence]. *Zeitschrift für Psychologie, 202*, 95–132.

Guevara, M. L. (1994). *Alienation und Selbstkontrolle: Das Ignorieren eigener Gefühle* [Alienation and self-control: Ignoring one's own feelings]. Berne, Switzerland: Lang.

Guinote, A., Judd, C. M., & Brauer, M. (2002). Effects of power on perceived and objective group variability: Evidence that more powerful groups are more variable. *Journal of Personality and Social Psychology, 82*, 708–721.

Gupta, B. S., & Nagpal, M. (1978). Impulsivity (sociability and reinforcement in verbal operant conditioning. *British Journal of Psychology, 69*, 203–206.

Gurack, E. (1978). *Die Entwicklung des Fähigkeitskonzepts im Vorschulalter* [The development of the ability concept at preschool age]. Unpublished Diplom thesis, University of Bochum, Germany.

Haase, C. M., Heckhausen, J., & Köller, O. (2007). Goal engagement during the school-work transition: Beneficial for all, particularly for girls. *Journal of Research on Adolescence.*

Haber, R. N. (1958). Discrepancy from adaptation level as a source of affect. *Journal of Experimental Psychology, 56*, 370–375.

Haber, R. N., & Alpert, R. (1958). The role of situation and picture cues in projective measurement of the achievement motive. In J. W. Atkinson (Ed.), *Motives in fantasy, action, and society* (pp. 644–663). Princeton, NJ: Van Nostrand.

Hackman, J. R., & Porter, L. W. (1968). Expectancy theory predictions of work effectiveness. *Organizational Behavior and Human Performance, 3*, 417–426.

Haffner, S. (2003). *Historische Variationen* [Historical variations]. Munich, Germany: dtv.

Haider, M. (1969). Elektrophysiologische Indikatoren der Aktiviertheit [Electrophysiological indicators of activation]. In W. Schönpflug (Ed.), *Methoden der Aktivierungsforschung* (pp. 125–156). Berne, Switzerland: Huber.

Halisch, C., & Halisch, F. (1980). Kognitive Voraussetzungen frühkindlicher Selbstbewertungsreaktionen nach Erfolg und Misserfolg [Cognitive prerequisites of self-evaluative reactions after success and failure in early childhood]. *Zeitschrift für Entwicklungspsychologie und Pädagogische Psychologie, 12*, 193–212.

Halisch, F. (1986). *Operante und respondente Verfahren zur Messung des Leistungsmotivs* [Operant and respondent measures for the assessment of need for achievement]. Munich, Germany: Max Planck Institute for Psychological Research.

Halisch, F., & Geppert, U. (2001a). Motives, personal goals, and life satisfaction in old age: First results from the Munich Twin Study (GOLD). In *Trends and prospects in motivation research* (pp. 389–409). Dordrecht, Netherlands: Kluwer.

Halisch, F., & Geppert, U. (2001b). Genetic vs. environmental determinants of traits, motives, self-referential cognitions, and volitional control in old age: First results from the Munich Twin Study (GOLD). In *Trends and prospects in motivation research* (pp. 359–387). Dordrecht, Netherlands: Kluwer.

Halisch, F., & Heckhausen, H. (1977). Search for feedback information and effort regulation during task performance. *Journal of Personality and Social Psychology, 35*, 724–733.

Halisch, F., & Heckhausen, H. (1988). Motive-dependent vs. ability-dependent valence functions for success and failure. In F. Halisch & J. van den Bercken (Eds.), *Intentional perspectives on achievement and task motivation.* Lisse, Netherlands: Swets & Zeitlinger.

Halisch, F., & Kuhl, J. (Eds.). (1986). *Motivation, intention, and volition.* Berlin, Germany: Springer.

Hamburg, D. A. (1963). Emotions in the perspective of human evolution. In P. H. Knapp (Ed.), *Expression of emotions in man* (pp. 300–317). New York: International University Press.

Hamilton, J. O. (1974). Motivation and risk-taking behavior. *Journal of Personality and Social Psychology, 29*, 856–864.

Hamilton, V. L. (1980). Intuitive psychologist or intuitive lawyer? *Journal of Personality and Social Psychology, 39*, 767–772.

Hamilton, W. D. (1964). The genetical evolution of social behavior. *Journal of Theoretical Biology, 7*, 17–52.

Hansen, R. D., & Stonner, D. M. (1978). Attributes and attributions: Inferring stimulus properties, actors' dispositions, and causes. *Journal of Personality and Social Psychology, 36*, 657–667.

Harackiewicz, J. M., Barron, K. E., & Elliot, A. (1998). Rethinking achievement goals: When are they adaptive for college students and why? *Educational Psychologist, 33*(1), 1–21.

Harackiewicz, J. M., Barron, K. E., Tauer, J. M., & Elliot, A. (2002). Predicting succes in college: A longitudinal study of achievement goals and ability measure as predictors of interest and performance from freshman year through graduation. *Journal of Educational Psychology, 94*, 562–575.

Harackiewicz, J. M., & Elliot, A. (1993). Achievement goals and intrinsic motivation. *Journal of Personality and Social Psychology, 65*, 904–915.

Harcourt, A. H. (1987). Dominance and fertility among female primates. *Journal of Zoology, 213*, 471–487.

Harcourt, A. H. (1989). Social influences on competitive ability: Alliances and their consequences. In V. Standen & R. A. Foley (Eds.), *Comparative socioecology – The behavioural ecology of humans and other mammals* (pp. 223–242). Oxford, UK: Blackwell.

Hardy, K. R. (1957). Determinants of conformity and attitude change. *Journal of Abnormal and Social Psychology, 54*, 289–294.

Hardyck, J. A., & Braden, M. (1962). Prophecy fails again: A report of a failure to replicate. *Journal of Abnormal and Social Psychology, 65*, 136–141.

Harlow, H. F. (1950). Learning and satiation of response in intrinsically motivated complex puzzle performance by monkeys. *Journal of Comparative and Physiological Psychology, 43*, 289–294.

Harlow, H. F. (1953). Motivation as a factor in the acquisition of new responses. In *Current theory and research in motivation: A symposium.* (pp. 24–49). Lincoln: University of Nebraska Press.

Harlow, H. F. (1971). *Learning to love.* San Francisco: Abbion.

Harlow, H. F., & Harlow, M. H. (1966). Learning how to care. *American Scientist, 54,* 244–272.

Harlow, H. F., & Zimmermann, R. (1959). Affectional responses in the infant monkey. *Science, 130,* 421–432.

Harmon-Jones, E. (2000). Cognitive dissonance and experienced negative affect: Evidence that dissonance increases experienced negative affect even in the absence of aversive consequences. *Personality and Social Psychology Bulletin, 26,* 1490–1501.

Harmon-Jones, E., & Harmon-Jones, C. (2002). Testing the action-based model of cognitive dissonance: The effect of action-orientation on post-decisional attitudes. *Personality and Social Psychology Bulletin, 28,* 711–723.

Harris, B. (1979). Whatever happened to little Albert? *American Psychologist, 34,* 151–160.

Harris, J. R. (1995). Where is the child's environment? A group socialization theory of development. *Psychological Review, 102,* 458–489.

Harter, S. (1974). Pleasure derived from cognitive challenge and mastery. *Child Development, 45,* 661–669.

Harter, S. (1978). Effectance motivation reconsidered. *Human Development, 21,* 34–64.

Hartshorne, H., & May, M. A. (1928). *Studies in the nature of character (Vol. 1). Studies in deceit.* New York: Macmillan.

Hartshorne, H., & May, M. A. (1929). *Studies in the nature of character (Vol. 2). Studies in service and self-control.* New York: Macmillan.

Hautzinger, M. (1994). Action control in the context of psychopathological disorders. In J. Kuhl & J. Beckmann (Eds.), *Volition and personality: Action versus state orientation* (pp. 209–215). Seattle, WA: Hogrefe.

Havighurst, R. J. (1953). *Human development and education.* London: Longmans.

Hayashi, T., & Yamauchi, K. (1964). The relation of children's need for achievement to their parents' home discipline in regard to independence and mastery. *Bulletin of Kyoto Gakugei University, A25,* 31–40.

Hebb, D. O. (1946). On the nature of fear. *Psychological Review, 53,* 259–276.

Hebb, D. O. (1949). *The organization of behavior.* New York: Wiley.

Hebb, D. O. (1953). Heredity and environment in mammalian behavior. *British Journal of Animal Behavior, 1,* 43–47.

Hebb, D. O. (1955). Drives and the C. N. S. (conceptual nervous system). *Psychological Review, 62,* 243–254.

Heckhausen, H. (1955). Motivationsanalyse der Anspruchsniveau-Setzung [Motivational analysis of the setting of levels of aspiration]. *Psychologische Forschung, 25,* 118–154.

Heckhausen, H. (1960). Die Problematik des Projektionsbegriffs und die Grundlagen und Grundannahmen des Thematischen Auffassungstests [The problems surrounding the concept of projection and the basic assumptions of the Thematic Apperception Test]. *Psychologische Beiträge, 5,* 53–80.

Heckhausen, H. (1963a). *Hoffnung und Furcht in der Leistungsmotivation* [Hope and fear in achievement motivation]. Meisenheim(Glan, Germany: Hain.

Heckhausen, H. (1963b). Eine Rahmentheorie der Motivation in zehn Thesen [A framework theory of motivation in ten theses]. *Zeitschrift für experimentelle und angewandte Psychologie, 10,* 604–626.

Heckhausen, H. (1964a). Über die Zweckmäßigkeit einiger Situationsbedingungen bei der inhaltsanalytischen Erfassung der Motivation [On the suitability of some situational conditions in the content-based assessment of motivation]. *Psychologische Forschung, 27,* 244–259.

Heckhausen, H. (1964b). Entwurf einer Psychologie des Spielens. *Psychologische Forschung, 27,* 225–243.

Heckhausen, H. (1965). Leistungsmotivation [Achievement motivation]. In H. Thomae (Ed.), *Handbuch der Psychologie* (Vol. II, pp. 602–702). Göttingen, Germany: Hogrefe.

Heckhausen, H. (1967). *The anatomy of achievement motivation.* New York: Academic Press.

Heckhausen, H. (1968). Achievement motive research: Current problems and some contributions toward a general theory of motivation. In W. J. Arnold (Ed.), *Nebraska Symposium on Motivation, 1968* (pp. 103–174). Lincoln: University of Nebraska Press.

Heckhausen, H. (1969). *Allgemeine Psychologie in Experimenten* [General psychology in experiments]. Göttingen, Germany: Hogrefe.

Heckhausen, H. (1972). Die Interaktion der Sozialisationsvariablen in der Genese des Leistungsmotivs [The interaction of socialization variables in the genesis of the achievement motive]. In C. F. Graumann (Ed.), *Handbuch der Psychologie* (Vol. 7/2, pp. 955–1019). Göttingen, Germany: Hogrefe.

Heckhausen, H. (1973). Intervening cognitions in motivation. In D. Berlyne & K. B. Madsen (eds.), *Pleasure, reward, and preference* (pp. 217–242). New York: Academic Press.

Heckhausen, H. (1974a). *Leistung und Chancengleichheit* [Achievement and equality of opportunity]. Göttingen, Germany: Hogrefe.

Heckhausen, H. (1974b). *Motivationsanalysen* [Analyses of motivation]. Berlin, Germany: Springer.

Heckhausen, H. (1975a). *Effort expenditure, aspiration level and self-evaluation before and after unexpected performance shifts.* Unpublished manuscript, University of Bochum, Germany.

Heckhausen, H. (1975b). Fear of failure as a self-reinforcing motive system. In I. G. Sarason & C. Spielberger (Eds.), *Stress and anxiety* (Vol. II, pp. 117–128). Washington, DC: Hemisphere.

Heckhausen, H. (1977a). Achievement motivation and its constructs: A cognitive model. *Motivation and Emotion, 1*(4), 283–329.

Heckhausen, H. (1977b). Motivation: Kognitionspsychologische Aufspaltung eines summarischen Konstrukts [Motivation: Splitting a summary construct along the lines of cognitive psychology]. *Psychologische Rundschau, 28,* 175–189.

Heckhausen, H. (1978). Selbstbewertung nach erwartungswidrigem Leistungsverlauf: Einfluß von Motiv, Kausalattribution und Zielsetzung [Self-evaluation after unexpected performances: Influence of motives, causal attributions, and goal selection]. *Zeitschrift für Entwicklungspsychologie und Pädagogische Psychologie, 10,* 191–216.

Heckhausen, H. (1980). *Motivation und Handeln* [Motivation and action]. Berlin, Germany: Springer.

Heckhausen, H. (1981). Neuere Entwicklungen in der Motivationsforschung [Recent developments in motivation research]. In W. Michaelis (Ed.), *Bericht über den 32. Kongreß der Deutschen Gesellschaft für Psychologie, Zürich 1980* (pp. 325–335). Göttingen, Germany: Hogrefe.

Heckhausen, H. (1982). The development of achievement motivation. In W. W. Hartup (Ed.), *Review of child development research* (pp. 600–668). Chicago: The University of Chicago Press.

Heckhausen, H. (1983a). Motivationsmodelle: Fortschreitende Entfaltung und unbehobene Mängel [Models of motivation: Progressive development and remaining shortcomings]. In W. Hacker, W. Volpert, & M. V. Cranach (Eds.), *Kognitive und motivationale Aspekte der Handlung* (pp. 9–17). Berlin, Germany: VEB Deutscher Verlag der Wissenschaften.

Heckhausen, H. (1983b). Entwicklungsschritte in der Kausalattribution von Handlungsergebnissen [Developmental stages in the causal attribution of action outcomes]. *Kindliche Erklärungsmuster: Entwicklungspsychologische Beiträge zur Attributionsforschung, 1,* 49–85.

Heckhausen, H. (1984a). Attributionsmuster für Leistungsergebnisse: Individuelle Unterschiede, mögliche Arten und deren Genese [Attribution patterns for performance outcomes: Individual differences, possible types, and their development]. In F. E. Weinert & R. H. Kluwe (Eds.), *Metakognition, Motivation und Lernen* (pp. 133–164). Stuttgart: Kohlhammer.

Heckhausen, H. (1984b). Emergent achievement behavior: Some early developments. In J. Nicholls (Ed.), *Advances in achievement motivation* (pp. 1–32). Greenwich, CT: JAI Press.

Heckhausen, H. (1987a). Wünschen – Wählen – Wollen [Wishing – weighing – willing]. In H. Heckhausen, P. M. Gollwitzer, & F. E. Weinert (Eds.), *Jenseits des Rubikon: Der Wille in den Humanwissenschaften* (pp. 3–9). Berlin, Germany: Springer.

Heckhausen, H. (1987b). Perspektiven einer Psychologie des Wollens [Perspectives on a psychology of the will]. In H. Heckhausen, P.M. Gollwitzer, & F.E. Weinert (Eds.), *Jenseits des Rubikon: Der Wille in den Humanwissenschaften* (pp. 121–142). Berlin, Germany: Springer.

Heckhausen, H. (1987c). Vorsatz, Wille und Bedürfnis: Lewins frühes Vermächtnis und ein zugeschütteter Rubikon [Intention, will, and need: Lewin's early legacy and a missed Rubicon]. In H. Heckhausen, P. M. Gollwitzer, & F. E. Weinert (Eds.), *Jenseits des Rubikon: Der Wille in den Humanwissenschaften* (pp. 86–96). Berlin, Germany: Springer.

Heckhausen, H. (1989). *Motivation und Handeln* [Motivation and action] (2nd ed.). Berlin, Germany: Springer.

Heckhausen, H. (1991). *Motivation and action.* New York: Springer-Verlag.

Heckhausen, H., & Gollwitzer, P. M. (1987). Thought contents and cognitive functioning in motivational versus volitional states of mind. *Motivation and Emotion, 11,* 101–120.

Heckhausen, H., Gollwitzer, P. M., & Weinert, F. E. (Eds.). (1987). *Jenseits des Rubikon: Der Wille in den Humanwissenschaften* [Beyond the Rubicon: The will in the behavioral and social sciences]. Berlin, Germany: Springer.

Heckhausen, H., & Halisch, F. (1986, July). *"Operant" versus "respondent" motive measures: A problem of validity or of construct?* Paper presented at the 21st International Congress of Applied Psychology, Jerusalem, Israel.

Heckhausen, H., & Kuhl, J. (1985). From wishes to action: The dead ends and short cuts on the long way to action. In M. Frese & L. Sabini (Eds.), *Goal-directed behavior: Psychological theory and research on action* (pp. 134–160, 367–395). Hillsdale, NJ: Erlbaum.

Heckhausen, H., & Meyer, W. U. (1972). Selbständigkeitserziehung und Leistungsmotiv [Raising children to be independent and the achievement motive]. *Forschungsgemeinschaft, 4,* 10–14.

Heckhausen, H., & Rheinberg, F. (1980). Lernmotivation im Unterricht, erneut betrachtet [A new look at motivation to learn in the classroom]. *Unterrichtswissenschaft, 8,* 7–47.

Heckhausen, H., & Roelofsen, I. (1962). Anfänge und Entwicklung der Leistungsmotivation: (I) Im Wetteifer des Kleinkindes [Origins and development of achievement motivation: (I) In the competition of infancy]. *Psychologische Forschung, 26,* 313–397.

Heckhausen, H., Schmalt, H.-D., & Schneider, K. (1985). *Achievement motivation in perspective.* New York: Academic Press.

Heckhausen, H., & Strang, H. (1988). Efficiency under maximal performance demands: Exertion control, an individual-difference variable? *Journal of Personality and Social Psychology, 55,* 489–498.

Heckhausen, H., & Wagner, I. (1965). Anfänge der Entwicklung der Leistungsmotivation: (II) In der Zielsetzung des Kleinkindes. Zur Genese des Anspruchsniveaus [Origins and development of achievement motivation: (II) In the goal setting of infancy. Development of the level of aspiration]. *Psychologische Forschung, 28,* 179–245.

Heckhausen, J. (1987a). Balancing for weaknesses and challenging developmental potential: A longitudinal study of mother-infant dyads in apprenticeship interactions. *Developmental Psychology, 23,* 762–770.

Heckhausen, J. (1987b). How do mothers know? Infants' chronological age or infants performance as determinants of adaptation in maternal instructions? *Journal of Experimental Child Psychology, 43,* 212–226.

Heckhausen, J. (1988). Becoming aware of ones competence in the second year: Developmental progression within the mother-child dyad. *International Journal of Behavioral Development, 11,* 305–326.

Heckhausen, J. (1989). Normatives Entwicklungswissen als Bezugsrahmen zur (Re)Konstruktion der eigenen Biographie [Normative developmental knowledge as a framework for (re)constructing one's own biography]. In P. Alheit & E. Hörning (Eds.), *Biographisches Wissen: Beiträge zu einer Theorie lebensgeschichtlicher Erfahrung* (pp. 202–282). Frankfurt, Germany: Campus.

Heckhausen, J. (1990). Erwerb und Funktion normativer Vorstellungen über den Lebenslauf: Ein entwicklungspsychologischer Beitrag zur sozio-psychischen Konstruktion von Biographien [Acquisition and function of normative conceptions about the life course: A developmental psychology approach to the socio-psychological construction of biographies]. *Kölner Zeitschrift für Soziologie und Sozialpsychologie, 31,* 351–373.

Heckhausen, J. (1991). Adults' expectancies about development and its controllability: Enhancing self-efficacy by social comparisons. In R. Schwarzer (Ed.), *Self-efficacy: Thought control of action* (pp. 107–126). Washington, DC: Hemisphere.

Heckhausen, J. (1993). The development of mastery and its perception within caretaker-child dyads. In D. Messer (Ed.), *Mastery motivation in early childhood: Development, measurement and social processes* (pp. 55–79). New York: Routledge.

Heckhausen, J. (1997). Developmental regulation across adulthood: Primary and secondary control of age-related challenges. *Developmental Psychology, 33,* 176–187.

Heckhausen, J. (1999). *Developmental regulation in adulthood: Age-normative and sociostructural constraints as adaptive challenges.* New York: Cambridge University Press.

Heckhausen, J. (2000a). Evolutionary perspectives on human motivation. *American Behavioral Scientist, 43,* 1015–1029.

Heckhausen, J. (2000b). Developmental regulation across the life span: An action-phase model of engagement and disengagement with developmental goals. In J. Heckhausen (Ed.), *Motivational psychology of human development: Developing motivation and motivating development* (pp. 213–231). Oxford, UK: Elsevier.

Heckhausen, J. (2002a). Transition from school to work: Societal opportunities and the potential for individual agency. *Journal of Vocational Behavior, 60,* 173–177.

Heckhausen, J. (2002b). Developmental regulation of life-course transitions: A control theory approach. In L. Pulkkinen & A. Caspi (Eds.), *Paths to successful development: Personality in the life course* (pp. 257–280). Cambridge, UK: Cambridge University Press.

Heckhausen, J. (2005). Competence and motivation in adulthood and old age: Making the most of changing capacities and resources. In A. Elliot & C. S. Dweck (Eds.), *Handbook of competence and motivation* (pp. 240–256). New York: Guilford Press.

Heckhausen, J., & Baltes, P. B. (1991). Perceived controllability of expected psychological change across adulthood and old age. *Journal of Gerontology: Psychological Sciences, 46,* 165–173.

Heckhausen, J., & Brim, O. G. (1997). Perceived problems for self and others: Self-protection by social downgrading throughout adulthood. *Psychology and Aging, 12,* 610–619.

Heckhausen, J., Chang, E. S., Chen, C., & Greenberger, E. (2007). *Optimistic goal selection and control striving during the transition after high school.* Manuscript submitted for publication.

Heckhausen, J., Dixon, R. A., & Baltes, P. B. (1989). Gains and losses in development throughout adulthood as perceived by different adult age groups. *Developmental Psychology, 25,* 109–121.

Heckhausen, J., & Dweck, C. S. (1998).(Eds.). *Life span perspectives on motivation and control.* Mahwah, NJ: Erlbaum.

Heckhausen, J., & Farruggia, S. P. (2003). Developmental regulation across the life span: A control-theory approach and implications for secondary education. *British Journal of Educational Psychology, Monograph series II: Psychological aspects of education – Current trends.* Leicester, UK: British Psychological Society.

Heckhausen, J., & Hosenfeld, B. (1988, October). *Lebensspannenentwicklung von normativen Vorstellungen über Lebensspannenentwicklung* [Life-span development of normative conceptions about life-span development]. Paper presented at the 36th Congress of the Deutsche Gesellschaft für Psychologie, Berlin, Germany.

Heckhausen, J., & Krüger, J. (1993). Developmental expectations for the self and most other people: Age grading in three functions of social comparison. *Developmental Psychology, 29,* 539–548.

Heckhausen, J., & Schulz, R. (1993). Optimisation by selection and compensation: Balancing primary and secondary control in life span development. *International Journal of Behavioral Development, 16*(2), 287–303.

Heckhausen, J., & Schulz, R. (1995). A life-span theory of control. *Psychological Review, 102*(2), 284–304.

Heckhausen, J., & Schulz, R. (1999a). The primacy of primary control is a human universal: A reply to Gould's critique of the life-span theory of control. *Psychological Review, 106*(3), 605–609.

Heckhausen, J., & Schulz, R. (1999b). Biological and societal canalizations and individuals' developmental goals. In J. Brandstädter & R. Lerner (Eds.), *Action and self development: Theory and research through the life span* (pp. 67–103). London: Sage.

Heckhausen, J., Schulz, R. & Wrosch, C. (1998). Developmental regulation in adulthood: Optimization in primary and secondary control – A multiscale questionnaire (OPS-Scales) [Technical report]. In J. Heckhausen & C. S. Dweck (Eds.), *Motivation and self-regulation across the life span* (pp. 50–77). New York: Cambridge University Press.

Heckhausen, J., & Tomasik, M. J. (2002). Get an apprenticeship before school is out: How German adolescents adjust vocational aspirations when getting close to a developmental deadline. *Journal of Vocational Behavior, 60,* 199–219.

Heckhausen, J., Wrosch, C., & Fleeson, W. W. (2001). Developmental regulation before and after a developmental deadline: The sample case of "biological clock" for childbearing. *Psychology and Aging, 16,* 400–413.

Heider, F. (1946). Attitudes and cognitive organization. *Journal of Psychology, 21,* 107–112.

Heider, F. (1958). *The psychology of interpersonal relations.* New York: Wiley.

Heider, F. (1960). The Gestalt theory of motivation. In M. R. Jones (Ed.), *Nebraska Symposium on Motivation, 1960* (pp. 145–172). Lincoln: University of Nebraska Press.

Heine, S. J., Lehman, D. R., Markus, H. R., & Kitayama, S. (1999). Is there a universal need for positive self-regard? *Psychological Review, 106,* 766–794.

Heinz, W. R. (1999). *From education to work: Cross-national perspectives.* New York: Cambridge University Press.

Heinz, W. R., Krüger, H., Rettke, U., Wachtveitl, E., & Witzel, A. (1985). *Hauptsache eine Lehrstelle: Jugendliche vor den Hürden des Arbeitsmarkts* [The main thing is having an apprenticeship: Young people and the hurdles of the labor market]. Weinheim, Germany: Beltz.

Held, T. (1986). Institutionalization and deinstitutionalization of the life course. *Human Development, 29,* 157–162.

Helmke, A. (1987). Entwicklung lern- und leistungsbezogener Motive und Einstellungen: Ergebnisse aus dem SCHOLASTIK-Projekt [Development of learning- and achievement-related motives and attitudes: Findings from the SCHOLASTIK project]. In F. E. Weinert & A. Helmke (Eds.), *Entwicklung im Grundschulalter* (pp. 59–76). Weinheim, Germany: Beltz.

Helmke, A., & Weinert, F. E. (1997). Bedingungsfaktoren schulischer Leistungen [Conditional factors of school achievement]. In F. E. Weinert (Ed.), *Psychologie des Unterrichts und der Schule* (Enzyklopädie der Psychologie, Themenbereich D, Serie I: Pädagogische Psychologie) (Vol. 3, pp. 71–176). Göttingen, Germany: Hogrefe.

Helson, H. (1948). Adaptation level as a basis for a quantitative theory of frames of reference. *Psychological Review, 55,* 297–313.

Helson, H. (1964). *Adaptation-level theory.* New York: Harper & Row.

Helson, H. (1973). A common model for affectivity and perception: An adaption-level approach. In D. E. Berlyne & K. B. Madsen (Eds.), *Pleasure, reward, preference* (pp. 167–188). New York: Academic Press.

Henemann, H. H., & Schwab, D. P. (1972). Evaluation of research on expectancy theory of employee performance. *Psychological Bulletin, 78,* 1–9.

Henle, M. (1944). The influence of valence on substitution. *Journal of Psychology, 17,* 11–19.

Hentsch, A. (1992). *Motivationale Aspekte des Malens: Eine Anreizanalyse* [Motivational aspects of painting: An analysis of incentives]. Unpublished Diplom thesis, University of Heidelberg, Germany.

Hepper, P. G. (1994). Long-term retention of kinship recognition established during infancy in the domestic dog. *Behavioural Processes, 33*, 3–14.

Hermann, M. G. (1980). Assessing the personalities of Soviet politburo members. *Personality and Social Psychology Bulletin, 6*, 332–352.

Hermans, H. J. M. (1970). A questionnaire measure of achievement motivation. *Journal of Applied Psychology, 54*, 353–363.

Hess, E. H. (1962). Ethology. In T. M. Newcomb (Ed.), *New directions in psychology* (Vol. I). New York: Holt, Rinehart and Winston.

Hess, W. R. (1954). *Das Zwischenhirn: Syndrome, Lokalisationen, Emotionen* [The interbrain: Syndromes, localizations, emotions]. Basel, Switzerland: Schwabe.

Hesse, F. W., Spies, K., & Lüer, G. (1983). Einfluß motivationaler Faktoren auf das Problemlöseverhalten im Umgang mit komplexen Problemen [Influence of motivational factors on problem-solving behavior in the context of complex problems]. *Zeitschrift für experimentelle und angewandte Psychologie, 30*, 400–424.

Hetzer, H. (1931). *Kind und Schaffen: Experimente über konstuktive Betätigung im Kleinkindalter* [Children and creative work: Experiments on constructive activity in young childhood]. Jena, Germany: Fischer.

Heyman, D., Dweck, C. S., & Cain, L. (1992). Young children's vulnerability to self-blame and helplessness. *Child Development, 63*, 391–403.

Heyman, D., Gee, C. L., & Giles, J. W. (2003). Preschool children's reasoning about ability. *Child Development, 74*, 516–534.

Heyn, S., Schnabel, U., & Röder, P. M. (1997). Von der Options- zur Realitätslogik. Stabilität und Wandel berufsbezogener Wertvorstellungen in der Statuspassage Schule-Beruf [Stability and change of career-related values at the school-to-work transition]. In A. Meier, U. Rabe-Kleberg & K. Rodax (Eds.), *Jahrbuch Bildung und Arbeit '97: Transformation und Tradition in Ost und West* (S. 281–305). Opladen: Leske and Budrich.

Heyns, R. W., Veroff, J., & Atkinson, J. W. (1958). A scoring manual for the affiliation motive. In J. W. Atkinson (Ed.), *Motives in fantasy, action, and society* (pp. 205–218). Princeton, NJ: Van Nostrand.

Hidi, S. (2000). An interest researcher's perspective: The effects of extrinsic and intrinsic factors on motivation. In C. Sansone & J. M. Harackiewicz (Eds.), *Intrinsic and extrinsic motivation* (pp. 311–339). San Diego, CA: Academic Press.

Hiemisch, A., Ehlers, A., & Westermann, R. (2002). Mindsets in social anxiety: A new look at selective information processing. *Journal of Behavior Therapy and Experimental Psychiatry, 33*, 103–114.

Higgins, E. T. (1987). Self-discrepancy: A theory relating self and affect. *Psychological Review, 94*, 319–340.

Higgins, E. T. (1997). Beyond pleasure and pain. *American Psychologist, 52*, 1280–1300.

Higgins, E. T., & Silberman, I. (1998). Development of regulatory focus: Promotion and prevention as ways of living. In J. Heckhausen & C. S. Dweck (Eds.), *Motivation and self regulation across the life span* (pp. 78–113). New York: Cambridge University Press.

Higgins, R. L., Snyder, C. R., & Berglas, S. (Eds.). (1990). *Self-handicapping: The paradox that isn't*. New York: Plenum.

Hillgruber, A. (1912). Fortlaufende Arbeit und Willensbetätigung [Continuous work and use of volition]. *Untersuchungen zur Psychologie und Philosophie, 1*, 6.

Himmi, T., Boyer, A., & Orsini, J. C. (1988). Changes in lateral hypothalamic neuronal activity accompanying hyper- and hypoglycemias. *Physiology & Behavior, 44*, 347–354.

Hinde, R. A. (1974). The study of aggression: Determinants, consequences, goals, and functions. In J. de Wit & W. W. Hartup (Eds.), *Determinants and origins of aggressive behavior* (pp. 3–27). The Hague, Netherlands: Mouton.

Hiroto, D. W., & Seligman, M. E. P. (1975). Generality of learned helplessness in man. *Journal of Personality and Social Psychology, 31*, 311–327.

Hodoka, A., & Fincham, F. D. (1995). Origins of children's helpless and mastery achievement patterns in the family. *Journal of Educational Psychology, 87*, 375–385.

Hofer, J., & Chasiotis, A. (2004). Methodological considerations of applying a TAT-type picture-story test in cross-cultural research: A comparison of German and Zambian adolescents. *Journal of Cross-Cultural Psychology, 35*, 224–241.

Hoffmann, J. (1993). *Vorhersage und Erkenntnis: Die Funktion von Antizipationen in der menschlichen Verhaltenssteuerung und Wahrnehmung* [Prediction and insight: The function of anticipation in human behavioral control and perception]. Göttingen, Germany: Hogrefe.

Hoffmann, N. (1998). *Zwänge und Depressionen: Pierre Janet und die Verhaltenstherapie* [Compulsions and depressions: Pierre Janet and behavioral therapy]. Heidelberg, Germany: Springer.

Hogan, J., & Hogan, J. (1995). *Hogan Personality Inventory Manual*. Tulsa, OK: Hogan Assessment Systems.

Hogan, J., & Ones, D. S. (1997). Conscientiousness and integrity at work. In R. Hogan, J. Johnson, & S. Briggs (Eds.), *Handbook of personality psychology* (pp. 849–870). San Diego, CA: Academic Press.

Hogan, R. (1996). A socioanalytic perspective on the five-factor model. In J. S. Wiggins (Ed.), *The five-factor model of personality: Theoretical perspectives* (pp. 163–179). New York: Guilford Press.

Hogan, R. (1981). *Transitions and the life course*. New York: Academic Press.

Hokoda, A., & Fincham, F. D. (1995). Origins of children's helpless and mastery achievement patterns in the family. *Journal of Educational Psychology, 87*, 375–385.

Holder, W. B., Marx, M. N., Holder, E. E., & Collier, G. (1957). Response strength as a function of delay in a runway. *Journal of Experimental Psychology, 53*, 316–323.

Holland, J. L. (1997). *Making vocational choices: A theory of vocational personalities and work environments*. Englewood Cliffs, NJ: Prentice Hall.

Holowka, S., & Petitto, L. A. (2002). Left hemisphere cerebral specialization for babies with babbling. *Science, 297*, 1515.

Hoppe, F. (1930). Untersuchungen zur Handlungs- und Affektpsychologie. IX. Erfolg und Misserfolg [Studies of the psychology of action and affect. IX. Success and failure]. *Psychologische Forschung, 14*, 1–63.

Hörhold, M., & Walschburger, P. (1997). Depressive Störung als Ausdruck misslingender Handlungskontrolle: Überprüfung einer psychophysiologischen Belastungsdiagnostik [Depressive disorders as an expression of failed action control: Testing a psychophysiological assessment]. *Zeitschrift für Klinische Psychologie: Forschung und Praxis, 26*, 31–27.

Hormuth, S. E. (1986). The sampling of experience in situ. *Journal of Personality, 54*, 262–293.

Horner, M. S. (1974a). Performance of men in noncompetitive and interpersonal competitive achievement-oriented situations. In J. W. Atkinson & J. O. Raynor (Eds.), *Motivation and achievement* (pp. 237–254). Washington, DC: Winston.

Horner, M. S. (1974b). The measurement and behavioral implications of fear of succes in women. In J. W. Atkinson & J. O. Raynor (Eds.), *Motivation and achievement* (pp. 91–117). Washington, DC: Winston.

Hosenfeld, B. (1988). *Persönlichkeitsveränderungen im Erwachsenenalter aus der Sicht Jugendlicher* [Personality changes in adulthood from the perspective of adolescents]. Unpublished doctoral dissertation, Free University of Berlin, Germany.

Housten, D. M. (1995). Vulnerability to depressive mood reactions: Retesting the hopelessness model of depression. *British Journal of Social Psychology, 34*, 293–302.

Hovland, C. I., & Sears, R. R. (1938). Experiments on motor conflict: I. Types of conflict and their modes of resolution. *Journal of Experimental Psychology, 23*, 477–493.

Hudley, C., & Graham, S. (1993). An attributional intervention to reduce peer directed aggression among African-American boys. *Child Development, 64*, 124–138.

Hull, C. L. (1930). Knowledge and purpose as habit mechanisms. *Psychological Review, 37*, 511–525.

Hull, C. L. (1932). The goal and maze learning. *Psychological Review, 39*, 25–434.

Hull, C. L. (1933). Differential habituation to internal stimuli in the albino rat. *Journal of Comparative Psychology, 16*, 255–273.

Hull, C. L. (1934). The concept of the habit-family hierarchy, and maze learning. *Psychological Review, 41*, 33–54; 134–152.

Hull, C. L. (1943). *Principles of behavior.* New York: Appleton-Century-Crofts.

Hull, C. L. (1952). *A behavior system: An introduction to behavior theory concerning the individual organism.* New Haven, CT: Yale University Press.

Hundertmark, J. (1990). *Entwicklungsbezogene Intentionen im Lebenslauf: Selbstbild und normative Entwicklungsvorstellungen als Einflußfaktoren* [Development-related intentions across the lifespan: The role of self-related and normative conceptions].Unpublished Diplom thesis, Technical University of Berlin, Germany.

Hundertmark, J., & Heckhausen, J. (1994). Entwicklungsziele junger, mittelalter und alter Erwachsener [Developmental goals in young, middle, and old adulthood].

Zeitschrift für Entwicklungspsychologie und Pädagogische Psychologie, 26, 197–217.

Hunt, J. M. V. (1965). Intrinsic motivation and its role in psychological development. In D. Levine (Ed.), *Nebraska Symposium on Motivation: Vol. 13* (pp. 189–282). Lincoln: University of Nebraska Press.

Hyland, M. E., Curtis, C., & Mason, D. (1985). Fear of success: Motive and cognition. *Journal of Personality and Social Psychology, 49*, 1669–1677.

Ikemoto, S., & Panksepp, J. (1999). The role of nucleus accumbens dopamine in motivated behavior: A unifying interpretation with special reference to reward-seeking. *Brain Research Reviews, 31*(1), 6–41.

Insel, T. R. (1997). A neurobiological basis of social attachment. *American Journal of Psychiatry, 154*(6), 726–735.

Insel, T. R., Winslow, J. T., Wang, Z., & Young, L. J. (1998). Oxytocin, vasopressin, and the neuroendocrine basis of pair bond formation. *Advances in Experimental Medicine and Biology, 449*, 215–224.

Irani, B. G., & Haskell-Luevano, C. (2005). Feeding effects of melanocortin ligands – A historical perspective. *Peptides, 26*(10), 1788–1799.

Irle, M., & Krolage, J. (1973). Kognitive Konsequenzen irrtümlicher Selbsteinschätzung [Cognitive implications of erroneous self-evaluations]. *Zeitschrift für Sozialpsychologie, 4*, 36–50.

Irwin, F. W. (1953). Stated expectations as functions of probability and desirability of outcomes. *Journal of Personality, 21*, 329–339.

Irwin, F. W. (1971). *Intentional behavior and motivation: A cognitive theory.* Philadelphia: Lippincott.

Izard, C. E. (1971). *The face of emotion.* New York: Appleton-Century-Crofts.

Izard, C. E. (1977). *Human emotions.* New York: Plenum.

Jackson, D. N. (1974). *Manual for the Personality Research Form.* Goshen, NY: Research Psychology Press.

Jackson, L. A., & Larrance, D. T. (1979). Is a "refinement" of attribution theory necessary to accommodate the learned helplessness reformulation? A critique of the reformulation of Abramson, Seligman & Teasdale. *Journal of Abnormal Psychology, 88*, 681–682.

Jackson, S. A., & Eklund, R. C. (2002). Assessing flow in physical activity: The flow state scale 2 and dispositional flow scale 2. *Journal of Sport and Exercise Psychology, 24*, 133–150.

Jacobs, B. (1958). A method for investigating the cue characteristics of pictures. In J. W. Atkinson (Ed.), *Motives in fantasy, action, and society* (pp. 617–629). Princeton, NJ: Van Nostrand.

Jagacinski, C. M., & Nicholls, J. G. (1987). Competence and affect in task involvement and ego involvement: The impact of social comparison information. *Journal of Educational Psychology, 79*, 107–114.

Jagacinski, C. M., & Nicholls, J. G. (1990). Reducing effort to protect perceived ability: They'd do it but I wouldn't. *Journal of Educational Psychology, 82*, 15–21.

James, W. (1890). *The principles of psychology (2 vols).* New York: Holt.

James, W. (1892). *Psychology: The briefer course.* New York: Holt.

Janke, W., Erdmann, G., & Kallus, W. (1985). *Stressverarbeitungsfragebogen (SVF)* [Stress management questionnaire (SVF)]. Göttingen, Germany: Hogrefe.

Janos, O., & Papouek, H. (1977). Acquisition of appetition and palpebral conditioned reflexes by the same infants. *Early Human Development, 1*, 91–97.

Jaudas, A., & Gollwitzer, P. M. (2004, April). *Führen Vorsätze zu Rigidität im Zielstreben?* [Do implementation intentions lead to rigidity in goal pursuit?] Paper presented at the symposium "Recent developments in research on implementation intentions" at the 46th meeting of the Tagung experimentell arbeitender Psychologen (TeaP), Giessen, Germany.

Jemmott, J. B., III (1982). *Psychosocial stress, social motives and disease susceptibility.* Unpublished doctoral dissertation, Harvard University, Cambridge, MA.

Jemmott, J. B. (1987). Social motives and susceptibility to disease: Stalking individual differences in health risks. *Journal of Personality, 55*, 267–298.

Jemmott, J. B., Borysenko, J. Z., Borysenko, M., McClelland, D. C., Chapman, R., Meyer, D., & Benson, H. (1983). Academic stress, power motivation, and decrease in salivary secretory immunoglobulin A secretion rate. *Lancet*, 1400–1402.

Jemmott, J. B., & Locke, S. E. (1984). Psychosocial factors, immunologic mediation, and human susceptibility to infections diseases: How much do we know? *Psychological Bulletin, 95*, 78–108.

Jenkins, S. R. (1994). Need for achievement and women's careers over 14 years: Evidence for occupational structure effects. *Journal of Personality and Social Psychology, 53*, 922–932.

Jenkins, T. N., Warner, L. H., & Warden, C. J. (1926). Standard apparatus for the study of animal behavior. *Journal of Comparative Psychology, 6*, 361–382.

Jennings, K. D. (1991). Early development of mastery motivation and its relation to the self-concept. In M. Bullock (Ed.), *The development of intentional action: Cognitive, motivational and interactive processes. Contributions to human development* (pp. 1–13). Basel, Switzerland: Karger.

Jones, E. E. (1976). How do people perceive the causes of behavior? *American Scientist, 64*, 237–246.

Jones, E. E., & Davis, K. E. (1965). From acts to dispositions: The attribution process in person perception. In L. Berkowitz (Ed.), *Advances in experimental social psychology* (Vol. 2, pp. 219–266). New York: Academic Press.

Jones, E. E., & McGillis, D. (1976). Correspondent inferences and the attribution cube: A comparative appraisal. In J. H. Harvey, W. J. Ickes, & R. F. Kidd (Eds.), *New directions in attribution research* (Vol. 1, pp. 387–420). Hillsdale, NJ: Erlbaum.

Jones, E. E., & Nisbett, R. E. (1971). *The actor and the observer: Divergent perceptions of the causes of behavior.* New York: General Learning.

Jones, E. E., Worchel, S., Goethals, G. R., & Grumet, J. F. (1971). Prior expectancy and behavioral extremity as determinants of attitude attribution. *Journal of Experimental and Social Psychology, 7*, 59–80.

Jones, E. E., Rock, L., Shaver, K. G., Goethals, G. R., & Ward, L. M. (1968). Pattern of performance and ability attribution: An unexpected primacy effect. *Journal of Personality and Social Psychology, 10*, 317–340.

Jones, H. E., & Jones, M. C. (1928). A study of fear. *Childhood Education, 5*, 136–143.

Jones, S. C. (1973). Self- and interpersonal evaluations: Esteem theories versus consistency theories. *Psychological Bulletin, 79*, 185–199.

Jopt, U.-J. (1974). *Extrinsische Motivation und Leistungsverhalten* [Extrinsic motivation and achievement behavior]. Unpublished doctoral dissertation, University of Bochum, Germany.

Joule, R. V., & Beauvois, J.-L. (1998). Cognitive dissonance theory: A radical view. *European Review of Social Psychology, 8*, 1–32.

Jucknat, M. (1938). Leistung, Anspruchsniveau und Selbstbewußtsein [Achievement, level of aspiration, and self-confidence]. *Psychologische Forschung, 22*, 89–179.

Jung, C. G. (1936/1990). *Typologie* [Typology]. Munich, Germany: dtv.

Jungermann, H., Pfister, H.-R., & May, R. S. (1994). Competing motivations or changing choices: Conjectures and some data on choice-action consistency. In J. Kuhl & J. Beckmann (Eds.), *Volition and personality: Action versus state orientation* (pp. 195–208). Seattle, WA: Hogrefe.

Junker, E. (1960). *Über unterschiedliches Behalten eigener Leistungen* [On the differing retention of one's own achievement]. Frankfurt, Germany: Waldemar Kramer.

Kafka, F. (1986). *Briefe an Milena* [Letters to Milena]. Frankfurt am Main: Fischer.

Kästele, G. (1988). *Anlage- und umweltbedingte Determinanten der Handlungs- und Lageorientierung nach Misserfolg im Vergleich zu anderen Persönlichkeitseigenschaften* [Genetic and environmental determinants of failure-related action and state orientation in comparison with other personality traits]. Unpublished doctoral dissertation, University of Osnabrück, Germany.

Kagan, J. (1988). The meanings of personality predicates. *American Psychologist, 43*, 614–620.

Kagan, S. (1981). Ecology and the acculturation of cognitive and social styles among Mexican American children. *Hispanic Journal of Behavior Sciences, 3*(2), 111–144.

Kahneman, D., & Tversky, A. (1979). On the interpretation of intuitive probability: A reply to Jonathan Cohen. *Cognition, 7*, 409–411.

Kahneman, D., & Tversky, A. (1984). Choices, values, and frames. *American Psychologist, 39*, 341–350.

Kammer, D. (1983). Eine Untersuchung der psychometrischen Eigenschaften des deutschen Beck-Depressionsinventars (BDI) [An investigation of the psychometric properties of the German Beck Depression Inventory (BDI)]. *Diagnostica, 29*, 48–60.

Kammer, D., & Stiensmeier-Pelster, J. (1987). Depressive Attribuierung: Eine Standortbestimmung [Depressive attribution: The state of the art]. In M. Ameland (Ed.), *Bericht über den 35. Kongress der Deutschen Gesellschaft für Psychologie in Heidelberg* (Vol. 2, pp. 557–566). Göttingen, Germany: Hogrefe.

Kanfer, R. (1990). Motivation theory and industrial and organizational psychology. In M. D. Dunnette & L. M. Hough (Eds.), *Handbook of industrial and organizational psychology* (pp. 75–170). Palo Alto, CA: Consulting Psychology Press.

Karabenick, J. D., & Heller, K. A. (1976). A developmental study of effort and ability attributions. *Developmental Psychology, 12*, 559–560.

Karabenick, S. A. (1972). Valence of success and failure as a function of achievement motives and locus of control. *Journal of Personality and Social Psychology, 21*, 101–110.

Karabenick, S. A., & Yousseff, Z. I. (1968). Performance as a function of achievement level and perceived difficulty. *Journal of Personality and Social Psychology, 10*, 414–419.

Karasawa, M., Little, T. D., Miyashita, T., Mashima, M., & Azuma, H. (1997). Japanese children's action-control beliefs about school performance. *International Journal of Behavioral Development, 20*, 405–423.

Karau, S. J., & Williams, K. D. (1993). Social loafing: A meta-analytic review and theoretical integration. *Journal of Personality and Social Psychology, 65*, 681–706.

Kaufmann, I. C., & Rosenblum, L. A. (1969). The reaction of separation from mother on the emotional behavior of infant monkeys. *Annals of the New York Academy of Science, 159*, 681–695.

Kaye, K. (1977a). Thickening thin data: The maternal role in developing communication and language. In M. Bullowa (Ed.), *Before speech: The beginning of interpersonal communication* (pp. 191–206). Cambridge, UK: Cambridge University Press.

Kaye, K. (1977b). Toward the origin of dialogue. In H. R. Schaffer (Ed.), *Studies in mother-infant interaction* (pp. 89–117). New York: Academic Press.

Kazén, M., Baumann, N., & Kuhl, J. (2003). Self-infiltration vs. self-compatibility checking in dealing with unattractive tasks and unpleasant items: The moderating influence of state vs. action orientation. *Motivation and Emotion, 27*, 157–197.

Kazén, M., & Kuhl, J. (2005). Intention memory and achievement motivation: Volitional facilitation and inhibition as a function of affective contents of need-related stimuli. *Journal of Personality and Social Psychology, 89*, 426–448.

Keenan, J. P., Nelson, A., O'Connor, M., & Pascual-Leone, A. (2001). Self-recognition and the right hemisphere. *Nature, 409*, 305.

Keeney, R. L., & Reiffa, H. (1976). *Decisions with multiple objectives: Preferences and value tradeoffs.* New York: Wiley.

Kehr, H. M. (2004a). Implicit(explicit motive discrepancies and volitional depletion among managers. *Personality and Social Psychology Bulletin, 30*, 315–327.

Kehr, H. M. (2004b). Integrating implicit motives, explicit motives, and perceived abilities: The compensatory model of work motivation and volition. *Academy of Management Review, 29*, 479–499.

Keller, H. (1997a). Entwicklungspsychopathologie: Das Entstehen von Verhaltensproblemen in der frühesten Kindheit. [Developmental psychopathology: The emergence of behavioral problems in infancy]. In H. Keller (Ed.), *Handbuch der Kleinkindforschung* (pp. 625–641). Berne, Switzerland: Huber.

Keller, H. (1997b). Kontinuität und Entwicklung [Continuity and development]. In H. Keller (Ed.), *Handbuch der Kleinkindforschung.* (pp. 235–258). Berne, Switzerland: Huber.

Keller, H. (1997c). Evolutionary approaches. In J. Berry, Y. Poortinga, & J. Panndey (Eds.), *Handbook of cross-cultural psychology, theory and method* (Vol. 1, pp. 215–255). Boston: Allyn & Bacon.

Keller, H. (2000). Human parent-child relationships from an evolutionary perspective. *American Behavioral Scientist, 43*, 957–969.

Keller, H., & Gauda, G. (1987). Eye contact in the first months of life and its developmental consequences. In H. Rauh & H.-C. Steinhausen (Eds.), *Psychobiology and early development (advances in psychology)* (pp. 129–143). Amsterdam: North-Holland.

Keller, H., Lohaus, A., Völker, S., Cappenberg, M., & Chasiotis, A. (1999). Temporal contingency as a measure of interactional quality. *Child Development, 70*, 474–485.

Keller, H., Lohaus, A., Völker, S., Elben, C., & Ball, J. (2003). Warmth and contingency and their relationship to maternal attitudes toward parenting. *Journal of Genetic Psychology, 164*, 275–292.

Kelley, H. H. (1967). Attribution theory in social psychology. In D. Levine (Ed.), *Nebraska Symposium on Motivation* (pp. 192–238). Lincoln: University of Nebraska Press.

Kelley, H. H. (1971). *Attribution in social interaction.* New York: General Learning.

Kelley, H. H. (1972). *Causal schemata and the attribution process.* New York: General Learning.

Kelley, H. H. (1973). The process of causal attribution. *American Psychologist, 28*, 107–128.

Kelley, H. H., & Michela, J. L. (1980). Attribution theory and research. *Annual Review of Psychology, 31*, 457–501.

Kelly, G. (1962). Comments on J. Brehm "Motivational effects of cognitive dissonance." In M. P. Jones (Ed.), *Nebraska Symposium on Motivation* (pp. 78–81). Lincoln: University of Nebraska Press.

Keltner, D., Gruenfeld, D. H., & Anderson, C. (2003). Power, approach, and inhibition. *Psychological Review, 110*, 265–284.

Keltner, D., & Robinson, R. J. (1996). Extremism, power, and the imagined basis of social conflict. *Current Directions in Psychological Science, 5*, 101–105.

Keltner, D., & Robinson, R. J. (1997). Defending the status quo: Power and bias in social conflict. *Personality and Social Psychology Bulletin, 23*, 1066–1077.

Kemmler, L. (1957). Untersuchungen über den frühkindlichen Trotz [Studies on defiance in early childhood]. *Psychologische Forschung, 25*, 279–338.

Kenrick, D. T., Li, N. P., & Butner, J. (2003). Dynamical evolutionary psychology: Individual decision rules and emergent social norms. *Psychological Review, 110*, 3–28.

Kendrick, K. M. (2004). The neurobiology of social bonds. *Journal of Neuroendocrinology, 16*(12), 1007–1008.

Keverne, E. B., & Curley, J. P. (2004). Vasopressin, oxytocin and social behaviour. *Current Opinion in Neurobiology, 14*(6), 777–783.

Keverne, E. B., & Kendrick, K. M. (1994). Maternal behaviour in sheep and its neuroendocrine regulation. *Acta Paediatrica, 397*(Suppl), 47–56.

Keverne, E. B., Martensz, N. D., & Tuite, B. (1989). Beta-endorphin concentrations in cerebrospinal fluid of monkeys are influenced by grooming relationships. *Psychoneuroendocrinology, 14*(1–2), 155–161.

Killcross, S., Robbins, T. W., & Everitt, B. J. (1997). Different types of fear-conditioned behaviour mediated by separate nuclei within amygdala. *Nature, 388*(6640), 377–380.

King, J. E., & Figueredo, A. J. (1997). The five-factor model plus dominance in chimpanzee personality. *Journal of Research in Personality, 31*, 257–271.

King, L. A. (1995). Wishes, motives, goals, and personal memories: Relations of measures of human motivation. *Journal of Personality, 63*, 985–1007.

Kipnis, D. (1972). Does power corrupt? *Journal of Personality and Social Psychology, 24*, 33–41.

Kipnis, D. (1974). The powerholder. In J. T. Tedeschi (Ed.), *Perspectives on social power* (pp. 82–122). Chicago: Aldine.

Kipnis, D. (1976). *The powerholders.* Chicago: The University of Chicago Press.

Kircher, T. T. J., Brammer, M., Bullmore, E., Simmons, A., Bartels, M., & David, A. S. (2002). The neural correlates of intentional and incidental self processing. *Neuropsychologia, 40*, 683–692.

Kirschbaum, C., Wolf, O., Wippich, W., & Hellhammer, D. (1996). Stress- and treatment-induced elevations of cortisol levels associated with impaired declarative memory in healthy adults. *Life Science, 58*, 1475–1483.

Klandermans, P. G. (1983). Rotter's I-E-scale and socio-political action-taking: The balance of 20 years of research. *European Journal of Social Psychology, 13*, 399–415.

Klein, S. B., Cosmides, L., Tooby, J., & Chance, S. (2002). Decisions and the evolution of memory: Multiple systems, multiple functions. *Psychological Review, 109*, 306–329.

Kleinbeck, U. (1975). *Motivation und Berufswahl* [Motivation and occupational choice]. Göttingen, Germany: Hogrefe.

Kleinbeck, U. (1996). *Arbeitsmotivation: Entstehung, Wirkung und Förderung* [Work motivation: Origins, effects, and promotion]. Weinheim, Germany: Juventa.

Klineberg, D. (1938). Emotional expression in Chinese literature. *Journal of Abnormal and Social Psychology, 33*, 517–520.

Klinger, E. (1967). Modelling effects on achievement imagery. *Journal of Personality and Social Psychology, 7*, 49–62.

Klinger, E. (1971). *Structure and functions of fantasy.* New York: Wiley.

Klinger, E. (1975). Consequences of commitment to and disengagement from incentives. *Psychological Review, 82*, 1–25.

Klinger, E. (1977). *Meaning and void: Inner experience and the incentives in people's lives.* Minneapolis: University of Minnesota Press.

Klüver, H., & Bucy, P. C. (1937). "Psychic blindness" and other symptoms following bilateral temporal lobectomy in rhesus monkeys. *American Journal of Physiology, 119*, 352–353.

Klüver, H., & Bucy, P. C. (1939). Preliminary analysis of functions of the temporal lobes in monkeys. *Archives of Neurology and Psychiatry, 42*, 979–1000.

Koch, S. (1956). Behavior as "intrinsically" regulated: Work notes towards a pre-theory of phenomena called "motivational." In M. R. Jones (Ed.), *Nebraska Symposium on Motivation* (pp. 42–87). Lincoln: University of Nebraska Press.

Koch, S. (Ed.) (1959–1963). *Psychology: A study of science.* New York: McGraw Hill.

Kochanska, G., Coy, K. C., & Murray, K. T. (2001). The development of self-regulation in the first four years of life. *Child Development, 72*, 1091–1111.

Kock, S. E. (1965). *Företagsledning och motivation*. Svenska Handeinshögskolan, Affärsekonomiska Förlagsförenigen, Helsingfors.

Kock, S. E. (1974). Företagsledning och motivation. *Nordisk Psykologi, 26*, 211–219.

Koepp, M. J., Gunn, R. N., Lawrence, A. D., Cunningham, V. J., Dagher, A., Jones, T., Brooks, D. J., Bench, C. J., & Grasby, P. M. (1998). Evidence for striatal dopamine release during a video game. *Nature, 393*(6682), 266–268.

Koestner, R., & McClelland, D. C. (1990). Perspectives on competence motivation. In L. Pervin (Ed.), *Handbook of personality theory and research* (pp. 527–548). New York: Guilford Press.

Koestner, R., Weinberger, J., & McClelland, D. C. (1991). Task-intrinsic and social-extrinsic sources of arousal for motives assessed in fantasy and self-report. *Journal of Personality, 59*, 57–82.

Koestner, R., Zuckerman, M., & Koestner, J. (1987). Praise, involvement and intrinsic motivation. *Journal of Personality and Social Psychology, 53*(2), 383–390.

Kohli, M. (1981). Zur Theorie der biographischen Selbst- und Fremdthematisierung [Theory of biographical accounts of the self and others]. In J. Matthes (Ed.), *Lebenswelt und soziale Probleme: Verhandlungen des 20. Deutschen Soziologentages* (pp. 502–520). Frankfurt, Germany: Campus.

Kohut, H. (1979). *Die Heilung des Selbst* [Healing the self]. Frankfurt, Germany: Suhrkamp.

Köller, O. (2000). *Leistungsgruppierung, soziale Vergleiche und selbstbezogene Fähigkeitskognitionen in der Schule* [Ability grouping, social comparisons, and self-related ability cognitions in school]. Habilitationsschrift, Univeristy of Potsdam, Germany.

Köller, O., Trautwein, U., Lüdtke, O., & Baumert, J. (2006). Zum Zusammenspiel von schulischer Leistung, Selbstkonzept und Interesse in der gymnasialen Oberstufe [On the interplay of academic achievement, self-concept, and interest in upper secondary schools]. *Zeitschrift für Pädagogische Psychologie, 20*, 27–39.

Konner, M. J. (1981). Evolution of human behavioral development. In R. H. Monroe, R. L. Monroe, & B. B. Whiting (Eds.), *Handbook of cross-cultural human development* (pp. 3–51). New York: Garland.

Koole, S. L. (2000). *Positivity in self-evaluation*. Unpublished doctoral dissertation, Free University of Amsterdam, Netherlands.

Koole, S. L. (2004). Volitional shielding of the self: Effects of action orientation and external demand on implicit self-evaluation. *Social Cognition, 22*, 117–146.

Koole, S. L., & Jostmann, N. (2004). Getting a grip on your feelings: Effects of action orientation and social demand on intuitive affect regulation. *Journal of Personality and Social Psychology, 87*(6), 974–989.

Koole, S. L., Smeets, K., Van Knippenberg, A., & Dijksterhuis, A. (1999). The cessation of rumination through self-affirmation. *Journal of Personality and Social Psychology, 77*, 111–125.

Kornadt, H.-J. (1982a). Band 1: Empirische u. theoretische Untersuchungen zu einer Motivationstheorie der Aggression und zur Konstruktvalidierung eines Aggressions-TAT [Volume 1: Empirical and theoretical studies on a motivational theory of aggression and on the construct validation of an aggression TAT]. *Aggressionsmotiv und Aggressionshemmung*. Berne, Switzerland: Huber.

Kornadt, H.-J. (1982b). Grundzüge einer Motivationstheorie der Aggression [Outline of a motivational theory of aggression]. In R. Hilke & W. Kempf (Eds.), *Aggression* (pp. 86–111). Berne, Switzerland: Huber.

Kornadt, H.-J., Eckensberger, L. H., & Emminghaus, W. B. (1980). Cross-cultural research on motivation and its contribution to a general theory of motivation. In H. C. Triandis (Ed.), *Handbook of Cross-Cultural Psychology (Vol. 3: Basic processes)* (pp. 223–321). Boston: Allyn & Bacon.

Kosfeld, M., Heinrichs, M., Zak, P. J., Fischbacher, U., & Fehr, E. (2005). Oxytocin increases trust in humans. *Nature, 435*(7042), 673–676.

Krampen, G. (1987). Differential effects of teacher comments. *Journal of Educational Psychology, 79*, 137–146.

Krantz, D. L., & Allen, D. (1967). The rise and fall of McDougall's instinct doctrine. *Journal of the History of the Behavioral Sciences, 3*, 326–338.

Krapp, A. (1999). Intrinsische Lernmotivation und Interesse: Forschungsansätze und konzeptuelle Überlegungen [Intrinsic learning motivation and interest: Research approaches and conceptual considerations]. *Zeitschrift für Pädagogik, 45*, 387–406.

Krapp, A. (2001). Interesse [Interest]. In D. H. Rost (Ed.), *Handwörterbuch Pädagogische Psychologie* (2nd ed., pp. 286–293). Weinheim, Germany: PVU.

Krapp, A., Hidi, S., & Renninger, K. (1992). Interest, learning and development. In K. A. Renninger & S. Hidi (Eds.), *The role of interest and development* (pp. 3–25). Hillsdale, NJ: Erlbaum.

Krau, E. (1982). Motivational feedback loops in the structure of action. *Journal of Personality and Social Psychology, 43*, 1030–1040.

Krebs, J. R. (1980). Optimal foraging, predation risk and territory defense. *Area, 68*, 83–90.

Krech, D., Crutchfield, R. S., & Ballachey, E. L. (1962). *Individual in society*. New York: McGraw-Hill.

Krohne, H. W. (1988). Erziehungsstilforschung: Neuere theoretische Ansätze und empirische Befunde [Child-rearing research: New theoretical approaches and empirical results]. *Zeitschrift für Pädagogische Psychologie, 2*, 157–172.

Krohne, H. W. (1996). *Angst und Angstbewältigung* [Anxiety and coping with anxiety]. Stuttgart, Germany: Kohlhammer.

Krug, S. (1976). Förderung und Änderung des Leistungsmotivs: Theoretische Grundlagen und deren Anwendung [Fostering and modifying the achievement motive: Theoretical fundamentals and their application]. In H.-D. Schmalt & W.-U. Meyer (Eds.), *Leistungsmotivation und Verhalten* (pp. 221–247). Stuttgart, Germany: Klett.

Krüger, H. (1978). *Anfänge der Entwicklung des Anstrengungskonzepts im Kindergartenalter* [Early development of the effort concept at kindergarten age]. Unpublished Diplom thesis, University of Bochum, Germany.

Krüger, J., & Heckhausen, J. (1993). Personality development across the adult life span: Subjective conceptions versus cross-sectional contrasts. *Journal of Gerontology: Psychological Sciences, 48*, 100–108.

Krüger, J., Heckhausen, J., & Hundertmark, J. (1995). Perceiving middle aged adults: Effects of stereotype-congruent and incongruent information. *Journal of Gerontology: Psychological Sciences, 50B*, 82–93.

Kruglanski, A. W. (1989). *Lay epistemics and human knowledge: Cognitive and motivational bases*. New York: Plenum.

Kruglanski, A. W. (Eds.). (1996). *Social psychology: A handbook of basic principles* (pp. 329–360). New York: Guilford Press.

Kubinger, K. D., & Ebenhöh, H. (1996). *Arbeitshaltungen (AHA): Objektiver Persönlichkeitstest* [Work styles: Objective personality test]. Mödling, Austria: Schuhfried.

Kubinger, K. D., & Litzenberger, M. (2003). Zur Validität der Objektiven Persönlichkeits-Test-Batterie "Arbeitshaltungen" [On the validity of the objective personality test battery "Work Style"]. *Zeitschrift für Differentielle und Diagnostische Psychologie, 24,* 119–133.

Külpe, O. (1893). *Grundriß der Psychologie. Auf experimenteller Grundlage dargestellt* [Outlines of Psychology. Based upon the Results of Experimental Investigation]. Leipzig, Germany: Wilhelm Engelmann.

Kuester, J., & Paul, A. (1989). Reproductive strategies of subadult barbary macaque males at Affenberg Salem. In A. E. Rasa, C. Vogel, & E. Voland (Eds.), *The sociobiology of sexual and reproductive strategies* (pp. 93–109). London: Chapman & Hall.

Kuhl, J. (1977). *Meß- und prozeßtheoretische Analysen einiger Person- und Situationsparameter der Leistungsmotivation* [Personal and situational determinants of achievement motivation: Computer simulation and experimental analysis]. Bonn, Germany: Bouvier.

Kuhl, J. (1978a). Situations-, reaktions- und personbezogene Konsistenz des Leistungsmotivs bei der Messung mittels des Heckhausen TAT [Situation-, reaction-, and person-related consistency of the achievement motive measured using Heckhausen's TAT]. *Archiv für Psychologie, 130,* 37–52.

Kuhl, J. (1978b). Standard setting and risk preference: An elaboration of the theory of achievement motivation and an empirical test. *Psychological Review, 85,* 239–248.

Kuhl, J. (1981). Motivational and functional helplessness: The moderating effect of state vs. action orientation. *Journal of Personality and Social Psychology, 40,* 155–170.

Kuhl, J. (1982). The expectancy-value approach in the theory of social motivation. In N. T. Feather (Ed.), *Expectations and actions: Expectancy-value models in psychology* (pp. 125–162). Hillsdale, NJ: Erlbaum.

Kuhl, J. (1983). *Motivation, Konflikt und Handlungskontrolle* [Motivation, conflict, and action control]. Berlin, Germany: Springer.

Kuhl, J. (1984). Motivational aspects of achievement motivation and learned helplessness: Toward a comprehensive theory of action control. In B. A. Maher & W. B. Maher (Eds.), *Progress in experimental personality research* (Vol. 13, pp. 99–171). New York: Academic Press.

Kuhl, J. (1987). Action control: The maintenance of motivational states. In F. Halisch & J. Kuhl (Eds.), *Motivation, intention, and volition* (pp. 279–291). Berlin, Germany: Springer.

Kuhl, J. (1994). Action versus state orientation: Psychometric properties of the Action-Control-Scale (ACS-90). In J. Kuhl & J. Beckmann (Eds.), *Action control: From cognition to behavior* (pp. 47–59). Toronto, Ontario, Canada: Hogrefe.

Kuhl, J. (1996). Wille und Freiheitserleben: Formen der Selbststeuerung [The will and perceived freedom: Forms of volition]. In J. Kuhl & H. Heckhausen (Eds.), *Enzyklopädie der Psychologie: Motivation, Volition und Handlung* (Series IV, Vol. 4, pp. 665–765). Göttingen, Germany: Hogrefe.

Kuhl, J. (1998). Wille und Persönlichkeit: Von der Funktionsanalyse zur Aktivierungsdynamik psychischer Systeme [Volition and personality: Functional analysis of self-regulation]. *Psychologische Rundschau, 49,* 61–77.

Kuhl, J. (2000a). A functional-design approach to motivation and volition: The dynamics of personality systems interactions. In M. Boekaerts, P. R. Pintrich, & M. Zeidner (Eds.), *Self-regulation: Directions and challenges for future research* (pp. 111–169). New York: Academic Press.

Kuhl, J. (2000b). A theory of self-development: Affective fixation and the STAR model of personality disorders and related styles. In J. Heckhausen (Ed.), *Motivational psychology of human development: Developing motivation and motivating development* (pp. 187–211). New York: Elsevier.

Kuhl, J. (2000c). The volitional basis of personality systems interaction theory: Applications in learning and treatment contexts. *International Journal of Educational Research, 33,* 665–703.

Kuhl, J. (2001). *Motivation und Persönlichkeit: Die Interaktion psychischer Systeme* [Motivation and personality: The interaction of psychological systems]. Göttingen, Germany: Hogrefe.

Kuhl, J., & Baumann, N. (2000). Self-regulation and rumination: Negative affect and impaired self-accessibility. In W. Perrig & A. Grob (Eds.), *Control of human behavior*

mental processes and consciousness: Essays in honor of the 60th birthday of August Flammer (pp. 283–305). New York: Wiley.

Kuhl, J., & Beckmann, J. (1983). Handlungskontrolle und Umfang der Informationsverarbeitung: Wahl einer einfachen (nicht optimalen) Entscheidungsregel zugunsten rascher Handlungsbereitschaft [Action control and scope of information processing: Selection of a simplified (non-optimal) decision rule to achieve fast readiness for action]. *Zeitschrift für Sozialpsychologie, 14,* 241–250.

Kuhl, J., & Beckmann, J. (1985). *Action control theory: From cognition to behavior.* New York: Springer.

Kuhl, J., & Beckmann, J. (1994a). *Volition and personality: Action versus state orientation.* Seattle, WA: Hogrefe.

Kuhl, J., & Beckmann, J. (1994b). Alienation: Ignoring one's preferences. In J. Kuhl & J. Beckmann (Eds.), *Volition and personality: Action versus state orientation.* Seattle, WA: Hogrefe.

Kuhl, J., & Blankenship, V. (1979). The dynamic theory of achievement motivation: From episodic to dynamic thinking. *Psychological Review, 86,* 141–151.

Kuhl, J., & Fuhrmann, A. (1998). Decomposing self-regulation and self-control: The volitional components checklist. In J. Heckhausen & C. Dweck (Eds.), *Life span perspectives on motivation and control* (pp. 15–49). Mahwah, NJ: Erlbaum.

Kuhl, J., & Goschke, T. (1994). State orientation and the activation and retrieval of intentions from memory. In J. Kuhl & J. Beckmann (Eds.), *Volition and personality: Action versus state orientation* (pp. 127–152). Toronto, Ontario, Canada: Hogrefe.

Kuhl, J., & Helle, P. (1986). Motivational and volitional determinants of depression: The degenerated intention hypothesis. *Journal of Abnormal Psychology, 95,* 247–251.

Kuhl, J., & Kaschel, R. (2004). Entfremdung als Krankheitsursache: Selbstregulation von Affekten und integrative Kompetenz [Alienation as a determinant of symptom formation: Self-regulation of affect and integrative competence]. *Psychologische Rundschau, 55,* 61–71.

Kuhl, J., & Kazén, M. (1994). Self-discrimination and memory: State orientation and false ascription of assigned activities. *Journal of Personality and Social Psychology, 66,* 1103–1115.

Kuhl, J., & Kazén, M. (1999). Volitional facilitation of difficult intentions: Joint activation of intention memory and positive affect removes Stroop interference. *Journal of Experimental Psychology: General, 128,* 382–399.

Kuhl, J., & Kazén, M. (2003). Handlungs- und Lageorientierung: Wie lernt man, seine Gefühle zu steuern? [Action and state orientation: How do people learn to control their feelings?] In J. Stiensmeier-Pelster & F. Rheinberg (Eds.), *Diagnostik von Motivation und Selbstkonzept.* Göttingen, Germany: Hogrefe.

Kuhl, J., & Kazén, M. (2004). *Impress them or convince them? Sales performance, social needs and psychological well-being as a function of histrionic vs. action oriented personality.* Manuscript submitted for publication.

Kuhl, J., & Scheffer, D. (1999). *Der operante Multi-Motiv-Test (OMT): Manual* [The operant Multi-Motive Test (OMT): Manual]. University of Osnabrück, Germany.

Kuhl, J., & Völker, S. (1998). Entwicklung und Persönlichkeit [Development and personality]. In H. Keller (Ed.), *Lehrbuch der Entwicklungspsychologie* (pp. 207–240). Berne, Switzerland: Huber.

Kuhl, J., & Weiß, M. (1994). Performance deficits following uncontrollable failure: Impaired action control or global attributions and generalized expectancy deficits? In J. Kuhl & J. Beckmann (Eds.), *Volition and personality: Action versus state orientation.* Seattle, WA: Hogrefe.

Kukla, A. (1972a). Attributional determinants of achievement-related behavior. *Journal of Personality and Social Psychology, 21,* 166–174.

Kukla, A. (1972b). Foundations of an attributional theory of performance. *Psychological Review, 79,* 454–470.

Kukla, A. (1978). An attributional theory of choice. In L. Berkowitz (Ed.), *Advances in experimental social psychology* (Vol. 11, pp. 113–144). New York: Academic Press.

Kummer, H. (1995). Causal knowledge in animals. In D. Sperber, D. Premack, & A. James Premack (Eds.), *A causal cognition* (pp. 26–39). Oxford, UK: Clarendon Press.

Kun, A. (1977). Evidence for preschoolers' understanding of causal direction in extended causal sequences. *Child Development, 49,* 218–222.

Kun, A., Parsons, J. E., & Ruble, D. (1974). The development of integration processes using ability and effort information to predict outcome. *Developmental Psychology, 10* (5), 721–732.

Kun, A., & Weiner, B. (1973). Necessary versus sufficient causal schemata for success and failure. *Journal of Research in Personality, 7,* 197–207.

Kunda, Z. (1999). *Social cognition: Making sense of people.* Cambridge, MA: MIT Press.

Kunde, W., Koch, I., & Hoffmann, J. (2004). Anticipated action effects affect the selection, initiation and execution of actions. *Quarterly Journal of Experimental Psychology. Section A: Human Experimental Psychology, 57A,* 87–106.

Lacey, J. I. (1969). Somatic response patterning and stress: Some revisions of activation theory. In M. H. Appley & R. Trumbull (Eds.), *Psychological stress: Issues and research* (pp. 14–39). New York: Appleton.

Lang, F. R. (2001). Regulation of social relationship in later adulthood. *Journal of Gerontology, Psychological Sciences, 56B,* 321–329.

Lang, F. R. (2004). Social motivation across the life span. In F. R. Lang & K. L. Fingerman (Eds.), *Growing together: Personal relationships across the lifespan* (pp. 341–367). New York: Cambridge University Press.

Lang, F. R., & Heckhausen, J. (2001). Perceived control over development and subjective well-being: Differential benefits across adulthood. *Journal of Personality and Social Psychology, 81,* 509–523.

Lang, F. R., & Heckhausen, J. (2002). Stabilisierung und Kontinuität der Persönlichkeit im Lebensverlauf [Stabilization and continuity of personality across the lifespan]. In J. B. Asendorpf (Ed.), *Enzyklopädie der Psychologie (Vol. C/V/3). Soziale, emotionale und Persönlichkietsentwicklung* (pp. 525–562). Göttingen, Germany: Hogrefe.

Lang, F. R., & Heckhausen, J. (2006). Developmental changes of motivation and interpersonal capacities across adulthood: Managing the challenges and constraints of social contexts. In C. Hoare (Ed.), *The Oxford handbook of adult development and learning* (pp. 149–166). Oxford, UK: Oxford University Press.

Lang, F. R., Reschke, F. S., & Neyer, F. J. (2006). Social relationships, transitions and personality development across the life span. In D. K. Mroczek & T. D. Little (Eds.), *Handbook of personality development* (pp. 445–466). Mahwah, NJ: Erlbaum.

Lang, P. J., Bradley, M. M., & Cuthbert, B. H. (1999). *International Affective Picture System (IAPS): Technical manual and affective ratings.* Gainesville: NIMH Center for the Study of Emotion and Attention, University of Florida. *(this reference to Lang et al. replaces the one to CEA, please substitute in master reference list)*

Lange, L. (1888). Neue Experimente über den Vorgang der einfachen Reaktion auf Sinneseindrücke [New experiments on the process of simple reaction to sense impressions]. *Philosophische Studien, 4,* 479–510.

Langens, T. A. (2001). Predicting behavior change in Indian businessmen from a combination of need for achievement and self-discrepancy. *Journal of Research in Personality, 35,* 339–352.

Langens, T. A. (2002). *Tagträume, Anliegen und Motivation* [Daydreams, personal goals, and motivation]. Göttingen, Germany: Hogrefe.

Lansing, J. B., & Heyns, R. W. (1959). Need affiliation and frequency of four types of communication. *Journal of Abnormal and Social Psychology, 58,* 365–372.

Latané, B., Williams, K., & Harkins, S. (1979). Many hands make light the work: The causes and consequences of social loafing. *Journal of Personality and Social Psychology, 37,* 822–832.

Lawler, E. E. (1968). A correlational-causal analysis of the relationship between expectancy attitudes and job performance. *Journal of Applied Psychology, 52,* 462–468.

Lawler, E. E., & Porter, L. W. (1967). Antecedent attitudes of effective managerial job performance. *Organizational Behavior and Human Performance, 2,* 122–142.

Lawrence, D. M., & Festinger, L. (1962). *Deterrents and reinforcement: The psychology of insufficient reward.* Stanford, CA: Stanford University Press.

Lawrence, P. R., & Nohria, N. (2002). *Driven: How human nature shapes our choices.* San Francisco: Wiley.

Lazarus, R. A., & Launier, R. (1979). Stress-related transactions between person and environment. In L. A. Pervin & M. Lewis (Eds.), *Perspectives in interactional psychology* (pp. 287–372). New York: Plenum.

Lazarus, R. S. (1968). Emotion and adaption: Conceptual and empirical relations. In W. J. Arnold (Ed.), *Nebraska Symposium on Motivation* (pp. 175–270). Lincoln: University of Nebraska Press.

Lazarus, R. S. (1984). On the primacy of cognition. *American Psychologist, 39,* 124–129.

Lazarus, R. S., Opton, E. M., Nomikos, M. S., & Rankin, N. D. (1965). The principle of short-circuiting of threat: Further evidence. *Journal of Personality, 33,* 622–635.

Le Magnen, J., & Tallon, S. (1966). La periodicité spontanée de la prise d'aliments ad libitum du rat blanc. *Journal de Physiologie, 58,* 323–349.

Lecci, L., Karoly, P., Briggs, C., & Kuhn, K. (1994). Specificity and generality of motivational components in depression: A personal projects analysis. *Journal of Abnormal Psychology, 103,* 404–408.

LeDoux, J. (1995). Emotion: Clues from the brain. *Annual Review of Psychology, 46,* 209–235.

LeDoux, J. (1996). *The emotional brain.* New York: Touchstone.

LeDoux, J. E. (2002). *The synaptic self.* New York: Viking.

Lee, F. K., Sheldon, K. M., & Turban, D. B. (2003). Personality and the goal-striving process: The influence of achievement goal patterns, goal level and mental focus on performance and enjoyment. *Journal of Applied Psychology, 88,* 256–265.

Leeper, R. W. (1935). The role of motivation in learning: A study of the phenomenon of differential motivational control of the utilization of habits. *Journal of Genetic Psychology, 4b,* 3–40.

Lefcourt, H. M. (1976). *Locus of control: Current trends in theory and research.* New York: Wiley.

Lehmann, H. C., & Witty, P. A. (1934). Faculty psychology and personality traits. *American Journal of Psychology, 46,* 486–500.

Leibowitz, S. F., Weiss, G. F., Walsh, U. A., & Viswanath, D. (1989). Medial hypothalamic serotonin: Role in circadian patterns of feeding and macronutritient selection. *Brain Research, 503,* 132–140.

Lengfelder, A., & Gollwitzer, P. M. (2001). Reflective and reflexive action control in patients with frontal brain lesions. *Neuropsychology, 15,* 80–100.

Leon-Villagra, J., Meyer, W. U., & Engler, U. (1990). Ability judgments based on praise: A developmental psychology study. *Zeitschrift für Entwicklungspsychologie und Pädagogische Psychologie, 22* (1), 54–74.

Lepper, M. R., Greene, D., & Nisbett, R. E. (1973). Undermining children's intrinsic interest with extrinsic rewards: A test of the overjustification hypothesis. *Journal of Personality and Social Psychology, 28,* 129–137.

Lerner, R. M. (2002). *Concepts and theories of human development* (3rd ed.). Mahwah, NJ: Erlbaum.

Lerner, R. M., & Busch-Rossnagel, N. A. (1981). *Individuals as producers of their development: A life-span perspective.* New York: Academic Press.

Lersch, P. (1938). *Aufbau des Charakters* [Structure of the character]. Leipzig, Germany: Barth.

Lersch, P. (1951). *Aufbau der Person* [Structure of the person] (4th ed. of *Aufbau des Charakters*). Munich, Germany: Barth.

LeVay, S., & Hamer, D. H. (1994). Evidence for a biological influence in male homosexuality. *Scientific American, May,* 44–49.

Leventahl, H. (1984). A perceptual-motor theory of emotion. In L. Berkowitz (Ed.), *Advances in Experimental Social Psychology* (Vol. 17, pp. 117–182). New York: Academic Press.

Levesque, J., Fanny, E., Joanett, Y., Paquette, V., Mensour, B., Beaudouin, G., Leroux, J.-M., Borugouin, P., & Beauregard, M. (2003). Neural circuitry underlying voluntary suppression of sadness. *Biological Psychiatry, 53,* 502–510.

Levine, A. S., & Billington, C. J. (1997). Why do we eat? A neural systems approach. *Annual Review of Nutrition, 17,* 597–619.

Levine, A. S., & Billington, C. J. (2004). Opioids as agents of reward-related feeding: A consideration of the evidence. *Physiology & Behavior, 82* (1), 57–61.

Levine, A. S., Kotz, C. M., & Gosnell, B. A. (2003). Sugars and fats: The neurobiology of preference. *Journal of Nutrition, 133* (3), 831S–834S.

Lewin, K. (1922). Das Problem der Willensmessung und das Grundgesetz der Assoziation. II [The problem of measuring volition and the law of association. II]. *Psychologische Forschung, 2,* 65–140.

Lewin, K. (1926a). Untersuchungen zur Handlungs- und Affekt-Psychologie I.: Vorbemerkungen über die psychischen Kräfte und Energien und über die Struktur der Seele [Studies of the psychology of action and affect. I: Preliminary remarks on the psychic powers and energies and the structure of the soul]. *Psychologische Forschung, 7,* 294–329.

Lewin, K. (1926b). Untersuchungen zur Handlungs- und Affekt-Psychologie II.: Vorsatz, Wille und Bedürfnis [Studies of the psychology of action and affect. II: Intent, volition, and need]. *Psychologische Forschung, 7,* 330–385.

Lewin, K. (1931a). *Die psychologische Situation bei Lohn und Strafe* [The psychological elements in rewards and punishment]. Leipzig, Germany: Hirzel.

Lewin, K. (1931b). Environmental forces in child behavior and development. In C. Murchison (Ed.), *Handbook of child psychology* (pp. 94–127). Worcester, MA: Clark University Press.

Lewin, K. (1932). Ersatzhandlung und Ersatzbefriedigung [Substitute action and substitute satisfaction]. *Bericht über den 12. Kongreß der Deutschen Gesellschaft für Psychologie, Hamburg, 1931* (pp. 382–384). Jena, Germany: Fischer.

Lewin, K. (1934). Der Richtungsbegriff in der Psychologie: Der spezielle und allgemeine hodologische Raum [The concept of direction in psychology: Special and general hodological space]. *Psychologische Forschung, 19,* 249–299.

Lewin, K. (1935). *A dynamic theory of personality: Selected papers.* New York: McGraw-Hill.

Lewin, K. (1936). *Principles of topological psychology.* New York: McGraw-Hill.

Lewin, K. (1938). *The conceptual representation and the measurement of psychological forces.* Durham, NC: Duke University Press.

Lewin, K. (1939). Field theory and experiment in social psychology. *American Journal of Sociology, 44,* 868–897.

Lewin, K. (1942). Field theory of learning. *Yearbook of National Social Studies of Education, 41,* 215–242.

Lewin, K. (1943). Defining the "field at a given time." *Psychological Review, 50,* 292–310.

Lewin, K. (1946a). Action research and minority problems. *Journal of Social Issues, 2,* 34–46.

Lewin, K. (1946b). Behavior and development as a function of the total situation. In L. Carmichael (Ed.), *Manual of child psychology* (pp. 791–844). New York: Wiley.

Lewin, K. (1947). Group decision and social change. In E. E. Maccoby, T. M. Newcomb, & E. L. Hartley (Eds.), *Readings in social psychology* (pp. 197–211). New York: Holt, Rinehart and Winston.

Lewin, K. (1951). *Field theory in social science.* Chicago: The University of Chicago Press.

Lewin, K. (1963). *Feldtheorie in den Sozialwissenschaften* [Field theory in the social sciences]. Berne, Switzerland: Huber.

Lewin, K., Dembo, T., Festinger, L., & Sears, P. S. (1944). Level of aspiration. In J. McHunt (Ed.), *Personality and the behavior disorders* (Vol. 1, pp. 333–378). New York: Ronald.

Lewis, M., & Brooks-Gunn, J. (1979). Toward a theory of social cognition: The development of the self. In *Social interaction and communication during infancy: New directions for child developmen* (pp. 1–20). New York: Plenum.

Lewis, M., & Goldberg, S. (1969). Perceptual-cognitive development in infancy: A generalized expectancy model as a function of the mother-infant interaction. *Merrill-Palmer Quarterly, 15*, 81–100.

Lewis, M., & Ramsay, D. (2002). Cortisol response to embarrassment and shame. *Child Development, 73*, 1034–1045.

Li, N. P., Bailey, J. M., Kenrick, D. T., & Linsenmeier, J. A. W. (2002). The necessities and luxuries of mate preference. *Journal of Personality and Social Psychology, 82*, 947–955.

Libet, B. (1985). Unconscious cerebral initiative and the role of conscious will in voluntary action. *Behavioral and Brain Sciences, 2*, 529–566.

Lieberman, M. D. (2003). Reflective and reflexive judgment processes: A social cognitive neuroscience approach. In J. P. Forgas, K. R. Williams, & W. V. Hippel (Eds.), *Social judgments: Implicit and explicit processes* (pp. 44–67). New York: Cambridge University Press.

Liebert, R. M., & Morris, L. W. (1967). Cognitive and emotional components of text anxiety: A distinction and some initial data. *Psychological Reports, 20*, 975–978.

Lienert, G. (1969). *Testaufbau und Testanalyse* [Test design and test analysis]. Weinheim, Germany: Beltz.

Lindsley, D. B. (1957). Psychophysiology and motivation. In M. R. Jones (Ed.), *Nebraska Symposium on Motivation, 1957* (pp. 44–105). Lincoln: University of Nebraska Press.

Lindworsky, J. (1923). *Der Wille: Seine Erscheinung und seine Beherrschung* [The will: Its emergence and its mastery] (3rd ed.). Leipzig, Germany: Barth.

Linnenbrink, E. A., & Pintrich, P. R. (2003). The role of self-efficacy beliefs in student engagement and learning in the classroom. *Reading and Writing Quarterly: Overcoming Learning Difficulties, 19*, 119–137.

Linville, P. W. (1987). Self-complexity as a cognitive buffer against stress-related illness and depression. *Journal of Personality and Social Psychology, 52*, 663–676.

Lippitt, R. (1940). An experimental study of the effect of democratic and authoritarian group atmospheres. *University of Iowa Studies in Child Welfare, 16*, 45–195.

Lissner, K. (1933). Die Entspannung von Bedürfnissen durch Ersatzhandlungen [Relieving needs by substitute actions]. *Psychologische Forschung, 18*, 218–250.

Little, B. R. (1983). Personal projects: A rationale and method for investigation. *Environment and Behavior, 15*, 273–309.

Little, B. R. (1989). Personal projects analysis: Trivial pursuits, magnificent obsessions, and the search for coherence. In D. M. Buss & N. Cantor (Eds.), *Personality psychology: Recent trends and emerging directions* (pp. 15–31). New York: Springer.

Little, B. R. (1999). Personal projects and social ecology: Themes and variations across the life span. In J. Brandstädter & R. Lerner (Eds.), *Action and self-development: Theory and research through the life span* (pp. 197–221). Thousand Oaks, CA: Sage.

Little, T. D. (1988). Sociocultural influences on the development of children's action-control beliefs. In J. Heckhausen & C. S. Dweck (Eds.), *Motivation and self-regulation across the life span* (pp. 281–315). New York: Cambridge University Press.

Little, T. D. (1998). Self-regulation and school performance: Is there optimal level of action-control? *Journal of Experimental Child Psychology, 70* (1), 54–74.

Little, T. D., & Lopez, D. (1997). Regularities in the development of children's causality beliefs about school performance across six sociocultural contexts. *Developmental Psychology, 33*, 165–175.

Little, T. D., Lopez, D., Oettingen, G., & Baltes, P. B. (2001). A comparative-longitudinal study of action-control beliefs and school performance: On the role of context. *International Journal of Behavioral Development, 25*, 237–245.

Little, T. D., Oettingen, G., Stetsenko, A., & Baltes, P. B. (1995). Children's action-control beliefs about school performance: How do American children compare with German and Russian children? *Journal of Personality and Social Psychology, 69*, 686–700.

Little, T. D., Stetsenko, A., & Maier, H. (1999). Action control beliefs and school performance: A longitudinal study of Moscow children and adolescents. *International Journal of Behavioral Development, 23*, 799–823.

Litwin, G. H. (1966). Achievement motivation, expectancy of success, and risk-taking behavior. In J. W. Atkinson & N. T. Feather (Eds.), *A theory of achievement behavior* (pp. 103–115). New York: Wiley.

Litwin, G. H., & Stringer, R. A. (1968). *Motivation and organizational climate*. Boston: Harvard University, Graduate School of Business Administration, Division of Research.

Locke, E. A. (1968). Toward a theory of task motivation and incentives. *Organizational Behavior and Human Performance, 3*, 157–189.

Locke, E. A. (1975). Personnel attitudes and motivation. *Annual Review of Psychology, 26*, 457–480.

Locke, E. A., & Latham, G. P. (1990). *A theory of goal setting and task performance*. Englewood Cliffs, NJ: Prentice Hall.

Locke, E. A., & Latham, G. P. (2002). Building a practically useful theory of goal setting and task motivation – A 35 year odyssey. *American Psychologist, 57*, 705–717.

Locke, E. A., & Shaw, K. N. (1984). Atkinson's inverse-U curve and the missing cognitive variables. *Psychological Reports, 55*, 403–412.

Loehlin, J. C. (1989). Partitioning environmental and genetic contributions to behavioral development. *American Psychologist, 44*, 1285–1292.

Logan, G. D., Schachar, R. J., & Tannock, R. (1997). Impulsivity and inhibitory control. *Psychological Science, 8*, 60–64.

Lopez, D. F., Little, T. D., Oettingen, G., & Baltes, P. B. (1998). Self regulation and school performance: Is there optimal level of action-control? *Journal of Experimental Child Psychology, 70*, 54–74.

Lorberbaum, J. P., Newman, J. D., Horwitz, A. R., Dubno, J. R., Lydiard, R. B., Hammer, M. B., Bohning, D. E., & George, M. S. (2002). A potential role for thalamocingulate circuitry in human maternal behavior. *Biological Psychiatry, 51*, 431–445.

Lorenz, K. (1935). Der Kumpan in der Umwelt des Vogels. *Journal für Ornithologie, 83*, 137–213.

Lorenz, K. (1937). Über die Bildung des Instinktbegriffs [On the construction of the concept of instinct]. *Naturwissenschaften, 25*, 289–331.

Lorenz, K. (1943). Die angebotenen Formen möglicher Erfahrung [The forms of potential experience]. *Zeitschrift für Tierpsychologie, 5*, 235–409.

Lorenz, K. (1950). The comparative method of studying innate behavior patterns. In Society for Experimental Biology (Ed.), *Physiological mechanisms in animal behavior* (pp. 221–268). New York: Academic Press.

Lorenz, K. (1966). Ethologie, die Biologie des Verhaltens [Ethology, the biology of behavior]. In F. Gessner & L. V. Bertalanffy (Eds.), *Handbuch der Biologie* (Vol. II, pp. 341–559). Frankfurt, Germany: Athenäum.

Lovejoy, C. D. (1981). The origin of man. *Science, 211*, 341–350.

Lowell, E. L. (1950). *A methodological study of projectively measured achievement motivation.* Unpublished master's thesis, Wesleyan University, Middletown, CT.

Lowell, E. L. (1952). The effect of need for achievement on learning and speed of performance. *Journal of Psychology, 33,* 31–40.

Lowin, A. (1967). Approach and avoidance: Alternate modes of selective exposure to information. *Journal of Personality and Social Psychology, 6,* 1–9.

Luginbuhl, J. E. R., Crowe, D. H., & Kahan, J. P. (1975). Causal attribution for success and failure. *Journal of Personality and Social Psychology, 31,* 86–93.

Luhmann, N. (1975). *Macht* [Power]. Stuttgart, Germany: Enke.

Lund, B., Rheinberg, F., & Gladasch, U. (2001). Ein Elterntraining zum motivationsförderlichen Erziehungsverhalten in Leistungskontexten [Teaching parents how to reduce children's fear of failure]. *Zeitschrift für Pädagogische Psychologie, 15,* 130–142.

Lundy, A. (1985). The reliability of the Thematic Apperception Test. *Journal of Personality Assessment, 49,* 141–145.

Lundy, A. (1988). Instructional set and Thematic Apperception Test validity. *Journal of Personality Assessment, 52,* 309–320.

Luria, A. R. (1973). *The working brain: An introduction to neuropsychology.* New York: Basic Books.

Luria, A. R., & Homskaya, E. D. (1964). Disturbances in the regulative role of speech with frontal lobe lesions. In J. M. Warren & K. Akert (Eds.), *The frontal granular cortex and behavior* (pp. 353–371). New York: McGraw-Hill.

Lütkenhaus, P. (1984). Pleasure derived from mastery in three-year olds: Its function for persistence and the influence of maternal behavior. *International Journal of Behavioral Development, 7,* 343–358.

Lütkenhaus, P., & Bullock, M. (1991). *Die Entwicklung von funktionalen und deklarativen Aspekten des Selbstkonzeptes bei Kleinkindern* [The development of functional and declarative aspects of the self-concept in toddlers]. Paper presented at the 8th Tagung Entwicklungspsychologie, Berne, Switzerland.

Lütkenhaus, P., Grossman, K. E., & Grossman, K. (1985). Transactional influences of infants' orienting ability and maternal cooperation on competition in three-year-old children. *International Journal of Behavioral Development, 80,* 257–272.

MacDonald, K. (1988). *Social and personality development: An evolutionary synthesis.* New York: Plenum.

MacDonald, K. (1992). Warmth as a developmental construct: An evolutionary analysis. *Child Development, 63,* 753–773.

Machiaovelli, N. (1532). *Il principe* [The prince] (L. Ricci, Trans.). New York: McGraw Hill).

MacIver, D. J., Stipek, D. J., & Daniels, D. H. (1991). Explaining within-semester changes in student effort in junior high school and senior high school courses. *Journal of Educational Psychology, 83,* 201–211.

Macrae, C. N., Bodenhausen, G. V., Milne, A. B., & Jetten, J. (1994). Out of mind but back in sight: Stereotypes on the rebound. *Journal of Personality and Social Psychology, 67,* 808–817.

Macrae, C. N., Hewstone, M., & Griffiths, R. J. (1993). Processing load and memory for stereotype-based information. *European Journal of Social Psychology, 23,* 77–87.

MacTurk, R. H., & Morgan, G. A. (1995). *Mastery motivation: Origins, conceptualization and applications. Advances in applied developmental psychology* (Vol. 12). Westport, CT: Ablex.

Madsen, K. B. (1959). *Theories of motivation.* Copenhagen, Denmark: Munksgaard.

Madsen, K. B. (1974). *Modern theories of motivation.* Copenhagen, Denmark: Munksgaard.

Maehr, M. L. (1974). Culture and achievement motivation. *American Psychologist, 29,* 887–896.

Maehr, M. L., & Kleiber, D. (1981). The graying of achievement motivation. *American Psychologist, 36,* 787–793.

Magnusson, D., & Endler, N. S. (Eds.). (1977). *Personality at the crossroads: Current issues in interactional psychology.* Hillsdale, NJ: Erlbaum.

Mahler, W. (1933). Ersatzhandlungen verschiedenen Realitätsgrades [Substitute actions on various levels of reality]. *Psychologische Forschung, 18,* 27–89.

Mai, S. (2004). *Erfolg im Verkauf – Entwicklung und Evaluation eines kognitiv-behavioralen Trainings* [Success in sales – Development and evaluation of a cognitive behavioral training program]. Unpublished doctoral dissertation, University of Hildesheim, Germany.

Maier, G. W., & Brunstein, J. C. (1999). *Action versus state orientation and disengagement from unrealistic goals.* Poster presented at the 107th annual convention of the American Psychological Association, Boston, MA.

Major, B. (1980). Information acquisition and attribution processes. *Journal of Personality and Social Psychology, 39,* 1010–1023.

Malmo, R. B. (1959). Activation: A neurophysiological dimension. *Psychological Review, 66,* 367–386.

Mandler, G. (1975). *Mind and emotion.* New York: Wiley.

Mandler, G., & Sarason, S. B. (1952). A study of anxiety and learning. *Journal of Abnormal and Social Psychology, 47,* 166–173.

Mann, P. E., & Bridges, R. S. (2001). Lactogenic hormone regulation of maternal behavior. *Progress in Brain Research, 133,* 251–262.

Mansson, H. H. (1969). The relation of dissonance reduction to cognitive, perceptual, consummatory, and learning measures of thirst. In P. G. Zimbardo (Ed.), *The cognitive control of motivation* (pp. 78–97). Glenview, IL: Scott, Foresman.

Marbe, K. (1915). Der Begriff der Bewusstseinslage [The concept of mindset]. *Fortschritte der Psychologie und ihrer Anwendungen, 3,* 27–39.

Marini, M. M. (1984). Age and sequencing norms in the transition to adulthood. *Social Forces, 63,* 229–244.

Markus, H. M., & Kitayama, S. (1991). Culture and the self: Implications for cognition, emotion and motivation. *Psychological Review, 98,* 224–253.

Marrow, A. J. (1938). Goal tensions and recall: I. *Journal of General Psychology, 19,* 3–35.

Marsh, H. W. (1989). Age and sex differences in multiple dimensions of self-concept: Preadolescence to adulthood. *Journal of Educational Psychology, 81,* 417–430.

Marsh, H. W., Byrne, B. M., & Shavelson, R. J. (1988). A multifaceted academic self-concept: Its hierarchical structure and its relation to academic achievement. *Journal of Educational Psychology, 80,* 366–380.

Marsh, H. W., Cairns, L., Relich, J., Barnes, J., & Debus, R. L. (1984). The relationship between dimensions of self-attribution and dimension of self-concept. *Journal of Educational Psychology, 76,* 3–32.

Marszal-Wisniewska, M. (2002). Model of volitional and temperamental influences on everyday functioning. *Polish Psychological Bulletin, 33,* 151–157.

Martin, A. J., Marsh, H. W., & Debus, R. L. (2001). A quadripolar need achievement representation of self-handicapping and defensive pessimism. *American Educational Research Journal, 38,* 583–610.

Martin, L. L., & Tesser, A. (1989). Toward a motivational and structural theory or ruminative thought. In J. S. Uleman & J. A. Bargh

(Eds.), *Unintended thought* (pp. 306–326). New York: Guilford Press.

Martin, L. L., & Tesser, A. (1996). Some ruminative thoughts. In R. S. Wyer, Jr. (Ed.), *Advances in social cognition* (Vol. 9, pp. 1–47). Mahwah, NJ: Erlbaum.

Martinez, J. A. (2000). Body-weight regulation: Causes of obesity. *Proceedings of the Nutritional Society, 59* (3), 337–345.

Martire, J. C. (1956). Relationship between the self-concept and differences in the strength and generality of achievement motivation. *Journal of Personality, 24*, 364–375.

Maslow, A. H. (1954). *Motivation and personality*. New York: Harper.

Maslow, A. H. (1968). *Toward a psychology of being*. New York: Van Nostrand.

Mason, A., & Blankenship, V. (1987). Power and affiliation motivation, stress, and abuse in intimate relationships. *Journal of Personality and Social Psychology, 52*, 203–210.

Massimini, F., & Carli, M. (1991). Die systematische Erfassung des Flow-Erlebens im Alltag [The systematic assessment of flow experience in everyday life]. In M. Csikszentmihalyi & I. S. Csikszentmihalyi (Eds.), *Die außergewöhnliche Erfahrung im Alltag: Die Psychologie des Flow-Erlebens* (pp. 291–312). Stuttgart, Germany: Klett-Cotta.

Matsuzawa, T. (2003). The AI project: Historical and ecological contexts. *Animal Cognition, 6* (4), 199–211.

Matthews, G., & Gilliland, K. (1999). The personality theories of H. J. Eysenck and J. A. Gray: A comparative review. *Personality and Individual Differences, 26*, 583–626.

Mayer, J. D., & Salovey, P. (1993). The intelligence of emotional intelligence. *Intelligence, 17*, 433–442.

Mayer, K. U. (1986). Structural constraints on the life course. *Human Development, 29*, 163–170.

Mayer, K. U., & Carroll, G. (1987). Jobs and classes: Structural constraints on career mobility. *European Sociological Review, 3*, 14–38.

Mayer, K. U., & Müller, W. (1986). *The state and the structure of the life course. Human development and the life course: Multidisciplinary perspectives* (pp. 217–245). Hillsdale, NJ: Erlbaum.

Mayr, E. (1974). Behavior programs and evolutionary strategies. *American Scientist, 62*, 650–659.

Mazur, A. (1985). A biosocial model of status in face-to-face primate groups. *Social Forces, 64*, 377–402.

Mazur, A., & Booth, A. (1998). Testosterone and dominance in men. *Behavioral and Brain Sciences, 21*, 353–397.

McAdams, D. P. (1979). *Validation of a thematic coding system for the intimacy motive.* Unpublished doctoral dissertation, Harvard University, Cambridge, MA.

McAdams, D. P. (1980). A thematic coding system for the intimacy motive. *Journal of Research in Personality, 14*, 413–432.

McAdams, D. P. (1982a). Intimacy motivation. In A. J. Stewart (Ed.), *Motivation and society* (pp. 133–171). San Francisco: Jossey-Bass.

McAdams, D. P. (1982b). Experiences of intimacy and power: Relationship between social motives and autobiographical memories. *Journal of Personality and Social Psychology, 42*, 292–302.

McAdams, D. P., & Constantian, C. A. (1983). Intimacy and affiliation motives in daily living: An experience sampling analysis. *Journal of Personality and Social Psychology, 45*, 851–861.

McAdams, D. P., Healy, S., & Krause, S. (1984). Social motives and patterns of friendship. *Journal of Personality and Social Psychology, 47*, 828–838.

McAdams, D. P., & McClelland. D. C. (1983). *Social motives and memory.* Unpublished manuscript, Harvard University, Department of Psychology, Cambridge, MA.

McAdams, D. P., & Powers, J. (1981). Themes of intimacy in behavior and thought. *Journal of Personality and Social Psychology, 40*, 573–587.

McAdams, D. P., & Vaillant, G. E. (1982). Intimacy motivation and psychosocial adjustment: A longitudinal study. *Journal of Personality Assessment, 46*, 586–593.

McArthur, L. A. (1972). The how and what of why: Some determinants and consequences of causal attribution. *Journal of Personality and Social Psychology, 22*, 171–193.

McArthur, L. A. (1976). The lesser influence of consensus than distinctiveness information on causal attribution. *Journal of Personality and Social Psychology, 33*, 733–742.

McClelland, D. C. (1951). *Personality.* New York: Holt, Rinehart and Winston.

McClelland, D. C. (1953). *The achievement motive.* New York: Appleton-Century-Crofts (Irvington/Wiley).

McClelland, D. C. (1958a). Methods of measuring human motivation. In J. W. Atkinson (Ed.), *Motives in fantasy, action, and society* (pp. 7–42). Princeton, NJ: Van Nostrand.

McClelland, D. C. (1958b). Risk taking in children with high and low need for achievement. In J. W. Atkinson (Ed.), *Motives in fantasy, action, and society* (pp. 306–321). Princeton, NJ: Van Nostrand.

McClelland, D. C. (1961). *The achieving society.* Princeton, NJ: Van Nostrand.

McClelland, D. C. (1965). N achievement and entrepreneurship: A longitudinal study. *Journal of Personality and Social Psychology, 1*, 389–392.

McClelland, D. C. (1970). The two faces of power. *Journal of International Affairs, 24*, 29–47.

McClelland, D. C. (1971). *Assessing human motivation.* New York: General Learning.

McClelland, D. C. (1975). *Power: The inner experience.* New York: Irvington.

McClelland, D. C. (1976). New introduction. In D. C. McClelland (Ed.), *The achieving society.* New York: Irvington.

McClelland, D. C. (1978). Managing motivation to expand human freedom. *American Psychologist, 33*, 201–210.

McClelland, D. C. (1979). Inhibited power motivation and high blood pressure in men. *Journal of Abnormal Psychology, 88*, 182–190.

McClelland, D. C. (1980). Motive dispositions: The merits of operant and respondent measures. In L. Wheeler (Ed.), *Review of personality and social psychology* (Vol. 1, pp. 10–41). Beverly Hills, CA: Sage.

McClelland, D. C. (1982). The need for power, sympathetic activation, and illness. *Motivation and Emotion, 6*, 31–41.

McClelland, D. C. (1984a). Motives as sources of long-term trends in life and health. In D. C. McClelland (Ed.), *Motives, personality, and society.* New York: Praeger.

McClelland, D. C. (1984b). The empire-building motivational syndrome. In D. C. McClelland (Ed.), *Motives, personality, and society: Selected papers* (pp. 147–174). New York: Praeger.

McClelland, D. C. (1985a). How motives, skills, and values determine what people do. *American Psychologist, 41*, 812–825.

McClelland, D. C. (1985b). *Human motivation.* Glenview, IL: Scott, Foresman.

McClelland, D. C. (1987a). *Human motivation.* New York: Cambridge University Press.

McClelland, D. C. (1987b). Biological aspects of human motivation. In F. Halisch & J. Kuhl (Eds.), *Motivation, intention, and volition* (pp. 11–19). Berlin, Germany: Springer.

McClelland, D. C. (1989). Motivational factors in health and disease. *American Psychologist, 44*, 675–683.

McClelland, D. C. (1995). Achievement motivation in relation to achievement-related recall, performance, and urine flow, a marker associated with release of vasopressin. *Motivation and Emotion, 19*, 59–76.

McClelland, D. C. (1999). *Human motivation* (6th ed.). Cambridge, UK: Cambridge University Press.

McClelland, D. C., Alexander, C., & Marks, E. (1982). The need for power, stress, immune function, and illness among male prisoners. *Journal of Abnormal Psychology, 91*, 61–70.

McClelland, D. C., Atkinson, J. W., Clark, R. A., & Lowell, E. L. (1953). *The achievement motive*. New York: Appleton-Century-Crofts.

McClelland, D. C., & Boyatzis, R. E. (1982). The leadership motive pattern and long term success in management. *Journal of Applied Psychology, 67*, 737–743.

McClelland, D. C., Clark, R. A., Roby, T. B., & Atkinson, J. W. (1949). The projective expression of need for achievement on thematic apperception. *Journal of Experimental Psychology, 39*, 242–255.

McClelland, D. C., Davis, W. N., Kalin, R., & Wanner, E. (1972). *The drinking man*. New York: Free Press.

McClelland, D. C., Davidson, R. J., Floor, E., & Saron, C. (1980). Stressed power motivation, sympathetic activation, immune function, and illness. *Journal of Human Stress, 6*, 11–19.

McClelland, D. C., Davidson, R. J., Saron, C., & Floor, E. (1980). The need for power, brain norepinephrine turnover, and learning. *Biological Psychology, 10*, 93–102.

McClelland, D. C., & Franz, C. E. (1992). Motivational and other sources of work accomplishment in mid-life: A longitudinal study. *Journal of Personality, 60*, 680–707.

McClelland, D. C., & Jemmott, J. B. (1980). Power motivation, stress, and physical illness. *Journal of Human Stress, 6*, 6–15.

McClelland, D. C., Koestner, R., & Weinberger, J. (1989). How do self-attributed and implicit motives differ? *Psychological Review, 96*, 690–702.

McClelland, D. C., & Liberman, A. M. (1949). The effects of need for achievement on recognition of need related words. *Journal of Personality, 18*, 236–251.

McClelland, D. C., Locke, S. E., Jemmot, J. B., Kraus, L., Williams, R. M., & Valeri, C. R. (1985). *Motivational syndromes associated with natural killer cell activity and illness*. Unpublished manuscript, Harvard University, Cambridge, MA.

McClelland, D. C., Maddocks, J. A., & McAdams, D. P. (1985). The need for power, brain noradrenaline turnover, and memory. *Motivation and Emotion, 9*, 1–10.

McClelland, D. C., & Miron, D. (1979). The impact of achievement motivation training in small businesses. *California Management Review, 21* (4).

McClelland, D. C., Patel, V., Stier, D., & Brown, D. (1987). The relationship of affiliative arousal to dopamine release. *Motivation and Emotion, 11*, 51–66.

McClelland, D. C., & Pilon, D. A. (1983). Sources of adult motives in patterns of parent behavior in early childhood. *Journal of Personality and Social Psychology, 44*, 564–574.

McClelland, D. C., Ross, G., & Patel, V. (1985). The effect of an academic examination on salivary norepinephrine and immunoglobuline levels. *Journal of Human Stress, 11*, 52–59.

McClelland, D. C., & Teague, G. (1975). Predicting risk preference among power related tasks. *Journal of Personality, 43*, 266–285.

McClelland, D. C., & Watson, R. I. (1973). Power motivation and risk-taking behavior. *Journal of Personality, 41*, 121–139.

McClelland, D. C., & Winter, D. G. (1969). *Motivating economic achievement*. New York: Free Press.

McCrae, R. R., & Costa, P. T. (1987). Validation of the five factor model of personality across instruments and observers. *Journal of Personality and Social Psychology, 52*, 81–90.

McCrae, R. R., & Costa, P. T. (1997). Conceptions and correlates of openness to experience. In R. Hogan, J. Johnson, & S. Briggs (Eds.), *Handbook of personality psychology* (pp. 826–848). San Diego, CA: Academic Press.

McCrae, R. R., Costa, P. T., Hrebickova, M., Ostendorf, F., Angleitner, A., Avia, M. D., Sanz, J., Sanchez-Bernardos, M. L., Kusdil, M. E., Woodfield, R., Saunders, P. R., & Smith, P. B. (2000). Nature over nurture: Temperament, personality and life span development. *Journal of Personality and Social Psychology, 78* (1), 173–186.

McDougall, W. (1908). *An introduction to social psychology*. London: Methuen.

McDougall, W. (1932). *The energies of men*. London: Methuen.

McGuire, W. J. (1966). The current status of cognitive consistency theories. In S. Feldman (Ed.), *Cognitive consistency* (pp. 1–46). New York: Academic Press.

McKeachie, W. J. (1961). Motivation, teaching methods, and college learning. In M. R. Jones (Ed.), *Nebraska Symposium on Motivation, 1961* (pp. 111–142). Lincoln: University of Nebraska Press.

McReynolds, P. (Ed.). (1971). *Advances on psychological assessment* (Vol. 2). Palo Alto, CA: Science and Behavior Books.

Meaney, M., Aitken, D., van Berkel, C., Bhatnagar, S., & Sapolsky, R. (1988). Effect of neonatal handling on age-related impairments associated with the hippocampus. *Science, 239*, 766–768.

Mehrabian, A. (1969). Measures of achieving tendency. *Educational and Psychological Measurement, 29*, 445–451.

Mehrabian, A. (1970). The development and validation of measures of affiliative tendency and sensitivity to rejection. *Educational and Psychological Measurement, 30*, 417–428.

Mehrabian, A. (1972). *Nonverbal communication*. Chicago: Aldine-Atherton.

Mehrabian, A., & Ksionzky, S. (1974). *A theory of affiliation*. Lexington, MA: Heath.

Meins, E. (1999). Sensitivity, security, and internal working models: Bridging the transmission gap. *Attachment and Human Development, 1*, 325–342.

Meltzoff, A. N., & Moore, M. (1977). Imitation of facial and manual gestures by human neonates. *Science, 198*, 75–78.

Meltzoff, A. N., & Moore, M. (1994). Imitation, memory, and the representation of persons. *Infant Behavior, 17*, 83–100.

Mertin, M. (1994). *Aufmerksamkeitszuwendung bei vorgenommenen Gelegenheiten* [Focusing attention as intended]. Unpublished Diplom thesis, Max Planck Institute for Psychological Research, Munich, Germany.

Metalsky, G. I., Halberstadt, L. J., & Abramson, L. Y. (1987). Vulnerability to depressive mood reactions: Toward a more powerful test of the diatheses – stress and causal mediation components of the reformulated theory of depression. *Journal of Personality and Social Psychology, 52*, 386–393.

Metalsky, G. I., Joiner, T. E., Hardin, T. S., & Abramson, L. Y. (1993). Depressive reactions to failure in a naturalistic setting: A test of the hopelessness and self-esteem theories of depression. *Journal of Abnormal Psychology, 102*, 101–109.

Metcalfe, J., & Jacobs, W. J. (1998). Emotional memory: The effects of stress on "cool" and "hot" memory systems. *Psychology of Learning and Motivation, 38*, 187–222.

Meumann, E. (1908/1913). *Intelligenz und Wille* [Intelligence and volition]. Leipzig, Germany: Quelle & Meyer.

Meyer, G. J., Finn, S. E., Eyde, L. D., Kay, G. G., Moreland, K. L., Dies, R. R., Eisman, E. J., Kubiszyn, T. W., & Reed, G. M. (2001). Psychological testing and psychological assessment: A review of evidence and issues. *American Psychologist, 56,* 128–165.

Meyer, W.-U. (1972). *Überlegungen zur Konstruktion eines Fragebogens zur Erfassung von Selbstkonzepten der Begabung* [Thoughts on the construction of a questionnaire to assess self-concepts of ability]. Unpublished manuscript, University of Bochum, Germany.

Meyer, W.-U. (1973a). Anstrengungsintention in Abhängigkeit von Begabungseinschätzung und Aufgabenschwierigkeit [Intended effort as a function of evaluations of ability and task difficulty]. *Archiv für Psychologie, 125,* 245–262.

Meyer, W.-U. (1973b). *Leistungsmotiv und Ursachenerklärung von Erfolg und Mißerfolg* [The achievement motive and causal attribution of success and failure]. Stuttgart, Germany: Klett.

Meyer, W.-U. (1976). Leistungsorientiertes Verhalten als Funktion von wahrgenommener eigener Begabung und wahrgenommener Aufgabenschwierigkeit [Achievement-oriented behavior as a function of self-concept of ability and perceived task difficulty]. In H.-D. Schmalt & W.-U. Meyer (Eds.), *Leistungsmotivation und Verhalten* (pp. 101–135). Stuttgart, Germany: Klett.

Meyer, W.-U. (1978). *Der Einfluss von Sanktionen auf Begabungsperzeptionen* [The influence of sanctions on perceptions of own ability] (pp. 71–87). Bielefelder Symposium über Attribution. Bielefeld, Germany.

Meyer, W.-U. (1984a). *Das Konzept von der eigenen Begabung* [Self-concept of ability]. Berne, Switzerland: Huber.

Meyer, W.-U. (1984b). Das Konzept von der eigenen Begabung: Auswirkungen, Stabilität und vorauslaufende Bedingungen [Self-concept of ability: Effects, stability, and antecedent conditions]. *Psychologische Rundschau, 35,* 136–150.

Meyer, W.-U. (1987). Perceived ability and achievement-related behavior. In F. Halisch & J. Kuhl (Eds.), *Motivation, intention, and volition* (pp. 73–86). Berlin, Germany: Springer.

Meyer, W.-U. (1988). Die Rolle von Überraschung im Attributionsprozeß [The role of surprise in the attribution process]. *Psychologische Rundschau, 39,* 136–147.

Meyer, W.-U., Heckhausen, H., & Kemmler, L. (1965). Validierungskorrelate der inhaltsanalytisch erfaßten Leistungsmotivation guter und schwacher Schüler des dritten Schuljahres [Validation correlates of the achievement motivation of good and poor third grade students as measured by picture content analysis]. *Psychologische Forschung, 28,* 301–328.

Meyer, W.-U., Mittag, W., & Engler, U. (1986). Some effects of praise and blame on perceived ability and affect. *Social Cognition, 4,* 293–308.

Meyer, W.-U., Niepel, M., Rudolph, U., & Schützwohl, A. (1991). An experimental analysis of surprise. *Cognition and Emotion, 5,* 295–311.

Meyer, W.-U., Niepel, M., & Schützwohl, A. (1994). Überraschung und Attribution [Surprise and attribution]. In F. Försterling & J. Stiensmeier-Pelster (Eds.), *Attribution: Grundlagen und Anwendungen* (pp. 105–122). Göttingen, Germany: Hogrefe.

Meyer, W.-U., Reisenzein, R., & Dickhäuser, O. (2004). Inferring ability from blame: Effects of effort- versus liking-oriented cognitive schemata. *Psychology Science, 46,* 281–293.

Meyer, W.-U., Schützwohl, A., & Reisenzein, R. (1993). *Einführung in die Emotionspsychologie: Bd. 1. Die Emotionstheorien von Watson, James und Schachter* [Introduction to the psychology of emotion: Vol. 1. The emotion theories of Watson, James und Schachter]. Berne, Switzerland: Huber.

Meyer, W.-U., Schützwohl, A., & Reisenzein, R. (1999). *Einführung in die Emotionspsychologie. Bd. II: Evolutionspsychologische Emotionstheorien* [Introduction to the psychology of emotion: Vol. 2. Evolutionary psychology theories of emotion]. Berne, Switzerland: Huber.

Meyer, W.-U., & Starke, E. (1982). Seeking information about one's own ability in relation to self-concept of ability: A field study. *Personality and Social Psychology Bulletin, 8,* 501–507.

Michalski, N. (2004). *Die Wirkung von Vorsätzen in kritischen Situationen im Tenniswettkampf* [The effects of implementation intentions in critical situations in tennis competitions]. Unpublished Diplom thesis, University of Konstanz, Germany.

Michotte, A. E. (1912). Note à propos de contributions recentes à la psychologie de la volonté. *Études de Psychologie, 1,* 193–233.

Michotte, A. E. (1954). *Autobiographie. Extrait de "Psychologica Belgia."* Louvain, Belgium: Editions Nauwelaerts.

Michotte, A. E., & Prüm, E. (1910). Étude expérimentale sur le choix volontaire et ses antecédents immediats. *Archives de Psychologie, 10,* 119–299.

Midlarsky, E. (1968). Aiding responses: An analysis and review. *Merrill-Palmer Quarterly, 14,* 229–260.

Mierke, K. (1955). *Wille und Leistung* [Volition and achievement]. Göttingen, Germany: Hogrefe.

Milana, S. A. (1981). The effects of naturally occurring depression and induced mood states on social skill. *Dissertation Abstracts International, 42,* 2541.

Milburn, M. A. (1978). Sources of bias in the prediction of future events. *Organizational Behavior and Human Performance, 21,* 17–26.

Miller, A. T. (1985). A developmental study of the cognitive basis of performance impairment after failure. *Journal of Personality and Social Psychology, 49,* 529–538.

Miller, A. T. (1987). Changes in self academic self concept in early school years: The role of conceptions of ability. *Journal of Social Behavior and Personality, 2,* 551–558.

Miller, A. T., & Hom, H. (1990). Influence of extrinsic and ego incentive value on persistence after failure and continuing motivation. *Journal of Educational Psychology, 82,* 539–545.

Miller, A. T., & Hom, H. (1997). Conceptions of ability and the interpretation of praise, blame and material rewards. *Journal of Experimental Education, 65,* 163–177.

Miller, D. T. (1976). Ego involvement and attribution for success and failure. *Journal of Personality and Social Psychology, 34,* 901–906.

Miller, D. T., & Ross, M. (1975). Self-serving biases in the attribution of causality: Fact or fiction? *Psychological Bulletin, 82,* 213–225.

Miller, K. S., & Worchel, P. (1956). The effects of need-achievement and self-ideal discrepancy on performance under stress. *Journal of Personality, 25,* 176–190.

Miller, N. E. (1941). An experimental investigation of acquired drives. *Psychological Bulletin, 38,* 534–535.

Miller, N. E. (1944). Experimental studies of conflict. In J. M. Hunt (Ed.), *Personality and the behavioral disorders* (Vol. I, pp. 431–465). New York: Ronald.

Miller, N. E. (1948). Studies of fear as an acquirable drive: I. Fear as motivation and fear-reduction as reinforcement in the learning of new responses. *Journal of Experimental Psychology, 38*, 89–101.

Miller, N. E. (1951). Learnable drives and rewards. In S. S. Stevens (Ed.), *Handbook of experimental psychology* (pp. 435–472). New York: Wiley.

Miller, N. E. (1956). Effects of drugs on motivation: The value of using a variety of measures. *Annals of the New York Academy of Science, 65*, 318–333.

Miller, N. E. (1959). Liberalization of basic S-R concepts: Extensions to conflict behavior, motivation, and social learning. In S. Koch (Ed.), *Psychology: A study of a science* (Vol. II, pp. 196–292). New York: McGraw-Hill.

Miller, N. E. (1961). Analytical studies of drive and reward. *American Psychologist, 16*, 739–754.

Miller, N. E. (1963). Some reflections on the law of effect produce a new alternative to drive reduction. In M. R. Jones (Ed.), *Nebraska Symposium on Motivation, 1963* (pp. 65–112). Lincoln: University of Nebraska Press.

Miller, N. E., & Dollard, J. (1941). *Social learning and imitation.* New Haven, CT: Yale University Press.

Milne, S., Orbell, S., & Sheeran, P. (2002). Combining motivational and volitional interventions to promote exercise participation: Protection motivation theory and implementation intentions. *British Journal of Health Psychology, 7*, 163–184.

Milner, P. (1970). *Physiological psychology.* New York: Holt, Rinehart and Winston.

Mischel, T. (1970). Wundt and the conceptual foundations of psychology. *Philosophical and Phenomenological Research, 31*, 1–26.

Mischel, W., Cantor, N., & Feldman, S. (1996). Principles of self-regulation: The nature of willpower and self-control. In E. T. Higgins & A. W. Kruglanski (Eds.), *Social psychology: Handbook of basic principles* (pp. 329–360). New York: Guilford Press.

Mischel, W., & Gilligan, C. (1964). Delay of gratification, motivation for the prohibited gratification, and responses to temptation. *Journal of Abnormal and Social Psychology, 69*, 411–417.

Mischel, W., & Shoda, Y. (1995). A cognitive-affective system theory of personality: Reconceptualizing situations, dispositions, dynamics, and invariance in personality structure. *Psychological Review, 102*, 246–268.

Mischel, W., & Shoda, Y. (1998). Reconciling processing dynamics and personality dispositions. *Annual Review of Psychology, 49*, 229–258.

Mischel, W., Shoda, Y., & Smith, R.E. (2004). *Introduction to personality* (7th ed.). New York: Wiley.

Mitchell, T. R. (1974). Expectancy models of job satisfaction, occupational preference and effort: A theoretical, methodological, and empirical appraisal. *Psychological Bulletin, 81*, 1053–1077.

Mitchell, T. R. (1982). Expectancy-value models in organizational psychology. In N. T. Feather (Ed.), *Expectations and actions: Expectancy-value models in psychology* (pp. 293–312). Hillsdale, NJ: Erlbaum.

Mitchell, T. R., & Albright, D. (1972). Expectancy theory predictions of job satisfaction, job effort, job performance, and retention of naval aviation officers. *Organizational Behavior and Human Performance, 8*, 1–20.

Mitchell, T. R., & Biglan, A. (1971). Instrumentality theories: Current uses in psychology. *Psychological Bulletin, 76*, 432–454.

Mittag, H.-D. (1955). Über personale Bedingungen des Gedächtnisses für Handlungen [On the personal conditions of memory for actions]. *Zeitschrift für Psychologie, 158*, 40–120.

Modell, J. (1980). Normative aspects of American marriage timing since World War II. *Journal of Family History, 5*, 210–234.

Modell, J., Fürstenberg, F. F. J., & Hershberg, T. (1976). Social change and transitions to adulthood in historical perspective. *Journal of Family History, 1*, 7–32.

Modell, J., Fürstenberg, F. F. J., & Strong, D. (1978). The timing of marriage in the transition to adulthood: Continuity and change. *American Journal of Sociology, 84*, 120–150.

Mogenson, G. J., Jones, D. L., & Yim, C. Y. (1980). From motivation to action: Functional interface between the limbic system and the motor system. *Progress in Neurobiology, 14*, 69–97.

Molden, D. C., & Dweck, C. S. (2000). Meaning and motivation. In C. Sansone & J. M. Harackiewicz (Eds.), *Intrinsic and extrinsic motivation* (pp. 131–159). San Diego, CA: Academic Press.

Moller, A. C., & Elliot, A. J. (2006). The 2 × 2 achievement goal framework: An overview of empirical research. In A. V. Mitel (Ed.), *Focus on educational psychology research* (pp. 307–326). New York: Nova Science.

Moneta, G. B., & Csikszentmihalyi, M. (1996). The effect of perceived challenges and skills on the quality of subjective experience. *Journal of Personality, 64*, 274–310.

Monson, T. C., & Snyder, M. (1977). Actors, observers, and the attribution process. *Journal of Experimental Social Psychology, 13*, 89–111.

Morgan, C. D., & Murray, H. A. (1935). A method for investigating fantasies: The Thematic Apperceptive Test. *Archives of Neurological Psychiatry, 34*, 289–306.

Morgan, C. T. (1943). *Physiological psychology.* New York: McGraw-Hill.

Morris, J. S., Öhman, A., & Dolan, R. J. (1998). Conscious and unconscious emotional learning in the human amygdala. *Nature, 393*(6684), 467–470.

Moruzzi, G., & Magoun, H. W. (1949). Brain stem reticular formation and activation of the EEG. *EEG and Clinical Neurophysiology, 1*, 455–473.

Mosher, D. (1968). Measurement of guilt in females by self-report inventories. *Journal of Consulting and Clinical Psychology, 32*, 690–695.

Moulton, R. W. (1958). Notes for a projective measure of fear of failure. In J. W. Atkinson (Ed.), *Motives in fantasy, action, and society* (pp. 563–571). Princeton, NJ: Van Nostrand.

Moulton, R. W. (1965). Effects of success and failure on level of aspiration as related to achievement motives. *Journal of Personality and Social Psychology, 1*, 399–406.

Mowrer, H. O. (1939). A stimulus-response analysis of anxiety and its role as a reinforcing agent. *Psychological Review, 46*, 553–565.

Mowrer, H. O. (1947). On the dual nature of learning: A reinterpretation of "conditioning" and "problem-solving." *Harvard Educational Review, 17*, 102–148.

Mowrer, H. O. (1960). *Learning theory and behavior.* New York: Wiley.

Müller, G. E., & Pilzecker, A. (1900). *Experimentelle Beiträge zur Lehre vom Gedächtnis* [Experimental contributions to memory research]. Leipzig, Germany: Barth.

Münsterberg, H. (1888). *Die Willenshandlung: Ein Beitrag der physiologischen Psychologie* [Volitional acts: A contribution to physiological psychology]. Freiburg, Germany: Moler.

Muraven, M., & Baumeister, R. (2000). Self-regulation and depletion of limited resources: Does self-control resemble a muscle? *Psychological Bulletin, 126*, 247–259.

Muraven, M., Tice, D. M., & Baumeister, R. F. (1998). Self-control as a limited resource: Regulatory depletion patterns. *Journal of Personality and Social Psychology, 74*, 774–789.

Murphy, S. T., & Zajonc, R. B. (1993). Affect, cognition and awareness: Affective priming with optimal and suboptimal stimulus exposures. *Journal of Personality and Social Psychology, 64*, 723–739.

Murray, E. J., & Berkun, M. M. (1955). Displacement as a function of conflict. *Social Psychology, 51*, 47–56.

Murray, H. A. (1933). The effect of fear upon estimates of the maliciousness of other personalities. *Journal of Social Psychology, 4*, 310–329.

Murray, H. A. (1938). *Explorations in personality.* New York: Oxford University Press.

Murray, H. A. (1943). *Thematic Apperceptive Test Manual.* Cambridge, MA: Harvard University Press.

Murstein, B. I., & Pryer, R. S. (1959). The concept of projection: A review. *Psychological Bulletin, 56*, 353–374.

Nakamura, J. (1991). Optimales Erleben und die Nutzung der Begabung [Optimal experience and making use of talent]. In M. Csikszentmihalyi & I. S. Csikszentmihalyi (Eds.), *Die außergewöhnliche Erfahrung im Alltag: Die Psychologie des Flow-Erlebens* (pp. 326–334). Stuttgart, Germany: Klett-Cotta.

Neiss, R. (1988). Reconceptualizing arousal: Psychobiological states in motor performance. *Psychological Bulletin, 103*, 345–366.

Nelson, E. E., & Panksepp, J. (1998). Brain substrates of infant-mother attachment: Contributions of opioids, oxytocin, and norepinephrine. *Neuroscience and Biobehavioral Reviews, 22*(3), 437–452.

Nelson, R. J. (2005). *An introduction to behavioral endocrinology* (3rd ed.). Sunderland, MA: Sinauer Associates.

Nesse, R. M. (2000). Is depression an adaptation? *Archives of General Psychiatry, 57*, 14–20.

Nesse, R. M. (2001). *Evolution and the capacity for commitment. Volume III in the Russell Sage Foundation Series on Trust.* New York: Sage.

Neugarten, B. L. (1979). Time, age, and the life cycle. *American Journal of Psychiatry, 136*, 887–894.

Neugarten, B. L., Moore, J. W., & Lowe, J. C. (1965). Age norms, age constraints and adult socialization. *American Journal of Sociology, 70*, 710–717.

Neumann, J., & Morgenstern, O. (1944). *Theory of games and economic behavior.* Princeton, NJ: Princeton University Press.

Newell, A., & Rosenbloom, P. S. (1981). Mechanisms of skill acquisition and the law of practice. In J. R. Anderson (Ed.), *Cognitive skills and their acquisition* (pp. 1–55). Hillsdale, NJ: Erlbaum.

Newtson, D. (1974). Dispositional inference from effects of actions: Effects chosen and effects foregone. *Journal of Experimental Social Psychology, 10*, 489–496.

Nicholls, J. G. (1975). Causal attributions and other achievement-related cognitions: Effects of task outcome, attainment value, and sex. *Journal of Personality and Social Psychology, 31*, 379–389.

Nicholls, J. G. (1976). Effort is virtuous, but it's better to have ability: Evaluative responses to perceptions of effort and ability. *Journal of Personality and Social Psychology, 10*, 306–315.

Nicholls, J. G. (1978). The development of the concepts of effort and ability, perception of own attainment, and the understanding that difficult tasks require more than ability. *Child Development, 49*, 800–814.

Nicholls, J. G. (1984a). Achievement motivation: Conceptions of ability, subjective experience, task choice, and performance. *Psychological Review, 91*, 328–346.

Nicholls, J. G. (1984b). Conceptions of ability and achievement motivation. In R. Ames & C. Ames (Eds.), *Student motivation* (pp. 39–73). Orlando, FL: Academic Press.

Nicholls, J. G. (1985). Development and its discontents: The differentiation of the concept of ability. In J. G. Nicholls (Ed.), *The development of achievement motivation* (pp. 185–218). Greenwich, CT: JAI Press.

Nicholls, J. G. (1989). *The competitive ethos and democratic education.* Cambridge, MA: Harvard University Press.

Nicholls, J. G., & Miller, A. T. (1983). The differentiation of the concepts of difficulty and ability. *Child Development, 54*, 951–959.

Niederberger, U., Engemann, A., & Radtke, M. (1987). Umfang der Informationsverarbeitung bei Entscheidungen: Der Einfluss von Gedächtnisbelastung und Handlungsorientierung [Scope of information processing in decision making: The impact of load and action orientation]. *Zeitschrift für Experimentelle und Angewandte Psychologie, 34*, 80–100.

Nietzsche, F. (1878). *Menschliches, allzumenschliches* [Human, all-too-human] (H. Zimmern, Trans.). Dover Publication.

Niitamo, P. (1999). *"Surface" and "depth" in human personality: Relations between explicit and implicit motives.* Helsinki, Finland: Finish Institute of Occupational Health.

Nisbett, R. E., & Borgida, E. (1975). Attribution and the psychology of prediction. *Journal of Personality and Social Psychology, 32*, 932–943.

Nisbett, R. E., Borgida, E., Crandall, R., & Reed, H. (1976). Popular induction: Information is not necessarily informative. In J. Carroll & J. Payne (Eds.), *Cognitive and social behavior* (pp. 113–133). Hillsdale, NJ: Erlbaum.

Nisbett, R. E., & Wilson, T. D. (1977). Telling more than we can know: Verbal reports on mental processes. *Psychological Review, 84*, 231–259.

Nolen-Hoecksema, S., Girgus, J. S., & Seligman, M. E. P. (1992). Predictors and consequences of childhood symptoms: A 5-year longitudinal study. *Journal of Abnormal Psychology, 101*, 405–422.

Nolen-Hoeksema, S., Parker, L., & Larson, J. (1994). Ruminative coping with depressed mood following loss. *Journal of Personality and Social Psychology, 67*, 92–104.

Norman, D. A. (1980). Twelve issues for cognitive science. *Cognitive Science, 4*, 1–32.

Norman, D. A., & Shallice, T. (1986). Attention to action: Willed and automatic control of behavior. In R. J. Davidson, G. E. Schwartz, & D. Shapiro (Eds.), *Consciousness and self-regulation: Advances in research* (Vol. 4, pp. 1–18). New York: Plenum.

Novak, T. P., & Hoffman, D. L. (1997, July). *Measuring the flow experience among web users.* Paper presented at the Interval Research Corporation, Vanderbilt University, Nashville, Tennessee.

Nurmi, J. E. (1992). Age differences in adult life goals, concerns and their temporal extension: A life course approach to future-oriented motivation. *International Journal of Behavioral Development, 15*, 487–508.

Nurmi, J. E., & Salmela-Aro, K. (2002). Goal construction, reconstruction and depressive symptoms in a life-span context: The transition from school to work. *Journal of Personality, 70*, 385–420.

Nurmi, J. E., Salmela-Aro, K., & Koivisto, P. (2002). Goal importance and related achievement beliefs and emotions during the transition from vocational school to work: Antecedents and consequences. *Journal of Vocational Behavior, 60*, 241–261.

Nygard, R. (1975). A reconsideration of the achievement motivation theory. *European Journal of Social Psychology, 5*, 61–92.

Nygard, R. (1977). *Personality, situation, and persistence.* Oslo, Norway: Universitetsforlaget.

Nygard, R. (1982). Achievement motives and individual differences in situational specificity of behavior. *Journal of Personality and Social Psychology, 43*, 319–327.

Ochsner, K. N., Bunge, S. A., Gross, J. J., & Gabrieli, J. D. (2002). Rethinking feelings: An fMRI study of the cognitive regulation of emotion. *Journal of Cognitive Neuroscience, 14*(8), 1215–1229.

O'Connor, P., Atkinson, J. W., & Horner, M. S. (1966). Motivational implications of ability grouping in schools. In J. W. Atkinson & N. T. Feather (Eds.), *A theory of achievement motivation* (pp. 231–248). New York: Wiley.

O'Doherty, J., Kringelbach, M. L., Rolls, E. T., Hornak, J., & Andrews, C. (2001). Abstract reward and punishment representations in the human orbitofrontal cortex. *Nature Neuroscience, 4*(1), 95–102.

Oettingen, G. (1996). Positive fantasy and motivation. In P. M. Gollwitzer & J. A. Bargh (Eds.), *Psychology of action: Linking cognition and motivation to behavior* (pp. 236–259). New York: Guilford Press.

Oettingen, G. (1997). *Psychologie des Zukunftsdenkens* [The psychology of thinking about the future]. Göttingen, Germany: Hogrefe.

Oettingen, G. (2000). Expectancy effects on behavior depend on self-regulatory thought. *Social Cognition, 18*, 101–129.

Oettingen, G., & Gollwitzer, P. M. (2000). Das Setzen und Verwirklichen von Zielen [Goal setting and goal striving]. *Zeitschrift für Psychologie, 208*(3–4), 406–430.

Oettingen, G., & Gollwitzer, P. M. (2001). Goal setting and goal striving. In A. Tesser & N. Schwarz (Eds.), *The Blackwell handbook of social psychology* (pp. 329–347). Oxford, UK: Blackwell.

Oettingen, G., Pak, H. J., & Schnetter, K. (2001). Self-regulation of goal-setting: Turning free fantasies about the future into binding goals. *Journal of Personality and Social Psychology, 80*, 736–753.

Öhman, A., Fredrikson, M., Hughdal, K., & Rimmö, P. A. (1976). The premise of equipotentiality in human classical conditioning: Conditioned electrodermal responses to potentially phobic stimuli. *Journal of Experimental Psychology: General, 105*, 313–337.

Olds, J. (1955). Physiological mechanisms of reward. In M. R. Jones (Ed.), *Nebraska Symposium on Motivation, 1955* (pp. 73–139). Lincoln: University of Nebraska Press.

Olds, J. (1958). Satiation effects in self-stimulation of the brain. *Journal of Comparative and Physiological Psychology, 51*, 675–679.

Olds, J. (1969). The central nervous system and the reinforcement of behavior. *American Psychologist, 24*, 114–132.

Olds, J., & Milner, P. (1954). Positive reinforcement produced by electrical stimulation of septal area and other regions of rat brain. *Journal of Comparative Physiological Psychology, 47*, 419–427.

Olds, J., & Olds, M. (1965). Drives, rewards, and the brain. In T. N. Newcomb (Ed.), *New directions in psychology* (Vol. II, pp. 327–404). New York: Holt, Rinehart and Winston.

Olweus, D. (1976). Der "moderne" Interaktionismus von Person und Situation und seine varianzanalytische Sackgasse [The "modern" interactionism of person and situation and the impasse of variance analysis]. *Zeitschrift für Entwicklungspsychologie und Pädagogische Psychologie, 8*, 171–185.

Orbell, S. (2003). Personality systems interaction theory and the theory of planned behavior: Evidence that self-regulatory volitional components enhance enactment of studying behavior. *British Journal of Social Psychology, 42*, 95–112.

Orbell, S., Hodgkins, S., & Sheeran, P. (1997). Implementation intentions and the theory of planned behavior. *Personality and Social Psychology Bulletin, 23*, 945–954.

Orbell, S., & Sheeran, P. (2000). Motivational and volitional processes in action initiation: A field study of the role of implementation intentions. *Journal of Applied Social Psychology, 30*, 780–797.

Orpen, C. (1983). Risk-taking attitudes among Indian, United States, and Japanese managers. *Journal of Social Psychology, 120*, 283–284.

Ortony, A., Clore, G. L., & Collins, A. (1988). *The cognitive structure of emotions.* Cambridge, UK: Cambridge University Press.

Orvis, B. R., Cunningham, J. D., & Kelley, H. H. (1975). A closer examination of causal inference: The role of consensus, distinctiveness, and consistency information. *Journal of Personality and Social Psychology, 32*, 605–616.

Oster, G., & Alberch, P. (1982). Evolution and bifurcation of developmental programs. *Evolution, 36*, 444–459.

Ovsiankina, M. (1928). Die Wiederaufnahme unterbrochener Handlungen [The resumption of interrupted activities]. *Psychologische Forschung, 11*, 302–379.

Oyegbile, T. O. and Marler, C. A. (2005). Winning fights elevates testosterone levels in California mice and enhances future ability to win fights. *Hormones and Behavior 48*, 259–267.

Packard, M. G., Cornell, A. H., & Alexander, G. M. (1997). Rewarding affective properties of intra-nucleus accumbens injections of testosterone. *Behavioral Neuroscience, 111*, 219–224.

Pajares, F. (1996). Self-efficacy beliefs in academic settings. *Review of Educational Research, 66*, 543–578.

Palfai, T. P. (2002). Action-state orientation and the self-regulation of eating behavior. *Eating Behaviors, 3*, 249–259.

Palfai, T. P., McNally, A. M., & Roy, M. (2002). Volition and alcohol-risk reduction: The role of action orientation in the reduction of alcohol-related harm among college student drinkers. *Addictive Behaviors, 27*, 309–317.

Pang, J. S., & Schultheiss, O. C. (2005). Assessing implicit motives in U.S. college students: Effects of picture type and position, gender and ethnicity, and cross-cultural comparisons. *Journal of Personality Assessment, 85*(3), 280–294.

Panksepp, J. (1998). *Affective neuroscience: The foundations of human and animal emotions.* New York: Oxford University Press.

Panksepp, J. (2003). Feeling the pain of social rejection. *Science, 302*, 237–239.

Papoušek, H. (1967). Experimental studies of appetitional behavior in human newborns and infants. In H. W. Stevenson, E. H. Hess, & H. L. Rheingold (Eds.), *Early behavior: Comparative developmental approaches* (pp. 249–277). New York: Wiley.

Papoušek, H., & Papoušek, M. (1975). Cognitive aspects of preverbal social interaction between human infants and adults. In M. Hofer (Ed.), *Parent-infant interaction* (pp. 241–269). Amsterdam: Elsevier.

Papoušek, H., & Papoušek, M. (1987). Intuitive parenting: A dialectic counterpart to the infant's integrative competence. In J. D. Osofsky (Eds.), *Handbook of infant development* (2nd ed., pp. 669–720). New York: Wiley.

Parsons, J. E., & Ruble, D. (1977). The development of achievement-related expectancies. *Child Development, 48*, 1075–1079.

Passman, R. H., & Erck, T. (1978). Permitting maternal contact through vision alone: Films of mothers for promoting play and locomotion. *Developmental Psychology, 14*(5), 512–516.

Patten, R. L., & White, L. A. (1977). Independent effects of achievement motivation and overt attribution on achievement behavior. *Motivation and Emotion, 1*, 39–59.

Paul, R. (2001). The school-to-work transition: A cross-national perspective. *Journal of Economic Literature, 39*, 34–92.

Pavlov, I. P. (1927). *Conditioned reflexes.* London: Oxford University Press.

Peak, H. (1955). Attitude and motivation. In M. R. Jones (Ed.), *Nebraska Symposium on Motivation, 1955* (pp. 149–189). Lincoln: University of Nebraska Press.

Pecina, S., Cagniard, B., Berridge, K. C., Aldridge, J. W., & Zhuang, X. (2003). Hyperdopaminergic mutant mice have higher "wanting" but not "liking" for sweet rewards. *Journal of Neuroscience, 23*(28), 9395–9402.

Peck, J. W., & Blass, E. M. (1975). Localization of thirst and antidiuretic osmoreceptors by intracranial injections in rats. *American Journal of Physiology, 5*, 1501–1509.

Pekrun, R. (1993). Entwicklung von schulischer Aufgabenmotivation in der Sekundarstufe: Ein erwartungswert-theoretischer Ansatz [Development of task-related motivation in secondary school: An expectancy-value approach]. *Zeitschrift für Pädagogische Psychologie, 7*, 87–98.

Pennebaker, J. W. (1993). Putting stress into words: Health, linguistic, and therapeutic implications. *Behaviour Research and Therapy, 31*, 539–548.

Penner, D. D., Fitch, G., & Weick, K. E. (1966). Dissonance and the revision of choice criteria. *Journal of Personality and Social Psychology, 3*, 701–705.

Perin, C. I. (1942). Behavioral potentiality as a joint function of the amount of training and the degree of hunger at the time of extinction. *Journal of Experimental Psychology, 30*, 93–113.

Perloff, L. S., & Fetzer, B. K. (1986). Self-other judgements and perceived vulnerability of victimization. *Journal of Personality and Social Psychology, 50*, 502–510.

Pérusse, D. (1993). Cultural and reproductive success in industrial societies: Testing the relationship at the proximate and ultimate levels. *Behavioral and Brain Sciences, 16*, 267–322.

Pérusse, D. (1994). Mate choice in modern societies: Testing evolutionary hypotheses with behavioural data. *Human Nature, 5*, 255–278.

Pervin, L. A. (Ed.). (1989). *Goal concepts in personality and social psychology.* Hillsdale, NJ: Erlbaum.

Peterson, B. E., & Stewart, A. J. (1993). Generativity and social motives in young adults. *Journal of Personality and Social Psychology, 65*, 186–198.

Peterson, C., & Seligman, M. E. P. (1984). Causal explanations as a risk factor for depression: Theory and evidence. *Psychological Review, 91*, 347–374.

Peterson, C., Semmel, A., von Baeyer, C., Abramson, L. Y., Metalsky, G. I., & Seligman, M. E. P. (1982). The attributional style questionnaire. *Cognitive Therapy and Research, 6*, 287–299.

Pfaffmann, C. (1982). Taste: A model of incentive motivation. In D. W. Pfaff (Ed.), *The physiological mechanisms of motivation* (pp. 61–97). New York: Springer.

Pfänder, A. (1911). Motive und Motivation [Motives and motivation]. In A. Pfänder (Ed.), *Münchener Philosophische Abhandlungen (Festschrift für Theodor Lipps)* (pp. 163–195). Leipzig, Germany: Barth.

Pfaus, J. G., Damsma, G., Wenkstern, D., & Fibiger, H. C. (1995). Sexual activity increases dopamine transmission in the nucleus accumbens and striatum of female rats. *Brain Research, 693*(1–2), 21–30.

Pfister, R. (2002). *Flow im Alltag* [Flow in everyday life]. Berne, Switzerland: Lang.

Phares, E. J. (1976). *Locus of control in personality.* Morristown, NJ: General Learning.

Piaget, J. (1936). *Le naissance de l'intelligence chez l'enfant.* Neuchâtel, Switzerland: Delachaux et Nestlé.

Piaget, J. (1952). *The origins of intelligence in children.* New York: International University Press.

Pikowsky, B. (1988). Lob im Unterricht: Lehrer- und Schülerkognitionen im Vergleich [Praise in school classes: Comparison of teacher and student cognitions]. *Zeitschrift für Pädagogische Psychologie, 2*, 251–257.

Pintrich, P. R., & De Groot, E. (1990). Motivational and self-regulated learning components of classroom academic performance. *Journal of Educational Psychology, 82*, 33–40.

Pintrich, P. R., & Garcia, T. (1991). Student goal orientation and self-regulation in the college classroom. In M. Maehr & P. R. Pintrich (Eds.), *Advance in motivation and achievement: Goals and self-regulatory processes* (Vol. 7, pp. 371–402). Greenwich, CT: JAI Press.

Pizzagalli, D. A., Regard, M., & Lehmann, D. (1999). Rapid emotional face processing in the human right and left brain hemispheres: An ERP study. *NeuroReport, 10*, 2691–2698.

Plath, D. W., & Ikeda, K. (1975). After coming of age: Adult awareness of age norms. In T. R. Williams (Ed.), *Socialization and communication in primacy groups* (pp. 107–123). The Hague, Netherlands: Mouton.

Plomin, R. (2004). Genetics and developmental psychology. *Merrill-Palmer Quarterly, 50*, 341–352.

Plomin, R., DeFries, J. C., Craig, I. W., & McGuffin, P. (Eds.). (2003). *Behavioral genetics in the postgenomic era.* Washington, DC: American Psychological Association.

Plomin, R., & Roew, D. C. (1979). Genetic and environmental psychology. *Developmental Psychology, 15*, 62–72.

Plutchi, R. (1980). *Emotion: A psychoevolutionary synthesis.* New York: Harper & Row.

Pomerantz, E. M., & Ruble, D. (1997). Distinguishing multiple dimensions of conceptions of ability: Implications for self-evaluations. *Child Development, 68*, 1165–1180.

Poppe, P. (2002). *Nutzung von Kovariationsinformationen im Attributionsprozess: Ein Vergleich depressiver und nichtdepressiver Erwachsener* [Use of covariation information in the attribution process: A comparison of depressive and nondepressive adults]. Unpublished Diplom thesis, University of Gießen, Germany.

Poppe, P., Stiensmeier-Pelster, J., & Pelster, A. (2005). *Attributionsstilfragebogen für Erwachsene* (ASF-E) [Attribution style questionnaire for adults (ASF-E)]. Göttingen, Germany: Hogrefe.

Porter, L. W., & Lawler, E. E. (1968). *Managerial attitudes and performance.* Homewood, IL: Irwin-Dorsey.

Porter, R. H. (1998). Olfaction and human kin recognition. *Genetica, 104*(3), 259–263.

Pösl, I. (1994). *Wiederaufnahme unterbrochener Handlungen: Effekte der Bewusstseinslagen des Abwägens und Planens* [Mindset effects on the resumption of disrupted activities]. Unpublished Diplom thesis, University of Munich, Germany.

Posner, M. I., & Rothbart, M. K. (1992). Attentional mechanisms and conscious experience. In A. D. Milner & M. D. Rugg (Eds.), *The neuropsychology of consciousness* (pp. 91–111). New York: Academic Press.

Postman, L., & Solomon, R. L. (1949). Perceptual sensitivity to completed and incompleted tasks. *Journal of Personaiity, 18*, 347–357.

Poulin, M., Haase, C. M., & Heckhausen, J. (2005). Engagement and disengagement across the life-span: An analysis of two process models of development regulation.

In W. Greve, K. Rothermund, & D. Wentura (Eds.), *The adaptive self: Personal continuity and intentional self-development* (pp. 117–135). Göttingen, Germany: Hogrefe & Huber.

Pribram, K. H. (1976). Self-consciousness and intentionality. In G. E. Schwartz & D. Shapiro (Eds.), *Consciousness and self-regulation: Advances in research* (Vol. 1, pp. 51–100). New York: Wiley.

Pritchard, R. D., & Sanders, M. S. (1973). The influence of valence, instrumentality, and expectancy of effort and performance. *Journal of Applied Psychology, 57,* 55–60.

Pruitt, D. J., & Insko, C. A. (1980). Extension of the Kelley attribution model: The role of comparison-object consensus, target-object consensus, distinctiveness, and consistency. *Journal of Personality and Social Psychology, 39,* 39–58.

Puca, R. M. (2001). Preferred difficulty and subjective probability in different action phases. *Motivation and Emotion, 25,* 307–326.

Puca, R. M., & Schmalt, H. (2001). The influence of the achievement motive on spontaneous thoughts in pre- and postdecisional action phases. *Personality and Social Psychology Bulletin, 27,* 302–308.

Pusey, A., Williams, J., & Goodall, J. (1997). The influence of dominance rank on the reproductive success of female chimpanzees. *Science, 277,* 828–831.

Pyszczynski, T. A., & Greenberg, J. (1987). Toward an integration of cognitive and motivational perspectives on social inference: A biased hypotheses-testing model. In L. Berkowitz (Ed.), *Advances in experimental social psychology* (Vol. 20). San Diego, CA: Academic Press.

Radloff, L. (1977). The CES-D scale: A self report depression scale for research in the general population. *Applied Psychological Measurement, 1,* 385–401.

Ramey, C., & Finkelstein, N. (1978). Contingent stimulation and infant competence. *Journal of Pediatric Psychology, 3,* 89–96.

Rank, O. (1945). *Will therapy and truth and reality.* New York: Alfred A. Knopf.

Rapaport, D. (1959). The structure of psychoanalytic theory: A systematizing attempt. In S. Koch (Ed.), *Psychology: A study of a science* (Vol. III, pp. 55–183). New York: McGraw-Hill.

Rapaport, D. (1960). On the psychoanalytic theory of motivation. In M. R. Jones (Ed.), *Nebraska Symposium on Motivation, 1960* (pp. 173–247). Lincoln: University of Nebraska Press.

Raps, C. S., Peterson, C., Reinhard, K. E., Abramson, L. Y., & Seligman, M. E. P. (1982). Attributional style among depressed patients. *Journal of Abnormal Psychology, 91,* 102–108.

Rasch, G. (1960). *Probabilistic models for some intelligence and attainment tests.* Copenhagen, Denmark: Nielson & Lydicke.

Raup, R. B. (1925). *Complacency, the foundation of human behavior.* New York: Macmillan.

Raven, B. H. (1974). The comparative analysis of power and power preference. In J. T. Tedeschi (Ed.), *Perspectives on social power.* Chicago: Aldine.

Raynor, J. O. (1969). Future orientation and motivation of immediate activity: An elaboration of the theory of achievement motivation. *Psychological Review, 76,* 606–610.

Raynor, J. O. (1974). Future orientation in the study of achievement motivation. In J. W. Atkinson & J. O. Raynor (Eds.), *Motivation and achievement* (pp. 121–154). Washington, DC: Winston.

Raynor, J. O., & Entin, E. E. (1982). *Motivation, career striving and aging.* Washington, DC: Hemisphere.

Raynor, J. O., & Roeder, G. P. (1987). Motivation and future orientation: Task and time effects for achievement motivation. In F. Halisch & J. Kuhl (Eds.), *Motivation, intention, and volition* (pp. 61–71). Berlin, Germany: Springer.

Reif, M. (1970). *Leistungsmotivation in Abhängigkeit vom Erziehungsverhalten der Mutter* [Achievement motivation as a function of the mother's parenting]. Unpublished Diplom thesis, University of Bochum, Germany.

Reitman, W. R. (1960). Motivational induction and the behavioral correlates of the achievement and affiliation motives. *Journal of Abnormal and Social Psychology, 60,* 8–13.

Remy, K. (2000). *Entwicklung eines Fragebogens zum Flow-Erleben* [Development of a questionnaire on flow experience]. Unpublished Diplom thesis, University of Bielefeld, Germany.

Rescorla, R. A. (1968). Probability of shock in the presence and absence of CS in fear conditioning. *Journal of Comparative and Physiological Psychology, 66,* 1–5.

Rescorla, R. A. (1972). Informational variables in Pavlovian conditioning. In G. H. Bower (Ed.), *The psychology of learning and motivation* (pp. 1–46). New York: Academic Press.

Rescorla, R. A., & Wagner, A. R. (1972). A theory of Pavlovian conditioning: Variations in the effectiveness of reinforcement and nonreinforcement. In A. H. Black & W. Prokasy (Eds.), *Classical conditioning II: Current theory and research* (pp. 64–99). New York: Appleton.

Resnik, S. M. Gottesman, I. I., & McGue, M. (1993). Sensation seeking in opposite-sex twins: An effect of prenatal hormones? *Behavior Genetics, 23,* 323–329.

Rethorts, S. (1994). Attribution und Emotion in der sportpsychologischen Forschung [Attribution and emotion in sports psychology research]. In F. Försterling & J. Stiensmeier-Pelster (Eds.), *Attributionstheorie* (pp. 163–183). Göttingen, Germany: Hogrefe.

Reuman, D. A. (1982). Ipsative behavioral variability and the quality of thematic apperceptive measurement of the achievement motive. *Journal of Personality and Social Psychology, 43,* 1098–1110.

Reuman, D. A., Alwin, D. F., & Veroff, J. (1984). Assessing the validity of the achievement motive in the presence of random measurement error. *Journal of Personality and Social Psychology, 47,* 1347–1386.

Revelle, W. (1986). Motivation and efficiency of cognitive performance. In D. R. Brown & J. Veroff (Eds.), *Frontiers of motivational psychology* (pp. 107–127). Berlin, Germany: Springer.

Revelle, W., & Michaels, E. J. (1976). The theory of achievement motivation revisited: The implications of inertial tendencies. *Psychological Review, 83,* 394–404.

Reynolds, W. F., & Anderson, J. E. (1961). Choice behavior in a T-maze as a function of deprivation period and magnitude or reward. *Psychological Reports, 8,* 131–134.

Rheinberg, F. (1975). Zeitstabilität und Steuerbarkeit von Ursachen schulischer Leistung in der Sicht des Lehrers [Temporal stability and controllability of the causes of school outcomes from the teacher's perspective]. *Zeitschrift für Entwicklungspsychologie und Pädagogische Psychologie, 7,* 180–194.

Rheinberg, F. (1980). *Leistungsbewertung und Lernmotivation* [Achievement evaluation and motivation to learn]. Göttingen, Germany: Hogrefe.

Rheinberg, F. (1989). *Zweck und Tätigkeit* [Purpose and activity]. Göttingen, Germany: Hogrefe.

Rheinberg, F. (1991). Flow-experience when motorcycling: A study of a special human condition. In R. Brendicke (Ed.), *Safety, environment, future: Proceedings of the*

1991 International Motorcycle Conference (pp. 349–362). Bochum, Germany: IfZ.

Rheinberg, F. (1993). *Anreize engagiert betriebener Freizeitaktivitäten. Ein Systematisierungsversuch* [An attempt to systematize the incentives of leisure time activities]. Unpublished manuscript, University of Potsdam, Germany.

Rheinberg, F. (1995). *Motivation*. Stuttgart, Germany: Kohlhammer.

Rheinberg, F. (1996). Flow-Erleben, Freude an riskantem Sport und andere "unvernünftige" Motivationen [Flow experience, enjoyment of dangerous sports and other "unwise" motivations]. In J. Kuhl & H. Heckhausen (Eds.), *Motivation, Volition und Handlung. Enzyklopädie der Psychologie C/IV/4* (pp. 101–118). Göttingen, Germany: Hogrefe.

Rheinberg, F. (2001). Bezugsnormorientierung [Reference norm orientations]. In D. Rost (Ed.), *Handwörterbuch Pädagogische Psychologie* (pp. 55–62). Weinheim, Germany: Beltz.

Rheinberg, F. (2002a). Freude am Kompetenzerwerb, Flow-Erleben und motivpassende Ziele [Enjoyment of learning, flow experience and motive-congruent goals]. In M. V. Salisch (Ed.), *Emotionale Kompetenz entwickeln* (pp. 179–206). Stuttgart, Germany: Kohlhammer.

Rheinberg, F. (2002b). *Motivationale Kompetenz* [Motivational competence]. Paper presented at the 22nd Colloquium on Motivational Psychology (MPK), Siegen, Germany. Retrieved July 12, 2007, from www.psych.uni-potsdam.de/people/rheinberg/personal/lectures-d.html.

Rheinberg, F. (2004a). *Motivationsdiagnostik* [Measurement of motivation]. Göttingen, Germany: Hogrefe.

Rheinberg, F. (2004b, July). *Motivational competence and flow-experience*. Paper presented at the 2nd European Conference of Positive Psychology, Verbania, Italy. Retrieved July 12, 2007, from www.psych.uni-potsdam.de/people/rheinberg/personal/lectures-d.html.

Rheinberg, F. (2006). *Motivation* (6th ed.). Stuttgart, Germany: Kohlhammer.

Rheinberg, F., Duscha, R., & Michels, U. (1980). Zielsetzung und Kausalattribution in Abhängigkeit vom Leistungsvergleich [Goal setting and causal attribution as a function of performance comparisons]. *Zeitschrift für Entwicklungspsychologie und Pädagogische Psychologie, 12*, 177–189.

Rheinberg, F., Iser, I., & Pfauser, S. (1997). Freude am Tun und/oder zweckorientiertes Schaffen? Zur transsituativen Konsistenz und konvergenten Validität der Anreiz-Fokus-Skala [Doing something for fun and/or for gain? Transsituational consistency and convergent validity of the Incentive Focus Scale]. *Diagnostica, 42*, 174–191.

Rheinberg, F., & Krug, S. (2005). *Motivationsförderung im Schulalltag* [Fostering motivation in school] (3rd ed.). Göttingen, Germany: Hogrefe.

Rheinberg, F., Lührmann, J.-V., & Wagner, H. (1977). Bezugsnormorientierung von Schülern der 5. bis 13. Klassenstufe bei der Leistungsbeurteilung [Reference norm orientations in 5th to 13th graders]. *Zeitschrift für Entwicklungspsychologie und Pädagogischer Psychologie, 9*, 90–93.

Rheinberg, F., & Manig, Y. (2003). Was macht Spaß am Graffiti-Sprayen? Eine induktive Anreizanalyse [What is enjoyable about graffiti spraying? An inductive incentive analysis]. *Report Psychologie, 4*, 222–234.

Rheinberg, F., Manig, Y., Kliegl, R., Engeser, S., & Vollmeyer, R. (2007). Flow bei der Arbeit, doch Glück in der Freizeit: Zielausrichtung, Flow und Glücksgefühle [Flow at work, but happiness at leisure: Goal directedness, flow and feelings of happiness]. *Zeitschrift für Arbeits- und Organisationspsychologie, 51*, 105–115.

Rheinberg, F., Schmalt, H., & Wasser, I. (1978). Ein Lehrerunterschied, der etwas ausmacht [A difference between teachers that matters]. *Zeitschrift für Entwicklungspsychologie und Pädagogische Psychologie, 10*(1), 3–7.

Rheinberg, F. & Tramp, N. (2006) Anreizanalyse intensiver Nutzung von Computen in der Freizeit [Analysis of the incentive for intensive leisure-time use of computers]. *Zeitschrift für Psychologie, 214*, 97–107.

Rheinberg, F., & Vollmeyer, R. (2003). Flow-Erleben in einem Computerspiel unter experimentell variierten Bedingungen [Flow experience in a computer game under experimentally controlled conditions]. *Zeitschrift für Psychologie, 114*, 161–170.

Rheinberg, F., & Vollmeyer, R. (2004). Flow-Erleben bei der Arbeit und in der Freizeit [Flow experience at work and in leisure time]. In J. Wegge & K.-H. Schmidt (Eds.), *Förderung von Arbeitsmotivation und Gesundheit in Organisationen* (pp. 163–180). Göttingen, Germany: Hogrefe.

Rheinberg, F., Vollmeyer, R., & Burns, B. D. (2000). Motivation and self-regulated learning. In J. Heckhausen (Ed.), *Motivational psychology of human development: Developing motivation and motivating development* (pp. 81–108). Amsterdam: Elsevier.

Rheinberg, F., Vollmeyer, R., & Engeser, S. (2003). Die Erfassung des Flow-Erlebens [Measuring flow experience]. In J. Stiensmeier-Pelster & F. Rheinberg (Eds.), *Diagnostik von Motivation und Selbstkonzept* (Tests and Trends Vol. 2, pp. 261–279). Göttingen, Germany: Hogrefe.

Rheinberg, F., & Weich, K. (1988). Wie gefährlich ist Lob? Eine Untersuchung zum "paradoxen Effekt" von Lehrersanktionen [How risky is it to praise students? A study concerning "paradox effects" of teachers' sanctions]. *Zeitschrift für Pädagogische Psychologie, 2*, 227–233.

Rheingold, H., & Eckerman, C. (1969). The infant's free entry into a new environment. *Journal of Experimental Child Psychology, 8*(2), 271–283.

Rholes, W. S., Blackwell, J., Jordan, C., & Walters, C. (1980). A developmental study of learned helplessness. *Developmental Psychology, 16*, 616–624.

Rholes, W. S., &. Ruble, D. (1984). Children's understanding of dispositional characteristics of others. *Child Development, 55*, 550–560.

Richter, C. P. (1927). Animal behavior and internal drives. *Quarterly Review of Biology, 2*, 307–343.

Riemann, R., Angleitner, A., & Strelau, J. (1997). Genetic and environmental influences on personality: A study of twins reared together using the self- and peer-report NEO-FFI scales. *Journal of Personality, 65*, 449–475.

Riksen-Walraven, J. M. (1978). Effects of caregiver behavior on habituation rate and self-efficacy in infants. *International Journal of Behavioral Development, 1*, 105–130.

Rind, B., & Kipnis, D. (1999). Changes in self-perception as a result of successfully persuading others. *Journal of Social Issues, 55*, 141–156.

Rindfuss, R. R., Swicegood, C. G., & Rosenfeld, R. A. (1987). Disorder in the life course: How common and does it matter? *American Sociological Review, 52*, 785–801.

Rinn, W. E. (1984). The neuropsychology of facial emotions: A review of the neurological and psychological mechanism for producing facial expressions. *Psychological Bulletin, 95*, 52–77.

Riskind, J. H. (1984). They stoop to conquer: Guiding and self-regulatory functions of physical posture after success and failure.

Journal of Personality and Social Psychology, 47, 479–493.

Roberts, B. W., & Caspi, A. (2003). The cumulative continuity model of personality development: Striking a balance between continuity and change in personality traits across the life course. *Understanding human development: Dialogues with lifespan psychology* (pp. 183–214). Dordrecht, Netherlands: Kluwer.

Robinson, T. E., & Berridge, K. C. (2000). The psychology and neurobiology of addiction: An incentive-sensitization view. *Addiction, 95*(Suppl 2), S91–S117.

Roe, A., & Siegelman, M. (1964). The origin of interests. *APGA Inquiry Studies, 1*, 98.

Rogers, C. R. (1961). *On becoming a person: A therapist's view of psychotherapy*. Boston: Houghton Mifflin.

Rogers, E. M., & Svenning, L. (1969). *Modernization among peasants: The impact of communication*. New York: Holt, Rinehart and Winston.

Rogers, R. D., & Monsell, S. (1995). Costs of a predictable switch between simple cognitive tasks. *Journal of Experimental Psychology, 124*, 207–231.

Rogoff, B., & Wertsch, J. (1984). Children's learning in the "zone of proximal development." *New Directions for Child Development, 23*.

Röhrle, B., Hedke, J., & Leibold, S. (1994). Persönliche Projekte zur Herstellung und Pflege sozialer Beziehungen bei depressiven und nicht-depressiven Personen [Personal projects serving the establishment and maintenance of social relations in depressive and nondepressive adults]. *Zeitschrift für Klinische Psychologie, 23*, 43–51.

Rokeach, M. (1973). *The nature of human values*. New York: Free Press.

Rolls, E. T. (1999). *The brain and emotion*. Oxford, UK: Oxford University Press.

Rolls, E. T. (2000). The orbitofrontal cortex and reward. *Cerebral Cortex, 10*(3), 284–294.

Rolls, E. T. (2004). The functions of the orbitofrontal cortex. *Brain and Cognition, 55*(1), 11–29.

Rolls, E. T. (2005). Taste, olfactory, and food texture processing in the brain, and the control of food intake. *Physiology & Behavior, 85*(1), 45–56.

Roney, J. R., Mahler, S. V., & Maestripieri, D. (2003). Behavioral and hormonal responses of men to brief interactions with women. *Evolution and Human Behavior, 24*, 365–375.

Rook, K., Sorkin, D., & Zettel, A. (2004). Stress in social relationships: Coping and adaptation across the lifespan. In F. R. Lang & K. L. Fingerman (Eds.), *Growing together: Personal relationships across the lifespan* (pp. 210–239). Cambridge, UK: Cambridge University Press.

Rosahl, S. K., Tennigkeit, M., Kuhl, J., & Haschke, R. (1993). Handlungskontrolle und langsame Hirnpotentiale: Untersuchungen zum Einfluss subjektiv kritischer Wörter (Erste Ergebnisse) [Action control and slow brain potentials: Studies on the impact of subjectively emotional words (first findings)]. *Zeitschrift für Medizinische Psychologie, 2*, 1–8.

Rose, M. (1991). *Evolutionary biology of aging*. New York: Oxford University Press.

Rose, R. M., Holaday, J. W., & Bernstein, I. S. (1971). Plasma testosterone, dominance rank, and aggressive behavior in male rhesus monkeys. *Nature, 231*, 898–904.

Rosen, B. C. (1959). Race, ethnicity, and the achievement syndrome. *American Sociological Review, 24*, 47–60.

Rosen, B. C., & D'Andrade, R. (1959). The psychosocial origins of achievement motivation. *Sociometry, 22*, 185–218.

Rosenbaum, R. M. (1972). *A dimensional analysis of the perceived causes of success and failure*. Unpublished doctoral dissertation, University of California, Los Angeles.

Rosenberg, G. J. (1956). Cognitive structure and attitudinal affect. *Journal of Abnormal and Social Psychology, 53*, 367–372.

Rosenberg, M. (1965). *Society and the adolescent self-image*. Princeton, NJ: Princeton University Press.

Rosenzweig, S. (1933). Preferences in the repetition of successful and unsuccessful activities as a function of age and personality. *Journal of Genetic Psychology, 42*, 423–441.

Rosenzweig, S. (1941). Need-persistive and ego-defensive reactions to frustration as demonstrated by an experiment on repression. *Psychological Review, 48*, 347–349.

Rosenzweig, S. (1943). Experimental study of "repression" with special reference to need-persistive and ego-defensive reactions to frustration. *Journal of Experimental Psychology, 32*, 64–74.

Rosenzweig, S. (1945). Further comparative data on repetition choice after success and failure as related to frustration tolerance. *Journal of Genetic Psychology, 66*, 75–81.

Rösler, H.-D. (1955). Über das Behalten von Handlungen schwachsinniger und normaler Kinder [Retention of actions by feeble-minded and normal children]. *Zeitschrift für Psychologie, 158*, 161–231.

Ross, L. (1977). The intuitive psychologist and his short-comings: Distortions in the attribution process. In L. Berkowitz (Ed.), *Advances in experimental social psychology* (Vol. 10, pp. 173–220). San Diego, CA: Academic Press.

Rotenberg, V. S. (1993). Richness against freedom: Two hemisphere functions and the problem of creativity. *European Journal for High Ability, 4*, 11–19.

Rotenberg, V. S. (2004). The peculiarity of the right hemisphere function in depression: Solving the paradoxes. *Progress in Neuro-Psychopharmacology and Biological Psychiatry, 28*, 1–13.

Rothermund, K., & Brandstädter, J. (2003a). Coping with deficits and losses in later life: From compensatory action to accommodation. *Psychology and Aging, 18*, 896–905.

Rothermund, K., & Brandstädter, J. (2003b). Depression in later life: Cross sequential patterns and possible determinants. *Psychology and Aging, 18*, 80–90.

Rotter, J. B. (1954). *Social learning and clinical psychology*. Englewood Cliffs, NJ: Prentice Hall.

Rotter, J. B. (1955). The role of the psychological situation in determining the direction of human behavior. In M. R. Jones (Ed.), *Nebraska Symposium on Motivation, 1955* (pp. 245–269). Lincoln: University of Nebraska Press.

Rotter, J. B. (1960). Some implications of a social learning theory for the prediction of goal directed behavior from testing procedures. *Psychological Review, 67*, 301–316.

Rotter, J. B. (1966). Generalized expectancies for internal versus external control of reinforcement. *Psychological Monographs, 80*(1, Whole no. 609), 1–28.

Rotter, J. B. (1982). Social learning theory. In N. T. Feather (Ed.), *Expectations and actions* (pp. 241–260). Hillsdale, NJ: Erlbaum.

Rotter, J. B., Chance, J. E., & Phares, E. J. (1972). *Applications of a social learning theory of personality*. New York: Holt, Rinehart and Winston.

Rotter, J. B., Liverant, S., & Crowne, D. P. (1961). The growth and extinction of expectancies in chance controlled and skilled tasks. *Journal of Psychology, 52*, 161–177.

Rotter, J. B., Seeman, M. R., & Liverant, S. (1962). Internal versus external control of reinforcements: A major variable in behavior theory. In W. F. Washburn (Ed.), *Decisions, values, and groups* (Vol. 2, pp. 473–516). New York: Pergamon.

Rovee, C. K., & Fagan, J. (1976). Extended conditioning and 24 hour retention in infants. *Journal of Experimental Child Psychology, 21,* 1–11.

Rozin, P. (1976). The evolution of intelligence and access to the cognitive unconscious. In J. M. Sprague & A. N. Epstein (Eds.), *Progress in psychobiology and physiological psychology* (pp. 245–277). New York: Academic Press.

Ruble, D. N., Boggiano, A., Feldman, N. S., & Loebl, J. H. (1980). A developmental analysis of the role of social comparison in self-evaluation. *Developmental Psychology, 16,* 105–115.

Ruble, D. N., & Feldman, N. S. (1976). Order of consensus, distinctiveness, and consistency information and causal attribution. *Journal of Personality and Social Psychology, 34,* 930–937.

Ruble, D. N., & Martin, C. L. (2002). Conceptualization, measuring and evaluation the developmental course of gender differentiation: Compliments, queries and quandaries. *Monographs of the Society for Research in Child Development, 67*(269), 148–166.

Ruble, D. N., Parsons, J. E., & Ross, M. (1976). Self-evaluative responses of children in an achievement setting. *Child Development, 48,* 1362–1368.

Rudolph, U., Roesch, S. C., Weiner, B., & Greitmeyer, T. (2004). Responsibility and help-giving: A meta-analytic review. *Cognition and Emotion, 18,* 815–848.

Ruhland, D., & Feld, S. (1977). The development of achievement motivation in black and white children. *Child Development, 48,* 1362–1368.

Russell, B. (1938). *Power.* London: Allen & Unwin.

Russell, J. A., & Carroll, J. M. (1999). On the bipolarity of positive and negative affect. *Psychological Bulletin, 125,* 3–30.

Ryan, R. M., & Deci, E. L. (2000). When rewards compete with nature: The undermining of intrinsic motivation and self-regulation. In C. Sansone & J. M. Harackiewicz (Eds.), *Intrinsic and extrinsic motivation* (pp. 14–54). San Diego, CA: Academic Press.

Ryan, R. M., Kuhl, J., & Deci, E. (1997). Nature and autonomy: An organizational view of social and neurobiological aspects of self-regulation in behavior and development. *Development and Psychopathology, 9*(4), 701–728.

Sadalla, E. K., Kenrick, D. T., & Vershure, B. (1987). Dominance and heterosexual

attraction. *Journal of Personality and Social Psychology, 52,* 730–738.

Sader, M., & Keil, W. (1968). Faktorenanalytische Untersuchungen zur Projektion der Leistungsmotivation [Factor analytic studies on the projection of achievement motivation]. *Archiv für die gesamte Psychologie, 120,* 25–53.

Sader, M., & Specht, H. (1967). Leistung, Motivation und Leistungsmotivation: Korrelationsstatistische Untersuchungen zur Leistungsmotivmessung nach Heckhausen [Achievement, motivation and achievement motivation: Correlational studies on achievement motivation after Heckhausen]. *Archiv für die gesamte Psychologie, 119,* 90–130.

Salamone, J. D. (1994). The involvement of nucleus accumbens dopamine in appetitive and aversive motivation. *Behavioural Brain Research, 61,* 117–133.

Sameroff, A. J. (1983). Developmental systems: Contexts and evolution. *Handbook of Child Psychology, 1*(4), 237–294.

Sanford, R. N. (1937). The effects of abstinence from food upon imaginal processes: A preliminary experiment. *Journal of Psychology, 3,* 145–159.

Sanford, R. N., & Risser, J. (1948). What are the conditions of self-defensive forgetting? *Journal of Personality, 17,* 244–260.

Sansone, C., & Harackiewicz, J. M. (2000). *Intrinsic and extrinsic motivation.* San Diego, CA: Academic Press.

Sansone, C., & Smith, J. L. (2000). Interest and self-regulation: The relation between having to and wanting to. In C. Sansone & J. M. Harackiewicz (Eds.), *Intrinsic and extrinsic motivation* (pp. 343–372). San Diego, CA: Academic Press.

Sansone, C. D., Sachau, A., & Weir, C. (1989). Effects of instruction on intrinsic interest: The importance of context. *Journal of Personality and Social Psychology, 57,* 819–829.

Sapolsky, R. M. (1987). Stress, social status, and reproductive physiology in free-living baboons. In D. Crews (Ed.), *Psychobiology and reproductive behavior: An evolutionary perspective* (pp. 291–322). Englewood Cliffs, NJ: Prentice Hall.

Sapolsky, R. M. (1992). *Stress, the aging brain, and the mechanism of neuron death.* Cambridge, MA: MIT Press.

Saucier, G., & Goldberg, L. (1996). The language of personality: Lexical reflections on the five-factor model. In J. S. Wiggins (Ed.), *The five-factor model of personality: Theoretical perspectives* (pp. 21–50). New York: Guilford Press.

Sawusch, J. R. (1974). Computer simulation of the influence of ability and motivation on test performance and cumulative achievement and the relation between them. In J. W. Atkinson & J. O. Raynor (Eds.), *Motivation and achievement* (pp. 425–438). Washington, DC: Winston.

Scarr, S., & McCartney, K. (1983). How people make their own environments: A theory of genotype-environment effects. *Child Development, 54,* 424–435.

Schachter, S. (1959). *The psychology of affiliation.* Stanford, CA: Stanford University Press.

Schacter, D. L. (1987). Implicit memory: History and current status. *Journal of Experimental Psychology: Learning, Memory, and Cognition, 13,* 501–518.

Schallberger, U. (2000). *Qualität des Erlebens in Arbeit und Freizeit: Eine Zwischenbilanz* [Quality of experience in work and leisure: An interim assessment]. Berichte aus der Abteilung Angewandte Psychologie, No. 31. Zürich, Switzerland: University of Zürich.

Schallberger, U., & Pfister, R. (2001). Flow-Erleben in Arbeit und Freizeit: Eine Untersuchung zum Paradox der Arbeit mit der Experience Sampling Method [Flow experiences in work and leisure: An experience sampling study about the paradox of work]. *Zeitschrift für Arbeits- und Organisationspsychologie, 45,* 176–187.

Scheffer, D. (2000). *Entwicklungsbedingungen Impliziter Motive: Bindung, Leistung und Macht* [Developmental conditions of implicit motives: Affiliation, achievement, and power]. Doctoral dissertation, University of Osnabrück, Germany. Retrieved July 12, 2007, from http://elib.ub.uni-osnabrueck.de/publications/diss/E-Diss150˙thesis.pdf.

Scheffer, D. (2003). *Die Messung impliziter Motive* [The measurement of implicit motives]. Göttingen, Germany: Hogrefe.

Scheffer, D. (2005). *Implizite Motive* [Implicit motives]. Göttingen, Germany: Hogrefe.

Scheffer, D., & Kuhl, J. (2006). *Erfolgreich motivieren* [Successful motivation]. Göttingen, Germany: Hogrefe.

Scheffer, D., Kuhl, J., & Eichstaedt, J. (2003). Der Operante Motiv-Test (OMT): Inhaltsklassen, Auswertung, psychometrische Kennwerte und Validierung [The Operant Motive Test (OMT): Categories, interpretation, psychometric properties, and validation]. In F. Rheinberg & J. Stiensmeier-Pelster (Eds.), *Diagnostik von Motivation und Selbstkonzept* (pp. 151–168). Göttingen, Germany: Hogrefe.

Scheier, M. F., & Carver, C. S. (1985). Optimism, coping and health: Assessment and implications of generalized outcome expectancies. *Health Psychology, 4,* 219–247.

Scherer, K. R. (1981). Über die Vernachlässigung der Emotion in der Psychologie [On the neglect of emotion in psychology]. In M. Michaelis (Ed.), *Bericht über den 32. Kongress der Deutschen Gesellschaft für Psychologie, Zürich 1980* (pp. 304–317). Göttingen, Germany: Hogrefe.

Scherer, K. R. (1984). On the nature and function of emotion: A component process approach. In K. R. Scherer & P. Ekman (Eds.), *Approaches to emotion* (pp. 293–317). Hillsdale, NJ: Erlbaum.

Schiefele, U. (1996). *Motivation und Lernen mit Texten* [Motivation and learning from texts]. Göttingen, Germany: Hogrefe.

Schiefele, U., & Köller, O. (2001). Intrinsische und extrinsische Motivation [Intrinsic and extrinsic motivation]. In D. H. Rost (Ed.), *Handwörterbuch Pädagogische Psychologie* (pp. 304–310). Weinheim, Germany: Beltz.

Schiefele, U., & Rheinberg, F. (1997). Motivation and knowledge acquisition: Searching for mediating processes. In M. L. Maehr & P. R. Pintrich (Eds.), *Advances in motivation and achievement* (Vol. 10, pp. 251–301). Greenwich, CT: JAI Press.

Schiefele, U., & Urhahne, D. (2000). Motivationale und volitionale Bedingungen der Studienleistung [Motivational and volitional conditions of college outcomes]. In U. Schiefele & K.-P. Wild (Eds.), *Interesse und Lernmotivation: Untersuchungen zu Entwicklung, Förderung und Wirkung* (pp. 183–205). Münster, Germany: Waxmann.

Schlenker, B. R., & Leary, M. R. (1982). Social anxiety and self-presentation: A conceptualization and model. *Psychological Bulletin, 92,* 641–669.

Schmajuk, N. A., & Buhusi, C. V. (1997). Stimulus configuration, occasion setting, and the hippocampus. *Behavioral Neuroscience, 111,* 235–257.

Schmalt, H. (1975). Independence training and various aspects of achievement motivation. *Zeitschrift für Entwicklungspsychologie und Pädagogische Psychologie, 7,* 24–37.

Schmalt, H.-D. (1973). Die GITTER-Technik – ein objektives Verfahren zur Messung des Leistungsmotivs bei Kindern [The Grid technique – an objective technique to measure children's achievement motivation]. *Zeitschrift für Entwicklungspsychologie und Pädagogische Psychologie, 5,* 231–252.

Schmalt, H.-D. (1976a). *Das LM-GITTER. Handanweisung* [The AM-Grid. Manual]. Göttingen, Germany: Hogrefe.

Schmalt, H.-D. (1976b). *Die Messung des Leistungsmotivs* [Measurement of the achievement motive]. Göttingen, Germany: Hogrefe.

Schmalt, H.-D. (1978). Machtmotivation [Power motivation]. *Psychologische Rundschau, 30,* 269–285.

Schmalt, H.-D. (1979). Leistungsthematische Kognitionen. II: Kausalattribuierungen, Erfolgserwartungen und Affekte [Achievement-related cognitions. II: Causal attributions, expectancies of success, and affect]. *Zeitschrift für Experimentelle und Angewandte Psychologie, 26,* 509–531.

Schmalt, H.-D. (1986). Das Machtmotiv und Verantwortlichkeitsattribution für interpersonale Ereignisse [The power motive and attribution of responsibility for interpersonal events]. *Psychologische Beiträge, 28,* 533–550.

Schmalt, H.-D. (1987). Power motivation and the perception of control. In F. Halisch & J. Kuhl (Eds.), *Motivation, intention, and volition* (pp. 101–113). Berlin, Germany: Springer.

Schmalt, H.-D. (1996). Zur Kohärenz von Motivation und Kognition [The coherence of motivation and cognition]. In J. Kuhl & H. Heckhausen (Eds.), *Enzyklopädie der Psychologie. Motivation, Volition und Handeln* (pp. 241–273). Göttingen, Germany: Hogrefe.

Schmalt, H.-D. (1999). Assessing the achievement motive using the Grid technique. *Journal of Research in Personality, 33,* 109–130.

Schmalt, H.-D. (2003). *Leistungsmotivation im Unterricht: Über den Einsatz des LM-Gitters in der Schule* [Achievement motivation in the classroom: Implementing the AM Grid in schools]. In J. Stiensmeier-Pelster & F. Rheinberg (Eds.), *Diagnostik von Motivation und Selbstkonzept* (pp. 105–127). Göttingen, Germany: Hogrefe.

Schmalt, H. D., & Langens, T. (1999). *Projective, semiprojective and self-report. Measures of human motivation predict private cognitive events: Strivings, memories, and daydreams.* Unpublished manuscript, University of Wuppertal, Germany.

Schmalt, H.-D., & Sokolowski, K. (2000). Zum gegenwärtigen Stand der Motivdiagnostik [The current status of motive measurement]. *Diagnostica, 46,* 115–123.

Schmalt, H.-D., & Sokolowski, K. (2004). Motivation. In H. Spada (Ed.), *Allgemeine Psychologie* (3rd ed.). Berne, Switzerland: Huber.

Schmalt, H.-D., Sokolowski, K., & Langens, T. (2000). *Das Multi-Motiv-Gitter (MMG)* [The Multi-Motive Grid (MMG)]. Lisse, Netherlands: Swets.

Schmidt, F. L. (1973). Implications of a measurement problem for expectancy theory research. *Organizational Behavior and Human Performance, 10,* 243–251.

Schnackers, U., & Kleinbeck, U. (1975). Machtmotiv und machtthematisches Verhalten in einem Verhandlungsspiel [The power motive and power-related behavior in a con game]. *Archiv für Psychologie, 127,* 300–319.

Schneider, E. L., & Rowe, J. (1990). *Handbook of the biology of aging.* San Diego, CA: Academic Press.

Schneider, K. (1971). *Leistungs- und Risikoverhalten in Abhängigkeit von situativen und überdauernden Komponenten der Leistungsmotivation: Kritische Untersuchungen zu einem Verhaltensmodell* [Achievement-related and risk-taking behavior as a function of situational and enduring components of achievement motivation: Critical investigations of a behavioral model]. Unpublished doctoral dissertation, University of Bochum, Germany.

Schneider, K. (1973). *Motivation unter Erfolgsrisiko* [Motivation under the risk of success]. Göttingen, Germany: Hogrefe.

Schneider, K. (1974). Subjektive Unsicherheit und Aufgabenwahl [Subjective uncertainty and task choice]. *Archiv für Psychologie, 126,* 147–169.

Schneider, K. (1996). Intrinsisch (autotelisch) motiviertes Verhalten – dargestellt an den Beispielen des Neugierverhaltens sowie verwandter Verhaltenssysteme (Spielen und leistungsmotiviertes Handeln) [Intrinsically (autotelically) motivated behavior – The examples of curiosity and related behavioral systems (playing and achievement-motivated behavior)]. In J. Kuhl & H. Heckhausen (Eds.), *Motivation, Volition und Handlung: Enzyklopädie der Psychologie C/IV/4* (pp. 119–153). Göttingen, Germany: Hogrefe.

Schneider, K., & Dittrich, W. (1990). Evolution und Funktion von Emotionen [Evolution and the function of emotions]. In K. R. Scherer (Ed.), *Enzyklopädie der Psychologie: Psychologie der Emotion* (pp. 41–114). Göttingen, Germany: Hogrefe.

Schneider, K., & Heckhausen, H. (1981). Subjective uncertainty and task preference. In H. I. Day (Ed.), *Advances in intrinsic motivation and aesthetics* (pp. 149–167). New York: Plenum.

Schneider, K., & Kreuz, A. (1979). Die Effekte unterschiedlicher Anstrengung auf die Mengen- und Güteleistung bei einer einfachen und schweren Zahlensymbol-aufgabe [The effects of effort on the quantity and quality of performance outcomes on easy and difficult number symbol tasks]. *Psychologie und Praxis, 23*, 34–42.

Schneider, K., & Schmalt, H.-D. (1994). *Motivation* (2nd ed.). Stuttgart, Germany: Kohlhammer.

Schneider, K., & Schmalt, H.-D. (2000). *Motivation* (3rd ed.). Stuttgart, Germany: Kohlhammer.

Schneider, K., & Schmalt H.-D. (2002). *Motivation* (4th ed.). Stuttgart, Germany: Kohlhammer.

Schneider, K., & Unzner, L. (1992). Preschoolers' attention and emotion in an achievement and an effect game: A longitudinal study. *Cognition and Emotion, 6*, 37–63.

Schneider, K., Wegge, J., & Konradt, U. (1993). Motivation und Leistung [Motivation and achievement]. In J. Beckmann, H. Strang, & E. Hahn (Eds.), *Aufmerksamkeit und Energetisierung: Facetten von Konzentration und Leistung* (pp. 101–131). Göttingen, Germany: Hogrefe.

Schneider, R. J., Hough, L. M., & Dunnette, M. D. (1996). Broadsided by broad traits: How to sink science in five dimensions or less. *Journal of Organizational Behavior, 17*, 639–655.

Schnierla, J. C. (1959). An evolutionary and developmental theory of biphasic processes underlying approach and withdrawal. In M. R. Jones (Ed.), *Nebraska Symposium on Motivation, 1959* (pp. 1–42). Lincoln: University of Nebraska Press.

Schöne, C., Dickhäuser, O., Spinath, B., & Stiensmeier-Pelster, J. (2004). Zielorientierung und Bezugsnormorientierung: zum Zusammenhang zweier Konzepte [Goal orientation and reference-norm orientation: Two related constructs?]. *Zeitschrift für Pädagogische Psychologie, 18*, 93–99.

Schore, A. N. (2003). *Affect regulation and the repair of self.* New York: Norton.

Schoenfeld, W. N. (1950). An experimental approach to anxiety, escape, and avoidance behavior. In P. M. Hoch & J. Zubin (Eds.), *Anxiety* (pp. 70–99). New York: Grune & Stratton.

Schroth, M. L. (1988). Relationships between achievement-related motives, extrinsic conditions, and task performance. *Journal of Social Psychology, 127*, 39–48.

Schubert, C. (1986). *Motivationsanalysen zur Interaktion mit Computern* [Motivational analyses of interaction with computers]. Unpublished Diplom thesis, University of Heidelberg, Germany.

Schülein, J. A. (1989). Symbiotische Beziehungen und gesellschaftliche Entwicklung [Symbiotic relations and societal development]. *Psyche, 43*, 1007–1028.

Schüler, J. (2002). *Ein hierarchisches Modell der Anschlussmotivation: Hoffnung-auf-Anschluss und Furcht-vor-Zurückweisung und die Selbstregulation von Zielsetzungen* [A hierarchical model of affiliation motivation: Hope for affiliation and fear of rejection and self-regulation of goal setting]. Doctoral dissertation, University of Wuppertal, Germany. Retrieved July 13, 2007, from http://elpub.bib.uni-wuppertal.de/edocs/dokumente/fb03/diss2002/schueler/f030202.pdf.

Schuler, H., & Prochaska, M. (2000). Entwicklung und Konstruktvalidierung eines berufsbezogenen Leistungsmotivationstests [Development and construct validation of a job-related achievement motivation test]. *Diagnostica, 46*, 61–72.

Schultheiss, O. C. (in press). Implicit motives. In O. P. John, R. W. Robins & L. A. Pervin (Eds.), *Handbook of Personality: Theory and Research.* (3 ed.). New York: Guilford.

Schultheiss, O. C. (2001a). *Manual for the assessment of hope of success and fear of failure: English translation of Heckhausen's need achievement measure.* Unpublished manuscript, University of Michigan at Ann Arbor.

Schultheiss, O. C. (2001b). An information processing account of implicit motive arousal. In M. L. Maehr & P. Pintrich (Eds.), *Advances in motivation and achievement: Vol. 12. New directions in measures and methods* (pp. 1–41). Greenwich, CT: JAI Press.

Schultheiss, O. C. (2007). A biobehavioral model of implicit power motivation: Arousal, reward and frustration. In E. Harmon-Jones & P. Winkielman (Eds.), *Fundamentals of social neuroscience* (pp. 176–196). New York: Guilford Press.

Schultheiss, O. C., & Brunstein, J. C. (1999). Goal imagery: Bridging the gap between implicit motives and explicit goals. *Journal of Personality, 67*, 1–38.

Schultheiss, O. C., & Brunstein, J. C. (2001). Assessment of implicit motives with a research version of the TAT: Picture profiles, gender differences and relations to other personality measures. *Journal of Personality Assessment, 77*, 71–86.

Schultheiss, O. C., & Brunstein, J. C. (2002). Inhibited power motivation and persuasive communication: A lens model analysis. *Journal of Personality, 70*, 553–582.

Schultheiss, O. C., & Brunstein, J. C. (2005). An implicit motive perspective on competence. In A. J. Elliot & C. S. Dweck (Eds.), *Handbook of competence and motivation* (pp. 31–51). New York: Guilford Press.

Schultheiss, O. C., Campbell, K. L., & McClelland, D. C. (1999). Implicit power motivation moderates men's testosterone responses to imagined and real dominance success. *Hormones and Behavior, 36*, 234–241.

Schultheiss, O. C., Pang, J. S., Torges, C. M., Wirth, M. M., & Treynor, W. (2005). Perceived facial expressions of emotion as motivational incentives: Evidence from a differential implicit learning paradigm. *Emotion, 5*(1), 41–54.

Schultheiss, O. C., & Rohde, W. (2002). Implicit power motivation predicts men's testosteron changes and implicit learning in a contest situation. *Hormones and Behavior, 41*, 195–202.

Schultheiss, O. C., Wirth, M. M., Torges, C. M., Pang, J. S., Villacorta, M. A., & Welsh, K. M. (2005). Effects of implicit power motivation on men's and women's implicit learning and testosterone changes after social victory or defeat. *Journal of Personality and Social Psychology, 88*(1), 174–188.

Schultz, W. (1998). Predictive reward signal of dopamine neurons. *Journal of Neurophysiology, 80*(1), 1–27.

Schultz, W., Dayan, P., & Montague, P. R. (1997). A neural substrate of prediction and reward. *Science, 275*, 1593–1599.

Schulz, R., & Curnow, C. (1988). Peak performance and age among superathletes: Track and field, swimming, baseball, tennis and golf. *Journal of Gerontology: Psychological Sciences, 43*, 113–120.

Schulz, R., & Heckhausen, J. (1996). A life-span model of successful aging. *American Psychologist, 51*, 702–714.

Schulz, R., Wrosch, C., & Heckhausen, J. (2002). The life-span theory of control:

Issues and evidence. In S. Zarit, L. Pearlin, & K. W. Schaie (Eds.), *Personal control in social and life course contexts: Societal impact on aging* (pp. 233–262). New York: Springer.

Schunk, D. H. (1982). Effects of effort attributional feedback on children's perceived self-efficacy and achievement. *Journal of Educational Psychology, 74*, 548–556.

Schur, W., & Weick, G. (1999). *Wahnsinnskarriere* [Mind-blowing career]. Frankfurt, Germany: Eichhorn.

Schuster, B., Ruble, D. N., & Weinert, F. E. (1998). Causal inferences and the positivity bias in children: The role of the covariation principle. *Child Development, 69*, 1577–1596.

Schwartz, B. (1974). On going back to nature. *Journal of Experimental Analysis of Behavior, 21*, 183–198.

Schwarz, N. (1990). Feeling as information: Informational and motivational functions of affective states. In E. T. Higgins & R. M. Sorrentino (Eds.), *Handbook of motivation and cognition: Foundations of social behavior* (Vol. 2, pp. 527–561). New York: Guilford Press.

Schwarzer, R. (1994). Kausalattributionen als gesundheitsbezogene Kognitionen [Causal attributions as health-related cognitions]. In F. Försterling & J. Stiensmeier-Pelster (Ed.), *Attributionstheorie*. Göttingen, Germany: Hogrefe.

Schwarzer, R., & Jerusalem, M. (1982). Selbstwertdienliche Attributionen nach Leistungsrückmeldungen [Self-serving attributions after performance feedback]. *Zeitschrift für Entwicklungspsychologie und Pädagogische Psychologie, 14*, 47–57.

Schweiger Gallo, I., Achtziger, A., & Gollwitzer, P. M. (2003, September). *Vorsatzeffekte bei der Kontrolle von Emotionen* [Effects of implementation intentions in the control of emotions]. Paper presented at the Fachtagung Sozialpsychologie, Heidelberg, Germany.

Schweiger Gallo, I., & Gollwitzer, P. M. (2004, April). *Die vorsatzgesteuerte Inhibition der Emotion Ekel* [Inhibiting the emotion of disgust by means of implementation intentions]. Paper presented at the symposium "Recent developments in research on implementation intentions" at the 46th meeting of the Tagung experimentell arbeitender Psychologen (TeaP), Giessen, Germany.

Schweiger Gallo, I., Keil, A., Mc Culloch, K. C., Rockstroh, B., & Gollwitzer, P. M. (forthcoming). *Strategic Automation of Emotion Control.*

Scott, W. A. (1956). The avoidance of threatening material in imaginative behavior. *Journal of Abnormal and Social Psychology, 52*, 338–346.

Sears, R. R. (1950). Personality. *Annual Review of Psychology, 1*, 105–118.

Sears, R. R., Maccoby, E. E., & Levin, H. (1957). *Patterns of child rearing*. Evanston, IL: Row Peterson.

Sechenow, I. (1863). The reflexes of the brain. *Medizinsky Vestnik*. In I. Sechenow, Selected works (pp. 263–336). Amsterdam: Bonset, 1968.

Sedikides, C., & Strube, M. J. (1997). Self-evaluation: To thine own self be good, to thine own self be sure, to thine own self be true, and to thine own self be better. *Advances in Experimental Social Psychology, 29*, 209–269.

Seidenstücker, G., & Seidenstücker, E. (1974). Contribution to a computer evaluation of the Thematic Achievement Motivation Test by Heckhausen. *Psychologische Beiträge, 16*, 68–92.

Seifert, A. (2001). *Fairness leicht gemacht: Zur Rolle von Diskrepanzprozessen in der vorsatzgesteuerten sozialen Urteilsbildung* [How to be fair: The role of discrepancy processes and implementation intentions with regard to social judgments]. Unpublished doctoral dissertation, University of Konstanz, Germany.

Seligman, M., & Maier, S. F. (1967). Failure to escape traumatic shock. *Journal of Experimental Psychology, 74*(1), 1–9.

Seligman, M. E. P. (1970). On the generality of the laws of learning. *Psychological Review, 77*, 406–428.

Seligman, M. E. P. (1971). Phobias and preparedness. *Behavior Therapy, 2*, 307–320.

Seligman, M. E. P. (1975). *Helplessness: On depression, development, and death*. San Francisco: Freeman.

Seligman, M. E. P., Abramson, L. Y., Semmel, A., & von Baeyer, C. (1979). Depressive attributional style. *Journal of Abnormal Psychology, 88*, 242–247.

Selz, O. (1910). Die experimentelle Untersuchung des Willensaktes [The experimental study of the volitional act]. *Zeitschrift für Psychologie, 57*, 241–270.

Selz, O. (1913). *Über die Gesetze des geordneten Denkverlaufs* [On the laws of ordered thought processes]. Stuttgart, Germany: Spemann.

Semmer, N. (1995). Die Komplexität der Motivation [The complexity of motivation]. *Psychoscope, 16*(19), 11–15.

Settersten, R. A., & Hagestad, G. (1996). What's the latest? Cultural age deadlines for family transition. *Gerontologist, 36*, 178–188.

Seward, J. P. (1942). Note on the externalization of drive. *Psychological Review, 49*, 197–199.

Seward, J. P. (1951). Experimental evidence for the motivating function of reward. *Psychological Bulletin, 48*, 130–149.

Shah, J. Y., Friedman, R., & Kruglanski, A. W. (2002). Forgetting all else: On the antecedents and consequences of goal shielding. *Journal of Personality and Social Psychology, 83*, 1261–1280.

Shah, J. Y., & Kruglanski, A. W. (2000). The structure and substance of intrinsic motivation. In C. Sansone & J. M. Harackiewicz (Eds.), *Intrinsic and extrinsic motivation* (pp. 105–127). San Diego, CA: Academic Press.

Shah, J. Y., & Kruglanski, A. W. (2003). When opportunity knocks: Bottom-up priming of goals by means of means and the effects on self-regulation. *Journal of Personality and Social Psychology, 84*, 1109–1122.

Shaklee, H. (1983). Causal schemata: Description or explanation of judgment processes? A reply to Fiedler. *Journal of Personality and Social Psychology, 45*, 1010–1012.

Sheeran, P., & Orbell, S. (1999). Implementation intentions and repeated behavior: Augmenting the predictive validity of the theory of planned behavior. *European Journal of Social Psychology, 29*, 349–369.

Sheeran, P., & Orbell, S. (2000). Using implementation intentions to increase attendance for cervical cancer screening. *Health Psychology, 19*, 283–289.

Sheeran, P., Webb, T. L., & Gollwitzer, P. M. (2005). The interplay between goals and implementation intentions. *Personality and Social Psychology Bulletin, 31*, 87–98.

Sheffield, F. D., & Campbell, B. A. (1954). The role of experience in the "spontaneous" activity of hungry rats. *Journal of Comparative and Physiological Psychology, 47*, 97–100.

Sheffield, F. D., & Roby, T. B. (1950). Reward value of non-nutrive sweet taste. *Journal of Comparative and Physiological Psychology, 43*, 471–481.

Sheffield, F. D., Roby, T. B., & Campbell, B. A. (1954). Drive reduction versus consummatory behavior as determinants of reinforcement. *Journal of Comparative and Physiological Psychology, 47*, 349–355.

Sheffield, F. D., Wulff, J. J., & Backer, R. (1951). Reward value of copulation without sex drive reduction. *Journal of Comparative and Physiological Psychology, 44,* 3–8.

Sheldon, K. M., & Elliot, A. J. (1999). Goal striving, need satisfaction, and longitudinal well-being: The self-concordance model. *Journal of Personality and Social Psychology, 76,* 482–497.

Sheldon, K. M., Elliot, A. J., Kim, Y., & Kasser, T. (2001). What is satisfying about satisfying events? Testing 10 candidate psychological needs. *Journal of Personality and Social Psychology, 80,* 325–339.

Sherrington, C. S. (1906). *The integrative action of the nervous system.* New Haven, CT: Yale University Press.

Shipley, T. E., & Veroff, J. (1952). A projective measure of need for affiliation. *Journal of Experimental Psychology, 43,* 349–356.

Short, J. -A. C., & Sorrentino, R. M. (1986). Achievement, affiliation, and group incentives: A test of the overmotivation hypothesis. *Motivation and Emotion, 10,* 115–131.

Showers, C. J., & Kling, K. C. (1996). Organization of self-knowledge: Implications for recovery from sad mood. *Journal of Personality and Social Psychology, 70,* 578–590.

Siebert, T., & Vester, T. (1990). *Zur Anreizstruktur des Musizierens: Motivationsanalyse einer Tätigkeit* [The incentive structure of playing a musical instrument]. Unpublished Diplom thesis, University of Heidelberg, Germany.

Siegler, R. S. (2002). Variability and infant development [Special issue: Variability in infancy]. *Infant Behavior and Development, 25,* 550–557.

Simmons, R. (1924). The relative effectiveness of certain incentives in animal learning. *Comparative Psychology Monographs, 2*(Serial no. 7).

Simon, H. A. (1957). *Models of man.* New York: Wiley.

Singh, D. (1970). Preference for bar-pressing to obtain reward over freeloading in rats and children. *Journal of Comparative and Physiological Psychology, 73,* 320–327.

Singh, S. (1979). Relationships among projective and direct verbal measures of achievement motivation. *Journal of Personality Assessment, 43,* 45–49.

Skinner, B. F. (1935). Two types of a conditional reflex and a pseudotype. *Journal of General Psychology, 12,* 66–77.

Skinner, B. F. (1938). *The behavior of organisms: An experimental approach.* New York: Appleton-Century.

Skinner, B. F. (1953). *Science and human behavior.* New York: Macmillan.

Skinner, B. F. (1968). *The technology of teaching.* New York: Appleton-Century-Crofts.

Skinner, E. A. (1990). Age differences in dimensions of perceived control during middle childhood: Implications for developmental conceptualizations and research. *Child Development, 61,* 1882–1890.

Skinner, E. A. (1996). A guide to constructs of control. *Journal of Personality and Social Psychology, 71,* 549–570.

Skinner, E. A., Chapman, M., & Baltes, P. B. (1988). Control, means-ends, and agency beliefs: A new conceptualization and its measurement during childhood. *Journal of Personality and Social Psychology, 54,* 117–133.

Slavin, R. E. (1995). *Cooperative learning* (2nd ed.). Boston: Allyn & Bacon.

Smith, A. A. (1953). An electromyographic study of tension in interrupted and completed tasks. *Journal of Experimental Psychology, 46,* 32–36.

Smith, C. P. (Ed.). (1969). *The origin and expression of achievement-related motives in children* (pp. 102–150). New York: Sage.

Smith, C. P. (Ed.). (1992). *Motivation and personality: Handbook of thematic content analysis.* New York: Cambridge University Press.

Smith, C. P., & Feld, S. C. (1958). How to learn the method of content analysis for n achievement, n affiliation, and n power. In J. W. Atkinson (Ed.), *Motives in fantasy, action, and society* (pp. 685–818). Princeton, NJ: Van Nostrand.

Smith, D. A. (1971). Lateral hypothalamic stimulation: Experience and deprivation as a factors in rat's licking of empty drinking tubes. *Psychological Science, 23,* 329–331.

Smith, R. E. (2003). The costs of remembering to remember in event-based prospective memory: Investigating the capacity demands of delayed intention performance. *Journal of Experimental Psychology: Learning, Memory, and Cognition, 29,* 347–361.

Smock, C. D. (1957). Recall of interrupted and non-interrupted tasks as a function of experimentally induces anxiety and motivational relevance of the task stimuli. *Journal of Personality, 25,* 589–599.

Sokolov, E. N. (1958). *Vospriiate i uslovny refleks.* Moscow, Russia: University of Moscow Press.

Sokolov, E. N. (1963). *Perception and the conditioned reflex.* New York: Macmillan.

Sokolowksi, K. (1993). *Emotion und Volition* [Emotion and volition]. Göttingen, Germany: Hogrefe.

Sokolowski, K. (1986). *Kognitionen und Emotionen in anschlussthematischen Situationen* [Cognitions and emotions in affiliative situations]. Unpublished doctoral dissertation, University of Wuppertal, Germany.

Sokolowski, K. (1992). Entwicklung eines Verfahrens zur Messung des Anschlussmotivs [Development of a technique to measure the affiliation motive]. *Diagnostica, 38,* 1–17.

Sokolowski, K. (1997). Sequentielle und imperative Konzepte des Willens [Sequential and imperative theories of volition]. *Psychologische Beiträge, 39,* 346–369.

Sokolowski, K. (2002). Emotion. In W. Prinz & J. Müsseler (Ed.), *Allgemeine Psychologie* (pp. 337–384). Heidelberg, Germany: Spektrum Akademischer Verlag.

Sokolowski, K., & Kehr, H. M. (1999). Zum differentiellen Einfluss von Motiven auf die Wirkungen von Führungstrainings (MbO) [Differential impact of motive dispositions on the effects of management trainings (MbO)]. *Zeitschrift für Differentielle und Diagnostische Psychologie, 20,* 192–202.

Sokolowski, K., & Schmalt, H.-D. (1996). Emotionale und motivationale Einflussfaktoren in einer anschlussthematischen Konfliktsituation [Emotional and motivational influences in an affiliation-related conflict situation]. *Zeitschrift für Experimentelle Psychologie, 18,* 461–482.

Sokolowski, K., Schmalt, H.-D., Langens, T., & Puca, R. M. (2000). Assessing achievement, affiliation, and power motives all at once: The Multi-Motive-Grid (MMG). *Journal of Personality Assessment, 74,* 126–145.

Sokolowski, K., Schmitt, S., Jörg, J., & Ringendahl, H. (1997). Anschlussmotiv und Dopamin: Ein Vergleich zwischen Parkinson- und Rheumaerkrankten anhand implizit und explizit gemessener Motive [Implicit versus explicit affiliation motives and dopamine concentration: A comparison of parkinsonian and arthritis patients]. *Zeitschrift für Differentielle und Diagnostische Psychologie, 18,* 251–259.

Solomon, R. L., & Wynne, L. C. (1953). Traumatic avoidance learning: Acquisition in normal dogs. *Psychological Monographs, 67*(Whole no. 354).

Sørensen, A. B. (1986). Social structure and mechanisms of life-course processes. *Human development and the life course: Multidisciplinary perspectives* (pp. 177–197). Hillsdale, NJ: Erlbaum.

Sorrentino, R. M., Hanna, S. E., & Roney, C. J. R. (1992). Uncertainty orientation. In C. P. Smith (Ed.), *Motivation and personality: Handbook of thematic content analysis* (pp. 428–439). New York: Cambridge University Press.

Sorrentino, R. M., & Hewitt, E. C. (1984). The uncertainty-reducing properties of achievement tasks revisited. *Journal of Personality and Social Psychology, 47*, 884–899.

Sorrentino, R. M., Roney, C. J. E., & Hewitt, E. C. (1988). Information value versus affective value and achievement behavior. In F. Halisch & J. H. L. van den Bercken (Eds.), *International perspectives on achievement and task motivation*. Lisse, Netherlands: Swets & Zeitlinger.

Sorrentino, R. M., & Sheppard, B. H. (1978). Effects of affiliation-related motives on swimmers in individual versus group competition: A field experiment. *Journal of Personality and Social Psychology, 36*, 704–714.

Sorrentino, R. M., & Short, J.-A. (1977). The case of the mysterious moderates: Why motives sometimes fail to predict behavior. *Journal of Personality and Social Psychology, 35*, 478–484.

Sorrentino, R. M., Short, J. C., & Raynor, J. O. (1984). Uncertainty orientation: Implications for affective and cognitive views of achievement behavior. *Journal of Personality and Social Psychology, 46*, 189–206.

Spangler, G., Bräutigam, I., & Stadler, R. (1984). Handlungsentwicklung in der frühen Kindheit und ihre Abhängigkeit von der kognitiven Entwicklung und der emotionalen Erregbarkeit des Kindes [Behavioral development in early childhood and its dependence on the cognitive development and emotional excitability of the child]. *Zeitschrift für Entwicklungspsychologie und Pädagogische Psychologie, 16*, 181–193.

Spangler, W. D. (1992). Validity of questionnaire and TAT measures of need for achievement: Two meta-analyses. *Psychological Bulletin, 112*, 140–154.

Spangler, W. D., & House, R. J. (1991). Presidential effectiveness and the leadership motive profile. *Journal of Personality and Social Psychology, 60*, 439–455.

Spence, J. T., & Helmreich, R. L. (1978). *Masculinity and femininity*. Austin: University of Texas Press.

Spence, K. W. (1956). *Behavior theory and conditioning*. New Haven, CT: Yale University Press.

Spence, K. W. (1960). *Behavior theory and learning: Selected papers*. Englewood Cliffs, NJ: Prentice Hall.

Spence, K. W., Farber, T. E., & McFann, H. H. (1956). The relation of anxiety (drive) level to performance in competitional and non-competitional paired-associates. *Journal of Experimental Psychology, 52*, 296–305.

Spence, K. W., & Runquist, W. N. (1958). Temporal effects of conditioned fear on the eye-lid reflex. *Journal of Experimental Psychology, 55*, 613–616.

Spinath, B., & Stiensmeier-Pelster, J. (2003). Goal orientation and achievement: The role of ability self-concept and failure perception. *Learning and Instruction, 13*, 403–422.

Spirito, A., & Hartford, K. (1990). Social skills and depression in adolescent suicide attempters. *Adolescence, 25*, 543–552.

Squire, L. R. (1992). Memory and the hippocampus: A synthesis from findings with rats, monkeys, and humans. *Psychological Review, 99*, 195–231.

Squire, L. R., & Zola, S. M. (1996). Structure and function of declarative and nondeclarative memory systems. *Proceedings of the National Academy of Sciences of the United States of America, 93*(24), 13515–13522.

Sroufe, L. A. (1977). Weariness of strangers and the study of infant development. *Child Development, 48*, 731–746.

Sroufe, L. A. (1979). The coherence of individual development: Early care, attachment and subsequent developmental issues. *American Psychologist, 34*, 834–841.

Sroufe, L. A., & Waters, E. (1977). The ontogenesis of smiling and laughter: A perspective on the organization of development in infancy. *Psychological Review, 83*, 173–189.

Stahl, M. J. (1983). Achievement, power, and managerial motivation: Selecting managerial talent with the job choice experience. *Personnel Psychology, 36*, 775–789.

Stayton, D. F., Hogan, R., & Ainsworth, M. D. (1971). Infant obedience and maternal behavior: The origins of socialization reconsidered. *Child Development, 42*(4), 1057–1069.

Steele, R. S. (1977). Power motivation, activation, and inspirational speeches. *Journal of Personality, 45*, 53–64.

Steiner, M. (2006). *Motivationale Kompetenz und Anreize im Badminton* [Motivational competence and intentives in badminton]. Unpublished Lizensiat thesis, University of Zürich, Switzerland.

Steller, B. (1992). *Vorsätze und die Wahrnehmung günstiger Gelegenheiten* [Intentions and grasping favorable opportunities]. Munich, Germany: tuduv.

Steller, B. (1992). *Vorsätze und die Wahrnehmung günstiger Gelegenheiten* [Implementation intentions and the perception of viable opportunities to act]. Tuduv: Munich, Germany.

Stern, W. (1935). *Allgemeine Psychologie auf personalistischer* Grundlage [General psychology: From the personalistic standpoint]. The Hague, Netherlands: Martinus Nijhoff.

Sternberg, R. J. (2003). WICS: A model of leadership in organizations. *Academy of Management Learning and Education, 2*, 386–401.

Stevens, L., & Jones, E. E. (1976). Defensive attribution and the Lelley cube. *Journal of Personality and Social Psychology, 34*, 809–820.

Stewart, A. J., & Chester, N. L. (1982). Sex differences in human social motives: Achievement, affiliation, and power. In A. J. Stewart (Ed.), *Motivation and society* (pp. 172–218). San Francisco: Jossey-Bass.

Stiensmeier, J., Kammer, D., Pelster, A., & Niketta, R. (1985). Attributionsstil und Bewertung als Risikofaktoren der depressiven Reaktion [Attribution style and evaluation as risk factors for depressive symptoms]. *Diagnostica, 31*, 300–311.

Stiensmeier-Pelster, J. (1988). *Erlernte Hilflosigkeit, Handlungskontrolle und Leistung* [Learned helplessness, action control, and achievement]. Berlin, Germany: Springer.

Stiensmeier-Pelster, J. (1989). Attributional style and depressive mood reactions. *Journal of Personality, 57*, 581–599.

Stiensmeier-Pelster, J. (1994). Choice of decision-making strategies and action versus state orientation. In J. Kuhl & J. Beckmann (Eds.), *Volition and personality, action versus state orientation* (pp. 167–176). Göttingen, Germany: Hogrefe.

Stiensmeier-Pelster, J. (1995). Eine attributionale Analyse elterlichen Erziehungsverhaltens [An attributional analysis of parenting behavior]. In K. Pawlik (Ed.), *Bericht über den 39. Kongress der Deutschen Gesellschaft für Psychologie* (Vol. 2, pp. 445–450). Göttingen, Germany: Hogrefe.

Stiensmeier-Pelster, J. (2004). *Die Suche nach und das Nachdenken über Ursachen* [Searching for and reflecting on causes]. Unpublished manuscript, Department of Psychology, University of Giessen, Germany.

Stiensmeier-Pelster, J., & Grüner, S. (2005). *Reattributionsstraining: Ein Leitfaden* [Reattribution training: A guide]. Unpublished manuscript, Department of Psychology, University of Giessen, Germany.

Stiensmeier-Pelster, J., & Assimi, S. (2002). Attributionale Analyse aggressiven Verhaltens bei Jungen und Mädchen [Attributional analysis of aggressive behavior in boys and girls]. In M. Baumann, A. Keinath, & J. F. Krems (Eds.), *Experimentelle Psychologie* (p. 65). Regensburg, Germany: Roderer.

Stiensmeier-Pelster, J., Balke, S., & Schlangen, B. (1996). Lern- versus Leistungszielorientierung als Bedingungen des Lernfortschritts [Learning goal orientation vs. performance goal orientation as determinants of learning progress]. *Zeitschrift für Entwicklungspsychologie und Pädagogische Psychologie, 28,* 169–187.

Stiensmeier-Pelster, J., & Gerlach, H. (1997). Aggressives Verhalten bei Kindern und Jugendlichen aus attributionstheoretischer Sicht [Aggressive behavior of children and adolescents from an attributional point of view]. *Zeitschrift für Pädagogische Psychologie, 11,* 203–209.

Stiensmeier-Pelster, J., & Grüner, S. (2005). *Reattributionsstraining: Ein Leitfaden* [Reattribution training: A guide]. Manuscript submitted for publication.

Stiensmeier-Pelster, J., Kammer, D., & Adolphs, J. (1988). Attributionsstil und Bewertung bei depressiven versus nichtdepressiven Patienten [Attribution style and evaluation in depressive versus nondepressive patients]. *Zeitschrift für Klinische Psychologie, 17,* 46–54.

Stiensmeier-Pelster, J., Reisenzein, R., & Martini, A. (1995). The role of surprise in the attribution process. *Cognition and Emotion, 9,* 5–31.

Stiensmeier-Pelster, J., & Rheinberg, F. (Eds.). (2003). *Diagnostik von Motivation und Selbstkonzept* [Diagnosis of motivation and self-concept]. Göttingen, Germany: Hogrefe.

Stiensmeier-Pelster, J., & Schürmann, M. (1991). Attributionsstil als Risikofaktor der depressiven Reaktion bei Kindern [Attribution style as a risk factor for depressive symptoms in children]. *Zeitschrift für Entwicklungspsychologie und Pädagogische Psychologie, 23,* 318–329.

Stiensmeier-Pelster, J., Schürmann, M., Eckert, C., & Pelster, A. (1994). *Attributionsstil-Fragebogen für Kinder und Jugendliche (ASF-KJ)* [Attribution style questionnaire for children and adolescents (ASF-KJ)]. Göttingen, Germany: Hogrefe.

Stipek, D. (1996). Motivation and instruction. In D. C. Berliner & R. C. Calfee (Eds.), *Handbook of educational psychology* (pp. 85–113). New York: Macmillan.

Stipek, D., & Daniels, D. (1990). Children's use of dispositional attributions in predicting the performance and behavior of classmates. *Journal of Applied Developmental Psychology, 11,* 13–28.

Stipek, D., & Gralinski, J. H. (1996). Children's beliefs about intelligence and school performance. *Journal of Educational Psychology, 88,* 397–407.

Stipek, D., & Hoffman, J. (1980). Development of children's performance-related judgements. *Child Development, 51,* 912–914.

Stipek, D., & Kowalski, P. (1989). Learned helplessness in task-orienting versus performance-orienting testing conditions. *Journal of Educational Psychology, 81*(3), 384–391.

Stipek, D., Recchia, S., & McClintic, S. (1992). Self-evaluation in young children. *Monographs of the Society for Research in Child Development, 57*(1).

Stipek, D., & Tannatt, L. (1984). Children's judgments of their own and peers' academic competence. *Journal of Educational Psychology, 76,* 75–84.

Stipek, D. J., & Decotis, K. (1988). Children's understanding of the implications of causal attributions for emotional experiences. *Child Development, 59,* 1601–1616.

Stone, P. J., Dumphy, D. C., Smith, M. S., & Ogilvie, D. M. (1966). *The general inquirer.* Cambridge, MA: MIT Press.

Stricker, E. M., & Verbalis, J. G. (2002). Hormones and ingestive behaviors. In J. B. Becker, S. M. Breedlove, & D. Crews (Eds.), *Behavioral endocrinology* (2nd ed., pp. 451–473). Cambridge, MA: MIT Press.

Stroebe, W., Eagly A. H., & Stroebe, M. S. (1977). Friendly or just polite? The effect of self-esteem on attributions. *European Journal of Social Psychology, 7,* 265–274.

Stuchlikova, I., & Man, F. (1999). Motivational structure of state and action oriented alcoholics. *Studia Psychologica, 41,* 63–72.

Stumpf, H., Angleitner, A., Wieck, T., Jackson, D. N., & Beloch-Till, H. (1985). *Deutsche Personality Research Form (PRF)* [German Personality Research Form (PRF)]. Göttingen, Germany: Hogrefe.

Stutz, A. M., Morrison, C. D., & Argyropoulos, G. (2005). The agouti-related protein and its role in energy homeostasis. *Peptides, 26*(10), 1771–1781.

Sueton Tranquilinas. De vita Caesarum.

Sullivan, H. S. (1953). *The interpersonal theory of psychiatry.* New York: Norton.

Sullivan, R. M., Wilson, D. A., Wong, R., Correa, A., & Leon, M. (1990). Modified behavioral and olfactory bulb responses to maternal odors in preweanling rats. *Brain Research. Developmental Brain Research, 53*(2), 243–247.

Surber, C. F. (1980). The development of reversible operations in judgments of ability, effort and performance. *Child Development, 51,* 1018–1029.

Sutherland, R. W., & Rudy, J. W. (1989). Configurational association theory: The role of hippocampal formation in learning, memory and amnesia. *Psychobiology, 17,* 129–144.

Sutton, S. K., & Davidson, R. J. (1997). Prefrontal brain asymmetry: A biological substrate of the behavioral approach and inhibition systems. *Psychological Science, 8,* 204–210.

Svenson, G. R., Oestergren, P.-O., Merlo, J., & Rastam, L. (2002). Action control and situational risks in the prevention of risks HIV and STIs: Individual, dyadic, and social influences on consistent condom use in a university population. *AIDS Education and Prevention, 14,* 515–531.

Swithers, S. E., & Martinson, F. A. (1998). Habituation of oral responding in adult rats. *Behavioral Neuroscience, 112*(1), 213–224.

Taira, K., & Rolls, E. T. (1996). Receiving grooming as a reinforcer for the monkey. *Physiology & Behavior, 59*(6), 1189–1192.

Taub, E., & Berman, A. J. (1968). Movement and learning in the absence of sensory feedback. In S. J. Freedman (Ed.), *The neuropsychology of spatially oriented behavior* (pp. 173–192). Homewood, IL: Dorsey.

Tauer, J. M., & Harackiewicz (1999). Winning isn't everything: Competition, achievement orientation, intrinsic motivation. *Journal of Experimental Social Psychology, 35*, 209–238.

Taylor, J. A. (1953). A personality scale of manifest anxiety. *Journal of Abnormal and Social Psychology, 48*, 285–290.

Taylor, J. A., & Spence, K. W. (1952). The relationship of anxiety level to performance in serial learning. *Journal of Experimental Psychology, 44*, 61–64.

Taylor, S. E., & Brown, J. (1988). Illusion and well-being: A social-psychological perspective on mental health. *Psychological Bulletin, 103*, 193–210.

Taylor, S. E., & Brown, J. (1994). Positive illusions and well-being revisited: Separating fact from fiction. *Psychological Bulletin, 116*, 21–27.

Taylor, S. E., & Gollwitzer, P. M. (1995). Effects of mindset on positive illusions. *Journal of Personality and Social Psychology, 63*, 213–226.

Taylor, S. E., Neter, E., & Wayment, H. A. (1995). Self-evaluation processes. *Personality and Social Psychology Bulletin, 21*, 1278–1287.

Teachman, J. D., & Heckhert, A. (1985). The impact of age and children on remarriage. *Journal of Family Issues, 6*, 185–203.

Teevan, R. C., & McGhee, P. E. (1972). Childhood development of the fear of failure motivation. *Journal of Personality and Social Psychology, 21*, 345–348.

Terhune, K. W. (1968a). Motives, situation, and interpersonal conflict within Prisoner's Dilemma. *Journal of Personality and Social Psychology, Monograph Supplement 8*, 1–24.

Terhune, K. W. (1968b). Studies of motives, cooperation, and conflict within laboratory microcosms. *Buffalo Studies, 4* (1), 29–58.

The Oxford English Dictionary (2007). Volume IX. Oxford: Clarendon Press.

Thierry, D. (2004). Financial compensation at work: A motivational mess? In J. Wegge & K.-H. Schmidt (Eds.), *Förderung von Arbeitsmotivation und Gesundheit in Organisationen*. Göttingen, Germany: Hogrefe.

Thomae, H. (Ed.). (1965). *Handbuch der Psychologie. Allgemeine Psychologie II: Motivation* [Handbook of psychology. Germany psychology II: Motivation]. Göttingen, Germany: Hogrefe.

Thomas, E. A. C. (1983). Notes on effort and achievement oriented behavior. *Psychological Review, 90*, 1–20.

Thompson, R. (1987). Development of children's inferences of the emotions of others. *Developmental Psychology, 22*, 124–131.

Thompson, R., Gupta, S., Miller, K., Mills, S., & Orr, S. (2004). The effects of vasopressin on human facial responses related to social communication. *Psychoneuroendocrinology, 29*, 35–48.

Thorndike, E. L. (1898). Animal intelligence: An experimental study of associative processes in animals. *Psychological Review, Monographs Supplement 5*, 551–553.

Thorndike, E. L. (1911). *Animal intelligence.* New York: Macmillan.

Thorndike, E. L. (1913). *Educational psychology.* New York: Teachers College Press.

Thrash, T. M., & Elliot, A. J. (2002). Implicit and self-attributed achievement motives: Concordance and predictive validity. *Journal of Personality, 70*, 729–755.

Thurstone, L. L. (1937). Ability, motivation, and speed. *Psychometrika, 2*, 249–254.

Tiedens, L. Z., & Fragale, A. R. (2003). Complementarity in dominant and submissive nonverbal behavior. *Journal of Personality and Social Psychology, 84*, 558–568.

Tinbergen, N. (1951). *The study of instinct.* London: Oxford University Press.

Toates, F. M. (1981). The control of ingestive behavior by internal and external stimuli: A theoretical review. *Appetite, 2*, 35–50.

Toates, F. M. (1986). *Motivational systems.* Cambridge, UK: Cambridge University Press.

Tolman, E. C. (1926). The nature of fundamental drives. *Journal of Abnormal and Social Psychology, 20*, 349–358.

Tolman, E. C. (1932). *Purposive behavior in animals and men.* New York: Appleton-Century.

Tolman, E. C. (1951). A psychological model. In T. Parsons & E. Shils (Eds.), *Toward a general theory of action* (pp. 279–361). Cambridge, MA: Harvard University Press.

Tolman, E. C. (1952). A cognition motivation model. *Psychological Review, 59*, 389–400.

Tolman, E. C. (1959). Principles of purposive behavior. In S. Koch (Ed.), *Psychology: A study of a science* (Vol. II, pp. 92–157). New York: McGraw-Hill.

Toman, W. (1960). On the periodicity of motivation. In M. R. Jones (Ed.), *Nebraska Symposium on Motivation, 1960* (pp. 80–96). Lincoln: University of Nebraska Press.

Tomasik, M. J. (2003). *Adjusting goal aspirations when getting close to a developmental deadline: The role of primary and secondary control strategies.* Unpublished Diplom thesis, Free University of Berlin, Germany.

Tomkins, S. S. (1962). *Affect, imagery, and consciousness. Vol. 1. The positive affects.* New York: Springer.

Tomkins, S. S. (1970). Affect as the primary motivational system. In M. Arnold (Ed.), *Feelings and emotions* (pp. 101–111). New York: Academic Press.

Tomkins, S. S. (1981). The quest for primary motives: Biography and autobiography of an idea. *Journal of Personality and Social Psychology, 41*, 306–329.

Trevarthen, C. (1977). Descriptive analyses of infant communicative behavior. In H. R. Schaffer (Ed.), *Studies in mother-infant interaction* (pp. 227–270). London: Academic Press.

Trevarthen, C. (1980). *The foundations of intersubjectivity: Development of interpersonal and cooperative understanding in infants. The social foundations of language and thought: Essays in honor of J. S. Bruner.* Toronto, Ontario, Canada: McLeod.

Trevarthen, C., & Aitken, K. J. (2001). Infant intersubjectivity: Research, theory, and clinical applications. *Journal of Child Psychology and Psychiatry and Allied Disciplines, 42*, 3–48.

Trevarthen, C., & Hubley, P. (1978). Secondary intersubjectivity: Confidence, confiding, and acts of meaning in the first year. *Action, gesture, and symbol: The emergence of language* (pp. 183–229). London: Academic Press.

Triandis, H. C. (1972). *The analysis of subjective culture.* New York: Wiley.

Triandis, H. C. (1997). Cross-cultural perspectives on personality. In R. Hogan, J. Johnson, & S. Briggs (Eds.), *Handbook of personality psychology* (pp. 440–464). San Diego, CA: Academic Press.

Triemer, A. (2001). *Ambulantes psychophysiologisches 24-Stunden-Monitoring zur Erfassung von arbeitsbezogenen Stimmungen und Emotionen* [Ambulant psychophysiological 24-hour monitoring to assess work-related mood and emotion]. Unpublished doctoral dissertation, Technical University of Dresden, Germany.

Triemer, A., & Rau, R. (2001). Stimmungskurven im Arbeitsalltag – eine Feldstudie [Mood curves at normal working days – A field study]. *Zeitschrift für Differentielle und Diagnostische Psychologie, 22*, 42–55.

Trivers, R. L. (1971). The evolution of reciprocal altruism. *Quarterly Review of Biology, 46*, 35–57.

Trope, Y. (1975). Seeking information about one's own ability as a determinant of choice among tasks. *Journal of Personality and Social Psychology, 32*, 1004–1013.

Trope, Y. (1980). Self-assessment, self-enhancement, and task preference. *Journal of Experimental Social Psychology, 16*, 116–129.

Trope, Y. (1983). Self-assessment in achievement behavior. In J. M. Suls & A. G. Greenwald (Eds.), *Psychological perspectives on the self* (Vol. 2, pp. 93–121). Hillsdale, NJ: Erlbaum.

Trope, Y. (1986a). Identification and inferential processes in dispositional attribution. *Psychological Review, 93*, 239–257.

Trope, Y. (1986b). Testing self-enhancement and self-enhancement theories of achievement motivation: A reply to Sohn's critique. *Motivation and Emotion, 10*, 247–261.

Trope, Y. (1986c). Self-enhancement and self-assessment in achievement behavior. In R. M. Sorrentino & E. T. Higgins (Eds.), *Handbook of motivation and cognition: Foundations of social behavior* (pp. 350–378). New York: Guilford Press.

Trope, Y., & Brickman, P. (1975). Difficulty and diagnosticity as determinants of choice among tasks. *Journal of Personality and Social Psychology, 31*, 918–926.

Trötschel, R., & Gollwitzer, P. M. (2004). Verhandlungsführung – Psychologische Grundlagen [Negotiation – Psychological fundaments]. In G. Sommer & A. Fuchs (Eds.), *Lehrbuch Konflikt- und Friedenspsychologie* (pp. 158–177). Weinheim, Germany: Beltz, PVU.

Trudewind, C. (1975). *Häusliche Umwelt und Motiventwicklung* [Home environment and motivation]. Göttingen, Germany: Hogrefe.

Trudewind, C. (1982a). The development of achievement motivation and individual differences: Ecological determinants. In W. W. Hartup (Ed.), *Review of child development research* (Vol. 6, pp. 669–703). Chicago: The University of Chicago Press.

Trudewind, C. (1982b). Der ökologische Ansatz in der Erforschung der Leistungsmotivgenese [The ecological approach in research on the development of the achievement motive]. In L. Vaskowics (Ed.), *Umweltbedingungen familialer Sozialisation* (pp. 168–203). Stuttgart, Germany: Enke.

Trudewind, C. (1987). The role of toys and games in an ecological approach to motive development. In F. Halisch & J. Kuhl (Eds.), *Motivation, intention, and volition* (pp. 179–199). Berlin, Germany: Springer.

Trudewind, C. (2000). Curiosity and anxiety as motivational determinants of cognitive development. In J. Heckhausen (Ed.), *Motivational psychology of human development: Developing motivation and motivating development* (pp. 15–38). New York: Elsevier.

Trudewind, C., Brünger, T., & Krieger, K. (1986). Parental expectations and the development of achievement motivation. In J. H. van den Bercken, E. DeBruyn, & T. Bergen (Eds.), *Achievement and task motivation* (pp. 179–200). Lisse, Netherlands: Swets & Zeitlinger.

Trudewind, C., & Husarek, B. (1979). Mutter-Kind-Interaktion bei der Hausaufgabenbetreuung und die Leistungsmotiventwicklung im Grundschulalter: Analyse einer ökologischen Schlüsselsituation [Mother-child interaction in homework supervision and the development of the achievement motive in primary school age: Analysis of a key ecological situation]. In H. Walter & R. Oerter (Eds.), *Ökologie und Entwicklung* (pp. 229–246). Stuttgart, Germany: Klett.

Trudewind, C., & Schneider, K. (1994). Individual differences in the development of exploratory behavior: Methodological considerations. In H. Keller, K. Schneider, & B. Henderson (Eds.), *Curiosity and exploration* (pp. 151–176). Berlin, Germany: Springer.

Trudewind, C., Unzner, L., & Schneider, K. (1997). Die Entwicklung der Leistungsmotivation [The development of achievement motivation]. In H. Keller (Ed.), *Handbuch der Kleinkindforschung* (pp. 587–622). Berne, Switzerland: Huber.

Trudewind, C., & Windel, A. (1991). Elterliche Einflussnahme auf die kindliche Kompetenzentwicklung: Schulleistungsentwicklung und ihre motivationale Vermittlung [Parental influence on the development of child competence: Development of school achievement and its motivational antecedents]. In R. Pekrun & H. Fend (Eds.), *Schule und Persönlichkeitsentwicklung* (pp. 131–148). Stuttgart, Germany: Enke.

Tucker, D. M., & Williamson, P. A. (1984). Asymmetric neural control systems in human self-regulation. *Psychological Review, 91*, 185–215.

Tuerlinckx, F., De Boeck, P., & Lens, W. (2002). Measuring needs with the Thematic Apperception Test: A psychometric study. *Journal of Personality and Social Psychology, 82*, 448–461.

Tulving, E. (1985). How many memory systems are there? *American Psychologist, 40*, 495–501.

Tupes, E. C., & Christal, R. C. (1992). Recurrent personality factors based on trait ratings. *Journal of Personality, 60*, 225–252.

Tweer, R. (1976). *Das Ökonomieprinzip in der Anstrengungskalkulation: Eine entwicklungspsychologische Untersuchung* [The parsimony principle in the calculation of effort: An investigation from the perspective of developmental psychology]. Unpublished Diplom thesis, University of Bochum, Germany.

Twenge, J. M., & Campbell, W. K. (2001). Age and birth cohort differences in self-esteem: A cross temporal meta-analysis. *Personality and Social Psychology Review, 5*, 321–344.

Tzourio-Mazoyer, N., De Schonen, S., Crivello, F., Reutter, B., Aujard, Y., & Mazoyer, B. (2002). Neural correlates of woman face processing by 2-month-old infants. *NeuroImage, 15*, 454–461.

Uhlenberg, P. (1974). Cohort variations in family life cycle experiences of U.S. females. *Journal of Marriage and Family, 36*, 284–292.

Uleman, J. S. (1966). *A new TAT measure of the need for power.* Unpublished doctoral thesis, Harvard University, Cambridge, MA.

Uleman, J. S. (1971). Dyadic influence in an "ESP study" and TAT measures of the needs for influence and power. *Journal of Personality Assessment, 35*, 248–251.

Uleman, J. S. (1972). The need for influence: Development and validation of a measure, and comparison with the need for power. *Genetic Psychology Monographs, 85*, 157–214.

Undeutsch, U., & Hermans, H. (1976). *Leistungsmotivationstest für Jugendliche (LMT-J)* [Achievement motivation test for adolescents]. Göttingen, Germany: Hogrefe.

Ungless, M. A. (2004). Dopamine: the salient issue. *Trends in Neuroscience, 27*, 702–706.

Uvnaes-Moberg, K. (1998). Oxytocin may mediate the benefits of positive social interaction and emotions. *Psychoneuroendocrinology, 23*, 819–835.

Valentine, C. W. (1930). The innate bases of fear. *Journal of Genetic Psychology, 37*, 394–419.

van Lawick-Goodall, J. (1968). The behavior of free-living chimpanzees in the Gombe Stream Area. *Animal Behavior Monographs, 1*, 161–312.

van Lawick-Goodall, J. (1975). The behavior of the chimpanzee. In G. Kurth & I. Eibl-Eibesfeldt (Eds.), *Hominisation und Verhalten*. Stuttgart, Germany: Fischer.

van Overwalle, F., & Heylighen, F. (1995). Relating covariation information to causal dimensions through principles of contrast and invariance. *European Journal of Social Psychology, 25*, 435–455.

Veroff, J. (1957). Development and validation of a projective measure of power motivation. *Journal of Abnormal and Social Psychology, 54*, 1–8.

Veroff, J. (1969). Social comparison and the development of achievement motivation. In C. P. Smith (Ed.), *Achievement-related motives in children* (pp. 46–101). New York: Sage.

Veroff, J. (1982). Assertive motivations: Achievement versus power. In D. G. Winter & A. J. Stewart (Eds.), *Motivation and society*. San Francisco: Jossey-Bass.

Veroff, J. (1992). Power motivation. In C. P. Smith (Ed.), *Motivation and personality: Handbook of thematic content analysis* (pp. 278–285). Cambridge, UK: Cambridge University Press.

Veroff, J., Atkinson, J. W., Feld, S. C., & Gurin, G. (1960). The use of thematic apperception to assess motivation in a nationwide interview study. *Psychological Monographs, 74* (12, Whole no. 499).

Veroff, J., Depner, C., Kulka, R., & Douvan, E. (1980). Comparison of American motives: 1957 versus 1976. *Journal of Personality and Social Psychology, 39*, 1249–1262.

Veroff, J., & Feld, S. C. (1970). *Marriage and work in America*. New York: Van Nostrand-Reinhold.

Veroff, J., Reuman, D., & Feld, S. C. (1984). Motives in American men and women across the adult life span. *Developmental Psychology, 20*, 1142–1158.

Veroff, J., & Veroff, J. B. (1972). Reconsideration of a measure of power motivation. *Psychological Bulletin, 78*, 279–291.

Volling, B. L., McElwain, N. L., Notaro, P. C., & Herrera, C. U. (2002). Parents' emotional availability and infant emotional competence: Predictors of parent-infant attachment and emerging self-regulation. *Journal of Family Psychology, 16*, 447–465.

Vollmeyer, R., & Rheinberg, F. (2003, August). *Task difficulty and flow*. Paper presented at the biennial EARLI conference, Padova, Italy.

Vontobel, J. (1970). *Leistungsbedürfnis und soziale Umwelt* [Need for achievement and the social environment]. Berne, Switzerland: Huber.

Vroom, V. H. (1964). *Work and motivation*. New York: Wiley.

Vuilleumier, P., Richardson, M. P., Armony, J. L., Driver, J., & Dolan, R. J. (2004). Distant influences of amygdala lesion on visual cortical activation during emotional face processing. *Nature Neuroscience, 7* (11), 1271–1278.

Vygotski, L. S. (1978). *Mind in society: The development of higher psychological processes*. Cambridge, MA: Harvard University Press.

Waddington, C. H. (1957). *The strategy of the genes*. London: Allen & Unwin.

Wadsworth, M., &. Ford, D. (1983). Assessment of personal goal hierarchies. *Journal of Counseling Psychology, 30*, 514–526.

Wagner, R. (1969). Levels of symbolization in adolescent adjustment patterns. *International Journal of Symbology, 1* (1), 67–74.

Wahba, M. A., & House, R. J. (1974). Expectancy theory in work and motivation: Some logical and methodological issues. *Human Relations, 27*, 121–147.

Wainer, H. A., & Rubin, I. M. (1971). Motivation of research and development entrepreneurs: Determinants of company success. In D. A. Kolb, I. M. Rubin, & J. McIntire (Eds.), *Organizational psychology* (pp. 131–139). Englewood Cliffs, NJ: Prentice Hall.

Walker, E. L. (1969). Reinforcement – The one ring. In J. T. Trapp (Ed.), *Reinforcement and behavior* (pp. 47–62). New York: Academic Press.

Walker, E. L. (1973). Psychological complexity and preference: A hedgehog theory of behavior. In D. E. Berlyne & K. B. Madsen (Eds.), *Pleasure, reward, preference* (pp. 65–97). New York: Academic Press.

Walker, E. L., & Heyns, R. W. (1962). Conformity and conflict of needs. In E. L. Walter & R. W. Heyns (Eds.), *Anatomy for conformity* (pp. 54–68). Belmont, CA: Wadsworth.

Wallen, K. (2001). Sex and context: Hormones and primate sexual motivation. *Hormones and Behavior, 40* (2), 339–357.

Walschburger, P. (1994). Action control and excessive demand: Effects of situational and personality factors on psychological and physiological functions during stressful transactions. In J. Kuhl & J. Beckmann (eds.), *Volition and personality* (pp. 233–266). Seattle: Hogrefe & Huber Publishers.

Walster, E. (1964). The temporal sequence of post-decision processes. In L. Festinger (Ed.), *Conflict, decision, and dissonance* (pp. 112–127). Stanford, CA: Stanford University Press.

Warden, C. J., Jenkins, T. N., & Warner, L. H. (1936). *Comparative psychology*. New York: Ronald.

Wasna, M. (1970). *Die Entwicklung der Leistungsmotivation* [The development of achievement motivation]. Munich, Germany: Reinhardt.

Watson, D. (1982). The actor and the observer: How are their perceptions of causality divergent? *Psychological Bulletin, 92*, 682–700.

Watson, D., & Clark, L. A. (1997). Extraversion and its positive emotional core. In R. Hogan, J. Johnson, & S. Briggs (Eds.), *Handbook of personality psychology* (pp. 767–793). San Diego, CA: Academic Press.

Watson, D., Clark, L. A., & Tellegen, A. (1988). Development and validation of brief measures of positive and negative affect: The PANAS scales. *Journal of Personality and Social Psychology, 54*, 1063–1070.

Watson, D., & Tellegen, A. (1985). Toward a consensual structure of mood. *Psychological Bulletin, 98*, 219–235.

Watson, D., Wiese, D., Vaidya, J., & Tellegen, A. (1999). The two general activation systems of affect: Structural findings, evolutionary considerations, and psychobiological evidence. *Journal of Personality and Social Psychology, 76*, 820–838.

Watson, J. B. (1913). Psychology as the behaviorist views it. *Psychological Review, 20*, 158–177.

Watson, J. B. (1919). *Psychology from the standpoint of a behaviorist*. Philadelphia: Lippincott.

Watson, J. B. (1924). *Behaviorism*. New York: People's Institute Company.

Watson, J. B., & Morgan, J. J. B. (1917). Emotional reactions and psychological experimentation. *American Journal of Psychology, 28*, 163–174.

Watson, J. B., & Rayner, R. (1920). Conditioned emotional responses. *Journal of Experimental Psychology, 3*, 1–14.

Watson, J. S. (1966). The development and generalization of contingency awareness in early infancy: Some hypotheses. *Merrill-Palmer Quarterly, 12*, 123–135.

Watson, J. S. (1972). Smiling, cooing, and "The Game." *Merrill-Palmer Quarterly, 18*, 323–339.

Watson, J. S., & Ramey, C. (1972). Reactions to response contingent stimulation in early infancy. *Merrill-Palmer Quarterly, 18*, 219–228.

Watt, H. J. (1905). Experimentelle Beiträge zu einer Theorie des Denkens [Experimental contributions to a theory of thought]. *Archiv für die gesamte Psychologie, 4*, 289–436.

Webb, T. L., & Sheeran, P. (2003). Can implementation intentions help to overcome ego-depletion? *Journal of Experimental Social Psychology, 39*, 279–286.

Weber, M. (1904). Die protestantische Ethik und der Geist des Kapitalismus [The Protestant ethic and the spirit of capitalism]. *Archiv für Sozialwissenschaft und Sozialpolitik, 20*, 1–54.

Weber, M. (1921). *III. Abteilung. Wirtschaft und Gesellschaft. 1. Die Wirtschaft und die gesellschaftlichen Ordnungen und Mächte. Grundriss der Sozialökonomik* [Economy and society. 1. The economy and social powers and structures] (New ed. 1964). Tübingen, Germany: Mohr-Siebeck.

Weber, M. (1947). *The theory of social and economic organization. The theory of social and economic organization* [1st American Edition (A. M. Henderson & T. Parsons, Trans.)]. Oxford University Press: New York, NY.

Wegge, J., Quaeck, A., & Kleinbeck, U. (1996). Zur Faszinationskraft von Video- und Computerspielen bei Studenten: Welche Motive befriedigen die "bunte Welt am Draht"? [The fascination of video and computer games among students]. In K. Bräuer & U. Kittler (Eds.), *Pädagogische Psychologie und ihre Anwendungen* (Vol. 2, pp. 51–76). Essen, Germany: Die blaue Eule.

Wegner, D. (1994). Ironic processes of mental control. *Psychological Review, 101*, 35–52.

Wegner, D. M., & Wheatley, T. (1999). Apparent mental causation: Sources of the experience of will. *American Psychologist, 54*, 480–492.

Weinberger, J., & McClelland, D. C. (1990). Cognitive versus traditional motivational models: Irreconcilable or complementary? In E. T. Higgins & R. M. Sorrentino (Eds.), *Handbook of motivation and cognition: Foundations of social behavior* (Vol. 2, pp. 562–597). New York: Guilford Press.

Weinberger, J., & Silverman, L. H. (1987). Subliminal psychodynamic activation: A method for studying psychoanalytic dynamic propositions. In R. Hogan & H. Jones (Eds.), *Perspective in personality* (Vol. 2, pp. 251–287). Greenwich, CT: JAI Press.

Weiner, B. (1965a). Need achievement and the resumption of incompleted tasks. *Journal of Personality and Social Psychology, 1*, 165–168.

Weiner, B. (1965b). The effects of unsatisfied achievement motivation on persistence and subsequent performance. *Journal of Personality, 33*, 428–442.

Weiner, B. (1966). Role of success and failure in the learning of easy and complex tasks. *Journal of Personality and Social Psychology, 3*, 339–344.

Weiner, B. (1967). Implications of the current theory of achievement motivation for research and performance in the classroom. *Psychology in the School, 4*, 164–171.

Weiner, B. (1970). New conceptions in the study of achievement motivation. In B. Maher (Ed.), *Progress in experimental personality research* (Vol. 5, pp. 67–109). New York: Academic Press.

Weiner, B. (1972). *Theories of motivation.* Chicago: Markham.

Weiner, B. (1974). *Achievement motivation and attribution theory.* Morristown, NJ: General Learning.

Weiner, B. (1979). A theory of motivation for some classroom experiences. *Journal of Educational Psychology, 71*, 3–25.

Weiner, B. (1980). A cognitive (attribution) – emotion – action model of motivated behavior: An analysis of judgments of help-giving. *Journal of Personality and Social Psychology, 39*, 186–200.

Weiner, B. (1985a). An attributional theory of achievement motivation and emotion. *Psychological Review, 92*, 548–573.

Weiner, B. (1985b). "Spontaneous" causal thinking. *Psychological Bulletin, 97*, 74–84.

Weiner, B. (1986). *An attributional theory of motivation and emotion.* New York: Springer.

Weiner, B. (1992). *Human motivation.* London: Sage.

Weiner, B. (1994). Sünde versus Krankheit [Sin versus illness]. In F. Försterling & J. Stiensmeier-Pelster (Eds.), *Attributionspsychologie* (pp. 1–25). Göttingen, Germany: Hogrefe.

Weiner, B. (1995). *Judgments of responsibility. A foundation for a theory of social conduct.* New York: Guilford Press.

Weiner, B., Frieze, I. H., Kukla, A., Reed, L., Rest, S., & Rosenbaum, R. M. (1971). *Perceiving the causes of success and failure.* New York: General Learning.

Weiner, B., Heckhausen, H., Meyer, W.-U., & Cook, R. E. (1972). Causal ascriptions and achievement behavior: A conceptual analysis of effort and reanalysis of locus of control. *Journal of Personality and Social Psychology, 21*, 239–248.

Weiner, B., & Kukla, A. (1970). An attributional analysis of achievement motivation. *Journal of Personality and Social Psychology, 15*, 1–20.

Weiner, B., Kun, A., & Benesh-Weiner, M. (1980). The development of mastery, emotions, and morality from an attributional perspective. *Minnesota Symposia on Child Development, 13*, 103–129.

Weiner, B., & Peter, N. (1973). A cognitive-developmental analysis of achievement and moral judgments. *Developmental Psychology, 9*, 290–309.

Weiner, B., & Schneider, K. (1971). Drive versus cognitive theory: A reply to Boor and Harmon. *Journal of Personality and Social Psychology, 18*, 258–262.

Weinert, A. B. (2001). Berufsorientierungstest [Career orientation test]. In H. Wottawa & W. Sarges (Eds.), *Handbuch Wirtschaftspsychologischer Testverfahren* (pp. 125–130). Lengerich, Germany: Pabst.

Weinert, F. E. (1991). Vorwort zur deutschsprachigen Ausgabe [Preface to the German edition]. In M. Csikszentmihalyi & I. S. Csikszentmihalyi (Eds.), *Die außergewöhnliche Erfahrung im Alltag: Die Psychologie des Flow-Erlebens* (pp. 7–9). Stuttgart, Germany: Klett-Cotta.

Weisfeld, G. E., & Beresford, J. M. (1982). Erectedness of posture as an indicator of dominance or success in humans. *Motivation and Emotion, 6*, 113–131.

Weiss, A., King, J. E., & Enns, R. M. (2002). Subjective well-being is heritable and genetically correlated with dominance in chimpanzees (*Pan troglodytes*). *Journal of Personality and Social Psychology, 83*, 1141–1149.

Weiss, A., King, J. E., & Figueredo, A. J. (2000). The heritability of personality factors in chimpanzees (*Pan troglodytes*). *Behavior Genetics, 30*, 213–221.

Weisz, J. R. (1983). Can I control it? The pursuit of veridical answers across the life span. In P. B. Baltes & O. G. Brim (Eds.), *Life-span development and behavior (Vol. 3)* (pp. 233–300). Orlando, Forida: Academic Press.

Weisz, J. R., Yeates, K. O., Robertson, D., & Beckmann, J. C. (1982). Perceived contingency of skill and chance events: A developmental analysis. *Developmental Psychology, 18*, 898–905.

Welker, W. L. (1956). Some determinants of play and exploration in chimpanzees. *Journal of Comparative and Physiological Psychology, 49*, 84–89.

Wells, G. L., & Harvey, J. H. (1977). Do people use consensus information in making causal attributions? *Journal of Personality and Social Psychology, 35,* 279–293.

Wendt, H. W. (1955). Motivation, effort, and performance. In D. C. McClelland (Ed.), *Studies in motivation* (pp. 448–459). New York: Appleton-Century-Crofts.

Wendt, H. W. (1967). Verhaltensmodelle des Nichtwissenschaftlers: Einige biographische und Antriebskorrelate der wahrgenommenen Beziehung zwischen Erfolgswahrscheinlichkeit und Zielanreiz [Models of a nonscientist's behavior: Some biographical and motivational correlates of the perceived relationship between the probability of success and incentive value]. *Psychologische Forschung, 30,* 226–249.

Wentzel, K. R. (1989). Adolescent classroom goals, standards for performance and academic achievement: An interactionist perspective. *Journal of Educational Psychology, 81* (2), 131–142.

Wertlieb, D., Weigel, C., & Feldstein, M. (1987). Measuring children's coping. *American Journal of Orthopsychiatry, 57* (4), 548–560.

West, M. M., & Konner, M. J. (1976). *The role of the father: An anthropological perspective.* New York: Wiley.

Westergaard, G. C., Suomi, S. J., Higley, J. D., & Mehlman, P. T. (1999). Csf 5-hiaa and aggression in female macaque monkeys: Species and interindividual differences. *Psychopharmacology, 146* (4), 440–446.

Wheeler, M. A., Stuss, D. T., & Tulving, E. (1997). Toward a theory of episodic memory: The frontal lobes and autonoetic consciousness. *Psychological Bulletin, 121,* 331–354.

White, G. M. (1980). Conceptual universals in interpersonal language. *American Anthropologist, 82,* 759–781.

White, R. W. (1959). Motivation reconsidered: The concept of competence. *Psychological Review, 66,* 297–333.

White, R. W. (1960). Competence and the psychosexual stages of development. In M. R. Jones (Ed.), *Nebraska Symposium on Motivation, 1960* (pp. 97–140). Lincoln: University of Nebraska Press.

Wicklund, R. A., & Brehm, J. W. (1976). *Perspectives on cognitive dissonance.* Hillsdale, NJ: Erlbaum.

Wicklund, R. A., & Gollwitzer, P. M. (1982). *Symbolic self-completion.* Hillsdale, NJ: Erlbaum.

Wicklund, R. A. (1986). Orientation to the environment versus preoccupation with human potential. In R. M. Sorrentino, & E. T. Higgins (Eds.), *Handbook of motivation and*

cognition: Foundations of social behavior (pp. 64–95). New York, NY: Guilford Press.

Wiese, B. S. (2000). *Berufliche und familiäre Zielstrukturen* [Occupational and family goal structures]. Münster, Germany: Waxmann.

Wiese, B. S., & Freund, A. M. (2000). The interplay of work and family in young and middle adulthood. In J. Heckhausen (Ed.), *Motivational psychology of human development: Developing motivation and motivating development* (pp. 233–249). New York: Elsevier.

Wiese, R. A., & Rompré, P. P. (1989). Brain dopamine and reward. *Annual Review of Psychology, 40,* 191–225.

Wigfield, A., & Eccles, J. S. (1997). Changes in children's competence beliefs and subjective task values across the elementary school years. *Journal of Educational Psychology, 89,* 451–469.

Wigfield, A., & Eccles, J. S. (2000). Expectancy-value theory of achievement motivation. *Contemporary Educational Psychology, 25,* 68–81.

Wigfield, A., Eccles, J. S, Yoon, K. S., & Harold, R. D. (1997). Change in children's competence beliefs and subjective task values across the elementary school years: A 3-year study. *Journal of Educational Psychology, 89,* 451–469.

Williams, D. R., & Williams, H. (1969). Auto-maintenance in the pigeon: Sustained pecking despite contingent non-reinforcement. *Journal of the Experimental Analysis of Behavior, 12,* 511–520.

Williams, G. C. (1957). Pleitropy, natural selection, and the evolution of senescence. *Evolution, 11,* 398–411.

Williams, S. B. (1938). Resistance to extinction as a function of the number of reinforcements. *Journal of Experimental Psychology, 23,* 506–521.

Wilson, E. O. (1980). *Sociobiology: The abridged edition.* Cambridge, MA: Belknap(Harvard.

Wilson, T. D. (2002). *Strangers to ourselves: Discovering the adaptive unconscious.* Cambridge, MA: Harvard University Press.

Wilson, T. D., Lindsey, S., & Schooler, T. Y. (2000). A model of dual attitudes. *Psychological Review, 107,* 101–126.

Wine, J. (1971). Test anxiety and direction of attention. *Psychological Bulletin, 76,* 92–104.

Wine, J. (1982). Evaluation anxiety: A cognitive-attentional construct. In H.

W. Krohne & L. C. Laux (Eds.), *Achievement, stress, and anxiety* (pp. 207–219). Washington, DC: Hemisphere.

Wingfield, J. C., Hegner, R. E., Dufty, A. M., & Ball, G. F. (1990). The "challenge hypothesis": Theoretical implications for patterns of testosterone secretion, mating systems, and breeding strategies. *The American Naturalist, 136,* 829–846.

Winslow, J. T., & Insel, T. R. (2002). The social deficits of the oxytocin knockout mouse. *Neuropeptides, 36* (2–3), 221–229.

Winter, D. G. (1967). *Power motivation in thought and action.* Unpublished doctoral thesis, Harvard University, Cambridge, MA.

Winter, D. G. (1973). *The power motive.* New York: Free Press.

Winter, D. G. (1987a). Enhancement of an enemy's power motivation as a dynamic of conflict escalation. *Journal of Personality and Social Psychology, 52,* 41–46.

Winter, D. G. (1987b). Leader appeal, leader performance, and the motive profiles of leaders and followers: A study of American presidents and elections. *Journal of Personality and Social Psychology, 52,* 196–202.

Winter, D. G. (1988). The power motive in women – and men. *Journal of Personality and Social Psychology, 54,* 510–519.

Winter, D. G. (1991a). *Manual for scoring motive imagery in running text* (3rd ed.). Unpublished scoring manual, University of Michigan at Ann Arbor.

Winter, D. G. (1991b). Measuring personality at a distance: Development of an integrated system for scoring motives in running text. In R. Hogan (Series Ed.) & D. Ozer, J. M. Healy, & A. J. Stewart (Vol. Eds.), *Perspectives in personality: Vol. 3B. Approaches to understanding lives* (pp. 59–89). London: Jessica Kingsley.

Winter, D. G. (1993). Power, affiliation, and war: Three tests of a motivational model. *Journal of Personality and Social Psychology, 65,* 532–545.

Winter, D. G. (1996). *Personality: Analysis and interpretation of lives.* New York: McGraw-Hill.

Winter, D. G. (2001). Measuring Bush's motives. Proceedings of the International Society for Political Psychology. *ISPP News,* 8–9.

Winter, D. G., & Barenbaum, N. B. (1985). Responsibility and the power motive in women and men. *Journal of Personality, 53,* 335–355.

Winter, D. G., John, O. P, Stewart, A. J., Klohnen, E. C., & Duncan, L. E. (1998). Traits and motives: Toward an integration of two traditions in personality research. *Psychological Review, 105*, 230–250.

Winter, D. G., & Stewart, A. J. (1977). Power motive reliability as a function of retest instructions. *Journal of Consulting and Clinical Psychology, 45*, 436–440.

Winter, D. G., & Stewart, A. J. (1978). Power motivation. In H. London & J. Exner (Eds.), *Dimensions of personality* (pp. 391–447). New York: Wiley.

Winter, D. G., Stewart, A., John, O. P., Klohnen, E. C., & Duncan, L. E. (1998). Traits and motives: Toward an integration of two traditions in personality research. *Psychological Review, 105*, 230–250.

Winter, D. G., & Wiecking, F. A. (1971). The new Puritans: Achievement and power motives of New Left radicals. *Behavioral Science, 16*, 523–530.

Winterbottom, M. R. (1953). The relation of childhood training in independence to achievement motivation. *Dissertation Abstracts, 13*, 440–441.

Winterbottom, M. R. (1958). The relation of need for achievement to learning experiences in independence and mastery. In J. W. Atkinson (Ed.), *Motives in fantasy, action and society* (pp. 453–478). Princeton, NJ: Van Nostrand.

Wirth, M. M., Welsh, K. M., & Schultheiss, O. C. (2006). Salivary cortisol changes in humans after winning or losing a dominance contest depend on implicit power motivation. *Hormones and Behavior, 49* (3), 346–352.

Wise, R. A., & Rompré, P.-P. (1989). Brain dopamine and reward. *Annual Review of Psychology, 40*, 191–225.

Witkowski, T., & Stiensmeier-Pelster, J. (1998). Performance deficits following failure: Learned helplessness or self-esteem protection? *British Journal of Educational Psychology, 37*, 59–71.

Wittling, W. (1990). Psychophysiological correlates of human brain asymmetry: Blood pressure changes during lateralized presentation of an emotionally laden film. *Neuropsychologia, 28*, 457–470.

Woike, B. A. (1995). Most memorable experiences: Evidence for a link between implicit and explicit motives and social cognitive processes in everyday life. *Journal of Personality and Social Psychology, 68*, 1081–1091.

Woike, B., Gershkowich, I., Piorkowski, R., & Poco, M. (1999). The role of motives in the content and structure of autobiographical memory. *Journal of Personality and Social Psychology, 76*, 600–612.

Woike, B., & Poco, M. (2001). Motive-related memories: Content, structure, and affect. *Journal of Personality, 69*, 391–415.

Wolters, C. A. (2003). Regulation of motivation: Evaluating an underemphasized aspect of self-regulated learning. *Educational Psychologist, 38*, 189–205.

Wood, D. J., Bruner, J. S., & Ross, G. (1976). The role of tutoring in problem solving. *Journal of Child Psychology and Psychiatry, 17*, 89–100.

Wood, R. E. (1986). Task complexity: Definition of the construct. *Organizational Behavior and Decision Processes, 37*, 60–82.

Wood, R. E., & Locke, E. A. (1990). Goal setting and strategy effects on complex tasks. In B. Staw & L. Cummings (Eds.), *Research in organizational behavior* (Vol. 12, pp. 73–110). Greenwich, CT: JAI Press.

Wood, R. E., Mento, A. J., & Locke, E. A. (1987). Task complexity as a moderator of goal effects: A meta-analysis. *Journal of Applied Psychology, 72*, 416–425.

Woodson, J. C. (2002). Including "learned sexuality" in the organization of sexual behavior. *Neuroscience and Biobehavioral Reviews, 26*, 69–80.

Woodworth, R. S. (1918). *Dynamic psychology.* New York: Columbia University Press.

Worchel, P. (1957). Adaptability screening of flying personnel: Development of a self-concept inventory for predicting maladjustment. ASAF School of Aviation Medicine Report, No. 56–62.

Wright, R. (1994). *The moral animal: Evolutionary psychology and everyday life.* New York: Vintage Books.

Wright, R. A. (1996). Brehm's theory of motivation as a model of effort and cardiovascular response. In P. M. Gollwitzer & J. A. Bargh (Eds.), *The psychology of action: Linking cognition and motivation to behavior* (pp. 424–453). New York: Guilford Press.

Wrosch, C., & Freund, A. (2001). Self-regulation of normative and non-normative developmental challenges. *Human Development, 44* (5), 264–283.

Wrosch, C., & Heckhausen, J. (1999). Control processes before and after passing a developmental deadline: Activation and reactivation of intimate relationship goals. *Journal of Personality and Social Psychology, 77*, 415–427.

Wrosch, C., & Heckhausen, J. (2002). Perceived control of life regrets: Good for young and bad for old adults. *Psychology and Aging, 17*, 340–350.

Wrosch, C., Heckhausen, J., & Lachman, M. E. (2000). Primary and secondary control strategies for managing health and financial stress across adulthood. *Psychology and Aging, 15*, 387–399.

Wrosch, C., Miller, G. E., Scheier, M. F., & de Pontet, C. (2007). Giving up on unattainable goals: Benefits for health? *Personality and Social Psychology Bulletin, 33*, 251–265.

Wrosch, C., Scheier, M. F., Miller, G. E., Schulz, R., & Carver, C. S. (2003). Adaptive self-regulation of unattainable goals: Goal disengagement, goal reengagement and subjective well-being. *Personality and Social Psychology Bulletin, 29* (12), 1494–1508.

Wrosch, C., Schulz, R., & Heckhausen, J. (2002). Health stresses and depressive symptomatology in the elderly: The importance of health engagement control strategies. *Health Psychology, 21* (4), 340–348.

Wrosch, C., Schulz, R., & Heckhausen, J. (2004). Health stresses and depressive symptomatology in the elderly: A control-process approach. *Current Directions, 13*, 17–20.

Wundt, W. (1874). *Grundzüge der physiologischen Psychologie* [Principles of physiological psychology]. Leipzig, Germany: Engelmann.

Wundt, W. (1894). Über psychische Causalität und das Princip des psychophysischen Parallelismus [On psychic causality and the principle of psychopsychic parallelism]. *Philosophische Studien, 10*, 1–124.

Wundt, W. (1896). *Grundriß der Psychologie* [Outlines of psychology]. Leipzig, Germany: Engelmann.

Wynne-Edwards, K. E. (2001). Hormonal changes in mammalian fathers. *Hormones and Behavior, 40*, 139–145.

Yamaguchi, S., & Ninomiya, K. (2000). Umami and food palatability. *Journal of Nutrition, 130* (4 Suppl), 921–926.

Yarrow, L. J., McQuiston, S., MacTurk, R. H., McCarthy, M. E., Klein, R. P., & Vietze, P. M. (1983). Assessment of mastery motivation during the first year of life: Contemporaneous and cross-age relationships. *Developmental Psychology, 19*, 159–171.

Yerkes, R. M., & Dodson, J. D. (1908). The relation of strength of stimulus to rapidity of habit-formation. *Journal of Comparative and Neurological Psychology, 18*, 459–482.

Yerkes, R. M., & Morgulis, S. (1909). The method of Pavlov in animal psychology. *Psychological Bulletin, 6*, 257–273.

Young, L. J., & Insel, T. R. (2002). Hormones and parental behavior. In J. B. Becker, S. M. Breedlove, D. Crews, & M. M. McCarthy (Eds.), *Behavioral endocrinology* (2nd ed., pp. 331–369). Cambridge, MA: MIT Press.

Young, P. T. (1936). *Motivation of behavior: The fundamental determinants of human and animal activity.* New York: Wiley.

Young, P. T. (1941). The experimental analysis of appetite. *Psychological Bulletin, 38,* 129–164.

Young, P. T. (1949). Food-seeking drive, affective process, and learning. *Psychological Review, 56,* 98–121.

Young, P. T. (1959). The role of affective processes in learning and motivation. *Psychological Review, 66,* 104–125.

Young, P. T. (1961). *Motivation and emotion: A survey of the determinants of human and animal activity.* New York: Wiley.

Yussen, S., & Kane, P. (1985). Children's conceptions of intelligence. In S. R. Yussen (Ed.), *The growth of reflection in children* (pp. 207–241). New York: Academic Press.

Zajonc, R. B. (1968). Cognitive theories in social psychology. In G. Lindzey & E. Aronson (Eds.), *Handbook of social psychology* (Vol. I, 2nd ed., pp. 320–411). Reading, MA: Addison-Wesley.

Zajonc, R. B. (1980). Feeling and thinking: Preferences need no inferences. *American Psychologist, 35,* 151–175.

Zak, P. J., Kurzban, R., & Matzner, W. T. (2005). Oxytocin is associated with human trustworthiness. *Hormones and Behavior, 48* (5), 522–527.

Zeaman, D. (1949). Response latency as a function of the amount of reinforcement. *Journal of Experimental Psychology, 39,* 466–483.

Zehr, J. L., Maestripieri, D., & Wallen, K. (1998). Estradiol increases female sexual initiation independent of male responsiveness in rhesus monkeys. *Hormones and Behavior, 33,* 95–103.

Zeigarnik, B. (1927). Über das Behalten von erledigten und unerledigten Handlungen [The retention of completed and uncompleted activities]. *Psychologische Forschung, 9,* 1–85.

Zepelin, H., Sills, R. A., & Heath, M. W. (1986–87). Is age becoming irrelevant? An exploratory study of perceived age norms. *International Journal of Behavioral Development, 24,* 241–256.

Ziegler, A., & Heller, K. A. (2000). Effects of an attribution retraining with female students gifted in physics. *Journal of the Education of the Gifted, 23,* 217–243.

Ziegler, A., & Stöger, H. (2004). Evaluation of an attributional retraining (modeling technique) to reduce gender differences in chemistry instruction. *High Ability Studies, 15,* 63–83.

Zimbardo, P. (ed.) (1969). *The cognitive control of motivation.* Glenview, IL: Scott, Foresman.

Zimmerman, B. J., & Kitsantas, A. (1997). Developmental phases in self-regulation: Shifting from process goals to outcome goals. *Journal of Educational Psychology, 89,* 29–36.

Zuckerman, M., & Lubin, B. (1965). *Multiple Affect Adjective Checklist: Today form.* San Diego, CA: Educational and Industrial Testing Service.

Zumkley, H. (1978). *Aggression und Katharsis* [Aggression and catharsis]. Göttingen, Germany: Hogrefe.

Zurbriggen, E. L. (2000). Social motives and cognitive power-sex associations: Predictors of aggressive sexual behavior. *Journal of Personality and Social Psychology, 78,* 559–581.

Index